A Historical Companion to Postcolonial Literatures – Continental Europe and its Empires

A Historical Companion to Postcolonial Literatures – Continental Europe and its Empires

Edited by

Prem Poddar, Rajeev S. Patke and Lars Jensen

Regional Editors

John Beverley, Charles Forsdick, Pierre-Philippe Fraiture, Ruth Ben-Ghiat, Theo Dh'aen, Lars Jensen, Birthe Kundrus, Elizabeth Monasterios, Phillip Rothwell

Edinburgh University Press

Edinburgh University Press Ltd
22 George Square, Edinburgh

www.euppublishing.com

First published in hardback by Edinburgh University Press in 2008

Typeset in 10/12 Goudy
by Servis Filmsetting Ltd, Stockport, Cheshire, and
printed and bound in Great Britain by
CPI Antony Rowe, Chippenham, Wiltshire

A CIP record for this book is available from the British Library

ISBN 978 0 7486 2394 5 (hardback)
ISBN 978 0 7486 4482 7 (paperback)

Contents

THE NETHERLANDS AND ITS COLONIES

SPAIN, LATIN AMERICA AND THE PHILIPPINES

Preface

by Walter D. Mignolo

Literature, fiction and history have been closely interlinked in Western culture from the period of Greek theatre and epic through the period when the Roman *trivium* and *quadrivium* were established to the European Renaissance. But during the Renaissance a kind of 'deviation' or 'turn' can be said to have taken place when Spanish explorers and adventurers came into contact and conflict with the indigenous peoples of the Caribbean, in Tawantinsuyu and Anáhuac. Those people were neither familiar with Greek and Latin, nor with European concepts of poetry, drama, epic, history, etc. To say that they were not familiar with the two languages of Classical Europe, nor with the literacy and the system of written genres that was embodied by, and embedded in, that tradition, means simply that they were not familiar with a specific kind of literariness and culture, and not that they were 'barbarians'. Likewise, the Europeans who came upon the 'New World' were unfamiliar with the languages, societies and cultures of the Americas, but they were in the privileged position to invent 'Indians' as a new identity (as well as 'Black' to homogenise Africans enslaved and transported to the New World), and degraded them by attributing to them less than human qualities. However, as invaders, they had the chance and the incentive to learn unfamiliar languages and acquaint themselves with unfamiliar societies and cultures in a manner and for reasons that did not apply to the native inhabitants of the continents and regions to which Europeans went in their pursuit of exploration. In Anáhuac, the Aztec had built a magnificent civilisation over a long period of time, whose narrative was recounted and chanted in Nahuatl and painted in a variety of *amoxtly* (later called codices and codex by Europeans learned in Latin and Greek). It is now recognised that the Aztecs were not alone in an enterprise that was recorded in the Mayan region and also in Tawantinsuyu. Likewise, later, the huge populations of slaves inducted into the Americas and the Caribbean by Europeans from Africa developed oral modes of narration and memorial construction and transmission to which we find indirect references in texts written by missionaries and by British and French travellers. These complex developments represent some of the most significant aspects of the experiences generated by the encounter between the 'Old' and 'New' worlds all over the Americas and the Caribbean.

What happened in the sixteenth and seventeenth centuries in the 'New' world in the West was reproduced in Asia and Africa, when Europeans (with the British, the Dutch and the French as the most successful among them) transformed various kinds of commercial enterprises into full-fledged undertakings that combined colonisation with claims of the civilising mission of Europe in the world. In British India, the final vestiges of the Mughal Sultanate (1526–1803) were the target of supersession; likewise, in the Americas, the Incanate in Tawantinsuyu, and the Tlatoanate in Anahuac were structures and institutions that the Spanish set about dismantling and supplanting with their own system of governance. In the eighteenth century, the world witnessed the increasing influence of Britain and the British East India Company in western imperial expansion. The Company was the virtual ruler of large parts of India until 1858, when the British government took direct control over the territories controlled by the Company. Although local rulers continued to exist in various pockets scattered over the Indian subcontinent, direct control by Britain over India brought the Mughal Sultanate to its demise. The Mughal Sultanate was a mosaic of cultures, languages and religions. The Sultans were of course Muslim, but a vast majority of the population was Hindu. Persian and native Indian themes were part of that mosaic. Art thrived during this time because it was a very rich and important part of Mughal culture, and much valued by most of the Mughal Sultans. Consider what happened when the British gained control and English became part of that mosaic, as the language of the latest foreign rulers. Whatever was narrated, sung or written in that locale, was certainly different from what was written and narrated in England. Over time, colonialism changed the societies and cultures of the colonised as well as the colonisers. However, the coloniser maintained control and the changes and transformations in India were far more significant than the changes and transformations of England. Today immigration from India to England (as well as from Africa or the Middle East) to other countries of the European Union could help to understand the meaning and feelings of having one's own territory invaded by foreigners, be they British in India or Indians and Pakistanis in Britain.

As with the British narrative, we can also follow related and parallel narratives of Western imperial expansion through Asia, Africa and Oceania from the perspective of French colonialism, Belgian, German, Italian and Portuguese colonialism as well. Likewise, it is possible to examine the consequences of Western imperial cultural expansion in relation to Russia, China and Japan. Such examples suffice to identify what this 'historical companion' sets out to illuminate: while literary histories were written within Western empires, and in the national-imperial languages, the rich, dense, trans-cultural and inter-cultural experiences and subjectivities of *colonial subjects* were silenced or made exotic (as in Orientalism). Post-colonial literatures, post-colonial histories, post-colonial theory and criticism emerged, at the end of the twentieth century, as scholarly enterprises (both in the ex-colonies and in European imperial territories) to redress mono-topic representations and mis-representations of local histories in the world that were being invaded by subjects embedded in European local history and elevated to universality. Literary histories and narratives of European nations either ignored or marginalised colonial subjects and subjectivities, as people without letters, without literature and without history.

This 'historical companion' attempts to illuminate the 'postcolonial literatures' of the continental European empires. That is a monumental task, as evident from the size of this companion. We must keep in mind that despite the global reach of continental European imperial/colonial expansion, the relations between imperial and colonial cultures extend well beyond Europe. For example, Russia and the Soviet Union and the colonies and republics in Central Asia and the Caucasus as well as China and Japan had colonies of their own in East Asia, which were modelled on Western continental imperialism. Africa, on the other hand – both the Maghreb and Sub-Saharan Africa – were regions constantly traversed, encroached upon and colonised by Spain, Portugal, France, England, Italy and Belgium. To look at a map of colonial Africa is to see a re-production of the colours of a map of Western Europe in the Southern continent.

In this context, this historical companion to continental post-colonial literatures is unique. It provides a wealth of analysis and information about Belgium and its colonies; Spain and its colonies in America and the Philippines; Denmark and its colonial possessions; and the French colonial empire. The colonising ambitions of Germany, Italy, the

Netherlands and Portugal complete the cast of continental colonisers and present the entire assembly in a wonderful mis-en-scène.

It is a true 'companion' that invites trans-cultural readings of trans-cultural literatures. 'Trans-cultural' is used here in the restricted sense of literature written in the borders of colonial experiences of imperial domination. A literature that is 'trans-cultural' in this sense is a liberating reading experience; a literature that dwells between the imperial language of the 'colonial turn' and the mixed experiences, memories and subjectivities that have to deal with the colonial wound.

Acknowledgements

We owe a special debt of gratitude to Jackie Jones at Edinburgh University Press, who supported this project from conception to completion with unfailing enthusiasm, patience and professionalism, as did Mairead McElligott, and her editorial team, which included James Dale, Catriona Murray and Nicola Wood.

David Johnson gave invaluable help and advice in conceptualising the book. In Aarhus, Bjarne Bendtsen and Ole Laursen contributed enormously to the Chronology. Cheralyn Mealor was always there as a sounding board on many issues. Dominic Rainsford was encouraging all along. In London, Prem would like to thank the Institute of Commonwealth Studies at the School of Advanced Study, University of London for a fellowship that facilitated some of the work.

In Singapore, Rajeev is grateful for the forbearance shown by family and friends for absenting himself from daily felicities whenever the call to work on the project proved more compelling.

In Copenhagen, Lars specifically would like to thank Karen Langgård for coming up with ideas for further contributors, and his colleagues at Cultural Encounters, Roskilde University, for their contributions to the volume. A special thanks to Julia Suárez Krabbe for helping out in the Spanish section, and acting as a go-between.

Putting together a book of this size and scope is a collaborative project, in which our section editors have shown themselves resourceful in the teams they have helped us put together, indefatigable in following up on detail and overview, and infinitely patient in coaxing work from busy scholars to urgent deadlines: without their consistent and steady input, this project would have never been completed. We are also grateful to each and every contributor, whose scholarship and capacity to accommodate a wealth of detail within relatively narrow limits has helped us keep this book within manageable proportions. We are grateful for the electronic resources made available by Wikipedia, which have helped us in the preparation of our maps; and to the Tate Gallery, London, for permission to use 'Scramble for Africa' (2003) by Yinka Shonibare as an emblematic image for our project.

Editors

General Editors

Prem Poddar

Prem Poddar is currently Research Fellow at Southampton University and has held the position of Associate Professor of Postcolonial Studies at Aarhus University for many years. He has published widely on culture and nationalism, and is the author of *Violent Civilities* (Aarhus University Press, 2002) and *Postkolonial Contra-Modernitet: Immigration, Identitet, Historie* (Modtryk Forlag, 2004). He has also edited *Translating Nations* (Aarhus University Press, 2000), *A Historical Companion to Postcolonial Thought* (Columbia University Press, 2005) and *Empire and After: Englishness in Poscolonial Perspective* (Berghahn Books, 2007). He is now working on a monograph on the passport and completing a book entitled *Invented Futures: Fin de siècle Fantasies*.

Rajeev S. Patke

Rajeev S. Patke teaches at the National University of Singapore. He is the author of *The Long Poems of Wallace Stevens* (Cambridge University Press, 1985) and *Postcolonial Poetry in English* (Oxford University Press, 2006). He has edited *Europe in Post-Colonial Narratives* for *The European Legacy* (2002), and co-edited *Complicities, Connections and Divisions: Literatures and Cultures of the Asia-Pacific Region* (Peter Lang, 2003) and *Institutions in Cultures: Theory and Practice* (Rodopi, 1996). He is currently co-authoring *The Routledge Concise History of Southeast Asian Writing in English* (forthcoming).

Lars Jensen

Lars Jensen is a lecturer at Cultural Encounters, Roskilde University. His two most recent publications are *Unsettling Australia: Readings in Australian Cultural History* (Atlantic Books, 2005), and a Danish introduction to Edward Said's *Orientalism*, co-written with John Botofte. He is currently working on a book on the intersections between Cultural Studies and Postcolonial Studies.

Section Editors

Belgium and its Colonies: Pierre-Philippe Fraiture

Pierre-Philippe Fraiture is Associate Professor in the Department of French Studies at the University of Warwick, where he teaches Francophone and French literatures. He is the author of two monographs on the relationship between fiction, ethnography and imperialism: *Le Congo belge et son récit à la veille des indépendances. Sous l'empire du royaume*, coll. in 'Critiques Littéraires' (Éditions L'Harmattan, 2003), and *La mesure de l'autre. L'Afrique subsaharienne et le roman ethnographique de Belgique et de France* (Honore Champion, 2007).

Denmark and its Colonies: Lars Jensen
See above

France and its Colonies: Charles Forsdick
Charles Forsdick is James Barrow Professor of French at the University of Liverpool. He is author of *Victor Segalen and the Aesthetics of Diversity* (Oxford University Press, 2000) and *Travel in Twentieth-Century French and Francophone Cultures* (Oxford University Press, 2005), and co-editor of *Francophone Postcolonial Studies: A Critical Introduction* (Arnold, 2003). He is currently completing monographs on the representation of Toussaint Louverture and on the Swiss travel writer Ella Maillart, and co-editing a volume on *Postcolonial Thought in the Francophone World*.

Germany and its Colonies: Birthe Kundrus
Birthe Kundrus is Professor of History at the University of Oldenburg and Senior Researcher at the Hamburg Institute for Social Research. She is the author of *Kriegerfrauen: Familienpolitik und Geschlechterverhältnisse im Ersten und Zweiten Weltkrieg* (Christians, 1995) and *Moderne Imperialisten: Das Kaiserreich im Spiegel seiner Kolonien* (Böhlau, 2003). She is also the editor of *Kolonialphantasien: Zur Kulturgeschichte des Deutschen Kolonialismus* (Campus, 2003).

Italy and its Colonies: Ruth Ben-Ghiat
Ruth Ben-Ghiat is Chair of the Department of Italian Studies and Professor of Italian Studies and History at New York University. She is the author of *Fascist Modernities: Italy 1922–1945* (University of California Press, 2001), co-editor, with Mia Fuller, of *Italian Colonialism* (Palgrave, 2005), and editor of *Gliimperi: dall'antichita all'eta contemporanea* (forthcoming).

The Netherlands and its Colonies: Theo D'haen
Theo D'haen is Professor of American Literature at K. U. Leuven University and Emeritus Professor of English and American Literaure at Leyden University. He has published widely on literatures in European languages, especially on (post)modernism and (post)colonialism. Recent books include *Contemporary American Crime Fiction* (Palgrave, 2001), *Configuring Romanticism* (Editions Rodopi, 2003), *How Far Is America From Here?* (Editions Rodopi, 2005), and *Cultural Identity and Postmodern Writing* (Editions Rodopi, 2006).

Portugal and its Colonies: Phillip Rothwell
Phillip Rothwell is Associate Professor of Portuguese at Rutgers University. He is author of *A Postmodern Nationalist: Truth, Orality and Gender in the Work of Mia Couto* (Bucknell University Press, 2004) and *A Canon of Empty Fathers: Paternity in Portuguese Narrative* (Bucknell University Press, 2007). He is executive editor of *ellipsis: The Journal of the American Portuguese Studies Association*.

Spain, Latin America: John Beverley, Elizabeth Monasterios; Philippines: Rajeev S. Patke
John Beverley teaches in the Department of Hispanic Languages and Literatures at the University of Pittsburgh. He was a founding member of the Latin American Subaltern Studies Group. His most recent books include *The Postmodernism Debate in Latin America*

(Duke University Press, 1995), *Subalternity and Representation* (Duck University Press, 1999; Spanish trans. 2004), *From Cuba* (Duke University Press, 2004), and *Testimonio: On the Politics of Truth* (University of Minnesota Press, 2005). He co-edits with Sara Castro Klaren the University of Pittsburgh Press series, *Illuminations: Cultural Formations of the Americas*. He is working on pre-national concepts of territoriality in the Americas in the eighteenth century.

Elizabeth Monasterios is Associate Professor of Andean Studies and Latin American Poetry, and currently Chair of the Department of Hispanic Languages and Literatures at the University of Pittsburgh. In 2006 she founded a new series in Latin American cultural theory studies: *Entretejiendo crítica y teoría cultural latinoamericana*. She is a contributing editor for the *Handbook of Latin American Studies* and has co-ordinated a section for the *Literary Cultures of Latin America. A Comparative History* (Oxford University Press, 2004). She authored *Dilemas de la poesía latinoamericana de fin de siglo: Jaime Saenz y José Emilio Pachecho* (Plural Editores, 1997), and a series of edited books and essays published in Bolivia, Canada, Europe and the United States. She is preparing a book on the Andean Avant-Garde.

List of Maps

Map I   World Colonisation 1550

United Kingdom

France

Portugal

Spain

Russia

Turkey

A Selective Chronology of Historical and Literary Events

Year	Regions	Historical Event	Literary Event
756	Spain	Abd ar-Rahman's emirate in Cordova	
793	England	Vikings plunder Lindisfarne convent	
874	Iceland/Faeroe Islands	Norwegians settle in Iceland and Faeroe Islands	
875	Greenland/North Atlantic	Gunnbjørn in Greenland	
878	England	Danelaw in England	
912–61	Spain	Caliphate in Cordova	
1013	England	Swein Forkbeard conquers England (ruled by Danes until 1042)	
1066	England	William the Conqueror beats Harald Godvinson at Hastings	
1071	Italy	Norse conquer southern Italy	
c. 1170–1400	Iceland/North Atlantic	Icelandic and Norse sagas	
1271–95	Asia	Marco Polo's journeys to China	
1299	Middle East	Osman Empire founded by Osman I	
c. 1300	Middle East	Osman Empire in Asia Minor	
1345	Middle East/Europe	Ottoman Turks make their first crossing into Europe	
1380–1814	North Europe	Denmark and Norway united	
1415	Portugal/Africa	Portuguese capture Ceuta (North Africa)	
1427	Atlantic	Discovery of Azores by Portuguese	
1441	Portugal/Africa	Start of slave trade	
1445	Portugal/Africa	Portuguese reach Cape Verde	
1453	Middle East	Constantinople conquered by Ottoman Turks	
1471	Portugal/Africa	Portuguese on Gold Coast	
1473	North Atlantic	Kristian I organises expeditions to Greenland and Labrador	
1482	Portugal/Africa	First voyage of Diogo Cão	

Year	Regions	Historical Event	Literary Event
1487	Portugal/Africa	Bartolomeu Dias rounds Cape of Good Hope	
1492	Europe	Spanish conquest of Granada Expulsion of Jews from Spain	
1492	The Americas	Columbus reaches 'New World'	
1493	Caribbean	Settlement of Hispaniola	
1494	South America	Portugal and Castile partition exploration and exploitation of the world (East and West of c. 50 degrees meridian resp.)	
1497–98	Asia	Vasco da Gama makes first Portuguese voyage to and from India	
1499	South America	Italian navigator Amerigo Vespucci sights coast of South America	
1500	South America	Portuguese navigator Pedro Álvares Cabral accidentally reaches and then seizes Brazil	
1503	Caribbean	First sugar mill in Hispaniola	
1505	Asia	Portuguese in Ceylon	
1510	India	Afonso de Albuquerque conquers city of Goa	
1510–50	The Americas	Spanish ship large quantities of gold from New World to Spain	
1511	The Americas	First Spanish settlement on American mainland	
1511	Asia	Portuguese in Java and Malacca	
1512	The Americas	Arrival of first bishop from Europe in the Americas	
1513	The Americas	Spanish conquistador Vasco Núñes de Balboa discovers Pacific Ocean	
1514	South America	Spanish missionary Bartolomé de Las Casas begins work in support of better treatment of indigenous peoples of the Americas	
1516	South America	Portuguese begin sugar cultivation in Brazil	
1516	South America		Garcia de Resende, *Cancioneiro Geral*
1519–21	Central America	Cortés and his Spaniards destroy Aztec empire and begin building Mexico City	
1521	Asia	Portuguese Ferdinand Magellan explores islands now known as	

Year	Regions	Historical Event	Literary Event
		Philippines, approaching them from Pacific Ocean	
1524	North America	Giovanni da Verrazano lands in Carolinas and explores northwards	
1526	Africa	Congolese king Mbemba Nzinga protests to Portugal's Joao III that Portuguese merchants are selling his people as slaves to Brazilian sugar planters	
1529	Europe	Siege of Vienna Ottoman expansion in Central Europe stopped	
1532–6	South America	Pizarro conquers Incas	
1530s	South America	Spanish conquest of New Granada (Colombia)	
1532			Francisco de Vitoria, *Doctrina sobre los indios*
1534	North America	Jacques Cartier undertakes first voyage to New France	
1536	South America	Buenos Aires established by Spanish	
1537		Jesuit Order founded	
1541	South America	Spanish settlement of Chile	
1542	Far East	First European contact (Portuguese) with Japan	
1542	Asia	Spanish name Philippines islands and claim them as colonies	
1549	Asia	Jesuits in Japan	
1552	Spanish Caribbean		Bartolomé de las Casas, *Brevísima relación de la destrucción de las Indias*
1552	Portugal		Luís de Camões, *The Lusiads*
1557	Asia	Portuguese in Macau	
1560s	The Americas	First epidemic of European-borne diseases in Brazil	
1564	North America	Spanish missionaries introduce grapes to California	
1565	North America	Florida colonised by Pedro Menendez de Aviles	
1565	Asia	First Spanish settlement in Philippines	

Year	Regions	Historical Event	Literary Event
1570	Portugal/Africa	Portuguese establish a colony in Angola	
1571	Europe	Battle of Lepanto Holy League fleet defeats Ottoman fleet	
1572	Asia	Establishment of Manila, as a port to facilitate shipping of goods from Asia across Pacific to Mexico and thence to Spain	
1573		Franciscans arrive in Florida	
1574	Spanish Empire		Juan Ginés de Sepúlveda, *Demócrates Segundo o de las justas causas de la guerra contra los indios*
1578		Battle of Alcácer Quibir Death of Portugal's King Sebastião	
1580–1640		Spanish dominion over Portuguese territories	
c. 1585	Mexico		Diego Muñoz Camargo, *Historia de Tlaxcala*
1588	Europe	Defeat of Spanish Armada by British	
1595	Holland/Asia	Dutch explorer Cornelis de Houtmanpice discovers a new sea route to Indonesia: beginning of Dutch spice trade	
c. 1598	South America		*Dioses y hombres de Huarochirí. Narración quechua recogida por Francisco de Avila*
1601	Holland	Dutch East India Company founded	
1608	North America	Quebec founded by Samuel de Champlain	
1609	North America	Dutch East India Company sponsors Henry Hudson's exploration of North America	
1609	North America	First tobacco plantations in Virginia	
1610	Asia		Tomas Pinpin prints the first book to be published in the Philippines

Year	Regions	Historical Event	Literary Event
1611	Europe	Foundation of French East India Company	Shakespeare's *The Tempest* first performed in London
1614	Japan	Christian missionaries expelled from Japan	
1614	Portugal		Fernão Mendes Pinto, *The Travels of Mendes Pinto* (Portuguese)
1615	Asia	Netherlands seize Moluccas from Portugal / English defeat a Portuguese armada off coast of Bombay	
1618–48	Europe	Thirty Years War	
1619	North America	Dutch bring first slaves from Africa to North America	
1620	Europe/Asia	Tranquebar in southern India becomes a Danish colony (sold to Britain in 1845)	
1621	Holland	Formation of Dutch West India Company	
1635	Caribbean	French claim Martinique and Guadeloupe	
1641–8	Dutch Empire	Dutch occupy Luanda	
1652	Africa	Dutch establish colony at Cape of Good Hope	
1654	Central America	Dutch leave Brazil	
1671	Caribbean	St Thomas becomes Danish colony	
1673	Asia	French trading post established at Pondicherry	
1683	Europe	Battle of Vienna / Beginning of decline of Ottoman Empire	
1685	Caribbean		Publication of *Code noir*
1695	Caribbean	Spain cedes Hispaniola to French	
1703–4	Asia: Philippines		Aquino de Belen, *Pasyon*
1717	Atlantic	English and French slave trading companies begin slave trade with Spanish colonies in Americas	
1718	Caribbean	St John becomes Danish colony	
1721	Greenland	Hans Egede arrives in Greenland to begin (re)colonisation	

Year	Regions	Historical Event	Literary Event
1733	Caribbean	Denmark buys St Croix from France	
1755	Portugal	Lisbon earthquake kills 10,000–30,000, and shakes confidence of Europe	
1755	Middle East	Earthquake in northern Persia killing 40,000	
1755	North America	Acadians deported by British from Nova Scotia	
1759	Portugal	Expulsion of Jesuits from Portuguese territory	
1763	North America	Spain cedes Louisiana Territory to France	
1766	Europe	King Charles III expels Jesuits from Spanish Empire	Jean-Jacques Rousseau, *Confessions*
1767	Spanish Empire	Expulsion of Jesuits from Spanish territories	
1775–83	North America	War of American Independence	Immanuel Kant, *Critique of Pure Reason*
1788	France		Amis des Noirs founded in France
1789	France	French Revolution	Declaration of the Rights of Man adopted by French assembly
1789	Europe	Austrian Netherlands (Belgian provinces) declare independence from Vienna	
1789	Britain		*The Interesting Narrative of the Life of Olaudah Equiano, or Gustava Vassa*
1790	Britain		Edmund Burke, *Reflections on the Revolution in France*
1791	France	French National Assembly grants political rights to all blacks and mulattoes born in freedom, but not to slaves	
1791–1803	Caribbean	Haitian Revolution	
1792	Denmark	Danish ban on slave trade to come into effect from 1803	
1793	France	The Reign of Terror Execution of Louis XVI and Marie Antoinette	

Year	Regions	Historical Event	Literary Event
		France declares war against Britain	
1794	France	Convention abolishes slavery Fall of Robespierre	
1795–1815	Africa	Dutch lose control of Cape Colony, S. Africa to British	
1803	North America	The Louisiana Purchase: France sells territory to US	
1804	Caribbean	Creation of Republic of Haiti	
1804	France	Napoleon crowned emperor	
1805	Europe	Battle of Trafalgar	
1807	Portugal/Brazil	First Napoleonic invasion of Portugal/ transfer of Portuguese Royal Court to Brazil	
1807	Britain	Abolition of slave trade in British Empire	
1811	South America	Independence for Paraguay	
1814	Europe	Kingdom of the Netherlands created	
1814–15	Europe	Congress of Vienna	
1815	South America	Brazil attains status of kingdom Independence for Uruguay (ruled by Brazil until 1828)	
1815	Europe	Battle of Waterloo	
1816	South America	Independence for Argentina	
1817	France	France bans slave trade	
1818	South America	Independence for Chile	
1820	Europe	Revolutions in Spain, Portugal and Italy	
1821	C. America	Independence	
1821	Spain	Spain abolishes slave trade	
1821	Greece	Greek War of Independence	
1822	South America	Independence for Brazil	
1823	The Americas	Monroe Doctrine	
1823–54	South America/ Caribbean	Spanish American states abolish slavery (Spanish colonies: Puerto Rico 1872–3 and Cuba 1886)	
1825	South America	Simon Bolivar wins independence for territories now known as Venezuela, Colombia, Panama (until 1903), Ecuador, Peru and Bolivia	
1826	Europe		Alexander von Humboldt, *Essai politique sur l'île de Cuba*

Year	Regions	Historical Event	Literary Event
1830	North Africa	Initial French occupation of Algeria	
1830–4	Africa	Dutch-descended Boers make 'Great Trek' into Natal	
1832	Cuba		Juan Francisco Manzano, *Autobiografía*
1833	Britain	Emancipation Act passed in Britain	
1836	Sweden	Sweden abolishes slavery	
1838	Asia: Philippines		Francisco Baltazar, *Florante at Laura*
1842	Pacific	Tahiti becomes French protectorate	
1845	South America		Domingo Faustino Sarmiento, *Facundo: civilisación y barbarie*
1846	Sweden	Sweden abolishes slave trade	
1846–8	Mexico/North America	Mexican–American War	
1848	Europe	Revolutions all over Europe Denmark abolishes slavery Second abolition of slavery in French Empire	
1850	Denmark		B. S. Ingemann, *Araberen i Konstantinopel*
1851	Asia/Europe		Richard Burton, *Goa, and the Blue Mountains: Or, Six Months of Sick Leave*
1851	France		Gérard de Nerval, *Le Voyage en Orient*
1853	Pacific	French arrive in New Caledonia	
1853–5	France		Joseph Arthur Comte de Gobineau, *Essai sur l'inegalité des races humaines*
1857	South America: Brazil		José Martiniano de Alencar, *O Guarany*
1860	Italy	Italian unification	
1860	Holland		Multatuli (Eduard Douwes Dekker), *Max Havelaar*

Year	Regions	Historical Event	Literary Event
1861–5	North America	American Civil War	
1861–7	Mexico	French intervention in Mexico	
1861–90	North America	Indian Wars	
1860s	South America		Castro Alves (Brazil) writes abolitionist poems
1863	Holland	Holland abolishes slave trade	
1864	Europe	Denmark loses Schleswig and Holstein in war against Prussia and Austria	
1864–70	South America	War of Triple Alliance	
1865	Caribbean	Jamaica Rebellion	
1866	Europe	Austria defeated by Prussia Prague Peace	
1867	Europe		Karl Marx *Das Kapital*
1867	North America	Knights of the White Camelia formed in Louisiana	
1867–1918	Germany	German Empire	
1868	Middle East	Opening of Suez Canal	
1868	Mexico		Ignacio Manuel Altamirano, *Clemencia*
1870–1	Europe	Franco-Prussian War	
1870–90	South America	Unrest in Argentina	
1871	Europe	Paris Commune	Giuseppe Verdi, *Aida*
1872–9	Argentina		José Hernández, *Martín Fierro*
1872	Africa		Henry Morton Stanley, *How I Found Livingstone*
1873	Africa	Zanzibar's public slave markets close	
1873–4	Spain	First Spanish Republic	
1874–7	Africa	Stanley's journeys	
1879–83	South America	War of Pacific between Bolivia and Chile	
1880s–1914	Africa	Scramble for Africa	
1881	Brazil		Machado de Assis, *Memórias Póstumas de Brás Cubas*
1881–8	Germany		Karl May, *Orientzyklus*
1882	Spanish Caribbean		Manuel de Jesus Galván, *Enriquillo*

Year	Regions	Historical Event	Literary Event
1882–1902	Middle East	First mass Jewish migrations to Palestine, largely from East Europe	
1883–4	Africa	German colonisation of south-west Africa	
1884–5	Europe	Berlin Conference	
1885	Africa	German colonisation of parts of East Africa (until 1917) Congo private property of Belgian king Leopold II (until 1908) 3–22 million Congolese killed as a result of ruthless extraction of natural resources	
1885	Russia	Nathan Birnbaum coins term 'Zionism'	
1886	Europe	Slavery abolished in Spanish colonies	Gabriele D'Annunzio, Isaotta Guttadàuro ed altre poesie
1887	Europe	Founding of World Zionist Organization	
1887	Asia/Europe		Jose Rizal, Noli Me Tangere
1887	Europe		Emilio Salgari, La Favorite del Mahdi
1888	South America	Brazil abolishes slavery	
1889–97	South America	Unrest in Brazil	
1889	Philippines		Newspaper La Solidaridad starts publication in Manila
1889	Mexico		Clorinda Matto de Turner, Aves sin nido
1890	Africa/Europe	Ultimatum clash between British and Portuguese	
1890	North America	Wounded Knee Massacre	
1891	Philippines		Jose Rizal, El Filibusterismo
1891	Cuba		José Marti, Nuestra América
1891	Europe		Frieda von Bülow, Der Konsul
1896	Asia	Spanish execute José Rizal for promoting insurrection in Philippines	

Year	Regions	Historical Event	Literary Event
1896	Europe/Africa	Theodor Herzl, Zionist leader, asserts need for a Jewish State as a solution to European anti-Semitism Italy beaten in Abyssinia	Frieda von Bülow, *Tropenkoller*
1897	Asia	Kiachow (China) becomes a German Protectorate (until 1914)	
1897	France	Dreyfus Affair	
1897	Germany		Peter Altenberg, *Ashante*
1898	Caribbean/Asia	Spanish–American War. Spain loses her last colonies in Americas	
1899	Pacific	German colonisation of Western Samoa (until 1914)	
1899	Asia	Spanish cede Philippines to USA	
1899–1902	South America	War of the Thousand Days in Columbia	
1899–1902	Africa	Boer War	
1900	China	Boxer Rebellion	
1900	Mexico		José Enrique Rodo, *Ariel*
1901	Middle East		Code of Hammurabi discovered
1902	Africa	Benin becomes a French colony (until 1960)	
1903	Middle East	Anglo-Palestine Bank established as principal financial institution of Jewish community in Palestine	
1904	Germany		Hanna Christaller, *Alfreds Frauen*
1904–5	Asia	Russian–Japanese War	
1904–8	Africa	Herero massacre in German south-west Africa	
1904–14	Middle East	Second wave of Jewish migrants from Russia and Poland to Palestine	
1905	North Europe	Norway obtains independence from Sweden after 91 years of union	
1905	USA		Mark Twain, *King Leopold's Soliloquy*
1905–6	Africa	Tangier Crisis (First Moroccan Crisis)	

Year	Regions	Historical Event	Literary Event
1906	Germany/Africa		Gustav Frenssen, *Peter Moors Fahrt nach Südwest*
1905–7	Africa	Maji-Maji War in German East Africa	
1905–9	Russia	Pogroms killing estimated 50,000 Jews	
1907	Africa		Victor Segalen, *Les Immémoriaux* (pub. 1995)
1907	Germany		Else Lasker-Schüler, *Die Nächte Tino von Bagdads*
1908	Africa/Europe	Congo to Belgian state	
1909	Middle East	Establishment of Tel Aviv as a Jewish city	
1910–24	Mexico	Mexican Revolution	
1911	Africa	Morocco divided between French and Spanish Agadir Crisis Italy conquers Tripoli	
1911	Germany/Africa		Richard Küas, *Vom Baum der Erkenntnis*
1911–12	Europe		Gabriele D'Annunzio, *Le canzoni delle gesta d'oltremare*
1912	Germany/Africa		Clara Brockmann, *Briefe eines Mädchens aus Südwest*
1914	Central America	Opening of Panama Canal	
1914	Denmark		Mathias Storch, *singnagtugaK* (*A Greenlander's Dream*)
1914	Uruguay		Delmira Agustini, *El Rosario de Eros*
1915	Mexico		Mariano Azuela, *Los de abajo*
1915–16	Turkey	Allied defeat at Gallipoli	
1915–17	Europe	Armenian genocide	
1916	Europe		Lenin, *Imperialism, the Highest Stage of Capitalism* (Russian)
1916–18	Middle East	Arab Revolt	
1917	Middle East	Balfour Declaration by British promises Jews a homeland	

Year	Regions	Historical Event	Literary Event
		in Palestine	
		British conquer Baghdad and Jerusalem	
1917	Russia	Russian Revolutions End of Romanov Empire	
1917	Denmark/Caribbean	Danish West Indian colonies sold to USA	
1918	Europe	First World War ends and terminates German and Austro-Hungarian Empires	
1918	Peru		César Vallejo, *Heraldos negros*
1919	Europe	Versailles Treaty (end of German Empire)	Oswald Spengler, *Untergang des Abendlandes*
1919	South America		Alcides Arguedas, *Raza de bronce*
1919–23	Middle East	Third wave of mass Jewish migrations to Palestine	
1919–26	North Africa	Rif War: Spanish defeat Rif Kabyles in northern Morocco	
1919–33	Germany	Weimar Republic	
1920	Germany		Erich Scheurmann, *Der Papalagi*
1921	Africa		Herman Grégoire, *Makako, singe d'Afrique* René Maran, *Batouala, véritable roman nègre*
1921	Germany		Willy Seidel, *Der Buschhahn*
1921	Middle East	Arab anti-Jewish riots	
1922	Middle East	Britain is given mandate for Palestine by League of Nations	T. E. Lawrence, *Seven Pillars of Wisdom*
1923	Turkey	End of Ottoman Empire; proclamation of Turkish Republic by Mustafa Kemal Atatürk	
1923–30	Spain	Primo de Rivera Spanish dictator	
1924–9	Middle East	Fourth wave of Jewish migrations to Palestine	
1924	South America		Luis Ambrosio Morante, *Tupac-Amarú, drama en*

Year	Regions	Historical Event	Literary Event
			cinco actos, año de 1821
			Oswald de Andrade, *Pau-Brasil*
			Pablo Neruda, *poemas de amor y una canción desesperada*
1925–7	Central America	Nicaraguan Civil War	
1926	Africa/Europe		Bakary Diallo, *Force-Bonté*
			Marie-Louis Delhaise-Arnould, *Amedra: Roman de mœurs nègres du Congo belge*
1926	Europe		Hans Grimm, *Volk ohne Raum*
1926	South America		Ricardo Güiraldes, *Don Segundo Sombra* Peruvian journal: *Boletín Titicaca* (active to 1930)
1927	Europe		Paul Morand, *Magie noire* Knud Rasmussen, *Across Arctic America (5th Thule Expedition)*
1928	South America		José Carlos Mariátegui, *Siete ensayos de inter pretación de la realidad Peruana* Luis E. Valcárcel, *Tempestad en los Andes*
1928	Turkey	Turkey becomes secular: Islam no longer in the constitution as state religion	Halide Edib, *The Turkish Ordeal*
1928	Germany	Völkerschau, Stuttgart	
1928	USA		Nella Larson, *Quicksand*
1929	USA		Nella Larson, *Passing*
1929–39	Europe/Middle East/ North America	Fifth wave of Jewish migrations to Palestine	
1929	Middle East	Arab riots in Hebron	

Year	Regions	Historical Event	Literary Event
1930	Asia	Yen Bay rebellion, Vietnam	
1930	Africa		Tshekisho Plaatje, *Mhudi* (first novel from an African writer)
1930	Europe		Willy Seidel, *Der Buschhahn, Ein Roman aus der Deutsch-Samoa*
1930	South America		Carlos Drummond de Andrade (Brazil), *Alguma poesia* Uriel García (Peru), *El nuevo indio*
1930s	Europe/Caribbean		Négritude movement in France, North Africa and the Caribbean
1930–1	Belgium		Hergé, *Tintin au Congo*
1930–7	Turkey	Turkey suppresses Kurdish revolts	
1930s–74	Portugal	New State régime	
1931	Africa	Famine in Niger due to French use of forced labour to build roads and railways	
1931	France	Colonial Exhibition, Paris	
1931	Peru		César Vallejo, *Tungsteno*
1931–9	Spain	Second Spanish Republic	
1932	Africa		Henri Drum, *Luéji ya kondé*
1932	France		Céline, *Voyage au bout de la nuit*
1933	Japan/Europe	Japan and Germany leave League of Nations	
1933	Germany		Franz Werfel, *Die vierzig Tage des Musa Dagh*
1934	France		Michel Leiris, *L'Afrique fantôme*
1934	Portugal		Fernando Pessoa, *Message*
1934	South America		Jorge Icaza, *Huasipungo*
1934	Turkey	Women get right to vote and to abandon veil	

Year	Regions	Historical Event	Literary Event
1935	Europe		Clément Charoux, *Ameenah: Roman mauricien* Hergé, *L'Oreille cassée* Pierre Ryckmans, *Allo! Congo! Chroniques Radiophoniques*
1935	Caribbean		Aimé Césaire uses the term Négritude in *L'Étudiant noir*
1935	South America		Ciro Alegría (Peru), *La serpiente de oro* Víctor Raúl Haya de la Torre, *¿A dónde va Indoamérica?*
1935–6	Africa	Italy conquers Ethiopia (Abyssinia)	
1936–9	Middle East	Arab anti-Jewish revolt in Palestine	
1936	Europe/Africa		Jeanne Maquet-Tombu, *Le Siècle marche*
1936–9	Spain	Spanish Civil War	
1936	Germany		Adolf Hitler, *Mein Kampf*
1937	Middle East	Peel Commission recommends partition of Palestine into Jewish and Arab sections	
1937	Italy	Italy leaves League of Nations	
1937	Denmark		Karen Blixen *Den afrikanske farm*
1938	Africa		Paul Hazoumé, *Doguicimi*
1938	Middle East	Woodhead Commission advises against partition recommended by Peel Commission	
1938	Turkey	Death of Atatürk	
1939	Europe	Italy attacks Albania	Jørgen-Frantz Jacobsen, *Barbara*
1939	Caribbean		Aimé Césaire, *Cahier d'un retour au pays natal*
1939	Middle East		Aharon Appelfeld, *The Story of a Life*

Year	Regions	Historical Event	Literary Event
1939–45	Europe	Holocaust: mass extermination of Jews by Nazis	
1939–78	Spain	Franco régime	
1940	Europe	Britain occupies Iceland	
1941	Peru		Ciro Alegría, *El mundo es ancho y ajeno*
1942	Germany	Wannsee Conference planning *Endlösung der Judenfrage* (Final Solution to the Jewish Question)	
1942	France		Albert Camus, *L'etranger* (*The Stranger*)
1944	Caribbean		Jacques Roumain, *Gouverneurs de la rosée*
1944	Iceland/Denmark	Iceland cancels union with Denmark and becomes a republic	
1944	Africa	Free French forces and representatives of France's African colonies meet at Brazzaville	
1944	Denmark		Pâvia Petersen, *Niuvertorutsip pania*, (*The Trading Station Manager's Daughter*)
1944	South America		Jorge Luis Borges, *Ficciones*
1945	Africa/France		Léopold Sédar Senghor, *Chants d'ombre*
1946	French Empire	Creation of the Union Française, and 'departmentalisation' of former colonies	
1946	Africa		Egide Straven, *Kapiri-Pi. Roman africain*
1946	Faeroe Islands/Denmark	Faeroe Islands in a shock referendum votes in favour of independence from Denmark	
1946	Poland	Pogrom of Polish Jews surviving Holocaust at Kielche, 14 July	
1947	Middle East	UN General Assembly approves a partition plan for Palestine that is accepted by Jews but rejected by Arabs	

Year	Regions	Historical Event	Literary Event
1947	Africa	French massacres in Madagascar. Estimates of number of victims vary from a few thousands to more than 300,000	Pierre Ryckmans, *Barabara*
1948	Africa		Paul Lomami-Tshibamba, *Ngando (Le crocodile)*
1948	Europe	Universal Declaration of Human Rights	*Anthologie de la nouvelle poésie nègre et malgache*, ed. Léopold Sédar Senghor Jean-Paul Sartre, 'Orphée Noir'
1948	Middle East	State of Israel established, followed by war with Egypt, Syria, Jordan, Lebanon and Iraq	
1948	Faeroe Islands	Faeroe Islands granted home rule	
1948	Argentina		Ernesto Sábato, *El Túnel*
1949	Africa	Massacres in Cote d'Ivoire killing 100,000 Apartheid laws passed in South Africa	Fernando de Castro Soromenho, *Terra morta*
1949	Caribbean		Alejo Carpentier, *El reino de este mundo*
1949	Portugal		José Régio, *El-Rei Sebastião: Teatro*
1949	Middle East	Jerusalem is divided between Israel and Jordan; mass immigrations to Israel	
1949	South America		Miguel Ángel, *Hombres de maiz*
1950	Caribbean		Joseph Zobel, *La Rue cases-nègres*
1950	France		Marguerite Duras, *Un Barrage contre le Pacifique*
1951	Middle East	Persia nationalises oil industry	
1952	Europe		Frantz Fanon, *Peau noire, masques blancs*
1952–60	Africa	Mau Mau Uprising in Kenya	
1953	Africa		Camara Laye (Guinea), *L'Enfant noir* (French)
1953	Greenland	Greenland changes from colony to Danish county	

Year	Regions	Historical Event	Literary Event
1954	Africa		Henri Cornélus, *Kufa*
1954	Asia	French defeated at Dien Bien Phu	
1955	Africa/USA		Robert Ruark, *Something of Value*
1955	Caribbean		Aimé Césaire, *Discours sur le colonialisme*
1955	Turkey		Yaşal Kemal, *Memed, My Hawk*
1956	Middle East	Egypt nationalises Suez Canal Israel invades Sinai	
1956	Africa	Independence for Tunisia and Morocco	Kateb Yacine, *Nedjma*
1956	Europe	Soviet Union crushes uprisings in Poland and Hungary	
1956	Brazil		João Guimarães Rosa, *Grande Sertão: Veredas*
1957	Africa	Independence for Ghana	Ousmane Sembène, *Le Docker noir*
1957	Caribbean		Aimé Césaire, *Et les chiens se taisaient*
1957	Middle East	Israel withdraws from the Gaza Strip	
1957	South America		Gamaliel Churata, *El Pez de Oro*
1958	Africa		Chinua Achebe, *Things Fall Apart*
1958	Africa	Afrikaner-ruled South Africa becomes independent of British rule	
1959	Africa		Bernard Dadié, *Un Nègre à Paris* Frantz Fanon, *L'An V de la révolution algérienne* Marcel Tinel, *Le Monde de Nzakomba*
1959	Europe		André Schwarz-Bart, *Le Dernier des Justes*
1959	Mexico		Carlos Fuentes, *La región más transparente*

Year	Regions	Historical Event	Literary Event
1960	Africa	Zaire (formerly the Belgian Congo) becomes independent from Belgium	Ousmane Sembène, *Les Bout de bois de dieu*
1960	Europe/Africa		Daniel Gillès, *La Termitière*
1960	South America		Clarice Lispector, *Laços de família*
1960	Europe/Africa		Joseph Esser, *Matuli, fille d'Afrique*
1960	Turkey	Military coup overthrows democratic government	
1961	Africa		António Agostinho Neto, *Poemas*
1961	Asia		Orlando da Costa, *O Signo da Ira*
1961	Portugal/India/Africa	Uprisings against Portuguese colonialism in Angola Goa ceases to be a Portuguese colony	
1961	Europe		F. Fanon, *Les Damnés de la terre*
1961	Germany	Berlin Wall erected	
1961	Africa		Cheikh Hamidou Kane, *L'Aventure ambiguë*
1961	Caribbean	Bay of Pigs	
1961	France	Massacre in Paris of pro-Algerian demonstrators, 17 October	
1961	South America		José María Arguedas, *Los Ríos Profundos*
1962	Africa	Evian Accords: Algeria becomes independent from French rule	Assia Djebar, *Les Enfants du nouveau monde*
1962	Caribbean	Cuban Missile Crisis	
1963	Africa	Kenya becomes independent from British rule	Jean Ikelle-Matiba, *Cette Afrique-la!*
1964	Africa		José Luandino Vieira, *Luuanda: Short Stories of Angola* (Portuguese)
1964	Caribbean		Edouard Glissant, *Le quatrième siècle*
1964	Middle East	The Palestine Liberation Organization established by the Arab League	

Year	Regions	Historical Event	Literary Event
1965	Africa	Rhodesia declares independence	
1965–73	Asia	Vietnam War	
1965	Africa		James Ngugi, *The River Between* Thomas Kanza, *Sans rancune*
1966	Africa		Albert Memmi, *La Libération du Juif* Flora Nwapa, *Efuru* (first novel by a woman writer from Africa)
1966	Middle East		Aziz Nesin, *Istanbul Boy* (Turkish) S.Y. Agnon is declared joint winner of the Nobel Prize for Literature
1966	South America		Arturo Borda, *El loco* Carolina María de Jesús, *Child of the Dark* (Portuguese) Mario Vargas Llosa, *La Casa Verde*
1967	Africa		Aimé Césaire, *Une saison au Congo* (French)
1967	Denmark		Thorkild Hansen, *Slavernes kyst*
1967	Middle East	The Six-Day War: Israel wrests control of several Arab-occupied regions	
1967	South America		Gabriel García Márquez, *Cien años de soledad*
1968	Caribbean		Aimé Césaire, *Une tempête*
1968	Africa	Independence for Equatorial Guinea (from Spain)	Ahmadou Kourouma, *Les Soleils des indépendances* Malian Yambo Ouologuem, *Le Devoir de violence* Kwame Nkrumah, *The Beautiful Ones Are Not Yet Born*

Year	Regions	Historical Event	Literary Event
1968	Caribbean		Marie Chauvet, *Amour, colère, folie*
1968	Europe		Conor Cruise O'Brien, *Murderous Angels* Thorkild Hansen, *Slavernes skibe* (*Ships of Slaves*)
1969	Africa		Luís Bernardo Honwana, *We Killed Mangy-Dog and Other Mozambique Stories* (Portuguese)
1969	Cuba		Heberto Padilla, *Fuera del juego*
1969	Peru		Mario Vargas Llosa, *Conversación en la Catedral*
1970s	Africa	Angola and Mozambique become independent from Portuguese rule	
1970	Denmark		Thorkild Hansen, *Slavernes øer* (*Islands of Slaves*)
1971	Africa		Kofi Awonoor, *This Earth, My Brother*
1971	Cuba		Roberto Fernández Retamar, 'Calibán'
1971	Europe		Antonio Gramsci, *Selections from the Prison Notebooks*
1971	South America		José María Arguedas, *El zorro de arriba y el zorro de abajo* José Watanabe, *Album de Familia*
1972	Caribbean		Simone Schwarz-Bart, *Pluie et vent sur Télumée Miracle*
1972	Europe		André Schwarz-Bart, *La Mulâtresse solitude*
1973	Middle East	Egypt and Syria attack Israel	
1973	South America	Allende's fall in Chile	
1974	Africa		António Agostinho Neto, *Sagrada Esperança*

Year	Regions	Historical Event	Literary Event
1974	Portugal	Carnation Revolution in Portugal ends nearly five decades of dictatorship	
1974	Paraguay		Augusto Roa Bastos, *Yo el Supremo*
1975	Africa	Angola, Cape Verde, São Tomé e Príncipe, Guinea Bissau and Mozambique gain independence from Portugal	
1975	Mexico		Carlos Fuentes, *Terra Nostra*
1975	Middle East	UN passes resolution equating Zionism with racism	
1976	Africa		Cheikh Anta Diop, *The African Origin of Civilization* (French)
1976	Asia		Francisco Borja da Costa, *Revolutionary Poems in the Struggle Against Colonialism: Timorese Nationalist Verse*
1976	South America		Manuel Puig, *El beso de la mujer araña*
1977	Africa		Grégoire Pessaret, *Émile et le destin*
1978	Central America	Sandinista Revolt in Nicaragua	
1978	Europe		Ivan Reisdorff, *L'Homme qui demanda du feu* Uwe Timm, *Morenga*
1979	Africa		Mariama Bâ, *Une si longue lettre* Sony Labou Tansi, *La Vie et demie* Valentin Yves Mudimbe, *L'Écart* Williams Sassine, *Le Jeune homme de sable*
1979	Portugal/Africa		António Lobo Antunes, *South of Nowhere* (Portuguese)

Year	Regions	Historical Event	Literary Event
1979	Caribbean		César Leante, *Los guerrilleros negros* René Depestre, *Le Mât de cocagne*
1979	Middle East	Israel signs peace treaty with Israel Islamic Revolution in Iran USSR invades Afghanistan	
1979	Greenland	Greenland achieves home rule	
1980	Africa		Pepetela, *Mayombe*
1980	Caribbean		Axel Gauvin, *Quartier trois lettres*
1980	Portugal		Alexandre Herculano, *Eurico, o Presbítero*
1981	Africa		Nadine Nyangoma, *Le Chant des fusillés* Paul Lomami-Tshibamba, *Ngemena*
1981	Caribbean		Edouard Glissant, *Le Discours antillais*
1982	Africa		Emmanuel Dongala, *Jazz et vin de palme*
1982	Europe		Fernando Pessoa, *The Book of Disquiet Composed by Bernardo Soares* Teolinda Gersão, *Paisagem Com Mulher e Mar ao Fundo*
1982	Middle East	Israel launches attack in southern Lebanon; withdraws from most parts by 1983	Amos Oz, *In the Land of Israel* (Hebrew)
1982	Chile		Isabel Allende, *La casa de los espíritus*
1983	Africa	Mauritania abolishes slavery – the last country in the world to do so	Mehdi Charef, *Le Thé au harem d'Archi Ahmed* Michèle Rakotoson, *Le Bain des reliques: Roman malgache* (pub. 1988) Omer Marchal, *Afrique,Afrique* Tété-Michel Kpomassie,

Year	Regions	Historical Event	Literary Event
1983	Central America	US invasion of Grenada	*L'Africain du Grœnland* Rigoberta Menchú, *I, Rigoberta Menchu: An Indian Woman in Guatemala*
1984	Africa		Pepetela, *Yaka* Touati Fettouma, *Printemps désespéré*
1984	France		Didier Daeninckx, *Meurtres pour mémoire*
1984	North America		J. Poulin, *Volkswagen Blues*
1984	South America		Julio Cortázar, *Nicaragua tan violen tamente dulce*
1985	Africa		Assia Djebar, *L'Amour, la fantasia* Tahar Ben Jelloun, *L'Enfant de sable*
1985	Caribbean		Dany Laferrière, *Comment faire l'amour avec un nègre sans se fatiguer*
1985	Europe		Jacques de Decker, *La Grande roué*
1986	Africa		Mpoyi Buatu, *La re-Production*
1986	Caribbean		Maryse Condé, *Moi, Tituba, sorcière noire de Salem*
1986	Portugal		José Saramago, *The Stone Raft* (Portuguese) José Saramago, *The Year of the Death of Ricardo Reis* (Portuguese)
1987	Africa		Calixthe Beyala, *C'est le soleil qui m'a brûlée* Chinua Achebe, *Anthills of the Savannah* Tahar Ben Jelloun, *La Nuit sacrée*

Year	Regions	Historical Event	Literary Event
1987	Caribbean		Daniel Maximin, *Soufrières* Raphaël Confiant, *Marisosé*
1987	Germany		Aly Diallo, *Die Täuschun*
1987	Mexico/USA		Sandra Cisneros, *My Wicked, Wicked Ways*
1987	Middle East	Violent protests by Palestinians in the West Bank and Gaza Strip	
1988	Africa		Lina Magaia, *Dumba Nengue: Run for your Life: Peasant Tales of Tragedy in Mozambique* (Portuguese) U. Xitu, *The World of 'Mestre' Tamoda*
1988	Canada/France		Anne Hébert, *Le Premier Jardin*
1988	Middle East	Independent state of Palestine proclaimed by the Palestinian National Council	
1988	Pacific	The Matignon Accords grant considerable autonomy to New Caledonia	
1988	Portugal		António Lobo Antunes, *The Return of the Caravels: A Novel* (Portuguese) Lídia Jorge, *A Costa dos Murmúrios*
1989	Africa		Azouz Begag, *Béni ou le paradis privé* Manuel Alegre, *Jornada de África: Romance de Amor e Morte do Alferes Sebastião* Maryse Condé, *Traversée de la mangrove*
1989	Central America	US Panama campaign	
1989	Germany	Fall of Berlin Wall	
1989	Portugal		José de Sousa Saramago, *História*

Year	Regions	Historical Event	Literary Event
			do Cerco de Lisboa Manuel Alegre, *Jornada de África: Romance de Amor e Morte do Alferes Sebastião*
1989	South America		Alvaro Mutis, *La nieve del Almirante*
1989	Vietnam/France		Kim Lefèvre, *Métisse blanche*
1990	Caribbean		Edouard Glissant, *Poétique de la relation*
1990	Africa/Portugal		Filinto de Barros, *Kikia Matcho*
1990	Italy/Africa		Pap Khouma, *Io, Venditore di elefanti* Salah Methnani, *Immigrato*
1990	Portugal		Almeida Faria, *O Conquistador*
1990	Vietnam/France		Kim Lefèvre, *Retour à la saison des pluies*
1991	Africa		Assia Djebar, *Loin de Médine* Saidou Moussa Bâ, *La promessa di Hamadi*
1991	Europe	Collapse of the Soviet Union	Erminia dell'Oro, *L'abbandono: Una storia Eritrea*
1991	French Polynesia		Chantal Spitz, *L'Ile des rêves écrasés*
1991	Germany		Amma Darko, *Der verkaufte Traum*
1991	Italy/Africa		Mohamed Bouchane, *Chiamatemi Alì*
1991	South America		Raúl Agudo Freites, *Miguel de Buría*
1992	Caribbean		Patrick Chamoiseau, *Texaco*
1992	Denmark		Peter Høeg, *Frøken Smillas fornemmelse for sne*
1993	Africa		Domingas Samy, *A Escola*

Year	Regions	Historical Event	Literary Event
1993	Europe		Gisèle Pineau, *La Grande Drive des esprits*
			Erminia dell'Oro, *Asmara addio*
			Mohsen Melliti, *Pantanella: canto lungo la strada*
			Nassera Chorha, *Volevo diventare bianca*
			Ribka Sibhatu, *Aulò: Canto poesia dell'Eritrea*
1993	Middle East	Israel and the PLO sign the Oslo Peace Treaty	
1993	South America		Miguel Arroyo, *El reino de buria*
1993	Vietnam/France		Linda Lê, *Calomnies*
1994	Africa	Democracy in South Africa	Fatima Mernissi, *Dreams of Trespass: Tales of a Harem Girlhood* (French)
1994	Europe		Mário de Carvalho, *Um Deus Passeando pela Brisa da Tarde*
			Miguel Medina, *Além do Mar*
			Shirin Fazel, *Lontano da Mogadiscio*
1994	Caribbean	US military intervention in Haiti	Patrick Chamoiseau, *Chemin d'école*
1994	South America		Fernanda Farias de Albuquerque, *Princesa*
1995	Africa		Abdulai Sila, *A Última Tragédia*
			Mohammed Dib, *La Nuit sauvage*
			Mohsen Melliti, *I bambini delle rose*
1996	Caribbean		Edwidge Danticat, *Breath, Eyes, Memory*
1996	Europe		António Lobo Antunes, *Manual*

Year	Regions	Historical Event	Literary Event
			dos Inquisidores
			Sven Lindqvist, *Exterminate All the Brutes*
1996	North America		Bernard Assiniwi, *La Saga des Béothuks*
1997	Africa		Assia Djebar, *Les Nuits de Strasbourg* Yolande Mukagasana, *La Mort ne veut pas de moi*
1997	Europe		Fesum Brhan, *L'ombra del poeta* Jarmila Očkayovà, *Verrà la vita e avrà i tuoi occhi* Ronan Bennett, *The Catastrophist*
1998	Africa		Rosária da Silva, *Totonya*
1998	Caribbean		Patrick Chamoiseau, *L'Esclave vieil homme et le molosse*
1998	French Polynesia		Flora Devatine, *Tergiversations et Rêveries de l'ecriture orale: Te Pahu a Hono'ura*
1998	South America		Rosana Crispim, *Il mio corpo traduce molte lingue*
1998	North America		Barbara Kingsolver, *The Poisonwood Bible*
1999	Africa		Amara Lakhous, *Le cimici e il pirata* R. D. Carvalho, *Vou lá Visitar Pastores*
1999	Germany		Hans J. Massaquoi, *Destined to Witness: Growing up Black in Nazi Germany*
1999	Middle East		Amin Maalouf, *Ports of Call*
2000	Africa		Ahmadou Kourouma, *Allah n'est pas obligé*

Year	Regions	Historical Event	Literary Event
2000	Asia		Smari Abdel Malek, *Fiamme in paradiso* Luís Cardoso, *The Crossing: A Story of East Timor* (Portuguese)
2000	Caribbean		Yanick Lahens, *Dans la maison du père*
2000	Europe		Gëzin Hadjdari, *Antologia della pioggia* Ron Kubati, *Va e non torna*
2000	Middle East	The Camp David Summit	
2001	Africa		Bahassan Adamodjy, *Milandos de um Sonho* Lília Momplé, *Neighbours: The Story of a Murder* (Portuguese)
2001	Europe		Alejandro Leiva Wenger, *Till vår ära*
2001	France/Africa	Loi Taubira, recognising slavery as a crime against humanity	Fatou Diome, *La Préférence nationale*
2001	Italy/Africa		Jadelin Mabiala Gangbo, *Verso la notte BAKONKA*
2001	Middle East		Muin Madih Masri, *Il sole d'inverno*
2002	Africa		José Eduardo Agualusa, *Creole* (Portuguese) Kossi Komla-Ebri, *Imbarrazzismi I* Paulina Chiziane, *Niketche. Uma História de Poligamia*
2002	Middle East	Israel launches a major military offensive in the West Bank	
2003	Africa		Mbacke Gadji, *Kelefa: la prova del pozzo*
2003	Europe		Fatou Diome, *Le Ventre de l'Atlantique* Gerhard Seyfried, *Herero*

Year	Regions	Historical Event	Literary Event
			Igiaba Scego, *La nomade che amava Alfred Hitchcock*
2003	New Caledonia		Nicolas Kurtovitch, *Le Piéton du dharma*
2003	Turkey		Orhan Pamuk's *My Name is Red* wins the IMPACV Dublin Literary Award
2004	Africa		J. M. G. Le Clézio, *L'Africain* Werewere Liking, *La Mémoire amputée*
2004	Europe		Jonas Hassen Khemiri, *Ett öga rött*
2004	New Caledonia		Pierre Gope, *La Parenthèse*
2004	South America		Christiana de Caldas Brito, *Qui e là racconti*
2004	Vietnam/France		Linda Lê, *Kriss*
2005	Middle East	Israel completes unilateral disengagement plan in the Gaza Strip	
2005	Europe	In France, the controversial 23 February law includes a clause obliging educators to teach the benefits of colonisation	Jeff Janoda, *Saga: A Novel of Medieval Iceland* Marjaneh Bakhtiari, *Kalla det vad fan du vill*
2005	Vietnam/France		Linda Lê, *Le Complexe de Caliban*
2006	Africa		Aminata Fofana, *La luna che mi seguiva* Mia Couto, *A Sleepwalking Land* (1992, Portuguese)
2006	Europe		Jonas Hassen Khemiri, *Montecore: En unik tiger*
2006	Middle East	The militant Hamas party wins legislative elections; a UN study reports the plight of inhabitants in the Gaza Strip as 'intolerable'	Orhan Pamuk wins the Nobel Prize for Literature

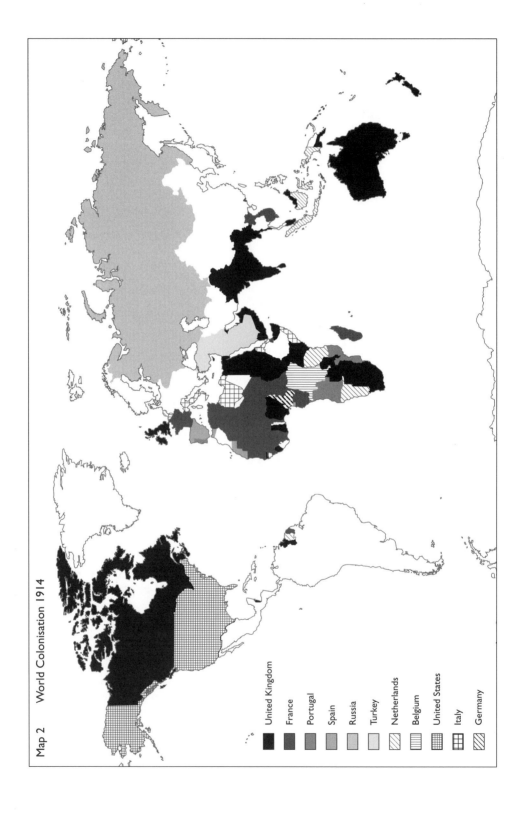

Map 2   World Colonisation 1914

United Kingdom
France
Portugal
Spain
Russia
Turkey
Netherlands
Belgium
United States
Italy
Germany

Introduction: Postcolonial Europe

> *I met History once, but he ain't recognise me.*
>
> Derek Walcott

The relation between history and postcoloniality might be described, after Walter Benjamin's notes 'On the Concept of History', as a series of images that flash up 'at the moment of their recognisability', which threaten to disappear 'in any present that does not recognise itself as intended' in those images. What that signifies for a compilation like this one, which follows upon *A Historical Companion to Postcolonial Literatures in English* (2005), is that we hope readers will want to use this book not like a reference work that narrates events in the mode of 'once upon a time', or 'the way it really was', but as a series of refractions that bend the light of history, historiography and literary writing onto the many twisted links between colonial and postcolonial experiences, predicaments, mindsets, institutions and systems of thought, belief and action.

These refractions are grouped in terms of the several European nations that colonised many diverse peoples and regions, for varying periods of time, and with effects that are still with us today in a variety of obvious, concealed, mutated or vestigial ways. They seek to reinsert something of the traditions of the oppressed, which teach us, as Benjamin wrote in the dark times of Nazi rule over Europe, 'that the 'state of emergency' in which we live is not the exception but the rule'. Through the various entries collected under each section, the *Companion* hopes to underline the 'presentness' of historical detail, its enormous and urgent relevance to what we think of as the continuous present. This present is always aimed at some near or distant future: nonce-words such as 'progress' and 'modernity' are set as markers on the paths that peoples and nations walk in the hope that what they seek will redeem the pasts that had such futures in their sights.

The *Companion* hopes to reinforce an additional recognition: that boundaries pertaining to languages and nations – while they make for convenience and neatness of conspectus and survey – misrepresent the complexity of what happened when several European nations sent men and ships, technologies, ideas, beliefs and desires, over many centuries, across the oceans to explore, trade, conquer, settle, Christianise, exploit and 'civilise'. The *Companion* assembles the Belgian, Danish, French, German, Italian, Dutch, Portuguese and Spanish (as well as Latin American and Filipino) narratives of colonial institutions and practices, persons, events and legacies, not merely within the covers of a single book, but also as a constellation of related interactions between peoples and practices. The significance of this collation and contextualisation is deepened when individual sections are read contrastively rather than in isolation. We hope that the *Companion* thus answers to the felt need for grounding postcolonial studies in historical awareness, and for grounding historical awareness of modern colonialism and its continued impact on contemporary realities in a comparative context that is mindful of the literary dimension.

Our compilation is meant to complement *A Historical Companion to Postcolonial Literatures in English*, edited by Prem Poddar and David Johnson (Edinburgh University

Press, 2005), which covered the postcolonial dimensions of the literary legacies of the British Empire. The two books share a sense of the interconnectedness between postcolonial texts and their historical contexts. As with the first *Companion*, we have commissioned entries by a large number of scholars from around the world in order to convey a sense of the multiplicity of literatures and histories in whose creation continental Europe and its languages and literary traditions played a major role. In addressing issues that cross many regions, languages and time periods, we have drawn on the scholarship of several linguistic and academic cultures, thus hoping to enrich the anglophone awareness of global issues with insights derived from a range of modern scholarship that falls ordinarily outside the scope of anglophone readers. The entries are grouped under sections that correspond to each of the European empires. At all points throughout the *Companion*, connections, parallels and inter-relationships between these empires are identified and discussed; in doing so, we hope to open up new possibilities for correlation and interaction between anglophone and continental European understandings of postcolonial literatures, histories and the politics of contemporary societies and cultures. The additional long essays on Turkey, Sweden, Russia, the Jewish Diaspora and the contemporary 'Clash of Civilisations' aim to broaden the scope of our concerns, by crossing and recrossing the borders that stitch together a notion of Europe constantly redefined in relation to its many and changing 'others'.

We hope that the *Companion* will provide a useful tool for grounding postcolonial studies in historical awareness, and grounding historical awareness of modern colonialism, and its continued impact on contemporary realities, in a comparative context that is mindful of the literary dimension to the historicity of experience. Our enterprise contends with a very long time-frame and a hugely variegated field of events and activities. Continental Europe in the era of European imperialism – a period extending from 1492 to the decolonisation that began after World War II – constitutes a vast and heterogeneous field. Confronted by this scale of diversity, one might well ask: why attempt to encompass such widely different cultural experiences, epochs, languages and histories in a single book? Our answer is that it is both possible and desirable to identify common and contrastive traits between the various colonial processes and formations initiated and partially shaped by the different continental European imperial powers, just as it is possible and necessary to identify common and contrastive traits in the phases of twentieth-century decolonisation and nationhood.

The *Companion* also provides a set of historical genealogies for several phenomena such as migration, modernisation and the historical pathologies of contemporary mass violence. Thus, for instance, it is worth noting that the various histories of continental European colonialism are constituted by and around the fact of endemic and systemic violence to a degree that has been given no more than reluctant recognition by European cultural historians. That is one reason why it has proved very difficult to come up with histories and historiographies that could deal with five centuries of exploitation from any kind of common perspective. The Spanish massacre of millions of Native Americans in the Caribbean and Latin America recorded in its early stages by las Casas, the much later German genocide of the Herero people in south-west Africa, the Italian use of indiscriminate mass killings in their colonial wars in the early part of the twentieth century, the Dutch policy of violent *transmagrasi* in Indonesia, and the Belgian atrocities in the Congo have not figured prominently in the national histories of the respective countries, nor are they seen as central – at times they are hardly considered relevant to the concerns of national historiography – nor for that matter are they given adequate recognition as constitutive elements in the articulations of national identity. Our *Companion* goes some way towards reinscribing such narratives into the texture of a larger common fabric of historical experience.

This volume also underlines the many ways in which traces of colonial pasts define modern European nations in fundamental terms. One of the most obvious ways in which this is noticeable is in the monumental buildings that still stand as vestiges of the former imperial glory of all the European capitals, buildings funded by profits from slavery and colonial plunder. More centrally, and sometimes less obviously, many of the central concerns of contemporary European societies – migration, trans-nationalism, the integration (or not) of diasporic communities, multiculturalism, xenophobia and racism – are made less incomprehensible through a careful interrogation of their colonial pasts. By bringing together apparently disparate but partially congruent historical narratives, our *Companion* reinforces the fundamental relevance of historical memory to contemporary life.

The perspective enjoined by Benjamin recognises that the task of historicising the past is misdirected if it pursues an 'objective' category of knowledge; instead, it is meant to enlist narrative to the task of politicising the present in the sense of showing the many ways in which issues of action, choice, motive and representation, in the arena of nationhood and of societies today, are always necessarily and deeply implicated in the history of related choices, motives and representations during that part of the global past which gets recognised (and misrecognised) as European colonialism.

The myriad details that constitute the micro-narratives of Europe's history of global domination and the subsequent narratives of postcolonial nationhood also remind us that it is not simply or primarily the future that has claims upon us in any given present, but also the past, whose irretrievability can be redeemed whenever the present experiences the shock of recognition which constitutes in itself a realisation of a specific unfulfilled potentiality from that past which finds its realisation in the present. Historical knowledge, like literary experience, enacts an ethics of reading and action. The past matters because we owe it recognition. How Europe colonised peoples, how that changed Europe and those peoples, and how the changed world now looks back on those pasts matters in every here and now where the book finds its readers.

Prem Poddar, Rajeev Patke and Lars Jensen

REFERENCES

Benjamin, Walter (2003), *Walter Benjamin: Selected Writings, Volume 4: 1938–1940*, ed. Howard Eiland and Michael W. Jennings, trans. Edmund Jephcott, Howard Eiland et al., Cambridge, MA and London: The Belknap Press of Harvard University Press.

Poddar, Prem and David Johnson (2005) (eds), *A Historical Companion to Postcolonial Literatures in English*, Edinburgh: Edinburgh University Press.

Belgium and its Colonies

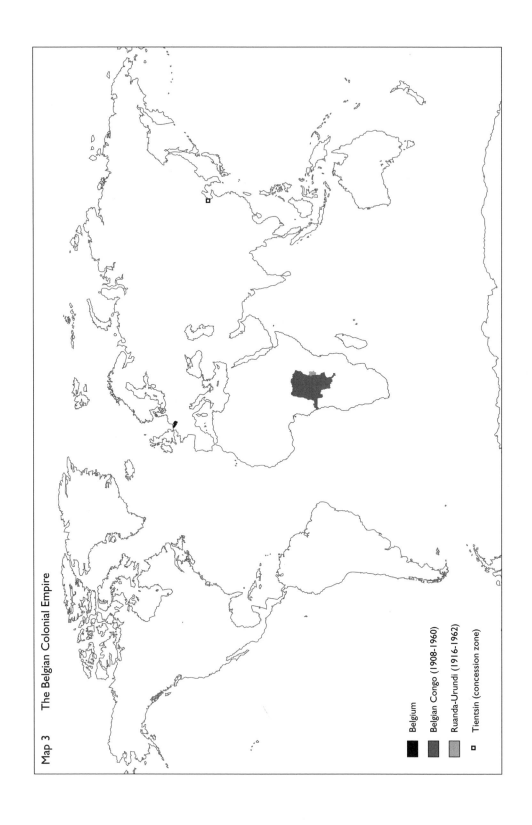

Map 3   The Belgian Colonial Empire

Belgium

Belgian Congo (1908-1960)

Ruanda-Urundi (1916-1962)

Tientsin (concession zone)

Belgium and its Colonies: Introduction

Belgium and parts of Central Africa – the present Democratic Republic of the Congo (RDC), Rwanda and Burundi – have shared a short but significant common history. The Congo Free State (CFS) – the Belgian Congo from 1908 to 1960 – was officially attributed to Leopold II, King of the Belgians (1865–1909), as a result of the notorious Berlin Conference (1884–5). After World War I and the subsequent demise of the Deutsch Ost-Afrika, 'Ruanda-Urundi', as it was called, was put under a League of Nations mandate and was ruled by Belgium from 1919 until 1962.

In the history of modern colonialism, Belgium, a young nation-state which had been created in 1830 – barely fifty years before the Scramble for Africa – was the most unlikely candidate for imperial grandeur. Despite its formidable economic and industrial prosperity, Belgium was never powerful enough to take on, exploit and administer a domain eighty-one times larger than its national territory. This disproportion between the project and the available resources has until today shaped the very nature of the three African post-colonial states. Leopold II had the ambition of using the Congo as a tool to strengthen the somewhat precarious basis of the Belgian nation and dispel the growing tensions between the ruling French-speaking upper middle class and the rising working class. His imperial venture was, however, badly received by those that he dismissed as '*les avocats de la petite Belgique*'. This lack of internal support had two major consequences. Firstly, Belgian colonialism was never a truly national, nor assimilationist project. Contrary to France where the idea of the so-called *plus grande France* entered the national consciousness from the interwar period onwards, the analogous concept of *communauté belgo-congolaise* remained in Belgium overall inoperative or, at best, peripheral. Secondly, as his personal resources were not limitless, the king had to rely heavily on international capital. As a consequence, he leased out, in the framework of the infamous concessionary régime, large portions of the Congolese territory to European and American industrialists who during the Red Rubber scandal, but also after the takeover of the CFS by Belgium in 1908, continued to curtail the power of the colonial administration (and that of the subsequent postcolonial régimes) and exert unsustainable pressure on local populations. The relative disempowerment of the administration was also compounded by the presence of Christian missionaries, often from Roman Catholic orders, who were understandably not always inclined to endorse and implement policies laid down by state officials. The Congo and Ruanda-Urundi were therefore more the reflection of Belgian internal conflicts (religious, linguistic and ideological) than the expression of a concerted and homogeneous national project.

This lack of homogeneity on the part of the colonial power was somehow mirrored by the very fragmented nature of the Congo (but not of the much smaller kingdoms of Burundi and Rwanda). In spite of some cultural unity (de Heusch; Vansina), and the prevalence of the Bantu element, the territory was, and still is, an eminently heterogeneous whole. In the neo-colonialist speech that he gave at the ceremony marking the end of Belgian colonialism on 30 June 1960, Joseph Kasavubu, the first President (1960–5) of the Republic of Congo, noted that one of the benefits of Belgian rule had been to unify the country. Whether he was right is of course very debatable, particularly if one considers that the history of the region (including Rwanda and Burundi) since independence has been one of protracted and bloody ethnic wars and genocides. The territory that Leopold II seized was as vast as Western Europe and shared, therefore, no resemblance with the oft-quoted 'blank space' to which Conrad alluded ethnocentrically. This colonial venture amalgamated human communities which had hitherto lived independently. What is now referred to as the Democratic Republic of the Congo is an incredibly diverse territory. Anthropologists have so far identified more than 360 different ethnic groups (Boone) and registered several hundred languages in the territory. Behind this mosaic, however, the country is also characterised by a number of larger cultural areas – such as the Luba, Kuba, Lunda – encompassing several smaller ethnic groups. These entities have, over the centuries, cohabited often antagonistically with one another and, for this reason, their geographical positioning has evolved and has never had the permanency that colonial ethnic mapping had first assumed (see van Overbergh). The boundaries that resulted from the Berlin Conference were the most radical signs of the denial, on the part of its Western co-signatories, of Central African history. This territorial reconfiguration reflected the ethnocentric belief that Africa, as Mudimbe demonstrated it (1994), was a *terra nullius*, that is, a no man's land, which presented the opportunity of being unambiguously converted into Western modernity. This economic, political and religious conversion was staged as a new beginning and the period before 1885 arbitrarily dismissed as 'pre-colonial'. These redefinitions were the rhetorical weapons of a systematic dismembering of local history and geography. Behind the new map of Central Africa, the co-signatories of the Berlin Conference had deliberately suppressed other histories, partly because they did not reflect the newly-rearranged territory. Some political and cultural entities, such as the Lunda or the Kongo domains, to name but two, could not be accommodated under the new régime. Their respective extension cut across the arbitrary divides separating French, Belgian, Portuguese and British colonial possessions.

   The Kingdom of Kongo (located in West Central Africa, in an area including portions of Angola, Cabinda, the Republic of Congo and the Democratic Republic of the Congo) was a powerful political and military player well before the establishment of Portuguese trading posts on the western coasts of Sub-Saharan Africa in the fifteenth century, with extensive commercial links stretching as far as the Indian Ocean. In the colonial historiography (for example, de Bouveignes), the former African kingdom is often presented as the success story of early colonisation. What is highlighted in these accounts is the conversion of the Kongo royal family to Catholicism in 1491 and the subsequent renaming of the capital city from Mbanza-Kongo to San Salvador. This encounter, however, had a much more sinister consequence as it provided Portugal with the basis on which the slave trade from Africa to Brazil would gradually develop, contribute to Portuguese prosperity and, conversely, deprive the Kongo of a vital workforce, whilst exacerbating the oligarchic nature of the dynasty. The Portuguese did not introduce the slave trade in the region but they dramatically accelerated its practice. The ravages of slavery were such that by the seventeenth century the kingdom was considerably weakened and progressively lost its regional significance. Although the dynasty was kept alive until 1914, the ancient Kongo was shared out between French, Portuguese and Belgian colonial powers after the Berlin Conference. Kongo nationalism, however, remained a force to be reckoned with, most notably in 1921 during the events surrounding the arrest, trial and imprisonment of Simon Kimbangu, the 'modern Kongo prophet' noted by Wyatt Mac Gaffey (1983), and in the period immediately before the decolonisation of the Belgian Congo, with the creation of ABAKO by Kasavubu.

The Lunda dynasty had, overall, a similar trajectory. It originated from southern Katanga (present Shaba) but from the seventeenth century onwards, after adopting the Luba political structure, it was able to expand territorially and bring other chiefdoms under its domination in an area spreading from northern Angola, north-western Zambia and the southern portion of the Democratic Republic of the Congo. It established a large network of client states. Less powerful chiefs were eager to be associated with Lunda overlords for two main reasons. Firstly, their submission meant that they became part of the Lunda sacred lineage. Secondly, they also benefited economically as the Lunda had exclusive access to trade routes. As Jan Vansina remarks, 'The new political pattern which evolved around 1600 in the Lunda capital could be taken over by any culture [and] its diffusion was to condition until 1850 the history and the general cultural evolution of a huge area'. By the middle of the nineteenth century, the Lunda hegemony was indeed starting to disintegrate as other dominant, and mainly nomadic ethnic groups such as the Chokwe and the Lwena, rose to prominence. The Lunda dynasty did not disappear – it still exists today – but its influence receded dramatically.

When the Scramble for Africa began in the last two decades of the century, the co-signatories of the Berlin Conference were therefore faced with a relative power vacuum. The downfall of former Central African nations such as the Kongo or the Lunda reinforced the popular claim that the region was indeed an ahistorical no-man's land (see Victor Hugo's famous remark: '*L'Afrique n'a pas d'histoire . . . Allez, Peuples! emparez-vous de cette terre. Prenez-la. A qui? A personne.*'). For the Catholic Church, the opening of new African territories was seen as an opportunity to revive evangelisation in western Congo, and also to take up the even more challenging task of putting a halt to the rapid expansion of Islam in the eastern part of the territory (in the Great Lakes region). This modern age crusade also aimed at eradicating slavery, a practice that had been reawakened by Muslim traders and proselytes from the Sudan. Leopold II, who was a staunch advocate of the Church in his own country, used this argument further to legitimise his ambitions and, in order to achieve his goal, he joined forces with the French anti-slavery activist Cardinal Lavigerie who made sure that his *ordre des pères blancs* became the main converting agency in the eastern provinces of the colony.

Despite this tendency to deny Central African history and to present Leopold's colonisation as the beginning of time, the colonial régime was also eager, when it served its overall strategy, to promote the idea of African historicity and, consequently, to rewrite African historiography. Two concrete examples will help us to understand this colonial propensity to engineer the past in order to meet present political objectives. When the CFS was founded, the Lunda influence was, as said before, in stark decline. CFS administrators, and subsequently Belgian officials, chose, however, to offer their support to the Lunda royal family in order that it might restore its lost prestige in exchange for co-operation. In this exercise, the colonial power actively promoted, within the strictly corseted framework of Belgian rule, the historical rights of the former Lunda 'empire' over its 'natural' vassals (see Bustin). The Lunda political organisation and power structure had been praised by European travellers (see Carvalho) and was seen as the perfect vehicle to strengthen Belgian control over the territory and to try out indirect rule in the Katanga province. There was, however, also an ulterior motive. Since the 1840s, Lunda hegemony had been repeatedly challenged by the Chokwe who had, effectively, become the most prominent regional power. The Chokwe were more martially minded than the Lunda and were, as a consequence, regarded as unruly by the colonial power. They were also nomadic and their constant movements in and out of the CFS destabilised the permanency of the newly rearranged geography that had emerged from the Berlin Conference. They needed, therefore, to be subdued and there was, until the 1930s, a constant effort on the part of colonial historiography to establish, sometimes on the basis of a partial reinterpretation of Bantu myths of origins (see Fraiture 2007), the Lunda precedence over other ethnic groups.

The second example of ethnic engineering practised by the colonial power has had up to the present day much more sinister consequences in that it has been responsible for the second genocide of the twentieth century in Rwanda and is also regarded as one of the key obstacles to the resolution of the (ongoing) bloody armed conflict between the DRC and its neighbours. Before the colonisation of Burundi and Rwanda by the Germans, Tutsis and Hutus, the two main communities, cohabited peacefully and were, as Colette Braeckman argues (1996), not fixed categories. The divide, as Braeckman contends, was more socio-economic than strictly ethnic. The Germans, and then the Belgians, however, after World War I, exacerbated the differences between the Hutus and the Tutsis in order to consolidate their domination. Under the Belgian mandate, ethnicity became the main prism through which the two groups were catalogued, fixed and controlled. Until independence the Mwami, the Tutsi king, was used as a tool to secure the implementation of Belgian indirect rule over Ruanda-Urundi. From the 1950s onwards, however, the Hutus, who made up 85 per cent of the population, started resenting this overt discrimination. According to Braeckman, the Hutu–Tutsi ethnic divide, as it was imagined and reconstructed by Belgians, is the reflection of a typically Belgian conflict imported – or 'tropicalised' as Ndaywel (1998) puts it – into Central Africa. At this point, it is important to note that Ruanda-Urundi was regarded by the Catholic Church as one of its success stories in terms of evangelisation. This conversion was carried out by missionaries who were, for the most, of Flemish extraction. They felt sympathetic towards the Hutus' plight in that they were able to compare it to their own cultural under-representation and discrimination in Belgium. There lies one of the most essential differences between French and Belgian colonialisms. In French colonies, the French language became the tool and symbol of the assimilationist policy. In the Belgian Congo and Ruanda-Urundi, on the other hand, the use of French (although it remained the predominant language) had, potentially, far-reaching political consequences. In their teaching and preaching, Flemish missionaries resorted, as a consequence, to local languages that they studied and used to disseminate their faith.

The Hutu–Tutsi conflict was, therefore, not only fuelled by the colonial ambition to secure Belgian control over the territory but, more controversially, also by the linguistic (or ethnic) divide at the heart of Belgian society. This antagonism between irredentist and unitary factors constitutes, ultimately, the background against which Belgium and its former colonies have developed since decolonisation. After the collapse of the empire, the gap between French-speaking and Flemish-speaking communities widened in Belgium and after more than forty years of institutional dismembering of the former centralised state, it is debatable whether or not they still have a common future. The same basic forces – unity, irredentism and ethnic struggles – have also shaped the histories of the Congo, Rwanda and Burundi up to the present day. Until 1965, Congolese decolonisation was marred by the Katanga secession. In his long 'reign' (1965–97) Mobutu applied, in the name of territorial unity (and with the backing of Western investors), the *divide et impera* principle that had characterised the Belgian administration in the colonial period. Since the 1990s, the ethnic question has re-emerged even more dramatically and triggered off a cycle of bloody violence that no change of régime (the Kabila father and son in the

Congo, Kagame in Rwanda) or international conference has managed to contain, let alone stop.

It is ironic, however, despite the many fractures induced by Belgian colonialism and its aftermath, the Belgian Congo remains one of the few manifestations (alongside Tintin and the national debt, one could sarcastically add) which involved a large-scale national mobilisation. The former colony has retained in the national psyche some symbolic currency. In November 2006, the RTBF, the French-speaking public television, announced in a carefully planned and edited hoax that the Flemish parliament had voted in favour of partition. The news resulted in short-lived waves of panic. In their fabricated account, the journalists also reported that the royal couple, Albert II and Paola, had fled the country and taken refuge in Kinshasa.

Pierre-Philippe Fraiture

LITERARY WORKS

Drum, Henri (1932), *Luéji ya kondé*, Brussels: Éditions de Belgique.

Esser, Joseph (1957), *Légende africaine. Iyanza, héros national nkundo*, Paris: Presses de la Cité.

Marchal, Omer (1983), *Afrique, Afrique*, Paris: Fayard.

Mpoyi-Buatu (1986), *La Re-Production*, Paris: L'Harmattan.

Mudimbe, Valentin Yves (1979), *L'écart*, Paris: Présence Africaine.

Mukagasana, Yolande and Patrick May (1997), *La Mort ne veut pas de moi*, Paris: Fixot.

Ngal, Georges (1984) [1975], *Giambatista Viko ou le viol du discours africain*, Paris: Hatier.

Ngoye, Achille Flor (1993), *Kin-la-joie, Kin-la-folie*, Paris: L'Harmattan.

Ruti, Antoine (1997), *Le Fils de Mikeno*, Lubumbashi, Éditions Impala.

Salkin, Paul (1926), *L'Afrique centrale dans cent ans. Le problème de l'évolution noire*, preface by Maurice Delafosse, Paris: Payot.

HISTORIES

Boone, Olga (1973), *Carte ethnique du Congo, quart Sud-Quest, Tervuren*: MRAC.

Bouveignes, Olivier de (1948), *Les anciens rois de Congo*, Namur: Grands Lacs.

Braeckman, Colette (1996), *Terreur africaine. Burundi, Rwanda, Zaïre: les racines de la violence*, Paris: Fayard.

Bustin, Edouard (1975), *Lunda under Belgian Rule. The Politics of Ethnicity*, Cambridge, MA: Harvard University Press.

Carvalho, Henrique A. Dias de (1890), *Etnografia e historia tradicional dos povos da Lunda*, Lisbon: Imprensa Nacional.

Fraiture, Pierre-Philippe (2007), *La Mesure de l'autre. Afrique sub-saharienne et roman ethnographique de Belgique et de France (1918–1940)*, Paris: Honoré Champion, 'Bibliothèque de Littérature Générale et Comparée'.

Heusch, Luc de (1972), *Le Roi ivre ou l'origine de l'état*, collection 'Les Essais', clxxiii, Paris: Gallimard.

Mac Gaffey, Wyatt (1983), *Modern Kongo Prophets*, Bloomington, IN: Indiana University Press.

Mudimbe, Valentin Yves (1988), *The Invention of Africa: Gnosis, Philosophy, and the Order of Knowledge*, Bloomington, IN and London: Indiana University Press.

Mudimbe, Valentin Yves (1994), *The Idea of Africa*, Bloomington, IN and London: Indiana University Press and James Currey.

Ndaywel è Nziem, Isidore [1996] (1998), *Histoire générale du Congo. De l'héritage ancien à la République Démocratique*, Paris and Brussels: Duculot.

Overbergh, Cyrille van (1907), *Les Mayombe (État Ind. du Congo)*, Brussels: Albert Dewit
    Éditeur & Institut International de Bibliographie.
Vansina, Jan (1966), *Kingdoms of the Savanna*, Madison, WI: University of Wisconsin Press.

Anthropology and Ethnography

The history of Belgian anthropology was until recently a 'missing link' in scientific research. The period 1882–1925 has now been studied in detail, but a clear view of the more recent period is still lacking. The inauguration of the Anthropological Society of Brussels (SAB) in 1882 can be seen as the starting point of Belgian anthropology. This Society concentrated on physical anthropology and was influenced by French anthropologists like Paul Broca and Paul Topinard. Members of the SAB such as Léon Vanderkindere, Emile Houzé and Victor Jacques first worked on the 'Other' within Western society, a very broad category that included labourers, women, criminals and prehistoric men. They also dealt with the history of Belgium, which they defined within a racial discourse. Researchers measured the intellectual capacities of Flemish people in the North and Walloons in the South on the basis of several physical characteristics, which were often used partially to make a claim for Flemish or Walloon superiority. After the Belgian colonisation of the Congo, the methods of physical anthropology were exported to the colony, where skulls were collected and living Congolese were measured. Studying the many races in the Congo, however, made plain that a clear distinction between races based on physical characteristics was hard to prove. The SAB remained influential until the end of the nineteenth century, but due to internal weaknesses, physical anthropology lost its predominant role in Belgian anthropology.

After 1885 Belgian anthropologists became more interested in colonial ethnography. The Société d'Études Coloniales (SEC), a society that specifically concentrated on the study of the colony and united the first colonisers, was inaugurated in 1894. The first ethnographic studies were structured according to standardised queries and concentrated on material culture. The first ethnographic exhibitions in Belgium were organised in connection with the World Exhibitions in Antwerp (1885 and 1894) and Brussels-Tervuren (1897). In all three cases a 'Negro village' was erected, which for many visitors became their first encounter with the colony. The organisation of the colonial exhibitions led to the installation of the first permanent colonial museum in Tervuren with the support of King Leopold II (1898). It marked the starting point of a flourishing colonial ethnography. Tervuren Museum curators like Théodore Masui, Alphonse de Haulleville and Émile Coart were influenced by British and American evolutionism. Evolutionists considered Congolese culture to be a living example of an earlier evolutionary stage that was comparable with European prehistory. The ethnographers in Tervuren were less pessimistic than the members of the SAB and found that the evolution of Congolese culture showed traces of civilisation, which gave rise to a hopeful future.

The new (and present-day) museum building, came into being at the time of the World Exhibition in Brussels-Tervuren in 1910. Joseph Maes, who led the Department of Ethnography single-handedly, was an adherent of German diffusionism and tried to reconstruct the complete history of the Congolese economy by mapping the dispersion of material culture and defining cultural areas or zones. He was also the first curator of the Africa Museum in Tervuren to travel to the Congo, where he led an ethnographic expedition in the south of the Belgian colony (1913–14). In a similar move to the physical anthropologists, however, Maes tried to adjust data to an existing theory instead of analysing the data first and drawing conclusions afterwards. The classification of his collected objects did not result in a clear view of the elusive past. Mixed areas soon replaced pure ethnic zones once Maes tried to map his results. Like Masui, Coart and de Haulleville, he defended the link between Congo and Egypt, a presupposition that led to serious attacks by his successors.

One of these, Frans M. Olbrechts, began his academic career in 1925 as a student at Columbia University in New York as a postdoctoral fellow under the guidance of Franz Boas. This marked the start of a new chapter in the history of Belgian anthropology. With the support of the Bureau of Ethnology, Olbrechts was able to conduct fieldwork among Native Americans like the Cherokee, Onondaga and Tuscarora. After his return to Belgium he became head of the Department of Ethnography at the Musée Cinquantenaire in Brussels. Olbrechts also taught ethnology at the Rijksuniversiteit Gent, where he later on established the Centre for the Study of African Art. Olbrechts was influenced by functionalism, diffusionism and the historical method of Boas. Several of his students, like Albert Maesen, Marie Louise Bastin and Hugette van Geluwe, later on conducted research at the Africa Museum of Tervuren. Maesen even accompanied Olbrechts during his expedition to the Ivory Coast (1938–39). In the 1950s Maesen travelled to Congo where he collected more than 8,000 objects. He was to succeed Olbrechts as director of the museum in 1958 and became a professor at the Katholieke Universiteit Leuven (KUL) where he held a chair in material culture. Still, initiatives were seldom coherent and a general view was lacking. Other students of Olbrechts like Daniel Biebuyck, who conducted fieldwork in eastern Congo (1949–53), moved to the United States.

It was only after 1970 that universities took over the leading role in Belgian anthropology. The first teaching of ethnography and anthropology at universities dates back to 1908, when Edouard de Jonghe started an institut colonial that was part of the École de Commerce. In 1973 a separate Department of Social and Cultural Anthropology was inaugurated at the KUL. On the French speaking side of the country the Université Libre de Bruxelles started the Centre d'Anthropologie Culturelle. As stated above, the history of Belgian anthropology after 1925 remains largely unstudied. Mention should be made, however, of the very important contributions made by Luc de Heusch, one of Belgium's foremost disciples of Claude Lévi-Strauss, and those of Jan Vansina. Finally, Belgian cultural anthropology owes much of its development to the more empirical and less theoretically grounded work of missionaries. Figures such as Gustav Hulstaert, Victor Roelens and Pacide Tempels have had a lasting impact in the field of ethnography, paremiology, linguistics and folklore.

Maarten Couttenier

LITERARY WORKS
Delhaise-Arnould, Marie-Louis (1926), *Amedra. Roman de mœurs nègres du Congo belge*, Brussels: Renaissance d'Occident.
Drum, Henri (1932), *Luéji ya kondé*, Brussels: Éditions de Belgique.
Esser, Joseph (1960), *Matuli, fille d'Afrique*, Brussels and Paris: Elsevier.
Mudimbe, Valentin Yves (1979), *L'Écart*, Paris: Présence Africaine.

HISTORIES
Bogers, Koen and Patrick Wymeersch (1987), *De Kongo in de Vlaamse Fiktie en Reisverhalen*, Brussels: Afrika Studie- en Dokumentatiecentrum.

Couttenier, Maarten (2005), *Congo Tentoongesteld. Een geschiedenis van de Belgische antropologie en het museum van Tervuren (1882–1925)*, Leuven: Acco.

Fraiture, Pierre-Philippe (2007), *La Mesure de l'autre. Afrique subsaharienne et roman ethnographique de Belgique et de France (1918–1940)*, Paris: Éditions Champion.

Mudimbe, Valentin Yves (1988), *The Invention of Africa: Gnosis, Philosophy, and the Order of Knowledge*, Bloomington, IN and London: Indiana University Press.

Petridis, Constantijn (2001), *Frans Olbrechts 1899–1958. Op zoek naar kunst in Afrika.* Antwerpen: Etnografisch Museum Antwerpen.

Pirotte, Jean (1973), *Périodiques missionnaires belges d'expression française. Reflets de cinquante années d'évolution d'une mentalité 1889–1940*, Louvain: Publications Universitaires de Louvain.

Vellut, Jean-Luc (1994), 'Ressources scientifiques, culturelles et humaines de l'africanisme en Belgique. Perspectives sur un patrimoine d'outre-mer et sa mise en valeur', *Cahiers Africains* 9-10-11: 115–44.

Anti-colonial Resistance in the Former Belgian Colonies

The Democratic Republic of the Congo, Republic of Rwanda, and Republic of Burundi have different histories of anti-colonial resistance movements, due to the different conditions under which each became a colony of Belgium. The largest of the three former colonies, Congo, was not at first a colony, but a private domain of King Leopold II before becoming a colony in 1908. Congo was annexed to Belgium under the Charte Coloniale Belge, whereas Rwanda and Burundi were under the control of the German Residency in colonial German East Africa from 1890 to 1919. During World War I, the areas that are now Rwanda and Burundi were occupied by the Belgian Force Publique (the colonial army), and in 1919 they became a Belgian-controlled League of Nations mandate under the name of Ruanda-Urundi. In 1946, Ruanda-Urundi became a United Nation's trust territory overseen by Belgium. Rwanda and Burundi became separate governing entities in April 1962, after delegates from the two countries failed to reach an agreement on a common independent future.

The historians B. Jewsiewicki and Georges Nzongola-Ntalaja differentiate among various stages of anti-colonial resistance. They distinguish between the primary rebellion, which was directed against the initial European presence and the slave trade in the earliest colonial period, and such collective anti-colonial uprisings as religious movements, rural peasant rebellions and urban trade unionism. The former were isolated and regional and the latter were the forerunners that led to the nationalist and independence movements in Congo, Rwanda and Burundi. Anti-colonial resistance in the Congo can be attributed to a state of constant oppression experienced through the social, political and economic policies of King Leopold, the Belgian colonial government, and the concessions and enterprises that were supported by the government: the *corvée* or forced labour practices (in ivory, rubber and mineral extraction), which were driven by cruel punishment, such as the loss of limbs or flogging with the *chicotte*; *porterage*; compulsory crop farming and taxes; the *chefferie* system, in which local leaders were chosen not according to tradition, but for their loyalty to Belgian colonial authorities; and racial segregation.

Similar to the anti-colonial uprisings in Congo, the sources of rural rebellions in Ruanda-Urundi often stemmed from the same issues of *corvée* and compulsory farming and taxes, but also from a growing ethnic divide between Tutsi and Hutu, with the colonial privileging of one group over the other in education and politics. During the German Residency and throughout the Belgian military rule and colonial supervision of Rwanda and Burundi, 'divide and rule' policies included radically reshaping and hierarchising ethnic groups to conform to European standards of categorisation and efficiency. The most unfortunate heirs to this German, and later Belgian creation of castes, were the Hutu, Tutsi and Twa groups in Burundi and Rwanda. Before World War I, pockets of anti-colonial resistance were formed to oppose the German colonial consolidation of independent chiefdoms into one unified kingdom. Chiefs Kilima and Maconco espoused anti-colonial resistance to these German policies, and German colonial troops intervened against them in October 1905, burning all the villages on their path through Kilima's chiefdom. Colonial forces attacked the independent chiefdoms of Kanugunu and Busokoza in 1906 and 1908, respectively. Although interregnum fighting was not unknown to the region, the 1908 policies of German Governor-General von Rechenberg and Resident Captain Fonck increased the tension by recognising, contrary to tradition, a single *mwami* (king). Until World War I, pockets of anti-colonial resistance existed in what is now the north-east regions of Burundi, where Chiefs Mbanzabugabo and Busokoza refused colonial Germany's policy of consolidation. After World War I, the major acts of anti-colonial resistance by autochthonous people were directed against the Belgian *chefferie* system in rural areas, where local leaders were chosen according to the pre-established German system of loyalty to colonial authorities. Historian René Lemarchand identifies four major regions in Burundi and Rwanda where anti-colonial activities stemmed from a confluence of these forces as well as from the economic devastation and natural disasters. He also sees these revolts as precursors to contemporary ethnic conflicts in the two nations.

Mistreatment and oppression coupled with economic hardships in the early 1920s and early 1930s in Congo paved the way for the anti-colonial syncretic mass religious movements of Maria N'koï, the *kitawala*, and Simon Kimbangu. Maria N'koï (Marie aux léopards) in 1915 led a peasant revolt in the south, preaching that the incarnation of the ancestors would intervene to throw the white colonists out and bring in the reign of the righteous in a new world. The *kitawala* movement was also messianic in nature and promised a new order free from 'white' rule, but practised non-violence as a tactic against the oppressive colonial régime and policies. The Kimbanguist movement of the Eglise de Jésus-Christ sur la Terre par le Prophète Simon Kimbangu (EJCSK) was religious in origin, but became politicised after the arrest and life imprisonment of its founder Simon Kimbangu in 1921. In addition, the fight for religious recognition of the movement led its members to become active in the fight for civil and democratic rights. While these religious leaders did not directly link social and economic emancipation to political freedom, the insurrections they led were in regions most permeated by European economic and social programmes, and their beliefs were founded on the idea of a new social order promising that the departure of the white colonists would bring about equal distribution of wealth and social equity. These ideals can be found in similar syncretic religious movements in Rwanda and Burundi, and they also became the basis for later anti-colonial revolts in the decolonisation phase.

Characterised as messianic resistance movements, the rural revolts in Ruanda-Urundi were named after their leaders and often based on a notion of a return to a pre-colonial rule of local kingdoms with an 'ideal king', called *anti-roi* by historians. The Rubengebenge revolt began under German colonial rule in 1912 and continued through to 1922, when Ruanda-Urundi was under Belgian supervision. The Inamuvyeyi Nyavyinshi revolt (1922) took place in the north on the Kagera river, near the border of what is now Rwanda.

Historian Joseph Gahama relates that the Runyota-Kanyarufunzo revolt (1922) was messianic in nature, invoking the spirit of Kiranga (a god favourable to kingship). It came on the heels of a consolidation of power in the Buyenzi region and a catastrophic disease killing 80 per cent of the local cattle. It gained strength from a peasantry angered by road and marshland *corvées* and obligatory coffee growing. Runyota led this rural uprising under the banner of 'righteous anger'.

By 1929, the Belgian colonial administration had begun consolidating more small independent chiefdoms to maintain better control of the regions. In Burundi, primarily Bezi and Batare princes (*ganwa*) vied for control, yet demands of *corvée* and taxes by these new chiefs for the colonial government, along with economic hardships on the local peasant populations, created rural unrest in the north-west Ndora region in 1932. In what has become known as the Inamujandi revolt (1934), named after its leader, an elderly woman Inamujandi (or Mujande), protesters burned Christian mission schools and hundreds of huts before being crushed by Force Publique troops. In Rwanda, the German and Belgian colonial policies of country consolidation under one king (*mwami*) were also met with resistance. In the April 1912 campaign led by German Resident Gudovius in northern Rwanda to suppress Chief Ndungutse's rebellion (which was supported by followers of Muhumusa, wife of a Chief and a messianic-style leader of her own rebellion in 1911), colonial troops attacked Ndungutse and his village with orders to burn the village, crops and settlements, and kill all those who resisted. The Belgians encountered the same kind of resistance in the northern Rukiga region.

In the Congo, where there were many regional anti-colonial uprisings in the 1930s, colonial administrators and missionaries documented more rural uprisings among the peasants who were forced to work in the *corvée* or were made to cultivate crops by colonial and corporate orders. In 1931, local growers destroyed cotton plants in the Ndengese region in opposition to forced cultivation practices. In May 1931, the Pende uprising in Kwilu, which then formed part of the Kwango district, was the first collective action taken by a group of peasants (*coupeurs de fruit*) and an ethnic group (Pende) against both the Belgian administration and colonial agricultural industries. Even though slave labour had been abolished legally, as a result of the pressure from the international abolitionist Congo Reform Association in 1897–8, the colonial administration turned a blind eye to company-based *corvées*, which still existed and included forced labour for road building and village relocation. The Pende uprising of the *coupeurs de fruit* was the result of several factors: the fall in palm prices by some 50–60 per cent; imposition of annual taxes which remained the same even though wages decreased significantly; and the continuation of forced labour by the Huileries du Congo Belge (HCB). The swift reprisals by the Force Publique claimed at least 500 Congolese lives.

After several uprisings throughout the 1930s, the Belgian authorities constructed exile or *relégation* camps to contain insurgents. But organised rebellions among Congolese workers continued during the 1940s, immediately before the rise of pan-African independence movements of the 1950s, and can be traced again to the cumulative effect of living under colonial rule and economic hardships imposed on the Congolese during World War II. In December 1941, miners working for Union Minière du Haut Katanga went on strike in Elisabethville (Lumumbashi) demanding equal treatment. The Force Publique repressed the strikers killing 40–60 miners and injuring countless others. Miners in Manono working for Géomines went on strike using *kitawala* principles of non-violence, demanding better working conditions and higher salaries. The strike of dock workers in Matadi, the port city at the mouth of the Congo river, in November 1945, stopped ocean-going traffic. Although none of the worker-based anti-colonial movements called for the end of colonial rule, they helped identifying the economic and social practices that would become touchstones of the independence movement. However, an earlier uprising, the February 1944 mutiny of Congolese conscripted soldiers in the Force Publique at the garrison in Luluabourg (Kananga), nearly crippled the entire colonial enterprise when the soldiers brought into question the authority of white Belgian officers over black African soldiers. Such sentiment threatened Belgian power at all levels, and the mutiny was quickly brought under control for fear that its ideas of racial discrimination might spill over into the general population and create widespread unrest.

When the French President, Charles de Gaulle, offered independence to the French colonies in West Africa in 1945, it triggered a greater drive for pan-African independence movements in the Belgian colonies. In 1956, several leaders including Patrice Lumumba and Joseph Kasavubu gained political prominence as members of a group of anti-colonial leaders who sent a memorandum to Governor-General M. Cornélis of the Belgian Congo, demanding independence and African participation in governance, citing among other things the desire to have the same kind of democratising policies of local elections that had begun in 1953 and 1956 in Ruanda-Urundi. Even though Brussels had created rudimentary local elections in Ruanda-Urundi, colonial caste policies had caused educational, political and social dominance of the Tutsi. In March 1957, a group of nine Hutu intellectuals wrote an anti-colonial manifesto ('Bahutu Manifesto') criticising the Belgian system of governance, demanded a greater voice in local governance and the abandonment of the caste system. From this manifesto developed several anti-colonial political parties, including the Mouvement Social Muhutu (MSM), supported by the Catholic Church, and organised by Grégoire Kayibanda, who later became the first President of independent Rwanda in 1962; the Association pour la Promotion Sociale de la Masse (APROSOMA), which was also committed to the democratisation of Rwanda, but through a mass movement regardless of caste affiliation; and the Union Nationale Rwandaise (UNAR) organised by François Rukeba, which was anti-Belgian and pro-traditionalist and monarchist, especially after the death of King Mutara. In September 1959, Kigali became the centre for a flurry of anti-colonial meetings and the creation of new political parties, including a progressive democratic group called Rassemblement Démocratique Ruandais (RADER) led by Chief Bwanakweli and Kayibandi's new party, the Parti du Mouvement de l'Emancipation Hutu (PARMEHUTU). In November 1959, anti-colonial rioting and inter-ethnic violence swept the country, but was suppressed by Belgian forces after the colonial government rejected a plan for the *mwami* to restore order. The political unrest resulted in tens of thousands of refugees fleeing the country and set the pattern for future violence between ethnic groups. A Belgian-assisted coup d'état on 28 January 1961 in Gitarama placed a republican government in Rwanda. However, the Hutu élite of the PARMEHUTU (although aided by colonial authorities) strategically renamed a local auxiliary administrative post as 'prefect', forcing the Residency to come to terms with anti-colonial sentiment and to announce the changes in the political power structures.

In Burundi, two main political parties from the dynastic traditions of the Batare and Bezi *chefferies* furthered the progress of the anti-colonial movement in the late 1950s. In 1957, Chief Léopold Bihumugani organised the Parti de l'Unité et du Progrès National (UPRONA), after a group of chiefs sent a petition to the UN Visiting Mission protesting the colonial administration's interference in the traditional role of the monarch. The next leader of UPRONA, university-educated Prince Louis Rwagasore, who was more militant in his anti-colonial stance, insisted upon immediate independence from Brussels, and monarchical legitimacy. Rwagasore's anti-Belgian rhetoric cemented a mixed-ethnic popular and rural nationalist movement until his assassination in 1961. In contrast to Rwagasore's programme, the Parti Démocratique Chrétien (PDC) was not militant in its approach to self-governance, rather the PDC's sense of nation-building was anti-colonial in its desire for a slow economic emancipation and political freedom from Brussels. Burundi became a constitutional monarchy in August 1962 that lasted until 1966 and like Rwanda has suffered from inter-ethnic violence.

In the Congo, the ban on political parties until 1957 limited anti-colonial collective actions. Trade unionism was accepted as a legal form of organisation from 1946 and was a conduit for such future independence leaders as Patrice Lumumba. Due to the restrictive measures for the creation of any Congolese political organisations, other anti-colonial resistance alliances often organised around ethnic or regional groups, which ultimately led to political fragmentation during the final push for independence in the late 1950s. The earliest such group formed was Joseph Kasavubu's ABAKO (Alliance des Bakongo) based around Leopoldville (Kinshasa) in 1950. Later came LUKA (Union Kwangolaise pour l'Indépendence et la Liberté) in the Kwango district; UNIMO (Union Mongo) in the Equateur; BALUBAKAT (Association des Baluba du Katanga) in the Katanga; and the MSM (Mouvement Solidaire Muluba) in the Kasai. They all became political contenders during the first elections in 1959. The Parti National du Progrès (PNP) was a creation of the Belgian colonial authorities and was not respected by leaders of the African-organised anti-colonial resistance groups. Antoine Gizenga's Parti Solidaire Africain (PSA) and Patrice Lumumba's Mouvement National Congolais (MNC), formed in 1958, both espoused a policy of unification and did not identify themselves with one region, thus creating an alliance of working class, peasantry and the *évolués*. The participation in the All African Peoples' Conference in Accra, Ghana, in 1958, intensified Congolese anti-colonial activities and solidified aspirations for independence. September 1959 marked the date of an important joint memorandum by the ABAKO and PSA parties, which other parties joined later, delivered to the colonial authorities. It stated their refusal to participate in anti-democratic local elections in December. But the decisive anti-colonial revolt in Congo took place on 4 January 1959 when the ABAKO party's request to meet was denied. An uncontainable riot in Leopoldville (Kinshasa) followed, which lasted three days and caused severe damage to European property, Catholic missions and social centres. This led to the arrival of local police forces, the Force Publique and Belgian paratroopers to support Belgian colonial rule and violently to suppress the uprising. Under pressure to negotiate a settlement, Belgian authorities agreed to set independence day for 30 June 1960. Decolonisation was rapid. The anti-colonial resistance begun only some decades earlier in rural regions had become transformed into a mass movement for independence which brought colonial rule to an end.

Carina Yervasi

LITERARY WORKS
Conrad, Joseph (1902), *Heart of Darkness*, Edinburgh and London: Blackwood and Sons.
Cornélus, Henri (1954), *Kufa*, Brussels: Renaissance du Livre.
Debertry, Léon (1953), *Kitawala*, Elisabethville: Essor du Congo.
Gillès, Daniel (1960), *La Termitière*, Paris: Gallimard.
Walschap, Gerard [1953] (1956), [*Oproer in Congo*] *Insurrection au Congo*, Brussels: Elsevier.

HISTORIES

Adi, Hakim and Marika Sherwood (2003), *Pan-African History: Political Figures from Africa and the Diaspora since 1787*, London and New York: Routledge.

Anyang' Nyong'o, Peter (ed.) (1987), *Popular Struggles for Democracy in Africa*, London and New Jersey: Zed Books.

Ewans, Martin (2002), *European Atrocity, African Catastrophe: Leopold II, the Congo Free State and its Aftermath*, London: RoutledgeCurzon.

Gahama, Joseph (1983), *Le Burundi sous administration belge*, Paris: Karthala.

— (1985), 'La révolte de Runyota-Kanyarufunzo au Burundi (1922)', *Société et Pouvoirs dans l'Afrique des Grands Lacs* 3: 23–39.

James, C. L. R. (1969), *A History of Pan African Revolt*, Washington, DC: Drum and Spear Press.

Jewsiewicki, Bogumil (1976), 'La Contestation social et la naissance du prolétariat au Zaire au cours de la première moitié du XXè Siècle', *Canadian Journal of African Studies* 10 (1): pp. 47–70.

Kanza, Thomas (1972), *Conflict in the Congo: The Rise and Fall of Lumumba*, Harmondsworth: Penguin African Library.

Lemarchand, René (1994), *Burundi: Ethnocide as Discourse and Practice*, Cambridge: Woodrow Wilson Center Press and Cambridge University Press.

— (1970), *Rwanda and Burundi*, New York: Praeger Publishers.

— (1964), *Political Awakening in the Belgian Congo*, Berkeley, CA: University of California Press.

Louis, William Roger and Jean Stengers (eds) (1968), *E. D. Morel's History of the Congo Reform Movement*, London: Clarendon Press.

Markowitz, Marvin D. (1970), 'The Missions and Political Development in the Congo', *The Journal of the International African Institute* 40 (3): 234–7.

Morel, Edmund Dene (1904), *King Leopold's Rule in Africa*, London: William Heinemann.

Nelson, Samuel H. (1994), *Colonialism in the Congo Basin, 1880–1940*, Athens, OH: Center for International Studies.

Nzongola-Ntalaja, Georges (2002), *The Congo from Leopold to Kabila: A People's History*, London and New York: Zed Books.

Prunier, Gérard (1995), *The Rwanda Crisis: History of a Genocide*, New York: Columbia University Press.

Simbandumwe, Samuel S. (1992), 'Understanding the Role of a Modern Prophet in Kimbanguist Hymns', *History of Religions* 32 (2): 165–83.

Welch, Claude E. (1980), *Anatomy of Rebellion*, Albany, NY: State University Press of New York.

Witte, Ludo de [1999] (2001), *The Assassination of Lumumba*, London and New York: Verso.

Woddis, Jack (1960), *Africa: The Roots of Revolt*, New York: The Citadel Press.

The 'Arab Campaign'

This armed conflict, which took place from 1892 to 1894, can be described as the war that was fought by Leopold II's Congo Free State against the so-called 'Arabs', Swahili or Afro-Arabs from Zanzibar and the coastal region of East Africa, who had settled in eastern Congo as they became involved in the search for slaves and ivory. Unlike most colonial conflicts, the purpose of the 'Arab Campaign' was not the subjugation of an enemy native population. Instead, it was more a struggle between two rival powers competing for the possession of the interior of the Congo and the control of the ivory trade, which constituted an important source of income at the time.

The conflict broke out as a result of the defection of a significant number of African auxiliaries who worked for the Afro-Arabs. This brought about a reversal in the balance of power in favour of the Congo Free State. These allies of the Congo Free State were deployed in the wider context of military operations as well as in the sphere of logistics and provisioning. On the side of the Congo Free State, around 10,000 men were directly or indirectly involved in various military operations, with 60,000 to 70,000 on the side of the Afro-Arabs, who never managed to combine their forces. The army of the Congo Free State was very similar to that of the Afro-Arabs as far as composition and organisation were concerned because of the low number of cadre personnel. Various auxiliary forces operated, mostly within a very loose structure, together with a small nucleus of what could be called 'professional soldiers'. Around half the fighters on the Afro-Arab side lost their lives, compared with 2,000–3,000 on the side of the Congo Free State.

There is no doubt that the 'Arab Campaign' is highly significant to the history of the Congo. The military and political subjugation of the Afro-Arabs enabled the Congo Free State to annexe an area that made up about a third of its territory, and this – with a minimum of resources – ended up shaping the face of present-day Congo. Furthermore, the settling of the 'Arab question' safeguarded future profits and hence the continued existence of Leopold II's colonial enterprise.

The long-distance trade to the east coast basically came to an end, and the Congo Free State to a large extent gained control of the ivory trade. The spoils of war – at least twenty tonnes of ivory – also generated substantial profits. In 1895, Antwerp rivalled London as the primary ivory market in the world.

More than 6,000 prisoners of war, the majority of whom were conscripted into the Force Publique, produced major savings in the budget for the recruitment of foreign soldiers and workers. This in turn created the space for the intensification of the rubber trade, which required a vast number of armed personnel to impose rubber production by force. Here lies most probably the explanation of the spectacular rise in rubber harvesting from 1895 onwards, with all its dramatic consequences for the population groups involved.

Philippe Marechal

LITERARY WORKS
Grégoire, Herman (1921), *Makako, Singe d'Afrique*, Paris: La Renaissance du Livre.
Straven, Egide (1946), *Kapiri-Pi. Roman africain*, Brussels: La Renaissance du Livre.

HISTORIES
Bennett, Norman R. (1986), *Arab versus European. Diplomacy and War in Nineteenth-Century East Central Africa*, New York and London: Holmes and Meier.
Ceulemans, P. (1959), *La Question arabe et le Congo (1883–1892)*, Brussels: Académie Royale des Sciences Coloniales.
Hinde, Sidney Langford (1897), *The Fall of the Congo Arabs*, London: Methuen.
Marechal, Philippe (1992), *De 'Arabische' campagne in het Maniema-gebied (1892–1894). Situering binnen het kolonisatieproces in de Onafhankelijke Kongostaat*, Tervuren: The Royal Museum for Central Africa.

Vellut, Jean-Luc (1984), La Violence armée dans l'état Indépendant du Congo. Ténèbres et clartés dans l'histoire d'un état conquérant, *Cultures et Développement* 16: 3–4, 671–707.

Colonial and Postcolonial Exhibitions in Belgium (1885–2005)

Between 1885 and 1958, ten international exhibitions with noteworthy colonial sections were held in Belgium. The 'colonial' sections of these universal and international exhibitions of the late nineteenth century and the early twentieth century had several objectives. Firstly, to promote the economic potential of the Congo; secondly, to justify Belgian presence in the colony as a means of introducing civilisation and eradicating slavery; and, finally, to emphasise the civilising influence of the Europeans in contrast with the barbarous nature of the 'Other'. The phenomenon of living exhibits, fashionable in Belgium since the mid- to late nineteenth century, manifested itself in the form of 'Congolese' going about their tasks in reconstructions of villages. These experiences continue to shock us perhaps more than the conditions of recruitment and the accidental deaths.

The dates of the largest recreation of Congolese life under the patronage of King Leopold II (1897), and of the first exposition of the Belgian Congo (1910), are also two moments in which the Museum of Tervuren began to take shape, first as the Museum of the Congo (1898–1909) and then as the Museum of the Belgian Congo (1910–60). The material culture of the Congo occupied an important position in this museum. The attention given to these cultures by curators was inevitably reductive, commensurate to the ignorance towards them and to the mistaken way in which they were represented. Plaster figures of ethnographic groups, a technique intended to liven up the shows, helped the West form a popular image of the peoples represented as primitive, naïve or helpless. Paradoxically, the existence of a strong artistic sense in the Congo was underlined in the same exhibition space.

Remaining in the tradition of the first exhibitions, Gent 1913 was particularly notable for the *Panorama du Congo*, a gigantic naturalist and post-impressionist painting by Alfred Bastien and Paul Mathieu, which attempted to place the Congo in its modern and natural context, from the port-town Matadi to the equatorial forest. The great art déco exhibitions which followed, Antwerp 1930 and Brussels 1935, demonstrated the pride that was taken in the development of Belgian Africa.

After the trauma of the first atomic bombs and at the height of the Cold War, the 1958 exhibition was dedicated to mankind, and its mission in a pacific world, in a better world. Belgian Africa took up eight hectares and included seven palaces and pavilions dedicated to the ecomonic, industrial, scientific and spiritual domains of the Belgian Congo. Despite its modern presentation, the tone of the exhibition was set by the Minister of the Colonies Auguste Buisseret's speech, a high point of paternalism at a time when the general atmosphere was of decolonisation. A further contributor to this tone was *Congorama*, a film presented in a multimedia environment which glorified the colonial project, only a few weeks before the riots of January 1959 in Leopoldville.

In 1985, twenty-five years after decolonisation, the UROME (Union Royale Belge pour le Congo et les pays d'Outre-Mer) exhibition continued the tradition of pride towards Belgian actions in the world, especially the colonial project in the Congo and Cooperation in Zaire (1885–1985). Cent Ans de Regards Belges, of a totally different ilk, was the first of the new critical exhibitions which characterised the end of the twentieth century and the beginning of the twenty-first. Beginning with an idea from the film director Balufu

Bakupa Kanyinda, it explored 100 years of images taken from books, photography, film, cartoons, the plastic arts, school textbooks, lithographs and postal stamps. In visiting it, the public became aware of the impregnation of Belgian society by these images, charged with stereotypes and with racism, and gained the intellectual tools needed to analyse them and distance themselves from them.

Further exhibitions confronted the moral stance of their time with that of the past. Het museum van de Natie (The Museum of the Nation), an unconventional and politically committed project, offered a reflection on Belgian colonisation and the Congo's recent history whilst focusing on the Museum of Tervuren which it placed in both the new federal Belgium and in postmodern, multicultural and multimedia society.

The exhibition ExitCongoMuseum, Un Siècle d'Art avec ou sans Papiers, investigated the way in which ethnographical collections – fragments of the Congolese cultural heritage – found their way to the Musée Royal de l'Afrique Centrale and how, once there, they were presented, studied and interpreted. It also looked into how the journey colonialisation brought upon them played a role in initiating Belgians to the Congo in general. That is, in being removed from the environment which gave them meaning and placed in a European museum, they were transformed into anonymous objects of contemplation according to European aesthetic norms, into props of colonial propaganda and into the elements constituting the creation of a popular European image of the Congo.

Two years later, the exhibition La Mémoire du Congo, Le Temps Colonial, was the preliminary step needed for a calm renovation of the Musée Royal de l'Afrique Centrale. This exercise in democratisation, combining diachronic and thematic approaches, rested on the recent advances in historical research around the world. The exhibition began with a journey into the long history of Central Africa, in order to explain to visitors that colonisation did not take place in a vacuum; after this, they were taken to the Congo Free State, the Belgian Congo and, finally, to Mobutu's Zaire.

If we consider the reactions that these exhibitions provoked, it seems clear that the passions and emotions of the colonial period are still very much alive. A public debate based around the exhibition and a conference on colonial violence, organised by the museum, made it clear that Belgian society is still divided between those who defend colonisation as a civilising movement, and those who see it as one of – notably cultural – violence, and of humiliation. The debate is also present in Congolese society, which is divided between a qualified acceptance of the Belgian colonial project and its rejection.

The year 2005 ended with the appearance of an erudite essay by Maarten Couttenier on the representation of the Congo in which parallels are drawn between the history of the Tervuren Museum and that of Belgian anthropology.

Sabine Cornélis

LITERARY WORKS

Daeninckx, Didier (1998), *Cannibal*, Paris: Verdier.

Decker, Jacques de (1985), *La grande roué*, Paris: Grasset.

Morand, Paul (1927), *Magie noire*, Paris: Ferenczi.

Simenon, Georges (1976), 'L' Heure du nègre, in G. Simenon, À la recherchè de l' homme nu. Mes Apprentissages 2, Paris: Union Générale d' Éditions, pp. 45–106.

HISTORIES

Asselberghs, H. and D. Lesage (1999), *Het museum van de natie. Van kolonialisme tot globalisering*, Brussels: Yves Gevaert.

Corbey, R. (1989), *Wildheid en beschaving. De Europese verbeelding van Afrika*, Ambo: Baarn.

Couttenier, Maarten (2005), *Congo tentoongesteld. Een geschiedenis van de Belgische antropologie en het museum van Tervuren (1822–1925)*, Leuven and Tervuren: ACCO-MRAC.

Jacquemin, Jean-Pierre (2000), *Notre Congo/Onze Kongo. La propagande coloniale belge: fragments pour une étude critique*, Brussels: CEC.

Vellut, Jean-Luc (2005) (ed.), *La Mémoire du Congo. Le temps colonial*, Tervuren: Editions Snoeck/Musée Royal de l'Afrique Centrale.

Wynants, Maurits (1997), *Des Ducs de Brabant aux villages congolais. Tervuren et l'exposition coloniale de 1897*, Tervuren: Musée Royal de l'Afrique Centrale.

Zaïre 1885–1985. Cent ans de regards belges, Brussels: CEC.

Comics and the Belgian Congo

The history of comics in the Belgian Congo (or during Mobutu's period, Zaire) begins with Hergé's *Tintin au Congo* (1931). Commissioned by a pro-colonial Catholic newspaper publisher, Hergé's racialised images are less shocking if situated within the full range of inter-war visual images that appeared in print. 'Cannibal humour' caricatures were common, a genre best known for its highly racialised, slapstick icons of primitive cannibals stirring human body parts in immense cooking pots. A former colonial agent, Fernand Dineur, also published a comic album about Belgian colonial life, *Tif et Tondu au Congo* (1939).

The first Congolese-produced comics were printed in a Catholic colonial newspaper seeking a Congolese reading public in the early 1930s; others followed in the 1950s. In the post-war period, semi-didactic comics for Congolese audiences proliferated. Printed in official and missionary news media, their official and missionary producers imagined that Congolese audiences would not notice their racial slurs and racialised semiotics. The longest lasting was *Mbumbulu*, which first appeared in *Nos Images* (1946) and later in album form (1956). Colonial advertising companies also appealed to Congolese consumers with more deracialised comic messages, such as Klim milk and Aspro pill advertisements. Catholic missionary producers turned from comics-in-print to comics-on-screen, with a popular Matamata and Pilipili film series, whose Laurel and Hardy-like characters became a postcolonial comic series, produced by Mongo Sisé.

An urban youth culture began to develop in the postwar period, as did colonial concerns about delinquency and unemployment. The coded language and subculture known as 'Hindu-Bill' that developed among the disaffected, wry youth owed inspiration in part to American Westerns and comics, and continued into the postcolonial period. New comic forms exploded in the Congo from about the time Hergé arranged to have *Tintin au Congo* reprinted for the Congolese in the *Zaire* magazine in 1969. The range included rather dull development comics; the use of serial, caricatured juxtapositions in popular paintings; a promotional comic on Mobutu's life story; and ephemeral street comics. The emergence in the early 1970s of a comic-producing subculture featured a semi-savage-looking school teacher known as Apolosa. At the same time Apollo dances and Kinshasa's 'Pepsi generation' pressed back against Mobutu's first authenticity campaigns. The now world-famous, 'popular' painter, Chéri Samba, took part in this explosion of street comics in Kinshasa, and later moved on to serial art paintings. Belgian development agencies and the French cultural attaché agency attempted to capture Congolese comic artists and audiences for postcolonial development and co-operation agendas. These efforts encouraged the formation of comic artist associations, as well as comic workshops, courses, exhibits and contests. The most independent, Kinshasa-based comic artist, the wry and feisty political commentator, Mfumu'eto, began producing ephemeral comic book series in Lingala in about 1985. Especially as Mobutu's grip unravelled in the early 1990s, Mfumu'eto's 'zines' entered public consciousness with potent political comments about sorcery, money, sex and the state. A pretentious, sugar daddy big man figure with a sumptuous car transforms himself into a boa in his bedroom, proceeding to consume his sexual prey, a young, married woman, who has accepted his invitation home. Soon, the woman-eating boa is vomiting up his meal as cash, and money fills his bedroom, as the shocked city people read this unfolding news. The major postcolonial Congolese comic producer to enter metropolitan production is Barly Baruti, who resided for years in Brussels. He began by producing development comics before moving into African art gangster themes. Many of his glossy French-language albums are readily available in Belgium and France.

Nancy Rose Hunt

HISTORIES
Denis, Benoît (1995), 'Aller voir ailleurs si j'y suis. Hergé, Michaux, Simenon', *Textyles* 12: 121–36.
— (2007), 'Hergé-Simenon, Thirties', in Nathalie Aubert, Pierre-Philippe Fraiture and Patrick McGuinness (eds), *From Art Nouveau to Surrealism. Belgian Modernity in the Making*, Oxford: Legenda, pp. 110–27.
Frey, Hugo (2004), 'Contagious Colonial Diseases in Hergé's *The Adventures of Tintin*', *Modern and Contemporary France* 12 (2): 177–88.
Maurin, Marie-Rose (1993), '*Tintin au Congo* ou la nègrerie en clichés', in Pierre Halen and János Riesz (eds), *Images de l'Afrique et du Congo/Zaïre dans les lettres françaises de Belgique et alentour*, Brussels: Textyles-éditions, pp. 151–62.
Mbiye, Lumbala (1993), 'Les Images du Noir et du Congo/Zaïre dans les aventures de Jimmy Tousseul', in Pierre Halen and János Riesz (eds), *Images de l'Afrique et du Congo/Zaïre dans les lettres françaises de Belgique et alentour*, Brussels: Textyles-éditions, pp. 163–78.

Évolués

In the wake of World War II, the Belgian Congo produced a class of white-collar workers, including civil servants, known as *évolués* (from the French, literally 'evolved' or 'developed'), from which the leadership of the nationalist movement emerged. The rise of this new Congolese middle class was precipitated by the Nazi occupation of Belgium which prevented the colonial administration from recruiting civil servants and skilled workers from the homeland. The consequent labour shortfall was exacerbated by the departure of many Europeans, previously established in the Congo, to join the Allied cause. The skilled jobs which remained, were, by default, filled by Congolese who had hitherto occupied positions as low-level functionaries. With their new social status the *évolués* took their place as the new vanguard of Congolese civil society.

In the late 1940s and early 1950s, the increasing politicisation of the *évolués* and their desire to extend their influence beyond urban areas was to contribute to a climate of social unrest suitable to the development of nationalist sentiment. The rise of nationalist feeling was also fermented by the heavy demands made upon the rural masses during the war and the impact of post-war constitutional reforms in neighbouring French-speaking territories. Unlike many of its counterparts, the Belgian colonial administration paid only lip-service to post-war pressure for reform on the part of the international community and did not grant any significant political concessions to the Congolese until the mid-1950s. Instead, it instituted a series of limited social and cultural reforms aimed at the new African urban élite. These included the establishment of clubs, newspapers, radio and film programmes and a monthly newspaper, *La Voix du Congolais* (from 1945).

In 1948, the colonial administration introduced a 'social merit card' (*carte du mérite civique*, later superseded by *immatriculation*) for those Africans considered sufficiently culturally 'evolved' to be treated like Europeans. By 1958, only 1,557 Congolese had qualified for this status. However, as the limitations of its benefits with respect to promotion, pay and social status became evident, its effect was to alienate its beneficiaries from their colonial patrons.

When the Congolese did begin to formulate nationalist demands, their only available channels of expression were cultural, social and ethnic. The result was a proliferation of non-political associations, headed by prominent *évolués*, which functioned as the breeding ground for future key political players, as well as providing the leadership structures, organisational models and constituencies for the political parties that would come into being after 1956.

Associations based on ethnic kinship started to appear in the late 1940s and 1950s, as a result of post-war mass migration to the cities. Established by *évolués*, these aimed at preserving ethnic affiliations within expanding urban contexts and at increasing the social, economic and cultural status of their particular ethnic communities. Chief amongst these was the Alliance des Bakongo (ABAKO), whose main objectives were the unification, preservation and spread of the Kikongo language and whose members were drawn exclusively from the Kongo and Kongo-related ethnic groups. A second type of association, alumni associations (*associations d'anciens élèves*), enabled their most prominent members, who would later form political parties (such as future President Joseph Kasavubu and Prime Minister Patrice Lumumba) to gather a critical mass of advisers and collaborators. The third type of association, the *cercles d'études et d'agrément pour évolués*, was set up exclusively for *évolués*, with the stated aim of improving the intellectual, social, moral and physical formation of its members. In 1956, most *évolués* had left these *cercles* in order to direct their energy to the newly created political parties, whose total number had reached 317, with a combined membership of 15,245.

In 1955, a plan for the progressive political, social and economic emancipation of the Congo over a thirty-year period was devised by the Belgian, Professor A. J. Van Bilsen. Although summarily dismissed by the colonial administration (despite being tuned to their interests), the plan was embraced by a group of Catholic *évolués*, who produced the first, albeit moderate, official public expression of anti-colonial rhetoric in the form of a manifesto that endorsed the plan. It was followed by a second, much more radical manifesto, which was to function as the precipitating factor behind the general political awakening of the Congolese. Penned by a group of Bakongo *évolués* affiliated to ABAKO, it vehemently repudiated the Van Bilsen plan, dismissed any solution short of immediate self-government and urged the formation of political parties.

In 1957, with the introduction of a major local government reform (the so-called *statut des villes*), the Congolese were given their first taste of democracy. In a matter of months, the ethnic associations were transformed into political organisations, which maintained the same leadership structures, dominated by *évolués*. Under the leadership of Joseph

Kasavubu, ABAKO was transformed into a major vehicle of anti-colonial protest. Another party, the Mouvement National Congolais (MNC), emerged as the most powerful vector of territorial nationalism. It distinguished itself from the ABAKO and other ethnic groups, whose appeal was limited to their ethnic constituencies. When Patrice Lumumba took up its helm in 1958, the MNC was transformed into a radical militant force.

With the rise of anti-colonialist sentiment, the term *évolué* was abandoned in favour of *intellectuel*. When Belgium suddenly capitulated in January 1959 after the riots in Leopoldville, and arranged for the Congo to become an independent republic, the *intellectuels* were well positioned to take advantage of the flight of Belgian civil servants and army officers. They rapidly entered the senior executive ranks of the civil service and the national and provincial ministerial offices. But because Belgium had been slow to introduce higher education to the colony, the new ruling élite did not include a single Congolese lawyer, doctor or judge. At this point, the universities of Lovanium and Elisabethville, which were not established until the mid-1950s, had accepted fewer than 500 Congolese students. As a result, at the dawn of independence there were only thirty Congolese holding university degrees, a factor which further exacerbated the chaotic transition to self-rule.

Priscilla Ringrose

LITERARY WORKS

Cornélus, Henri (1954), *Kufa*, Brussels: Renaissance du Livre.
Lomami Tshibamba, Paul (1981), *Ngemena*, Yaoundé: Éditions Clé.
Kanza, Thomas [1965] (2006), *Sans rancune*, Paris: L'Harmattan.
Mutombo, Dieudonné (1954), *Victoire de l'amour*, Leverville: Bibliothèque de l'Étoile.
Naigisiki, Joseph-Saverio (1950), *Escapade ruandaise. Journal d'un clerc en sa trentième année*, Brussels: Éditions Georges A. Deny.

HISTORIES

Anstey, Roger (1966), *King Leopold's Legacy: The Congo under Belgian Rule 1908–1960*, London, New York and Ibadan: Oxford University Press.
Dunn, Kevin C. (2003), *Imagining the Congo: The International Relations of Identity*, New York: Palgrave MacMillan.
Gondola, Ch. Didier (2002), *The History of Congo*, Westport, CT and London: Greenwood Press.
Nzongola-Ntalaja, Georges (2002), *The Congo from Leopold to Kabila: A People's History*, London and New York: Zed Books.
Tshimanga, Charles (2001), *Jeunesse, formation et société au Congo/Kinshasa 1890–1960*, Paris: L'Harmattan.

Historiography: The Belgian Congo

The history of the Belgian Congo, which was written until relatively recently by non-African scholars, was characterised before the late 1960s by two dominant schools. Imperialists and apologists, described by Coquery-Vidrovitch and Jewsiewicki (1986) as 'ethnocentric nationalists', praised Leopold II and defended the Belgian colony from 'moral' crusaders (Arnaut and Vanhee 2001). Liberal or revisionist historians such as Cornevin, Massoz, Stengers, Vansina and Vellut were critical of the colonial project. In the early 1970s

African scholars like Ndaywel and Obenga began to publish. They challenged not only the conclusions of earlier historians but also their historical method. Although some historians are independent of any school whilst the views of others evolve, a key difference exists between non-African (also referred to as Africanists) and African scholars. The historiography of the Belgian Congo begins with the first collections of personal testimony from explorers, administrators and missionaries. Then follows the non-African scholars, while more recently publications have been increasingly written by the Congolese themselves.

The primary sources from the late nineteenth century explorations and the Congo Free State ruled by Leopold II from 1885 until 1908 are the accounts of explorers, in particular Stanley, and the records of Catholic and Protestant missionaries describing the traditions of the local people and documenting their oral history. Pre-eminent among the administrators, officials and individuals recording the events of that period were two non-Belgians: the Englishman, Morel; and Roger Casement, an Irish-born British consular official. Morel investigated trade between the Congo and Belgium from 1901. Casement submitted a report to the British Foreign Office in 1905 that led to public and official pressure on Leopold II.

Public debate between 1906 and 1908 became more agitated in Belgium and internationally. In 1906 the Belgian lawyer, Cattier, presented evidence of brutalities. Morel and Casement published 'The Crime of the Congo' (1909) with Conan Doyle, who was a member of the Congo Reform Association; and Mark Twain published 'King Leopold's Soliloquy' in 1905. Some missionaries such as Guinness (1890), Sjöblom (1897), Vermeersch (1906) and Johnson (1908) also condemned and reported abuses.

In Belgium, Stanley's extensive records led imperialist and apologist historians to argue that Leopold acquired the Congo to benefit Belgium politically and economically (Perier 1936). Revisionist or liberal historians commented that Leopold and his collaborators used Belgium's weakness to build the Congo Free State. Ascherson suggests that the Congo was a means to transform a politically vulnerable Belgium with major colonising states on its borders. Ascherson also scrutinises the actions of Belgian politicians such as Banning and Lambermont, who had argued from 1894 for state annexation of Leopold's personal estate. Further, he investigates public opposition to the acquisition of the colony. He connects the failures of post-1960 Congo to establish a political identity acceptable to its people, to invent its nationhood and to create a recognisable leadership of all its main ethnic groups back to the Belgian colonialism under Leopold.

Slade concentrates on the English-speaking missions in the Congo state, but Belgian missionaries were also active, and in 1937 Boelaert and Hulstaert set up the Æquatoria Centre, which focused on culture, language and the pre-colonial and colonial history of the central Congo basin. De Boeck (1987) confirms that the missionaries did not share the administration's views. They founded stronger relationships with the natives due largely to their superior command of the local languages.

Morel's accounts and Casement's 1903 diary and 1905 report have sparked later debates amongst historians. Martelli and Goffin rebuff their allegations and fiercely criticise the authors whilst Jadot finds the abuses detailed to be exaggerated. O'Síocháin and O'Sullivan argue for the authenticity of Casement's diary and the accuracy of the report. The 'moral' crusaders bring additional evidence of abuse (Marchal 1999), asserting that Europeans have a duty to report historical events, especially those that have been 'forgotten' (De Boeck 1987).

In 1908, the Belgian government acquired the Belgian Congo. Stengers (1980) describes a time of stability spanning 1908 to 1956 and a period of instability prior to independence

(1956–60). Goffin, Jadot and Martelli saw the Belgian Congo as a model colony. Perier (1936) was enraptured in his admiration of *la mise en valeur* of the Belgium Congo. Of these and other accounts, Stengers asks: '*Sont-ils aveugles?*' (1980). By contrast the Belgian Congo represents for Wastiau a rigid, authoritarian, paternalistic and hierarchical régime controlled by a colonising country that allowed amnesia to rule its past. Martelli (1964) reduces the Congo's independence movement to a bid by the *évolués* and the unstable Patrice Lumumba to jump on the nationalist bandwagon of the newly independent Congo-Brazzaville.

Ndaywel (1999) regrets that between independence and the 1970s, African studies, such as that of Mendiaux, focused on the political and economic history of the Congo from a Belgian perspective and for a Belgian audience. However, several scholars stood apart, in particular Vellut and Verhaegen.

Belgian missionaries, notably Schumacher, Hulstaert and Boelaert, worked intensively on the history of the Congo, at times to the annoyance of Church authorities. Boelaert registered the arrival of the first white people in the region of Wangata, and village life during the period of rubber harvesting before 1908. In general, the missionaries recorded oral statements from natives that depict with precision the brutalities inflicted. Their records illuminate parts of the collective memory of the colonised. Boelaert recommends that historians peruse these resources.

New leading Africanists emerged from the early 1960s at the National University of Zaire and included Cahen, de St Moulin, Cornevin, Jewsiewicki, Stengers, Van Noten, Vansina and Vellut. They actively participated in the debate on imperialism, moved away from the European cultural context, included oral tradition as a historical source (Coquery-Vidrovitch and Jewsiewicki 1986), and trained young Congolese historians (Ndaywel 1999).

Arnaut and Vanhee (2001) identify three historical trends: positivist academicism, imperial historiography, and the 'moral' crusades. Vellut (2001) distinguishes between professional historians providing source-based historical analysis from those who comment on the abuses alone, whom he sees as purveyors of '*Greuelgeschichte*' (atrocities history). Marchal (1999) is cited as one example of this category. Stengers advocates a more measured approach which, whilst acknowledging the régime's maltreatment of indigenous people, stresses the importance of resisting 'the temptation to describe the Congo and its people as purely a European enterprise' and notes 'that the role of historians is to understand not judge' (1980).

Vansina argues (Vellut 2001) that too many non-African historians have tried to influence the research agenda of African historians and to impose on them historiographies generated in the West. Chrétien emphasises the importance of pre-nineteenth century '*historiolalie*' (the oral transmission of history) for today's debate on the Congo, concluding that early history is crucial to understand colonial and postcolonial times. He argues that the role of historians is 'not to negotiate the truth' but to make available and to analyse all the historical elements, including oral history, missionary records and events, to help the country find its identity (Chrétien 1992). Ndaywel also believes that oral history has a continuing role to play and suggests that African historians are best qualified to assess the corpus of oral tradition.

De Boeck (1987), writing on the Force Publique, stresses the importance of not discussing abuses during the colonial period in a way that mitigates them. Vansina criticises the 'extremely positivist methodology' of revisionist Belgium-based academics of the 1970s and 1980s that eschews engagement with the moral assessments of colonial history (Arnaut and Vanhee 2001). In reply, Vellut (2001) points out that the reticence of Stengers, Massoz and others about putting violence centre-stage in their narratives must not be construed as a denial of that violence, but rather as a will to present history in a way that invites readers to draw moral conclusions for themselves.

Lumumba declared in 1960 that 'history will one day tell its story . . . Africa will one day write its own history' (Ndaywel 1999), thereby inviting his compatriots to adopt a new perspective in writing history. From the early 1970s, newly trained Congolese historians began to write their own history from an African perspective. They captured elements that non-indigenous historians, not having been culturally immersed in the area, could not (Ndaywel 1999).

Ndaywel notes that the first African historians in the 1970s inevitably adopted an 'outside in' approach to writing African history, since they sought to correct what had already been written by the non-Africans. Following Lumumba's lead, he advocates examining the past from the 'inside out' not the 'outside in' (1999). Akyeampong (2003) agrees as long as it is not forgotten that 'Africa is part of a larger world', whilst Emongo urges Congolese historians to consider the history already written by non-African Africanists. Through an analogy between the crimes of the Congo as reported by Conan Doyle and those of post-independence, Emongo observes that African history will have a place in the future only if the past is accurately written.

External constraints curb historical research by Congolese on the Belgian Congo. As De Boeck (1987) notes, many African scholars are cautious in reporting events because it might be unsafe politically to do so. Today serious financial limitations on research in Congolese universities impact negatively on historical studies.

Mumbanza (1986) judges history to be useful only to historians and specialists. He claims that historical debate is foreign to Zairian society and serves solely to widen the gap between political and historical debates. M'Bokolo warns against debate focusing more on historiography and historical methods than on the historical events themselves. This seems to be particular to the history of the Belgian Congo. Vanhee calls on historians to adopt a holistic and dynamic approach, to engage in a more moderate and balanced dialogue that involves African and non-African experts; he advocates collective collaboration, of which the edited volume by M'Bokolo is an example. Thus the objectives and achievements of Congolese scholars and Africanists may be different but they are not incompatible.

Postcolonial literature in the Democratic Republic of the Congo (also known as Congo-Kinshasa, Republic of the Congo [1960–5], Democratic Republic of the Congo [1966–71], Zaire [1971–1997]) is disseminated via Congolese and Parisian publishing houses, primarily Union des Écrivains du Zaïre (UEZA), Belles Lettres, Mont-noir, Saint-Paul-Afrique, L'Harmattan and Centre Africain de Littérature. UEZA and Mont-noir received government backing from the Mobutu dictatorship. At this time literature was censored and writers, such as Matala Mukadi Tshiakatumba, were persecuted. There is therefore a body of 'littératures soumises et déférentes' (Ngandu 1995) which may inflect the representation of the Belgian Congo. Literature is treated extensively in the annual review *Annales Æquatoria*, a 1980 relaunch of the *Æquatoria* journal (1937–62) set up by the Belgian missionaries, Boelaert and Hulstaert, to study the Congo's indigenous languages and cultures, and in the monthly *Congo-Afrique: Economie – Culture – Vie Sociale*, founded in 1960. Les Archives et Musée de la Littérature in Brussels, directed by Marc Quaghebeur, holds a rich fund of postcolonial francophone Congolese literature.

V. Y. Mudimbe explores the individual's inner strife between religious faith and political engagement, Western education and ancestral roots in *Entre les eaux: Dieu, un prêtre, la révolution* (1973), *Le bel immonde* (1976), and *Shaba deux. Les carnets de Mère Marie Gertrude* (1989). In the autobiographical *Les Corps glorieux des mots et des êtres* (1994), Mudimbe describes his realisation that he has never been fully liberated from the *cadre bénédictin de mon enfance*. Although the political engagement treated in his fiction is contemporary, the protagonists' characters are shaped by the religious and educational institutions of the Belgian Congo, in which – like the author himself – they were born.

The Martiniquan Aimé Césaire dramatises the Congo's transition into independence in *Une Saison au Congo* (1966). His Patrice Lumumba writes poetry and is ridiculed for it. This double-bind illustrates the predicament of a number of Congolese writers grappling with the colonial period. The transitional period is also treated by Justine M'Poyo Kasa-Vubu in *Kasa-Vubu et le Congo indépendant* (1997). This is a biography of her father, Joseph Kasa-Vubu, who, before becoming first president of the Democratic Republic of the Congo was from 1954 President of the Association of Bakongo (ABAKO), a cultural society influential in the independence movement.

Maguy Kabamba, born in 1960 in East DR Congo and educated at Lubumbashi, Mons and Toronto, charts in the fictional *La Dette coloniale* (1995) Europe's attractiveness to the Congolese of the 1990s as a place for work and education, the disillusionment that ensues when the protagonist actually moves from Africa to Belgium, and the changes in the Congolese as they adapt to their new environment. Within the community of disaffected young Congolese in Mons, the protagonist encounters a nihilistic desire to extract from the white community reparation, in the form of petty crime and working the benefits system, for what is perceived as its colonial debt.

André Cnockaert writes of '*un public congolais qui garde bien en mémoire les heures sombres de son histoire coloniale*' and this is reflected in the country's literature from 1960.

Pascale Stacey and Victoria Reid

LITERARY WORKS
Césaire, Aimé (1966), *Une Saison au Congo*, Paris: Présence Africaine.

Mudimbe, Valentin Yves (1989), *Shaba deux: Les carnets de Mère Marie Gertrude*, Paris: Présence Africaine.

— (1994), *Les Corps glorieux des mots et des êtres: esquisse d'un jardin africain à la bénédictine*, Paris: Présence Africaine.

Ngandu, Pius Nkashama (1995), *Le Livre littéraire: bibliographie de la littérature du Congo (Kinshasa)*, Paris: L'Harmattan.

Quaghebeur, Marc and Emile van Balberghe (eds) (1992), *Papier blanc, encre noir: cent ans de culture francophone en Afrique centrale (Zaïre, Rwanda et Burundi)*, 2 vols, Brussels: Labor.

The University of Western Australia (2004), 'Women Writers of the Democratic Republic of the Congo' <http://www.arts.uwa.edu.au/aflit/CountryZaireEN.html> [30 July 2006].

HISTORIES
Akyeampong, Emmanuel (2003), 'The African Voice in African Studies Today'. Keynote Address at the Listening (Again) for the African Past Conference, 24 Oct., Cambridge, MA: Smith College, Harvard University.

Arnaut, Karel and Hein Vanhee (2001), 'History Facing the Present: An Interview with Jan Vansina', in *H-NET.ORG*, 1 November 2001 <http://www.h-net.org/~africa/africaforum/VansinaInterview.htm> [accessed 30 July 2006].

Chrétien, Jean-Pierre (1992), 'Le Défi de l'intégrisme ethnique dans l'historiographie africaniste. Le cas du Rwanda et du Burundi', *Politique Africaine* 46 (June): 71–83.

Coquery-Vidrovitch, Catherine and Bogumil Jewsiewicki (1986), 'African Historiography in France and Belgium: Traditions and Trends', in B. Jewsiewicki and D. Newbury (eds), *African Historiographies: What History for Which Africa?*, London: Sage Publications, pp. 139–50.

De Boeck, Guy (1987), *Baoni, les révoltes de la force publique sous Léopold II, Congo 1895–1908*, Anvers: EPO.

Ndaywel è Nziem, Isidore [1997] (1999), *Histoire générale du Congo: de l'héritage ancien à la république démocratique*, Louvain-la-Neuve: Duculot, édition Africaine.

Perier, Gaston-Denys (1936), *Le Congo vu par les Belges*, Brussels: Éditions de l'INR.

Stengers, Jean (1980), *Congo: mythes et réalités, 100 ans d'histoire*, Louvain-la-Neuve: Duculot.

Vellut, Jean-Luc (2001), 'Jan Vansina on the Belgian Historiography of Africa: Around the Agenda of a Bombing Raid. A Reply to "History Facing the Present: An Interview with Jan Vansina"', in *H-NET.ORG*, 1 November 2001 <http://www.h-net.org/~africa/africaforum/Vellut.htm> [accessed 30 July 2006].

Imperial Policy

A Belgian empire came into existence only in 1908, when the Belgian parliament took over the Congo Free State, which thus became the Belgian Congo, from King Leopold II of the Belgians. The Berlin Congress of 1884–5 had recognised Leopold's personal control of a territory some eighty times bigger than his European kingdom, covering one-thirteenth of the African landmass. Although he never set foot there, he ran the Congo as a private enterprise, extracting wild rubber by brutal coercion, killing or maiming countless Africans. The régime was memorialised in Joseph Conrad's *Heart of Darkness* (1902). Suitably indemnified by his own parliament, Leopold bowed to mounting international pressure. Thereafter, Belgian colonialism was broadly comparable to that of other European powers, though it might have surprised many Congolese that Belgium was considered a more 'fit' colonial power than Germany, which was stripped of its colonial empire by the Versailles Treaty. In 1923, Belgium thus acquired Ruanda-Urundi, formerly part of German East Africa, under League of Nations mandate (and, from 1945, as a UN Trusteeship Territory).

Erasing memories of Leopold's Congo, Belgian officials aspired to run a 'model colony', and yet the Belgian colonial state has been seen as a paradigmatic 'Bula Matari' (Crusher of Rocks, so named after the explorer, Henry Morton Stanley), subjecting Africans to state power through taxation, forced labour, and a harsh régime of corporal punishment and imprisonment only phased out in the 1950s. The Belgian Congo was more intensively administered than other colonial empires; by independence, the élite 'Territoriale' numbered some nineteen hundred administrators, mostly recruited since 1945 (Dembour 2000). Belgian authority was mediated through a network of chiefdoms, ostensibly following British patterns of 'indirect rule', but in which chiefs were reduced to salaried officials. The 'Platonist' ethos of Belgian late colonial rule, aptly characterised by the left-wing historian (and ex-colonial official), Thomas Hodgkin, was:

> implicit in the sharp distinction, social and legal, between Belgian philosopher-kings and the mass of African producers; in the conception of education as primarily concerned with the

transmission of certain unquestioned and unquestionable moral values . . . in the belief that
the thought and behaviour of the mass is plastic and can be refashioned by a benevolent, wise
and highly trained élite; that the prime interest of the mass is in welfare and consumer goods –
football and bicycles – not liberty; and in the conviction that it is possible, by expert administration, to arrest social and political change. (1956)

These 'philosopher-kings' presided over a benign 'welfare' colonialism, embracing inclusive primary (but not secondary or higher) education, and the most extensive system of
health care in colonial (and probably postcolonial) Africa. Administration was only one
element in an interlocking 'trinity' of colonial institutions, alongside Church and big
business. More than 5 million of 15 million Congolese were declared Christians, four-
fifths of them Catholics, ministered to by some 6,000 missionaries and growing numbers
of African priests and religious. The Congo was booming, and its mining interests (diamonds, copper, tin, uranium and other minerals) and cotton production subsidised health
and education to the extent that metropolitan development funding was deemed unnecessary (unlike British or French Africa). This self-containment extended to the political
sphere, as Belgian politicians and public evinced little interest in colonial affairs, and
a toothless Colonial Council in Brussels oversaw a carefully balanced status quo. Only
a handful of Congolese attended Belgian universities, and so-called *évolués* had
little contact with worldwide intellectual and political currents, and no legal outlet for
political activism.

Decolonisation was always more rapid and thorough than the colonial power envisaged,
but the Belgian case took this to extremes. In 1955, a university professor controversially
suggested that Congolese political 'emancipation' might be achieved within thirty years.
In 1958, an official working group proposed elaborate political reforms to start this process –
without mentioning eventual independence. King Baudouin supplied the missing word in
January 1959, following riots in Leopoldville (Kinshasa), although the promise of independence was still conditional and long-term, according to an implied Belgian 'model' of
gradual decolonisation. The resulting explosion in political activity was barely contained
by elections held in December 1959, contested by dozens of brand-new political parties,
although few commanded more than a local or personal following. At a Round Table in
Brussels in January–February 1960, nationalist parties formed an unexpected, temporary
united front, and insisted on independence on 30 June 1960. Belgian acquiescence in this
fait accompli was eased by the knowledge that the official, military and commercial pillars
of Belgian power remained in place. However, immediately following independence,
Congolese troops in the Force Publique mutinied against their Belgian officers, and the vast
majority of officials and settlers fled. Although the Congo was thus 'Africanised' at a stroke,
in effect Congolese decolonisation now stretched over several years. Very rapidly, two separate statelets seceded, Katanga and South Kasai, both founded on ethnic distinctiveness
backed by strong mining interests. Moïse Tshombe's Katanga shared not only a long border
and access to rich copper deposits with Northern Rhodesia (Zambia), but also the potential for independent 'multi-racial' (that is, settler-dominated) statehood. In September
1960, President Joseph Kasavubu dismissed his Prime Minister, Patrice Lumumba, leading
to the latter's arrest, escape, capture and murder, with CIA connivance. The death of the
man seen variously as the champion of African liberation and the puppet of Soviet imperialism drove a split between Leopoldville and Lumumba's north-eastern stronghold of
Stanleyville (Kisangani), and despite the internationalisation of the Congo crisis
through UN intervention, it took until 1964 to stitch the country back together under an

increasingly kleptocratic régime unrecognisable from the abortive Belgian-style parliamentary democracy of June 1960.

In Ruanda-Urundi, Belgian immobilism was inflected by the colonial power's responsibilities to the UN Trusteeship Council. However, reforms initiated in the mid-1950s merely tampered with the shifting complexities of the social, ethnic (or 'caste') and ideological distinction between 'aristocratic' Tutsis and 'peasant' Hutus, a distinction which Belgian policy tended to make rigid and absolute, but with widely differing outcomes in the separate kingdoms of Rwanda and Burundi. Facing Belgian hostility, a strong Burundian nationalist party emerged headed by the king's son, Prince Louis Rwagasore, and achieved independence in 1962, despite Rwagasore's assassination in late 1961 on his chief rivals' orders. National unity was thus preserved under monarchical rule, although a 'Hutu awakening' (Lemarchand 1970: 343) was beginning at independence. In Rwanda, Belgian officials tempered traditional support of Tutsi chiefs, but frustrated the expectations of an emerging Hutu 'counter-élite'. Following a wave of Hutu violence directed against Tutsis in November 1959, Belgian repression was chiefly aimed at Tutsi counter-violence, and hereafter Belgian backing of Hutus against Tutsis (who favoured immediate independence) became ever more blatant under military rule. In January 1961, a hegemonic Hutu movement declared the Republic, and this revolution was ratified by UN-monitored elections in September 1961, in circumstances pregnant with future violence.

Martin Shipway

LITERARY WORKS

Drum, Henri (1931), *Les Coloniaux*, Brussels: Éditions de Belgique.
Grégoire, Herman (1921), *Makako, singe d'Afrique*, Paris: La Renaissance du Livre.
Mathelin de Papigny (1922), Hyppolite de, *Le Coup de bambou*, Brussels: Luycks.
Reisdorff, Ivan [1978] (1995), *L'Homme qui demanda du feu*, Brussels: Labor.
Ryckmans, Pierre [1947] (1991), *Barabara*, Lubumbashi: Ed. Impala.

HISTORIES

Ageron, Charles-Robert and Marc Michel (eds) (1995), *L'Ere des décolonisations: Actes du Colloque d'Aix-en-Provence*, Paris Karthala.
Dembour, Marie-Bénédicte (2000), *Recalling the Belgian Congo: Conversations and Introspection*, New York and Oxford: Berghahn.
Hodgkin, Thomas (1956), *Nationalism in Colonial Africa*, London: Frederick Muller.
Lemarchand, René (1970), *Rwanda and Burundi*, London: Pall Mall Press.
Shipway, Martin (2007), *Decolonization and its Impact: A Comparative Approach to the End of Colonial Rule*, Oxford: Blackwell.
Young, Crawford (1994), *The African Colonial State in Comparative Perspective*, New Haven, CT and London: Yale University Press.

Simon Kimbangu

Simon Kimbangu was born in 1887 (or 1889) in Nkamba, in the Lower-Congo. He was educated at the Wathen Baptist Missionary Society Mission in Ngombe Lutete. In March 1921, he started to perform miraculous acts such as healings and resurrections, and to reject witchcraft. He claimed that he was acting under the influence of *Mpeve* (the Spirit); he also interpreted the Bible freely and prophesied the overthrow of the colonial order. Thus he appeared like a *ngunza* (prophet) and a *mvuluzi* (saviour). Consequently, a great number of pilgrims from the whole of Lower-Congo and Leopoldville left their missions and their jobs to go to Nkamba. Soon Kimbangu was accused by the colonisers of incitement to xenophobia and incivility, but above all, he was suspected of being the tool of a Protestant and 'Anglo-Saxon' plot against the state. On 12 September 1921, Kimbangu was arrested, then court-martialled and sentenced to death, a penalty which was commuted to life imprisonment.

From 1922, the Kimbanguists were deported to 'relegation camps'. Despite the repression, the movement survived and recruited new members amongst the Bakongo people of the French Congo and the Portuguese Congo (Angola). In these areas, it was also regarded as a vehicle for Kongo ethnonationalism which aspired to the restoration of the old Kingdom of Kongo that had been brought down in 1665 and divided in 1885 (Berlin Conference). During this process, it diversified and generated several movements, which were variously organised, but all more radical (and labelled as *ngunzistes* [prophetics]).

Kimbangu died a recluse in 1951. The banning of the movement was lifted by official order in December 1959. The previous year the movement had become 'Église de Jésus-Christ sur la Terre par le Prophète Simon Kimbangu' (EJCSK). Diangienda, Kimbangu's youngest child, received the title of *mfumu a nlongo* (spiritual leader). In 1969, the EJCSK became a member of the World Council of Churches and it gained status as an independent Church in Zaïre in 1971. Diangienda died in 1992 and during his brother's (Dialungana) spiritual leadership, the EJCSK went through several mutations, such as the revival of the Kongo ethnicity, millenarianism and the upsurge of healing acts. When Dialungana died in 2001, Simon Kimbangu Kiangani – the oldest of Kimbangu's grandchildren – took on the role of spiritual leader. Since then, Kimbanguism has been characterised by deep divisions.

                                                                                      Anne Mélice

LITERARY WORKS
Diantantu, Serge (2002–4), *Simon Kimbangu*, 2 vols, Amfreville-La-Mivoie: Mandala AfricaBD Éditions.
Elebe, Philippe (1972), *Simon Kimbangu ou le messie noir*, Paris: Nouvelles Editions Debresse.
Maquet-Tombu, Jeanne (1936), *Le Siècle marche*, Bruxelles: Office de Publicité.
Salkin, Paul [1926] (2001), *L'Afrique centrale dans cent ans*, Bruxelles: Archives et Musée de la Littérature Éditions.
Valleys, Anne (1991), *Coup de bambou*, Paris: Payot.

HISTORIES
Asch, Susan (1983), *L'Église du prophète Simon Kimbangu*, Paris: Karthala.
Diangienda Kuntima, Joseph (1984), *L'Histoire du kimbanguisme*, Kinshasa: Ed. Kimbanguistes.
Mac Gaffey, Wyatt (1983), *Modern Kongo Prophets*, Bloomington, IN: Indiana University Press.
Martin, Marie-Louise (1975), *Kimbangu. An African Prophet and his Church*, Oxford: Basil Blackwell.
Mélice, Anne (2001), 'Le Kimbanguisme: un millénarisme de la terre aux cieux', *Bulletin des Séances Académie Royale des Sciences d'Outre-Mer* 47 (suppl.): 35–54.

Raymaekers, Paul and Henri Desroche (1983), *L'Administration et le sacré (1921–1957)*, Bruxelles: Académie Royale des Sciences d'Outre-Mer.

Sinda, Martial (1972), *Le Messianisme congolais et ses incidences politiques*, Paris: Payot.

Vellut, Jean-Luc (2005), *Simon Kimbangu. 1921: de la prédication à la déportation. Les sources*, vol. 1, Bruxelles: Académie Royale des Sciences d'Outre-Mer.

Leopold II

King Leopold II (1835–1909), succeeded his father, King Leopold I, to the Belgian throne in 1865. During his reign, Belgium experienced great industrial development and colonial expansion. Outside Belgium, Leopold is chiefly remembered as the founder and sole owner of the Congo Free State, and for the brutal exploitation of its population in his pursuit of resources such as rubber and ivory. He is held responsible for the deaths of millions of Africans.

In his youth Leopold travelled extensively. Returning from Egypt and Greece in 1860 he presented the Belgian Minister of Finance, Frère Orban, with a piece of marble from the Acropolis. Leopold's portrait was mounted in the middle and surrounded by the inscription: *Il faut à la Belgique une colonie* (Belgium needs a colony). The gift was a first sign of the future king's overwhelming passion for colonisation. After he ascended the throne in 1865 he invested a large amount of his inheritance in the building of the Suez Canal, a venture that proved very lucrative and which prompted him to consider further colonial projects.

Leopold firmly believed that a country without a colony would never achieve historical significance and worked tirelessly to acquire colonial territory. However, the Belgian government considered colonialism anachronistic and was not interested in pursuing the King's colonial dreams. Realising that he could not count on governmental support, Leopold developed a new strategy, and founded a holding company. To help legitimise his operation he organised a geographical conference in Brussels in 1876, at which he proposed the creation of the Association Internationale Africaine (AIA), which later became the Comité d'Études pour le Haut Congo, and finally the Association Internationale du Congo (AIC). The AIA's sole purpose was to provide a front for the King's colonial activities, giving him an officially recognised and seemingly philanthropic platform from which to operate. In 1879 the King employed the explorer Henry Morton Stanley to establish a colony in the Congo region. Far from being a philanthropic mission, Stanley's expedition was simply part of the wider 'Scramble for Africa' that would lead to the division of Africa at the Berlin Conference of 1884–5. At this diplomatic gathering, representatives from fourteen countries recognised Leopold (who was himself not present) as sovereign of most of the area to which he and Stanley had laid claim. The King's private colony was given the name 'État Indépendant du Congo' or 'Congo Free State' (later the Belgian Congo, then upon independence Zaire, today the Democratic Republic of the Congo), an area eighty-one times larger than Belgium, which Leopold was free to rule as his own personal property.

Leopold's Congo Free State was not to last. Reports of the outrageous exploitation and widespread abuse of the population, especially in the rubber industry, led to the formation of an international protest movement in the early 1900s. Many prominent writers took part in the condemnation of Leopold's treatment of the Congo, including Arthur Conan Doyle, Booker T. Washington and Mark Twain. Estimates of the death toll range from 5 miillion to 15 million and many historians consider the atrocities to constitute genocide. Finally, in 1908, the Belgian Parliament compelled the King to cede the Congo Free State to Belgium and the King's private property became a Belgian colony.

As a constitutional monarch, the King had no power to determine government policy but he did succeed in promoting many pet projects. He was committed to safeguarding Belgium's neutrality which he believed required a large standing army (especially considering the perceived danger of Napoleon III). Many Belgians referred to Leopold II as the 'king-builder'. The King's urban and architectural ambitions were linked to the exploitation of the Congo Free State and his desire to be the figurehead of a 'great nation'. However, the Belgians did not share Leopold's love of spending money on grand buildings. To overcome resistance to his plans he claimed his funds were donated by 'benefactors', whereas in fact they came from the Domaine de la Couronne, the large territory in the Congo from which he was able to draw all profit without the knowledge of the Belgian government. Of the many oversized monuments that were constructed in Brussels under Leopold's reign, the most grandiose was the Cinquantenaire – a collection of huge structures commemorating the fiftieth anniversary of Belgium's independence in 1880. It took fifty years to build, and was finally completed some twenty years after the King's death. The other grand architectural project was the Palais de Justice which required the demolition of some 3,000 houses. Further buildings commissioned included urban projects in Ostend and Antwerp, the Royal Glasshouses, the Japanese tower, the Chinese pavilion, several country estates and most notably the Colonial Museum in Tervuren, built in 1897 as part of the World Exhibition. This ostentatious edifice on the outskirts of Brussels was linked to the Cinquantenaire by a huge tree-lined avenue.

King Leopold II remains a controversial figure: whilst undoubtedly a highly intelligent man and a shrewd strategist, he used his talents ruthlessly to exploit the Congo. Still viewed as a 'great king' by many Belgians, in recent years historians have come to reveal the greed and corruption that also characterised the second king of the Belgians.

Lieve Spaas

LITERARY WORKS
Conrad, Joseph (1902), *Heart of Darkness*, Edinburgh: Blackwood.
Straven, Egide (1946), *Kapiri-Pi. Roman africain*, Brussels: La Renaissance du Livre.
Tinel, Marcel (1959), *Le Monde de Nzakomba*, Bruxelles: La Renaissance du Livre.
Twain, Mark (1905), *King Leopold's Soliloquy*, Boston, MA: The P. R. Warren Co.

HISTORIES
Ascherson, N. (1963), *The King Incorporated: Leopold the Second and the Congo*, London: Granta Books.
Emerson, Barbara (1979), *Leopold II of the Belgians: King of Colonialism*, London: Weidenfeld and Nicolson.
Hochschild, Adam (1998), *King Leopold's Ghost: A Story of Greed, Terror, and Heroism in Colonial Africa*, New York: Houghton Mifflin Company.
Mpoyi-Buatu, Thomas (1986), *La Re-production*, Paris: L'Harmattan.
Pakenham, Thomas (1991), *The Scramble for Africa: 1876–1912*, London: Weidenfeld and Nicolson.
Stengers, Jean (1989), *Congo, mythes et réalités. 100 ans d'histoire*, Paris; Louvain-la-Neuve: Éditions Duculot.

Patrice Émery Lumumba

Patrice Émery Lumumba (1925–61), a Congolese leader of the nationalist independence movement against Belgian colonialism and co-founder of the Mouvement National Congolais (MNC) in 1958, was the first Prime Minister of what is now the Democratic Republic of the Congo from June 1960 until September 1960, when he was removed from office by a confluence of forces under the direction of President Joseph Kasavubu, Colonel Joseph Désiré Mobutu, and Belgian and American officials.

Lumumba was born in Onalua in the Katako-Kombe district of Sankuru in the Kasai province of the Belgian Congo and educated by Protestant missionaries. He was registered as an *évolué* and worked as a postal clerk and as a charismatic salesman, an image made famous first in Aimé Césaire's play *Une Saison au Congo* (1967) and then in Raoul Peck's biographical film *Lumumba* (2000). He became active in the independence movements in the mid-1950s and began a career as a journalist and writer, editing a Congolese postal workers' newspaper *L'Écho*, and writing for *La Voix du Congolais*, *La Croix du Congo* and the Belgium-based, *L'Afrique et le Monde*. In 1956, he sent a manuscript to Brussels entitled, *Le Congo, terre d'avenir est-il menacé?* (published posthumously in 1961). His anti-colonial ideas brought him to the attention of Belgian officials who thought they might redirect his political activism by inviting him to visit Brussels in 1956. After his arrest in 1957, on trumped-up charges of embezzlement, he returned to Leopoldville (Kinshasa) and gained political prominence as one of a group of anti-colonial leaders who sent a memorandum to M. Cornelis, the Governor-General of the Belgian Congo, demanding independence and African participation in governance. Later that year, he helped found MNC and attended the All African Peoples' Conference in Accra organised by George Padmore and convened by Kwame Nkrumah in the independent nation of Ghana to study the question of African independence. He was subsequently arrested for anti-colonial activities in 1959 about the same time that the government in Brussels revealed a five-year plan for independence. Despite being in prison, Lumumba was elected Prime Minister. In 1960 Lumumba was released from prison to attend a conference in Brussels at which the date for independence was moved up to June of that same year. On 23 June 1960, the first government of Congo was established by Lumumba and Kasavubu. At the independence day ceremonies on 30 June, Lumumba gave his famous speech about the daily denigration and humiliation of the Congolese by Belgian colonists.

In September 1960, United Nations troops arrived to quell unrest in Congo, but Lumumba was put under house arrest after a coup d'état led by Mobutu (later President Mobutu Sese Seko) and supported by Kasavubu. These two leaders in turn were supported by Belgium and the USA in their attempts to eliminate Lumumba. The United Nations troops positioned outside Lumumba's home to protect him did not see him escape in late 1960. He was re-arrested by Mobutu's soldiers on 1 December 1960 during his failed attempt to reach supporters in Stanleyville (Lumumbashi). United Nations Secretary General Dag Hammarskjöld appealed to Kasavubu to make sure that Lumumba was treated humanely. However, Lumumba was delivered with two other MNC leaders, Maurice Mpolo and Joseph Okito, from the military prison in Thysville to his enemy, Katanga seces- sionist leader Moïse Tshombe. Lumumba was tortured, and executed along with Mpolo and Okito by Katangese soldiers, while under the supervision of Tshombe and Belgian officers in the mineral-rich province of Katanga, on 17 January 1961. His death was not announced until three weeks later.

Many historians and political scientists consider the assassination of Lumumba as the event that has most profoundly affected post-independent Africa and led to violence and upheaval in Congo. Historian Madeleine Kalb examined hundreds of cross-continental cables from the 1950s and 1960s and determined that the CIA and President Eisenhower conspired to poison Lumumba and were aware of Belgian activities surrounding Lumumba's death. In *The Assassination of Lumumba* Belgian historian, Ludo de Witte, used the same data as a book that had exonerated Belgium, to conclude that the Belgian government was deeply involved in Lumumba's death. In 2002, after an extensive parliamentary investigation, the Belgian government issued an apology to the Congolese people and released a statement accepting 'moral responsibility' for the murder of Patrice Lumumba. Remembered by nationalist leaders as a fallen giant, Lumumba is often hailed in politically engaged literature and film of the African diaspora for his important principles of African independence and unity. He is celebrated in the philosophical writings of Jean-Paul Sartre; in photos, paintings, and *pagne* designs in the films of Ousmane Sembene; as the subject of two films by Raoul Peck and a play by Aimé Césaire; and is featured most recently in a novel by Barbara Kingsolver.

Carina Yervasi

LITERARY WORKS

Bennett, Ronan (1997), *The Catastrophist*, New York: Simon and Schuster.

Canel, Fausto (1961), *El Congo 1961* [film].

Césaire, Aimé [1967] (1968), *A Season in the Congo*, New York: Grove Press, Inc. (Evergreen).

Iguh, Thomas (n. d.), *The Last Days of Lumumba: The Late Lion of the Congo*, Onitsha: Membership Book-Shop.

Kingsolver, Barbara (1998), *The Poisonwood Bible*, New York: HarperCollins Publishers, Inc.

O'Brien, Conor Cruise (1968), *Murderous Angels: A Political Tragedy and Comedy in Black and White*, Boston and Toronto: Little, Brown and Company (An Atlantic Monthly Press Book).

Peck, Raoul (1992), *Lumumba: La mort du prophète* [film].

Peck, Raoul (2000), *Lumumba* [film].

Sartre, Jean-Paul [1963] (2001), 'The Political Thought of Patrice Lumumba', in *Colonialism and Neocolonialism*. trans. Azzedine Haddour, Steve Brewer and Terry McWilliams, London and New York: Routledge, pp. 156–200.

HISTORIES

Kalb, Madeleine (1982), *The Congo Cables: The Cold War in Africa – From Eisenhower to Kennedy*, New York: Macmillan.

Kanza, Thomas (1972), *Conflict in the Congo: The Rise and Fall of Lumumba*, Harmondsworth: Penguin African Library.

Lumumba, Patrice [1961] (1962), *Congo, My Country*, London: Pall Mall Press and Barrie and Rockliff.

Van Lierde, Jean (ed.) [1963] (1972), *Lumumba Speaks: The Speeches and Writings of Patrice Lumumba, 1958–1961*, Boston and Toronto: Little, Brown and Company.

Witte, Ludo de [1999] (2001), *The Assassination of Lumumba*, London and New York: Verso.

Missionaries in the Congo: The First 120 years

Missionaries from Belgium have had a significant impact on society and the way it has evolved in the Congo. Indeed Stenger suggests that Catholic evangelisation was probably the most successful mission in Africa in the nineteenth and early twentieth centuries. Their contribution was distinctive; they were often distinguished as teachers, doctors and in other ways. At first largely supportive of the colonial enterprise, the missionary impulse has developed to a point at which the Catholic Church can now be seen, at least in the areas in which it is most active, as an alternative State, providing services in place of an unreliable or absent civil authority.

Belgian missionaries arrived in the Congo region at the end of the nineteenth century at the request of King Leopold II and Pope Leo XIII and, according to Marchal (1999), to counterbalance Protestant missions already present. In 1906, they agreed a convention under which Catholic missions created schools and evangelised, for which they received land free in perpetuity.

The religious orders present included the Pères Blancs Scheutistes, based in Katanga from 1886 with missions in Lusaka and Baudouinville. Jesuits settled in the Kwango region from 1892 and Trappists and Prémontrés in the Ruki and Uele regions respectively. Passionists arrived from Belgium in 1930. The Congolese were said to fear the Jesuits most for their methods of recruiting children.

Between 1885 and 1960, the Belgian missionaries were engaged in *la mission civilisatrice*. This was first and foremost a Christianisation that included education and evangelisation. Stenger notes that, even after the missionaries continued to work for '*une oeuvre nationale, de civilisation et de mise en valeur*'.

Mpangala argues that this 'civilising' mission, underpinned by racist ideology, was a necessary instrument because it was believed that the African mind was 'pre-logical, non-conceptual and dominated by emotional thinking'. He suggests that the missionaries' ideology of ethnicity, regionalism and religious antagonism divided Africans amongst themselves.

Christian evangelisation tended to require repudiation of all previous religious beliefs. But Colle's 1913 studies of the Baluba led him to acknowledge a spiritual philosophy onto which Christianity could be grafted, whilst Tempels, inspired by the Bantu, suggested similar views in 1943. Boelaert (1946) judged these initiatives 'inconceivable'. These contrary approaches were reconciled in the Passionists, who believed in an indigenous clergy with their own Church.

Until 1954, the school educational programme for confessional and non-confessional schools was mainly in the hands of the Scheutists. Secondary education was offered to the Congolese only from 1939.

The Scheutists had little formal educational training. They wrote the majority of their schoolbooks in vernacular languages or in a language of trade aiming to reach the widest audience and area. Vinck (1999) suggests that their respect for local languages and culture derived from the fact that they themselves belonged to the Flemish cultural minority in Belgium. He argues that their educational booklets played a significant role in balancing colonialism and thereby contributed to the independence movement.

Not less important was the missionaries' medical work. By 1960 each mission had a dispensary. Nuns worked in hospitals. For example Les Filles de la Charité was attached to Mama Yemo's clinic in Mbandaka.

Belgian missionaries also wrote histories. In 1937, Hulstaert and Boelaert founded and ran the periodical *Æquatoria* for twenty-five years. Topics for discussion ranged from the social consequences of the colonial régime, its jurisdiction, education and Christianisation. These occasionally offended their superiors in Belgium. The journal was relaunched by Claessens and Vinck under the name *Annales Æquatoria* in 1979–80. Today the Centre Æquatoria library holdings are broad and include Hulstaert's collection of over 500 school-books.

Until 1939 so close was the relationship between state, Church and administration that Massoz (1994) speaks of the 'triple alliance'. But some missionaries contested Leopold's colony. The Jesuit Vermeersch in 1906 and the Scheutist Varonsly in 1895 expressed concerns about colonial excess.

The war in 1939 added different pressures. Jans authorised the publication of a news bulletin that was strongly critical of the European war. In 1940 Leclercq accused the Axis and the Allies alike of grave errors. There was a group of missionary *objecteurs de conscience* including Boelaert and Hulstaert. In 1941, Boelaert blamed 'selfish citizenship [for] making democracy inefficient and corrupt'. Hulstaert strongly condemned the publication of propaganda leaflets urging wider participation in rubber harvesting as a war effort. Censorship gave the Congolese limited access to information about the war. This did not prevent Boelaert, Hulstaert and de Jans from expressing their views in *Le Coq Chante*, a journal written in vernacular languages and French.

In 1954 ecclesiastics such as Duclos, Mosmans and Philips urged the Church to distance itself from the state. Massoz (1994) suggests that the Church realised that only through disengagement from the 'triple alliance' could it prosper in an independent state. In 1956 the Church formally declared itself independent, financially and politically.

In 2005, only nineteen Europeans trained to join the mission (lavigerie.org 2006). There are Belgian missions in the Congo such as the Bethsaïde Centre in Sud-Kivu, Aprofime in Goma (North-Kivo), SOS Handicapé in Lubumbashi, and the Damian Foundation in Kinshasa. There is a Passionist mission. By contrast the number of Congolese priests is increasing.

Nevertheless the Church is vulnerable. In August 1999, six priests and nuns were killed in Bukavu by rebel soldiers. The Church seeks also to be a mediator. For example, in April 2006 Bukavu diocese published a call for peace condemning the intimidation and insecurity engendered by 'men in uniforms', asking those responsible: '*est-ce une fatalité de vivre ainsi ou peut-on vivre autrement?*' and inviting local, national and international politico-military authorities to reflect on the consequences of the violence inflicted on the population.

But Vinck (1999) argues that religion is still used for political power and submission. He has posited links between education, power and the actual behaviour of the postcolonial authorities. Noting that all protagonists in contemporary Congo were educated with colonial textbooks, he asserts a direct relationship between the attitudes of uncontrolled domination and religious submission. In his view, the second republic (1965–90) continued, but without enduring success, to express the same authoritarian principles. Most schoolbooks presented power and authority not as a democratic interpretation, but as deriving from God and dividing into religious and civic self-ruling sectors. Vinck believes that, as a result, democratic political structures and rules imposed by 'la loi fondamentale' in 1960, as a basis for an independent state, were never effective.

Today the Church in the Congo, along with civil society as a whole, has been obliged to shoulder some of the responsibilities usually exercised by the state. In spite of its ethnocentric self-confidence and its denial of African religions in the early stages of Belgian colonisation, Christian missions have contributed, from the 1940s onwards to the renewal of Congolese civil society.

Pascale Stacey

LITERARY WORKS
Bolombo, G. (1954), *Kavwanga*, Namur: Éditions Grands Lacs.
Bontinck, François (1951), *Emmanuel*, Bolongo: n. p.
Halen, Pierre (2006), *Approches du roman et du théâtre missionnaire*, Bern: Peter Lang.
Pessaret, Grégoire (1977), *Émile et le destin*, Brussels: Max Arnold.

HISTORIES
Boelaert, E. (1946), 'La Philosophie Bantoue selon le R. P. Placide Tempels' avec une réaction de la part de Tempels, www.aequatoria.be [accessed 9 Jan. 2007].
Marchal, J. (1999), 'Première partie: Histoire de la colonisation belge du Congo, 1876–1910', www.cobelco.org [accessed 7 April 2006].
Massoz, M. (1994), *Le Congo des Belges 1908–1960*, Liège: Michel Massoz.
Pirotte, Jean (1973), *Périodiques missionnaires belges d'expression française: reflets de cinquante années d'évolution d'une mentalité, 1889–1940*, Louvain: Bibliothèque de l'Université.
Vinck, H. (1999), 'Livrets scolaires coloniaux: Méthodes d'analyse – approche herméneutique', www.aequatoria.be [accessed 29 Nov. 2006].

Mobutu

Mobutu Sese Seko Nkuku Ngbandu Wa Za Banga (14 October 1930, Congo – 7 September, 1997, Morocco) was the President of the Democratic Republic of the Congo (named Zaire under Mobutu's rule) from 1965 to 1997 and his rule remains one of the world's most notorious examples of dictatorship and kleptocracy. A former colonel and member of Lumumba's Mouvement National Congolais, he nevertheless participated actively in the 1960 coup d'état which overthrew Lumumba (then, the Prime Minister) in favour of Joseph Kasavabu (then, the President). Supported at that time by the CIA and the Belgians – who wanted to remove Lumumba from power (considered pro-Soviet and thus, dangerous for them) and saw in Mobutu the figure of the an ally in the Cold War – Mobutu, feeling invested with new powers, provoked another coup d'état in November 1965 to dismiss Kasavabu. From then on, Mobutu imposed a one-man rule, a unitary state, with no political party at all at first. Later there emerged the Popular Movement of the Revolution (MPR) whose main claims were nationalism, revolution and authenticity, whose membership was obligatory for all civilians and which was the only legal political party of the country until 1991. Despite all the challenges to his rule, Mobutu consolidated his power and legitimacy with force, violence and by dilapidating the country's wealth through mismanagement and mostly, by institutionalising corruption. His devastating rule came to an end when he started losing the support of his former allies (France, Belgium, USA and China mainly) and of his people, and when he was finally overthrown in 1997 by Laurent-Désiré Kabila supported by the Tutsi governments of Rwanda, Burundi and Uganda.

Priscilla R. Appama

LITERARY WORKS
Achebe, Chinua [1987] (1997), *Anthills of the Savannah*, New York: Anchor Books.
Labou Tansi, Sony (1979), *La Vie et demie*, Paris: Seuil.
Lopès, Henri [1982] (2003), *Le Pleurer-rire*, Paris: Présence Africaine.
Naipaul, V. S. [1979] (1989), *A Bend in the River*, New York: Vintage.
U Tam'si, Tchicaya (1979), *Le Destin glorieux du Maréchal Nnikon Nniku, Prince qu'on sort*, Paris: Présence Africaine.

HISTORIES
Braeckman, Colette (1992), *Le Dinosaure, le Zaïre de Mobutu*, Paris: Fayard.
Dungia, Emmanuel (1993), *Mobutu et l'argent du Zaïre: les révélations d'un diplomate ex-agent des services secrets*, Paris: L'Harmattan.
Janssen, Pierre (1997), *A la cour de Mobutu*, Paris: Michel Lafon.
Nguza Karl-i-Bond, Jean (1982), *Mobutu ou l'incarnation du mal zaïrois*, London: Rex Collings.
Schatzberg, Michael G. (1991), *The Dialectics of Oppression in Zaire*, Bloomington, IN: Indiana University Press.
Schatzberg, Michael G. (1991), *Mobutu or Chaos?* Lanham, MD: University Press of America.
Wrong, Michela (2002), *In The Footsteps of Mr Kurtz: Living on the Brink of Disaster in Mobutu's Congo*, London: Harper Perennial.

Narratives of Empire: (Post)colonial Congo

What is now the Democratic Republic of the Congo is an immense country, comprising several hundred ethnic groups, and as many languages. It is a country famous for its traditional plastic arts, as well as for its oral traditions. Its modern culture, especially music, is also renowned.

The Congo today finds itself in a complex linguistic situation: in addition to French, the official language since independence, Tshiluba, Kikongo, Kiswahili and Lingala are widely-spoken national languages. Congolese languages, in fact, grew in influence during colonialism; for example, the continent's first African language radio station has been broadcasting from Leopoldville since 1948, although the project began in 1933. If literature has been written mainly in French, theatre and chanson have also developed in Lingala and Kiswahili; as for fiction writing in an African language, the main language used more recently is Tshiluba.

The Congo, which covers the valley of the Congo river, borders, in the East, the volcanic area of the Great Lakes and, in the South-East, the savannahs of southern Africa. Its borders were established at the end of the 1870s, the time of the founding of the Congo Free State by the journalist and explorer Stanley and the administrators sent on a private basis by Leopold II (also constitutional King of the Belgians). It was a complex period, characterised by exploration and problems in setting up enterprises, armed conflict against slavery and against rebel soldiers, missionary and political outreach.

The 'Belgian Congo' only officially came into existence in 1908 as a result of pressure from, amongst others, Great Britain. Human relations were characterised by a general racist paternalism, reinforced by the wish to select colonial personnel and to avoid 'poor whites'. Indirect rule, separating urban sectors from the 'native lands', went alongside a favourable attitude to the indigenes in both administration and culture. The relative importance of basic education, especially when overseen by the missionaries (and conducted in African languages), the notable development of transport and industrial production infrastructure, but also of scientific literature in all fields, including ethnography and linguistics, all went hand in hand with a form of intellectual and symbolic entrapment. The régime was ill-equipped to adapt to the rapidly changing post-war world. Its legacy was a double memory of prosperity (in fact more fragile than it seemed) and iniquity, due to the slow and limited integration of the colonised peoples into the material benefits of the system, and into the exercise of responsibility.

With independence in 1960, the republic went though a great many troubles – rebellions, fragmentation, civil war – and finally the dictatorship of Colonel Mobutu, whose régime lasted until the late 1990s. During these years, the country changed its name to Zaire; its only political party preached a return to national 'authenticity'. If on balance the first years after independence were not entirely negative, economic 'Zairianisation' turned out to be a fiasco. Overall, the 'model colony' of the 1950s, with its strong economic potential, had by the end of the twentieth century become a country drained, beholden to armed groups, a state of lawlessness denounced by the writer Bolya in *L'Afrique, le maillon faible* (2002). The number of intelligent young people and the amount of capital going abroad was considerable. The infrastructure was devastated, but not national feeling, nor the hope of a return to prosperity.

FROM CONRAD TO BOLYA: THE INTERNATIONALE OF CHAOS
If the colonial period was relatively short, Belgians were active in the Congo before 1908. There were, however, never enough volunteers: in the same way that he had had to source some of his capital from overseas, especially in Great Britain, the King had to rely mainly on the services of Italians and Scandinavians.

The degree of international intervention was further reinforced, in the period of the independent state, by two ideological or political factors. The humanitarian aspect, first of all, marked the debates on what was still a terra incognita that Europeans aimed to free from the Arab slave trade. The reality of this trade was denounced by Livingstone and many others. On the other hand, the generosity of those who vowed to fight it and who called it a new 'crusade' against 'barbarity', did not mean that the humanitarian question could not serve as a shield for a campaign aiming at territorial conquest and economic exploitation. The situation was more complex, however, than this preliminary analysis suggests. The Act of Berlin did not separate the 'civilising' objectives from the clauses relating to commercial freedom in the Congo: at the time the 'Free State' was seen as an open territory, where commerce would introduce progress, simultaneously showing what unfettered liberalism was supposedly capable of.

The establishment of the colonial system began with the funding of a minimum state apparatus and the setting up of customs charges and taxes: the royal coffers were not bottomless. Transport alone, with the construction of a titanic railway between Matadi and Kinshasa, on top of the human cost, demanded huge financial support. The risk of failure explains the Free State's relaxed attitude in giving over markets to private companies without having, or creating, the means of controlling them. This plunder economy led to the violence of *Red Rubber*. The work of D. van Groenweghe (*Rood Rubber*, 1985) tells us precisely what to make of these exactions, which had already been the object of an independent enquiry commission in 1906.

The scandal lasted a decade, during which the Western press made a lot of fuss over the Congo. This had important consequences in literature. Well-known writers, first of all, became engaged in denunciations of the régime: before A. Conan Doyle's *Crime of the Congo* (1909), Mark Twain's satire *King Leopold's Soliloquy* (1905) began a tradition of anti-Leopoldian caricatures, which continued as far as *Het leven en de werken van Leopold II* (1970) by the Flemish writer Hugo Claus. But the work that has left the most lasting impression today is Joseph Conrad's *Heart of Darkness* (1899). Of course, the anti-colonialism of this tale is counterbalanced by a racism that most notably Chinua Achebe has denounced. Conrad's work has become an iconic text which has been retold in con-temporary African cultural history, for example in the context of child soldiers in Sierra Leone, and more generally, of course, as a universal parable of evil.

From Conrad to Graham Greene's *A Burnt-Out Case* (1960), V. S. Naipaul's *A Bend in the River* (1979), to Alberto Moravia (*La Donna Leopardo*, 1991), the referent of the 'prim-itive forest' has been used many times to figure savagery, dereliction, chaos, entropy, every-thing that is opposed to civilisation or threatens with regression. Other forms of literature have also played an important role here, whether they be comic strips like the *Tiger Joe* series from the 1950s, adventures for the young like *Les Démons des cataractes* (H. Vernes, Bob Morane collection, 1957), or even spy novels like *Panique au Zaïre* (G. de Villiers, SAS collection, 1978). In Belgian literature, beyond several Georges Simenon novels – espe-cially *Le Coup de lune* (1933), where the action takes place in Gabon – it is really the novel *Kufa* (1955) by Henri Cornélus, as well as George Duncan's stories – *Blancs et noirs* (1949) – that are inspired in this way. This is what has been called critical exoticism, a simultane-ously ideological and stylistic vision of a tragic scene whose issues are more metaphysical than realistic. The media's resurrection of this mythical discourse in the context of the crisis in Africa poses an obvious problem of an ethical nature, but also of a political one, since some photographs were taken on the basis of information that itself was deformed by the myth.

From the 1980s onwards a few Congolese writers attempted to join this tradition them-selves in the context of 'new African writing'. Bolya Baenga, in *Cannibale* (1986), which opens with an epigraph taken from Conrad, or Pius Ngandu Nkashama, in *Le Pacte de sang* (1984), do not, however, limit themselves to illustrating a mythical figure of chaos: via lit-erary means certainly far removed from documentary, they evoke the tragic lives of popu-lations abandoned to neglect and despair. V. Y. Mudimbe's latest novel, *Shaba deux* (1989), probably his major work, simultaneously evokes the same Congo and the same universal tragedy, but by using a style of writing that is very different in its sobriety from that of the authors mentioned above.

The historical pessimism often symbolised by the 'shadow' figure is not limited to the modern era, however: a close reading of *Ngando* (1948) – a masterpiece and the first work of Congolese literature by Paul Lomami-Tshibamba – shows that this preoccupation was also present in the oral tradition. *Ngando* reveals itself as a colonial product in a passage where it praises colonisation; if the story denounces the régime's repressive side, it is even more critical of human impotence to guard against the forces of evil, which it sees as always ready to intervene.

THE ANTI-EXOTIC TRADITION

Colonial literature, in the proper sense, is principally defined in opposition to the exotic, whether this be the traveller's clichés or the critical exoticism mentioned above. The colo-nial vision, logically speaking, not only should not consider the colony as 'elsewhere', nor the colonised people as 'Other', but rather rests on a confidence in the human being's promethean ability to assure 'development' and 'progress'. Above all, this entails a confidence in history. If the novel *Ngando* sidesteps the colonial logic of its time, it is less through the image of police suppressing the unemployed, than by the absence of this confidence.

The colonial corpus in part avoids the simplicity of the 'civilising' discourse because it is literature. It rather plays the role of a bad conscience for this discourse. Colonial fiction indeed lists the obstacles that the colonial enterprise as a whole encountered. In many cases, the confidence is maintained regardless; in others, more numerous as time goes on, doubt, even despair, eventually overcome it.

The famous cartoon *Tintin au Congo* (1931), not written by a colonial author, is the paragon of this confidence being maintained, both in history and in language. At the same time, it illustrates the paternalistic stereotypes that were dominant at the time: here is a racism that is expressed inside a group, in contrast to the exclusive racism that we find in Conrad. In literary fiction, this confidence is best represented by a novella written by the future Governor-General P. Ryckmans: *Barabara*, published belatedly in 1947. The story is set around the construction of a road in Burundi in the 1920s; the colonised people appear only marginally, but still have nothing in common with the caricatured version found in Hergé. Here we have the challenge presented by a long-term project, performed in a disinterested manner by a single man across the mountain, a man who is at the centre of this parable of 'the action of the energetic man in a new country'. The republishing of this story in the Congo in 1991 can be explained by the idealism of its values, and as such it becomes a paradoxical counter narrative to the corrupt Mobutu régime.

Colonial fiction, which begins in Dutch with *Ook een ideaal* (1896) by Pieter Danco, and in French with *Udinji* (1905) by C. A. Cudell, is not always straightforward colonialist: and becomes even less and less so with time. Thus, in the novel *L'Arrêt au carrefour* (1936), the painter Henri Kerels begins to doubt the values of Western society. In his novellas (*Apéritifs*, 1934), the magistrate Joseph-Marie Jadot shows a profound scepticism concerning the process of cultural integration. *Oproer in Congo* (1953) by G. Walschap, and a great novel like *Le Crépuscule des ancêtres* (1948), published in Leopoldville by René Tonnoir, are already African novels thanks to their essential interest in a Congolese society in rapid transition. In the age of independence, this preoccupation is even more pronounced in novels such as *La Termitière* (1960) by Daniel Gillès and *Matuli* by Joseph Esser (1960). After a period of relative obscurity, the colonial memory resurfaces in Belgium with works like those of Grégoire Pessaret and Michel Massoz. An exemplary novel, *L'Homme qui demanda du feu* (1978) by Ivan Reisdorff, is a sort of affective and political appraisal of the colonial enterprise and, finally, of its historical failure, understood in terms of the violence which broke out at the Great Lakes from the end of the 1950s. At once postcolonial (because of its date of publication, and definitely for its retrospective point of view) and colonial (because of the period discussed and by the foregrounding of an European administrator whose dream of becoming integrated in a new country fails to materialise), this novel demonstrates that easy labels are insufficient.

The field of Congolese literature

Approaching literature from a more material base provides a more solid perspective. The progressive formation of a literary field in the Congo can be observed from the end of the nineteenth century. It began with the printing of reviews and the establishment of a local-language theatre, on the initiative of missionaries. From the period between the wars, whilst a colonial literature essentially aimed at the Belgian market that was developing, we also see the activities of the *'amis de l'art indigène'* develop in the Congo – which would encourage the writing down of oral tradition – and those of the '*cercles d'évolués*'. A pocket edition, the 'Bibliothèque de l'Étoile' went on to play an essential role in the spread of written material, including the first modern fiction written by a Congolese. Colonial cultural life would become much more structured after 1945, with the activities of associations such as l'Union Africaine des Arts et des Lettres, which had been exclusively European, slowly opening up to Congolese participation. Cultural reviews such as *Brousse* or *Jeune Afrique* provide evidence of this evolution. *La Voix du Congolais*, official newsletter of the *évolués*, whose editor-in-chief was the poet Bolamba, also played a key role.

However, in 1960 the Congo had only one university graduate, Thomas Kanza, author of essays and of an autobiographical novel: *Sans Rancune* (1965). But things changed rapidly: Lovanium University had been opened in 1954, Elisabethville University in 1956. Throughout the 1960s, young poets formed many different active circles, like Clémentine Faïk-Nzuji and her group La Pléiade. Les Éditions du Mont Noir, a little later, were to centre a remarkable editorial momentum around V. Y. Mudimbe. Political power tried not to be left behind, notably supporting *Belles-lettres*. Of course, this flowering was to be countered by the drift towards autocracy, which pushed a number of intellectuals either to join militant groups, or to go into exile.

The Congolese diaspora's big names – V. Y. Mudimbe, G. Ngal, P. Ngandu – should not, however, make us forget the writers who remained in the country, whose production was furthermore widely read, notably in schools. Zamenga is the most famous, prolific author of popular literature mostly distributed through the 'Saint-Paul' network. He is far from being the only one: before also fleeing into exile, authors such as Charles Djungu-Simba or Pie Tshibanda whose books unfortunately remained out of the public domain had a literary impact totally separate from that of the authors published in the west.

These material reasons, today, continue to limit not only access to books, but also to constrain the secondary and tertiary institutions responsible for teaching of and carrying out research in literature. Meanwhile, however, young authors in the Congo and abroad continue to emerge and deliver new books for the market, in all sectors of publishing.

Pierre Halen

LITERARY WORKS

Tshitungu Kongolo, Antoine (ed.) (2000), *Au Pays du Fleuve et des Grands Lacs. Tome 1: chocs et rencontres des cultures (de 1885 à nos jours)*, Brussels: Archives et Musée de la Littérature.

Jago-Antoine, Véronique and Antoine Tshitungu Kongolo (eds) (1994), *Dits de la nuit. Anthologie de contes et légendes de l'Afrique centrale (Zaire, Rwanda et Burundi)*, Brussels: Labor.

Halen, Pierre (ed.) (1994–1995), *Littérature (La-) coloniale. I: de l'amour aux colonies, de son récit.*, Brussels: Editions Le Cri.

Lomami-Tshibamba, Paul [1948] (1982), *Ngando (Le Crocodile)*, Paris and Kinshasa: Présence Africaine and Lokolé.

Masegabio, Philippe (Masegabio Nzanzu Mabelemadiko) [1976] (1982), *Zaïre écrit. Anthologie de la poésie zaïroise de langue française*, Tübingen and Kinshasa: Horst Erdmann Verlag and Dombi Diffusion.

HISTORIES

Fraiture, Pierre-Philippe (2003), *Le Congo belge et son récit francophone à la veille des indépendances. Sous l'empire du royaume*, coll. 'Critiques Littéraires', Paris: L'Harmattan.

Halen, Pierre (1993), *Le petit Belge avait vu grand. Une littérature coloniale*, coll. 'Archives du Futur', Brussels: Labor.

Halen, Pierre and János Riesz (eds) (1993), *Images de l'Afrique et du Congo-Zaïre dans les lettres belges de langue française et alentour. Actes du colloque de Louvain-la-Neuve, 4–6 février*, Brussels: Textyles-Éditions.

Périer, Gaston-Denys (1944), *Petite Histoire des lettres coloniales de Belgique*, Brussels: J. Lebègue–Office de Publicité.

Riva, Silvia [2000] (2006), *Nouvelle Histoire de la littérature du Congo-Kinshasa*, coll. 'L' Afrique au Coeur des Lettres', trans. C. Fort, prefaces by V. Y. Mudimbe and Marc Quaghebeur, Paris, Budapest, Torino, Kinshasa and Ouagadougou: L'Harmattan.

Quaghebeur, Marc and Émile van Balberghe (eds) (1992), *Papier blanc, encre noire. Cent ans de culture francophone en Afrique centrale (Zaïre, Rwanda et Burundi)*, coll. 'Archives du Futur', 2 vol, Brussels: Labor.

The Red Rubber Scandal

The Red Rubber Scandal, the name given to the events arising from rubber collecting in the then Congo Free State, has become synonymous with images of abuse of colonial power in the early twentieth century. With recent publications such as Adam Hochschild's best seller *King Leopold's Ghost: A Story of Greed, Terror and Heroism in Colonial Africa* in 1998, King Leopold's régime, and its lasting legacy on this central African country, have been brought once again into the public arena.

The Congo Free State, which contained the now Democratic Republic of the Congo, was the personal fief of King Leopold II of Belgium from its conception in 1885, following the Berlin Conference, until its annexation by the Belgian state in 1908. Leopold's desire for a colony in order to establish Belgium within Europe, and for financial reward, was so profound that the legacy of his merciless régime resonates a century later as an extreme of political instability and financial corruption. Under his rule, the quest for rubber and other valuable natural resources caused a régime of terror, murder, mutilation and slavery to be imposed.

Leopold was fortunate to have acquired his colony at the beginning of the rubber boom. Following Dunlop's invention of the pneumatic tyre, rubber was in high demand, and Leopold found the Congo Free State to be a golden goose in a new technological era, where rubber became a worldwide necessity for developments such as car tyres, telephone cables and telegraph wires. Rubber very soon overtook ivory as the Congo's most valuable export.

The rubber was produced by wild vines and collected through a demanding process by the native Congolese, who were expected to amass a target volume per day. As Leopold's needs increased, so too did his demands, regardless of the difficult nature of the process. The wild vines, once tapped, died, which meant the workers had to penetrate much further each time into the jungle. In order to ensure the targets were met, Leopold drafted for his notorious Force Publique a ruthless army, whose use of guns and the *chicotte* (a whip made of hippopotamus hide) allowed them to punish, kidnap, rape and torture workers and their families. Perhaps the most lasting images of the Force Publique and their reign of terror can be found in the photos of severed hands and feet, which resulted from the practice of cutting limbs from victims in order to account to the white officers for the bullets spent on killing.

Eventually and inevitably, the rubber boom created a competitive world market, and Leopold's position in this market became more and more open to public investigation. Any rumours of ill-treatment, questionable profits, or suspicious stories emerging from the Congo Free State were quashed by Leopold through bribes, denials, counter-accusations and dismissals. He even created the Commission for the Protection of the Natives, which existed in name alone as proof of the king's 'benevolent' colonial rule, all of which secured Leopold's lucrative success until the turn of the century.

However, that time also marked the turn of Leopold's good luck, when mass opinion began to rise against him, as he encountered an opponent who refused to be silenced. E. D. Morel, a young Liverpool shipping clerk – whose suspicions were roused by the quantity of rubber coming from, and the quantity of ammunition going to, the Congo – sounded the alarm to the British public regarding the running of Leopold's rubber yielding colony. Morel's awareness of African affairs and economics, which was a result of his part-time jour-nalistic career, meant that he had a steady foundation on which to build a lasting campaign against the ruler of the Congo Free State. Morel was particularly insistent and vocal in his campaign and left his post at the shipping company in 1900 – after his first published arti-cles on the Congo appeared in *The Speaker* – to devote himself fully to this endeavour. After Morel had suceeded in forcing a British inquiry into the running of the Congo Free State in 1903, the British government sent their consul, Roger Casement, to the Congo to inves-tigate these claims of slavery and corruption. On his return, he met with Morel and urged him to create a Congo Reform Association. Casement's now famous 1903–4 Congo Report, although diluted by the British government, told of population decline, abuse and out-and-out slavery in Leopold's Congo. Joseph Conrad's famous colonial novella *Heart of Darkness* published in 1902 – a story based on his own experiences on the Congo river which became, and remains, a chilling view of colonial barbarity, murder and plunder – and the publication by the Congo Reform Association of Mark Twain's satirical *King Leopold's Soliloquy* in 1905, further accelerated the growth in public concern about the Congo. The Congo Reform Association's message had spread throughout Europe and the United States and had put great pressure on the Belgian government to investigate. In response, Leopold was forced to send a commission of inquiry to the Congo Free State, which, contrary to the wishes and interventions of the king, returned in 1905 with evi-dence vindicating Casement's claims in his report, and supporting the accusations of the Congo Reform Association.

With the findings of the commission, the writing was on the wall for the Belgian monarch. The signatories of the Berlin Act of 1885 now had a responsibility to act. The only real solution was for Belgium to take over from Leopold in governing the Congo, and so finally, and after much discussion, Belgium did just that in 1908, renaming it the Belgian Congo. By this time, however, the competitive market had produced cheaper providers of rubber, in South America and Asia, triggering humanitarian scandals of their own, and the Congo rubber trade, because of its previous bad management and this new market, was no longer profitable in the now Belgian Congo.

Aisling Campbell

LITERARY WORKS
Bennet, Ronan (2000), *The Catastrophist*, Chicago, IL: Simon and Schuster.
Césaire, Aimé (2001), *Une Saison au Congo*, Paris: Seuil.
Conrad, Joseph (1902), *Heart of Darkness*, Edinburgh and London: Blackwood and Sons.
Joris, Lieve (1995), *Mon Oncle du Congo* [*Terug naar Congo*], Paris and Arles: Actes Sud.
Naipaul, V. S. (1979), *A Bend in the River*, London: Picador.

Twain, Mark (1905), *King Leopold's Soliloquy*, Boston, MA: The P. R. Warren Co.
Vialette, Alexandre (1991), *Les Fruits du Congo*, Paris: Gallimard.

HISTORIES
Ascherson, Neal (2001), *The King Incorporated*, London: Granta Books.
Gidé, André (1955), *Voyage au Congo*, Paris: Gallimard.
Hochschild, Adam (1998), *King Leopold's Ghost: A Story of Greed, Terror and Heroism in Colonial Africa*, New York: Houghton Mifflin Company.
Loadman, John (2005), *Tears of the Tree – The Story of Rubber: A Modern Marvel*, Oxford: Oxford University Press.
O'Síocháin, Seamus (2001), *The Eyes of Another Race*, Dublin: University College Dublin Press.
Wrong, Michaela (2002), *In the Footsteps of Mr Kurtz*, London: Harper Perennial.

The Rwandan Genocide of the 1990s

Between 6 April and July 1994, 1 million Rwandan citizens were killed. The vast majority of these victims belonged to the Tutsi socio-ethnic group. They were not exterminated by military means, but by their neighbours, most of whom they already knew. They were massacred with machetes, small arms and explosive devices, and were hunted through the swamps by dogs. Catholic churches became the graveyard of tens of thousands of people and the corpses were thrown into the latrines of ordinary families. People who had been living together for decades, sharing the same poverty, the same language, the same culture and religion became enemies. This was not a war nor an accident but the result of a psychological, political and military preparation, with deep roots in the history of the country.

In pre-colonial Rwanda, the Tutsis, who were cattle breeders with different physical features to the Hutus, had dominated the more numerous Hutu labourers. Belgian colonialists practised indirect rule in what was a protectorate, and relied on the Tutsis to help them in the administration. They changed sides before independence, when the Tutsi élite tried to negotiate the departure of their white 'masters'. The Belgians then started to support the Hutus, and assisted them on the eve of independence in 1962. The Belgians also approved the expulsion of tens of thousands of Tutsis who became refugees in the neighbouring countries. Inside Rwanda, the remaining Tutsis, a minority of 15 per cent, became second-class citizens and were the victims of discrimination and massacres. In 1990, young Tutsis from the diaspora launched a military attack across the Ugandan border, claiming their right to return to the homeland of their parents. They enjoyed the support of the Ugandan Army, in which they had served, helping President Museveni to gain power. The régime of President Habyarimana, which was supported by the army of Zaire and by French soldiers, tried to resist the assaults of the Rwanda Patriotic Forces (RPF). But under pressure from the international community, Habyarimana was forced to negotiate with the RPF and with the democratic opposition. The peace agreement, signed in Arusha in August 1993, had expressed the hope that power would be shared through a government of national unity and that the government army and the rebel army would merge. This agreement, however, was never genuinely accepted by the President and his supporters who secretly prepared the genocide. When UN soldiers were deployed in the country under the supervision of the Canadian general Romeo Dallaire, hardliners had begun recruiting militias among the jobless and the destitute youth, who formed the Interhahamwe (those who fight together). Small arms were bought in China, other military equipment was secretly delivered by France, despite the embargo, and a million machetes were distributed to the Interhahamwe gangs, who had lists of the Tutsi civilians, all of whom were considered as accomplices of the RPF. A psychological campaign was an intrinsic part of the preparation for the killings. Extremist newspapers described the Tutsis as 'cockroaches'. A hate radio station, Radio Mille Collines, was created with private funds collected within the ranks of the presidential hardliners. The régime, however, was under heavy pressure from the international community, and on 6 April, the shooting down of the plane of the President, who was coming back from another meeting in Tanzania with his Burundian counterpart, marked the start of the killings. Within hours, political personalities were systematically killed, opening the way for the hardliners, who could operate under the cover of an interim government.

For 100 days, Rwandan citizens were trapped in a 'killing machine': the Tutsis were hunted and massacred, the Hutus were forced to participate in the killing, and instead of fighting the RPF which had resumed its military operations, the army and the gendarmerie took part in the mass murder. After the execution of ten Belgian soldiers from the UN force, on 7 April, foreigners were evacuated by Belgian and French troops, but nothing was done to stop the killing of the Rwandans. On 15 April, the Security Council decided to withdraw most of the UN contingent, leaving General Dallaire without any significant forces. On 22 June, France decided to launch single-handedly the controversial 'Opération Turquoise', whose allegedly humanitarian purposes had been questioned since it had been conceived. For three months Turquoise established a 'safety zone', which in the end was used less by surviving Tutsis than by fleeing Hutus. When the RPF troops entered Kigali in the first days of July the country was a graveyard: houses were demolished, corpses were lying everywhere, the Hutu government had fled with the archives, bank reserves and military equipment. The purpose of the Hutu authorities, military and civilian alike, was to regroup themselves in huge refugee camps established in Kivu and supported by humanitarian aid. International public opinion, which had thus far been largely indifferent to the genocide of the Tutsis, mobilised itself after a much publicised cholera outbreak in Goma that killed 40,000 refugees. The RPF troops were also accused of committing crimes, which gave the Hutu refugees reasons for refusing to re-enter the country.

After the genocide, the RPF tried to form a coalition government with Hutu politicians who had signed the Arusha agreement, but the former rebel movement had the upper hand and the then Minister of Defence, Paul Kagame, was the real strong man of the country.

It took some time for the international community to help the 300,000 orphans, the thousands of widows, the 120,000 prisoners in the crammed jails. Finally an international tribunal (ICTR) was created in Arusha, where the perpetrators of the genocide were transferred and sentenced, but no death penalty was inflicted upon them.

In Rwanda, a new constitution was adopted which banned the divisive tendencies of the past and prevented citizens from defining themselves as Hutus and Tutsis, in an attempt to reverse the brainwashing of decades. For more than ten years, former Hutu militias and soldiers, together with their civilian relatives, stayed in neighbouring Zaire, later the Democratic Republic of the Congo, refusing to go back to Rwanda. Their presence in the Congo gave the Kigali régime an excuse to invade, conquer and exploit Zaire. The suffering of Rwanda was exported to the Congo where the effects of war caused the loss of more than 3 million people.

Colette Braeckman

LITERARY WORKS

Broqueville, Huguette de (1997), *Uraho? Es-tu toujours vivant?*, Grace-Hollogne: Éditions Mols.

Mukagasana, Yolande (1997), *La Mort ne veut pas de moi*, Paris: Fixot.

Nyangoma, Nadine (1981), *Le Chant des fusillés*, Dakar: Nouvelles Éditions Africaines.

Pessaret, Grégoire (1977), *Émile et le destin*, Brussels: Max Arnold.

Richard, Pierre-Olivier (1994), *Moi, Alexandre Pivoine de Mortinsart, Ambassadeur au Rwanda*, Herstae: Pimm's Editions.

HISTORIES

Braeckman, Colette (1994), *Rwanda. Histoire d'un génocide*, Paris: Fayard.

Hatzfeld, Jean (2006), *Machete Season. The Killers in Rwanda Speak*, trans. Linda Coverdale, preface by Susan Sontag, London: Picador.

Richard, Pierre-Olivier (1997), *Casques bleus, sang noir. Rwanda 1994-Zaïre: Un génocide en spectacle*, Antwerp: EPO.

André Ryckmans

As the son of the Governor-General Pierre Ryckmans, André Ryckmans (Louvain 1929 – Congo 1960), spent several years of his childhood in the colony. His father believed in colonial imperialism as a project of reforming the Other 'respectfully' (Fraiture 2003: 46). Yet, unlike his father, Ryckmans' work as a colonial administrator would take him beyond the official orders of his superiors.

Ryckmans had intimate knowledge of the Kikuyu language and, when asked by the administration to translate and categorise the proverbs used in the traditional courts in the period 1956 to 1959, he used anthropological proceedings such as group interviews and staged fictitious trials. He thus investigated the use of proverbs under the guidance of the Kikuyu judges (Ryckmans 1992). When ordered to confront the rising Kimbaguisme in the Bakongo, his knowledge about the dynamics of social power led him to put an end to all direct contact between colonial authorities and the Kimbanguist leaders, which slowly corroded the power of the authorities (Ryckmans 1995). Symptomatically for Ryckmans' position, he understood the importance of the sect as a unique space for the colonised, yet he never considered the sect's legitimate movements of resistance but found that they manipulated and exploited their followers.

During the riots in Leopoldville in January 1959, André Ryckmans' strategy was verbal mediation without the use of force. When the new policy in the Belgian Congo, promising independence for the first time, was made public on 13 January, he was infuriated by the imprecise formulas and took it upon himself to translate the text into Kikuyu (Kestergat 1961). Ryckmans worked hard to convince his superiors to hire African assistant administrators who could take over as administrators once independence was a fact. In August 1959, he convinced the Governor-General, Schoeller, that the Bakongo should be granted independence as a province in a future federation, both to assure social and political order and to show the sincerity of Belgian policy. The idea, however, was dismissed by the Belgian government.

Following the round table conference in Brussels in 1960, Ryckmans became increasingly frustrated by the absence of any thorough preparation for independence. He decided to go beyond his orders and began to transfer formal administrative responsibilities to

Africans. In Brussels, the authorities tried to take disciplinary action against the administrator. Yet Ryckmans' commitment to increase African autonomy did not represent a critique of the colonial project, but was based on the pragmatic judgement that this was how the colonial mission (respectful reformation) could be effectuated and concluded. Following the military rebellion on 6 July 1960, Ryckmans was arrested. He was profoundly affected when he found that local acquaintances in the Bakongo had joined in with the rebels and cheered at his arrest. After his release he engaged in helping various people, both Europeans and Africans, who were persecuted by the rebelling army. On 17 July he and a colleague were arrested while seeking to pick up refugees. They were brought to a military base in Thysville where they were interrogated, beaten and – by accident, it appears – shot to death.

Heidi Bojsen

LITERARY WORKS
Esser, Joseph (1960), *Matuli, fille d'Afrique*, Brussels and Paris: Elsevier.
Reisdorff, Ivan [1978] (1995), *L'Homme qui demanda du feu*, Brussels: Labor.

HISTORIES
Fraiture, Pierre-Philippe (2003), *Le Cong belge et son récit francophone á la veille des indépendances:. Sous l'empire du royaume*, Paris: L'Harmattan.
Kestergat, Jean (1961), *André Ryckmans*, Brussels: Charles Dessart.
Lemarchand, René (1964), *Political Awakening in the Belgian Congo*, Berkeley and Los Angeles, CA: University of California Press.
Ryckmans, André [1969] (1992), 'Introduction' in André Ryckmans and C. Mwelanzambi, *Droit coutumier africain. Proverbes judiciaires Kongo (Zaïre)*, Paris and Mbandaka: Aequatoria and L'Harmattan.
Ryckmans, Geneviève (1995), *André Ryckmans, un territorial du Congo Belge. Lettre et documents 1954–1960*, Paris and Louvain-la-Neuve: L'Harmattan.

Pierre Ryckmans

Pierre Ryckmans (1891–1959) was born into a bourgeois Catholic family from Antwerp. After studying law as well as Thomist philosophy at the University of Louvain, he left Belgium in 1915 to join the colonial troops in Cameroon and East Africa, first as an administrator, then as a resident of Urundi. In 1925, he became Royal Commissioner *ad interim* for Ruanda-Urundi, the Belgian mandate territories. Known as Rikimasi, he was respected for being an extraordinary and efficacious leader, who insisted on sincerity and on the importance of understanding and communicating with the people. He was familiar with several African languages such as Lingala, Bahia, Swahili and Kirundi.

Returning to his home country in 1928, he wanted to make Belgium aware of its responsibilities towards its colony and territories in Central Africa. In his quest to make the Congo, its populations, and the problems of colonial administration better known, he gave lectures and radio talks which were published under the name *Allo! Congo!*. His recent African experience and the authority of his talks were appreciated by the general public. He taught colonial law at the Catholic University of Louvain and the Colonial University of Antwerp and published *La politique coloniale* (1934) and *Dominer pour servir* (1931 and 1948). This latter book explains his view that to dominate in order to serve provides both the excuse and the justification for the colonial conquest, and to serve Africa was to civilise it. In the second part of the book, he demonstrates his emphasis on the idea that grasping the way Africans – and more specifically people in Urundi – live, think and behave and in understanding their value systems, is central to becoming a successful colonial administrator. His genuine love for Africa and its people appears also in his collection of short stories *Barabara*.

In 1934, Ryckmans became Governor-General of the Congo, a position he held until the end of World War II, thanks to his leadership style and uncanny ability to anticipate future developments. During this period he succeeded in improving the country's adverse economic situation. When War broke out, he committed the colony to the British side. As a result, the Congolese Army fought against the totalitarian régimes, and the industries (in particular the mining sector) intensified their production to supply the Allies. In July 1946, before leaving the Congo, he gave a conference talk in which he urged Belgium to provide financial assistance for its 'colonial offspring'.

From 1946 on, he was the Belgian representative at the United Nations General Assembly and then served on the Trusteeship Council where he defended Belgian colonial work until 1957.

Thérèse de Raedt

LITERARY WORKS

Ryckmans, Pierre (1935), *Allo! Congo! Chroniques Radiophoniques*, Brussels: L'Édition Universelle.
— (1945), *Messages de guerre*, Brussels: F. Larcier.
— (1946a), *Vers l'Avenir: problèmes coloniaux de demain*, n.p.: n.p.
— (1946b), *Étapes et jalons*, Brussels: F. Larcier.
— (1947a), *Barabara*, Brussels: F. Larcier.
— (1947b), *A l'autre bout du monde*, Brussels: F. Larcier.
Ryckmans, Pierre and Jacques Vanderlinden (1988), *Inédits de P. Ryckmans*, Brussels: Académie Royale des Sciences d'Outre-Mer.

HISTORIES

Fraiture, Pierre-Philippe (2003), *Le Congo belge et son récit francophone à la veille des indépendances. Sous l'empire du royaume*, Paris: L'Harmattan.
Ryckmans, Pierre (1931), *Dominer pour servir*, Brussels: Albert Dewit.
— (1934), *La Politique coloniale*, Louvain: Éditions Rex.
— (1948), *Dominer pour servir*, Brussels: L'Édition Universelle.
Vanderlinden, Jacques (1994), *Pierre Ryckmans 1891–1959. Coloniser dans l'honneur*, Brussels: De Boeck Université.

The Scramble for the Congo

When, in October 1996, an unknown movement calling itself AFDL (Alliance des Forces Démocratiques pour la Libération du Congo) crossed the borders of Rwanda and entered the Kivu province in what was then the Zairian state, a country still ruled by President Mobutu, nobody foresaw that a political earthquake was about to take place.

The invaders were made up of a combination of Rwandan and Ugandan forces. They claimed they had the right to intervene in Kivu in order to destroy the Hutu refugee camps because they regarded them as a threat to the new régime in Rwanda, now led by the Tutsis of the Rwandan Patriotic Front. Among them were also a significant number of Congolese of Tutsi origin, called Banyamulenge (from the name of a hill in South Kivu), as well as Congolese opponents to the Mobutu régime living in the neighbouring countries, including their spokesperson Laurent Désiré Kabila.

Mobutu's army did not resist and the rapid advance of the rebel movement was spectacular. In May 1997, after only seven months of fighting, the rebels entered Kinshasa and forced Mobutu to flee the country. Kabila became the new President. The military movement soon appeared to be an 'African joint venture', as Rwanda, Uganda and Angola had joined forces to topple the dictator. Zimbabwe provided financial assistance. But when Kabila took it upon himself to behave like the president of an independent country, rejecting the tutelage of his friends and foreign advisors, and defied the Western powers through nationalist measures, he was removed.

With the silent approval of the international community, a new war broke out in August 1998 launched once more by Rwandan and Ugandan troops who again inspired two 'liberation movements' with Congolese proxies, the 'Rassemblement Congolais pour la Démocratie' and the 'Mouvement Congolais pour la Libération'. Other African countries, however, changed sides: Angola and Zimbabwe did not support the toppling of Kabila, who had joined the SADC (Southern African Development Conference) and did not approve the idea of this tutelage of Congo by its eastern neighbours. The unexpected intervention of their troops prevented the new rebels from seizing Kinshasa.

From 1998 to 2002, when a peace agreement was signed in South Africa, Congo was divided in three zones, controlled respectively by the two rebel movements and the government. In January 2001, President Kabila was assassinated by his guards as a result of an international conspiracy. His favourite son, Joseph, took power and started to negotiate with the invaders, becoming more accommodating towards Western powers. In the meantime, it emerged that despite the toppling of Kabila, Rwanda and Uganda (strongly supported by London, Washington and foreign companies) had another agenda: they needed Congolese resources for their own development, and started the extraction of gold, diamond, timber and a new mineral, used in the information technologies, the columbite tantalite, (coltan) which is abundant in the forests of Kivu. Zimbabwe also tried to exploit local resources, mainly diamonds, to pay for its military efforts.

The partition eventually failed because the foreign occupation deteriorated into a humanitarian disaster (the death of 3.5 million civilians provoked an international outrage); because Belgium, the former colonial power, became deeply involved in the negotiations in order to stop the war; and, thirdly, because Joseph Kabila appeared more flexible towards Western interests than his father. Ultimately, the partition also failed because the Congolese people themselves refused this solution and inspired a resistance movement, the Mai Mai, which fought fiercely against the occupation armies.

                                                                                    Colette Braeckman

LITERARY WORKS
Le Carré, John (2006), *The Mission Song*, London: Little, Brown and Co.
Yamusangie, Frederick (2003), *Full Circle*, iuniverse.com.

HISTORIES
Berkeley, Bill (2001), *The Graves Are Not Yet Full: Race, Tribe, and Power in the Heart of Africa*, New York: Basic Books.

Braeckman, Colette (1996), *Terreur africaine. Burundi, Rwanda, Zaïre: Les racines de la violence*, Paris: Fayard.

Tippu Tip

Tippu Tip (c.1830–1905) was born Hamed bin Muhammed el Murjebi in Zanzibar. Between 1860 and 1890, through a combination of trade and force, he established control over vast areas of East Africa. Although he had inherited African blood from a great-great-grandmother, Tippu Tip considered himself an Arab and had no hesitation in following his father and grandfather into the highly profitable trade in African slaves and ivory. Despite the efforts of the British Consul and European missionaries, the slave trade was flourishing, and even the announcement by Zanzibar's Sultan Barghas in 1876 that the export of slaves was to end, had little effect. Between 1880 and 1890 record numbers of slaves were bought and sold in the Upper Congo region, bringing huge wealth to traders like Tippu Tip.

A combination of skilful negotiation and tactical force made Tippu Tip into the most successful trader in East Africa. From his base in Zanzibar he made increasingly lengthy expeditions into the interior, initially around Lake Tanganyika, and later further inland from his base at Kasongo. Both respected and feared, eventually he was to control an area half the size of Europe. His power and influence made him useful to the great European explorers of the day, towards whom he was generally friendly. In July 1867 he met David Livingstone, then sick and with few provisions. Although Livingstone was shocked by the cruelty of the slave trade, he was grateful for Tippu Tip's kindness to him and travelled with the trader's caravan for three months.

In October 1876 Tippu Tip met Henry Morton Stanley, then on his second expedition and searching for the Congo river. Aware of the trader's influence, Stanley persuaded him to provide an escort for three months. However, disease, attacks from hostile tribes, and the difficulties of the terrain saw the trip end with accusations and recriminations. Despite this, in 1887 Tippu Tip agreed to help Stanley on his expedition up the Congo river to rescue Emin Pasha. However, according to Stanley, the problems encountered by the expedition, which took much longer than anticipated and cost the lives of many of those involved, were due to Tippu Tip's failure to provide the 600 porters promised.

Despite his strained relationship with Stanley, Tippu Tip was quick to realise the inevitable expansion of the European powers in Africa and maintained friendly relations with them, even offering protection to the missionaries who disapproved of his slave trading. From 1887 to 1890 he served the Belgian King, Leopold, as Governor of the Congo Free State. But his abiding loyalty was to the Sultans of Zanzibar, and it was to Zanzibar that he finally returned when in 1890 Germany and Britain agreed control of the region.

Fiona Barclay

HISTORIES

Brode, Heinrich [1903] (2000), *Tippu Tip: The Story of his Career in Zanzibar and Central Africa*, Zanzibar: Gallery Publications.

Farrant, Leda (1975), *Tippu Tip and the East African Slave Trade*, London: Hamish Hamilton.

Livingstone, David (1874), *The Last Journals of David Livingstone, in Central Africa, from 1865 to his Death*, London: J. Murray.
Renault, François, (1988), *Tippo Tip. Un potentat arabe en Afrique centrale au XIXe siècle*, Paris: Société Française d'Histoire d'Outre-mer.
Stanley, Henry M. [1899] (1988), *Through the Dark Continent*, 2 vols, Mineola, NY: Dover.

Denmark and its Colonies

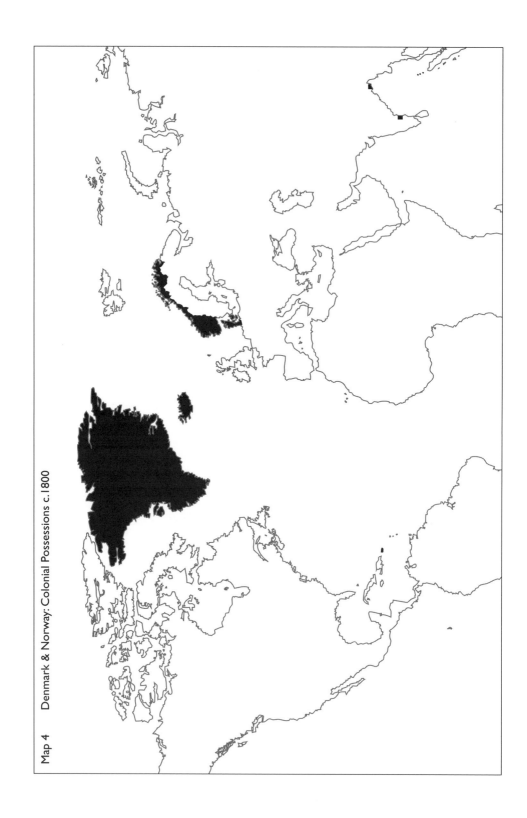

Map 4   Denmark & Norway: Colonial Possessions c.1800

Denmark and its Colonies: Introduction

In the general history of European imperialism and the creation of colonial administrations around the globe Denmark does not occupy a particularly prominent place. Its colonies were small in terms of population and, with the notable exception of Greenland, territory. But Denmark was an active partner in virtually all aspects of European imperialism, from exploration to trading posts, colonial administrations to slave possession; particularly in the second half of the 1700s it developed a lucrative trade in goods and slaves in the shadow of the larger European powers' engagement in major warfare over colonial possessions and monopolies on trade (see the entry on the Danish Charter Companies). So, the question is if anything other than relative size singles out Denmark for its particular brand of imperialism? Probably not, but what does distinguish each and every European imperial power from the others, is the particular culture around imperialism that grew out both of the imperial experiences with the colonised world, and that imperialism's relationship to nationalism.

What is characteristic of postcolonial Denmark then? To me it represents a historical engagement with Danish history, and its relative lack of attention to the importance of Danish colonies as a formative influence on Danish history and Danish national identity. This lack of attention from national historiographers towards the colonies and the idea of Denmark as part of an overseas imperial enterprise is matched by an equally underrated significance granted to the remnants of the Danish empire, Greenland and the Faeroe Islands, as a formative influence on contemporary Danish history. Yet the idea of the ungrateful and somehow lacking citizen (and therefore never quite ready for autonomy) from that bit on the North Atlantic, is an easily activated reaction from the average Dane interpellated through education, media representation and the Danish political establishment. The other side of the contemporary excavation of a post-imperial stress syndrome is the discourse on the migrant Other, as it takes place on all levels of Danish society. Arguably, the focus on the 'ill-adapting' or downright 'unsuited' migrant Other has contributed to the removal of the focus from the North Atlantic Other at least in its manifest political discourse. Nonetheless, the representations of both the 'semi-domestic' and migrant Other follow a remarkably similar pattern, where the unquestioned, rational, pragmatic and well-intended Dane is positioned against an Other who remains trapped by his or her own culture, tradition and/or religion. In particular in the current climate the national self is continuously constructed as being under siege from a haunting Other with nothing to offer the national self. The presence of others, 'semi-domestic' as well as migrants, is at the moment an extremely formative influence on definitions of a Danish identity. This cannot be seen only as a consequence of demographic change, as other periods in Danish history have had equally large migrant waves.

Simon Gikandi has lucidly described how British identity was in fact shaped decisively by events and developments in its colonies, in particular India. There was no Jewel in the Danish Crown, but there is a remarkable continuity in the way in which Denmark has looked differently at its tropical and Arctic possessions. This became absolutely clear when it came to recruiting contributors for this volume. Hence it was extremely difficult to find anyone willing to write on aspects which are historically relevant to, say, both Greenland and the Danish West Indies (now the US Virgin Islands). This compartmentalisation of research, of course, partly reflects the specific interests of historians, anthropologists and so on, but it also reflects a reluctance to see how such historical situations were connected to an overall attitude, and policy, back in Copenhagen. To take but one example, Hinrich Rink was on the global, naval Galathea expedition in 1845–7, which had instructions to search for and record important natural resources en route, and to make one last-ditch attempt to establish a Danish colony on the Nicobar Islands. The same Hinrich became perhaps the most important colonial administrator of Greenland in the nineteenth century. No one to my knowledge has taken an interest in this connection, but the important point here is that this is a single instance of a much wider pattern; a pattern which feeds into a wider narrative about relative insignificance and therefore relative innocence about the Danish empire. In the preface to Leif Svalesen's book on the slave ship *Fredensborg*, Erik Gøbel writes that the Danish part of the slave transportation was only 1 per cent out of a total number between 12 million and 15 million from 1450 to 1870. It is important, however, to keep in mind that Denmark itself was small, and that the transportation of slaves on Danish ships took place in a shorter period; so the size and relative intensity differs from Gøbel's overall assessment. Considering the 85,000 slaves Gøbel estimates that Danish ships sailed across the Atlantic, it is hard to see this as a negligible activity.

There is, however, in postcolonial terms a different and equally important aspect to this question. That is the question of how the Danish participation in the general European imperialism is understood today, outside its more specific contexts. Here we can turn to the extremely important French language account of colonialism, *Le Livre noir du colonialisme*, where the Danish Foreign Minister and widely recognised intellectual, Per Stig Møller, has written the preface to the Danish translation of this book. Møller comments that 'colonialism is a black chapter in the history of human kind'. Why 'history of human kind' rather than European history, when this is what the book is about? Even more curious is the fact that although Møller mentions the Danish colonies in the tropics, Tranquebar, West Africa and the Caribbean, he says nothing about the North Atlantic colonies. This is in spite of the fact that Greenland ceased to be a Danish colony only in 1953, and as such it would seem far more relevant to talk of the relative late decolonisation phase of this part of the Danish empire. This process is still not over, since the Faeroe Islands and Greenland are still reluctant members of the Danish Commonwealth (*Rigsfællesskabet*). The argument that Møller does not bring out in this context, but which has to be implicitly there, is that Greenland was somehow not a colony that could be compared with its tropical 'sisters'. Here Møller's omission of Greenland can again be connected to the argument that the Danish empire was smaller, less violent, and made less money than the other empires did from their colonies. Yet, interestingly enough it is impossible to find a European imperial power that would not make exactly the same argument about *their* empire. Greenland occupies a central discursive space in this narrative, because it, or rather the Danish handling of it, is supposed to show that Greenland is the perfect illustration that Denmark always had the best interests of its colonised at heart. This imperial policy has come under increasing criticism, interestingly enough in a parallel move with the increased demands for Greenlandic and Faroese independence. The formal Danish colonial policy in Greenland finished with the inclusion of Greenland in the Danish Commonwealth, a move that has in recent years been proved not to be the result of a Danish wish to grant independence to its colonies, but, on the contrary, to be the result of increased UN intervention on behalf of remaining colonies in the decolonisation phase of the 1940s and 1950s. The archives have furthermore revealed that the actions of the Danish government and its civil servants were dishonest. Greenlanders were deliberately kept in the dark, in violation of the rules laid down by the UN, and, in fact, the inclusion of Greenland in the Danish Commonwealth served mainly to protect the interests of a shrinking Danish realm and to improve Denmark's standing within NATO. The American desire for base facilities in Thule in North Greenland allowed the Danish government to punch above its weight and have influence disproportionate to its position, size and contribution to NATO. Despite the introduction of home rule for Greenland in 1979 (the Faeroese had been granted home rule in 1948) defence and foreign policy combined with the overall economic policy continue to put heavy restrictions on Greenlandic self-determination. The argument used by the Danish government (and largely uncontested by the Danish population at large, the Danish media or Danish intellectuals) is that Denmark has nothing to be ashamed of in its dealings with Greenland, as Denmark each year transfers large amounts of money to Greenland and its home rule government. This interpretation, of course, leaves out of the equation the fact that Denmark has had a de facto discount membership of NATO because it offered (or rather did not resist) American presence in Greenland's north, that Denmark has profited from the traffic in goods to Greenland, and that thousands of Danes have earned sizable amounts of money in Greenland (they were paid a higher salary than the locals) for example during the modernisation period after World War II.

The Faeroe Islands have fought through the political channels for independence for some years now, and the remarkable comments of a Danish Prime Minister, who said in 2000, 'If you slam the door I will slam the till', speaks volumes about the customary arrogance with which the Danish administration still chooses to deal with what it otherwise prefers to call 'equal partners' in the Danish Commonwealth. So, the postcolonial evidently comes in the Danish case both through the unequal relationship which is not only a product of a past imperial-colonial bind, but is actually also still being acted out today.

A last historiographical consideration, postcolonial Denmark deals with the questions of a national blindspot – a perception of Denmark as if its territorial borders were evidence of a largely unchanged holistic Danish identity, easily separated from its neighbouring countries. Here again there is a temporal and a spatial dimension. The temporal dimension challenges through the reading of Danish history, how Denmark not only has both grown and shrunk in size, but as a consequence of that fluctuation has also included areas where other languages were spoken. So, the self-assuring view that Denmark's borders are natural as well as territorial because they demarcate where Danish historically has been spoken, has only, and even then not completely, been the situation since the end of World War I. Apart from this contradictory representation, such a proposition also ignores that dialects from different parts of the country are as different, at times even more so, from each other as Danish is from Swedish or Norwegian. It comes as no surprise that the Danish state secured the relative linguistic homogeneity of its population through the teaching in schools of standard Danish, and left the dialects to die away slowly.

The idea about the one-to-one correspondence between the natural (through language) as well as territorial demarcation of Denmark has been used also to single out the migrant Other as 'naturally' different and therefore simply not proper material for Danishness. The common narrative here speaks of holistic Denmark being challenged by migrant Others, through the arrival of low-paid labour from southern Europe and the Middle East from the 1960s. The one option on offer was assimilation, the discursive term being used now is integration, but assimilation is still what is meant by the Danish majority led (on) by the political and media establishment. This narrative of historical homogeneity is easily disturbed by the presence in Danish history of many other migrant groups, such as Jews, Romani, Huguenots, Poles, Swedes and so on (see entry Denmark: Migrancy). Here also the Faeroese and Greenlanders occupy a peculiar space: they are not recognised as minorities because that would grant them certain rights in relation to issues of self-determination and discrimination.

This volume enables scholars researching various European colonial and post-imperial histories to find out what happened in other parts of Europe. One of the crucial obstacles to more comparative work, which might help remove some of the national blindspots, is language. In the Danish case the problem is a combined one of too few non-Danish scholars being able to read Danish, and a general lack of available material in English. This constitutes a serious problem for scholars eager to familiarise themselves with postcolonial Denmark, and, as the reader will see from the list of Danish references, it has also been a problem for the contributors to this volume. It is quite often difficult to come up with any references in English at all, let alone any that follow a postcolonial trajectory. In Danish the problem is that even though there exists a wealth of archival material on the former colonies, the vast majority of the work that has been done with this material suffers from a lack of attention to the power paradigm which the Danish state spread over its possessions. This is accompanied by a general lack of knowledge about what postcolonial criticism has achieved in particular in relation to making a critique of the British Empire, and to a lesser extent of the other major European empires.

Translation into English by Lars Jensen

Lars Jensen

Histories

Bregnsbo, Michael and Kurt Villads Jensen (2004), *Det danske imperium: storhed og fald*, Copenhagen: Aschehoug.

Brøndsted, Johannes (ed.) (1952–3), *Vore gamle tropekolonier*, 2 vols, Copenhagen: Westermann.

Petersen, Sophie (1946), *Danmarks gamle tropekolonier*, Copenhagen: Det Kgl. Danske Geografiske Selskab.

Skaale, Sjúrdur (2004), *The Right to National Self-Determination*, Leiden: Martinus Nijhoff Publishers.

West, Hallbera and Maria Amalia Heinesen (2004), *Kilder til Færøernes og Grønlands historie*, Torshavn: Færoya Fródskaparfelag.

Abolition of Slavery

In 1998, when the 150th anniversary of Governor Peter von Scholten's proclamation of the end of slavery in the Danish West Indies was celebrated in the Virgin Islands, it was marred by the protest and last minute withdrawal by prominent Danish politicians. In Denmark a group of Danish scholars attended a symposium on the Danish West Indian slave society, and papers from this symposium were later published. In the preface to the volume the editor regrets the absence of scholars from the Virgin Islands, and the resulting Danish bias to the volume, but says the Virgin Islands scholars were unable to attend the Danish symposium because of their participation in the celebrations in the Virgin Islands. Why their contributions could not subsequently be included for publication since the volume was not published until 2001, is cause for speculation.

Official Denmark, helped by some historians, and history books for Danish school children, has long prided itself on the fact that it was the first Western country to abolish slave trade in 1792 (although this did not come into effect until 1803), and on the humanitarian attitude of Governor von Scholten, who set the slaves free in 1848. In fact, von Scholten's proclamation was the result of a slave rebellion and in the longer term inevitable in light of the abolition of slavery by the British. When the Danish slave trade and slavery during the era of the Middle Passage is discussed, attention is drawn to the relatively small number of slaves shipped by Danish companies. While it is obviously important to present accurate facts, it is also a curious feature of Danish historians to draw attention to the comparative insignificance of Danish participation in the slave trade, which presumably has little effect on the question of morality. The same acute attention is seldom applied to the equally relative small size of Denmark in European terms with relation to population, and the shorter Danish involvement in the trade which would also put natural limits on the Danish contribution.

Lars Jensen

HISTORIES
Hall, Neville A. T. (1992), *Slave Society in the Danish West Indies: St Thomas, St John and St Croix*, ed. B. W. Highman, Mona: University of the West Indies Press.
Holsoe, Svend Einar (2001), 'A View of the Emancipation Rebellion on St Croix: 150 Years Later', in *Fra slaveri til frihed*, Copenhagen: Nationalmuseet, pp. 115–35.
Olwig, K. F. (1985), *Cultural Adaptation and Resistance on St John: Three Centuries of Afro-Caribbean Life*, Gainesville, FL: University of Florida Press.
Paiewonsky, I (1987), *Eyewitness Accounts of Slavery in the Danish West Indies*, St Thomas: Self-Aristographics.
Tyson, George F. and Arnold R. Highfield (eds) (1994), *The Kamina Folk: Slavery and Slave Life in the Danish West Indies*, St Thomas: The Virgin Islands Humanities Council.

Anthropology, Greenland and Colonialism

Danish anthropology or ethnology as an exhibition and research activity at what later became the Danish National Museum originated and developed independently of Danish colonialism during the second half of the nineteenth century, a time when only Greenland remained as a real Danish colony. The function of anthropology was to support the construction of Danish national history as part of the construction of a Danish national identity. During the 1830s, archaeology was separated from historical studies, and during the same period national history changed from being the history of kings to the history of the people. In accordance with the spirit of the romantic period, the history of the people before written history – conceived at the time as 'heathen times' – was to be established by archaeology. Because they only had material remains as a basis for reconstructing early prehistory, scholars also had to rely on anthropological collections and descriptions of 'savages' or 'primitive peoples' in order to be able to reconstruct the social and cultural life of early Danes. An anthropological collection was thus established as a study collection for the archaeologists in the newly established National Museum. As the technology of primitive peoples was comparable to prehistoric technology, archaeologists thought the same to be the case with social and cultural life in general. This belief was built into the evolutionary constructions of civilisation of the Enlightenment philosophers, and thus the archaeologists were able to reconstruct the social and cultural origins and developments during what was regarded as parallel to philosophical ideas about savagery and barbarism. In Denmark these periods were idealised, and Greenlandic social and cultural conditions served to illustrate the earliest human conditions and thus, as a hunting culture, to illustrate the earliest Stone Age culture in Denmark. The colonial system had no direct relevance in this connection (Høiris 1986).

Few people in Denmark involved in the colonial administration knew anything about the culture of Greenland. Most important among those who did was Heinrich Johannes Rink (1819–93), a physicist and chemist who took part in the Danish scientific global expedition on the ship *Galathea* from 1845 to 1847. Apart from scientific exploits, the expedition's instructions included the handing over of the colony of Tranquebar in India to the British and, as a proposed compensation, investigating the possibilities for establishing a new Danish colony on the Nicobar Islands – the expedition warmly recommended this to the King, but the proposal was never realised. During his stay on the Nicobar Islands, Rink contracted malaria or 'climate fever' and returned home. Shortly afterwords, he was sent to Greenland to do mineralogical research. Between 1858 and 1868 he was Inspector of South Greenland (the highest administrative official in the colonial administration in Greenland). Knowing the fate of indigenous peoples in different parts of the world and especially America, he was worried that the Greenlanders, like the American Indians, would become extinct, and he saw the anarchy created by the Danish colonial strategy as a direct threat to the Greenlanders' survival. He was specifically referring to the fact that in order to Christianise the Greenlanders, the Danish authorities had fought and removed or killed the *angakoks* (Greenlandic shamans), who, as the most central authorities, had played a key role in making people observe those customs and laws that centuries of experience had proved necessary for survival under such extreme natural conditions.

The authority of the *angakok* had secured the respect for customs and laws and he himself had been a person with exceptional knowledge about the laws of nature, weather conditions, conditions for hunting and human nature in general. Normally, the *angakok*, according to Rink, would be the best hunter among the men and he often passed on his knowledge through fairytales, myths and legends. Religion was his system of sanctions and the most rational customs and laws, and those most essential to survival were closely connected to religion. Dissidents were corrected in song duels where public opinion settled the dispute. But Danish mission activities disrupted this practice and both song duels and the *angakoks* were removed, after which society fell into disarray. Sons no longer showed respect for the hunting experience of their fathers and no longer learned to hunt; women lost their respect for their husbands and behaved very badly. The traditional sharing system ceased, and people sold individually to the traders and sometimes they even sold so much of their fur that they did not have enough left to make their own tools. Under such conditions there was no surplus for the poor and weak. The leadership of the *angakok* was replaced by the leadership of Europeans, but due to their lack of knowledge of Greenlandic language and culture and frequent replacements, they could not fulfil this leadership role. Their demands to the Greenlanders were inconsistent, and in reality the laws introduced were meant only to protect Danish interests. But there was still hope, according to Rink. His advice to the Danish government was that the colonial government should help those in most need and simultaneously re-establish the traditional system of production to stimulate household independence. This was to be done by supporting the rich hunters and entrusting skilled natives with the leadership of local societies. Thus, order could be re-established. The natives should have both money and spiritual authority, and the Europeans should fall back and only function as overseers without the authority to intervene in ways that would weaken the authority of the native leaders. Rink gave as the reason why only native leaders should be used the physical hazards associated with the economic activities in Greenland, which demanded hard discipline, something that in turn necessitated the hunter's extreme independence. Finally, in order for this system to function smoothly, Greenland needed to be protected from the intrusion of private interests, so it was important to preserve the commercial monopoly in Greenland. Rink's analysis and advice were not in vain. In 1862 the so-called *forstanderskaber* (directorships) were introduced in Greenland, and in 1863 support was given to expand Greenlandic production (Rink 1966–7, 1865 and 1877).

In the early decades of the twentieth century, anthropology developed as an academic discipline within cultural geography, and Greenland, or more precisely Eskimo culture, came into focus again. Inspired by German anthropogeography and cultural history, the origins of Eskimo culture became the most important anthropological subject, and until the 1960s only very rarely did anthropological analyses refer to Greenland's status as a colony or, after 1953, as a Danish county. And when Greenland was mentioned as a colony it was merely to emphasise that the Danish colonial administration functioned only to make life as good as possible for the Greenlanders, or it was used to put pressure on the Danish government to grant financing for research and exploration in Greenland. And finally, in the 1930s, scientific expeditions to East Greenland were an important political activity to secure the area as part of the Danish colony in the Danish-Norwegian conflict concerning the ownership of East Greenland.

Two themes were important to Danish anthropological investigations in Greenland before the 1960s: the origins of Eskimo culture and whether the settlement routes in Greenland had gone north or south around the island. In order to solve these questions, artefacts, list of words and myths were collected on anthropological and archaeological expeditions; the widest ranging of these was Knud Rasmussen's (1879–1933) famous fifth Thule expedition. All the collections were analysed at the National Museum, which was regarded as a cultural laboratory, and with its collections from not only all of Greenland, but also nearly all Inuit groups along the northern coast of America and inland Canada, the National Museum in Denmark had the most complete anthropological and archaeological collection in the world. Consequently, the museum became the centre for international studies of the cultural history and material culture of the Eskimos between 1925 and 1960.

Eskimo research was also carried out at the University of Copenhagen, where a chair in 'Greenlandic (Eskimo) Language and Culture' was established in 1920. William Thalbitzer (1873–1958) became the first Professor after a bitter conflict between this famous linguist and the Ethnographic Collection scholars at the National Museum over the publication of Gustav Holm's (1849–1940) work from Ammassalik. Thalbitzer had visited Greenland to do fieldwork several times, and like Rink he was critical of the execution of Danish colonialism in Greenland, but not of colonialism itself. In 1907, Thalbitzer claimed that European clothes caused colds because they were not adapted to the Arctic climate. He added that the Greenlanders needed doctors more than priests and that the mission caused ruptures in the intellectual life of the Greenlanders. Finally, he could not see why it was so urgent to baptise the Greenlanders that the colonial officials had forced them together in large communities, in spite of such serious consequences as hunger because of too much pressure on the local hunting and fishing resources (Thalbitzer 1907). After Thalbitzer's resignation, the institute continued doing ethnographic, linguistic and archaeological research similar to that conducted by the National Museum.

During the 1970s, the Institute of Eskimology grew and the new young assistant professors became deeply involved in the political processes that ended in Greenland home rule in 1979. Contemporary Greenland became the subject of research, and anthropologists among the staff were doing critical work on themes like modernisation and identity formation, based on extensive fieldwork. Robert Petersen, a native Greenlander and one of few Greenlanders with an academic degree, became a full professor with language as his main subject, and he was also deeply involved in structuring the new Greenland. He may be credited with the establishment of a Greenlandic university in the capital of Nuuk, Ilisimatusarfik. In 1968, the anthropologists Helge Kleivan (1924–83) and Jens Dahl took the initiative to establish what is now a worldwide organisation, the International Work Group of Indigenous Affairs (IWGIA), to defend the general and human rights of indigenous people. Since then IWGIA has grown enormously and received international recognition. Also the two institutes of anthropology in Copenhagen and Aarhus conducted intensive fieldwork in the small local societies from the 1960s through to the 1980s, studying the modernisation which had spread all over Greenland, and critically analysing both the general policy towards Greenland and its effects on local societies in a more or less Marxist perspective focusing on imperialism, colonialism and neo-colonialism.

After the establishment of home rule in Greenland, the interest in anthropological research diminished in Denmark and the Institute of Eskimology was reduced in staff and students and its very existence threatened. Greenland gained its own national museum, Nunatta Katersugaasivia Allagaateqarfialu, and a great number of the Danish collections were transferred there. With its own national museum and university and with major reductions in the Danish allocations for doing cultural research in Greenland, the Danish Research Ministry regarded it as the duty of the Greenlanders themselves to conduct and especially finance cultural and historical research in Greenland.

Ole Høiris

HISTORIES

Høiris, Ole (1986), *Antropologien i Danmark*, Copenhagen! Nationalmuseets Fozlag.

Rink, Heinrich J. (1865), *Bemærkninger angaaende den grønlandske comissions betænkning af 23de juli 1863*, Copenhagen.

Rink, Heinrich J. (1877), *Om en nødvendig foranstantning til bevarelse af Grønland som dansk biland*, Copenhagen.

Rink, Heinrich J. [1862] (1966–7), 'Om aarsagen til Grønlændernes og lignende af jagt levende nationers materielle tilbagegang ved berøring med europæerne', *Folk* 8–9: 224–41.

Thalbitzer, William (1907), 'Eskimokulturen ved angmassalik. Iagttagelser fra et ophold i Østgrønland 1905–6', *Geografisk Tidsskrift* 19: 56–70.

WEBSITES

History of Eskimology: http://eskimologi.ku.dk/omuddannelsen/eskimologis_historie/
IWGIA: http://www.iwgia.org/sw617.asp
Ilisimatusarfik: http://www.ilisimatusarfik.gl/
National Museum of Greenland: http://www.natmus.gl/en/

Charter Companies

In a book published in 1946 the Danish colonial historian, Sophie Petersen, makes the acute observation that Copenhagen has retained many traces of its highly prosperous period in the second half of the 1700s. Such remarks have since disappeared from books on Danish history, which inevitably focus on history being produced as a consequence of largely domestic factors.

However, Denmark did enjoy great prosperity in the 1700s and it was caused, not so much by the direct possession of colonies as by the wider trading activities brought on by European imperialism. The profits of the mercantilistic period reached Denmark through the hands of the Charter Companies. There were about twenty of these over a period of 200 years, and their lives were characterised by cycles of boom and bust. It was Dutch influence and rivalry which sparked off the first round of Danish Charter Companies in the early 1600s. Danish sailors went on Dutch expeditions to the East Indies, and Dutch speculators contacted the Danish king with a view to opening up a trading post in India. Some of the operations were initially small in scale, quite literally one-ship missions to establish a trading post. Eventually the operational ground of the Charter Companies would mirror Danish colonial possessions as they established themselves in Greenland (1619, 1636 and 1747), Iceland (1619, three subsequent companies 1733–74), West Africa (1625, 1636, 1671, 1765 and 1781), Morocco (1778), the Caribbean (1652, 1671 and 1778), and particularly India, where the most successful of the Danish Indian Charter Companies was established in 1732. With the loss of Denmark's international position after the Napoleonic Wars, the Danish Charter Companies slowly disappeared or were taken over by the British. In the North Atlantic Danish colonies a royal trading monopoly took over, which was abolished in Iceland and the Faeroe Islands in the 1850s, but not until 1950, in Greenland, and even then the company retained many of its privileges.

The Danish colonies were small in terms of population and (with the exception of Greenland) territory. The Charter Companies largely controlled the administration of the colonies during the companies' most influential periods. The contact between Denmark and its colonies was sporadic at best, which provided for long periods of relatively extensive autonomy for the local commander. The Charter Companies were a quasi-private enterprise, as investors were made up of a mixture of merchants, both Danish and other Europeans (in particular, Dutch merchants), while the King was often the main investor. The nature of the arrangement meant that the Danish state would intervene both to protect its colonial possessions from rival nations and to protect its investments. Even as late as 1845 there was a last attempt to locate a possible new colony in the Nicobar Islands, when it was clear that Britain would monopolise the trade with India itself.

Lars Jensen

HISTORIES

Brøndsted, Johannes (ed.) (1952–3), *Vore gamle tropekolonier*, 2 vols, Copenhagen: Westermann.

Feldbæk, Ole (1969), *India Trade under the Danish Flag 1772–1808*, Odense: Scandinavian Institute of Asian Studies Monograph Series.

— (1986), *Danske handelskompagnier 1616–1843*, Copenhagen: Selskabet for Udgivelser af Kilder til Dansk Historie.

Larsen, Kay (1907–8), *De Dansk-Ostindiske koloniers historie*, 2 vols, Copenhagen: Peter Hansen.
Petersen, Sophie (1946), *Danmarks gamle tropekolonier*, Copenhagen: H. Hagerups Boghandel.

Colonial Exhibitions

Colonial exhibitions in Denmark can be traced to the seventeenth century. In 1605 several Inuit were kidnapped on the expedition ordered by Christian IV to 'rediscover' Greenland. They created widespread public excitement on arrival in Copenhagen, and were displayed to the royal court. More were kidnapped in 1606, and there were later attempts; three women arriving in 1654 were made to dance ballet for the court. During the 1600s the court collected other living subjects for its amusement and service; 'Blackamoors' (from the West Indies and Gold Coast) and Turks provided entertainment alongside 'freaks' and exotic animals. Ethnographic artefacts were also collected for the royal Kunstkammer.

In 1724, following the establishment of the first Danish mission in Greenland, two Inuit men, Pooq and Qiperoq, encouraged by the missionary Hans Egede, travelled to Denmark. They were presented to the court and, to promote interest in Greenland, a grand public spectacle was arranged in which they paddled kayaks and hunted ducks on the canals of central Copenhagen. When Pooq (baptised Christian) returned to Denmark in 1728 with his family and other companions, they became a major public attraction (their doorkeeper profiting by charging admission) (Bertelsen 1945). Several of the Inuit later taken to Denmark would also be displayed at court.

In the late nineteenth and early twentieth centuries, exhibitions of 'exotic' people were extremely popular. Frequent large-scale exhibitions (for example, Nubians, Sioux Indians, Cannibals, Mahdi's warriors, Senegambians, Bedouins, Indians, Chinese) were held in the capital, many at Tivoli and at the Copenhagen Zoo. The German, Carl Hagenbeck, who began this tradition touring Europe with human and animal exhibits, arranged many of these. The exhibitions supposedly portrayed the authentic life of those on display, and were not without erotic interest (Andreassen 2003). These spectacles staged the Orientalist construction of the non-European as a primitive, exotic 'Other'. Victor Cornelins, a West Indian boy exhibited in the 1905 Colonial Exhibition at Tivoli, described how being displayed in a cage (to prevent him wandering around other exhibits) increased spectators' interest.

Exhibitions of living subjects and/or ethnographic objects did not merely serve as entertainment; they were strategic, promoting colonial interests. International colonial exhibitions exemplified this, for instance, Denmark's exhibition on Greenland at the 1931 Exposition Coloniale in Paris.

Ideas of race and evolution propagated at 'living exhibitions' were also structuring principles of ethnographic exhibitions in museums. Items from the Kunstkammer were rehoused in the world's oldest ethnographic museum in 1841 (later the National Museum's Ethnographic Collection), and classified according to stages of civilisational progress. The collection was greatly expanded in the twentieth century with expeditions to Greenland, Central Asia and North Africa. Ethnographic exhibitions continued to present other cultures in terms of temporal backwardness, thus legitimising colonialism's 'civilising mission'.

Cheralyn Mealor

LITERARY WORKS
Høeg, Peter (1997), *Miss Smilla's Feeling for Snow*, trans. F. David, London: The Harvill Press.

HISTORIES
Andreassen, Rikke (2003), 'The 'Exotic' as Mass Entertainment: Denmark 1878–1909', *Race & Class* 45 (2): 21–38.
Bertelsen, A. (1945), 'Grønlænderne i Danmark', *Meddelelser om Grønland* 145(2) special issue.
Cornelins, V. (1977), *Fra St Croix til Nakskov*, Odense: Frimodts Forlag.
Harbsmeier, Michael (2002), 'Bodies and Voices from Ultima Thule: Inuit Explorations of the Kablunat from Christian IV to Knud Rasmussen', in M. Bravo and S. Sörlin (eds), *Narrating the Arctic*, Canton, MA: Watson Publishing International.
Høiris, Ole (1986), *Antropologien i Danmark: museal etnografi og etnologi 1860–1960*, Copenhagen: Nationalmuseets Forlag.

Creolisation

Within linguistics the term 'creolisation' has been used to describe encounters and interchanges between different languages. Creolisation has also been theorised by Caribbean intellectuals (Glissant, Benítez-Rojo, Brathwaite, Ortiz among others) as a concept that describes the dynamics of cultural signifying systems and practices in the Caribbean in a way that focuses on the complexity of social agency throughout the particular history of the region while revealing the shortcomings of colonialist conceptions of race, territory, history and their legacies, even if the term has also been applied in other contexts. Among the various etymological meanings attributed to the word 'creole', it is perhaps 'to grow' and 'to raise' that are particularly important when referring to creolisation within the three Caribbean islands that were colonised by the Danes: St Thomas (1666), St Jan (St John) (1718) and St Croix (1733). Until 1755 it was notably private trading companies which inscribed the Caribbean islands into the Danish imperial territory through the general 'growing' and 'raising' of profits in a trade that involved goods from Iceland and Greenland and, most importantly, slaves from the Gold Coast.

The history of creolisation in the former Danish islands presents several distinctive features. Only a few of the settlers in the Danish Caribbean were Danes. Most had a Dutch background and others had various European backgrounds. The Afro-Caribbean slaves exercised a particular kind of social power in the relationship with the Euro-Caribbeans because of the pronounced fear of slave riots and rebellions. More importantly, within a generation or two, the slaves formed their own internal communities and trading economies. As food shortages were was often a problem, Euro-Caribbeans became dependent on this economy. During the nineteenth century, slaves became increasingly aware of the possibility of using the court system as a forum for resistance against social injustice. Sexual relations between Euro- and Afro-Caribbeans and the economic and social success of the freemen and women (freed slaves and their descendants) were instrumental in the formation of a distinct creolisation within the official conceptualisation of a racial hierarchy. The best-known example may be the wealth and influence of Anna Heegaard, the companion of Governor Peter von Scholten. Even after the abolition of slavery, social creolisation continued as a struggle for social justice. Significant examples that caused changes in social order and practices and ideas about race are the rebellion of the Afro-Caribbean workers in 1878, the strike in Charlotte Amalie on St Thomas in 1892, the political activism of David Hamilton Jackson of St Croix, in Denmark and on the islands, the founding of the Labour Union in 1915 by George Morehead, and the strike of the coal workers in 1916. After the islands were sold to the USA in 1916, Afro-Caribbean immigrants contributed to the Harlem Renaissance. However, within the islands, cultural and social order was now marked by the use of St Thomas as a military base. Although racial segregation had been legally abolished already in 1834 – *before* the abolition of slavery in 1848 – the Afro-Caribbean population was now facing a body of administrators and military personnel that were trained in working within segregationist ideologies.

Heidi Bojsen

LITERARY WORKS
Hertz, Henrik [1836] (1998), *De frifarvede*, Copenhagen: Dansk Vestindisk Selskab/Poul Kristensens Forlag.
Larson, Nella (1928), *Quicksand*, New York and London: Knopf.
Larson, Nella (1929), *Passing*, New York and London: Knopf.

HISTORIES
Brathwaite, Edward K. (1971), *The Development of Creole Society in Jamaica 1770–1820*, Oxford: Clarendon.
Glissant, Édouard [1981] (1989), *Caribbean Discourse*, trans. Michael Dash, Charlottesville, VA: The University Press of Virginia.
Guirty, Geraldo (1989), *Harlem's Danish-American West Indies, 1899–1964*, New York: Vantage Press.
Holsoe, Svend and John MacCollum (eds) (1993), *Danish Presence and Legacy in the Virgin Islands*, Frederiksted Saint Croix: Saint Croix Landmarks Society.
Nielsen, Per (2004), 'Opfattelser af race og klasse i Dansk Vestindien', *Nationalmuseets Arbejdsmark*, 209–29.
Olwig, Karen Fog (1985), *Cultural Adaption and Resistance on St John: Three Centuries of Caribbean Life*, Gainesville, FL: University of Florida Press.

The Greenlandic Colonial Administration

The Danish government took over responsibility for trade in West Greenland in 1726, and in 1776 formed the Royal Greenlandic Trade Company (known as KGH: Det Kongelige Grønlandske Handelskompani). KGH maintained a trade monopoly until the end of World War II. During the late eighteenth century KGH established colonies along the West Greenlandic coast, which up to the 1950s were divided into two provinces each headed by a governor who reported directly to the KGH administration in Copenhagen.

Until 1908 both trade and administration were the responsibility of KGH. The Danish colonial attitude towards Greenland was isolationist and paternal, and aimed to protect the Inuit seal-hunting culture. KGH kept Greenland closed off from the rest of the world, and even Danish citizens were not allowed to enter Greenland without a permit. The Royal Ordinance's instructions of 1782 focused on European trade with the Greenlander and the regulation of other kinds of intercourse between Greenlanders and outsiders. This situation changed around 1860, when the Danish state introduced councils with Greenlandic participation in every factory district. Up to 1950, three distinct periods can be identified: 1862–1910 was the time of the Boards of Guardians; 1911–25 was the period of the Municipal Councils and the Provincial Councils; and in 1925 District Councils were added. From 1925 to 1950, therefore, there were three levels: local, district (factory) and provincial. In 1950, municipalities were introduced to what was formerly the factory district level and the two Provincial Councils were made into one. Councils now existed on only two levels.

The establishment of the Boards of Guardians in the 1860s owed much to the Governor of South Greenland, H. Rink, who was amongst the first to criticise the policy of increased westernisation and commercialisation in Greenland. He argued that Greenlanders had to take responsibility for their own lives, like they had before the Danes colonised Greenland in 1721. Western 'luxury goods' had spoiled the Greenlanders, and they had forgotten the old ways of hunting and taking care of their kinsmen. The Boards of Guardians were seen by Rink as a platform for political reform from which Greenlandic representatives could restore their self-confidence and increase the pride of the seal hunters. The members were Greenlanders as well as Danes, while the Municipal Councils mostly had Greenlandic members. The participation of Greenlanders in politics still had a long way to go.

After World War II Denmark ended its isolationist policy towards Greenland. Emphasis was placed on social welfare as a part of 'modernisation'. On Danish Constitution Day, 5 June 1953, Greenland was incorporated into the Kingdom of Denmark, and was granted two seats in the Danish Parliament. This brought a formal end to Greenland's colonial status, and Greenland became a Danish province. East Greenland and Thule in northernmost West Greenland were not integrated into the general political and administrative system of Greenland until the beginning of the 1960s.

Mette Rønsager

LITERARY WORKS
Høeg, Peter [1992] (1997), *Miss Smilla's Feeling for Snow*, trans. F. David, London: Harvill Press.

HISTORIES
Forchhammer, Soeren (2001), 'Political Participation in Greenland in the 19th Century, State Hegemony, and Emancipation', *The Northern Review* 23: 38–58.
Harhoff, Frederik (1994), *Rigsfællesskabet*, Aarhus: Klim.
Marquardt, Ole (1999), 'A Critique of the Common Interpretation of the Great Socio-Economic Crisis in Greenland 1850–1880: The Case of Nuuk and Qeqertarsuatsiaat', *Études Inuit Studies* 23 (1): 9–34.
Nuttall, Mark (1994), 'Greenland: Emergence of an Inuit Homeland', in Minority Rights Group (ed.), *Polar Peoples. Self-Determination and Development*, London: Minority Rights Publications, pp. 1–28.

Greenlandic Writers

The Danish colonisation of Greenland was responsible for making Greenlandic (an Inuit language) a written language used as language of instruction in missions and schools. Both the Danish mission and the Moravian Brethren wrote hymn books in Greenlandic.

From the mid-nineteenth century the oral tradition was written down by the Greenlanders themselves. A newspaper was published from 1861 onwards (that is, 200 pages per year written by Greenlanders in Greenlandic). In the late nineteenth century Greenlandic hymns began to be set down in a literary fashion. After 1900, national songs and other European literary genres were consciously appropriated by the Greenlanders themselves to their own needs. The various forms of oral tradition, however, were not transferred to literature. Ethnic demarcation took place through themes and language. On a par with the newspapers, the literature became an important space for the internal Greenlandic debate on socio-political issues. Both media became important elements in the nation-building process of twentieth-century Greenland, first when it was a colony, then as part of Denmark and finally under home rule. Themes in the first half of the century included negotiations over how to define Greenlandic identity, how to imagine future developments, how to depict 'heathen' forefathers in light of the fact that most Greenlanders were now born within the Christian faith.

The Danification policy from 1953 triggered off a protest movement which peaked in the late 1970s and early 1980s. Protest lyrics attacking Danish rule were used (with Danish or English translation) to convey the political messages. Many of these lyrics appeared as songs issued in albums, thereby reaching many.

When home rule had been introduced in 1979, Danification was replaced with Greenlandification. After a decade Greenlandic officially was no longer considered a threatened language. An increasing number of literary works were published. However, from the late 1980s younger readers began to complain that Greenlandic literature did not address their lives. Some contemporary works do have a very conservative moral outlook, while older literature presupposes better knowledge of Christianity than the younger generation has. In an age of the internet, satellite TV and DVDs, the challenge for the authors is serious. Meanwhile politicians seem to think that literature should be self-financing. In any given population only a few per cent will buy and read literature. In Greenland this percentage has to be found amongst roughly 50,000 mother-tongue speakers of Greenlandic. It is important for any language (and its culture) that it is literary and creative, and that the world is represented through the local tongue. This is even more important in Greenland, where in film and video production local production is still almost non-existent. Greenlandic literature in the twentieth century is a postcolonial literature that deals with nation building. In general, it describes how things are among Greenlanders. The Danes are the significant Others, who are left unmentioned in most cases.

Asked as citizens Greenlanders will still think that Greenlandic literature should go on in this postcolonial way. But as readers they want thrillers, romance, in depth psychological plots and so on. This discrepancy (along with a deal with of young literary talents) has been a problem for some time now, but imminent change is in the air. There has been a recent emergence of a written Greenlandic thriller genre, which has grown out of an old oral genre (typically starting with disappointed people seeking evil supernatural power through a hermit existence in the wilderness). Further, increasing focus in the community on individuality and on social problems from a non-ethnic-national perspective is mirrored in a new, but steadily growing testimony literature and in literary works closely bound up with personal problems such as psychological and physical violence in relationships, incest and child abuse, alcoholism and homophobia. Most of these works are not sophisticated, but may pave the way for something better. This is also apparent in explicitly ethnic-national works, where humour is beginning to emerge as well.

Parallel to the literary production many song lyrics have been written since the 1970s. Less confined by ethno-national stereotypes although protest lyrics kicked off the movement, this form has attracted new young writers. Now young rappers are criticising their parents for many forms of neglect.

While published literary works in general are written in Greenlandic and very few in Danish, in recent years two young Greenlandic singers have written (or co-written) their lyrics in English. It is a growing tendency that many new literary works, together with some older ones, appear in Danish translation (one of the reasons being that some Greenlanders have Danish as their mother tongue as a result of the Danification period), but virtually nothing has been translated into English (for Danish translations, see Langgård 2003). Compared to European literatures the Greenlandic one is both of very recent date and small. Compared to the other Inuit areas it is exceptionally old and both substantial and impressive in breadth and size.

Karen Langgård

CRITICAL WORKS
Berthelsen, Christian (1986), 'Greenlandic Literature', *Arctic Anthropology* 23: 339–45.
Langgård, Karen (2003), 'Mellem globalisering, nation building og individets dagligdag på godt og ondt. – Den nyeste grønlandske litteratur i teksthistorisk lys ud fra en postkolonial vinkel', *Nordica* 20: 263–300.
— (2004), 'Litteraturen er folkets øjne, ører og mund', in Birgitte Jacobsen et al., *Grønlænder og global*, Nuuk: Ilisimatusarfik, pp. 95–162.
— (2004), 'Identity and Interethnic Relations – seen through Research in the Greenlandic Language and in the Greenlandic Literature', in Michèle Therrien (ed.), *Dynamics and Shifting Perspectives. Arctic Societies and Research*, Nuuk: Ilisimatusarfik, pp. 19–35.
— (2005), 'Literature, Greenlandic', in Mark Nuttall (ed.), *Encyclopedia of the Arctic*, New York: Routledge, pp. 1184–6.
Pedersen, Birgit Kleist (2005), 'Young Greenlandic Writers in the Public versus the Anonymous Space', in Jenny Fossum Grønn (ed.), *Nordic Voices*, Oslo: NORBOK, pp. 56–9.

N. F. S. Grundtvig

N. F. S. Grundtvig (1783–1872) represents a towering figure in Danish intellectual, religious and national history. He was primarily concerned with ideas of nation and people, although interestingly enough he never wrote a Danish history, but rather three world histories. He wrote and spoke passionately about the Danish nation, but the intellectual influences on his thinking came from abroad, particularly from John Locke. More than anything, however, Grundtvig was a religious thinker, who spent a great many of his early years in isolation from mainstream religious and political thought. It was nationalism that brought him into the limelight, partly though his ability to appeal to the masses, mostly peasants in mid-nineteenth century Denmark. It was Grundtvig's thoughts on peasant education which led to the establishment of the first Danish Folk High School. His interest in peasant education was coupled with his strong support for the absolute monarchy. When the pressure for democratic reform forced a new constitution to be written, Grundtvig became an active politician who sat in the Danish Parliament.

Central to Grundtvig's ideas on nationalism was a common language, culture, history and territory. This went against the contemporary structure of society in mid-nineteenth-century Denmark, which included a significant part of current northern Germany, that had an important influence in the political power structure of Danish society, and also meant that around 40 per cent of the Danish population was German-speaking. Grundtvig's four criteria play an important role in contemporary discussions about Danish national identity, particularly in populist right-wing politics, but also more broadly in the debates concerning the rights of immigrants to be taught their mother tongue, and to practise their own culture. Furthermore the emphasis on territoriality continues to smack of an organic Danish identity unproblematically rooted in the Danish soil, as opposed to that of immigrants, whose identity and loyalty are frequently questioned. The Faeroe Islands and Greenland, as well as Greenlanders and Faeroese people living in Denmark, constitute a particular problem for this kind of self-definition. Hence in the early 1950s UN questions concerning the colonial desire for greater autonomy or independence were rejected with the Danish government's representative's remark that the Greenlanders and Faeroese felt they were Danish.

Grundtvig devoted little time to the Danish colonies, albeit he was an active member of an anti-slavery committee in Copenhagen. This committee was formed after the establishment of an English committee, which sought to set up sister organisations in continental Europe, partly out of humanitarian concern, partly out of an anxiety over unequal conditions for plantation owners in the Caribbean in particular. Grundtvig was more outspoken on the issue of slavery than actively instrumental in its eventual abolition in 1848.

Lars Jensen

HISTORIES

Allchin, A. M. (1997), *Grundtvig. An Introduction to his Life and Work*, Aarhus: Aarhus University Press.

Allchin, A. M., D. Jasper, J. H. Schjørring and K. Stevenson (eds) (1993), *Heritage and Prophecy: Grundtvig and the English-Speaking World*, Aarhus: Aarhus University Press.

Broadbridge, E. and L. Jensen (eds) (1984), *N. L. A Grundtvig Anthology*, Viby: Centrum.

Bugge, Knud Eyvin (2003), *Grundtvig og slavesagen*, Aarhus: Aarhus University Press (contains a short English summary).

Knudsen, Johannes (ed.) (1976), *N. F. S. Grundtvig, Selected Writings*, Philadelphia, PA: Fortress.

Thyssen, A. P. and Christian Thodberg (eds) (1983), *N. F. S. Grundtvig: Tradition and Renewal*, Copenhagen: Det danske Selskab.

Thorkild Hansen and the Critique of Empire

Prior to the 1960s and the emergence of documentary fiction and politically engaged literature, Denmark's colonial history and the Danish slave trade were distant and romanticised episodes in the historical consciousness. Modern Denmark is not generally regarded as a colonial power engaged in the subjugation of indigenous peoples in distant colonies – and certainly not when measured against the imperial legacies of neighbouring Europeans. However, in the 1960s, when the civil rights movement in the USA began to create a global awareness of racial injustices, and when massive popular movements in Western Europe began to expose the role of Western imperialism in the developing world, a critique of imperialism emerged in Danish documentary literature; in the works of Danish writer Thorkild Hansen (1927–89), this critique is sharply focused on Denmark's colonialist legacy. In this regard, Thorkild Hansen's contribution is unique in Danish letters; it is also remarkable in terms of sheer volume: Hansen published several substantial documentary works dealing with controversial or forgotten chapters in Denmark's imperialist past.

Prior to the publication of a remarkable trilogy of works by Thorkild Hansen, *Slavernes kyst* (*The Slave Coast*, 1967), *Slavernes skibe* (*The Slave Ships*, 1968) and *Slavernes øer* (*The Slave Islands*, 1970), Denmark's involvement in slave trading and slavery on West Indian colonies was an obscure chapter in the national past. One sentence by popular Danish historian Palle Lauring in his *Danmarkshistorie* (1960, translated as *A History of the Kingdom of Denmark*) illustrates quite well the official and widely held view: 'Denmark had put a stop to the import of Negro slaves on its West Indian Islands in 1792 – the first country in the world to forbid slave-trading' (1960b). Thorkild Hansen's extensively researched and masterfully narrated 'Slave Trilogy' may be read as a corrective to the cursory treatment which Denmark's involvement in the slave trade has received in popular and textbook histories. In Hansen's words in the opening volume of the trilogy:

> Skole bøgernens lille oplysning om, at Danmark var det første land, som afskaffede slavehandelen. Tusinder af mænd, kvinder og børn. Og bagefter en enkelt sætning. Som er forkert. (1960a) [The textbook's little piece of information about the fact that Denmark was the first country to abolish the slave trade. Thousands of men, women and children. And in the end a single sentence. Which is incorrect.]

While it is tempting to read the Slave Trilogy solely as an attack on imperialism and Danish complicity with the atrocities of slave-trading and slavery, the trilogy also demonstrates the author's dedication to the process of investigating and recreating a historical reality. In a decade when the USA was in the spotlight for its racist treatment of African Americans, Thorkild Hansen shifted the focus to his own home-front and touched a sensitive nerve in the national conscience. Indeed, the award to Hansen of the Nordic Council's literary award in 1971 for *Slavernes øer* appeared politically motivated; the commission (part of the Nordi Council) called the work 'an example of the wealthy countries' exploitation of the impoverished countries . . . illustrated with historical expertise and powerful artistry' (quoted in Hansen 1982).

Slavernes kyst, the first volume of the trilogy, offers a history of 'Danish Guinea' (southeastern Ghana), where the Danish state maintained five forts for the purpose of enslaving Africans as labourers for its West Indian colonies. The second volume, *Slavernes skibe*, describes the dreadful conditions aboard the slave ships which transported African prisoners from the forts to the colonies in the West Indies, where they were sold on the auction block to Danish plantation owners. Of the tens of thousands of Africans transported, Hansen estimates that one fifth perished in the packed holds of the ships which drifted across the windless 'Middle Passage'. *Slavernes øer*, the final volume, is a tour de force, that dramatises the entire history of the Danish West Indies, which included the islands of St Croix, St Jan and St Thomas (now the US Virgin Islands), from the arrival of the first colonists in 1671 to the sale of the islands to the USA in 1917 for $25 million.

Although Thorkild Hansen refused to subscribe to the narrowly defined leftist political ideology of the 1960s, his major documentary works dealing with little-known episodes in Denmark's history of exploration and colonialism share some of the common concerns of this period. To some degree, these documentary novels articulate the newly awakened interest in Western ventures into 'exotic' parts of the world. Focusing on nearly forgotten explorers, scientific expeditions and commercial ventures in Denmark's imperial past, Hansen constructed very engaging historical narratives about the Danish expedition to Yemen in 1761–7 headed by Carsten Niebuhr, *Det lykkelige Arabien* (1962; *Arabia Felix*, 1964) and about the ill-fated seventeenth-century Danish voyage led by captain Jens Munk to discover a Northwest Passage through North America, *Jens Munk* (1965; *The Way to Hudson Bay*, 1970). Hansen was an early proponent and master of documentary fiction; his major works published in the 1960s became best-sellers in his native Denmark and were extremely popular throughout Scandinavia. The political climate of the period with its new awareness of Western neo-colonial influence in the developing world may have encouraged writers such as Hansen (as well as Per Olav Enquist and Per Olaf Sundman in Sweden) to seek answers to current problems through historical inquiries into earlier European colonialist ventures.

Similar to Johannes V. Jensen in some respects, Thorkild Hansen is one of the great travellers in modern Danish letters; his works reach back into history and out into the far corners of the globe. His method, which involves extensive research into authentic documents as well as first-hand expeditions to the historical sites, was highly innovative in his day. Hansen deliberately walked a tightrope between fact and fiction, demonstrating his great skill as a novelist as well as his impressive talent as an historian. More daring and provocative than other documentary writers of the period, he undertook ambitious and controversial topics while challenging the disciplinary boundaries between history and fiction with all the hazards involved. In Hansen's final documentary block-buster, which deals with Norwegian Nobel Laureate and Nazi-sympathiser Knut Hamsun, *Processen mod Hamsun* (*The Case against Hamsun*, 1978), this controversial mixture of fact and fiction provoked considerable public debate.

Nonetheless, Hansen's three major documentary projects of the 1960s contribute a significant 'revisionist' perspective on Denmark's colonialist past. At the same time, Hansen's documentary fiction articulates some of the philosophical concerns of modern historiography. Similar to other Scandinavian documentary works of this period which depict historical expeditions or ventures, an existentialist quest is embedded in Thorkild Hansen's narratives. This quest depicted by the author is historical as well as epistemological; the reader is invited to share in the difficulties involved in any historical inquiry into the past – and in this case, into questions regarding Denmark's imperialist past.

Marianne Stecher-Hansen

LITERARY WORKS

Hansen, Thorkild (1962), *Det lykkelige Arabien: en dansk ekspedition 1761–67*, Copenhagen: Gyldendal; trans. James and Kathleen McFarlane (1964) as *Arabia Felix: The Danish Expedition of 1761–1767*, New York: Harper and Row; London: Collins, 1964.

— (1967), *Slavernes kyst*, illust. Birte Lund, Copenhagen: Gyldendal; trans. Kari Dako as *Coast of Slaves* (2002) as Accra: Sub-Saharan Publishers.

— (1968), *Slavernes skibe*, illust. Lund, Copenhagen: Gyldendal; trans. Kari Dako (2003) as *Ships of Slaves*, Accra: Sub-Saharan Publishers.

— [1965] (1969), *Jens Munk*, 2 vols, Copenhagen: Gyldendal; trans. and abr. James McFarlane and John Lynch (1970) as *North West to Hudson Bay: The Life and Times of Jens Munk*, London: Collins; republished (1970) as *The Way to Hudson Bay: The Life and Times of Jens Munk*, New York: Harcourt, Brace and World.

— (1970), *Slavernes øer*, illust. Lund, Copenhagen: Gyldendal; trans. Kari Dako (2004) as *Islands of Slaves*, Accra: Sub-Saharan Publishers.

— (1978), *Processen mod Hamsun*, 3 vols, Copenhagen: Gyldendal.

— (1982), *Søforhør: nærbillede af Thorkild Hansen*, Copenhagen: Lindhardt and Ringhof.

Hansen, Thorkild and Peter Seeberg (1965), *Jens Munks minde-ekspedition*, Copenhagen: Gyldendal.

Histories

Lauring, Palle (1960a), *Danmarkshistorie*, Copenhagen: Forum.

— (1960b), *A History of the Kingdom of Denmark*, trans. David Hohnen, Copenhagen: Høst and Søn.

Said, Edward W. (1994), *Culture and Imperialism*, New York: Knopf.

Stecher-Hansen, Marianne (1997), *History Revisited: Fact and Fiction in Thorkild Hansen's Documentary Works*, Columbia, SC: Camden House.

— (1999), 'Thorkild Hansen', in Marianne Stecher-Hansen (ed.), *Twentieth-Century Danish Writers*, Dictionary of Literary Biography 214 (Gale Group): 134–47.

Historiography

Generally speaking, the imperial past has been largely neglected, underestimated and ignored in modern Danish historiography. Modern Danish identity and self-image has traditionally been formed by the traumatic defeat in the war of 1864 against Prussia and Austria where the duchies of Schleswig and Holstein were lost; and furthermore, Denmark was left as a weak and small state soon to be threatened in its very existence by the overwhelmingly dominant, recently united and aggressive Germany. Consequently, in order to survive as an independent nation, Denmark had to rely on non-military means. A strategy to secure national coherence to help the Danish nation survive was developed during the last decades of the nineteenth and first decades of the twentieth centuries stressing allegedly typically Danish values such as democracy, popular culture and education, social equality and welfare. This was meant to secure internal peace, consensus and co-operation between different classes, and it stressed pacifism and co-operation with the other Scandinavian peoples. Denmark's past as a multinational conglomerate state, a dominant Northern European and Baltic power and her many wars against Sweden, not to mention her status as a North Atlantic and tropical colonial power, did not fit in very well with Denmark's post-1864 self-image. Thus, this history was more or less superseded and instead Denmark's position as a weak, peaceful and defenceless minor power after 1864 was projected back onto the past in Danish historiography. Before 1864 and especially in Danish historiography during the Middle Ages and early modern time the various territories belonging to the Danish crown had certainly been mentioned and often used to glorify king and nation. Furthermore, royal art and heraldry had traditionally reflected the King of Denmark's desire to see himself and to be seen by others as a ruler over a composite, multi-territorial and multinational state.

After 1864, however, Danish histories has focused overwhelmingly on the geographical territory which comprised the present state of Denmark, and the territories which had previously belonged to the Danish conglomerate state were underestimated and only mentioned when absolutely necessary to understand Danish political development, for example, the Kalmar Union or the cessation of Norway in 1814. In social and cultural historiography, however, focus was exclusively on present-day Denmark with no references to the other territories. This national historiography was shared by historians of very varied political and ideological persuasion. Conservatives, liberals and Marxists, usually saw the world quite differently. However, practically all of them had the territory of the present day state named Denmark as their frame of reference, which excluded the territories of the comprehensive conglomerate state of former ages. Hence the liberally revisionist synthesis of the general history of Denmark by the Danish historian Erik Arup (1876–1951) in the 1920s and 1930s deliberately and provocatively placed the peasantry in the centre of historiography instead of kings and statesmen, while an attempt to write a Marxist history of Denmark in the early modern age was characteristically given the title *Class Struggle within the History of Denmark*.

The Viking age did not fit in so well with the post-1864 self-image either, at least not the conquering and settling elements (in present-day France and especially in present-day England) whereas a strong interest in that age as part of the Nordic (and thus non-Germanic) cultural heritage developed. In the historiography of the countries that were under Viking dominance, the tendency has been to describe the Vikings as looting and pillaging pirates, whereas Danish historiography has preferred to focus on them as traders and settlers. This picture is becoming more nuanced, but, as the Viking age is now more than 1,000 years ago; as power relationships between present-day Denmark and the present-day states of those former stamping grounds of the Vikings have now changed radically; and as Denmark has now become a minor power, that age can hardly be said to be top of today's political agenda.

Estonia was sold by the king of Denmark in 1347 and the isle of Ösel (in Estonian: Saarema) off the Estonian coast ceded by Denmark to Sweden in 1645 and not much about this is remembered in Denmark. In Estonia, however, the country's former belonging to the Danish crown is still relevant and was invoked during Estonia's struggle for independence from Russia in the 1980s and 1990s to underline Estonia's long historical connections with the Nordic countries and, more broadly, to the West.

The provinces of Scania, Halland and Blekinge were Danish provinces until they were conquered by Sweden in 1658. In spite of several later Danish attempts to reconquer those provinces they remain Swedish today. In Denmark, this has now long been accepted as a matter of fact; and in Scania, Halland and Blekinge, the same is true. However, as a result of growing regionalism and an acute feeling of being on the Swedish periphery in relation to Stockholm (whereas Denmark and her capital Copenhagen are much closer), these provinces are now rediscovering their Danish past. Here the brutal Swedification process which Scania, Halland and Blekinge were subjected to after 1658 has been used as an argument in constructing a regional identity and in gaining more regional self-autonomy.

As for the native historiography of the successor states of the Danish empire from the nineteenth century onwards, first and foremost Norway, Iceland and to some extent Schleswig and Holstein, the period of Danish rule has, of course, not been forgotten. However, emphasis has been placed on the internal development and relations of each particular territory that later became an independent successor state rather than on comparative studies integrating the other parts of the Danish kingdom. Furthermore, the government and foreign policy of the Danish state has only been described insofar as it had an impact on the territories of the later successor states, whereas the state as a whole and how it acted and appeared externally has been ignored. The historiography of the successor states often had a strong anti-Danish tendency with thinly veiled accusations against Denmark of political and cultural suppression and financial exploitation.

The many modern general histories of Denmark usually only describe the present-day state of Denmark. This is not to say that the history of other parts of the state especially Greenland and the tropical areas in Asia, Africa and the West Indies has been ignored. In fact, much has been written about these colonies by Danish historians, but in independent volumes supplementing the general histories of Denmark. They have tended to see the Danish presence in the tropics as exotic, fascinating and entertaining (this applies especially to the West Indies) without asking questions about, for example, the connection between the acquisition of these colonies and the general politics 'at home' in Denmark, the economic impact of these colonies on Denmark or the interaction between politics at home and in the colonies. By and large, however, the colonies have remained invisible. This must be seen as a result of the 1864 trauma but it also reflects the fact that the colonial past is not and has never been a big issue on the Danish political agenda. Firstly, the Danish colonies were only trade colonies, not emigration colonies, which meant only very small segments of the Danish population had any direct connections or relations with them. Secondly, the number of Danish speakers within the tropical colonies was small, the European population here was first and foremost English-speaking so that questions of Danish identity in the colonies were less pressing and no policies of Danification were ever implemented (apart from in Greenland). Thirdly, for these reasons, when Denmark gave up her colonies, Danish civil servants and military personnel went home and few other Danish speakers were left behind and thus the memory of Danish rule dwindled in the former colony where a new European colonial power was now ruling. Fourthly, during the period which in Western historiography is called the Age of Imperialism (1870–1914) Denmark had already begun to dismantle her tropical overseas empire: the colonies in India had been sold to Britain in 1845, the one in Africa in 1850. The Danish West Indies were incurring increasing losses and a genuine but futile attempt at selling them to the USA had been made in 1867. Fifthly, the populations of the Danish overseas colonies were small and so were the areas of the colonies (apart from that of Greenland). They were not colonies of mass emigration or immigration and they were given up and taken over by other Western powers at an early stage during the height of European imperialism. Danish tropical colonial rule has thus more or less been erased from public memory, the more so as the populations of the colonies were small and no immigration from them took place.

As in many other Western European states, immigration from Third-World countries has become a big issue on the political agenda. However, in the Danish context these immigrants do not come from areas which used to be Danish colonies. Consequently, the link between immigration and postcolonialism is not direct in Denmark in the way it is in Britain or Portugal. Problems originating from Denmark's former role as an imperial or colonial power appear only occasionally on the Danish political agenda today. Notable exceptions include the covert and equivocal nuclear policy of the Danish government in Greenland during the Cold War, the high-handed treatment of the Greenlandic population by the Danish authorities during the modernisation process of the 1950s and 1960s, and the Faeroese feeling of being politically and financially unfairly treated within the present 'Danish Commonwealth'. Occasionally, desires for additional autonomy and maybe even independence in due course are uttered by Greenlandic and Faeroese political representatives. And when the 150th anniversary of the abolition of black slavery in the Danish West Indies was celebrated in 1998, local black political leaders asked for an official apology, a demand that was not fulfilled and caused astonishment and lack of understanding in Denmark, where the colonial past was considered as nothing but past. A more lengthy political affair between Denmark and the (since 1944) fully independent Iceland took place during the 1960s and early 1970s, when relationships between Denmark and Iceland were strained by the Icelandic request for the return of valuable Icelandic mediaeval manuscripts, collected in the eighteenth century and donated to the University of Copenhagen. They were considered of great cultural value for this newly independent nation. The University of Copenhagen as well as large segments of the Danish literati were against this, even if other parts of Danish society (such as a majority in the Danish parliament) and Danish public opinion were in favour. Only after prolonged public debate and two rulings by the Danish Supreme Court were the manuscripts returned to Iceland, from 1971 onwards. This affair stirred up much more political commotion than academic affairs usually do, but the matter was not simply academic. The return of the manuscripts was considered a necessary step to restore political relations between Denmark and Iceland.

In recent decades, a new trend in Danish historiography has emerged. This trend tends to describe the Danish state of former ages as a whole, to analyse how this conglomerate state acted and appeared externally and how the various territories of the state interacted internally, even if much still needs to be analysed. The reasons for this turn have probably to do with the fact that the Danish nation-state (a construction from the decades after 1864) is being challenged by globalisation, increasing European integration and growing multiculturalism as a consequence of Third-World immigration. Historians are looking at the past in new ways and asking new questions.

Michael Bregnsbo

HISTORIES

Bregnsbo, Michael and Kurt Villads Jensen (2004), *Det danske imperium. Storhed og fald*, Copenhagen: Aschehoug.

Feldbæk, Ole and Ole Justesen (1980), *Kolonierne i Asien og Afrika*, Copenhagen: Politikens Forlag.

Hornby, Ove (1980), *Kolonierne i Vestindien*, Copenhagen: Politikens Forlag.

Østergård, Uffe (1992), 'Det danske rige – statshistorie eller nationalistisk historie', in *Europas ansigter. Nationale stater og politiske kulturer i en ny, gammel verden*, Copenhagen: Munksgaard Rosinante, pp. 29–50.

Home Rule

Home rule refers to autonomy achieved by colonies, usually in the process of achieving independence from a former imperial power. Generally, it has operated as a means by which nationalist movements could pressure imperial powers into recognising that imperial rule is neither necessarily benevolent nor to the benefit of the colonials. However, it has also served as a policy of containment by which imperial powers have sought to stem the tide of resistance to imperial rule. This is the case in the Danish context, where home rule has a chequered and extended history that refers to quite different degrees of autonomy for the former colonies Greenland, Iceland, the Faeroe Islands and the Danish Virgin Islands.

In contemporary terms the highest profile case has been Greenland's achievement of a formalised control over its domestic affairs (albeit with specific limitations in the economic, foreign policy and defence areas) in 1979. The Greenlandic demand for autonomy has in its various shapes and forms a long history, but in its modern form it rose as a protest movement against the modernisation programme initiated by the Danish government after World War II, when Denmark moved quickly to re-establish its sovereignty over Greenland after five years of isolation caused by the German occupation of the 'motherland'. While the modernisation process' stated purpose was to bring Greenland 'up' to the level of Danish 'civilisation', it brought also, through the deployment of Danish artisans and administrators, an acute awareness to the Greenlanders that they were second-class citizens in their own country. This recognition paved the way in the 1960s for a radical nationalist group of young Greenlanders. In the 1970s the Greenlandic protest against the Danish administration's paternalistic attitude culminated in the referendum for Danish membership of the EC, which Denmark voted in favour of, while Greenland and the Faeroe Islands voted against.

A commission was set up to explore ways of structuring a future Greenlandic autonomy, and in 1979, Greenlandic home rule was introduced. Certain elements in the Danish-Greenlandic agreement remained highly contentious issues, including the question concerning sovereignty over mineral resources. Since 1979, the home rule government has increased its area of jurisdiction. However, the sensitive areas of foreign policy and defence still rest with the Danish government, although it has committed itself to consultations with the Greenlandic government over such issues related to Greenland, such as the Thule Base.

The Faeroe Islands came under Danish sovereignty after Norway lost them in the wake of the Napoleonic Wars. The local parliament in the Faeroe Islands (the Lagting) and in Iceland (the Althing) were both abolished as the Danish king consolidated his power over the smaller realm. At the time of the national-liberal awakening in Denmark, the Lagting (1852) and the Althing (1843) were re-established albeit with fairly limited powers and under centralised control from Copenhagen. In Greenland, a paternalistic Danish council was set up in 1862, and in the Danish West Indies in 1865. A nationalist movement in both the Faeroe Islands and Iceland (but also by colonial nationalists resident in Copenhagen) in the last decades of the nineteenth century, pushed, particularly in Iceland, for greater autonomy. Iceland won important concessions from the Danish government in 1874, but it also had to surrender important concessions in return. The most thorny issue was the Danish demand that the minister for Iceland must submit laws and decisions to the Danish Council of State for royal approval.

The Icelandic nationalist movement took advantage of a radical régime change in Denmark (1901), to push for the Icelandic minister as a genuine representative of the Icelandic community. In Greenland political-administrative changes brought an increased, though still indirect, influence to Greenlanders in local matters. In 1908 a commission was established to look into Iceland's future status in the Danish realm. The resulting proposal was rejected by the Icelanders, but in 1918 a personal union between Denmark and Iceland was agreed upon, which made Iceland into a separate state, under the Danish crown. The treaty was to run for twenty years, after which it could be annulled by either party. The Icelanders took advantage of the German occupation to annul the treaty in 1940, and formally declared its independence in 1944. The Danish king had no alternative but to accept this, after a referendum overwhelmingly supported Icelandic independence.

The Faeroe Islands took a similar road after World War II when they won a referendum on independence from Denmark in 1946. However, this referendum was subsequently rejected by the Danish government. As compensation the Faeroese were granted home rule (1948), while Greenland's status as a Danish colony was abolished (1953) and the island became 'integrated' into the Danish realm. There were several reasons for this, one of the more important the Danish reluctance to have the UN scrutinise Danish submissions on the Greenlandic progress towards independence, which were demanded by the UN in the context of a general emphasis on decolonisation.

Lars Jensen

HISTORIES

Alfredsson, Gudmundur (1982), 'Greenland and the Law of Political Decolonization', *German Yearbook of International Law*, vol. 25, Berlin: Duncker and Humblot, pp. 290–308.

Karlsson, Gunnar (2000), *Iceland's 1100 Years: The History of a Marginal Society*, London: Hurst and Company.

Naurby, Torben (1996), *No Nation is an Island: Language, Culture and National Identity in the Faroe Islands*, Aarhus: SNAI – North Atlantic Publications.

Skaale, Sjúrdur (ed.) (2004), *The Right to National Self-Determination: The Faroe Islands and Greenland*, Leiden: Martinus Nijhoff Publishers.

West, Hallbera and Heinesen, Maria Amalia (2004), *Kilder til Færøernes og Grønlands historie*, Torshavn: Føroya Fródskaparfelag.

Migrancy

In the public and political eye, the archetypal immigrant in present-day Denmark is a relatively newly arrived Muslim man – or his son. A growing section of the population, the press and a broad swathe of the political spectrum associate him as well as his son with unemployment, crime, religious fanaticism, oppression of women and a general hostility towards Danish society or 'Danish values'. Migration is, however, not exclusively a post-war phenomenon, and according to statistics the Muslim male meets competition from other genders, orientations and faiths (including other Islamic denominations). 'The immigrant' in the public eye, then, is not entirely synonymous with immigrants.

The modern migration régime is a feature of the nation-state as it developed in the nineteenth century. In the largely immobile and divided social environment of the diminishing Danish empire, movement in itself was an object of control. Workers migrating for casual labour opportunities were submitted to control measures regardless of their place of birth, and with reference to the possible disturbances they might cause. In 1875 workers born in Denmark were exempted from control, but border controls and residence permits did not appear until well into the twentieth century (1911 and 1926 respectively). Since then residence and working permits have been issued by the state. In the late eighteenth century most of the migrant workers originated in Germany and Sweden. From the beginning of the twentieth century Polish-speaking groups from the province of Galicia in Austria-Hungary began to arrive. In 1901, 3.3 per cent of the Danish population were non-nationals; in Copenhagen it was 6.9 per cent. Between World War I and the late 1960s immigration was negligible, especially since refugees – overwhelmingly Jewish – fleeing the totalitarian régimes of the 1930s were not admitted into the country.

Contrary to most of the other European empires, post-war migration to Denmark has not been dominated by migrants from the (former) colonies. Or more to the point, the (political) questions attached to migration are not associated with inhabitants of the former colonies, since Greenland was officially included in the state in 1953, and since the national imagining has long forgotten the imperial past. Due to their status as Danish citizens and hence non-immigrants, people originating in Greenland are not counted as a separate group for statistical purposes, and consequently, general knowledge of the living conditions of this group is scarce.

When 'guest workers' arrived in Denmark in the late 1960s, their presence was seen as a completely new and alien phenomenon. The workers were generally single men, who took up jobs in the heavy industries, and were suspiciously watched by the trade unions in case their presence undermined the conditions of the Danish workers. They left home and families in the countryside of Turkey, Yugoslavia and Morocco, and the towns (mainly) of Pakistan. Excluding Pakistan, most of the workers grew up in minority communities in their home state: they were Kurds, Berbers and (Muslim) Macedonians. In the early 1970s economic recession set in, and the borders were closed to new migrating workers. The families of those who had already arrived, however, gradually joined their men in Denmark. In 1980 immigrants and their descendants comprised 3 per cent of the population.

During the 1980s another feature of the outside world arrived at the borders of the country, refugees. Denmark had since the 1960s received refugees from UN camps, but now refugees began to cross the world, and arrived individually. Tamils escaping from the Sri Lankan civil war, and Iranian and Iraqi young men fleeing the war between the two states were among the first so-called spontaneous refugees who came to Denmark. Others have followed in the wake of wars and conflicts around the world. Today the largest groups of immigrants (including refugees and EU citizens) originate in Turkey, Iraq, Germany, Lebanon and Bosnia. (Germany, of course, is not considered part of any immigration problem.) The total number is still low, however, compared to other European states: immigrants and their descendants made up 8.4 per cent of the population in January 2005, or half that of neighbouring Sweden.

State measures to prevent immigration of any form have, since the late 1980s, become ever more draconian. Denmark has on several occasions been a pioneer in the art of inventing new measures that deny or prevent refugees or other groups of immigrants access to the country. The practice of fining companies which transport persons without the required travel documents, was for instance originally 'made in Denmark', but quickly spread to the rest of the EU countries. Up until the mid-1990s these measures were generally directed towards admission controls, where the right of family reunification as well as the right of asylum have gradually and systematically been undermined. Since the late 1990s focus has been directed towards the rights of migrants already living in the country. Universal welfare rights to subsistence have been reduced for newcomers to the country, who now receive less in social benefits than the population at large – the politicians argue, that this will both force the minorities into the labour market *and* prevent further immigration to Denmark.

The 2006 'cartoon wars', sparked off by caricature drawings of the prophet Mohammed in the Danish newspaper *Jyllandsposten*, placed Denmark and her admission/integration policies temporarily at the top of the world's news agenda. The *Washington Post* reported on 8 February 2006:

> This country of 5.4 million people, including about 200,000 Muslims, has long viewed itself as a haven for all views and faiths. But skyrocketing immigration in the 1990s spurred a backlash that culminated in the November 2001 election of Prime Minister Anders Fogh Ramussen.

For most observers, the Danish 'tough on immigration and tough on immigrant policies' are identified with the year 2001. This is, however, only true in a limited sense. Immigration and partly also integration policies in Denmark have since the 1980s followed an increasingly tight and tough scheme. While this has increased quantitatively, it hardly constitutes a qualitative change. What has changed, however, is the political and public rhetoric. From the late 1990s the former 'soft humanitarian rhetoric' has been replaced by open othering of the immigrant population, and immigration-talk has become a focal bone of contention.

Kirsten Hvenegård-Lassen

BIBLIOGRAPHICAL NOTE
No overall migrant histories have been produced in English or in Danish, although smaller episodic accounts of specific migrant groups have been written.

Missions in the Danish-Norwegian Colonies

Colonialism in the Danish-Norwegian double monarchy was not formally connected with ideas about Lutheran mission. Trade was the predominant and accepted reason for expansionism. However, several of the colonial projects were from the beginning or became after a while closely connected to missionary activities. The approach to mission varied much depending on the type of colony and internal conditions in regard to the relationship between colonial authorities, local authorities and/or colonial subjects. None of the colonial mission fields was alike, but generally, mission was a consequence of and not a reason for colonialism, and private initiatives preceded state mission. The Protestant state Church held a religious monopoly, and was in the seventeenth century dominated by an orthodox Lutheran approach to Christianity that focused strongly on internal religious control. God had chosen the king, and the king needed good Christian subjects. As a consequence the only initiative concerning mission in the seventeenth century was connected to internal colonialism: the attempt to convert Sami in the Finnmark, an area claimed for Norway but having a frontier status. By including the Sami in Christianity their subjection to the king would be underlined. The attempt to convert the Sami was furthermore connected with a general fight against witchcraft in northern Europe in the seventeenth century. The Sami were 'natural' suspects. From 1715 the mission to the Sami was systematised and administered by the Mission Board, an official office founded in 1714.

   Greenland was formally seen as part of the Norwegian realm, and as such, belonging to the Danish-Norwegian king. Since the dying out of the mediaeval Norse settlement around 1500 there had been no contact, but in 1721 the pastor Hans Egede was allowed by the King to go to Greenland to trade with and convert the Inuit population. He settled in the most populous part, western Greenland, where all mission took place until 1900. Eastern and northern Greenland were left alone until this time. Shortly after its beginning Egede's mission was challenged by the emergence of the pietistic movement, which influenced a substantial number of the Danish clergy from around 1670 as well as the Kings Frederik IV (1699–1730), and Christian VI (1730–46). Among pietists ideas about mission were important. This paved the way for more mission initiatives in the Danish colonies. The Moravian Church, sprung from the pietistic movement in Europe, began a mission in Greenland in 1733, and it existed side by side with Egede's mission, but with many conflicts between the two. The Moravian Church based its missions around the world on close contacts between converts and missionaries and strict supervision of the converts. By the middle of the nineteenth century western Greenlanders were Christian and members of either the Danish-Lutheran or the Moravian Churches. The Moravian mission left Greenland in 1900 and members went over to the Lutheran Church.

A true pietistic mission began in 1705 at the trading post Tranquebar on the Coromandel Coast of India with two missionaries from the pietistic seminar in Halle. The mission was supported by the state, but run from Halle. It expanded in southern India through the eighteenth century. The average of converts was a few hundreds a year. From the end of the century it declined, and was in 1847 replaced by the Leipzig mission. The pietistic mission focused, like the Moravian missions, on personal instruction, and the education of local teachers and missionaries was an important part of the strategy. Reading the Bible was central in religious instruction. In principle all layers of society were targeted but in practice it was mostly poorer people who were attracted to the mission. From the beginning, the mission was strongly supported by the King and administration in Copenhagen, an interest not seen in regard to other mission fields. A reason might be different attitudes towards different non-Europeans. Indians were seen as relatively civilised, and therefore, perhaps, more ready for conversion. Moravian missionaries took part in attempts to colonise the Nicobar Islands in 1768. They also had a few missionaries in Tranquebar. However, the pietistic mission was always the most important.

The first mission in the Danish West Indies was established on private initiative by the Moravian Church in 1732, even though a limited number of conversions had taken place during the early years of the colony. The Moravian mission focused on personal religiosity and made place for African-Caribbean agency within the Church hierarchy. Even though the Moravian system recognised cultural differences among African Caribbeans according to ethnic origin, the Church played a major part in the cultural creolisation in the colony because of its emphasis on de-Africanisation as part of the mission, its strict attitude towards non-Christian acts and beliefs, and its frequent use of excommunications to promote a true Christian lifestyle. The Danish Lutheran state Church made an attempt to found a mission focusing on children from 1755, but its lack of success is reflected in the fact that Moravian teachers were chosen for the slave school system founded in 1839. In 1835 97 per cent of the African Caribbean population were members of a Christian congregation. Church affiliation mirrored the diverse Euro-Caribbean population, created by the open settlement policy practised in the Danish West Indies. The most popular churches among African Caribbeans were the Moravian (35 per cent) and the Catholic (32 per cent) Churches, followed by the Anglican (20 per cent) and the Lutheran (9 per cent) Churches. A handful belonged to the Methodist and Dutch Reformed Churches. Catholic and Anglican missionary activity is so far unresearched. Mission in the Danish West Indies was, together with Greenland, the most successful numerically.

The Danish-Norwegian settlements on the West African coast were small trading posts, not colonies. Mission was never part of the plan for coexistence with the local population, but from 1722 there existed a school for the children of Danish-Norwegian men living at the fort and African women, where the teaching of Christianity was central. In the 1760s a few Moravian missionaries arrived as part of a larger plan of colonisation and development of plantations. The whole project was very unsuccessful and the mission quickly died out. A similar project was initiated in the 1830s, where a few missionaries from the Basle Evangelical Missionary Society settled at the Danish fort as well as in the countryside.

A general description of from the Denmark-Norway mission is that it had a qualitative rather than a quantitative focus. Furthermore, a general tendency was that the numerically successful missions were not tied to the colonial administration but were based on private initiative, even if the king and authorities in Copenhagen supported it. The pietistic focus on personal religiousness led to a predominantly, but not uniformly, personal approach to mission, in the sense that most missions in the Danish-Norwegian realm were based on close personal contact between missionaries and converts, and focused on wholehearted conversions and strict control of converts and their life styles.

Louise Sebro

HISTORIES

Crantz, David (1767), *The History of Greenland: Containing a Description of the Country, and its Inhabitants: and Particularly a Relation of the Mission, Carried on for above these Thirty Years by the Unitas Fratrum, at New Herrnhut and Lichtenfels, in that Country. Trans. from the High-Dutch, and Illustr. with Maps and other Copper-plates*, London.

Egede, Hans Saabye (1818), *Greenland: Being Extracts from a Journal kept in that Country in the Years 1770 to 1778 by H. Egede Saabye. To which is Prefixed an Introduction; Containing some Accounts of the Manners of the Greenlanders, and of the Mission in Greenland. And Illustrated by a Chart of Greenland by G. Fries*, Copenhagen.

Highfield, Arnold R. (1994), 'Patterns of Accommodation and Resistance: The Moravian Witness to Slavery in the Danish West Indies', *Journal of Caribbean History* 28 (2): 138–64.

Oldendorp, C. G. A. (1987), *History of the Mission of the Evangelical Brethren on the Caribbean Islands of St. Thomas, St. Croix, and St. John*, Arnold A. Highfield and Vladimir Barac (eds), Ann Arbor, MI: Karoma Publishers.

Sensbach, John F. (2005), *Rebecca's Revival. Creating Black Christianity in the Atlantic World*, Cambridge, MA and London: Harvard University Press.

Weihe, Hans-Jørgen Wallin (1999), *'Social Work' and Missionary Work as Part of the Power Game: A Discussion through Two Examples: Hans Egede, Missionary in Greenland 1721–1736 and the Norwegian Saami Mission in Finnmark – the Period of Establishment of Missions and Social Services 1888–1900*, Lund: Socialhögskolan.

Modernisation of Greenland

During the German occupation of Denmark (1940–5), the local Danish administration in Greenland was cut off from Denmark. As a consequence, Greenland was administered by Danish civil servants in Greenland, and all goods were imported from the USA. The presence of American goods exposed the Greenlanders to an outside world from which the Danish administration had sought to 'protect' the Greenlanders.

After the war it was apparent that a return to the previous policy of isolation was impossible and fears that the American presence in Greenland could actually put an end to the Danish colonial administration, together with Denmark's wish to be struck off the UN's list of countries with colonies, prompted the Danish government to embark on a modernisation of Greenland. This made the Danish presence more overt and gave the Greenlanders the idea that they were on the way to being treated on an equal footing.

The start of this first major modernisation of Greenland since the arrival of Hans Egede in 1721 and the changes in the 1830s marked the end of the formal Danish colonisation of Greenland. A change of the Danish constitution in 1953 gave Greenland the status of an integrated part of the kingdom of Denmark, and opened up the island to new investments, through the two ten-year development plans called G50 (for the 1950s) and G60 (for the 1960s).

To the Danish government it was obvious something had to be changed in Greenland after World War II, but not so obvious what the changes should be. The discussions ended with the idea of intensifying the process of equalisation and of putting an end to formal colonisation through a massive Danish economic investment in the infrastructure of Greenland. Never in history had so much been brought from Denmark to Greenland.

In a long-term perspective the process of modernising Greenland after World War II was another step in a modernisation process started by Hans Egede's arrival in 1721, but the process has over the years been marked by two conflicting views of Greenland and its people.

THE EARLY IMAGINED EQUALITY

The first imagined relationship between Greenland and Denmark, with the former as an equal and integrated part of the Nordic people's lands, dates back to the Norse settlements in Greenland from 985 and this was kept alive right up to 1832. Even when Hans Egede started his modernisation in the shape of the formal colonisation of Greenland in 1721, it was with clear reference to the old brotherhood of the Norse, who were at that time still believed to be living in Greenland.

From 1721 it had been an object in itself to find the Norse in order to convert them from Catholicism to the Lutheran belief and that remained the main goal during the first 111 years of the Danish colonisation of Greenland. This period can be characterised as a parasitic colonialism in respect of the Inuit people. They were exploited and christened but they were not the primary goal for the colonisation.

THE PERCEPTUAL SHIFT IN 1832

The end of the Napoleonic Wars (1807–14) signalled intensified efforts to find the Northwest Passage. Under this banner, the Danish King, Frederik VI, in 1828 equipped an expedition that had as its goal to go as high up along the east coast of Greenland as possible. The aim was to secure Danish sovereignty, to map the coastline, and to look for evidence of an earlier Norse settlement, in the last place left to look for them.

W. A. Graah (1793–1863) was appointed as the expedition leader, and on his return to Denmark his conclusion was clear: there had never been any Norse settlements on the east coast. The only existing remains of Norse colonies had already been found on the west coast. It was now clear there were no surviving descendants of the Norse people.

In 1832, after Graah's conclusion had been made public in the book he wrote about the expedition, the Danish colonisers suddenly found themselves without a primary goal for the colonisation of Greenland. This forced the administrators over the following years to rethink the Danish colonisation of Greenland. A totally new imagined relationship between Denmark and Greenland had to be invented.

THE DANISH BURDEN

The result of the perceptual shift that Graah's conclusion gave birth to, was that the character of Danish colonialism in Greenland changed through the 1830s from parasitic to intensive colonisation with the 'upbringing' of the Greenlanders as its new primary goal.

The inspiration for this new imagined relationship between Denmark and Greenland – ever since that time described 'as the Danish burden' – was found in a new theory, 'social evolutionism', that spread across Europe in the first part of the nineteenth century, where the colonial subject was thought of as a child to be brought up by the enlightened European. This new approach was in clear contrast to the eighteenth century's Enlightenment theories.

Today, there are no obvious changes in the Danish imagined relationship between Denmark and Greenland. It is still imagined to be the burden of Denmark to help Greenland. Today the help is mostly in the shape of funds transferred (400 million Euros each year).

In its stereotypical depiction Denmark sees this more or less as a philanthropic donation because of the Danish obligation to help Greenland. This polished self image has become dented in recent years, as it has become more and more clear that Denmark also gains considerably from its engagements in Greenland. Many jobs occupied by Danes both in Greenland and in Denmark directly depend on the Danish engagement in Greenland, and it has been established through an officially commissioned report that Denmark has had a discounted membership of NATO, due to its sovereignty over the strategically important Greenland.

GREENLAND TAKES OVER

The change after 1832 of the imagined relationship created new power relations between Denmark and Greenland. Up until the constitutional change in 1953 Denmark had principal sovereignty over political decisions concerning Greenland. After 1953 the political power was to a greater extent than before transferred from Denmark to Greenland, a political process that culminated with the introduction of the home rule government in 1979. The political process was accompanied by a Greenlandic perceptual shift away from the imagined Danish-Greenlandic common project of modernisation, produced among other things by the realisation that Greenlanders did not receive equal treatment in spite of what they had been told during almost 130 years – since the 1830s.

In 1979 the home rule system was conceived of by many as the final destination. However, at the turn of the millennium Greenland experienced a revival of nationalism, which was accompanied by calls for independence. An internal Greenlandic commission – 'Selvstyrekommissionen' (The Commission for Own Government) – worked from 1999 until 2003 when it handed over its report. One of the results of that commission's work was the establishment of a Danish-Greenlandic 'Selvstyrekommission'.

It is becoming more and more obvious that the Danish preferred narrative of its obligations towards 'the poor, helpless, primitive' people struggling for survival high up in the cold North – an image created in the 1830s and still very much alive in Denmark – is proving a difficult hurdle to get over, in the fight by Greenlanders to determine their own condition for modernisation.

Klaus Georg Hansen

HISTORIES
Gad, Finn (1970–82), *The History of Greenland*, London: C. Hurst.
Gad, Ulrik Pram (2005), *Dansksprogede grønlænderes plads i et Grønland under grønlandisering og modernisering: en diskursanalyse af den grønlandske sprogdebat – læst som identitetspolitisk forhandling*, Copenhagen: Afdeling for Eskimologi og Arktiske Studier, Københavns Universitet.
Lidegaard, Mads (1992), *Kilder til Grønlands historie 1950–1980*, Nuuk: Atuakkiorfik.
— (1973), *Ligestilling uden lighed: en oversigt over det statsretlige forhold mellem Grønland og Danmark*, Copenhagen: Schultz.
Lorentzen, Jørgen, Einar Lund Jensen and Hans Christian Gulløv (eds) (1999), *Inuit, kultur og samfund: en grundbog i eskimologi*, Aarhus: Systime.

Narratives and Fictions of Empire

In *Out of Africa* (1937), Denmark's most famous colonialist, Karen Blixen (1885–1962), recounts the conviction of her houseboy, Kamante, that the book she was writing had no cover to hold it together, and so would not be 'a good book'. Blixen's farm was in British East Africa, but her book's scattered papers are reminiscent of the odds and ends of territories from the North Atlantic to the Indian Ocean that constituted the Danish Empire. Blixen's unbound pages also suggest that the colonising process and aftermath are as much about imaginings and narratives as they are about territory. And they remind us that the book as material object is the apparatus that invests certain stories with authority, and makes possible their dissemination over the disparate spaces of empire.

The absence of a coherent narrative of the Danish Empire is not simply a result of geographical space between its territories, or of the temporal disjunction between the transience of the so-called 'tropical colonies', and the enduring historical entanglements between Denmark and its North Atlantic protectorates. It is also a function of the linguistic, formal and material criteria by which a narrative is adjudged to constitute literature worthy of translation, dissemination and canonisation. Denmark's successive losses of contiguous territory in 1814 and 1864 loomed larger in the popular imagination than the surrender of its far-flung colonies. The task of the nineteenth-century Danish novelist and historian was therefore to re-imagine the Danish nation as small and homogeneous. The linear historical time of the classic novel, which Benedict Anderson sees as essential to popular conceptions of the modern nation-state, was harnessed in Denmark to suture the rump Danish territory to a Nordic past, not to the geographically-disparate colonial lands that remained. As Hans Hauge (2003) has commented, writing a postcolonialist literary history of Denmark therefore entails looking hard, and reading for absences.

Arguably the most direct engagement with Denmark's colonial history was undertaken by Thorkild Hansen (1927–89) in his documentary and historiographical works. Hansen's trilogy on the Danish slave trade (1967–70) employs literary strategies to produce a 'revisionist historiography' of Denmark's involvement in slavery and its claim to have been the first European power to abolish it in 1792 (Stecher-Hansen 1997). Hansen juxtaposes firsthand accounts by Danish colonialists with established historical authorities, exposing the latter as complicit in creating the national myth of benevolent colonialism. His fragmented narratives gesture to the silence imposed on the slaves by coolly recounting the conditions of their existence, not by fabricating a voice for them. Hansen's polyphonic approach anticipates the recent turn in Denmark to 'postnational' historiography and meta-history. For example, Søren Mørch's *Den sidste Danmarkshistorie* (*The Last History of Denmark*, 1996) uses autobiography and micro-history to expand 'Danish' history tentacularly around the globe. In launching his narrative with his own schoolboy memory of meeting Victor Cornelins, a black Danish-trained teacher from St Croix, Mørch subverts the title of the 1952 standard work on the colonies, *Vore gamle tropekolonier* (*Our Old Tropical Colonies*). Cornelins' narrative presence renders the colonies neither unproblematically 'ours', nor 'old'.

While the trajectories of Denmark's slave ships have been excised from popular history, the movement across the North Atlantic of the foundational texts of Nordic culture is fundamental to the imaginative construction of historical links with the lost colony of Iceland. The manuscripts of Old Icelandic sagas had been preserved in the museums and libraries of Copenhagen during the period of Danish sovereignty, but in the nineteenth century came to function as fetishised artefacts in narratives of Icelandic nationhood and of common Norse heritage, not least in Danish school history books. They were returned to Iceland from 1971. The drawn-out negotiations over the return of the manuscripts crystallised a historical teleology of the Icelandic nation-state: a golden age of civilisation and literary production from the ninth to the thirteenth centuries, followed by a dark age of colonisation by Denmark, and eventual restoration of national independence. The counter-argument shifted the focus from a paternalistic need to protect the precious arte-facts from the vicissitudes of Icelandic neglect, to an emphasis on their transnational status as literary-historical creations of Norse emigrants.

The Faeroe Islands offer the most obvious examples of Denmark's empire 'writing back' in the twentieth century. Central to the development of Faeroese literature has been the political and creative interplay of Danish and Faeroese as languages of state and culture. The centripetal pull of Copenhagen University for Faeroese students spawned Dano-Faeroese collaboration on Faeroese philology and folk culture in the nineteenth century; the conse-quent renaissance of the Faeroese language informed the ambivalence of William Heinesen towards the canonisation of his own Danish-language novels. He anticipated his rumoured nomination as Nobel Laureate in 1981 by arguing that the advancement of Faeroese culture would best be served by honouring Faeroese-language literature. Nevertheless, Faeroese lit-erature opens up an interlingual, liminal space within the Danish canon, as suggested by the translational, transnational afterlife of Jørgen-Frantz Jacobsen's historical novel *Barbara* (1939; trans. 1948 and 1992). Though the bilingual Jacobsen wrote *Barbara* in Danish, its translation into Faeroese by the islands' national poet, Christian Matras, gained such canonical status that the most recent English translation – a bestseller amongst interna-tional visitors to Tórhavn's tourist office – used both texts as its composite source.

Greenlandic narrative production has been dominated by the material and existential divide between 'traditional' colony and 'modern' coloniser. Kirsten Thisted has shown how the early, nationalist Greenlandic novel harnesses postcolonial mimicry to blend local experience with the coloniser's literary form. The Danish colonial discourse of tutelage and historical progress towards modernity is espoused in literary conceits such as the dream of a 'civilised' Greenland of 2105 in the novel *singnagtugaK* (*A Greenlander's Dream*, 1914) by Mathias Storch (1883–1957), and Pâvia Petersen's (1904–43) motif of the struggle to inte-grate a mixed genealogical heritage in *Niuvertorutsip pania* (*The Trading Station Manager's Daughter*, 1944).

The theme of cultural hybridity is reworked in the Dane Peter Høeg's international best-seller *Miss Smilla's Feeling for Snow* (1994). This novel's self-consciously hybrid narrator morphs the imagined limits of the nation to encompass a fictionalised Greenlandic tundra, and maps out an intercultural cityscape where the people of the Danish *pagus* still gather, though now as a vulnerable Greenlandic underclass. *Smilla* remains a lodestone for con-temporary scholars attempting to remap Danish literature and history in the context of the postcolonial condition writ large, not least because it situates the experience of cultural hybridity and the intercultural encounter within a 'glocalised' national space.

Høeg's material is often said to rework Blixen's colonial sensibilities for a postcolonial age. In *Out of Africa*, Blixen explains to Kamante that her stories will become a book in Europe, where people will 'fix it all up together'; it is in refusing to fix together a stable, comprehensive, Eurocentric narrative that certain contemporary Danish writers and his-torians most obviously engage with the postcolonial. It falls to the coming generation of Danish writers of diverse ethnic origins to 'stitch together' the narrative genres that will relate a heterogeneous national history of Denmark.

                                                                                    Claire Thomson

LITERARY WORKS
Blixen, Karen [1937] (1954), *Out of Africa*, London: Penguin.
Høeg, Peter [1992] (1994), *Miss Smilla's Feeling for Snow*, trans. F. David London: Harvill Press.
Jacobsen, Jørgen-Frantz [1939] (1993), *Barbara*, Norwich: Norvik Press.

Histories

Brøndsted, Johannes (ed.) (1952), *Vore gamle tropekolonier*, Copenhagen: Gyldendal.

Hauge, Hans (2003), *Post-Danmark: politik og æstetik hinsides det nationale*, Copenhagen: Lindhardt and Ringhof.

Mørch, Søren (1996), *Den sidste Danmarkshistorie. 57 fortællinger af fædrelandets historie*, Copenhagen: Gyldendal.

Poddar, Prem and Cheralyn Mealor (2000), 'Danish Imperial Fantasies: Peter Høeg's *Miss Smilla's Feeling For Snow*', in Prem Poddar (ed.), *Translating Nations. The Dolphin*, no. 30, Århus: Aarhus University Press, pp. 161–202.

Pálsson, Gísli (1995), *The Textual Life of Savants. Ethnography, Iceland, and the Linguistic Turn*, Chur: Harwood Academic Publishers.

Stecher-Hansen, Marianne (1997), *History Revisited: Fact and Fiction in Thorkild Hansen's Documentary Works*, Columbia, SC: Camden House.

Orientalism and Exoticism

The Danish Empire, which started to collapse around 1800, was centred in the Baltic and North Atlantic regions with a limited network of trading posts and smaller settlements in Asia, Africa and the Caribbean. Direct contacts with the Oriental world were therefore limited and thus more immediately comparable to those of Germany with individual scholars, writers, artists, adventurers and traders following in the well-trodden paths of British and French armies of soldiers and academicians.

In 1761 the Danish King, Frederik V, sent an ill-fated but scientifically successful expedition to Arabia, led by the German scholar Carsten Niebuhr, who returned with the first detailed account of the peoples of the Arabian peninsula and especially about the many local forms of Islam, including the emergence of Wahhabism. Before Niebuhr, the only introduction to Islam and Muhammad in Danish was *Hero-Tales* by Ludvig Holberg (1684–1754), the leading Scandinavian exponent of the Enlightenment, in which Muhammad, based partly on contemporary European writers, partly on travellers' accounts of the Muslim world, was still seen with the eyes of mediaeval Christianity as a false prophet. Unlike earlier biographers, however, Holberg recognised how Muhammad's life and work had contributed in a significant and positive way to the unfolding of the human spirit through history.

The new era of philology began in Denmark with Rasmus Rask, the discoverer of the Indo-European family of languages, who took his obsessive quest for linguistic unity as far as India. He wrote dissertations about ancient Oriental languages and helped decipher Old Persian, but unlike the father of Semitics, Ernst Renan, he avoided Eurocentric prejudices about the languages he studied. He was followed by a number of internationally acclaimed Orientalists in the nineteenth century, including Frantz Buhl, whose historical biography of Muhammad from 1903 is still considered reliable, while Johannes Østrup was preoccupied with the contemporary Islamic world, realising its growing importance to the West.

Earlier writers and painters like Hans Christian Andersen travelled only as far as Constantinople. While other European powers expanded outwards, Denmark's size and importance shrank with the loss of Norway (1814) and Schleswig-Holstein (1864), making the country reinvent itself as an ancient nation-state vulnerable to attacks from abroad, an Israel of the North according to the nationalist theologian N. F. S. Grundtvig, whose Christian world histories condemned the Oriental peoples to irrelevance at best.

In this atmosphere the international movement of Orientalism failed to ignite the Danish popular imagination in the same way as Egyptomania or Japanism did in metropolitan Paris or London, the only exception being Tivoli, the amusement park in Copenhagen, founded in 1843 by the Algerian-born writer-architect Georg Carstensen, where Arab-inspired ballets by August Bournonville were performed in the shade of Oriental food palaces. In literature the mystical allure of the Orient itself first appears in Adam Oehlenschläger's 1805 version of *Allddin* about the power of poetic intuition, symbolised by the magical oil lamp. While English and French writers went to the Orient, Danish writers like B. S. Ingemann, St. St. Blicher and Christian Winther rather chose to integrate the Orient with mediaeval Danish history, the period where modern Danish identity supposedly had its roots, in the shape of exotic strangers such as Gypsies and Jews, usually endowed with magical and sexual powers, who, like the main character's Jewish object of desire in Nobel Laureate Johannes V. Jensen's novel *The Fall of the King* (1900–1), always function as destructive forces.

Because of Denmark's close cultural and political connections to Germany and Russia, a strong interest in Buddhist Central Asia developed at the end of the nineteenth century, resulting in live exhibits of Central Asian village life in Copenhagen Zoo, and Ole Olufsen's dramatic expeditions to the Pamir region in the 1890s, which became the last European incursion into Russian Central Asia until the collapse of the Soviet Union, and made Copenhagen University a stronghold for Buddhist studies. Buddhism also made its mark in Danish literature with another Nobel Laureate, Karl Gjellerup, whose novels explored Indian philosophy and especially reincarnation. Orientalism as an academic discipline is today, according to Edward Said's definition, divided between traditional Orientalist philology and theology at Copenhagen and Aarhus universities and American-inspired Middle East Studies at the University of Southern Denmark with the focus on the Middle East as a source of crises, terrorism and immigration.

John Botofte

Literary Works
Andersen, Hans Christian [1842] (2002), *A Poet's Baza: A Journey to Greece, Turkey and Up the Danube*, Toronto: Scholarly Book Services.
Ingemann, B. S. (1850), *Araberen i Konstantinopel*, Copenhagen: Reitzel.

Histories
Oxfeldt, Elisabeth (2005), *Nordic Orientalism. Paris and the Cosmopolitan Imagination 1800–1900*, Copenhagen: Museum Tusculanum Press.
Folsach, Brigitte von (1996), *I Halvmånens skær. eksempler på skildringer af den Nære Orient i dansk kunst og litteratur omkring 1800–1875*, Copenhagen: Davids Samling.
Simonsen, Jørgen Bæk (2004), *Islam med danske øjne*, Copenhagen: Akademisk Forlag, København.

Race and Ethnicity, Greenland

To the Norse population in Greenland Inuit were *skraellings* (small weaklings); and in the later European tradition they were trolls, pygmies or savage men. After 1721 Greenlanders appeared to the Europeans as individual human beings, converting to Christianity. An increasing number of mixed marriages were seen in the colonised West Greenland. Inuit culture had always been open to out-group sexual intercourse. However, some of the children from mixed marriages did not socialise into the hunting culture and became a burden on the colonisers. The rules in 1782 constraining European personnel included rules for marriages too, on one hand to avoid expense but on the other to maintain Christian morality by allowing marriage rather than cohabitation.

A high death-rate among kayakers created a surplus of women. Mixed relationships solved part of this problem in the northern part of West Greenland. In the southern part of West Greenland the Moravian Brethren had their missionary stations. They did not permit mixed marriages in their communities, a circumstance that led to a demographic crisis.

In general, native Greenlanders received less salary for equal work, but had easier access to the subsistence economy. However, the money earned by Greenlanders working for the mission or the trade had a widespread impact on most families in Greenland.

The colonial authorities classified the native population from the 1820s till 1901 as 'crossbreeds' (with more or less European blood in their veins) or Greenlanders, but the decisive criteria were culture and way of life. In general crossbreeds with fathers who were factors or missionaries were raised as Danes, the rest as Greenlanders. The latter would either get a job in the trade or the mission or they would add to the number of low-skilled hunters who regardless of their descent were considered a problem by all.

From the Inuit oral tradition we can tell that Inuit had ethnic awareness. European contact added the concepts of king and kingdom and later of national awareness, and paved the way for an evolving Greenlandic national consciousness in the late nineteenth century (dominated by Danish ideas about a linguistically homogeneous country). An ideal Greenlander – at least from 1861 onwards, where we have the Greenlandic newspaper as a source – was a good seal hunter and a good Christian, while the linguistic criterion was non-explicit. After 1900 the development of new trades created an intense debate about ethnic-national identity in newspapers and fiction. The progressive proposal was to use the mother tongue, history and love for the country as ethnic-national identity criteria. However, the Greenlanders wanted at the same time more foreign language competence (Danish). Mere thoughtless imitation was distinguished from deliberate appropriation of European culture. Greenlanders found inspiration for socio-political and cultural development in Knud Rasmussen's Greenlandic translation of a book about evolution, while his works about Inuit still influence Danish thinking about Greenlanders as noble natives whom civilisation unfortunately ruined.

In the nineteenth century parts of the Danish administration considered further breeding of a mixed race a desirable physical as well as intellectual development in Greenland. Anthropological studies were carried out – and in the 1920s civil servants in the Danish governmental departments were influenced by eugenics. Such cultural theories were not unfamiliar among Greenlanders. Augo Lynge, a leading Greenlandic intellectual and politician stressed in newspapers that Greenlanders were already of mixed descent. He made the hero of his 1931 novel a fair man of mixed descent, with a more impulsive dark-haired helper. In a novel from 1944, Pavia Petersen lets the daughter of a mixed marriage live out the message. The Danish father pleads for more secular education, while the mother wishes for a more intimate Christianity. The daughter's answer is that she cannot do without any of these. The same author wrote in 1934 that this literary genre had spread from Antiquity to all races. Greenlandic literature in this period focused on nation building as a domestic issue, with few references to the significant Danish Other.

Greenland's altered state, from colony to Danish province in 1953, was followed by modernisation and Danification. The successful fight against tuberculosis meant an increasing number of schoolchildren. This in turn led to the import of more Danish teachers to Greenland. Construction works brought a huge number of Danish workers to Greenland. The increase of Danes in Greenland also resulted in a dramatic rise in mixed relationships. One of the consequences of this development was a Danish-speaking minority of Greenlanders whose presence threatened the traditional ethnic-national demarcation symbol, the language. Furthermore, wage differentials defined by birthplace, but very much correlating with ethnicity, created great discontent, and were highly instrumental in the process that ended with the establishment of home rule (1979). The process was mirrored in Greenlandic literature too, most overtly in protest lyrics, some of which were composed in Danish, while most of the rest were translated into Danish in order to get the message through to the Danes. For some years during the transition to home rule, the need for a decolonisation of the mind meant a need for a sharp demarcation from the former coloniser, leaving little or no space for the Danish-speaking offspring from mixed marriages. In general the common Greenlandic way of thinking at that time continued to operate with a binary division of the population. The theme for discussion (including literary works) was how to expel non-Inuit cultural parts of contemporary culture in Greenland and find a way back to a more Inuit rooted culture.

The years after home rule was established have witnessed a slow decolonisation characterised by a balancing between an ethnic-national desire for a homogeneous Greenlandic-speaking permanent population and a more or less pragmatic and democratic acceptance of the fact that the population is not homogeneous, but on the contrary – especially in Nuuk – includes a minority of Danish-speaking Greenlanders and a Danish minority group with a long presence in Greenland (not to mention the many Danes coming to Greenland for short-term stays). In everyday communication there is still a dichotomy between Greenlanders and Danes, where language operates as the basic ethnic-national symbol and definition. At the same time everyone knows that reality is much more complex. In general the tone of public debates is sober, thanks to the fact that it has become part of the Greenlandic culture to adhere to human rights and minority rights while simultaneously nourishing the postcolonial wish for Greenlandification (that is, less dependency on a foreign labour force and increasing linguistic Greenlandification). Furthermore, recent years have brought back an acknowledgement of the need for competence in foreign languages and brought an increasing awareness of being part of a global society.

Karen Langgård

Histories

Bravo, Michael and Sverker Sörlin (eds) (2002), *Narrating the Arctic*, Nantucket, MA: Science History Publications.

Gad, Finn (1974), *Fire detailkomplekser i Grønlands historie 1782–1808*, Copenhagen: Nyt Nordisk Forlag, Arnold Busck.

Langgård, Karen (1998), 'An Examination of Greenlandic Awareness of Ethnicity and National Self-Consciousness through Texts produced by Greenlanders 1860s–1920s', *Études Inuit Studies* 22 (1): 83–107.

— (2003), 'Language Policy in Greenland', in Joseph Brincat, Winfred Boeder and Thomas Stoltz (eds), *Purism in Minor Languages, Endangered Languages, Regional Languages And Mixed Languages*, Bochum: Universitätsverlag Dr. N. Brockmeyer, pp. 225–55.

Marquardt, Ole (1998), 'Reservation, Westernisation or Annihilation', in Ingi Sigurdsson Ingi and Jón Skaptason (eds), *Aspects of Arctic and Sub-Arctic History*, Reykjavik: University of Iceland Press.

— (2002), 'Greenland's Demography 1700–2000: The Interplay of Economic Activities and Religion', *Études Inuit Studies* 26 (2): 47–69.

Knud Rasmussen

The writer and arctic explorer, Knud Johan Victor Rasmussen, born in Ilulissat (Jakobshavn) Greenland in 1879, was the son of Danish priest Christian Rasmussen and wife Sophie L. S. Fleischer, of partly Greenlandic descent. In Ilulissat he received a mixed Greenlandic and Danish upbringing, and spoke both languages fluently. Upon finishing his education in Denmark, Knud Rasmussen returned to Greenland in 1902–4 with the Danish literary Greenland expedition to north-western Greenland, whose goal was to contact the Polar Eskimos in the Thule area. The Thule expedition resulted in Rasmussen starting a local trading station, and contributed to securing north-western Greenland for Denmark; and both financed and lent its name to Knud Rasmussen's seven Thule expeditions undertaken in the period between 1912 and 1933.

The best known expedition is the fifth Thule expedition from Greenland to the Pacific Ocean, with the purpose of visiting all of the Eskimo peoples and examining their travel paths. The expedition met with great national interest and acclaim, and contributed to Denmark becoming a centre for ethnographic Eskimo and polar research. It also established Rasmussen as a polar researcher and a national hero. Rasmussen's scientific work covered geography, ethnography, folklore, literature and religion. On his travels he collected ethnographica and archaeological artefacts, as well as languages, songs, myths and tales from the entire Eskimo area.

The results were presented in both scientific works and in more popular form, where the genres would blend into personal, saga-like stories with more focus on the journey than on scientific results. While these popular writings helped to make Rasmussen a household name, they also helped shape the public image of Eskimo peoples.

It is remarkable that Rasmussen presented his scientific results in both Greenlandic and Danish. He had a romantic notion of Eskimos as enviably free and 'noble savages', and his expeditions took place at a time of colonial expansion and national quests. Hence, the goal of his expeditions was to secure as well as colonise certain land areas for Denmark. The march of civilisation was inevitable, Rasmussen felt, and Denmark's role in this was to ease the transition of primitive people into civilisation. It was a role that the nationally disposed polar researcher regarded as important. Due to this and to the aforementioned circumstances such as his mixed Danish/Greenlandic descent and upbringing, and his ability to speak fluently in both languages, Knud Rasmussen was a natural born translator between Eskimo/Greenlandic and Danish/European cultures, and he represented Denmark at the court in The Hague in the dispute between Denmark and Norway about territorial rights to north-east Greenland.

During the seventh Thule expedition to Ammassalik in 1933 Rasmussen fell ill; he was brought to Denmark where he died shortly afterwards. Today his work still holds great significance. His focus on the kinship between Eskimo people has played an important role for the Inuit communities, and his collection and dissemination of Greenlandic myths and tales has been instrumental in gaining recognition of oral storytelling as a part of Greenlandic cultural history, and consequently for the formation of Greenlandic identity.

Nanna Folke Olsen

Literary Works

Rasmussen, Knud (1905), *Nye mennesker*, Copenhagen: Gyldendal.
— (1909), *Avángarnisalerssârutit: oqalualât kuisimángitsut upernaviup avangnâne ivnângar-ngup erpâne pivdlugit*, Copenhagen: A. Rosenberg.
— (1915), *Report of the First Thule Expedition 1912*, Copenhagen: Meddelelser om Grønland.
— (1921), *Eskimo Folktales*, Copenhagen: Christiania.
— (1927a), *Report of the Second Thule Expedition for the Exploration of Greenland from Melville Bay to Long Fjord, 1916–1918*, Copenhagen: Meddelelser om Grønland.
— (1927b), *Across Arctic America: Narrative of the Fifth Thule Expedition*, Fairbanks, AK: University of Alaska Press.
— (1933), *Palos Brudefærd*, Ammassalik: Palladium A/S in co-operation with Ammassalik Museum.
— (1934–5), *Mindeudgave*, 3 vols, Copenhagen: Gyldendal.

Histories

Frederiksen, Kurt L. (1995), *Kongen af Thule*, Copenhagen: Rhodos.
Freuchen, Peter (1961), *I Sailed with Rasmussen*, New York: Viking Press.
Hastrup, Kirsten (2000), 'Menneskesyn: kultur, race og Knud Rasmussen', Electronic publication for Center for Kulturforskning Århus Universitet. www.hum.au.dk/ckulturf/pages/publications/kh/mrk.pdf
Høiris, Ole (1988), *Antropologien i Danmark. Museal Etnografi og Etnologi 1860–1960*, Copenhagen: Nationalmuseets Forlag.
Pedersen, Kennet (1998), 'Is-interferenser. København som verdenshovedstad for den etnografiske eskimoforskning i perioden 1900–1940', in Thomas Söderqvist, Jan Faye, Helge Kragh and Frans Allan Rasmussen (eds), *Videnskabernes København*, Copenhagen: Roskilde Universitets Forlag.
Thisted, Kirsten (ed.) (2005), *Grønlandsforskningen. Historie og perspektiver*, Copenhagen: Det Grønlandske Selskab.

Thule

Thule is the European name given to a hill on the remote coast of north-western Greenland, and to the surrounding district. The Greenlandic/Inughuit name of the hill is Uummannaq, which was also the name of the historical settlement inhabited by the Inughuit hunter community until their forced relocation by the Danish government in 1953. The area has been inhabited by human hunters for approximately 4,000 years and contemporary Inughuit, one of the smallest and northernmost human societies today are acknowledged as descendants of these early inhabitants. The first recorded encounter between Inughuit and European visitors in recent history is John Ross' short-term visit in 1818 during his expedition to search for the Northwest Passage. In 1902–4, Knud Rasmussen conducted an ethnographic expedition to Thule and in 1909–10, a missionary station and trading station were established, commencing a Danish colonial presence in Thule. In 1927, Knud Rasmussen established the Thule Hunters' Council with the purpose of protecting the Inughuit from Danish and European influences on their indigenous cultural, social and economic practices.

In 1941, during the German occupation of Denmark, the first American-Danish Defence Agreement authorised the establishment of a American-Danish weather station in Thule, enabling US military presence in northern Greenland. After World War II the Defence Agreement of 1951 affirmed the Danish acceptance of American troops in Greenland and Thule Air Base was established. The presence of the air base led to Inughuit concerns over their long-term ability to remain relatively self-supporting. The proximity of the base to the Inughuit was also a concern to the Americans and the Danish authorities and in the spring of 1953, the Danish authorities chose to relocate the Inughuit from Uummannaq to Qaanaq, an old settlement approximately 150 kilometres further north, an area where game was less prolific. In 1985, Danish scholars Jens Brøsted and Mads Fægteborg published 'Fangerfolk og militæranlæg', documenting that the relocation in 1953 was done without proper consultation with the Inughuit. Two government commissions failed to place final responsibility for the relocation. In 1996, Hingitaq 53 ('the Discarded 53') was formed, an Inughuit organisation, which launched legal proceedings against the Danish state. They claimed land rights and permission to hunt in the Thule district along with compensation for the relocation. In 1999, the Danish Eastern High Court recognised the relocation had been forced upon the locals and that the Inughuit was an indigenous people in 1953. However, the compensation was markedly lower than the amount claimed by Hingitaq 53 and land rights to Thule district were denied. Hingitaq 53 appealed to the Danish Supreme Court which in 2003 upheld the verdict of the lower court, but withdrew the recognition of Inughuit as an indigenous people. In 2004 Hingitaq 53 took the case to the European Court of Human Rights. Other important events connected to Thule are the American military's storage of nuclear bombs in Thule in 1950s and 1960s, contrary to Danish official policy of no nuclear weapons on Danish soil, and the exposure of Inughuit and Danish workers to radioactive radiation.

Pia Krüger Johansen

Histories

Brøsted, Jens and Mads Fægteborg (1987), *Thule – fangerfolk og militæranlæg*, 2nd edn, Copenhagen: Jurist- og Økonomiforbundets Forlag.

Dragsdahl, Jørgen (2001), 'The Danish Dilemma', *Bulletin of the Atomic Scientists* 57: 5 <http://www.bullatomsci.org/issues/2001/so01/so01dragsdahl.html> [accessed 19 February 2003].

Lynge, Aqqaluk (2000), *The Right to Return. Fifty Years of Struggle by Relocated Inughuit in Greenland*, Nuuk: Atuagkat.

Malaurie, Jean (2001), *Call of the North: An Explorer's Journey to the North Pole*, New York: Abrams.

Wulff, Steen (2005), 'The Legal Bases for the Inughuit Claim to their Homelands', *International Journal on Minority and Group Rights* 12: 63–92

Tropical Colonies

In the seventeenth century, following the examples of especially the Dutch and English merchants, the united kingdom of Denmark-Norway established colonies in India, the West Indies, and on the Gold Coast of Africa. In comparison to the size of the other European colonial empires, the Danish-Norwegian one remained, however (with the territorial exception of Greenland), rather small. Nevertheless the tropical colonies came to play an important role in the building of Danish merchant capitalism in the eighteenth century, the Ostindisk Kompagni in 1616 also forming the first Danish private company, where King Christian IV virtually forced the larger merchants to subscribe for shares. Of tropical colonies, the Indian ones in Tranquebar and Serampore and the African ones in Ghana were sold to England in the 1840s, while the West Indian Virgin Islands were sold to the USA in 1917.

From the time of the Viking age, the Danish-Norwegian kings claimed sovereignty over the North Atlantic, including Greenland. Five hundred years after the Viking chief Eric the Red during his exile from Norway founded the Vineland settlement in Canada, an expedition under the leadership of Pinning and Pothorst was sent out by King Christian I to search for a Northwest Passage to India. In 1472, twenty years before Columbus discovered America, this expedition reached the St Lawrence River and New Foundland, but failed in its mission to discover any Northwest Passage. In 1619, a fresh attempt was made when King Christian IV dispatched Jens Munk with two ships in a renewed attempt to find this fabled route which could deliver to the Danish-Norwegian throne a tax income from European shipping to and from the Indies – in similar fashion to the lucrative tax on international ship cargoes to and from the Baltic countries. However, this expedition also failed. After visiting the Hudson Bay, the crew contracted scurvy and met with serious trouble in the pack ice. Jens Munk, with only two other surviving sailors, barely managed to reach Bergen on one of his ships. This marked the end of Danish-Norwegian attempts to discover a Northwest Passage to India.

From then, economic resources were directed at equipping ships bound for the Indian colony Tranquebar, which had been established in 1620 on the southern Coromandel Coast by Admiral Ove Giedde, with the assistance of the Dutch merchant Roland Crappe. From the local prince or *naik* of Tanjore, the Danes along with the already present Portuguese shared a monopoly on all trade with Europe. For many years Tranquebar functioned as a military stronghold and the fort, Dansborg, became a storage place for coveted tropical products, acquired locally, at other Indian localities, and in South-East Asia. In 1706, Tranquebar housed the first Protestant mission in India which soon clashed with the local colonial administration, when during conflicts the missionaries sided with the local population. In Tranquebar as well as in Serampore in Bengal, the Danes established a town after the European model, and in Serampore missionaries opened what was to become the first modern university in Asia.

In the West Indies, St Thomas was claimed in 1625, but it took time to establish regular contacts and consolidate the trading company. In 1648, St Jan and in 1733 also St Croix were annexed. On all three islands, the indigenous Caribbean population was already extinct when occupied by the Danes. Danish and Norwegian debt slaves and criminals were, with very limited success, converted into workers or given plantation land along with planters from foreign nations, in order to grow the coveted sugar and tobacco to sell in Copenhagen. In 1697, the first Danish-Norwegian slave ship arrived from the Gold Coast and for roughly 100 years, the triangular trade between Copenhagen, Africa and the West Indies continued. In 1792, the Danish government abolished all slave trade, and slave transports on Danish-Norwegian ships after 1803. Slavery as such was, however, not abolished until 1848 when a slave demonstration caused the Governor-General, Peter von Scholten, simply to proclaim all slaves to be free.

In 1658, the first attempt to gain a foothold in the Gold Coast of West Africa to obtain ivory and gold was made, but here, too, it was difficult to maintain regular contact, not least because Denmark-Norway was involved in wars in Europe. Fort Christiansborg was constructed on land obtained from the local king in Accra and it became the main Danish-Norwegian military stronghold on the coast as well as a reception camp for slaves awaiting shipment to the West Indies. From 1790 to 1808, as a consequence of the abolition of the Danish slave trade, private investors tried to establish plantations inland to grow coffee, cotton, sugar and oil palms, but because of wars between the local tribes, the ten plantations were finally abandoned.

One characteristic of Danish-Norwegian overseas activities was the relatively strong involvement of the King in the promotion of colonialism. Merchant capital seems to have been too small and underdeveloped, and the investment required needed a big player like the crown to put capital into the enterprise which at times even took over the trade company and the administration of the colonies. Only in the eighteenth century does Danish colonial trade seem to have functioned more normally. In Tranquebar and Serampore, the items in demand were rather few: silver, lead and guns in exchange for Indian textiles and pepper; on the African Gold Coast mirrors, spirits, watches, iron bars and Indian textiles were traded for slaves. In the West Indies, the income generated by the importing of African slaves was used to buy sugar and tobacco for the home markets. Equally characteristic of the Danish-Norwegian Empire was its ability to take advantage of wars between the larger imperial countries in the second half of the eighteenth century, offering foreign trade under the neutral Danish flag.

During colonialism, cultural impact from the colonies and other overseas connections were to be observed in stately homes, where Indian and Chinese styles were fashionable. Modern migration from the tropical colonies to Denmark-Norway has been negligible, making these two countries comparatively ethnically homogeneous. Relations with former tropical colonies are few, these days, outside historical and anthropological research into cultural encounters during colonialism and the practical work of NGOs and museums to preserve Ghana-Danish, Indo-Danish, or West Indian-Danish cultural heritage in relation to buildings and plantations.

Esther Fihl

LITERARY WORKS AND FILMS
Bidstrup, Ole (ed.) (1992), *Kunstnere i tropesol*, Dansk Vestindisk Selskab in co-operation with Nikolaj Udstillingsbygning.
Hansen, Thorkild (1967–70), *Slavernes kyst. Slavernes skibe. Slavernes øer*. 3 vols, Copenhagen: Gyldendal.
Kjærulff-Schmidt, Palle (1987), *Peter von Scholten*. Crone Film Production – Metronome Production.

HISTORIES
Brøndsted, Johannes (1966), *Vore gamle tropekolonier*, Copenhagen: Fremad.
Fihl, Esther (1984), 'Some Theoretical and Methodological Consideration on the Study of Danish Colonialism in Southeast India', *FOLK* 26: 51–66.
Feldbæk, Ole (1969), *India Trade under the Danish Flag 1772–1808*, Monograph Series no. 2. Copenhagen: Scandinavian Institute of Asian Studies.
Hall, Neville A. T. (1992), *Slave Society in the Danish West Indies*, Mona: University of West Indies Press.
Olwig, Karen Fog (1985), *Cultural Adaptation and Resistance on St John*, Gainesville, FL: University of Florida Press.

Viking Settlements in Iceland, Faeroe Islands, and Greenland, and Danish Arctic Exploration

The Faeroe Islands and Greenland are the only remaining parts of a once vast Danish empire. But, actually, the islands became a part of the Danish Empire by chance. They were not conquered or discovered by order of the Danish king. They were not cultivated on behalf of the king. Instead the islands were populated by chieftains and their voluntary followers, who moved from primarily Norway in pursuit of better farmland and as a result of power struggles in Norway. In the thirteenth century all the islands became a part of the Norwegian kingdom. In 1380 a personal union of Norway and Denmark was established, but in 1536 Norway was officially incorporated into the Danish kingdom (the kingdom Denmark-Norway) and thus also were the islands in the North Atlantic. In Greenland the Norse disappeared in the fifteenth century. Norway and Denmark never de facto became one kingdom but Iceland, the Faeroe Islands and Greenland remained a part of the dominion of the Danish king while the rest of the Norwegian kingdom was lost to Sweden in 1814 as a result of the Napoleonic Wars.

The Vikings from Denmark, Norway and Sweden pillaged all across Europe and even found opportunity to settle. They possessed the technology and sufficient navigational know-how to enable them to travel across the Atlantic Ocean. Thus, in the ninth century Norwegian farmers and chieftains set out to take new land in the North Atlantic. Why they were so adventurous still remains to be explained but trade and commodities were among the important factors. Conventional wisdom and a look at a map tell us that the Faeroe Islands were populated first, then Iceland – both in the second half of the ninth century – and finally Greenland around the turn of the millennium. From Greenland and Iceland the Norse then went on to the American continent (Newfoundland), although without realising they had discovered a new continent. The Norse probably considered Newfoundland an extension of habitable lands and fjords stretching from Norway over the Shetlands, Orkneys, Faeroes, Iceland and Greenland.

The wealthier of the first settlers had their own ships and were able to maintain contact and trade with the homeland on their own. Since none of the islands had any trees, after a short period of settlement it proved nearly impossible to maintain the ships. Due to their isolation the settlements had to be self-reliant in most ways, but the islands' limited resource base forced the settlers to depend on import of many items and goods, such as iron. In the long run it was necessary for the settlers to find ways to meet the heavy cost of these imported materials. It also meant the islanders became more and more dependent on foreign merchants.

The Norse settlements on the Faeroe Islands, Iceland and Greenland were much alike – even though they adapted to the different conditions of the local environments. The Norse were the first to cultivate the islands. The end of the tenth century marked the culmination of several hundred years of high temperatures in Northern Europe, and the Greenlandic soil had never been cultivated by previous Eskimo cultures. The Norse farmer who arrived at the south-western part of Greenland would have seen an uninhabited land with lush fields suitable for the same kind of farming he knew from Norway. In the extreme north-western and eastern parts of Greenland an Eskimo culture known as Dorset remained until the late thirteenth century. However, it was not until the early thirteenth century that the Eskimo culture known as Thule, which now inhabits Greenland, made its way from the North American continent to the northernmost parts of the island.

The Norse established a farming society based upon the raising of domestic animals: cows, goats and especially sheep, supplemented with whatever could be caught from the sea or along the shores. Fish, birds and, especially in the Greenlandic case, seals provided part of the diet. The Norse farms generally consisted of a core, where the buildings, farmhouses, outhouses, kitchen gardens and refuse piles were located. There were enclosed cultivated infields close to the farms which were used for growing hay needed for winter fodder and, if possible, grain. There were also uncultivated outfields used for pasture, and for turf and peat cutting. Turf was an important building material. Neither the Faeroese nor the Icelandic way of life changed much before the nineteenth century. Establishing a Norwegian-style farming society in Greenland bordered on the impossible and the settlement was small: perhaps only 2,000–5,000 inhabitants in all compared to the Icelandic population which has been estimated at up to 70,000 at one point. All archaeological excavations show that the Norse maintained their original lifestyle in Greenland, even though they had to eat more marine food. Analyses of the surviving bones of the Norse in Greenland even show that marine food constituted up to 80 per cent of their diet towards the end of the Norse settlement period. The Norse disappeared from Greenland in the fifteenth century. Many have attempted to explain why, but no one explanation has been found. In the eighteenth century the Danish king recolonised the island with the help of the missionary, Hans Egede. The main export goods from the Faeroe Islands were woollen products and fish. Iceland's primary export article was *wadmal*, homespun cloth, and fish. The voyage to Greenland was more perilous but the potential profits for merchants were also greater. Greenland mainly exported items of high value: walrus tusks, along with other products from the walrus, and luxury items like white falcons. While the settlers on the Faeroe Islands and Iceland could produce the export goods at home the Greenlandic Vikings had to acquire their trading goods on dangerous hunting trips to the North (Nordsetur, in Disko Bay and further north).

The societies were highly differentiated, one symbol of power and wealth being the amount of cattle one possessed. The wealthiest and most powerful chieftains were those who arrived at the islands first and therefore had been able to take possession of large pieces of the best land (*landnám*). The initial consolidation period was, in Iceland, followed by stiff competition for power among the wealthy chieftains during the eleventh, twelfth and thirteenth centuries. There is no reason to believe that the situation was different in Greenland or the Faeroe Islands. The influence of the Catholic Church and the Norwegian king changed the dynamics.

When the Norse first came to the islands most were still pagan but around 1000 Christianity became the official religion. In the early twelfth century the islands each gained their own bishopric – at first subject to Lund (in Denmark) but in the middle of the twelfth century they became subject to Trondheim. Through the Church (and the crown) the islands were economically and culturally linked to each other and Northern Europe – not least because the islanders now had to pay tithe. As was the case elsewhere the clerics quickly came to play a substantial role in the society and we have much for which to thank their ledgers and scholarship, not least the sagas. The sees became the centres of the islands, cultural and otherwise. It is noteworthy that no Norse Greenlander was ever elected bishop of Gardar. This indicates that the establishment of the Episcopal see did not happen at the request of the Greenlandic settlers, but rather as a result of the Roman Church's desire to strengthen the Church's organisation.

In the twelfth century the Faeroe Islands, Iceland and Greenland were persuaded to pay tribute to the Norwegian king, that is they became part of the Norwegian kingdom. The political influence was concentrated in fewer hands. The King wanted to make sure that all goods were landed in Norway so he could tax them. Changes in the economic condi-tions in Europe from 1300 made the Greenlanders increasingly dependent on direct trade with the king. The Scandinavian markets could now provide enough skins and hides and Europe no longer demanded the Greenlandic walrus tusk. As a result, the official Norwegian trade ceased completely at the beginning of the fifteenth century. That might have been the final blow to the Norse settlement in Greenland.

ARCTIC EXPLORATION

The Northwest Passage was the name of a fabled sea route north and west around the American continents. If found it would be a far shorter route to the Far East. The poten-tial economic gains were then as now huge. Between the end of the fifteenth century and the twentieth century, many attempts were made to find the passage. Many died trying. The Danish King, Christian IV, also backed an attempt. In 1619 the nobleman Jens Munk set sail with three ships. The ships got caught in the ice in Hudson Bay and one by one the crew died. The captivating story of the dreadful voyage is known because Jens Munk mirac-ulously managed to return in 1620 along with two of his shipmates in the smallest of the ships and brought his diary home. In the end it was the Norwegian explorer Roald Amundsen who first managed to sail through the passage in 1906.

Greenland was never forgotten and as late as the eighteenth century it was still believed that the Norse had survived. Ships did continually reach Greenland without the required permission. From time to time there was talk of sending expeditions to Greenland. In 1605, 1606 and 1607 Christian IV did actually send out expeditions to find the lost Norse of yore and in 1654 King Frederik III issued a special thirty-year grant to sail to Greenland which resulted in trading expeditions in 1652–4.

Another attempt to find the Norse was made the early eighteenth century. Sanctioned by the King of Denmark and Norway, and sponsored by a company in Bergen for trade with Greenland which Norwegian priest, Hans Egede himself had founded (the trade later passed to the Royal Greenland Trading Company of Copenhagen), Egede sailed to Greenland in 1721, accompanied by his wife and children. Smallpox and political misfor-tunes almost killed off the colony in Greenland in its infancy. Egede converted many Eskimos to Christianity, established commerce with Denmark, and not least caused the establishment of a permanent Danish presence in Greenland.

Danish expeditions explored Greenland and the polar region in the nineteenth and the twentieth centuries. These expeditions were dangerous and conducted under the most primitive conditions. Among the notable were the expeditions led by Fridthjof Nansen, Ludvig Mylius-Erichsen, and Knud Rasmussen. Initially the primary goal was to chart Greenland. One example is the expedition of 1906–7 led by Ludvig Mylius-Erichsen, to chart the north-eastern regions of Greenland. However, Mylius-Erichsen and his two com-panions did not return to their ship before winter set in and they all died in November 1907. One of the bodies was found along with the diary that told of their fate. The expe-dition had secured valuable results which were later published.

In 1878 the Commission for Scientific Exploration in Greenland was established, which still exists. In 1854 the first cryolite had been shipped from Greenland and later the quarry provided the state with substantial revenue. It is no wonder, then, that the first order of business was systematic geological and mineralogical exploration. The expeditions were often interdisciplinary, with biology, geology, archaeology, anthropology and astronomy among the fields of research. World War II more or less brought an end to these and in recent years government backing has diminished. The focus today is on possible sources of income: gold, diamonds, oil and so on. Valuable minerals can be extracted from the Greenlandic rocks but the costs of retrieving them are so high that it until now has not been profitable.

Lasse Wolsgård

LITERARY WORKS

Hreinsson, Vidar (1997), *The Complete Sagas of the Icelanders*, Reykjavik: Leifur Eiríksson Publishing.

Høeg, Peter [1992] (1997), *Miss Smilla's Feeling for Snow*, trans. F. David, London: Harvill Press.

Janoda, Jeff (2005), *Saga: A Novel of Mediaeval Iceland*, Chicago, IL: Academy Chicago Press.

HISTORIES

Bravo, Michael and Sverker Sorlin (eds) (2002), *Narrating the Arctic: A Cultural History of Nordic Scientific Practices*, Canton, MA: Watson Publishing International.

Hansen, Thorkild (1970), *North West to Hudson Bay: The Life and Times of Jens Munk*, London: Collins.

Jones, Gwyn (1984), *A History of the Vikings*, Oxford: Oxford University Press.

Jones, Gwyn and Robert McGhee (1986), *The Norse Atlantic Saga: Being the Norse Voyages of Discovery and Settlement to Iceland, Greenland and North America*, Oxford: Oxford University Press.

Page, R. I. (1995), *Chronicles of the Vikings: Records, Memorials and Myths*, Toronto: Toronto University Press.

France and its Colonies

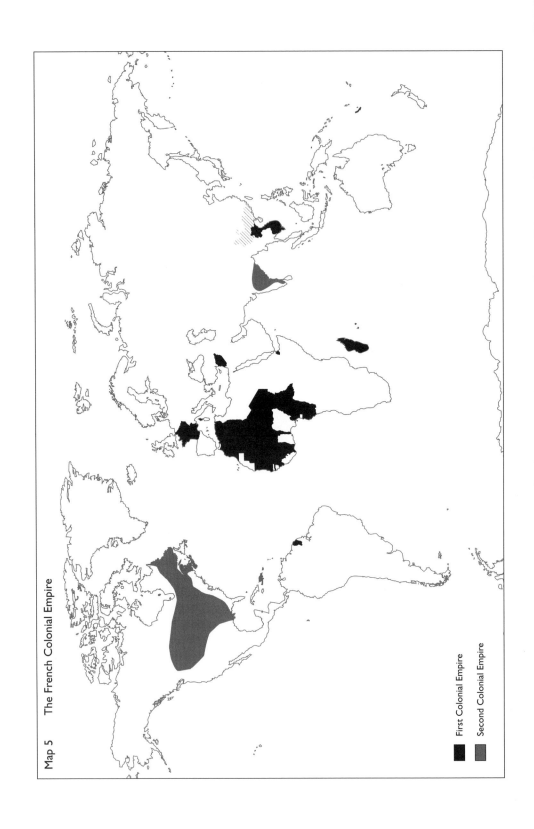

Map 5   The French Colonial Empire

First Colonial Empire

Second Colonial Empire

France and its Colonies: Introduction

There was not a single French Empire. Nor, for the millions of people (colonising, colonised, or somewhere in between) whose lives were implicated in and affected by French imperial expansion, were there unified, monolithic experiences of empire. It is for this reason that a rigorous historical contextualisation, addressing the regional and chronological specificities associated with colonial contact, is essential for any nuanced reading of postcolonial literatures in French. Drawing primarily on French-language thinkers (both anti-colonialists, such as Césaire and Fanon, and poststructuralists, such as Cixous, Derrida and Foucault), postcolonial criticism has provided a series of 'key concepts' in the light of which literary texts may be analysed (Ashcroft, Griffiths and Tiffin 1998); it is the task of the reader or critic, however, to negotiate the interplay between the universalist pretensions of any such critical approach and the groundedness of our objects of study in specific or singular sets of circumstances (Hallward 2001).

The entries that follow address this challenge by outlining key themes that connect, across historical and geographical diversity, the existence and experience of those whose everyday lives were (and are) affected by colonialism and its aftermath; at the same time, however, they offer an introduction to the variability of such phenomena at different chronological moments and in different geographical locales. Robert Aldrich, in the subtitle of his *Greater France* (1996), proposes 'A History of French Overseas Expansion' (my emphasis), and there were indeed various formations – judicial, ideological and social – whose role was progressively to impose unity on a heterogeneous range of colonial 'possessions'. These included such diverse phenomena as the Code Noir (1685), the Third Republic doctrine of assimilation (and the 'Plus Grande France' it was supposed to forge), the colonial education system (also developed under Jules Ferry and applied to a lesser or greater degree across French colonial societies): the role of legislative, administrative and ideological apparatus such as these was to police the links between France and its colonies, as well as to consolidate the internal structures of the colonies themselves. (It is also important to note that, despite efforts to fragment anti-colonial movements, these also operated across different colonies, forming radically alternative globalised structures [Young 2001].) What Aldrich's own study reveals, however, is that beneath the monolithic sense of a single colonial history there exists a proliferation of plural colonial histories. It is the evolution and progressive transformation of institutions and ideologies, whose theoretical status is often challenged by their more partial and pragmatic application in the field, that suggests the need for an approach to French colonialism that reveals its specific formations in particular regions, at individual sites and at distinct chronological moments. Postcolonial criticism may, through comparative analysis, illuminate certain continuities between and within colonial or historically postcolonial situations, but there is a need for thorough historical contextualisation to test such often abstract continuities and to judge to what extent their literary manifestations may converge with or diverge from them.

In seeking to explore the historical context of francophone postcolonial literatures, a number of provisos are therefore necessary. Firstly, those interested in colonial histories and in their representation in postcolonial literatures must also be aware that history does not begin with colonial contact. Indeed, challenging the endeavours of much colonial literature to relegate pre-colonial cultures to a prehistorical moment (Miller 1985), many postcolonial authors, particularly in the period leading up to and immediately following decolonisation, used their writing to salvage, resurrect and reassert those elements of their indigenous culture eroded and destroyed by imperial expansionism. (Negritude and Haitian *noirisme* are clear examples of these processes.) Secondly, there is a need to avoid a reductively linear history of empire that presents, for instance, the replacement of an Ancien Régime imperialism with its post-revolutionary, republican counterpart. Although Napoleon's humiliations in Egypt and Saint-Domingue forced him to abandon any planned expansion into the Ottoman Empire and North America, remnants of the pre-revolutionary empire (in India and the Indian Ocean, as well as the Caribbean itself) persisted alongside territories annexed and appropriated throughout the nineteenth century, and it is some of these *vieilles colonies* – most notably French Guiana, Guadeloupe, Martinique and Reunion Island – that maintain a direct constitutional connection with France as the DOM-ROMs (Départements et Régions d'Outre-Mer), France's residual overseas territories. Finally, recent developments in historiography encourage an approach to French colonial history that avoids, in the distinction of (former) coloniser and (former) colonised, any perpetuation of a hierarchised, binary, neo-colonial relationship of centre and periphery. In an influential essay, Cooper and Stoler have outlined the ways that 'metropole and colony, coloniser and colonised, need to be brought into one analytic field' (1997), and their agenda has been addressed by a new generation of historians concerned not so much with traditional comparatism as with the exploration of more complex transnational connections underpinning a wider 'francophone postcolonial' space (Conklin 1997; Jennings 2001; Mann 2003).

There has been much discussion around the meaning and spelling of the adjective 'postcolonial' (Ashcroft 1996), with Chris Bongie's variation on the term – 'post/colonial' – providing one of the clearest refutations of any sense of chronological compartmentalisation. For Bongie, the notion of the 'post/colonial' signifies an 'intimate (dis)connection of the colonial and the postcolonial' (1998). It is in the light of such an analysis of interconnectedness and disconnectedness, of complex entanglements, that we might best understand the crucial twentieth-century story of how the 'francophone' world – with that epithet including, but not privileging, France itself – became postcolonial. The destabilising experience of World War I on thousands of colonial troops (*tirailleurs indigènes*) had considerable implications for twentieth-century anti-colonial movements. Brought to France, the country vaunted by colonial education and other forms of propaganda as the apogee of civilisation, they had witnessed not a society regulated by republican and Enlightenment values but the barbarity of the front. Moreover, the justification of the war as a struggle to protect smaller nations permitted the nurturing of early aspirations to national independence that became increasingly apparent in the highly politicised and closely policed colonial populations of 1920s Paris (Miller 1998). The 1931 colonial exhibition at Vincennes represented a final attempt to win over the still largely apathetic French population to the cause of the empire, but this exoticist spectacle – despite the vast crowds who visited it, and the very minor hostility it provoked (Norindr 1996) – came much too late (Ageron 1997). A new generation of African and Caribbean students, completing their education in Paris, began to forge – around the loose concept of Negritude – a pan-African, transatlantic activism that would call into question, whilst exposing the racist foundations of, the philosophical assumptions underpinning colonialism.

The experience of World War II, during which France once again relied on its colonial troops in a number of fields of battle, led to a last-ditch attempt to transform the empire – formulated at Brazzaville in 1944 as the Union Française (itself created in 1946) – into the means of salvaging national esteem on a world stage. As Aimé Césaire outlined, however, in his magisterial *Discours sur le colonialisme* (1955), rapid decolonisation was the logical outcome of the anti-fascist struggle in which the Allies had recently been engaged. French reluctance to accept the inevitability of this process led to increasingly vicious attempts to maintain power over its colonies (Benot 2001). Whilst VE Day was celebrated in mainland France (8 May 1945), French troops perpetrated the massacres of anti-colonial demonstrators in the Sétif and Constantine regions of Algeria that form the core of Kateb Yacine's *Nedjma* (1956). When, two years later, in 1947, a insurrection in Madagascar was put down with even more ferocious brutality, it became increasingly apparent that France's withdrawal from its overseas territories would prove to be a violent one. Troops deployed in the liberation of France, many of whom originated in the colonies, travelled to Indo-China to wage a harsh and ultimately unsuccessful campaign against Ho Chi Minh's Vietnamese nationalist forces. Shortly after French forces been defeated at Dien Bien Phu in 1954 (and just as France's Indian possessions were reunited with newly independent India), the Algerian War of Independence broke out, heralding an eight-year conflict that saw high numbers of fatalities on the Algerian as well as the French side. Such talk of sides is, however, misleading, for the war did not lend itself to Manichean divisions. Algerians were divided over independence, with considerable numbers of *harkis* rallying to the French cause (Enjelvin 2003); at the same time, a pro-independence movement rapidly emerged in France, led by prominent intellectuals such as Jean-Paul Sartre. General de Gaulle, returned to power at this time of national crisis, presided over the dismantling of France's colonial empire: following referenda in the Sub-Saharan African colonies in 1958, a progressive, constitutional passage to independence was granted. Under pressure from the Far Right (embodied in the OAS group), no such solution was broached for Algeria, the war for whose independence led to a traumatic historical experience whose afterlives still shape French and Algerian society today.

At the end of the war in 1962, France entered a period of postcoloniality, although any rhetoric of a 'clean break' with the past was undermined by the complex reality of empire's aftermath. On the one hand, the end of empire was accompanied by large population shifts that had a considerable demographic impact on metropolitan France itself. Not only were thousands of *Harkis* and *pieds-noirs* repatriated from Algeria, creating social tensions that remain unresolved today, but also a generation of colonial officials and administrators were forced, in Hermann Lebovics' terms, to 'bring the Empire back home' (2004), shaping contemporary France in often unexpected ways. On the other hand, what purported to be a chronologically 'postcolonial' moment proved to be distinctly 'neo-colonial': France maintained the 'confettis' of its empire, constituted by the DOM-TOMs, scattered departments and territories in the Caribbean, the Pacific and the Indian Ocean (as well as, in the Atlantic, the seemingly anomalous Saint-Pierre et Miquelon off Newfoundland); at the same time, through the organisation of la Francophonie and schemes such as co-opération, a sphere of influence was maintained in former parts of the empire, some of whose financial dependence on France reconfigured rather than replaced previous colonial relationships. France's recent or continued involvement in the domestic politics of a range of its former colonies – for example, Rwanda, Morocco, the Ivory Coast and Haiti – suggests that imperial or strategic ambitions survive, and that the imbrications of former coloniser in the affairs of the former colonised remain persistent.

In many ways, such continued connections are far from surprising. It was the linguistic legacies of French imperialism – and the continued use of French, at least by postcolonial élites – that permitted the establishment of la Francophonie and France's continued intervention in the national education systems of its former colonies; the migratory flows of people – primarily for the purposes of work – have led to the further entanglement of postcolonial histories, transforming – for instance – France and Algeria into a 'transpolitical' space (Silverstein 2004); and perhaps most notably, the unequal but nevertheless shared experience of empire has led, in the postcolonial era, to a reflection on the processes of colonial memory (and of memory's connections to postcolonial identity: see Aldrich 2005; Blanchard and Bancel 2006; Rioux 2006). After decades of an apparent national obsession with the fratricidal conflicts by which it was divided during the Nazi occupation (1940–4), a process dubbed by Henry Rousso as its 'Vichy syndrome', France has – in the twenty-first century – turned its attention to the colonial past. Collective, official amnesia in the aftermath of the traumatic Algerian War of Independence could not disguise the proliferation of multiple, individual memories, a subject addressed in Michael Haneke's 2005 film *Hidden* (*Caché*). A series of events – the recognition, in 1999, that the Algerian conflict had actually been a 'war'; General Paul Aussaresses' admission of the use of torture, in 2000; the 2001 inauguration, by the Mayor of Paris Bertrand Delanoë, of a memorial to the victims of the 1961 massacre of FLN demonstrators in Paris – triggered debates and associated publications regarding the legacies of the colonial past (Macmaster 2002). The current 'Algeria syndrome' may be seen, however, to have detracted attention from other areas of colonial history – and the memories with which these are related. The Indo-Chinese War, and the humiliating French defeat at Dien Bien Phu which signalled its end, play an unsurprisingly minor role in national memory: despite a ceremony at Les Invalides, the battle's fiftieth anniversary in 2004 was inevitably eclipsed by the sixtieth anniversary of the Normandy landings (Cooper 2004); and increased attention to the history of slavery has done little to illuminate the continuing neo-colonial ties that link France to its remaining overseas departments in the Caribbean.

It is perhaps the memorialisation of slavery that reveals in particular the continually contested nature of colonial history and memory. Whereas those in the Caribbean remember the experience of enslavement and efforts at its resistance, the metropolitan commemoration remains focused on abolition, epitomised by figures such as Victor Schoelcher (whose remains were removed to the Pantheon, alongside those of Félix Eboué, in 1949). The abolition of slavery in 1848 is seen as the result of a principally philanthropic process, an interpretation that ignores the significance of the Haitian Revolution (as well as other, less successful slave rebellions) whilst conveniently obscuring the fact that an initial abolition, voted by the Convention in 1794, had been overturned by Napoleon in 1802. The inauguration of a national slavery remembrance day (10 May) and the constitution of a Comité pour la Mémoire de l'Esclavage aim to raise public consciousness of the role of slavery in French history, but many feel that the aim of a 'shared memory' remains a distant hope, with such a model representing more a theoretical approach than actual evidence of any postcolonial rapprochement of former coloniser and colonised.

Literature represents a clear response to such colonial and postcolonial dilemmas, imagining connections between history and the present, and often gesturing – in what Edouard Glissant has dubbed a 'prophetic vision of the past' (2005) – towards 'refashioned futures' (Scott 1999). As with other postcolonial literatures, there exists rich criticism devoted to the discussion of ways of reading material in French. While some insist on the need for rigorous historical and cultural contextualisation (Serrano 2005), others stress the singularity of literature and its privileged standing as a particularly complex form of historical discourse (Harrison 2003). It is perhaps most useful to understand literary texts as elements in a larger colonial (and postcolonial) 'archive' (Richards 1993): a grasp of the historical situation from which they emerged and with which they engage is essential, but their literariness permits what Joan Dayan (1995), in her work on Haiti, has described as 'literary fieldwork', by which she outlines a means of accessing aspects of culture, history and memory that might otherwise be lost in more 'empirical' sources. Literature – as is the case, it should be added, with cinema, whose educational and memorial role in countries with high rates of illiteracy should not be underestimated – is, therefore, a key means of writing back into history those whom official, and even unofficial, histories have often ignored, such as women and enslaved people. While national historiographies have often contributed, as adjuncts to ideology, to 'silencing the past' (Trouillot 1995), postcolonial literatures have played a key role in history's progressive postcolonial recovery.

Charles Forsdick

Histories

Ageron, Charles-Robert (1997), 'L'Exposition coloniale de 1931: Mythe républicain ou mythe impérial?', in Pierre Nora (ed.), *Les Lieux de mémoire*, vol. 1, Paris: Gallimard/Quarto, pp. 493–515.

Aldrich, Robert (1996), *Greater France: A History of French Overseas Expansion*, Basingstoke: Palgrave.

— (2005), *Vestiges of the Colonial Empire in France: Monuments, Museums and Colonial Memories*, New York: Palgrave Macmillan.

Ashcroft, Bill (1996), 'On the Hyphen in Post-Colonial', *New Literatures Review* 32: 23–32.

Ashcroft, Bill, Gareth Griffiths and Helen Tiffin (1998), *Key Concepts in Post-Colonial Studies*, London: Routledge.

Benot, Yves [1994] (2001), *Massacres coloniaux 1944–1950: La IVe République et la mise au pas des colonies françaises*, Paris: La Découverte.

Blanchard, Pascal and Nicolas Bancel (eds) (2006), *Culture post-coloniale 1961–2006: traces et mémoires coloniales en France*, Paris: Autrement.

Bongie, Chris (1998), *Islands and Exiles: The Creole Identities of Post/Colonial Literature*, Stanford, CA: Stanford University Press.

Conklin, Alice L. (1997), *A Mission to Civilize: The Republican Idea of Empire in France and West Africa, 1895–1930*, Stanford, CA: Stanford University Press.

Cooper, Frederic and Ann Laura Stoler (eds) (1997), *Tensions of Empire: Colonial Cultures in a Bourgeois World*, Berkeley, CA: University of California Press.

Cooper, Nicola (2004), 'Dien Bien Phu: Fifty Years On', *Modern and Contemporary France* 12 (4): 445–57.

Dayan, Joan (1995), *Haiti, History, and the Gods*, Berkeley, CA and London: University of California Press.

Enjelvin, Géraldine (2003), 'Les Harkis en France: Carte d'identité française, identité harkie à la carte?', *Modern and Contemporary France* 11 (2): 161–73.

Glissant, Edouard (2005), *Monsieur Toussaint: A Play*, trans. J. Michael Dash and Edouard Glissant, Boulder, CO and London: Lynne Riener.

Hallward, Peter (2001), *Absolutely Postcolonial*, Manchester and New York: Manchester University Press.

Harrison, Nicholas (2003), *Postcolonial Criticism: History, Theory and the Work of Fiction*, Cambridge: Polity.

Jennings, Eric T. (2001), *Vichy in the Tropics: Pétain's National Revolution in Madagascar, Guadeloupe, and Indochina, 1940–1944*, Stanford, CA: Stanford University Press.

Lebovics, Herman (2004), *Bringing the Empire Back Home: France in the Global Age*, Durham, NC and London: Duke University Press.

MacMaster, Neil (2002), 'The Torture Controversy (1998–2002): Towards a New History of the Algerian War?', *Modern and Contemporary France* 10 (4): 449–59.

Mann, Gregory (2003), 'Locating Colonial Histories: Between France and West Africa', *American Historical Review* April 2005 <http://www.historycooperative.org/journals/ahr/110.2/mann.html> [accessed 20 Oct. 2006].

Miller, Christopher (1985), *Blank Darkness: Africanist Discourse in French*, Chicago, IL: University of Chicago Press.

— (1998), *Nationalists and Nomads: Essays on Francophone African Literature and Culture*, Chicago, IL and London: University of Chicago Press.

Norindr, Panivong (1996), *Phantasmatic Indochina. French Colonial Ideology in Architecture, Film and Literature*, Durham, NC and London: Duke University Press.

Richards, Thomas (1993), *The Imperial Archive: Knowledge and the Fantasy of Empire*, London: Verso.

Rioux, Jean-Pierre (2006), *La France perd la mémoire*, Paris: Perrin.

Serrano, Richard (2005), *Against the Postcolonial: 'Francophone' Writers at the Ends of French Empire*, Lanham, MD and Oxford: Lexington Books.

Scott, David (1999), *Refashioning Futures*, Princeton, NJ: Princeton University Press.

Silverstein, Paul (2004), *Algeria in France: Transpolitics, Race and Nation*, Bloomington, IN: Indiana University Press.

Trouillot, Michel-Rolph (1995), *Silencing the Past: Power and the Production of History*, Boston, MA: Beacon Press.

Young, Robert J. C. (2001), *Postcolonialism: An Historical Introduction*, Oxford: Blackwell.

The Algerian War

The Algerian War of Independence began on 1 November 1954, when the newly formed FLN (Front de Libération Nationale) launched guerrilla attacks on military and police targets. The early stages of the war saw polarisation and radicalisation of opinion, and a rapid escalation of violence on both sides. Prominent incidents in this first phase included the vote in the French parliament in March 1956 that granted 'special powers' to the French military in Algeria; the kidnapping in October 1956 of FLN leader Ben Bella, who eventually came to power in 1962; and the 'Battle of Algiers', a period of conflict in 1956–7 comprising a wave of attacks and general strikes orchestrated by the FLN and its violent suppression by battalions of parachutists. That military victory for the French proved, in the longer term, a propaganda victory for Algeria, focusing international attention on the war and the French Army's systematic use of torture. In May 1958, rebellious actions by the French Army in Algeria led to the end of the vacillant Fourth Republic and the return to power of de Gaulle. Like his predecessors he initially underestimated the momentum of the independence movement, but by 1959 he had begun to speak of Algerian self-determination, and in June 1960 effectively recognised the GPRA (Gouvernement Provisoire de la République Algérienne). Political progress was slowed by hard-liners including the *colons* (or *pieds-noirs*) who threw up barricades in Algiers in January 1960, and the generals who joined the pro-French-Algeria OAS (Organisation Armée Secrète), with its plans to assassinate de Gaulle. He survived a putsch in Algiers in April 1961 and signed the Evian agreements with the GPRA on 18 March 1962, which led to full independence in July 1962.

The most detailed account of the war in English is still Horne's *A Savage War of Peace*, though its tone now sounds a little dated and – like much of the historiography – it is Eurocentric. The legacy of the war remains fiercely contested, and recent works (historical, literary and cinematic) have revived debates around torture, the fate of the *harkis* (Algerians who fought with the security forces, and many of whom were killed in the violence that continued after July 1962) and the slaughter in Paris in 1961 of pro-FLN demonstrators.

It is a peculiarity of Algerian literary history that the first great wave of Algerian literature, by writers such as Mohammed Dib, Mouloud Feraoun, Mouloud Mammeri and Kateb Yacine, predates not only independence but the war. Kateb's classic *Nedjma*, though published in 1956, was largely written earlier, and like other works of the era it emphasises the importance for the nationalist movement of the Sétif massacres of 8 May 1945, when Algerian demonstrators at an Armistice Day procession were shot by members of the security forces. Most major works on the war have been published in France and in French; exceptions include French-language texts published in Algeria by SNED (Société Nationale d'Édition et de Diffusion), and successful Arabic-language texts by Tahar Ouettar (also spelled as Wattar) and Ahlam Mosteghanemi.

Nicholas Harrison

LITERARY AND CINEMATIC WORKS
Djebar, Assia (1962), *Les Enfants du nouveau monde*, trans. as *Children of the New World* (2005) Marjolijn de Jager, New York: The Feminist Press.
Etcherelli, Claire (1969), *Élise ou la vraie vie*, trans. as *Elise, or the Real Life* (1970) June P. Wilson and Walter Benn Michaels, London: Deutsch.
Feraoun, Mouloud [1962] (2000), *Journal, 1955–1962: Reflections on the French-Algerian War*, ed. and intro. James D. Le Sueur; trans. Mary Ellen Wolf and Claude Fouillade, Lincoln, NE: University of Nebraska Press.
Fanon, Frantz (1959), *L'An V de la révolution algérienne*, trans. as *A Dying Colonialism* (1980) Haakon Chevalier, London: Writers and Readers.
Pontecorvo, Gillo (director) (1966), *The Battle of Algiers*, Algeria and Italy: Casbah Films and Igor Film.

HISTORIES
Dine, Philip (1994), *Images of the Algerian War: French Fiction and Film, 1954–1992*, Oxford: Clarendon.
Horne, Alistair [1977] (2002), *A Savage War of Peace: Algeria 1954–1962*, London: Pan Macmillan.
Harbi, Mohammed and Benjamin Stora (eds) (2004), *La Guerre d'Algérie: 1954–2004, La fin de l'amnésie*, Paris: Robert Laffont.
Ruedy, John (2005), *Modern Algeria: The Origins and Development of a Nation*, 2nd edn, Bloomington and Indianapolis, IN: Indiana University Press.
Thénault, Sylvie (2005), *Histoire de la guerre d'indépendance algérienne*, Paris: Flammarion.

Anthropology and Ethnography

Napoleon's campaign in Egypt (1798–99) was a crucial moment in the emergence of erudite anthropological research in France. In the first part of the nineteenth century, writers such as Chateaubriand, Nerval and Hugo brought other civilisations into mainstream literature. Henceforth, literature and anthropology became closely interrelated. This privileged relationship was further activated by the French colonial expansion of the late nineteenth century. In the development of anthropology as an autonomous discipline, the role of the Third Republic was indeed vital, even though significant predecessors such as Louis Faidherbe, notably in his work on Senegal, were instrumental in laying down the foundations of the new science. From the creation of the Trocadéro Museum of Ethnography in 1878 until its replacement by the Musée de l'Homme in 1937, the ethnographer, once an ill-defined figure, became a key interpreter of indigenous cultures. In this institutional recognition, it is important to underscore Maurice Delafosse' role. Delafosse began his colonial career in the French Sudan from where he contributed to the transformation of ethnography. Delafosse, who was able to maintain strong connections with Paris-based university scholars such as E.-T. Hamy, engineered a rapprochement between anthropological theory and practice. There had been hitherto a clear divide between the collectors of anthropological items and data (the ethnographers) and those (usually university dons) who took on the more rewarding task of interpreting these materials. Delafosse refused to ascribe racial diversity to polygenic factors. He was convinced of the scientific legitimacy of the monogenic thesis and embraced the tenets of Durkheimian sociology. Inspired by Marcel Mauss, he refuted the *primitif-civilisé* dichotomy and this posture generated, most notably in his *Haut-Sénégal-Niger* (1912), a more relativist set of paradigms that were to influence ethnographic enquiries until the advent of structuralism.

Colonial literature in France went also through a process of gradual transformation. Critics demanded more realistic representations of indigenous people; they were calling for a *nouvel exotisme* that would disseminate among the French public a more authentic knowledge of the colonies, based on the view that colonial authors needed to be direct observers of local practices. Victor Segalen's *Les Immémoriaux* (1907) paid close attention to Maori customs, oral tradition, cosmogony, rites and religious beliefs, and was regarded as the desired recipe for fictions about the empire. As a consequence, Segalen was labelled in colonial circles as the 'French Kipling'. This ethnographic posture is central to the understanding of fictional imagination from or about the empire until decolonisation. From the 1920s anthropology became a two-edged sword as it exposed, on the one hand, the complicit relationship between colonial power and knowledge and, on the other, the possibility of revealing colonised others in their complexity. After the controversy produced by the anti-colonial Goncourt prize-winning novel *Batouala* (1921) by the black Franco-Caribbean writer René Maran, French colonial authors with ethnographic credentials launched a campaign against Maran. In this critique, they attacked Maran for his purported lack of ethnographic authenticity and claimed that their own narratives had more successfully captured the essence of the indigenous world view.

The interwar period can be regarded as the golden age of anthropology. In 1925 the Institute of Ethnology of the Sorbonne was created by Marcel Mauss, Lucien Lévy-Bruhl and Paul Rivet, under the auspices of the Ministry of the Colonies. This official recognition fuelled a number of state-funded events such as the Colonial Exhibition of Vincennes

(1931) and the Dakar-Djibouti (1931–3) mission led by Marcel Griaule. The discipline also fed the discussions of the avant-garde cenacle le Collège de Sociologie. At the same time, the instigators of the *Négritude* movement engaged in a far-reaching literary and philosophical reflection on black cultural identity. In this debate, the progenitors of the movement explicitly praised *The Voice of Africa* (1913) by the German ethnologist Leo Frobenius as a work which restored the cultural dignity of Africa. Anthropology, however, also came under harsh criticism during this period. In *L'Afrique fantôme* (1934), Leiris, who had been Griaule's secretary in the Dakar-Djibouti expedition, produced a damning account of the mission, deploring the lack of respect for African cultures and the predatory nature of ethnography. In 1938, Paul Hazoumé, a professional ethnographer from Dahomey, wrote *Doguicimi*, a voluminous novel in which ethno-historic materials were used to highlight the failure of the French universalist project in western Africa. Implicitly, this ambitious book also argued that ethnography as a discipline reflects the inequality and paternalism of the colonial system in that it establishes a hierarchy between local informants and Western ethnographers, regarded as intruders whose usurped authority can be bypassed.

This idea of the misappropriation and misinterpretation of other cultures by French anthropologists has retained up to the present day its potency in the works by many francophone novelists such as Edouard Glissant, Patrick Chamoiseau, Maryse Condé, Abdelkebir Khatibi, Valentin Yves Mudimbe or even J.-M.-G. Le Clézio and Didier Daeninckx. After World War II, the discipline was submitted to renewed criticisms. In *Tristes tropiques* (1955), Lévi-Strauss lampooned the discipline for its exotic propensities. Later, in *The Wretched of the Earth* (1961), Fanon criticised the tendency of colonial Africanists to produce, in the name of authenticity, fossilised images of colonised cultures. This concern had already been voiced in 1950 in *Les Temps modernes* by Leiris who urged his contemporaries to devote more attention to the study of the effects of traditional myths and rites on the daily experiences of the so-called *évolués*. In this area, it is fiction, rather than anthropology per se, which took the lead and proved the most innovative. Writers such as Sembene Ousmane, Ahmadou Kourouma, Mongo Beti, Cheikh Hamidou Kane or more contemporary figures such as Calixthe Beyala or Azouz Begag have produced a rich network of narratives focusing on protagonists – in the former empire or in France – torn between the legacy of tradition and the advent of a globalised world. This tension has also reflected the evolution of anthropology in the last thirty years. The discipline no longer focuses solely on otherness to expose human and cultural diversity.

Pierre-Philippe Fraiture

LITERARY WORKS

Chamoiseau, Patrick [1992] (1997), *Texaco*, trans. Rose-Myriam Réjouis and Val Vinokurov, London: Granta.

Hazoumé, Paul (1938), *Doguicimi*, Paris: Maisonneuve and Larose.

Le Clézio, J. M. G. (2004), *L'Africain*, Paris: Mercure de France.

Maran, René [1921] (1973), *Batouala: veritable roman nègre/ Batouala*, trans. Barbara Beck and Alexandre Mboukou, London: Heinemann.

Mudimbe, Valentin Yves (1979), *L'Écart*, Paris: Présence Africaine.

Segalen, Victor (1907), *Les Immémoriaux*, trans. as *A Lapse of Memory* (1995) Rosemary Arnoux, Brisbane: Boombana.

Ousmane, Sembene [1973] (1976), *Xala*, trans. Clive Wake, London: Heinemann.

HISTORIES

Bataille, George (1988), *The College of Sociology (1937–39)*, ed. Denis Hollier, trans. Betsy Wing, Minneapolis, MN: University of Minnesota Press.

Clifford, James (1988), *The Predicament of Culture. Twentieth-Century Ethnography, Literature and Art*, Cambridge, MA and London: Harvard University Press.

Coundouriotis, Eleni (1998), *Claiming History. Colonialism, Ethnography and the Novel*, New York: Columbia University Press.

Forsdick, Charles (2000), 'L'Exote mangé par les hommes', in Charles Forsdick and Susan Marson (eds), *Reading Diversity: Lectures du divers*, Glasgow: Glasgow French and German Publications, pp. 5–24.

Fraiture, Pierre-Philippe (2005), '*Batouala*: véritable roman d'un faux ethnographe?', *Francofonía* 14: 23–37.

Gaillard, Gérald (ed.) (2004), *Routledge Dictionary of Anthropologists and Ethnologists*, London: Routledge.

Miller, Christopher L. (1985), *Blank Darkness: Africanist Discourse in French*, Chicago, IL and London: University of Chicago Press.

Mudimbe, Valentin Yves (1988), *The Invention of Africa: Gnosis, Philosophy and the Order of Knowledge*, Bloomington, IN and London: Indiana University Press.

Sibeud, Emmanuel (2002), *Une Science impériale pour l'Afrique. La construction des savoirs africanistes en France (1878–1930)*, Paris: EHESS.

Anti-colonialism

Anti-colonialism is an active, wilful, politicised attempt to end colonial rule, as opposed to the politically neutral process 'decolonisation' (Rothermund 2006). In the francophone world there are two distinct periods of anti-colonial struggle: 1789–1940 and 1945–62. The first period was inaugurated by the Haitian Revolution. The 1945–62 period fits into a wider, anti-colonial move against Europe that ran for thirty years, 1945–75, ending with the independence of the Portuguese colonies, Angola and Mozambique. Though much has been written on the twentieth-century experience of decolonisation in the francophone world, much less has been forthcoming on the character, nature and actions of the various anti-colonial movements that shook France's empire to the core. A comparative historical overview of these movements reveals the ways in which the anti-colonial label serves to synthesise, and at the same time mask, the disparities between the very different situations and reactions pertaining in the various colonies and protectorates under France's dominion.

Within the twentieth-century French Empire there were two major types of colonialism for anti-colonialists to fight against: settler colonialism (as in Algeria and the Caribbean); and/or 'protectorate/dependency colonialism' (as in Morocco and Tunisia). It was in the latter that successful decolonisation came more smoothly, as often the national bourgeoisie was already firmly in power, but independence was not inevitable. The French Republic had established a policy of cultural assimilation in its empire, to differing degrees in different regions and countries: it was where assimilationist policies were most entrenched in colonial ideology – in the case of France, the republican *mission civilisatrice* – that anti-colonialism was most heavily repressed and that, by turn, anti-colonialism moved towards more drastic and widespread confrontations. Often this led to the need for a national liberation army, the Army of National Liberation in Algeria (ALN) or the Viet Minh in Vietnam. In the latter it was geo-political intransigence, rather than assimilationist settler colony mentality (as in Algeria), that fuelled the anti-colonial forces. Hence the need for a nationalist ideology as a means to encourage an anti-colonial movement (Fanon 1961).

Of the five categories of anti-colonial resistance – resistance to conquest, rebellions against European rule, movements of religious revivalism, nationalist constitutional moves towards decolonisation, national liberation struggles (Young 2001) – francophone colonies experienced all to different degrees. The first was a predominantly pre-twentieth-century phenomenon, though the Rif War in 1925 was effectively a repelling of a joint French–Spanish attempt to conquer an untamed mountain region of Morocco. The other four can be found in all aspects of post-war anti-colonial resistance to empire.

Once begun anti-colonialism spread rapidly. If Tunisia and Morocco surround Algeria geographically, they also exclude Algeria from the relative ease with which they were given formal independence in the mid-1950s. They illustrate, at the same time, the 'domino effect' of anti-colonial struggle. For, although both countries were never colonised (they were French protectorates), their accession to independence from France – obvious as early as 1953 – was bound to encourage the insurgency in Algeria; and France's ignominious military defeat at Dien Bien Phu in Vietnam in May 1954 merely compounded the 'domino effect': the 1 November uprising in the Aurès region of southern Algeria, though planned for months, was triggered with stunning effect. Similarly, throughout Sub-Saharan Africa and across the Sahara itself, the 'domino effect' is unmistakeable as Algeria became the pole of anti-colonial struggle in the second half of the 1950s. Anti-colonial forces in the very different countries in francophone Africa united within a pan-Africanist identity. However, during the post-war period of anti-colonial struggle, it was not Africa which led the way, despite the patent bankruptcy of French colonial rule there, but former Indo-China. In September 1945, following the defeat of the Japanese forces, Ho Chi Minh proclaimed Vietnam independent, and Cambodia and Laos followed suit. Indeed, the anti-colonial movements of the second half of the twentieth century were unleashed, in part, because of one huge profound historical injustice: France and its colonies had been helped to liberate themselves from Nazi occupation precisely by their colonial subjects, through the hard work and sacrifice of *tirailleurs sénégalais* and Algerians alike; and both saw the harsh repression meted out by France at the end of the war: 'the victim became the butcher' (Sartre in Alleg 1958).

Lenin and the Third International had defined and propelled anti-colonialism with the formation of the Comintern in 1919 and this was a major moment in the development of anti-colonialism into anti-imperialism's critique of capitalism. Across the late 1920s (first in China) and throughout the 1930s, communist parties, including those in France and in her colonies, were diverted, if not dissuaded, from demanding independence for the sake of Stalin's geo-political priorities (Merle 2003). Indeed, for many activists, the anti-colonial struggle in Algeria began only in 1945. If the traditional anti-colonial parties in Europe failed to take seriously their historic mission to spread freedom and justice in the colonies, it was, specifically in relation to the Algerian anti-colonial struggle, Trotskyites, anarchists, left-libertarians (Evans 1997; Boulouque 2003), not to mention Church and pacifist groups (Ahmad 1992), who joined with the indigenous anti-colonial movements; to the point that the political wing of Algerian anti-colonial struggle, the Front de Libération Nationale (FLN), based in France with its French Internationalist allies, was described as '7th *wilayah*' of Algeria's army and the crucial element in France's final capitulation. Nevertheless, unlike the first wave of anti-colonialism in the eighteenth and nineteenth centuries, it was the 'autochtones' (indigenous people) (with some French enlightened help) who ended France's colonial system.

The 'softer' wing of anti-colonialism – uniting future Senegalese president and poet Léopold Senghor with Jean Rous – argued that the *Union française* could be slowly unravelled to give independence eventually. While France fought hard to resist the anti-colonial war in Algeria, Charles de Gaulle was forced in 1958 to accede to the vigorous anti-colonialist demands across French-speaking Sub-Saharan Africa, allowing a certain amount of autonomy within the French community: the only dissenter in the referendum was Sékou Touré's Guinea-Conakry. The same year, a moderate anti-colonial activist, Ferhat Abbas, was installed as the first president of the provisional Algerian government, now residing in Tunis. The other key year for the success of the various anti-colonial struggles in the French-speaking world is 1960, with full independence granted to Cameroon, Togo, Mali, Madagascar, Zaire (now RDC), Upper Volta (now Burkina Faso), Chad, Ivory Coast, the Congo, Gabon and Senegal, followed by Rwanda and finally Algeria in July 1962. All of these countries had seen some form of anti-colonial resistance: the FLN in Algeria, the CNO guerillas in the Cameroons between 1955 and 1962; but also most countries developed anti-colonial movements after 1945, and many joined the 'Rassemblement Démocratique Africain' under Ivorian leader Félix Houphouët-Boigny. Algeria was nevertheless a very different case. Not only was it part of France, with three French *départements* (counties); it was also home to a million French settlers (the *pieds-noirs*) and to rich landowning colonialists. Like the British in Kenya faced with the Mau-mau rebellion, France met the rebellion of 1954 with extreme repression; similarly, the ways and means of anti-colonial resistance had its own lethal, if selective, responses.

It is perhaps ironic that France is shown to be the central pin of the anti-colonial struggle. Not only did metropolitan France have a tight rein on its very different colonies, it was also on the mainland, ultimately, that the anti-colonial wars of independence were won. Desertions against the war in Indo-China were famously defended by Sartre (in the case of the sailor Henri Martin in 1950); *rappelés* (reservists) also deserted when called to fight in Algeria in 1955 and famously 20,000 revolted in their barracks in 1956; French anti-colonialists such as Maurice Audin were abducted, tortured and murdered by the French far right; in September 1960, 121 French intellectuals signed a petition demanding the right for French soldiers to desert the war in Algeria (though some refused to sign due to the FLN's own use of repression); Michel Raptis (aka Pablo), influenced by C. L. R. James and a leading member of the Trotskyite Fourth International, lent determined political (and uncritical) support to Algeria's struggle. French anti-colonialists during the Algerian War were radicalised by the experience of anti-fascism during World War II and by two main sources, the novels of Algerians Mohammed Dib and Kateb Yacine, and left-leaning French publications such as *Esprit*, *France-Observateur* and *Les Temps modernes* (Evans 1997). André Mandouze was a left-wing Catholic involved in the anti-colonial struggle, and other militant 'worker-priests' also joined the anti-war networks in France. If France's anti-colonialists took their role seriously, then other traditional and more natural anti-colonialist forces failed. Though highly critical of the French Army's methods, neither the French Communist Party, nor the Socialist SFIO under Guy Mollet as Prime Minister of France advocated Algerian independence, and both parties voted for the French Army's special powers in 1956.

The other principal aspect of francophone anti-colonialism is that the heroic period of struggle coincided with the Cold War. The anti-colonial movements and outcomes in Congo-Brazzaville (formerly French Congo) and Congo-Kinshasa (formerly the Belgian Congo) illustrate this bi-polar move towards independence. On the northern side of the River Congo, the Belgian colonial authorities engineered the brutal liquidation (quite literally, in a tub of acid) of the radical anti-colonial leader Patrice Lumumba, replacing him with Sese Mobutu and thereby staving off a clean sweep of the region by Moscow-backed governments. Indeed the 'Red Revolution' of 1958, on the south side of the Congo river in Brazzaville, was precisely what the Cold War West wanted to avoid: a mineral-rich area of Central Africa falling into the sphere of influence of the (then) Soviet Union. The haemorrhage in 1956 of activists and intellectuals from the PCF (including the Martiniquan poet and politician Aimé Césaire), following the Soviet invasion of Hungary (itself a distinctly colonialist and imperialist act), and the victory of Mao in 1949 in China and then Guevara and Castro in Cuba in 1959, led to a new hybrid form of anti-colonial theories, loosely called '*Tiers-Mondisme*' (Third-Worldism) and defined at the Bandung Conference in 1955. Anti-colonialism in France then came of age in the 1960s. The massacres by French police in Paris of Algerian anti-colonial protestors (17 October 1961) and then student anti-war protestors at Charonne tube station (in 1962) radicalised a new generation who would gather at François Maspero's bookshop, support his publishing house and read the journal *Partisans*, all of which culminated in the anti-Vietnam war and May 1968 movements.

Most of Africa's anti-colonial movements were tied to some form of (so-called) Marxist theory of social emancipation, the irony being that the leaderships of the movements were, by and large, wholly unable to institute socialism (with the possible exception of Ben Bella in Algeria), if for the simple reason that working-class and peasant classes were subordinated in the anti-colonial struggle, in favour of a militaristic, nationalistic (if pan-Africanist in theory) approach which risked establishing a 'stages' approach to social liberation (Stafford 2003). Fanon, for example, was exasperated by the FLN's lack of internationalism in the Algerian anti-colonial movement. Thus 'the historical role of Marxism in the history of anti-colonial resistance remains paramount as the fundamental framework of postcolonial thinking', though the Marxist ideas dominant in any anti-colonial movement, grouping or faction could be as varied as the individuals involved in the action: the crucial relationship between anti-colonialism and Marxism was that the fight against European imperialism was also a struggle for social change and human progress, but also a distinct attempt to modify the perceived 'Eurocentrism' of orthodox Marxist theory and praxis (Young 2001). Under the auspices of the Cold War, many of the anti-colonial movements fell financially, militarily and then politically under the aegis of Moscow and/or Beijing, to the point that any radical Marxist critique of these Marxist deformations was repressed by the anti-colonial leaderships (witness the FLN's and the Viet Minh's purging of Trotskyites). Another error was for the left to believe that, given the social nature of anti-colonial nationalism, social change was 'intrinsic' to, inevitable in, the very metropolitan centres of empire, France and Europe's heartlands (Ahmad 1992). What is described as 'revolutionary anti-colonialism' is in fact a set of contradictions illustrated by the anti-colonial wars in Vietnam (French and then American), which resulted in nothing but misery and then starvation for much of the Indo-Chinese peninsula, in-fighting and economic disaster in Cambodia, rigid Stalinism in Vietnam; and Algeria was different only in that economic destitution was replaced by vicious civil war in the 1990s.

Anti-colonial struggle was a 'riven terrain' (Ahmad 1992), with communal, tribal and sectarian division within anti-colonial movements underscored by deep political division. The FLN, itself a loose grouping, was deeply hostile to the Messalists. Messali Hadj had been the founder of the Étoile Nord-Africaine in the 1930s influenced by Comintern anti-imperialism, and then moved away from communism to found the Parti Populaire Algérien and finally the Mouvement pour le Triomphe des Libertés Démocratiques. In the Katanga region of Zaire the local tribes were co-opted by Mobutu against Lumumba. Thus, 'divide and rule' was a well-worn colonialist tactic, successful in the Belgian Congo (ex-Zaire, now RDC), but not so effective in Algeria, where the only widespread example of France winning indigenous people to their side was the 'Harki' forces, though this was often an economic arrangement which did not exclude force or chance, not dissimilar to some collaborationists during the Nazi occupation of France.

A number of key writings in French emerged from the heroic period of anti-colonial struggle. Fanon, Memmi, Amrouche and Césaire use the speech and essay form to denounce colonial control, with Césaire promoting *Négritude* (a form of black pride) as an antidote to the racism and depersonalisation caused by the colonial system, and Fanon the idea of a violent, Hegelian fight to the death, with a new humanity emerging from the anti-colonial victory. All francophone anti-colonialist intellectuals were beholden to Sartre, who inspired (1948) cultural resistance against colonialism, leading to 'cultural nationalism' (whether black nationalist, pan-Africanist or Arab nationalist, and more recently Créolist in the Caribbean). In the hands of colonised writers, language itself became a form of anti-colonialist action; either by using a language not compatible with nor tolerated by France, or by using French in a 'literary' manner and sending it back to the metropolitan centre radicalised, redefined and reused (Césaire 1995). However, it was always events that inspired the theory and theories of anti-colonialism.

The Caribbean anti-colonial movement did not fare so well as Africa's nor the British Caribbean's, with France's Caribbean territories being incorporated into the mainland as counties (*départements*), a sign of how assimilated the islands had become over four centuries and of the concomitant lack of an indigenous middle class (Guérin 1956). After the 1948 'departmentalisation' of Guadeloupe, Guyane and Martinique, a racial incident in the last of these in 1959 provoked riots in Fort-de-France in which three young Martiniquan demonstrators were shot dead. This led to the founding of the 'Front Antillo-Guyanais' by Glissant, Niger (aka Béville) and Manville, demanding freedom for Caribbeans, but dissolved by de Gaulle in 1961 (when Glissant was expelled from Guadeloupe back to France). The Créolité movement was the product of this struggle for independence, inspired by the Kanak in New Caledonia whose anti-colonial militancy shook France in the 1980s; and Martinique and the French Caribbean have since maintained a strong anti-colonial spirit that extends to parts of France's mainland. The uprising in the French suburbs of November 2005 is indeed part of a *'fracture coloniale'* (Blanchard et al. 2005), but also suggests that anti-colonialism is today a globalised and politicised, anti-imperialist movement.

Andy Stafford

LITERARY WORKS

Césaire, Aimé (1939), *Cahier d'un retour au pays natal*, trans. as *Notebook of a Return to the Native Land* (1995) Mireille Rosello with Annie Pritchard, Newcastle-upon-Tyne: Bloodaxe Books.

— (1955), *Discours sur le colonialisme*, trans. as *Discourse on Colonialism* (1972) Joan Pinkham, New York: Monthly Review Press.

Dib, Mohammed (1995), 'The Savage Night', in *The Savage Night*, trans. C. Dickson, Lincoln, NE and London: University of Nebraska Press, pp. 47–73.

Fanon, Frantz (1961), *Les Damnés de la terre*, trans. as *The Wretched of the Earth* (1967) Constance Farrington, Harmondsworth: Penguin.

Laye, Camara (1953), *L'Enfant noir*, trans. as *The Dark Child* (1959) James Kirkup, London: Collins.

Mammeri, Moulud (1992), *L'Opium et le bâton*, Paris: La Découverte.

Sartre, Jean-Paul [1948] (1963), *Black Orpheus*, Paris: Gallimard.

Sembene, Ousmane (1960), *Les Bouts de bois de Dieu*, trans. as *God's Bits of Wood* (1995) Francis Price, London: Heinemann.

Yacine, Kateb (1956), *Nedjma*, Paris: Seuil.

HISTORIES

Ahmad, Aijaz (1992), *In Theory. Classes, Nations, Literatures*, London: Verso.

Alleg, Henri (1958), *La Question*, trans. as *The Question* (2006) James D. Le Sueur, Lincoln, NE: University of Nebraska Press.

Biondi, Jean-Pierre (with Gilles Morin) (1992), *Les Anticolonialistes (1881–1962)*, Paris: Robert Laffont.

Blanchard, Pascal, Nicholas Bancel and Sandrine Lemaire (eds) (2005), *La Fracture coloniale*, Paris: La Découverte.

Boulouque, Sylvain (2003), *Les Anarchistes français face aux guerres coloniales*, Lyons: Atelier de Création Libertaire.

Chaliand, Gérard (1977), *Revolution in the Third World. Myths and Prospects*, Hassocks: Harvester Press.

Enwezor, Okwui (2001), *The Short Century: Independence and Liberation Movements in Africa 1945–1994*, Munich and New York: Prestel.

Evans, Martin (1997), *Memory of Resistance. French Opposition to the Algerian War (1954–1962)*, Oxford: Berg.

Fanon, Frantz [1959] (1970), *A Dying Colonialism*, Harmondsworth: Penguin.

Guérin, Daniel (1956), *Les Antilles décolonisées*, Paris: Présence Africaine.

Merle, Marcel (2003), 'L'Anti-colonialisme', in Marc Ferro (ed.), *Le Livre noir du colonialisme. XVIe-XXIe siècle: De l'extermination à la repentance*, Paris: Robert Laffont, pp. 815–61.

Rothermund, Dieter (ed.) (2006), *The Routledge Companion to Decolonization*, London: Routledge.

Sartre, Jean-Paul (1964), *Situations V: Colonialisme et néo-colonialisme*, trans. as *Colonialism and Neocolonialism* (2001) Azzedine Haddour, Steve Brewer, Terry McWilliams, London and New York: Routledge.

Stafford, Andy (2003), 'Frantz Fanon, Atlantic Theorist. Or: Decolonisation and Nation-State in Postcolonial Theory', in C. Forsdick and D. Murphy (eds), *Francophone Postcolonial Studies*, London: Arnold, pp. 166–77.

Young, Robert J. C. (2001), *Postcolonialism: An Historical Introduction*, Oxford: Blackwell.

Colonial Administration

'Assimilation can be considered the traditional colonial doctrine of France . . . Not only did assimilation appeal to the French love of order, belief in man's equality, and ever-present desire to spread French culture; it also appeared to provide for a uniform colonial administration' (Betts 2005). Assimilation has been variously defined but essentially is taken to mean the integration of overseas territories within the motherland to create a 'Greater France', in which local society and people are remade in the image of the population of the mother country so that they become French in all but the colour of their skin. The pursuit of this objective would appear to imply the imposition, as Betts' statement above suggests, of rationally conceived, uniform political and administrative structures, modelled on those of the metropole. Yet the gap between this ideal image of the administration of France's colonial empire and the untidy reality on the ground could hardly be greater: in practice, France's empire lacked organisational coherence, its administrative structures were frequently ramshackle and its administrators often exerted nominal authority over vast swathes of territory about which they knew little and often understood less. This slowly began to change, as the École Coloniale produced more colonial administrators and their training became more professional, but lack of staff and resources and frequent transfers of personnel from one posting to another often rendered the pursuit of a consistent policy impracticable.

However, it was not only at the periphery, in the colonies themselves, that ideal and reality diverged. In Paris, there was no single ministry in charge of the colonial empire. The Naval Ministry was responsible for the colonies until a colonial ministry was finally created in 1894, but even after this date control of the colonies remained dispersed between the Ministry of the Interior, which was responsible for Algeria (Algeria was officially not a colony but administered as an integral part of metropolitan France), the Foreign Ministry, which was responsible for the protectorates (since they were technically independent entities under French protection), and the Ministry of Colonies, which covered the rest of the empire (remaining something of a Cinderella ministry since in practice it had to share responsibility for some areas of colonial policy with other ministries, notably finance and war).

At the next level of the administration, there was again diversity. Governors-General headed the administrations in Algeria, Indo-China, French West Africa (AOF – Afrique Occidentale Française); Madagascar and French Equatorial Africa (AEF – Afrique Equatoriale Française); with governors or lieutenant-governors at the head of each of the territories within these federations. The protectorates, on the other hand, were headed by a resident or a resident-general. Further diversity was added in 1919, when France acquired the former German colonies of Togo and Cameroon, together with Syria and the Lebanon, under a League of Nations mandate. Although Paris was not formally given sovereignty over these territories and was required to submit regular reports to the League of Nations on economic, social and political conditions in them, in practice it ruled the former as extensions of AOF and AEF respectively, while a French high commissioner in Beirut took charge of the latter. The 'old colonies' of the Caribbean and the Four Communes of Senegal had elected local councils and also elected representatives to parliament in Paris. Everywhere else, colonised populations – apart from the tiny minority who 'earned' French citizenship – had no political rights and were subject to the *indigénat* (native administrative code), which gave French officials powers to punish indigenous peoples for a wide range of offences including failure to obey orders and showing disloyalty to France.

Below the governors-general and governors were the true 'rulers of empire', in Cohen's phrase (1971): the *commandants de cercle*, assisted in some of the more populous or important regions by *chefs de subdivision*. Initially military men, as their name suggests, the colonial administration was progressively civilianised following the creation of the École Coloniale in 1887. The *commandants de cercle* had wide-ranging powers: they implemented government decrees, made decisions on local regulations, oversaw the census, collected taxes, were responsible for law and order, supervised development projects, including the development of schools and health centres, and generally acted as the local representatives of the French state. Below them were the African village chiefs and canton chiefs (chiefs appointed by the French administration), who were charged with executing the instructions of the *commandant* or his assistant.

This approach to colonial rule, where authority was in theory handed down from Paris via a pyramidal structure to the local chiefs and which in principle provided very little scope for local initiative, has been described as 'direct rule'. Characterised as typically French, it has been contrasted to the British approach of 'indirect rule', which was supposed to involve governing colonised peoples through their own political institutions by taking local rulers into partnerships with the colonial administration, and was portrayed by its apologists as less destructive of indigenous authority than the French system of direct rule. Some commentators have, however, questioned how different the British and French approaches were in practice (Kiwanuka 1970). They point out that lack of resources and the diversity of the actual situations on the ground made a uniform, one-size-fits-all approach impossible. Poor communications, their distance from the centres of power, the enormous gulf between European and indigenous cultures and the manifest impossibility of assimilating such vast and heterogeneous areas into a single 'Greater France' meant that French officials had more or less sole responsibility for the day-to-day running of their administrative region. In these conditions, there was in practice considerable scope for local initiative.

These situations changed with the reconfiguration of empire after World War II. The colonial empire became the French Union, the 'old colonies' in the Caribbean, together with the Indian Ocean island of Réunion, became overseas departments and as such were henceforth administered as integral parts of metropolitan France, and in the rest of the colonial empire there was a renewed emphasis on integrating the colonies – now renamed 'Overseas France' – with the metropole. This meant enhanced political representation in the French parliament in Paris and increased investment in colonial economic and social development, which in turn led to a major new influx of French officials and specialists – from accountants and planners to engineers and agricultural technicians – to promote and implement the development plans. The increased bureaucratisation of colonial rule that resulted, together with the dramatic improvement in communications, meant that French colonial officials were no longer, in the words of Hubert Deschamps (1975), the 'kings of the bush'.

Tony Chafer

LITERARY WORKS (MEMOIRS BY COLONIAL ADMINISTRATORS)
Clauzel, Jean (1989), *Administrateur de la France d'outre-mer*, Paris: Jeanne Laffite/A. Barthélemy.
Delavignette, Robert (1946), *Service africain*, Paris: Gallimard.
Deschamps, Hubert (1975), *Roi de la brousse. Mémoires d'autres mondes*, Nancy: Berger-Levrault.
Gauthereau, Raymond (1986), *Journal d'un colonialiste*, Paris: Seuil.

HISTORIES
Betts, Raymond F. (2005), *Assimilation and Association in French Colonial Theory, 1890–1914*, Lincoln, NE: University of Nebraska Press.
Clauzel, Jean (ed.) (2003), *La France d'outre-mer (1930–1960): Témoignages d'administrateurs et de magistrats*, Paris: Karthala.
Cohen, William B. (1971), *Rulers of Empire: The French Colonial Service in Africa*, Stanford: Hoover Institution Press.
Crowder, Michael (1964), 'Indirect Rule: French and British Style', *Africa: Journal of the International African Institute* 34 (3): 197–205.
Kiwanuka, M. Semakula (1970), 'Colonial Policies and Administrations in Africa: The Myths of the Contrasts', *African Historical Studies* 3 (2): 295–315.

Colonial Education

As France formalised its imperial presence around the world in the last decades of the nineteenth century, the role of education in colonisation moved to centre stage. In 1890, Pierre Foncin, Inspector-General for Public Instruction, summed up education as the *sine qua non* of conquest. Referring to the struggle to consolidate French rule in North Africa he warned: 'We will never be masters of Algeria until Algeria speaks French' (Ruscio 2002). Here and throughout the empire the primary objective of the 'civilising mission' was to assimilate local cultures into the universalist culture of Greater France.

Between 1870 and 1918 the French set up a colonial education system consisting mainly of rural primary schools designed to deliver a basic education and some French language skills to indigenous people, and technical schools designed to train artisans for employment in the colonial economy. Secondary schools were opened in major towns where an indigenous élite was prepared for training as auxiliary doctors, teachers or administrators in the colonial civil service. High flyers (parliamentary deputies and future presidents) were sent to French universities to complete their education.

Underpinning the system was an ideology of conquest tempered by the republican ideal of equality of opportunity which held that all children had a right to basic formal education irrespective of race and religion. In practice access would depend on the race and gender of the applicant. With respect to religion, both in Africa and Indo-China education was ostensibly secular and not designed to confront Buddhism or Islam head on, but rather to supersede them with an alternative credo of republican universalist values. Meanwhile the Catholic Church maintained over 1,000 mission schools in Indo-China alone to promote the faith through education. As regards race, fewer than one in twenty black African children were registered in schools in the colonial period compared with around one in ten Asian children. Gender was a factor of intense discrimination. By 1946 girls counted for fewer than one in ten indigenous schoolchildren in the French colonies.

In theory the French school curriculum was universal, although in practice colonial curricula were often adapted to local conditions. In Indo-China teachers were given a curriculum to deliver which acknowledged the value of Asian cultures but positioned French culture as more progressive and modern. French schooling in Algeria was administered as part of France, and so developed differently from the system in other parts of the empire, but here also it accommodated the colonisers' vision of the external environment. Segregated schools were introduced in 1870 keeping European children separate from Arab and Berber pupils, a situation which prevailed until the end of the 1930s. The legacy of French colonial education remains particularly evident, however, in the former French colonies of Sub-Saharan Africa, where access to schooling remains low, the numbers of girls in schools are among the lowest in the world, and reliance on France for funding and higher education persists.

In the literary works listed below, Camara Laye's autobiographical novel recounts his colonial education in French Guinea in Koranic primary and French secondary schools. In *Ambiguous Adventure*, we see the negative cultural ramifications of a colonial education on the central character. Bâ's work reveals the complex relationship between Western education and patriarchal social structures while delivering a more positive verdict on the legacy of French education in Senegal.

Claire Griffiths

LITERARY WORKS

Bâ, Mariama (1979), *Une si longue lettre*, trans. as *So Long a Letter* (1981) Modupé Bodé-Thomas, London and Portsmouth, NH: Heinemann.

Laye, Camara (1953), *L'Enfant noir*, trans. as *The Dark Child* (1959) James Kirkup, London: Collins.

Kane, Cheikh Hamidou (1961), *L'Aventure ambiguë*, trans. as *Ambiguous Adventure* (1972) Katherine Woods, London: Heinemann.

HISTORIES

Barthel, Diane (1985), 'Women's Educational Experience under Colonialism: Toward a Diachronic Model', *Signs* 7 (1): 137–54.

Conklin, Alice L. (1997), *A Mission to Civilize: The Republican Idea of Empire in France and West Africa*, Stanford, CA: Stanford University Press.

Ha, Marie-Paule (2003), 'From "Nos ancêtres, les gaulois" to "Leur culture ancestrale": Symbolic Violence and the Politics of Colonial Schooling in Indochina', *French Colonial History* 3: 101–17.

Kelly, Gail P. (1984), 'The Presentation of Indigenous Society in the Schools of French West Africa and Indochina, 1918–1938', *Comparative Studies in Society and History* 26 (3): 523–42.

Ruscio, Alain (2002), *Le Credo de l'homme blanc*, Brussels: Editions Complexe.

Creolisation and Creoleness

The signifier 'Creole' is a notoriously elastic one, whose origins, evolution and disputed meanings testify to a protracted anxiety around identity in postcolonial – and most markedly in post-slavery – societies. The term originates in the Portuguese *crioulo*, meaning a slave born in his master's house, and derives from the Portuguese *criar*, 'to breed' or 'to bring up', a verb which can in turn be traced to the Latin *creare*, 'to create'. While the Portuguese term refers to the native slave, the meaning shifted as the lexeme passed into Spanish (*criollo*), and came to designate a person of European descent, born and raised in a colonial territory. The term Creole later came to describe all people, European or not, who are native to such areas, although as Chaudenson notes, there are regional exceptions to this usage (1995). In its general application today, creoleness is at once a racial, a cultural and a linguistic descriptor, although the use of the substantive 'Creole' to designate a specific language is by far the most recent of the three usages.

From a linguistic perspective, creolisation occurs when two or more languages converge to form a new, indigenous language. The new form evolves from a pidgin to a creole when it becomes the mother tongue of a second generation. French-based Creoles are spoken in the Caribbean (Guadeloupe, Martinique and, most widely, Haiti, where Creole is the official language), in North America (Louisiana), and in the Indian Ocean (Réunion, Mauritius, the Seychelles). In its more general application, creolisation refers to the process of intense, unpredictable and often violent cultural mixing that occurred on the plantation during slavery, and in its aftermath. While linguists such as Valdman and Chaudenson stress the link to slavery, creolisation in anthropological terms has come to describe any coming together of diverse cultural traits or elements, usually in the context of a colonial situation, to form a distinct culture with new features. For this reason, the islands of

Polynesia, because of their history of colonisation and forced assimilation, are also considered as Creole.

In the context of French colonialism, the plantation can be seen as a primary crucible of creolisation. However, the years which succeeded departmentalisation in 1946, when Martinique, Guadeloupe and Réunion were officially assimilated to the *métropole*, saw the beginnings of a rapid process of decreolisation, accelerated by the dominance of the republican education system and the increasing grip of the French media. Since the 1970s, there has been a concerted effort to counter this process and to rehabilitate Creole language and culture. This period saw the growth of writing in Creole (for example Raphaël Confiant in Martinique; Alex Gauvin in Réunion), although the phenomenon has remained marginal. This linguistic and cultural recreolisation has been contested by some, who see the valorisation of Creole as an anachronistic and nostalgic reaction, and one which risks elevating the period of slavery.

In the contemporary French Caribbean, and to a lesser extent, the Indian Ocean, the terms 'creolisation' and 'creoleness' have an undeniably cultural ring. They stand as two of the privileged terms in a highly theorised, and often polemical, identitarian debate. The democratic, all-encompassing reach of the term 'Creole' has been mobilised most notably in the Martinican *Créolité* movement. In their high-profile manifesto *In Praise of Creoleness*, Bernabé et al. explicitly choose not to define the term 'Creole' (1989), thus strategically side-stepping the issue of its referential scope. Rather, they describe creoleness in vague terms as an 'open specificity' and as a 'kaleidoscopic totality' (1989). Such an emphasis on hybridity and syncretism has been instrumental in the widespread appeal of the movement, which sits more easily within a postcolonial paradigm than the supposedly more essentialist *Négritude*. This inclusivity allows the *créolistes* in turn to declare 'a Creole solidarity with all African, Mascarene, Asian and Polynesian peoples who share the same anthropological affinities as we do – our Creoleness' (1989). And yet, although the authors claim in this manifesto to transcend the restrictive categories of race, critics have shown how far racial categories are reinforced in this articulation of creoleness (Bongie 1998). At the textual level, creolisation takes on a particular meaning for these writers as well. Rather than writing in the Creole which they claim to champion – a pursuit which Confiant has abandoned, and in which Chamoiseau never engaged – the *Créolité* authors write instead in a French heavily marked by Creole lexis and syntax.

Less prescriptive, perhaps, is Edouard Glissant's preference for the term *créolisation*, elaborated in *Le Discours antillais* and in *Poétique de la relation*. With its insistence on an endless dynamic process, Glissant argues that *créolisation* avoids the temptations of essentialist or exclusivist thought more satisfactorily than the static-sounding *Créolité*. While Glissant celebrates the infinite vistas of interrelating, which allow for the definitive deconstruction of 'pure' identities on a global scale, the *créolistes* declare that 'the world is evolving into a state of creoleness' (Bernabé et al. 1989). All would therefore agree that the Caribbean functions as a prototype of a much larger global phenomenon.

Maeve McCusker

LITERARY WORKS

Bernabé, Jean, Patrick Chamoiseau and Raphaël Confiant (1989), *Eloge de la créolité / In Praise of Creoleness*, Paris: Gallimard.
Chamoiseau, Patrick (1994), *Chemin-d'école*, trans. as *School Days* (1997) Linda Coverdale, Lincoln, NE: University of Nebraska Press.
Confiant, Raphaël (1987), *Marisosé*, Schoelcher: Presses Universitaires Créoles.

Gauvin, Axel (1980), *Quartier trois lettres*, Paris: L'Harmattan.

— (1984), *Kartyé trwa lèt*, Saint Denis: Ziskakan-ASPRED.

Glissant, Edouard (1981), *Le Discours antillais*, trans. as *Caribbean Discourse. Selected Essays* (1989) J. Michael Dash, Charlottesville, VA: University Press of Virginia.

— (1990), *Poétique de la relation*, trans. as *Poetics of Relation* (1997) Betsy Wing, Ann Arbor, MI: University of Michigan Press.

HISTORIES

Balutansky, Kathleen M. and Marie-Agnès Sourieau (eds) (1998), *Caribbean Creolization. Reflections on the Cultural Dynamics of Language, Literature and Identity*, Gainesville, FL and Bridgetown: University Press of Florida and University Press of the West Indies.

Bongie, Chris (1998), *Islands and Exiles. The Creole Identities of Post/Colonial Literature*, Stanford, CA: Stanford University Press.

— (2003), '"Of Whatever Colour": (Dis)locating a Place for the Creole in Nineteenth-Century French Literature', in Charles Forsdick and David Murphy (eds), *Francophone Postcolonial Studies. A Critical Introduction*, London: Arnold, pp. 35–45.

Brathwaite, Kamau (1971), *The Development of Creole Society in Jamaica, 1770–1820*, Oxford: Oxford University Press.

Brooks, Jane (1999), 'Challenges to Writing Literature in Creole: The Cases of Martinique and Guadeloupe', in Sam Haigh (ed.), *An Introduction to Caribbean Francophone Writing. Guadeloupe and Martinique*, Oxford: Berg, pp. 119–34.

Chaudenson, Robert (1995), *Les Créoles*, Paris: Presses Universitaires de France.

— (2001), *Creolization of Language and Culture*, London and New York: Routledge.

Lionnet, Françoise (1993), '*Créolité* in the Indian Ocean: Two Models of Cultural Diversity', *Yale French Studies* 82 (1): 101–12.

Valdman, Albert (2000), 'Creole, the Language of Slavery', in Doris Y. Kadish (ed.), *Slavery in the Caribbean Francophone World. Distant Voices, Forgotten Acts, Forged Identities*, Athens, GA and London: University of Georgia Press, pp. 143–63.

Decolonisation

Debates about French decolonisation have focused on the question of how much control France exerted over the process as a whole, and over its pace of change in particular. In 1944–5, a colonial consensus prevailed in France, which held that it was thanks to the empire that France had emerged from World War II as a victorious power. However, this did not mean that the need for reform in the colonies was ignored. In response partly to African support for Free France, a reform programme for Sub-Saharan Africa was announced at the Brazzaville Conference of January 1944. This conference has been seen as evidence of the French commitment to decolonisation, but no African political leader was present, and the conference produced a final declaration which unequivocally ruled out the prospect of 'self-government' (although it did speak of Africans' 'participation' in their own affairs). In 1946 the French Empire became the 'French Union', comprising metropolitan France and the colonies, and territorial assemblies with limited power were set up in the colonies. The French Union was intended to prevent the development of a militant, anti-French nationalism, but the pace of decolonisation soon exceeded the gradualism implicit in this project.

The examples of Algeria and Indo-China, in particular, challenge the model of a peaceful transfer of power. In May 1945, nationalist protests at Sétif in Algeria were put down at the expense of several thousand lives, while in 1946 negotiations between the French government and Vietnamese nationalists gave way to war. France withdrew from Indo-China after suffering the first defeat of a Western army by an anti-colonial liberation movement, at the battle of Dien Bien Phu in May 1954. The case of Algeria also suggests that France was forced into decolonisation by revolts in the colonies. While it can be argued that the French Army was not defeated militarily in the war in Algeria between 1954 and 1962, the political, economic and diplomatic cost of the war led President de Gaulle to conclude that to prevent Algerian independence would only cause division and instability in France.

Further evidence that the pace of decolonisation was determined by factors beyond France's control can be seen in the internationalisation of the process. In April 1955, the first conference of non-aligned nations took place at Bandung in Indonesia. Attended by the newly-independent former colonies, with an Algerian nationalist delegation in attendance by invitation, this conference marked the emergence of a 'Third-World' bloc as a significant new voice in international affairs. The international recognition, notably at the United Nations, that it afforded those still campaigning against French colonial rule undoubtedly contributed to decolonisation; from 1958 the Algerian provisional government successfully exploited this internationalisation of the colonial question, while France came under increasing pressure to concede independence. By 1960 the French Union had come to an end and the overseas territories of French West Africa and French Equatorial Africa had split into fourteen independent states; Algerian independence in 1962 marked the end of France's status as a colonial power.

Stephen Tyre

LITERARY WORKS

Camus, Albert (1957), 'L'Hôte', in *L'Exil et le royaume*, trans. as 'The Guest', in *Exile and the Kingdom* (1958) Justin O'Brien, London: Penguin, pp. 65–82.

Duras, Marguerite (1950), *Un Barrage contre le Pacifique*, trans. as *The Sea Wall* (1959) Antonia White, London: John Spencer.

Etcherelli, Claire (1969), *Élise ou la vraie vie*, trans. as *Elise, or the Real Life* (1970) June P. Wilson and Walter Benn Michaels, London: Deutsch.

Servan-Schreiber, Jean-Jacques (1957), *Lieutenant en Algérie*, trans. as *Lieutenant in Algeria* (1958) Ronald Matthews, London: Hutchinson.

HISTORIES

Betts, Raymond (1991), *France and Decolonisation*, London: Macmillan.

Chafer, Tony (2002), *The End of Empire in French West Africa: France's Successful Decolonization?*, Oxford: Berg.

Clayton, Anthony (1994), *The Wars of French Decolonization*, London: Longman.

Connelly, Matthew (2002), *A Diplomatic Revolution*, Oxford: Oxford University Press.

Kahler, Miles (1984), *Decolonization in Britain and France: The Domestic Consequences of International Relations*, Princeton, NJ: Princeton University Press.

Thomas, Martin (2001), 'France Accused: French North Africa before the United Nations, 1952–1962', *Contemporary European History* 10: 91–121.

White, Dorothy (1979), *Black Africa and de Gaulle: From the French Empire to Independence*, University Park, PA and London: Pennsylvania State University Press.

Exploration and Travel

Travel and exploration constituted a fundamental impulse for the European imperial project. Greater curiosity about the globe encouraged the Renaissance world in particular to harness its technological and scientific knowledge to geographical aims, thereby heralding the globalised age we now live in. By the end of the nineteenth century, and the height of colonial expansion, the relationship between science, exploration and literature had been consolidated and was crucial in shaping the way colonising cultures saw themselves and others. Although French explorers and travellers never quite attained the reputation of their British counterparts, the 'scientific' expeditions of figures such as Louis Antoine de Bougainville (Pacific), René Caillié (West Africa) and the French sponsored Savorgnan de Brazza (Congo) helped to confirm the mutually beneficial relationship between exploration, 'knowledge' acquisition and the expansionist objectives of colonialism. From a literary perspective, these voyages also helped to establish the image of the male, Western explorer/traveller as an intrepid and heroic adventurer pitted against the dangers of primitive, hostile landscapes. With the foundation of the Société de Géographie (1821), increased colonial ambitions following the conquest of Algeria, and the growing importance of different fora (public exhibitions, popular and learned journals) for disseminating accounts by explorers, public curiosity abut 'exotic' landscapes and radical otherness was progressively aroused. In such a climate, cross-fertilisation between explorers and creative writers became inevitable, and the stylistic embellishment of staid, scientifically 'truthful' narratives contributed to the development of travel literature. Imaginary rewritings of travellers' testimonies or the adopting of exoticist tropes in various fictional genres were frequently influenced by the tastes and preoccupations of the French public. And if the accounts of explorers and travellers represented a source of inspiration for imaginary journeys, they arguably also inspired writers to become travellers themselves (Gérard de Nerval, Ernest Psichari, Michel Leiris) or indeed explorers (Arthur Rimbaud, Pierre Loti, Victor Segalen).

A significant problem with travel and travel literature's relationship with colonisation is that it gave rise to dominant definitions of these terms that led to the marginalisation of other types of traveller and travel literature. For example, the tendency to associate travel and exploration with individual male heroic endeavour has meant that important female travellers such as Isabelle Eberhardt and Alexandra David-Néel have been neglected. In addition, other types of movement, notably the counter movement of colonised/formerly colonised subjects journeying outside their own countries to France and beyond, are all too rarely registered as exploration or travel. Yet, to take the example of francophone Africa alone, soldiers, students, politicians, housewives, labourers, illegal immigrants and even tourists have been travelling to the West, and narrating their experiences through different forms, since the early decades of the twentieth century. The perspective provided by these texts reveals the complex nature of cultural exchange and offers a vital insight into the shifting conditions of travel over the decades. Indeed, it is arguable that a fuller picture of travel, exploration and the strategies employed to represent otherness is gained only when such texts are read against and alongside Western narratives of travel.

Aedín Ní Loingsigh

LITERARY WORKS

Dadié, Bernard (1959), *Un Nègre à Paris*, trans. as *An African in Paris* (1994) Karen C. Hatch, Urbana, IL: University of Illinois Press.

Kpomassie, Tété-Michel (1980), *L'Africain du Grœnland*, trans. as An African in Greenland
    (1983) James Kirkup, London: Secker and Warburg.
Leiris, Michel (1934), *L'Afrique fantôme*, Paris: Gallimard.
Nerval, Gérard de [1851] (1980), *Voyage en Orient*, 2 vols, Paris: Garnier-Flammarion.

HISTORIES
Brunschwig, Henri (1969), 'French Exploration and Conquest in Tropical Africa from
    1865 to 1898', in Peter Duignan and L. H. Gann (eds), *Colonialism in Africa*, vol. 1,
    Cambridge: Cambridge University Press, pp. 132–64.
Elliott, Jane (2005), 'The Choosers or the Dispossessed? Aspects of the Work of Some
    French Eighteenth-Century Pacific Explorers', in Annick Foucrier (ed.), *The French
    and the Pacific World, 17th–19th Centuries*, Aldershot: Ashgate, pp. 279–301.
Fonkoua, Romuald (1998), *Les Discours de voyage*, Paris: Karthala.
Mortimer, Mildred (1990), *Journeys through the French African Novel*, Portsmouth, NH and
    London: Heinemann and James Currey.

France in Asia and the Indian Ocean

The French colonial encounter with Asia took place over a period of 300 years and across
a vast geographical area. Various French empires have encompassed, at different times, the
island of Madagascar (in the far West of the Indian Ocean), the Mascarenes Islands, five
trading posts on the subcontinent of India, and the territory known as l'Indochine
Française in South-East Asia. The historical narrative of the French colonial presence in
Asia and the Indian Ocean does not easily conform to that historiographical practice
which neatly divides the French imperial project into two discrete periods or movements:
the old colonies of the *Ancien Régime* and the new colonies of the nineteenth century.
Whilst this periodisation, favoured by anglophone and francophone historians alike
(Aldrich 1996 and Girardet 1978), certainly highlights the distinct imperial focal points
(India under the *Ancien Régime*, and South-East Asia in the nineteenth century), it
neglects both political and geographical continuities in the French involvement with Asia.
Changing political attitudes in the *métropole* inevitably result in differently plotted histories of French intervention in India, the Indian Ocean and South-East Asia. Nevertheless,
all colonial projects show evidence of three defining factors: trade; an awareness of competing colonialisms (notably that of the British); and the function of Asia as an *ailleurs rêvé*
for the metropolitan French imagination.

INDIA
By the time of the *de jure* secession of the five French *comptoirs* (or trading posts) in 1962,
the French presence in India had persisted for almost 300 years – longer than in certain
areas of metropolitan France, notably Nice and Savoy. This notwithstanding, the public
amnesia evident in modern metropolitan France towards its former small possessions in
India is a source of much regret to the limited number of French historians working on the
Établissements Français de l'Inde (Decraene 1994). For anglophone postcolonial critics and
French historians alike, India is generally perceived as an exclusively British affair, the
'jewel in the crown', an assumption which is reflected by literary production. Catherine
Clément, for example, a writer more readily associated with *écriture féminine*, has produced
a postcolonial narrative of the end of British colonial rule and the partition of the

subcontinent in 1947 which seeks to foreground the previously silent colonial 'Other' whilst inscribing the history of India, and the biography of Gandhi, within an overtly feminist and maternal rhetoric (1993). To date, no text written in French has sought to eschew the binaries of orthodox colonial discourse and narrate the history of the French colonial encounter from a postcolonial perspective; rather, nostalgia for a lost empire predominates (Vincent 1983). The history of the *comptoirs* remains marginal to metropolitan narratives of colonial history, as indeed the *comptoirs* themselves were to the colonial project of the nineteenth and early twentieth centuries.

The French colonial encounter with India began through trade. La Compagnie des Indes was founded in 1664, although significant gains in Indian territory were not achieved until 1673 with the establishment of a trading post at Pondicherry. This was followed by the creation of *comptoirs* at Chandernagor (1688), Mahé (1721), Yanaon (1731) and Karikal (1739). The apogee of the French presence in India, however, is closely linked to the biography of one man, Joseph-François Dupleix. During his governorship of Pondicherry (1742–54), and benefiting from the spread of hostilities between the British and French from Europe to the Indian subcontinent, French control increased to cover a vast territory in the South, including a large part of the Deccan peninsula, the Carnatic region and the province of Masulipatam. The machinations of the government in Paris, and the internal politicking of the Compagnie des Indes, which precipitated Dupleix's eventual recall to metropolitan France in 1754, curtailed the further advancement of French influence and control. In the course of the Seven Year War the principal French *établissements*, which were poorly defended after the collapse of Dupleix's political strategy, were quickly taken over by the English. The Treaty of Paris of 1763 restored the original five *comptoirs* to French control, but stipulated that it be limited to these areas alone. Occupied again by the British in 1778 and 1793, the *comptoirs*, with a total surface area of 500 square kilometres but geographically discrete, were definitively returned to the French in 1814.

During the nineteenth century the French presence on the subcontinent remained insignificant and isolated. Aside from serving as a 'laboratory experiment' for assimilation policies post-1880 (Weber 1996), the primary significance of the *comptoirs* was a cultural one within the litany of French colonial possessions recited by French schoolchildren under the Third Republic. The decolonisation of India by the British in 1947, however, fundamentally challenged the status of the French. France clung on to the *comptoirs* for seven more years, but the combined effects of Chandernagor's decision by referendum to secede (1949), a blockade of the French territories by the Indian government, and anti-French demonstrations by the Indian Congress in Pondicherry, encouraged the French government to reopen negotiations with their Indian counterparts. These negotiations led to France's de facto withdrawal from her Indian possessions on 1 November 1954, although the Treaty of Cession remained without ratification by the Assemblée Nationale until 12 July 1962 after the end of the Algerian conflict.

INDIAN OCEAN

The history of the French presence in the Indian Ocean, like that on the subcontinent itself, is often treated as a footnote to French colonial history. Trade (chiefly the creation of spice and sugar plantations) was a potent motivating factor behind the establishment in 1642 of an earlier Compagnie des Indes on the uninhabited Île Bourbon (later the Île Bonaparte and finally renamed Réunion), the creation of a settlement on the Île de France (Mauritius) in 1715, and the annexation of the Seychelles archipelago in 1756. By the middle of the eighteenth century the Île de France had become the base of the later

Compagnie des Indes, although all the islands retained a strategic importance in light of their position on global shipping lanes. After the collapse of the company in 1767, the Île de France became a crown colony, before being seized, along with the Île Bourbon, by the British in 1810. In the Treaty of Paris settlement (1814–15) the Île Bourbon (Réunion) was restored to France, to which it still belongs, whilst Britain retained the Île de France.

The sugar plantations established in the eighteenth century relied on slave labour, with the majority of workers coming from East Africa. The abolition of slavery in the wake of the 1848 French Revolution led to 63,000 slaves being freed on Réunion and replaced by low-paid Indian and Chinese workers. This mélange of national identities, languages and dialects in the Mascarenes (French, British, African, Indian and Chinese) is reflected in its literature from both the colonial and postcolonial eras. The Mauritian Clément Charoux's 1935 novel, *Ameenah*, for example, explores *métissage*, whilst Axel Gauvin's 1980 novel, *Quartier trois-lettres*, uses Creole language.

If the longevity of the *comptoirs* and Réunion contradicts the neat division of French colonial history into *les vieilles colonies* and *les nouvelles colonies*, the history of French presence in Madagascar lends itself more readily to such a periodisation. While French trading ships had visited the island since the sixteenth century, attempts by the Compagnie des Indes Orientales to establish a settlement there failed in 1665, and throughout the eighteenth and early nineteenth centuries sporadic trading contact did not develop into colonisation. French claims to Madagascar were not seriously renewed until the 1880s, when the French fought with the island's dominant Merina people. An attempt to impose a protectorate resulted in intermittent warfare until 1896 when Madagascar was formally annexed as a French colony. After the successful repression of the 1904 rebellion, the colonial authorities considered Madagascar 'pacified'.

This situation continued until March 1947 when separatist riots occurred, sparked by the falling prestige of the French during the British occupation of the island during World War II and the example of the Indian independence movement. Violent suppression by the French authorities of the March revolution only confirmed Malagasy determination for independence, which was eventually achieved in June 1960.

INDO-CHINA

The creation of Indochine, the *perle* of the colonial project under the Third Republic, was not initially the result of a coherent policy. Until the middle of the nineteenth century, Jesuitical missionary interests were the prime factor behind French intervention in the countries which were to become Indochine. The British acquisition of Hong Kong in 1842, however, reawakened the French desire for a trading base in South-East Asia. The history of French intervention in Indo-China assumes many narrative forms (conquest, pacification or the protection of missionaries), but between 1860 and 1890 the pursuit of territory was inseparable from colonial rivalry, particularly after France's defeat by Prussia in 1870. The political boundaries of Indo-China were formally established in 1887, when the French government created the Union Indochinoise. Of the constituent areas, Cochinchine was ruled by a governor-general from Saigon, whilst Annam, Tonkin and Laos (after 1893) were protectorates. The Vietnamese monarchy was allowed to survive.

The policies of *mise en valeur* which were imposed on Indochine aimed to create a unified, homogenised state that was both politically and culturally French. Although the imposition of 'Frenchness' was moderated by the eventual adoption of a policy of association as opposed to assimilation (Cooper 2001), *mise en valeur* included urban planning and educational reforms. In the *métropole*, as demonstrated by the spectacular recreation of

Angkor Wat at the 1931 Parisian Exposition Coloniale, Indochine was France's showpiece colony. Protests by Indo-Chinese students in Paris against the French suppression of the Yen Bay uprising (February 1930), and the French-educated Ho Chi Minh's consolidation of the Vietnamese Communist Party (1931), with its aim of a completely independent Vietnam, however, fundamentally contradicted the official image of benevolent and popular French rule.

It was the events of World War II which precipitated the end of colonial rule. In June 1940 the Governor-General of Indo-China, Catroux, was forced to cede to Japanese demands for military footholds. France later recognised Japanese interests in the area in return for acknowledgement of French sovereignty in Indo-China. Nevertheless, the Japanese continued to infiltrate Indo-China, a process culminating in an attempt to seize sovereignty in March 1945. De Gaulle's response was the creation of the Fédération Indochinoise; meanwhile, Ho Chi Minh and his guerrillas came to power in Tonkin and proclaimed the birth of the Democratic Republic of Vietnam (September 1945). In this confused situation, the Fourth Republic launched its first colonial war, which it eventually lost after the miscalculations and defeat of Dien Bien Phu (May 1954). With the Geneva Accords of July 1954, Vietnam was divided along the seventeenth parallel and the last French troops withdrew from Indo-China in 1955.

Unpopular amongst French intellectuals (Sorum 1977), *la sale guerre d'Indochine* was largely overlooked by the rest of the population (Cooper 2001). Since 1990, however, there has been revived metropolitan cinematic and literary interest in Indochine. Despite earlier counter-narratives (notably Marguerite Duras' *Un barrage contre le Pacifique* (1950), which relates the failure of the colonial dream and *mise en valeur*), this revival, arguably, has perpetuated a nostalgic colonial vision of Indochine as an *ailleurs rêvé* (Norindr 1996). It is only very recent novels, such as that by the Vietnamese-born Linda Lê (*Kriss* 2004), which challenge dominant narratives and prevailing strategies of historical representation, auguring a different form of literary engagement with the French colonial encounter.

Kate Marsh

LITERARY WORKS

Charoux, Clément (1935), *Ameenah: roman mauricien*, Port-Louis: The General Printing and Stationary Company.

Clément, Catherine (1993), *Pour l'amour de l'Inde*, trans. as *Edwina and Nehru: A Novel* (1996) Annie Mathews and Nandita Aggarwal, New Delhi: Penguin.

Duras, Marguerite [1950] (1959), *Un barrage contre le Pacifique*, trans. as *The Sea Wall* Antonia White, London: John Spencer.

Gauvin, Alex (1980), *Quartier trois-lettres, roman réunionnais*, Paris: Éditions L'Harmattan.

Lê, Linda (2004), *Kriss*, Paris: Christian Bourgois.

Rakotoson, Michèle [1983] (1988), *Le Bain des reliques: roman malgache*, Paris: Karthala.

Vincent, Rose (1983), *Le Temps d'un royaume: Jeanne Dupleix, 1706–1756*, Paris: Éditions du Seuil.

HISTORIES

Aldrich, Robert (1996), *Greater France: A History of French Overseas Expansion*, London: Macmillan.

Brocheux, Pierre and Daniel Hémery (2001), *Indochine, la colonisation ambiguë 1858–1954*, Paris: La Découverte.

Chane-Kune, Sonia (1993), *Aux Origines de l'identité réunionnaise*, Paris: L'Harmattan.

Cooper, Nicola (2001), *France in Indochina: Colonial Encounters*, Oxford: Berg.
Decraene, Philippe (ed.) (1994), *Trois siècles de présence française en Inde*, Paris: CHEAM.
Girardet, Raoul [1972] (1978), *L'Idée coloniale en France de 1871 à 1962*, Paris: Pluriel.
Norindr, Panivong (1996), *Phantasmatic Indochina: French Colonial Ideology in Architecture, Film and Literature*, Durham, NC: Duke University Press.
Rabermananjara, Raymond W. (2000), *Madagascar: l'affaire de Mars 1947*, Paris: L'Harmattan.
Sorum, Paul Clay (1977), *Intellectuals and Decolonization in France*, Chapel Hill, NC: University of North Carolina Press.
Weber, Jacques (1996), *Pondichéry et les comptoirs de l'Inde après Dupleix: la démocratie au pays des castes*, Paris: Denoël.

France in North America

The binary oppositions between 'France' and 'America' engendered by recent events such as the Iraq War, or by current French cultural nationalism, belie nearly five centuries of entwined histories. Far from constituting picturesque remnants of a French empire lost in 1759–63, various francophone spaces in contemporary North America constitute living, dynamic realities which continue to evolve. Any account of the French in North America must therefore engage with histories of exploration and settlement, interactions with English/British, Spanish and also African and Native American cultures, the emergence of a French-speaking nation in Quebec, at least two French diasporas within the continent itself, and a constant flow of migrants buffeted and shaped by historical upheaval.

The French were, in fact, the first European nation to open up the vast interior of the North American continent to European exploration and settlement, largely due to their command of the entrance to the two great river systems. The three voyages of the St Malo mariner Jacques Cartier in the years 1534 to 1542, during which he sailed up the St Lawrence to native settlements at present-day Quebec City and Montreal, and recognised the region as 'Canada' (probably from the Huron-Iroquois word for 'village'), mark the beginning of this process. Permanent French settlement on the mainland began only when the emergence of a lucrative fur trade with the natives meant there was a reason to return, Cartier having failed to find either a passage to Asia or any gold. Posts were established at Tadoussac on the St Lawrence in 1599, and then a more substantial enterprise, marking the foundation of Acadia, began in present-day Maine in 1604, moving to Port-Royal in present-day Nova Scotia the following year. The foundation of Quebec dates to 1608, when Samuel de Champlain established the colony 'where the river narrows' (*kebec* in Algonquin). Over the next 150 years the French carved out a vast but under-populated empire – New France – from this core on the St Lawrence.

The fur trade continued to be the mainstay of the colony's economy, constituting 50 per cent of all exports and spawning profound cultural transformations. The French made military alliances with the Huron and Montagnais native groups in the fur-rich areas north of the St Lawrence against their traditional enemies, the Iroquois, to the South, who became allies of the British. Montreal, founded in 1642 as a religious centre (the Jesuits arrived in New France in 1629), was also closer to western trade routes and became the fur capital. Society in New France, organised after 1663 like any region of France, was based on the hierarchical and feudal seigneurial system, with a population of *habitants* living off agriculture (bolstered by the transportation of *filles du roy* in the 1660s and 1670s to correct the gender imbalance), and of urban administrative and military élites, along with artisans. This *Ancien Régime* arrangement both favoured a co-operative and corporatist relation to allied native groups, and saw its authority wither when the demands of the fur trade propelled young men into the interior and into native societies, as *voyageurs* transporting goods back and forth, and as illicit *coureurs de bois*, who often 'went native' and co-mingled in every sense with native people, giving rise to a distinct ethnic group, the Métis, who played an important role in the history of francophone Manitoba, birthplace of the prominent francophone writer Gabrielle Roy (1909–83).

The fall of New France in 1759–63 at the climax of the Seven Years' War was the inevitable outcome of both numbers (a maximum of 70,000 Canadiens to over 1.5 million British settlers on the east coast) and a willingness by the French government to abandon it in favour of the far more lucrative Caribbean territories. However, this was not the end of a (transformed) 'French' presence. With the departure of the French élites (apart from the clergy), the *Canadiens* maintained a distinct and then flourishing culture, bolstered by the Quebec Act of 1774 (promulgated by a British government anxious to short-circuit any alliance with rebellious American colonists to the South), and by the *revanche des berceaux* during which an astronomical birth rate over the next century, with numbers doubling every twenty-five years, led to a Quebec population of 1.2 million by 1871. This numbers game of majorities and minorities determined the politics of Canada from the start, with the influx of empire loyalists from the new United States in the 1780s, and with European immigration in the nineteenth century, provoking various institutional responses from 1791, and democratic rebellions in 1837–8. Canadian Confederation in 1867 at least gave French-Canadians a territorial majority in the province of Quebec, where, after 1837, clerical-nationalist élites, increasingly out of kilter with social and industrial realities, dominated political life until 1960. The 'Quiet Revolution' of that decade impelled a process of modernisation and secularisation which culminated in the strongly federalist 'French power' of Pierre Elliott Trudeau (Prime Minister of Canada 1968–79 and 1980–4), with his vision of a bilingual Canada, and the 1976–85 and 1994–2003 governments of the nationalist Parti Québécois which organised and lost two referendums on sovereignty in 1980 and 1995. Eighty-two per cent of the just over 7 million population of Quebec in 2006 are French-speaking, with laws regulating the language of commercial signage and of immigrants' school education. The metropole of Montreal, 68 per cent French-speaking, has in particular undergone a renaissance since the early 1990s, and is leading the province into a competitive position in the world economy, largely based on its bilingualism and function as bridge between North America and Europe. Quebec's rich cultural production explores the distinctiveness of its history but also its interaction with the world. Names that can be picked out are those of Anne Hébert (1916–2000), whose novels such as *Kamouraska* (1970) and *Le Premier Jardin* (1988) trouble Quebec's national narratives via gender; Michel Tremblay (b. 1942), whose plays and novels articulate the concerns and language of the Montreal working class and a sexual *demi-monde*; and the filmmakers Denys Arcand (b. 1941), winner of the best foreign-language film Oscar for *Les Invasions barbares* in 2004, and Robert Lepage (b. 1957), whose international renown in theatre is accompanied by, and has generated, a corpus of five feature films in which his home town of Quebec City usually plays a central role. In addition, cultural debates in Quebec since 1980 have been preoccupied with questions of hybridity and *transculture* – producing important reflections by writers such as Régine Robin (b. 1939) – as Quebec nationalism, and its opponents, come to grips with the reality of a multi-ethnic society. There is also some literary production by native authors, notably the playwright Yves Sioui Durand (b. 1951), and novelist Bernard Assiniwi (1935–2000). There are also 1 million French-speakers in Canada living outside Quebec; along with the Franco-Québécois they constitute around 24 per cent of the Canadian population, and constitute the national Association des Communautés Francophones et Acadiennes.

The fate of the Acadians represents the first important diasporic movement of French peoples within the continent. A distinct culture and society had emerged after 1632, characterised by the desalination of marshes for agriculture, and flourished despite its vaguely defined borders and conflict with the English/British which led to definitive British rule with the 1713 Treaty of Utrecht. In 1755, when their leaders refused to swear an unconditional oath of allegiance to the crown in the context of the Seven Years' War, most of the population (around 12,000–13,000) were deported, dispossessed and scattered round the Atlantic world (this is the subject, of course, of the American poet Longfellow's *Evangeline* of 1847), an event known as *le grand dérangement*. Some, however, eventually returned to what are now the Maritime Provinces, but to more remote areas – the coast and the north of New Brunswick – rather than their original settlements in Nova Scotia. A cultural and political renaissance eventually took place due to the creation of a francophone higher education institution there in the late nineteenth century, and further advances have been made since 1960 that have ensured the future of this North American francophone society distinct from that of Quebec. The most famous Acadian writer is Antonine Maillet (b. 1929), whose *Pélagie-la-charrette* won the Prix Goncourt in 1979.

Famously, one of the destinations of the dispersed Acadians was Louisiana, where they settled in pastureland or swamps. They inserted themselves into a culture already marked by half a century of French colonial rule. René-Robert Cavelier de La Salle (1643–87), a French adventurer who had settled near Montreal, had been the first European to reach the mouth of the Mississippi, claiming and naming 'Louisiana' – a swathe of territory stretching from the Great Lakes to the Gulf of Mexico and west to the Rockies – for France in 1682. The founders of the colony of Louisiana (1699) and then New Orleans (1718) were in fact Canadians: the first Governor-General, the French naval officer Pierre le Moyne, sieur d'Iberville (1661–1706) and his brother, Jean-Baptiste Le Moyne, sieur de Bienville (1680–1767). They used their Canadian experience to strike up alliances with native groups such as the Choctaws, on which the early colony depended for survival. The arrival of the first slaves after 1719 to work tobacco plantations also contributed to the emergence of a distinct frontier culture in which race relations were relatively fluid, partly due to the shortage of white French women despite the importation of dowry-bearing *filles à la cassette*. The French relied on Africans' skill in cultivating rice and the processing of dyes, and recruited most of their slaves from one ethnic group, the Bambara of Senegambia, which in turn created and helped perpetuate a cohesive African culture among the slaves of Louisiana. The Frenchness of the territory was paradoxically strengthened under Spanish rule (1763–1800), when better governance led to an expanded economy and encouragement of new settlers, most of whom were French-speaking, hence the influx of up to 3,000 Acadians which reached its peak in 1785. The present period of American sovereignty following the Louisiana Purchase of 1803 was initially marked by a strengthened French-speaking culture, as more than 10,000 refugees from Saint-Domingue and the Haitian revolution arrived, including slaves and free people of colour. New Orleans in the first half of the nineteenth century was therefore more typical of a three-tiered Caribbean society than that of North America. In addition, many 'foreign French' also emigrated to Louisiana from France itself, often fleeing the political upheavals of the era. One of these, Charles Testut (1818–92), wrote a key anti-slavery novel, *Le Vieux Salomon* (1858, published 1872), just one example of the thriving francophone literature of the period. Indeed, the first literary works published by African Americans were in French: Victor Séjour (1817–74) was the son of a refugee from Saint-Domingue, publishing an anti-slavery short story, *Le Mulâtre*, in Paris in 1837, spending the rest of his life there as a successful playwright. *Les Cenelles*, published in New Orleans in 1845, is the first anthology of poetry by African-Americans. This literature died out in the first decade of the twentieth century. Racial polarisations – such as segregationist 'Jim Crow' legislation – in the aftermath of the American Civil War meant that white Creoles (the descendants of French and Spanish settlers who had sought to perpetuate *Ancien Régime* aristocratic lifestyles) threw their lot in with the now majority white Americans, thus denying their multi-racial heritage.

The use of the French language was also affected by the banning of its use in state schools after 1922. During the early years of their presence, Acadians/Cajuns had been looked down upon by the Creoles. In the twentieth century, they became the main repository of the French language in Louisiana, but in a context of economic marginalisation and a loss of social and cultural cohesiveness. A small land-owning gentry, generally assimilated to English, was vastly outnumbered by a largely dirt poor army of landless sharecroppers. Poor Creoles in the countryside in turn assimilated to Cajun culture, key elements of which were music (zydeco, for example, was born out of the adjacency of white Cajun and black tenants), cuisine and oral traditions. Not until 1968 did the state of Louisiana begin to promote the French language, with the creation of CODIFIL (Council for the Development of French in Louisiana), and although this measure favours standard French, since 1970 there has been a Cajun renaissance in terms of cultural activity, particularly poetry and theatre. Cajun French speakers, largely concentrated in the South-West, number about 260,000, forming 6 per cent of the population of Louisiana.

The second major French diaspora within North America was that of those Québécois – approximately 900,000 in number – who emigrated to the United States in the late nineteenth and early twentieth centuries, principally to work in the textile mills of New England. The Depression and World War II stopped further substantial immigration from Quebec, and post-war upward mobility and suburbanisation put an end to the concentrated populations of the 'little Canadas', and widespread assimilation to English ensued. Only since the 1970s has a kind of ethnic revival taken place, with Franco-Americans claiming a place in the politics of ethnicity and memory in the United States, and producing the first francophone literary works since the 1930s (Robert B. Perreault, *L'Héritage*, 1983; Normand Beaupré, *Le Petit Mangeur de fleurs*, 1999).

To these internal movements within North America must, of course, be added those movements of French transatlantic migration in addition to the colonists of New France and Louisiana. First among these were the Huguenots after the Revocation of the Edict of Nantes in 1685, many of whom, unable to settle in French Catholic lands, ended up in Protestant North America. The California gold rush of 1849–50 spurred the arrival of 25,000–30,000 French, and for a time San Francisco had a thriving French quarter. Many of these immigrants were from the impoverished and marginalised South-West of France. Indeed, many French Basques, after supplying the mining communities, went into livestock raising in California, western Nevada, and elsewhere in the American far West. As befits the most populous state, California has the highest numbers of residents of French descent or born in France. In all, over 13 million Americans are of French descent, and in the 2000 census 1.6 million people claimed to speak French at home, the third largest language group after those who spoke Spanish or Chinese. In places like Florida, where

444,000 people are of French or French-speaking descent, new zones of intercultural contact are being formed, especially in the southern part of the state, between French nationals, French-Canadians fleeing winter (132,000), the new influx of Haitians (234,000), and Anglo-Saxon and Hispanic Americans. Finally, it should not be forgotten that there is a part of North America over which France has sovereignty, the *collectivité territoriale* of St Pierre et Miquelon in the Gulf of St Lawrence, whose 6,500 inhabitants of mostly Breton, Norman and Basque descent encapsulate in microcosmic form the specificities and transformations of the French in North America. The French in North America may be less numerous than the British and Spanish, but their diversity testifies to a diasporic, centrifugal version of Frenchness, understanding of which provides an essential corrective to centripetal national myth-making on both sides of the Atlantic.

Bill Marshall

Literary Works

Arceneaux, Jean (1980), *Cris sur le bayou: naissance d'une poésie acadienne en Louisiane*, trans. as *Je suis cadien* (1994) Sheryl St Germain, Merrick, NY: Cross-Cultural Communications.

Assiniwi, Bernard (1996), *La Saga des Béothuks*, trans. as *The Beothuk Saga: A Novel* (2001) Wayne Grady, Toronto: McLelland and Stewart.

Hébert, Anne (1988), *Le Premier Jardin*, trans. as *The First Garden* (1990) Sheila Fischman, Toronto: House of Anansi Press.

Ledoux, Denis (ed.) (1990), *Lives in Translation: An Anthology of Contemporary Franco-American Writers*, Lisbon Falls, ME: Soleil Press.

Maillet, Antonine (1979), *Pélagie-la-charrette*, trans. as *Pélagie-la-charrette* (1982) Philip Stratford, London: Calder.

Robin, Régine (1983), *La Québécoite*, trans. as *The Wanderer* (1997) Phyllis Aronoff, Montreal: Alter Ego Editions.

Roy, Gabrielle (1945), *Bonheur d'occasion*, trans. as *The Tin Flute* (1948) Hannah Josephson, London: Heinemann.

Séjour, Victor (1844), *Diegarias*, trans. as *The Jew of Seville* (2002) Norman R. Shapiro, Urbana and Chicago, IL: University of Illinois Press.

Shapiro, Norman (ed.) (2004), *Creole Echoes: The Francophone Poetry of Nineteenth-Century Louisiana*, trans. Norman R. Shapiro, intro. and notes M. Lynn Weiss, Urbana and Chicago, IL: University of Illinois Press.

Tremblay, Michel (1968), *Les Belles-Soeurs*, trans. as *The Guid Sisters: Three Plays* (2001) Bill Findlay, Martin Bowman, John van Burek and Bill Glassco, London: Nick Hern Books.

Histories

Desroches, Vincent (2003), 'Quebec and Postcolonialism', *Québec Studies* 35 (spring/summer) special edition.

Brasseaux, Carl A. (1987), *The Founding of New Acadia: The Beginnings of Acadian life in Louisiana, 1765–1803*, Baton Rouge, LA: Louisiana State University Press.

— (1992), *Acadian to Cajun: Transformation of a People, 1803–1877*, Jackson, MS: University Press of Mississippi.

Brault, Gérard J. (1986), *The French Canadian Heritage in New England*, Hanover, NE: University Press of New England.

Eccles, W. J. (1998), *The French in North America 1500–1783*, East Lansing, MI: Michigan State University Press.

Griffiths, N. E. S. (2004), *From Migrant to Acadian: A North American Border People, 1604–1755*, Montreal: McGill-Queen's University Press.

Hall, Gwendolyn Midlo (1992), *Africans in Colonial Louisiana: The Development of Afro-Creole Culture in the Eighteenth Century*, Baton Rouge, LA: Louisiana State University Press.

Hirsch, Arnold R. and Joseph Logsdon (eds) (1992), *Creole New Orleans: Race and Americanization*, Baton Rouge, LA: Louisiana State University Press.

Linteau, Paul-André, Jean-Claude Robert and René Durocher (1983), *Quebec: A History 1867–1929*, trans. Robert Chodos, Toronto: Lorimer.

— (1991), *Quebec since 1930*, trans. Robert Chodos and Ellen Garmaise, Toronto: Lorimer.

Trudel, Marcel (1973), *The Beginnings of New France*, trans. Patricia Claxton, Toronto: McLelland and Stewart.

France in the South Pacific

Historians of the French presence in the South Pacific identify four principal motivations behind France's colonial designs upon the diverse island territories and peoples over which it achieved dominion: nationalist prestige through imperial compass; geo-strategic purchase in the world's largest ocean and last theatre of colonial competition; economic aspirations in a promising arena of trade; cultural expansionism to create *la France australe* in an empire lacking colonies of settlement. This 'France' is the nation-state-economy. Understood as 'the eldest daughter of the Church', France also entered the Pacific as the Marist missionary society, crucially exercising a fifth 'French' motivation, the Catholic evangelisation of Pacific souls, pursued in tandem with territorial acquisitions for the nation. These motivations persist across 150-odd years of France's Pacific presence: small islands first collected to compensate for the loss of the American colonies continue to bolster France's global stature; the imperative to control seaways and harbours at the peak of maritime trade and imperial rivalry foreshadows the imperative to maintain the nuclear capability tested at Moruroa and Fangataufa atolls (1966–96); the dream of a vast 'new Mediterranean', despite all the commercial and trade disappointments to date, is revived as recently as 1986 (see Gomane et al.), while Pacific possessions give France the world's third largest 'exclusive economic zone'; New Caledonia, France's best hope for a settler colony, never became the French New Zealand but is now poised to attract thousands of intra-republic migrants to an expanding nickel economy; missionaries supported by French arms and administration had great conversion success, and churches remain committed, providing significant educational frameworks alongside under-funded state systems. Perpetual ambivalence about the viability of its heavily subsidised Pacific possessions notwithstanding, France's motivations for establishing them have enduring force.

Granted these continuities of motivation, the territorially, culturally and politically disparate nature of those scores of islands, unevenly colonised by monarchy and republic, means that there is no one 'French Pacific' nor any coherent 'France' engaging uniformly with all 'French' possessions. A history of particularism in the Pacific sees France adapt to contingencies to realise various localised ambitions for territorial influence or control. Witness, for example: the accommodations of the 1842 protectorate, empowering the three pre-eminent chiefs of Uvea (Wallis) and Futuna, and acknowledging the Catholic Church (hence the so-called Wallisian theocracy), arrangements reaffirmed after conversion to 'territory' status (1961–2); the concessions to Tahiti's Pomare state after imposition of the protectorate (1842) and official recognition of Protestantism there (1860), the 'omnipotence' of the governor in the period of the Établissements Français d'Océanie (EFO, until 1957), and the unusual 'internal autonomy' granted to French Polynesia (1984); the wholesale annexation of the cultivable, non-Christianised Grande Terre of New Caledonia (1853) for penal then free settlement, prompting the 'containment' – unique in the empire – of the resistant indigenous peoples upon reserves (1872–1946), and, now, the Noumea Accord (1998), granting a singular status within the Fifth Republic, that of substantial and irreversible autonomy; or again, the minimal-state plantation colony of the New Hebrides (from 1865), and the 'Pandamonium' of the Condominium with Britain (1905 to Vanuatu's independence in 1980).

Differing original causes for interest in the different territories (trade station, harbour, geo-strategic pawn, sop to the Catholic lobby, mixed-economy settler colony) explain this multiply French and multiply Pacific 'French Pacific'. It also results from variation amongst indigenous régimes and cultures: Wallis and Futuna, 250 kilometres apart, affiliated with Tonga and Samoa, respectively, but largely Catholic by 1841, were amenable to the protectorate; the EFO grouped five major archipelagos, presenting numerous different indigenous régimes when the French approached, with Tahitian royalty deeply implicated in British Protestantism, but betrayed by rivals; the six main islands of New Caledonia presented myriad micro-states, speaking thirty-six languages, without over-arching politico-military alliances to match French incursions; the New Hebrides encompassed seventy inhabited islands and some hundred languages, whose customary chiefdoms, overall, never ceded control because Anglo co-occupation deterred full French colonisation. In the absence of a concerted French drive into arguably the most politico-culturally atomised region on earth, the diversity of colonial outcomes is unsurprising. The New Hebrides knew little colonial conflict or dispossession and obtained independence relatively easily – although not without fractures – thanks to the British factor. In the two territories sustaining most economic and colonial investment, Tahiti – where resistance to the protectorate involved years of conflict (1844–7) – and New Caledonia – which saw recurrent counter-colonial/colonial violence up to the Great Rebellion of 1878–9, and massive dispossession of Kanak lands – post-war independence movements command the state's attention, especially that of 'Kanaky'. Contrastingly, Wallis-Futuna is militantly pro-dependency, having experienced no devastation. The Marquesas, whose population was almost annihilated by contact, are culturally estranged from Tahitian Polynesia and are also pro-dependency.

Two generalisations suggest themselves: that France has been non-committal vis-à-vis its Pacific possessions, yet (sometimes brutally) reluctant to relinquish them; and that no 'French Pacific' identity has emerged, despite dialogue between indigenous-nationalist movements in Tahiti-Te Ao Mā'ohi, New Caledonia-Kanaky and Vanuatu. Colonial non-committalism has failed equitably to deliver the nation's benefits to Pacific citizens, but also failed to deliver Pacific peoples entirely to France: cultural survival animates the colonies that France always overlooked.

In literary culture, educational neglect and isolation from France impede developments, but, once postcolonial literatures emerge (1970s-1980s), they represent indigenous cultures and languages, insistently and variously: in declamations of *'tahitianité'* in Tahitian-language poetry (Hiro); in Tahitian and Paicî inflections of *lingua-franca* poetry (Devatine,

Gorodé); in relentless concern for '*oralité*' and memory; and in complaints against the erosion of ancestral culture by urbanisation and cash-materialism (Hiro, Spitz, Gorodé, Gope). New Caledonia and Tahiti are the literary power-houses. Counter-colonial militancy invests all forms. Jean-Marie Tjibaou's 1975 performance piece, 'Kanaké' – predating Tjibaou's independence leadership – establishes the New Caledonian nexus between postcolonial critique and literary creation, rejoined when Gorodé memorialises the independence struggle of the 1980s within a polyvocal novel of urban marginalisation, and when Gope's *mise-en-scène* embodies the post-Accord corruption, by indigenous mandarins, of both tradition and Tjibaou's political invention. Meanwhile, Kurtovitch's poetry minimalises non-indigenous presence in listening, openness and witnessing. In the first Tahitian novel, Spitz rejects the exoticism generated by Bougainville's 'New Cythera' in order to assert the contemporary potency of Mā'ohi speech, resisting militarist violation of ancestral lands and passéism alike. Tahitian identity now also assumes written and francophone form, whether it persists as soul (Hiro) or is a 'culture in the making' (Devatine).

Amanda Macdonald

LITERARY WORKS

French Polynesia
Devatine, Flora (1998), *Tergiversations et rêveries de l'écriture orale: Te Pahu a Hono'ura*, Papeete: Au Vent des Îles.
Hiro, Henri (1982), 'Henri Hiro' (selection of poems), *Mana* (Fiji) 7: (1) (special issue on Tahitian poetry): 34–74.
Spitz, Chantal [1991] (2003), *L'Île des rêves écrasés*, Châteauneuf-le-Rouge: Vents d'Ailleurs.

New Caledonia
Gope, Pierre (2004), *La Parenthèse*, Nouméa: Eds Traversées.
Gorodé, Déwé (2005), *L'Épave*, Nouméa: Madrépores.
Kurtovitch, Nicolas (2003), *Le Piéton du dharma*, Nouméa: Grain de Sable.

HISTORIES
Aldrich, Robert (1993), *France and the South Pacific since 1940*, Houndsmill and London: Macmillan.
Deckker, Paul de and Pierrre-Yves Toullelan (eds) (1990), *La France et le Pacifique*, Paris: Société Française d'Histoire d'Outre-Mer.
Fève, Guy (ed.) (1997), *Polynésie, Polynésiens, hier et aujourd'hui*, Paris: L'Harmattan.
Foucrier, Annick (ed.) (2005), *The French and the Pacific World, 17th–19th Centuries: Explorations, Migrations and Cultural Exchanges*, Aldershot: Ashgate.
Gomane, Jean-Pierre, Jean-Louis Guibert, André Martin-Pannetier and Georges Ordonnaud (1986), *Le Pacifique, 'nouveau centre du monde'*, Paris: Berger-Levrault.
Henningham, Stephen (1992), *France and the South Pacific: A Contemporary History*, Sydney: Allen and Unwin.
'Littératures du Pacifique', *Île en île*, http://www.lehman.cuny.edu/ile.en.ile/pacifique/paroles.html
Maclellan, Nic and Jean Chesnaux (1998), *After Moruroa: France in the South Pacific*, Melbourne and New York: Ocean Press.

Roberts, Stephen H. (1929), *History of French Colonial Policy (1870–1925)*, vol. 1, London: P. S. King and Son.

Thomas, Martin (2005), *The French Empire between the Wars: Imperialism, Politics and Society*, Manchester: Manchester University Press.

Francophone

The use of the term 'francophone' transcends its strict meaning of 'French-speaking' in a number of ways. Originally coined by the geographer Onésime Reclus (1837–1916) to denote a community of people linked by the common French language, the term 'Francophonie', and the movement associated with it, developed above all in the aftermath of French decolonisation. Its moment of birth is usually situated with the publication of an issue of the review *Esprit* in March 1962, to which a number of leading intellectuals and political leaders from the newly independent colonies contributed pieces, extolling the notion of a francophone community, built not just on the common French language, but also on a set of shared universal values, associated with the humanism of the Enlightenment. Unlike the British Commonwealth, the impetus for this movement came from the formerly colonised themselves. The French eschewed an active role in the movement, preferring to maintain bilateral relations with their former colonies, while at the same time appreciating the importance of a proactive policy to maintain and indeed promote the French language and culture outside the borders of the Hexagon.

In its early stages, Francophonie was primarily an intellectual movement, in which ideas, rather than institutions, were paramount. Indeed, at the outset, the whole movement was bathed in an extreme form of idealism, in which the relations of domination between coloniser and colonised were replaced by a vision of universal harmony, from which any conflict was banished. The French language and French culture were seen as the keys to universal values and the passport to participation on the world stage.

Institutional development was, however, not totally absent. With the active support of the Canadians, in 1961 the AUPELF (Association des Universités Partiellement ou Entièrement de Langue Française), now known as AUF (Agence Universitaire de la Francophonie), was the first important institution to be set up, to encourage contacts and co-operation between French-speaking academics. This was followed in 1969 with the establishment of the ACCT, which had as its purpose the fostering of cultural and technological co-operation and which went on to become the main operating agency of Francophonie. By the beginning of the 1980s, a number of francophone bodies had been established in piecemeal fashion, bringing together particular types of functionaries, sectors or interest groups across the French-speaking world.

The character of Francophonie was to change fundamentally when François Mitterrand, elected to the French presidency in 1981, grasped the potential of the movement and decided that France should henceforth play a leading role in it. With the organisation of the first francophone summit at Versailles in 1986, the process of establishing coherent overarching institutional structures was set in train, although it would take many years for it to adopt a permanent, administrative apparatus to oversee and direct its various activities. This was finally achieved following the Hanoi summit of 1997, with the creation of the OIF (Organisation Internationale de la Francophonie) and the election of Boutros Boutros-Ghali, former UN General Secretary, as its first Secretary-General, now succeeded by Abdou Diouf, a former president of Senegal.

At the same time, the ideological content of the movement underwent a number of transformations, in line with French preoccupations to maintain its role on the world stage. Increasingly, it was seen as a valuable counterweight to the growing global power of the USA. From being valued in its own right as the vehicle of rational, Enlightenment humanism, the French language became an instrument with which to challenge the predominance of the English language and American cultural hegemony. The role of Francophonie as a bastion from which to wage the defence of *l'exception française* became increasingly important at the time of the GATT negotiations in 1993, particularly in the domain of audiovisual cultural products. The importance of 'diversity' as a major plank of francophone ideology grew from its prominence as the key slogan of the Mauritius Francophone summit in 1993. Indeed, it soon evolved from the defence of French language and culture into an often eloquent plea for a broader defence of cultural diversity *per se*, including the importance of safeguarding multilingualism across the planet. This was, of course, in stark contrast to the continued application of a strictly homogeneous, indivisible and universalist interpretation of the French republican model in the Hexagon itself. On the other hand, it was strictly in line with the foreign policy favoured by President Jacques Chirac, as one of encouraging 'multipolarity', to counterbalance the hegemony of a single superpower.

In its new political dimension, Francophonie has broadened its appeal to include new member countries, not formerly part of the French colonial empire, in particular, a number of Eastern European countries (for up-to-date information on membership, policies, institutions and summits, see: www.francophonie.org). In the process, the importance of the French language as the unifying factor of the community has receded to some extent, with the Charte de la Francophonie not requiring any language qualification from its members.

At the same time, it must also be recognised that there has always been considerable ambivalence attached to the francophone concept, where the relation to the French language of the populations involved has been varied and often problematical. The number of native, mother-tongue speakers of French has always constituted a minority, with French more characteristically serving as the language of an administrative or intellectual élite, most notably in the African countries. Furthermore, the French language has also been tainted, most particularly in a country such as Algeria, by its association as the language of the former colonial power. Yet, notwithstanding its problematic status, it has been striking, that, contrary to the predictions of writers such as Albert Memmi, the French language has not been evinced by other, national languages, but, on the contrary, has even increased its take-up in some of the former colonies, most notably Algeria itself, where there are now far more French-speakers than at the time of colonisation. The quality and vigour of the literature produced by writers, who have their origins outside metropolitan France, also cannot be denied, even it the status of this 'francophone' literature continues to prove an ongoing subject of debate.

Margaret A. Majumdar

LITERARY WORKS

Chamoiseau, Patrick [1992] (1997), *Texaco*, trans. Rose-Myriam Réjouis and Val Vinokurov, New York: Pantheon Books.

Djebar, Assia (1997), *Les Nuits de Strasbourg*, Arles: Actes Sud.

Khatibi, Abdelkebir (1971), *La Mémoire tatouée: autobiographie d'un décolonisé*, Paris: Denoël.

Meddeb, Abdelwahab (1986), *Phantasia*, Paris: Sindbad.

Ouologuem, Yambo (1968), *Le Devoir de violence*, trans. as *Bound to Violence* (1971) Ralph Manheim, London: Heinemann.

Poulin, J. [1984] (1988), *Volkswagen Blues*, trans. Sheila Fischman, Toronto: McClelland and Stewart.

HISTORIES
Barrak, Anissa et al. (2004), *Diversité culturelle et mondialisation*, Paris: Éditions Autrement.
Forsdick, Charles and David Murphy (eds) (2003), *Francophone Postcolonial Studies: A Critical Introduction*, London: Arnold.
Majumdar, Margaret A. (ed.) (2002), *Francophone Studies*, London and New York: Arnold and Oxford University Press.
Maugey, Axel (2003), *Francophonie et dialogue des cultures*, Montreal: Humanitas.
Moura, Jean-Marc (1999), *Littératures francophones et théorie postcoloniale*, Paris: Presses Universitaires Françaises.
Salhi, Kamal (ed.) (2003), *Francophone Postcolonial Cultures: Critical Essays*, Lanham, MD: Lexington Books.

Francophone Black Atlantic

When France colonised the Caribbean territories of Guadeloupe, Martinique, French Guiana and Saint-Domingue (Haiti), it was very much engaged in North America as well. France established its first permanent colony in 1608 at Quebec City, and then colonised St Christopher in 1625, followed by Guadeloupe and Martinique in 1635. This initiated the erasure of the region's indigenous Indians and their replacement by a majority black, slave-based population. Quebec and the francophone Caribbean islands of Guadeloupe and Martinique are also linked by the peculiar parallelism of their existing status: Quebec, a francophone province within an anglophone country; the Caribbean islands, French departments overseas.

By 1760 the British had conquered New France, and in 1793 the lieutenant-governor of Upper Canada presented a bill to the government to abolish slavery, which was unanimously passed. From this point on black slaves in the USA saw Canada as a place of freedom and many escapees reached there through the 'underground railroad'. The Haitian Revolution broke out in 1799, and national independence in 1804 produced the second sovereign nation in the New World. Repercussions of this event were felt in France; as royalists sought to undermine the incipient revolution, the workers and peasants who stormed the Tuileries and struck out at tyranny and oppression were both inspired by and responding to the depredations of slavery. The love of *liberté*, *égalité* and *fraternité* that they espoused in the *métropole* was directly linked to the transatlantic formation of New World identities. Ultimately, all slaves in all French territories were freed by the Convention during the French Revolution in 1794; slavery was reinstated by Napoleon in 1802, and emancipation was only finalised in 1848.

The new century saw a passion for black culture sweep through Paris. Authors such as René Maran, the Goncourt-Prize-winning author of *Batouala*, became important conduits in the 1920s and 1930s between the francophone black world and black America. Such transatlantic cultural connections drove the publication in 1928 of the folklore collection *Ainsi parla l'oncle* by Haiti's Dr Jean Price-Mars, and oversaw the birth of the Negritude movement, marked by the appearance in 1939 of Martiniquan Aimé Césaire's landmark text *Cahier d'un retour au pays natal*. This inspired black Caribbean writers like Frantz Fanon to counter the transatlantic legacies of colonialism; his revolutionary writings centred on the Algerian War of Independence of 1954–62. Meanwhile, French Caribbean departmentalisation in 1946 led to increased levels of literary production.

The 1980s saw the theorisation of the Black Atlantic extended even further; Edouard Glissant's *antillanité* or 'Caribbeanness', formulated in *Le Discours antillais* (1981), draws on the common Caribbean heritage of uprooting, transformation and cultural exchange to forge a composite identity, where historical patterns of pluralism undergird a new geopolitical framework for French Caribbean expression. By contrast, the *Éloge de la créolité* (1989) by the Martiniquan authors Raphaël Confiant and Patrick Chamoiseau and the Guadeloupean linguist Jean Bernabé draws on the compound linguistic and cultural structures of the Creole language to valorise the diversity inherent in the Caribbean mosaic over Western universalism's singular perspective. Today, the work of North America-based Haitian writers such as Dany Laferrière and Edwige Danticat continue to expand the geographical, linguistic and cultural frontiers of the francophone Black Atlantic.

H. Adlai Murdoch

LITERARY WORKS

Bernabé, Jean, Patrick Chamoiseau and Raphaël Confiant (1989), *Éloge de la créolité*, Paris: Gallimard.

Césaire, Aimé (1939), *Cahier d'un retour au pays natal*, trans. as *Notebook of a Return to the Native Land* (2001) Clayton Eshleman and Annette Smith, Middletown, CT: Wesleyan University Press.

Danticat, Edwige (1994), *Breath, Eyes, Memory*, New York: Vintage.

Glissant, Edouard (1981), *Le Discours antillais*, trans. as *Caribbean Discourse: Selected Essays* (1989) J. Michael Dash, Charlottesville, VA: University Press of Virginia.

Laferrière, Dany (1985), *Comment faire l'amour avec un nègre sans se fatiguer*, trans. as *How to Make Love to a Negro* (1991) David Homel, London: Bloomsbury.

Maran, René (1921), *Batouala: veritable roman nègre*, trans. as *Batouala* (1973) Barbara Beck and Alexandre Mboukou, London: Heinemann.

HISTORIES

Chamoiseau, Patrick and Raphaël Confiant (1991), *Lettres Créoles: Tracées antillaises et continentales de la littérature, 1635–1975*, Paris: Hatier.

Dash, J. Michael (1995), *Edouard Glissant*, New York: Cambridge University Press.

Fabre, Michel (1991), *From Harlem to Paris: Black American Writers in France, 1840–1980*, Urbana, IL: University of Illinois Press.

Edwards, Brent Hayes (2003), *The Practice of Diaspora: Literature, Translation, and the Rise of Black Internationalism*, Cambridge, MA: Harvard University Press.

Gilroy, Paul (1993), *The Black Atlantic*, Cambridge, MA: Harvard University Press.

Williams, Dorothy W. (1997), *The Road to Now. A History of Blacks in Montreal*, Montreal: Véhicule Press.

Francophone Caribbean

Although historically France has had a strong influence in other islands such as Dominica, Saint Lucia, Grenada and Tobago, today the francophone Caribbean is generally understood to include the overseas departments of Guadeloupe, Martinique and Guiana, and the independent republic of Haiti.

The history and geography of French Guiana distinguish it from the other territories. Situated between Surinam and Brazil on the north-east coast of South America, and with a vast, forested hinterland, Guiana proved a far more difficult land to colonise than the Caribbean islands. Most of its 157,000 inhabitants live on the Atlantic coastal strip, which, since the 1670s, has been the locus of French settlement. Long underdeveloped as a colony, the French first made serious attempts to settle in Guiana in 1763, after losing much of their other American territory. Guiana's reputation as the white man's grave was consolidated when 6,000 of the 10,000 French emigrants died from hunger, malaria and yellow fever. Despite these difficulties, and despite the relative ease with which slaves could escape to, and remain undiscovered in the vast forests, plantation slavery was established. After short periods of Portuguese and British control, France took definitive possession of Guiana in 1817.

France's earliest Caribbean possessions were, however, Martinique (1631) and Guadeloupe (1635), and it was here that the patterns of French colonial trade were first implemented: the island economies existed to produce goods – especially sugar – for export to France and other parts of Europe, while the islands were almost completely dependent on France for manufactured commodities. As in virtually all other Caribbean islands, contact with Europeans decimated the Amerindian population. Faced with a workforce shortage, and after the failure of a scheme to import indentured labourers from France, the French began to import African slaves, on whose labour the plantation economy prospered. Thus was created the rigid colour and class hierarchy that still to some extent characterises these Caribbean islands: a white planter class enjoyed the fruits of its wealth, while the *petits blancs*, or poor whites felt themselves racially superior to the *affranchis*, the free coloureds, who in turn were regarded to be of higher status than the slaves. Until 1685, when Louis XIV introduced the notorious Code Noir, the treatment of slaves was largely left to the whims of individual planters. Ostensibly intended to limit planters' punitive excesses, the Code Noir in fact instituted an extremely harsh penal system, and effectively reinforced the slave owners' powers by further commoditising slaves as human merchandise, transferable according to the will of the owner. With such a degree of control over the workforce, the colonies prospered, so much so that by the time of the Seven Years, War (1756–63), France was prepared to trade most of its North American possessions with Britain if it could retain control of its Caribbean colonies.

The French Revolution in 1789 exacerbated existing tensions between the white planters and the free coloureds, and between the colony and the metropolitan government. In France, Abbé Grégoire and the abolitionist Société des Amis des Noirs promoted the extension of *liberté, égalité, fraternité* to slaves, while in the colonies the slaves themselves saw an opportunity to end their bondage. Most dramatically, in Saint Domingue (Haiti), a slave revolt broke out in August 1791, which would lead finally to the declaration of Haitian independence on 1 January 1804. The National Convention in France first abolished slavery in 1794, largely in order to provide recruits for an army to repel the British, who took advantage of the unstable situation by annexing the French Caribbean colonies, with the support of the French planters, who colluded with the British in an attempt to bring back slavery. In 1802, the French regained control of Martinique and Guadeloupe, and Bonaparte immediately re-established slavery as a means of meeting the labour shortages on the sugar plantations, and thereby of reinvigorating the faltering colonial economy.

The same year, Bonaparte sent to the Caribbean islands the most significant expedition ever to have left French shores. In Guadeloupe, the 3,000-strong army was countered by a less numerous force of black soldiers, led by the legendary Martiniquan and former French Army officer Louis Delgrès, who finally led his men to a mass suicide, rather than give up their claims to liberty.

During the nineteenth century, the French at once ostracised Haiti as a nation of barbaric blacks, and promoted an assimilationist policy in its remaining territories, as part of its self-styled 'civilising mission' to the colonies. The accent was now on centralising power in the metropole, and on exporting French ideas, culture and language to the overseas territories, so that the people of those lands might identify more closely with the *mère patrie* and its values. France's desire to keep a strict control over its black subjects' bodies and minds is illustrated in the fact that it did not finally end slavery until 1848, fully ten years after emancipation in the British colonies. Voting rights in the elections of the Second Republic (1848–51) were extended to ex-slaves in the French colonies, who now had the status of free men and French citizens. As in other Caribbean islands, the end of slavery led to new labour supply problems for planters, and in Guadeloupe especially, this led to the arrival of indentured labourers from India. The presence of significant numbers of Indians in Guadeloupe, coupled with the increasingly complex Creole society, meant that social hierarchies became less rigidly stratified on that island than on Martinique, which largely retained its characteristic three-tiered social class and colour structure. On both islands, the image of France as a benevolent motherland has been an enduring and effective way of perpetuating loyalty among French Caribbean peoples who, much like their counterparts in the British islands, willingly enlisted to fight in both world wars.

In Guiana, the end of slavery signalled a new direction, quite different from that of the islands. In 1852, Napoleon III designated Guiana as France's principal penal colony, a status it retained for almost a century. Intended as at once an attempt to clear France's overcrowded prisons, and a means of populating the colony, the success of the French policy was once again compromised by disease, and of the 70,000 convicts sent to Guiana, only 5,000 returned to France alive.

The marriage of the French Caribbean to France was finalised in the 1946 *loi de départementalisation*, the act that finally transformed the colonies, along with Réunion, and Algeria (until its independence in 1962), into fully-integrated French departments. Backed in Martinique by the communist *député* and mayor of Fort-de-France, Aimé Césaire, in Guiana by Gaston Monnerville, and in Guadeloupe by Paul Valentino, departmentalisation was welcomed as the only viable solution to the long-standing problems of poverty and underdevelopment. The few dissenting voices feared a further loss of control over the local economy, and more centralised power. These fears were soon realised as ever greater numbers of French goods came into local markets, further weakening the departments' economic independence. In Martinique and Guadeloupe in particular, these economic problems have been compounded by the decline in local agricultural industries, and the islands are today more or less completely economically dependent on the metropole, importing 95 per cent of their goods from Europe.

The departmentalisation process led to an even greater centralisation of political power in France. Instead of feeling more attached to France, post-departmentalisation French Caribbeans have often felt themselves to be the poor relations, feelings exacerbated by their not assuming full social rights until the 1980s. Resentment has at times turned into violent protest: the popular riots in 1959 in Fort-de-France, Martinique were directed against the presence of white metropolitan French, who had become scapegoats for the frustrations and humiliations of departmentalisation. In Guadeloupe, too, in 1967, pro-independence groups and ordinary Guadeloupeans were involved in strikes and riots. In the 1970s and 1980s, there was a series of bombings in Guadeloupe, which helped consolidate its reputation as the rebellious counterpart to its respectable, more assimilated sister island. Such angry protests aside, the various independence movements have never enjoyed general support, and the more moderate drive for greater autonomy has gained greater favour. In 1981, more power was given to the overseas departments as part of the French Socialist Party's regionalist policies. This movement towards political autonomy continued in 2000, when the overseas departments' orientation law (*le projet de loi d'orientation des DOM*) was ratified, bringing local control to a range of economic, social, political and cultural affairs.

Even if France's Caribbean citizens enjoy a higher standard of living than virtually all of their island neighbours, the departments' economies are very weak: the effects of the high cost of living are exacerbated by perennially high unemployment rates. Consequently, there is a longstanding pattern of migration towards the metropole. Between 1961 and 1981 four official emigration plans were introduced with the dual aims of reducing the population surplus in the Caribbean departments, and of meeting the labour shortages in certain sectors of the French metropolitan economy. Emigration from Guiana is less significant than in the islands; indeed the South American department has seen successive waves of immigration, from its neighbours Brazil, Guyana and Surinam, and also from other francophone or creolophone lands such as Haiti and Saint Lucia. In all, Guiana has over twenty diverse ethnic groups. Martinique's population, by contrast, is far less diverse, and retains much of its historical stratification.

Despite, or indeed because of the departments' continued attachment to France, they have produced some of the most accomplished writers and intellectuals of the whole Caribbean region. The perceived threats to Creole language, cooking, costume, carnival and dance have, moreover, led to movements to protect the cultural heritage. Each of the French Caribbean territories has its own distinctive, if related, traditions of writing. Arguably, the major (male) contemporary thinkers and writers of the French Caribbean have come from Martinique: from Aimé Césaire's Négritude movement in the 1940s and 1950s, Frantz Fanon's trenchant anti-colonialism, Édouard Glissant's theories of *antillanité*, to Bernabé, Chamoiseau and Confiant's contemporary Créolité movement, Martiniquans have been the most prominent in resisting cultural assimilation. On the other hand, however, Guadeloupe can lay claim to some of the finest women writers in the Caribbean, the most prominent of whom are Maryse Condé, Simone Schwarz-Bart and Gisèle Pineau. Often, the works of these women writers call into question or deflate the more oracular tendencies of male Caribbean authors. In addition, Guadeloupe has produced some fine male intellectuals, such as Guy Tirolien, Paul Niger, Sonny Rupaire and Daniel Maximin. Guianese literature is significantly less developed than that of the islands, even if one of its earliest figures, Léon Gontran Damas was, with Césaire and Léopold Sédar Senghor, one of the founding fathers of the Négritude movement. A post-Négritude literary movement was slow to develop in Guiana; it was not until the 1970s, with the appearance of the poets Serge Patient and Elie Stephenson and the founding of the literary magazine *La Torche* that a more distinctly Guianese poetics began to emerge. Perhaps this relatively undeveloped literary tradition is a sign of Guiana's more profoundly creolised culture, and of a less-threatened Creole aesthetic there. In the island departments, the spectre of French assimilationism looms more immediately, and there is a heightened awareness of the dangers of surrendering the historically-created Creole culture to a French policy that by its nature gives with one hand, and takes away with the other.

Martin Munro

LITERARY WORKS

Césaire, Aimé (1983), *Aimé Césaire: The Collected Poetry*, trans. Clayton Eshleman and Annette Smith, Berkeley, CA: University of California Press.

Chauvet, Marie (1968), *Amour, colère, folie*, Paris: Gallimard.

Condé, Maryse (1986), *Traversée de la mangrove*, trans. as *Crossing the Mangrove* (1995) Richard Philcox, New York: Anchor Books; Doubleday.

Danticat, Edwige (1996), *Breath, Eyes, Memory*, London: Abacus.

— (2000), *The Farming of Bones*, London: Abacus.

— (2004), *The Dew Breaker*, New York: Alfred A. Knopf.

Depestre, René [1979] (1990), *Le Mât de cocagne*, Paris: Gallimard.

Fanon, Frantz (1952), *Peau noire, masques blancs*, trans. as *Black Skin, White Masks* (1967) Charles Lam Markmann, New York: Grove Press.

Frankétienne [1974] (2004), *Ultravocal*, Paris: Éditions Hoëbeke.

Glissant, Édouard (1964), *Le Quatrième siècle*, trans. as *The Fourth Century* (2001) Betsy Wing, Lincoln, NE: University of Nebraska Press.

Lahens, Yanick (2000), *Dans la maison du père*, Paris: Le Serpent à Plumes.

Maximin, Daniel (1981), *L'Isolé soleil*, trans. as *Lone Sun* (1989) Clarisse Zimra, Charlottesville, VA: University Press of Virginia.

— (1987), *Soufrières*, Paris: Seuil.

— (1995), *L'Île et une nuit*, Paris: Seuil.

Roumain, Jacques (1944), *Gouverneurs de la rosée*, trans. as *Masters of the Dew* (1947) Langston Hughes and Mercer Cook, New York: Reynal and Hitchcock.

Trouillot, Lyonel (2004), *Bicentenaire*, Arles: Actes Sud.

Zobel, Joseph (1950), *La Rue cases-nègres*, trans. as *Black Shack Alley* (1980) Keith Q. Warner, London: Heinemann.

HISTORIES

Aldrich, Robert (1996), *Greater France: A History of French Overseas Expansion*, Basingstoke: Macmillan.

Bernabé, Jean, Patrick Chamoiseau and Raphaël Confiant (1989), *Eloge de la créolité*, Paris: Gallimard.

Burton, Richard D. E. and Fred Reno (eds) (1995), *French and West Indian: Martinique, Guadeloupe, and French Guiana Today*, Basingstoke: Macmillan.

Dash, J. Michael (1981), *Literature and Ideology in Haiti, 1915–1961*, London and Basingstoke: Macmillan.

— (1998), *The Other America: Caribbean Literature in a New World Context*, Charlottesville, VA and London: University Press of Virginia.

Gallagher, Mary (2002), *Soundings in French Caribbean Writing since 1950: The Shock of Space and Time*, Oxford: Oxford University Press.

Glissant, Édouard [1981] (1989), *Caribbean Discourse: Selected Essays*, Charlottesville, VA: University Press of Virginia.

Sutton, Paul (ed.) (1991), *Europe and the Caribbean*, Basingstoke: Macmillan.

Haiti

The Republic of Haiti occupies the western third of the island of Hispaniola, which was originally populated by the Arawak/Taino indigenous groups. Columbus claimed the island for Spain in 1492, and for nearly 200 years the feudal *encomienda* system prevailed, whereby native people paid mandatory tributes to the Spanish in return for religious instruction and ostensible protection. As the indigenous labour force died out, African slaves were brought to the colony. French pirates and buccaneers seized and occupied neighboring La Tortue; in the 1697 Treaty of Ryswick, Spain ceded the western part of Hispaniola to France. The labour-intensive sugar industry replaced coffee as the major export, and the importation of slaves intensified. By 1789 Saint-Domingue was the world's most productive and wealthy colony. 'La perle des Antilles' accounted for two-thirds of French foreign trade and supplied more than half of Europe's sugar, plus coffee, indigo and cotton. This prosperity depended on an increasingly precarious balance of power among the approximately 40,000 whites, 30,000 mulattos and freed blacks, and 450,000 slaves, who continuously resisted the system.

The subsequent Haitian Revolution (1791–1804) was simultaneously a war of social, racial, civil and international dimensions, ultimately becoming a war for national liberation. It comprised three general stages: first, a civil war engulfed the whites, pitting those without power against those seeking to maintain the status quo. As the French Revolution unfolded, whites in Saint-Domingue who expected colonial self-rule spread revolutionary ideas in the colony; delegates attended the Estates-General meeting in France, but their interests and goals clashed with those of the revolution. Soon thereafter, mulattos began to fight for equality with whites, and finally, the black slaves struggled against both groups to pursue their freedom. On 14 August 1791 the legendary ceremony of Bois-Caïman took place, triggering the slaves' general uprising and allowing the masses to enter into the politics of the modern world system. Britain and Spain joined the struggle to prevent the spread of revolution to their colonies: the former supported French plantation owners, whereas the latter assisted black revolutionary leaders, and France sided with the mulattos. Many interests thus competed for the allegiance of the masses, and eventually all races battled on every front.

Slavery was officially abolished in Saint-Domingue in 1793 (then by the National Convention in France in 1794). Toussaint Louverture, ex-slave and revolutionary leader, was appointed Governor-General. Although in 1801 he established the island's autonomy under French suzerainty, Napoleon Bonaparte sent a punitive expedition under Leclerc to restore colonial power and reintroduce slavery the following year. Toussaint was captured and exiled to France in June 1802; he died in the Fort-de-Joux prison on 7 April 1803. Outside of Haiti, Toussaint is generally regarded as the foremost Haitian revolutionary figure. Toussaint remains controversial, however, because, according to some, he betrayed the Haitian people by suppressing the popular *vodou* religion, establishing strict codes requiring former slaves to remain on plantations, and allying himself with France. Jean-Jacques Dessalines (considered a founding father by Haitians) proclaimed Independence on 1 January 1804, and the new black republic readopted its indigenous name of Haiti, or 'mountainous land'. Although some 150,000 had died during the revolution, thousands of others were disabled, and the economy was in shambles, the French colonial system had been uprooted, the Atlantic economic circuit shifted, and entirely new social and political structures established. 'Haitian independence presented a radical challenge to colonialism, to slavery and to the associated ideology of white racialism' (Nicholls 1996).

The aftermath of the revolution saw a civil war and continued political turmoil for Haiti, unrecognised by a hostile international community and left out of the Industrial Revolution. Other slaveholding powers, fearing insurgency elsewhere, imposed a *cordon sanitaire* around Haiti. Henri-Christophe ruled the northern part of the country, proclaiming himself King (1807–20), while Alexandre Pétion governed a separate republic in the south (1807–18). Pétion contributed substantial military and economic aid to Simón Bolívar's revolutionary efforts; he also reinforced patterns of subsistence agriculture that isolated peasants from cities, the government and the external world. Jean-Pierre Boyer subsequently reunified the Republic of Haiti, attempted land reform, paid 40 million francs to France in exchange for recognition of Haiti's independence, and occupied neighbouring Santo-Domingo (1822–24). The notorious Faustin Soulouque, or Emperor Faustin I, ruled from 1847 to 1859. Increasing political instability marked the latter half of the nineteenth century. France and Germany dominated Haiti's economy until the American occupation (1915–34), which complicated existing racial tensions.

Claiming to represent the 'Black Power' movement, François 'Papa Doc' Duvalier took command in 1957. He formed the 'Tontons Macoutes' corps (1958), declared himself President-For-Life (1964), and was succeeded by his son Jean-Claude upon his death (1971). Although the Duvaliers' brutal régime was a difficult period socially and politically, an outpouring of literary and cultural production occurred both within Haiti and in the diaspora, where many intellectuals fled. Mass uprisings forced 'Baby Doc' Duvalier from power in 1986; a series of military governments followed, and in 1990 Jean-Bertrand Aristide won presidential elections in a landslide. He was overthrown by a military coup and exiled seven months after being sworn in. A worldwide embargo was imposed on Haiti; as many as 4,000 or more people were killed. Aristide returned to govern in 1995, was followed by René Préval, and then re-elected. During Haiti's highly anticipated bicentennial year, Aristide was ousted from office with the support of France and the USA, and an interim government established. Préval was re-elected President in February 2006.

Mariana Past

LITERARY WORKS

Alexis, Jacques-Stephen (1955), *Compère Général Soleil*, trans. as *General Sun, My Brother* (1999) Carrol F. Coates, Charlottesville, VA: University Press of Virginia.

Carpentier, Alejo (1949), *El Reino de este mundo*, trans. as *The Kingdom of this World* (1957) Harriet de Onís, New York: Knopf.

Césaire, Aimé (1963), *La Tragédie du Roi Christophe*, trans. as *The Tragedy of King Christophe* (1970) Ralph Manheim, New York: Grove Press.

Price-Mars, Jean (1928), *Ainsi parla l'oncle: essais d'ethnographie*, trans. as *So Spoke the Uncle* (1983) Magdaline W. Shannon, Washington, DC: Three Continents Press.

Roumain, Jacques (1944), *Gouverneurs de la rosée*, trans. as *Masters of the Dew* (1947) Langston Hughes and Mercer Cook, New York: Reynal and Hitchcock.

HISTORIES

Berrou, Raphaël and Pradel Pompilus (1975–7), *Histoire de la littérature haïtienne, illustrée par les textes*, 3 vols, Port-au-Prince: Éditions Caraïbes.

Dash, J. Michael (1981), *Literature and Ideology in Haiti, 1915–1961*, Totowa, NJ: Barnes and Noble Books.

Fick, Carolyn (1990), *The Making of Haiti: The Saint-Domingue Revolution from Below*, Knoxville, TN: University of Tennessee Press.
Geggus, David Patrick (2002), *Haitian Revolutionary Studies*, Bloomington, IN: Indiana University Press.
James, C. L. R. [1938] (1963), *The Black Jacobins*, 2nd edn, New York: Vintage Books.
Nicholls, David [1979] (1996), *From Dessalines to Duvalier: Race, Colour and National Independence in Haiti*, New Brunswick, NJ: Rutgers University Press.

Historiography

The historiography of French colonialism has frequently been a reflection of French debates about the benefits or disadvantages of colonial rule. From the nineteenth century's glorifications of imperialism as a symbol of progress and civilisation, to the French government's law of 23 February 2005 requiring that colonial history be taught in a 'positive' manner in French schools, the writing and teaching of the history of French colonialism have often been enlisted in the defence of the nation's colonial project. Outside France, historians of French colonialism were somewhat more distanced from the sometimes polemical nature of the subject as written and taught in France, but works by non-French scholars frequently echoed the debates of the Hexagon or betrayed the limitations imposed by incomplete access to sources.

For much of the colonial period, 'colonial history' amounted to the history of French colonial rule. Colonial policies, colonial governors and expeditions of discovery and conquest were appropriate subjects for the historian. The colonies, however, did not fit so easily into this conception of history. Indeed, according to common justifications of colonial rule, the colonies did not have pre-colonial pasts worthy of historians' attention; the period before French rule had been one of stagnation or even regression, and if 'progress' had been achieved under French control, then the history of recent changes in the lives of the colonial subjects was essentially the same as the history of French colonial rule. In the postcolonial period, a synthesis of these two interpretations has slowly emerged, with a new generation of colonial historians considering not only the impact of French colonial rule on the peoples of the empire, but also the empire's impact on France. This synthesis has had the welcome effect of integrating 'French' and 'colonial' histories, doing much to remove a neo-colonial separation of the centre from the periphery which had characterised colonial history in the age of imperialism.

During the colonial period, French historical writing about the empire was overwhelmingly supportive of colonialism, and in many cases in fact served to justify French rule. The intellectual foundations of this kind of historical writing can be found in the Enlightenment's notions of progress and civilisation. In the decades preceding the French conquest of Algiers in 1830, for example, histories of Algiers depicting an uncivilised land in the grip of piracy and despotism helped create the liberal and intellectual support for colonialism in North Africa. In the era of French colonial expansion and consolidation, historical writing about the colonies' past – which was seen by supporters of the French colonial project as fundamentally different from the narrative of progress that they saw in European history – legitimised imperial rule. It is important, however, to understand that for all their Eurocentrism, the French colonial histories of the imperial age were not mere ideological tracts produced for the sole purpose of justifying European hegemony. Although they reflect the prevailing views of their time, many such works were written by colonial administrators or by scientific or geographic experts, and accordingly offered a well-informed perspective on the French colonial project which can still be useful to historians.

The inter-war period was the apogee of French colonialism, when the nineteenth century's relative indifference to the colonial project among the French people gave way to a more overt triumphalism. The most hagiographic and celebratory histories of French colonialism date from this era, notably the period around the centenary of the conquest of Algeria in 1930 and the 1931 Colonial Exhibition in Paris. The six-volume history of French colonialism produced by Gabriel Hanotaux and Alfred Martineau between 1929 and 1934 exemplifies the enlistment of history in the promotion of colonial rule. Therefore, the 1930s can be seen as both the high-water mark of pro-colonial history, with a peak in the production of celebratory and hagiographic work, and as the turning-point after which anti-colonial voices gradually began to emerge.

World War II is seen with justification as the catalyst for decolonisation. Just as the defeat and occupation of metropolitan France shattered the myth of French invincibility, so the loss of prestige suffered by France called into question the notion of a French mission to spread progress and civilisation which had underpinned French colonial history. For the most part, however, critical views on France's colonial history at this stage were expressed by those outside the academic community, intellectuals like Frantz Fanon and Jean-Paul Sartre becoming the vanguard of anti-colonialism during the period of decolonisation. Although some professional historians, such as the North African specialist Charles-André Julien, publicly supported anti-colonialism and took a more objective stance in their published work, colonial history remained for the most part a conservative discipline.

Decolonisation marks a turning-point in the historiography of French colonialism. With colonialism now in the past, the process of reassessment could be conducted in a more dispassionate manner. Historians' attention turned first to the period of expansion between 1870 and World War I. Henri Brunschwig questioned the assumption that economic motives lay behind imperialism at this time, and suggested that it was ideology, especially the myth of the civilising mission, that had allowed the supporters of French colonialism to prevail in the face of opposition and indifference in Paris. In an argument which has remained influential, Brunschwig claimed that an expansionist nationalism was exported from France to the colonies, and refuted the idea that imperialism had 'civilised' the colonised peoples, concluding that they would have followed the same path whether or not they had been subject to direct European control. It is surely no coincidence that this statement of scepticism about the discourse of improvement and progress which had prevailed during the age of imperialism appeared in 1960, the year of Sub-Saharan African independence. It was echoed by the important works of Charles-Robert Ageron, Christopher Andrew and A. S. Kanya-Forstner in the 1970s. Ageron pioneered work on public opinion and colonialism, seeking to establish if the French had been united in enthusiastic support for empire, while Andrew and Kanya-Forstner developed the notion of a 'colonial lobby' which exerted pressure in parliament on behalf of colonial – mainly economic – interests and attempted to persuade public opinion of the benefits of imperial expansion. These works produced a more nuanced history of French colonialism, demonstrating that while many did believe that colonialism brought progress to the colonised and economic benefits to metropolitan France, these ideas were never universally taken for granted and imperialism had had its critics as well as its supporters. Colonialist ideology also came under scrutiny, with Raoul Girardet, previously one of the strongest defenders of Algérie française among the academic community, producing an important work on *L'Idée coloniale en France de 1871 à 1962* (1971). Covering subjects like 'the challenge to the West' and 'colonial humanism', Girardet's work amounted to an attempt to analyse and take seriously the ideologies and assumptions that underpinned French colonialism.

In addition to these interpretive works on the French colonial experience as a whole, the period after decolonisation also gave rise to authoritative works on the former colonies. Although the often painful process of decolonisation in the French empire might be expected to have dissuaded historians from investigating the nation's colonial past, during the 1970s and 1980s the study of non-European history expanded and provided a focal point for scholars more sympathetic to the colonised than the colonisers. Catherine Coquery-Vidrovitch and Jean Suret-Canale wrote detailed studies of Sub-Saharan Africa, Charles-Robert Ageron became recognised as the foremost French historian of colonial Algeria, and Pierre Brocheux analysed Indo-China under French rule. The leaders of the anti-colonial liberation campaigns also began to receive scholarly attention in this period, notably through Benjamin Stora's work on Algerian nationalism. These works all provided a counterweight to the focus on the colonisers and the colonialist assumptions that had dominated colonial-era history, but it is worth noting that by the 1980s it is possible to detect a revival of popular and academic interest in colonialism. The Denoël publishing house launched a series on *L'aventure coloniale de la France* with a four-volume survey of French colonialism published between 1987 and 1990 which testified to this interest, as did the growing number of memoirs and essays published by those who had pursued careers in the empire, notably officers and administrators keen to offer their versions of the end of colonialism in Algeria. During the late 1980s and the 1990s, partly due to the gradual declassification of archives and the development of the Centre des Archives d'Outre-Mer in Aix-en-Provence, decolonisation became a distinct area of study. Non-French historians were among the first to work on French decolonisation, which is perhaps an indication of the French reluctance to open old wounds in this domain, particularly with regard to the war in Algeria.

Algeria had not been entirely absent from French writing on the colonial past between 1962 and the early 1990s, but the majority of works published on the Algerian War of Independence in France were popular history with a pro-colonial orientation, or the memoirs and polemics of those who had been on the losing side in Algeria. Throughout the 1970s and 1980s, essays with titles like *Decadence, Imposture and Tragedy* and *Will We Be Understood at Last* kept painful memories alive among Algérie française veterans, while sympathetic publishers continued to produce works of nostalgia for a lost Algeria. Since the 1990s, however, the war in Algeria has been the most lively and high-profile area of French historical research on colonialism. In 1992 the thirty-year restriction on access to archive documents expired and although many files remained classified or uncatalogued, this provided a new impetus to a generation of historians for whom the war in Algeria was a subject for historical enquiry rather than simply a troublesome memory. Already in 1991, Benjamin Stora's *La Gangrène et l'oubli* had documented the 'national amnesia' about the war, while in 1992 the film *La Guerre sans nom*, with accompanying book, featured veterans talking for the first time about their experiences as conscripts in Algeria and made a significant contribution to ending this 'amnesia.'

Since 1992, in addition to a seemingly never-ending stream of memoirs and essays about the war, several important historical works on Algeria have appeared. These have focused on hitherto taboo subjects such as the French Army's use of torture, amply documented in Raphaëlle Branche's *La Torture et l'armée pendant la guerre d'Algérie*, and the killing of up to 200 Algerian protesters by the police in Paris in 1961. Thus, the revival of interest in the Algerian War – which may be explained not only by the emergence of a new generation without personal memories of the war but also by the increasing importance and visibility of North African immigrants and their descendants in French politics and society – has shed light on many of the unsavoury aspects of French colonial practice. However, historians have also offered a series of new interpretations and innovative methodological and conceptual approaches to colonial history through this work on Algeria. The British historian Martin Evans used oral history to reclaim the undocumented story of French opposition to the Algerian War. American historians employed the methodology of diplomatic history to argue that decolonisation was much more than a simple confrontation between France and Algeria, with the French ability to control the process of change constrained by the internationalisation of colonial questions during the Cold War. The Algerian side of the story was explored by the French historian Gilbert Meynier's pioneering work on the Algerian National Liberation Front. This revival of interest in the war in Algeria during the 1990s therefore significantly enhanced historians' understanding of French decolonisation and suggested important new interpretative perspectives; it also brought 'colonial' history back into the French historical spotlight.

The main beneficiaries of this renewed focus on colonial history have been the burgeoning field of memory studies, and a series of stimulating new directions in the history of colonialism. The progress made in the field of memory with regard to Algeria is demonstrated by the proliferation of works on the war as experienced by former settlers (*pieds-noirs*), veterans, women and other groups, and by the focus on representations of the conflict in areas such as popular culture and education. Interest in memory has spread beyond the Algerian War, as shown by the revival of scholarship on Indo-China to coincide with the fiftieth anniversary of independence, and by Jennifer Cole's study of memories of colonial repression in Madagascar which provided important theoretical insights about history and memory in the colonial context. The opening of archives has also made possible a series of detailed studies on aspects of colonial policy, many of which have suggested important new directions for future research. Alice Conklin and Patricia Lorcin have revived interest in colonial ideology by looking at how the civilising mission shaped colonial rule and fed into the discourses of power which sustained it. Works such as Owen White's study of miscegenation and Elizabeth Thomson's study of colonial society with special emphasis on women, have filled many gaps in our knowledge of how the colonial ideologies 'made in France' translated into social policy in the colonies. The question of 'representations' and the 'colonial imagination' has informed much interdisciplinary work, such as that of Nicola Cooper on Indo-China and Matt Matsuda on the South Pacific. These approaches complement the traditional colonial historians' attention to political or economic factors; the study of the mental world of both the colonisers and the colonised reflects the tendency towards re-examination of colonialism both as it was experienced in the colonies and as it was represented in France.

Finally, it is perhaps fitting that in a postcolonial era, attention has recently turned to the impact of colonialism on metropolitan France. Works on colonial and postcolonial immigration have been complemented by reflections on the relationship between the French republic and its imperial hinterlands. Echoing similar developments in the historiography of British imperialism over the past two decades, historians have begun to explore the infiltration of imperial themes into French popular culture, the ways in which the idea of empire was promoted in France, and the responses of French intellectuals to colonialism. At the heart of these inquiries has been what some see as a fundamental contradiction between the French republican principles and imperial ideology, which raises important questions about the supposedly colour-blind nature of French republicanism and the effects that colonialism has had on the shaping of French identities. It seems likely that this recent development will open up important new perspectives which will allow historians to continue writing colonialism into French history.

Stephen Tyre

LITERARY WORKS

Camus, Albert (1994), *Le Premier Homme*, trans. as *The First Man* (1994) David Hapgood, London: Hamish Hamilton.

Césaire, Aimé (1955), *Discours sur le colonialisme*, trans. as *Discourse on Colonialism* (1972) Joan Pinkham, New York: Monthly Review Press.

Chamoiseau, Patrick (1997), *Écrire en pays dominé*, Paris: Gallimard

Fanon, Frantz (1961), *Les Damnés de la terre*, trans. as *The Wretched of the Earth* (1967) Constance Farrington, Harmondsworth: Penguin.

Memmi, Albert (1957), *Le Portrait du colonisé*, trans. as *The Colonizer and the Colonized* (1990) Howard Greenfeld, London: Earthscan.

Sartre, Jean-Paul (1964), *Situations V: Colonialisme et néo-colonialisme*, trans. as *Colonialism and Neocolonialism* (2001) Azzedine Haddour, Steve Brewer and Terry McWilliams, London and New York: Routledge.

HISTORIES

Ageron, Charles-Robert (1978), *France coloniale ou parti colonial?*, Paris: Presses Universitaires de France.

Andrew, Christopher and Alexander Kanya-Forstner (1971), 'The French "Colonial Party": Its composition, aims and influence, 1885–1914', *Historical Journal* 14: 99–128.

Branche, Raphaëlle (2001), *La Torture et l'armée pendant la guerre d'Algérie*, Paris: Gallimard.

Brocheux, Pierre and Daniel Hémery (1995), *Indochine: La colonization ambiguë, 1858–1954*, Paris: La Découverte.

Brunschwig, Henri (1960), *Mythes et réalités de l'impérialisme colonial français 1871–1914*, trans. as *Colonialism 1871–1914 Myths and Realities* (1966) W. G. Brown, London: Pall Mall Press.

Cole, Jennifer (2001), *Forget Colonialism: Sacrifice and the Art of Memory in Madagascar*, Berkeley, CA: University of California Press.

Conklin, Alice (1997), *A Mission to Civilize: The Republican Idea of Empire in France and West Africa, 1895–1930*, Stanford, CA: Stanford University Press.

Cooper, Nicola (2001), *France in Indochina: Colonial Encounters*, Oxford: Berg.

Coquery-Vidrovitch, Catherine (1985), *Afrique noire: permanences et ruptures*, trans. as *Africa: Endurance and Change South of the Sahara* (1988) David Maisel, Berkeley, CA: University of California Press.

Evans, Martin (1997), *The Memory of Resistance: French Opposition to the Algerian War (1954–1962)*, Oxford: Berg.

Girardet, Raoul (1972), *L'Idée coloniale en France de 1871 à 1962*, Paris: La Table Ronde.

Hanotaux, Gabriel and Alfred Martineau (1929–33), *Histoire des colonies françaises et de l'expansion de la France dans le monde*, Paris: Plon.

Julien, Charles-André (1952), *L'Afrique du nord en marche: nationalismes musulmans et souveraineté française*, Paris: Julliard.

Matsuda, Matt (2005), *Empire of Love: Histories of France and the Pacific*, Oxford: Oxford University Press.

Meynier, Gilbert (2002), *Histoire intérieure du F.L.N.*, Paris: Fayard.

Prochaska, David (1990), *Making Algeria French: Colonialism in Bône, 1870–1920*, Cambridge: Cambridge University Press.

Rioux, Jean-Pierre (ed.) (1990), *La Guerre d'Algérie et les Français*, Paris: Fayard.

Ruscio, Alain and Serge Tignères (2005), *Dien Bien Phu: mythes et réalités. Cinquante ans de passions françaises*, Paris: Les Indes Savantes.

Stora, Benjamin (1991), *La Gangrène et l'oubli: La mémoire de la guerre d'Algérie*, Paris: La Découverte.

Suret-Canale, Jean (1964), *Afrique noire: II, l'ère coloniale 1900–1945*, Paris: Éditions Sociales.

Thomson, Elizabeth (2000), *Colonial Citizens: Republican Rights, Paternal Privilege, and Gender in French Syria and Lebanon*, New York: Columbia University Press.

White, Owen (1999), *Children of the French Empire: Miscegenation and Colonial Society in French West Africa, 1895–1960*, New York: Oxford University Press.

Imperial Policy

The first of France's two overseas empires collapsed at the end of the eighteenth century, leaving only a few fragments of empire in the Caribbean and some small trading posts in Senegal, India and Saint-Pierre-and-Miquelon. The process of rebuilding an overseas empire started with the seizure of Algiers in 1830 and continued throughout the nineteenth century, culminating in 1912 with the establishment of the Moroccan protectorate. By this time France had acquired an empire second only in size to that of Great Britain, having established claims to large areas of Africa and South-East Asia and to a number of islands in the Indian and Pacific Oceans.

The acquisition of empire in the nineteenth century was not the product of any deliberate or sustained strategy; indeed, there was no Colonial Ministry until 1894. Rather, it was an incremental process, not controlled by Paris but led by a motley collection of colonial enthusiasts that included explorers, military men, fortune seekers, missionaries and traders. During the 1840s and 1850s France established various colonial outposts (*points d'appui*) on the coast of Africa and South-East Asia and laid claim to a number of islands (for example, Mayotte 1841, Tahiti 1842, New Caledonia 1853). France also began to expand its influence in Algeria into the interior during this period. However, it was not until after the Franco-Prussian War of 1871 that a more sustained forward policy of territorial occupation began to be pursued in Sub-Saharan Africa and South-East Asia. This 'new imperialism' is usually associated with Prime Minister Jules Ferry, although by the time he intervened much of the actual staking out of new territorial claims had already been undertaken by men on the ground, often acting on their own initiative. Nonetheless, Ferry gave explicit support to France's new policy of colonial expansion, which he justified by reference to a combination of economic demands, political motives and the 'civilising mission'. Protectorates were established over Tunisia in 1881 and Tonkin in 1883. The Ferry government fell in 1885 following a clash with Chinese troops in Tonkin, but despite this setback further formalisations of French control of overseas territories followed: the government-general of Indo-China was created in 1887, that of French West Africa (Afrique Occidentale Française) in 1895, Madagascar in 1896 and French Equatorial

Africa (Afrique Équatoriale Française) in 1910. In the face of widespread public indifference to colonial expansion, this process was driven forward in Paris largely by the *parti colonial* (colonial lobby), comprising a heterogeneous group of colonial enthusiasts.

The assumed racial and cultural superiority of the colonisers was used to legitimise colonial conquest. By denying or ignoring the existence of indigenous cultures, French governments justified colonial occupation through the use of force, whether actual or threatened. Even in those cases where treaties were signed, no one could pretend that the balance of power between the coloniser and the colonised was an equal one. The reality of occupation was the extensive expropriation of land and/or labour, denial of political rights, exploitation of natural resources and cultural and religious confrontation, resulting often in widespread resistance to French rule. It was the everyday implications of these French imperial policies that form the basis of many literary works.

Tony Chafer

LITERARY WORKS
Diallo, Bakary [1926] (1985), *Force-Bonté*, Paris: ACCT/ Nouvelles Éditions Africaines.
Gueye, Amadou Lamine (1966), *Itinéraire africain*, Paris: Présence Africaine.
Kane, Cheikh Hamidou (1961), *L'Aventure ambiguë*, trans. as *Ambiguous Adventure* (1972) Katherine Woods, London: Heinemann.
Mapaté-Diagne, Ahmadou (1920), *Les Trois Volontés de Malick*, Paris: Larousse.
Maran, René (1921), *Batouala: Véritable roman nègre*, trans. as *Batouala* (1973) Barbara Beck and Alexandre Mboukou, London: Heinemann.

HISTORIES
Chafer, Tony and Amanda Sackur (eds) (2002), *Promoting the Colonial Idea: Propaganda and Visions of Empire in France*, Basingstoke: Palgrave.
Gann, Lewis H. and Peter Duignan (eds) (1969–75), *Colonialism in Africa 1870–1960*, 4 vols, London: Cambridge University Press.
Gifford, Prosser and William Roger Louis (1971), *France and Britain in Africa. Imperial Rivalry and Colonial Rule*, London and New Haven: Yale University Press.
Meyer, Jean, Jean Tarrade and Annie Rey-Goldzeiguer (1991), *Histoire de la France coloniale 1. Des origines à nos jours*, Paris: Armand Colin.
Cooke, James J. (1973), *New French Imperialism 1880–1910: The Third Republic and Colonial Expansion*, Newton Abbott: David and Charles.
Persell, Stuart M. (1983), *The French Colonial Lobby, 1889–1938*, Stanford, CA: Hoover Institution Press.
Mahir, Saul and Patrick Royer (2001), *West African Challenge to Empire: Culture and History in the Volta-Bani Anticolonial War*, Athens, OH: Ohio University Press.

Internal Colonialism

France was already undergoing a process of cultural centralisation before the 1789 revolution, but this increased as a result of Jacobin state centralism during the revolutionary era. At the same time, an overt campaign of 'linguistic terror' emerged against languages other than French (Brunot 1937). Nineteenth-century steps towards colonial integration of provinces and regions peaked in the 1830s (when Algerian colonisation began) and the 1880s. Such moves were in step with African colonisation, and used similar methods in the area of education (particularly to enforce the speaking of French). François-Auguste de Romieu (1800–55) proposed 'a sort of colonial régime' to remedy the paucity of French-speakers and combat the mentality he encountered in Brittany (1831; see Balcou and Le Gallo 1987). Similar crusading statements by state functionaries and *intellectuels* have been noted in the various regions down to the present day. Fear of armed 'natives' motivated the diversion of an army raised in Brittany away from Paris in 1870, an event bitingly commemorated by Tristan Corbière's poem 'Pastorale de Conlie'. Bretons, Normans and other rural dwellers were considered uncivilised and a disgrace to enlightened France.

Elements of colonial discourse can be found in the nineteenth-century travel writing of such writers as Mérimée, Michelet, Stendhal, Flaubert, and in novels by Balzac and Hugo which stress the ignorance and backwardness of the provincial peoples. The romantic cliché of the empty land, ready for *francisation*, can also be viewed as another colonial trope. Corbière subverted this derogatory view in statements where he poses as 'Bâtard de Créole et de Breton' (see his poem 'Paris', 1873), laying claim to a regional hybridity. Poet Armand Robin (Brittany) furthered this subversion, expanding it to include mechanisms of state power. Xavier Grall, Paol Keineg (Brittany), Robert Lafont and René Nelli (Occitania) stress the destructive effects of linguistic dispossession, cultural alienation and exile, while at the same time criticising the excesses and absurdities of centralisation.

Some of the first applications of the colonial model to peripheral regions and territories annexed by France in the course of its history date from the time of the Algerian War of Independence (1954–62). Elements of this analysis were present in nationalist political movements in Brittany before then. (Anti-)colonial terminology was more widely used from the 1960s, however, particularly in relation to Brittany (Lebesque 1970) and Occitania (Lafont 1971). It stressed the authoritarian nature of French republicanism, the economic desertification of the regions and the quaint stereotypes to which regional cultures were confined. The principal effects of French colonisation within the state borders of France have been: expansion of administrative power, led by an élite from outside the historical region; economic exploitation and disempowerment of the regions; political centralisation in Paris; and, above all, linguistic and cultural imperialism leading to cultural uniformisation.

Éamon Ó Ciosáin

LITERARY WORKS

Corbière, Tristan (1873), *Les Amours jaunes*, Paris: Librairie du XIXe Siècle; Glady Frères.
Grall, Xavier (1981), *Solo et autres poèmes*, Quimper: Calligrammes.
— [1965] (1986), *Le Rituel breton, poème lyrique*, Quimper: Calligrammes.
Keineg, Paol (1982), *Le Poème du pays qui a faim*, Taulé: Bretagnes.
Lebesque, Morvan (1970), *Comment peut-on être Breton?*, Paris, Seuil (see esp. Chaps 3–5).
Robin, Armand [1940] (1970), *Ma Vie sans moi*, Paris: Gallimard.

HISTORIES

Balcou, Jean and Yves Le Gallo (eds) (1987), *Histoire culturelle et littéraire de la Bretagne*, 3 vols, Paris and Geneva: Champion and Slatkine (see esp. vols 1 and 2).
Brunot, Ferdinand (1937), *Histoire de la langue française Volume IX, la Révolution et l'Empire*, Paris: Armand Colin.
Citron, Suzanne (1987), *Le Mythe national*, Paris: Éditions Ouvrières.
Jeanjean, Henri (2000), 'La Décolonisation française et le mouvement occitaniste', *Mots Pluriels* 16, see http://www.arts.uwa.edu.au/Motspluriels/MP1600hjj.html

Lafont, Robert (1971), *Décoloniser en France. Les régions face à l'Europe*, Paris: Gallimard.
— (1993), *La Nation, l'état, les régions*, Paris: Berg International (see esp. section on 'Le Colonialisme intérieur', pp. 81–90).
Williams, Heather (2003), ' "Séparisianisme", or internal colonialism', in Charles Forsdick and David Murphy (eds), *Francophone Postcolonial Studies: A Critical Introduction*, London: Arnold, pp. 102–11.

Massacres

The links between colonialism and various forms of violence are persistent and long-standing. In the *Ancien Régime* empire, the successful institution and perpetuation of slavery in the Caribbean depended on the deployment of generalised and often trivialised violent practices that dehumanised enslaved people and attempted, despite constant resistance and even revolt, to deny their active agency. Atlantic slavery may itself be seen as a result of the genocide – through disease and massacre – of the indigenous populations of the Caribbean, and increasing attention is being paid to the destruction of First Peoples as a result of French expansionism in North America. According to Olivier Le Cour Grandmaison, it was, however, under the republican empire that such violence – and in particular the massacre – was actively and systematically yoked to the practices of colonial expansion. The most prominent nineteenth-century instances of such an overt policy are found in the annexation of Algeria, with the notorious *enfumades* of General Bugeaud represented in Assia Djebar's *L'Amour, la fantasia* (1985).

Jean-Paul Sartre (1964) was one of the first to suggest that the use of massacre was systematic throughout French colonial expansion, and Yves Benot (2001) has revealed the ways in which such violence was entrenched as the inevitability of decolonisation became apparent in the aftermath of World War II. The increasing brutality of the Algerian War explains in part this strategy, but recent access to relevant archives has permitted exploration of the ways in which regional variations within decolonisation conceal a common set of colonial ideologies and practices in which the repeated use of massacre was widespread. The French Fourth Republic relied heavily on violent suppression of any manifestations of anti-colonialism in its overseas possessions (as well as, latterly, at home) in order to protect the coherence of empire. Some of the more prominent of these massacres – Thiaroye (Senegal) in 1944, Sétif (Algeria) in 1945, Madagascar in 1947 and Paris in 1961 – have attracted sustained literary attention and are the subject of a series of novels, plays and poems. Kateb Yacine's *Nedjma* (1956), for instance, explores the ways in which the Algerian massacres of 1945 played a central role in its author's own personal evolution and in the development of Algerian nationalism. More recently, the postcolonial massacres that occurred during the 1994 Rwandan genocide have inspired a project entitled 'Rwanda: Écrire par devoir de mémoire', involving ten contemporary writers including Boubacar Boris Diop, Tierno Monenembo, Véronique Tadjo and Abdourahman Ali Waberi.

Charles Forsdick

Literary Works
Daeninckx, Didier (1984), *Meurtres pour mémoire*, trans. as *Murder in Memoriam* (1984) Liz Heron, London: Serpent's Tail.
Diop, Boubacar Boris (1981), *Le Temps de Tamango, suivi de Thiaroye terre rouge*, Paris: L'Harmattan.

Djebar, Assia (1985), *L'Amour, la fantasia*, trans. as *Fantasia, an Algerian Cavalcade* (1993) Dorothy S. Blair, Portsmouth, NH: Heinemann.

Kateb, Yacine (1956), *Nedjma*, Paris: Seuil.

Lallaoui, Mehdi (2001), *Une nuit d'octobre*, Paris: Éditions Alternatives.

Rahimanana (2001), *Nour, 1947*, Paris: Le Serpent à Plumes.

Sartre, Jean-Paul (1964), *Situations V: Colonialisme et néo-colonialisme*, trans. as *Colonialism and Neocolonialism* (2001) Azzedine Haddour, Steve Brewer and Terry McWilliams, London and New York: Routledge.

Sassine, Williams (1976), *Wirryamu*, Paris: Présence Africaine.

HISTORIES

Benot, Yves [1994] (2001), *Massacres coloniaux 1944–1950: la IVᵉ république et la mise au pas des colonies françaises*, Paris: La Découverte.

Einaudi, Jean-Luc [1991] (2001), *La Bataille de Paris: 17 octobre 1961*, Paris: Seuil.

Marc Ferro (ed.) (2003), *Le Livre noir du colonialisme. XVIe-XXIe siècle: De l'extermination à la répentance*, Paris: Laffont.

El Kenz, David (ed.) (2005), *Le Massacre, objet d'histoire*, Paris: Gallimard.

House, Jim and Neil MacMaster (2006), *Paris 1961: Algerians, State Terror and Memory*, Oxford: Oxford University Press.

Le Cour Grandmaison, Olivier (2005), *Coloniser, Éxterminer: sur la guerre et l'état colonial*, Paris: Fayard.

Levene, Mark and Penny Roberts (eds) (1999), *The Massacre in History*, New York and Oxford: Berghahn.

Planche, Jean-Louis (2006), *Sétif 1945. Histoire d'un massacre annoncé*, Paris: Perrin.

Tronchon, Jacques (1986), *L'Insurrection malgache de 1947: essai d'interprétation historique*, Paris: Karthala.

Migrancy

In postcolonial critical discourse, migrancy – with its associations of rootlessness, exile and hybridity – has come to embody the very indeterminacy said by some critics to define the postcolonial condition. However, this focus on a generalised, and sometimes ahistorical notion of migrancy has frequently given rise to geographical simplifications that ignore the different identities of the migrant and underplay the reasons for, and complex nature of, the mobility triggered by colonisation. The international nature of French colonisation triggered not just the inward movement of (former) colonial subjects to France and other destinations but also the outward movement of French citizens to the colonies. Literary texts and literary history provide an extraordinary insight into the reasons for this migrancy and the multidirectional nature of its flow. For example, the importance of the outward movement of French personnel (military, administrative, religious, educational) to the colonies is underscored by numerous texts from the colonial era. The encounter between French and 'Other' cultures which such texts document also suggests the development of contact zones which would in turn influence the development of the centripetal migration of colonised subjects to France. Indeed Bakary Diallo's autobiographical portrait of a Senegalese soldier in France, *Force-Bonté*, Ousmane's Socé's depiction of a Senegalese 'native exhibit' in the 1931 Exposition Coloniale, *Mirages de Paris*, and Taos Amrouche's account of a female Tunisian student in Paris,

Jacinthe noire, all suggest some of the diverse reasons for migration to France during the colonial era.

However, whether we are dealing with colonial or postcolonial migrancy to or from the colonies, it is crucial not to elide fundamental distinctions between migrants themselves. Although migrancy may well be underwritten by a universal notion of exile and *déracinement*, issues of class, ethnic identity and gender all play a fundamental role in shaping the migrant experience. Literary representations have played a vital role in questioning neat assumptions and highlighting the ways in which socio-economic realities and power relations structure migrant experiences. To take the example of French Indo-China, a careful comparison of André Malraux's *La Voie royale*, Gabrielle Vassal's *Mes trois ans d'Annam* (the journal of a privileged British-born wife of a French doctor) and Marguerite Duras' auto-fictional descriptions of the life of her impoverished, white, widowed mother in colonial Indo-China reveals the impossibility of proposing a homogeneous portrait of the French overseas colonial migrant. Together, these texts reveal how, despite their relatively privileged position and overlapping trajectories, French citizens in the colonies had differential access to power, status and wealth based on gender and professional identity.

With regard to post/colonial movement *to* France, literature has also contributed greatly to our understanding of important similarities and distinctions between different experiences of migrancy. For example, representations of the colonised by formerly colonised intellectual migrants to France invariably foreground an exilic dimension. The central migrant characters of novels such as Cheikh Hamidou Kane's *L'Aventure ambiguë* (1960) and Pham Van Ky's *Des Femmes assises çà et là* (1964) are united by a profound sense of cultural alienation provoked by the clash between their culture of origin and the racism and intolerance of a French culture they had believed to be more 'progressive'. It would be wrong to assume, however, that post/colonial literature has upheld the tenuous distinction between the 'poetic' nomadism of the intellectual migrant and the implicitly less complex psychological reality of the socio-economic migrant. For example, texts such as Rachid Boudjedra's *Topographie pour une agression caractérisée* (1975) are powerful articulations of the cultural and mental trauma of the voiceless subjects of postcolonial mass migration whose movement frequently tends to be explained solely in terms of modern capitalist developments. Other texts, such as Driss Chraïbi's *Les Boucs* (1955) and Ousmane Sembene's *Le Docker noir* (1956), are careful to show that, despite the very different backgrounds of the educated intellectual and illiterate labourer, migrancy can reveal, in highly unexpected ways, how their respective psychological and cultural realms overlap.

If colonial texts about migrancy (whether to or from France) call into question neat divisions between 'centre' and 'periphery' and their respective associations with unqualified notions of 'modernity' and 'tradition', postcolonial literary representations of migrancy have raised important questions about citizenship, cultural integration and national literatures. 'Immigrant' literature in particular has received a growing amount of critical attention, much of it focused on works by 'Beur' authors, but also on texts by Sub-Saharan African and Caribbean authors such as Calixthe Beyala, Alain Mabanckou and Gisèle Pineau. With its emphasis on questions of social and cultural integration in post-war France, its portrayal of conflicting hybrid identities and its interrogation of the concept of 'home', this literature illustrates how migrancy still underwrites much of what we have come to recognise as contemporary diasporic culture in France. But by embracing plurality and multiculturalism, such writing has also been hugely influential in developing a critical discourse that moves us beyond narrow definitions of a unified or essentialist 'national' literary culture.

While the significance of migrancy and the transformative impact of inward and outward migration on French culture are now widely accepted in critical discourse, less well-known, perhaps, is the centrifugal migration of colonised and formerly colonised subjects to other destinations. The geographical spread of colonial and postcolonial migrations makes it impossible to provide an exhaustive account of the axes of movement involved, but examples might include the migration of rural populations to urban locations within colonised territories, the transatlantic (Africa–Americas) movement depicted in Lamine Diakhaté's *Chalys d'Harlem* (1978) and Maryse Condé's *Hérémakhonon* (1976) or the type of Caribbean migration to North America exemplified in the life, and certain works, of writers such as Dany Laferrière. However, whatever the routes concerned, what is significant is the continued relevance of literary representations of migrancy for our understanding of the multidirectional nature of contemporary cultural flows.

Aedín Ní Loingsigh

LITERARY WORKS

Amrouche, Taos (1947), *Jacinthe noire*, Paris: Charlot.

Boudjedra, Rachid (1975), *Topographie idéale pour une agression caractérisée*, Paris: Denoël.

Chraïbi, Driss (1955), *Les Boucs*, trans. as *The Butts* (1985) Hugh A. Harter, Boulder, CO: Lynne Rienner.

Condé, Maryse (1976), *Hérémakhonon*, trans. as *Heremakhonon* (1999) Richard Philcox, Boulder, CO: Lynne Rienner.

Diakhaté, Lamine (1978), *Chalys d'Harlem*, Dakar: Nouvelles Éditions Africaines.

Diallo, Bakary [1926] (1985), *Force-Bonté*, Paris: ACCT/ Nouvelles Éditions Africaines.

Kane, Cheikh Hamidou (1961), *L'Aventure ambiguë*, trans. as *Ambiguous Adventure* (1972) Katherine Woods, London: Heinemann.

Malraux, André (1935), *La Voix royale*, trans. as *The Royal Way* (1935) Stuart Gilbert, London: Random House.

Sembene, Ousmane (1956), *Le Docker noir*, trans. as *Black Docker* (1987) Ros Schwartz, London: Heinemann.

Van Ky, Pham (1964), *Des Femmes assises çà et là*, Paris: Gallimard.

Vassal, Gabrielle (1912), *Mes trois ans d'Annam*, Paris: Hachette.

HISTORIES

Blanchard, Pascal and Nicolas Blanchard (1998), *De l'indigène à l'immigré*, Paris: Gallimard.

Edwards, Brent Hayes (2003), *The Practice of Diaspora: Literature, Translation, and the Rise of Black Internationalism*, Cambridge, MA and London: Harvard University Press.

Hargreaves, Alec G. and Mark McKinney (eds) (1997), *Post-Colonial Cultures in France*, London and New York: Routledge.

Manceron, Gilles (2003), *Marianne et les colonies: une introduction à l'histoire coloniale de la France*, Paris: La Découverte.

Narratives and Fictions of Empire

France has a long and rich tradition of writing about its non-European 'Other': from Montaigne to Diderot to Verne, French literature has consistently engaged with the cultures that it encountered overseas in a fashion that ranges from curious exoticism to the 'scientific' racism that became the norm in the nineteenth century (for example, in the works of Gobineau and Renan). However, France's colonial possessions have occupied a relatively minor place in French literature; the 'fact' of empire does not enjoy the same role within nineteenth-century French literature that it does in British literature; from the deportation to Australia of Jack Magwitch in Charles Dickens' *Great Expectations*, to Rider Haggard's African adventures (*King Solomon's Mines* and *She*), and Rudyard Kipling's stories of imperial India (*Kim*).

In an exploration of the potential historical reasons that might explain these differences, it seems evident that the 'broken' nature of France's colonial history has played its part. For France 'lost' virtually all of its *Ancien Régime* empire to the British in the aftermath of the Seven Years' War (1756–63): this means that empire was a more ambiguous issue for the French than it was for the British, whose sense of imperial grandeur went from strength to strength as the nineteenth century progressed. Even after the French began to rebuild an empire in the mid-to-late nineteenth century, there appears to have been reluctance on the part of French authors to write about the colonies. For example, the hugely popular exotic novelist Pierre Loti rarely if ever set his work in France's colonies. One exception is his novel *Le Roman d'un spahi* (1881), which relates the tragic story of a French soldier who dies in France's West African wars: for many critics, the colonial setting of the work destroys the power and attraction of the exotic so present elsewhere in Loti's work. The French colonial expansion of this period was largely fuelled by a small, but powerful, coalition of right-wing military and business interests, which meant that empire was a vastly contested issue in France until early in the twentieth century. For instance, the campaigning journalist and politician Paul Vigné d'Octon published a widely read book, *La Gloire du sabre* (1900), which castigated French military adventurism in Africa, focusing on the brutality of the infamous Voulet-Chanoine expedition of 1898. It was not until the conquest was complete that the colonies became an accepted part of the political landscape, a process reinforced by the participation of colonial troops in the defence of the metropolitan 'homeland' in World War I.

When something called *littérature coloniale* finally emerges in France at the beginning of the twentieth century, it explicitly defines itself in opposition to exotic literature. The novelist and colonial administrator in Algeria, Robert Randau, soon became one of the major theorists of French colonial literature. He believed that exoticism was the literature of mere 'tourists', who knew little of the lands that they visited, whereas colonial literature was written by those who had lived in the colonies and were thus able to present a more realistic and 'scientific' account of France's civilising mission. This opposition between exotic literature and colonial literature has remained an important feature of French critical debates, whereas in Britain colonial and exotic literatures are generally argued, especially within the field of postcolonial studies, to be inextricably intertwined.

By the 1930s, and particularly in the aftermath of the hugely successful Exposition Coloniale of 1931, which finally forged a place for the empire in the French popular imagination, there was great demand for fictional and journalistic accounts of life in France's colonies: through its mix of information and entertainment, the Exposition fuelled a desire for what might be termed a 'colonial exotic'. However, there remained a concern that France remained unable to produce its own equivalent to Kipling, a writer who could cement the empire in the popular imagination. The ambiguity of the French attitude towards Kipling, and the British Empire in general, had already been illustrated by the hugely successful novel, *Dingley, l'illustre écrivain* (1902), by Jean and Jérôme Tharaud. Kipling is thinly disguised as Dingley, an egotistical and pompous individual, obsessed with both his own and his nation's destiny; in its excessive critique of Kipling, the novel reveals the enduring French rivalry with, and jealousy of, the British.

Although the 1930s marked the apogee of French colonialism and the glorification of empire, it would be misguided to think that all criticism of colonialism had simply disappeared with the completion of colonial conquest at the turn of the century. The anticolonialism of the Parti Communiste Français (PCF) and of the Surrealists, who organised a counter-exhibition denouncing the Exposition Coloniale, may have represented a marginalised position within French society, but less radical critiques of the excesses of colonialism were able to reach a wide audience. A work often described as the first anti-colonial novel in French is René Maran's *Batouala* (1921). Maran was a colonial administrator, originally from the French Caribbean, and his novel is an ironic and deeply ambiguous representation of French colonial (mis)rule, although later critics have also commented on the recurrence within the work of colonial stereotypes of Africans. In his journalistic reportage, *Voyage au Congo* (1927), the celebrated French author, André Gide, denounces French colonial exploitation, as does Louis-Ferdinand Céline in his novel, *Voyage au bout de la nuit* (1932). Criticism also emerged from unlikely sources: Michel Leiris, who participated in the official, scientific mission from Dakar to Djibouti, describes the pillage and destruction brought about by the European presence in Africa, in his monumental work, *L'Afrique fantôme* (1934).

Of course, it was not only the French who forged narratives and fictions of empire. By the early part of the twentieth century, a growing number of texts written by the colonised themselves began to appear. Two texts by ex-colonial soldiers, the infamous *tirailleurs sénégalais*, offer hugely contrasting visions of French colonialism. Bakary Diallo's *Force-Bonté* (1926) is an autobiographical account of the author's voyage from lowly shepherd to servant of the powerful (but good) French Empire; however, despite the glowing terms used to describe French colonialism, the text also acts as an unconsciously ironic commentary on French colonial hypocrisy, as Diallo suffers horrific injuries in World War I but is refused citizenship by the country that he had helped to defend. Lamine Senghor's neglected text *La Violation d'un pays* (1927) provides an outright attack on colonialism; in this polemical tale, Senghor, who was close to the PCF, depicts French colonialism as a violent enterprise designed to rape the colonies of their natural resources.

The 1930s witnessed a less radical but far more influential response to empire by the colonised. A group of black students from Africa and the Caribbean came together to forge the concept of Negritude, which countered colonialist stereotypes about black people and sought to forge a positive vision of an essential pan-African identity. Closely associated with the Martiniquan, Aimé Césaire, and the Senegalese, Léopold Sédar Senghor (not to be confused with Lamine Senghor), Negritude constituted an enabling concept for a generation of colonised intellectuals, and found its most powerful literary expression in Césaire's epic poem, *Cahier d'un retour au pays natal* (1939). Another hugely important, but less well-known, colonised text from the 1930s is Ousmane Socé's *Mirages de Paris* (1937), which relates the story of an educated African who attends the 1931 Exposition Coloniale, and, as its title suggests, becomes disillusioned at the inferior status accorded to the colonised.

The post World War II period witnessed the rapid development of literature from the colonies. Semi-autobiographical texts such as Mouloud Feraoun's *Le Fils du pauvre* (1950) and Camara Laye's *L'Enfant noir* (1953) relate the stories of Africans who have been 'assimilated' by their progression through the colonial education system. However, more radical and aggressive texts would soon appear, attacking the entire imperial project rather than simply seeking its reform. Kateb Yacine's *Nedjma* (1956) uses the French massacre of thousands of civilians at Sétif and Guelma in May 1945 as the platform for a highly experimental novel, which mythologises the independence struggle as a quest for the mysterious woman of the title who represents Algeria. In his novel, *Les Bouts de bois de dieu* (1960), Ousmane Sembene also takes a real event, the West African railway strike of 1947–8, as the canvass for an epic-realist portrait of the anti-colonial nationalist movement, which he presents as nothing less than the transformation of African society as a whole.

In his polemical text, *Discours sur le colonialisme* (1955), Aimé Césaire denounces several centuries of European racism and compares colonialism to the barbarism of the Nazis. The Tunisian Albert Memmi presents a more balanced but no less powerful account of the relationship between coloniser and colonised in *Portrait du colonisé* (1957). Perhaps the most powerful anti-colonial voice is that of Martiniquan psychiatrist Frantz Fanon (a former student of Césaire), whose work has been central to the development of postcolonial studies. In *Peau noire, masques blancs* (1952), Fanon discusses the mental trauma of colonialism for the colonised in the French Caribbean, for whom assimilation into the republic means wearing a white 'mask'. After transferring to a psychiatric hospital in Algeria in the early 1950s, Fanon rallied to the cause of the Algerian independence movement, le Front de Libération Nationale (FLN), in its war of independence against France. Fanon soon became the FLN's most eloquent spokesman and, in a series of passionate essays, of which *Les Damnés de la terre* (1961) has been the most influential, he denounces the hypocrisy and violence of French colonialism, and calls for the development of a new humanism, which would reflect the lives and cultures of people of all colours.

Amongst the various French voices raised against colonialism, the philosopher Jean-Paul Sartre enjoyed a prominent role. He was at the forefront of opposition to the war in Algeria and he sponsored the work of colonised authors such as Senghor and Fanon by writing prefaces to their work (although the ambiguity of this process has been explored by recent critics). Sartre's anti-colonial stance contrasts with the position of Albert Camus, his erstwhile collaborator within the existentialist 'movement'. Camus was born and raised in Algeria and he felt a strong attachment to his homeland. As a young, left-leaning writer in the 1930s, he had distanced himself from Randau and the *roman colonial*, and had sought to forge a new Algerian literature, with a group of friends, who became known as the École d'Alger. However, Camus was unable to support calls for Algerian independence, for Algeria was his home. Consequently, many postcolonial critics have taken their lead from Edward Said in viewing Camus' work as inextricably bound up in the French colonial enterprise, while critics in France have generally taken the opposite approach, choosing to divorce Camus from his colonial context. In recent years, there has developed a more nuanced approach to Camus's work, which acknowledges the colonial context within which he wrote and seeks to explore the ambiguity of his position as Algerian *and* French. (A similar process is under way in relation to Marguerite Duras' novels on her childhood in Indo-China.)

In the post-independence period, formerly colonised authors continued to create narratives of empire, in order to reassess the legacy of colonialism. Alongside important historical work, there have been countless memoirs – the multi-volume collections of Amadou Hampâté Bâ and Birago Diop – and works of fiction – Emmanuel Dongala, *Le Feu des origines* (1987), Ahmadou Kourouma, *Monnè, outrages et défis* (1990). In France itself, there continued to be a political and historical reflection on French colonialism but it often seemed as though a general amnesia had settled over the popular imagination. The popular detective novelist Didier Daeninckx was one of the first authors to revisit the legacy of empire in his work. Daeninckx uses the Exposition Coloniale as a means of exploring French attitudes towards race, in his novel, *Cannibale* (1998), as has Eric Orsenna. Daeninckx's novel, *Meurtres pour mémoire* (1984), uncovers the 'forgotten' history of the *Bataille de Paris* on 17 October 1961, when a peaceful FLN demonstration was brutally suppressed by the police. Several hundred protestors were killed and their bodies thrown into the Seine in a brutal act of repression that was never acknowledged by the French authorities. The *Bataille de Paris* was subsequently revisited by the Franco-Algerian author, Leïla Sebbar, in her novel, *La Seine était rouge* (1999), and it forms the backdrop to the recent *Palme d'Or*-winning film, *Caché* (2005). This uncovering of the particularly traumatic legacy of the Algerian War has been a marked feature of French culture since the late 1990s: Algerian-born French authors, such as Jacques Derrida and Hélène Cixous, have begun to explore the repressed memories of their Algerian childhood, while many Algerian authors, Assia Djebar in particular, have consistently examined the shared history of France and Algeria in their work. Although the emergence of these texts might suggest that a mature reflection on empire may now be possible, other factors indicate that, in fact, colonial nostalgia may be on the rise: the infamous February 2005 law, which sought to oblige history teachers to promote 'the benefits of colonialism' and the creation of museums celebrating *l'Algérie Française* suggest that the struggle over the memory of empire is only just beginning.

David Murphy

Literary Works

Camus, Albert (1939), *L'Etranger*, trans. as *The Outsider* (1961) Stuart Gilbert, Harmondsworth: Penguin.

Duras, Marguerite (1984), *L'Amant*, trans. as *The Lover* (1985) Barbara Bray, London: Collins.

Daeninckx, Didier (1984), *Meurtres pour mémoire*, trans. as *Murder in Memoriam* (1984) Liz Heron, London: Serpent's Tail.

Daeninckx, Didier (1998), *Cannibale*, Lagrasse: Verdier.

Gide, André (1927), *Voyage au Congo*, Paris: Garnier-Flammarion.

Kane, Cheikh Hamidou (1961), *L'Aventure ambiguë*, trans. as *Ambiguous Adventure* (1972) Katherine Woods, London: Heinemann.

Maran, René (1921), *Batouala: Véritable roman nègre*, trans. as *Batouala* (1973) Barbara Beck and Alexandre Mboukou, London: Heinemann.

Orsenna, Eric (1988), *L'Exposition coloniale*, Paris: Seuil.

Sebbar, Leïla (1999), *La Seine était rouge*, Paris: Thierry Magnier.

Sembene, Ousmane (1960), *Les Bouts de bois de Dieu*, trans. as *God's Bits of Wood* (1995) Francis Price, London: Heinemann.

Histories

Baumgart, Winfried (1982), *Imperialism: The Idea and Reality of British and French Colonial Expansion*, Oxford: Oxford University Press.

Fanon, Frantz (1961), *Les Damnés de la terre*, trans. as *The Wretched of the Earth* (1967) Constance Farrington, Harmondsworth: Penguin.

Girardet, Raoul (1972), *L'Idée coloniale en France de 1871 à 1962*, Paris: Hachette.

Loutfi, Martine Astier, *Littérature et colonialisme: L'Expansion coloniale vue dans la littérature romanesque française, 1871–1914*, Paris and The Hague: Mouton.

Memmi, Albert (1957), *Le Portrait du colonisé*, trans. as *The Colonizer and the Colonized* (1990) Howard Greenfeld, London: Earthscan.

Said, Edward W. (1993), *Culture and Imperialism*, London: Vintage.

Sartre, Jean-Paul (1964), *Situations V: Colonialisme et néo-colonialisme*, trans. as *Colonialism and Neocolonialism* (2001) Azzedine Haddour, Steve Brewer and Terry McWilliams, London and New York: Routledge.

Todorov, Tzvetvan (1989), *Nous et les autres: Réflexions sur la diversité humaine*, trans. as *On Human Diversity: Nationalism, Racism and Exoticism in French Thought* (1993) Catherine Porter, Cambridge, MA: Harvard University Press.

Vigné d'Octon, Paul [1900] (1984), *La Gloire du sabre*, Paris: Quinette.

Negritude

The term *Négritude* or Negritude applies both to the cultural movement which emerged through the work of a small group of black poets and intellectuals based in Paris in the 1930s and to the ideology which could be inferred from their writings and their art. The core message of the movement was that black people should actively counter negative images circulating within Western society, by asserting and celebrating their unique cultural, spiritual and racial identity. Ideologically, therefore, Negritude owed much to the intellectual influence of transatlantic campaigners like W. E. B. Du Bois as well as to the Harlem Renaissance of the 1920s which had employed the same strategy of celebrating black cultural identity as a counter to the racism of North American society. In effect, Negritude exploited the same essentialist notions that racists had themselves used, as Sartre recognised when he approvingly dubbed it 'an anti-racist racism'. The notion of a brotherhood of black peoples belonged to a confrontational logic that was no doubt tactically justified in a context of resistance to colonial oppression, but later generations would come to reject it as simplistic and sterile.

Aimé Césaire (1913–) and Léopold Sédar Senghor (1906–2001) are generally acknowledged as founders of the *Négritude* movement. They were students together in Paris in the 1930s where, with Léon Damas, they founded the short-lived but influential review *L'Étudiant noir* in 1935. They also collaborated with Alioune Diop in the creation of the highly successful review *Présence Africaine* in 1947. Helped in the beginning by André Breton, Césaire went on to achieve prominence as a poet, playwright and essayist, firstly with his epic *Cahier d'un retour au pays natal* and thereafter with numerous collections of poetry, plays and essays, including a major study of Toussaint Louverture. Since 1947 he has combined his literary work with a career in politics. For over four decades he held his seat as *député* in the French Assembly and the post of mayor of Fort de France. Senghor too combined a highly successful literary career with periods of high political office. His output included numerous collections of poetry and a series of prose essays, *Libertés* (6 vols), on a range of cultural, political and philosophical themes (Volumes 1 and 3 include his own writings on *Négritude*). He was elected to the Académie Française in 1983. In recent years, the political positions of both Césaire and Senghor have been increasingly questioned by a younger generation of intellectuals: the former for his position on independence for the Antilles and the latter for the highly dependent relationship maintained with France under his presidency.

Patrick Corcoran

LITERARY WORKS

Césaire, Aimé (1955), *Discours sur le colonialisme*, trans. as *Discourse on Colonialism* (1972) Joan Pinkham, New York and London: Monthly Review Press.

— (1983), *Aimé Césaire: The Collected Poetry*, trans. Clayton Eshleman and Annette Smith, Berkeley, CA: University of California Press.

— (1969), *Une Tempête*, trans. as *A Tempest* (2000) Philip Crispin, London: Oberon.

— (1939), *Cahier d'un retour au pays natal*, trans. as *Notebook of a Return to the Native Land* (2001) Clayton Eshleman and Annette Smith, Middletown, CT: Wesleyan University Press.

Senghor, Léopold Sédar (ed.) (1948), *Anthologie de la nouvelle poésie nègre et malgache de langue française*, preface J.-P. Sartre, Paris: Presses Universitaires de France.

— (1964), *Liberté I: Négritude et Humanisme*, Paris: Seuil.

— (1973), *Poèmes*, Paris: Seghers.

HISTORIES

Arnold, A. James (1981), *Modernism and Negritude: The Poetry and Poetics of Aimé Césaire*, Cambridge, MA: Harvard University Press.

Jack, Belinda (1996), *Negritude and Literary Criticism: The History and Theory of 'Negro-African' Literature in French*, London: Greenwood Press.

Kesteloot, Lilyan (1991), *Black Writers in French: A Literary History of Negritude*, Washington, DC: Howard University Press.

Miller, Christopher (1998), *Nationalists and Nomads: Essays on Francophone African Literature and Culture*, Chicago, IL: University of Chicago Press (esp. pp. 1–54).

Wilder, Gary (2005), *The French Imperial Nation-State: Negritude and Colonial Humanism between the Two World Wars*, Chicago, IL: University of Chicago Press.

Neo-colonialism

Neo-colonialism is the theory of continued political and economic control in former colonies, and was first defined by Sartre (1964). In 1965 the Ghanaian anti-colonial leader Kwame Nkrumah defined it thus: '[T]he State . . . is, in theory, independent and has all the outward trappings of international sovereignty[;] [i]n reality its economic system and thus political policy is directed outside' (1966). This could be applied to France's relationship with its former colonies; as recently as 2005, French troops in Côte d'Ivoire were attacked in the streets of Abidjan as 'neo-colonial' aggressors supporting a corrupt régime. France has increasingly used its former colonial status to impose its (and the European Union's) will on (so-called) postcolonial countries especially in Africa. Senegal in the 1970s was a good example of a victim of French and European 'neo-colonial' control under the guise of 'co-operation' (N'Dongo 1976). Neo-colonialism has been sent up in a range of African and Caribbean novels in French, beginning with the work of Ouologuem, and then of Depestre, Sony Labou Tansi, Mimouni and Sembene.

Neo-colonialism may also manifest itself in different patterns of dependency. In 1946 France divided its colonial territories into 'counties' and 'territories', the former – Guyane, Martinique, Guadeloupe and La Réunion called 'DOM' ('Départements d'Outre-Mer') – being attached to the metropolitan mainland of France, and the rest 'TOM' ('territoires'), which soon all became independent (with the exceptions of the Pacific islands in Polynesia and Wallis and Futuna). The incorporation of the DOM into

France proper and the continuation of the TOM status in the Pacific have merely encouraged the neo-colonial tag.

The classic statement, and then critique, of neo-colonialism points out that, like the
USA which created colonies 'without hoisting a flag', to 'some extent, after 1965, France
has at times emulated this policy in black Africa'; indeed 'economic bonds' have survived,
perpetuating dependence 'in another form', and 'to the joint benefit of the mother countries and of the new local middle classes' (Ferro 1997). Algeria (as in the case of the British
West Indies) organised direct exchanges of workers (to the motherland) and 'consultants'
to the ex-colonies. Algerians in 1993 are quoted as saying that the 'élites' who took over
after decolonisation do not govern the country: it is the military and FLN-state: 'So we have
not stopped being occupied.' Thus there has been a new, second form of neo-colonialism
during 'the thirty glorious years' of post-decolonisation for European ex-colonial powers. If
the first privileged continued economic ties with the mother country, the second form now
consists of 'the institutionalisation of the connivance between the new leaders of the
colonies and the political or financial circles in the colonial countries' (Ferro 1997).

'Dependency' and 'unequal' theorists such as Gunder Frank and Samir Amin, who
describe the neo-colonialist world as divided between the rich 'North' and the exploited
'South', seem not to have been vindicated, for trade in the post-war period began simply,
and quite sharply, to avoid poorer regions of the world (Callinicos 1994). Indeed, in today's
globalised economy, 'neo-colonialism' could be applied equally to other parts of the world.
Kelly (1995) suggests, for instance, that France itself stood in the immediate post-war
period 'in a neo-colonial client relationship' with the United States, paying 'for modernity
by acceptance of American domination'.

Andy Stafford

LITERARY WORKS
Depestre, René (1979), *Le Mât de Cocagne*, trans. as *The Festival of the Greasy Pole* (1990)
    Carrol F. Coates, Charlottesville, VA: University Press of Virginia.
Mimouni, Rachid (1982), *Le Fleuve détourné*, Paris: Laffont.
Ouologuem, Yambo (1968), *Le Devoir de violence*, trans. as *Bound to Violence* (1971) Ralph
    Manheim, London: Heinemann.
Sembene, Ousmane (1981), *Le Dernier de l'empire*, trans. as *The Last of the Empire* (1983)
    London: Heinemann.
Tansi, Soni Lab'ou (1979), *La Vie et demie*, Paris: Seuil.

HISTORIES
Callinicos, Alex (1994), 'Imperialism Today', in Alex Callinicos, John Rees, Chris
    Harman and Mike Haynes, *Marxism and The New Imperialism*, London: Bookmarks,
    pp. 11–66.
Dumont, René (1966), *False Start in Africa*, London: Sphere.
Ferro, Marc (ed.) (1997), *Colonization. A Global History*, London: Routledge.
Kelly, Mike (1995), 'Fast Cars, Clean Bodies', in *French Cultural Studies* 6 (3): 413–18.
N'Dongo, Sally (1976), '*Coopération' et néo-colonialisme*, Paris: Maspero.
Nkrumah, Kwame [1965] (1966), *Neo-colonialism. The Last Stage of Imperialism*, New York:
    International Publishers Co. Ltd.
Sartre, Jean-Paul (1964), *Situations V: Colonialisme et néo-colonialisme*, trans. as *Colonialism
    and Neocolonialism* (2001) Azzedine Haddour, Steve Brewer and Terry McWilliams,
    London and New York: Routledge.

North Africa and the Middle East

The complex cultures of North Africa and the Middle East have been formed by successive civilisations of which the most important resulted from the Arab conquests and the consequent Islamisation that began in the seventh century AD. What followed over the next 1,200 years was not the imposition of a single, all-embracing régime, culture or monolithic religion, but the absorption of further Arab invasions, the rise and fall of different dynasties, the evolution and political exploitation of different theological movements within Islam and much artistic and scientific innovation. This evolution continued under the Ottoman Empire that had effective control over the eastern and southern coasts of the Mediterranean (excluding Morocco) by 1535. By the beginning of the nineteenth century, Ottoman rule was largely nominal in North Africa and had been entirely usurped by Muhammad'Ali in Egypt during his period as pasha (1805–48). It was against this background that France established its colonial presence in the course of the nineteenth century through different modalities of intervention, including military invasion (Algeria) and the exploitation of debt repayments and local conflict (Morocco and Tunisia). Once in situ, French imperialism took on a variety of forms: intensive colonisation in Algeria; protectorates in Morocco and Tunisia; a League of Nations mandate in Syria and Lebanon.

FRENCH IMPERIALISM IN THE EASTERN AND SOUTHERN MEDITERRANEAN
Though Napoleon's expeditionary force invaded Egypt in 1798 and remained until 1805, it can largely be seen as the opening of a new campaign in the war with Britain. Once peace was restored within Europe in 1815, European powers began to seek new markets, cheaper sources of raw materials and outlets for investment. By at least 1825, France had established a consular and commercial presence across the Mediterranean from Mount Lebanon to Morocco. Trading terms and conditions were largely determined by European powers who combined negotiation with the threat of military intervention. In 1830, French forces attacked Algiers in order to shore up popular support in France for the restoration monarch Charles X. Viewed retrospectively this event was to determine France's future presence in North Africa. The invasion was carried out under the pretext of ridding the Mediterranean of piracy and of restoring French honour in a dispute over French debts claimed by the exasperated *dey* (the title of the ruler) of Algiers. The conquest of Algiers was swift and its future became the subject of debate when the July Revolution of 1830 replaced Charles X with the parliamentary monarch, Louis Philippe. The ad hoc arrival of colonial settlers along with trading interests and a concern to compete with British imperialism meant that Algiers became the base for a colony that was eventually integrated into metropolitan France. The most significant early resistance to French colonisation was by 'Abd al-Qādir (Abdelkader) who, after a number of military and diplomatic successes, surrendered to General Bugeaud in 1847, following French scorched-earth tactics and the withdrawal of Moroccan support. He remained an important symbol for Algerian resistance. Further uprisings took place in the early 1850s but were local in scale, and large areas of Algeria were run by the military officers of the *Bureaux arabes* by the 1860s. Assia Djebar's novel, *L'Amour, la fantasia* (1985) captures moments from this period within a narrative that juxtaposes autobiographical fragments, the invasion of 1830 and the War of Independence.

With Algeria more or less secured, France was able to concentrate on expanding its presence across North Africa. The period 1850–80 was marked by the accumulation of enormous debts by modernising rulers in Egypt, Tunisia and Morocco. This led to Western governments insisting on the repayment of loans drawn down from banks such as the Crédit Mobilier and the Erlanger banking house. By 1869 Tunisia was bankrupt and an international financial committee (made up of British, French and Italian representatives) was imposed upon the country's government. Tunisia's incremental transformation into a French protectorate was accelerated and completed between 1881 and 1883. The *bey* (the title of the ruler) remained as nominal head of state but France was in effective control of finances and foreign relations. Morocco retained its uncertain independence until 1912 when France divided the country with Spain with the agreement of Great Britain.

In the Ottoman controlled Mount Lebanon region of Syria, France, by adopting a policy of protecting the Christian Maronite community, was able to exercise considerable political influence. This influence was reinforced after the region witnessed the massacre of Maronites in 1860 by Druze Muslims who sought to protect their traditional ascendancy. As Ottoman attempts to protect the Maronites were inadequate, French forces intervened and the Organic Regulation of 1861 was drafted giving the area autonomy under a Christian governor appointed by the Ottoman sultan. French influence was further reinforced by the establishment of French schools such as the Université de Saint-Joseph founded by the Jesuits in Beirut in 1875.

The final decades of the nineteenth century saw the consolidation of the French colony in Algeria after the last major uprising, led by Muhammad al-Moqrani in 1871, was suppressed. Following the insurrection, the administration of the colony was ceded to a civilian authority and over the next thirty years the legal, administrative and social structures of French Algeria took definitive shape. The institutions were designed to benefit the colonists and to discriminate against the indigenous population. Europeans and, after 1870, indigenous Jews, enjoyed the rights of French citizenship; Algerians who wished to remain Muslim were excluded from citizenship. Vast areas of land were appropriated by European colonists after the insurrection of 1871. By 1900 one-sixth of the population was of European origin.

By contrast, in Egypt, a country that retained a degree of autonomy until the imposition of the British protectorate in 1882, French influence was such that throughout the reign of Muhammad'Ali (1805–48) many government cadres were trained by the French and sometimes educated in France. France was viewed as a counterweight to British control: in 1854 Ferdinand de Lesseps was granted a concession to construct the Suez Canal and when a system of mixed courts was introduced in 1875, it was based on the French civil code. The importance of French cultural influences should not be underestimated. The majority of foreign language schools were French and provided education to writers such as Albert Cossery in the 1920s. However, the rise of Arab nationalism, and Nasser's leadership of Egypt during and after the Suez crisis of 1956 that involved French, British and Israeli forces against the Egyptians, dimmed the prestige of French culture.

NATIONALISM AND THE WARS OF INDEPENDENCE

World War I (1914–18) brought about the collapse of the Ottoman Empire. During the war, Britain encouraged Arab nationalism within Arab areas under Ottoman control but secretly drew up an agreement with France (the Sykes–Picot Agreement of 1916) that envisaged French control of Lebanon and Syria and British control of Transjordan and Palestine. The secret agreement was given a semblance of international sanction when in 1920 the League of Nations incorporated the division under its mandate system. The French mandate involved the expansion of Lebanon at the expense of Syria and was welcomed by the Maronite community. Charif Majdalani's historical novel, *Histoire de la grande maison* (2005), gives an insight into the pro-French perspective of the Christian community in the 1920s. The mandate was especially resented in Syria where there was an insurrection in 1925–7 and, after further confrontations in 1945, France recognised Syrian independence in 1946. Lebanon gained its independence during World War II after British forces confronted the pro-Vichy administration in Beirut in 1943.

Meanwhile, in Algeria, Morocco and Tunisia opposition to French imperialism took a number of diverse forms. In Morocco, the interior was the scene of the Rif War that lasted from 1921 until 1926 and involved tribal forces led by Abd el-Krim. Thereafter, national-ist sentiment either continued to be channelled through tribal groupings or, increasingly, focused on the sultan. The presence of British and American troops during World War II galvanised opposition and led to the founding of the Istiqlāl (Independence) Party in 1943. Moroccan independence was finally conceded in 1956 due to the astute leadership of the sultan, Muhammad V, and after civil unrest and violence.

In Tunisia, opposition to the French protectorate was routed through a single party. The Destour (Constitution) Party, formed in 1920, had its roots in the Young Tunisian move-ment. Under the leadership of Habib Bourguiba the Neo-Destour Party was formed in 1934 in an effort to establish a broader, more popular, base. Bourguiba remained as the head of the party until the French, embroiled in the War of Independence in Algeria, and having already conceded independence to Morocco, agreed to the formation of a republic in 1956 with Bourguiba as President, a position he held until 1987. The impact of France's protec-torates in Morocco and Tunisia, and the modernising policies in the 1940s and 1950s, are given allegorical form by the Moroccan novelist Driss Chraïbi in *La Civilisation, ma mère!* . . . (1972). Their psychological effects are trenchantly critiqued by the Tunisian writer Albert Memmi in novels and essays including *La Statue de sel* (1953) and *Portrait du colonisé* (1957).

Where Moroccans could focus on the sultan and Tunisians had the unifying force of a single party and leader, Algerian nationalism was composed of at least three strands. One strand developed from the modernising revival of Islam in the 1920s that led Sheikh Abd al-Hamid ben Badis to found the Association des Oulémas in 1931. It was popular amongst the rural classes and, initially, it looked for the extension of French citizenship to all Algerians. A second strand was the largely secular and liberal Young Algerian movement which, though loosely organised, had Ferhat Abbas at its head. The movement attracted members of the indigenous élite who, at first, campaigned for French citizenship. Finally, there was a strand of radical nationalism associated with Messali Hadj, a founding member of the independence party, Étoile Nord-Africain (ENA), in 1926. The first two strands moved towards the idea of complete independence after metropolitan efforts to extend the democratic franchise in Algeria were persistently thwarted by the colonial administration in the 1930s and 1940s. This political frustration was compounded by the memory of the massacre of thousands of Algerians in May 1945 following anti-colonial riots in Sétif, Constantine and Guelma and by the kind of urban and rural poverty that Mohammad Dib represents in novels such as *Le Métier à tisser* (1957). But it is Kateb Yacine's novel *Nedjma* (1956) that brilliantly brings Algeria's colonial past to bear upon the tensions of the 1950s. It was at this time that a mil-itant group formed the Front de Libération Nationale (FLN) and instigated the War of Independence in November 1954. It was brought to an end in 1962.

POST-INDEPENDENCE

Since independence, the largely authoritarian governments of North Africa, Egypt and the Middle East have sought to put in place industrial and agricultural reforms, and educational and administrative structures, that would answer nationalist expectations. The decline of secular Arab nationalism following the 1967 Arab–Israeli war coincided with growing dissatisfaction with poverty, high unemployment, a housing shortage and agricultural decline. These problems were aggravated by a rising population, national debt and the economic recession of the mid-1970s.

In Algeria the official policy of 'Arabisation' was especially resented by the Berbers of Kabylia who wanted their language to be officially recognised. The demonstrations and strikes that characterised the 'Berber Spring' of March–April 1980 were contained by the FLN government but the resentment persisted. The protests of 1988, however, were general as people protested against abuses of power and sought better economic and social conditions. The government responded with violence, demonstrators were killed. Disenchantment with the political class led to a void that radical Islam exploited. Violent attacks against the army and their supporters began in the late 1980s. Rattled by popular discontent and by the ascendancy of radical Islam, the government demonstrated greater tolerance and allowed free elections. The strategy backfired, however, as the first round of elections saw the Front Islamique du Salut (FIS) poll well in December 1991. The second round was cancelled. The violence that ensued ravaged Algeria throughout the 1990s and resulted in the death of over 100,000 people. Boualem Sansal's novel, *Le Serment des barbares* (1999), is an anatomy of this tragic period and the myths that sustain the FLN and FIS.

Lebanon was also devastated by a civil war. Andrée Chedid's novel *La Maison sans racines* (1985) alternates between Beirut in 1932 and the outbreak of the civil war in 1975. The bloody after-tremors of the war lasted until the 1990s and included the Israeli invasions of 1978 and 1981. France, Italy and the United States sent troops in a failed attempt to impose a peace that eventually emerged following a long period of UN intervention. The war left over 150,000 dead and pushed almost a quarter of the population to emigrate. The Lebanese economy was shattered but is now recovering its old dynamism.

In 1976, Morocco annexed the former Spanish territory of Western Sahara. This was resisted by Polisario guerrillas who sought independence and were supported by Algeria. Though tensions between Algeria and Morocco have eased, the matter remains unresolved despite, as yet, unsuccessful UN attempts to organise a plebiscite. This external conflict did not ease social pressures within Morocco. The demonstrations and riots that erupted in 1981, for example, left hundreds dead. Indeed, the ruling élites across the region remain unable to provide adequate employment, housing or hope to a young population. Emigration, which has been a reality and solution for many North Africans, Syrians and Lebanese since the late nineteenth century (see Amin Maalouf's account of his Lebanese family's history in *Origines* [2004]), has become increasingly difficult and, even when successful, can lead to complex issues as explored by the Moroccan novelist Tahar Ben Jelloun in *Partir* (2006).

Patrick Crowley

LITERARY WORKS

Ben Jelloun, Tahar (2006), *Partir*, Paris: Gallimard.

Chedid, Andrée (1985), *La Maison sans racines*, Paris: Flammarion.

Chraïbi, Driss (1972), *La Civilisation, ma mère! . . .* trans. as *Mother Comes of Age* (1984) Hugh A. Harter, Washington, DC: Three Continents Press.

Dib, Mohammad (1957), *Le Métier à tisser*, Paris: Seuil.

Djebar, Assia (1985), *L'Amour, la fantasia*, trans. as *Fantasia: An Algerian Cavalcade* (1989) Dorothy Blair, London: Quartet.

Kateb, Yacine [1956] (1961), *Nedjma*, trans. Richard Howard, New York: Braziller.

Maalouf, Amin (2004), *Origines*, Paris: Bernard Grasset.

Majdalani, Charif (2005), *Histoire de la grande maison*, Paris: Seuil.

Memmi, Albert (1957), *Le Portrait du colonisé*, trans. as *The Colonizer and the Colonized* (1990) Howard Greenfeld, London: Earthscan.

Sansal, Boualem (1999), *Le Serment des barbares*, Paris: Gallimard.

HISTORIES

Abun-Nasr, Jamal M. (1975), *A History of the Maghrib*, Cambridge: Cambridge University Press.

Ezran, Maurice (1998), *La France en Égypte: Histoire et culture*, Paris and Montreal: L'Harmattan.

Ganiage, Jean and Jean Martin (1994), *Histoire contemporaine du Maghreb*, Paris: Fayard.

Issawi, Charles (1982), *An Economic History of the Middle East and North Africa*, New York: Columbia University Press.

Khalaf, Samir G. (2002), *Civil and Uncivil Violence in Lebanon: A History of the Internationalization of Communal Conflict*, New York: Columbia University Press.

Thompson, Elizabeth (2000), *Colonial Citizens: Republican Rights, Paternal Privilege and Gender in French Syria and Lebanon*, New York: Columbia University Press.

Orientalism and Exoticism

The terms Orientalism and exoticism are frequently seen as synonymous, being employed to describe colonial representations of non-European cultures, which designate those cultures as inferior and monolithic, reinforcing a perceived centre/periphery hierarchy. While the construct of 'the Orient' exists in works that predate colonisation, Orientalism is most frequently associated with a heterogeneous corpus of artistic and scholarly works produced during the period of French and British colonial expansion eastwards from the beginning of the nineteenth century until the end of World War II. French Orientalism focuses primarily on North Africa and – particularly from the 1870s – 'Indo-China'. French colonial activity in North Africa was initiated by Napoleon's invasion of Egypt in 1798, though the first conquest of France's second phase of empire was that of Algiers in 1830. Colonial expansion intensified after France's defeat by Prussia in 1871. Literary examples of French Orientalism include, amongst others, Lamartine's *Voyage en Orient*, Flaubert's *Salammbô* and Loti's *Un pèlerin d'Angkor*. While Orientalist texts are historically and regionally diverse, they have in common their reduction of certain territories and their inhabitants to their representative parts, which they firmly locate in space and time, maintaining the illusion of the distance between the constructed identities of self and Other. Exoticism is frequently equated with this process of 'othering', or reduction and definition of non-European cultures as absolutely and essentially 'different' from European cultures, for colonial ends. However, while Orientalism and exoticism overlap, the terms do not coincide entirely. A conflation of Orientalism and exoticism obscures the latter's semantic flexibility; unlike Orientalism, exoticism is not inextricably bound to a one-way perception and representation of 'otherness'. Before the period of colonial expansion, exoticism had been understood as a relative concept. A desire to return to the neutral understanding of exoticism can be discerned in the work of Victor Segalen, from which 'difference' emerges not as inherent and monolithic but as diverse and inassimilable.

Postcolonial literature in French engages with and contests both exoticism and Orientalism (the latter may be seen as a specific brand of colonial exoticism). In the work of Leïla Sebbar (of Franco-Algerian descent) and of the francophone Algerian writer Assia Djebar, Orientalist images, such as Delacroix's *Femmes d'Alger dans leur appartement* (1834), are reappropriated and reused to articulate the specificity and diversity of their postcolonial female identities. Other postcolonial writers reappropriate not the exoticist image itself but the *concept* of exoticism, renegotiating its seemingly rigid definition as a colonial term. Literature by writers such as Bernard Dadié and Rachid Boudjedra enacts an 'inversion' of exoticism, whereby France itself becomes the site of the post/colonial traveller's desire. However, distinct from literature in the tradition of Montesquieu's *Lettres persanes*, such literature highlights the complexity of 'returning' the Westerner's exoticising gaze, owing to residual traces of colonial power relations.

Siobhán Shilton

LITERARY WORKS

Boudjedra, Rachid (1975), *Topographie idéale pour une agression caractérisée*, Paris: Denoël.
Dadié, Bernard (1959), *Un Nègre à Paris*, trans. as *An African in Paris* (1994) Karen C. Hatch, Urbana, IL: University of Illinois Press.
Djebar, Assia (1980), *Femmes d'Alger dans leur appartement*, Paris: Des Femmes.
Flaubert, Gustave (1863), *Salammbô*, Paris: Michel Lévy Frères.
Lamartine, Alphonse de (1835), *Souvenirs, impressions, pensées et paysages pendant un voyage en Orient (1832–1833)*, Brussels: Louis Hauman et Comp. Libraires.
Loti, Pierre [1911] (1989), *Un pèlerin d'Angkor*, Paris: La Nompareille.
Sebbar, Leïla (1982), *Shérazade: 17 ans, brune, frisée, les yeux verts*, Paris: Stock.
Segalen, Victor (1978), *Essai sur l'exotisme*, trans. as *Essay on Exoticism* (2002) Yaël Schlick, Durham, NC: Duke University Press.

HISTORIES

Donadey, Anne (2001), *Recasting Postcolonialism: Women Writing between Worlds*, Portsmouth, NH: Heinemann.
Pratt, Mary Louise (1992), *Imperial Eyes: Travel Writing and Transculturation*, London and New York: Routledge.
Said, Edward [1978] (1995), *Orientalism: Western Conceptions of the Orient*, Harmondsworth: Penguin.
Santaolalla, Isabel (ed.) (2000), *'New' Exoticisms: Changing Patterns in the Construction of Otherness*, Amsterdam: Rodopi.

Race and Ethnicity

Race and ethnicity are both terms that fail to account for at once the simplicity and complexity of the social and historical dimensions in which they are used. Hargreaves rightly speaks of 'race' (there is no race other than the human race), acknowledging that the very use and existence of the concept 'race' *within* human society is linked to racial discrimination; and the definition of ethnicity, a less suspect concept, insists upon the group identification that this implies (1995). Since the increase of non-European (and non-Christian) migration to Europe coterminous with the post-war period, these two terms have earned wider currency, applied as they are in France to Maghrebi, African and South Asian populations leaving behind France's colonies and looking for work in the metropolitan centre. Indeed, after the United States, France has been traditionally, as a proportion of its population, the greatest acceptor of immigration in the world, a welcoming *terre d'asile* (land of asylum) since the French Revolution. France still has the highest proportion of mixed marriages in Europe, and its republican values promote the equality of any French individual before the law, in a progressive, non-communitarian way, preferring integration to multiculturalism (Pierrot 1998; Rosello 2003), and hesitating over affirmative action (Amselle 2003). However, there are two major problems in the republican model: firstly, the access to French citizenship is fraught with difficulties of bureaucracy, exclusivity and inconsistency, and secondly, there is a 'blindspot' within the French state to racial discrimination (Chapman and Frader 2004).

The ghettoisation of mainly North Africans, Africans and Caribbeans has afflicted minority peoples disproportionately in France, leading to a spiral in which housing, schooling and local job opportunities combine to provide a perennially-limited outlook for social advancement (Hargreaves 1995), graphically described by Charef (1983). The search for employment and lack of decent affordable housing has encouraged the French social services to build rapidly, in the belt of wastelands around major cities and near major workplaces, self-contained, cheap and quickly-erected tower-block accommodation in which to house a new immigrant workforce, replacing the communist-dominated suburbs with a black population (Stovall 2003). After World War II France needed a large workforce to rebuild the country, even to the point of welcoming illegal immigration (Silverman 1992), and its colonial (and then postcolonial) subjects have provided this service since, with the tragedies described by Sembene (1962). Despite this post-war phenomenon, it is important to stress that France has relied on foreign labour since the nineteenth century (Fysh and Wolfreys 2003). Despite the integration, even assimilation, into French society that these peoples ended up achieving, this was not without 'racial' and 'ethnic' tension with the host population; indeed, just as economic crisis following the oil crisis of 1973 brought about a sharp increase in racist attacks in France (Ben Jelloun 1984), so economic crises at the end of the nineteenth and in the first half of the twentieth century increased discrimination against other nationalities. In other words, France in modern times has regularly shown a contradictory attitude towards foreign populations, both welcoming in times of need and, in times of economic crisis, ready to see different cultural groupings played off against each other (of which the occupation and collaboration with Nazi Germany were an extreme example).

Indeed, history plays a crucial role in the experience of minorities in France, especially in relation to war and the decolonisation of empire. As a parachutist in the Algerian War Le Pen was an unrepentant torturer, the Parisian police chief and former official in Algeria, Maurice Papon, was responsible for the massacre of 200 Algerians in the Seine in October 1961. Those Algerians who fought on the side of the French (the *harkis*) have fared little better, denounced by their compatriots and forgotten by France. Nevertheless, historic moments such as the anti-fascist immigrant network, the MOI, during World War II, the founding in 1949 of the Mouvement contre le Racisme et pour l'Amitié entre les Peuples (MRAP) and the discovery of anti-colonialism by anti-racists around the same time (Lloyd 1998), the agitation against the Algerian and then Vietnam Wars and then the uprising of May 1968, all allowed a glimpse of unity between workers and students from different cultural backgrounds (described by Etcherelli [1969]), an experience that paved the way for the slow demand for equality across the 1970s and 1980s, including the 'Marche des beurs' for equality and justice in 1984, the founding of SOS-Racisme and the 'Touche pas à mon pote' (Leave my mate alone) campaign, of GISTI, of the anti-fascist 'Ras l'front'. The 1990s saw an 'ethnic' population now tired of promises of integration, equality and representation (Bouamama 1994). Pride in ethnicity is evident in francophone writing (Beyala 1987), although pigmentocracy has not disappeared, especially in the Caribbean (Fanon 1952), and inter-racial disputes are in evidence in France. In a country where black and Asian people are rarely visible (either in political representation or in the media), the appointment in 2005 of the Franco-Algerian writer Azouz Begag as Minister for 'Exclusion' was an important step, and suggests further that immigrant populations have an important role to play in French politics (Wihtol de Wenden 1994).

Andy Stafford

LITERARY WORKS

Begag, Azouz (1989), *Béni ou le paradis privé*, Paris: Seuil.
Beyala, Calixthe (1987), *C'est le soleil qui m'a brûlée*, trans. as *The Sun hath Looked upon Me* (1996) Marjolijn de Jager, London: Heinemann.
Charef, Mehdi (1983), *Le Thé au harem d'Archi Ahmed*, trans. as *Tea in the Harem* (1989) Ed Emery, London: Serpent's Tail.
Daeninckx, Didier (1984), *Meurtres pour mémoire*, trans. as *Murder in Memoriam* (1984) Liz Heron, London: Serpent's Tail.
Etcherelli, Claire (1969), *Élise ou la vraie vie*, trans. as *Elise, or the Real Life* (1970) June P. Wilson and Walter Benn Michaels, London: Deutsch.
Fanon, Frantz (1952), *Peau noire, masques blancs*, trans. as *Black Skin, White Masks* (1986) Charles Lam Markman, London: Pluto.
Sembene, Ousmane (1974), *Tribal Scars and Other Stories*, trans. Len Ortzen, London: Heinemann.

HISTORIES

Amselle, Jean-Loup (2003), *Affirmative Exclusion. Cultural Pluralism and the Rule of Custom in France*, Ithaca, NY: Cornell University Press.
Ben Jelloun, Tahar (1984), *Hospitalité française*, Paris: Seuil.
Bouamama, Said (1994), *Dix ans de marche des beurs*, Paris: Desclée de Brouwer.
Chapman, Herrick and Laura Frader (eds) (2004), *Race in France: Interdisciplinary Perspectives on the Politics of Difference*, Oxford: Berghahn.
Fysh, Peter and Wolfreys, Jim [1998] (2003), *The Politics of Racism in France*, London: Macmillan.
Hargreaves, Alec (1995), *Immigration, 'Race' and Ethnicity*, London and New York: Routledge.
Lloyd, Catherine (1998), *Discourses of Anti-Racism in France*, Aldershot: Ashgate.
Pierrot, Alain (1998), 'Le Multiculturalisme: Un langage faussement correct', in G. Ferréol (ed.), *Intégration, lien social et citoyenneté*, Lille: Septentrion, pp. 229–61.
Rosello, Mireille (2003), 'Tactical Universalism and New Multiculturalist Claims in Postcolonial France', in Charles Forsdick and David Murphy (eds), *Francophone Postcolonial Studies*, London: Arnold, pp. 135–44.
Silverman, Maxim (1992), *Deconstructing the Nation: Immigration, Racism and Citizenship in Modern France*, London: Routledge.
Stovall, Tyler (2003), 'From Red Belt to Black Belt: Class and Urban Marginality in Twentieth Century Paris', in Sue Peabody and Tyler Stovall (eds), *The Color of Liberty. Histories of Race in France*, Durham, NC: Duke University Press, pp. 351–69.

Taguieff, Pierre-André (1998), *La Couleur et le sang. Doctrines racistes à la française*, Paris: Mille et Une Nuits.

Wihtol de Wenden, Catherine (1994), 'France: Immigrants as Political Actors', in Martin Baldwin-Edwards and Martin Schain (eds), *The Politics of Immigration in Western Europe*, Ilford: Frank Cass, pp. 91–109.

Religion

The links between religion and colonialism are both long-standing and complex. Missionary activity often accompanied, or even preceded, military and commercial expansion, with Christianity in particular operating (often unofficially) as one element of the 'civilising mission' that served as an alibi for the annexation and control of vast portions of the French Empire. Indigenous religions were often targeted as 'primitive', although in certain regions – such as Indo-China – they were more actively tolerated. Religion thus serves not only as a means of understanding pre-colonial cultures, but also reveals the complex transformations and associated syncretism that resulted from colonial contact.

Christian missionaries benefited, then, from the favourable climate created by European colonialism. Urbanisation, Western culture and civilisation, science and technology all played a major role, but the missionaries themselves were additionally equipped with a range of practical, evangelical strategies. They preached salvation, offering various humanitarian services that included the rehabilitation of enslaved people and the socially disadvantaged. Medical care played an equally effective part in disposing many traditional adherents to accept the Christian message, as did pastoral visits and vocational training for young men and women. The promotion of formal school education proved to be by far the most viable and effective instrument of conversion developed by Christian missionaries among many traditional African groups. Thousands of young men and women who attended such schools also received instruction in the faith, accepted baptism while at school and so broke the ancestral covenant with traditional deities. It was not too long before the missionaries of the different mainstream Christian groups began to harvest the fruit of their vigorous evangelical efforts. On the other hand, as a universalist religion, Islam has confronted indigenous religious systems whose solutions to problems of interpretation, social structure and fertility have often appeared more effective to the local community. The relevance and immediacy of esoteric cults and the figurative art of shrines, which in theory fundamentalist Islam rejects, have clearly not diminished under the impact of Muslim practice. Indigenous religious systems, embedded in particular social formations and economic activities, have therefore rarely been eliminated by contact with Islam. The process of Islamisation has more often produced creative adaptations of traditional categories (including Maraboutism in North and West Africa). Wider socio-economic changes have more abruptly destroyed the cultural nexus in which indigenous beliefs thrived. Where this has happened, Islam has often been the beneficiary, but rarely the sole cause.

Across the Atlantic, under the Ancien Régime, the Caribbean peoples had been devastated by new epidemic diseases introduced by the Europeans and the Africans imported as slaves, whose own lives were régimented by slavery and the demands of profit-minded Europeans. While the dominant religions on the Caribbean islands are all variants of Christianity, a few religions have developed as a result of African slaves combining their spiritual practices with the beliefs of their captors. These Creole religions were most often practised on French and Spanish islands where Roman Catholicism was the religion of the whites, the best-known of them being the *vaudou* (commonly spelled 'voodoo' or 'vodun') practised in Haiti. This kind of blending of religions extends beyond the Caribbean, regardless of whether postcolonial identities revolve strictly around religion. The primal religions of Africa are, by definition, not world religions with missionary and expansionist goals, that is, not competitors with Christianity. Their tenacity and the resilience of their traditional rituals and spiritual practices nevertheless pose a challenge to a religion like Islam, with its holistic demands on its followers. The elimination of pagan practices has therefore been a theme of Muslim reformists, and featured strongly in early missionary literature. It has been the ideological intent of Islam to present itself convincingly as more essentially African, despite having a history of repudiating many aspects of African cultures. However, in many African cultures, social groups have identified themselves with other religious systems, such as totemic symbols, and established a sense of continuity between nature and Man through belief systems marked by animistic tendencies. By contrast, in the monotheism of the Islamic and Judeo-Christian tradition, God existed before the creation of anything else. Interestingly, the Jewish impact on identity in many parts of the francophone world has taken a variety of forms, the most important of which are the actual presence of Jews in those regions, the direct religious impact of Judaism, the indirect impact of Judaism through Christianity and Islam, Jewish experiences as a comparative metaphor for Africa, and the Jewish economic and political penetration of Africa, especially in the twentieth century.

The advent and spread of Islam and Christianity has precipitated a different kind of religious situation in contemporary Africa. A vast majority of the population have abandoned the religions of their ancestors to convert to one or other of the missionary faiths now present on the continent. Despite the many problems and difficulties confronting such converts, it is indisputable that both Christianity and Islam have sunk deep roots in Africa. The religious desire for the sacred has survived the move away from traditional cultures, characterised by the dominant role of a single religion, towards the current pluralism. The Jewish presence in Africa, though more modest than that of the Arabs, reveals a specificity of its own. North Africa has accommodated clusters of Sephardic Jews, mainly immigrants from Spain and Portugal who went to Africa in the fifteenth and sixteenth centuries, and Ashkenazi Jews, from Northern and Eastern Europe, who emigrated to Africa in the nineteenth and twentieth centuries. The largest Jewish community today is in Morocco, home, before the creation of Israel, to more than a quarter of a million Jews. However, every Arab-Israeli war created new fears among Moroccan Jews, leading them to flee and thus reducing very considerably their presence there. In Algeria, a mass exodus of the Jewish population, who acquired French citizenship through the Cremieux Decree of 1870, began in 1962 after the conclusion of the Evian Agreements, which secured Algerian national independence. In Tunisia, the island of Jerba is inhabited by a mixed Jewish-Berber population, whose unique culture raises questions about where the boundaries of the nation should be drawn and demands a re-examination of who belongs and who is excluded. Berbers, Jews and – in Egypt – Copts identify themselves with the interests of a minority not only out of principle, but also out of an awareness that, in order to gain attention and acceptance, they need to occupy a position on the periphery that allows them to retain their own character, while contributing to the overall development of society.

North and Sub-Saharan African indigenous religious cultures have shared certain common experiences by virtue of their similar, antagonistic relationships to the dominant colonial or postcolonial hegemonic cultures, which have generally sought to marginalise them. It is assumed that ideological unity is most likely to be achieved by secularism, either due to the nature of the cultures themselves or due to the French legacy of *laïcité*; but in the last few decades, religion has assumed greater social, and even political, importance in many parts of North Africa. Islam, for example, has reasserted itself as a symbol of identity in the independent countries that occupy the territories of what were once the large unitary states of Numidia or Tamazgha in the North and Guinea or the Yolofs in the West. In part, Islam's role in defining identities follows directly from the failure of other post-independence ideologies, especially Nasserism, Boumedienism, Bourguibism, Baathism, Senghorism and, to some extent even, the materialism of the liberal capitalism that has inspired the kingdom of Morocco. However, Berbers have cultures that are sometimes much more deeply rooted in religious experience than that of the Arab-Muslim population. They have traditions, almost comparable with Confucianism, that make their civilisation notable for its secularity. Collective celebrations and commemorations have, for instance, played a crucial role in the emerging sense of identity found among local and regional populations and indeed the 2 million Berbers living in France.

The general set of problems explored by the literature of recent years concerns the ways in which people from North and Sub-Saharan Africa interpret and appropriate their own religious history to address current issues and difficulties that their own religious traditions face. Some writers and scholars from these regions have appropriated the sacred texts and histories of their own religious traditions, namely Islam, Christianity and Judaism, as they construct their contrasting visions for these religions in the modern world. For example, Mariama Bâ, Assia Djebar and Fatima Mernissi combine various principles from modern feminism, including the equality of the sexes, with certain traditional Islamic principles, such as the unity of believers before God, as they construct their distinctive feminist-oriented visions of Islam in the contemporary world. Tahar Ben Jelloun, Edmond Amran El Maleh, Mohamed Arkoun, Jean Amrouche and Léopold Sédar Senghor combine humanism and modern notions of human rights and democracy with Christian, Judaic and Islamic principles of social justice in order to construct their contrasting visions of these religions, which emphasise freedom and liberty. The contribution made by Jewish-North African writers is particularly noticeable in the development of North African literature in French. Various Jewish writers (Albert Memmi, Annie Cohen, Hélène Cixous and Edmond Amran El Maleh) have created a highly specific rhetoric, which combines simultaneously their Jewishness and their North Africanness.

In Francophone North America, there has been religious equality in Canada ever since the exclusive claims of the Church of England to be the established Church in the British North American colonies were defeated. The ultramontane tendencies of some of the French-Canadian Roman Catholic clergy led them, on occasion, to attempt to dictate to French-Canadian citizens how they should vote. But on each occasion an appeal to Rome by more liberal-minded French-Canadians brought about a moderation of the clerical attitude. In the 1960s, Quebecois society underwent the greatest liberalisation movement in its history, akin to May 1968 in France. Although at present there is no state religion and freedom of worship is sanctioned by law, the majority of the population being Catholics, the relations between Church and state are, as a rule, harmonious. Although the hierarchy and clergy are customarily treated with due consideration, Church influence over public order, education at every level, agriculture, colonisation and even industry, has been wiped out by the Quiet Revolution.

Kamal Salhi

LITERARY WORKS

Amrouche, Fadhma A. M. (1968), *Histoire de ma vie*, trans. as *My Life Story* (1989) Dorothy S. Blair, New Brunswick: Rutgers University Press.

Bâ, Mariama (1979), *Une si longue lettre*, trans. as *So Long a Letter* (1981) Modupé Bodé-Thomas, London and Portsmouth, NH: Heinemann.

Ben Jelloun, Tahar (1987), *La Nuit sacrée*, trans. as *The Sacred Night* (1989) Alan Sheridan, London: Quartet.

— [1985] (1988), *L'Enfant de sable/ The Sand Child*, trans. Alan Sheridan, London: Quartet.

Djebar, Assia (1991), *Loin de Médine*, trans. as *Far from Madina* (1994) Dorothy S. Blair, London: Quartet.

Memmi, Albert (1962), *Portrait d'un juif: L'Impasse*, trans. as *Portrait of a Jew* (1962) Elisabeth Abbott, New York: Orion Press.

— 1966, *La Libération du juif*, trans. as *The Liberation of the Jew* (1966) Judy Hyun, New York: Orion Press.

— (1953), *La Statue de sel*, trans. as *The Pillar of Salt* (1992) Edouard Roditi, Boston: Beacon Press.

Mernissi, Fatima (1990), *Sultanes oubliées: Femmes chefs d'état en Islam*, trans. as *The Forgotten Queens of Islam* (1993) Mary Jo Lakeland, Minneapolis, MN: University of Minnesota Press.

— (1994), *Dreams of Trespass. Tales of a Harem Girlhood*, Reading, MA: Addison-Wesley.

Touati, Fettouma (1984), *Le Printemps désespéré*, trans. as *Desperate Spring* (1987) Ros Schwartz, London: Women's Press.

HISTORIES

Bangura, Ahmed S. (2000), *Islam and the West African Novel*, Boulder, CO: Lynne Rienner Publishers.

Chouraki, André (1985), *Histoire des juifs en Afrique du nord*, Paris: Hachette

Dejeux, Jean (1986), *Le Sentiment religieux dans la littérature maghrébine de langue française*, Paris: L'Harmattan.

Erickson, John (1998), *Islam and Postcolonial Narrative*, Cambridge: Cambridge University Press.

Gauvreau, Michael (2005), *The Catholic Origins of Quebec's Quiet Revolution, 1931–1970*, Quebec: McGill-Queen's University Press.

Isichei, Elizabeth (1995), *A History of Christianity in Africa: From Antiquity to the Present*, Trenton, NJ: Africa World Press.

Kalu, O. U. (1980), *The History of Christianity in West Africa*, London: Longman.

Majid, Anouar (2000), *Unveiling Traditions: Postcolonial Islam in a Polycentric World*, Durham, NC: Duke University Press.

Mernissi, Fatima (1975), *Beyond the Veil: Male-Female Dynamics in a Modern Muslim Society*, Cambridge, MA: Schenkman.

— (1991), *Women in Islam: An Historical and Theological Inquiry*, trans. Mary Jo Lakeland, Oxford: Basil Blackwell.

— (1996), *Women's Rebellion and Islamic Memory*, London: Zed Books.

Moir, John S. (1959), *Church and State in Canada West: Three Studies in the Relation of Denominationalism and Nationalism, 1841–1867*, Toronto: University of Toronto Press.

Nielsen, Jorgen (1992), *Religion and Citizenship in France and the Arab World*, London: Grey Seal.

Ranger, Terence O. and Isaria Kimambo (1972), *The Historical Studies of African Religion*, Berkeley, CA: University of California Press.

Slavery and Abolition

Slavery was introduced in the French Caribbean in the first half of the seventeenth century, and by the eighteenth century had been extended to include such territories as Guyana, Reunion (then Ile Bourbon) and New Orleans. It was at its height between 1716 and 1774, at which point it was supplying 20,000 African slaves a year to the French colonies. The plantation economy was based primarily on the cultivation, refinement and export of sugar cane. There were, however, significant variations in the experience of slavery across the French-owned islands. Until 1740, for example, Martinique was by far the most important customer of the slave ships. It was overtaken later in the century, however, by Saint-Domingue (Haiti), whose independence struggle (1791–1804), leading to the foundation of the first black republic, involved the abolition of slavery during the French Revolution (1794) and its reimposition by Napoleon (1802). Slavery would not be definitively abolished in the remaining French colonies until 1848.

Many intellectuals feel that dominant accounts of the abolition of slavery unduly emphasise the role of the metropole, by insisting on the impact of the *philosophes* and the French Revolution, or by elevating the benign intervention of the French abolitionist Schœlcher, while underplaying the importance of local rebels such as Louis Delgrès. Such accounts similarly overlook the cumulative effects of *marronnage*, the phenomenon of runaway slaves, which destabilised the plantation economy. While some critics (Burton 1997) have disputed the actual extent of *marronnage* in the French Caribbean, it functions as a powerful symbolic presence in art and culture, and is most fully explored in the novels of Édouard Glissant. Recent historical work, notably that carried out by the Comité Devoir de Mémoire (the Committee for the Duty of Memory) in Martinique, has insisted on the widespread resistance to slavery across the islands of the Caribbean, and has reasserted the agency of the slaves themselves.

The traumas of slavery – crystallised in such horrors as the Middle Passage, slave infanticide and suicide, and in the brutal treatment of captured runaways – continue to haunt the Caribbean imaginary, and the subject remains oppressively present and yet, often, curiously marginal in Antillean writing.

Maeve McCusker

LITERARY WORKS

Césaire, Aimé (1956), *Et les chiens se taisaient*, Paris: Présence Africaine.

Chamoiseau, Patrick (1997), *L'Esclave vieil homme et le molosse*, Paris: Gallimard.

Condé, Maryse (1986), *Moi, Tituba, sorcière noire de Salem*, trans. as *I Tituba, Black Witch of Salem* (1992) Richard Philcox, Charlottesville, VA and London: University Press of Virginia.

Glissant, Édouard (1964), *Le Quatrième Siècle*, trans. as *The Fourth Century* (2001) Betsy Wing, Lincoln, NE: University of Nebraska Press.

HISTORIES

Burton, Richard (1997), *Le Roman marron. Études sur la littérature martiniquaise contemporaine*, Paris: L'Harmattan.

James, C. L. R. [1938] (1963), *The Black Jacobins. Toussaint Louverture and the San Domingo Revolution*, London: Vintage Books.

Kadish, Doris Y. (ed.) (2000), *Slavery in the Caribbean Francophone World. Distant Voices, Forgotten Acts, Forged Identities*, Athens, GA and London: The University of Georgia Press.

Pétré-Grenouilleau, Olivier (2004), *Les Traites négrières. Essai d'histoire globale*, Paris: Gallimard.

Price, Richard (1976), *The Guiana Maroons. A Historical and Bibliographical Introduction*, Baltimore, MD: The Johns Hopkins University Press.

Rochmann, Marie-Christine (2000), *L'Esclave fugitif dans la littérature antillaise*, Paris: Karthala.

Segal, Ronald (1995), *The Black Diaspora*, London and Boston: Faber and Faber.

Sub-Saharan Africa

The French colonial enterprise in Sub-Saharan Africa was, in large part, a product of the late nineteenth-century 'Scramble for Africa'. Between 1880 and World War I, the French Republic conquered vast swathes of the continent, which it governed as two separate administrative regions, l'Afrique Occidentale Française (AOF) and l'Afrique Equatoriale Française (AEF): AOF comprised what would become the independent states of Senegal, Mauritania, Mali, Burkina Faso, Guinea, Ivory Coast, Benin, Togo and Niger, while AEF was comprised of Cameroon, Gabon, Chad, Central African Republic and Congo. The French military and commercial presence in Africa long pre-dated the nineteenth century; France's involvement in the slave trade had led to the establishment of trading *comptoirs* along the West African coast, particularly in the Senegambian region. However, by the 1850s, France had just four small bases in this area: the *quatre communes* of Saint-Louis, Gorée, Dakar and Rufisque.

France's colonial conquest of Africa began in earnest under General Louis Faidherbe, Governor of Senegal from 1854 to 1861, who extended French control inland from its coastal possessions. By the 1880s, the full-scale conquest of Africa was under way in a series of bloody wars, which destroyed the social, political and cultural fabric of life for countless millions of Africans. This brief reminder of the violence that accompanied the French conquest of Africa provides a necessary counter-balance to France's colonial discourse of its 'civilising mission'. The vision of a largely benign France inculcating African schoolchildren with a love for the ideals of the republic and the history of *nos ancêtres, les Gaulois* has proved extremely tenacious not only in the French popular imagination but also amongst educated Africans themselves. It is as though the French colonial enterprise erred solely in its excessive attachment to its own culture, which led it to assimilate its subjects into the 'universal' culture of the republic. However, if one looks beyond colonial discourse, it becomes clear that France never genuinely attempted the assimilation of its 'natives'; indeed, for much of the colonial period, only 1 per cent–2 per cent of (male) African children attended French schools. The fact that the African relationship to French language and culture has been so central to much francophone African literature is thus less a comment on the nature of French colonialism than on the education and class background of African writers themselves.

The earliest Sub-Saharan African texts in French emerged from Senegal, France's oldest African colony. Inhabitants of the *quatre communes* were granted French citizenship at the beginning of the Third Republic and were able to elect a deputy who represented them in the French Assemblée Nationale; they were thus closely tied to the socio-cultural values of the colonial metropolis, which is not to suggest that they were completely 'alienated' from their own, local culture. Rather, early Sub-Saharan African texts deal with French colonialism as a given, with which African culture is obliged to find some form of accommodation: David Boilat's *Esquisses sénégalaises* (1853) is, as its title suggests, a series of sketches of the different ethnic groups of Senegal written by a *Métis* priest, who, although his aim is the conversion of these 'heathens', displays admiration and respect for certain of the cultures he describes; *Les trois volontés de Malick* (1920) by the schoolteacher Ahmadou Mapathé-Diagne is a simple children's story describing the benefits of French colonialism, but it does not advocate total assimilation, and seeks rather to find common ground between African and French 'values'.

Senegal's position as an 'old' colony gave it a privileged status that did not extend beyond the boundaries of the *quatre communes*. France's subjects in Senegal, as well as elsewhere in its African colonies, had no such rights until after World War II, and their lives were governed by the codes of *l'indigénat*, or direct colonial military rule. In Equatorial African colonies such as the Congo, there was a hugely exploitative form of colonialism, which sought to bleed the land of its precious raw materials, especially rubber. Consequently, Equatorial African colonies lagged behind their West African counterparts in terms of infrastructure and education, which meant that, for the first half of the twentieth century, francophone African literature was primarily a West African phenomenon. When Equatorial Africa did start to produce its own literature in French, authors such as the Cameroonians Ferdinand Oyono and Mongo Beti reflected the harshness of French colonialism in their writing.

Negritude, the first major 'school' of African writing, which emerged in the 1930s, is closely associated with the Senegalese poet (and later President from 1960 to 1980), Léopold Sédar Senghor. Negritude is a pan-Africanist concept, which seeks to counter colonialist stereotypes of Africa, and promote the positive expression of an essential black identity. Negritude writers were above all educated Africans, and colonialism appears in their work as a cultural clash, which they attempt to reconcile through their writing. For, alongside Negritude, Senghor believed in the values of *francité*, a manner of expression shared by all French-speakers: writing in French thus gives expression to a profound Franco-African hybridity, in which the values of French and African 'civilisation' could co-exist.

Camara Laye's *L'Enfant noir* (1953) is often viewed by critics as the archetypal text of Negritude. An autobiographical novel about an idyllic rural childhood, the text nostalgically documents various aspects of 'traditional' African life. As the protagonist grows up and excels within the colonial education system, he follows the well-worn path from village to town to colonial metropolis. However, the text is not merely the nostalgic evocation of a romanticised past; it is a literary intervention by an educated African that seeks to reconcile his 'traditional' African past with his francophone African present: Negritude looks forwards as much as it looks backwards. Cheikh Hamidou Kane's classic novel, *L'Aventure ambiguë* (1961), although closely associated with Negritude, dramatises the cultural encounter between Africa and Europe in a much darker fashion than the reconciliation and celebration of the values of blackness and *francité* that one finds in Senghor or Laye. Kane's protagonist Samba Diallo is taken from the harsh but spiritually enlightening rigours of the Koranic school and initiated into the cold, rational logic of the French education system. Samba cannot reconcile the competing sets of values provided by his schooling, which leads to a profound sense of alienation and, ultimately, death: French colonialism creates a form of mental trauma that afflicts its colonised subjects.

The novels of Ousmane Sembene and Mongo Beti act as powerful counter-balances to the vision of Negritude: indeed, Beti famously described *L'Enfant noir* as a 'roman rose', a rose-tinted account of African life under colonialism. Sembene and Beti are virulently anti-colonial authors who attack the injustice and hypocrisy at the heart of colonial rule. Beti's novel *Le pauvre Christ de Bomba* (1956) is a darkly ironic account of missionary activity in Cameroon, which deftly undermines the European discourse of cultural superiority through the use of comedy. Sembene's most famous novel, *Les Bouts de bois de Dieu* (1960), is a fictionalised account of the West African railway strike of 1947–8; through its epic portrayal of the strike, the novel underlines the powerful social(ist) dimension of the nationalist anti-colonial movement.

All of France's Sub-Saharan African colonies negotiated their independence in 1960, except for Guinea, which opted to leave the 'French Community' in 1958. This independence was achieved largely through peaceful means, although for much of the post-war period, anti-colonial resistance often met with fierce repression. After the initial optimism at the ending of colonial rule, there soon developed a sense of anger and disillusionment at the corruption of many of the new regimes, as well as at the continued interference by the French in African affairs: the era of neo-colonialism had begun.

The anti-colonial authors Sembene and Beti also provide an important link to the concerns of the writers of the post-independence period. Using a range of media – literature and cinema for Sembene, literature and journalism for Beti – both writers explore the situation facing the continent after the departure of the imperial powers. In *Xala* (1973), which he later remade as a powerful film, Sembene viciously satirises the African bourgeoisie, who are presented as a parasitic class, ruling Africa on behalf of their former colonial masters. Beti's *Main basse sur le Cameroun* (1972) is a devastating critique of the neo-colonial situation in his homeland, written in a hybrid style mixing journalism and fiction.

The two texts most closely associated with the growing sense of post-colonial disillusionment are Ahmadou Kourouma's *Les Soleils des indépendances* and Yambo Ouologuem's *Le Devoir de violence*, both of which were first published in the 'revolutionary' year of 1968. As well as crystallising the sense of confusion, pain and disappointment at the advent of neo-colonialism, these novels are also extremely innovative, developing new linguistic and narrative strategies, which depart from the predominantly realist texts of their predecessors. As its title suggests, *Le Devoir de violence* is primarily concerned with the oppressive nature of the fictional African society of Nakem: in a comic appropriation of the oral epic tradition, Ouologuem charts the despotism of generations of African rulers who prey on the *négraille*. A similar process is at work in Kourouma's novel, which creates a hybrid French prose style through, what at the time, was perceived as the direct translation of Malinké into French, but which later critics have, in fact, shown to be the 'invention' of a hybrid, Franco-African literary language.

The profound rupture in African literary traditions created by Ouologuem and Kourouma paved the way for a generation of younger writers who emerged in the 1970s. Their texts explore nightmarish visions of African society, and are often written from the perspective of profoundly disturbed protagonists. In *Le Jeune Homme de sable* (1979), Williams Sassine traces the 'disintegration' of a former student radical. Emmanuel Dongala uses deft irony in the short stories of *Jazz et vin de palme* (1982) to satirise the (supposedly Marxist) one-party regime in the Congo. (The one-party state had progressively become the norm across the continent in the decades following independence.) Perhaps the most celebrated writer of this era is Sony Labou Tansi, whose experimental style pushed the African novel in ever more innovative directions. *La Vie et demie* (1979), his most acclaimed novel, is a highly inventive and grimly comic work, which takes the violence of a fratricidal African state to ever more absurd extremes.

Women writers began to emerge in the 1970s, with autobiography enjoying a privileged role, as in Nafissatou Diallo's *De Tilène au plateau* (1976). The major breakthrough for women writers came with the publication of Mariama Bâ's epistolary novel, *Une si longue lettre* (1979), which gives voice to the thoughts and feelings of a middle-aged, educated woman coming to terms with the death of her polygamous husband. Since the 1980s, a range of female voices has been heard, which explore the specificity of African women's experiences. Amongst the most acclaimed authors is Calixthe Beyala, whose work has consistently explored the nature of sexuality and gender in Africa.

The development of African women's writing is a clear sign of the changes taking place within various francophone African societies. However, it is worth noting that many female authors such as Beyala live in Europe, where they enjoy a freedom of expression that they may not find at home. Indeed, many African writers – from Mongo Beti to Tierno Monénembo – have found greater freedom to express themselves from 'exile' in France, where most African novels continue to be published (Présence Africaine and L'Harmattan are the two major specialist African publishers), although new African-based publishing houses are emerging after the short-lived experiments of the 1970s. (Publishing in African languages has been an important but marginalised activity.) Beyala's later work has increasingly focused on the black experience in France, in texts such as *Le Petit Prince de Belleville* (1992). This has also proven a rich terrain for other French-based African authors: Fatou Diome's collection of short stories, *La Préférence nationale* (2001) provides a sardonic take on the everyday racism encountered by educated African women in eastern France. Although this indicates the persistence of a colonial axis, centred on Paris, other axes are now emerging. Over the past two decades, more and more African writers – for example, Emmanuel Dongala and Alain Mabankcou – have made careers teaching in colleges across the United States and Canada.

Although there has in recent years been a greater focus on smaller, individual narratives, African writers have also continued to engage with the grand narratives of African history: Dongala and Kourouma have penned extremely important novels in recent years on the civil wars that have affected Congo and the Ivory Coast, focusing in particular on the tragic role of child soldiers; similarly, a group of African writers, including Véronique Tadjo, Tierno Monénembo and Boris Diop, contributed to the 'Devoir de Mémoire' project, which sought to promote a specifically African reflection on the Rwandan genocide of 1994. Although Sub-Saharan African literature in French enjoys a precarious existence in terms of its audience and its reliance on French publishing houses, these works attest to its continuing vitality and importance.

David Murphy

LITERARY WORKS

Bâ, Mariama (1979), *Une si longue lettre*, trans. as *So Long a Letter* (1981) Modupé Bodé-Thomas, London and Portsmouth, NH: Heinemann.

Beyala, Calixthe (1987), *C'est le soleil qui m'a brûlée*, trans. as *The Sun Hath Looked Upon Me* (1996) Marjolijn de Jager, London and Portsmouth, NH: Heinemann.

Diome, Fatou (2001), *La Préférence nationale*, Paris: Présence Africaine.

Dongala, Emmanuel (1982), *Jazz et vin de palme*, Paris: Hatier.

Kane, Cheikh Hamidou (1961), *L'Aventure ambiguë*, trans. as *Ambiguous Adventure* (1972) Katherine Woods, London: Heinemann.

Kourouma, Ahmadou (1968), *Les Soleils des indépendances*, trans. as *The Suns of Independence* (1981) Adrian Adams, London: Heinemann.

— (2000), *Allah n'est pas obligé*, trans. as *Allah is not obliged* (2006) Frank Wynne, London and Portsmouth, NH: Heinemann.

Sassine, Williams (1979), *Le Jeune Homme de sable*, Paris: Présence Africaine.

Sembene, Ousmane (1960), *Les Bouts de bois de Dieu*, trans. as *God's Bits of Wood* (1995) Francis Price, London: Heinemann.

Senghor, Léopold Sédar (1990), *Œuvre poétique*, Paris: Seuil.

Tansi, Sony Labou (1979), *La Vie et demie*, Paris: Seuil.

HISTORIES

Aldrich, Robert (1996), *Greater France: A History of French Overseas Expansion*, London: Palgrave.

Betts, Raymond (1961), *Assimilation and Association in French Colonial Theory*, New York and London: Columbia University Press.

Conklin, Alice (1997), *A Mission to Civilize: The Republican Idea of Empire in France and West Africa, 1895–1930*, Stanford, CA: Stanford University Press.

De Benoist, Joseph-Roger (1982), *L'Afrique occidentale française de Brazzaville (1944) à l'indépendance (1960)*, Dakar: Nouvelles Éditions Africaines.

Echenberg, Myron J. (1991), *Colonial Conscripts: The 'Tirailleurs Sénégalais' in French West Africa, 1857–1960*, Portsmouth, NH and London: Heinemann and James Currey.

Gifford, Prosser and Roger Louis (eds) (1971), *France and Britain in Africa: Imperial Rivalry and Colonial Rule*, New Haven, CT and London: Yale University Press.

— (eds) (1982), *Decolonization and African Independence*, New Haven, CT and London: Yale University Press.

Vaillant, Janet G. (1990), *Black, French and African: A Life of Léopold Sédar Senghor*, Cambridge, MA and London: Harvard University Press.

Tirailleurs Sénégalais

The corps of *tirailleurs sénégalais* was founded in 1857 by Louis Faidherbe, the Governor-General of l'Afrique de l'Ouest Française (AOF). Frustrated by the lack of troops arriving from France as well as by the poor resistance of those received to tropical conditions, he sought to develop indigenous African régiments within the French Army. These consisted initially of enslaved men purchased under a system of *rachat* (literally, 'buying back') from their African owners, but this source was progressively supplemented by prisoners of war and local recruits. By the late nineteenth century, NCOs were increasingly drawn from indigenous ruling élites. Despite their name, the *tirailleurs* were not exclusively Senegalese, and were drawn from throughout West and Central Africa (coming in particular, for instance, from the Bambara of present-day Mali). From 1905 onwards, the strategic importance of these indigenous troops increased as they were deployed to police revolts throughout French possessions in Africa (for example the Rif War of the 1920s) and to continue annexation of territory (including that of Morocco 1908–14).

Charles Magnan's *La Force noire* (1910) argued for an expansion of the *tirailleurs'* role, and conscription (in 1915) and financial inducements for volunteers led to a rapid expansion of numbers after 1914 to supplement the regular French Army at the front during World War I. In 1916, seventeen battalions of *tirailleurs* were involved in the Battle of the Somme, and by that time, 120,000 African troops in all were serving in the French Army. An effort to recruit 50,000 additional men was met by resistance in parts of West Africa, but Blaise Daigne, a Senegalese deputy in the French parliament, was persuaded by the promise of certain privileges for veterans (reduced taxes, guaranteed work and even French citizenship) and encouraged a further 60,000 troops to enrol.

Of the almost 200,000 *tirailleurs* active during World War I, 163,000 were stationed in France. Over 30,000 of these died in action, often having been deployed in situations where French troops might have refused to serve. Such sacrifice created a sense of a *dette de sang* (blood debt), the inadequate recognition of which continues to trigger debates about mutual obligation (Mann 2006). World War I permitted the professionalisation of the *tirailleurs*, and troops from North and Central Africa later fought during World War II, most notably in the North African and Italian campaigns. Poor treatment during demobilisation in conjunction with a progressive *blanchissement* (whitening) of the French Army at the liberation led to a series of mutinies, culminating in the massacre of *tirailleurs* at Thiaroye in Senegal in December 1944 (represented by Ousmane Sembene in his 1988 film *Camp de Thiaroye*).

Although the Central and West African *tirailleurs* are the most prominent in literary representations, troops from Algeria served in the Crimean and Franco-Prussian Wars (1870), and colonial troops were also recruited elsewhere, such as in Madagascar and Indo-China, with their individual régiments named after the territory in which they were recruited (*tirailleurs malagaches*, *tirailleurs annamites*, and so on). Algerian, Moroccan and Senegalese units also served in the liberation of France (see Rachid Bouchareb's 2006 film *Indigènes*) as well as in Indo-China until the fall of Dien Bien Phu, operating subsequently as part of the French forces during the Algerian War of Independence (1954–62).

Charles Forsdick

LITERARY WORKS
Cousturier, Lucie (1920), *Des inconnus chez moi*, Paris: La Sirène.
Diallo, Bakary [1926] (1985), *Force-Bonté*, Paris: ACCT/ Nouvelles Éditions Africaines.
Kane, Cheikh Hamidou (1961), *L'Aventure ambiguë*, trans. as *Ambiguous Adventure* (1972) Katherine Woods, London: Heinemann.

HISTORIES
Echenberg, Myron (1991), *Colonial Conscripts: The Tirailleurs Senegalais in French West Africa, 1857–1960*, Portsmouth, NH: Heinemann.
Magnin, Charles (1910), *La Force noire*, Paris: Hachette.
Mann, Gregory (2006), *Native Sons: West African Veterans and France in the Twentieth Century*, Durham, NC and London: Duke University Press.
Onana, Charles (2003), *La France et ses tirailleurs: enquête sur les combattants de la République*, Paris: Duboiris.
Riesz, Janos (1996), 'The *Tirailleur Sénégalais* Who Did Not Want To Be A "Grand Enfant": Bakary Diallo's *Force Bonté* (1926) reconsidered', *Research in African Literatures* 27 (4): 157–79.

Women's Histories

Rather than try to be comprehensive, this article will refer to scholarly works whose theoretical and methodological approaches provide examples of the most important ways of studying women, gender and sexuality in France and its former empire. Where literary works are concerned, it will emphasise major texts by a few of the most influential writers whose work is available in English.

The term 'women's histories' often designates studies of the women of France's former colonies, as in Catherine Coquery-Vidrovitch, *African Women* (1997); Patricia Lorcin, 'Teaching Women' (2004); and David Barry Gaspar and Darlene Hine (eds), *More than Chattel* (1996), which has four chapters on the French Caribbean, including colonial New Orleans. 'Women's histories' also refers to studies of the French, Belgian and Swiss women who participated in the colonising process, however indirectly, as travellers, nurses, teachers, scholars and homemakers, as in Denise Brahimi, *Femmes arabes et soeurs musulmanes* (1984) and two works by Bénédicte Monicat, 'Autobiography and Women's Travel Writing' (1994) and *Itinéraires de l'écriture au féminin* (1996).

Yet the term also refers to studies that use gender as a significant category of analysis, usually in conjunction with the analysis of other axes of identity such as social class, ethnicity, race and sexuality. Rather than focusing exclusively on women, such studies may deal mainly with gendered relations between colonisers and colonised (showing, for instance, how colonised men were often feminised in colonial discourses) or with gender relations within each of those groups. Examples include work that focuses on the domestic sphere as a key site of colonial domination, as in Julia Ann Clancy-Smith and Frances Gouda (eds), *Domesticating the Empire* (1998) as well as J. P. Daughton, *An Empire Divided* (2006), which takes account of gender in examining the role of missionaries in shaping French colonialism in Africa, Asia and the South Pacific. Other examples are Elizabeth Thompson, *Colonial Citizens* (2000) and Lisa McNee, 'The Languages of Childhood' (2004), which considers the ways gender hierarchies shaped the colonial education system and cast African women as adult children.

Certain women's histories highlight the difficulty of defining the field of francophone studies as well as the drawbacks of remaining strictly within its bounds in feminist scholarship. For example, the renowned historian of early modern France, Natalie Zemon Davis, has also studied New France in the sixteenth and the first half of the seventeenth centuries, drawing on the colonial archive of Jesuit writings in French as well as studies of Amerindian women, cultures and societies. In 'Iroquois Women, European Women' (1994), an essay that in fact deals as well with Algonquin, Montagnais and Huron women, Davis writes:

> I want to look at the Amerindian women of the eastern woodlands [of New France] in terms of historical change – and not just change generated by contact with Europeans, but by processes central to their own societies. I want to insist on the absolute simultaneity of the Amerindian and European worlds, rather than viewing the former as an earlier version of the latter, and make comparisons less polarised than the differences between 'simple' and 'complex' societies. I want to suggest interactions to look for in the colonial encounter other than the necessary but overpolarised twosome of 'domination' and 'resistance' . . .

Apart from its interest as a study of gender and empire in the early modern period, an area that is still relatively neglected in francophone postcolonial studies, Davis' essay is notable for its use of a method that has become a hallmark of the discipline, one that problematises the categorical opposition, consolidated during the Enlightenment, between 'modern' and 'traditional' societies, while also granting that indigenous peoples in the Americas (and implicitly, indigenous peoples everywhere) have their own particular histories of consciousness, religious and cultural expression, political organisation and economic production. And of course, in order to glimpse these other histories, the scholar must consider languages and cultures that are not francophone.

In the years since the publication of Davis' 1994 essay, this method has come to be known as one that recognises the existence of 'alternative modernities'. Laura Rice takes up this idea in *Of Irony and Empire* (2006), examining the complex relationship between the social imaginary of colonisers and that of the colonised, while also considering gender as a central force in colonial and postcolonial encounters. Rice's work in progress involves collecting the life stories of rural and Bedouin women in Tunisia. Working in concert with large-scale international development agencies such as the Association for Women's Rights in Development, Rice aims to empower poor women by helping to make their voices heard, and by respecting their self-understanding as well as their world view. Rice's work has obviously entailed learning Arabic/Tunisian dialect. But more than this, it has entailed reconceptualising 'francophone' scholarship in such a way as to incorporate rural Tunisian women's personal narratives into a larger study of women and literacy in the Maghreb, one that takes account of the ways literacy is represented in literature and other discourses of the region. Rice's work complements the myriad publications of the Moroccan feminist sociologist Fatima Mernissi, some of which are collected in *Women's Rebellion and Islamic Memory* (1996). A final example of truly original work that addresses francophone societies while exceeding the bounds of francophone studies is Sara Johnson's '*Cinquillo* Consciousness' (2005), which shows how slaves used music and dance as modes of counter-hegemonic inter-island communication that crossed barriers of language, culture and geography.

Where critical analyses of sexuality and heteronormativity are concerned, Jarrod Hayes' *Queer Nations* (2000) is a pioneering work. Also notable is Mary Jean Green's *Marie-Claire Blais* (1995), which includes discussions of the many utopian and dystopian lesbian communities represented in Blais' novels (often set mainly in Montreal). Scholarly studies of francophone women writers abound. *Postcolonial Subjects* (Mary Jean Green et al. 1996) gives the most comprehensive overview of the subject and includes fine essays by leading critics in the field. Other exemplary works include Françoise Lionnet, *Postcolonial Representations* (1995); Odile Cazenave, *Rebellious Women* (2000); Nicki Hitchcott, *Women Writers in Francophone Africa* (2000); Anne Donadey, *Recasting Postcolonialism* (2001); Suzanne Rinne and Joëlle Vitiello (eds), *Elles écrivent des Antilles* (1997); Renée Larrier, *Francophone Women Writers* (2000); Miriam J. A. Chancy, *Framing Silence* (1994); Sarah Barbour and Gerise Herndon, *Emerging Perspectives on Maryse Condé* (2006); and Ernstpeter Ruhe, *Assia Djebar* (2001).

On immigration, Odile Cazenave's *Afrique sur Seine* (2005) is excellent. Also, two anthologies, both edited by Susan Ireland and Patrice J. Proulx, provide helpful introductions to francophone 'immigrant' writing: *Immigrant Narratives in Contemporary France* (2001) and *Textualising the Immigrant Experience in Contemporary Quebec* (2004). Although these anthologies are not centrally concerned with gender, they feature a number of feminist analyses focused on women writers. Moreover, the latter volume, which includes essays on Quebec writers with cultural ties to Haiti, Iraq, Lebanon, China and Vietnam, dovetails with other work cited in this article, insofar as it moves beyond the familiar contours of francophone studies.

Works offering a cultural studies perspective on gender in francophone postcolonial literature and/or culture (as opposed to more narrowly defined historical or literary perspectives) include Winifred Woodhull, *Transfigurations of the Maghreb* (1993); Mireille Rosello, *France and the Maghreb* (2005); Kathryn Robson and Jennifer Yee, *France and 'Indochina'* (2005); and Elizabeth Ezra, *The Colonial Unconscious* (2000).

Let us conclude by citing some of the most important francophone literary texts that have been translated into English and that deal specifically with women's histories. The Cameroonian-born Ivoirian Werewere Liking's *It Shall Be of Jasper and Coral* (2000) should be read alongside her most recent, as yet untranslated novel *La Mémoire amputée* (2004), which deals with the long history of struggle by African women who have been devalued in the West and sometimes in their own societies, but who will surely be the ones to alter the face of Africa for the better in the age of globalisation.

Assia Djebar deserves mention here as well. A historian and a filmmaker, Djebar is also a prolific and highly talented writer with an international reputation. Her *Fantasia, an Algerian Cavalcade* (1989) deals with histories of Algerian women from the time of the French conquest in 1830 to the present, as they have been told by those women themselves, and as they have been imagined in the writings of nineteenth-century European military officers and travellers, as well as Orientalist authors and painters such as Eugène Fromentin and Eugène Delacroix. The novel also draws attention to the histories that have been forever lost, and to the stories told to the author about the women who fought or were 'damaged' in Algeria's anti-colonial war against France (1954–62).

Maryse Condé's *Crossing the Mangrove* (1995), like Gisèle Pineau's *The Drifting of Spirits* (1999), reflects on the legacy of slavery and colonialism in present-day Guadeloupe, while also paying close attention to the specific histories and struggles of women on the island. Both writers explore the intricate relations between African and European cultures in Guadeloupe, as well as the means by which those relations are continually reworked, notably in storytelling. Condé's *Crossing the Mangrove* is notable also for its reflection on inter-island connections, including the history of East Indian indentureship in the Caribbean; the migrations of poor Haitians seeking work on neighbouring islands; and pan-African political alliances that link Guadeloupe to independence struggles in Africa, especially Angola's belated fight against Portugal, which continued into the 1970s.

Like Maryse Condé, André Schwarz-Bart ties the history of women in Guadeloupe to other histories of struggle, in *A Woman Named Solitude* (1973), in particular the Jews' struggle to survive the Holocaust (not to mention their enslavement in Ancient Egypt, which was noted by enslaved Christianised Africans in the Caribbean). In preparing to write this novel, the author conducted research and collected oral histories with his black Guadeloupean wife, Simone Schwarz-Bart, on a legendary leader of slave revolts in eighteenth-century Guadeloupe. The result is a beautiful text that helped to rewrite the history of slavery as one in which slaves were both keenly aware of their oppression and were continually taking steps to resist it and to end it. This novel is also remarkable for its poignant articulation of the (necessarily imagined) history of the consciousness of enslaved Africans and 'fresh water slaves' born in the New World, as well as the painful processes of identity formation, de-formation and re-formation under slavery and colonialism. The novel carefully explores various liberatory transformations of consciousness in periods of *marronage*, while also evoking responses to the reinstitutionalisation of slavery in the French Empire from 1802 to 1848. Schwarz-Bart addresses fundamental feminist issues of female friendship, love relationships, pregnancy, childbirth and motherhood, in their material, psychological and symbolic dimensions. He also directly confronts issues such as the rape of black women and the appropriation of their children by slave masters. Along similar lines, Simone Schwarz-Bart's *The Bridge of Beyond* (1974) is noteworthy for its imaginative account of generations of Guadeloupean women – their family lives, their sources of strength, and their struggle to survive and to adapt to new forms of oppression in the wake of emancipation.

Few texts by women writers from the former Indo-China have been translated into English, the notable exception being Linda Lê's *Slander* (2000). In many respects Lê resists identification as a 'postcolonial writer', although her *Le Complexe de Caliban* (2005) does address questions of language, identity, the loss of loved ones, and the role of literature in the postcolonial world. By contrast, Kim Lefèvre's *Métisse blanche* (1989) and *Retour à la saison des pluies* (1990) deal directly with themes generally associated with postcolonial literature, such as mixed-race identity, exile, and the real or imagined return to the homeland.

Last, let us cite Quebec writer Marie-Claire Blais' *Anna's World* (1985), as impressive for its form and style as for its look at the wisdom of an adolescent girl, painfully acquired in her struggles with her family and her travels with drifters, drug addicts and dealers, and various other people crushed or rejected because of their race, their poverty, or their inability (or refusal) to accept what passes for 'normality' in Canada and the USA. This novel manages to forge meaningful links between the groups in wealthy countries who suffer from the abuse of power by governments and corporations, and peoples in the Third World who suffer considerably more, and differently, from this abuse.

Winifred Woodhull

LITERARY WORKS

Blais, Marie-Claire (1985), *Anna's World*, trans. Sheila Fischman, Toronto: L. and O. Dennys.

Condé, Maryse (1995), *Crossing the Mangrove*, trans. Richard Philcox, New York: Anchor Books.

Djebar, Assia (1989), *Fantasia, an Algerian Cavalcade*, trans. Dorothy S. Blair, London: Quartet Books.

Lê, Linda (1996), *Slander*, trans. Esther Allen, Lincoln, NE: University of Nebraska Press.

— (2005), *Le Complexe de Caliban*, Paris: Christian Bourgois.

Lefèvre, Kim (1989), *Métisse blanche*, Paris: Bernard Barrault.

— (1990), *Retour à la saison des pluies*, Paris: Bernard Barrault.

Liking, Werewere (2000), *It Shall Be of Jasper and Coral; and, Love-across-a-Hundred Lives: Two Novels*, trans. Marjolijn de Jager, Charlottesville, VA: University Press of Virginia.

— (2004), *La Mémoire amputée*, Abidjan: Nouvelles Éditions Ivoiriennes.

Pineau, Gisèle (1999), *The Drifting of Spirits*, trans. Michael Dash, London: Quartet Books.

Schwarz-Bart, André (1973), *A Woman Named Solitude*, trans. Ralph Manheim, San Francisco, CA: D. S. Ellis.

Schwarz-Bart, Simone (1974), *The Bridge of Beyond*, trans. Barbara Bray, London: Heinemann.

HISTORIES

Barbour, Sarah and Gerise Herndon (eds) (2006), *Emerging Perspectives on Maryse Condé: A Writer of Her Own*, Trenton, NJ: Africa World Press.

Brahimi, Denise (1984), *Femmes arabes et soeurs musulmanes*, Paris: Tierce.

Cazenave, Odile (2000), *Rebellious Women: The New Generation of Female African Novelists*, Boulder, CO: Lynne Rienner Publishers.

— (2005), *Afrique sur Seine: A New Generation of African Writers in Paris*, Lanham, MD: Lexington Books.

Chancy, Miriam (1994), *Framing Silence: Revolutionary Novels by Haitian Women*, Newark, NJ: Rutgers University Press.

Clancy-Smith, Julia Ann and Frances Gouda (eds) (1998), *Domesticating the Empire: Race, Gender, and Family Life in French and Dutch Colonialism*, Charlottesville, VA: University Press of Virginia.

Coquery-Vidrovitch, Catherine [1994] (1996), *African Women: A Modern History*, trans. Beth Gillian Raps, Boulder, CO: Westview Press.

Daughton, J. P. (2006), *An Empire Divided: Religion, Republicanism, and the Making of French Colonialism, 1880–1914*, Oxford: Oxford University Press.

Davis, Natalie Zemon (1994), 'Iroquois Women, European Women', in Margo Hendricks and Patricia Parker (eds), *Women, Race, and Writing*, London: Taylor and Francis Ltd, pp. 243–58.

Donadey, Anne (2001), *Recasting Postcolonialism: Women Writing between Worlds*, Portsmouth, NH: Heinemann.

Ezra, Elizabeth (2000), *The Colonial Unconscious: Race and Culture in Interwar France*, Ithaca, NY: Cornell University Press.

Gaspar, Barry David and Darlene Clark Hine (eds) (1996), *More than Chattel: Black Women and Slavery in the Americas*, Bloomington, IN: Indiana University Press.

Green, Mary Jean (1995), *Marie-Claire Blais*, New York: Twayne.

— et al. (ed.) (1996), *Postcolonial Subjects: Francophone Women Writers*, Minneapolis, MN: University of Minnesota Press.

Hayes, Jarrod (2000), *Queer Nations: Marginal Sexualities in the Maghreb*, Chicago, IL: University of Chicago Press.

Hitchcott, Nicki (2000), *Women Writers in Francophone Africa*, Oxford: Berg.

Ireland, Susan and Patrice J. Proulx (eds) (2001), *Immigrant Narratives in Contemporary France*, Westport, CT: Greenwood Press.

— (2004), *Textualising the Immigrant Experience in Contemporary Quebec*, Westport, CT: Praeger.

Johnson, Sara (2005), '*Cinquillo* Consciousness: The Formation of a Pan-Caribbean Musical Aesthetic', in Tim Reiss (ed.), *Music, Writing and Caribbean Unity*, Trenton, NJ: Africa World Press, pp. 35–58.

Larrier, Renée (2000), *Francophone Women Writers of Africa and the Caribbean*, Gainesville, FL: University Press of Florida.

Lionnet, Françoise (1995), *Postcolonial Representations: Women, Literature, Identity*, Ithaca, NY: Cornell University Press.

Lorcin, Patricia (2004), 'Teaching Women and Gender in *France d'Outre-Mer*: Problems and Strategies', *French Historical Studies* 27 (2): 293–310.

McNee, Lisa (2004), 'The Languages of Childhood: The Discursive Construction of Childhood and Colonial Policy in French West Africa', *African Studies Quarterly* 7 (4), web.africa.ufl.edu/asq/v7/v7i4a2.htm

Mernissi, Fatima (1996), *Women's Rebellion and Islamic Memory*, trans. Emily Agar, London: Zed Books.

Monicat, Bénédicte (1994), 'Autobiography and Women's Travel Writing in Nineteenth-Century France', *Gender, Place, and Culture: A Journal of Feminist Geography* 1: 61–70.

— (1996), *Itinéraires de l'écriture au féminin. Voyageuses du 19e siècle*, Amsterdam: Rodopi.

Rice, Laura (2006), *Of Irony and Empire: The Transcultural Invention of Contemporary North Africa*, Albany, NY: State University of New York Press.

Rinne, Suzanne and Joëlle Vitiello (eds) (1997), *Elles écrivent des Antilles: Haïti, Guadeloupe, Martinique*, Paris: L'Harmattan.

Robson, Kathryn and Jennifer Yee (eds) (2005), *France and 'Indochina': Cultural Representations*, Lanham, MD: Lexington Books.

Rosello, Mireille (2005), *France and the Maghreb: Performative Encounters*, Gainesville, FL: University Press of Florida

Ruhe, Ernstpeter (ed.) (2001), *Assia Djebar*, Würzburg: Könighausen and Neumann.

Thompson, Elizabeth (2000), *Colonial Citizens: Republican Rights, Paternal Privilege, and Gender in French Syria and Lebanon*, New York: Columbia University Press.

Woodhull, Winifred (1993), *Transfigurations of the Maghreb: Feminism, Decolonisation, Literatures*, Minneapolis, MN: University of Minnesota Press.

Germany and its Colonies

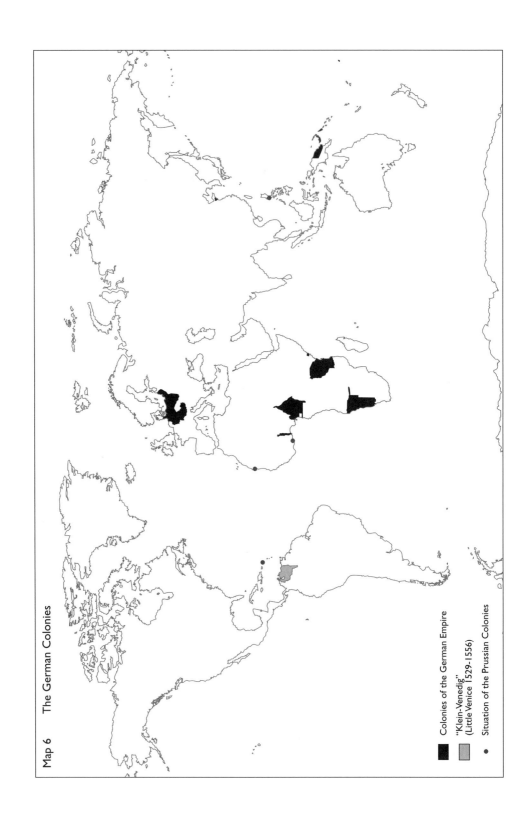

Map 6   The German Colonies

■   Colonies of the German Empire

■   "Klein-Venedig"
     (Little Venice 1529–1556)

●   Situation of the Prussian Colonies

Germany and its Colonies: Introduction

The inclusion of a section on Germany in a handbook on the colonial past and postcolonial present of continental Europe is not an easy undertaking, for there has only lately been a significant upswing in research on German colonial history. The amount of scholarly attention that has been devoted to the German colonies in recent years is somewhat surprising. The German colonial empire lasted for a very brief period, beginning in the mid-1880s and ending in 1918, when Germany relinquished its overseas possessions 'to the Allied and associated main powers' (article 119 of the Versailles peace agreement) following its defeat in World War I. In the face of increasing pressure from parts of the country's bourgeoisie to establish German colonies, the first Chancellor of the Reich, Otto von Bismarck, aimed to limit the state's role to an absolute minimum, in favour of initiatives from private enterprise. The shift to more active 'world politics' began in the 1890s, under the reign of Wilhelm II. The colonies acquired consisted of territories that other imperial countries had no desire to annex: Cameroon, German East Africa, German South-West Africa, and Togo in Africa; German Samoa and German New Guinea in the Pacific; and Kiaochow in China (see the respective entries). The total area was relatively limited and much of it embraced desert and sparsely populated jungle. Very few Germans were attracted to the prospect of settling in these colonies. At the height of the German colonial period, on the eve of World War I, fewer than 18,000 settlers lived in the German overseas possessions. Overall, in spite of the parsimonious approach of the German government, the administrative costs of empire considerably exceeded revenues, and trade between Germany and its colonies never reached 1 per cent of total German foreign trade.

What then are the reasons for the current interest in colonial studies? Significant factors are the (no-longer-quite-so) new paradigm of the 'cultural turn' and international colonial and postcolonial studies. Moreover, this interest is a response to globalisation and the prevalent rhetoric of global connectedness (see the entry on 'Historiography'). Colonialism is now understood to be a phenomenon of the history of interdependence, the effects of which were felt in the colonising countries as well as the colonies themselves, albeit to varying degrees and in divergent ways (see the entry on 'Colonialism and African and Afro-German Writing'). European modernity would be unthinkable without colonialism; colonialism is an integral element of Western societies, including German society. The brevity of formal German colonial rule does not mean that German colonialism was irrelevant. On the contrary: recent research has drawn an unfamiliar portrait of both the German Kaiserreich and post-1918 German societies, in which the exotic and the colonial seem to have played more than a subordinate role.

Scholars from the USA were the first to begin scrutinising German colonial and postcolonial history. Susanne Zantop's work in the field of literary studies offered important inputs, uncovering the German pre-colonial fantasies that 'provided Germans an arena for creating an imaginary community and constructing a national identity'. Moreover, her results revealed that the historical caesuras of 1884 or 1918 did not, in fact, mark decisive turning points. Long before 1884, German merchants, missionaries, voyagers, scholars and traders travelled beyond the borders of Europe (see the entries on 'West Africa'; 'Missions'; and 'Slavery, the Slave Trade and Abolition'), and an active lobby campaigned for German imperial engagement. By 1900, supporters of German colonial involvement – as well as opponents – could be found in all political camps, including the ranks of the Social Democrats. The German public was not only fascinated with the country's own overseas possessions: beginning in the eighteenth century, an 'Orientalism' (see the entry on 'Orientalism') emerged and flourished that reached its height with Goethe's 'West-Eastern Divan' in the nineteenth century, and also materialised later in the trips made by Kaiser Wilhelm II to the Orient, and the construction of the Baghdad Railway; and in the nineteenth century, similar phases of popular projection focused on Rome and Greece in antiquity as well as China and Egypt. The same period saw an upsurge of interest in Central and Eastern Europe, areas in which Germans had formerly settled; annexation of these territories was a political demand championed by right extremists with *völkisch* views from 1900 onwards. Whether and how these very diverse expansionist tendencies were related to (or competed with) one another is controversial (see the entry on 'Historiography'; and van Laak 2005). Although Germany's history as a colonial power ended in 1918 (see the entry on 'Versailles Conference'), the influence of colonial desires and projections was still felt, and proved to be astonishingly persistent under varying historical conditions. Thus, one unique feature of German colonialism is the way in which decolonisation occurred in 1918, namely, as a result of confrontation with the other imperial powers, rather than after conflicts with the colonised peoples.

New approaches to research on these issues are characterised by three elements. First, there is a focus on the local practices of colonial rule that expressly incorporates the perspectives and actions of the colonised peoples. A second theme is the interactive nature of relations between these peoples and the colonial powers. A third aspect emphasises the significance of cultures outside of Europe for the self-perception of Western European 'civilisation'. Various entries in this volume are devoted to retracing the influence of colonialism in the metropolises. Although the protectorates were hardly profitable economically, except for a few individual entrepreneurs (and hopes that they would lure millions of German settlers were not fulfilled), they did serve as a foil onto which personal as well as collective desires and concepts were projected, which ranged from the notion of 'New Germanys' overseas, to the mission of disseminating the achievements of civilisation in the name of medicine and Christianity, to a space for adventure, or for the concrete designs of scholars, planners, civil servants and women's organisations. This conglomerate of phantasmagoric desires, absolute pretensions to power, and their unrestrained pursuit regularly lead to conflicts with the indigenous societies that ended all too often in extreme forms of violence (see the entries on 'Anticolonial Struggles'; 'Herero/Nama Genocide'). Imperial 'self-fulfilment' at the expense of those who were colonised affected not only the annexed states but also Germany. Colonialism left its mark on such diverse spheres as literature (see the entry on 'Colonial Literature'), film (Baer, Fuhrmann, Nagl, Nganang, Schönert, Struck), the academic world (see the entry on 'Anthropology and Ethnography'), advertising (Ciarlo), urban topography (see the entry on 'Colonial Monuments') and exhibitions (see the entry on 'Commercial Ethnographic Exhibitions'). Clubs and associations influenced political and administrative planning and the demands of the women's movement (see the entry on 'Women's Histories'). Moreover, subjects from the (former) colonies, especially those in Africa, immigrated to Germany – although not in significant numbers due to the abrupt end of German colonial rule (see the entries on 'Colonial Migration and the Law'; 'Black Germans'; also see Amenda 2006). In short, colonialism found its way into the emotions and thoughts of German society (see the entry on 'Colonial Culture and the Colonial Impacts on Culture in Germany').

The astonishing persistence of racist constructions of difference with colonial connotations is especially apparent in the media and in the tourism sector, and also in the educational system (see Berman 2004; and articles in the journal *Stichproben*). To what extent such constructions have influenced the political thought and cultural identity of Germans, and how significant they have been in the total context of factors that created difference and identity, including, for example, anti-Semitism, is a question that remains controversial and awaits further investigation. Meanwhile, a dispute has developed over possible connections between violent practices and mentalities in the German colonies and the National Socialist occupation of Eastern Europe (see the entries on 'Historiography'; 'NS-Colonialism' and 'Herero/Nama Genocide'). It would appear as if there is now a tendency to take this approach too far and link nearly every key aspect of German society to imperialism, colonialism and their repercussions, as if to overcompensate for decades in which these dimensions were neglected. Nevertheless, this process of grappling with the significance of Germany's colonial past also highlights the political relevance of this field of research. Scholars, artists, writers and others who play an active part in contemporary civil society have initiated a variety of activities and discussions aimed at establishing an enduring politics of memory and reconciliation in Germany. One example is the campaign for an official apology for the genocide perpetrated against the Herero in Namibia, or for payment of compensations by the German government in that context; a further example is provided by the efforts to have streets in Germany renamed that today continue to bear unchallenged the names of colonial conquerors like Hermann von Wissmann or Carl Peters. In our digital age, the media used in such projects are quite diverse. Felix Axster, Heike Hartmann, Astrid Kusser and Susann Lewerenz initiated an exhibition focusing on postcards in the visual culture of German colonialism. There are also several websites on the colonial past of specific German cities or regions, including Hamburg, Hanover and Freiburg.

This new interest and the new perspectives developed in the field indicate that much work is still in the making, so far yielding tentative results on a broad spectrum of issues. To date, research on German colonialism is characterised by its interdisciplinary and international nature. For a reference volume like this – which aims to offer readers an informative, concise survey of the current status of a particular field – the seemingly unsystematic status of current work-in-progress on German colonialism and the risk of highlighting aspects that may later prove to be of marginal significance is problematic. Because the body of knowledge about German colonial history is constantly growing, some contributions may already be outdated when this compendium is published; in other cases, topics may be eclipsed by themes later considered 'more important', while others might have been left out which later times might consider relevant. In this respect, our section is a review of the current state of affairs in the field of German colonial/postcolonial studies, and although this may be said of other sections as well, the portrayal of work on Germany is presumably of an even more tentative nature.

Beyond the criteria set by the editors, what systematic considerations should determine which entries to include and which to leave out? Keeping in mind the limited space available, we have decided to reproduce the current landscape of publications and to offer readers both core topics and themes that may seem marginal, such as board games (see the entry on 'African Playground') or languages (see the entry on 'The Language Question'). Carefully-researched work has already been completed on these themes, as well as e.g. for the Askari myth (see the entry on 'Askari and Askari myth') whereas the investigation of topics such as 'Sport and Colonialism' (the focus of Gertrud Pfister's work) or 'Exoticism and Empire in German Education, 1871–1914' (a study by Jeff Bowersox) are still under way. But the hard facts are also included: the Berlin Conference, which was decisive for the further course of events in Africa; a characterisation of the German colonial administration; the principles of colonial education overseas as well as in the German Reich; colonial revisionism between the two world wars; and various aspects of racism during the heyday of imperialism. In this sphere as well, important work is still in the making, or has just been completed; some examples are studies on the Reichstag elections of 1907, in which racism and anti-socialism were intertwined (Sobich 2007); on discourse about Africa in German-language literature from the eighteenth to the twentieth century (Fiedler 2005; Simo 2002); on the European Enlightenment (Lüsebrink 2006); on German colonial critique (Robin Krause is currently exploring this topic); or on the Third-World and Africa policies pursued by both Germanys between 1948 and 1990 in the context of Cold War rivalries (Berman 2004; Hein 2006; Schriftenreihe 1995–; projects by Katrina Hagen and Young-sun Hong). Despite invitations to colleagues from the former German colonies to contribute to this volume, the section unfortunately lacks any work by these authors. In general, scholars from Africa and Asia – and especially female colleagues – remain under-represented in research on German colonialism; while the reasons for this are complex, existing power structures within academia no doubt constitute one factor.

What, then, characterised German colonialism; what can be considered to distinguish it from the colonial systems of other European nations? One might answer: for the most part, its non-existence. The phase of colonial rule, in the strict sense, was brief and differed from the colonial periods of other nations with respect to the zeal apparent in Germany's attempts to catch up with the great powers, France and Great Britain (Eckert 2007; Gründer 2004; van Laak 2005; Speitkamp 2005). The result was a certain lack of planning on the part of the German bureaucracy, and a constant habit of improvising, which did not end when Bernhard Dernburg was appointed State Secretary for Colonial Affairs in 1907. Thus, developments in the German protectorates were at times more exaggerated, more intense, and only rarely more low-key than in the other European colonies. As a general tendency, however, the findings that have been accumulated thus far for European imperialism also apply to the German Reich. Among these characteristic elements are, for example, the sexualised metaphor of the conquest; the considerable significance of prestige; a constant vacillation between self-affirmation and perceived threat by the foreign Other; the pronounced de facto caste system in the colonies; the 'white woman' as a guarantor of culture; and the limited influence of policies formulated in European capitals (in this case, Berlin) on the local practice of colonial rule. As elsewhere, inequality, segregation, paternalism and condescension (see the entry on 'Hybridity and Race Relations') as well as systematic exploitation and slave labour were the trademarks of dealings with indigenous cultures in the German colonies. Moreover, German colonies shared traits with the colonies of other European states: the structural instability of colonial domination; and a hegemonic order that unfailingly demonstrated outward strength and yet was invariably marked internally by fragility and possible disintegration. In order to gloss over this discrepancy, and the uncertainties, misunderstandings and deceptions it produced, colonists as well as parts of the administration repeatedly resorted to acts of violence, which in turn engendered the resistance of the colonised peoples. Furthermore, colonial domination was initially limited to a thin network of stations, most of them located along the coastlines, with a few outposts in the interior. Just as control of the colonial territories was achieved in stages, so were attempts to subjugate the population only gradually crowned with success. It would appear that in the German colonies (and especially in Africa – the situation in the South Pacific was different) the colonial state was far from representing a reliable political order. But this, too, is a characteristic that German colonialism shares with other European powers. Moreover, many German colonial concepts – such as the German equivalent of 'bride ships', which sent potential wives to the colonists, or the prohibitions on immigration to the colonies for those deemed undesirable – were patterned after the practices of other imperial powers and thus in effect 'hybrid' phenomena.

To sum up: German society, like the societies of Britain, France or Spain, is a postcolonial society. Although the epoch of colonial rule was quite short, the 'colonial' mentalities and practices that developed in Germany even without formal colonial possessions continue to have a lasting effect up to the present day. This echo is clearly marked by the persistent self-imagination of German society as a 'white' collective. Recognition of this phenomenon and the desire further to explore its implications has lead to a renaissance of 'colonial' themes in Germany that is especially apparent among younger historians. Modern approaches from cultural studies originally developed in the United States have been adopted and adapted to new issues. Contextualising phenomena in broader societal, socio-economic and political landscapes on a European and a global level is another, increasingly important direction of research. To this day, one process by which 'Europe' is constituted is by delimiting its borders and its difference with respect to the Near East, Africa or the Muslim world. In the years to come, those who seek to uncover the traces of national colonialism will no doubt attempt to analyse what unique features have resulted – especially in comparison to the other European colonial powers – from Germany's special constellation as a country with a long history of colonialism without colonies and a short imperial phase.

Birthe Kundrus

HISTORIES

Amenda, Lars (2006), *Fremde–Hafen–Stadt. Chinesische Migration und ihre Wahrnehmung in Hamburg 1897–1972*, Hamburg: Doelling und Galitz.

Ames, Eric, Marcia Klotz and Lora Wildenthal (eds) (2005), *Germany's Colonial Pasts*, Lincoln, NE and London: University of Nebraska Press.

Baer, Martin (2001), 'Von Heinz Rühmann bis zum Traumschiff: Bilder von Afrika im deutschen Film', in Susan Arndt (ed.), *AfrikaBilder. Studien zu Rassismus in Deutschland*, Münster: Unrast, pp. 253–70.

Berman, Nina (2004), *Impossible Missions. German Economic, Military, and Humanitarian Efforts in Africa*, Lincoln, NE and London: University of Nebraska Press.

Ciarlo, David (forthcoming), *Consuming Race, Envisioning Empire: Colonialism and German Mass Culture, 1887–1914*.

Eckert, Andreas (2005), 'Sport und Kolonialismus in Afrika', *Geschichte in Wissenschaft und Unterricht* 56 (10): 565–79.

— (2006), *Kolonialismus*, Frankfurt am Main: Fischer.

— (2008), *Geschichte des deutschen Kolonialismus*, Munich: Beck.

Fiedler, Matthias (2005), *Zwischen Abenteuer, Wissenschaft und Kolonialismus. Der deutsche Afrikadiskurs im 18. und 19. Jahrhundert*, Cologne: Böhlau.

Fuhrmann, Wolfgang (2002), 'Der Kinema in Afrika', in Frank Kessler and Sabine Lenk (eds): *Grüße aus Viktoria: Film-Ansichten aus der Ferne*, Basle: Stroemfeld Roter Stern, pp. 117–38.

Gründer, Horst (2004), *Geschichte der deutschen Kolonien*, 5th edn, Stuttgart: UTB.

Hein, Bastian (2006), *Die Westdeutschen und die Dritte Welt. Entwicklungspolitik und Entwicklungsdienste zwischen Reform und Revolte 1959–1974*, Munich: Oldenbourg.

Laak, Dirk van (2005), *Über alles in der Welt. Deutscher Imperialismus im 19. und 20. Jahrhundert*, Munich: Beck.

Lüsebrink, Hans-Jürgen (ed.) (2006), *Das Europa der Aufklärung und die außereuropäische koloniale Welt*, Göttingen: Wallstein.

Nagl, Tobias (2005), 'Louis Brody and the Black Presence in German Film Before 1945', in Patricia Mazon and Reinhild Steingrover (eds), *Not So Plain as Black and White: Afro-German Culture and History, 1890–2000*, Rochester, NY: University of Rochester Press, pp. 109–135.

Nganang, Alain Patrice (2001), 'Der koloniale Sehnsuchtsfilm: vom lieben "Afrikaner" deutscher Filme in der NS-Zeit', in Susan Arndt (ed.), *AfrikaBilder: Studien zu Rassismus in Deutschland*, Münster: Unrast, pp. 232–52.

Poley, Jared (2005), *Decolonisation in Germany. Weimar Narratives of Colonial Loss and Foreign Occupation*, Bern: Peter Lang

Schöning, Jörg (ed.) (1997), *Triviale Tropen. Exotische Reise- und Abenteuerfilme aus Deutschland 1919–1933*, Munich: edition text + kritik.

Schriftenreihe (1995–), Series: *Die DDR und die Dritte Welt*, Münster: Lit.

Simo, David (ed.) (2002), *Die Erfahrungen des Imperiums kehren zurück. Inszenierungen des Fremden in der deutschen Literatur*, Leipzig: Leipziger Universitäts – Verlag.

Sobich, Frank O. (2007), *'Schwarze Bestien, rote Gefahr'. Rassismus und Antisozialismus im Deutschen Kaiserreich*, Frankfurt am Main: Campus.

Speitkamp, Winfried (2005), *Deutsche Kolonialgeschichte*, Stuttgart: Reclam.

Stichproben. Wiener Zeitschrift für kritische Afrikastudien 6 (2006), No 10.

Struck, Wolfgang (2004), '"Du hörst nachts die Trommeln dröhnen, doch du wirst nie verstehn". Konstruktionen des Fremden', in Julia Bayer, Andrea Engl and Melanie Liebheit (eds), *Strategien der Annäherung. Darstellungen des Fremden im deutschen Fernsehen*, Bad Honnef: Horlemann, pp. 16–29.

— (2005), '"Ein renegatisches Machtabenteuer unter den Negern". Der phantasierte Kolonialismus der literarischen Moderne in Deutschland', in Axel Dunker (ed.), *(Post-) Kolonialismus und Deutsche Literatur. Impulse der angloamerikanischen Literatur- und Kulturtheorie*, Bielefeld: Aisthesis, pp. 179–202.

African Playground

Playing is both a symbolic and a mediating activity in which players can rehearse various roles. Each game provides training and practice in its allegedly non-utilitarian and unconstraining form and content. Like many other common cultural pursuits, games may bear the traces of colonial violence; they are – even if latently and unconsciously – a form of 'colonial memory'.

The most popular role-playing games for German children around 1900 included not only 'cops and robbers' and 'Indians and trappers' but also 'Hereros and German troops'. In the *Jungdeutschlands Pfadfinderbuch*, the veteran 'African' Maximilian Bayer recommended this 'simple, lively war game' as appealing to the romantic fantasy of German boy scouts. The book, a German version of Robert Baden-Powell's *Scouting for Boys*, was first published in 1909. In each subsequent edition, episodes from German South-West Africa gradually replaced those based on Baden-Powell's examples from the Boer War and India.

In such war games played outdoors, but also in re-enactments of the colonial conflicts with stereoscopes or tin figures, the reference to real historic events in the colonies was fairly unambiguous and blunt. In board and card games, however, colonial relationships were articulated with somewhat more subtlety. While travellers brought games from various parts of the world back to Europe (for example, the Indian *pachisi* became popular in England, where it was called 'India' or 'Ludo', and in Germany, where it was known as 'Mensch ärgere Dich nicht'), European game manufacturers incorporated the new colonies into their products. Following the invention of lithography and the introduction of colour printing, the production of board and parlour games became a true industry in the second half of the nineteenth century. These games were produced in editions of several hundred thousand. A veritable boom in the establishment of toy companies – 250 in Nuremberg alone in 1909 – coincided with the creation of the German state and colonial expansion. Of note among these manufacturers were Jacob Wolf Spear and Otto Robert Maier. The latter brought out in 1884 his first parlour game based on Jules Verne's novel *Around the World in Eighty Days*. The titles of many of these games with their spiral-shaped, goal-directed journeys betray their colonial character, for example, 'The Race for the Carolinas' (1885), or 'Journey to the German Colonies' (1908). Such board games were less concerned with strategy than with imprinting knowledge about contemporary colonial activities through the regular repetition of the game: the programmed journey sharpened the players' awareness of the newly partitioned map. The educational qualities were most strongly foregrounded in the lotto and happy families' games popular among the middle classes. The imparting of geographical and historical knowledge were important components of such games as 'Kolonial-Quartett', produced by the women's section of the German Colonial Society.

The majority of games, however, emphasised their communicative and playful elements, and were none too scrupulous in their presentation of colonial affairs. With card games like 'Kamerun-Spiel' (1885), the whole family could 'learn' about the inhabitants of the new German colonies. In assigning cards bearing portraits of the indigenous Duala to activities and attributes, players were rewarded or penalised. The country's population were stereotypically characterised as submissive supporters of German commercial enterprises and inland expeditions or as malicious trouble-makers and thieves. The German at home quickly learned to recognise his or her Cameroon subjects, and for the duration of the game could act pretty much like a colonial ruler. An apparently harmless leisure activity for the whole family functioned perfectly to instil and sanction the colonial social order.

Nana Badenberg

LITERARY WORKS/GAMES

Das Kamerun-Spiel oder King Bell und seine Leute (1885), Leipzig: Moritz Ruhl. *My thanks to the Deutschen SPIELEmuseum e.V., Chemnitz for providing an example of the game.*

Frauenbund der Deutschen Kolonialgesellschaft (ed.) (2006), *Deutsches Kolonial-Quartett*, Hannover: Wittmann and Leysner (also a game) http://www.traditionsverband.de/download/pdf/bastelsatz_kolonial.pdf. 18 (shows the cards) [accessed Nov. 2006].

Lion, Alexander (ed.) [1911] (1913), *Jungdeutschlands Pfadfinderbuch*, 4th edn, Munich: Gmelin.

Reise in die deutschen Kolonien (c. 1904), Ravensburg: Maier.

Histories

Badenberg, Nana (2004), 'Spiel um Kamerun. Kolonialismus in Brett- und Gesellschaftsspielen', in Alexander Honold and Klaus R. Scherpe (eds), *Mit Deutschland um die Welt. Eine Kulturgeschichte des Fremden in der Kolonialzeit*, Stuttgart: Metzler, pp. 86–94.

Anthropology and Ethnography

While 'anthropology' remains acceptable shorthand for the fields of archaeology, ethnology, linguistics and physical anthropology in English, they have been recognised as distinct, if interconnected, disciplines in the German tradition. During the nineteenth century, the terms *Ethnologie* (ethnology) and *Ethnographie* (ethnography) were used almost interchangeably. *Völkerkunde* (also ethnology), which became the dominant term by the turn of the century, eclipsed neither. All were roughly commensurate to today's cultural anthropology – but none of them were exact equivalents. Moreover, different people used the terms in different ways. In some cases, *Völkerkunde* and *Ethnologie* continued to be used interchangeably well into the twentieth century. In other cases, the distinction was made between *Völkerkunde*, as a science focused on people who were illiterate before their exposure to European expansion, and *Ethnologie* as a science that included literate peoples as well. In either case, the term *Anthropologie* was reserved for physical anthropology, which was considered the natural history of man, in the nineteenth century, or the comparative biology of man, by the third decade of the twentieth century.

Initially, physical anthropology dominated these emerging disciplines. When the German Society for Anthropology, Ethnology and Prehistory was founded in 1869, it was the leading association of its kind in Central Europe and physical anthropology was at its centre. The anthropological section of the society drew on a large, older contingent of supporters dominated by physicians interested in morphological studies of skeletons and skulls. It also had its own publication, the *Archiv für Anthropologie*, founded in 1863. However, when the Berlin section of the society published its first issue of the *Zeitschrift für Ethnologie*, Adolf Bastian, the leading figure in German ethnology until his death in 1905, felt the need to distinguish ethnology from physical anthropology: culture was the ethnologists' realm. That distinction remained in place up to World War I.

The institutions that supported these disciplines were not centralised. Museums rather than universities became the dominant institutional setting for the ethnographic sciences during the imperial period, which influenced the kind of ethnology that took shape – one focused on material culture and widespread collecting. These museums were meant to encompass the entire world, displaying artefacts organised according to geographical rather than evolutionary principles, and with little or no place for physical anthropology. That exclusion contributed to the institutional and professional crisis of physical anthropology by the early twentieth century, and helped to maintain the separation of these fields.

The professionalisation of these disciplines and a series of generational shifts provide us with a clear periodisation: the domination of Humboldtian visions, travel literature, and scattered collecting in the period before 1868; the foundation of major associations and institutions dominated by Rudolf Virchow and Adolf Bastian between 1868 and 1905; a radical generational shift in the leading positions in ethnology and anthropology during the following decade, which introduced more highly trained and bureaucratically subservient scientists as well as theories of diffusion and biological anthropology; and the decline of ethnology and the museums in the inter-war years and the rise of physical anthropology and race science funded by government institutions.

H. Glenn Penny

HISTORIES

Fischer, Hans (ed.) (1998), *Ethnologie: Einführung und Überblick*, 4th edn, Berlin and Hamburg: Reimer.

Penny, H. Glenn and Matti Bunzl (eds) (2003), *Worldly Provincialism: German Anthropology in the Age of Empire*, Ann Arbor, MI: University of Michigan Press.

Zimmerman, Andrew (2001), *Anthropology and Antihumanism in Imperial Germany*, Chicago, IL: University of Chicago Press.

Zwernemann, Jürgen (1983), *Culture History and African Anthropology: A Century of Research in Germany and Austria*, Stockholm: Uppsala.

Anti-colonial Struggles

The German colonial empire lasted for only a short period (1884–1918). Anti-colonial struggles, therefore, were primary resistance movements which occurred as initial violent reactions and post-pacification revolts. They have to be distinguished from nationalist mass movements. Nonetheless, these struggles had a great impact on the politics of the colonial authorities, and also affected African policy later.

Initial resistance to German influence contributed to the breakdown of Otto von Bismarck's system of commercial companies. The German East Africa Company, which possessed a *Schutzbrief* for German East Africa (EA), caused an uprising in 1888 when attempting to gain control over the intermediate trade of the Arab coastal people. The Herero in German South-West Africa (SWA), disappointed by the lack of German protection against the Nama, cancelled their treaty in 1888. In both cases, the German government was not only forced to dispatch troops, but also to assume direct responsibility for the colony.

Until the turn of the century, especially in German Africa (EA, SWA, Cameroon and Togo), colonial troops were waging numerous wars of conquest. Although they did not meet with unified resistance because of pre-colonial rivalries, the troops occasionally faced severe local resistance as for example in the Hehe Wars in EA. The Hehe, not willing to give up their control of the caravan route, defeated a German expeditionary force in 1891 and put up resistance for seven years.

The established colonial orders in SWA, Cameroon and EA were almost simultaneously threatened by uprisings, which in the cases of the Herero and the Nama rebellion in SWA (1904–8) as well as the Maji-Maji rebellion in EA (1905–7) escalated into large-scale colonial wars. The Herero uprising, mainly caused by the destruction of their socio-political order, was suppressed by a war of extermination, whilst the Nama waged a protracted guerrilla war until 1908. The Maji-Maji rebellion in south-eastern EA opposed the colonial order as such. The cult of the holy water ('maji') made it possible to transcend ethnic-political limitations. The *Schutztruppe* responded with a strategy of scorched earth. Up to 200,000 Africans died in these wars.

These struggles were highly controversial issues in the German parliament. As a consequence, the Chancellor, Bernhard Bülow, dissolved the Reichstag and new elections were held in January 1907 (*Hottentottenwahlen*). Economic considerations and a *negererhaltende Politik*, a policy of 'preserving negroes', were the basis for protective measures in EA also as a part of security policy, whereas in SWA, the colonial policy still aimed at the total control of the people.

These anti-colonial struggles had also effects on the postcolonial world. In Tanzanian nationalistic historiography and politics, the independence movement of the Tanganyika African Peoples Union is regarded as the direct successor of the Maji-Maji rebellion. The personality cult of the leaders of the Herero and Nama rebellion are still important for the organisation and identity of these groups. African resistance against the suppression and exploitation on the part of imperial Germany was a central theme of East German historiography, which identified West Germany with the heritage of German colonial rule. Today, the German government is confronted with Herero calls for an official apology for the committed genocide.

Tanja Bührer

LITERARY WORKS
Seyfried, Gerhard (2003), *Herero*, Frankfurt am Main: Eichborn.
Timm, Uwe (1978), *Morenga*, Munich: Verlag Autoren Edition.
Witbooi, Hendrik (1982), *Afrika den Afrikanern! Aufzeichnungen eines Nama-Häuptlings aus der Zeit der deutschen Eroberung Südwestafrikas 1884–1894*, Berlin and Bonn: Dietz.

HISTORIES
Bald, Detlef (1976), 'Afrikanischer Kampf gegen koloniale Herrschaft', *Militärgeschichtliche Mitteilungen* 19: 23–50.
Becker, Felicitas (2004), 'Traders, "Big Men" and Prophets: Political Continuity and Crisis in the Maji Maji Rebellion in Southeast Tanzania', *The Journal of African History* 45 (1): 1–22.
Becker, Felicitas and Jigal Beez (eds) (2005), *Der Maji-Maji-Krieg in Deutsch-Ostafrika. 1905–1907*, Berlin: Ch. Links.
Hull, Isabel V. (2004), *Absolute Destruction. Military Culture and the Practices of War in Imperial Germany*, Ithaca, NY and London: Cornell University Press.
Zimmerer, Jürgen and Joachim Zeller (2006), *Genocide in German South-West Africa. The Colonial War (1904–1908) in Namibia and its Aftermath*, London: Merlin Press.

Askari and Askari Myth

In 1889, Germany asserted formal control over its East African colonial territory and provoked African coastal rulers to war. To defeat the forces of the coastal élites, and to bring East Africa under military control, the experienced military explorer Major Hermann von Wissmann requested and received his government's permission to recruit close to 800 African soldiers to form a small expeditionary force. This force, later known as the *Schutztruppe für Deutsch-Ostafrika*, drew on African soldiers recruited from Egypt, Somalia, the Swahili coast and south-eastern Africa. The Germans referred to their African soldiers as *askari*, a word of Arabic origin meaning 'police' or 'soldier'. These *askari*, led by German officers, defeated the forces of the coastal élites in the Abushiri War of 1889–90.

With the coast secured, the force pushed into the East African interior during the 1890s. In an endless series of campaigns, the *Schutztruppe* waged war with local powers, defeating some, forming alliances with others. As they established outposts throughout the territory now claimed as German East Africa, the *askari* became the most visible representatives of German power to African civilians. The *askari* quickly developed a reputation as a highly skilled, brave and loyal yet brutal force in the service of Germany's colonial aspirations. Their major test came in 1905, when the territorial expanse and diversity of peoples involved in the anti-colonial Maji-Maji War caught German officials by surprise. The *askari* again proved reliable and ruthlessly effective, finally defeating the last Maji-Maji fighters in 1907. Observers on all sides reported their violent battlefield excesses, but their loyalty and cohesion during the crisis proved the critical factor for German officers in post-war reporting on *askari* performance.

In 1914, when World War I began in Europe, an expanded force of *askari* defended the colony from Allied conquest. Under the leadership of General von Lettow-Vorbeck, they conducted a mobile war of retreat, using scorched-earth tactics that again exacted a harsh toll on African lives and livelihoods. Having successfully evaded the Allied forces for over four years, Lettow's force surrendered in November 1918 upon receiving word of the European armistice.

After the war and the seizure of German colonies in the Versailles settlement, colonial revisionists clamoured for the return of the colonies, citing Germany's supposed past glories as a model coloniser. A potent icon used to demonstrate Germany's fitness to recover its colonies was the figure of the 'loyal *askari*'. In countless publications, colonial revisionists cultivated a myth that proclaimed the virtues of their brave and loyal *askari* who stuck by Lettow-Vorbeck until the bitter end, despite experiencing horrible privations and dangers. Their familiar image circulated widely in Weimar and Nazi print and performance culture. Staring stoically back from photographic or artistic representations, their exploits described at length in romantic colonial memoirs, the image of the loyal *askari* stood for Germany's former and future role as a coloniser among its European peers. Yet consideration of *askari* identities as soldiers and colonial subjects in German East Africa, and their actual role in African history beyond the myth, remained largely obscure until recently.

Michelle Moyd

LITERARY WORKS

Lettow-Vorbeck, Paul von (1920), *Heia Safari! Deutschlands Kampf in Ostafrika*, Leipzig: v. Hafe and Koehler Verlag.

HISTORIES

Bechhaus-Gerst, Marianne (2007), *Treu bis in den Tod: Von Deutsch-Ostafrika nach Sachsenhausen – eine Lebensgeschichte*, Berlin: Links Verlag.

Mann, Erick J. (2002), *Mikono ya damu: 'Hands of Blood': African Mercenaries and the Politics of Conflict in German East Africa, 1888–1904*, Frankfurt: Peter Lang.

Michels, Stephanie (2004), 'Askari – treu bis in den Tod? Vom Umgang der Deutschen mit ihren schwarzen Soldaten', in Marianne Bechhaus-Gerst and Reinhard Klein-Arendt (eds), *AfrikanerInnen in Deutschland und schwarze Deutsche – Geschichte und Gegenwart*, Münster: Lit, pp. 171–86.

Nigmann, Ernst (1911), *Geschichte der Kaiserlichen Schutztruppe für Deutsch-Ostafrika*, Berlin: Mittler und Sohn.

Pesek, Michael (2005), *Koloniale Herrschaft in Deutsch-Ostafrika: Expeditionen, Militär und Verwaltung seit 1880*, Frankfurt am Main: Campus.

Berlin Conference

The Berlin Conference has often been regarded as the beginning of the partition of Africa. Yet the 'Scramble for Africa' started well before it. The French occupied Tunis in 1881. In 1882, a British protectorate was established in Egypt. Parts of the West African coast, the lower Niger, and the Congo Basin were disputed spheres of interest. All these developments raised fears of exclusion from trade opportunities through exclusive domination by other nations. Anglo-French rivalry provided an opportunity for the German Chancellor Otto von Bismarck to invite the French to co-ordinate foreign policy, by convening a conference on African issues. After the foundation of imperial Germany in 1871, the strategy of Bismarck's foreign policy had been to divert tensions away from Europe. Other goals of the planned conference included curtailing Britain's supremacy in world affairs and keeping open large areas of Africa to international trade.

The conference, which took place in Berlin from 15 November 1884 to 27 February 1885, was attended by delegates from Germany, Austria-Hungary, Belgium, Denmark, Spain, the United States, France, Great Britain, Italy, the Netherlands, Portugal, Russia, Sweden and the Ottoman Empire. According to diplomatic tradition, the 'civilised' powers claimed unilateral control over non-European territories. In this respect the conference reflected the tacit agreement on violent conquests that followed afterwards. Disagreement on different issues arose between those powers that already possessed territories in Africa and those that did not. The latter demanded freedom of navigation and free trade, whereas the former, especially France and Portugal, claimed sovereignty over their possessions. Britain generally supported free trade, but still reserved sovereign rights on the lower Niger.

The participants finally agreed on a formula for future occupations of the African coast. In addition, freedom of trade in the Congo Basin as well as freedom of navigation on the Niger and the Congo was stipulated, but on the latter an international commission should be established. The initiative to neutralise the Congo Basin in the eventuality of war resulted in the meaningless formula of *neutralité facultative*. The humanitarian issues – the suppression of the slave trade and the limiting of the spirits traffic – were of limited value. Apart from the main agenda of the conference, numerous bilateral settlements were negotiated. Of great importance for Central Africa was the fact that almost all participants recognised the private international association under the patronage of Belgium King Leopold II as a representative of a sovereign power.

Whatever the Conference intended, in the following years almost the whole of Africa was occupied. The International Congo Commission never convened, freedom of navigation was left to the responsibility of the river powers that abused their privileges of sovereignty to establish monopolies. But it was King Leopold II's Congo that showed the greatest discrepancy between the claims of free trade and philanthropic mission and the reality of a murderous system of forced labour. The liberal spirit of the conference and the free trade ideology were an expression of European imagination rather than historic reality.

Tanja Bührer

HISTORIES
Förster, Stig, Wolfgang Mommsen and Ronald Robinson (eds) (1988), *Bismarck, Europe, and Africa: The Berlin Africa Conference 1884–1885 and the Onset of Partition*, Oxford: Oxford University Press.

Hochschild, Adam (1998), *King Leopold's Ghosts: A Story of Greed, Terror, and Heroism in Colonial Africa*, New York: Houghton Mifflin Company.

Pakenham, Thomas (1991), *The Scramble for Africa, 1876–1912*, London: Weidenfeld and Nicolson.

Black Germans

Research on the history of blacks in Germany is relatively recent, and there remain many gaps in the historical record. In the early modern period, individual Africans began to be imported as ornamental household servants. Records of black prostitutes, sea-men and travelling entertainers go back at least as far as the eighteenth century. From the mid-eighteenth century onwards a number of young men of African origin were sponsored for training as skilled workers in Germany. In the same period, the growth of a relatively cosmopolitan aristocratic and civic culture allowed for notable individual careers, such as those of the Ethiopian-born Viennese courtier Angelo Soliman (c. 1721–96) and the Ghanaian Anton Wilhelm Amo (c. 1700–5?), a university lecturer in philosophy.

After the founding of a colonial empire in 1884, young Africans were again sponsored for training by missionary societies and by businesses with branches operating in the colonies. Until 1900, the government actively promoted visits of members of the African élites to Germany, in the hope of developing a native colonial administration. Employment in ethnographic exhibitions also enabled Africans to visit the metropolis. And individuals made their own way there, often as members of the increasingly international workforce in the German merchant fleet. The occupational profile of those who remained in Germany was varied, including work in transport and industry, as small businessmen, as language assistants in university departments, and as performers – often in shifting combinations.

In the face of discriminatory legislation and practices, they had families and maintained social networks. A number of men of this generation were active in challenging the colonial régime even before World War I. After 1918, their networks became the basis for mutual aid associations, and also for organised politics; between 1927 and 1933, some of them were active in the Comintern-influenced Anti-Imperialist League and in the League for the Defence of the Negro Race. Alongside the children of this generation, a second group of German-born 'blacks' emerged between 1919 and 1927: the 400–500 children of German women and African soldiers stationed with the French occupying forces in the Rhineland (*Rheinlandbastarde*). Under the National Socialist régime (1933–45) black Germans were subject to varying forms and degrees of discrimination and persecution. Most of the *Rheinlandbastarde* were forcibly sterilised. A number of black Germans were able to survive as performers in the colonial films and other spectacles favoured by the régime. As a group, however, they were formally identified as racial aliens and excluded from normal schooling and careers. They were easy targets for prosecution under the miscegenation laws and for assignment to the most demanding and degrading forms of forced labour.

Post-1945 developments increased the numbers and public visibility of black Germans. In Western Germany, about 5,000 children were born to German women as the result of relationships with African and African-American servicemen. They were the objects of public debate and informal discrimination during their formative years. In the 1980s, it was to a considerable extent the reception of the African-American experience among this generation (notably young women) that inspired the growth of a black German self-consciousness and politics. In the GDR, the majority of resident blacks were contract workers from Mozambique (15,000 in 1989), Namibia and Angola. They were officially discouraged from mixing with Germans or starting families, and where the majority population was aware of their presence at all, they tended to be regarded with suspicion as competitors for scarce consumer goods. After reunification in 1990, blacks were often victims of the steadily increasing incidence of racist violence, which was disproportionately concentrated in the new federal states (former GDR). The challenge of reunification provided a powerful impulse for the consolidation of black political and cultural associations (1990 Initiative Schwarze Menschen in Deutschland / ISD-Bund e.V.). Since 2000, continued tightening of controls in respect of immigration and asylum rights for newcomers has contrasted with the celebration of the historic native black presence on the part of the liberal media and government agencies, pursuing a vision of a harmonious multicultural Germany.

Eve Rosenhaft

Histories

AntiDiskriminierungsBüro (ADB) (ed.) (2004), *The BlackBook. Deutschlands Häutungen*, Frankfurt am Main: IKO, Verlag für Interkulturelle Kommunikation.

Blackshire-Belay, Carol Aisha (ed.) (1996), *The African-German Experience. Critical Essays*, Westport, CT and London: Praeger.

Campt, Tina (2004), *Other Germans. Black Germans and the Politics of Race, Gender, and Memory in the Third Reich*, Ann Arbor, MI: University of Michigan Press.

Fehrenbach, Heide (2005), *Race after Hitler. Black Occupation Children in Postwar Germany and America*, Princeton, NJ: Princeton University Press.

Kuck, Dennis (2003), '"Für den sozialistischen Aufbau ihrer Heimat?" Ausländische Vertragsarbeitskräfte in der DDR', in Jan C. Behrends, Thomas Lindenberger and Patrice G. Poutrous (eds), *Fremde und Fremd-Sein in der DDR. Zu historischen Ursachen der Fremdenfeindlichkeit in Ostdeutschland*, Berlin: Metropol, pp. 245–57.

Lemke Muniz de Faria, Yara-Colette (2002), *Zwischen Fürsorge und Ausgrenzung. Afrodeutsche 'Besatzungskinder' im Nachkriegsdeutschland*, Berlin: Metropol.

Martin, Peter (2001), *Schwarze Teufel, edle Mohren. Afrikaner in Geschichte und Bewußtsein der Deutschen*, Hamburg: Hamburger Edition.

Martin, Peter and Christine Alonzo (eds) (2004), *Zwischen Charleston und Stechschritt. Schwarze im Nationalsozialismus*, Hamburg and Munich: Dölling und Gallitz.

Oguntoye, Katharina (1997), *Eine afro-deutsche Geschichte. Zur Lebenssituation von Afrikanern und Afro-Deutschen in Deutschland von 1884 bis 1950*, Berlin: Verlag Christine Hoffmann.

Opitz, May, Katharina Oguntoye and Dagmar Schultz (eds) (1992), *Showing Our Colors. Afro-German Women Speak Out*, Amherst, MA: University of Massachusetts Press.

http://www.bpb.de/themen/X5FI94,0,0,Afrikanische_Diaspora_in_Deutschland.html [accessed 18 Nov. 2006].

Cameroon

In July 1884 a treaty signed by the chiefs of the coastal port of Douala and the Chancellor Bismarck's emissary, Gustav Nachtigal, established Germany's claim to what became the colonial territory of Cameroon. Thirty years later, in September 1914, combined British and French military forces invaded Cameroon, putting an end to German rule in this portion of Africa. Such a brief occupation provided no opportunity for Germany to draw much profit from Cameroon and left Cameroonians with a heritage of mainly French and partially British acculturation. Yet the developments of those three decades provided important elements of the German colonial experience and created a distinctive modern identity for Cameroonians.

As with almost all contemporary African states, the very geographic definition of Cameroon derives from the original partition of the continent among European powers. In the course of subsequent international manoeuvring, and especially during the divisions that arose among mandate powers following World War I, the boundaries of Cameroon shifted a number of times. However, after independence in 1960 and reunification in 1961, the new Republic of Cameroon very closely resembled the contours of the old *Schutzgebiet* (protectorate) 'Kamerun'.

It took the German régime almost twenty years and numerous military campaigns, to extend its political control from the coast to the inland frontiers of Cameroon. This small-scale if often quite bloody colonial warfare left little impression on public consciousness in the metropole. Cameroon, instead, was notorious for an endless series of scandals involving abuses of power in already occupied zones. These events began with a mutiny of imported Dahomean (Beninois) police troops in 1893. The long-serving (1895–1907) Governor Jesco von Puttkamer received constant criticism for his brutality against Duala chiefs and overly-close relations with plantation and trading companies and was finally removed for smuggling his mistress into the territory on a bogus passport. Missionaries, officials, merchants and plantation owners continually engaged in public battles over the treatment of Africans recruited to work on European-owned land. Finally, one month before the Germans left, they publicly executed the ex-Paramount Chief Rudolph Duala Manga Bell, as the last episode of a lengthy dispute over segregation and land expropriation in the city of Douala.

Among Cameroonians, the memory of German rule remains surprisingly positive. There were several major rebellions against this colonial régime, but mainly in remote southern and south-western areas of the south and southwest assigned as concessions to monopoly trading companies (which raised their own financial scandals in Germany). A small but significant group of Africans gained power and prestige as government approved chiefs. Many of them (and numerous lower level black functionaries in the colonial administration) received German education, and some of them (including Duala Manga Bell) even continued their studies in Germany.

Cameroonian pro-German sentiment may also be explained as a counter to later colonial régimes, especially that of France. During the independence era it has been furthered by aid, education and cultural efforts on the part of both the West and East German régimes. Perhaps the very rarity and short duration of German colonial rule has given it a somewhat mythic quality in Cameroonian self-representation.

Ralph A. Austen

LITERARY WORKS
Grimm, Hans (1931), *Der Ölsucher von Duala; ein afrikanisches Kriegstagebuch*, Hamburg: Deutsche Hausbücherei.
Ikellé-Matiba, Jean (1963), *Cette Afrique-là!*, Paris: Présence Africaine.

HISTORIES
Austen, Ralph A. and Jonathan Derrick (eds) (1999), *Middlemen of the Cameroon Rivers: The Duala and their Hinterland, c. 1600–c. 1960*, Cambridge: Cambridge University Press.

Hausen, Karin (1970), *Deutsche Kolonialherrschaft in Afrika: Wirtschaftsinteressen und Kolonialverwaltung in Kamerun vor 1914*, Zurich: Atlantis.

Ndumbe, Kum'a III (ed.) (1986), *L'Afrique et l'Allemagne de la colonisation á la cooperation, 1884–1986 (Le cas du Cameroun)*, Yaoundé: editions Africavenir.

Rudin, Harry R. (1938), *Germans in the Cameroons*, New Haven, CT: Yale University Press.

Stoecker, Helmuth (ed.) (1960), *Kamerun unter deutscher Kolonialherrschaft*, Berlin: Rütten u. Loening.

Wirz, Albert (1972), *Vom Sklavenhandel zum kolonialen Handel: Wirtschafsräume und Wirtschaftsformen in Kamerun vor 1914*, Zurich: Atlantis.

Colonial Administration

Lasting for only thirty years the German Empire never managed to establish a colonial administration in its own right and as the institutional power centre for colonial policy. For the first twenty years, the Department for Colonial Affairs (Kolonialabteilung) was part of the Foreign Office. After the disastrous colonial wars of the early twentieth century, and the colonial crises which they caused in Germany, in 1907 a Colonial Office (Kolonialamt) was established under Secretary Bernhard von Dernburg. After his time in office he had only three successors, Friedrich von Lindequist (1910–11), Wilhelm Solf (1911–18) and Johannes Bell (1919–20), who was already a minister without land when Germany's colonial empire was abandoned in the Treaty of Versailles.

The short period of existence is one of the reasons why central colonial officials never succeeded in effectively gaining control over German colonial policy. Competing institutions in Berlin, and centrifugal tensions between the imperial centre and colonial representatives 'on the spot', in the colonies, prevented the formulation and enactment of a clearly defined policy, and the creation of conditions suitable for implementing any such policy. Even Bernhard Dernburg, commonly regarded as the moderniser of German colonial policy, who established a benevolent approach to 'native policy', failed to create more than a public relations coup by stating that the 'natives are the most important asset in our colonies'. Even if we leave aside the fact that he endorsed some of the most brutal native ordinances in German South-West Africa, which attempted nothing less than total control and social engineering of African colonial subjects, his benevolent appeal fell mostly on deaf ears in the colonies. Looking at colonialism overseas, no change in policy can be detected and this fact reflects on the history of German central colonial administration. Developments on the spot proved to be much more decisive in shaping colonial rule than decisions in Berlin-Wilhelmstraße.

This can partly be explained by the history of the German colonial service. At the time of acquiring colonies, in the mid-1880s, no colonial administration existed. Personnel had to be recruited from other institutions. Notably, it was the military that provided most of the staff of the early colonial administration in the colonies, followed by the Foreign Office. Members of both services never completely lost their allegiance to their original masters. Split loyalties were the consequence. It was also due to this history that important aspects of colonial policy, such as international relations, and military defence, both against invasion and 'uprisings', remained the domain of the Foreign Office and the Military High Command (Großer Generalstab). This added to the difficulties experienced by colonial administrators in formulating a stringent policy.

The German central colonial administration was not powerless; it played an important role in creating and shaping public opinion at home, and it intervened in many fields of colonial policy, although to what extent it was successful has to be dealt with on a case-by-case basis. As part of Germany's fight against the 'colonial guilt question', and its attempt to regain its colonies in 1924, a colonial office was re-established as a department of the Foreign Office. However, without an empire to govern, it did little more than symbolise for a short while Germany's claim to world power status.

Jürgen Zimmerer

HISTORIES

Gründer, Horst (2004), *Geschichte der deutschen Kolonien*, 5th edn, Stuttgart: UTB.

Hubatsch, Walter (ed.) (1983), *Grundriß zur deutschen Verwaltungsgeschichte 1815–1945*, vol. 22, Bundes-und Reichsbehörden, Marburg an der Lahn: Johann-Gottfried-Herder-Institut.

Voigt, Rüdiger (ed.) (2001), *Kolonialisierung des Rechts. Zur kolonialen Rechts- und Verwaltungsordnung* (Schriften zur Rechtspolitologie, Bd 11), Baden-Baden: Nomos.

Colonial Culture and Colonial Impacts on Culture in Germany

In the German context, for a long time, colonialism was addressed only within the dimensions of political colonial rule and was thus restricted to the annexed territorial areas of the so-called 'protectorates' (*Schutzgebiete*). In this way it could be argued that since colonialism had been short-lived and spatially both limited and fragmented, colonial rule had never played a significant role in German culture; and that the loss of the colonies during World War I left no lasting effects. More recent research, however, emphasises the colonial dimension in areas of society not directly involved in national colonial politics, in settings both within and also outside Germany itself. In the deep structure of the colonial period, psychological, religious and ideological attitudes, 'acquired racism' and cultural stereotypes contributed to the climate of opinion on political and military colonial questions, while also being influenced themselves by political developments. Seen this way, colonialism is a dominant cultural phenomenon. Bearing in mind the shared origin of the terms colonialism and culture in the Latin *colere* ('till', 'grow', 'cultivate'), it is even a key metaphor of cultural dealings.

Within the German Empire, colonial themes developed concomitantly with modernisation. Colonial goods such as chocolate, tobacco and coffee reflected a growing area of foreign trade relations, and significant innovations were made in both the production and the distribution of these exotic products. From about 1890, advertising posters and automats, for example for chocolate and cigarettes, became a basic, everyday feature of modern life, while simultaneously evoking aristocratic pleasure rituals. The rise in travel to distant parts of the world and of tourism in general was bound up with the popularisation of exotic countries and ways of life. Even those who did not travel could find information and entertainment in the rapidly growing number of travel guides, prominent among which was Karl Baedeker's series, still being published today. In the ethnographic museums opened from the middle of the nineteenth century in Munich, Berlin, Hamburg, Bremen, Leipzig, Stuttgart, Vienna, Frankfurt and Cologne, visitors were offered a three-dimensional presentation of how lives were lived overseas, along with panoramas and dioramas, each with its own geographic and ethnographic arrangement. One commercially very successful permanent exhibition was the collection of the Hamburg furnishing company, Umlauff, which specialised in the import and adaptation of ethnographica.

Another opportunity to encounter the foreign and the strange was provided by the slide shows given by famous travellers, first in the Berlin 'Urania', later also in evening and adult education schools. Zoological gardens were also laid out to both entertain and to teach. Prominent among these was the Hagenbeck Zoo in Hamburg, which was also a pioneer in the staging of ethnographic shows.

The aesthetic impact of such exhibits lay in the cultural contrast made with exotic worlds and their inhabitants ('us' versus 'them'), and in the allure of presenting what was taboo to civilised European cultural norms (for example, public nudity). Some shows were tied in very directly to colonial interests, such as the Berlin Trade Exhibition of 1896, which displayed fruits, coffee and furniture manufactured from tropical woods from the African colonies to stimulate the public's support, and create potential buyers for German involvement in the colonies.

Tangible economic and political interests were also pursued even where the Reich was not directly involved in territorial rule, for example among the German settlers in Palestine (whose cultural significance was underscored by Kaiser Wilhelm II during his visit to Jerusalem, though no political demands were made on the then existing colonial power, Britain); and in the building of the 'Baghdad Railway', which was laid by German firms and almost exclusively financed with German capital, and ran right through Anatolia, with an extension planned into Mesopotamia and to the Arabian Gulf. In addition to its economic and political dimensions (collaboration with Turkey, the setting up of an international consortium of firms), this project also stimulated the power fantasies of Germany's planners; among its cultural benefits were the excavations in Turkey and Mesopotamia, with Oriental Studies becoming a major discipline in German archaeology.

                                                                                    Alexander Honold

HISTORIES

Heyden, Ulrich van der and Joachim Zeller (eds) (2002), *Kolonialmetropole Berlin. Eine Spurensuche*, Berlin: Berlin Edition.

Honold, Alexander and Oliver Simons (eds) (2002), *Kolonialismus als Kultur. Literatur, Medien, Wissenschaft in der deutschen Gründerzeit des Fremden*, Tübingen und Basle: Francke.

Honold, Alexander and Klaus R. Scherpe (eds) (2004), *Mit Deutschland um die Welt. Eine Kulturgeschichte des Fremden in der Kolonialzeit*, Stuttgart: Metzler.

Kundrus, Birthe (ed.) (2003), *Phantasiereiche. Zur Kulturgeschichte des deutschen Kolonialismus*, Frankfurt am Main: Campus.

Thode-Adora, Hilke (1989), *Für fünfzig Pfennig um die Welt. Die Hagenbeckschen Völkerschauen*, Frankfurt am Main and New York: Campus.

Thomas, Nicholas (1994), *Colonialism's Culture. Anthropology, Travel and Government*, Princeton, NJ: Princeton University Press.

Colonial Education

During Germany's colonial period, the term 'colonial education' was associated with two projects: first, the development of an elementary school education for the colonised; and second, the mission of an ideological education at home, aiming to turn young Germans into active and committed representatives of the colonial empire.

By the mid-nineteenth century, European educational measures were already established in all subsequent German colonies (except Kiaochow) by Christian missionary societies. After 1884, school education became a vital question as well for state politics in the so-called protectorates. The first government school was founded in Cameroon in 1887. But German missionary societies differed from colonial administrators regarding goals, methods and scales of the education measures. While the missions pursued a sustainable religious and moral education for broad sections of the population in the respective regional language, the rather short-term efforts of the government and the colonial administration aimed first and foremost at teaching in German and training selected indigenous assistants for office jobs and colonial troops. Neither of these groups cared for local needs or for existing educational traditions in the colonies.

A widespread distribution of government schools turned out to be unattainable for reasons of cost. Thus, in 1898, the German government made an effort to increase its influence on the activities of the missionary societies by linking state subsidies for the often badly-equipped mission schools to a German language curriculum, following the British model of indirect rule. Besides religious education, especially in the mission schools, the primary purpose of colonial education measures was literacy. The linguistic studies of the missionaries and the school primers written by them in indigenous languages laid the foundations for a far-reaching media change to the predominantly oral indigenous cultures. At the same time, they served as a source of knowledge for the colonial power and were used in the training of future colonial officials. By 1911, 1,682 evangelical and 916 Catholic mission schools existed in the German colonies with approximately 142,000 pupils compared to only 112 government schools with approximately 7,000 pupils (see Schlunk 1914).

In addition to this education policy in the colonies, state and private colonial propagandists encouraged the 'colonial education' of the youth back home. From as early as 1892, the German colonies were part of the Prussian school curriculum within the framework of geography classes. After the turn of the century, teaching of colonial topics was increasingly integrated into other school subjects as well. The German Colonial Society and other colonial associations tried to gain influence on the curriculum by editing and disseminating teaching material. While this domestic colonial education had its last and final revival in the revisionist colonial propaganda under Nazi rule, it remains an unfinished task in academic educational research and cultural-political analysis to reflect upon the colonial tradition of present education work abroad.

Sven Werkmeister

LITERARY WORKS
Achebe, Chinua (1958), *Things Fall Apart*, London: Heinemann.
Ngugi, James [1965] (1979), *The River Between*, London: Heinemann.

HISTORIES
Adick, Christel and Wolfgang Mehnert (eds) (2001), *Deutsche Missions-und Kolonialpädagogik in Dokumenten. Eine kommentierte Quellensammlung aus den Afrikabeständen deutschsprachiger Archive 1884–1914*, Frankfurt am Main: IKO Verlag für Interkulturelle Kommunikation.
Altbach, Philip G. and Gail Paradise Kelly (eds) (1984), *Education and the Colonial Experience*, 2nd rev. edn, New Brunswick: Transaction Books.
Mehnert, Wolfgang (1993), 'Regierungs- und Missionsschulen in der deutschen Kolonialpolitik (1885–1914)', *Bildung und Erziehung* 46 (3): 251–65.

Schlunk, Martin (1914), *Das Schulwesen in den deutschen Schutzgebieten*, Hamburg: Friedrichsen.

Werkmeister, Sven (2004), 'Koloniale Erziehung. Montag, 25. Juni 1906: Der erste Schultag in Fumban/Kamerun', in Alexander Honold and Klaus R. Scherpe (eds) (2004), *Mit Deutschland um die Welt. Eine Kulturgeschichte des Fremden in der deutschen Kolonialzeit*, Stuttgart: Metzler, pp. 347–56.

Colonial Literature: Narratives and Fiction of Empire

In German history, the word 'imperial' is closely bound up with the traditional term, the 'Reich', a concept implying not only territorial expansion and possession, but also assuming an imaginary continuity with the Roman/Christian Empire and its programme. In the modern period, this meant that the nation's ideological claims to leadership remained intact precisely *because* its territorial body and its borders no longer were. Thus the occupation by Napoleonic troops became the springboard from which the Romantics after 1860 called for a renewal of German national culture. Goethe's *Wilhelm Meisters Wanderjahre* (*Wilhelm Meister's Travels*) articulates the pioneering spirit that drove emigration to America (found as an anagram in the fictional character 'Makarie'), citing the lack of living space and work consequent to increasing industrialisation as the incentives for such departures. The figure of the emigrant seeking his fortune in America moves from the works of Kürnberger and Vischer right through to Kafka's novel *Der Verschollene* (*America*). As a counterbalance to the loss of one's 'own' ground, as a consequence of these ocean passages and overseas experiments, Gustav Freytag's anti-Semitic family saga, *Soll und Haben* (*Debit and Credit*), stakes out Germany's territorial self-assertion in the East, where it must use force if necessary to defy both the Slavic 'human flood' and Jewish capital.

The craving for adventure, and dreams of conquest, played an important role in popular travel literature (Balduin Möllhausen, Karl May). In the last thirty years of the nineteenth century, geographical discoveries (the source of the Nile, the Kilimanjaro, the Amazon, the South Seas) and their heroes filled the pages of family magazines like *Gartenlaube* (*The Arbour*) and *Über Land und Meer* (*Across Land and Sea*). These magazines were the most important literary medium of modernity. The novels of Theodore Fontane appeared first in such magazines in serial form, works which, and particularly *Der Stechlin* (*The Stechlin*), on careful reading resonate with the German colonial experience. In the twentieth century, many authors continued to take up exotic themes and foreign settings, without necessarily contributing directly to German colonial politics: China was used by Brecht and Döblin; Brazil by Heinrich Mann, Döblin, and Robert Müller; Mexico and Japan by Max Dauthendey; Egypt by Rilke and Thomas Mann. These writers were more concerned with the fantasies of flight of Europeans tired of civilisation, the seductions of a free life under southern suns. Some authors, though, stressed that these exotic journeys could be dangerous, and lead to fatal diseases, as in Thomas Mann's novella, *Tod in Venedig* (*Death in Venice*). Another version of the exotic threat more closely associated with colonisation is found in Frieda von Bülow's 1896 novel, *Tropenkoller* (*Tropical Spleen*), set in German East Africa. For a German colonial officer, more dangerous even than malaria and sleeping sickness (against which German scientific heroes fought in numerous second-rate novels) is the problem of losing one's reason, and indulging in orgies of cruelty. An extremely critical and brutal variation of this situation, namely the torture of a prisoner by a colonial officer, and the latter's eventual suicide using a flesh-engraving device, is described in an alienated form in Kafka's story *In der Strafkolonie* (*In the Penal Colony*). In 1930, Hermann Broch in the first part of the *Die Schlafwandler* (*The Sleepwalkers*) trilogy describes in retrospect the colonial dimension of political life in 1888. In this novel, the Prussian officer Joachim von Pasenow plays with the idea of joining the colonial troops, and visits an 'Indian Panorama' on Leipziger Straße.

German colonial literature in a more narrow sense is represented by works illustrating life in the protectorates, predominantly in German South-West Africa and in German East Africa. A relevant example here is Gustav Frenssen's 1906 novel, *Peter Moors Fahrt nach Südwest* (*Peter Moor's Journey to the South-West*), which describes the annihilation of the rebelling Herero and Nama from the perspective of a colonial soldier. The author's descriptions of Africa are not based on any personal experience, but are drawn entirely from newspaper reports and the accounts of eye-witnesses. In Hans Grimm's epic *Volk ohne Raum* (*A People without Space*), which sets out an ideological programme for German expansion during the Nazi period, the colonial mission is presented as the consequence of German overpopulation in a 'Reich', which has become too small. Uwe Timm's 1983 novel, *Morenga*, can be read as a counter-text to the militant line represented in Frenssen's colonial narrative. Employing historical documents, Timm exposes the calculated politics of extermination by the German troops, while also giving aesthetic expression to the strangeness of Africa. This book contributed to reviving the debate about German guilt and responsibility in the former colonies, and to an engagement with the cultural consequences of German colonialism.

Alexander Honold

LITERARY WORKS

Bülow, Frieda von (1896), *Tropenkoller. Eine Episode aus dem deutschen Kolonialleben*, Berlin: Fontane.

Frenssen, Gustav (1906), *Peter Moors Fahrt nach Südwest. Ein Feldzugsbericht*, Berlin: Grote.

Grimm, Hans (1926), *Volk ohne Raum*, Munich: Langen.

Holm, Orla (i.e. Dorrit Zuern) (1909), *Ovita. Episode aus dem Hereroland*, Dresden: Reissner.

Kafka, Franz [1914] (1994), *In der Strafkolonie. Gesammelte Werke*, ed. Hans-Gerd Koch, Frankfurt am Main: Fischer, vol. 1, pp. 159–96.

Kandt, Richard (1904), *Caput Nili. Eine empfindsame Reise zu den Quellen des Nils*, Berlin: Reimer.

Timm, Uwe (1983), *Morenga*, Cologne: Kiepenheuer and Witsch.

HISTORIES

Benninghoff-Lühl, Sibylle (1983), *Deutsche Kolonialromane 1884–1914 in ihrem Entstehungs- und Wirkungszusammenhang*, Bremen: Übersee-Museum.

Berman, Russel (1998), *Enlightenment or Empire. Colonial Discourse in German Culture*, Lincoln, NE and London: University of Nebraska Press.

Friedrichsmeyer, Sara, Sara Lennox and Susanne Zantop (eds) (1997), *The Imperialist Imagination. German Colonialism and its Legacy*, Ann Arbour, MI: Michigan University Press.

Honold, Alexander and Oliver Simons (eds) (2002), *Kolonialismus als Kultur. Literatur, Medien, Wissenschaft in der deutschen Gründerzeit des Fremden*, Tübingen und Basle: Francke.

Honold, Alexander and Klaus R. Scherpe (eds) (2004), *Mit Deutschland um die Welt. Eine Kulturgeschichte des Fremden in der Kolonialzeit*, Stuttgart: Metzler.

Noyes, John K. (1992), *Colonial Space, Spatiality in the Discourse of German South West Africa 1884–1915*, Chur etc.: Harwood Academic Publishers.

Warmbold, Joachim (1982), *'Ein Stückchen deutsche Erd'* . . .'. *Deutsche Kolonialliteratur. Aspekte ihrer Geschichte, Eigenart und Wirkung, dargestellt am Beispiel Afrikas*, Frankfurt am Main: Haag and Herchen.

Zantop, Susanne (1997), *Colonial Fantasies. Conquest, Family, and Nation in Precolonial Germany (1770–1870)*, Durham, NC: Duke University Press.

Colonial Migration and the Law

During the thirty years of German colonial rule, regulating migration became a key element in establishing a colonial legal order based on ethno-cultural difference. Migration occurred between different geo-judicial boundaries (within a colony, between different German colonies, between Germany and the colony of another colonial power, between a German colony and the German metropole), and for various motives (labour, education). Migrants included people with distinct judicial status (German citizens, citizens of other nations, 'colonial subjects') and specified ethnological features ('white', 'black', 'Chinese', 'native'). Right from the beginning of German colonial rule, the colonial administration issued a corpus of decrees aimed at harnessing these facets of colonial migration to supply the workforce necessary in tropical colonies, and to provide an appropriate socio-economic habitat for German migrants who came to the colonies. Thus attempts to regulate colonial migration judicially can be regarded as a true reflection of the ways in which German colonialism was organised as a racial state.

At the level of German federal law the colonies were defined neither as part of the homeland nor as a foreign country. This separate judicial sphere could exist because the German constitution did not apply in the colonies. Thus German executive power, represented both by the central colonial administration in Berlin and by its local branches in the colonies, could enact legislation in the colonies that was well outside the metropole's law code. As such, restrictions on migration could be justified even when German citizens were concerned, and despite the fact that freedom of movement had been guaranteed in Prussia and Germany since 1867 and 1870 respectively. However, because of a ubiquitous fear of colonial labour shortage, the bulk of decrees concerning migration applied to local as well as inter-colonial labour markets. Socio-politically, the countless decrees all aimed to establish a compromise between the interests of private enterprises, with their mostly ruthless labour recruitment practices, and the interests of the German colonial state in avoiding local resistance and depopulation of entire regions.

Some features in colonial migration restrictions deserve special mention, namely those concerning movements between the colonies and the metropole. Although one of the main justifications for becoming a colonial power was channelling migration of Germans to a piece of land overseas under German jurisdiction, not all German emigrants were welcome in the colonies. Whereas the colonial administration was keen on attracting independent artisans, farmers and trades people through a variety of special programmes, after around 1900 it imposed a series of restrictions on any 'whites', including German citizens, who might eventually become wage-dependant. The general fear was that such emigrants would devolve into a 'poor white' segment of the colonial society, eventually losing their distinctiveness as 'whites' vis-à-vis non-white communities. Conversely, also around the turn of the century, successive colonial administrations began systematically to restrict

the migration of 'non-white' colonial subjects to the German metropole. But as the imperial government had no interest in instituting general immigration restrictions for colonial
subjects to Germany at the level of imperial law, the local colonial administrations issued
case-specific decrees such as the general 'ban on the emigration of natives out of the colony'
to Germany, or, when interests of Germans were involved, the 'ban on taking native servants out of the colony' (1900) and the 'ban on exporting natives for ethnographic exhibitions' (1901). In summary, between the turn of the century and World War I, the German
colonial administration sought to establish a legal order which limited movements of
whites and non-whites to and from the colonies, thus furthering the intended segregation
of the socio-cultural spheres of racially defined groups.

Despite all intentions to establish separate socio-cultural spheres for whites and non-
whites, migration obviously occurred. So far, the most thoroughly studied example of such
migration is that of Africans (mainly from Cameroon or Togo, and a few inhabitants of the
other African and South Pacific colonies) who migrated to the Germany metropole, either
temporarily, or for good. Because these immigrants were not specifically recorded upon
entry or during their stays, there are no exact figures on how many resided in Germany until
1914 or thereafter. However, archival sources based on police records and other biased
materials lead to estimates of more than 500 (including their offspring). Reasons for such
immigration to the metropole were manifold, such as pursuing an education, following
colonial officers as servants, or acting as members of colonial or anthropological exhibits.

From a judicial perspective the presence of these colonial migrants in Germany was
undefined, because they were not citizens (with the exception of those few who became
naturalised German citizens). But neither were they foreigners or 'natives': the latter category only formally applied within the context of the colonies. In the years leading up to
World War I, the German government, pressured by radical nationalist groups and the
colonial administration, attempted to formalise this undefined status of being 'native', but
without any palpable result. After World War I, this ambiguous legal state was further complicated for the roughly fifty colonial migrants who stayed in Germany after Germany lost
its colonial possessions. They now became 'natives' of another colonial power (for example
Great Britain, France, Australia) under the umbrella of the League of Nations. Similarly,
the National Socialist state never regulated their legal status through an internationally
binding judicial agreement. In the logic of the National Socialist régime the existence of
these migrants required only an ethnological definition; they would be classified under the
Nuremberg Law of 1935 as members of 'foreign blood', and were prohibited marriage with
'Aryans'. Although colonial migrants were now unequivocally defined on racial grounds
within the context of the National Socialist racial state, no convincing evidence has yet
appeared that they were systematically persecuted as a group beyond the scope of the
Nuremberg Laws, as was the case with other racially defined groups.

Pascal Grosse

HISTORIES

Bechhaus-Gerst, Marianne Klein-Arendt and Rüdiger Klein-Arendt (eds) (2004),
AfrikanerInnen in Deutschland und schwarze Deutsche-Geschichte und Gegenwart,
Münster: Lit.

Campt, Tina, Pascal Grosse and Yara-Colette Lemke-Muniz de Faria (1998), 'Blacks, Germans
and the Politics of Colonial Imagination, 1920–1960', in Sara Friedrichsmeyer, Sara
Lennox, Susanne Zantop (eds), *The Imperialist Imagination. German Colonialism and its
Legacy*, Ann Arbor, MI: University of Michigan Press, pp. 205–29.

Die Deutsche Kolonialgesetzgebung (1884–1910), Berlin: Ernst Siegfried Mittler und Sohn.

Gilman, Sander (1982), *On Blackness without Blacks: Essays on the Image of Blacks in Germany*, Boston, MA: G. K. Hall.

Grosse, Pascal (2000), *Kolonialismus, Eugenik und bürgerliche Gesellschaft in Deutschland, 1850–1918*, Frankfurt am Main: Campus.

— (2002), 'Koloniale Lebenswelten in Berlin, 1885–1945', in Ulrich van der Heyden and Jürgen Zeller (eds), *Kolonialmetropole Berlin. Eine Spurensuche*, Berlin: Berlin Edition, pp. 195–203.

— (2003), 'Zwischen Privatheit und Öffentlichkeit. Kolonialmigration in Deutschland, 1900–1940', in Birthe Kundrus (ed.), *Phantasiereiche. Der deutsche Kolonialismus in kulturgeschichtlicher Perspektive*, Frankfurt am Main: Campus Verlag, pp. 91–109.

Kundrus, Birthe (2003), *Moderne Imperialisten. Das Kaiserreich im Spiegel seiner Kolonien*, Cologne and Weimar: Böhlau.

Oguntoye, Katharina, May Opitz and Dagmar Schultz (eds) (1986), *Farbe bekennen. Afrodeutsche Frauen auf den Spuren ihrer Geschichte*, Berlin: Orlanda-Verlag.

Rüger, Adolf (1975), 'Imperialismus, Sozialreformismus und antikoloniale demokratische Alternative. Zielvorstellungen von Afrikanern in Deutschland im Jahre 1919', *Zeitschrift für Geschichtswissenschaft* 23(1): 293–308.

Sadji, Uta (1987), 'Höhere Tochter in der Kaiserstadt Berlin. Gespräche mit Maria Diop', *Etudes Germano-Africaines* 5: 145–52.

Stengel, Karl Freiherr von (1886), *Die staats-und völkerrechtliche Stellung der Deutschen 'Kolonien' und ihre zukünftige Verfassung*, Berlin: Verlag des Deutschen Kolonialvereins.

Wildenthal, Lora (2001), *German Women for Empire, 1884–1945*, Durham, NC: Duke University Press.

Colonial Monuments

Even today, monuments in Germany, Africa and the Pacific region bear witness to the fact that between 1884 and World War I the German Reich was one of the European colonial powers. One such monument is the equestrian statue in Windhoek (Namibia). Another is the huge brick statue of an African elephant in Bremen that used to be known as the Colonial Monument (Kolonial-Ehrenmal).

The colonial monuments erected in the metropole before World War I served to popularise and propagate the colonial idea, with its connotations of greatness, national prestige and world-power. The aim of commemorating 'great German colonial pioneers' such as Hermann von Wissmann, or Carl Peters, or soldiers who had fallen in the colonies, was to strengthen German identification with the overseas colonial empire.

The cult of the hero in the colonies was not just about mourning Germans who had perished there. The monuments erected in those territories were first and foremost signs of hegemony, symbolic appropriations of the conquered space. The aim was to make the foreign possessions German; the monuments demonstrated the German Reich's claim to its protectorates. The monuments were built to endure for generations and to convey the message of the supremacy of the imperial race to the subjugated native populations in the colonies, who were to be made to forget that they had once themselves been masters in their lands. The repressive imposition in the colonies of European commemorative culture as an instrument of cultural domination and social oppression went hand in hand with the suppression of indigenous history and culture. The colonised societies did not, however, passively accept the break with their traditions that the colonial power tried to force upon them. They actively countered such cultural imperialism in innovative and subversive ways: they appropriated German commemorative culture and reinterpreted it in light of their own traditions and for their own purposes, thus refusing the colonial power's claim to a monopoly on representation and interpretation. Eloquent examples can be found in the Herero and Witbooi-Nama in Namibia, whose memorial culture (for example, the annual Herero Day in Okahandja) was an important element in the anti-colonial struggle against the authoritarian colonial state.

After the early end of Germany's colonial empire in 1919, the old colonial monuments, and the new ones that were created until the end of the 1930s, became shrines for the German colonial movement, where its supporters would rally and disseminate neo-colonial propaganda. Monuments in former German colonial territories were taken down by the new mandate powers, and handed over to the German authorities. The statues were then put up again in Germany.

Exceptions to these practices are the colonial monuments in what used to be South-West Africa (now Namibia). Many of the German settlers were not repatriated but allowed to stay after World War I, and the new mandate power, South Africa, left all the monuments standing. They remain part of the historical and political topography of the country to this very day. Even after Namibia gained independence in 1990, they were not destroyed, as many whites had feared.

After the end of World War II in 1945, many of the colonial and military monuments still standing were taken down, including all those in East Germany. In the context of the ensuing worldwide process of decolonisation, the old Eurocentric view of the world and history was eroded. In West Germany, monuments were toppled. Some colonial monuments were relegated to museums; others were rededicated as anti-colonial, usually as a result of efforts by Third World and solidarity groups. Among those now commemorated were the local people killed in the colonial wars, who had until then been banished from memory. The symbolic upgrading of African, Pacific and Chinese victims was an attempt to remove the guilt of crimes committed in the name of Germany in its colonies. In Germany's official state commemoration practices today, colonialism plays no role, or at most a marginal one.

Joachim Zeller

HISTORIES

Colonial Monuments and Participative Art – Cultures of Remembrance, Myths, Antitheses, Inversions, by Jokinen, Visual Artist: http: //www.afrika-hamburg.de [accessed 18 November 2006].

Speitkamp, Winfried (2000), 'Kolonialherrschaft und Denkmal. Afrikanische und deutsche Erinnerungskultur im Konflikt', in Wolfram Martini (ed.), *Architektur und Erinnerung*, Göttingen: Vandenhoeck and Ruprecht, pp. 165–90.

Zeller, Joachim (2000), *Kolonialdenkmäler und Geschichtsbewußtsein. Eine Untersuchung der kolonialdeutschen Erinnerungskultur*, Frankfurt am Main: IKO Verlag für Interkulturelle Kommunikation.

— (2004), 'Kolonialkrieg und Denkmal. 100 Jahre Politik mit der Erinnerung', in Larissa Förster, Dag Henrichsen and Michael Bollig (eds), *Namibia-Deutschland: Eine geteilte Geschichte. Widerstand, Gewalt, Erinnerung*, Cologne: Edition Minerva, pp. 124–43.

Colonial Revisionism

After Germany was defeated in World War I, it faced the loss of its colonies due to the Versailles Treaty. The Allies argued that the Germans had demonstrated their inability to colonise, especially by mistreating their colonised subjects. In Germany, this line of reasoning was countered by a wave of protest. The former Governor of German East Africa, Heinrich Schnee, called the Allied accusations a 'colonial guilt lie' (*koloniale Schuldlüge*), analogous to the revisionist term 'war guilt lie' (*Kriegsschuldlüge*). Colonial revisionism thus centred upon the regaining of power over the former colonies, and could be seen as part of the general revisionist movement against the Versailles settlement in post-World War I Germany.

Colonial revisionism worked mainly on two different levels: based on the assumption that the colonies were vital for the German nation for economic, geo-political, and bio-political reasons, it was a political movement with the aim of re-establishing Germany as a colonial power. On a more symbolic level, it was a discourse of national humiliation and victimisation, which simultaneously established a myth of German military power and colonial achievements. Colonial revisionist propaganda spread narratives of the alleged loyalty of the colonised subjects which were designed to prove the 'accomplishments' of the German colonial past. The most popular of these narratives was the myth of the loyal *askari* soldier, which referred to the campaign of the East African Schutztruppe under Paul von Lettow-Vorbeck in World War I. Apart from the supposed devotion of the black soldiers to their white commanders, the *askari* myth claimed that Lettow-Vorbeck's Schutztruppe had been undefeated at the end of war, in spite of the British troops' superiority in numbers.

In the early post-war period, colonial revisionism enjoyed widespread support in the population and nearly the whole political spectrum. When Lettow-Vorbeck and his Schutztruppe paraded through the Brandenburg Gate upon their arrival in Berlin in March 1919, they were welcomed as heroes; in the same month, the National Assembly (Nationalversammlung) voted 414 to 7 against the loss of the colonies, and in April 1919, approximately 3.8 million Germans signed similar protest notes. While colonialism had been a disputed issue during the Wilhelmine Empire, the campaign against the Versailles Treaty succeeded in making it a 'national project' at a time when German colonial rule had already ended.

In the course of the 1920s, a number of new colonial associations were established. These groups, however, consisted mainly of former colonialists, and their total number did not exceed 35,000 to 40,000 in the Weimar Republic. In 1922, they joined together as the umbrella organisation 'Colonial Reich Working-Group' (*Koloniale Reichsarbeitsgemeinschaft*). The rest of the population grew increasingly indifferent to the topic. Indeed, soon only the colonial associations continued insistently to demand the return of the colonies. They criticised the government for being too moderate, and a number of prominent colonial revisionists joined the NSDAP before 1933.

In the second half of the 1930s, colonial revisionism had a revival, although Nazi colonial ambitions focused primarily on Eastern Europe rather than Africa. With the end of the National Socialist régime, colonial revisionism in the sense of concrete colonial ambitions finally came to an end. However, certain elements from colonial revisionist thinking are part of German memory even today. The belief that the Germans were good colonisers who built roads, railway lines, schools and hospitals and who were – and still are – generally liked by the population seems to be widely held up to the present day.

Susann Lewerenz

LITERARY WORKS
Grimm, Hans (1926), *Volk ohne Raum*, Munich: Langen-Mueller.
Lettow-Vorbeck, Paul von (1920), *Heia Safari! Deutschlands Kampf in Ostafrika*, Leipzig:
    Hase and Koehler.
Schnee, Heinrich (1924), *Die koloniale Schuldlüge*, Munich: Süddeutsche Monatshefte.

HISTORIES
Hildebrand, Klaus (1969), *Vom Reich zum Weltreich. Hitler, NSDAP und koloniale Frage
    1919–1945*, Munich: Fink.
Laak, Dirk van (2004), *Imperiale Infrastruktur. Deutsche Planungen für eine Erschließung
    Afrikas 1880 bis 1960*, Paderborn: Schoeningh.
Rogowski, Christian (2003), ' "Heraus mit unseren Kolonien!" Der Kolonialrevisionismus
    der Weimarer Republik und die "Hamburger Kolonialwoche" von 1926', in Birthe
    Kundrus (ed.), *Phantasiereiche. Zur Kulturgeschichte des deutschen Kolonialismus*,
    Frankfurt am Main and New York: Campus Verlag, pp. 52–60.
Rüger, Adolf (1991), 'Das Streben nach kolonialer Restitution in den ersten
    Nachkriegsjahren', in Helmuth Stoecker (ed.), *Drang nach Afrika. Die deutsche kolo-
    niale Expansionspolitik und Herrschaft in Afrika von den Anfängen bis zum Verlust der
    Kolonien*, 2nd edn, Berlin: Akademie-Verlag, pp. 262–83.
Schmokel, Wolfe W. (1964), *Dream of Empire: German Colonialism, 1919–1945*, New
    Haven, CT and London: Yale University Press.

Colonialism and African and Afro-German Writing

As a result of losing its colonies after World War I, Germany did not face a colonial legacy
in ways like that of, for example, France and Britain. With the exception of today's
Namibia, the German language no longer plays a significant role in formerly German-
colonised territories. Intellectuals and authors from these areas rarely expressed their
thoughts in the German language; for the most part, Germany was not at the centre of their
critical writings. Intellectuals and artists from Africa, however, moved to Germany before,
during and after decolonisation and articulated their views in German. Other Africans or
Afro-Americans discussed the German presence in Africa or their experiences in Germany
in other languages.

One of the earliest examples of German-language literature and autobiographies by
authors with origins in German-colonised countries are the autobiographies of Sayyida
Salima bint Sa'id bin Ahmad Al Bu-Sa'id (1844–1924), who was a daughter of the sultan
of Zanzibar. She married an agent of a German mercantile firm, moved with him to
Hamburg, and was later known under her married name, Emily Ruete. An important publication that brought attention to the tenacity of racist and colonialist thought in German
society was *Farbe bekennen* (Oguntoye et al. 1996). Writings and films by, for example, May
Ayim and Fatima El-Tayeb, articulate Afro-German views of life in Germany. Another
group of texts includes autobiographies and novels of individuals who were born in
colonised or decolonised countries and came to Germany to study and work. Their
commentary on German society reveals the difficulties they encountered while living in
Germany. With regard to non-literary writings, the tremendous output of intellectuals from
decolonised countries is significant. Dissertations, theses and other scholarly work, such as
the African studies publications coming out of Bayreuth University or the yearbooks of the

Afrikanisch-Asiatische Studienförderung in Göttingen, amount to significant postcolonial contributions in the German language.

Another group of writings includes literature and autobiographies composed in non-German languages that articulate a critique of German colonialism. An outstanding example is Swahili historiographic poetry about German colonial rule in East Africa. Drawing on Swahili traditions of praise poems and narrative poems, this historiographic poetry is vivid testimony to a cruel occupation. It chronicles battles, death and destruction, and presents a deep sense of humiliation, anger at defeat and helplessness in light of an overwhelming occupying power (Miehe et al. 2002). Other examples of writings about the German colonial period can be found in countries such as Cameroon, Togo and Namibia; yet more material of this kind still needs to be located and published. Another type of non-German writing is represented by Hans J. Massaquoi's English-language autobiographical account of his everyday life experiences as a black child growing up in Nazi Germany. Finally, autobiographical novels by Amma Darko and Aly Diallo (texts that were translated from English and French but first published in German) also belong to this growing body of texts about contemporary intercultural relations.

Studies evaluating this significant corpus of texts are slow to emerge in Germany, mostly because of a lack of historical knowledge about colonialism, the fact that comparative knowledge is undervalued, and because of the enduring refusal to understand Germany as an immigrant society.

Nina Berman

LITERARY WORKS AND AUTOBIOGRAPHIES

Ayim, May (1997), *Grenzenlos und unverschämt*, Berlin: Orlanda Frauenverlag.

Bisimana, Nsekuye (1985), *Müssen die Afrikaner den Weissen alles nachmachen?*, Berlin: Quorum.

Darko, Amma (1991), *Der verkaufte Traum*, Stuttgart: Schmetterling.

Diallo, Aly (1987), *Die Täuschung*, Frankfurt am Main: Nexus.

El-Tayeb, Fatima and Angelina Maccarone (1999), *Alles wird gut*, Berlin: Orlanda Frauenverlag. Film, 1999.

Kwalanda, Miriam, with Birgit Theresa Koch (1999), *Die Farbe meines Gesichts: Lebensreise einer kenianischen Frau*, Frankfurt am Main: Eichborn.

Massaquoi, Hans J. (1999), *Destined to Witness: Growing up Black in Nazi Germany*, New York: Morrow.

Mazimpaka, Thomas (1997), *Ein Tutsi in Deutschland: Das Schicksal eines Flüchtlings*, Leipzig: Evangelische Verlagsanstalt.

Oji, Chima (1992), *Unter die Deutschen gefallen: Erfahrungen eines Afrikaners*, Wuppertal: Hammer.

Ruete, Emily (Sayyida Salima bint Saʿid bin Ahmad Al Bu-Saʿid (1886), *Memoiren einer arabischen Prinzessin*, reprinted (1989) as *Leben im Sultanspalast: Memoiren aus dem 19. Jahrhundert*, Frankfurt am Main: Athenäum.

HISTORIES

Ashcroft, Bill, Garett Griffiths and Helen Tiffin (eds) (1989), *The Empire Writes Back: Theory and Practice in Post-Colonial Literatures*, London: Routledge.

Keil, Thomas (2003), *Die postkoloniale deutsche Literatur in Namibia (1920–2000)*, Ph.D. diss. Stuttgart. http://elib.unistuttgart.de/opus/volltexte/2003/1495/ [accessed 19 Nov. 2006].

Miehe, Gudrun, Katrin Bromber, Said Khamis, Ralf Großerhode and Hilke Meyer-Bahlburg (eds) (2002), *Kala Shairi: German East Africa in Swahili Poems*, Cologne: Köppe.

Oguntoye, Katharina and Dagmar Schultz (eds) (1986), *Farbe bekennen: Afro-Deutsche Frauen auf den Spuren ihrer Geschichte*, Berlin: Orlanda Frauenverlag.

Riesz, János (2000), 'Autor/innen aus dem schwarzafrikanischen Kulturraum', in Carmine Chiellino (ed.), *Interkulturelle Literatur in Deutschland: ein Handbuch*, Stuttgart: Metzler, pp. 248–62.

Wright, Michelle M. (2004), *Becoming Black: Creating Identity in the African Diaspora*, Durham, NC: Duke University Press.

Commercial Ethnographic Exhibitions: *Völkerschauen*

Starting with the age of overseas discoveries, Europe has a long tradition of putting people on display who were considered ethnically and culturally different or 'exotic'. The early seafarers presented Native Americans, and later Inuit and Pacific Islanders as human specimens at the royal courts and country fairs. While some were introduced into noble society as individuals, others play-acted in front of painted sceneries, or elaborately created settings that were considered typical pursuits of their culture. Following the European paradigms of their times and local origins, the discourse of their presentation could cover any continuum between 'wild man' and 'noble savage'.

In Germany, *Völkerschauen* were mainly a small-scale, but wide-spread phenomenon till the last quarter of the nineteenth century. From the 1870s, influenced by the big London shows, by successful American impresarios (P. T. Barnum, 'Buffalo Bill' Cody) and by freak shows putting 'exotic' people on display, some enterprises (for example, the Hagenbeck company), elaborated them to logistically sophisticated, highly mobile, ethnographically detailed spectacles with intricate background sceneries and dramaturgy. Commercial *Völkerschauen* peaked between the 1880s and 1914; hundreds of troupes, sometimes comprising several hundred participants, went on tour all over Europe, drawing large crowds. Accordingly, their impact on the masses was much greater than that of the relatively few and immobile trade and colonial exhibitions. *Völkerschauen* gradually lost significance after World War I due to the upsurge of sophisticated films depicting exotic worlds. The Nazis put an end to them, but tried to concentrate black Germans in a colonial propagandistic Africa Show.

Völkerschauen could be seen in zoos, fun parks, exhibition areas, at fairs, theatres or pubs. The two main attractions were performances – usually including dances, music and fighting – and 'villages', where visitors could roam freely, observe alleged 'daily life', and buy souvenirs. Some organisers went to great lengths to provide 'authentic' ethnographic objects, fauna, flora and background sceneries, thus creating for the spectators the illusion of travel to the depicted area.

Anthropologists, musicologists and linguists were usually granted extra performances, and given the chance to use troupe members as study objects or informants, thus trying to enhance the sparse data bases of their young disciplines, but often getting trapped in circular reasoning due to the unreliable ethnic origin of troupe members. Museums profited by ethnographic objects used or produced during the shows.

The scarce reliable sources about troupe members' lives and views suggest financial considerations as the main motive for participating – often repeatedly – in *Völkerschauen*, sometimes, but not always, out of deprivation or colonial oppression in their regions of origin. Some troupe members became small-scale *Völkerschau* impresarios themselves.

The essence of *Völkerschauen* was the evocation of an ethnic 'Other', which constituted a projection screen of private and public ideologies and fantasies. This was not limited to non-Europeans – there were *Völkerschauen* with Swedish peasants, for example. In contrast to German colonial exhibitions with their explicit educative aims, commercial *Völkerschauen* were business. Accordingly, they did not *create* new stereotypes, but rather *reinforced* and *perpetuated* images of ethnic 'Others' that had been in existence for centuries. Portraits of *Völkerschau* participants formed part of the race charts of Germany's most influential encyclopaedia, *Brockhaus*, till the 1950s. And there was a continuity of personnel and expertise from the *Völkerschauen* towards German (and, through emigration, the USA) film industry in conjuring exotic worlds (for example, UFA, Fritz Lang).

Hilke Thode-Arora

LITERARY WORKS
Altenberg, Peter (1897), *Ashantee*, Berlin: S. Fischer.
Horváth, Ödon von (1932), *Kasimir und Karoline*, Frankfurt am Main: Suhrkamp.
Jahn, Hanns Henny (1949–61), *Fluß ohne Ufer. Roman in drei Teilen*, Frankfurt: Europäische Verlagsanstalt.
Scheurmann, Erich (1920), *Der Papalagi: die Reden des Südseehäuptlings Tuiavii aus Tiavea*, Zurich: Verlag Tanner und Staehelin.
Stinde, Julius (1897), *Hotel Buchholz. Ausstellungserlebnisse der Frau Wilhelmine Buchholz*, Berlin: Freund and Jeckel.

HISTORIES
Debusmann, Robert and János Riesz (eds) (1995), *Kolonialausstellungen. Begegnungen mit Afrika?* Frankfurt am Main: IKO Verlag für Interkulturelle Kommunikation.
Höpp, Gerhard (ed.) (1996), *Fremde Erfahrungen. Asiaten und Afrikaner in Deutschland, Österreich und in der Schweiz bis 1945*, Berlin: Das Arabische Buch.
Lewerenz, Susann (2006), *Die Deutsche Afrika-Schau (1935–1940). Rassismus, Kolonialrevisionismus und postkoloniale Auseinandersetzungen im nationalsozialistischen Deutschland*, Frankfurt am Main and New York: Peter Lang Verlag.
Schöning, Jörg (ed.) (1997), *Triviale Tropen: Exotische Reise- und Abenteuerfilme aus Deutschland 1919–1939*, Munich: edition text + kritik
Thode-Arora, Hilke (1989), *Für fünfzig Pfennig um die Welt. Die Hagenbeckschen Völkerschauen*, Frankfurt and New York: Campus.

German East Africa

German East Africa (today's Tanzania) was Germany's second largest colony. Although German merchants had been active in Zanzibar and along the East African coastline during the 1870s and 1880s, they evidently felt safe under the protection of a few British administrators and the Arabic merchants dominating the East African trade business at the time and never officially asked for political or military protection from the German state. Thus, in the end, it was colonial ideology alone that led to the founding of German East Africa.

By the time the first German colonisers arrived in the early 1880s, East Africa had been shaped by a highly developed transnational economic system, largely based on slaves, ivory and cloves, even though the inner region beyond the coastline remained largely unexplored. That the region eventually became a German colony was mainly the work of one person; Carl Peters, a trained historian and self-declared philosopher. In 1883, Peters founded the 'Society for German Colonisation', and managed to collect enough money to organise an expedition to East Africa, where he intended to establish a 'German India'. With no support from the German government, he first stepped onto the African continent in September 1883, and began a nine-week march into the inner region. During this trip, which he and his three German friends survived more due to luck than skill, he managed to convince some of the local leaders to sign bizarre 'contracts' that he had formulated. With these papers he went back to Berlin in early 1884, as proof of his 'founding' of a new colony. Although Chancellor Bismarck was anything but an enthusiastic colonialist, he felt the establishment of a colony in the region to be diplomatically advantageous. Bismarck declared the papers to be official German contracts of protection (*Schutzverträge*), and thus the colony of German East Africa was formally founded. Contrary to expectations, Peters never became governor of the new colony. He was released from colonial duty in 1896, after it was made public that he had killed two of his African servants and, without reason, burned several African villages while he had been the leader of a colonial outpost in the Kilimanjaro region in the winter of 1891–2. The public announcement of these events, and Peters' release from duty, were perceived as Germany's biggest colonial scandal.

Although East Africa quickly became Germany's most prestigious colonial project (after German South-West Africa; today's Namibia), until 1889, colonial administration and settlement were limited to the coastline. During the 1890s German military expeditions started to conquer and explore the inner region, constantly fighting African and Arabic resistance in an ongoing guerrilla war with thousands of mostly African victims. At the same time German and Indian settlers began to establish farms and plantations in relatively safe areas and 'employed' African workers. Since there was no official regulation of labour conditions in the colony until 1905, many Africans worked on these plantations in a quasi-slavery system under the control of the military administration. When, in 1905, a new tax system was introduced, according to which Africans had to pay in cash and no longer in kind, many were forced into unpaid public labour, building streets and railroads for the colonial government. This became the major social origin for the uprising of 1905 that was later called the Maji-Maji War. The German administration had to deploy its entire military force to suppress the uprising, leaving at least 80,000 Africans dead.

After the Maji-Maji War, the new Governor, Albrecht von Rechenberg, together with the missions, tried to transform German East Africa from a settler colony into a pure trading colony, envisioned as an open market for German, Indian, Arabic and African products and exchanges. Von Rechenberg even imagined allowing Africans political representation and, to a certain degree, participation in the administration of the colony. However, official German colonial politics as well as the views of the German public made such reforms impossible. Thus, even though the colony developed quite well economically and by 1914 had even established a relatively impressive education system, the great majority of Africans still worked under conditions closer to slavery than to a modern labour system.

An important aspect of the situation, in the years before and during World War I, was the military integration of Africans and the organisation of black colonial troops trained in their own, as well as in European, methods of warfare. The success of this particular form of integration was evident in the fact that although British forces quickly occupied all other German colonies, General Lettow-Vorbeck and his *Askari* troops were able to defend

German East Africa up to the end of the war. After the defeat of Germany, and the stricture against any further colonial activity, the largest part of East Africa came under the protection of the League of Nations, and de facto under British rule, until its final declaration of independence as the state of Tanzania in 1964. The mandate for Burundi and Rwanda went to Belgium. In the South, the *Kionga Triangle*, which later was known as Mozambique went to Portugal.

In the general context of Germany's colonial and postcolonial history, German East Africa represents – more than the other African colonies – the ideological and even phantasmagoric side of the German colonial consciousness. From its legendary founder Carl Peters, through the 'magical' and violent Maji-Maji War, and the myths around Lettow-Vorbeck and his 'loyal', quasi-German Africans, the colony's history remained an important as well as ambiguous source for the German colonial and postcolonial imagination. The colonial revisionists of the Weimar Republic, and even more so the National Socialists, produced a vast amount of literature and popular imagery about the history of German East Africa, which quickly turned it into a symbol representing most of the hopes, fears and fantasies of German colonialism.

Christian Geulen

Literary Works
Bülow, Frieda von (1896), *Tropenkoller. Eine Episode aus dem deutschen Kolonialleben*, Berlin: Fontane.
Olden, Balder (1927), *Ich bin Ich. Der Roman Carl Peters*, Berlin: Universitas.

Histories
Becker, Felicitas (2005), *Der Maji-Maji-Krieg in Deutsch-Ostafrika 1905–1907*, Berlin: Links.
Deutsch, Jan-Georg (2006), *Emancipation without Abolition in German East Africa, c. 1884–1914*, Oxford: James Currey.
Kaniki, M. H. Y. (ed.) (1980), *Tanzania under Colonial Rule*, London: Longman.
Perras, Arne (2004), *Carl Peters. A Political Biography*, New York: Oxford University Press.
Pesek, Michael (2005), *Koloniale Herrschaft in Deutsch-Ostafrika: Expeditionen, Militär und Verwaltung seit 1880*, Frankfurt am Main: Campus.

German New Guinea

With the explorations of Louis Antoine de Bougainville and James Cook, the South Pacific region referred to at the time as the South Sea captured the fancy of the German public. Of special significance were the accounts of Georg Forster, a German naturalist and travel writer who accompanied Cook on his second voyage from 1772 to 1775 and recorded his observations in *A Voyage Round the World*. Around 1800, utopian projects that sought to realise alternative lifestyles arose, the majority of them on Tahiti. The longings underlying such plans continued to find their expression, over the course of the years to follow, in the visual arts and various areas of literature, resulting in a number of dramas and novels. Tattooing was a practice that fascinated many German writers, among them Adolf Loos, around 1900. While Polynesians – and especially the Samoans – were described as exhibiting classic beauty, intelligence and a noble character, the Melanesian population was frequently characterised as 'ugly' and 'wild' but 'nonetheless somehow noble'.

From about the mid-nineteenth century, the islands of the South Pacific also began attracting the attention of German trading companies. Trade with numerous islands was established and maintained by Johann Cesar Godeffroy and Son – a company that dealt in copra – as well as its successor firm, the Deutsche Handels- und Plantagengesellschaft (from 1878), and Robertson and Hernsheim (from 1876). In most cases these companies co-operated with the local mission societies and thus established a relatively secure basis for the legitimation of a German protectorate. The German New Guinea Company, founded by banker Adolph von Hansemann and other German financial magnates, concentrated its efforts in the 1880s on acquiring the north-eastern part of the island; Australia had been given the southern section, and the West already belonged to Dutch India. As in the case of other German colonies, this New Guniea colonial society was at first granted sovereign rights, but relinquished them successively until, in 1898–9, the German state assumed the task, albeit unwillingly, of extending the protectorate.

Gradually, Britain and Germany demarcated their respective spheres of interest in the Pacific. Besides Emperor Wilhelm's Land (New Guinea), the neighbouring Bismarck Islands – including New Mecklenburg, New Hanover and New Pomerania – as well as the Bougainville island group and Buka (both of the Solomon Islands), Nauru and the Marshall Islands became German possessions. Following defeat in the war against the USA in 1899, Spain sold Germany the Carolinas, Marianas and Palau Islands, which at the time had a total area of 2,376 square kilometres. In 1911, the native population of these formerly Spanish islands was estimated to be about 600,000. The white population amounted to 301 in 1901. By 1914, this number had risen to 1,137; the largest subgroup was made up of missionaries, followed by planters, traders and government officials.

Administration of the German South Sea possessions bore the stamp of Governor Albrecht Hahl, who ruled from 1902 to 1914. In contrast to the racial arrogance of many colonial administrators in Africa, the policies practised by Hahl, like those of Wilhelm Solf on Samoa, were aimed at 'developing the typically indigenous, the characteristically local' (Hiery 2001) and maintaining these traits through circumspect modernisation. Thus, people of 'mixed blood' were encouraged to participate in economic and social life; the influential Emma Forsyth was a renowned case in point. Hahl integrated local figures into the colonial administration, for example, as *luluais*, local officials who mediated between the colonial administration and the native population. In exchange for privileges such as autonomous jurisdiction with respect to civil law and misdemeanours, these officials were obliged, as the executive arm of the colonial authorities, to participate in levying taxes or drafting inhabitants to help construct roads. At the same time, Hahl protected the land rights of indigenous inhabitants and promoted cultivation of cash crops by establishing 'native plantations' for coconut palms. Such trade structures in the South Sea colonies were a further element that distinguished these overseas possessions from far more conflict-plagued German settlement projects in Africa. Nonetheless, worker recruitment practices and the treatment of indigenous as well as non-indigenous plantation workers, most of whom were Chinese, constitute the most violent chapters of German history in the South Sea. In response to isolated uprisings by the indigenous populations, the German colonial administration sent out warships on punitive expeditions. Moreover, the large numbers of missionaries at work in these colonies as representatives of various German and French, Catholic and Protestant mission societies were instrumental in implementing colonial rule, economically as well as politically. Missionaries owned some of the largest estates in the German South Sea colony. Nevertheless, German colonial rule had by no means penetrated the entire region. Although a series of anthropological, geographical and ethnological expeditions were carried out, they did not result in the establishment of comprehensive formal control. Administrative authority was more or less limited to the coastal areas of a few islands. The transnational character of colonial hegemony was more evident in the South Sea – where imperial powers observed the policies of their European neighbours, sought models to emulate, and at times co-operated with one another – than on the African continent.

In the early phases of World War I, Australian troops occupied Emperor Wilhelm's Land, the Bismarck Islands, the Solomon Islands and Nauru. The Carolinas, Marianas, Palau Islands and the Marshall Islands were occupied by Japanese units virtually without a fight. In 1920, the League of Nations placed the region under Japanese and Australian mandate.

Birthe Kundrus

Literary Works and Biographies

Chamisso, Adelbert (1986), *A Voyage Around the World with the Romanzov Exploring Expedition in the Years 1815–1818 in the Brig Rurik*, Honolulu: University of Hawai'i Press.

Forster, Georg (2000), *A Voyage Round the World*, ed. Nicholas Thomas and Oliver Berghof, Honolulu: University of Hawai'i Press.

Gerstäcker, Friedrich (1950), *In der Südsee*, Dusseldorf: Droste.

Kotzebue, August von (1840), *Bruder Moritz, der Sonderling. Oder: die Colonie für die Pelewinseln* (1791), in idem, *Theater* von *Kotzebue*, vol. 3, Leipzig and Wien: Kummer/Klang.

Loos, Adolf (1962), *Sämtliche Schriften in 2 Bänden*, ed. Franz Glück, Vienna and Munich: Herold.

Müller, Robert (1919), *Das Inselmädchen. Novelle*, Munich: Roland.

Nolde, Emil (1965), *Welt und Heimat (1913–1918)*, Cologne: DuMont Schauberg.

Histories

Gerd Hardach (1990), *König Kopra. Die Marianen unter deutscher Herrschaft*, Stuttgart: Steiner.

Hempenstall, Peter J. (1978), *Pacific Islanders under German Rule. A Study in the Meaning of Colonial Resistance*, Canberra: Australian National University Press.

Hiery, Hermann Joseph (1995), *The Neglected War. The German South Pacific and the Influence of World War I*, Honolulu: University of Hawai'i Press.

— (1997), *European Impact and Pacific Influence. British and German Colonial Policy in the Pacific Islands and the Indigenous Response*, London: Tauris Academic Studies.

— (ed.) (2001), *Die deutsche Südsee 1884–1914. Ein Handbuch*, Paderborn: Schöningh.

Küchler Williams, Christiane (2004), *Erotische Paradiese. Zur europäischen Südseerezeption im 18. Jahrhundert*, Göttingen: Wallstein.

German Samoa

Samoa is an illustration of the assessment that 'trade . . . was the foundation of the German colonial experiment' (Hempenstall 1978). The German trading company Johann Cesar Godeffroy and Son established a Samoan office in 1857. Taking advantage of power struggles that divided the indigenous élites, the imperial powers Germany, Britain and the USA increasingly extended their spheres of influence in the decades that followed. A tripartite accord reached in 1899 formalised division of the archipelago between the three, with Britain renouncing its claims to parts of Samoa in exchange for control of other islands in the South Pacific; the German flag was raised in the Samoan capital of Apia on 1 March 1900.

The islands of Western Samoa – the last colony to be acquired by Germany – covered a mere 2,570 square kilometres. With a non-European population of less than 40,000, and never more than 300 German citizens (as well as about the same number of residents from other European countries), the German administrative bureaucracy at no time exceeded fifty officials. The islands were insignificant from the perspective of naval strategy. Wilhelm Solf, Governor of German Samoa from 1900 to 1911, championed the notion of a cultural mission of European colonialism and, like his colleague Albrecht Hahl in German New Guinea, was committed to enforcing German rule with a minimum of coercion and to allowing the indigenous population to participate in the colony's prosperity. Thus, his first goal was to resolve Samoa's internal conflicts, abolish the monarchy, and then instal German rule in its place, while otherwise leaving the existing power structure in place virtually unchanged. Although Solf determined the general direction of domestic as well as foreign policies, the orders set down by the *faipule* – indigenous representatives who were paid by the German administration – in their respective districts was, for the most part, entirely up to them, as long as they did not challenge German hegemony. Traditional judicial authorities were also incorporated into the German administrative system to an extent not found in any other German colony. Parts of the civil jurisdiction were delegated to indigenous judges. Samoans sat on the bench with colonial officials in conflicts over land, marriage and family affairs; and criminal cases remained for the most part in the hands of traditional courts.

Poll taxes were introduced and their acceptance was enhanced by the promise that the resulting funds would be used to finance the costs of native administration. The Germans did not exploit the Samoans as a source of labour for plantations that cultivated copra, the islands' export staple; instead, Chinese labourers were imported. Strict limits were placed on the appropriation of land for European-owned plantations. With these paternalistic policies and a economic orientation that also aimed to foster voluntary indigenous co-operation by offering material incentives, Governor Solf increasingly came into conflict with the intentions of settlers in Samoa and interested parties in the German Reich.

The question of 'mixed marriages' also became a focus of conflict. Most planters had liaisons with Samoan women, but Solf was determined to prevent an increase in the numbers of children of mixed ancestry. In contrast to Africa, however, the question of mixed marriages failed to mobilise racist prejudice to a significant extent. Solf, who felt he could not enforce such an intermarriage ban as long as he was Governor of Samoa, promptly enacted the prohibition from the safe distance of far-off Berlin in 1912, after he was appointed a state secretary in the German Colonial Office. Whereas in the settler colony German South-West Africa the ban had been retroactive, children from existing mixed marriages were considered legitimate descendents of white Germans. Samoans who spoke German fluently and demonstrated that they had a European educational background could apply for recognition as so-called 'cultural Germans' who were on an equal footing with other Germans.

New Zealand occupied West Samoa at the beginning of World War I and controlled the islands based on mandates from the League of Nations (1920–46) and the United Nations (1946–62), until Samoa regained independence in 1962.

Birthe Kundrus

LITERARY WORKS

Benkard, Christian (1888), *In ferner Inselwelt*, 2 vols, Stuttgart: Deutsche Romanbibliothek.

Scheurmann, Erich (1919), *Paitea und Ilse. Eine Südseegeschichte*, Berlin: Grote.

Seidel, Willy (1930), *Der Buschhahn, Ein Roman aus der Deutsch-Samoa*, Munich: Müller.

HISTORIES

Firth, Stewart (1990), *German Regulation and Employment of Plantation Labour in Samoa, 1864–1914*, Adelaide: Flinders University of South Australia.

Hempenstall, Peter John (1978), *Pacific Islanders under German Rule. A Study in the Meaning of Colonial Resistance*, Canberra: Australian National University Press.

Hiery, Hermann Joseph (1995a), *The Neglected War. The German South Pacific and the Influence of World War I*, Honolulu: University of Hawai'i Press.

— (1995b), *Das Deutsche Reich in der Südsee (1900–1921). Eine Annäherung an die Erfahrungen verschiedener Kulturen*, Göttingen: Vandenhoeck and Ruprecht.

— (ed.) (2001), *Die deutsche Südsee 1884–1914. Ein Handbuch*, Paderborn: Schöningh.

Wareham, Evelyn (2002), *Race and Realpolitik. The Politics of Colonisation in German Samoa*, Frankfurt am Main: Lang.

German South-West Africa

Unlike Germany's other colonies, German South-West Africa was seen primarily as a settler colony. This was especially apparent after Theodor Leutwein arrived in the colony on 1 January 1894, when the state assumed a more active role in promoting white (in particular, German) settlement in the territory. Prior to Leutwein, development in the colony had been largely left to concessionary companies which did not possess the means to make the region safe and productive. In light of this situation, as well as in response to public concerns over the perceived value of the colonies, Imperial Chancellor Caprivi sent Leutwein to South-West Africa to bring order to the territory and turn it into an economically useful possession.

In order to transform the area into an economically self-sufficient, profitable German possession, Leutwein pursued a policy of making peace with the indigenous populations and promoting German settlement. Toward this end, Leutwein began expanding the colonial bureaucracy (away from the previous military structure), as a means of ensuring the rule of law and facilitating a methodical economic exploitation of the territory. The latter undermined the former, for an integral component of attracting European colonists was the expropriation of African land and livestock. Ultimately, Leutwein's system and the overall exploitative treatment of the indigenous populations led to the 1904 Herero and Nama revolts against German colonial rule.

The brutal German response to these acts nearly decimated the Herero and Nama, and resulted in the first genocide of the twentieth century. After they had been crushed, a new period in German colonial rule was ushered in. Essentially, few restraints existed to prevent an almost complete exploitation of the Nama and Herero peoples. New regulations were issued to control Africans, and their land and cattle was expropriated. These new rules not only destroyed African economic independence and forced them into dependency on European employers, they also introduced legal discrimination, by distinguishing between 'non-natives' and 'natives'.

As German authority became more firmly established in South-West Africa after 1907, two major issues arose. One was the settler demand for more control over Africans and colonial affairs in general. The other one was miscegenation. They both revolved around notions of German masculinity, and the extent of state control. Settler efforts to achieve a greater voice in colonial governance starkly exposed their status in the territory as 'dependent masters'. The power of the state was also evident in the proscriptions introduced to ban interracial marriages, and to exclude those Europeans who crossed the racial divide. Such unions and the children of such relations were perceived both in the colony and in the metropole as threats to German hegemony, especially because of German citizenship laws. These official measures found support in the private sector, which also sought to prohibit these sexual relations.

Nearly one year after the outbreak of World War I in 1914, German colonial troops surrendered to South Africa. As with Germany's other overseas possessions, South-West Africa became a mandate after the war and remained under South African control until gaining its independence in 1990 as Namibia.

Daniel J. Walther

LITERARY WORKS

Brockmann, Clara (1912), *Briefe eines Mädchens aus Südwest*, Berlin: Mittler and Son.
Eckenbrecher, Margarethe von (1940), *Was Afrika mir gab und nahm. Erlebnisse einer deutschen Frau in Südwestafrika 1902–1936*, 8th edn, Berlin: Mittler and Son.
Frenssen, Gustav (1914), *Peter Moor: A narrative of the German Campaign in South-West Africa*, trans. Margaret May Ward, London: Archibald Constable.
Grimm, Hans (1926), *Volk ohne Raum*, Munich: A. Langen.
Timm, Uwe (2003), *Morenga*, trans. Breon Mitchell, New York: New Directions.

HISTORIES

Bley, Helmut (1996), *Namibia under German Rule*, Hamburg: Lit.
Drechsler, Horst (1986), *'Let us Die Fighting'. The Struggle of the Herero and Nama against German Imperialism (1884–1915)*, Berlin: Akademie-Verlag.
Krüger, Gesine (1999), *Kriegsbewältigung und Geschichtsbewußtsein. Realität, Deutung und Verarbeitung des deutschen Kolonialkriegs in Namibia 1904 bis 1907*, Göttingen: Vandenhoeck and Ruprecht.
Walther, Daniel (2002), *Creating Germans Abroad. Cultural Policies and National Identity in Namibia*, Athens, OH: Ohio University Press.
Zimmerer, Jürgen (2002), *Deutsche Herrschaft über Afrikaner. Staatlicher Machtanspruch und Wirklichkeit im kolonialen Namibia*, Hamburg: Lit.

Herero/Nama Genocide

The War of imperial Germany against the Herero and Nama in German South-West Africa (today, Namibia) from 1904 to 1908 was arguably one of the most brutal colonial wars ever fought in history. Together with the Maji-Maji War in German East Africa (1905–7), this war symbolised both the hubris and the utter failure of the German colonial project. What was supposed to prove the (superior) colonising skills of the Germans fell apart as a project within twenty years of Germany's colonial experience.

The war, which began on 12 January 1904, did not so much change the German colonial policy of subjugation and dispossession of Germany's African subjects as accelerate it. The war was the consequence of Germany's attempt at creating a white settler colony in southern Africa. Although the level of violence and destruction the war brought to the fore was not inevitable, conflict between the inhabitants of the land and the intruders was. Several factors combined their effect in leading to the war. First, there was competition over control of land; then, there were problems created by the 'master race' attitude adopted towards the local people by German traders and settlers, which culminated in killings and rapes. Inevitably, these provoked reactions. In addition, there was the German plan of social engineering, of dispossessing the African population, and of transforming them into an easily accessible 'black' workforce.

The war itself, despite, or even because of, the successful way in which the Herero (and later the Nama) fought, quickly developed into a war of annihilation and outright genocide. Herero warriors were shot upon capture; Herero men, women and children were driven into the desert to die of thirst. After the Nama had entered the war against Germany, they too became targets of the German policy of extermination. Survivors, both Herero and Nama, were put in concentration camps, where they were – at least partially – subjected to a policy of annihilation by deliberate neglect. It is this policy of elimination that makes this war the first genocide of the twentieth century and the first genocide in German history.

This judgement raises the question about possible similarities, links and continuities between the Herero and Nama genocide and Nazi expansionist and exterminatory policies. There are obviously no easy answers. European genocides are far too complex as events to be reducible to simple equations. We can neither state a causal link, nor can we ignore the formative influence that colonialism had on Nazi policies. Germany's colonial and eastward expansion was based on similar notions of race and space. Both attempted to create an 'ideal' German settler state based on the subjugation or even elimination of the original population. Colonialism offered important precedents, and a cultural archive of ideas and reservoir of practices from which inspirations could be drawn roughly a generation later.

For the Herero and the Nama, the war and the system of total control that the German administration introduced meant tremendous individual and cultural loss. In a clandestine process, the Herero slowly reinvented their own history and recreated social structures that had been severed by the war. In Namibia today there remain different attitudes towards the genocide. Whereas the Herero (and to a lesser extent the Nama), who are descendants of the primary victims, demand recognition and reparation, the Namibian government, dominated by Ovambo, refuses to single out specific victim groups, and integrates Herero and Nama warriors in the attempt to sustain a unified national anti-colonial resistance movement. Many white Namibians of German descent simply deny the scale or impact of the atrocities. The German government, however, in 2004 officially apologised for the genocide, although refusing the payment of any reparations.

Jürgen Zimmerer

LITERARY WORKS
Gustav Frenssen (1906), *Peter Moors Fahrt nach Südwest: Ein Feldzugsbericht*, Berlin: Grote.
Timm, Uwe (1978), *Morenga*, Munich: Verlag Autoren Edition.

HISTORIES
Gewald, Jan-Bart (1999), *Herero Heroes, A Socio-Political History of the Herero of Namibia, 1890–1923*, Oxford: James Currey.

Hull, Isabel V. (2004), *Absolute Destruction. Military Culture and the Practices of War in Imperial Germany*, Ithaca, NY and London: Cornell University Press.

Krüger, Gesine (1999), *Kriegsbewältigung und Geschichtsbewußtsein. Realität, Deutung und Verarbeitung des deutschen Kolonialkriegs in Namibia 1904–1907*, Göttingen: Vandenhoeck and Ruprecht.

Melber, Henning (ed.) (2005), *Genozid und Gedenken. Namibisch-deutsche Geschichte und Gegenwart*, Frankfurt am Main: Brandes and Apsel.

Zimmerer, Jürgen (2001), *Deutsche Herrschaft über Afrikaner. Staatlicher Machtanspruch und Wirklichkeit im kolonialen Namibia*, Hamburg: Lit.

Zimmerer, Jürgen and Joachim Zeller (2007), *Genocide in German South-West Africa. The Colonial War of 1904–1908 and its Aftermath*, London: Merlin Press.

Historiography

The historiography of German colonialism can be conveniently divided into three phases. The leading perspectives and methodological approaches differed in each period, as did the political thrust of engagement with the colonial past. At the risk of simplification, one can identify three main currents, each articulating scholarly concerns with the broader socio-political context: a politically revisionist literature in the 1920s; a critical social history of colonialism in the 1970s; and a postcolonial historiography since the 1990s.

After the Versailles Treaty of 1919 had handed over German overseas possessions to the mandate powers, German historians joined broad segments of the public in lamenting the loss of the colonial empire. This is not to say that there had not been research into issues of colonialism before 1919. But while the colonies had always been a subject for novels and the arts, and also created interest among anthropologists and legal scholars, historians had only occasionally devoted their attention to what was considered to be the 'New Germany'. In general, this did not change after 1919. The most important publications of the time, like the *German Colonial Lexicon* by former Governor of German East Africa Heinrich Schnee (1920), were produced outside the universities. The general concern was to thwart the Versailles dictum of German colonial crimes (what Schnee had termed the *Kolonialschuldlüge*). Most studies of colonialism, therefore, must be seen as attempts to prove the colonial merits of Germany and to pave the way for further colonial engagement. Due to the preoccupation with political revision, the international scholarship of the time (for example, Townsend 1930) was largely ignored by German historians.

More thorough, and less hagiographic, research into German colonialism did not start before the late 1960s. After several decades of relative neglect, the worldwide process of decolonisation, in combination with the general and critical re-examination of German history since the Fischer controversy, spawned heated debates and new scholarship of the colonial period. The re-evaluation of German colonialism was part of a larger international trend, and it was undertaken from different locations. In particular, East German scholarship played a crucial role in posing new questions and initiating source-based research (see Stoecker 1977 for an overview). These works proved to be a major influence for West German historians, as were the works by American scholars (Gann and Duignan 1978; Smith 1978). In addition, historians based in Tanzania used archival materials in Dar-es-Salaam and produced some of the most important studies of the colonial period (in particular Iliffe 1969).

Earlier scholarship had focused on issues of foreign policy and military encounters. The bulk of research produced since the 1960s was in the field of social history. As a result, some problems that had hitherto preoccupied historians – like Bismarck's sudden turn towards an active politics of colonial acquisition in 1884 – now receded into the background. Instead, the focus now was on the structural dimension of social, political and economic developments. From this perspective, a number of important studies were published that inquired into the social and political history of the colonial movement (Bade 1975), the role of parties and mass organisations, economic imperialism (Schinzinger 1984), missions and education (Gründer 1982), administration and colonial control, and local resistance. The last concern was not least an expression of the anti-imperialist impulse and pro-Third-World politics that was behind much of the scholarship at the time. Above all German East Africa (Tanzania) was the object of several comprehensive analyses, dealing with occupation, administration and resistance (Loth 1968; Iliffe 1969) as well as economic development and exploitation (Tetzlaff 1970; Bald 1970). In addition, several works were published on the history of German South-West Africa (Namibia), with the Herero war as a central concern (Drechsler 1966; Bley 1968), and Cameroon (Hausen 1970; Wirz 1972). The close connection with the decolonisation process and the political drive behind this kind of scholarship is further illustrated by the fact that most studies focused on Africa, while the German presence in the Pacific and in China received much less coverage. The majority of these works was infused with a strong emphasis on Africanist knowledge and an attention to local agency and forms of resistance. At the same time, however, most authors implicitly operated with a diffusionist model of the colonial encounter. Accordingly, the main decisions and essential factors contributing to colonial expansion were internal to German society. All potential 'weapons of the weak' notwithstanding, in its core colonialism remained a metropolitan affair. This was particularly evident in the highly influential study by Hans-Ulrich Wehler (1969), which was on the surface a close and detailed reconstruction of the political mechanisms leading to colonial expansion. At an analytical level, Wehler's controversial book was a powerful argument for a reading of German colonialism as a form of social imperialism. According to this point of view, not only was the colonial endeavour intended to grant access to the necessary resources to fuel the German economy, but it was also meant to provide Bismarck's rule with new and additional appeal. It was alleged that the collective project of overseas expansion supplied oppositional groups, in particular the discontented working class, with a national purpose, and diverted their attention away from urgent material concerns. By thus exporting internal problems abroad, the 'counter utopia' of imperial glory furthered social integration and the pacification of the lower strata of German society.

Wehler's book used the example of colonial expansion to discuss crucial antagonisms in the social fabric of German society. His main concern, in the last instance, was not with the colonies but with the class conflicts and structural problems in the metropolis. In this respect, his book is a typical example of the German historiography of colonialism in the 1970s. While many case studies dealt specifically with the colonial periphery, the general framework in which they were conceived was the search for the long-standing, structural defects of German society. Through concepts such as militarism, imperialism and class interests, historians linked the history of colonialism to a master narrative that viewed the German path into modernity essentially as a *Sonderweg*.

In the two decades to follow, interest in the subject of colonialism gradually declined. There have been, to be sure, a few important studies. But in general, after the anti-imperialist rhetoric of the new left had subsided, colonial history was not high on the agenda of historians in Germany. Comparatively speaking, the period of a mere thirty years of existence made the German colonial empire seem marginal and ephemeral. Instead, the focus on the Holocaust as the central and unavoidable fact (if not *telos*) of German history has preoccupied historians, and for a long time occluded their interest in colonialism. Moreover, until recently, there was little by way of a diasporic presence from formerly colonised peoples in Germany to remind Germans of past violence or to claim recognition for itself as an integral part of German history.

Since the late 1990s, however, the fortunes of colonial studies have again been on the rise. This must be seen as a response, above all, to globalisation and the prevalent rhetoric of global connectedness. In particular, the neo-colonial tendencies of the post-Cold War order were conducive to a renewed interest in the history of colonialism and its connection to a prehistory of globalisation. The academic expression of this consciousness was the success of postcolonial studies that now began to exert their influence in Germany as well (Conrad and Randeria 2002). The attraction of probing into the history of colonialism was further enhanced by the general calls for overcoming national history and experimenting with transnational forms of historiography.

Whereas the scholarship of the 1970s had a clear focus on the social history of colonialism, the bulk of work since the late 1990s can be subsumed under the label of cultural history. The paradigm shift of the discipline as a whole thus translated, in the field of colonialism, into an interest in issues of hybridity, memory and representation. It is impossible to subsume the wealth of recent scholarship under a few convenient headings. Apart from new syntheses with a regional scope, it is nevertheless possible to say that four areas have received particular attention in recent work.

While scholarship in the 1970s has done much to assess the organisational structures and social composition of the colonial movement, more recent work has focused especially on colonial discourse and issues of representation. In the spirit of much of postcolonial studies dedicated to what can be called a 'decolonisation of representation', many studies in the past few years have been preoccupied with unearthing the rhetoric and discursive practices that fundamentally shaped the colonial project in Germany. Through analyses of an 'imperialist imagination' (Friedrichsmeyer et al. 1998), historians and scholars from other disciplines are looking for patterns of epistemology and social practice within the German colonial mind. They find these patterns in the literature and popular culture of the time, in exhibitions and *Völkerschauen*, but also in scientific and political texts. The colonial expansion, seen from this vantage point, was not only a military and political strategy, but in the first place must be understood as the effect of a culture of colonialism broadly conceived (Zantop 1997; Honold and Simons 2002; Kundrus 2003a; Honold and Scherpe 2004).

A second and related field is the inquiry into colonial knowledge. A variety of disciplines – like anthropology, geography, linguistics, tropical medicine, eugenics and others – flourished in the context of the colonial encounter. In these studies, knowledge is not only seen as a prerequisite of European supremacy, but at the same time, following Foucault and Edward Said, as deeply implicated in the logics of power and difference. The notion of difference is also at the heart of a third area of concern, namely identities and memory. As a number of studies have demonstrated, colonial discourse was characterised by a set of binary oppositions that served to reinforce essentialised notions of race, class, nation, gender and sexuality (El-Tayeb 2001). The colonial experience, however, worked towards unsettling these assumptions. The dichotomous structure of race, for example, was questioned by a variety of practices that the colonial government sought to confine through ethnic segregation and legislation against miscegenation (Wildenthal 2001; Kundrus 2003b). The legacy of this history of hybridity, however, continues both to shape the identities of individuals and to undermine unreflected assumptions of 'Germanness' (Campt 2004).

The issue of memory is also central in a fourth debate that is centred around questions of violence, war and genocide. The atrocities committed in the German colonies did not go unnoticed by contemporaries and led to critical discussions in the Reichstag. In current scholarship, it is the Herero war of 1904 in particular that has commanded the attention of historians. Taking Hannah Arendt's early insights into the connection between imperialism and fascism as a point of departure (Arendt 1955), authors like Jürgen Zimmerer have probed into the complex issue of continuities between the Herero genocide and the Holocaust of the 1940s. While it seems futile to deny a connection between colonial and European genocide entirely, the question remains as to why, in other imperialist countries, colonial violence did not lead to a genocidal politics within (Zimmerer and Zeller 2007).

These four areas of interest do not exhaust the scope of recent scholarship on German colonialism, but they can be taken as representative of some of the overarching tendencies of this research. First, colonialism is not confined to the thirty years of the colonial empire. Colonial fantasies and imaginations reach back into the eighteenth century (Zantop 1997), while revisionism and neo-colonial projects continued long after the empire had been formally dissolved in 1919 (van Laak 2004; van Laak 2005). Second, the geographical reach of imperial ambitions clearly transcended the formal colonial empire. In particular, the expansion – both politically and mentally – into the European East has in recent studies been interpreted as a form of colonialism (Kopp 2001; Furber 2003; Ther 2004). This perspective contributes both to a Europeanisation of German colonialism, and to the unsettling of the unspoken assumption that colonies are divided from the imperial centre by racial difference and by an ocean. Third, the colonial encounter did not only deeply affect the colonised societies, but also had important repercussions in the metropolis: the empire strikes back (even if this crucial insight of postcolonial studies may harbour the danger of unduly focusing on the German side of the colonial divide). By attempting to situate colony and metropole within a single analytical field, recent historians have done much to demonstrate that colonialism was not a marginal adventure but rather an integral part of German history.

Sebastian Conrad

HISTORIES

Arendt, Hannah (1955), *Elemente und Ursprünge totaler Herrschaft*, Frankfurt: Europäische Verlagsanstalt.

Bade, Klaus J. (1975), *Friedrich Fabri und der Imperialismus der Bismarckzeit. Revolution, Depression, Expansion*, Zurich: Atlantis.

Bald, Detlef (1970), *Deutsch-Ostafrika 1900–1914. Eine Studie über Verwaltung, Interessengruppen und wirtschaftliche Erschließung*, Munich: Weltforum Verlag.

Bley, Helmut (1968), *Kolonialherrschaft und Sozialstruktur in Deutsch-Südwestafrika 1894– 1914*, Hamburg: Leibniz.

Campt, Tina M. (2004), *Other Germans. Black Germans and the Politics of Race, Gender, and Memory in the Third Reich*, Ann Arbor, MI: University of Michigan Press.

Conrad, Sebastian and Shalini Randeria (eds) (2002), *Jenseits des Eurozentrismus. Postkoloniale Perspektiven in den Geschichts- und Kulturwissenschaften*, Frankfurt: Campus.

Drechsler, Horst (1966), *Südwestafrika unter deutscher Kolonialherrschaft. Der Kampf der Herero und Nama gegen den deutschen Imperialismus (1884–1915)*, East Berlin: Akademie-Verlag.

El-Tayeb, Fatima (2001), *Schwarze Deutsche. Der Diskurs um 'Rasse' und nationale Identität 1890–1933*, Frankfurt: Campus.

Friedrichsmeyer, Sara, Sara Lennox and Susanne Zantop (eds) (1998), *The Imperialist Imagination. German Colonialism and its Legacy*, Ann Arbor, MI: Michigan University Press.

Furber, David (2003), '*Going East'. Colonialism and German Life in Nazi-Occupied Poland*, Buffalo, NY: unpublished Ph.D.

Gann, Lewis H. and Peter Duignan (eds) (1978), *African Proconsuls. European Governors in Africa*, Stanford, CA: Free Press.

Gründer, Horst (1982), *Christliche Mission und deutscher Imperialismus. Eine politische Geschichte ihrer Beziehungen während der deutschen Kolonialzeit (1884–1914) unter besonderer Berücksichtigung Afrikas und Chinas*, Paderborn: Schöningh.

Hausen, Karin (1970), *Deutsche Kolonialherrschaft in Afrika. Wirtschaftsinteressen und Kolonialverwaltung in Kamerun vor 1914*, Zurich: Atlantis.

Honold, Alexander and Klaus Scherpe (eds) (2004), *Mit Deutschland um die Welt. Eine Kulturgeschichte des Fremden in der Kolonialzeit*, Stuttgart: Metzler.

Honold, Alexander and Oliver Simons (eds) (2002), *Kolonialismus als Kultur. Literatur, Medien, Wissenschaft in der deutschen Gründerzeit des Fremden*, Tübingen: A. Francke Verlag.

Iliffe, John (1969), *Tanganyika under German Rule, 1905–1912*, Cambridge: Cambridge University Press.

Kopp, Kristin (2001), *Contesting Borders. German Colonial Discourse and the Polish Eastern Territories*, Berkeley, CA: unpublished Ph.D.

Kundrus, Birthe (ed.) (2003a), *Phantasiereiche. Zur Kulturgeschichte des deutschen Kolonialismus*, Frankfurt: Campus.

— (2003b), *Moderne Imperialisten. Das Kaiserreich im Spiegel seiner Kolonien*, Cologne: Böhlau.

Laak, Dirk van (2004), *Imperiale Infrastruktur. Deutsche Planungen für eine Erschließung Afrikas 1880 bis 1960*, Paderborn: Schöningh.

— (2005), *Über alles in der Welt. Deutscher Imperialismus im 19. und 20. Jahrhundert*, Munich: C. H. Beck.

Loth, Heinrich (1968), *Griff nach Ostafrika. Politik des deutschen Imperialismus und anti-kolonialer Kampf. Legende und Wirklichkeit*, East Berlin: Deutscher Verlag der Wissenschaften.

Schinzinger, Francesca (1984), *Die Kolonien und das Deutsche Reich. Die wirtschaftliche Bedeutung der deutschen Besitzungen in Übersee*, Stuttgart: Steiner.

Schnee, Heinrich (1920), *Deutsches Koloniallexikon*, 3 vols, Leipzig: Quelle and Meyer.

Smith, Woodruff (1978), *The German Colonial Empire*, Chapel Hill, NC: University of North Carolina Press.

Stoecker, Helmuth (ed.) (1977), *Drang nach Afrika. Die koloniale Expansionspolitik und Herrschaft des deutschen Imperialismus in Afrika von den Anfängen bis zum Ende des zweiten Weltkrieges*, East Berlin: Akademie-Verlag. Published in English in 1986 as *German Imperialism in North Africa*.

Tetzlaff, Rainer (1970), *Koloniale Entwicklung und Ausbeutung. Wirtschafts- und Sozialgeschichte Deutsch-Ostafrikas*, Berlin: Duncker and Humblot.

Ther, Philipp (2004), 'Deutsche Geschichte als imperiale Geschichte. Polen, slawophone Minderheiten und das Kaiserreich als kontinentales Empire', in Sebastian Conrad and Jürgen Osterhammel (eds), *Das Kaiserreich transnational. Deutschland in der Welt 1871–1914*, Göttingen: Vandenhoeck and Ruprecht, pp. 129–48.

Townsend, Mary E. (1930), *The Rise and Fall of Germany's Colonial Empire 1884–1918*, New York: Macmillian.

Wehler, Hans-Ulrich (1969), *Bismarck und der Imperialismus*, Cologne: Kiepenheuer and Witsch.

Wildenthal, Lora (2001), *German Women for Empire, 1884–1945*, Durham, NC: Duke University Press.

Wirz, Albert (1972), *Vom Sklavenhandel zum kolonialen Handel. Wirtschaftsräume und Wirtschaftsformen in Kamerun vor 1914*, Zurich: Atlantis.

Zantop, Susanne (1997), *Colonial Fantasies. Conquest, Family, and Nation in Precolonial Germany (1770–1870)*, Durham, NC: Duke University Press.

Zimmerer, Jürgen (2001), *Deutsche Herrschaft über Afrikaner. Staatlicher Machtanspruch und Wirklichkeit im kolonialen Namibia*, Hambürg: Lit.

Zimmerer, Jürgen and Joachim Zeller (2007), *Genocide in German South-West Africa. The Colonial War of 1904–1908 and its Aftermath*, London: Merlin Press.

Hybridity and Race Relations

All colonial societies were confronted with the challenge of organising the cohabitation of the races. Colonies that were comparatively tolerant in matters of race rubbed shoulders with districts subjected to strict racial segregation by their colonial rulers. The problem was worse within those colonial settlements where a group of colonisers strove permanently to secure land and other resources for themselves at the cost of the indigenous population.

German colonial settlements comprised German South-West Africa (GSWA), German East Africa (GEA) and Samoa. At the beginning of German colonial rule, the 'miscegenation' of German men and indigenous women was 'tolerated' within the colonies. Due to the scarcity of white women, it was considered hard to avoid. Unions that endured were mainly with wealthy women. Such unions facilitated social integration, and linguistic and cultural adaptation, and they enabled the colonisers to establish themselves economically. Marriages either took place according to the local tradition, especially on Samoa, or in accordance with German law, as in GSWA. As far as the Chinese population of Kiaochow was concerned, it was thought to be decadent, but the Chinese were also regarded as heir to an advanced ancient culture. Therefore, it was occasionally even possible for a German woman to settle down there with her (wealthy) Chinese husband (Klein 2004).

The number of marriages between white men and indigenous women never exceeded the number of 150 at any time in all of the German colonies. From 1904, during the great revolts in the African dependencies, marital unions as well as the general 'mixing of the races' were subjected to criticism. These forms of integration were now regarded as a threat to power politics and as an overstepping of the boundaries. Also, 'mixed people' were perceived as dissatisfied: while they considered themselves above the Africans, they were not accepted as equals by white people; as a consequence, they were expected to strive for freedom from white rule in order to rise to the top of the social hierarchy on their own. Besides, interracial marriages and 'miscegenated' children challenged the colonisers' desire for control: their very bodies bore testimony to the possibility of bridging the gap between the races. The debate also included aspects of gender insofar as the interethnic unions were regarded as proof of the physical and moral degeneration of German men, imperilling German predominance as well as German prestige. As a consequence, the demand arose for a clear division between colonisers and colonised. The prohibition of interracial marriages in GSWA (1905), and in GEA (1906) represented the first step toward a reduction of 'mixed people'. In addition, many schools and kindergartens in GSWA no longer admitted 'miscegenated' children. As a sort of precautionary intervention, colonial associations attempted to motivate German women to emigrate to GSWA (Wildenthal 2001). However, the educational reform centres for the 'racially mixed', which had been established by the missions, remained untouched. The Protestant mission first installed such a centre in Okahandja (1904), and a second one in Keetmanshoop (1907), while the Catholic mission founded an institute in Klein-Windhuk (1902). Both Catholics and Protestants were in agreement that 'mixed people' had to be given a special education, allowing them at least to aspire to occupations at the margins of white society, and thereby preventing a rebellion – which the missionaries expected would happen if the 'mixed people' were treated simply as 'indigenous people' as the majority of the settlers demanded. After the revolt, power politics became more influenced by racial ideology. Settlers as well as government officials embraced these views. 'Racial mixture' was now regarded as a threat to German tradition (*Volkstum*). The missionaries resisted this perception for several years, but as World War I approached, they, too, began to adopt the prevailing opinion, particularly the Protestant missionaries. Protestant educational institutions were closed in 1912 and 1915 (Becker 2004).

In 1912, the debate rekindled as the Colonial Permanent Secretary Wilhelm Solf established an interdict on interracial marriages in Samoa. Solf's decree provoked angry disapproval. Unions between colonisers and indigenous women had been considered almost natural, in part because the people of Samoa, especially the women, were judged more positively than the people of Sub-Saharan Africa. The majority of the German Legislative Assembly (the Reichstag), remained unimpressed by the demands voiced by Solf, the colonial associations and the lobby of African settlers, and parliament passed a resolution which, by contrast, demanded that the lawfulness of interracial marriages be explicitly protected by the legislator. In 1913, the new law on citizenship proved to be similarly 'colourblind', as it continued to extend German citizenship to any German's foreign spouse (Gosewinkel 2001). Decrees within the dependencies remained valid until the end of the German colonial era. However, although they reflected a negative development in the social climate (Kundrus 2003), they were not able actually to influence legislation within the Kaiserreich (the German Empire).

The German colonial novel dealt with 'racial mixture' in various forms. Most authors judged it to be a great evil, threatening the identity of the ruling white class and weakening the dual organisation of colonial society. In these novels, people of 'mixed race' were either ignored, treated as inadmissible, or represented as beings unfit for life, without any prospect for a future. Other texts, however, underlined the fascination that 'mixed people' could evoke as forerunner of a 'third race' and a new society (Samulski 2004).

Frank Becker

LITERARY WORKS

Grimm, Hans (1913), 'Wie Grete aufhörte ein Kind zu sein', in Hans Grimm, *Südafrikanische Novellen*, Frankfurt am Main: Rütten and Loening.

Küas, Richard (1911), *Vom Baum der Erkenntnis*, Leipzig: Paul List.

Scheurmann, Erich (1936), *Zweierlei Blut*, Munich: Ludendorffs Verlag.

Seidel, Willy (1921), *Der Buschhahn*, Leipzig: Insel-Verlag.

Zieschank, Frieda (1923): *Ein verlorenes Paradies*, Leipzig: E. Haberland.

HISTORIES

Becker, Frank (ed.) (2004), *Die "Bastardheime" der Mission. Zum status der Mischlinge in der kolonialem Gesellschaft Deutsch-Südwestafrikas*', in idem (ed.), *Rassenmischehen–Mischlinge–Rassentrennung. Zur Politik der Rasse im deutschen Kolonialreich*, Stuttgart: Franz Steiner Verlag, pp. 184–219.

Gosewinkel, Dieter (2001), *Einbürgern und Ausschließen. Die Nationalisierung der Staatsangehörigkeit vom Deutschen Bund bis zur Bundesrepublik Deutschland*, Göttingen: Vandenhoeck and Ruprecht.

Klein, Thoralf (2004), 'Rasse–Kultur–soziale Stellung: Konzeptionen des 'Eingeborenen' und koloniale Segregation in Kiautschou', in Frank Becker (ed.), pp. 304–28.

Kundrus, Birthe (2003), *Moderne Imperialisten. Das Kaiserreich im Spiegel seiner Kolonien*, Cologne: Böhlau.

Samulski, Roland (2004), 'Die 'Sünde' im Auge des Betrachters. Rassenmischung und deutsche Rassenpolitik im Schutzgebiet Samoa 1900 bis 1914', in Frank Becker (ed.), pp. 329–56.

Wildenthal, Lora (2001), *German Women for Empire, 1884–1945*, Durham, NC and London: Duke University Press.

Kiaochow

The murder of two German missionaries in November 1897 gave Germany the long awaited excuse for the occupation of the Jiaozhou Bay in the North Chinese province of Shandong. Thereafter, the Chinese Empire was forced to sign a treaty in March 1898, which granted the German Reich a ninety-nine-year lease of a small territory around the bay. With this treaty Germany also secured so-called concessions or rights to build railways and to exploit coal mines in Shandong province. The province was now considered by the German Reich as her 'sphere of influence' in China. Although Kiaochow, as the territory was named, was formally a leasehold, Germany treated it as nothing less than a colony. German interests in China were by no means limited to the leased territory itself. The construction of a railway line to the provincial capital Jinan, and the opening of coal mines along the railway, were the beginning of a larger German economic, cultural and political plan to dominate the entire Shandong province.

After the occupation, Kiaochow was placed under the jurisdiction of the naval ministry. It was the only German colony ever run by a branch of the military. The role given to the Navy had far-reaching consequences for the German colonial project in China. Kiaochow was to be turned into a 'model colony', a colony that would demonstrate a specific new approach to colonialism. 'Model colony' meant making Kiaochow a showcase for modern cultural, scientific and technological achievements. The navy put huge resources into the building of the new city of Qingdao, and a new urban infrastructure, including railway connections and port facilities. More significantly, this concept also implied the establishment of an exemplary economic and social order. The Navy saw in Kiaochow the opportunity to realise its economic and social ideals, and to demonstrate its efficiency at running a colonial society along military patterns. Unlike Hong Kong, the British crown colony in China, Kiaochow was under tight supervision by the naval ministry, with almost no room left for any form of self-administration. The colonial economy was centrally managed by state authorities focusing on the establishment of large-scale industries (coal, iron and steel) of military significance. This colonial policy aimed at erecting a military industrial base in

Kiaochow, which would provide the basis for the future military prowess of Germany in East Asia. Life in this colonial society was tightly controlled and systematically engineered with the aim of establishing clear-cut social structures. There was no mingling of different races or different social groups (like soldiers and civilians). Kiaochow was divided into different zones for the various ethnic and social groups. The main city of the colony, Qingdao, was exclusively reserved for Europeans, while Chinese workers were settled in newly constructed suburbs. The legal system, too, made a fundamental distinction between Chinese and Europeans. Local common law was applied to the 'natives', while German law (with its courts and legal proceedings) was exclusively applied to Europeans.

In the beginning, the occupation of Kiaochow was met with fierce Chinese resistance. Boycotts, protests, as well as violent upheavals in the surrounding areas all document the resentments against the foreign occupation in the first years of German rule. In later years, relations with the Chinese population improved somewhat as the colonial authorities were now more willing to give Chinese representatives (elected in public ballots) a say in the economic affairs of the colony. After the completion of major constructions for the infrastructure of the colony and the hinterland (railway, mines, harbour), around 1907, an economic upswing began, which started to transform the colony into a busy marketplace connecting the hinterland to national and international markets reaching from East Asia to Europe.

Kiaochow was acquired from China for ninety-nine years, but the grand colonial project ended abruptly. The rising imperialist power in Asia, Japan, used the opportunity of World War I to declare war on Germany in August 1914. In September 1914, Japanese ships and troops attacked the colony and overwhelmed the German station after some fighting.

Klaus Mühlhahn

Literary Works

Lindenberg, Paul (1899), *Fritz Vogelsang: Die Abenteuer eines deutschen Schiffsjungen in Kiautschou*, Berlin: F. Dümmler.

Schrameier, Wilhelm (1915), *Kiautschou. Seine Entwicklung und Bedeutung. Ein Rückblick*, Berlin: Curtius.

Uthemann, Walter and Fürth Uthemann (1911), *Tsingtau: Ein kolonialhygienischer Rückblick auf die Entwicklung des deutschen Kiautschougebietes*, Leipzig: Barth.

Histories

Hinz, Hans-Martin and Christoph Lind (eds) (1998), *Tsingtau – Ein Kapitel deutscher Kolonialgeschichte in China, 1897–1914*, Berlin: Deutsches Historisches Museum.

Leutner, Mechthild (ed.) with Klaus Mühlhahn (1997), *'Musterkolonie Kiautschou'. Die Expansion des Deutschen Reiches in China. Deutsch-chinesische Beziehungen 1897–1914. Eine Quellensammlung*, Berlin: Akademie Verlag.

Mühlhahn, Klaus (2000), *Herrschaft und Widerstand in der 'Musterkolonie' Kiautschou: Interaktionen zwischen China und Deutschland 1897–1914*, Munich: Oldenbourg.

Schrecker, John. E. (1971), *Imperialism and Chinese Nationalism: Germany in Shantung*, Cambridge, MA: Harvard University Press.

The Language Question

The term 'language question' (*Sprachenfrage*) was coined during the Kaiserreich (the German Empire) to refer to questions of language policy in the German colonies. Due to the co-existence of numerous local languages, it remained controversial until the end of the colonial period, whether or not the introduction of unified languages could stabilise colonial authority, and whether indigenous languages or German were preferable for this purpose. These discussions were related to ongoing fundamental debates on language policy in the late nineteenth century. The nationalistic coupling of the terms 'people', 'culture' and 'language', accompanied by the xenophobic demand for 'linguistic hygiene' were closely related issues, and reflected contemporary attempts to establish a standardised international language.

In 1900, the Romantic paradigm of the identity of a people's language and mind was discussed in increasingly nationalistic terms. The Allgemeine Deutsche Sprachverein (General German Language Society) in particular, founded in 1885, promoted a radical 'language purity', and opposed the use of foreign words. While the activities of the society were aimed primarily at the situation at home, its members also observed and commented with discontent on the linguistic development of their language in the colonies. Apart from these highly ideological concerns, more practical considerations about establishing a standardised language for international traffic and trade were discussed. Though artificial language projects like Esperanto, designed in 1887 by Lazarus Ludwik Zamenhof, were committed to the idealistic cause of global communication, nationalistic voices demanded measures for the promotion of German as a world language. Aside from whimsical projects such as a grammatically and lexically simplified 'World German', presented by the linguist Adalbert Baumann in 1915 during World War I, it was above all the language policy in the colonies which promised to strengthen Germany's imperial influence linguistically.

Controversial discussions persisted among colonial administrators, mission societies, linguists and representatives of colonial settlers concerning the best strategy to use for strengthening German power within the colonies, in comparison with the other European imperial powers. Missionaries and linguists opposed a German lingua franca in the colonies and called for more thorough research of the indigenous languages. However, many settlers rejected this option, since they feared losing their local positions of power. In contrast, the German Colonial Society argued that long-term power interests could be secured only through a comprehensive expansion of the German language. The question of whether a lingua franca would prove advantageous in the colonies remained controversial. On the one hand, it promised large administrative benefits; on the other hand, there were fears that it could facilitate widespread indigenous uprisings.

Due to the different political conditions in the colonies, the German language established itself as a colloquial language only in the settler colony of South-West Africa, and nowadays Namibia still has a significant German-speaking community, predominantly of German descent. Yet even today, the central aspects of the 'language question' – administrative, nationalistic and politico-cultural – are predominant in the discourse about language requirements for foreigners in Germany. In opposition to this prejudice, recent migrant literature like the 'Kanak Sprak' movement questions the underlying ideal of a 'pure' German language.

Sven Werkmeister

LITERARY WORKS
Rock, Zé do (1997), *Fom Winde ferfeelt. Welt-Strolch macht Links-Shreibreform*, Munich: Piper.
Zaimoglu, Feridun (1995), *Kanak Sprak. 24 Mißtöne vom Rande der Gesellschaft*, Hamburg: Rotbuch-Verlag.
— (2001), *Kopf und Kragen. Kanak-Kultur-Kompendium*, Frankfurt am Main: S. Fischer.

HISTORIES

Ashcroft, Bill, Garett Griffiths and Helen Tiffin (1989), *The Empire Writes Back: Theory and Practice in Post-Colonial Literatures*, London: Routledge.

Böhm, Michael Anton (2003), *Deutsch in Afrika. Die Stellung der deutschen Sprache in Afrika vor dem Hintergrund der bildungs- und sprachpolitischen Gegebenheiten sowie der deutschen Auswärtigen Kulturpolitik*, Frankfurt am Main: Lang.

Calvet, Louis-Jean (1974), *Linguistique et colonialisme. Petit traité de glottophagie*, Paris: Payot.

Mehnert, Wolfgang (1974) 'Zur "Sprachenfrage" in der Kolonialpolitik des deutschen Imperialismus', *Vergleichende Pädagogik* 10 (1): 52–60.

Werkmeister, Sven (2004), 'Die verhinderte Weltsprache. 16. Dezember 1915: Adalbert Baumann präsentiert "Das neue, leichte Weltdeutsch"', in Alexander Honold and Klaus R. Scherpe (eds) (2004), *Mit Deutschland um die Welt. Eine Kulturgeschichte des Fremden in der deutschen Kolonialzeit*, Stuttgart: Metzler, pp. 464–72.

Missions

German mission societies operated in all German colonies, like other European mission societies. The primary object of the fourteen Protestant German mission societies, such as the Leipzig Mission, the Moravians (Herrnhuter Mission), the Berlin Mission Society, the Basel Mission (which had most of its supporters in South Germany), the North German Mission Society or the Rhenish Mission Society, to name just a few, was to spread Christianity. The beginning of a new and modern mission movement in Germany, as well as in the subsequent colonies, dates from the first third of the nineteenth century. The impetus came from the Protestants and was influenced by a new kind of pietism and by the idea of awakening. The personal striving for spiritual perfection went hand in hand with social commitment. In German colonies, German branches of Catholic associations also got involved in the Christianising mission. Most of them had their head offices in Rome: they included the Hünfeld Oblates, the Franciscan and Salesian Missions, and the Hiltrup Mission.

The mission movements of both denominations had a large number of participants, especially from the lower middle classes, who assumed a critical attitude towards modernity, and advocated peasant and artisan ideals. Their ambition was to protect family and community, and to accustom the African and Asian 'heathens' to virtues like diligence, discipline and orderliness. The costs that many missionaries, their wives and families had to bear were material distress, disease and often an early death.

Apart from religious duties, social work, healthcare, schooling and scholarship formed the work of missionaries. The missionary schools aimed to spread Christian attitudes among adolescents and to deprive them of the religious influence of their native culture, in order to acquire local helpers in the task of spreading Christianity, but also to train the children in technical skills of the kind which could be of use to the missions. Several German missionaries had scholarly ambitions as well. They often studied the mother tongues of the ethnic groups they were operating among, and transformed the spoken languages into written ones by translating the Bible. Both religions expressed intransigent disapproval of Islam, which was regarded as a serious competitor.

The role of missionaries during the process of European colonisation is still being debated in colonial historiography and mission work: were they 'pioneers of colonialism' or 'advocates of the natives'? In German colonies, the missionaries placed themselves between the colonial administration and the colonised; they had to decide whether to co-operate with, or to oppose, governmental expectations. Furthermore, missions owning large estates, plantations, ranches and workshops became an important economic factor, and contributed to the development of capitalist methods and wage work. On the one hand, through their Europeanisation of indigenous societies, missions remained part of the colonial system; but on the other hand, they also remained organisations pursuing their own interests and values, for example opposing the colonial administration on questions such as the alcohol trade, forced labour and corporal punishment. In these cases, their paternalistic intervention eased the severities of colonial rule. Ironically enough, most African leaders of liberation movements were educated in missionary schools.

The reports of missionary men and women in the form of letters, diaries, bills, station or personal files are still available in the archives and libraries of the mission societies. Some of the missionaries even published their experiences and observations. Today, these materials are important sources for many fields of African studies.

Ulrich van der Heyden

HISTORIES

Altena, Thorsten (2003), '*Ein Häuflein Christen mitten in der Heidenwelt des dunklen Erdteils'. Zum Selbst- und Fremdverständnis protestantischer Missionare im kolonialen Afrika 1884–1918*, Münster: Waxmann.

Gründer, Horst (1982), *Christliche Mission und deutscher Imperialismus. Eine politische Geschichte ihrer Beziehungen während der deutschen Kolonialzeit 1884–1914 unter besonderer Berücksichtigung Afrikas und Chinas*, Paderborn: Schöningh.

Heyden, Ulrich van der and Jürgen Becher (eds) (2000), *Mission und Gewalt. Der Umgang christlicher Missionen mit Gewalt und die Ausbreitung des Christentums in Afrika und Asien in der Zeit von 1792 bis 1918/19*, Stuttgart: Steiner

Heyden, Ulrich van der and Holger Stoecker (eds) (2005), *Mission und Macht im Wandel politischer Orientierungen. Europäische Missionsgesellschaften in politischen Spannungsfeldern in Afrika und Asien zwischen 1800 und 1945*, Stuttgart: Steiner.

Oermann, Nils Ole (1999), *Mission, Church and State Relations in South-West Africa under German Rule (1884–1915)*, Stuttgart: Steiner.

NS-Colonialism

Judging from the enormous number of publications – and also films – dealing with African topics in the 1930s, the popular expectations that NS-colonialism was confronted with must have been high. In fact a revived colonialism appears to have been a salient aim of the Third Reich's foreign policy, and regaining African territories definitely ranked among the most popular fantasies of fascist Germany. With Hitler in power, however, 'classical' colonialism had few chances of realisation. Furthermore, the popularity of the colonial option derived from the all too evident 'injustice' perpetrated by the Allies in forcing Germany to withdraw from its colonies after 1918, and proclaiming them as Allied mandates. Many Germans refused to accept the allegation of the Versailles Treaty, that before 1914, German colonisers had been unsuccessful altogether. Instead, many Germans expected to be reinvolved in the 'colonising mission' sooner or later. Moreover, Wilhelminian imperialists held that having colonies abroad would be imperative for a powerful German nation state. But National Socialists, who were predominantly younger than traditional imperialists, preferred to conquer 'living space' (*Lebensraum*) in Eastern Europe.

In his book *Mein Kampf*, Hitler had called for diverting the 'eternal migration of Germans to the South' towards an eastern direction. Despite the meagreness of his comments on colonial matters (and point 3 of the NSDAP programme, in which colonies were demanded for Germany), colonial enthusiasts kept returning to Hitler's ideas. Hitler nourished colonial claims for the sake of maintaining political options in relation to France and Britain, in order to gain access to raw materials, and to demand 'equal chances of living' for Germany. Once in power, however, he forced the colonial movement into political conformity, and forged a Reichskolonialbund with colonial veteran Franz Ritter von Epp as its leader. A dramatically rising number of members (more than 2 million in 1943), and extensive planning for a future colonial empire in Africa, showed that the colonial idea was still vigorously alive in Germany.

Countless publications, in the form of personal recollections, travel diaries and novels suggested a return of Germans to Africa as early as possible (Dinglreiter 1935; Kaempffer 1940). The colonial movement was also inspired by the Italians, who had occupied Abyssinia in 1935, and thus established an African empire rather quickly. It was highly symbolic that National Socialists misused the title of an early colonial novel, Hans Grimm's *People without Space* (*Volk ohne Raum*, 1926), as a slogan for claiming *Lebensraum* in Eastern Europe. But these projects differed from the colonialism of the past in terms of spatial directions and in colonising methods as well. The 'General Plan for the East' (*Generalplan Ost*) ruthlessly disregarded the indigenous people of Poland, the Ukraine and Russia, and completely ignored their human rights, while European colonialism since the turn of the century had started critically to examine their methods of treating colonised people. Although the German colonial planning of the 1930s and 1940s obviously manifested racism and anticipated some aspects of 'apartheid', it was still rooted in Eurocentric international law and diplomacy. By contrast, the ideas of 'living space' in the East and of the Holocaust were conceptualised as 'final battles of races' (*rassischer Endkampf*). As early as 1951, Hannah Arendt suggested a continuity between Wilhelminian imperialism and National Socialist warfare in Eastern Europe, although more is needed now by way of evidence to define similarities and contrasts between the two. In general, colonialism in Africa ranked among the less urgent NS targets.

Dirk van Laak

LITERARY WORKS

Dinglreiter, Senta (1935), *Wann kommen die Deutschen endlich wieder? Eine Reise durch unsere Kolonien in Afrika*, Leipzig: Koehler and Amelang.

Grimm, Hans (1926), *Volk ohne Raum*, Munich: Langen-Mueller.

Hitler, Adolf (1936), *Mein Kampf*, Berlin: Eher.

Kaempffer, Adolf (1940), *Das erste Jahr. Roman des kolonialen Morgen*, Braunschweig, Berlin and Hamburg: Westermann.

HISTORIES

Crozier, Andrew J. (1988), *Appeasement and Germany's Last Bid for Colonies*, London: Macmillan.

Hildebrand, Klaus (1969), *Vom Reich zum Weltreich: Hitler, NSDAP und koloniale Frage 1919–1945*, München: Fink.

van Laak, Dirk (2004), *Imperiale Infrastruktur. Deutsche Planungen für eine Erschliessung Afrikas 1880 bis 1960*, Paderborn: Schöningh.

Linne, Karsten (2002), *'Weisse Arbeitsfuehrer' im 'kolonialen Ergaenzungsraum'. Afrika als Ziel sozial-und wirtschaftspolitischer Planungen in der NS-Zeit*, Münster: Monsenstein and Vannerdat.

Schmokel, Wolfe W. (1964), *Dream of Empire: German Colonialism, 1919–1945*, New Haven, CT and London: Yale University Press.

Orientalism

German-speaking countries never acquired colonial territory in the Middle East or northern Africa, but the longer history of direct political, military and economic interaction between German-speaking countries and different states and empires of the Middle East produced a large corpus of cultural and literary commentary on the relations between the two spheres.

The distinct German relationship to the Middle East is visible in writings produced during the Crusades. Initially, German writers expressed their support for these wars in enthusiastic ways; reflecting the Holy Roman Empire's decreasing interest in the Crusades, however, they increasingly composed poems and epics that were critical of them, and painted a sympathetic picture of Middle Eastern people. In the following centuries, the Ottoman Empire posed a larger threat for German-speaking territories than, for example, for France and England. Correspondingly, German images of Turks created during this period were more virulent, and remained so until Ottoman power declined in the course of the eighteenth century. A clearly positive image of the Middle East developed in German culture during the Enlightenment period and into the early nineteenth century, at a time when the Ottoman Empire no longer threatened German territories, and before European colonial powers began occupying Middle Eastern areas.

The brief time of Germany's congenial engagement with cultures and religions of the Middle East was followed by a period in which ideologies of superiority and domination, such as nationalism, racism and 'the civilising mission' prevailed. Even though Germany never became a colonial power in the Middle East, it expanded its political, economic and even military influence in the region. At times German policy in the Middle East supported colonised peoples in their struggle for independence from colonial domination, an aspect that distinguishes German strategy from that of other European powers and highlights the interdependency of the European states. Writings by Achim von Arnim, Franz Grillparzer, Karl May and Hugo von Hofmannsthal reflect aspects of the dominant belief systems. The oeuvre of Else Lasker-Schüler, on the other hand, which embodies the notion of 'the Jew as Oriental', offers a critique of established ideologies but also exemplifies the modern German enthusiasm for the Middle East that corresponds to diplomatic efforts geared at strengthening local populations vis-à-vis their colonisers.

The period after World War II brought two new aspects to the fore, namely the repercussions of the Holocaust on the German attitude concerning the Middle East and the effects of large-scale migration from Middle Eastern to German-speaking countries. Writings by authors originally from the Middle East changed the German literary landscape; the works of Emine Svegi Özdamar, Said, Salim Alafenisch, Rafik Schami and Feridun Zaimoglu, for example, articulate the various dimensions of the contemporary German–Middle Eastern encounter.

Whereas issues related to immigration are comparable to processes under way in France and Britain, the German case continues to be distinct in light of specific historical events (such as the Holocaust), long-standing relations (for example, with the Ottoman Empire and then Turkey), and German notions of citizenship and culture. The plethora of images and representations engaging themes related to the changing interconnections between

Germany and the Middle East highlights the material realities of the range of extant literary and other cultural production.

Nina Berman

Literary Works

Lasker-Schüler, Else [1907] (1919), *Die Nächte Tino von Bagdads*, Berlin: Cassirer.

Lessing, Gotthold Ephraim (1779), *Nathan der Weise*, Berlin: Voss.

May, Karl [1881–8] (1990), *Orientzyklus*, Zurich: Haffman.

Özdamar, Emine Sevgi (1992), *Das Leben ist eine Karawanserei*, Cologne: Kiepenheuer and Witsch.

Eschenbach, Wolfram von [1215] (1994), *Willehalm: Nach der Handschrift 857 der Stiftsbibliothek St Gallen*, ed. Joachim Heinzle, Tübingen: Niemeyer.

Goethe, Johann Wolfgang von (1819), 'West-Östlicher Divan', in Erich Trunz (ed.) (1981), *Goethes Werke*, vol. 2, Munich: Beck, pp. 7–270.

Histories

Berman, Nina (1997), *Orientalismus, Kolonialismus und Moderne. Zum Bild des Orients in der deutschsprachigen Kultur um 1900*, Stuttgart: Metzler.

Kontje, Todd (2004), *German Orientalisms*, Ann Arbor, MI: University of Michigan Press.

Mangold, Sabine (2004), *Eine 'Weltbürgerliche Wissenschaft'. Die deutsche Orientalistik im 19. Jahrhundert*, Stuttgart: Franz Steiner Verlag.

Özyurt, Senol (1972), *Die Türkenlieder und das Türkenbild in der deutschen Volksüberlieferung vom 16. bis zum 20. Jahrhundert*, Munich: Fink.

Schwanitz, Wolfgang G. (ed.) (2004), *Germany and the Middle East, 1871–1945*, Princeton, NJ: Markus Wiener.

Wilson, W. Daniel (1984), *Humanität und Kreuzzugsideologie um 1780. Die 'Türkenoper' im 18. Jahrhundert und das Rettungsmotiv in Wielands 'Oberon', Lessings 'Nathan' und Goethes 'Iphigenie'*, New York: Peter Lang.

Race and Ethnicity

Racism was an essential component in the justification for European colonial supremacy. In Germany, the racist perception of colonial hegemony was characterised by two distinct and sometimes even competing semantics: the idea of a 'cultural mission' (*Kulturmission*) developed in the eighteenth century; and the modern concept of 'social Darwinism'.

German colonial rule was legitimised between 1884 and 1914–18 by the belief widely held in anthropological and philosophical academic circles that Western civilisation provided an example for the rest of the world. A system for classifying the varieties of humanity in terms of their cultural environment was developed during the Enlightenment. This belief found expression in the publication of various authors (for example, Fabri, Hübbe-Schleiden), who were seeking to drum up support for a German colonial adventure to underline the specific cultural task of the Reich. Two basic assumptions were vital for this kind of racism: the idea of a difference between the colonising 'educators' and the colonised 'people', who were regarded as being 'educable'; and the view that colonisation was in some way a humanitarian cultural act. But meanwhile colonial discourse was increasingly influenced by social Darwinist argumentation, which meant a shift to a more biological and no longer dynamic, but static understanding of *race*. In particular the colonial wars in German

South-West and German East Africa were accompanied and justified by a colonial rhetoric which rejected any possibility of a 'cultural mission'. Although this view gained support from both settlers in the colonies and their representatives in Germany, especially the Pan-German League, the reform of colonial politics from 1906–07 onwards signalled to a certain degree a return to traditional 'educational' semantics. It was driven by colonial criticism of missionary societies, political parties such as the Centre Party (Zentrumspartei), the Social Democrats and the left-wing liberals. This form of colonial racism dominated the colonial mental map up till the beginning of the Third Reich.

The German colonial discourse demonstrates once more the dynamics of racism and the deployment of the notion of the 'colonial Other'. The constructions of white superiority found their way not only into everyday expressions and representations, but also into academic and political discourses, by way of colonial novels (see Frenssen, Grimm, Lettow-Vorbeck) and through schoolbooks, advertising and other popular portrayals. Today we are confronted with a paradoxical process: Whereas on the one hand there is a growing sensitivity regarding all forms of racism – due to new concepts of migration, integration and citizenship – on the other hand racist beliefs continue – in self-conscious or subliminal form.

Michael Schubert

LITERARY WORKS

Frenssen, Gustav (1906), *Peter Moors Fahrt nach Südwest. Ein Feldzugsbericht*, Berlin: Grote.

Grimm, Hans (1926), *Volk ohne Raum*, Munich: Langen.

Lettow-Vorbeck, Paul (1920), *Heia Safari! Deutschlands Kampf in Ostafrika*, Leipzig: Hase and Koehler.

HISTORIES

Becker, Frank (ed.) (2004), *Rassenmischehen-Mischlinge-Rassentrennung. Zur Politik der Rasse im deutschen Kolonialreich*, Stuttgart: Steiner.

Ciarlo, David M. (2003), *Rasse konsumieren. Von der exotischen zur kolonialen Imagination in der Bildreklame des Wilhelminischen Kaiserreichs*, in Birthe Kundrus (ed.) (2003), *Phantasiereiche. Zur Kulturgeschichte des deutschen Kolonialismus*, Frankfurt am Main: Campus-Verlag, pp. 135–79.

Martin, Peter (1993), *Schwarze Teufel, edle Mohren. Afrikaner in Bewußtsein und Geschichte der Deutschen*, Hamburg: Junius.

Fredrickson, George M. (2002), *Racism: A Short History*. Princeton, NJ: Princeton University Press.

Schubert, Michael (2003), *Der schwarze Fremde. Das Bild des Schwarzafrikaners in der parlamentarischen und publisistischen Kolonialdiskussion in Deutschland von den 1870er bis in die 1930er Jahre*, Stuttgart: Steiner.

Slavery, the Slave Trade and Abolition

Although German rulers on the whole did not take part in the early European expansion drive, controlled as it was by the Iberian monarchies of Portugal and Castile, some outstandingly rich merchant families, such as the Welsers and Fuggers from Augsburg, received important slave trade privileges. They were bankers to the Spanish crown and participated highly successfully in the emerging global trade. Thus, for instance, the Welsers brought some 4,000 slaves from Africa (Cape Verde and São Tomé) via Seville or directly to the Americas. The

Welsers also possessed sugar plantations on the Canary Islands and on the island of La Española (today Dominican Republic and Haiti) that were run using significant quantities of slave labour. In 1528, the Emperor Charles V signed a *capitulación* (a type of contract with the crown), which gave these merchants access to the exclusive exploitation of territories in what today constitutes Venezuela (1528–56). Their administrators, the 'men on the spot', undertook massive raids for Indian slaves, whom they subsequently sold to the Caribbean Islands.

From the time of the Thirty Years War, the Duke of Courland (Jakob Kettler) and the Great Elector of Brandenburg (Friedrich Wilhelm) sought to institutionalise their participation in the slave trade between their African trading forts and the Caribbean. These efforts were partially successful, at least until the outbreak of the Spanish succession war (1701), but their attempt to establish a slave plantation economy in their Caribbean 'possessions' (in the Virgin Islands and Tobago) failed miserably. In addition, in the seventeenth, eighteenth and nineteenth centuries, German ships, sailors and captains from Friesland, Hamburg, Bremen and Schleswig took part in the Atlantic slave trade, mostly under Dutch or British control.

Generally speaking, after about 1100 BC, 'white' slavery or slave trading did not occur in German speaking territories, though serfdom and other forms of unfree labour were widespread. The first texts concerning modern forms of slavery appeared in Prussian and Austrian codes of law at the end of the eighteenth century. At the same time, merchants, captains and the nobility started to employ African slaves as servants and sailors; and in the courts of Germany, the so-called *Hof-Mohren* (court slaves, Mohr or Maure [saracen]) began to appear more frequently. They often worked as drummers or musicians, with typical names Antonio Congo, Rudolf August Mohr, Pietro Angelo Angiola or August Afrika. Some of them found employment as scholars and scientists, such as Anton Wilhelm Amo (c. 1700–53), the 'black philosopher' of Halle and Wittenberg. There was a vigorous debate in various quarters about the civil rights such persons possessed.

In nineteenth-century Germany, a strong anti-slavery movement (in contrast to Britain, the USA, France, Spain or the Latin American republics) failed to emerge, with the exception perhaps of the brief period between 1888 and 1890, when the anti-slavery propaganda employed by the Catholic and Protestant Churches was used by the authorities to justify German colonial expansion into Africa, particularly East Africa. On the other hand, German intellectuals had a great interest in the anthropology and economics of slavery and abolition and their writings had a significant impact. Thus, for instance, the works of Alexander von Humboldt (1760–1856), especially his essay 'The Island of Cuba', which appeared in 1826, played an important role in the Atlantic anti-slavery debate. It is also noteworthy that Karl Marx and Friedrich Engels were committed abolitionists.

In 1857, Prussia proclaimed a law according to which all slaves who set foot on Prussian territory were to be declared 'free'. Despite the prohibition of slavery in Prussia, it was not outlawed in the German Colonial Empire. In German East Africa, for instance, slavery was legally recognised and administratively enforced by the colonial authorities, although some preparations were made to eliminate eventually the 'evil institution'. Here, slavery as a legal institution was only abolished in 1922, when the League of Nations took over the administration of these areas following Germany's defeat in World War I.

Jan-Georg Deutsch and Michael Zeuske

LITERARY WORKS

Humboldt, Alexander von [1826] (1992), 'Essai politique sur l'île de Cuba', in Hanno Beck (ed.) *Cuba-Werk*, Humboldt-Studienausgabe Bd 3, Darmstadt: Wissenschaftliche Buchgesellschaft, pp. 154–69.

HISTORIES

Bade, Karl J. (1977), 'Antisklavereibewegung in Deutschland und Kolonialkrieg in Deutsch-Ostafrika 1888–1890: Bismarck und Friedrich Fabri', *Geschichte und Gesellschaft* 3 (1): 31–58.

Denzer, Jörg (2005), *Die Konquista der Augsburger Welser-Gesellschaft in Südamerika 1528– 1556. Historische Rekonstruktion, Historiografie und lokale Erinnerungskultur in Kolumbien und Venezuela*, Munich: Verlag C. H. Beck.

Deutsch, Jan-Georg (2006), *Emancipation without Abolition in German East Africa, c. 1884– 1914*, Oxford: James Currey.

Harding, Leonhard (1995), 'Die deutsche Diskussion um die Abschaffung der Sklaverei in Kamerun', in P. Heine and U. van der Heyden (eds), *Studien zur Geschichte des deutschen Kolonialismus in Afrika*, Pfaffenweiler: Centaurus, pp. 280–308.

Zeuske, Michael (2006), *Sklaven und Sklaverei in den Welten des Atlantiks, 1400–1940. Umrisse, Anfänge, Akteure, Vergleichsfelder und Bibliografien*, Münster, Hamburg and London: Lit.

Togo

The current territory of the state of Togo is a strip about 100 kilometres wide and 540 kilometres long extending from the west coast of Africa into the hinterland. When German and French diplomats fixed the borders of East and North Togo in 1897, the artificial division of population groups also marked the beginning of ethnic-political problems between the North and the South of Togo, which are still prevalent today.

By 1884, the coast of Togo had been integrated into the Atlantic trade for centuries. The three German administrators who secured the territory against French and British interests in 1884–5, through protection agreements with the local chiefs, could easily assume control over a prospering import-export trade; the customs duty covered the expenses of the administration. The first – economic – foundation stone of the 'model colony' (*Musterkolonie*) had been laid. *Ruhe und Ordnung* (peace and order) made up the second. No scandals, just minor rebellions: Togo with its effective administration was considered an example to other German colonies in Africa, which in contrast needed public money and suffered uprisings. The role of being a *Musterkolonie* frustrated projects for economic development because the administration had to earn the capital in advance of any investment. In contrast with neighbouring British and French colonies, the German administration, two-thirds of which belonged to the military, established governance officially based on racial privileges. About 100 German government employees (out of a population of 428 Germans, mainly missionaries and merchants, in 1914) ruled over a population of nearly 1 million people in 87,000 square kilometres. From about 1900 onwards, they were able to enforce their orders in the remotest village via mercenaries, chiefs and native employees acting as interpreters and clerks. These African élites had to follow instructions unconditionally, but participated in colonial power at the same time. The administration set up four government schools and eleven prisons in Togo. By exemplary punishment and demonstrative paternalism the people of Togo experienced how a minority gained the ability to rule over the majority.

German administrators had to leave Togo in August 1914. In 1914 France and Britain agreed to split the colony of Togo lengthwise. Whereas in the British mandate territory the majority voted for a connection with Ghana in 1956 (becoming independent in

1957), the larger part of the Togolese population opted for independence as a national state in 1960.

Peter Sebald

LITERARY WORKS

Asmis, Rudolf (1942), *Kalamba na m'putu. Koloniale Erfahrungen und Beobachtungen*, Berlin: Mittler.

Gruner, Hans and Peter Sebald (eds) (1997), *Vormarsch zum Niger. Die Memoiren des Leiters der Togo-Hinterland-Expedition 1894/95*, Berlin: Edition Ost.

Küas, Richard (1939), *Togo. Erinnerungen*, Berlin: Volksverb. d. Bücherfreunde.

Rentzell, Werner von (1922), *Unvergessenes Land: von glutvollen Tagen und silbernen Nächten in Togo*, Hamburg: Alster-Verlag.

HISTORIES

Erbar, Ralph (1991), *Ein 'Platz an der Sonne'? Die Verwaltungs- und Wirtschaftsgeschichte der deutschen Kolonie Togo 1884–1914*, Stuttgart: Steiner.

Jones, Adam and Peter Sebald (eds) (2005), *An African Family Archive. The Lawsons of Little Popo/Aneho (Togo) 1841–1938*, Oxford: Oxford University Press.

Marguerat, Yves (1992), *Lomé, une brève histoire de la capital du Togo*, Lomé: Edition Haho.

Oloukpona-Yinnon, Adjaï Paulin (1998), *Unter deutschen Palmen. Die 'Musterkolonie' Togo im Spiegel deutscher Kolonialliteratur (1884–1944)*, Frankfurt am Main: IKO Verlag für Interkulturelle Kommunikation.

Schuerkens, Ulrike (2001), *Du Togo allemande aux Togo et Ghana independents. Changement social sous régime colonial*, Paris: L'Harmattan.

Sebald, Peter (1988), *Togo 1884–1914. Eine Geschichte der deutschen 'Musterkolonie' auf der Grundlage amtlicher Quellen; mit einem Dokumentenanhang*, Berlin: Akademie-Verlag.

Trotha, Trutz von (1994), *Koloniale Herrschaft. Zur soziologischen Theorie der Staatsentstehung am Beispiel des 'Schutzgebietes Togo'*, Tübingen: Mohr.

The Versailles Conference

The German colonies were not the focal point of interest during the consultations on the peace treaties in Paris in 1919. Nevertheless, the differing war aims of the Allies did provide substantial occasions for conflict. The Japanese government regarded the conquests in Kiaochow and the Pacific as spoils of war. The South African sub-imperialists had already worked for the de facto assimilation of South-West Africa. In Namibia, after the German capitulation at Korab on 9 July 1915, a new South African administrative system was built up while the war was still in progress. In similar fashion, the Australian and New Zealand governments strove for the possession of New Guinea, and the neighbouring archipelago. These strivings were opposed by Wilson, who held a determinedly anti-colonial position, and sought primarily to strengthen the planned League of Nations, although he had no well-conceived alternative conception at his disposal.

Wilson's principled opposition to annexation policies was well-known in the British dominions. For this reason, during the preliminaries to the negotiations, General Smuts put forward the idea of a mandate system, which apparently fitted in well with Wilson's ideas. Territories were to be handed over for administration as mandates to the League of Nations, which was to be granted extensive supervisory powers. Smuts had developed this concept for a non-colonial context, namely the multi-ethnic states of Europe and the Ottoman Empire. During the discussions in the Supreme Council, the American president was forced to recognise that the German colonies had already effectively been distributed, and to take cognisance of the powerful resistance of the prime ministers of the dominions.

After hard negotiations a compromise was found which allowed Wilson to save face. The 'Draft Resolution in Reference to Mandatories' pointed out that the peoples of the former German colonies were not yet in a position to rule themselves and that the well-being and the development of these people was a sacred duty of the civilised nations. Guardianship was therefore to be placed in the hands of the advanced nations as mandatories of the League of Nations. All the German protectorates were placed under the mandate of the League of Nations, with the exception of Kiaochow, which had been leased from China. However, Kiaochow was not returned to China, but taken over by Japan.

Togo, Cameroon and East Africa were classified as B-mandates, South-West Africa and the Pacific areas as C-mandates, all of which were declared to be completely incapable of independent government. This amounted in fact to annexation by the victorious powers, as the administration of the territories was transferred in each case to the corresponding member state of the League of Nations.

On the German side it was clear at the moment of capitulation that the colonies had been lost. Nonetheless, the terms of the Versailles Treaty gave rise to widespread indignation in the German population, particularly as it was linked with a severe indictment. Lloyd George had expressly justified the mandate rule for the former German colonies with the proven inability of the German Empire to wield colonial power, in order to accommodate Wilson's moral position at least on paper. The political approval of colonialism was absolutely clear in Germany. In the years that followed, the heterogeneous colonial revisionist movement was able to instrumentalise Versailles as a symbol, and to fill it with new anti-parliamentarian contents which found approval far beyond the organisations of the political right wing.

Boris Barth

Histories

Barth, Boris (2003), *Dolchstoßlegenden und politische Desintegration. Das Trauma der deutschen Niederlage im Ersten Weltkrieg 1914–1933*, Dusseldorf: Droste.

Boemeke, Manfred Franz (1998), *The Treaty of Versailles. A Reassessment after 75 Years*, New York: Cambridge University Press.

Krumeich, Gerd (ed.) (2001), *Versailles 1919: Ziele-Wirkung-Wahrnehmung*, Essen: Klartext-Verlag.

Silagi, Michael (1977), *Von Deutsch-Südwest zu Namibia: Wesen und Wandlungen des völkerrechtlichen Mandats*, Ebelsbach: Gremer.

West Africa: 17th–18th Century

The western coast was the first region in Africa where almost all great European powers appeared and established trading bases in early modern times. West Africa saw no large colonies in the seventeenth and eighteenth centuries: these trading centres were built only along the shores or on large estuaries.

The Portuguese, as the first European merchants, established their trading companies in 1471. Initially, they mainly exported gold and ivory to Europe, but shortly afterwards, they started to consign Africans as slaves to America. Within a short time, this transatlantic slave trade became the major source of profit. In addition to the great European powers, even delegates of the German Duke of Kurland aspired to benefit from the slave trade. In the early 1680s, Elector Wilhelm of Brandenburg, called the Great Elector, planned a venture into this market. Adopting the Dutch pattern, he constructed harbours for ocean-going vessels, and built and purchased many ships, which sailed for the Gulf of Guinea. After talks with the African coastal population, and promising great wealth, despite tough competition from European colonial powers, the first *brandenburgische Afrikaexpedition* returned home with 100 pounds of gold and 10,000 pounds of ivory. An overseas trading company, the Churfürstliche Afrikanisch-Brandenburgische Compagnie, was founded in 1682.

In addition, Brandenburg built a fort called Großfriedrichsburg on the coast of former Gold Coast (today's Ghana) and from there, started to participate in the transatlantic slave trade. Agents of the Brandenburg state sold some 10,000 to 30,000 Africans as slaves to America. Today, the main fort on the border of Princess Town remains, and UNESCO has included it on the distinguished list of World Heritage Sites, along with all the other fortresses of the slave trade era on the coast of Ghana.

In addition to Großfriedrichsburg, Brandenburg and Prussia acquired two more overseas bases to facilitate its transatlantic slaves trade. One was the island of Arguin, situated close to the coast of today's Mauritania. It was mainly used for the gum trade. In 1721, it was conquered by the French, and the existing Prussian fortress was completely destroyed. The other was the Caribbean island of St Thomas, which was partly leased out to the Danes. This island was used as a 'reloading point' for the resale of slaves. In 1731, every Brandenburg and Prussian holding was confiscated by the Danes.

The Great Elector died in 1688. His successors had no stake in the 'African trade'. Their economic and military efforts concentrated on the continent of Europe. King Friedrich Wilhelm I of Prussia sold his African possessions to the Dutch East India Company in 1717. By a contract clause the new owner of Großfriedrichsburg was bound to 'send 12 negro boys, six of them decorated with golden chains' to the Prussian king. The arrival of these African children, who were consequently brought to Berlin and Potsdam, marked the historical beginning of the influx of Africans into Germany.

Ulrich van der Heyden

HISTORIES

Brooks, George E. (2003), *Eurafricans in Western Africa. Commerce, Social Status, Gender, and Religious Observance from the Sixteenth to the Eighteenth Century*, Athens, OH: Ohio University Press.

Heyden, Ulrich van der (1993), *Rote Adler an Afrikas Küste. Die bandenburgisch-preußische Kolonie Großfriedrichsburg an der westafrikanischen Küste*, Berlin: Brandenburgisches Verlagshaus.

Women's Histories

The colonised and colonisers of the German Colonial Empire each comprised both sexes, as well as various sexualities, and entailed the adoption of various sexual roles. The people in the colonies belonged to diverse cultures, and in some cases were neither indigenous nor German (for example, Indian commercial families in East Africa; Italian male labourers in

German South-West Africa). Colonial gender hierarchies were inextricable from the specificities of such cultural contexts. Tracing the lives of women in these societies and in the metropole leads to new histories and revisions of old ones.

The overwhelming majority of women whose lives intersected with German colonialism were colonised indigenous women in Africa, the Pacific and China. War, taxation and new forms of labour and consumption under German rule reshaped their lives. German policies also targeted women specifically, in areas such as domestic service, cohabitation, marriage (which was linked to citizenship, military service, and inheritance), prostitution and public health. Colonised women sometimes situated themselves directly at the interface of the colonial encounter, forming primary relationships with Germans as interpreters, businesswomen and other kinds of mediators, as cohabiting and marital partners, and as mission members. Finally, the colonial crucible of nationalism produced new gender roles for women.

German women, whether radical nationalist, conservative, liberal or feminist, saw promise in colonialism for improving their lives. They engaged in missionary and anti-slavery work, nursing, settlement policy, race purity agitation (for example, opposing marriages between Germans and colonial subjects) and in schools which prepared women for paid colonial careers. In doing so, they confronted German men's fantasies of gendered colonial conquest, which often wrote German women out of playing any role in colonial encounters. This struggle was expressed in, for example, debates about whether white women could acclimatise to the tropics to a sufficient degree to enable white family settlements. A consensus emerged that German women were preservers of whiteness and racial purity. This consensus simultaneously secured women's participation in colonial politics, and profoundly racialised it. Germany's loss of its colonies after 1919, which the Entente justified in terms of the perceived or alleged deficiencies of Germans as colonisers, only reinforced colonialist women's focus on racialised German culture. They remained active in the colonial movement, which sought to revise the Versailles Treaty, until the time of World War II.

Lora Wildenthal

Literary Works and Biographies

Brockmann, Clara (1910), *Die deutsche Frau in Südwestafrika. Ein Beitrag zur Frauenfrage in unseren Kolonien*, Berlin: E. S. Mittler.

Bülow, Frieda von (1891), *Der Konsul. Vaterländischer Roman aus unseren Tagen*, Dresden: Carl Reissner.

Christaller, Hanna (1904), *Alfreds Frauen: Novelle aus den deutschen Kolonien*, Stuttgart: Franckh.

Ruete, Emily (i.e. Sayyida Salme) (1993), *An Arabian Princess between Two Worlds. Memoirs, Letters Home, Sequels to the Memoirs. Syrian Customs and Usages*, ed. E. van Donzel, Leiden: E. J. Brill.

Histories

Grosse, Pascal (2006), *Colonialism, Eugenics and Civil Society in Germany, 1850–1918*, Ann Arbor, MI: University of Michigan Press.

Hendrickson, Hildi (1996), 'Bodies and Flags: The Representation of Herero Identity in Colonial Namibia', in Hildi Hendrickson (ed.), *Clothing and Difference: Embodied Identities in Colonial and Post-Colonial Africa*, Durham, NC: Duke University Press, pp. 157–88.

Krüger, Gesine (1999), *Kriegsbewältigung und Geschichtsbewusstsein: Realität, Deutung und Verarbeitung des deutschen Kolonialkrieges in Namibia 1904 bis 1907*, Göttingen: Vandenhoeck and Ruprecht.

Mead, Margaret (1960), 'Weaver of the Border', in Joseph B. Casagrande (ed.), *In the Company of Man. Twenty Portraits by Anthropologists*, New York: Harper and Bros, pp. 175–210.

Wildenthal, Lora (2001), *German Women for Empire, 1884–1945*, Durham, NC: Duke University Press.

Zantop, Susanne (1997), *Colonial Fantasies: Conquest, Family, and Nation in Precolonial Germany, 1770–1870*, Durham, NC: Duke University Press.

Italy and its Colonies

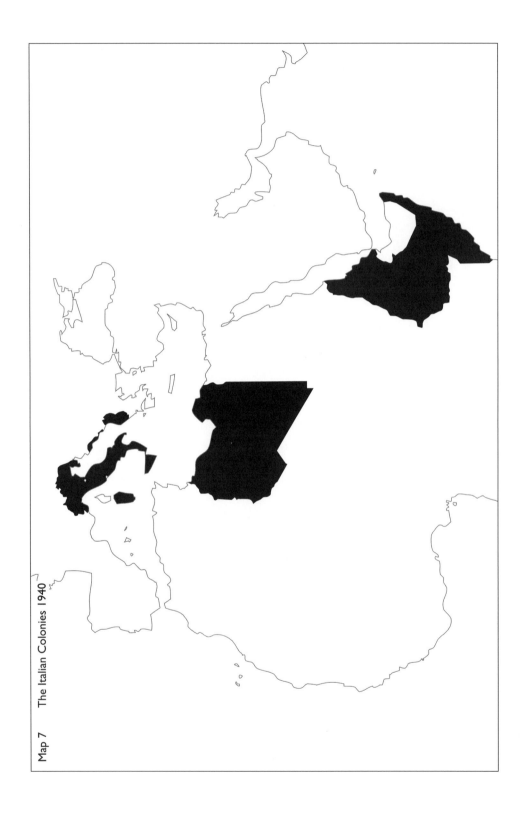

Map 7   The Italian Colonies 1940

Italy and its Colonies: Introduction

The history and consequences of Italian colonialism were until very recently little known in Italy and abroad, despite the lasting legacies of Italian imperial possessions that stretched from the Red Sea to the Mediterranean to the Adriatic. Italian colonialism is often linked to the expansionist foreign policy of Benito Mussolini, who ruled Italy as dictator from 1922 to 1943, but the foundation of Italian colonialism was laid during the liberal era, with the occupations of the East African countries of Eritrea (1890) and Somalia (1908) and the seizure of Ottoman-held Libya in 1912. Mussolini added the Aegean outpost of the Dodecanese Islands (1923), avenged the Italians' 1896 defeat at Adwa by occupying Ethiopia in 1935, and took control of Albania in 1939 as a precursor to the Italian wartime occupations of parts of Yugoslavia, Greece and France. Of all these imperial actions, only the takeover of Emperor Haile Selassie's Ethiopia has been well studied, primarily from the point of view of Italian military history, European diplomatic history and as an event which sparked African nationalism. The social, cultural, political and economic impact of the long years of Italian occupation in the Balkans and in East and North Africa is only now being delineated clearly.

Indeed, it has been argued that Italian colonialism has been doubly marginalised within the historical record (Andall et al. 2003; Ben-Ghiat and Fuller 2005). Mirroring Italy's faint presence within most accounts of modern Europe, Italy's imperial enterprises have received little attention in comparative colonial studies and in histories of the continent. Until very recently Italian colonialism also occupied a peripheral place within Italian national histories. The separation of the national and the colonial spheres was not unusual within the historiography of Europe: the study of the borrowings, reciprocal influences and parallel developments between metropoles and colonies is a relatively new phenomenon. Yet in the Italian case, the neglect of these 'tensions of empire' belied a deep investment in a larger culture of 'myths, suppressions [and] denials' (Del Boca 2003; Labanca, this volume) that was content to pass over the theme of Italian empire altogether, other than to indulge in nostalgic or neo-colonial evocations. Yet as Triulzi (2006), Andall and Duncan (2005), and Taddia (1988) have observed, memories of Italian colonialism were not so much repressed as displaced, in favour of narratives of an Italian 'exceptionalism' which distinguished between the exploitative and abusive nature of other imperial enterprises and the essential humanity of Italian colonisers and their policies of 'demographic colonialisation'. Such narratives of 'Italians as good people' (*Italiani brava gente*) proved tenacious, in part because they were embraced by much of the mainstream press and by many government institutions. The collective investment by Italian élites in sustaining the myth of Italian colonial exceptionalism was manifested in government policies that severely restricted scholars' access to important colonial archives for most of the post-war period, and in a general rejection of alternative framings of the histories and legacies of Italian colonialism. Thus not only was Italian colonialism little studied within Italy, until the 1990s (apart from the significant exceptions of Italian pioneers such as Giorgio Rochat and Del Boca) but comparative colonial scholars lacked the empirical data and fund of interpretative analyses that would allow for the study of the Italian case.

The lag in the study of Italian colonialism with respect to its French and British counterparts has also affected the study of the postcolonial period – the histories of Italy's former territories and the legacies of Italian colonialism in Italy. The concept of the postcolonial is itself continually in evolution and subject to contestation and debate (Loomba et al. 2005). Yet it can be safely used to denote an engagement with the aftermath of colonial rule and a conceptualisation of colonialisation and decolonisation as overlapping processes: regardless of the weight one places on the 'post' in 'postcolonial', there is clearly no clean and tidy break between the two historical eras. The historian Frederick Cooper argues accordingly for postcolonial narratives which are grounded in ethnographic and historical research: we cannot understand the complex internal and international dynamics of postcolonial societies, he contends, unless we have a thorough understanding of how these dynamics were shaped by decades of colonial occupations (Cooper 2005).

This point is particularly germane to the study of Italian postcolonialism. Much more research needs to be done on the colonial period before we can grasp its short-and long-term postcolonial effects. In Libya, Mu'ammar Qadhafi's 1969 revolution was framed as the continuation of the anti-colonial resistance led by 'Umar al-Mukhtar, who was made a martyr in the course of a ferocious Italian crackdown on that resistance in Cyrenaica in the late 1920s and 1930s (Jerary 2005). Yet we do not know enough about the social framework of Libyan resistance (and of Libyan collaboration), nor about the long-term social, economic, political and cultural effects of thirty years of Italian rule, nor, finally, about the consequences of that rule as manifested in relations between Libyans and Italians who remained in Libya until the expulsions of 1970. In Italy's former colonies in the Horn of Africa, contemporary conflicts between Ethiopia and Eritrea and between Ethiopia and Somalia are the most dramatic legacy of Italy's territorial reorganisations of East Africa and of Fascist colonial ideologies and practices of rule that intensified ethnic conflict (Calchi Novati 2005; Triulzi 2006). Throughout Italy's former empire, from the Dodecanese Islands to Eritrea, the lasting ambivalences toward and interiorisations of colonial cultures and values will be better understood as we come to know more about the social fabric of colonial existence (Iyob 2005; Triulzi 2006; Doumanis 1997).

Although none of the entries in this section are explicitly comparative, since the goal here is to provide the reader with succinct treatments of topics related to the history and culture of Italian colonialism and postcolonialism, the reader will gain a sense of how Italian colonialism differed from other European imperialisms and what the Italian case can tell us about imperialism in general. Yet I wish to present a brief overview of the particularities of Italian colonialism here, as a means of foregrounding themes which recur throughout the section and which suggest the limited applicability of Anglo-French models of imperialism to the Italian case.

The first particularity is certainly poverty. Paltry state resources hampered the realisation of ambitious land settlement schemes and limited private investment in the colonies. That same poverty fuelled Italians' anxieties about their country's backwardness with respect to other European powers, making the maintenance of authority and prestige central concerns. For Italians, empire was an escape route from a subordinate international position, a means of advertising Italian power and modernity. Yet Italian élites and colonial functionaries also worried constantly that Italian colonists were themselves too unschooled and subaltern to command effectively. In these obsessive concerns about prestige and image lies one peculiarity of the Italian 'civilising mission', which was directed as much toward Italian colonisers as towards the colonised.

Poverty had also made Italy a nation of emigrants since the country's unification, sending millions not only to North and South America, but also to French colonial territories such as Tunisia. Although these mass emigrations have been often treated as an issue of migration history, they were fundamental to the development of Italian colonialism and to any understanding of the relationship between Italian colonial and national identities over time. Italian colonialism was, in fact, a response to the phenomenon of mass emigration: during both liberal and fascist periods ideas of 'demographic colonisation' (using colonies to resettle large numbers of Italians who could not find work at home, thus stemming the flow of Italians abroad) found fortune as a distinctively Italian solution to imperial practice and ideology. Moreover, during the Fascist period in particular the colonies were seen as a means of 'bringing home' Italians who were already abroad, from the Americas to Europe to the French colonies of North Africa. Fascist imperial thinking thus posited not only the outward expansion of Italian influence – the claiming of foreign lands and seas as Italian – but also the reclaiming of Italians already abroad for the motherland. This diasporic quality of the Italian nation invites treatments of Italian national identity and Italian imperialism that look beyond linear exchanges between colony and metropole to include relations among the Italian metropole, Italian colonies and Italians who lived abroad under a variety of national and imperial sovereignties. The different 'tensions of empire' that mark the Italian case remind us of the limitations of national paradigms in accounting for the complexities of colonial histories.

The circumstances of the Italian Empire's demise, in the context of Italy's larger military defeat during World War II, also marks Italy off from other European colonial powers. Unlike the French and British Empires, which ended in a groundswell of nationalist revolts by their colonial subjects, the Italian Empire saw defeat by Europeans, first through military conquest and then by diplomatic fiat. The Allied powers had taken over Eritrea, Somalia and Libya as they routed Italy in Africa during World War II. Emperor Haile Selassie returned to rule Ethiopia, and Italy had to wait two years, until the ratification of the 1947 Paris Peace Treaty, for the confirmation that it had lost its colonies. The symbolic importance of empire for Italy – which had viewed the colonies as a means of gaining prestige with other European powers – is demonstrated by the fact that liberals, leftists and neofascists all participated in the intense campaign waged by the Italians between 1945 and 1947 to retain their colonies. In this circumstance, the Allied decision to deny these entreaties was experienced as a further injury to national pride. The way Italian colonialism ended, finally, meant that Italy did not undergo any real process of decolonisation. In Eritrea and Somalia, for example, the Italians were immediately replaced by a British military administration, and English quickly replaced Italian as the official language. This 'external decolonisation' (Andall 2005) at the hands of the Great Power the Fascists had hoped to become the equal of through its own imperial New Order left a legacy of humiliation that worked against Italians' acknowledgement of their colonial crimes, even as it fostered nostalgic attitudes towards the colonies that had been unjustly 'taken away'. In this climate, no real debate was carried out about the economic, moral and other costs of Italian imperialism, either in the immediate post-war period, or later on. On the African side, the Allied attempt to 'wipe clean' Italian colonialism added yet another layer of imperial interference but did not erase the cultural, linguistic and other effects of decades of Italian rule.

Finally, there is the question of colonial violence as it was experienced and remembered in the Italian case. Any comparative consideration of colonial violence is a difficult and perhaps fruitless exercise. Yet the longevity of the trope of Italians as the 'humane' colonisers, the general lack of knowledge about Italian colonialism, and the fact that the Italian Empire developed in the context of dictatorship as well as democracy warrant a few observations here. The first is that the colonies were from the start considered testing grounds for military technology and colonial violence, an opportunity to broadcast Italy's modernity and martial prowess to the rest of the world. Indeed, far from being 'more humane' than other Europeans, the Italians attain a primacy in military aggression when the colonial arena is factored in. The Italo-Turkish war over Libya, which was unified Italy's first 'national' war, garnered Italy the 'honour' of the first military use of air strikes and, three years before World War I, the first aerial bombings. In the 1920s, during Mussolini's régime, Italy was the first country to use gases widely in violation of the 1925 Gas Protocol. Gas was used in Libya and Eritrea throughout the 1920s, and in Ethiopia, not only in massive quantities during the 1935–6 war of conquest but throughout the late 1930s as an instrument of colonial rule. With the Ethiopian war, Italy also became the first European country to wage a large-scale war after World War I, a war that resulted in genocide. In the Cyrenaica region of Libya, between 1928 and 1932, the 'pacification' of resisting tribes was carried out through a combination of forced marches and mass detention in concentration camps that destroyed the local nomadic economy and lifestyle and caused the deaths of over 100,000 Libyans. From the Dodecanese Islands to Libya to Eritrea, the Italian state's colonial holdings were testing grounds for strategies of governance and repression that would characterise Italian domestic and occupied territories during World War II. The question of violence is but one example of how Italian history reads differently with Italian colonialism as part of its narrative. Italy's heavy early uses of chemical and aerial warfare, and the deeply destabilising effects of the Ethiopian invasion, beg a re-evaluation of the country's role in the history of twentieth-century European warfare and international relations.

These distinguishing features of Italian colonialism have had important postcolonial consequences. Fascist doctrines of colonial racism, Italian concerns with prestige in both liberal and Fascist eras, and the lack of a longstanding colonial culture led the Italians to adopt anti-assimilationist policies which forestalled the formation of an italophone colonial élite. Although many of Italy's colonial subjects learned to speak Italian, with the exception of the Dodecanese Islands, which underwent a forced 'Italianisation', formal teaching of Italian, and indeed all schooling, was very limited. Moreover, Italy's 'external decolonisation' meant that Italian did not remain the official language in any of Italy's former colonies. This situation contributed to the lack of debate in the first decades after World War II over Italy's responsibilities as an ex-colonial power, since no figure emerged from the former colonies to accuse the Italians in their own language, as Franz Fanon and others had done in France. The Fascists had also destroyed native élites by driving many of them into exile, as in Libya, or by targeting them for reprisal executions, as in Ethiopia. In the longer term this has produced a much smaller italophone community and, as in the case of a number of African italophone writers from the former French Empire, a community that has adopted Italian as a second European language, as a conscious alternative to writing in French. With the majority of Italy's contemporary immigrant population originating from countries other than Italy's former colonies, writing in Italian is a means for them to carry on a dialogue with one another that addresses their feelings of exclusion, their hopes for social and political integration, and their desire to create a hybridised language and a public of Italian readers that accepts formal and stylistic innovations (Parati 2005; Lombardi-Diop, this volume).

Italy's relative poverty with respect to other colonial powers and its status as a sending rather than receiving migrant nation until the 1970s has also greatly shaped its postcolonial existence. Whereas in post-war Britain and to a lesser extent in France and Holland colonial and later ex-colonial subjects made up the bulk of its labour migrant pool, in Italy migrants from its South served as the labour resource for its post-war economic boom of the late 1950s and 1960s, when they were not continuing to emigrate abroad. Libyans and East Africans did emigrate to Italy, often as individuals in the employ of repatriating Italians. Between 1940 and 1960 between 550,000 and 850,000 Italians returned from the colonies (Colombo and Sciortino 2004), and in the 1970s Eritreans and Ethiopians made up the second largest group of migrants residing in Italy. Yet by the 1990s migrants from Italy's ex-colonies had been far outnumbered by many other nationalities. The second generation of Eritreans and others whose parents once lived under Italian rule have maintained the pattern of not choosing Italy as their emigration destination (Pastore 2004; Andall 2005).

The particular concerns that shaped Italian colonial ideologies and policies, such as deleterious effects of Italian mass emigration and insecurities over Italy's European status, are visible today in restrictive contemporary Italian laws regarding nationality and immigration. A 1992 law reflected a desire to safeguard Italian nationality by considering it as something that may be 'passed on' even among those of Italian heritage who may never have set foot in Italy, but who form part of the Italian diaspora. This 'inclusionist' conception of nationality is juxtaposed with 'exclusionist' provisions in the same law that make it very difficult for foreign immigrants (including those of Italy's former colonial territories) to gain Italian citizenship even if they have lived legally in Italy for decades (Pastore 2004). Such contemporary state measures beg the question of Italy's responsibility as a former colonial power and of the exclusions Italians themselves faced as former immigrants. As Armando Gnisci has argued, Italy's willed repression of its colonial past and of the scale of Italian misery and mass emigration facilitates public support for such legislation (Gnisci 1999; Parati 2005). Certainly, it is difficult to draw firm conclusions about the relation between Italy's past as a colonial power and the anti-immigrant racism that marks its postcolonial era. Yet, as Andall has observed, Italy's treatment of its former subjects as a colonial power provides a framework for its treatment of immigrants as a postcolonial country (Andall 2005).

The entries that make up this section of the present volume are written by scholars who work in a range of disciplines, from history to Italian studies to political science to anthropology, and who come from Italy, from throughout the anglophone world, and from many of Italy's former colonies. Taken together, their short essays make clear that although Italian colonialism was more restricted in geographical scope and duration than the French and British Empires, it had no less impact on the development of metropolitan conceptions of race and of national identity, and it was certainly no less violent. As Andall and Duncan have cogently stated, Italy's colonial ideologies and practices are implicated in broader modes of Eurocentrism, and there is no history of Italian colonialism to be recovered without a sense of the wider context in which it took place (Andall and Duncan 2005). The present volume, which presents the Italian case alongside other European imperialisms and their aftermaths, will surely foster the inclusion of Italy in future comparative colonial and postcolonial research.

Ruth Ben-Ghiat

Histories

Andall, J. (2005), 'Immigration and the Legacy of Colonialism: The Eritrean Diaspora in Italy', in J. Andall and D. Duncan (eds), *Italian Colonialism: Legacy and Memory*, Bern: Peter Lang, pp. 191–216.

Andall, J. and D. Duncan (eds) (2005), *Italian Colonialism: Legacy and Memory*, Bern: Peter Lang.

Andall, J., C. Burdett and D. Duncan (2003), 'Introduction', *Journal of Modern Italian Studies* (special issue on Italian colonialism) 8 (3): 1–5.

Ben-Ghiat, R. and M. Fuller (2005), 'Introduction', in R. Ben-Ghiat and M. Fuller (eds), *Italian Colonialism*, New York: Palgrave, pp. 1–12.

Calchi Novati, G. (2005), ' "National Identities" as a By-Product of Italian Colonialism: A Comparison of Eritrea and Somalia', in J. Andall and D. Duncan (eds), *Italian Colonialism: Legacy and Memory*, Bern: Peter Lang, pp. 47–74.

Colombo, A. and G. Sciortino (2004), 'The Flows and the Flood: The Public Discourse on Immigration in Italy, 1969–2001', *Journal of Modern Italian Studies* 9 (1): 94–113.

Cooper, F. (2005), *Colonialism in Question: Theory, Knowledge, History*, Berkeley, CA: University of California Press.

Del Boca, A. (2003), 'The Myths, Suppression, Denials and Defaults of Italian Colonialism', in P. Palumbo (ed.), *A Place in the Sun. Africa in Italian Colonial Culture from Post-Unification to the Present*, Berkeley, CA: University of California Press, pp. 17–36.

Doumanis, Nicholas (1997), *Myth and Memory in the Mediterranean: Remembering Fascism's Empire*, New York: St Martins.

Gnisci, Armando (1999), 'Africa e mondi', *Rivista di Letteratura Italiana Comparata* 13: 47–57.

Iyob, R. (2005), 'From Mal d'Africa to Mal d'Europa? The Ties that Bind', in J. Andall and J. Duncan (eds), *Italian Colonialism: Legacy and Memory*, Bern: Peter Lang, pp. 255–82.

Jerary, Muhammad T. (2005), 'Damages Caused by the Italian Fascist Colonization of Libya', in R. Ben-Ghiat and M. Fuller (eds), *Italian Colonialism*, New York: Palgrave, pp. 203–8.

Loomba, A. et al. (eds) (2005), *Postcolonial Studies and Beyond*, Durham, NC: Duke University Press.

Parati, G. (2005), *Migration Italy: The Art of Talking Back in a Destination Culture*, Toronto: University of Toronto Press.

Pastore, F. (2004), 'A Community out of Balance: Nationality Law and Migration Politics in the History of Post-Unification Italy,' *Journal of Modern Italian Studies* 8 (3): 27–48.

Triulzi, A. (2006), 'Displacing the Colonial Event: Hybrid Memories of Postcolonial Italy', *Interventions: International Journal of Postcolonial Studies* 8 (3): 430–43.

Adwa

The Battle of Adwa, which was fought in Tigray, Ethiopia, on 1–2 March 1896, saw the defeat of an Italian expeditionary force by an imposing but poorly equipped army which

Emperor Menelik II of Ethiopia had successfully gathered to defend the integrity of his country. In the bloody battle, after the Italians invaded Ethiopia from the neighbouring Italian colony of Eritrea, several thousand newly recruited men from Italy, Eritrea and Ethiopia died in one day. The battle has long echoed in Ethiopia and abroad as the main symbol of Ethiopian unity and independence, and of African determination to resist colonial rule.

Yet the memory of Adwa has also followed other, very different, trajectories. In Italy, throughout the liberal period (1870–1922), the colonial defeat was perceived as intensely humiliating and eventually gave rise to Mussolini's revanchist occupation of Ethiopia in 1935–41, which was followed by an enduring amnesia in Italy of her colonial past. In Ethiopia, Adwa's national symbology has been recently revisited, notably on the occasion of the hundredth anniversary of the battle, which was celebrated in March 1996. It was pointed out then that Adwa's unquestioned external achievement – the Ethiopian struggle to maintain her independence – tended to ignore Adwa's internal and more pressing legacy. Menelik's confirmation of Italian control over Eritrea allowed him to partition the northern Ethiopian province of Tigray, thus weakening internal opposition to his rule. The division of Tigray facilitated his annexation of huge tracts of fertile land in the South-West, over which he exercised a form of internal 'colonial' rule. On the Eritrean side, where denial of independence during decolonisation and its annexation to Ethiopia resulted in a bloody war of liberation which lasted almost thirty years (1962–91), the memory of Adwa has been dismissed as part of Ethiopia's exclusionist collective memory. Thus the representation of Adwa in postcolonial times has changed dramatically.

This fluid counter-memory of Adwa – secretly nourished over the years and preserved both within Ethiopia's multi-layered society and in post-liberation Eritrea –flared up during the border conflict (1998–2000), which pitted Ethiopia against independent Eritrea over the old colonial border. The conflict, which ended in December 2000 after two years of a virulent 'war of words' and bloody border clashes, was often portrayed in Ethiopia as a replay of the attacks Italy had staged from neighbouring Eritrea in both the liberal and Fascist years. In February 1999, when the Eritrean troops were routed near the village of Badme, along the Tigray-Eritrea border, the Battle of Badme was promptly labelled 'the second Adwa'. The recent assignment of Badme to Eritrea by the independent border commission which was jointly appointed to adjudicate the legal dispute between the two countries has opened yet another chapter of Adwa's legacy, one infused with new national and local symbolisms.

Alessandro Triulzi

HISTORIES

Abdussamed A. and R. Pankhurst (eds) (1998), *Adwa Victory Centenary Conference 26 February-2 March 1996*, Addis Ababa: Institute of Ethiopian Studies, Addis Ababa University.

Del Boca, A. (ed.) (1997), *Adua. Le ragioni di una sconfitta*, Roma-Bari: Laterza.

Garima, H. (1999), *Adwa*, Mypheduh Films.

Labanca, N. (1993), *In marcia verso Adua*, Turin: Einaudi.

Mennasemay, M. (1997), 'Adwa: A Dialogue between the Past and the Present', *Northeast African Studies* (new series), 4 (2): 43–89.

Triulzi, A. (2003), 'Adwa: From Monument to Document', *Modern Italy* 8 (1): 95–108.

Albania

Albanian colonial and postcolonial experiences emerged from the historical relations between Italy and Albania, which were shaped by Italy's geo-political interest in controlling the access to the Adriatic Sea and expanding into the Balkans. In 1914, the Italian military invaded the country and controlled the city of Vlora and the strategic island of Sazan until 1920, when the Italians were moved out. However, after World War I, Italy's prominent interest in Albania was recognised by the Conference of Ambassadors and Albania finally became a de facto Italian protectorate, with Italy playing a key role in endorsing and actively sustaining the rule of King Zog.

Italian academic and political literature written before World War II downplayed Albania's social and political cohesiveness, highlighting historical and cultural relations between the two countries in order to justify Italy's claim to be Albania's 'natural' protector. On the Albanian side, the fact that historically Albanian nationalism emerged against the threat of assimilation and domination from neighbouring powers such as Greece and Serbia meant that Italy's overwhelming influence could be tolerated in the name of Albanian modernisation. Thus, depending on the geo-political circumstances, Italy was strategically constructed in Albania as a dangerous invader or as a modernising protector.

The experience of the Italian military occupation between 1939 and 1943 and of the ensuing anti-fascist partisan resistance became key themes in the construction of an Albanian national identity during the communist rule which lasted from the end of World War II through to 1991, well after the death of Enver Hoxha, its founding leader, in 1985. However, with the collapse of the régime in early 1991, Albania displayed a 'reaction-formation' to the official national-communist ideology's propagandistic emphasis on the threat of moral, social and economic decay posed by westernisation. Because of its resonance in Albanian culture and history and because of the fact that in communist times Italian television became the main window to the capitalist material and cultural landscape, Italy was once again culturally constructed as the embodiment of Albania's aspiration to be part of the West. Thus, in the first post-communist years, Italy became the imagined space on to which Albanians first projected their hopes and desires.

The mass arrivals of Albanians in 1991 and then again in 1997 were just the most spectacular events within a dramatic migratory flow which had its roots in the prolonged economic and political instability of the country during the 1990s. Within the wider context of the Italian media representation of migrants, Albanians are those who have been most intensely stigmatised by being constructed as prone to criminal behaviour and as lacking 'civilisation'. The arrival and presence of Albanian migrants came at a moment in which Italy was struggling to reorganise its national identity according to the parameters set by the process of European integration, which were based on economic reliability and the ability to control EU borders. Because of their common somatic traits and their resonance in Italy's past, Albanians became mirrors through which Italy recognised and rejected its own self-perceived backwardness, unreliability and lack of 'civilisation' in relation to its desire to be recognised as fully belonging to the West by other 'more northern' European states. In contemporary Albania, because of the increasing awareness of the levels of exploitation and stigmatisation endured by Albanian migrants in Italy and in other Western countries, both the identification of Italy with Albania's road to the West and the cultural construction of the latter in utopian terms have gradually faded away.

On the geo-political front, post-communist Albania became once more the battlefield for the competing interests of European powers, with Italy again invoking its special role. In fact, not only did Italy lead two military humanitarian campaigns –with full international endorsement – during the migratory and political crises of 1991 and 1997, but the country rapidly became and remains the politically most influential foreign country in Albania, as well as the major foreign investor and trade partner.

Nicola Mai

HISTORIES
Fischer, B. (1999), *Albania at War 1939–1945*, London: Hurst.
Mai, N. (2002), 'Myths and Moral Panics: Italian Identity and the Media Representation of Albanian Immigration', in R. D. Grillo and J. Pratt (eds), *The Politics of Recognising Difference: Multiculturalism Italian Style*, Aldershot: Ashgate, pp. 77–95.
— (2003), 'The Cultural Construction of Italy in Albania and Vice Versa: Migration Dynamics, Strategies of Resistance and Politics of Mutual Self-Definition across Colonialism and Post-Colonialism', *Modern Italy* 9 (1): pp. 77–94.
Schwandners-Sievers, S. B. and Fischer (2002) (eds), *Albanian Identities: Myth, Narratives and Politics*, London: Hurst.
Vickers, M. (1995), *The Albanians: A Modern History*, London and New York: I. B. Tauris.
Vickers, M. and J. Pettifer (1997), *Albania: From Anarchy to a Balkan Identity*, London: Hurst.

Anthropology and Ethnology

The study of Italian cultural anthropology for the colonial period has been little explored by post-World War II scholars, who until recently were not inclined to consider the contribution of the disciplines of anthropology and ethnology to colonial policies and culture. Academic anthropology of the colonial era largely assumed that human bones and bodies directly determined the level of civilisation of different races. Cultural and physical anthropology became two distinct disciplines only in the 1940s. In addition, Italian academic anthropology was for a long time an 'armchair' anthropology, with little attention devoted to ethnographic fieldwork.

Yet, towards the end of the 1800s, various professional anthropologists started to show a strong interest in the colonial process: even though most of them never travelled to the colonies in person, they collected ethnographic information and materials gathered by missionaries, colonial officers and civil servants. This 'first generation' of Italian academic anthropologists was mostly concerned with the description of the origin and racial classification of the different races inhabiting the Horn of Africa. In particular, the Ethiopians were believed to belong to the so-called Hamitic race, and the majority of Italian anthropologists writing at the beginning of 1900 agreed with the internationally shared assumption that because they had a supposedly superior civilisation, the Hamites were not 'real Africans', and thus placed their origin in Asia or in the Caucasian region. This belief conveniently implied that, if the Africans had once needed a foreign group (the Hamites) to improve themselves, they now similarly needed the Europeans. Most anthropologists stressed that the Hamites were from their origins a coloured race, while others pointed to the degenerating effect of their prolonged mixing with local and darker 'inferior' races. These interpretations led to a racial separation (both epistemological and political) between Europeans and Ethiopians. Only Giuseppe Sergi, a major figure of the early colonial period, insisted that there were no racial differences between the Europeans and the Hamites and that the very cradle of Western civilisation was in the Horn of Africa.

Academic studies were flanked by ethnographic documentation produced by non-professional ethnographers (such as travellers, missionaries, colonial officers and civil servants) through the colonial period. These amateur ethnographic studies were produced both out of personal curiosity and as a means of better policing the new subjects, and they often contain rich and detailed ethnographic information and first-hand cultural data on local groups. In a few cases, they represent a first attempt at ethnographic fieldwork, a methodological practice then uncommon in Italian academic anthropology.

During the Fascist period, methodological rigour was replaced by dogmatic assertions in anthropology (as well as in any other science or discipline) directly controlled or manipulated by the régime: free science and any expression of plural opinions were silenced. In addition, the establishment of the Empire in 1936 further reinforced the discipline's concern with physical issues. The new 'racial consciousness' and notions of Italian racial purity promoted by the fascist régime rested on a clear separation – on merely biological grounds – of citizens and subjects. Anthropologists like Guido Landra and Lidio Cipriani played an important role in dismantling Sergi's theory, which had a strong political dimension and threatened the régime's new paradigm of Italian superiority in relation to the Africans. Landra and Cipriani also participated in the drafting of the infamous Manifesto della Razza which asserted the inferiority of the African and the Jewish 'races'.

The involvement of the discipline with the forging of Fascist racial ideology had a strong impact on the development of Italian cultural anthropology after World War II. Cultural anthropology split then from physical anthropology and has kept away from any biological stance ever since. On the other hand, it has concentrated mainly on 'internal folklore' focusing mostly on the study of Italian popular culture.

Barbara Sòrgoni

HISTORIES

Dore, G. (1980), 'Antropologia e colonialismo italiano. Rassegna di studi di questo dopoguerra', *La ricerca Folklorica* 1: 129–32.

Grottanelli, V. (1977), 'Ethnology and/or Cultural Anthropology in Italy', *Current Anthropology* 18 (4): 493–614.

Sòrgoni, B. (2003), 'Italian Anthropology and the Africans: The Early Colonial Period', in P. Palumbo (ed.), *A Place in the Sun. Africa in Italian Colonial Culture from Post-Unification to the Present*, Berkeley and Los Angeles, CA: University of California Press, pp. 62–80.

Solinas, P. G. (1988a), 'Introduzione', *La Ricerca Folklorica* 18: 5–7.

— (1988b), 'Coscienza coloniale e affari indigeni: l'Africa italiana da Ferdinando Martini a Giacomo de Martino', *La Ricerca Folklorica* 18: 41–7.

Anti-colonial Resistance in Eastern Libya

The coming of European colonialism tipped the balance of power in the Sahara. First, French expansion into Bilad al-Sudan posed a threat to the influence of the native Sanusi order which had spread through lodges that provided education, courts, places of refuge and stations for trans-Sahara trade after the 1860s. A half-century of building a reformist social movement based on this innovative strategy of pan-Islamic education and trade had allowed the order to consolidate its social and political influence in its home base in eastern and southern Libya and beyond, into the Sahara. The Sanusi influence was very strong in eastern Libya, strong in Fezzan in the southern region, but weak in Tripolitania due to the dominance of the Ottoman state and military structure. When European imperialism began to expand into the Sahara and Libya, the Sanusi fought from 1897 to 1910 to defend their lodges against the French Army in what is today's Chad.

Although the Italian conquest of Libya began in 1911, only in 1932 did its army succeed in controlling the entire country. These years can be divided into three phases according to the conquest of territories. The first phase (1911–14), began with the Italian invasion of Libya in October of 1911, and was marked by their conquest of Tripolitania Jabal in 1913 and Fezzan in 1914. Although Sayyid Ahmad al-Sharif, the head of the Sanusi order, had invited the Ottomans into Sanusi territory in Cyrenaica in 1902 in order to benefit from the Ottoman Empire's legal, diplomatic and military status, the Ottomans were forced to leave the area in 1912 after being defeated by the Italians. To avoid further embarrassment, the Ottomans granted independence to Libyans before their withdrawal, clearing the way for the proclamation of an independent Sanusi state in 1913, with *jihad* as its ideology. The Sanusi role in the anti-colonial rebellions began in Fezzan and Jabal in November 1914, and spread throughout Tripolitania, and Italy's entry into World War I forced the Italians to make compromises, such as granting Libyans autonomy and self-rule between 1914 and 1922. Sanusi followers led the anti-colonial rebellion in Fezzan, but not in the Jabal and western Tripolitania where rival leaders to the Sanusi forces such as Khalifa Ben Askar, Ramadan al-Suwaythi and Sulyman al-Baruni were in charge of the resistance.

In the second phase, from 1915 to 1922, British-Sanusi relations also influenced Sanusi resistance against the Italians. The order had many followers in western Egypt, and in 1916 the Sanusi went to war with the British to preserve their influence there. Due to their modern weapons, the latter prevailed and the order's new leader, Sayyid Idris al-Sanusi, agreed to exile the militant pan-Islamic Sayyid Ahmad al-Sharif from Cyrenaica in return for British patronage. As Sayyid Ahmad's newly discovered personal papers indicate, he continued to diffuse his own brand of anti-colonial ideology among his followers, first from Turkey and then from Arabia, until his death in 1933. Under the British-backed leadership of Idris, the Sanusi signed three major truces with the Italian government, and the years 1916 to 1922 were a period of Italian conciliation toward the Sanusi, who had also increased their following among resistance fighters.

The 1916 agreement of al-Zuwaytina, which was ratified by the 1917 Treaty of 'Akrama, ended hostilities between the Italians and the Sanusis, recognised Italian sovereignty along the coast and Sanusi sovereignty in the hinterland, allowed for free trade but also the removal of 'troublemakers' from Cyrenaica (like Sayyid Ahmad al-Sharif), exempted Sanusi land and *zawiya* from taxes, and granted the Sanusi family and the senior Ikhwan monthly salaries from the Italian government, in exchange for a Sanusi agreement to disarm and disband their tribes. The al-Rajma treaty of 1920 reaffirmed the previous agreements.

The policies were changed during the third phase, from 1922 to 1932, which began with the advent of Italian Fascist rule in Italy. Benito Mussolini's government pushed up the colonial plan of the liberals to full scale, declaring that Libya was essential for settling

Italian peasants and thus that there was no room for compromise on this point; only force would succeed in clearing the land for settlement. Fascist imperialism threatened all non-collaborating groups, especially autonomous states, tribal confederations and peasants. Yet the Fascists' goal of conquering the hinterland was not as easy to accomplish as had been expected. Sayyid Idris al-Sanusi could not convince the tribes and middle-level commanders to give up their arms. Shaykh 'Umar al-Mukhtar, a senior Sanusi shaykh, led the opposition to these agreements. The leaders of this guerrilla war were veterans of the anti-colonial campaigns against the French in Chad and the British in Egypt. Many of them believed in Sayyid Ahmad al-Sharif's pan-Islamic anti-colonial ideology and came from lower-status Murabtin tribal backgrounds.

To crush this resistance, Italian military leaders used tactics unmatched in brutality at any other time during the colonial wars in Africa, such as sealing wells, confiscating herds, closing Libya's borders with Egypt, dropping rebels from airplanes, and finally, forcing 100,000 tribesmen and their families to leave their homes, consigning them to terrible concentration camps in the desert of Syrtica. In 1933 there were only 35,000 survivors of these camps. The colonialist goal was to separate the resistance from its social base. Toward this end, al-Mukhtar was eventually captured and hanged in 1931, and in January of 1932 four of his commanders were trapped along the Egyptian borders: one died, two were captured, and one escaped into Egypt.

At the end of this anti-colonial resistance eastern Libya was a devastated place. Thousands were exiled in Egypt, Chad, Syria and Turkey, and the Italian colonial programme started to build more settlements and infrastructure for Italians. This enforced peace ended with the battles of the Second World War in Eastern Libya. Cities were repeatedly destroyed, and many Libyans were recruited to fight for the Italian Empire first in Ethiopia and later on against the Allies in Egypt. The defeat of Italy in the war was an incentive to many Libyans, especially those from eastern Libya. Emir Idris al-Sanusi, who allied with the British in Egypt, convinced his followers to fight against the Italian and the German armies. This pragmatic alliance between the Sanusi leadership under Emir Idris was honoured by the British government, which was eager to protect its security in Egypt, and this paved the way for Libyan independence guided by the UN in 1951. The Sanusi leadership had an important role in this independence as Emir Idris became King Idris I and the eastern Libyan élite dominated the monarchy until 1969. Both the monarchy and Colonial Qadhdhafi, after he gained power in 1969, have represented their régimes as heirs to the anti-colonial resistance and its leader, 'Umar al-Mukhtar, as the father of the country. The monarchy focused on the fact that the al-Mukhtar was a Sanusi shaykh, while the Qadhdafi régime depicts him as an anti-Sanusi revolutionary hero and links him with Sayyid Ahmad al-Sharif, whom the monarchy ignored after his exile in Arabia. The struggle between history and memory has been a major trend in postcolonial Libya as the nationalist régimes select, suppress and appropriate historical memory to boost its legitimacy.

Ali Abdullah Ahmida

HISTORIES

Ahmida, A. A. (1994), *The Making of Modern Libya, State Formation, Colonialization, and Resistance, 1830–1932*, Albany, NY: State University of New York Press.

Anderson, L. S. (1986), *The State and Social Transformation in Tunisia and Libya, 1830–1980*, Princeton, NJ: Princeton University Press.

Barbar, A. (ed.) (1983), *'Umar al-Mukhtar*, Tripoli: Centre for Libyan Studies.

Anti-colonial Resistance in Italian East Africa

The Italians came late to Europe's empire building in Africa. Whereas the other major European imperial powers had begun the process centuries earlier, Italy arrived in force on the Eritrean coast only in 1869, in Somalia between 1885 and 1889, and in Libya in 1911. The capstone of fascist Italy's new empire, the conquest of Ethiopia, was set in place in 1936, but lasted only until the end of World War II, when its whole African edifice collapsed with the defeat of the Axis. The Italians thus had to deal with the residual effects of the rules of other imperial powers. They inherited a confusing situation marked, on the one hand, by shifting alliances and loyalties within a context of sporadic violence and opposition, and on the other, by a twenty-year war in Libya (1911–31) against such leaders as 'Umar al-Mukhtar and Ahmad al-Sharif; by the major rebellion of Sayyid Abdile Hassan (1900–4) in Somalia; and by the uprising led by the Dejazmatch Bahta Hagos, whose three-day rebellion in 1894 became part of Eritrean nationalist folklore.

Italy, in compensation for the French occupation of Tunisia in 1881(which Italy had coveted), was given leave to engineer a war with Turkey, which then allowed the Italians to invade the Libyan coast, itself under more or less effective Ottoman control since the seventeenth century. Resistance appeared almost immediately, mostly led by Sanusi notables (the Sanusi were a religious order and the ruling Libyan dynasty during much of the Ottoman period). The Arab resistance was complicated by Turkish financial and arms support to the Sanusi leaders, especially during World War I, when Turkey fought on the side of the Central Powers, and Italy alongside the Allies. Further complications arose with the arrival of the Tripolitanian nationalist, Ramadan al-Suwaythi, who had co-operated with the Italians and the Sanusi, and fought against both.

Italy entered Eritrea in 1869 by buying land from a local sultan at the port of Assab. It extended its occupation of the area until, in 1889, it had captured all of Eritrea and declared it a colony. Resistance, again, was general but sporadic and unco-ordinated, complicated by local notables who sought to use the Italians in their feuds with one another. The climate of resistance changed markedly, however, when the Italians, emboldened by their successful conquest of Eritrea, sought to seize Ethiopia and were defeated by the Emperor Menelik at the Battle of Adwa in 1896. The memory of that humiliation still rankled forty years later, when Italy attacked, and finally conquered, Ethiopia and its emperor, Haile Selassie. Ethiopia, which was supposed to be the centrepiece of Mussolini's Fascist empire, exposed the fragility of the 'Italian East African Empire', or AOI, which was repeatedly under attack by Ethiopian patriot militias until the restoration of the emperor to his throne by Allied forces. Fascist brutality in Ethiopia, Libya and Somalia gave rise to a determined anti-colonial resistance which also included former *askaris* from Eritrea and Somalia as well as Libyan *spahis* who turned their guns and training against Rome's hyperbolic directives in its second and last African war. Four years later, the Italians were forced to give up their dream of a 'place in the sun' and the avenging of their defeat by the imperial Ethiopian army in 1896. A half-century more was to elapse before the Italians acknowledged the atrocities committed during their brief and stormy African encounters, leading to a rethinking of the Italo-African encounter.

Finally, Somalia was acquired piecemeal by Italy through annexation and purchase from local sultans. Like Libya, Somalia was more or less ceded to Italy by the European powers, this time in compensation for not having received any of the colonies Germany had surrendered during World War I. Like Libya, Somalia had its major revolt led by a religious figure, Sayyid 'Abdile Hassan, head of the Salihiyya brotherhood. 'Abdille Hasan's revolt was finally crushed, but not until he had united many of the clans against the European invaders, and given heart to the sporadic resistance Italy faced until 1941.

Ruth Iyob

HISTORIES

Abbay, A. (1998), *Identity Jilted or Re-Imagining Identity?: The Divergent Paths of the Eritrean and Tigrayan Nationalist Struggles*, Lawrenceville, NJ and Asmara: The Red Sea Press.

Ahmida, A. A. (1994), *The Making of Modern Libya: State Formation, Colonization, and Resistance, 1830–1932*, Albany, NY: State University of New York Press.

Girmu, G. (1997), *Deghiat Bahta Hagos Segeneiti*, Asmara: MBY.

Hobsbawm, E. (1981), *Bandits*, New York: Pantheon Books.

Lewis, I. M. (1988), *A Modern History of Somalia: Nation and State in the Horn of Africa*, Boulder, CO and London: Westview Press.

Negash, T. (1997), *Eritrea and Ethiopia: The Federal Experience*, New Brunswick, NJ: Transaction Publishers.

Samatar, S. S. (1982), *Oral Poetry and Somali Nationalism: The Case of Sayyid Mahammad 'Abdile Hassan*, London and New York: Cambridge University Press.

Tareke, G. (1991), *Ethiopia: Power and Protest*, London and New York: Cambridge University Press.

Dodecanese Islands

The Dodecanese Islands, which are situated in the south-eastern corner of the Aegean Sea, formed part of Italy's colonial empire between 1912 and 1947. Italy's overriding interest in maintaining control of the Dodecanese was strategic. Military bases were established on the islands of Rhodes, Kos and especially Leros, as both liberal and Fascist régimes harboured much grander imperial ambitions in the eastern Mediterranean. In contrast to the preceding half-century, however, the inter-war years afforded few opportunities for colonial expansion in the region. Italian colonial authorities had greater success in exploiting the territory's propaganda potential. Italian munificence and imperial worth were showcased through development projects such as road works, urban construction and heritage building restoration. Such projects were particularly important for a small and unproven colonial contestant that was keen to earn a respectable status among Europe's major powers. The Dodecanese island group was particularly useful for propaganda purposes as it attracted many more visitors than any other part of the Italian colonial empire, and it was small enough for Italy's limited financial resources to make a profound impact.

In order to secure permanent possession, colonial authorities aimed to assimilate its mainly Greek population. Their chief weapon was language attrition. Italian was made compulsory in schools while teaching time dedicated to Greek was progressively reduced. In 1937 the high-ranking fascist Cesare de Vecchi, as Governor, banned Greek in schools entirely and severely restricted its usage in public. Such violations of local culture inevitably provoked widespread antipathy towards Italian rule and fostered various forms of furtive resistance, especially clandestine Greek schools. Resentment towards the régime increased during World War II, when wartime privations and the appropriation of essential foodstuffs by the Axis powers induced famine conditions. Italy effectively lost control of the islands in late 1943 to its Axis partner, and to Britain in March 1945. Italy was deprived of formal possession by peace terms imposed by the victorious Allies in February 1947.

Dodecanesian popular discourse since then has reflected the complexities of postcolonial memory that can often be found among former colonised subjects. Despite injustices suffered, the islanders would often speak of Italians in rather positive terms, thus appearing to support commonplace Italian claims that theirs was an unusually benign and benevolent form of colonialism. To a degree, such nostalgia was a function of postcolonial disappointments. Economic hardships that extended into the 1960s, and which provoked emigration to Athens, North America and Australia, placed colonial development programmes and the employment opportunities they provided in a new light. Locals even lamented the end of their subaltern status, as Dodecanesian society was adversely affected by the polarising nature of Greek politics during the early Cold War years. Memories of Italian rule served new purposes by the 1970s and 1980s, when mass tourism brought a marked degree of affluence, rampant development and an ostensible decline in moral values. Older Dodecanesians often claimed the Italians would have done much better than contemporary Greek authorities in prosecuting parking violations and enforcing closing times on bars and night clubs.

To a significant extent, however, Dodecanesian nostalgia did reflect a real admiration for Italian governance. Locals did appreciate useful material legacies such as the public buildings and sewerage systems, but they also appreciated the fact that individual Italians often refused to play the role of colonial master and engaged with locals on an equal social level, which served to mitigate the humiliation of foreign domination. Moreover, the islanders believed they shared similar cultural tastes and social values, which also made Italian domination more palatable. Since 1947 Dodecanesians have managed to accommodate nostalgia and resentment for the colonial past in a manner that reflects the ambiguities of that legacy.

Nicholas Doumanis

HISTORIES

Doumanis, N. (1997), *Myth and Memory in the Mediterranean*, London: Macmillan/St Martins.

— (2005), 'Italians as "Good Colonizers": Speaking Subalterns and the Politics of Memory in the Dodecanese', in R. Ben-Ghiat and M. Fuller (eds), *Italian Colonialism*, New York: Palgrave, pp. 221–32.

Carabott, P. (1993), 'The Temporary Italian Occupation of the Dodecanese: A Prelude to Permanency', *Diplomacy and Statecraft* 3 (2): 285–312.

Eritrea to 1935

Italy's interest in colonial issues coincided both with the unification of Italy (completed in 1871) and the opening of the Suez Canal in 1869. As is typical of the formation of colonies, the port of Assab was first bought by a shipping company (in 1869) and later handed over to the Italian state (1882). The entire Red Sea coastline, which was under Egyptian control, changed hands in 1882 when Britain took control of the country, ostensibly to assist Egypt in its financial crisis. Securely established in Assab and consistently supported by Britain, Italy quickly extended its possessions 600 miles along the coast. In the early months of 1885, Italy replaced the ineffectual Egyptian rule in and around Massawa. Moreover, through a dubious Italo-Ethiopian treaty of 1889, Italy acquired a small piece of the Ethiopian highlands. Thus in January 1890, the disparate possessions in the Red Sea were consolidated into a unified political entity that came to be known as Eritrea. Meanwhile, Italy soon realised that its first African colony (fondly described as *la colonia primogenita* [firstborn]) was of little value without the Ethiopian hinterland.

Attempts to lure the Ethiopian leadership to accepting Italian colonialism through a protectorate treaty led to a humiliating defeat at the Battle of Adwa (fought on 2 March 1896), which was the first significant war where a European power was thoroughly defeated by an African one. A disillusioned Italy was on the verge of abandoning its African colonial adventure if it had not been for the magnanimity of the Ethiopian authorities and the astute diplomacy of Ferdinando Martini, the first civilian Governor.

For the greater part of the colonial period Eritrea remained a poor substitute for Ethiopia. But until Italy could gain the opportunity of avenging its defeat at Adwa, the colony and its resources were exploited for what they could render. Eritrea, in fact, was destined to fulfil several functions. The possibility of using the colony for settlement was dropped early on, when it was realised that expropriation and confiscation of land would provoke serious resistance that could start a second Italo-Ethiopian war. As a result, the number of Italian colonists remained small and the total area confiscated from the Eritreans was about 7,000 hectares, insignificant by any measure.

Eritrea's primary function was to attract the export and import trade of northern Ethiopia and north-eastern Sudan. For such purposes an elaborate railroad system was built spreading from Massawa and Asmara to the frontiers of Ethiopia and Sudan. The communication infrastructure (both rail and road) was undoubtedly too big for the colony, but this was not considered to be a problem, since the idea of colonising Ethiopia at some future date was always present. The Italians were proud that by the end of 1920s they were able to attract up to 25 per cent of Ethiopian exports and imports. But this figure was so small that it did not in any significant manner affect the adverse imbalance between exports and imports of the colony.

The second function of Eritrea was as a source of colonial soldiers for the expansion of Italian imperial acquisitions in Somalia and Libya. From 1905 onwards, Eritrean soldiers were continuously present in Somalia and Libya. It could indeed be argued that the long consolidation of Italian rule, in Somalia and even more in Libya, was carried out without arousing any outcry of Italian public opinion because of the presence of Eritrean soldiers, who in contrast to their Italian counterparts, were agile in desert wars and cheap to recruit and maintain. As the largest employer in the colony, the colonial army may have provided jobs for up to 10,000 soldiers from the early decades of 1900 until the eve of the invasion of Ethiopia (1935).

The role of Eritrea as a source of colonial soldiers was at times deplored and at times condoned depending on the ideological climate in Rome. Italian investment was negligible and the colonial state did what it could to diversify the economic basis of the colony, which was by and large founded on the political economy of the colonial army. By 1932, the city of Asmara had about 3,000 Italian colonists and about 30,000 Eritreans. The most significant building was the cathedral of the Catholic Mission (entrusted to the Capuchin Order), which was completed in 1923. Most of the Italian community was made up of armed forces personnel, busy training Eritrean soldiers who were then sent on various missions to Somalia and Libya. There was a considerable scarcity of labour and the wage gap between Italian and Eritrean was in the range of 2 to 1.

The Fascist invasion of Ethiopia brought about fundamental changes in the Eritrean landscape. The city of Asmara was greatly revamped and by 1938 it had a total population of 98,000 out of whom 53,000 were Italians. The residence of the colonial governor and the cathedral, both located on the same street, were the nodal points around which the new city was built. Asmara was radically transformed from essentially an African city with a small Italian and European population into a predominantly Italian city. The high point of growth of Asmara took place between 1935 and 1940. During this period Italy invested billions of lire in highly prestigious projects such as the construction of cities and the maintenance of a metropolitan army that eventually may have numbered up to 468,000 men. Many Italians earned quite well and some of these earnings went to build beautiful villas in Asmara.

In the new Italian African imperial framework, of which Eritrea was destined to be the economic and financial centre, its proximity to Italy and the huge investments in communication infrastructure were important contributing factors. By the end of the 1930s, Eritrea alone had more commercial and industrial firms than all the provinces of the East African Empire put together. As most of the commercial and economic activities were in and around Asmara, situated in the Eritrean highlands – a small and relatively densely populated part of Eritrea – communication and contacts between Eritreans and Italians, in spite of racial laws, were bound to be close. The Eritrean highlands were not only geographically significant (they measured about 20,000 square kilometres) but were inhabited by communities who enjoyed protected land rights.

The second fundamental change was the destruction of the Eritrean subsistence economy. On the eve of the Italian invasion of Ethiopia, the colony of Eritrea was transformed into a huge recruitment ground for the colonial army. The 468,000 Italian soldiers who passed through Eritrea on their way to Ethiopia were bolstered by a 60,000-strong Eritrean colonial army. As most of those 60,000 Eritrean soldiers who accompanied the Italian Army into Ethiopia remained in Ethiopia, the indigenous agricultural sector, the mainstay of the majority of the population, was virtually abandoned. The Italian invasion of Ethiopia siphoned off about 40 per cent of the Eritrean labour force, the highest recruitment of colonial army per capita in Tropical Africa. Thus while a significant portion of the Eritrean population served the consolidation of Italian imperialism in Ethiopia, Eritrea became a veritable colony of settlement. On the eve of World War II, the Italians in Eritrea constituted about 12 per cent of the entire population of Eritrea. In comparison, the British community in Zimbabwe, another colony of settlement, was 6 per cent.

Eritrea's contribution to Italy's efforts to secure and maintain colonies in Africa was recognised. Within the framework of the racial laws, the Eritreans were accorded an identity that was denied to other subjects of the East African Empire. Whereas the other ethnic groups were to be addressed as subjects (*soggetti*) or as indigenous people (*indigeni*), the peoples of Eritrea were to be addressed as *Eritrei*. The reward for long service was the wedge that colonialism created between Eritreans and the other colonised populations in the Horn of Africa. This policy of distinguishing the Eritreans from their fellow Africans in the Italian East African Empire did eventually contribute to the later emergence of a separate Eritrean identity.

A sad component of this new Eritrean identity was the adoption of racist attitudes. To suit its purposes and to woo the Eritreans, Italy had, since the late 1920s, pushed the idea that the Eritreans were more developed than the rest of the Ethiopian population, thanks to their long colonisation by Italy. The active participation of Eritrean colonial soldiers in Ethiopia, the co-option of Eritreans in the consolidation of colonial rule in Ethiopia and the privileges (access to skills and jobs) that were reserved only for Eritreans led to the growth of a superiority complex. To be an Eritrean in the 1930s was to be a privileged colonial subject. Ironically, the occupation of Ethiopia created more avenues for Eritreans to be gainfully employed in the East African Empire than in Eritrea itself.

Tekeste Negash

HISTORIES

Iyob, R. (1995), *The Eritrean Struggle for Independence: Domination, Resistance, Nationalism, 1941–1993*, Cambridge: Cambridge University Press.
Negash, T. (1987), *Italian Colonialism in Eritrea, 1882–1941: Policies, Praxis and Impact*, Stockholm: Almqvist and Wiksell International.
Taddia, I. (1986), *L'Éritrea colonia, 1890–1952: paesaggi, strutture, uomini del colonialismo*, Milan: Franco Angeli.

Ethiopian War

On 2 and 3 October 1935, Italian soldiers crossed the Mareb river to invade Ethiopia. Thus began the Fascist campaign to vindicate the 1896 Italian defeat by the Ethiopians at Adwa. Although the fascist war on Ethiopia was in some ways a belated colonialist intervention it represents an important moment in the radicalisation of Italian Fascism. More generally, it brings about a further deterioration of the international climate, representing a serious defeat for the League of Nations that would bring Europe closer to another world war.

Italian commercial penetration of Ethiopia had slowed by the early 1930s and in 1932, in Rome, the Minister of Colonies, Emilio De Bono, prepared a plan for an attack on Ethiopia. Although the idea was purely theoretical at this point, in the coming years the advent of Adolf Hitler's rule in Germany, the effects of the 1929 economic crisis, and the need to increase Italian Fascism's international prestige all conspired to rouse interest in an invasion.

Although the Italian armed forces found De Bono's plan lacking (in part because it deprived them of a managerial role in the attack), and the king remained doubtful as late as 1934, Benito Mussolini supported it and negotiated with France to gain that country's guarantee of an official 'disinterest' in the event of a fascist aggression against Ethiopia (which was a League of Nations member). Fearing an Italian alliance with Germany, the French agreed to a 1935 (7 Jan.) accord; a week earlier, a confident Mussolini had already secretly directed the armed forces to prepare for a military invasion. Warning that nothing must be left to chance, the Duce authorised a massive military expedition on a scale that greatly exceeded traditional colonial operations.

A frontier incident with Ethiopia (at Ual-Ual, in November 1934) provided the excuse for Italy to launch its active war preparations. Months of military, diplomatic, colonial and propagandistic operations followed. The Italian population, whose favour toward the régime had been tested by the economic crisis, was bombarded by a co-ordinated cinema, radio and press campaign that juxtaposed Italian fascist modernity with the prehistoric state of Ethiopia. When Italian operations began and the League of Nations imposed sanctions on Italy, the régime held out the hope that conquest would bring Italians a new 'place in the sun'.

On the military level, the campaign lasted seven months. After the conquest of Adwa in October 1935 the commander-in-chief, De Bono, displeased Mussolini by waiting another month to conquer Macallè, and was promptly substituted by Marshal Pietro Badoglio. Badoglio, too, made Mussolini wait (no further operations were carried out until January 1936) but proved skilled at the kind of logistical preparations for a war on this scale. After defeating numerous Ethiopian counter-attacks, the Italians launched an offensive from the North (Battles of Mai Ceu and Lake Ascianghi) and the South (from Ganale Doria to Ogaden) that ultimately brought defeat to the valorous and large, but badly armed, Ethiopian Army. The Negus Haile Selassie was forced to flee from Ethiopia, and the conquest of Addis Ababa followed. Although Italian colonial troops had entered the capital on 3 May 1936, this fact was kept back in order to make the official date of the conquest coincide with the entry of Italian troops, led by Badoglio, on 5 May. By that time 330,000 Italian soldiers, 87,000 Eritrean and Libyan *askari*, 100,000 military workers, 90,000 beats, 10,000 machine guns, 1,100 cannons, 250 tanks and 350 aeroplanes were operating in Ethiopia. From those planes, onto Ethiopian soil, came not only conventional bombs, but bombs laden with chemical agents. The chemical weapons – superfluous to the victory–had been ordered by Mussolini in person, in a flagrant violation of the Geneva Protocol.

With such a ruthless war machine – which was in much worse shape than the régime's propaganda let on- Fascist Italy had little chance of losing to a traditionally-armed adversary. Yet this was also a useless victory, damaging to Italy and full of consequences for all of Europe. It was useless in part because Ethiopia, routed in May 1936, was never wholly 'conquered' or pacified: in the five years of Italian occupation, neither the anti-colonial resistance nor the insubordination of tribal heads and local population ever ceased. And for Italy it represented a 'victory' that, as Giorgio Rochat has commented (1971, 2005), brought much prestige but greatly weakened its preparation for European warfare. Leaving in its wake a train of illusions and a wrecked international order, the Ethiopian War gave Mussolini his empire but accelerated the march to world war.

Nicola Labanca

HISTORIES
Del Boca, Angelo (1965), *La guerra d'Abissinia 1935–1941*, Milan: Feltrinelli.
— (1982), *Gli italiani in Africa Orientale. La conquista dell'impero*, Roma-Bari: Laterza.
Rochat, G. (1971), *Militari e politici nella preparazione della campagna d'Etiopia. Studio e documenti 1932–1936*, Milan: Franco Angeli.
— (2005), 'The Italian Air Force in the Ethiopian War (1935–1936)', in R. Ben-Ghiat and M. Fuller (eds), *Italian Colonialism*, New York: Palgrave, pp. 37–46.

Fictions and Narratives of Empire

The production of literary works inspired by Italy's expansionist policy in the first part of the twentieth century, or by the memory of the nation's colonial adventure is, in comparison with Britain and France, limited. Among the most famous writers to celebrate Italian imperialism in the early years of the century were Gabriele D'Annunzio and Filippo Tommaso Marinetti. D'Annunzio's highly significant literary anticipation of Italian expansion into North Africa was his 1906 play *Più che l'amore* (*More than Love*). Marinetti's writing on Africa ran from his early work *Mafarka le futuriste* (*Mafarka the futurist*, 1909) through to his celebration of the Italian invasion of Ethiopia in *Poema africano della divisione 28 ottobre* ((*African Poem of the '28 October' Division*), 1937).

From an early stage Mussolini's Fascist régime attempted to encourage forms of literary production that would act as a kind of propaganda in demonstrating the distinctiveness of Italian imperialism, in disseminating knowledge about the colonies, and in involving large swathes of the population in the expansionist mindset. Writing about travel to the colonies proved a growth industry in the inter-war years with many well-known writers and journalists – including such names as Mario Appelius, Angelo Piccioli and Orio Vergani – composing lengthy accounts of journeys to Italy's growing empire. The association of this type of writing with the régime was strong and many of the explanations that were used to justify Italian imperialism were reproduced in these narratives of travel. The writer fulfilled the role of a witness who purported to observe the recovery of the glories of the Roman past, the opportunities for demographic expansion or the progress of the imposition of Italian 'civilisation'. In this kind of literature Italy's African possessions tended to be figured as a pastoral paradise or as an 'empire of work' peopled by the ideal types of Italian fascism. The militaristic character of the Italian Empire found expression in the publication of accounts, written by both journalists and soldiers, which glorified the violent acquisition of territory. Many writers felt no contradiction in composing alluring travel narratives while at the same time providing precise details of the suppression of resistance to Italian rule.

Other literary genres with potentially greater popular appeal proved more problematic as a means of disseminating the narratives of empire. As early as 1926 a national competition was organised to promote the colonial novel. The competition was won by Mario Dei Gaslini for his *Piccolo amore beduino* ((*A Small Bedouin Love Affair*), 1936), a story, set in Libya, of a relationship between an Italian officer and his Berber lover. Though it won the prize, the work – as various critics indicated both at the time and subsequently – betrayed a dependence on the exoticising language of the travel/adventure stories of the French writers Pierre Loti (1850–1923) or Pierre Benoit (1886–1962) that was not entirely consonant with the message that the régime sought to convey. Many journalists were among the writers who, in the inter-war years, attempted to convey through fiction some of the complexities of the contact between Italians and the subject populations of the Italian Empire. Arnaldo Cipolla established himself as one of the most prolific travel writers of his time, a colonial novelist and a successful writer of children's literature, able to use the genre – in works like *Balilla regale* (1935) – as a means of conveying an idea of the meaning of imperialism. Though most writers of colonial fiction were men, there were a number of women writers – most notably Augusta Perricone Violà – who contributed to the genre.

From the late 1920s and through the 1930s two of the most significant authors were Gino Mitrano Sani and Vittorio Tedesco Zammarano. Mitrano Sani's books, from his first work *E per i solchi millennari delle carovaniere* ((*Along the Millenarian Furrows of the Caravan Tracks*), 1936), were characterised by a vision of Africa as a space where the man of action, committed to the ideals of fascism, could exhibit his courage while serving as the agent of an advancing civilisation. If Sani's works were informed by a complex vision of Africa and involved – especially in *Femina somala* ((*Somali Woman*), 1933)–the depiction of an intimacy between colonisers and colonised, Zammarano's books from *Azanagò non pianse* (Azanagò Did Not Weep, 1934) onwards were more sensitive to the development of propaganda in the 1930s and maintained a strict racial distinction between their characters. What made Sani's works increasingly problematic and, in the view of Tomasello, effectively destroyed the possibility of a colonial literature, was the policy of racial segregation that was pursued with vigour by the régime in the wake of the invasion of Ethiopia. In the last years of fascism, any suggestion of a complex, multi-layered or indeed intimate contact between colonisers and colonised had become an unfitting subject for literary representation.

In the years after World War II and the dramatic end of Italy's short-lived empire, relatively few works have been published that have drawn inspiration from the nation's colonial past. Though Giovanni Comisso republished his pre-war writings on Africa and Pier Paolo Pasolini wrote on Eritrea (1973), the most substantial work of fiction to appear was Ennio Flaiano's *Tempo di uccidere* ((A *Time to Kill*), 1947), with its portrayal of the reality of the occupation of Ethiopia through the representation of the tragic and disguised consequences of a relationship between an Italian officer and an Ethiopian girl. Most of the writing that has appeared on Italy's former colonies has been in the form of collections of memories written by those who experienced the empire as settlers, soldiers, bureaucrats or indeed as children who spent their formative years in Libya or what was once Italian East Africa. One of the most revealing of these collections was Anna Maria Moglie's *Africa come amore* ((*Africa like Love*), 1978), but more recently the work of Erminia Dell'Oro in texts such as *Asmara addio* or *L'abbandono* ((*The Desertion*), 1991) has sought to consider the legacy of Italian colonialism. The latter text in particular uses fiction as a means of exploring the life histories of children of mixed race in postcolonial Eritrea.

Charles Burdett

HISTORIES

Andall, J. and D. Duncan (eds) (2005), *Italian Colonialism: Legacy and Memory*, New York: Peter Lang.

Palumbo, P. (2003), 'Orphans of Empire: Colonial Propaganda and Children's Literature during the Imperial Era', in P. Palumbo (ed.), *A Place in the Sun: Africa in Italian Colonial Culture from Post-Unification to the Present*, Berkeley, CA: University of California Press, pp. 225–51.

Polezzi, L. (2003), 'Imperial Reproductions: The Circulation of Colonial Images across Popular Genres and Media in the 1920s and 1930s', *Modern Italy* 8 (1): 31–49.

Tomasello, G. (2004), *L'Africa tra mito e realtà: storia della letteratura coloniale italiana*, Palermo: Sellerio.

Antonio Gramsci and the Southern Question

The writings of Antonio Gramsci have had a major impact on the interpretation and study of the colonial and postcolonial condition. This is not because Gramsci dedicated extensive attention either to Italian colonialism or to colonialism more generally in his *Prison Notebooks*. It is rather because his reflections on Italian history, and his engagement with the Italian Southern Question in particular, generated a set of concepts and critical tools that would prove exceptionally fruitful to the analysis of the colonial and postcolonial world. Gramsci's investigations of the differences and interrelations between the northern and southern parts of Italy – the Southern Question – were the matrix out of which he developed his noted theories of hegemony, passive revolution, the intellectuals and subalternity. In the field of Subaltern Studies, on the one hand, and in the work of Edward Said, on the other, these aspects of Gramsci's thoughts have played a decisive role.

The Subaltern Studies movement owes both its name and core theoretical inspiration to Gramsci's reflections on the historiography of the subaltern classes and related themes in the *Prison Notebooks*. The conceptual template of the founding editor of the Subaltern

Studies series, Ranajit Guha, is fundamentally Gramscian, evident not only in Guha's emphasis on subaltern themes but also in his abiding interest in what he identifies as the central problematic in the historiography of colonial India, the condition of 'dominance without hegemony' that nationalist élites exercised over the subaltern classes. The themes of subalternity, hegemony and passive revolution are also salient in the work of other Subaltern Studies scholars, most notably David Arnold and Partha Chatterjee.

Gramsci's influence on Edward Said – who helped to launch the field of postcolonial studies with *Orientalism* in 1978 – has been no less important. Said's conception of the worldly, secular critic, and his intellectual practice itself, was deeply indebted to Gramsci's theory of the intellectuals. At the same time, Gramsci's 'indispensable' concept of hegemony helped Said to conceive of Orientalism not simply as a discourse imposed by colonial force, but one that owes much of its strength and durability to an ongoing process of cultural reproduction within civil society. In his subsequent study *Culture and Imperialism*, Said emphasises Gramsci's relevance to the interpretation of imperialism with even greater force. Here Said argues that Gramsci's noted 1926 essay, 'Some Aspects of the Southern Question', provides a theoretical model for a form of 'contrapuntal' analysis of the relations between north and south, metropolis and periphery, white and native, across the globe. Said thus shows how the lessons Gramsci drew from Italian history, and from the Southern Question in particular, have shaped and sharpened our understanding of the colonial and postcolonial world.

It should be mentioned finally that scholars in the field of international relations and globalisation studies have also turned to Gramsci in recent decades. Robert Cox, Stephen Gill and Giovanni Arrighi in particular have drawn on Gramsci's theory of hegemony to illuminate questions of imperialism and global domination.

Nelson Moe

HISTORIES

Gramsci, Antonio (1971), *Selections from the Prison Notebooks*, ed. and trans. Q. Hoare and G. Nowell Smith, New York: International.
— (1994), 'Some Aspects of the Southern Question', in R. Bellamy (ed.), *Pre-Prison Writings*, trans. V. Cox, Cambridge: Cambridge University Press, pp. 313–37.
Guha, Ranajit (1988), 'Preface', in R. Guha and G. Chakravorty Spivak (eds), *Selected Subaltern Studies*, New York and Oxford: Oxford University Press, pp. 35–6.
— (1998), *Domination without Hegemony*, Cambridge, MA: Harvard University Press.
Moe, Nelson (2002), *The View from Vesuvius: Italian Culture and the Southern Question*, Berkeley, CA: University of California Press.

Haile Selassie

Born Ras (Duke) Tafari Makonnen, Haile Selassie I (1892–1975) ruled Ethiopia from 1916, when he was named Regent of the country, until 1974. During his long reign, Haile Selassie was seen by supporters as a progressive monarch while dissident intellectuals, students and army officers denounced him as a reactionary autocrat. Abroad, because of his prominent involvement in international affairs, Tafari was widely viewed as an African potentate of world standing. For people of the African diaspora, as ruler of black Africa's oldest sovereign nation, which traced its history back to biblical times, Ethiopia's king was an inspiring symbol of black power and pride. They often viewed him as a messianic figure divinely empowered to deliver African people worldwide from oppression.

Ras Tafari's image as an emblem of black authority and dignity began with his highly publicised and spectacular coronation in 1930. Black liberation fundamentalists saw his crowning, coming at the height of worldwide white hegemony, as fulfilment of the biblical prophecy, 'Ethiopia shall stretch forth its hands unto God'. Since the eighteenth century black theists, infused with a strong Ethiopian ethos drawn from scripture, had interpreted the verse as an omen of universal race redemption. In the United States, the emperor's coronation also prompted the emigration to Ethiopia of about a hundred black settlers, some of whom were black Jews from Harlem. In Jamaica, where black millennialists felt white rule would soon experience an apocalyptic end, the event stimulated the rise of the Rastafarian religious sect whose followers believed Ethiopia's new king was God incarnate.

News of Italy's invasion of Ethiopia in 1935 and reports of the emperor's valiant stand against Italian aggression made him a household name in black and white communities across the globe. Italian imperialism also provoked an especially loud outcry from the world's black populations who sought to organise moral, monetary and military support for beleaguered Ethiopia. The emperor's popularity among overseas blacks declined, however, after Ethiopia's defeat. His decision to flee Ethiopia and rumours of his denial of a Negro identity also subdued their enthusiasm. But African peoples acclaimed the emperor's restoration in 1941 and small numbers of black Americans went to Ethiopia in the post-war era to serve the government as technical advisers. In the 1950s and 1960s, His Majesty supported the struggle for African independence and the establishment of the Organization of African Unity in Addis Ababa, actions that bolstered his image as a champion of universal black rights. State visits overseas, which included contact with black American and Caribbean populations, reinforced impressions that Tafari closely identified with the freedom struggles of African people.

In April 1966, when Haile Selassie visited Jamaica, vast crowds including some 10,000 Rastafarians greeted the emperor, praising him as God incarnate. The royal visit gave the Rastas a great boost in prestige on the island and reinforced the group's interest in repatriation in Ethiopia on land the emperor had granted New World Africans in the name of the Ethiopian World Federation for their support of Ethiopia during the war with Italy. A modest number of Rastafarians have since resettled in 'Zion' (Ethiopia). A group also travelled to Addis Ababa in 1992 to a centennial commemoration of Haile Selassie's birthday. Although a military junta deposed the emperor in 1974 and later killed him, the sect insists that 'Jah' (Haile Selassie), remains alive and American blacks absorbed with classical Nile Valley civilisations retain a deep admiration for the 'Lion of Judah', Ethiopia's last emperor.

William R. Scott

HISTORIES

Barrett, L. Sr (1977), *The Rastafarians. Sounds of Cultural Dissonance*, Boston, MA: Beacon Press.

Greenfield, R. (1965), *Ethiopia*, New York: Frederick A. Praeger, Inc..

Marcus, H. G. (1987), *Haile Selassie I. The Formative Years, 1892–1936*, Berkeley, CA: University of California Press.

Pankhurst, R. (2001), *The Ethiopians: A History*, London: Blackwell Publishing.

Scott, William, R. (1993), *The Sons of Sheba's Race. African Americans and the Italo-Ethiopian War*, Bloomington, IN: Indiana University Press.

Historiography

To understand Italian colonial historiography one must depart from the concept that the colonies were, for both liberal and Fascist Italy, a resource that was out of proportion with the country's actual historical realities. This small Empire, made up of poor territories separated from one another by great distances and lasting only six decades (as compared to the Portuguese empire, which lasted six centuries) fostered a sense of national identity and made Italians feel modern, but produced little in the way of economic advantage for Italy.

Like other imperial regimes, liberal and Fascist Italian colonialism made use of big concessionaries and large-scale interest groups who had the ability to condition colonial policy. Yet the motor of Italian colonialism was the exportation of Italian labour. The sociologist Roberto Michels defined the Italian brand of colonialism as 'demographic imperialism,' and Lenin scorned it as 'ragamuffin imperialism'. Yet neither phrase takes into account the complexity of the 'on the spot' interactions that this labour-oriented colonialism generated between the Italians and native populations in Libya, Eritrea, Ethiopia, and Somalia, which has been the subject of new research.

Italian colonial historiography can be divided into several phases. In a first phase, from the end of World War I through the 1920s, Italian 'colonial historians' wrote primarily about early Italian colonial expansion in Eritrea, driven by the need to explain the Italian defeat at Adwa (1896). The late 1920s onward was a particularly golden phase for these 'colonial historians' who wrote during and for the Fascist regime. Studies on Fascism's colonial expansion in Libya, Somalia, and on the Ethiopian occupation suffered due to a culture of silence after 1945 about Italian colonialism and due to the lack of a public debate about decolonisation and the continued control of the 'colonial historians' lobby over many of the relevant archival collections relating to Italian colonialism. While occasional studies in the 1960s and 1970s challenged this silence, such as the pioneering works by Giorgio Rochat and Angelo Del Boca, it was only in the 1980s and 1990s that innovative work began to appear, fruit of a new generation born after the end of colonialism. Interest in Italian colonialism was also sparked by the Italy's move to restore a military presence abroad (peace-keeping or peace-enforcing operations in Iraq, Somalia, Kosovo, and Afghanistan), and the presence in Italy of many international migrants from black and Mediterranean Africa, from Asia and from Eastern Europe.

Only very recently have studies appeared that take a postcolonial or cultural studies approach to Italian colonialism. These are not always granted a warm reception in Italy, in part due to the lack of knowledge they show about Italian political and institutional history and in part due to the general reluctance of Italian historical studies to open itself to this kind of scholarship. And yet the attempts of these scholars, who are mostly of literary provenance, to look at the postcolonial production of Italians or migrants to Italy have shown the validity of new approaches.

Thus it can be said that with respect to other ex-imperial powers, Italy has had the slowest decolonisation of historical studies on colonialism. Indeed, great gaps remain in our knowledge of Italian colonialism, not only chronologically, but also geographically (Eritrea, which dates to the liberal years, is the best studied, along with Libya; Ethiopia and Somalia are still little studied) and thematically. Political and diplomatic histories were long favoured, while military history was neglected. Colonial discourses have attracted a certain attention in the last fifteen years among cultural historians, as expressed in literature, advertising, cinema, painting, architecture, and exhibition practices. Yet gender and urban history are only at the beginnings, and the economic and constitutional histories of Italian colonialism still await their analysts. Much remains to be done also in terms of the interchange between historians of imperialism and Africanists. Overall, it can be said that a new generation of scholars is radically changing the landscape of studies on Italian colonialism. New works by Africanists and by scholars of Italian colonial culture and society are contributing to a reintegration of the history of Italian colonialism into the national past.

REFERENCES

Andall, Jacqueline and Derek Duncan (eds) (2005), *Italian Colonialism: Legacy and Memory*, New York: Peter Lang.

Ben-Ghiat, Ruth and Mia Fuller (eds) (2005), *Italian Colonialism*, New York: Palgrave.

Del Boca, Angelo (1965), *La Guerra d'Abissinia 1935–1941*, Milan: Feltrinelli.

— (1976–1984), *Gli italiani in Africa Orientale*, 4 vols, Rome and Bari: Laterza.

— (1986–1988), *Gli Italiani in Libia*, 2 vols, Rome and Bari: Laterza.

— (1991), *I gas di Mussolini: Il fascismo e la Guerra d'Etiopia*, Rome and Bari: Laterza.

Goglia, Luigi and Fabio Grassi (1981), *Il colonialismo italiano da Adua all'impero*, Rome-Bari.

Labanca, Nicola. *Oltremare. Storia dell'espansione coloniale italiano* (Bologna: Mulino, 2002).

Palumbo, Patricia (2003), *A Place in the sun. Africa in Italian Colonial Culture from Post-Unification to the Present*, Berkeley: University of California Press.

Rochat, Giorgio (1973), *Il colonialismo italiano. Documenti*, Turin.

Nicola Labanca

Immigration

Immigration has constituted an integral and significant aspect of Italy's social and political history. Between 1876 and 1976, some 26 million Italians left Italy to work in other parts of the world, and, as a consequence, Italian emigrants and their descendents are widely dispersed across the globe. In terms of colonialism, however, when compared to the major European colonial powers, Italy's colonial empire was geographically limited. Thus, in the post-war period, Italy's experience would differ with respect to colonialism and migration trends occurring in other European countries. Firstly, Italy underwent an anomalous decolonisation process whereby it was dispossessed of its colonies by Allied forces. Secondly, Italy became an immigration receiving society at a later stage than Britain or France. This combination of historical circumstances has contributed to a range of migration typologies pertinent to any discussion about immigration and postcolonialism. These include the emigration of Italians to colonial as well as non-colonial territories, the decolonisation migration of Italians, the colonial migration of former subjects of 'Italian East Africa' to Italy and the contemporary migration of labour migrants to Italy.

In the late nineteenth and early twentieth centuries, some Italian politicians viewed the widespread emigration of Italians abroad as a potential form of Italian colonial expansion. The concept of ethnographic or demographic colonialism was utilised to refer to the possibility of integrating Italian migrant colonies abroad into the wider colonial empire. Ultimately, proposals to conflate ethnographic and traditional colonies failed, forcing its advocates to abandon the project of developing an Italian version of colonialism based on emigration. Compared to transatlantic migration to the Americas, or emigration to North Africa, the migration of Italians to Italy's colonial territories was certainly not extensive. In the 1920s, approximately 26,000 Italians settled in Libya and in 1935 approximately 4,000–5,000 Italians were living in Eritrea. In the 1920s, far more sizeable communities of Italians were settled in other African countries such as Egypt (49,000) and Tunisia (97,000). In other words, demographic colonial migration did not even replace traditional Italian labour migration to Africa. Italian migration to African or colonial territories has generally been marginalised in academic accounts of Italy's extensive labour diaspora. Under fascism, however, the issue of colonial migration resurfaced as the migration of Italians to the East African territories was an integral component of the fascist colonial project. It was during this period that the number of Italians migrating to Italian colonial territories began to rise. The majority of these emigrants came from working-class backgrounds and particularly from regions such as the Veneto and Emilia-Romagna. By 1941, the Italian community in Eritrea had grown to 73,000, while in Ethiopia, which Italy occupied in 1936, the Italian community was intensively developed over a short period of time, numbering 62,000 by 1940.

Italy's decolonisation process had both short-and long-term consequences in terms of migration. In fact, there were successive phases of Italian return migration linked to the different phases of decolonisation. In 1940, for example, approximately 9,000–15,000 Italians returned from Libya. The transitional decolonisation arrangements that were put in place for Somalia and Eritrea would also ultimately contribute to the migration of both Italians and former colonial subjects. Eritrea's federation to Ethiopia, following a period of British administration from 1941 to 1952, led to a protracted liberation war which culminated in formal independence in 1993. The changing political situation in Eritrea during this time meant that Italians returned not simply because of Italy's loss of control over the colony but also in response to the political conflict with Ethiopia.

In the postcolonial context, there was initially limited migration to Italy by its former colonial subjects. In the early post-war period, unlike those European countries that had partially filled their labour shortages through the recruitment and migration of nationals from colonised or previously colonised countries, Italy still had to contend with a surplus supply of labour. As a result, at a comparable time, significant numbers of Italians were actually fulfilling the labour market requirements of the more advanced European industrial economies, migrating to countries such as Switzerland, Germany and France. Italy arrived at a positive migration balance only in the early 1970s and this decade would in fact mark Italy's gradual but formal transition into a country of immigration. The inception of incoming labour migration had actually already begun in the 1960s. Firstly, colonial migration was present in the form of Eritrean women travelling to Italy to continue their employment as domestic workers with their returning Italian families. There was also new migration unrelated to the colonial context, such as the labour migration of women from the Cape Verde islands.

An overview of contemporary migration to Italy clearly demonstrates that nationals from Italy's former colonies represent a negligible numerical component of current labour migrants. In 2003, against a total of over 2 million foreign nationals legally resident in Italy, there were 6,312 Eritrean nationals; 5,148 Somali nationals; 5,137 Ethiopian nationals; and 1,087 Libyan nationals. These figures nevertheless disguise the evolution of recent migration trends. Although reliable data are lacking for the 1970s, it is estimated that Eritreans were the second largest group of migrants in Italy from outside Europe at this time. In addition, the Eritrean case cannot be categorised simply as a form of colonial labour migration despite the fact that the very migration of Eritreans was in no small part attributable to the mode of Italian decolonisation. The migration of Eritreans to Italy was also determined by political factors, as the thirty-year liberation war with Ethiopia produced large numbers of Eritrean refugees. Eritreans were not initially recognised as refugees in

Italy, and the dominance of domestic work as an employment niche meant that Italy would develop into more of a transit destination for Eritrean nationals. This accounts for the long-standing greater presence of women amongst Eritrean nationals settled in Italy as well as the presence of significant groups of Eritreans in countries such as Canada and the USA.

A striking aspect of Italy's immigration situation in the postcolonial context is the sheer diversity of the current ethnic groups currently living and working in the country. Since its inception, incoming labour migration has already undergone a series of transformations. In the 1970s, there was a substantial female migration from Cape Verde, Ethiopia/Eritrea and the Philippines. By the 1980s the countries of origin had diversified and Moroccans, Tunisians and Senegalese migrants emerged as numerically significant groups. In the post-Cold War period, migration from former communist countries has become dominant and at present the five largest minority groups in Italy are from Romania (239,426); Albania (233,616); Morocco (227,940); Ukraine (112,802); and China (100,109). A number of commentators have begun to question what – if any – impact the legacy of colonialism has on the contemporary approach to the new migrations, particularly given that most foreign nationals in Italy are from countries with no previous colonial link to the country. Much emphasis has been placed on the racist dimension of Italy's colonial past, while other writers have emphasised the absence of an extensive colonial tradition to explain Italy's difficulties in dealing with diverse cultures. In addition, against the prevalent view that the memory of colonialism is a repressed or latent memory in Italy, some scholars have begun to investigate the ways in which Italy and Italians did not in fact relinquish the memory and ambition of colonial rule even into the postcolonial period. For example, in relation to the issue of citizenship, the current immigration policy approach might be classified as a continuum of former colonial approaches. Under fascism, Italian racial policies ensured that both racial criteria and merit shaped decisions about Italian citizenship eligibility. In the immigration context too, citizenship has emerged as a contested issue. The reform of the Italian citizenship law in 1992 categorically re-asserted the hierarchical divide between Italians and Other, in much the same way that changing legislation in the fascist period sought to confirm hierarchies along racial lines. The law not only made it more difficult for non-European Union citizens to acquire citizenship (extending the residence period from five to ten years) but it also prioritised the blood route to citizenship, leaving access open to the third generation of Italians abroad. In the absence of full citizenship rights, even access to the local vote for labour migrants has proved to be politically controversial. Regional political and economic differentiation within Italy also creates a combination of diverse structures which impact on the general conditions of settled migrant workers. These include the dominant type of labour market activity in a particular region, the pervasiveness of the informal economy and the legitimisation of local racisms by centre-right parties. The postcolonial immigration context in Italy is thus marked by substantial diversity, both in terms of the migrants themselves but also in terms of the local context they encounter. How this diversity is managed at both the local and national level will have important implications regarding the nature of Italy's transformation into a genuinely multicultural society.

Jacqueline Andall

HISTORIES

Andall, J. and D. Duncan (eds) (2005), *Italian Colonialism: Legacy and Memory*, Oxford: Peter Lang.

Colombo, A. and G. Sciortino (eds) (2004), *Journal of Modern Italian Studies* 9 (1) (special issue).

Choate, M. (2003), 'From Territorial to Ethnographic Colonies and Back Again: The Politics of Italian Expansion, 1890–1912', *Modern Italy* 8 (1): 65–75.
Gabaccia, D. (2000), *Italy's Many Diasporas*, London: University College, London.

Italian East Africa

Italian East Africa (Africa Orientale Italiana, or AOI) refers to the short-lived federation (1936–42) of Eritrea and southern Somalia, Libya and parts of Ethiopia. Eritrea, the so-called first-born colony (*la colonia primogenita*) provided the manpower and launching pad for the pacification of both Somalia (1889–1905) and Libya (1911–31). Italian Somalia was the only colony that retained its links with the metropole as an Italian trust territory administered by a post-fascist Rome. Libya, conquered by the Italians during the war with Turkey, 1911–12, was known as the 'fourth shore'. Although it was geographically distant from the older Italian colonies on the shores of the Red Sea and Indian Ocean, the dream of transforming it into an extension of the metropole was never attained. Colonial *askaris* (native troops renowned for their ruthlessness in battle and clad in colourful uniforms reflecting the Italian penchant for fashion), today remain the repository of the lived experience of Italy's 'fleeting empire'.

Like the empire they served, Italy's various subjects – collaborators and opponents alike – remain buried under the historical detritus of Fascism. The achievements of this, Italy's latter-day attempt at empire-building – material as well as spiritual – remain hostage to the post-imperial metropole's unwillingness to confront its past and permit open examination of its colonial memory banks, not to mention those in Tripoli, Mogadishu and Asmara. A more sustained and sincere inquiry into the successes and failures of the AOI would fill the gaps that continue to distort contemporary perceptions of the colonial past. It would then be possible to identify the ties that bind the histories of the peoples of the AOI to each other and also to Rome. This, in turn, might provide the forum that could enable the post-1941 legatees of AOI – inhabiting the metropole and the former colonies – to acknowledge a shared past which has remained buried in the debris of Italy's African Empire. Confronting the past – in its entirety, rather than the selected fragments favoured by post-colonial metropolitan and national élite(s) – would yield a richer and more nuanced history of the now-submerged existence of an italophone Africa.

Despite its brevity, the dream of an African empire had long been in gestation in Italian imagination, in various manifestations, dating back to the mediaeval period. Italian 'Orientalists' resuscitated this dream during the Risorgimento and nurtured the early debates on colonial policies, which in turn promoted Italy's foothold in Africa in the latter half of the nineteenth century. Classical narratives of hegemonic conflicts in the Mediterranean provided the impetus for modern aspirations to colonial empire building. Whether inspired by the Punic Wars of Ancient Rome or goaded into competition by Ottoman success in establishing suzerainty over the recalcitrant communities of Arabs, Berbers and Afro-Arabs of the Mediterranean and the Red Sea coast, the dream of establishing an overseas empire has deep socio-economic and historical roots.

In the nineteenth century practical economic and political considerations dictated the trimming of the grandiose scope of the imagined Italian African Empire that would reign supreme over the Mediterranean, including, at its most outlandish, a swathe of Sahelian Africa stretching from the Guinea Coast to the Red Sea. Unfortunately, Italy, as a late-comer to the colonial table, had to settle for territories left over from the more powerful

European empire builders such as Britain, France, Germany, Belgium and even Spain. Pragmatism dictated a role for the newly established peninsular nation as one that could be entrusted with buffer zones separating the British empire from the French. Thus, with the blessing of Britain, Italy acquired Eritrea and southern Somalia – in essence limiting the French sphere of control to the tiny enclave of Djibouti and investing itself with the pedigree of a colonising nation.

The earlier vision of resuscitating a Roman Africa through the establishment of informal and formal mercantile communities from the Italian diaspora in North Africa had to be discarded in the face of the realities of European competitive empire building. Numerous treaties between Britain and France forced nineteenth-century Italian parliamentarians to discard the dream of (re)building an African empire over the ruins of Carthage. As a consequence, Italian settlements in Tunisia and Egypt remained diasporic communities rather than pioneers of colonial settlements. The facts on the ground included the indisputable French military capability to plant its tricolour over Tunisia, and the reign of the Union Jack over Anglo-Egyptian Sudan and Arabia Felix (Yemen). With only the Ethiopian Empire left as the obstacle in connecting its colonies in Eritrea and Somalia, Italy embarked on an ill-fated and badly executed invasion of Adwa in 1896 which brought it an ignominious failure and an enduring stain on its national honour. Faced with national uproar over its defeat at the hands of the African *negusse negaest* (king of kings) and the need to justify the continuation of its colonial enterprise, Italy turned its attention to the Mediterranean and to the Balkans. In the twentieth century, with the demise of the Ottoman empire, Italy finally acquired a precarious foothold on the African shores of the Mediterranean by claiming Tripolitania, Cyrenaica and Fezzan, which it later renamed Libya. Revenge on the Ethiopians, and the redemption (albeit temporary) of national honour lost at Adwa had to wait another thirty-nine years.

It was Italy's ill-luck that it not only arrived late to the nineteenth century's European imperial feast, but that Mussolini's fascism (after 1922) and its predatory strategy of empire building not only created the illusion of an empire but also a false vision of glory and power, which as it turned out, contained its own seeds of destruction. First, following the invasion of Ethiopia in October 1935 the corporatist state blended nineteenth-century Orientalists' mercantile aspirations with policies intended to appease both its peasantry's land hunger and its intelligentsia's demand for avenging the nation's defeat at Ethiopian hands at Adwa. Four years earlier, in 1931, the Libyan Sanusi rebellion had been crushed with extreme brutality using aerial bombings, poison gas, massacres and ethnic cleansing. That 'success' certainly fed the ambitions and enthusiasms of Italy's new empire builders. Moreover, in both Libya and Ethiopia, Eritrean *askaris* and Somali *dub'aat* – under Italian command – proved their mettle as warriors in expanding the frontiers of the new empire. Urban centres mushroomed in the heart of the old cities of Asmara, Mogadishu and Tripoli as well as surrounding areas. Railways were built and a new modernity hovered over the war-centred activities that linked command centres in the Mediterranean with those in the Red Sea and the Indian Ocean. A new generation of colonial subjects familiar with the rhetoric and realities of alien rule – who had witnessed the institutionalisation of racial laws and loss of privileges – emerged into adulthood under the shadow of fascist salutes.

Second, Mussolini's ill-fated alliance with Hitler led to the Allies' strategy of targeting Italy's soft underbelly – its re-configured African empire. After June 1936 Rome reorganised AOI as a single territory sub-divided into six administrative territories: Amhara, Eritrea, Galla-Sidama, Harrar, Shoa and an expanded Somalia that included the Ogaden. In 1940 British Somaliland was temporarily added to AOI until February 1941, when Allied forces penetrated Italian defences in Jubaland and successfully dislodged Italy from its foothold on the Indian Ocean. By May 1941, the AOI had been disarmed and placed under British military rule with its inhabitants ushered into an era of accelerated decolonisation with juridical statehood as a possible option. In the Italian metropole, however, the demise of the Fascist state was neither as speedy nor as salutary for its inhabitants. The loss of Italian sovereignty over its colonies was made ever more bitter by the landing of American troops (1943) in the Italian South, dividing the country into two halves: the North under the control of the Fascist-Nazi armies, with an accommodating South patrolled by Allied forces.

In July 1943 the Duce was stripped of his powers, a step unappreciated by his Nazi allies, who promptly reinstalled him as a puppet dictator in northern Italy. The presence of foreign rulers on Italian soil fuelled the ideological wars between fascists and anti-fascists and gave free reign to more localised hostilities. Divided by factional conflicts and the real battle between the country's two halves, Italy began its descent into civil war and mayhem. With the collapse of the state and the flight of the dictator to a Nazi-protected enclave in the North, the country was plunged into general violence with the Allies controlling the Italian South and attacking northward, while the remnants of Mussolini's corporatist state fought for survival. Thus the disintegration of the state, small and large-scale massacres of ideological groupings, the impoverishment of the population, and the brutality of Italian empire building now laid bare, all facilitated the disenchantment of the Italian populace with its long-held popular dream of ruling the Afro-Mediterranean world.

Interestingly enough, with the establishment of a post-war government, the dream of empire began to resurface when the second Berlusconi government (2001–6) initiated a selective, amnesic reconstruction of the history of AOI. The twenty-first century finds Italian intelligentsia, pundits – liberals as well as neo-fascists – and a postmodern polity faced with a colonial past which keeps them entangled in the Afro-Mediterranean world. At present, it would be unrealistic to deny that there are historical links to Italy's colonial past among the inhabitants of the AOI, including the Italian language and Italian cultural inheritances (for example, architecture, monuments, public works, cuisine or intellectual ties to Rome). The Berlusconi-era media romanticised these ties as *appartenenza* (senses of 'belonging'), highlighting a paternalistic Italian nostalgia for its 'lost' colonies and ignoring the complex relationships between postcolonial Eritreans, Somalis, Libyans and Ethiopians which continue to have salience in the political and economic arenas of the twenty-first century. More research into the genesis, development and demise of AOI, which would recognise the enduring ties between Italy and its former colonies would rectify the simplistic understanding of Italian empire building in the nineteenth and twentieth centuries. Doing so would also point to the gaps between Italy's colonial dreams and achievements and also identify the surprisingly strong lines that continue to nurture Italo-African relationships in the twenty-first century.

Italian colonialism in Africa was neither the brutal, unmitigated predator portrayed by those who see it through the lens of Mussolini's fascist state, nor the brief realisation of Italian dreams of political-cultural hegemonic benevolence as fantasised by the Berlusconi neo-romantics and Orientalists. In fact, it had elements of both – witness the agony of those who were its victims as well as the loyalty of those who were its beneficiaries and collaborators. The records of victims and collaborators are now finally being opened after decades of neglect, leading not only to a revival of academic Italian colonial studies, but also to a belated recognition of the extent to which long-buried political-cultural links between Italians, Eritreans, Somalis and Libyans remain salient.

Ruth Iyob

HISTORIES

Ahmida, A. (2005), *Forgotten Voices: Power and Agency in Colonial and Postcolonial Libya*, New York: Routledge.

Berhe, A. (2003), 'Revisiting Resistance in Italian-Occupied Ethiopia: The Patriots' Movement (1936–1941) and the Redefinition of Post-War Ethiopia,' in J. Abbink, M. Mirjam De Bruijn and K. van Walraven (eds), *Rethinking Resistance: Revolt and Violence in African History*, Leiden and Boston, MA: Brill.

Bosworth, R. J. B. (2002), *Mussolini*, Oxford: Arnold Publishers.

Del Boca, A. (1965), *The Ethiopian War, 1935–41*, Chicago, IL: University of Chicago Press.

Dirar, C. (2004), 'From Warriors to Urban Dwellers: Ascari and the Military Factor in the Urban Development of Colonial Eritrea', *Cahiers d'Études Africaines* XLIV (3): 533–57.

Hess, Robert L. (1966), *Italian Colonialism in Somalia*, Chicago, IL: University of Chicago Press.

Iyob, Ruth (2005), 'From Mal d'Africa to Mal d'Europa: The Ties that Bind, in J. Andall and D. Duncan (eds), *Italian Colonialism: Legacy and Memory*, Oxford and Bern: Peter Berg.

Ramm, A. (1944), 'Great Britain and the Planting of Italian Power in the Red Sea, 1868–1885,' *English Historical Review* 59: 234.

Santarelli, E., E. Rochat, R. Raniero and L. Goglia (1986), *Omar al-Mukhtar: The Italian Reconquest of Libya*, London: Darf Publishers, Ltd.

Tripodi, Paolo (1999), *The Colonial Legacy in Somalia: Rome and Mogadishu from Colonial Administration to Operation Restore Hope*, New York: St Martin's Press.

Italophone Literature

The term 'italophone literature' refers to an emerging body of literary works written in the Italian language by first generation immigrants and, in the last few years, by the second generation. Its most striking element is the plurality of its voices and points of view. Italy has, in fact, one of the largest pools of diverse immigrant communities, with approximately 3 million foreigners present in 2006 coming from regions of the world as different as Romania, Albania, Morocco, Tunisia, Senegal, China, Sri Lanka, the Philippines, Ecuador and Peru. The multicultural nature of italophone literature reflects this heterogeneous immigrant community.

Although many italophone writers come from countries that were former European colonies, most of them have not inherited the literary language from past colonial cultural systems. Contrary to other postcolonial literary traditions, italophone literature did not develop during colonial times. The lack of a state-run schooling system at secondary level in Italy's former colonies of the Horn of Africa (Eritrea, Ethiopia and Somalia) and Libya has prevented the formation of a postcolonial literary tradition. Unlike their French counterparts, Italian colonial policies were anti-assimilationist and discouraged Italianisation. Yet italophone writers, for the most part non-native speakers of Italian, have all chosen Italian as their only literary idiom.

Among the writers who learned Italian in their country of origin are the Eritrean poet Ribka Sibhatu, born in Asmara (Eritrea) and author of the bilingual (Tigrinya/Italian) collection *Aulò. Canto poesia dell'Eritrea* (1993) and the Eritrean-born poet Fesum Brhan, who has lived in Italy since 1984 and is the author of the poetry collection, *L'ombra del poeta* (1997). Other works by writers from Italy's former colonies include *Lontano da Mogadiscio*

(1994), by Somali expatriate Shirin Fazel, a memoir of political and cultural exile, and *Arrivederci a Mogadiscio* (1991) a long interview, written in the form of a political essay, with Somali political exile Mohamed Aden Sheikh, by Italian journalist Pietro Petrucci.

Direct reference to Italy's colonial history appears in the fictional and autobiographical work by writer Erminia dell'Oro, born in Asmara (Eritrea) of Italian parents. Her novel *L'abbandono: una storia Eritrea* (1991), set against the background of the Italian Fascist occupation, narrates the love story ending in human tragedy of an Eritrean woman abandoned by her Italian lover, and of her bi-racial daughter, struggling with her hybrid identity. The Italian colonial past is also evoked in her *Asmara addio* (1993), a memoir which reconstructs the idyllic and privileged life of Italian colonialists, from the 1930s Fascist imperial times to the 1950s nostalgic return of colonial expatriates and the 1970s struggle for Eritrea's independence.

The first stage in the development of italophone literature began with the appearance of autobiographical works that made known to the public the experience of Muslim immigrant men. Written in a journalistic style, the first novels were all co-authored by Italian editors, who recorded the immigrant's testimony and turned it into standard Italian. This act of linguistic mediation, at times highly controversial, often erased the traces of the original language and the authors' direct literary expression. Among the early works are: *Immigrato* (1990), by Tunisian writer Salah Methnani in collaboration with Mario Fortunato, *Io, Venditore di elefanti* (1990) by Senegalese Pap Khouma in collaboration with Oreste Pivetta; *Chiamatemi Alì* (1991) by Moroccan writer Mohamed Bouchane in collaboration with C. de Girolamo and D. Miccione.

These early texts recorded the often crude and violent encounter with Italian society through street-selling activities: drug addiction (*Io, venditore di elefanti*); alcohol abuse and urban dejection (*Immigrato*); and daily acts of racism encountered in a desperate search for odd jobs and self-dignity (*Chiamatemi Alì*) of male Muslim identities. The only exception to male voices is the autobiographical novel *Volevo diventare bianca* (1993), by French-born writer of Algerian origin Nassera Chorha, written in collaboration with Alessandra Atti di Sarro, a recording of the author's awakening to womanhood and to racial and cultural identity first in France and then in Italy.

The experience of migrant women emerged in later texts, such as the bilingual (Portuguese/Italian) autobiographical essay *Racordai* by Cape Verde journalist Maria de Lourdes Jesus (1996), and *Amanda Olinda Azzurra e le altre* (1998), a series of short stories that give voice to marginalised, lonely immigrant women, by Brazilian psychotherapist, playwright and performance artist Christiana de Caldas Brito, who has also published *Qui e là racconti* (2004). In her work, the Italian language expands to include idiomatic expressions, neologisms and syntactical structures that reflect the protagonists' socioeconomic conditions. Other works by Brazilian women writers include the poetry collection *Il mio corpo traduce molte lingue* (1998) by Rosana Crispim da Costa and the collection of short stories in bilingual (Portuguese/Italian) edition *Indagini in stato di quiete* (1998) by Rosete de Sà. Three female voices are also put on stage by Italy-born writer Valentina Acava Mmaka, in her theatrical piece *Io . . . Donna . . . immigrata volere dire scrivere* (2004). Noteworthy also is the shocking testimony *Princesa* (1994) by Fernanda Farias de Albuquerque, a Brazilian transvestite and prostitute writing from jail in collaboration with ex-Red Brigades prisoner Maurizio Jannelli. Italian journalist Raffaele Masto is editor and co-author of two autobiographical testimonies by African women, the story of Nigerian Safiya Hussaini Tungar Tudu (*Io, Safiya*, 2003) and Eritrean Feven Abreha Tekle (*Libera*, 2005).

In 1991, Moroccan and francophone writer Tahar Ben Jelloun published the tragic, real story of Jerry Masslo's death, killed in the tomato fields near Naples by an Italian mob, in *Dove lo stato non c'è* (written in collaboration with Egi Volterrani), thus bringing to the attention of a larger public the issue of racism in relation to migration. With the issuing of *La promessa di Hamadi* (1991) by Senegalese Saidou Moussa Bâ, written with a narrative language modelled on African oral forms, and the semi-autobiographical novel *Pantanella: canto lungo la strada* (1992) (originally written in Arabic and translated into Italian) by Tunisian writer Mohsen Melliti, whose narrative forms stem from the Arabic literary tradition, italophone literature moves away from the early journalistic style and begins to show signs of a significant hybridisation of its literary structure.

A second stage in the development of italophone literature started at the end of the 1990s, when immigrant writers relinquished the autobiographical genre and began writing fictional and poetic works directly in Italian. While experimenting with new narrative perspectives and poetic voices, italophone writers of the second wave concentrated less directly on the experience of immigration as a transitory event and more on the complex process of settlement and integration within Italian society. Their specific and often critical vision of Italy's socio-cultural rituals, together with the enrichment offered by their use of new literary and linguistic sources, constitute a great challenge to the future development of Italy's literary and cultural tradition.

During this second stage, new national authors emerged, many from the ex-communist countries, the Middle East and North Africa. The first group includes authors such as young Albanian writer Ron Kubati with his novels *Va e non torna* (2000) and *M* (2002); the Slovakian writer Jarmila Očkayovà with her novels *Verrà la vita e avrà i tuoi occhi* (1997), *L'essenziale è invisibile agli occhi* (1997), and *Requiem per tre padri* (1998); and the remarkable Albanian poet Gëzin Hadjdari (winner, among other prizes, of the prestigious Montale Prize for Poetry) with the poetry collections *Antologia della pioggia* (2000), *Erbamara Barihidhur* (2001), *Stigmate* (2002) and *Spine nere* (2004). Against essentialist notions of postcolonial divisions, Hadjdari refuses national affiliations and declares the Italian language as his sole fatherland.

Among the Middle Eastern and North African authors are Iraqi best-seller winning writer Younis Tawfik, with his novel *La straniera* (1999), also author of *La città di Iram* (2002); Palestinian writer Muin Madih Masri, with the novel *Il sole d'inverno* (2001); Syrian-born writer Yousef Wakkas, whose detention experience on a count of international drug trafficking is vividly rendered in the collection of short stories *Fogli sbarrati* (2002), and *Terra mobile* (2005); Algerian-born writer Smari Abdel Malek, author of the tragic novel, filled with Koranic prophecies, *Fiamme in paradiso* (2000); Algerian-born Amara Lakhous, author of *Le cimici e il pirata* (1999) and more recently, *Scontro di civiltà per un ascensore a Piazza Vittorio* (2006), a satirical thriller novel (whose setting and plot echo Carlo Emilio Gadda's *Quer pasticciaccio* (1957), but whose explicit Italian influence is Leonardo Sciascia) originally written in Arabic and rewritten in Italian by the author. Worthy of notice are also the parodies and satirical pieces by Kossi Komla-Ebri, *Imbarazzismi I* (2002) and *Imbarazzismi II* (2004); the novels, embedded within the oral and animistic tradition of Sub-Saharan writings, *Lo spirito delle sabbie gialle* (1999), *Pap Ngagne, Yatt e gli altri* (2000), *Kelefa: la prova del pozzo* (2003) by Senegalese writer Mbacke Gadji and *La luna che mi seguiva* (2006) by Guinea-born writer Aminata Fofana; Pap Khouma's *Nonno Dio e gli spiriti danzanti* (2005) and Mohsen Melliti's *I bambini delle rose* (1995).

Italophone literature is currently being written by second-generation immigrant writers. Among them are Italo-Congolese Jadelin Mabiala Gangbo who experiments with new narrative genres and has published iconoclastic novels such as *Verso la notte BAKONKA* (2001), and *Rometta e Giulieo* (2001), and Igiaba Scego, an Italian-born writer who has published a semi-autobiographical story, in Somali/Italian bilingual edition, *La nomade che amava Alfred Hitchcock* (2003), the novel *Rhoda* (2004), and many remarkable short stories. Of relevance also are the anthologies of short stories, such as *Italiani per vocazione* (2005) and *Pecore nere* (2005), by women writers such as Italo-Indians Gabriella Kuruvilla and Laila Wadia, Italo-Somalian Igiaba Scego and Italo-Egyptian Ingy Mubiayi.

With the exception of Tahar Ben Jelloun's *Dove lo stato non c'è* (published by the prestigious Einaudi), early italophone texts were issued by small and engaged publishers such as Fara, Sinnos, Besa, Datanews, Edizioni dell'Arco, and Sensibili alle Foglie, among others. The authors survived on the media scene thanks to the initiatives of cultural organisations (Arci, Caritas, La tenda, Manitese, and other NGOs) and small journals (*Il caffè, Nigrizia, Terre di mezzo*). Since 1995, the main outlet for italophone literary expression has been the Annual National Literary Prize promoted and organised by the Associazione Eks&Tra. The winning poetry and short stories are collected and edited by editors Roberta Sangiorgi and Alessandro Ramberti. Winners of the Eks&Tra prize include poets and writers from all over the world. Volumes so far issued are: *Le voci dell'arcobaleno* (1995), *Mosaici d'inchiostro* (1996), *Memorie in valigia* (1997), *Destini sospesi di volti in cammino* (1998), *Parole oltre i confini* (1999), *La nuova mappa dei popoli* (2001), *Anime in viaggio* (2002), *Il doppio sguardo, culture allo specchio* (2002), *Pace in parole migranti* (2003), *Impronte, scritture dal mondo* (2004), *La seconda pelle* (2004) and *Il cuore altrove* (2005).

Electronic publishing constitutes a new and extremely prolific outlet for italophone writings. Through web publications, immigrant writers are able to gain an easy, free and democratic access to publishing. Such visibility is not often available within the mainstream Italian cultural market. The website of the Associazione Eks&Tra offers a database of short stories and poems: www.eksetra.net. Other sites of interest, which include interviews with writers and literary texts are: http://digilander.libero.it/vocidalsilenzio/; the on-line literary magazines *El-Ghibli* at http://www.el-ghibli.provincia.bologna.it/; *Sagarana* at http://www.sagarana.net; Kúmácreaola at www.disp.let.uniroma1.it/kuma/kuma.html; *Il gioco degli specchi* at http://www.ilgiocodeglispecchi.org. Useful for bibliographical research is the database Basili, run by the Comparative Literature Department of the University of Rome la Sapienza, Basili, at http://www.disp.let.uniroma1.it/basili2001/

Cristina Lombardi-Diop

HISTORIES

Gnisci, A. (1998), *La letteratura italiana della migrazione*, Rome: Lilith Edizioni.

Lombardi-Diop, C. (2005), 'Selling/Storytelling: African Autobiographies in Italy', in J. Andall and D. Duncan (eds), *Italian Colonialism: Legacy and Memory*, Bern: Peter Lang, pp. 217–38.

Parati, G. (ed.) (1999), *Mediterranean Crossroads: Migration Literature in Italy*, Madison, WI: Fairleigh Dickinson University Press.

Parati, G. (2005), *Migration Italy: The Art of Talking Back in a Destination Culture*, Toronto: University of Toronto Press.

Portelli, A. (2001), 'Le origini della letteratura afroitaliana e l'esempio afroamericano', *L'ospite ingrato. Globalizzazione e identità*: 69–86.

Sangiorgi, R. (ed.) (2001), *Gli scrittori della migrazione*, Santarcangelo di Romagna: Eks&Tra Edizioni.

Land Expropriations

Like other colonisers, Italy expropriated land from the autochthonous populations to facilitate the formation of metropolitan land ownership and to have lands available for rural emigrants from the home country. The expropriations can be placed into three separate categories: 'sovereign' expropriations, in which lands belonging to pre-colonial state or government institutions were transformed into domanial properties; expropriations of a technical character, which asserted the ownership of the colonial state over uncultivated or abandoned lands (considered *res nullius*); expropriations of a political sort, which punished those who were opposed to colonial power. The Italian territories often followed the example of French colonial legislation in this sector.

The sudden and seemingly arbitrary way that expropriations were often decreed only increased discontent and opposition, which sometimes manifested itself in armed rebellions by the colonised populations. This happened in Eritrea, when the announcement that the best lands in the colony would be transformed into domanial territories brought on the revolt of Batha Agos (1894) and contributed to the failure of the first attempts at agricultural colonisation.

As an example of political expropriations one can cite the confiscation of the properties of the Negus, Haile Selassie, and of the families who had headed the resistance to the Italian occupation of Ethiopia (1936): in particular two huge properties of the reigning family, located in Oletta and in Bisfhoftù, were given to the Opera Nazionale Combattente (National Combattants' Organization) to allow for two Italian agricultural reclamations.

The recourse to expropriations was particularly notable in the Italian colony of Libya. In the first decade following the Italian conquest (1912) colonial properties were based on those inherited from the Ottoman state. Yet these properties (about 3,600 hectares in 1922) proved insufficient to support a colonial politics of economic control and the project of making the country an outlet for Italian emigration.

Under the governorship of Giuseppe Volpi, in 1922 and 1923 requisition decrees created lands for the first colonial agricultural settlements. One decree mandated that lands not cultivated for three years would transform into domanial lands; another confiscated lands from rebels and those who aided them. Through the application of these decrees the Fascist government acquired almost 70,000 hectares of land in Tripolitania for Italian colonisation. In Cyrenaica, where the Sanusi confraternity guided a long-lived resistance to Italian rule, expropriations were utilised to deprive the Sanusi of their assets, including buildings, furniture and lands almost as vast as those seized in Tripolitania.

The history of the high plains region during Fascist rule (Green Mountain, or *jabâl akhdâr*) can also be considered under the rubric of expropriation. The *jabâl* was a pastoral zone traditionally traversed by Bedouin tribes, but in order to defeat the armed resistance, the Fascists transferred all the tribes of the *jabâl* into concentration camps controlled by soldiers and forced them to remain there until 1933. This freed up the best lands of the Green Mountain for Fascist programmes of Italian colonisation: these lands, which were among those targeted by the Plan for Demographic Colonisation, were given to Italian farming families who emigrated from Italy.

The weight expropriations had in the formation of colonial land ownership in Libya is still debated among historians. Yet we can affirm that transforming uncultivated lands into colonial domanial territories often constituted in practice an expropriation that hurt the autochthonous population. Those lands, especially those destined for grazing use, formed part of a tribal land-use system based on indivisible property that proved to be irreconcilable with colonial interests and colonial law. Indeed, as had been the case in Algeria and other Maghrebian territories under French rule, this practice went together with the dissolution of tribal institutions already in motion but hugely accelerated by the Italian occupation.

With the end of the occupation a large part of the expropriated lands reverted to Libyan control. In Cyrenaica, once Italian colonists definitively left in 1942, lands were restored to their Libyan former owners, in particular to the members of the Sanusi family. In the independent state, some of these lands were involved in agricultural development plans, and some remained abandoned.

The revolutionary government ushered in by Mu'ammar Qadhafi's 1969 coup asserted the right to sequester the property of Italian citizens still living in Libya on the grounds that this had been illegally acquired during the colonial period. These property confiscations, and the expulsion of Italians from Libya, came with the decree of 21 July 1970. (The Libyan Jewish population was subject to the same confiscations and expulsions.) According to Libyan statistics, the Libyan government's expropriation of Italian property after 1970 totalled 37,000 hectares of land, which included 352 farms, as well as 1,750 urban properties and 500 properties for production or commercial use.

                                                                                            Federico Cresti

HISTORIES

Cresti, F. (1996), *Oasi di italianità. La Libia della colonizzazione agrarian tra fascismo, guerra, e indipendenza 1935–1956*, Turin: Società Editrice Internazionale.
Cresti, F. (2005), 'The Early Years of the Agency for the Colonization of Cyrenaica (1932–1935),' in R. Ben-Ghiat and M. Fuller (eds), *Italian Colonialism*, New York: Palgrave, pp. 73–82.
Segrè, C. (1974), *Fourth Shore. The Italian Colonization of Libya*, Chicago, IL: University of Chicago Press.

Land Settlements

The idea of using African territories as an outlet for that part of the population who could not be guaranteed a decent life at home had guided Italian colonialism since the inception of the scramble for Africa. The colonies would forestall the yearly mass emigration (in the hundreds of thousands) of Italians abroad which had started in the late nineteenth century and had continued through the first decades of the twentieth century.

In East Africa, following the Italian colonial occupations of Eritrea (1890), Somalia (1908) and Ethiopia (1935) several strategies were defined to channel Italian emigration to the colonial territories, chiefly through the creation of new agricultural settlements. While such settlements occasioned much state propaganda in the Fascist years, and a large bureaucracy, they were rather limited to scope and impact. According to official Fascist-era statistics (which are probably inflated), in the territories of Italian East Africa (Eritrea, Italian Somalia and Ethiopia) in 1940 there were about 31,000 Italian farmers, whose settlements occupied 113,000 of land. Even Eritrea, Italy's oldest colonial possession, only counted 150 metropolitan agricultural businesses operating there in 1939.

The importance of agricultural settlements was greater in Libya, where agrarian colonisation policies had gone through several phases since the 1912 Italian conquest of the country. In a first phase small-scale and private colonisation had been favoured, with domanial lands conceded to Italians at very low prices; and after 1922, private colonisation of a capitalistic nature that privileged well-funded and well-known agricultural businesses. After 1928 the state gave financial support to agricultural firms under conditions that would favour the hiring of metropolitan workers. But the poor results obtained by these methods convinced the Fascist government of the necessity of direct state intervention.

In 1932, when the Fascists had completed their so-called 'pacification' of the remaining rebel territories of the Cyrenaica region of Libya, the Agency for Colonisation (Ente della colonizzazione) was created as a parastatal institution charged with realising a large-scale project of population transfer and agricultural colonisation of all the available lands in the colony. (First titled the Agency for Colonisation of the Cyrenaica, it was later extended to encompass Tripolitania and finally all of Libya.) But it was under the leadership of Italo Balbo, who served as Governor of Libya after 1934, that this project was really actuated. In 1938, through a new Plan for the Intensive Demographic Colonisation of Libya, a vast web of new land settlements was created in the East, in the highland plains of Cyrenaica (*jabâl al-akhdâr*) and in the West, in the coastal and plains areas of Tripolitania. While the plan also foresaw a guided Muslim colonisation, with villages and settlements foreseen for the Libyan population as well, it revolved around the mass transfer of Italians to Libya. Starting in 1938, thousands of carefully selected Italian families were brought to Libya in an operation that received enormous publicity from the régime. Almost 30,000 colonists arrived in Libya in two waves of emigration in 1938 and 1939: these were to be but the first of many other mass transfers that in Fascist fantasy would produce almost 500,000 Italian residents by the mid-1950s.

World War II put an end to such plans and to the Fascist régime. After Italy entered the war in May 1940, plans for new settlements were put on hold, and in 1942, with Libya and the other colonies lost to the British, most Italian colonists and farmers were evacuated. In Cyrenaica, for example, the settlements were abandoned, and only partially used thereafter by the local populations. Several, though, became the nucleus of important agricultural concerns in independent Libya. In Tripolitania, in contrast, most of the settlements remained active even after the war, and in 1956 the Libyan government recognised the Italians' right to remain on the lands they had cultivated. Yet with the passing of time the Italian presence diminished in Libya, and in 1970, after Mu'ammar Qadhafi took power, the Libyan government seized the remaining settlements in Italian hands and expelled the last Italian ex-colonists from the country.

Federico Cresti

HISTORIES

Cresti, F. (1996), *Oasi di italianità. La Libia della colonizzazione agraria tra fascismo, guerra, e indipendenza 1935–1956*, Turin: Società Editrice Internazionale.

— (2005), 'The Early Years of the Agency for the Colonization of Cyrenaica (1932–1935)', in R. Ben-Ghiat and M. Fuller (eds), *Italian Colonialism*, New York: Palgrave, pp. 73–82.

Fowler, G. L. (1973), 'Decolonization of Rural Libya', *Annals of the Association of American Geographers* 63 (4): 490–506.

Larebo, H. (1994), *The Building of an Empire: Land Practice and Policy in Ethiopia, 1935–1941*, Oxford: Clarendon Press.

Moore, M. (1939), *Fourth Shore. Italy's Mass Colonization of Libya*, London: Routledge.

Segrè, C. (1974), *Fourth Shore. The Italian Colonization of Libya*, Chicago, IL: University of Chicago Press.

Libya

Even among postcolonial nations in general, Libya stands out for both its ambiguous statehood and its antagonistic relations with the West. Indeed, the theoretical hallmarks of the political philosophy of its ruler of thirty-seven years, Colonel Mu'ammar Qadhafi, are statelessness and decentralisation. Since the brutalities of Italian colonial rule (1911–43), but especially since the revolution of 1969, anti-(neo-)colonialism and anti-occidentalism have dominated the country's political experience. Qadhafi's opposition to the fundamentals of statehood is but one expression of his rejection of the West. In addition, Libya is composed of three disparate areas – Tripolitania and Cyrenaica on the coast, and the Fezzan in the interior – each of which has closer historical and geographical ties to its outer neighbours than to each other; a situation that contributes further to the weakness of the Libyan state's societal underpinnings. The three regions were unified only as recently as 1934 by the Italian government. In this respect, the country is a colonial concoction of Continental Europe. Recent decades have witnessed ongoing struggles to promote a Libyan identity that, if nothing else, can be rooted in anti-occidentalism.

Prior to Italian intervention, the Ottoman Empire's official control over the Libyan provinces only translated partially into effective control. Local dynasties, tribal groups and urban notables and merchants held much of the real power, and engaged in a complex balance of political and commercial interests. Meanwhile, Italy had achieved independence from foreign rule, and its own national unification, only in 1861. Its subsequent efforts to acquire colonies in East and North Africa stemmed more from a thirst for parity with other European nations than from solid military or financial resources with which to exploit such colonies. In particular, Italy's expansionists hoped to colonise Tunisia, both because of its proximity to Italy and because of the fact that it already held a large population of Italians. After France took over Tunisia in 1881, however, Italy turned its energies to East Africa, where it had already acquired a desultory foothold beginning in 1869. By the 1890s, Italy controlled its 'first-born' colony of Eritrea, as well as parts of Somalia; but the desire to acquire a North African colony persisted. After a period of gradual commercial penetration, Italy attacked Tripoli in late 1911. While this aggression was hardly on the scale of better-known and vaster colonial undertakings, it holds a significant place in world history, as the first use of aerial bombing.

Most Italians today are not aware of this primacy, but at the time Italy's attack was glorified as a great, modern accomplishment. In the words of Italy's celebrated poet Giovanni Pascoli: 'Was not [Italy] the first to beat her wings and rain death upon her enemy's camps?' In this as in many other instances, the North African conquest provided especially successful rhetorical fodder for Italian expansionists. To grasp the importance of the Libyan colony in modern Italian culture and politics, it is crucial to understand the Italians' particular justification for colonising a North African territory, namely, that Italians were merely regaining land to which they were legitimately entitled because it had long ago been part of the Roman empire. Those Italians hungry for colonies even saw colonisation as a historical mission rather than merely an entitlement. In any case, the notion of an Italian 'return' was at the heart of their rhetoric. In the same speech of 1911, Pascoli produced this vision most famously: 'We are close [to this land] . . . [we] were there before; we left signs that not even the Berbers, the Bedouins and the Turks have succeeded in erasing; signs of our humanity and civilisation, signs that indeed, we are not Berbers, Bedouins and Turks. We are returning.' This notion of return, both to the physical territory and to the Italian nation's distant 'Roman-ness' (*romanità*), also underlay the choice of the name 'Libya', which Italians revived from classical sources. Another description of Libya that captured Italians' imagination was as Italy's 'fourth shore' – coined by Gabriele d'Annunzio, arguably the most famous author of the period – to complement the Adriatic, Tyrrhenian and Ionian shores that define the Italian peninsula. At a more practical level, Italians pushing for conquest explained that the Libyan territories would be ideal for the settlement of tens of thousands of Italian farmers, who would transform Libya's ostensibly unproductive land into a 'breadbasket' for Italy. The few voices of opposition pointed out that Libya, instead, offered no more than a 'giant sandbox'; but to no avail.

Italian forces treated local resistance harshly from the start. How many Libyans were deported to, and died in, *confino* (internal exile) in Italy itself – for instance, on the island of Ustica, where the Marxist philosopher Antonio Gramsci was also confined – is a matter that has become the subject of serious study only recently, thanks to the opening of previously inaccessible archives. While Italian relations with Libya's minority populations (Jews, Maltese, Greeks, Albanians, Berber, Tuareg and other Sub-Saharan Africans) were generally stable, relations with the Arab Muslims were characterised simultaneously by a pattern of placating them officially (in order to appear as 'better' colonisers than the British or the French to international Muslim opinion) and a vicious war waged against the most co-ordinated Muslim body in Libya, and the de facto ruler of Cyrenaica – the Sanusi brotherhood, a prosperous religious, tribal, commercial and political network that systematically opposed foreign domination.

For a period between World War I (which depleted Italy's resources) and the beginning of Fascist rule in 1922, the grip of Italian government relaxed: both a Tripolitanian republic and a Cyrenaican parliament were formed by mutual consent with the Italians (1918–22 and 1920–23, respectively). But following the arrival of Governor Giuseppe Volpi, new aggressive and suppressive measures took over through the 1920s, ranging from extensive land expropriations to regulations limiting Libyans' rights to education and employment. Volpi's 'reconquest' of Tripolitania was more or less complete by 1923; the war on Cyrenaica continued for nearly a decade. This protracted assault was thoroughly destructive, and is viewed as a genocide by Libyan and foreign scholars alike. Under the command of Rodolfo Graziani – whose ruthlessness earned him the Libyan nickname of 'the butcher of Tripoli' – aerial campaigns intensified (and used chemical weapons, despite the 1925 Gas Protocol), and the Bedouin were stuffed into concentration camps, where they died of starvation and disease, if not execution by hanging. The war ended shortly after the rebel leader 'Umar al-Mukhtar was captured and hanged in 1931. Estimates of the casualties vary widely, but they begin at 70,000 dead as a direct result of battles, executions or starvation and disease. In addition, many other Libyans migrated to Egypt and Tunisia, further depleting the indigenous population. The highest overall estimates of total population loss due to Italian colonisation reach 1 million; most scholars assess the total to be between a quarter and a third of a million.

One reason Italians fought so fiercely for Cyrenaica was to gain control of the most fertile land in Libya, the Jabal Akhdar, long used by Bedouin to graze their livestock. In the wake of the resistance's collapse, Italy began to reorganise its colonial government to develop grand settlement schemes and bring Italian farmers there. In 1934, with the arrival of Governor Italo Balbo – an internationally renowned aviator and high-ranking Fascist – the provinces were integrated into the single colony of Libya. The northern provinces were run along national models, with a typical bureaucracy, and the southern territory remained under military command. Balbo gave the colony a certain glamour, at least for Italians: air shows and car rallies, and the Tripoli Trade Fair provided international publicity for what was now touted as a tourist 'destination' sporting gorgeous deserts and superb classical antiquities. His rule's theatricality was epitomised by the spectacular inauguration of the new trans-Libyan highway (the Litoranea Libica) in 1937, and in the course of Mussolini's attendance, the dictator being presented with the 'Sword of Islam' in an enactment of the government's philo-Islamic self-presentation. Balbo turned even the mass settlement of Italian farmers into highly publicised events, with the simultaneous transport from Italy of *i ventimila* ('the twenty thousand' settlers) in 1938 and a somewhat lesser number in 1939.

In this period of relative stability, Balbo reversed some of his predecessors' more damaging policies, creating the possibility of more effective rule by diminishing some of the well-entrenched indigenous resentment. He closed the concentration camps, gave amnesty to many Cyrenaicans, and released the last political prisoners in Tripolitania. He also created new schools for natives, commissioned the building of new mosques, and accorded Libyans the possibility of obtaining land concessions in Tripolitania on the same terms as Italians. Finally, with Mussolini's resistance, he began a small-scale programme of settlement villages for Libyan veterans who had served with the Italians in East Africa, in the less fertile edges of Cyrenaica.

In the course of World War II in Libya, Italians abandoned the Cyrenaican villages permanently; the settlers of Tripolitania, on the other hand, stayed through the 1960s. Italy's loss in the war led to its effective surrender of Libya in 1943, and official divestment of all colonies in 1947. Temporary government under the British Military Administration (in the coastal areas) and the French Military Administration (in the Fezzan) gave way in 1951 to the United Kingdom of Libya (later, the Kingdom of Libya), with Idris al-Sanusi on the throne. An extraordinary watershed in the country's history marked the eighteen years of Idris' rule. From an almost entirely illiterate country that was also one of the poorest in the world, Libya became one of the wealthiest after the discovery of oil in 1959. But this new wealth, rather than solving Libya's most pressing problems, exacerbated some of them. Corruption in government and finance undermined the functioning of the state, especially along lines of tribal alliances; and the fact that foreign oil companies were in charge of exploitation opened the doors to invasive foreign control. Idris, meanwhile, did not use his power to counter either of these trends, but rather allowed tribal interests to dominate internal affairs and got out of the way of the oil companies.

In this passive political climate, the revolution of 1969, of which Colonel Mu'ammar al-Qadhafi rapidly became the enduring charismatic leader, met with no opposition. The new government moved quickly to expel the remaining Italians and confiscate their land, and to complete the closing of the US Air Force base (although the process had begun earlier, the new régime took credit for it). Within the country, Qadhafi himself has retained vast political control, while taking the public position of a retired revolutionary. Different phases of the régime have seen intricate levels of surveillance and repression, as well as overt acts of brutality, all of which have yielded a persistent ambient fear on the part of citizens, who have no venue for political opposition. The régime, of course, is more notorious internationally for its support of terrorist movements, and specifically for attacks on foreign airliners such as the Pan Am flight that exploded over Lockerbie in Scotland. In recent years, however, the country has done an international about-face, paying damages to the families of victims; surrendering its programme to develop Weapons of Mass Destruction; and forging a new entente with the US, its most dogged opponent in past decades.

Meanwhile, due to the fact that Libya was not a country prior to Italian occupation as well as the fact that it was highly illiterate, there was no Libyan historiography of modern Libya

to speak of until the 1980s. This explains how one book concerning the Sanusiyya in relation to Italian colonisers – by anthropologist E. E. Evans-Pritchard, written in 1949 – served
for a few decades as a beacon of postcolonial scholarship. It must be kept in mind that the
book, in addition to being absolutely pro-Sanusi and anti-Italian, was also pro-British; thus
Libyans' acquaintance with postcolonial historiography was distinctly biased. Qadhafi's
régime, to counteract this void, opened universities, funded the postgraduate education overseas of many young Libyans, and created several research institutes, one of them specifically
devoted to reconstructing Libyans' experiences of, and resistance to Italian colonisation.
Using oral history methods, the Libyan Studies Centre (al-Markaz al-Jihad) has collected
thousands of hours of recorded interviews. Libyans' views of Italian rule, especially official
ones, have emphasised the memory of combat atrocities more than that of everyday life under
Italian colonialism. Indeed, such memories are hardly remote, as landmines in the desert
have continued to maim and kill civilians. But roads, sewage systems and other aspects of the
landscape and built environment are also reminders of the colonial past.

Despite strong commercial ties, relations between Libya and Italy have been strained.
Accords in the late 1990s introduced a new entente – leading, among other things, to
foreign scholars having access to colonial-era archives for the first time, and to scholarly
collaboration in the form of Italo-Libyan conferences and publications. More recent
events, however, have also provoked tensions anew between Libya and the former colonial
power. The Italian government maladroitly proposed sending Italian troops to Libya in
order to stem the flow of illegal immigrants who pass through Libyan territory (not surprisingly, this generous offer was rejected); and in February 2006, a deliberate provocation
on the part of a right-wing Italian politician provoked rioters in Benghazi to set fire to the
Italian Embassy there.

Aside from a dedicated minority of Italian scholars, most Italians have forgotten colonial Libya rather comfortably. The government has done its share to foster this amnesia, as
when Italian distribution of a highly realistic feature film on 'Umar 'al-Mukhtar (who
remains a key symbol of Libya's independence) and the war on Cyrenaica (*Lion of the
Desert*, 1980, by Mustapha Akkad) was halted by the Italian Ministry of Foreign Affairs; to
this day, it has been screened very few times in Italy, and only in the rarefied context of film
festivals. For Italians expelled from Libya in 1970, though, the colonial past remains a cause
for bitterness, as they have persistently tried to obtain compensation for their lost properties, and have been ignored by both governments. Some 'ex-Libyans' formed associations
(the most important one being the AIRL – Associazione degli Italiani rimpatriati dalla
Libia), and over the years, memoirs have been published in tiny print runs; such testimo-
nials are currently gaining a wider audience. Scholars and the public alike appear to be discovering a new interest in the colonial era, which has inspired new critical studies as well
as scholarly apologia and straightforward nostalgia.

Mia Fuller

HISTORIES

Ahmida, A. A. (2005), *Forgotten Voices: Power and Agency in Colonial and Postcolonial
Libya*, London: Routledge.
Anderson, L. (1991), 'Legitimacy, Identity, and History in Libya', in E. Davis and N. E.
Gavrielides (eds), *Statecraft in the Middle East: Oil, Historical Memory, and Popular
Culture*, Miami, FL: Florida University Press, pp. 71–91.
Baldinetti, A. (ed.) (2003), *Modern and Contemporary Libya: Sources and Historiographies*,
Rome: Istituto Italiano per l'Africa e l'Oriente.

Segrè, C. G. (1974), *Fourth Shore. The Italian Colonization of Libya*, Chicago, IL and
    London: University of Chicago Press.
Vandewalle, D. (2006), *A History of Modern Libya*, London: Cambridge University Press.
Wright, J. (1982), *Libya: A Modern History*, Baltimore, MD: Johns Hopkins University
    Press.

Orientalism

The extension of Edward Said's notion of Orientalism to the Italian context has helped
define a new strain of research on modern and contemporary Italy as both object and
subject of Orientalist discourses. It is thus possible to speak of an internal and an external
Orientalism. Italy's internal Orientalism originates from the making of the Italian nation
and the foundation of the Italian state. It refers to the discourse that constituted the historical dichotomy between the North and South of Italy since the inception of Italy's unification process in 1860. This internal Orientalist discourse stemmed from the perception
of the economic backwardness of the Mezzogiorno and then extended to a generalised
understanding of southerners and their culture as backward and degenerate. In political
treaties and economic studies by liberal political thinkers, government officials and parliamentary members such as Francesco Saverio Nitti, Giustino Fortunato, Sidney Sonnino,
Antonio de Viti de Marco, Ernesto Artom, Gaetano Salvemini and Pasquale Villari, Italy's
South, from being an object of study and an historical formation, was transformed into a
conceptual, monolithic entity described as ahistorical, morally corrupt and devoid of complexities and diversities. This polarised vision of the unredeemable otherness of the
Mezzogiorno, always defined in oppositional terms, contributed to the birth of the
'Southern Question' as the embodiment of the unrelenting difference between the North
and the South. Moreover, positivist thinkers such as Giuseppe Sergi, Alfredo Niceforo and
Cesare Lombroso applied Darwinian notions of biological degeneration to southerner peasants and subaltern classes, thus conflating racial and class prejudices. Lombroso, for
instance, linked southern Italians' dark complexion and cranial dimensions to their alleged
tendency to crime. This 'Africanisation' of Italian southern peasantry contributed to some
of the stereotypical images of *meridionali* as ethnically and biologically different from and
inferior to northern Italians.

   As a discursive formation, Italy's external Orientalism began in the eighteenth century
when young educated European travellers discovered Italy's monuments, artifacts of classical antiquity and landscape. The journey into Italy turned into a tourist commodity
when, in 1864, Thomas Cook began leading Europeans on the Grand Tour. These travels
produced many visual records and representations of Italian landscapes and cityscapes, as
well as travelogues and tourist guidebooks in which Italy figures as an exotic 'Other', and
its people as picturesque characters whose mannerisms and sensuality were linked to lin-
gering pagan prejudices or to religious fanaticisms.

   If internal and external Orientalist discourses are focused on the Italian peninsula, other
forms of Orientalism, involving faraway and exotic lands, also played a role within Italy's
literary and artistic imagination. From the nineteenth century on, a defined Orientalist
strain resonates in Italian travel writings and novels such as Edmondo De Amicis' *Marocco*
(1876), as well as Gabriele d'Annunzio's poetic collection *Isaotta Guttadàuro ed altre poesie*
(1886) (which included 'Sogno di una notte di primavera' a poem written in homage to a
passage from Gustave Flaubert's *Salammbò*). A taste for exoticising Orientalist *topoi* came

to Italian readers from the immensely popular fiction writer Emilio Salgari. Some of his most Orientalist works include *La favorite del Mahdi* (1887), *I predoni del Sahara* (1903), and *Le pantere di Algeri* (1903). In the nineteenth century, as Edward Said himself noted, Giuseppe Verdi's Egyptian *Aida* (1871) combined artistic brilliance and technical authority in order to produce an Orientalist fantasy realised through an immensely popular entertainment spectacle such as opera.

Scholars are only beginning to investigate the Orientalist paradigm within the Italian literary tradition. It has been argued that in the twentieth century, Egyptian-born Filippo Tommaso Marinetti, Giuseppe Ungaretti and Enrico Pea set the tone of Italy's literary modernism by incorporating their imaginary vision of the enchanted, composite and transnational reality of Alexandria of Egypt, their native city, into their words of freedom, assemblage, and decentred visual language. This modernist elaboration of Orientalist influences constitutes one of the streams of twentieth-century Orientalism. A negative form of Orientalist exoticism informs Guido Gozzano's India in *Verso la cuna del mondo* (1914–16), where a mosaic and a collage of geographical, religious and historical information derived from Orientalist literary sources construct India as the tombstone of the world, a museum in ruins. Such images of a decaying otherness also permeate Pier Paulo Pasolini's vision of India in his travelogue *L'odore dell'India* (1962) and more recently, Antonio Tabucchi's *Notturno indiano* (1984). At the opposite spectrum of a negative Orientalism, Pasolini's vitalistic vision of the Orient as a source of unbridled sexual impulses as seen in his film *A Thousand and One Nights* (1975) dates back to the early 1960s, when his interest shifted from the rural world of the Friuli to the urban world of Rome and then to Africa in the process of decolonisation. Pasolini's Africa is construed through a poetic invocation of instinctual and sexual liberation, to which he opposes Western classical rationalism and historicism. His film documentary project *Appunti per un Orestiade Africana* (1969) as well as his screenplay *Il padre selvaggio* (1975) all point in this direction.

Said's pivotal work *Orientalism* was translated into Italian for the first time only in 1991 but up to today it has not been of any relevance within Italy's cultural debates. The absence of a critical re-assessment of Italy's colonial experience in the Horn of Africa and in Libya may be accountable for such critical silence. Yet Italy's colonial enterprise saw the eager involvement of writers and intellectuals who travelled to the colonies and published their travel accounts in Italy's major newspapers. Edoardo Scarfoglio's *Abissinia 1888–1896* greatly influenced the intellectual milieu of Italy's Africanists. Journalists and political commentators disseminated the exoticising myth of the oversea colonies as a 'promised land' of abundance, plenitude and natural richness. But while in France the decline of fin-de-siècle Orientalism marked a shift in the nation's geo-political interest from North to Sub-Saharan Africa, within the Italian context a critique of Orientalism coincided with the inception of Italy's belated colonialism. D'Annunzio's Orientalist vanity was soon replaced by a militaristic and imperialist vision of Africa informed by his rereading of Classical Greek antiquity in his *Odi navali* (1892) and *Maia* (1903), and culminated in his strong imperialist verses of *Le canzoni delle gesta d'oltremare* (1911–12), which show the contamination of his aulic poetic language with military and journalistic chronicles describing the Libyan campaigns.

Under the Fascist régime, popular novels such as Arnaldo Cipolla's *Un'imperatrice in Etiopia* (1922); Mario dei Gaslini's *Piccolo amore beduino* (1926) (winner of the Prize for Best Colonial Novel), *Natisc fiore dell'oasi* (1928) and *I predoni della Sirte* (1929); Guido Milanesi's *La sperduta di Allah* (1927); Vittorio Tedesco Zammarano's *Auhér mio sogno* (1935); Mario Appelius' *Il cimitero degli elefanti*, (1927); Gino Mitrano Sani's *E per i solchi millenari delle carovaniere* (1926), *La reclusa di Giarabub* (1931) and *Femmina somala* (1933) popularised the genre of the colonial romance in which interracial love is staged against a highly exotic backdrop of wild deserts and palm trees. Colonial exotic novels provide a mix of Orientalist clichés and figures such as cruel and tyrannical Arab chiefs, treacherous Bedouins, languid and enamoured African women whose antagonists are sophisticated and cosmopolitan Italian women, and courageous officials on military duty. Although little scholarly work exists on Italy's colonial literature of the 1920s and 1930s, the study of the mass consumption of colonial novels offers insights into the nature of the appeal that the colonial experience had on the literate, middle-class constituencies of Italians who read them. Their fascination is probably linked to the pleasure offered by romantic exchanges, reciprocal or racially and politically impossible love affairs, heroism and death. One could argue that such stereotypical plots made of romance and loyalty to the state (which inevitably breaks the interracial romance and compels the hero to return home) enact the often conflictual tensions between an individualised sense of male hubris and the formation of a domesticated, nationalised Fascist male subjectivity. Colonial exotic novels thus contributed to the construction of an Italian model of citizenship assimilated within the national-colonial project and conforming to the Fascist régime's homogenisation of manhood.

Last but not least, a specifically female Orientalist discourse, often dissenting from the most clichéd *topoi* of exotic Orientalism, is found in works written by women as early as the 1840s. Worth of notice are Amalia Nizzoli's travel account *Memorie sull'Egitto* (1841); the remarkable travelogue (originally written in French) *Vita intima e vita nomade in Oriente* (1855) by patriot Cristina di Belgioioso; Annie Vivanti's *Terra di Cleopatra* (1925); Augusta Perricone Violà's *Ricordi somali* (1935); Anna Messina's *Cronache del Nilo* (1940); Fausta Cialente's *Cortile a Cleopatra* (1936) and *Ballata levantina* (1961); and more recently, Erminia dell'Oro's novels with an Orientalist colonial setting *Asmara addio* (1988) and *L'abbandono* (1991).

Cristina Lombardi-Diop

Histories

Becker, Jared M. (1990), 'D'Annunzio, Orientalism, and Imperialism', *Stanford Italian Review* 9 (1–2): 87–103.
Bongie, Chris (1991), *Exotic Memories: Literature, Colonialism, and the Fin de Siècle*, Stanford, CA: Stanford University Press.
Dickie, John (1999), *Darkest Italy*, New York: St Martin's Press.
Moe, Nelson (2002), *The View from Vesuvius: Italian Culture and the Southern Question*, Berkeley, CA: University of California Press.
Schneider, Jane (ed.) (1998), *Italy's Southern Question: Orientalism in One Country*, Oxford: Berg.
Said, Edward (1991), *Orientalismo*, Turin: Bollati Boringhieri.
Tomasello, Giovanna (1984), *La letteratura coloniale italiana dalle avanguardie al fascismo*, Palermo: Sellerio.

Racial Policies

The year 1938 is often identified as the start of racial policies in Italy. That year, a law was promulgated that initiated discriminatory and segregationist policies against all Italian citizens of the Jewish religion, who were henceforth referred to as members of the 'Jewish race'. Yet the chronology of official Italian racism becomes longer if we turn our attention to Italian colonial legislation. Governmental Acts in 1909 and 1914 discouraged marriage between Italian colonial officers and local women by forcing the former to retire and repatriate, while the 1908 colonial civil code made marriage between Italian women and native men virtually impossible. Inter-racial concubinage (only between Italian men and local women, since the opposite union was inconceivable) was tolerated provided that it was not openly acknowledged and only to avoid the more abhorred option of contracting legal marriage. Indeed, Italian men seldom expressed the wish to legalise their informal unions with local women. In addition, most of them did not legitimise their so-called 'mixed-race' offspring despite the fact that the law consented to it (at least until the proclamation of the Empire). The number of children abandoned by their Italian fathers in African colonies was extremely high. This shows that a hierarchical separation of citizens and subjects based on supposed racial differences was in place as a form of widely shared common sense and daily practice in the Italian colonial territory long before Fascist racial laws were imposed. The 1933 Regulation for the Administration of Eritrea and Somalia (L. 6.7.1932 n.999) is the first legal text to use the concept of 'race' as a juridical tool for the definition of political and social rights and status of colonial subjects. It represents the first attempt to classify individuals juridically on biological grounds, a tendency that would be further reinforced during the imperial period.

Despite the legal precedents discussed above, the racial laws of the imperial period mark an important shift in Italian colonial policy. The proclamation of the empire of Italian East Africa (Africa Orientale Italiana) in 1935 brought a series of new laws that introduced and enforced racial segregation within the colonial territory. Such segregation was essential to the maintenance of power within the changed imperial setting. With the conquest of Ethiopia, the colonial territory grew immensely (becoming four times that of Italy). A strict control of the native population – which now numbered about 8–10 million people – was perceived as impossible to achieve. Similarly, it was extremely difficult to prevent Italian citizens from 'going native'. As in other colonial contexts, when European supremacy became vulnerable, colonial governors responded by reinforcing the symbolic and practical separation between citizens and subjects. Thus, the 1936 decree on the administration of the Empire denied natives the possibility of obtaining Italian citizenship, while stating that Italian women who married local men would lose their citizenship. That same year natives were also denied access to public spaces and transport used by citizens. While in 1937 any type of informal inter-racial intimate relationships was forbidden, in 1938 the law was amended also to ban legal marriage between Italians and 'any other race' (thus including Italian Jews). In 1939 it was decreed that any behaviour considered detrimental to racial prestige could be punished with imprisonment, so introducing highly arbitrary principles into colonial jurisprudence. Finally, a 1940 law reassessed the juridical status of 'mixed-race' offspring, including them among the natives.

Apart from the case of Somalia, Italian presence in the Horn of Africa terminated in 1941. From that date and until the 1970s, Italian historiography either avoided a critical exploration of its colonial past or actively promoted the preservation of the myth of Italian colonialism as a 'good' one (*Italiani brava gente*). This belief in Italian colonisers as being more humane than British or French ones is still largely shared among the Italian population. Yet, the few existing studies on African perception of the colonial experience show that former colonial subjects have a very clear and vivid memory of the symbolic and practical violence of Italian colonial racism.

Barbara Sòrgoni

Histories

Barrera, G. (2003a), 'The Construction of Racial Hierarchies in Colonial Eritrea: The
    Liberal and Early Fascist Period (1897–1934),' in P. Palumbo (ed.), *A Place in the Sun.
    Africa in Italian Colonial Culture from Post-Unification to the Present*, Berkeley and Los
    Angeles, CA: University of California Press, pp. 81–115.
— (2003b), 'Mussolini's Colonial Race Laws and State-Settler Relations in Africa
    Orientale Italiana (1935–41),' *Journal of Modern Italian Studies* 8 (3): 425–43.
Del Boca, A. (2006), *Italiani, brava gente?*, Milano: Neri Pozza.
Pankhurst, R. (1969), 'Fascist Racial Policies in Ethiopia, 1922–1941', *Ethiopia Observer*
    12(4): 270–85.
Sòrgoni, B. (2002), 'Racist Discourses and Practices in the Italian Empire under Fascism',
    in R. Grillo and J. Pratt (eds), *The Politics of Recognising Difference: Multiculturalism
    Italian Style*, Aldershot: Ashgate, pp. 41–57.

The Sanusi Order or Sanusiyya, 1837–1932

The Sanusiyya emerged as the most influential socio-religious movement in North Africa
and the Sahara during the second half of the nineteenth century. The Sanusi Order was
founded by an urban Sharifian scholar from Algeria, Muhammad ibn Ali al-Sanusi (1787–
1859), better known as 'the Grand Sanusi'. He was a scholar who had studied in Algeria,
Morocco, Egypt, and al-Hijaz in Arabia. His order, the Sanusiyya, became one of many
resistance movements that appeared in the Middle East and North Africa during the eighteenth and nineteenth centuries. Among these movements were the Wahhabiyya in
Arabia, the Mahdiyya in Sudan, and the Sanusiyya in Cyrenaica and the Sahara.

The decline of the Oriental trade sparked the rise of these resistance movements, as in
the case of the Wahhabi movement in the eighteenth century. The Mahdiyya and the
Sanusiyya emerged as a reaction to the weakening of the Muslim states (Ottoman and
Egyptian), and to counter the British in the Sudan and the French in North Africa. Just as
Sufi movements had led the anti-Iberian attacks on Morocco in the sixteenth century, new
Sufi reformist movements such as the Sanusiyya and Mahdiyya took the initiative to organ-
ise local resistance against European imperialism in the late nineteenth century.

The Grand Sanusi was a committed intellectual influenced by his education and by his
travels in the Muslim world. He studied at Sufi Zawiya in Algeria and then attended the
Qarawiyyin University of Fez in 1805. At al-Qarawiyyin he became aware of Sufi and Shari'a
studies. In 1824, on his pilgrimage to Hijaz, he met his teacher, Ahmad ibn Idris al-Fasi
(1749–1837), a famous scholar who believed in reform and *ijtihad*, free scholarly interpretation of the Shari'a, a return to the original principles of Islam in the Qur'an and the Hadith,
and who criticised rigid *taqlid* (imitation) of the four Sunni schools of Islam. He chose to
settle in Cyrenaica, which had better political conditions than Hijaz, Egypt and Tripolitania.

Al-Sanusi's claim to be a *sharif* and his belief in the Qurayshi kinship qualification meant
he saw Ottoman sultans as illegitimate leaders of the faithful. Moreover, he was aware that
the Ottomans would not accept a rival social movement among rebellious tribesmen like
the one in Cyrenaica, which could threaten Ottoman sovereignty. While he remained on
good terms with the Ottomans through his representative in Benghazi, in 1856 he relocated to the remote oasis of Jaghbub to escape Ottoman influence and surveillance. Similar
reasons prompted his son, Muhammad al-Mahdi (1845–1902), to move the capital of the
order to Kufra, deep in the Sahara, in 1895.

Despite his long association with Sufism, al-Sanusi was critical of some Sufi practices and claims. He disputed the ideals of reaching God-like perfection and withdrawing from daily life, and argued instead that there are many paths to God and that no one must claim the ultimate truth, emphasising simple religious practice, work, production and a commitment to daily life. This reformist vision of Islam, combined with patience and sensitivity to tribal conditions, made the Grand Sanusi successful in building a strong social movement in Cyrenaica.

The ideology of the Sanusiyya stressed austerity, moral commitment and anti-colonial resistance. The main goal of the Sanusi was to build a coherent, unified community through education, work, self-reliance and dependence on local resources. The order was built on an Islamic model of the state – taxation, law, education and mobilisation for *jihad*. The Sanusiyya relied on the North African Sufi institute of *zawiya* or lodge, which began to emerge in the fourteenth century as Sufi orders assumed the leadership of the resistance against the Iberian crusade in Spain and North Africa. The *zawiya* was a place for worshipping, a centre for the followers of a given brotherhood, a sanctuary, and a shrine where the *murabuks* or founders of a brotherhood were buried. Al-Sanusi built his lodges in strategic places, either between tribal boundaries or along trading routes. He attracted tribes to him by providing education for children, a place for the arbitration of disputes, and by allocating land to tribesmen around the *zawiya*. His authority rested on his status as a religious man, a scholar, and a descendant of the Prophet, but it was equally important that he was not linked with any of the tribes of Cyrenaica.

By 1870 a Sanusi lodge was more than a place to worship. It was a mosque, a children's school, a residence of the *shaykh* of the lodge and his family, a guesthouse for travellers, an accommodation for caravans and refugees, and a storehouse for supplies and caravan goods. The Sanusiyya, comprising a de facto state, provided an elaborate socio-economic and legal organisation for the tribes and Sahara trade. The Sanusi network of lodges became an alternative communicational and administrative structure equivalent in strength to the Ottoman state bureaucracy and its town markets in Tripolitania.

The Sanusiyya's success as the major religious social movement in late nineteenth-century North Africa and the Sahara was due to the Sanusi's ability to transcend ethnic and local tribal identifications. The order provided a supratribal and ethnic institution for Sahara trade. It supplied the trade with a network of communicational and bureaucratic structures through its lodges and missionaries. This unity became a key to anti-colonial resistance – more so than in Tripolitania, where factionalism among the notables in the nineteenth century weakened the resistance and led to its defeat in 1922. In Cyrenaica the resistance continued, under Sanusi leadership, until 1932. The grandson of the founder of the Sanusi Order, Idriss al Muhdi al-Sanusi, became the first King of independent Libya from 1951 to 1969.

Ali Abdullah Ahmida

HISTORIES

Ahmida, A. A. (1994), *The Making of Modern Libya, State Formation, Colonialization, and Resistance, 1830–1932*, Albany, NY: State University of New York Press.

Anderson, L. S. (1986), *The State and Social Transformation in Tunisia and Libya, 1830–1980*, Princeton, NJ: Princeton University Press.

Vikor, K. S. (1995), *Sufi and Scholar on the Edge of the Desert*, Evanston, IL: Northwestern University Press.

Somalia before 1935

The Italian occupation of Somalia started in 1889, when after years of efforts and with the support of Great Britain, the Italian consul in Zanzibar acquired a small strip of land on the Benadir coast. The Italian possession on the Somali coast was granted to Vincenzo Filonardi, an Italian consul and entrepreneur. In 1895 Merca, Brava and Mogadishu were bought on concessionary terms (for twenty-five years) from the sultan of Zanzibar. Filonardi's company set out to exploit the resources of the hinterland but soon found out that its means were inadequate to the task. It survived only a few years before it was passed over to another Italian company in 1896. This new company that came to be known as La compagnia di Benadir faced similar financial problems and finally in 1905 the Italian state assumed official responsibility for the areas previously administered by commercial enterprise. The newly unified state of Italy was eager to support companies engaged in furthering its commercial interests. By 1905, Zanzibar was already under British rule, and the Italian colonisation of that part of Somaliland, which later came to be known as Italian Somaliland was carried out with the support of Great Britain.

Although Italy tried to delimit its possession by sending several expeditionary forces, its effective control of Somalia was limited to the coastal areas around Benadir until the beginning of the 1920s.

The rise of Fascism, which coincided more or less with the death of the Mullah, marked a new phase in the colonial relations between Italy and the Somalis. The Fascist state expected a great deal from its colonies and hoped that they would provide the mother country with tropical products. Consequently, the Italian state did what it could to develop the resource base of its semi-desert possession in Somalia. However, up to 1930, the only large-scale agricultural-industrial production remained the one created by the Duke of Abruzzi in 1920, which was colloquially known as Villabruzzi and funded mostly by Milanese capital.

Organised on 25,000 hectares of land some ninety kilometres north-west of Mogadishu, the Villabruzzi grew by 1935 into a successful agricultural consortium of over 30,000 hectares which employed about 4,000 people. Cotton, sugar and bananas were its main products. Most of the land under cultivation was bought. This was in sharp contrast with the imperial praxis of outright confiscation.

With its large labour force, the Villabruzzi looked like a microcosm of Somali society. The hectares devoted to cotton and sugar were cultivated by families organised in ethnic clans who owned their own garden plots, and were paid for their labour. The colonisers accepted the importance of the clan among the Somalis. The system of running a consortium in co-operation with the labour force was in large part based on the scarcity of workers and on the refusal of the Somalis to survive solely on labour wages. The Villabruzzi possessed an intricate road system (close to fifty kilometres) and electricity. Italian staff were quartered in villas according to rank. Less elaborate accommodation was provided for the Somalis who did clerical and technical work. A market and a series of small shops were placed at the centre of the village.

The Villabruzzi soon spawned imitations by other companies on the Genale and Juba. By the 1935, bananas superseded hides and skins as the prime export commodity from Somalia. The Villabruzzi was highly subsidised by the Italian fascist state which was all too eager to reward and subsidise enterprises that fell within its corporatist and autarchic policies. The famous bananas that Villabruzzi produced and exported to Italy were used to persuade the Italian population of the benefits of having colonies.

By 1935 the ports of Italian Somalia (Mogadishu, Chismayo and Brava) were transformed beyond recognition. Mogadishu was reorganised to house more than 50,000 newly arrived Italians. The invasion of Ethiopia, (the preparations for the war had started in earnest since 1932) was to transform Mogadishu (and to some extent the other Somali ports) from a small sleeping port into a busy town with a boisterous Italian population, mostly young members of both the Fascist Party and the Italian armed forces.

The creation of the Italian East African empire (Africa Orientale Italiana, or AOI) occasioned a great deal of rhetoric about Fascism's creation of a new Roman empire. By the end of 1935 Mogadishu had a population of about 30,000 Somalis and 20,000 Italians. Connected by road to the eastern parts of the empire, Somalia and Mogadishu were conceived as the eastern outlets of the Italian Empire.

Italian ambition to impose direct rule did give rise to a series of rebellions. However, the determination of the Fascist state to impose its rule and the generous/lenient way of treating defeated rebels finally led to a quite well centralised colonial rule. The extensive road and communication infrastructure first developed to extend its commercial and economic influence in eastern Ethiopia, contributed to the growth of an inchoate modern economy. However, the Somalis were expressly forbidden from engaging in economic activities that could compete with Italian firms. The introduction of the racial laws soon after the creation of AOI further curtailed the role of the Somalis in the economy of their country.

To ensure its survival, the Italian colonisers based their rule in Somalia on two cardinal principles: the preservation of the dominant clan/ethnic configuration and the respect of local religions. In the case of Somalia, Italy recognised Islam as the religion of the colony and did little to assist Catholic and other Christian denominations. The anti-clerical background of Fascism, despite the Lateran Pact of 1929 between the Vatican and the Italian state, was most probably a contributory factor.

Tekeste Negash

HISTORIES
Lewis, I. M. (1982), *A Modern History of Somalia: Nation and State in the Horn of Africa*, London: Longman.
Hess, R. (1968), *The Italian Colonization of Somalia*, Chicago, IL: University of Chicago Press.
Labanca, N. (2002), *Oltremare. Storia dell´espansione coloniale italiana*, Bologna: Mulino.
Cassanelli, L. C. and Bestelman (eds) (2000), *The Struggle for Land in Southern Somalia: The War Behind the War*, London: Hann.
Tripodi, P. (1999), *The Colonial Legacy in Somalia: Rome and Mogadishu from Colonial Administration to Operation Restore Hope*, Basingstoke: Macmillan.

Women's Histories

Women in Italian Africa are the subjects/objects through which Italy's particular brand of Orientalism unabashedly expressed fantasies of domination of the racialised 'Other'. Although it was Europe's newest state, Italy was no less endowed with imperial arrogance that manifested itself through official colonial propaganda promising a paradise of carnal pleasures. Italian colonial literature, postcards and cinematography represented the female subject as a sensual animal to be conquered, tamed and used as an adornment to the masculine ego of the coloniser. Naked women adorned travel posters and postcards while the ubiquitous Italian photographer in the colonies exposed the bodies of subjugated women of Eritrea, Somalia and Libya to the gaze of the colonial male. The verses and imagery in the (in)famous tunes of *Faccetta Nera*, *Africanina* and *Africanella* all attest to the central yet unenviable place accorded to the women of the colonies.

The imagery and rhetoric of the conquest of the colonies were conceptualised and articulated in gendered terms empowering the coloniser to take possession of the land and its women. The body of the African woman was celebrated as beautiful while simultaneously being denigrated as primitive. Colonial women were labelled as sirens who transformed the Italian male into a beast. Colonial logic ingeniously identified the syndrome of male bestialisation (*imbestialmento*), produced by exposure to the African sun and by the female colonial subject, which absolved the colonising male of sins of racial transgression and which justified concubinage throughout Italian Africa. Variously labelling the colonised women as *madamas* in the Horn and as *mabrukas* in North Africa, Italian colonisers left in their wake frozen images of sexual subjugation and humiliation of the female half of their subjects.

From 1921 to 1941, Fascist propaganda sought to break down the familial ties produced by Italo-African liaisons as well as the reciprocity of daily encounters between settlers and subjects. Colonial women of disparate cultures – from Tripolitania Cyrenaica and Fezzan in Libya; of the Benadir Coast, Majeerteen Sultanate and the Hobyo Sultanate; from the Savannah areas on the Ethio-Sudanese borders; the *altipiani* and Red Sea coastal areas to the Dahlak Archipelago – were all lumped into the single category of 'servants of the empire'.

With the demise of Italy's African Empire the indignities and atrocities inflicted on the colonised were expressed by the rejection of Italian trusteeship in the post-Fascist era. The one exception – Somalia's ten-year administration by Italy – was dictated more by fears of imperial Ethiopia's territorial claims. A number of excellent works emerged in the third quarter of the twentieth century that broke the silence on the colonial past and encouraged more dialogue on the legacy of gendered colonialism. Unfortunately, while one school of scholars has embarked on challenging colonial ideologies, the older and entrenched Orientalist school continues to produce knowledge embedded in hyperbole, lascivious imagery and rhetoric of the past. Pier Paolo Pasolini's *Fiore delle mille e una nottte* (*Arabian Nights*, 1974) exemplifies the inability of even Italy's anti-fascist radical intelligentsia to extricate itself from these colonial fantasies. Today, these images of naked women of Italian colonies in Africa continue to be circulated throughout the print and web-based mass media.

Ruth Iyob

HISTORIES

Barrera, G. (1996), 'Dangerous Liaisons: Colonial Concubinage in Eritrea 1890–1941,' *African Studies Program in Working Papers 1*.

Ben-Ghiat, R. (2001), *Fascist Modernities: Italy, 1922–1945*, Berkeley, CA: University of California Press.

Burgio, A. (ed.) (1999), *Nel nome della razza: il razzismo nella storia d'Italia, 1870–1945*, Bologna: il Mulino.

McClintock, A. (1991), *Imperial Leather: Race, Gender and Sexuality in the Colonial Context*, London: Routledge.

Sòrgoni, B. (1998), *Parole e Corpi: antropoligia, discorso giuridico e politiche sessuali interrazziali nella colonia Eritrea*, Naples: Liguori Editore.

The Netherlands and its Colonies

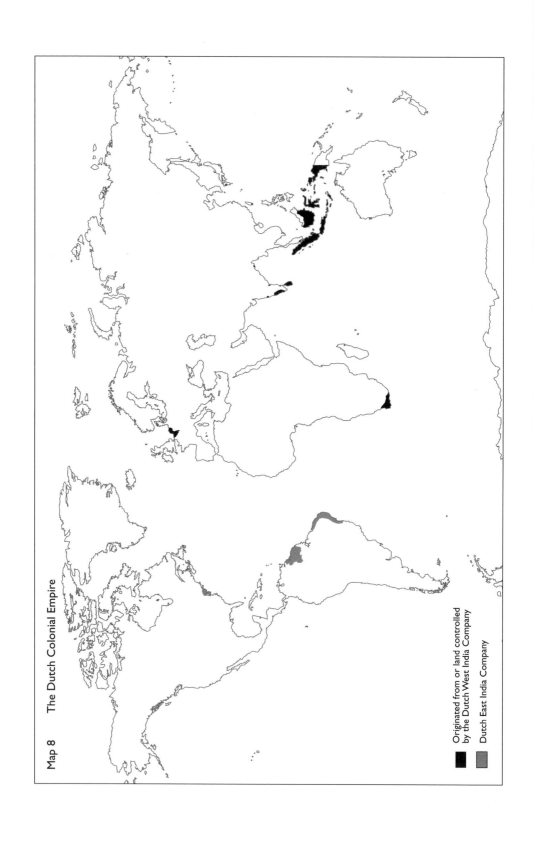

Map 8   The Dutch Colonial Empire

Originated from or land controlled
by the Dutch West India Company

Dutch East India Company

The Netherlands and its Colonies: Introduction

The Dutch burst on the colonial scene at the very beginning of the seventeenth century. They had just gained their de facto independence from the Spanish in the wars of religion then laying waste Europe. The sack of Antwerp by Spanish troops in 1585 had led to a vast exodus of financiers and tradesmen from that city. During the sixteenth century the main trading and financial hub of Western Europe, and of Protestants from what is (roughly) present-day Belgium, to the northern parts of what had until then been the Spanish Low Countries.

The influx of skilled labour and capital gave a tremendous boost especially to the counties of Holland and Zeeland, together forming the western parts of the present-day Netherlands. Amsterdam quickly replaced Antwerp as the trade and financial centre of north-western Europe; but many lesser towns such as Haarlem, Middelburg, Leyden and Rotterdam also developed rapidly. For their defence from the Spanish the Dutch were dependent upon the sea, and they quickly developed a powerful merchant navy, dominating the North Sea, and afterwards the oceans at large. During the so-called Dutch Golden Age, spanning roughly the first three quarters of the seventeenth century, the Dutch spread far and wide, colonising parts of three continents. In the Americas they first held present-day New York and the Hudson Valley, and parts of Brazil, and later the Netherlands Antilles and Suriname. In Asia they largely replaced the Portuguese, concentrating upon present-day Indonesia, but they also had settlements in Japan, present-day India, Taiwan and Ceylon. In Africa they at one time ruled most of present-day South Africa, and held forts and slaving and trading posts along the West African coast. Towards the end of the seventeenth and over the course of the eighteenth centuries the relatively small size of the Netherlands, also in terms of population as well as geographically and the rise of powerful rivals such as France, but especially Britain, led to the loss of the North American colonies, and of most of the Asian holdings outside present-day Indonesia. Brazil was lost to the Portuguese again, and strongholds along the West African coast fell to other powers, amongst them the slaving island of Goeree, near Dakar, which eventually went to the French. In the beginning of the nineteenth century South Africa was lost to the British. What finally remained were the East Indies, present-day Indonesia, the Dutch West Indies, present-day Suriname and the islands of Aruba, Curaçao and Bonaire, and half of Sint-Maarten/Saint-Martin.

In the Dutch East Indies it was the Dutch Verenigde Oost-Indische Compagnie or VOC (Dutch East India Company), founded in 1602, which established Dutch control under its ruthless Governor-General, Jan Pieterszoon Coen. In the course of the seventeenth century, the VOC eliminated all rivals and took control of the archipelago, and of the entire spice chain, from production in the Moluccas, through shipping from the colonial capital Batavia, to auction in Amsterdam. Batavia became the Asian capital of all VOC-operations east of the Cape, ruling a maritime and commercial empire that stretched from Deshima in Japan to the coast of Coromandel, and from Ceylon to the Moluccas. The success of this first multinational company lasted until its demise in 1799.

In the West Indies, the Dutch in 1630 seized Saint-Martin for its large salt deposits. After the Spanish had reconquered the island, the Dutch West India Company (WIC) took possession of Curaçao in 1634. Bonaire and Aruba were captured in 1636. The WIC colonised and governed the Leeward Islands until 1791. After 1648, Curaçao and Sint-Eustatius became centres for smuggling, privateering and the slave trade. Curaçao and Bonaire never developed plantations because of the arid climate. Dutch merchants and Sephardic Jewish merchants on Curaçao sold trade goods and slaves from Africa to the plantation colonies and the Spanish mainland. On Bonaire, the salt was exploited; and cattle were bred for trade and food on Curaçao.

In Africa, the Dutch, under Jan van Riebeeck, in 1652 established a settlement at the Cape of Good Hope with the purpose of providing fresh food, water and medical facilities to VOC-ships en route between the Netherlands and Asia. At the Cape a distinctive Dutch African or Boer order emerged. The so-called *trekboers* moved eastwards, and in 1779 the first of nine frontier wars broke out between white settlers and the Xhosa in the eastern Cape.

The Napoleonic period cost the Dutch a large part of their colonial empire. Thomas Stamford Raffles ruled the Dutch East Indies as Governor-General for the British between 1811 and 1816, but Dutch rule was restored by the Vienna Conference. Java and the other Dutch possessions in the archipelago now became part of a colony known as Nederlandsch Indië (the Netherlands Indies). In the West the British occupied Curaçao between 1801 and 1803, and from 1807 until 1816. South Africa came under British rule too during this period, and was definitively lost for the Dutch in 1815.

During the nineteenth century the Dutch, whose effective rule in Indonesia until then had largely been limited to parts of Java, Celebes (present-day Sulawesi), and Sumatra, moved to subdue the entire Indonesian archipelago. Indonesian resistance was systematically crushed. Java was turned into an enormous plantation system, growing crops for the European markets – tobacco, coffee, tea, sugar, indigo, quinine and of course the spices – under the so-called *cultuurstelsel* (cultivation system). This system of exploitation and cultivation has been the subject of fiery political and economic discussion ever since the publication of the anti-colonial novel *Max Havelaar, or the Coffee Auctions of the Dutch Trading Company* (1860) by the Dutch author Multatuli, penname for Edward Douwes Dekker. On the one hand, the Dutch were praised for running Indonesia like a model colony. On the other hand there were those who, like Multatuli, exposed the enormous human cost of this system. The key point of the whole system was the policy of the *batig slot*, the surplus made on the colonial budget, which was used to fund the economic development of the mother country. Over the nineteenth century, an estimated 1 billion guilders in colonial profits was used to build the railway system in Holland; and to fund the little war with Belgium in 1830, and even to fund the economic compensation for the abolition of slavery in the Caribbean and Suriname in 1863.

In the West Indies, Dutch administrators and merchants formed the white élite, Sephardim were the commercial élite. Poor whites and free blacks formed the nucleus of the small Creole middle class, slaves were the lowest class. Because of the absence of commercial, labour-intensive plantation agriculture, race relations were relatively good. The Roman Catholic Church played an important role in the repression of African culture, the legitimisation of slavery, and preparations for emancipation. Slave rebellions occurred in 1750 and 1795 on Curaçao and slavery was abolished in 1863. An independent peasantry did not arise because blacks remained economically dependent on their former owners.

The Cape remained a historical backwater for Europe until the British acquired it in 1815. This stimulated Afrikaner nationalism. From 1834 the 'Great Trek' of the Afrikaners into the interior of Africa led to bloody conflicts with the indigenous population, most famously with the Zulus at Blood River in 1838. In 1852 the Transvaal Boers were granted independence at the Sand River Convention, and in 1854 the trekkers were given British permission to establish two independent Boer republics. In the 1860s indentured labourers from India arrived to work on the sugar plantations on the east coast. The discovery of diamonds in the northern Cape in 1866–7 and gold on the Witwatersrand in 1886 almost overnight turned the colony into a valuable possession. Jewish, German, Greek, Portuguese and Italian immigrants flooded the country. The first (1880) and second (1899–1902) Anglo-Boer Wars brought the Boers to their knees, but only after 25,000 Boers – mainly women and children – had died in British concentration camps.

From 1900 on the policy of colonial exploitation in Indonesia was succeeded by the so-called *ethische politiek* (ethical policy), the Dutch equivalent of the 'white man's burden'. Heralded by Multatuli, the new idea was that the colonies should not merely be exploited but also developed. Colonial profits should be invested in the region itself. At the same time, this new ethical mission served as an excuse for the continuation of Dutch colonial rule, certainly in the eyes of its two main architects, Governor-General Van Heutsz, who effected the political unification of the archipelago under central control from Batavia, and his adjutant Hendrik Colijn, who later on became the most dominant Dutch politician of the pre-World War II period.

World War II spelled the end of the Dutch colonial empire in the East. In 1942 the Dutch were defeated in the Netherlands Indies by the Japanese, and they never recovered from this blow. After a three-year Japanese occupation, on 17 August 1945, the Indonesian leaders Sukarno and Hatta declared the independence of the new republic. Over the following years they bested the Dutch through guerrilla warfare and United Nations diplomacy. The Dutch officially handed over sovereignty in December 1949.

In the Dutch Antilles, the establishment of oil refineries on Curaçao and Aruba marked the beginning of industrialisation. Thousands of workers from the other Antillean islands and Suriname, civil servants from the Netherlands and Suriname, and trade minorities such as the Lebanese, Ashkenazim, Portuguese and Chinese flocked to the islands. Industrialisation ended colonial race relations. The Protestant and Sephardim élites on Curaçao retained their positions in commerce, civil service, and politics, but the black masses were no longer dependent on them for employment and land. The introduction of general suffrage in 1949 resulted in the formation of non-religious political parties, and the Catholic Church lost much of its influence. Within the state bureaucracy and the educational system, Antilleans replaced Dutch expatriates. Afro-Antillean cultural traditions were revalued, racial ideology was changed, and Papiamentu became the national language on Curaçao and Bonaire.

In 1910 the Union of South Africa became a self-governing dominion within the British Empire. Both Boer and Briton were represented in the cabinet, but not the indigenous black majority. Black dissatisfaction led to the formation of the African National Congress (ANC) in 1912. Afrikaner nationalism developed fast and in 1914 the National Party (NP) was founded. In 1948, the Afrikaner Nationalists under D. F. Malan gained power and immediately began to put into place a system of territorial, social and political segregation, known as 'apartheid'. This came to an end only when F. W. de Klerk, who in 1989 had become President, legalised the ANC, released Nelson Mandela, and began to negotiate a new political dispensation.

During the period of apartheid the Dutch, whose language is at the origin of the Afrikaans spoken in South Africa, studiously shunned any official or political involvement, even though there was at least some continued immigration from the Netherlands. Since the end of apartheid the Netherlands has shown a warm interest in South African politics, art and literature. Whereas during the period immediately after Indonesian independence a sense of loss pervaded Dutch society, summarised in the cliché '*Indië verloren, rampspoed geboren*' ('Indonesia lost means disaster'), and the colonial past of the Netherlands was routinely muted. Ever since the 1980s there has been a renewed interest in the East Indies, which expresses itself in numerous picture books glorifying *tempo doeloe*, and manifold manifestations, bazaars, cultural festivals, plus a rich literature evoking the Dutch involvement with Indonesia, most often written by the descendants of ex-colonials, themselves often of mixed descent. In Indonesia itself, Dutch has practically disappeared, as the Dutch, unlike the French or British, never imposed their language as the general instrument for administration or trade. Writing in Dutch in or from the former Dutch East Indies is therefore almost non-existent. In the West Indies Dutch continues as the language of administration, and also literature. There has also been large-scale immigration from the Dutch West Indies to the Netherlands. In general, European expansion, and Dutch colonial expansion in particular, are now avidly studied in the Netherlands, regularly still giving rise to controversies over the role the Dutch played in their former colonies.

> Luc Allofs, Annemie van Niekerk, Reinier Salverda and Theo Dh'aen

LITERARY WORKS
Multatuli [1860] (1982), *Max Havelaar, or the Coffee Auctions of the Dutch Trading Company*, Amherst, MA: University of Massachusetts Press.
Schoeman, Karel (1996), *Verkenning* (1998), *Verliesfontein* (2002), *Armosyn van die Kaap: voorspel tot vestiging, 1415–1651*, Cape Town: Human and Rousseau.
Venter, F. A. (1960), *Geknelde land* (1960), *Offerland* (1966), *Gelofteland* (1968), *Bedoelde land*, Cape Town: Tafelberg.

HISTORIES
Alofs, Luc and Leo Dalhuisen (1997), *Geschiedenis van de Antillen: Aruba, Bonaire, Curaçao, Saba, Sint Eustacius, Sint Maarten*, Zutphen: Walburg Pers.
Boxer, Charles (1965), *The Dutch Seaborne Empire*, New York: Alfred A. Knopf.
Davenport, T. R. H. and C. Saunders (2000), *South Africa: A Modern History*, London: Macmillan.
Resink, G. J. (1968), *Indonesia's History between the Myths. Essays in Legal History and Historical Theory*, The Hague: W. van Hoeve.
Taylor, Jean Gelman (2003), *Indonesia. Peoples and Histories*, New Haven, CT and London: Yale University Press.

Anthropology and Ethnography

EAST INDIES – INDONESIA
In the first part of the twentieth century, there was an unrivalled production of Dutch scholarly publications on practically all aspects of Indonesian culture. There were many active research institutes, but the two key centres responsible for this production were, in Leiden, the Koninklijk Instituut voor Taal- Land- en Volkenkunde (Royal Institute of

Anthropology and Linguistics), and in Batavia (now Jakarta), the Bataviaas Genootschap (Batavian Society).

Javanese culture, for example, was the focus of wide-ranging research activities in practically every field of the humanities and cultural disciplines. This has resulted in many standard works – on Hindu-Javanese art (N. J. Krom), *gamelan* and *kraton* ceremonies (J. Groneman), textiles and *batik* (G. E. Rouffaer and H. H. Juynboll), Javanese magic and the spiritual world (H. A. van Hien), *wayang* (J. Kats), traditional crafts (J. E. Jasper and Mas Pirngadie), history (W. Fruin-Mees), music (J. Kunst), language, literature and popular theatre (Th. Pigeaud). Many other Dutch scholars studied the religion, *adat* and traditions of the Javanese. Archaeologists such as Van Erp and Stutterheim investigated and restored the temples of Borobudur and Prambanan in central Java. When the Indian poet and Nobel Prize laureate Rabindranath Tagore visited the Borobudur temple in Central Java in 1927, they and others deeply impressed him by their 'love of knowledge' and 'warm-heartedness'. In 1935, the Sonobudoyo museum of Javanese antiquities was opened in Yogyakarta. The Java-Instituut played a key role here, and all this culminated in the encyclopaedic handbook *Land en volk van Java* (Lekkerkerker 1938). In Dutch journals and magazines such as *Djåwå, Cultureel Indië* and *Indië Oud en Nieuw* one could regularly read reports on these Javanese studies. Meanwhile the impact of Java on Dutch culture was studied by G. Brom in his *Java in onze kunst* (1931).

This Javanism, with its aristocratic worldview and its cultural, artistic, literary, scholarly, philological and historical-archaeological ramifications, was then the most highly developed form of Dutch Orientalism. Until 1942, this was the key to the political and cultural understanding between the Dutch colonial élite and the Javanese aristocracy it had co-opted into the administration of the Netherlands Indies. The central focus here was on the ancient Hindu-Javanese court culture of the self-governing principalities in central Java, in particular the refined and richly varied cultural traditions of the *kratons* in Solo and Yogyakarta. This was well researched as Johan Huizinga at the time studied the court culture of the Burgundians in his famous *The Waning of the Middle Ages*. But as a corollary, hardly any attention was paid to the contemporary, dynamic, mixed, vulgar, urban street culture of the Islamic common people in the poorer city *kampongs*.

In Leiden, at the same time, there was an immense programme of Indonesian legal studies and anthropology of law undertaken by van Vollenhoven, whose work, like that of so many Dutch Orientalists, was characterised by deep love and respect for the Indonesians and their language, culture, morals and customs. Linguists, anthropologists, historians, economists, ethnographers, literary scholars and philologists all followed suit, as did the vulcanologists, mining experts, geologists, doctors, cartographers, missionaries and many others. Their Orientalism and their lasting scholarly results have greatly contributed to the international renown of Dutch scholarship and have laid a basis on which other scholars have subsequently been able to build, notably Clifford Geertz's *Religion of Java* (1960) and *The Interpretation of Cultures* (1973), and Koentjaraningrat's *Javanese Culture* (1985).

It is an interesting question to ask to what extent these academics and their scholarly pursuits were complicit in the colonial enterprise. Was Snouck Hurgronje an enlightened scholar of Islam and Acheh, or was he really an accomplice in the Dutch war of subjugation against the Achenese? Were the founders of the Sonobudoyo museum freezing Javanese culture in time and representing it as a highly ornamental but static élite culture, or did they mean to contribute to the modernisation and revitalisation of traditional Javanese arts and crafts? There are Dutch libraries full of the most wonderful learning, erudition and understanding, in works produced by scholars with a deep love for all things Indonesian. Does their scholarship lose any of its quality and validity for having been produced under different historic, and in particular colonial conditions? The answer is not simple. The point here is rather that this critical question – free inquiry or complicity? – was never seriously explored in colonial days, and has had to wait till a much later date, in the postcolonial era.

Reinier Salverda

ANTHROPOLOGY IN THE DUTCH CARIBBEAN

Dutch Caribbean societies show characteristics similar to those of other former slave societies in the Americas in terms of social organisation, cultural customs and religious practices. Cultural forms and expressions are influenced by ethnic and racial provenance. Anthropological studies mark the Dutch Caribbean as an example of a plural society. Though the different social and ethnic orders do have contact with one another, there is little actual mixing. Each group sticks to its own religion, language and way of life. Rudolf van Lier's 1949 study of Suriname suggested the idea of a frontier society where contact with other groups triggers an acculturation process. René A. Römer (2000) explores the ongoing process of acculturation on Curaçao. He defines this phenomenon as the fusion of elements from different cultural sources which give birth to a new culture with characteristics of the various original cultures. In the case of the Netherlands Antilles these influences are Dutch, African, Latin American, Jewish, African and nowadays also North American. In Suriname, the main influences are of Amerindian, African, European and East Asian origin.

Anthropological studies of the Dutch Caribbean have largely concentrated on groups of African descent, such as the Creoles and the Maroons; the latter are descended from runaway slaves in Suriname. Their communities go back to the eighteenth century. The four main Maroon groups (Ndjukas, Saramaccan, Matawai, Boni), entered upon a truce with the Dutch colonial authorities in the late eighteenth century. This allowed them to settle outside the plantation zone. They have been the object of extensive scrutiny regarding the question of retention of African cultural form in the new world. The Herskovits analysis (1934) of the cultural life of Surinamese Maroon communities during the 1920s has been crucial in shaping later understandings of the formation and development of culture in former slave societies. Since the publication of their first findings, the question of the 'roots' of Afro-Caribbean cultures in the Dutch Caribbean has evolved into two schools of thought. One of these privileges the notion of a quick synthesis of African cultures in the New World through a process of creolisation. The other school highlights the retention and survival of African customs in spite of physical uprooting and geographical distance. Mintz and Price (1992) have argued that a uniquely creolised culture has evolved, showing African, Amerindian and European influences.

Among the Creole group, European and African influences attest to the possibility of cultural synthesis within the plantation system as black and whites were not hermetically separate. The fact that the black population far exceeded the white settlers in numbers also allowed for the development, often in secrecy, of a culture particular to the slave communities. For example, the *watramama* dance, a celebration of the water goddess, was forbidden by the slaveholders because of its supposedly seditious character. Still, it survived in secret performances. Stipriaan's research into the pattern of social relations on plantations underlines the informal ties which preceded biological ties. Symbolic or social foundations determined kinship. The term *sippi* was first used to describe the bond between slaves who had arrived on the same ship; later it was also used for slaves of a same plantation (Price 1973).

The existence of African-based religious systems in Curaçao and Suriname attests to the syncretic character of Dutch Caribbean societies. *Winti*, a belief system that relies on a cult of ancestors, rituals, the use of herbal medicines and supernatural forces to provide healing and relief emerged among slaves in Suriname. On Curaçao, spiritual sessions known as *Monamentu*, close to the Haitian *Vodun* and *Brúa* (Papiamentu for magic) have an important social function. Magic is used to appeal to supernatural forces to obtain results in a personal matter or predicament and is combined with chants, herbal medicines and rituals. African influences can be felt in musical forms (for example, *tambú*: both a dance and the instrument it is danced to, a drum) and in the story-telling tradition of *Anancy* tales.

Hitherto, relatively little anthropological attention has been paid to the Amerindian population of the Dutch Caribbean. Yet they were the first to be encountered by Spanish and English explorers to the region, and in Suriname their presence continues. Peter Hulme's extensive research into the representation of native Indians in travel accounts of the first explorers highlights how the early emphasis on the supposed opposition between peaceful Indians versus bloodthirsty cannibals shaped Europe's vision of the New World as a mythical Eldorado peopled with fantastic creatures. Hulme (1993, 1986), and with him Whitehead (1995), argue that these early views of the Caribbean obliterated the plural character of ethnic identities at the time of arrival of the Europeans. During the colonial and slave period the Amerindian population remained separate from the settlers and their plantations both culturally and geographically. Their societies continued to exist but had little interaction with the newer colonial society, save for contacts with runaway slave communities. Little is known about the Amerindian tribes prior to colonisation except through oral transmission of surviving groups and reconstruction based on archaeological finds. To this day, the remaining Amerindian tribes are to be found mainly in the Surinamese interior where Carib Indians and other indigenous peoples live alongside Maroons and Brazilian Garimpeiros mining for gold.

Patricia Krus

HISTORIES

Groot, Hans (2006), *Van de Grote Rivier naar het Koningsplein: het Bataviasch Genootschap van Kunsten en Wetenschappen, 1778–1867*, Ph.D. dissertation, Leiden University.

Herskovits, Melville J. and Frances S. Herskovits (1934), *Rebel Destiny: Among the Bush Negroes of Dutch Guiana*, New York: Whittlesey House.

Koentjaraningrat, R. M. (1985), *Javanese Culture*, Singapore: Oxford University Press.

Kuitenbrouwer, Maarten (2001), *Tussen oriëntalisme en wetenschap. Het Koninklijk Instituut voor Taal- Land- en Volkenkunde in historisch verband, 1851–2001*, Leiden: KITLV Press.

Mintz, Sidney and Richard Price (1992), *The Birth of African and American Culture: An Anthropological Perspective*, Boston, MA: Beacon Press.

Price, Richard (ed.) (1973), *Maroon Societies: Rebel Slave Communities in the Americas*, Garden City, NY: Anchor Press.

Whitehead, Neil (ed.) (1995), *Wolves from the Sea: Readings in the Anthropology of the Native Caribbean*, Leiden: KITLV Press.

Anti-colonial Resistance

EAST INDIES – INDONESIA

Just as the Arabs, the Portuguese and the Spanish before them, so the Dutch came to the Indonesian archipelago driven by their desire for the spice trade. They quickly established themselves as the dominant force, remaining in power from early in the seventeenth till the middle of the twentieth century. In the early part of the twentieth century there was a widespread belief amongst the Dutch that the whole archipelago had been theirs for some 350 years, and that they had always ruled it wisely, as a model colony, bringing law and order, justice, peace and trade, civilisation, progress and development to the girdle of emerald. But in actual fact, there have always been Indonesian rebellions and uprisings against the Dutch. As the Indonesian historian Sartono Kartodirdjo has said: 'The History of Java is the history of peasant revolt.'

During the Dutch East India Company (VOC) era (1602–1799), supremacy was established in the first half of the seventeenth century. When the Dutch arrived on Java, the spice trade was still concentrated in the sultanate of Bantam on the north-west coast of Java. But having established their own colonial capital, Batavia, some hundred miles to the east in the Jakarta area, the Dutch proceeded to strangle the Bantam trade through a permanent naval blockade. Similarly, they chased away the Portuguese, the Spanish and the British from the Moluccas. And when the Bandanese did not comply with the monopolistic clauses in the treaties the VOC had concluded with them, Jan Pieterszoon Coen took the island by force and extinguished the native population, thus establishing total control over the production of spices. The same approach was applied everywhere – trade where possible, but with a strong preference for Dutch domination and the elimination of any competition. All resistance appeared to be in vain, when, through total control over the Indonesian seas, the indigenous ports around the archipelago, especially Malacca and Macassar, were taken, and all foreign competition terminated.

Later that same century, the VOC became a powerful player in the interior of Java. Through skilful diplomacy, effective divide and rule, and the efficient use of superior military and naval forces, the unstoppable VOC managed to win victory for its native allies, but as these had usually been the weaker party in the conflict, they now became dependent on their new masters, the Dutch. In the eighteenth century, the VOC maintained its supremacy by the same means. Bantam was finished off, other local rulers were made dependent, and an uprising such as that of the Chinese gangs roaming the countryside around Batavia was repaid with the merciless week-long slaughter of all the Chinese living within its walls in 1745.

After the British intermezzo under Raffles, the Dutch were given back their eastern possessions, but they had to fight to regain control. The great Java war (1825–30), led by the Javanese prince Diponegoro, could only be brought to an end when the Dutch lured him into negotiations in Magelang, then captured and exiled him to Macassar. Even after this, however, the local population in Magelang continued to worship him and bring weekly offerings to the house where he had been taken prisoner. Such simple acts of passive resistance kept the memory of Diponegoro's heroic, if unsuccessful, fight alive, and for this reason the Javanese painter Raden Saleh was forbidden by the colonial government to visit Magelang in the 1880s, when he wanted to make a historic painting of Diponegoro's capture. Once it was finished, his painting was immediately taken to Holland, where for decades it hung as a trophy in one of the Dutch monarchy's outlying palaces, Bronbeek in Arnhem.

Throughout the nineteenth century and the first half of the twentieth centuries, the Dutch pursued a policy of establishing total control over the archipelago. From 1873, Dutch imperialism carried everything before it, with the subjugation, successively, of Acheh, the interior of Sulawesi, the islands of Lombok and Flores, and in the early years of the twentieth century, the bloody conquest of Bali. Dutch domination, the Pax Neerlandica and the political unification of the archipelago were achieved through the military campaigns of the Royal Netherlands Indies Army (KNIL, Koninklijk Nederlands Indisch Leger), with its use of modern weaponry and terror tactics against the native population.

Many Indonesians, however, bowed but never gave in. With the arrival of Indonesian nationalism, new uprisings followed, in the 1920s especially, which were as harshly as ever suppressed by the Dutch. However, there now was a new spirit of anti-colonial defiance, and in 1925 Mohammad Hatta could write that the violence used by the colonial Dutch showed they had lost the moral argument, and this heralded the end of their reign. But being more or less powerless themselves, the Indonesian nationalists, inspired by Gandhi's non-co-operation, focused on acts of passive, cultural and symbolic defiance against the Dutch – the idea of Indonesian unity and the use of the Indonesian language – while at the same time raising parliamentary questions in the People's Council (Volksraad), about the injustice and repression meted out to them.

After World War II, during the four years of the Indonesian war of independence (1945–49), the Dutch were confronted by widespread Indonesian guerrilla warfare. It was a very dirty war, with campaigns of terror and counter-terror raging everywhere. But the Indonesians also engaged in political and psychological warfare. Preserving the memory of those who had fought the Dutch in earlier wars, they built up a pantheon of heroes of the Indonesian revolution. They also sent artists into the villages, where they would perform *wayang* (shadow puppetry) plays about the Dutch-Indonesian conflict. Amongst the living, their leader Soekarno became a symbol of their political aspirations. For the Indonesians he was not only the man who proclaimed independence and the founding father of their republic, but also the charismatic *ratoe adil* (just ruler) known from ancient Javanese mythology.

For the Dutch, in contrast, Soekarno was the untrustworthy Javanese incarnate – a dangerous, opportunistic populist, a corrupt and incorrigible womaniser, and above all an Indonesian collaborator with the Japanese enemy. They believed, as they had done for a long time, that they knew what ordinary Indonesians wanted. Thus, to the end, they misjudged how successfully Indonesian leaders had mobilised native culture against the restoration and continuation of Dutch colonial rule.

Reinier Salverda

SOUTH AFRICA

The establishment of Dutch colonial rule at the Cape in 1652 was the beginning of the tumultuous contact between indigenous southern African people, especially the San and Khoikhoi, and West European culture. The Khoikhoi's attempts to hang onto their ancestral land, as well as the competition for grazing land, gave way to clashes. In 1779 the first of nine frontier wars broke out between white Afrikaans settlers pushing east and the Xhosa in the eastern Cape. South African colonial writing, most often in Afrikaans, often presents the Boer trekkers as either victims or heroes in their bloody encounters with the indigenous people, while writing in indigenous languages has tried to redress the balance.

Under the Union of South Africa, as of 1910, Boers and Brits were represented in the cabinet. The indigenous majority, however, was excluded. Black dissatisfaction led to the formation of the African National Congress (ANC) in 1912. Tension intensified and in 1913 the Natives Land Act was passed, limiting black land ownership to existing tribal territories. Afrikaner nationalism developed quickly and in 1914 the National Party (NP) was founded. Racial discrimination became increasingly evident when in 1936 all black people were removed from the common voters' roll in the Cape, and the Native Trust and Land Act restricted black people to only 13 per cent of the total land. In 1948, the Afrikaner Nationalists installed 'apartheid'; in 1949 racially mixed marriages were banned. In 1950 the Population Registration Act, the Group Areas Act, the Separate Representation of Voters Act, the Suppression of Communism Act and the Immorality Act were passed. The last prohibited sexual intercourse between different race groups; in 1953 the Bantu Education Act and Separate Amenities Act were passed. These laws fuelled international hostility and black resistance. The ANC launched its defiance campaign in 1952, and in 1955 the 'Freedom Charter' was adopted by the 'Congress of the People'. The government retaliated with more repressive laws, and in 1956 all coloured people were also removed from the voters' roll.

South Africa's resistance politics was further fuelled when in 1960 sixty-nine black people were killed at Sharpeville, while demonstrating against pass laws. This was followed with a flood of bans in the 1960s and 1970s. The ANC and Pan-Africanist Congress (PAC) were the first to be banned; world condemnation followed. South Africa was forced out of the Commonwealth and into becoming a republic in 1961. More international sanctions, such as the sports boycott, followed. The ANC formed an armed wing, Umkhonto weSizwe ('Spear of the Nation') and embarked on a campaign of limited sabotage that resulted in the arrest of Nelson Mandela and other activists. In 1964 Nelson Mandela, Walter Sisulu and others were sentenced for treason to life imprisonment on Robben Island. This was followed by decades of toughening of internal security.

The 1960s and 1970s saw an increase in the use of writing as a tool of protest against the apartheid régime, especially in the work of André P. Brink and Breyten Breytenbach. But later writers returned to this period in their work, for instance Karel Schoeman. Gradually the apartheid system became untenable, because of worker opposition and international sanctions. In the 16 June 1976 Soweto uprising against the imposition of Afrikaans in black schools 600 school children died. Successive states of emergency failed to break the resistance. International opprobrium and resistance mounted. In 1977 the United Nations Security Council imposed a mandatory arms embargo against South Africa; and in that year the death of PAC leader Steve Biko in prison caused an international uproar. The atrocities committed during this period came to light before the Truth and Reconciliation Commission installed after 1994. The victory of the ANC in the first democratic election on 27 April 1994 led South African writers to collect their experiences on this historic day in a volume entitled *S. A. 27 April 1994* (1994). On 10 May 1994 Nelson Mandela became the country's first black president. Soon after the elections international sanctions were lifted. The new constitution was signed into law on 10 December 1996.

Annemie van Niekerk

LITERARY WORKS

Breytenbach, Breyten [1983] (1985), *The True Confessions of an Albino Terrorist*, New York: Farrar, Strauss and Giroux.

Brink, André (1979), *A Dry White Season*, London: Allen Lane.

Krog, Antjie (1998), *Country of My Skull*, Cape Town: Random.

Toer, Pramoedya Ananta [1980] (1990–1), *The Buru Quartet* (*This Earth of Mankind*, *Child of All Nations*, *Footsteps*, and *House of Glass*), Harmondsworth: Penguin.

HISTORIES

Beinart, W. (1994), *Twentieth-Century South Africa*, Cape Town: Oxford University Press.

Davenport, T. R. H. and C. Saunders (2000), *South Africa: A Modern History*, London: Macmillan.

Kartodirdjo, Sartono (1966), *The Peasant Revolt of Banten in 1888: Its Conditions, Course and Sequel. A Case Study of Social Movements in Indonesia*, 's-Gravenhage: Nijhoff.

Legêne, Susan (1998), *De bagage van Blomhoff en Van Breugel: Japan, Java, Tripoli en Suriname in de negentiende-eeuwse Nederlandse cultuur van het imperialisme*, Amsterdam: Koninklijk Instituut voor de Tropen.

Worden, N. and C. Crais (1994), *Breaking the Chains: Slavery and its Legacy in the Nineteenth-Century Cape Colony*, Johannesburg: Witwatersrand University Press.

Edgar Cairo

The Surinamese author Edgar Cairo produced a large and varied oeuvre in the 1970s and 1980s comprising some twenty works, some several hundred pages long, and all written quickly. In 1968 he became a student of Dutch and General and Comparative Literature at Amsterdam University. Occasionally he published in two languages simultaneously, he himself translating his text from Sranan into Suriname-Dutch. Cairo was also an excellent performer of his own work.

It was his singular use of language that made him famous within Dutch-Caribbean literature. He fashioned a heavily regionalised Suriname-Dutch which was also labelled 'Cairoan', because it is unique to him. In theoretical reflections on the subject Cairo defended the use of 'Cairoan' over that of 'Algemeen Beschaafd Nederlands' (Standard Dutch) because of the former's supposedly superior ability to express Surinamese identity over and against the Dutch colonial heritage, and as a vehicle for a distinct Surinamese culture. Via his creolised Dutch, Cairo argued for a creolised 'buffer culture' as the meeting ground for the various ethnic and linguistic groups in Suriname and in the Netherlands. Suriname-Dutch would then serve as a symbol for what was proper to Suriname and at the same time enrich what the Curaçaon linguist and author Frank Martinus Arion has memorably called 'North Sea Dutch'.

Michiel van Kempen distinguishes between five stages in Edgar Cairo's use of language. In his early work Cairo uses pure Sranan and provides a translation into Dutch. Next, he uses Standard Dutch for the narrative passages, and Sranan for dialogues. Then he cobbles together his own form of Sranan–'Cairoan'. As his main reading public was increasingly made up of Europeans, he returned to Standard Dutch, but infused it with African idioms. Finally, he employed Standard Dutch again, but parodying Middle Dutch, and with all kinds of linguistic idiosyncracies.

Apart from the centrality of the language, a few themes also recur throughout Edgar Cairo's literary work. Cairo makes a plea for better contact and increased understanding between the diverse population groups, their languages and cultures, in Suriname. He often evokes the antagonism between Suriname and the Netherlands, and resistance toward the colonial heritage; and asks that attention be given to the minorities who have migrated to Europe. In a somewhat larger context he evokes the juxtaposition of an oppressed black culture with a hegemonic white one that becomes more pronounced due to tensions between Christianity and African derived *winti*-religions. Cairo also depicts past and present social and economic difficulties, the past leaving an indelible impression upon the present.

In *Jeje disi / Karakter's krachten* (1980) the Wi Egi Sani movement of Eddy Bruma is invoked. To put 'our own things first' (*onze eigen zaken*) is a concern that informs all of Cairo's work: asserting and defending vigorously what one considers right, in Suriname as in the Netherlands. Cairo does not argue in favour of segregation nor of assimilation or integration. What he wants is a doubly creolised 'buffer culture', in which black and white influence one another. Through his own migration from Suriname to the Netherlands, Cairo in the course of his career has evolved from a 'pure Sranan Man' to a 'Euro-Creole' who has had to learn how to survive as a member of a minority in the Netherlands.

At the height of his literary production Cairo was lauded as well as despised. Since he proclaimed himself the Messiah, at the end of the 1980s, his reputation has steeply declined, and his books now mostly go unread.

Wim Rutgers

Literary Works
Cairo, Edgar (1976), *Kollektieve schuld of wel Famir'man-Sani*, Baarn: Het Wereldvenster.
— (1977), *Adoebe lobi / Alles tegen alles*, Haarlem: In de Knipscheer.
— (1978), *Djari / Erven*, Haarlem: In de Knipscheer.
— (1979), *Koewatra Djodjo / In de geest van mijn kultuur*, Haarlem: In de Knipscheer.
— (1980a), *Jeje disi / Karakter's krachten*, Haarlem: In de Knipscheer.
— (1980b), *Mi boto doro / Droomboot havenloos*, Haarlem: In de Knipscheer.
— (1982), *Dat vuur der grote drama's*, Haarlem: In de Knipscheer.
— (1984), *Lelu! Lelu! Het lied der vervreemding*, Haarlem: In de Knipscheer.

History
Kempen, Michiel van (1990), 'Edgar Cairo', *Kritisch Lexicon von de Moderne Nederlandstalige Literatur* 36 (Feb.): 20.

Colonial Administration

East Indies – Indonesia
The colonial heritage of the Dutch in Indonesia is not overtly visible today. Still, there are still many infrastructural works, especially on Java – roads, bridges, railways, harbours, plantations, waterworks, cities, hospitals, palaces, jails, market places, houses – that date back to the Dutch era. The great *Postweg* stretches for a thousand kilometres from west to east across Java. It was constructed in the early 1800s under Governor-General Daendels at a cost of some 100,000 Javanese lives.

Dutch laws and administrative structures have been adopted into the Indonesian state system, just as many Dutch loan words are used in the Indonesian language. And of course, the Dutch colonial unification of the archipelago is continued in the Indonesian republic.

Dutch colonial administration had its beginnings in the seventeenth century, when the VOC established Batavia as the Asian capital of its seaborne empire. VOC jurisdiction covered the entire area east of the Cape, from Japan to South Africa. There were Dutch settlements in Malacca, Macassar, on Java and the Moluccas, in Sri Lanka, Coromandel and elsewhere in India, and all the way to Deshima in Japan. VOC law was collected and laid down in the so-called statute books. The administration was run by VOC officials; with the supreme Indies Council and the Dutch governor-general at the top. From Batavia, twice a year, he would report to the company directors, the so-called Heren XVII, in Amsterdam.

After the shortlived British conquest of Java, the Netherlands Indies was re-established as a colonial entity, run by the governor-general and his civil servants. The colony now reported to the Dutch government in The Hague. While it was still a maritime empire, it now also developed clear territorial ambitions, and in the course of the nineteenth century its domain continuously expanded until by the early twentieth century the political unification of the archipelago had been achieved under General (later Governor-General) J. B. van Heutsz (1851–1924).

Sometimes newly acquired areas were placed under direct Dutch rule; sometimes treaties or contracts were concluded (or renewed) with native rulers; sometimes – as in the Central Java Sultanates – areas were left under their own laws and customs, with the Dutch only represented by a political agent. The relevant regulations were laid down in *de Indische Staatsregeling* and collected in the *Wetboek van Nederlandsch Indië*.

On the whole, the system of government was a system of indirect rule – a pyramid of local rulers with their underlings, over which the Dutch administration was superimposed. Dutch colonial civil servants had to take an oath to defend the interests and well-being of their native subjects – and it was this oath that Multatuli's noble and ideal civil servant, assistant-resident Douwes Dekker, alias Max Havelaar, took a bit too seriously when he confronted the alleged corruption and extortion of his native colleague, the local ruler Raden Adipatti Karta Nata Negara (see Historiography). The oath embodies the ethical imperative of the Dutch civil servants and the *mission civilisatrice* for which they – as development aid workers *avant la lettere* – tirelessly worked.

The colonial civil service or Binnenlands Bestuur (BB) consisted of governors, residents, assistant-residents, controllers, book-keepers and administrators. As A. Alberts once remarked – they often acted a bit like the traditional feudal burgomasters in the Dutch countryside. In fact, many of them came from the same families of landed gentry in the eastern provinces of the Netherlands. A characteristic feature of their role was their paternalistic approach, which was recognised at the time of independence, when an Indonesian remarked: 'You have governed us well, but the problem is you have always only governed us and ruled over us, and never asked us what we thought or wanted.'

The colonial administration also made use of cultural instruments, both internally and externally. Inside the Netherlands Indies, there was the Kantoor voor de Volkslectuur (Office for Popular Literature), which aimed to modernise traditional Indonesian culture and literature. One of the most important vehicles of Dutch colonial cultural policy, it stimulated the development of new literary forms such as the Western novel in Indonesian literature. It also contributed enormously to the dissemination of standard Malay throughout the archipelago by using it in the journals and magazines, books, reports, brochures and translations it published and distributed through its library network. After independence its role as a publisher was continued by the Indonesian house Balai Pustaka.

For the outside world, the colonial administration invested in international image management, with regular presentations at the large Colonial World Exhibitions in London and Paris. The strongly Orientalist colonial image projected by the Dutch through the Balinese Pavilion and the Balinese dancers and musicians they sent to the World

Exhibition in Paris in 1931 (which, incidentally, inspired the Theatre of Cruelty of Antonin Artaud) generated much international praise and attention for the Netherlands East Indies as a modern model colony, even when the pavilion burned down before the end of the exhibition.

Reinier Salverda

The Dutch Caribbean

Until the late eighteenth century the Dutch Antilles and Suriname were administered by the Dutch West India Company (West Indische Compagnie, WIC), founded in 1621 by the Dutch Staten Generaal (States General). The WIC initiated the triangular trade and went on to play an important role in the slave trade from 1630 to 1730. Despite its monopoly on all Dutch trade and navigation between the Americas and Africa, the WIC faced strong competition from British and French companies and the Dutch market was not closed to foreigners. In Suriname, the WIC held half the shares – with the City of Amsterdam – of the Charter Society of Suriname (Geoctroyeerde Sociëteit van Suriname) which was responsible for the administration of Suriname until 1795 with a governor at its head. The society's policies were outlined by the Political Council (Politieke Raad) whose ten life-long members were nominated from among the colonists by the governor. The WIC was disbanded in 1792 and the society liquidated in 1795 when the Dutch state began to exercise direct authority. Subsequent political upheavals in Europe had direct consequences for the administration of the colonies.

During the Napoleonic occupation of the Netherlands the colonies were under French rule, and, after the French annexation of the Netherlands in 1810, under that of the 'Netherlands Department' of the French Overseas and Colonial Ministry. These changes affected only the Antilles, though, as Suriname had been invaded by the British, whose interim government lasted from 1799 to 1816 with a short break from 1802 to 1804. With the end of the Napoleonic occupation, the Netherlands became a kingdom. From 1815, colonial policy was the direct responsibility of King Willem I. To minimise administrative costs, the Dutch possessions in the Americas were merged administratively and placed under the responsibility of a single governor, based in Paramaribo, from 1828 onward. This arrangement proved unworkable because of the distance between the islands and Suriname. Eventually the colonies were split up again to form the Netherlands Antilles on the one hand and Suriname on the other, a format that continued unchanged until 1948. The Dutch Antilles became known as Curaçao and its Dependencies (Curaçao en zijn Onderdaanigheden). A Ministry of the Colonies was created in The Hague in 1848. The colonial administration policy fell under the responsibility of the States General to which the minister was answerable.

This new form of administration was followed by the introduction of a colonial constitution (Regeringsreglement) in 1865. This established a representative body, the Colonial Council (Koloniale Staten), a reform that marked an evolution in Dutch colonial attitudes: colonies came to be perceived as overseas territories whose people had the same rights and liberties as the population of the mother country. Still, the colony's governor and the colonial minister in The Hague continued to have the final say in all matters. Moreover, the composition of the body and the right to vote, based on poll tax, diminished the Colonial Council's representative character. The governor, appointed by the central government in The Hague, controlled all executive powers and enjoyed a legislative monopoly. He had a right of veto on proposals made by the Colonial Council and could carry through decisions made on his own. New statutory regulations, introduced in 1936, broadened internal autonomy through the founding of a largely elected local council in the Antilles, the Staten van Curaçao. Yet only 5 per cent of the total population was enfranchised; and the governor still held wide-ranging decision-making powers as the Colonial Council had no influence on his policies.

Throughout the colonial period a strong cultural divide prevailed between the Dutch Caribbean and the Netherlands. Compulsory education was introduced in 1876 which led to a gradual 'Dutchification' of the local cultures through teaching of and in the Dutch language. Newspapers printed in Dutch relayed information from the Netherlands to the colonies. Still, cultural ties were weak especially in the Dutch Antilles where the Dutch language never was very prominent. In Suriname Dutch culture held a more prominent place alongside various indigenous cultures. Population movements between the Caribbean and the Netherlands were limited due to the distances and the length of travel, while the population of the 'mother country' paid little attention to issues concerning the Dutch Caribbean.

During the colonial period, the colonies' financial situation was a major concern. After the abolition of slavery the Dutch colonial administration supported the agricultural sector by keeping the plantations afloat. In Suriname, the Dutch government provided yearly budget supplements to avoid financial collapse. After World War I the economic profile of the Dutch Antilles changed with the building of oil refineries. The oil industry spurred a rapid economic development and the islands were able to contribute financially to the Dutch treasury. In contrast, and notwithstanding American investments in the bauxite industry, Suriname was still considered an economic burden on the Dutch government, which even discussed the possibility of selling the colony to the US. World War II saw another change in Dutch colonial policy as ideas of political autonomy gradually emerged. In a speech made by Queen Wilhelmina in 1942, the Dutch sovereign alluded to the necessity of addressing the relationship between the Netherlands and its colonies (East Indies, Netherlands Antilles, Suriname) and suggested the possibility of autonomy within a reconstructed kingdom (see Decolonisation).

Patricia Krus

HISTORIES

Dew, Edward M. (1978), *The Difficult Flowering of Surinam: Ethnicity and Politics in a Plural Society*, The Hague: Martinus Nijhoff.

Fasseur, C. (1992), *The Politics of Colonial Exploitation. Java, the Dutch, and the Cultivation System*, Ithaca, NY: Cornell University Press.

Gaastra, F. S. (2003), *The Dutch East India Company. Expansion and Decline*, Zutphen: Walburg Pers.

Oostindie, Gert (2005), *Paradise Overseas: The Dutch Caribbean, Colonialism and its Transatlantic Legacies*, Oxford: Macmillan Caribbean.

Oostindie, Gert and Inge Klinkers (2003), *Decolonising the Caribbean: Dutch Policies in Comparative Perspective*, Amsterdam: Amsterdam University Press.

Counts of Orange

The Counts of Orange derived from a dynasty originating in the mediaeval principality of Orange in France that became inextricably involved with the history of the Netherlands. Members of the House of Orange became princes and served as *stadtholders*, or military governors, of the Dutch Republic. In 1815, the Netherlands became a monarchy under the house of Orange-Nassau.

Beginning in the twelfth century, Orange became a fief of the Holy Roman Empire as part of the kingdom of Burgundy. Henry III of Nassau-Breda (1483–1538) from Germany married Claudia of Châlon-Orange (1498–1521) from Burgundy. Henry III became *stadtholder* of Holland, Zeeland and Utrecht during the sixteenth century. Henry III's son, René of Châlon (1519–44), adopted the new surname 'Orange-Nassau'. He was succeeded by his nephew, William I of Orange (1533–84).

William I organised a Dutch revolt against Spanish rule, initiating the Eighty Years' War (1568–1648) and the creation of an independent Dutch state comprised of seven provinces (Holland, Zeeland, Utrecht, Gelderland, Overijssel, Friesland, Groningen). William I was assassinated and succeeded by his Protestant son, Maurice (1567–1625), who expanded Dutch territory. In 1585, Maurice became *stadtholder* of the Dutch Republic, engaging in a power struggle with a group of merchants led by Johan van Oldebarnevelt (1547–1619) who served as regents. Maurice was succeeded by his brother Frederick Henry (1584–1647), whose children married into important families, such as the Hohenzollerns of Prussia, the Nassaus of Friesland, and the Stuarts of England. Frederick Henry was succeeded by his son, William II (1626–50), who attempted to maintain authority following the Eighty Years' War. At William II's death, his wife was pregnant, but the regents declared the *stadtholderate* vacant.

The Princes of Orange had dominated the Dutch Republic, but they failed to control Dutch politics, in part because of religious differences, but also due to social and commercial traditions in the Netherlands that diminished aristocratic authority. The Dutch were experienced maritime traders within Europe; consequently, advanced Dutch trading networks laid the foundations for future European commercial growth overseas, and for the emergence of urbanisation and capitalist economies. Throughout the 1600s, the Dutch increased control over international trade in Asia, Africa and the Americas. The Princes of Orange were keen to invest in and sponsor such overseas ventures to increase their own wealth. However, the influx of wealth among merchants led to increased disparity between rich and poor.

In 1672, England and France attacked the Dutch Republic; William II's posthumous son, William III (1650–1702), became *stadtholder*. He repelled the attack and consolidated power. In 1677, he married Mary Stuart (1662–94), daughter of James II of Britain (1633–1701). In 1688, William and his wife, both Protestants, conspired with British nobles to depose Catholic James II. In 1689, William and Mary were crowned co-monarchs of England, Ireland and Scotland. William outlived his wife and died childless, ending the House of Orange and leaving Britain to his wife's sister.

The regents declared the *stadtholderate* vacant following disputes between the Frisian Nassaus and the Hohenzollerns over the rightful heir to the title Prince of Orange. William IV (1711–51) of the Frisian Nassaus became *stadtholder* of some Dutch provinces in 1722. Following France's invasion in 1747, William IV became *stadtholder* of the entire republic. Although William IV criticised the wealthy merchant class, he served as the Dutch East India Company's Director-General. William IV died in 1751, leaving his young son, William V (1748–1806), *stadtholder*. The regents dominated William V, whose tenure as *stadtholder* was a disaster. The Dutch East India Company declared bankruptcy and Britain declared war following Dutch recognition of the United States in 1776, a motion favoured by merchants hoping to expand their colonial enterprises at Britain's expense. The war ruined the Dutch Republic and led to revolutionary activity. Such wars whittled away at

Dutch colonial territories, weakening the Netherlands' position as an international maritime power. In 1795, France invaded, forcing William V into exile.

Following the French Empire's collapse in 1813, William V's son, William Frederick (1772–1843) became Prince Sovereign William I of the Netherlands. In 1815, Belgium and Luxembourg were added to his domains, creating the United Kingdom of the Netherlands. In 1830, Belgium began a successful bid for independence. In 1840, William I abdicated. His son, William II (1792–1849), accepted a constitution in 1848 limiting his power to avoid further revolutionary upheaval. His son, William III (1817–90) attempted to reassert royal authority. Upon William III's death, the House of Orange-Nassau's male line became extinct. His daughter, Wilhelmina (1880–1962), succeeded him. Luxembourg retained the Salic law barring females from inheriting its throne; consequently, the duchy passed to the House of Nassau-Weilburg.

Wilhelmina used her family's financial holdings to expand her investments, which encompassed industries in the United States and oil wells in the Indies, making her the first woman with a net worth exceeding 1 billion US dollars. During her lifetime, oil emerged as a major source of wealth and power, and the Dutch royal family is still the largest single shareholder of Royal Dutch Shell. Wilhelmina abdicated in favour of her daughter, Juliana (1909–2004), in 1948. Wilhelmina symbolised Dutch resistance to Nazism during World War II; consequently, controversy ensued in 1966 when her granddaughter, Beatrix (1938–), married Claus von Amsberg (1926–2002), a former member of the Hitler Youth and Wehrmacht. In 1980, Juliana abdicated in favour of Beatrix. In 2005, Forbes estimated the Queen's wealth at 4.7 billion dollars.

Eric Martone

Histories

Grew, Marion Sharpe (1947), *The House of Orange*, London: Methuen.
Rowen, Herbert A. (1988), *The Princes of Orange: The Stadtholders in the Dutch Republic*, New York: Cambridge University Press.
Schama, Simon (1977), *Patriots and Liberators: Revolution in the Netherlands, 1780–1813*, New York: Alfred A. Knopf.
— (1987), *The Embarrassment of Riches: An Interpretation of Dutch Culture in the Golden Age*, New York: Alfred A. Knopf.

Creolisation and Creoleness

East Indies – Indonesia

Creoles are people of European descent born in the colonies. In the Netherlands Indies, if both parents were Europeans, the children would be Europeans too. This was the case with important Indies writers such as Maria Dermoût and Hella Haasse. People in this category were often labelled 'Indisch', as distinct from true 'Dutch' people from the Netherlands. There was always a slight reserve about people who were Indisch. By law the governor-general had to be a Dutchman born in the Netherlands, which helps explain why the last one, Dr H. J. van Mook, a Dutchman born and bred in the Indies, was only made lieutenant-governor-general.

The Dutch community was always heavily male-dominated. Due to a shortage of European women, many children were of mixed race. A child's fortune depended on a white father's acknowledgement of paternity. If he recognised the child, it would be classed as European and would grow up with a European name, a European education and career, and live amongst Europeans. But if the father did not recognise the child, it would be a native Indonesian and would have to live the life of a native. The traumatic consequences this system could have are explored in Daum's novel *Aboe Bakar*, in which the English father John Silver, to spite his native concubine whom he suspects of infidelity, brings up their son as a European, but without officially recognising him, so that when the son comes of age, he is ejected from the European class and brought down to the status of a native.

Such 'Indos', as they were known, occupied an intermediate position in colonial society. In the course of history this position varied. Many mixed-race children were never recognised by their fathers, and many lived in deplorable conditions in the native villages. It took till the middle of the nineteenth century before this was recognised as a problem, and some action was taken by the colonial government to improve their position. From then on, however, there was also an increasing emphasis on whiteness. A colonial novel such as Johan Fabricius' *Halfbloed* (*Indo*) stereotypes the strong, white Dutchman who has just come out from Holland, a sharp contrast to the sensual coloured Indo girls with whom he fools around, and the indolent and weak Indo men, for whom the Dutch language had a wide variety of invective such as *blauwe* and *liplap*.

In the postcolonial era, Marion Bloem has rewritten this history in her novel, *Geen gewoon Indisch meisje*, creating a myth, very much like that of the Flying Dutchman, of the Eternal Indo who happens to have been present at all the important historical moments that define the Dutch colonial adventure in the Indonesian archipelago. Another reversal of colonial values can be seen in the furious debate in Holland throughout the 1990s over the question of who could truly call themselves Indisch, and whether for example a white writer such as Hella Haasse, who was born and bred in pre-war Indonesia, had any more right to call herself Indisch than a mixed-race Indo such as Siem Boon, the daughter of Tjalie Robinson, journalist penname for Jan Boon, who wrote fiction under his other *non de plume* Vincent Mahieu. A similar development can be traced when it comes to the creolisation of the Dutch language in the former East Indies.

From 1600 to 1950 a number of factors have shaped the colonial language policies of the Dutch. Historically, their settlements in the East Indies were never large. By 1795, there were no more than 543 Dutchmen living in Batavia, amidst a very large *mestizo* community, and the Dutch language had practically died out. Although in the nineteenth and twentieth centuries the colonial ruling class greatly increased in number, it always remained a small minority. In 1930 there were only 190,000 Europeans compared to an indigenous population of 18 million Indonesians. Dutch was the language of this small European governing class and their Indonesian associates; and Dutch language education was traditionally aimed at the children of this élite.

The Dutch language policy started from the premise that amidst the enormous linguistic diversity of the archipelago, Malay was the lingua franca, the commonly used language of contact. In 1864 it was therefore decided to disseminate this language – and not Dutch – throughout the colony. To this end, the colonial government stimulated the study, standardisation and modernisation of Malay, imposing it via its institutions, via education, the missions and the media, and via the literary works produced by the state publishers Balai Poestaka (Kantoor voor de Volkslectuur or Office for Popular Literature). In this respect, the Dutch pursued a non-chauvinistic cultural policy that consciously avoided the linguistic imperialism of the British and other European colonial powers.

For the Dutch language itself, however, the norm always remained the mother tongue as spoken by its European native speakers. As a consequence, all attempts to simplify the spelling of Dutch for the benefit of indigenous learners of the language were rejected. Creolisation in so-called 'Indo-Dutch' met with a sustained social and educational backlash. And 'pure' Dutch was often used as an instrument of social exclusion. The Dutch language thus became the symbol of colonialism, and when independence came, it was quickly abolished and replaced by Bahasa Indonesia as the official language of the Indonesian Republic. Dutch has today all but vanished from the archipelago, although there are still some 300 laws from the Dutch era, and Indonesian archives contain copious numbers of documents in Dutch.

This Dutch focus on purity of language and the outspoken prejudice against what was seen as an uneducated mishmash of languages, has been a major obstacle for the recognition (let alone the scholarly study) of creolised forms of the Dutch language. One either had to speak pure Dutch or pure Malay, and never mix the two languages. But in actual fact very many people did just that, and they have produced all kinds of linguistic mixtures, ranging between, on the one hand, Indisch Nederlands (the equivalent of Anglo-Indian), that is, colonial Dutch with a slight Indonesian accent and containing some loan words, and on the other hand, Petjoh, which was a heavily Indonesianised form of Dutch that was severely stigmatised socially in the colonial period.

Thanks to the literary works by Tjalie Robinson and Vincent Mahieu, the Dutch/Indonesian Narayan, who made great use of these colonial varieties of Dutch, and thanks also to the efforts of the annual Pasar Malam festival in The Hague, Petjoh today is rather more fashionable than it ever was in colonial days.

Reinier Salverda

The Dutch Caribbean

Although Dutch has been the official language of the Dutch Caribbean since 1676, the presence of a number of Creole languages used widely in private spheres as well as for cultural expression is a striking feature of the region. Suriname alone counts over twenty different languages. The dominance of Dutch is fairly recent. In colonial times, the white settlers were of Dutch, British, Portuguese and Spanish origin. Until the early nineteenth century, the number of Dutch speakers was small. From 1800 onwards, the rise of a coloured élite, often educated in Dutch schools in the Caribbean or in the Netherlands increased the number of Dutch speakers. In the post-emancipation era, the Dutchification of Suriname and the Netherlands Antilles intensified: Dutch became the compulsory language of education and administration. The process of cultural and political emancipation set in motion in the 1950s and 1960s triggered a renewed interest in Creole languages as means of expression for local cultures. The Dutch spoken in the Dutch Caribbean also shows significant differences in terms of grammar, pronunciation and lexis from the Dutch spoken in the Netherlands. Next to Dutch, the most widely spoken languages are Papiamentu (Netherlands Antilles) and Sranan (Suriname).

Netherlands Antilles

Papiamentu, or Papiamento, is the national language of Aruba, Bonaire and Curaçao. The term derives from *papuar*, meaning to talk, or chat in Portuguese, and Papiamentu indeed derives primarily from the Iberian languages Portuguese and Spanish. Linguists have traced its origins to fifteenth-century Western Africa where it became a lingua franca for Portuguese traders and the West African population. It developed further as the language travelled to the Caribbean with African slaves. There, interaction with other cultures and ethnic groups introduced words of Dutch, English, French and Arawak etymology. The creolisation of these linguistic elements also reflects the syncretic character of culture on the Netherlands Antilles. As a communication tool, Papiamentu has played a crucial role in unifying a variety of cultures of European, African, Amerindian and Asian origin. Originally a spoken language, attempts have been made to standardise Papiamentu, as the publication of dictionaries and grammars illustrates. Moreover, as the desire for political autonomy grew in the post-war years, Papiamentu came to be perceived as a means to affirm local cultural identity and distinctiveness. Today, it remains widely used as most inhabitants of Aruba, Bonaire and Curaçao speak Papiamentu as well as Dutch. Publication of books, novels, poetry, plays, songs, newspapers and the broadcast of radio and TV programmes in Papiamentu attest to the vitality of the language.

Suriname
The existence of over twenty Creole languages is testimony to the country's multicultural history. These languages can be divided in three distinct groups according to their origin: Amerindian (8), Creole (7) and Eurasian (4). The last group comprises Surinamese Dutch (the variant of Dutch spoken in Suriname which differs in lexis, syntax and phonetics from European Dutch), Sarnami (spoken by the Hindustani community), Javanese and Chinese (called Hakka in Suriname and originally from the Pearl river delta in southern China). The Creole group of languages includes Sranan Tongo, or Sranan (spoken by slaves and their descendents) and the languages spoken by the descendents of Maroon communities (Aluku, Saramaccan, Ndyuka among others). The remaining Creoles include the Amerindian languages from two distinct linguistic families: Cariban and Arawakan, which have small numbers of speakers.

Although now the lingua franca of Suriname, Sranan was originally the language of the population of black descent. Its name literally means 'Surinamese language' and it was first recorded around 1700 when it was known as 'Negerengels' or Negro English. It was used by European settlers, African slaves and Indians, and has a predominantly English etymological base with over 50 per cent of words of English origin. There are two theories to explain its origin. The first suggests that it originated in Africa and was brought to Suriname by African slaves. The second theory pinpoints its source in Suriname itself. Today, there are over 300,000 speakers of Sranan in Suriname and among the Surinamese population in the Netherlands. To some extent, the language is considered a symbol of unity in the post-independence nation. However, despite the introduction of an official spelling, and the publication of grammars, Sranan is not taught in school and apprenticeship of the language is carried on informally in family and social circles. Although used widely, Sranan's vocabulary is limited; hence the use of Dutch words to complement it.

The mainly Muslim labourers from Java developed their own language: Surinaams-Javaans. Among the indentured labourer Hindustani population, the different regional languages of India gave birth to Sarnami Hindoestani. They did not integrate very fast, as they stayed on in the plantation districts for a long period. Although dominant among groups of Hindustani descent, Sarnami slowly gave way to Sranantongo (or Sranan) as Hindustani labourers became more amalgamated into society.

Despite its status as lingua franca, Sranan has never attained the same cohesive power as Papiamentu in the Netherlands Antilles. This is partly due to Creole nationalism, which aimed to make Sranan the official language of all Surinamese, a move strongly rejected by non-Creole ethnic groups. In contemporary Suriname, bilingualism, and even trilingualism, is the norm. Next to Dutch, learnt at school, people will speak the language of their own ethnic group, and use Sranan to communicate with members of other ethnic communities. The presence of a large variety of languages encourages a high degree of code-switching. As Carlin (in, for example, Carlin and Arends 2002) has argued, the choice of language is also influenced by social and cultural factors.

Linguistic creolisation in the Dutch Caribbean has given birth to a large number of languages. The availability of cultural products such as plays, songs, fiction, poetry in the Creole languages testifies to their ongoing vitality. However, growing contacts between the Netherlands Antilles, Suriname and neighbouring countries have also intensified the use of English. For example, on Curaçao the local media use primarily Papiamentu and English. Proximity to Latin America has also triggered calls for the integration of Spanish as a national language. In Suriname, suggestions have been made to use English to fulfil the role of national language, a role no other language has been able to achieve. Still, for some this move towards Anglo-American and South American culture is perceived as a threat to the cultural survival of Creole languages.

Patricia Krus

SOUTH AFRICA

South Africa's oldest known inhabitants, the Khoesan, consisted of two subgroups: Southern Khoesan-speaking San (or Bushmen) and central Khoesan-speaking Khoekhoen (or Hottentots). The once widespread Khoesan languages eventually became extinct in what has been referred to as 'language genocide'. Dutch arrived with the establishment of a trading station by the VOC at the Cape in 1652. From 1658 slaves were imported from Madagascar, Mozambique, the East Indies and India, creating one of the most diverse slave populations in the world in terms of origin, religion, culture and language. This produced a layered linguistic situation at the Cape: the European immigrants spoke Dutch, German, French and Scandinavian languages, while the slaves brought with them Niger-Kordofanian languages, Malagasy (an Austronesian language), Indo-Aryan and Dravidian languages, and South-East Asian Austronesian, as well as non-Austronesian languages. In order to secure some degree of effective communication, mainly three 'contact languages' were used between slaves and colonists: Dutch, Asian Creole Portuguese and Malay. Khoekhoe and the languages spoken by the African and Asian slaves started influencing the Dutch of the colonists. At this juncture the first roots of Afrikaans as a new language became discernible.

Afrikaans developed rapidly. By the end of the seventeenth century the use of Dutch was mainly limited to written correspondence, official communication and 'civilised conversation' as well as the areas of church and education. An early version of Afrikaans was informally used on the farms and in ordinary day-to-day communication. Even though the exact origin of Afrikaans as a separate language is difficult to pinpoint, many sources identify the period between 1750 and 1775 as the crucial period, while others see it as an ongoing linguistic process continuing up to the beginning of the twentieth century.

After the colony had definitively passed into the hands of the British in 1815, a typically South African pronunciation of English developed. The Great Trek of the Dutch, known as 'Boers', during the nineteenth century into the interior of Africa had important consequences for the development of Afrikaans into a unique South African language. The Zuid-Afrikaansche Republiek (Transvaal) and the Oranje-Vrijstaat (Orange Free State) stuck to Dutch as their official language. From the 1820s indigenous languages were recorded by missionaries, with the help of local consultants. The first substantial writing in Afrikaans materialised in the first half of the nineteenth century through descendants of Muslim slaves, who used Arabic script in writing Islamic texts in Afrikaans. From 1860 onwards Afrikaans was increasingly used as a written language. In 1860 the 'Genootskap van Regte Afrikaners' was formed in order to promote the production of, for example, an Afrikaans translation of the Bible, an Afrikaans national anthem and an Afrikaans newspaper.

The Anglo-Boer War (1899–1902) ended with the English annexation of the republics. English became increasingly dominant in the business and industrial sphere. The major urbanisation of the late nineteenth century, with a massive influx of people from Europe, the USA and Australia, accompanied by the large-scale influx of black people into the mining areas, resulted in a unique mixture of foreign languages. Urban varieties of African languages also manifested themselves. A unique pidgin 'contact language' developed around the mines and in the urban areas, becoming known as Fanakalo.

Afrikaans was not officially recognised until 1925 when it replaced Dutch (which had been used for almost 270 years – from 1652 to 1925 – as a written language in South Africa) as an official language. Zuid-Afrika became Suid-Afrika. The Bantu Education Act, passed in 1953, had major consequences for linguistic development in South Africa. This law, controlling the syllabi and media of instruction, was a crucial factor in entrenching a permanent underclass of black people. The resistance against 'Bantu Education' and the language policy it imposed, culminated in 1976 in the Soweto uprisings. During these uprisings schoolchildren revolted against the imposition of Afrikaans in 'black' schools. The uprising spread throughout the country and Afrikaans increasingly became associated with racism and known as 'the language of the oppressor'. As such the struggle against apartheid also became a struggle against Afrikaans, the dominant language of the oppressive régime.

However, Afrikaans is the home language of many coloured people too, who were victims of apartheid. Kaapse Afrikaans (Kaaps), spoken by the 'Cape Coloured' community and the Cape Muslims, is based on the linguistic varieties of the early slave and Khoikhoi communities in the Western Cape.

In light of the fact that linguistic issues had always been closely related to political issues in South Africa, it came as no surprise that the political changeover brought about major linguistic changes for the country. With its new constitution (1996) and the Pan South African Language Board Act (1995) South Africa stands today in the forefront of promoting respect for other languages, multilingualism and the development of languages. South Africa has become the country with the most official languages (eleven) in the world. These are Zulu, Xhosa, Afrikaans, English, Tswana, Sotho (previously known as South Sotho), Pedi (also known as North Sotho), Tsonga, Swati, Venda and Ndebele. The dynamic language development of South Africa has not yet come to an end. The last decade has seen a major influx of people from other African states such as Mozambique, Zimbabwe, Malawi and Nigeria, but also from different parts of Europe. However, most South Africans can communicate in more than one language, with English as the most commonly spoken language in business and commerce.

Annemie van Niekerk

Literary Works
Bloem, Marion (1983), *Geen gewoon Indisch meisje*, Haarlem: In de Knipscheer.
Daum, P. A. (1893), *Aboe Bakar*, 's Gravenhage: Loman en Funke.
Debrot, Cola [1935] (1978), *Mijn zuster de negerin*, Amsterdam: De bezige bij.
Heerden, Etienne van (1986), *Toorberg*, Kaapstad: Talfelberg-Uitgewers Beperk.
Mahieu, Vincent (1996), *The Hunt for the Heart: Selected Tales from the Dutch East Indies*, Oxford: Oxford University Press.

Voorhoeve, J. and U. M. Lichtveld (eds) (1975), *Creole Drums: An Anthology of Creole literature in Surinam*, New Haven, CT: Yale University Press.

HISTORIES

Eckkrammer, Eva Martha (2003), 'On the Perception of "Creole" Language and Identity in the Netherlands Antilles', in Gordon Collier and Ulrich Fleischmann (eds), *A Pepper-pot of Cultures: Aspects of Creolization in the Caribbean*, Amsterdam: Rodopi, pp. 85–108.

Fouse, Gary C. (2002), *The Story of Papiamentu: A Study in Slavery and Language*, Lanham, MD: University Press of America.

Groeneboer, Kees (1998), *Gateway to the West. The Dutch Language in Colonial Indonesia 1600–1950. A History of Language Policy*, trans. Myra Scholz, Amsterdam: Amsterdam University Press.

Huigen, Siegfried and Jean Kommers (eds) (2004), *Interpretations of Colonial Representations*, Saarbrücken: Nijmegen Studies in Development and Cultural Change.

Mesthrie, Rajend (ed.) (2002), *Language in South Africa*, Cambridge: Cambridge University Press.

Migge, Bettina (2003), *Creole Formation as Language Contact: The Case of the Surinamese Creoles*, Amsterdam: Benjamins.

Critique of Imperialism/Anti-colonialism

EAST INDIES – INDONESIA

There has been a long tradition amongst the Dutch of critical discussion and rejection of their colonial enterprise.

In 1623, when the charter of the VOC was up for renewal, the former Governor-General, the learned merchant and diplomat, Admiral Sir Laurens Reael, severely questioned the humanity and wisdom of the VOC's activities in the East, and especially the ruthless behaviour of his successor, Jan Pieterszoon Coen, who had led the massacre of 1621 in the island of Banda-Neira, the first commercial genocide in history, driven entirely by greed and the desire to seal a monopoly over the spice trade. Again, in 1623, it was Coen who was behind the infamous Murder of Amboyna, when a group of Englishmen had been arrested, tortured, tried and hanged the next day, for their alleged attempt to take the Dutch fort Victoria. Similar criticisms had been voiced in Holland at the time, in pamphlets that decried the merciless inhumanity of Coen's executions, one of which is quoted in the twentieth-century colonial novel *John Company* by Arthur van Schendel.

Despite all these criticisms, the hardliners amongst the company's directors and in national politics won, and the VOC had its charter renewed. The critics, however, were not silenced. Again and again, down the centuries, Dutch commentators voiced grave concerns regarding the colonial enterprise in the East.

In the eighteenth century, at the time of the Enlightenment, there were critics such as the brothers Willem and Onno van Haren, Willem van Hogendorp and Jacob Haafner. In the nineteenth century this tradition was carried forward by Van Höevell, Multatuli, Roorda van Eysinga, C. Th. van Deventer, Daum and Alexander Cohen. In the twentieth century, too, many critics took up the issue, from van Kol, van den Brand and E. F. E. Douwes Dekker, through Henk Sneevliet, Jef Last and Marcel Koch to Willem Wertheim and

Poncke Princen. The list includes quite a few writers, from van Haren, Multatuli and Daum through Last and Du Perron to Szekely-Lulofs. A selection of their texts, containing many painful, gruesome, at times unbearable details, was published by Ewald Vanvugt in 1996.

In the twentieth century we find leading Indonesian thinkers taking up these critical themes and ideas. This is true in particular of the three leaders of the independence movement, Sjahrir, Hatta and Soekarno. Thus in 1928, when Mohammad Hatta, as leader of Perhimpunan Indonesia (the Indonesian Student Association) in the Netherlands (where he was studying at the time), had to appear before a Dutch court to defend his anti-colonial publications, he gave a well-thought-out critical analysis of Dutch imperialism, which was immediately published as a brochure, *Indonesië Vrij*. In 1930, when Soekarno was prosecuted in Bandoeng, he gave a majestic defence in which he quoted extensively from Kautsky, Jaurès, Schumpeter, Roland Holst, Troelstra, Sneevliet and many other European critics of imperialism. And later in the 1930s, we find Sjahrir, living in exile on the island of Banda-Neira, reading and commenting on the biography of Engels by Gustav Mayer, which he critically compares to Mehring's biography of Marx. The tragedy here is that a collection of texts on Indonesia, by leading twentieth-century critics of Dutch imperialism, *De roep om Merdeka* (*The Call for Freedom*), was published in Holland only long after Indonesia had become independent.

Reinier Salverda

SOUTH AFRICA

The establishment of Dutch colonial rule at the Cape was the beginning of the tumultuous contact between indigenous southern African people and West European culture. A portrayal of the history of this period as well as the time before the establishment of the colony up to 1733, is to be found in Karel Schoeman's *Armosyn van die Kaap: voorspel tot vestiging, 1415–1651* (2002). Dan Sleigh's *Eilande* (2002) deals with the arrival of the whites at the Cape.

The Cape remained a historical backwater for Europe until the British annexed it in 1795, in a climate of growing imperial rivalry between Britain, France and the Netherlands in the Indian Ocean. The emergent Boer society belonged to a new commercial and trading order with a developed consciousness regarding their race and status, yet still without the sense of an ideologically coherent nation. Novels relating to the colonial paradigm of the early nineteenth century include Elsa Joubert's *Missionaris* (1988) and *Verkenning* (1996) by Karel Schoeman. Both these novels refer to the colonisation of the interior and the efforts to convert the Khoi and San people to Christianity. In 1803 the Cape was retaken by the Batavian Republic, but the British reoccupied it in 1806. In 1815 Britain's colonial control of the Cape was finally sealed by treaty.

The Afrikaners despised British rule and their abolition of slavery in 1834. That same year Afrikaners, together with their African and coloured servants, embarked on the 'Great Trek' into the interior of Africa. This exodus was marked by many bloody conflicts between trekkers and the indigenous population, such as the clash with the Zulus at Blood River in 1838. The Afrikaans writer F. A. Venter wrote four novels with the Great Trek as their theme, entitled *Geknelde land* (1960), *Offerland* (1963), *Gelofteland* (1966) and *Bedoelde land* (1968). Some of the trekkers settled at Port Natal (later renamed Durban) where, from 1838, they governed their own republic of Natal. Five years later, however, Natal was proclaimed a British colony.

South African colonial writing often presents the Boer trekkers as either victims or heroes in their bloody encounters with the indigenous people. Thomas Mofolo's *Chaka*

(1925), written in South Soto, provides a counterview. Though influenced by Christian and Western psychological factors, he still speaks from an African insider perspective. Other historical novels about King Shaka written in indigenous languages include *Insila kaShaka* (*Shaka's Bodyguard*, 1930) by J. L. Dube and *UShaka* (1937) by R. R. R. Dhlomo.

The second Anglo-Boer War, also known as the South African War, erupted in 1899 when Paul Kruger (President of the Transvaal) and Cape Colony High Commissioner Lord Milner failed to resolve differences on *uitlander* rights. In 1902 the large British force brought the Boers to their knees, but only after 25,000 Boers – mainly women and children – had died in the British concentration camps. In 1902 the Peace of Vereeniging was signed and Transvaal and the Orange Free State became British colonies. Bill Nasson (1999) refers to the Anglo-Boer War as 'a war waged on the very edge of modern memory, inspiring a contemporary imaginative literature . . . not only in Dutch/Afrikaans and English, but also in European languages'. The title poem of the Afrikaans poet C. Louis Leipoldt's first collection, *Oom Gert vertel*, has an old man reflecting on how he sent two young men to the war, and how they were executed. Another poem, 'In die konsentrasiekamp', addresses the suffering in the camps. Most of the war writing of the time portrayed the Boers as heroically resisting the overpowering British troops. In his novel, *Verliesfontein* (1998), published a century after the war, Karel Schoeman provides a corrective by portraying the Boers as undisciplined instigators and troublemakers. Christoffel Coetzee's *Op soek na generaal Mannetjies Mentz* (1998) relates the story of a mysterious and notorious Boer general known for his cruelty against British as well as against Boers who wanted to surrender. Ingrid Winterbach, In *Niggie* (2002), portrays the stupidity and selfinterest of the Boers. Etienne van Heerden, in *Die swye van Mario Salviati* (2000), exposes a racially abusive Boer commando. These novels provide a view alternative to that of official history.

The 1960s and 1970s saw an increase in the use of writing as a tool of protest against the apartheid régime. André P. Brink's first politically engaged novel, *Kennis van die aand* (1973), was banned. In his *'n Droë wit seisoen* (*A Dry White Season*) (1979) Brink criticised the corrupt police and justice systems. The best-known anti-apartheid writer is probably Breyten Breytenbach, who was imprisoned for seven years as a terrorist. His poetry collections *'n Seisoen in die paradys* (1976) and *The True Confessions of an Albino Terrorist* (1984) refer to his prison experiences. Much contemporary writing still engages with this period, for example Karel Schoeman's *Die laaste Afrikaanse boek* (2002).

By the 1980s South Africa had become increasingly involved in the civil wars of its neighbours. All white men received compulsory military training after high school. Many fought in Angola, Mozambique, Namibia (then South West Africa), and Zimbabwe (then Rhodesia). These 'border wars' (*grensoorloge*) were inspired by South Africa's fear of communist rule on its doorstep. The South African Army also sought out and destroyed ANC bases in the neighbouring countries. This chapter of South African history is recorded in the local literary genre called 'border literature' (*grensliteratuur*). In the title story of Etienne van Heerden's collection *My Kubaan* (1983) an Afrikaans soldier pulls along 'his' Cuban prisoner of war on a chain. Other examples include van Heerden's 1984 *Om te awol*, Alexan der Strachan's *'n Wêreld sonder grense* (1984) and Louis Kruger's *'n Basis oorkant die grens* (1984).

John Miles' novel *Kroniek uit die doofpot* (1991) focuses on the corrupt police and judicial systems during the apartheid régime, especially in the 1980s. The true story on which this novel is based – that of a black policeman killed because of a conflict with a white colleague – was exposed at the Truth and Reconciliation Commission and reported on by

Antjie Krog in her book *Country of My Skull* (1999). One of the most prominent South African novels of the 1970s, reflecting on this tumultuous period in South African history, is Elsa Joubert's *Die swerfjare van Poppie Nongena* (1978). Francken and Renders (2005) explain how Joubert's book demonstrates the failure of apartheid. The novel narrates the true life history of the Xhosa woman, Poppie. *Die reuk van appels* (1993) by Mark Behr is set in 1974. It features the Afrikaans boy Marnus, who is cruelly exposed to all the cracks of immorality in the conservative armour of his father, a general in the South African army. *Triomf* (1994) by Marlene van Niekerk mercilessly debunks the notion of the Afrikaner family as the carrier of traditional Afrikaner values. Another novel dealing with identity issues is Elsa Joubert's *Die reise van Isobelle* (1995). The severe violence which marked the period between the abolition of apartheid and the first democratic elections often recurs as a theme in South African literature, for instance in Etienne van Heerden's *Die stoetmeester* (1993).

Annemie van Niekerk

LITERARY WORKS
Brink, André [1979] (1984), *A Dry White Season*, trans. J. Wilton, Harmondsworth: Penguin.
Dekker, Edward Douwes (Multatuli) [1860] (1982), *Max Havelaar; Or the Coffee Auctions of the Dutch Trading Company*, trans. Roy Edwards, Amherst, MA: University of Massachusetts Press.
Heerden, Etienne van (1993), *Die Stoetmeester*, Kaapstad: Talfelberg.
Joubert, Elsa (1978), *Die swerfjare van Poppie Nongena*, Kaapstad: Tafelberg.
Schendel, Arthur van [1932] (1983), *Jan Compagnie (John Company)*, Amherst, MA: University of Massachusetts Press.

HISTORIES
Beinart, W. (1994), *Twentieth-Century South Africa*, Cape Town: Oxford University Press.
Keegan, T. (1996), *Colonial South Africa and the Origins of the Racial Order*, Cape Town: David Philip.
Poeze, Harry and Henk Schulte Nordholt (eds) (1995), *De roep om Merdeka. Indonesische vrijheidlievende teksten uit de twintigste eeuw*, 's-Gravenhage: NOVIB.
Vanvugt, Ewald (1996), *Nestbevuilers. 400 jaar Nederlandse critici van het koloniale bewind in de Oost en de West*, Amsterdam: Babylon-De Geus.

December Killings

On 8 December 1982 the ruling military government seized fifteen prominent political opponents, trade union leaders, lawyers and intellectuals, and brutally executed them at the military headquarters in Paramaribo, Suriname. On the same day, a union building, a newspaper printing plant and two radio stations, alleged hot-beds of opposition, were blown up. This tragic episode, known as the December Killings (*December Moorden*), is perceived as a failure to establish true democracy in Suriname and considered the most traumatic event of the post-independence years.

Following independence in 1975, the political system, paralysed by continuous power struggles between government and opposition, was ineffective and marred by corruption. In 1980, the Surinamese government failed to fulfil its pledge to hold new elections while an ongoing union conflict within the armed forces intensified. Junior army officers felt dissatisfied, in particular on the issue of unionism which they wished to see implemented despite government objections. In response, officers mounted a campaign of strikes and radical actions from 1978 onwards, leading to the occupation of a military base in Paramaribo two years later. In retaliation, the government ordered the removal of the protesters who had demanded the release of three members of the military awaiting sentencing for their participation in the ongoing mutiny. On 25 February 1980, the eve of the sentencing, a group of army sergeants led by Desi Bouterse took power. At first the population welcomed the coup, believing forceful intervention could 'clean up' Surinamese politics. However, the self-appointed military government did not have a definite political programme and soon made clear it wished to hold onto its newly acquired power, if necessary by force.

In the months and years following the December Killings repression intensified as the government relied on violence, intimidation and press censorship. Decrees announced the suspension of parliament and constitution. The Dutch government froze its financial aid and the economy plummeted, leading to the growing isolation of the military government and mounting social unrest. In 1983 and 1984, trade unions put pressure on the military and obtained the replacement of Bouterse's government by a cabinet with no political affiliations, comprising representatives of the army, the industrial and commercial sectors, and the trade unions. Amidst further isolation on the international front, the military in power in 1985 offered to restore democracy as of 1987, in exchange for constitutional guarantees.

Although officially the responsibility for the killings has never been firmly established nor the events fully investigated, attempts have been made in this direction. In November 2000, following a complaint by relatives of the murdered victims, a court in Amsterdam ordered the opening of legal procedures against the former military leader Desi Bouterse. However, the Dutch Supreme Court repealed this decision arguing that international law and the limited jurisdiction of Dutch courts made it impossible to prosecute Bouterse. Moreover, the torture practices and the human rights violations the Bouterse régime allegedly committed did not constitute an offence under Dutch law at the time. This decision put an end to any further judicial procedures against Bouterse in the Netherlands. In Suriname, a commission was appointed, also in 2000, charged with investigating responsibility for the killings and the possibility of prosecution, thus paving the way for possible trials for the abuse of human rights, murder and torture.

Patricia Krus

LITERARY WORKS
Astrid Roemer (1997), *Lijken op Liefde*, Amsterdam: Arbeiders Pers.
Cynthia McLeod (2005), . . . *die Revolutie niet begrepen!*, Schoorl: Uitgeverij Conserve.

HISTORIES
Boerboom, Harmen and Joost Oranje (1992), *De 8 Decembermoorden: slagschaduw over Suriname*, 's Gravenhage: BZZTôH.
Brave, Iwan (2001), *Zolang ze praten, blijf ik: een boek over de vijftien slachtoffers van 8 December 1982*, Paramaribo: Organisatie voor Gerechtigheid en Vrede.
Breuning, Monique (1997), 'Foreign Policy in America's Backyard: Dutch and American Responses to the December 8th Murders in Suriname', *Acta Politica* 32 (3) (Autumn): 302–26.
Dew, Edward W. (1983), 'Suriname Tar Baby: The Signature of Terror,' in *Caribbean Review* 12 (1): 3–4, 34.

Elst, Richard van (2002), 'Universele Rechtsmacht over Foltering: bouterse en de Decembermoorden', *NJCM Bulletin* 27 (3): 208–24.
Zegveld, Liesbeth (2001), 'The Bouterse Case', *Netherlands Yearbook of International Law* 32: 97–118.

Decolonisation

East Indies – Indonesia

The end of the Dutch Empire in the East, when it came, was as unexpected as it was unstoppable. Unexpected, because as late as the 1930s, the then Governor-General of the Netherlands Indies had boasted: 'We, the Dutch, have been here for three hundred years; it will be another three hundred years before we are gone.' Unstoppable, because, when Sukarno and Hatta declared independence on 17 August 1945, the Dutch were in no position to counter this nationalist move.

The Dutch had come out of the war destroyed and impoverished; in the East Indies they had lost out against the Japanese in 1942; for three years their troops had suffered terribly in the Japanese POW camps; the liberation of the Dutch colonies was not a huge priority for the Allies. The Dutch, moreover, had no idea of the force of the nationalist movement, which they seriously underestimated, along with how much they themselves had lost in prestige and trust amongst the Indonesians, both because of their defeat by the Japanese and because of their severe political repression of the Indonesians before the war. After five years of German occupation, the political class in the Netherlands was badly out of touch with international developments.

Nevertheless, the Dutch decided to try and retake what they considered to be rightfully theirs. Initially, however, the two parties decided to talk, and those talks, led by Sjahrir as Indonesian Prime Minister and Schermerhorn, on behalf of the Dutch government, eventually led to the Linggadjati Agreement, which opened the way to a peaceful transition. This was not to be. Strong opposition, by colonial diehards in the Netherlands, and by militant nationalists in Indonesia, made it impossible for the agreement to be properly ratified. Diplomacy having failed, both parties resorted to armed conflict. Two major military campaigns – the so-called 'police actions' of 1947 and 1948 – were mounted by the Dutch to bring down the young Indonesian republic; to defeat its guerrilla army and restore law and order throughout the colony; and to gain as much territory as possible. The military gains were indeed considerable, but the Indonesian guerrilla army was never defeated, and the international community put great pressure on the Dutch to return to the negotiating table. What finally decided it was the American threat to exclude Holland from its Marshall Aid Programme, if the Dutch continued their military campaigns. Swift negotiations followed in 1949, which resulted in the Van Royen-Roem Agreement, and sovereignty was officially handed over to the Indonesian Republic in December 1949.

There was a messy coda, which took till 1962 to resolve. When the Dutch and Indonesians parted company in 1950, one issue remained unresolved, that of New Guinea, the large island in the East, inhabited by Papuan tribes. The Dutch hung onto this bastion, partly to retain some basis of influence in Asia, and partly to have a place where loyal natives, mixed race Indos and Christian Indonesians could be resettled so they would not come over to burden an already overcrowded and impoverished Holland.

From 1956 onwards, Sukarno exerted great pressure on the Dutch, breaking off diplomatic relations, expelling hundreds of thousands of Dutch descendants and mixed-race people still living in the republic, starting a new guerrilla war, and invoking the help of the United Nations and the United States. In the end, after a UN-supervised plebiscite amongst the Papuans, this led to the handover by the Dutch of this last colony to the republic in 1962.

On the Indonesian side, the rise and success of nationalism had other international effects. During their struggle with the Dutch, the Indonesian nationalists had strongly embraced the ideals of the new United Nations, to the extent that they included the Universal Declaration of Human Rights as a preamble in their own constitution. The Indonesians also joined the Non-Aligned Movement, and successfully organised the great Third World Conference in Bandung in 1955, which was attended by political leaders and heads of state from all over the world. And through the UN, Indonesian diplomats and legal scholars managed to get the notion of 'archipelago' enshrined in international maritime law.

On the Dutch side it has taken many years to come to terms with the loss of this colony. There was not just the loss of what many Dutch people had come to see as a paradise, but also a sense of being jilted, and of wounded pride. And it has taken the government till 2006 to accept 17 August 1945 – and not December 1949 – as the birth date of the Indonesian Republic.

The conflict has triggered an enormous literature. The series of official Dutch government documents relating to this conflict runs to twenty heavy volumes. Klooster's *Bibliography of the Indonesian Revolution* (1997) has 666 pages and contains over 7,000 titles. There is a large collection of primary documents and publications about this conflict in the British Library. Its catalogue, *The Indonesian Question* (2001), edited by Jaap Harskamp, has a further 1,500 titles of contemporary publications, amongst which are some 200 Dutch literary works relating to this conflict published between 1945 and 1950.

Reinier Salverda

Decolonisation in the Dutch Caribbean
After World War II, Dutch colonial policy shifted from the idea of a continued presence to a partial move towards autonomy and independence. Today, the Kingdom of the Netherlands consists of three parts: the Netherlands, the Netherlands Antilles and Aruba. Of the former colonies, only Suriname has achieved full political and economic autonomy, while Aruba has a separate status within the Kingdom. Although the Dutch government wished to achieve an 'exemplary decolonisation' in its Caribbean colonies, the process left much to be desired and can be divided into three major phases.

Phase I 1940–54: The birth of the Charter of the Kingdom of the Netherlands
During World War II, the Dutch Caribbean territories were under the protection of the Allied Forces. In a radio speech broadcast from London on 6 December 1942, Queen Wilhelmina introduced the notions of partnership, internal autonomy and shared solidarity between the Netherlands and its Caribbean possessions. From March 1947 on, a representative from Suriname and the Antilles sat on the Dutch Council of Ministers. It turned out that the territories wanted more autonomy and equal status, but rejected full political independence. Their status consequently changed from that of 'colonies' to 'overseas territories', and after nine years of negotiation they became equal and autonomous partners within the Kingdom of the Netherlands. The 'roundtable discussions' gave birth to the Charter of the Kingdom of the Netherlands (Statuut van het Koninkrijk der Nederlanden), promulgated in 1954. It remains largely unchanged today.

The charter was accepted as a fair compromise by the three countries now making up the Kingdom. Its sixty-one articles introduced parliamentary democracy, universal suffrage, a Dutch-style administration, and stressed the principles of autonomy, mutual assistance and solidarity. However, it also limited the number of affairs dealt with communally by restricting Surinamese and Antillean influence on the institutions of the Kingdom. There were also restrictions regarding nationality, defence, foreign affairs and the guarantee of good governance. Alongside the charter, the Ministerial Council of the Kingdom was created: a Dutch council of ministers with a plenipotentiary minister from each Caribbean country. The predominantly Dutch council retained final say over defence and foreign affairs policies, issues which would later motivate Suriname's demands for independence. The charter accepted the right to self-determination, and the relationship defined by the charter was not considered to be eternal. Lack of trust and mutual misunderstanding undermined the success of the relationship in the years to follow.

Phase II 1954–75: Suriname's independence
In this period the question of foreign policy proved contentious for the various members of the Kingdom. The Netherlands refused to make concessions on this point despite repeated demands made primarily by Suriname. Suriname and the Antilles had either to accept that the matter stood thus, or they had to opt for independence, a possibility which was at first cast aside by both countries. Development aid also became an important area of concern as the islands faced increasing economic difficulties from the mid-1950s on. The charter made financial assistance by the stronger partner mandatory. Soon the Dutch Antilles and Suriname discovered that economic dependence on the Netherlands also curtailed their political autonomy. Metropolitan involvement especially in education and cultural matters likewise fuelled local resentment. Though the Dutch government included a plenipotentiary minister for each part of the Kingdom – the Netherlands, the Dutch Antilles and Suriname – it spent very little time discussing Caribbean issues as the majority of the members were actually Dutch. The function of governor remained in place during this period. In the early 1960s for the first time native Caribbean governors were appointed.

With the acceleration of the independence process in Africa and the English-speaking colonies of the Caribbean, the once progressive Charter of the Kingdom of the Netherlands started to seem outdated. In Suriname, nationalism was on the rise among the Afro-Surinamese community, who wished for more autonomy in terms of foreign policy in the form of official representation in the region, and membership of international organisations. This position found little resonance in the Antilles. However, the 1969 Curaçao revolt brought a decisive change in Dutch policies. Political and social unrest caused by labour conflicts, resentment regarding unequally divided prosperity, and racial barriers, escalated into full-blown revolt on 30 May 1969. The crisis revealed a deep dissatisfaction with the issue of good governance as defined by the charter. In January 1970 the Dutch government began discussions with the overseas prime ministers. On 5 January 1972 a tripartite advisory 'kingdom commission' was set up to investigate possible alternatives to the existing situation, and to debate the thorny issues of nationality, development aid and defence.

The centre-left government led by Joop den Uyl that came to power in May 1973 in the Netherlands immediately announced its intention to start talks with the aim of granting full independence to the Dutch Caribbean 'overseas territories' before the end of the legislature in question, that is, by 1976. However, it needed to create support overseas.

Large-scale migration, especially from Suriname, also played a role in Dutch desire to accelerate the process, but this impatience only served to speed up and intensify migration. Things changed when the new Prime Minister for Suriname, Henck Arron, declared on behalf of the 'National Party Combination' (a combination of Afro-Surinamese parties and the Surinamese-Javanese KTPI, in office from November 1973) that Suriname would accept independence by the end of 1975 and this in spite of opposition from Hindustani leaders. The latter asked for a ten-year transition period to assist in the protection of human rights and the safeguarding of democracy. Den Uyl sided with the Surinamese government and ignored the opposition. In June 1975 a provisional agreement was reached, but negotiations continued until the actual transfer of power on 25 November 1975. Imminent independence again intensified the flow of migrants to the Netherlands. The fast pace of debate also led to growing social and racial tensions in Suriname as the opposition felt left out. Surinamese Hindustanis moved to the Netherlands in vast numbers. With an eye to financial aid, the parties eventually settled for 3.5 billion guilders, which is approximately €3.5 million. A compromise was also reached on migration: unlimited migration would be allowed for five years after independence, a provision which had disastrous consequences for the new country's human resources. On 13 November 1975, the Antillean Staten voted unanimously for the charter's amendment with regard to Suriname's independence. Governor Ferrier became the new republic's first President. To this day, the decolonisation process of Suriname is seen as an example of peaceful transition to independence, yet it is also criticised for its swiftness and its disregard for the opposition and for public opinion in Suriname. Independence has come to be seen as primarily motivated by self-interest on the side of the Dutch, but also as an inevitable step.

Phase III: The Antilles and Aruba after 1975

After the 1969 crisis which eventually led to Suriname's independence, the question of sovereignty also arose in the Antilles, where in general there was a strong desire to remain part of the Kingdom. With the exception of Aruba, which wanted to secede from the rest of the Antilles, the islands did not want independence. The Evertsz cabinet then in power in the Antilles agreed to a transfer of sovereignty only if it occurred in three stages: the realisation of internal self-governance for all six islands, a new form of co-operation between the islands, and, finally, the preparation for independence only when a reasonable level of economic development had been achieved. Today this tactic is seen as a smart move motivated by Evertsz's awareness of the economical frailty of the islands.

The Dutch wish to forge a united nation of the six Dutch Caribbean islands was unrequited, and both the Antillean and Dutch governments agreed to grant a 'status aparte' (separate status) to Aruba. This came into effect in 1986, and was to be followed by a full transfer of sovereignty ten years later. Aruba wanted to break away from 'Curaçao and onderhoorigheden', as it considered Curaçao as meddling in its affairs as well as ethnically different from itself. The Aruban call for separashon went back to the 1930s but became louder in the 1970s. Once the new status was implemented, however, it became clear that the Aruban government actually had no wish to become fully independent, but instead planned to remain inside the Kingdom of the Netherlands in a kind of commonwealth relationship. By 1990 an agreement was finally reached stating that independence would not become mandatory in 1996.

Though all three countries still within the Kingdom restated their wish to continue existing constitutional ties, the Dutch government expressed the wish to 'modernise' the charter, as the Dutch government found itself bound too much by it. By the 1990s the Dutch government had accepted the idea that decolonisation would not be achieved by the transfer of sovereignty. Consequently, it relaunched the debate on the charter and on the relationship between national and island autonomy and the responsibility of the government of the Kingdom. This continues to be a critical issue.

With Aruba as a separate country there was a new plenipotentiary prime minister for that country as well as a separate governor for the island. The Ministry of Antillean Affairs changed its name to include Aruba. However, this ministry was abolished in 1998, and its function was taken over by the renamed Ministry of the Interior and Kingdom Affairs. From 1998 to 2002 Caribbean affairs were managed by a state secretary. In 1993 Curaçao held a referendum on its future. The proposal to form a separate country was rejected by 86 per cent of the voters. Referenda in other parts of the Antilles yielded similar results. In 1999 the first Secretary of State for Kingdom Relations released a document entitled *Toekomst in Samenwerking* (*A Future in Co-operation*) which outlined measures for economic recovery and introduced conditions to be met to qualify for future Dutch assistance. In the Caribbean this document was perceived as a unilateral attempt to forge policy. Governments in the Antilles and the Netherlands eventually agreed that the International Monetary Fund would play the role of arbiter in the restructuring of the Antilles' finances and administration.

Under the charter's emphasis on the need for good governance questions of law enforcement, crime and money laundering have in fact strengthened ties between the countries of the Kingdom. Common policy-making has intensified the existing links. At the same time, in the early years of the twenty-first century the issues of development aid, migration, education and culture have also shown up the fragility of the original agreement.

Patricia Krus

HISTORIES

Cheong, Yong Mung (1982), *H. J. van Mook and Indonesian Independence. A Study of his Role in Dutch-Indonesian Relations 1945–1948*, The Hague: Martinus Nijhoff.

Kahin, George McTurnan (2003), *Nationalism and Revolution in Indonesia*, Ithaca, NY: Cornell University Press.

Oostindie, Gert and Inge Klinkers (2003), *Decolonising the Caribbean: Dutch Policies in Comparative Perspective*, Amsterdam: Amsterdam University Press.

Oostindie, Gert and Peter Verton (1998), 'Ki sorto di reino: What Kind of Kingdom? Antillean and Aruban Views and Expectations of the Kingdom of the Netherlands', *New West Indian Guide* 72 (1–2): 43–75.

Sartono Kartodirdjo (1997), 'The Decolonization of Indonesian Historiography: Perspectives and Trends', in P. J. Drooglever and M. J. B. Schouten (eds), *De Leeuw en de Banteng*, The Hague: ING, pp. 24–37.

The Dutch in the Caribbean

The Caribbean mainly consists of some 2,000 islands, only about fifty of which are inhabited. For some the Caribbean extends to all islands in, and all countries surrounding the Caribbean Sea; for others, all territories that once knew a plantation system and slavery. On this latter view, parts of Brazil and the south of the United States form part of the Caribbean. The most common definition of the Caribbean comprises the islands of the Caribbean Sea, Guiana, Suriname, French-Guiana, Belize and the coastal areas of Venezuela and Colombia.

There are some thirty countries in the Caribbean, with a total population of roughly 40 million. The area is multicultural and multilingual. European languages such as Spanish, English, French and Dutch are prominent. Regional variants include for instance West Indian Standard English, as well as island variations such as St Martin English, Bajan Creole English and Jamaican English. We also find Asian languages such as Chinese, Hindi and Javanese, including again variants thereof. Some languages find their origin in the region itself: French Créole in Haiti, Kweyòl in St Lucia, Papiamentu on the Dutch Leeward Islands, and Sranan and Sarnami in Suriname.

With more then 20 million speakers on the largest Caribbean islands – Cuba, the Dominican Republic and Puerto Rico – Spanish is the most important language of the Caribbean. English is the most widely disseminated, spoken in more than half of all Caribbean countries, but counts only 6 million speakers. French is the language of some 9 million Caribbeans, though it should be stressed that in Haiti, the largest 'French-language' country, 90 per cent of the population is monolingual in 'Créole'. In Suriname, in the Dutch Antilles, and in Aruba, Dutch is the first, second or third language of approximately half a million people.

The Caribbean covers 2,640,000 square kilometres, though only 10 per cent of this is land mass. Total land mass is 236,000 square kilometres, of which 444 square kilometres is Curaçao, 288 square kilometres is Bonaire, 34 square kilometres is the Dutch part of St Martin, and 192 square kilometres is Aruba. The distances from, for instance, the Bahamas and Belize to Barbados, from Paramaribo to Port au Prince or Puerto Rico are enormous. In other words, the Dutch part of the Caribbean is tiny.

Opinions differ as to the underlying unity – or not – of the region. There are many that emphasise the cultural and linguistic diversity of the countries and islands of the Caribbean, even if they do share the same tropical climate and a history of *conquista*, genocide and colonisation, the immigration of all kinds of Europeans as well as many Jews, an inhuman slave trade, the plantation system in which sugar was king, African slavery, eventual emancipation, and indentured labour in various parts of the region with the large-scale importation of Chinese, Indians and Indonesians. For centuries now the region has had a mixed population, with people of African descent forming a clear majority. Notions of 'Americanness' compete with those of 'Antillianity'. Most Caribbean countries opted for independence politically, and economically evolved from traditional rural societies to societies geared to industrialisation, service industries and, increasingly, tourism. History in the region follows the same trajectory. Caribbean literature strongly reflects these social developments. Michiel van Kempen's claim that 'Whoever writes Surinamese literature at the same time writes Surinamese history' holds true for the rest of the Caribbean.

The Dutch Antilles and Aruba have been separate countries within the Kingdom of the Netherlands since 1 January 1986. The Dutch Caribbean consists of two groups of islands: the so-called 'ABC-islands' of Aruba, Bonaire and Curaçao, forming the 'leeward' islands before the coast of Venezuela and the South American continent, and the 'windward' 'SSS-islands' of Saba, St Eustatius and St Martin, 500 miles to the North, in the Caribbean archipelago. St Martin is half Dutch, and half a French 'département d'outre mer' (Pizarro 1988).

The history of the Dutch Antilles is that of six islands that were joined by the whim of the European coloniser. The 'Dutch Antilles' is a Dutch concept, the Antillean first and foremost identifies with his or her specific island. After the Spanish *conquistadores* in the early sixteenth century had abducted the native Indian population, the islands were deemed uninteresting beacuse of a lack of precious ores. Consequently, they were labelled *islas inútiles*. The Dutch, in search of salt deposits for their herring trade and as a basis for privateering, in the 1730s occupied the islands without much opposition. Until the end of the eighteenth century the colony was administered by the Dutch West India Company. It was especially the northern Windward Islands that became the subject of European rivalries, with wars raging, and frequent changes of hand. 'The Golden Rock' St Eustatius (Statia) was a prosperous centre of commerce, a major trade depot, and an important distribution point for the slave trade. The French Revolution led to Dutch Caribbean possessions being temporarily occupied by other European powers, but in 1816 Dutch sovereignty was restored.

Government in the Dutch Caribbean underwent profound changes over the centuries. Initially, the colony was divided into 'leeward' and 'windward' islands. It was also united with Suriname and administered from Paramaribo. From 1848 the six islands were united as one territory, 'Curaçao' (and dependencies), a situation that would continue until 1954, though sometimes under different labels. In the meantime Indonesia had gained its independence. Already in December 1942 Queen Wilhelmina had announced a revision of colonial relations. This revision was enacted in the 'Statuut voor het Koninkrijk' ('Statute for the Kingdom') of 15 December 1954. This law granted the Dutch Antilles and Suriname home rule. After the social unrest of 'Thirty May 1969' in Curaçao, relations between the Netherlands and its West Indian colonies entered a new phase. In 1975 Suriname gained independence, and Aruba pursued a *status aparte*, that is, a special relationship with the other islands and the Netherlands. Aruba, economically doing well, wanted to remain part of the Kingdom, but also wished to be free of Curaçao, an ideal finally realised on 1 January 1986. From then the Kingdom comprised three countries: the Netherlands, the Dutch Antilles and Aruba. The Dutch Antilles and Aruba each have their own government and estates, a governor appointed by the Queen, and a minister plenipotentiary in The Hague (Aller 1994). If in the 1950s through to the 1970s the right to self-determination was primarily interpreted as the right to independence, as of the 1980s that same right came to be seen rather as the right to remain part of the Kingdom of the Netherlands. Regional developments, and specifically developments in Suriname, had made the islands think twice about pursuing outright independence. Mounting threats of international crime and the drugs trade, against which small countries have almost no defence, meant that the desire of these countries to remain inside the Kingdom of the Netherlands was respected by Venezuela, the United States and the Netherlands itself.

Initially a strategic possession, a slave depot, a centre of trade, and a traditional agricultural colony, Curaçao turned into a modern industrial society when Shell opened a refinery on the island in the early years of the twentieth century. Aruba followed a decade later. St Eustatius, the 'Golden Rock', went into steep decline after it was sacked by Admiral Rodney in 1781, and after the French occupation at the beginning of the nineteenth century. Over the last few decades all the islands have started to promote themselves as tourist paradises. St Martin and Aruba, particularly, have profited from American and European tourism. Curaçao, Aruba and St Martin have also gained reputations as financial service centres.

The original native Indian population of the Dutch Caribbean was decimated by the Spanish by means of deportation and outright extermination. Then came North European settlers, followed by Sephardic Jews from the middle of the seventeenth century on. The beginning of the infamous 'middle passage' so many West Africans made as slaves dates from the same period. Northern Europeans, Jews and West Africans made up the population of the islands both before and after emancipation in 1863. It was only with the coming of the oil early in the twentieth century that there occurred a relatively massive immigration of Ashkenazi Jews, British West Indians, Surinamese, Dutch, Portuguese and Lebanese. At present, more than forty nationalities or ethnicities make up the cultural melting-pot of the Dutch Antillean islands. Many inhabitants of the Dutch Windward Islands moved to the Dutch Leeward Islands. The growth of tourism on St Martin led to a considerable population increase there. Bonaire, Saba and St Eustatius continue to have a relatively small population.

In the meantime, there are also some 100,000 Antilleans and Arubans living in the Netherlands. So-called 'circular migration' has become a way of life for many citizens of the entire Kingdom of the Netherlands (Oostindie 1994).

It may sound strange for a Dutch colony, and indeed it also struck former and present-day colonials as such, but although Dutch is the official language of the ABC-islands, Papiamentu is actually the dominant national language there, while English is the more common language of the SSS-islands. Aruba is officially bilingual: Dutch and Papiamentu. The 250,000 inhabitants of the two Caribbean countries that are part of the Kingdom of the Netherlands use four languages: first Papiamentu, which serves as mother tongue, language of communication and national language on the ABC islands (and because of recent immigration it is also a minority language of St Martin). Second, English, which is the language common to the three Windward Islands (and because of the American refinery on Aruba it is also widely used on that island). Third, official Dutch and fourth, Spanish, as spoken in the mighty continent 'across the water'. In fact, on these islands Dutch is so much a 'foreign' language that there did not even arise a regional or local variant comparable to Suriname-Dutch ('Surinaams-Nederlands'). It also was not necessary: English and Papiamentu were already in place and widely used.

The present situation is rather paradoxical. On the one hand continuing ties with the Kingdom of the Netherlands also imply continuous exposure to meddling by the Dutch and the West in the form of 'a cultural bombardment by American mass media in particular; the comprehensive reach of an education modelled upon either American or European examples; the tilt toward emigration; [and] the influence of metropolitan centers and tourism' (Oostindie 1994). On the other hand these ties also make for stability: 'It is precisely because Aruba, Bonaire and Curaçao are relatively safely ensconced in a larger constitutional whole that they can afford (literally so!) to keep alive their very own language which, from an international point of view, is absolutely marginal' (Oostindie 1994).

(*Translations into English by Wim Rutgers*)

Wim Rutgers

HISTORIES

Aller, H. B. van (1994), *Van kolonie tot koninkrijksdeel; de staatkundige geschiedenis van de Nederlandse Antillen en Aruba (van 1634 tot 1994)*, Gröningen, Wolters-Noordhoff.

Kempen, Michiel van (2003), *Een geschiedenis van de Surinaamse literatuur*, Breda: Uitgeverij De Geus.

Oostindie, G. J. (1994), *Caraïbische dilemma's in een 'stagnerend' dekolonisatieproces*, Leiden: KITLV Uitgeverij.

Pizarro, Ana (1988), 'Reflections on the Historiography of Caribbean Literature', *Callaloo* 34: 173–85.

The Dutch in Colonial America: New Netherland, 1624–67

Following Henry Hudson's discovery of the region in 1609, about thirty Walloon speaking families (that is, originating from the southern-most and French-speaking part of the Low Countries, in present-day Belgium) established a trading colony (1624) in the area of modern Manhattan, Long Island, and along the banks of the Hudson river. Under the colonial administration of the Dutch West India Company (WIC) (founded in 1621) the colony grew into a population of 7,000–8,000 by the time of its annexation by England in the Treaties of Amsterdam (1664) and Breda (1667).

From the beginning, the colonists struggled with the WIC concerning the purpose of the settlement. Would the colony be limited to the sea-coast, and engage only in the trading of furs, and later tobacco? Would the company prevent it from establishing its own manufacturing markets (in textiles, for instance), and trade with New England? Or would it become a growing settlement for the eventual creation of a self-sustaining community? The colony was not of major economic importance to the company or the Dutch Republic. Consequently, it never developed its full potential as a settlement in the New World.

Perhaps the most important event in the colony's history was the purchase of Manhattan Island from the Native Americans for the price of 60 florins-worth of merchandise. This amount was equivalent to the price of a first-class ticket for the two-month sea voyage from the Dutch Republic to the Hudson. The Dutch called the natives *wilden* or 'savages' because the latter did not hold a belief comparable to Christianity and their customs in marriage and land ownership were different from the Dutch. The *wilden* were not given any rights in the colony. Initially, the relationships were fair. From 1643, tensions with the Native Americans escalated over issues of forced taxation and punishments for crimes against the colonists.

The most famous Dutch Director-General of the colony was Pieter Stuyvesant (1612–72), who governed from 1647 to 1664. He was a colourful figure, with a peg-leg as replacement for the leg he had lost in youthful military exploits. A charismatic yet headstrong leader, he was a strong supporter of free elementary education, a savvy merchant who introduced tea to the British colonies, and a staunch defender of the Dutch Reformed Church. He considered the Quakers as agitators and a threat to public order. He was bitterly opposed by more tolerant believers. His decision not to allow Jewish refugees into the colony was overruled by the civic leaders. He constantly rescinded orders from the officials in Amsterdam and was forced to appear before them on account of his insubordination. Despite his policies, the colony developed limited forms of representative rule and expanded considerably.

The Dutch-British wars brought about the demise of New Netherland. When the Duke of York appeared at New Amsterdam with a fleet of four ships, the colonists were unaware that only one of these was a proper man-of-war. Stuyvesant reluctantly surrendered, and on 8 September 1664 ceded the town to the British. York's brother, King Charles II, renamed it New York. However, the government in Amsterdam did not give up the fight, and battles continued until the Treaty of Breda in 1667, when the British gave up the Spice Islands in the future Indonesia to the Dutch in exchange for all New Netherland.

The historical legacy of the colony is still under debate. Some argue that its political development led to forms of religious tolerance, local political representation, and even served as an institutional model for the future United States of America. On this view the colony deserves praise for its stress on reason, tolerance and a pre-Jeffersonian encouragement of the moral right to rebel against illegitimate authority. Others argue that the colony varied little from its origins in the Netherlands. Though more religiously tolerant, it never became a magnet for people seeking refuge in America. Its social organisation, culture and political institutions were not radically reformed by the frontier experience.

Still, some of New Netherland's legacies are clear: American English has adopted many Dutch words such as 'golf', 'skate', 'skipper', 'Yankee', and 'yacht', to name just a few. Prominent Americans of Dutch descent include the poet Walt Whitman, the railway entrepreneur Cornelius Vanderbilt and presidents Martin van Buren, and Theodore and Franklin D. Roosevelt, with the last strongly conscious of his Dutch heritage. Most concretely, many geographic areas and settlements in the Hudson River Valley and New York City retain their Dutch names.

Richard C. Kagan

Histories

Jacobs, Jaap (2005), *New Netherland: A Dutch Colony in Seventeenth-Century America*, Netherlands: Brill.

Milton, Giles (1999), *Nathaniel's Nutmeg or The True and Incredible Adventures of the Spice Trader who Changed the Course of History*, New York: Farrar, Straus and Giroux.

Rink, Oliver A. (1986), *Holland on the Hudson: An Economic and Social History of Dutch New York*, Ithaca, NY and London: Cornell University Press.

Zee, Henri van der and Barbara van der Zee (1978), *A Sweet and Alien Land: The Story of Dutch New York*, New York: Viking Press.

The Dutch Colonisation of North America

The Dutch development of the New Netherland frontier in North America occurred in three distinct stages: exploration, 1609–14; trade, 1614–23; and settlement, 1624–64. Henry Hudson's expedition to North America proved the catalyst that began the Dutch colonisation of North America. In 1610, Emanuel van Meteren included the details of Hudson's voyage in his *History of the Netherlanders*. For Holland's merchants, van Meteren's history and the cargo from Hudson's ship illustrated the potential for a New Netherland fur market. Between 1611 and 1614, several ships, financed by merchants such as Arnout Vogels and the Pelgrom brothers, explored New Netherland.

The New Netherland Company was formed in 1614. Unlike the earlier and sporadic independent merchant activities, Holland's goal to establish a more robust and profitable presence in North America motivated the trading stage. Combined, Dutch and Indian objectives gave rise to Fort Nassau, Holland's first settlement in New Netherland.

The settlement phase occurred in two stages, 1624–50 and 1650–64. When the government monopoly granted to the New Netherland Company expired in 1617, several merchants resumed trade along the Hudson river. In 1620, threatened by the English and French, the New Netherland Company appealed for a second monopoly. Holland's government denied the request, but, bothered by the growing European presence, opted instead to create the Dutch West India Company. Holland's government granted the company a twenty-four year monopoly, agreed to provide troops and ships to protect any territory claimed, and provided nearly half a million dollars to fund the venture. In return, Holland's government expected the company to establish forts, settlements and trade routes, as well as to negotiate treaties and alliances with the rival European groups and native inhabitants. The Dutch West India Company elected to focus its market strategies on Africa, Brazil and the Caribbean, while adopting a policy of agricultural colonisation for New Netherland. By 1624, the company had sent thirty Walloon families, French Protestants from the southern Low Countries (present-day Belgium), and a multi-ethnic group of traders to build four trading posts in New Netherland. Unable to finance their Brazilian enterprise and at the same time fund the colony in New Netherland, the company decided to privatise settlement in the latter by initiating the patroonship programme in 1629. Under this, the company granted an investor land to finance and settle fifty colonists on within four years. In return, the patroon owned the land, and held jurisdiction over it.

By 1662, the Dutch had established several settlements, including Fort Orange (Albany), New Amsterdam (New York), Nieuw Utrecht, Nieuw Haerlem, Wiltwijck (Kingston), Schenectady and Nieuw Dorp (Hurley). Though it grew to 1,500 inhabitants, New Netherland paled in comparison to the English colonies which totalled nearly 30,000 people. In 1667, Holland lost New Netherland to England at the conclusion of the Second Anglo-Dutch War.

J. P. Alessi

LITERARY WORKS
Irving, Washington [1809] (1893), *Knickerbocker's History of New York*, New York and London: Putnam's.

HISTORIES
Jacobs, Jaap (1999), *Een zegenrijk gewest: Nieuw-Nederland in de zeventiende eeuw*, Amsterdam: Prometheus-Bert Bakker.
Ligtenberg, Lucas (1999), *De Nieuwe Wereld van Peter Stuyvesant*, Amsterdam: Balans.

The Dutch in Brazil, 1624–54

The first Dutch interest in Brazil dates back to the late sixteenth century, when the profitable and expanding Brazilian sugar trade attracted Dutch merchants. Unfortunately, the political conflict between Habsburg Spain and the rebellious Low Countries threatened Dutch participation in the Brazil trade since Portugal and its colonies had been incorporated into the Spanish Habsburg Crown in 1580. To weaken the finances of the Dutch rebels during the 1580s and 1590s, Spain repeatedly confiscated Dutch ships carrying Brazilian sugar and other commodities from the Spanish Habsburg Empire. Peaceful Dutch participation in the Brazilian sugar trade resumed and expanded during the twelve-year truce between Spain and the Dutch Republic from 1609 to 1621.

After the truce expired, peaceful Dutch commerce with Brazil was replaced by Dutch military aggression. In 1621, the States-General chartered the Dutch West India Company (WIC) as a commercial company that would control Dutch trade and colonialism in the Americas and West Africa. After the WIC had collected enough capital in 1623, the company directors launched an ambitious assault against Spanish Habsburg possessions in the southern Atlantic. By conquering the sugar growing provinces of north-eastern Brazil, the WIC hoped to secure the sugar trade and deliver a major blow to the Spanish Empire. In 1624, a WIC force occupied Salvador de Bahía, the Portuguese capital of Brazil and the main harbour of the Brazilian sugar trade. However, a Spanish and Portuguese relief expedition forced the Dutch to surrender Bahía a year later. Only after the WIC had collected

enough capital again through privateering in the Caribbean, including the capture of a
Spanish fleet loaded with Mexican silver in 1628, did the company directors plan a second
invasion of north-eastern Brazil.

In 1630, a WIC fleet and army attacked the weakly defended Brazilian sugar province of
Pernambuco. Although the WIC army quickly occupied the coastal towns of Recife and
Olinda, the Portuguese and their indigenous allies prevented the WIC troops from breaking out of their small beachhead. However, by 1635, combined naval and land-based operations of WIC forces had worn down the Portuguese resistance in Pernambuco and in the
neighbouring provinces of Paraíba, Itamaraca and Rio Grande. A considerable number of
moradores, Portuguese settlers, accepted WIC rule as long as their Catholic religion was
guaranteed by the Protestant Dutch. At the same time, about 7,000 Portuguese colonists,
their African slaves and Indian allies retreated to Bahía, from where they initiated a guerrilla war against the WIC forces.

WIC directors centralised the government of the colony by appointing the military
officer and nobleman Johan Maurits as Governor in 1636. Maurits was expected to defeat
the Portuguese guerrillas and to revitalise the weakened economy of the Dutch colony.
Although Maurits succeeded in driving the Portuguese guerrillas from Pernambuco in
1637, a WIC force failed to capture Bahía in May 1638. Maurits was more successful in
restoring the economy. In 1637, a WIC force sailing from Brazil took the strategic
Portuguese fort and slave port São Jorge da Mina on the Gold Coast of West Africa. This
conquest enabled the WIC to supply their Brazilian sugar plantations with West African
slaves. During Maurits' tenure as Governor, the arts and sciences also flourished in north-
eastern Brazil. Several landscape and portrait painters as well as the scientists Georg
Marcgraf and Willem Piso were part of Maurits' entourage in the twin capital cities of
Recife and Mauritsstad.

Dutch colonial society was characterised by ethnic and religious diversity. The free population consisted of a majority of Catholic *moradores* and a minority of Protestant WIC
employees, soldiers, sailors and free settlers. Much of the WIC personnel was of German,
English, French, Scottish or Scandinavian origin. Sephardic Jews made up a considerable
segment of the Recife population. The large enslaved population was comprised of recently
imported West African slaves. Tupi-speaking Indians from the coastal region and Tapuya-
speaking Indians from the interior also constituted a sizeable component of the north-
eastern Brazilian population.

The secession of Portugal from the Spanish Crown in 1640 initially appeared to
strengthen the Dutch colony in Brazil. The restored Portuguese kingdom was willing to
make an alliance with the Dutch Republic against the common Spanish enemy. However,
the WIC directors quickly instructed Maurits in 1641 to capture as many Portuguese possessions in Brazil and West Africa as possible before the Dutch-Portuguese alliance came
into effect in 1642. WIC forces successfully captured the northern Brazilian province of
Maranhão as well as the strategic Portuguese slave trade centre Luanda on the Angolan
coast. Although these conquests greatly angered the Portuguese, the WIC directors
recalled most WIC troops as well as Maurits himself from Brazil in 1644 as cost-saving
measures.

In the summer of 1645 a popular rebellion broke out among the *moradores* against WIC
rule. The *moradores*, who had never fully accepted the Protestant Dutch invaders, received
active support from Bahía-based guerrilla forces against the WIC. Because of the reduced
military strength of the WIC, the Portuguese rebels and guerrillas quickly regained most
parts of north-eastern Brazil. By the end of 1645, the WIC controlled only the coastal forts

and some parts of Rio Grande and Paraíba that were occupied by the indigenous allies of the Dutch. Although the WIC, with the support of the States-General, sent several thousand new soldiers to Brazil in 1648, the newly arrived troops suffered two humiliating defeats at the hands of the Portuguese in 1648 and 1649. After the Dutch Republic became preoccupied by a war with England in 1652, the Portuguese King sent a fleet to Recife to force the surrender of the weakened Dutch colony. Following the arrival of the Portuguese fleet at Recife in December 1653, the exhausted and demoralised WIC officials formally surrendered the city as well as all the other remaining WIC forts in Brazil to the Portuguese on 26 January 1654. After several years of negotiations, in 1661 the Portuguese agreed financially to compensate the Dutch for the loss of their short-lived colony in Brazil.

Mark Meuwese

HISTORIES

Boxer, Charles Ralph (1957), *The Dutch in Brazil, 1624–1654*, Oxford: Clarendon Press.

Ebert, Christopher (2003), 'Dutch Trade with Brazil before the Dutch West India Company, 1587–1621', in Johannes Postma and Victor Enthoven (eds), *Riches from Atlantic Commerce: Dutch Transatlantic Trade and Shipping, 1585–1817*, Brill: Leiden and Boston, pp. 49–75.

Heijer, Henk den (1994), *De geschiedenis van de WIC*, Zutphen: Walburg Pers.

Mello, José Antonio Gonsalves de (2001), *Nederlanders in Brazilië (1624–1654): De invloed van de Hollandse bezetting op het leven en de cultuur in Noord-Brazilië*, translated from the Portuguese by G. N. Visser, revised by B. N. Teensma, Zutphen: Walburg Pers.

Schalkwijk, Frans Leonard (1998), *The Reformed Church in Dutch Brazil (1630–1654)*, Zoetermeer: Boekencentrum.

The Dutch in Taiwan (1624–62)

The Dutch arrival in Taiwan was by default. When the Dutch East India Company (VOC) established its Asian headquarters at Batavia (present-day Jakarta) in 1618, it began to explore trade with China. Four years later, Cornelis Reijerson, with sixteen ships and 2,000 soldiers, surveyed south-western Taiwan, at that time known by its Portuguese name Formosa, for a few days, then established a trading port in the Pescadore Islands, closer to the Chinese mainland. Two years later, though, the Dutch were driven away by the army of the ruling Ming emperor. With mainland China unavailable, the Dutch established Fort Orange, later renamed Zeelandia, on Taiwan.

The Dutch were the first Europeans to establish administrative rule in Taiwan. In January 1625, the VOC appointed Martinus Sonck as the first Governor. He bought a tract of land from the Sinkan aborigines with fifteen pieces of cangan cloth. This property later developed into the city of Tainan. At the time, there were fewer than 2,000 Chinese living there, mainly pirates and fishermen who had fled the turmoil of mainland China.

The Dutch surveyed and mapped the coastal areas and the landholdings on Taiwan. They also established forts and ports in south-eastern and north-eastern Taiwan and engaged intensively in trade and the cultivation of the Tainan plain. Within a few years the Dutch had brought or encouraged settlers from China, whose numbers (mainly men) had reached 40,000–50,000 by the 1660s. Fishing, navigation and the cultivation of rice and sugar cane provided these immigrants with better opportunities to hold land and gain a living than what was available in Fujian province across the Taiwan Strait. Tonio

Andrade (2005) sees the relationship between the Dutch and the Chinese in those days as having led to the creation of a Sino-Dutch hybrid colony.

The Dutch ruled the south-western area of Taiwan, around Tainan and the Tainan plain, for forty-four years. Despite this brief rule, the Dutch became the originators of Taiwan's foreign trade with China, the Philippines, Japan and Europe. They exported their own rice, sugar, camphor, deer hides and tobacco, and served as entrepôt or trading centre for many other items, including Chinese porcelain, gold and silk. The Dutch did not encourage large-scale immigration from the motherland but relied on Chinese and aborigines. One estimate concludes that even at its peak the total Dutch population did not exceed 2,800, 2,200 of whom were soldiers (Wang I-shou 1980). The Dutch imposed exorbitant taxes, fees and legal restrictions upon the population.

Many of the local aborigines, mainly Austronesian tribes, did not accept Dutch rule and engaged in warfare that resulted in mutual slaughter. To ease tension with the aborigines and fulfil their proselytising mission, the Dutch converted the aborigines to Christianity, and transcribed their spoken languages into a phonetic script. Yet their attempts to befriend both the aborigines and the Chinese who had settled there resulted in failure. Their rule was brought to an end when a rebel from the ruling Ming Dynasty, Zheng Cheng-kong, better known as Koxinga in Western histories, descended on Tainan. At first he sought an alliance with the Dutch, possibly with an eye to returning to China with his fleet and army to conquer his homeland. Unfortunately, the Dutch miscalculated his military strength when they attacked Zheng's navy. The results were disastrous. Zheng allied with angry Chinese and aborigines to overthrow the Dutch, and established his own kingdom in 1662.

The Chinese nationalists view the Dutch as just another imperial-colonial power. The Taiwanese nationalists, though, have magnified the positive significance of Holland's brief rule over parts of Taiwan. They view Taiwan as an ocean nation which has developed through immigrants who have created multiple layers of culture and living experiences that have made of Taiwan a distinctive society. On this view, although the majority of the population on Taiwan indeed came from China, their experience in Taiwan has led to an identity that is uniquely Taiwanese, not Chinese. They look on the Dutch as a people who recognised the uniqueness of Taiwan long before the Chinese themselves paid any attention.

Richard C. Kagan

HISTORIES

Andrade, Tonio (2005), 'Pirates, Pelts and Promises: The Sino-Dutch Colony of Seventeenth-Century Taiwan and the Aboriginal Village of Favorlang', *Journal of Asian Studies* 64 (2) (May): 295–321.

Blussé, Leonard (1984), 'Dutch Protestant Missionaries as Protagonists of the Territorial Expansion of the VOC on Formosa', in Dick Kooiman, Otto van den Muizenberg and Peter van der Veer (eds), *Conversion, Competition and Conflict: Essays on the Role of Religion in Asia*, Amsterdam: Free University Press, pp. 155–84.

Hollman, Thomas O. (1991), 'Formosa and the Trade in Venison and Deer Skins', in Roderich Ptak and Dietmar Rothermund (eds), *Emporia, Commodities, and Entrepreneurs in Asian Maritime Trade, c. 1400–1750*, Beiträge zur Sudasienforschung, Sudasien-Institut, Universität Heidelberg, no. 141, Stuttgart: Franz Steiner, pp. 263–90.

Hsu Wen-hsiung (1980), 'From Aboriginal Island to Chinese Frontier: The Development of Taiwan before 1683', in Ronald G. Knapp (ed.), *China's Island*

Frontier: Studies in the Historical Geography of Taiwan, Honolulu: University of Hawaii Press, pp. 3–30.

Huber, Johannes (1990), 'Chinese Settlers against the Dutch East India Company: The rebellion led by Kuo-Huai-i on Taiwan in 1652', in Eduard B. Vermeer (ed.), *Development and Decline of Fukien Province in the Seventeenth and Eighteenth Centuries*, Leiden: E. J. Brill, pp. 265–96.

Knapp, Ronald G. (ed.) (1980), *China's Island Frontier: Studies in the Historical Geography of Taiwan*, Honolulu: University of Hawaii Press.

Kuepers, J. J. A. M. (1997), *The Dutch Reformed Church in Formosa 1627–1662: Mission in a Colonial Context*, Nouvelle Revue de Science Missionnaire: Immensee.

Oosterhof, J. L. (1985), 'Zeelandia, A Dutch Colonial City in Formosa (1624–1662)', in Robert Ross and Gerard J. Telkamp (eds), *Colonial Cities: Essays on Urbanism in a Colonial Context*, Dordrecht: Nijhoff, pp. 51–63.

Shepherd, John Robert (1993), *Statecraft and Political Economy on the Taiwan Frontier, 1600–1800*, Stanford, CA: Stanford University Press.

Wang I-shou (1980), 'Cultural Contact and the Migration of Taiwan's Aborigines: A Historical Perspective', in Ronald G. Knapp (ed.), *China's Island Frontier: Studies in the Historical Geography of Taiwan*, Honolulu: University of Hawaii Press, pp. 31–54.

Albert Helman

Albert Helman (1903–96) was the pen name of Lodewijk Alphonsus Maria Lichtveld. Helman was born in Suriname, to middle-class parents. At eighteen he was sent to the Netherlands to study. When leaving Suriname he had no intention of ever returning to the poverty-stricken and backward plantation colony. Still, the country 'where his navel string had been buried' would maintain its pull on him for the rest of his life.

In Holland Albert Helman became a teacher, a church organ player and a music critic. He began to study Dutch at university, but abandoned this because it 'bored him to death'. With his contemporaries Anton de Kom, the Antillean Cola Debrot and the slightly younger Rudie van Lier, Helman engaged with both Caribbean and Dutch literature. As such, this first generation of Dutch-Caribbean authors fulfilled a double role in the literary history of two countries. Eventually, the colonial 'mother country' proved just as unable to contain Helman's thirst for adventure and wandering as his native 'father country' had been. Helman seemed predestined to become a cosmopolitan. During the Spanish Civil War he was a war correspondent for the Dutch periodicals *N.R.C.* and *De Groene Amsterdammer*. He spoke out against Franco, and assumed the position of a non-party anarcho-socialist. From 1938 to 1939 he lived in Mexico. During World War II he participated, via literary and other means, in the Dutch resistance against the Germans.

Once the war was over, it was clear that major structural reforms were necessary in *De West*, as the Dutch Caribbean was customarily referred to in the mother country. Albert Helman was nominated Minister of Education and Public Health, and President of the Exchequer. He actively intervened in the cultural life of the colony, and founded the Office for Popular Literature and a language office; he also co-founded a music academy and a 'university without walls'. Helman then left for Washington, where he became Minister Plenipotentiary for the Kingdom of the Netherlands. After retirement he lived for many years on the Caribbean island of Tobago, and also spent long periods in various European countries.

Helman's work is characterised by a triple search: for the role the European 'mother' culture plays for him, for the continuing presence of the fatherland, and most importantly, for his own inner self .

Helman's 1926 debut *Zuid-Zuid-West* is an ode to the beauty of his country and its inhabitants, and at the same time a 'Multatulian' reproach against Holland: 'Without your love, without the love that is your duty . . . because all colonial possessions imply the deliberate assumption of a duty'. When Helman in 1983 wrote his historical study *De foltering van Eldorado; een ecologische geschiedenis van de vijf Guyana's* he had not yet changed his mind: 'The "civilised" world suffers from nothing so much as from half-knowledge and pseudo-insight. Its politicians and statesmen almost without exception are notorious blockheads . . . Let us rather turn to the poets that have so often – though equally often neglected during their lifetime – proven to have had a better idea of the present and the future than all the others.'

In his work, Helman remained committed to Suriname – it was a love– hate relationship without end, because although he could physically distance himself from his native country he never succeeded in mentally taking leave of it. It remained an object of study for him and fuelled his fiction. He published two important works on slavery. His well-known novel of slavery *De stille plantage* (1931), he later rewrote as the Vijverberg-Prize winning *De laaiende stilte* (1952): 'Pity this land that will never be yours . . . the locusts from the North will populate your woods and they will eat bare your fields, so bare that they will turn inside out the earth fathoms deep searching for more.' Helman continued writing into ripe old age. His copious oeuvre has not always been appreciated by his compatriots, who often think Helman too critical, too Westernised, too European. Helman has never exerted any direct influence upon younger writers. Undoubtedly, this would not have worried him as long as he had the feeling that he had stayed true to himself. Helman did not believe in national literatures – he was a cosmopolitan.

Translations into English by Wim Rutgers

Wim Rutgers

Historiography

EAST INDIES – INDONESIA

The Dutch maritime and colonial empire in South-East Asia was first established in the early part of the seventeenth century, and until the middle of the twentieth century it remained one of the great colonial powers in the world. But today, the history of the Dutch Empire in the East Indies (present-day Indonesia) is all but forgotten and ignored. From a comparative perspective, however, it is sufficiently unusual and different to merit attention and further study.

To begin with, over the centuries, the Dutch colonial possessions in the East Indies effected a complete transformation of the 'mother country'. The merchant empire in the 'emerald girdle' was a most profitable possession, and through the VOC (the Dutch East India Company, 1602–1799) and the Netherlands Indies (1814–1950), it made a contribution of fundamental importance to the economic development of the Dutch nation-state. The same is true in the political domain: the Dutch parliament gained its principal rights and powers in the nineteenth century in debates on colonial matters. We find the same again in the domain of knowledge and culture: from the publication of Van

Linschoten's *Itinerario* (1596) onwards, the Netherlands have been an important market for books on Asia, on travel, exotic peoples, countries and products, history, religions and languages. Surveying all this, the sociologist van Doorn concluded 'that the Indies, like it or not, form part of our national culture. The Indies live on in our writers, poets and painters, in scholarly research, in collections and museums in every field, and of course also in our historical consciousness.'

In the seventeenth century, VOC historians such as Hugo Grotius subscribed to the so-called Batavian myth, projecting the image of the honest Dutchman: simple, hard-working, tolerant and God-fearing but above all freedom-loving, focused on trade, and keen on law and regulation. This noble self-image lasted until the very end in 1945, when Meijer Ranneft wrote that 'the best of the Dutch character came out in the Indies: the calm, solid organisational ability, the love of freedom, religion and decency'.

But this self-image is strained to breaking point when we look at the legacy of the iron-fisted Governor-General Jan Pieterszoon Coen. Long seen in Holland as 'the founder of our colonial empire in the East', who had built Batavia on the ruins of a defeated Jakarta, the 'great man' who drove the English from the archipelago, the great icon of Dutch colonialism, the least we can say is that the Javanese and the English have retained a rather different image of this man.

From the early nineteenth century onwards, the colonial Dutch had a strong moral programme for their colonies. One of the foundation texts of the Dutch Empire is the great 'ethical' speech of the Dutch Governor-General van der Capellen in 1824, when he told the Indonesian natives – whom he regarded as children – that they should rejoice at being the subjects of the Dutch king, their 'benevolent father', who wanted to extend his fatherly love and concern for their welfare to them. In the domain of agriculture, this was followed in 1830 by the introduction on Java of the so-called *Cultuurstelsel* (cultivation system), for the forced production of crops like coffee, tea, indigo, sugar, spices and tobacco for the European market, at prices set by the colonial administration. This system required a well-organised infrastructure, an efficient administration, and effective maintenance of law and order. Thus, under Dutch control, Java came to be run as a 'model colony', as many foreign observers noted in the heyday of European imperialism. It is estimated today that in the nineteenth century the total benefit of this model colony for the motherland in Europe amounted to more than 1,250 million guilders.

The *Cultuurstelsel* is the subject of fierce criticism in the most important work of Dutch colonial literature, the novel *Max Havelaar or the Coffee Auctions of the Dutch Trading Company* (1860) by Multatuli (1820–87), which marked a key moment in Dutch literature and politics. In this respect – as Edward Said put it in his *Culture and Imperialism* – Multatuli's novel was a rare exception in nineteenth-century colonial debate, which almost exclusively focused on exploitation, profitability and management.

Many foreign observers, meanwhile, had nothing but praise for the way the Dutch ran Java as a 'model colony'. And today, the notion of the model colony still forms part of the cultural legacy from the colonial era. In the Netherlands at any rate, the self-image of the Dutch as enlightened and benevolent colonisers is known rather better than the many colonial wars, the repression necessary to sustain the Dutch Empire for so long, and the many black pages in that history, full of wars, intrigues, cunning, cruelty and treachery.

Throughout the nineteenth and twentieth centuries, colonial history – whether it was in the great source publications on Coen and the VOC or in Gerretson's majestic history of Royal Shell Oil Company – was written from a decidedly Hollando- and Eurocentric perspective. But from the 1930s onwards, a more comparative approach came to the fore, and in the works of van Leur, Vlekke and Resink we find a clear Indocentric angle on colonial historiography. The dominant view, however, was of the Indies as the symbol of 'the glory and grandeur of the Netherlands, which without the Indies would be an insignificant state.' Hence, at the time of decolonisation, the great fear of 'Indies lost, disaster the cost', as a popular political slogan had it. This could only strengthen the Dutch resolve to fight to the last in order to retain the Indies.

In the 1930s, too, Dutch repression of Indonesian political aspirations became unbearable. As the social-democrat Sutan Sjahrir, later the first Prime Minister of the Indonesian Republic, put it at the time: 'One day, the Dutch will be sorry that they have never pursued a cultural policy or a broad policy of reconciliation in this country.' Similarly, in 1950, the first Indonesian Vice-President, Mohammed Hatta, stated: 'Now, accounts have been settled. What is left is the old friendship.' But in 1979, the journalist and historian Mochtar Lubis came to a much more critical assessment: '[T]he Dutch came to the land beneath the rainbow to trade in spices. But their greed blinded them to the culture, dignity and human sense of honour of the Indonesians, and they brought destruction and death to whatever crossed their path, as if possessed by the devil.'

Reinier Salverda

THE DUTCH CARIBBEAN

Interest in the history of the Dutch Caribbean is a fairly recent phenomenon beyond the Dutch-speaking world, the availability of sources in languages other than Dutch hindering the work of most historians. The larger part of archival collections is held in the Netherlands. During the colonial period, the small size of the local élite and the distance from the metropolis offered little opportunity for historical writing at a local level. The diverse histories of the Dutch Antilles and Suriname also render any historical writing arduous. Many studies choose to concentrate on either one or more islands or on Suriname, the latter receiving the bulk of critical attention.

General studies

The first record of Dutch presence in the Caribbean appears in Joannes de Laet's (1644) *Historie ofte jaerlyk verhael van de verrichtingen der geoctroyeerde West-Indische Compagnie* (*History or Annual Account of the Activities of the West India Company*). This account – based on the now lost archive of the VOC and reprinted in the 1930s – traces the expeditions of the Dutch in Brazil and the Caribbean, and the conquest of Curaçao and its history from the early seventeenth century to the Napoleonic wars. Twentieth-century histories of the region include Cornelis Goslinga's three-part study *The Dutch in the Caribbean* (1971–90) which describes major events and concepts in Dutch Caribbean history but is criticised by Gert Oostindie for its supposed lack of methodological standards and its colonialist undertones. Dutch entrepreneurs were responsible for bringing sugar-making techniques from Brazil to the Caribbean and also dominated the slave trade (Postma and Enthoven 2003). The legal, moral and political circumstances surrounding the abolition of slavery have been outlined in Paasman and Oostindie (1998) and Emmer (1980).

Suriname

Until the early nineteenth century slaves made up 90 per cent of the population of the colony. The white population showed a significant degree of diversity with a significant number of Jewish settlers and transitory white groups. Consequently, before the twentieth century, local history was written by whites who were mostly visitors or temporary residents. The slave era was related in travel accounts, and in geographic, agronomic and ethnological studies that painted an optimistic picture of the plantation economy up until the economic crisis of the 1770s. The first major work was J. D. Herlein's (1718) *Beschryvinge van de volk-plantinge Zuriname* (*Description of the Colony of Suriname*) which covered the geography of the region, the Amerindian and slave populations and the sugar industry, and justified slavery because of the supposed inferiority of the Africans. However, by the mid-eighteenth century Suriname had gained a tainted reputation in the writings of Voltaire (*Candide*), Aphra Behn (*Oroonoko*), and John G. Stedman (*Narrative of a Five Year Expedition against the Revolted Negroes of Suriname*), who criticised the cruelty of planters.

Abolition signalled the ruin of the colony. Although the importation of indentured labour from the East Indies and British India allowed the plantations to survive economically, the colonies were rapidly overtaken by the East Indies. Abolition also increased social mobility and gave educated coloureds more opportunities in government. The introduction of education led to the emergence of a new group of non-white historians from the colony. A major text is Anton de Kom's *Wij slaven van Suriname* (*We Slaves of Suriname*) published in 1934. It is a fierce indictment of colonialism. The publication of R. A. J. van Lier's *Samenleven in een grensgebied* (1949) – translated into English as *Frontier Society* in 1971 – introduced the new notion of a 'frontier society', and approached slavery from a psychopathological angle. The book discusses the history of Suriname from the beginning of colonisation to the 1940s and includes all literature published on Suriname since colonisation.

The period after autonomy shows a divergence of interpretations and subject matters between Surinamese and Dutch historians (Oostindie, 1999). Studies focus mainly on Maroons, slavery and the plantation system, with nationalism a prominent topic in the 1950s and 1960s. Most historians of contemporary Suriname are expatriate Surinamese, Dutch or North American.

Since World War II there has been an important increase in publications and research on Suriname, mostly written in the Netherlands rather than in Suriname itself. Nevertheless, improved infrastructure in Suriname has helped promote research in history and the social sciences. Local archives are mostly scattered and often in a sorry state, but financial aid aims to improve that condition. Collections are microfilmed. In the Netherlands *Oso*, a journal for Surinamese culture and history, has been appearing since 1981. It contributes to the propagation of knowledge in this domain, thus further emancipating Surinamese historiography. In 2003 Michiel van Kempen published a magisterial and exhaustive two-volume *Geschiedenis van de Surinaamse literatuur*.

Netherlands Antilles and Aruba
Although the six Caribbean islands that the Dutch once possessed are invariably mentioned as a whole they are geographically dispersed and have individual histories. The islands' historiography is as fragmented as their topography and Curaçao, considered to be the main island, has received the larger portion of critical attention. Three studies were published in the first decades of twentieth century: Hamelberg (1901–9), Knappert (1932) and Menkman (1942). They document the islands' history and paved the way for later generations of historians. Hamelberg uses seventeenth- and eighteenth-century sources, as well as original archives. The study is colonial in tone. It is also the first work to present the histories of the Leeward and Windward Islands as separate.

Political autonomy saw an increase in historical interest but the scarcity of resources remained problematic. Johannes Hartog's *Geschiedenis van de Nederlandse Antilles* (1953–64) falls into in four monographs – *Aruba* (1953), *Bonaire* (1957), *Curaçao* (1961) and *De Bovenwindse eilanden* (1964). Wim Klooster's *Illicit Riches* (1998) depicts the role played by Curaçao and St Eustatius as warehouses from which a wide variety of products was shipped to other colonies during the period of the slave trade. In *Het patroon van de oude curaçaose samenleving*, Harry Hoetinck (1958) reconstructs patterns of social behaviour among whites, blacks and free coloureds, and analyses patterns of exclusion and creolisation and attitudes towards race and colour. This influential study introduces the concept of 'segmental interaction' as against that of a segmented society. Many of Hoetinck's concepts have been widely accepted. Like Hoetinck, Renkema (1981) emphasises the unique character of slavery on Curaçao, where the absence of large plantations stimulated contact between races and gave rise to a large coloured population. Race always remained an influential factor in social interactions though. Römer (1979) discusses the importance of colour in social relations and in gaining access to higher social classes in the post-emancipation era. A number of studies have focused on the social aspects of the economic boom addressing questions of demography, labour, unionism and migration: van Soest 1983, Römer 1979 and Allen and van Gelder 1990. Römer traces the development of an insular identity in Curaçao as a response to modernisation. The last decade of the twentieth century saw the emergence of scholarship on the cultural history of the islands, exploring various aspects such as the African origins and development of local culture in music, dance, language and religious practices (René V. Rosalia (1997), Wim Rutgers (1996)).

Patricia Krus

HISTORIES

Beinart, W. (1994), *Twentieth-Century South Africa*, Cape Town: Oxford University Press.

Keegan, T. (1996), *Colonial South Africa and the Origins of the Racial Order*, Cape Town: David Philip.

Klooster, Wim (1998), *Illicit Riches: Dutch Trade in the Caribbean 1648–1795*, Leiden: KITLV Press.

Ostindie, Gert (1995), *Fifty Years Later: Antislavery, Capitalism and Modernity in the Dutch Orbit*, Leiden: KITLV Press.

Soedjatmoko, Mohammad Ali, G. J. Resink and G. M. Kahin (eds) (1965), *An Introduction to Indonesian historiography*, Ithaca, NY: Cornell University Press.

Taylor, Jean Gelman (2003), *Indonesia. Peoples and Histories*, New Haven, CT and London: Yale University Press.

Immigration in the Netherlands: 1945 to the present

Close to 10 per cent of the Dutch population is born abroad (1.6 million immigrants). If we include their direct descendants the non-native population stands at close to 3.1 million. Of those non-natives just over half (1,668,000) are of non-Western origin. Non-Western immigration to the Netherlands after World War II can broadly be categorised into resettlement related to the Dutch colonial past and present; the recruitment of guest workers in the 1960s and 1970s; and the arrival of asylum seekers and refugees during the last two decades. Moreover, each of these categories has given rise to substantial subsequent immigration of family members and spouses. Until the end of the 1960s annual net migration (the balance of immigration and emigration) was often negative. The country was still suffering from the impact of the war and understood by the majority as a country of emigration to the New World. In the 1950s, 620,000 Dutch left their country (Garssen et al. 2005). However, since the end of the 1960s net migration has robustly remained positive until very recently. Yet, the self-perception of the Dutch nation has remained such that immigration is considered to be an anomaly rather than an integral part of a modern society. This perception has its impact on the measures employed by government aimed at regulating migration and integration processes.

(POST)COLONIAL IMMIGRATION

Until 1949, the present Republic of Indonesia was a Dutch colony. Japanese forces occupied it during World War II unhinging colonial rule. When the country became independent this caused substantial emigration of the Dutch colonial élite to the Netherlands. Also native Indonesians and persons of mixed descent who had been associated with Dutch rule felt compelled to leave the country. In all, approximately 300,000 persons arrived as a result of this process (Heering et al. 2002). At present 134,000 of these migrants still live in the Netherlands. Including their offspring, the Indonesian ethnic group comprises almost 400,000 individuals.

In 1954, the remaining Dutch colonies, Suriname and the Dutch West Indies (the Netherlands Antilles), became part of the Kingdom of the Netherlands. As a result all the inhabitants of these former colonies became Dutch nationals, which gave them too the right to live in the Netherlands. A growing number of people indeed migrated to the Netherlands in order to study or in other ways improve their situation. When Suriname became independent in 1975 those who lived in that country became Surinamese nationals, whereas those who had migrated to the Netherlands were given a choice. This forced many who considered Surinamese nationality the poorer option to move to the Netherlands shortly before independence took effect. Between 1975 and 1980 Surinamese citizens could still opt to become Dutch (again) if they resettled in the Netherlands. Many did so. As a consequence, during those years, Suriname lost a total of 80,000 inhabitants of a total population (in 1971) of 385,000. Presently the Surinamese-born population in the Netherlands numbers 188,000 and another 138,000 are their immediate descendants. The Surinamese population in the Netherlands is not ethnically homogeneous but comprises descendants of African slaves and Dutch (the Creoles), the East Indians (descendants of indentured labourers who arrived after slavery was abolished in 1863), and other smaller groups (notably Chinese and Javanese).

Still integral parts of the Kingdom are the autonomous island of Aruba and the other Dutch Antilles. The Netherlands is home to 84,000 people born on those Caribbean islands and another 47,000 have at least one parent born there. The first Antilleans to arrive were highly educated and integrated well into Dutch society. Presently Antillean immigration is seen by the government as a cause for concern for it often consists of poorly skilled young migrants (few of whom speak fluent Dutch) who arrive and tend to become marginalised.

GUEST WORKERS

During the 1960s and 1970s the Dutch economy was in dire need of additional manual labour. At first this was recruited from the northern Mediterranean countries but by far the largest numbers subsequently arrived from Turkey and Morocco. As the label suggests, the expectation of both these migrants and the Dutch government was that this was to be a temporary phenomenon. However, when economic decline set in as a result of the oil crises of the 1970s causing unemployment to rise considerably, many of these 'guest workers' stayed on. The government did not attempt to stimulate return and allowed family reunification to take place instead, which brought many newcomers to the country. This process gave rise to sizeable and still growing Turkish and Moroccan ethnic communities. In 1995 there were 264,000 inhabitants of Turkish origin in the Netherlands. A decade later their number had risen to 352,000, largely as a result of natural growth but also because of continued immigration (usually of people marrying children of the original migrants). Among the Moroccans too the numerical increase is significant: from 219,000 in 1995 to 306,000 over the same period.

Even though steadily improving, the structural integration into mainstream society of these migrants has been identified by government as insufficient, and policies to remedy this have been developed from the early 1980s. Most public debate, however, has centred on a presumed failed integration in cultural or religious terms.

ASYLUM SEEKERS AND REFUGEES
From the mid-1980s, immigration to the Netherlands diversified enormously as people started to seek asylum from a large number of countries. During the 1990s the number of asylum seekers was relatively high (compared to most other EU countries) and only since 2001 (with the introduction of a new Aliens Law) has the annual number of applicants returned to 1980s levels. Even though many asylum requests were and are being turned down, the Netherlands now is home to sizeable communities from the former Yugoslavia (76,000), Iraq (43,000), China (42,000), Somalia (25,000), the former Soviet Union (42,000), Afghanistan (36,000), Iran (28,000), Ghana (19,000), Pakistan (18,000), Vietnam (18,000); and there are many smaller such communities. In addition there is a significant (yet difficult to gauge or specify in character) group of irregular migrants, often individuals whose asylum request was rejected but who are also unable or unwilling to return home.

WESTERN IMMIGRANTS
Migrants arriving from the industrialised nations arrive for a variety of reasons but either economic activities or (re)union with a spouse appear to be the most prominent motives. In times of great mobility of tourists, students and others who travel internationally this should not surprise us. The Netherlands has been a popular destination for European migrants for some time, especially for Germans – 390,000 Dutch residents were either born in Germany or have at least one German parent.

Jeroen Doomernik

HISTORIES
CBS/Centraal Bureau voor de Statistiek (2004), *Allochtonen in Nederland 2004*, Voorburg/Heerlen: CBS.
Garssen, Joop, Han Nicolaas and Arno Sprangers (2005), 'Demografie van de allochtonen in Nederland', in *Bevolkingstrends*, Centraal Bureau voor de Statistiek, 3e kwartaal, pp. 96–117.
Heering, Liesbeth, Helga de Valk, Ernst Spaan, Corina Huisman and Rob van der Erf (2002), 'The Demographic Characteristics of Immigrant Populations in the Netherlands', in Werner Haug, Paul Compton and Youssef Courbage (eds), *The Demographic Characteristics of Immigrant Populations*, Strasbourg: Council of Europe Publishing (Population Studies No. 38), pp. 245–98.

Van Amersfoort, Hans and Mies van Niekerk (2006), 'Immigration as a Colonial Inheritance: Post-Colonial Immigrants in the Netherlands, 1945–2002,' *Journal of Migration and Ethnic Studies* 32 (3): 323–46.

Missionaries and Religion

East Indies – Indonesia

Throughout the time of Dutch colonial rule in Indonesia's history, religious factors have played an important role. In the contacts and conflicts between Christians and Muslims in the archipelago during this period, several historical patterns can be distinguished.

When the Dutch first came to the archipelago, the Muslims were already well established there. Their behaviour and religious practices were described with a mixture of curiosity and distancing, from Van Linschoten's *Itinerario* (1596) to Valentijn's encyclopaedic *Oud en Nieuw Oost Indië* (1722). These early reports and journals do not provide in-depth analysis, however, and one does not find anything like the thorough scholarly analysis of Hinduism in India and Sri Lanka written by theologians such as Baldaeus and Rogerius. The Dutch East India Company (VOC) was also active in these countries at the same time.

In those early days, Indonesian Muslims were seen by the Dutch as Respected Heretics. But when closer contact followed, this view changed and the theological home front in the Dutch Republic began to see Muslims rather as Detestable Heretics. This dogmatic line was taken by Grotius, Walaeus and especially Voetius, who rejected the tenets of Islam as unacceptable from the point of view of his own orthodox Protestant religion and theology. This rejection, based on vague and inaccurate information, remained the dominant view among Dutch theologians until well into the nineteenth century. The sole exception during the VOC period is the Leyden Arabist, Adrianus Relandus (1676–1718), whose *De Religione Mohammedica Libri Duo* (1705) contained a detailed Arabic catechism of Islamic doctrine with a commentary, in which he set out to correct widespread misinformation and misconceptions about Islam.

Once the VOC had taken hold in the Indonesian archipelago, its directors began to see Muslims as untrustworthy, fanatical and dangerous, in fact the greatest threat to Dutch trade and security in the East Indies. This attitude remained a constant in the Dutch approach to Islam for a very long time. Thus, whenever the Dutch were in a strong position, as in Sri Lanka, the Moluccas and Batavia, they banned Muslims from trading (cf. the *Batavia New Statutes* of 1776). But where they were not, the Dutch would practise the art of accommodation. This policy was driven by considerations of economic competition and political expediency more than anything else. For this reason, the directors did not allow Christian missionary activities to interfere with their commercial interests, and since they held the upper hand in the Church Council, both in Amsterdam and in Batavia, they usually had their way.

During the modern colonial period, from 1816 to 1942, Dutch rule expanded until it was firmly established throughout the archipelago. Along came feelings of European superiority, and a view of Islam as a backward and superstitious religion, in need of education and modernisation. This view of Muslims can also be found in many Dutch colonial novels, for example, Daum's *Aboe Bakar* (1893). And in a way, the current ill-informed and hostile comments on Islam by Dutch politicians such as Bolkestein, Fortuyn and Wilders, are merely a continuation of what has been a constant theme throughout colonial history.

In the early twentieth century, enlightened government advisors on native affairs, such as K. F. Holle, C. Snouck Hurgronje and G. A. J. Hazeu took a deep and scholarly interest in the situation of Indonesian Muslims, but at the same time they pursued a very Dutch agenda, aimed at economic development, modernisation and control within a secular colonial state. To guide and control the Indonesian Muslims, the Office for Native Islamic Affairs (Bureau voor Mohammedaansch-Inlandsche Zaken) was set up, to deal with matters such as the qualifications of religious teachers, the pilgrimage to Mecca, the supervision of those who wanted to study in Egypt, the regulations concerning religious marriages, Islamic law and jurisdiction, supervision of the mosques and many other issues that directly touched on the life of Indonesian Muslims.

For their part, the Indonesians reacted to the arrival of the Christians in the area in various ways, ranging from acceptance and approval to vigorous protest and rejection. From the seventeenth-century *Sejarah Melayu* and the *Babad Tanah Jawi* to the view of twentieth-century Islamic reformers such as Ahmad Dahlan and Haji Agus Salim, Islam has always been a potent factor in the political history of the archipelago, and Islamic factors clearly played a role in conflicts such as the Java War (1825–30), the Achinese War (1873–1914) and the Indonesian War of Independence (1945–49).

The twentieth century saw an increase in Christian missionary and educational activities, led by figures such as van Boetzelaer, Kraemer, Schuurman and van Lith, whose declared goal was to 'free the natives from their superstitions and backwardness'. These Dutch missionary activities were mostly aimed at the paganistic tribes in the Outer Territories, especially Sumatra, where the Bataks adopted Lutheranism, in Kalimantan where Catholic missionaries were active, in the Moluccas where Protestantism dominated, and in New Guinea, where Protestants and Catholics divided the spoils geographically, with the former in the North and the latter in the South, much as the situation was in Holland at the time. On Java, missionary work amongst the predominantly Muslim population has always been restricted. Salatiga in Central Java was an area of Protestant activity. In Solo, there was the institute of Pa van der Steur, which looked after abandoned orphans and gave them a good education. In the colonial cities many hospitals were set up by Christians, and there were important leprosy colonies run by Christians, as we know from the bestselling novel *Gods Geuzen* by Jan de Hartog. Meanwhile, though, the Catholic Church in Indonesia, well before World War II, successfully made the transition to an Indonesianised Church, and had a Javanese bishop in place by the time of the Japanese conquest in 1942.

Ever since Indonesian independence, Christianity has continued to spread at a considerably faster rate than in colonial times, to approximately 9 per cent of the population in the 1980 census. Within the secular Republic of Indonesia, it co-exists with other religions – 87 per cent of people are Muslim. The state ideology of *pancasila*, the system of inter-religious *musyawara*, and the national religious policy are all aimed at the prevention of inter-religious friction – and in this respect, they appear to continue the colonial policies developed by Snouck Hurgronje. But throughout the 1990s, there have been a number of very serious religious conflicts in various parts of the archipelago.

Reinier Salverda

THE DUTCH CARIBBEAN

> Every Catholic who leaves for the colonies of necessity takes with him the seal of Christianity.
> (F. J. Linnartz, *Amigoe* 13 May 1933)

Missionary novels provide an excellent touchstone for the changeover from colonial to postcolonial literature in Dutch. This literature (*missionaire en zendingsliteratuur*) was produced by European missionaries in their efforts to spread religious principles. As of the second half of the twentieth century the genre was taken up by Caribbean authors as a form of 'writing back'.

Within Dutch colonial literature, missionary tales go back to the end of the eighteenth and the beginning of the nineteenth centuries, and to the arrival of the printing press in the colonies. The printing press made it possible to spread God's word not just from the pulpit, but via locally produced material. Most missionaries, however, wrote about their experiences for the home front, in the form of letters home, or of memoirs published after their return. Next to an informative purpose these stories were also intended to help generate money for the missions. Before the advent of television they were the only source of information on 'that dark heathen world'. Missionary stories, published and disseminated either in the form of books or in popular magazines with telling titles such as *Berichten uit de Heidenwereld* (*Messages from the Heathen World*) and *De Godsdienstvriend* (*The Friend of Religion*) to a large extent determined how the colonies were perceived in Europe, and were therefore of major importance for the relationship between the mother country and the colonies.

At the beginning of the twentieth century Catholic missionaries had a virtual monopoly on literacy and literary life in the Dutch colonies in the Caribbean. They dominated the pulpit, education, the press and all social and community organisations. They studied local linguistic usage, local history and local folklore, and they were active as linguists and anthropologists. Edifying journalism and moralising stories were perceived as excellent means for religious proselytisation, but occasional poems, edifying *discursos*, travel stories, dialogues and letters, plays and serial stories also played their part.

Father Martin Legêne (1885–1954) wrote countless missionary novels about Suriname, where he worked from 1916 to 1930 as missionary to the Hindustani population. Legêne had earlier served in India, where he had become proficient in Hindi and Urdu. His Indian experience translates into a penchant for the Eastern mysticism which is typical of his novels.

According to F. J. Linnartz, who taught at St Thomas College on Curaçao, it was the duty of European missionaries to collaborate as brothers with the natives in order to spread and defend the tenets of Catholicism. Literature was particularly appropriate to this purpose:

> The Catholic novel can support Catholic thought, and bring its message home. The socially oriented Catholic novel can go to support, in fact is itself a manifestation of, Catholic social action. Average man can greatly benefit from good literature. A good novel not only provides entertainment; it also raises the reader out of his everyday limitations, and introduces him to the special world of the talented writer. In many cases he finds his own views confirmed or heightened. Sometimes he may change his views as a consequence of his reading experience. (*Amigoe* 13 May 1933)

Over and against the traditional literary genre of missionary literature, rooted in the staunch belief in the superiority of Western and Christian norms and values, there more recently arose a modern form of missionary literature that upholds the ideal of solidarity with the most oppressed inhabitants of the colonies. Conversion to Christianity often implied the break-up of families, social isolation, even exile. In the second half of the twentieth century Caribbean authors began rewriting the genre from the point of view of the new convert: Kees Neer with *Viottoe* (1949) and Edgar Cairo with *Dat vuur der grote drama's* (1982).

Cairo uses the Biblical Ham story as a point of departure for a complete overturn of the traditional missionary tale genre: 'You see, they say about us niggers, regardless of where we are, that we are heathens, born to serve idols in bowing down before them and worshipping them. But I tell you; it is the white Christians that are the true heathens.' The convert Akwembene, rebaptised Matthias, lives between two worlds. His conversion has not brought him freedom, but instead condemned him to a no-man's land: 'He did not understand his own negroes. A deep deep rift. The desperate rift of the colonies.' During the 1763 rising Pilgerhuth is plundered and burnt, the inhabitants slaughtered. Matthias, utterly confused, flees to the camp of the white colonials who welcome him as help against the rebellious blacks. Matthias is totally disoriented: 'He would keep on running, his spirit, his soul, is wood spirit! Through the woods, through the land. Run, run, run fleeing. Until the last negro's day!' In Pilgerhuth, once so prosperous a missionary post, wild nature and wild animals, reclaim their rights: 'The snake would again engender the snake. The tiger would claim a new domain. And the spider, Master Tarantula, would again tend its nets of spoil between the shrubbery, decay! Decay.' Everything is down again to a game of eat or be eaten. The 'harvest' of missonary work is nil.

The sub-genre of the Caribbean missionary tale, and its postcolonial rewritings, prove that the view of the colonies offered by Dutch temporary residents there, such as the missionaries, was not only very different from that held by writers on the colonies who themselves never left their Dutch homes, but also that it differed just as much from what Caribbeans subsequently wrote.

Wim Rutgers

Literary Works

Cairo, Edgar (1982), *Dat vuur der grote drama's*, Haarlem: In de Knipscheer.
Daum, P. A. (1894), *Aboe Bakar. Indische roman*, 's-Gravenhage: Loman en Funke.
Hartog, Jan de [1947] (1957), *The Spiral Road*, London: Hamish Hamilton.
Legêne, Peter Martin (1932), *Van boschnegers en roodhuiden*, 's-Garvenhage: J. N. Voorhoeve.
— (1941), *Langs diepe paden: Gods wondere weg met een Chinees in Suriname*, Zeist: Zeister Zendingsgenootschap der Evangelische Broedergemeente.
Kees Neer, Kees (1948), *Viottoe*, Utrecht: Spectrum.

Histories

Boelaars, H. W. J. M. (1991), *Indonesianisasi. Het omvormingsproces van de katholieke kerk in Indonesië tot de Indonesische katholieke kerk*, Kampen: Kok.
Boetzelaer van Dubbeldam, C. W. Th. van (1906), *De Gereformeerde Kerken in Nederland en de zending in Oost-Indie in de dagen der Oost-Indische Compagnie*, Utrecht: De Boer.
Lampe, Armando (2001), *Mission or Submission? Moravian and Catholic Missionaries in the Dutch Caribbean During the 19th Century*, Göttingen: Vandenhoeck and Ruprecht.
Linschoten, John Huighen van (1598), *His Discours of Voyages into ye Easte and West Indies*, London: John Wolfe.
Steenbrink, K. (1993), *Dutch Colonialism and Indonesian Islam. Contacts and Conflicts 1596–1950*, Amsterdam/Atlanta: Rodopi.

Narratives of Empire

DUTCH EAST INDIES – INDONESIA

The literatures of the Indonesian archipelago present an interesting challenge for comparative literature and postcolonial study. As Denys Lombard put it: '*Le champ qui s'ouvre ici au comparatisme est immense.*'

The field requires an international and comparative approach, and since 2002 this has been available in Theo D'haen's *Europa Buitengaats*, a comparative survey in which the Dutch colonial literatures of Indonesia, South Africa, Suriname and the Caribbean are presented together, in the international context of other European colonial literatures. D'haen's survey is an important step beyond the earlier standard works of Nieuwenhuys, *Mirror of the Indies* (1982), and *Troubled Pleasures. Dutch Colonial Literature from the East Indies, 1600–1950* (1996), by E. M. Beekman, which review only the Dutch colonial literature of the former Dutch East Indies. This is a very extensive literature, which is a veritable treasure-trove of information on life and culture in the colonial Indies, and contains some of the very best works ever produced in Dutch. Today, more than sixty years after Indonesian independence and the end of empire, Dutch literature of the former East Indies is as alive as it ever was, and it continues to be widely read in the Netherlands today, often in a framework of loss and nostalgia. Indeed, the post-independence era has enormously stimulated the production of so-called 'Indies' novels in the Netherlands.

The field offers a fruitful hunting ground for comparative investigation, as we can see in the case of the nineteenth-century Dutch colonial novelist P. A. Daum (1850–98), who was the first naturalist writer in Dutch literature. He was inspired by the French naturalism of Emile Zola, and he went on to translate and publish Kipling's stories in his Dutch newspaper in Batavia (present-day Jakarta) in the 1890s.

About a generation later, the first volume of Dutch poetry by the Javanese symbolist poet Noto Soeroto (1888–1951), entitled *Melatiknoppen* (*Jasmine Buds*, 1915), was inspired by Rabindranath Tagore's *Gitanjali* (1913). The connection between these two Asian poets came about through the Dutch translation of Tagore's poetry, which was made by a friend of W. B. Yeats, the Dutch poet Frederik van Eeden (1860–1932). In 1921, Noto Soeroto also wrote Tagore's biography, and we come full circle when we see that Tagore himself visited Java in the mid-1920s, where the two met at the sultan's court in Soerakarta, Central Java.

Then there is, in the post-war period, the Dutch Indies novelist Maria Dermoût (1888–1962), whose work is deeply indebted to the literary traditions, stories, legends, chronicles and oral narratives of Java and the Moluccas, while at the same time is intimately connected to that of contemporary modernists in English literature, such as Yeats, Eliot, Pound, the Sitwells and Elizabeth Bowen.

These various cases provide us with a good starting point for a comparative approach. Just as we already have Arnold's three-volume comparative *A History of Literature in the Caribbean* (1994–2001), we can now envisage an Indonesian companion volume, of the same archipelagic scope and with its focus on the literary and cultural traffic and exchange between South-East Asia and Europe. Java, after all, is one of the great crossroads of the world's civilisations, and the Indonesian archipelago has found representations in a wide range of Western literatures (cf. Savage 1984), in Dutch no less than in Russian (Braginsky and Diakonova 1999), in French (Dorleans 2001, Lombard 1993), in German literature (Seemann 2000), and in English fiction (Roff 1982).

All kinds of interesting cases would fall within the domain of such a comparative project. The Malay *pantun*, for example, is a traditional verse form that made its way to Europe in the early nineteenth century through the German-French romantic poet and explorer Adalbert von Chamisso (1781–1838). It was then incorporated, as *pantoum*, into that clarion call of high Orientalism, *Les orientales* (1829) by Victor Hugo (1802–85), after which it has followed a most remarkable artistic trajectory through the literatures of nineteenth- and twentieth-century Europe and into the music of Debussy and Ravel.

We also need an analysis comparing the martial attitudes and codes of honour expressed in nineteenth century Dutch novels written by officers of the Royal Netherlands Colonial Army (KNIL) and in du Perron's novel *Country of Origin* (1935), with those in Russian tales of the wars in the Caucasus or in French and English military novels of empire (such as *Beau Geste*).

More recently, the fascinating literary portrait given by V. S. Naipaul in his *Among the Believers* (1981), of the Indonesian poet Sitor Situmorang and his quest for a cultural identity that is both European and Indonesian, focuses on the cosmopolitanism he shares with the Dutch colonial writer Eddy du Perron, through whom he came into contact with a wide range of Dutch and European (especially French and Portuguese) literature, including the Dutch tropical poet J. J. Slauerhoff (1898–1936) and the sixteenth-century Portuguese poet Luis de Camoes (1524–80).

Then again, we find that around the time of Indonesian independence, the idea of 'world literature' was actively promoted by the nationalist leader and cultural critic, Sutan Sjahrir (1906–66). In the same period, interestingly, the work of the Indies-Dutch writer Tjalie Robinson (1911–74), whose naturalistic street tales set in mid-century Batavia/Jakarta, reminds us of the Malgudi-stories by the Indian author R. K. Narayan (1906–2001).

Over the past decade, a much more critical postcolonial approach has been developing, and this has already seen its first fruits in a range of studies by scholars such as Frances Gouda (*Dutch Culture Overseas*, 1995), D'haen and Termorshuizen (*De geest van Multatuli*, 1998) and Laura Ann Stoler (*Carnal Knowledge and Imperial Power*, 2002). But much remains to be done to develop further the systematic, critical-comparative and historical study of the colonial and postcolonial literatures of the Indonesian archipelago.

Reinier Salverda

THE DUTCH CARIBBEAN

To write a full-blown history of the Dutch Caribbean on the basis of whatever literary material has come down to our times is impossible. There simply is not enough of that, and what there is is too biased. The Dutch narratives of empire dealing with the Caribbean focus unilaterally on those instances when the colonies became entangled in repeated European brawls, and consequently fell prey to plunder or conquest.

Early novels about the Caribbean provide anthropological descriptions of the region and its inhabitants. Most famous in this respect are the works of Joannes de Laet (1625 and 1644), J. D. Herlein (1718), Jan Jacob Hartsinck (1770) and J. H. Hering (1779).

The Caribbean, with its vast sugar cane plantations, was at the heart of the slave economy. The Flushing (Vlissingen) ship's doctor D. H. Galandat, in his *Noodige onderrichtingen voor de Slaafhandelaaren* (*Useful Rules for Slave Traders*) of 1769 summarised matters as follows: 'There are many things that happen in the world that would not be permitted if they did not yield special profit.' Those who were accused of promoting this rationalist economic argument could always hide behind the reasoning that Africans in Africa were heathens and would always remain so, whereas they might turn into Christians if transported to the Caribbean as slaves. Bible texts backing up this view were not hard to find. Philip Fermin, in his *Nieuwe algemeene beschryving van de colonie van Suriname* (*New General Description of the Colony of Suriname*, 1770) listed four categories of slave provenance: condemned criminals, prisoners of war, children sold by their parents or people that sold themselves, and finally those that were born into slavery. The black theologian Jacobus Capitein in 1742 in a dispute upheld '*de slaverny, als niet strydig tegen de Christelyke Vryheid*' ('slavery as not in conflict with Christian liberty').

With the advent of the Enlightenment in the eighteenth century, and in its wake the rise of so-called spectatorial and pamphlet literature, slavery was increasingly criticised. First the excesses of the system were targeted, and shortly afterwards, the system itself. In 1731 minister Joannes Guiljelmus Kals advocated christening the slaves. The plantation owners' reaction was immediate: 'Allright, Minister! Let us convert those that have the same skin as we do, and the same Color, and let those accursed children of Cham go to the Devil; they are made to plant Coffe and Sugar for us.' The meddlesome minister, author also of *Neerlands Hooft- en Wortel-sonde, het verzuym van de bekeringe der Heydenen* (*The Capital and Root Sin of the Netherlands, or the Neglect to Convert the Heathens*, 1756), was soon removed from the colony. It is from foreign works such as Aphra Behn's *Oroonoko, or the Royal Slave* (1688), Voltaire's *Candide* (1759), and John Gabriel Stedman's work, *Narrative of a Five Years' Expedition against the Revolted Negroes of Surinam* (1796), translated into Dutch as *Reize naar Surinamen en door de binnenste gedeelten van Guiana* (1799), that the picture of Surinamese slavery as the most cruel in the entire region has come to us.

In the colony itself literature was practically absent. In the middle of the eighteenth century Governor Jan Jacob Mauricius bitterly complained about what he called the '*animum revertendi*' of the colonists, who according to him 'had no feelings for a country which they did not look upon as a true place of dwelling for themselves or their children, but rather as a foreign place, where they are merely passing through'. As to the arts in the colony he wrote: 'Its sour name, the sound it makes, already frightens the Muses, and the winged Horse flies backwards.' It was only at the end of the eighteenth and the beginning of the nineteenth centuries that there arose anything even remotely resembling a literary cultural life, with the arrival of the printing press; the first newspapers; the founding of a theatre; and the creation of a literary society, De Surinaamsche Lettervrienden (The Surinamese Friends of Letters) and its publications *Letterkundige Uitspanningen* (*Literary Entertainments*, 1785–7). Hendrik Schouten, a satirist, and the planter-poet Paul François Roos, with his pastoral poetry, merit mention.

Women, too, were active in the literary life of the colony in the late eighteenth century. In 1676–7 Elisabeth van der Woude recorded in a diary her experiences of the failed attempt at founding a colony. More important is the work of the already-mentioned Aphra Behn. Her 1688 *Oroonoko, or the Royal Slave* is an indictment of the slave trade and of the plantation system. Maria Sybilla Merian published *Metamorphosis insectorum Surinamensium, ofte Verandering der Surinaamsche insecten* (1719), the result of a visit to Suriname in 1699. Finally, there is Elisabeth Maria Post, with an anti-slavery novel entitled *Reinhart of Natuur en Godsdienst* (*Rinehart or Nature and Religion*, 1791–2).

It is worth noting that none of the authors mentioned holds canonical status within Dutch literature. They were mostly writing while 'passing through' the colony. Dutch literature on the Caribbean has always remained marginal, neither fully part of Caribbean literature nor of its European counterpart.

Wim Rutgers

South Africa

The Dutch and Portuguese developed a discourse about the Cape long before the Dutch established a settlement at this southern African location. This Cape discourse was characterised by a stereotypical and negative representation of the inhabitants of the Cape coastal area, who were described as dirty, uncivilised, lazy and unintelligent. On the other hand, the inhabitants of the interior were believed to be civilised people, belonging to a gold-rich kingdom, referred to as 'Monomotapa'. This kingdom and its inhabitants gained mythical proportions in early Portuguese and Dutch written and oral sources. The writing that emerged from later inland expeditions brought about substantial shifts in the 'Cape discourse', especially concerning the inhabitants of the interior. Nevertheless, throughout the period of colonial exploration in southern Africa, Dutch literary representation of the colony upheld a specific distinction between wildness and primitivism opposing order and civilisation. In this discourse, which systematically developed an attitude towards 'the country as object', the Cape became a construct of Dutch power – a discursive mechanism of power.

Prior to Dutch settlement and the introduction of writing to southern Africa, oral literature was the only literary form practised by the indigenous people. The period of written literature starts in 1652 when Jan van Riebeeck, on command of the Dutch East India Company (VOC), started a refreshment station at the Cape. The first manifestations of a Cape writing culture were in the form of VOC correspondence, writings about Cape flora, travelogues, geographical descriptions and a number of poems. The absence of printing facilities at the Cape meant that all early Cape writing was printed in the Netherlands. This was, of course, counter-productive for literary activity at the Cape.

A prominent genre of writing at the Cape during the initial years of Dutch settlement was the travel genre. Numerous travelogues and journals provide descriptions of the many inland expeditions. Noteworthy among them are those produced during Simon van der Stel's expedition (1685–6) in search of copper. In 1916 Godée Molsbergen collected a number of these journals in *Tochten naar het noorden 1652–1686* (*Journeys to the North 1652–1686*), the first of the four-part Van Linschoten series with the general title *Reizen in Zuid-Afrika in de Hollandsche tijd* (*Travels in South Africa in the Dark Period*).

In 1713 Peter Kolb (who lived at the Cape between 1705 and 1713) wrote what is still regarded as the most encompassing ethnographic source on the early Cape colony. *Capvt bonae spei hodiernvm* (*The Present State of the Cape of Good Hope*) was published in Nürnberg in 1719. Numerous fascinating journals documented inland expeditions. Interesting from both a linguistic and a literary point of view is Pieter Cloete's *Journaal van eenen landtogt die den ondergeteekende met den weledelen heer Mr Hendk Swellengrebel in den jare 1776 gedaan heeft* (1776) (*Journal of an Overland Journey . . . that the Author made together with the Most Honourable Gentleman Mr Hendrik Swellengrebel in the Year 1776*). This travel journal documents an inland journey starting in the region of Stellenbosch.

By the end of the eighteenth century the officials at the Cape had become increasingly known for their corruption, and a few free burghers resorted to writing as a tool of protest. Adam Tas, who had been born in 1668 in Amsterdam and who had arrived at the Cape in 1697, kept a journal (*Dagregister van den landbouwer Adam Tas*; *Journal of the Farmer Adam Tas*). His journal differed from the other Cape writing of the period because it was not written for official purposes. It is also the first to be concerned not with Dutch issues but to be locally focused. This journal exposes the monopolist managerial style and corrupt methods of the VOC at the Cape.

At the end of the eighteenth century the introduction of a printing press ushered in a new literary era. Gradually the local writing became more focused on a local readership.

Hence, it grew increasingly detached from Dutch influence. The first literary work by a South African and meant for the South African market was a poem by the Stellenbosch minister Meent Borcherd. The same *dominee* also produced the didactic poem *De Maan* (1802–3). Borcherd saw the colonists as the couriers of civilisation, order and Christianity to the Cape. In his early nineteenth-century poem, *Gedicht over de volkplanting van de Kaap de Goede Hoop* (*Poem on the Colony of the Cape of Good Hope*) the conventional distinction between order and chaos in Dutch writing about South Africa is evident.

From 1803 until 1806 the Cape went back to Dutch rule. Two reports of an inland journey to the eastern frontier during this period are particularly interesting. The first is by W. B. E. Paravicini di Capelli, a Dutch official, and is entitled *Joernaal en verbal eener landreisje in den jare 1803, door den gouverneur en generaal deezer Colonie J. W. Janssens door de binnenlanden van Zuijd Africa gedaan* (*Journal and Report of an Inland Trip through the Interior of South Africa made in the year 1803 by the Governor and General of this Colony, J. W. Janssens*). The second is by Dirk G. van Reenen, a wealthy farmer of the colony, and carries the title *Dag-Verhaal eener reize naar de binnenlanden van Africa beoosten de Kaap de Goede Hoop geleegen* (*Journal of a Trip to the Interior of Africa situated East of the Cape of Good Hope*). A comparison suggests that the Dutch and Afrikaans people, who during the seventeenth century had maintained a strong sense of relatedness, had gradually started drifting apart.

From the last quarter of the nineteenth century Afrikaans was increasingly used for publications, but it was only in the twentieth century that Afrikaans publications started to outnumber those in South African Dutch. Because Dutch South African texts after 1800 were produced within such a changed historical context, one can hardly refer to these any longer as 'narratives of the Dutch Empire in South Africa'.

During the period of 1920 to 1940 a pronounced ideological and thematic difference is evident between Afrikaans and English South African literature. Afrikaans literature promoted *die Afrikaanse gedagte* (Afrikaner ideology) which linked the Afrikaans language to its white users. The Afrikaans novel became thematically preoccupied with farm life and rural (*platteland*) South African society. The Boer was characterised as somebody who idealised the soil, the farm and rural existence. The Afrikaner's transition from farmer to townsman was thus portrayed as a traumatic happening for the Afrikaner community.

The most prominent writers of the Afrikaans *plaasroman* were D. F. Malherbe (*Die meulenaar*, 1926), Jochem van Bruggen (*Ampie* trilogy, 1924, 1928, 1942), Johannes van Melle (*Dawid Booysen*, 1933), Mikro (*Toiïngs* trilogy, 1934, 1935, 1944), C. M. van den Heever (*Groei*, 1933, *Gister*, 1941) and Abraham Jonker (*Die plaasverdeling*, 1932). Most portray the *platteland* as idyllic, and farm life as harmonious and in tune with the 'purity' of nature. The crisis on the *platteland* was depicted as a conflict between peasant and capitalist modes of production and conflicting values relating to land . Most of these novels portray capitalism as an evil construct. J. M. Coetzee sees the *plaasroman* as coming very close to 'the reactionary *Großstadtfeindschaft*, anticapitalism, anti-Semitism, and *Blut und Boden* ideology of the *Bauernroman*'. The *plaasroman* genre illustrates the Afrikaner's strong identification with rural living, in contrast to the urban background and commercial spirit of the British. As industry continued to outpace agriculture, the *plaasroman* was a way of idealising rural life. Later, some farm novels turned this tradition upside down. Wilma Stockenström's *Uitdraai* (1976), for instance, deals with love across the 'colour line'. More recently Marlene van Niekerk, in *Agaat* (2004), depicted the changed hierarchy between so-called maid and mistress, reflecting the historic transition that South Africa has been experiencing since the change of government. The love-hate relationship between the white woman and her coloured servant recalls the relationship between white Afrikaners and the Afrikaans-speaking coloured community during the years of apartheid.

After 1925 South Africa has remained a theme in Dutch literature and still plays a significant role in the Dutch self-image. Contemporary work reflecting this phenomenon includes *Het beloofde land* (1990) by Adriaan van Dis as well as *Moenie kyk nie* (1993) and *Een mond vol glas* (1998) by Henk van Woerden. The last provides an alternative biography of Tsafendas, the man who killed the South African Prime Minister and apartheid mastermind, Hendrik Verwoerd. Both these works by van Woerden also indicate a search for a personal attitude towards South Africa. Kader Abdolah's novel *Portretten en een oude droom* (2003) is another example. In this novel the main character, Dawoed, an Iranian refugee who lives in the Netherlands, travels through South Africa. His introduction to this newly freed country reminds him of his Persian comrades of before. The freedom of South Africa is juxtaposed to the situation in Iran.

Annemie van Niekerk

LITERARY WORKS

Brink, André (1993), *The First Life of Adamastor*, London: Secker and Warburg.

Couperus, Louis [1900] (1985), *The Hidden Force*, trans. A. Teixeira de Mattos, Amherst, MA: University of Massachusetts Press.

Haase, Hella S. (1992), *De heren van de thee*, Amsterdam: Querido.

Helman, Albert [1931] (1982), *De stille plantage*, 's Gravenhage: Nijgh en Van Ditmar.

Perron, Edgar Du [1935] (1984), *Country of Origin*, trans. F. Bulhof and E. Daverman, Amherst, MA: University of Massachusetts Press.

HISTORIES

Coetzee, J. M. (1988), *White Writing. On the Culture of Letters in South Africa*, Sandton: Radix Century Hutchinson South Africa.

Francken, Eep and Luc Renders (2005), *Skrywers in die strydperk. Krachtlijnen in de Zuid-Afrikaanse letterkunde*, Amsterdam: Uitgeverij Bert Bakker.

Huigen, Siegfried (1996), *De Weg Naar Monomotapa. Nederlandstalige representaties van geografische, historische en sociale werkelijkheden in Zuid-Afrika*, Amsterdam: Amsterdam University Press.

Huigen, Siegfried and Jean Kommers (eds) (2004), *Interpretations of Colonial Representations*, Saarbrücken: Nijmegen Studies in Development and Cultural Change.

Palencia-Roth, Michael (1997), 'Mapping the Caribbean; Cartography and the Cannibalization of Culture,' in James A. Arnold, *A History of Literature in the Caribbean*, vol. 3, Cross-Cultural Studies, Amsterdam and Philadelphia, PA: J. Benjamins, pp. 3–27.

Kempen, Michiel van (2003), *Een geschiedenis van de Surinaamse literatuur*, Dissertatie UvA 2002, Breda: Uitgeverij De Geus.

Nationalism/Nationhood

EAST INDIES – INDONESIA

During the nineteenth century anti-colonial resistance to the Dutch was widespread, but it was always local and – from the Java War (1825–30), through the Acheh War (from 1873), to the wars in Sulawesi and Lombok (1896) – these conflicts were fought out by local peoples in their own islands. By the beginning of the twentieth century, however, once the political unification of the archipelago had been effected by the Dutch, we see the beginnings of a new, pan-Indonesian resistance that was political in nature.

The awakening of a national, 'Indonesian' consciousness was marked by two native political movements in Java, Budi Utomo and Sarekat Islam, both founded in the early 1900s. They were encouraged by the colonial administration as part of the general 'ethical' movement towards modernisation, but they were also closely watched by the administration's native advisors. The term 'Indonesia' remained forbidden in the Dutch East Indies until 1942.

After these beginnings, there were three key moments in the further development of Indonesian nationalism until the successful establishment of the independent Indonesian republic we know today.

First of all, in 1913, the celebrations by the colonial Dutch of the centenary of Hollands' liberation from Napoleon triggered a critical Indonesian response in the short satirical pamphlet *Als ik eens Nederlander was* (*If I Were a Dutchman*) written by the Indonesian nationalist Suwardi Suryaningrat. For this pamphlet he was banished from the archipelago by the Governor-General. The pamphlet thus marks not only a new breath of life for Indonesian nationalism but at the same time the Dutch suppression of it.

During World War I, the Netherlands remained neutral and profited enormously from its colonial trade. But at the end of that war revolutions swept the world; the Indians had been promised their future independence by Lloyd George; and the Dutch Governor-General Van Limburg Stirum, in a concession to the Indonesians, instituted the so-called Volksraad or People's Council, a consultative assembly consisting of representatives, part elected, part appointed, from the three main constituencies in the population, the Dutch colonials, the Foreign Asians (Chinese, Indians and Arabs), and the native Indonesians. This assembly provided a forum for discussion, but the native Indonesian representatives were usually outmanoeuvred by the other two groups, or saw their ideas simply rejected by the colonial administration. Outside the assembly, however, popular support for the nationalist movement was growing by the day, stimulated especially by the arrival on the political scene in the 1920s of the charismatic nationalist leader Sukarno.

The second important date is 1928, when a group of young Indonesians, dissatisfied with the slowness of official politics, and angered by the increasing political repression, pledged their unanimous, pan-Indonesian support for the so-called Sumpah Pemuda or Oath of the Youth, coining the powerful slogan, 'One nation, one people, one language', that is, Indonesia. This declaration of Indonesian national aspirations, and the effective use of the Indonesian language as a symbol of those aspirations had a galvanising effect, not least in its rejection and boycott of the Dutch language (and by implication of Dutch colonial rule). The situation is comparable to what happened later in South Africa, when the Afrikaans language was seen, and rejected, as a symbol of the apartheid instigated by the Boers.

Meanwhile, Dutch political repression intensified throughout the 1930s. Intimidation, press censorship and prosecutions were standard. The episode of the house search in *Buiten het gareel* (*Out of Line*, 1940), the Dutch-language novel of the female Indonesian author Suwarsih Djojopoespito, shows how Indonesians were silenced. So effective was this repression in the 1930s that even the police complained that they no longer knew what was going on under the surface. In the background there were always the so-called 'extraordinary powers' that enabled persons 'considered dangerous to public law and order' to be detained or banished without trial. This was the fate suffered by the nationalist leadership triumvirate of Sukarno, Hatta and Sjahrir, but also by many ordinary Indonesians who were sent to perish in the infamous Boven-Digoel concentration camp in the swamps of New Guinea. These methods of a police state were used consistently by the colonial government right up to 1942 to suppress Indonesian nationalism.

The third big moment came on 17 August 1945, when Sukarno and Hatta officially declared the independence of the Republic of Indonesia. They became President and Vice-President respectively, while Sjahrir became the first Prime Minister. But the Dutch saw this as a Japanese-inspired puppet state, and demanded the restitution of what they considered to be rightfully theirs. However, whereas after 1813 the Dutch had, with the support of the Vienna Conference and Britain, successfully regained control over the archipelago, this time they failed to do so, even though they mounted their largest military force ever. Militarily they did establish control over large parts of the archipelago, but they never defeated the nationalist guerrilla forces. And politically they faced the clever international diplomacy of Sjahrir, who managed to outmanoeuvre the Dutch in the United Nations.

The rest, as they say, is history. Indonesian nationalism to this very day continues to be a potent political force for unity throughout the archipelago. All regionalist or secessionist movements – whether it was in the Moluccas in the 1950s, in Sumatra in the 1960s, or in Acheh ever since the early 1980s – have been defeated. In 1962, after a last little war of decolonisation with the Dutch, the republic took control of New Guinea (Irian Jaya). In 1975, the former Portuguese colony of East Timor was occupied by the Indonesians, but after years of terrible suffering for the Timorese, this annexation was brought to an end in the 1990s by an Australian/UN force. The Indonesians may have withdrawn their troops, but they continue to have control over the extremely valuable mineral resources in the seas around this tiny island.

Reinier Salverda

The Dutch Caribbean

In the Dutch Caribbean, the discourse of nation-building has focused on issues of national identity, language and political status. The 1930s saw the emergence of nationalism in the Caribbean, a movement which also took shape in the Dutch region but with varying results. While Suriname gained full independence in 1975, the Netherlands Antilles remain an integral part of the Kingdom of the Netherlands, thus rendering the nationalist project all the more arduous.

In Suriname, the development of a nationalist agenda first appeared in the Afro-Surinamese community. The publication of Anton de Kom's *Wij slaven van Suriname* in 1934 was the first attempt by an Afro-Surinamese author to affirm his Afro-Caribbean identity through the history of Suriname. De Kom's intellectual formation, however, took place outside Suriname among the black community of the Netherlands. His case illustrates how, in Suriname, the discourse of nationalism was shaped and influenced by expatriate Afro-Surinamese residing in the Netherlands where they became familiar with the ideas of Afro-Caribbean and African American thinkers. One particular group, Wi Egi Sani (Our Own Thing), formed in Amsterdam in the 1950s as a black students' and workers' movement, was influenced by the writings of Aimé Césaire and Léon Gontron Damas. Its members saw the need to assert the African roots of Surinamese culture and identity. In a sense, the nationalist movement was able to take shape outside of the colonies. Further, although World War II brought greater awareness for issues of democracy, and political representation as well as economic growth, the early exodus to the Netherlands had long-term consequences for the colonies' ability to gain independence. However, political affiliation and voting patterns were based on the personal appeal of candidates and their ethnic background. Indeed, although Suriname has been held up as an example of a plural society, the population was too segmented for an all-encompassing nationalist movement to take root. Creole nationalist intellectuals formed the Partij van de Nationalistische Republiek (National Republican Party) in 1961 and based their political agenda on the idea of cultural nationalism, the need to promote Afro-Caribbean Creole language, Sranan as national language, and the emancipation of Creole culture. This move was seen as cultural colonisation by other parties and reinforced ethnic awareness particularly among the Hindustani community.

The issue of independence was never a rallying point. In the post-war period, nationalist supporters demanded less colonial administration, more autonomy and greater decision powers. The case for full independence came in the early 1970s, and after much pressure from the Dutch authorities (see 'Decolonisation'). Moreover, the question of autonomy and independence revealed diverging national needs: for Creoles, independence was a means to affirm their own culture as the basis for Suriname's national culture. Among Hindustani, the ongoing Dutch presence was perceived as the only guarantee for securing their own political, economic and social emancipation. The fear of racial conflict as in Trinidad and Tobago or in British Guiana led to the realisation that calm and stability were necessary for the future of the country. But despite the belief in Suriname that political autonomy would facilitate the economic and cultural development of the country, political instability and economic difficulties in the post-independence years have increased tensions between the Afro-Surinamese, Hindustani, Maroon and Amerindian communities. Moreover, the emigration of the political and intellectual élite has also undermined the nation-building project in the long term.

The unstable economic and political situation in Suriname has had repercussions in the Netherlands Antilles on local politicians' stance regarding independence. Full political autonomy has been rejected in favour of a commonwealth status within the Kingdom of the Netherlands. Nationalist feelings nevertheless exist and focus on questions of racial identity and language. Moreover, Aruba's successful campaign to obtain a separate status (*status aparte*) within the kingdom also illustrates the existence of cultural differences between the islands despite the fact that successive Dutch governments have viewed them as a homogeneous entity. Aruba's *separashon*, or separation, was indeed an affirmation of its difference in terms of culture, language and identity (see 'Decolonisation'). On Aruba, underlining cultural and linguistic differences are prominent items on the nationalist agenda. Yet they are used to differentiate the local culture from that of Curaçao rather than the Netherlands.

On Curaçao, language, Papiamentu, is seen as a unifying element despite racial and ethnic differences. Ancestry and length of presence on the island are determining factors when assessing whether one belongs to the nation: newcomers and migrants from the era of industrialisation are not considered to be children of Curaçao (*Yu di Korsow*). This discrimination includes people of Afro-Surinamese descent despite the common African heritage. The Afro-Curaçaon discourse of nation is based on the idea of a shared history which gave birth to a unique culture, seen as the essence of the island's cultural heritage. The notion of *Di-nos-e-ta* ('This is ours'), the statement of an Afro-Curaçaon heritage, appeared in the 1970s and led to a debate on whether the island's history should be written from an Afro-Curaçaon perspective only. As far as language is concerned, the prominent position of Papiamentu within the nationalist discourse may have succeeded in achieving cultural and linguistic unity but only to the detriment of Dutch or even English. Lower linguistic proficiency in Dutch decreases the population's economic and employment chances.

Although English is not a dominant language in the Dutch Antilles, it is a necessary medium for regional integration and exchanges and may undermine further a nationalist agenda based on Papiamentu.

Like Suriname, the Netherlands Antilles are a transnational state, due to the large migrant community across the Atlantic in the Netherlands with which they still share cultural customs and language. Emigration and the need for substantial financial support from the Netherlands have made it difficult for a nationalist project to flourish or even survive. There have been no propositions for an alternative to the current situation. As a result, a radical nationalist discourse seems impossible. Despite this, the local political élite still shows a defensive attitude to the Dutch presence and influence on local policies and the economy. Dutch governmental policy concerning the political status of the Dutch Antilles poses a challenge to the nation-building project of the islands. Yet the political and intellectual élite are faced with the difficulty of finding elements on which to base their nationalist rhetoric. In the face of intensifying globalisation and the need to reinforce the Dutch Caribbean presence in the Americas, the long-term success of any nationalist discourse will need to channel attention to the idea of a common purpose for the Dutch-speaking Caribbean rather than focus on local rivalry and particularities.

Patricia Krus

LITERARY WORKS

Arion, Frank Martinus (1975), *Afscheid van de koningin*, Amsterdam: De bezige bij.

Djojopoespito, Suwarsih [1940] (1986), *Buiten het gareel*, 's Gravenhage: Nijgh en Van Ditmar.

Helman, Albert (1922), *Zuid-Zuid-West*, Amtserdam: Querido.

Toer, Pramoedya Ananta [1980] (1990–1), *The Buru Quartet (This Earth of Mankind, Child of All Nations, Footsteps*, and *House of Glass)*, Harmondsworth: Penguin.

Vianen, Bea (1971), *Strafhok*, Amsterdam: Querido.

HISTORIES

Aldrich, Robert and John Connell (1998), *The Last Colonies*, Cambridge: Cambridge University Press.

Anderson, Benedict (1991), *Imagined Communities. Reflections on the Origin and Spread of Nationalism*, London: Verso.

Anwar, Khaidir (1980), *Indonesian: The Development and Use of a National Language*, Yogyakarta: Gajah Mada University Press.

Hatta, Mohammad (1972), *Portrait of a Patriot. Selected Writings*, The Hague: Mouton.

Hoefte, Rosemarijn and Peter Meel (2001), *Twentieth-Century Suriname: Continuities and Discontinuities in a New World Society*, Leiden: KITLV Press.

Mrazek, R. (1994), *Sjahri: Politics and Exile in Indonesia*, Ithaca, NY: Southeast Asia Programme, Cornell University.

Orientalism/Exoticism

DUTCH EAST INDIES

One of the most enduring images of Indonesia in Dutch culture today is that of the mysterious 'girdle of emerald', the exotic paradise of a thousand islands, the land of the hidden force which puts its spell on anyone who has ever been there. The magic of the East – its enchanting qualities, its spices, smells and tastes, its music and dance, its incredible natural beauty and countless other seductions – can today still trigger feelings of deep longing amongst the Dutch for the paradise they have lost.

This powerful and essentially romantic image has a long history. Already in 1637 the Dutch writer van Heemskerk had included in his *Batavische Arcadia* (written in the vein of Philip Sidney's pastoral) a tale of *guna-guna* or Malay magic. In the Netherlands this magic is commonly known as 'the hidden force', which is the title of one of the most famous colonial novels, published in 1900 by Louis Couperus. The notion of 'hidden force' is also employed to advertise its Asian business by ABNAMRO Bank, itself the successor to the nineteenth-century colonial bank the Nederlandsche Handel Maatschappy of Multatuli's novel, *Max Havelaar*. In the same way, the Dutch Prime Minister, Balkenende, exhorted his fellow Dutchmen to be a bit more enterprising, a bit more inspired by the great past, saying that the country needed a bit more of the 'VOC spirit'.

This image runs very deep in Dutch culture. It is a commonplace which defines the colonial mindset inherited from the past, and which remains uncontested to this very day. To a large extent it has been shaped by the enduringly popular boys' novel, *De scheepsjongens van Bontekoe* (1929) by Johan Fabricus (translated as *Westward Ho!*), an all-time bestseller which is now being filmed. It presents a 'Boys Own' version of the colonial past that has put its stamp on the minds of generations of young Dutchmen, inspiring them to travel abroad and go on daring adventures while at the same time giving them an implicit sense of Western superiority.

It is in this way – as an exotic image coupled with a mindset that can only be described as colonial – that the colonial past is still alive and with us, more than half a century after the end of the Dutch Empire in the East. There is a pervasive presence in Dutch culture and politics, of things colonial – spices, *rijsttafel* dishes, gamelan music, the VOC (Dutch East India Company), the large number of colonial museums and other institutions, Javaanse jongens tobacco, *Indische meisjes* and their sensual appeal, the smells of the annual Pasar Malam Besar in The Hague, or the Chinese and Indonesian restaurants one can find in all but the smallest villages of the Netherlands. And in Dutch literature, the exotic fictions of the colonial past continue to inspire writers, from Hella Haasse just after the war to Helga Ruebsamen and Adriaan van Dis today.

In 2002, the foundation of the VOC was commemorated with a great exhibition in the Rijksmuseum in Amsterdam, 'The Dutch Encounter with Asia, 1600–1950'. For almost two centuries, from 1602 until its demise in 1799, the VOC, operating from Amsterdam, was the mainstay of the Dutch seaborne empire in Asia. Quite a few of its directors subscribed to the ideal of the *mercator sapiens*, the learned merchant, proclaimed in 1632 by Professor Caspar Barlaeus in Amsterdam. They were at the centre of a worldwide network of contact and exchange between VOC men working in many different fields of new knowledge – mapmakers, painters, geographers, interpreters, Bible translators, doctors, astronomers, and other colonial scientists such as the botanist of India's Malabar coast, Van Reede tot Drakenstein (1636–91), the expert on Asian languages Herbert de Jager (1636–94), the VOC historian Francois Valentijn (1666–1727) or Georg Rumphius (1627–1702), the founder of Indonesian botanical exploration.

But for all their interest – commercial as well as scholarly – in the natural world of the East, the Dutch for a very long time remained indifferent and unreceptive to Indonesian culture. Their envoys to sultans' courts in Central Java, for example, habitually described gamelan music as a cacophony, and Javanese dance as a strange, wild and unruly spectacle.

They also spread the enduring image of the Javanese as untrustworthy, dangerous and cruel, a *topos* that one can find already in van Linschoten's *Itinerario* of 1596.

When in the nineteenth century the Dutch began to take more of an interest in the peoples living in the archipelago, the crucial difference with the British approach in India was that Dutch colonial policies followed the Orientalists' view of East and West as essentially and totally different in culture. Thus, Dutch colonial civil servants did not go out to the East with a classical Oxford education, but were given an Orientalist training and had to learn one or two indigenous languages. And by the middle of the nineteenth century the Dutch explicitly rejected the educational and language policies of the British in India, and decided against offering a Western education to their Indonesian subjects.

In the process, an interesting mix of East and West developed. In Multatuli's work, for example, his Western, universalist ideals of justice and humanity are coupled with strongly exoticising tendencies in his representations of ordinary Javanese peasants.

A similar mix of East and West can be found in the ethical colonial policy which he heralded. Many leading Dutch ethicists of the 1920s and 1930s subscribed to a view of the Indonesians as Oriental and exotic 'Others', who were in need of education and civilisation. But their introduction to modernisation and Western civilisation would have to be effected under the umbrella of ethical policy and the Pax Neerlandica. At the same time, Dutch Javanists developed a strongly Orientalist image of Javanese and Balinese culture, very much along the lines of Huizinga's representation of Burgundian Court culture in his influential *The Waning of the Middle Ages* (1924), that is, as members of ancient, refined, aristocratic, feudal court cultures with venerable artistic traditions that needed study, protection and development.

Meanwhile, real Indonesians such as Sutan Syahrir, who claimed not otherness but equality, were faced with exclusion and repression, jail and exile. Such contradictions between the ethical and cultured idealism of the Dutch and the stark realities of their colonial practices are part of what Frances Gouda has called 'the cultural grammar of colonial rule'.

Reinier Salverda

THE DUTCH CARIBBEAN
Travel into the unknown is at the heart of exoticism. Unknown parts of the world, or ancient civilisations, are explored by travellers reporting on their discoveries. Painters opt for exotic scenes as subjects for their work. Technical developments enable travel to ever more remote parts of the globe. The Far East and the isles of the Pacific have invited intense interest. Yet, the Caribbean too became the object of exotic reveries, the islands playing the role of exotic backdrop to adventures that just as easily could have taken place anywhere else. It is especially non-resident authors, 'passing through' the Dutch Caribbean colonies that have exploited the islands for this purpose.

Jan Jacob Mauricius, Governor-General of Suriname from 1742 to 1751, complained that the colonists had no real feelings for the country they inhabited. Colonial authors constantly compared the colony to the mother country. Paul François Roos (Amsterdam 1751–Suriname 1805), in his *Surinaamsche mengelpoëzy* (*Surinamese Occasional Poetry*, 1804), has a character called Analoë, in a poem called 'Plantation Song' (*'Plantaadjezang'*), sing the praises of his new country Suriname which he compares favourably to Europe. Most colonials ended up staying in the colony. This was especially true of Curaçao which, with its dry climate and rocky soil, was less a plantation colony than Suriname, and where consequently it was more difficult to earn enough in a few years to be able to retire to the mother country. This fact fostered the emergence of a native cultural élite in Curaçao.

More important is the exoticising regionalist tradition of the Caribbean itself. If European authors looked at the Caribbean with exoticising and often also romanticising 'Western eyes', their Caribbean counterparts often adopted the same attitude in their writings about their region. Caribbean authors are reckoned to be 'exoticising' when they write in the same way authors foreign to the area would do. This results in stereotypical stories, full of references to European classics and foreign examples. Such authors prefer to dwell at large upon the idyllic nature and the tropical setting of the Caribbean. They are stories resembling those written in the 1920s and 1930s about the previous century; stories of adventure, passion, jealousy, fate, revenge, 'big houses', remote locales. The Curaçaoan writer Tuyuchi provides a good example with his numerous detective stories; and another example is Amador Nita, who in the 1950s produced a large number of novellas; short stories involving passionate and lustful love, prostitution, adultery, murder and revenge.

It is works such as these that made Frank Martinus Arion remark that Papiamentu literature focuses on 'love, romantic feelings and fate,' and that it is 'overly sentimental', wallows in 'religious feelings,' and is overloaded with 'typically Antillean anecdotes, customs and habits, and not least superstition'. These writers pay no attention to social or economic realities. It is only when exoticism turns into regionalism, concentrating on what is typical for Caribbean people in their everyday environments, that we see a return to the specificity of ancient and native cultural traditions.

Wim Rutgers

LITERARY WORKS
Dermoût, Maria [1958] (1983), *The Ten Thousand Things*, Afterword and Notes by E. M.
    Beekman, Amherst, MA: University of Massachusetts Press.
Dis, Adriaan van (1996), *My Father's War*, New York: The New Press.
Fabricius, Johan Wigmore, (1933) *Java Ho! The Adventures of Four Boys amid Fire, Storm
    and Shipwreck*, London: Methuen.
Haasse, Hella S. (1996), *Forever a Stranger and Other Stories*, Kuala Lumpur: Oxford in Asia.
Helman, Albert, (1931), *De stille plantage*, Amsterdam: Nijgh en Van Ditmar.

HISTORIES
Gouda, Frances (1995), *Dutch Culture Overseas: Colonial Practice in the Netherlands Indies,
    1900–1942*, Amsterdam: Amsterdam University Press.
Martinus, Frank Arion (1958), 'Schrijvers en muzikanten', in H. de Wit and J. van de
    Walle, *De Nederlandse Antillen in de actualiteit*, Amsterdam-Antwerpen: De
    Wereldbibliotheek, pp. 81–102.
Zandvliet, Kees (ed.) (2002), *The Dutch Encounter with Asia 1600–1950*, Amsterdam:
    Rijksmuseum/Zwolle: Waanders Uitgeverij.

Race and Ethnicity

EAST INDIES – INDONESIA
In the Netherlands Indies, race was enshrined in the basic state law by a three-way division of all colonial subjects into classes within a clear hierarchy: the Europeans (including the Japanese); the 'foreign Asians' (including Chinese, Indian and Arabic merchants); and the native Indonesians. The general principle was that each group would be left to

organise its life – family matters such as marriage, divorce and inheritance; property matters such as ownership, trade and bankruptcy – as much as possible according to its own customary laws and traditions. Thus, for the Europeans there was the civil and penal code of Dutch law, whereas the foreign Asians would follow Chinese or Arabic law, and the various native communities observed their own customary law or *adat*.

For the natives, this was an apartheid system which continued the traditional feudal hierarchies of Asian caste society, and which turned Indonesian natives into third-class subjects in their own land. At independence, the leaders of the new Indonesian Republic, inspired by the ideals of the French and American revolutions, ensured that the essential inequality of this colonial system was immediately abolished. In colonial times the system was, however, also used to protect the interests of the native Indonesians. For only they, and not the other two classes, could own land. Native land rights were recognised and respected under *adat* law, and this enlightened policy set the Netherlands Indies apart from the British colonies, where white settlers could always buy up and own vast tracts of native land, as a consequence of which indigenous tribes were often reduced to poverty in an ever-shrinking area.

The Europeans always had a privileged position at the top end of this system. Their category was not, however, completely exclusive. Thus, Japanese people were included in it, for, ever since the opening up of Japan by the Americans, Japanese people had enjoyed equal status with Europeans and other Westerners. And people from the other two classes, whether they were foreign Asians or natives, could accede to the European category by being 'equalised'. This was possible on condition that they had a certain income and education, could speak Dutch, and had a lifestyle comparable to those of Europeans (for example, they should be wearing shoes). They would then no longer be subject to indigenous customary law but to Dutch civil and penal jurisdiction. Christian Indonesians were also, to some extent at least, treated favourably. Most importantly – and this is another significant difference from the British Empire – mixed-race children could be recognised by their white fathers and would then count as Europeans.

Beyond enshrining the obvious colonial inequalities and having different kinds of regulation for different categories of people, the system did also give clear recognition to all kinds of cultural-anthropological differences between the many groups in society. And as it developed and grew, it provided a clear basic structure for what was an extraordinarily complex multiethnic, multilingual, multireligious and multicultural colonial society.

All this is not to say that there was no colour bar in the Netherlands Indies; because there clearly was, and there are many interesting instances that require further investigation. For example, for many Europeans of mixed-race descent, the colour of their skin was embarrassing and they would then often pretend to have had French or Italian ancestry, so as to explain away a skin that was not pure white. But in the 1930s, a leading Indonesian academic, Professor Achmad Djajadiningrat, rose to the highest post in the field of education and became a full member of the Council of the Indies, the highest administrative body in the colonial state. So, in the public domain, race clearly was not an insurmountable obstacle to a good career – probably due at least in part to the tradition of dual government, with a native élite co-opted into the colonial administration who gave their sons a Western education. But every Friday, after the Council of the Indies had finished its business meeting, the professor would excuse himself from coming along with his colleagues to their club, De Harmonie, which was whites-only and would not allow an exception even for such a high-ranking colonial official.

Conversely, it was certainly possible, at least in principle, for a white man to be called before a native court, for example in Central Java, which had its own Javanese jurisdiction, but when this happened, an outcry by whites against this insult to the position of Europeans usually put paid to the principle.

Other, often anecdotal evidence also points to well-established and widespread racial prejudice and taboo in Dutch colonial society. For example, young white girls would often be advised not to marry a native man, because they themselves would then be reduced to the status of a native, that is, they would lose all their rights as Europeans. In the 1930s, *Schuim van Goud*, a steamy Indies novel about a love affair between a white girl and a native boy was deemed so offensive that it was immediately banned. Native girls, on the other hand, were much in demand as concubines, but not for marriage. They were often abandoned when the white man found a white woman he could marry. But in the rare cases when a white man – for example, the writer Willem Walraven – actually married a native girl, this put him beyond the pale and cost him most of his European social contacts. Quite a few colonial novels depict the rivalry on the Indies marriage market between newly arrived European women, mixed-race Indo girls and the native Indonesian concubine or *nyai*. In doing so, these novels neatly reflect the prevailing attitudes and socio-cultural hierarchies of colonial society in the domain of sex and race.

Reinier Salverda

The Dutch Caribbean

As in other Caribbean and postcolonial societies, race and ethnicity form complex issues in the Dutch Caribbean with significant differences between the smaller islands and Suriname. While both the Netherlands Antilles and Suriname were originally populated with Amerindian peoples, the contemporary racial and ethnic make-up of the region reflects its history. During the slave period, Dutch colonial policy maintained a social, economic and legal distance between the black and white population, as well as between white and free coloureds. The latter were considered inferior to whites in spite of their free status. The scarcity of white women during and after the slave period triggered a high level of sexual relationships between white settlers and freed black women. The children of forced sexual relations between white planters and black female slaves were often freed, thus giving rise to a free coloured group. Although actually of mixed European and African descent, this group was considered 'Afro-Surinamese'.

The economic and agricultural crisis of the 1770s triggered changes in the racial hierarchy of Suriname due to a wave of white emigration. The free coloured élite came to occupy the places thus vacated. This was especially true for the coloured sons of white planters who had received a 'white' education in Suriname or Europe. Still, an informal colour hierarchy continued to prevail: the lighter the skin tone, the better. Throughout the nineteenth century light-skinned Creoles gained increasing influence in the administration and economy of the colony. These changes affected the social hierarchy and were also reinforced by the multiethnic composition of the white society. Early census records for the city of Paramaribo reflect the racial diversity of local society. In the plantation area blacks accounted for 90 per cent of the population, while the city of Paramaribo showed a wider demographic mix. At the end of the eighteenth century, the number of non-whites exceeded the number of whites. Women in particular formed the largest group of free coloureds and blacks.

The post-emancipation period saw the arrival of indentured labourers from British India, from China, and from the Dutch East Indies (present-day Indonesia). Between 1873 and

1917, 34,000 British Indians came to Suriname, joined between 1890 and 1938 by 32,600 East Indians. These groups brought along their own languages, religions and cultural customs. Labourers from Java were mainly Muslim, yet had different customs from the Indian Muslims. The larger portion of this group remained in the plantation districts longer than other indentured labourers. As a result they did not integrate as quickly. Of the 400,000 inhabitants of Suriname today, about 40 per cent are Hindustani, 27 per cent Creole, 15 per cent Javanese, 10 per cent Maroon, and 3 per cent Indian (that is 'Native American'). The remainder includes small minorities of Lebanese, Syrians, Chinese and Surinamese of mixed descent. The term 'Creole' in Suriname refers to people of African descent. The Maroon group descends from escaped plantation slaves. Nowadays, the emphasis is on ethnicity rather than on colour.

In the Netherlands Antilles, a different situation has emerged. Apart from Aruba, there is no Indian ('Native American') population left. The existing population is mostly of migrant origin and descendants from colonists and slaves. Moreover, during the slave period the numerical discrepancy between whites and blacks was less significant than in Suriname, and there has been little Asian immigration. Migration from the Caribbean and Latin America, however, was important during the twentieth century due to the booming oil and tourist industries.

On Curaçao, this largest and most important island, there quickly evolved a division between blacks and whites. The white population was also diverse and included Jews and Protestants, lower- and higher-class people. The separation from Dutch culture was important, and especially lower-class groups on the island had no wish to return to the Netherlands. From the 1920s onward the rapid development of the oil industry attracted new migrant populations. Dutch migrants occupied high positions, while Portuguese from Madeira, and Ashkenazy Jews from Eastern Europe accounted for the less skilled workforce. However, the majority of the new migrants came from Suriname, the Caribbean islands and Venezuela. There are also minority groups present in commerce, from the Middle East, China, India and Pakistan. Curaçao shows an extreme ethnic heterogeneity. Today there are about 160,000 inhabitants on the island, and the Afro-Caribbean group is no longer predominant. Colour does nevertheless play an important role, as does the fact of being born on the island.

Aruba experienced slavery on a much smaller scale than its Caribbean neighbours. The strong Indian ('Native American') roots and the proximity to Latin America pushed people to identify themselves with Venezuela and Colombia rather than with the Netherlands. As on Curaçao, the arrival of oil companies in the 1920s led to significant immigration. The population grew from 8,000 to 57,000 between 1920 and 1960. The largest group of migrant workers came from the British Caribbean. At first, migrants were separated from the rest of the local population as their living quarters were close to their place of work. Gradually, however, immigrant groups have integrated and after two generations most speak Papiamento (see 'Creolisation'). After 1960, the growth in tourism led to further migration to Aruba from mostly Spanish-speaking countries.

St Maarten experienced an even faster economic development than Aruba. During the period of slavery, slaves worked mainly on salt marshes and the difference in numbers of whites and blacks was small. A colour hierarchy, however, did exist. In contrast to other Dutch colonies, the white population was mainly of British descent and the local language was West Indian English. From the 1950s, tourism changed the racial and ethnic composition as the population grew from 5,000 to 80,000 by the early 1990s. Migration was mainly from English-speaking islands, Curaçao, Haiti and the Dominican Republic, as well as from

Europe, the US and Asia. The strongly heterogeneous character of the Dutch half of the island stands in sharp contrast to the situation in the French part of island, where, French influence dominates. The Dutch portion shows a strong British Caribbean and American influence. Social and economic differences exist between the different strata of society (affluent migrants and low wage workers). Nationality and citizenship are more important than ethnicity. Although migrants of British Caribbean or Haitian origins may share an Afro-Caribbean culture quite similar to the black locals, they do not possess the 'right' nationality.

Patricia Krus

LITERARY WORKS

Arion, Frank Martinus [1973] (1993), *Dubbelspel*, Amsterdam: De Bezige Bij.

Marugg, Tip [1958] (1994), *Weekendpelgrimage*, Amsterdam: De Bezige Bij.

Treffers, J. (1934), *Schuim van Goud*, Batavia: Kolff.

Vianen, Bea [1969] (1988), *Sarnami, hai*, Haarlem: In De Knipscheer.

Walraven, Willem (1979), 'Itih', in Rob Nieuwenhuys (ed.), *Memory and Agony. Dutch Stories from Indonesia*, Boston: Twayne.

HISTORIES

Benda-Beckman, C. E. von (ed.) (1986), *Anthropology of Law in the Netherlands. Essays on Legal Pluralism*, Dordrecht: Foris.

Boeke, J. H. (1961), *Indonesian Economics. The Concept of Dualism in Theory and Policy*, The Hague: Van Hoeve.

Hoefte, Rosemarijn (2001), 'The Development of a Multiethnic Plantation Economy: An Introduction to the History of Suriname from circa 1650 to 1900', in R. Hoefte and P. Meel (eds), *Twentieth Century Suriname: Continuities and Discontinuities in a New World Society*, Leiden: KITLV Press, pp. 1–22.

Oostindie, Gert (1996), 'Ethnicity, Nationalism, and the Exodus: The Dutch Caribbean Predicament', in Gert Oostindie (ed.), *Ethnicity in the Caribbean*, London: Macmillan, pp. 206–31.

Salverda, R. (1989), 'Dutch Legal Language in Indonesia', *Dutch Crossing. A Journal of Low Countries Studies* 38 (August): 32–45.

Race and Language in South Africa

South Africa has a population of more than 45 million people, comprising more than twenty ethnic groups. This diversity of cultures and languages has a dynamic history which can be traced back 100,000 years ago to South Africa's oldest known inhabitants, the Khoesan. This composite group consisted of two subgroups: southern Khoesan-speaking San (or Bushmen) and central Khoesan-speaking Khoikhoin (or Hottentots). The once widespread Khoesan languages eventually became extinct – this destruction was so immense that it has been referred to as 'language genocide' (Mesthrie 2002). A full understanding of these early race and language phenomena is limited because of the absence of early written sources. Written historical documentation materialised only once southern Africa came into contact with foreigners.

One of the key events influencing the language situation in modern South African history was the establishment of a trading station by the Dutch East India Company (VOC) at the Cape in 1652. This refreshment post soon turned into a colony. Tension over land and cattle between the colonists and the Khoesan forced the Dutch to find its labour force for the new colony from elsewhere. From 1658 slaves were imported from Madagascar, Mozambique, the East Indies and India, which according to Mesthrie (2002) created possibly one of the most diverse slave populations in the world in terms of origin, religion, culture and language. This diversity, added to the mix of European immigrants, and created a layered linguistic situation at the Cape: the European immigrants spoke Dutch, German, French and Scandinavian languages, while the slaves brought with them Niger-Kordofanian languages, Malagasy (an Austronesian language), Indo-Aryan and Dravidian languagues, and South-East Asian Austronesian, as well as non-Austronesian languages (den Besten 2004). In order to secure some degree of effective communication, mainly three 'contact languages' were used between slaves and colonists. These were Dutch, Asian Creole Portuguese and Malay, with variations over time and place. Despite the linguistic importance of Khoikhoi, this language was – mainly due to the dominant status of Dutch – never used as a contact language. However, during the course of time the languages spoken by the Khoekhoe and those spoken by the African and Asian slaves started influencing the Dutch of the colonists. At this juncture the first roots of Afrikaans as a new language became discernible.

Afrikaans developed rapidly. By the end of the seventeenth century the use of Dutch was mainly limited to written correspondence, official communication and 'civilised conversation' as well as the areas of church and education. An early version of Afrikaans was informally used on the farms and in ordinary day-to-day communication. Even though the exact origin of Afrikaans as a separate language is difficult to pinpoint, many sources identify the period between 1750 and 1775 as the crucial period, while others see it as an ongoing linguistic process continuing up to the beginning of the twentieth century (Roberge 2002).

In 1795 British forces took over the colony as a naval base, but handed it back to the Dutch in 1803, only to recapture it again in 1806. The strongest British influences came in 1820 with the arrival of a large group of settlers, settling mainly in the Eastern Cape. The British English used at the Cape could not withstand the new environment and other language influences, and gradually a typically South African pronunciation developed. The intrusion of the British into the Eastern Cape caused major tension with the Xhosa-speaking inhabitants of the area, giving rise to numerous frontier wars. The Dutch also were threatened and in 1834 started to move northwards. This 'Great Trek' introduced a new phase in European expansion (Mesthrie 2002) and gave way to the splitting off of the Afrikaners from their initial geographic identity as 'Dutch at the Cape'. The trek had important consequences for the development of Afrikaans into a unique South African language. In the 1850s the Dutch (then known as the 'Boers') who trekked northwards, established the Zuid-Afrikaansche Republiek (Transvaal) and the Oranje-Vrijstaat (Orange Free State), with Dutch as the official language.

For the indigenous South African languages this period represents a significant phase: from the 1820s indigenous languages were for the first time written down by missionaries, with the help of local consultants. The first substantial writing in Afrikaans materialised in the first half of the nineteenth century through initiatives of the descendants of Muslim slaves, who used Arabic script in writing Islamic texts in Afrikaans (Mesthrie 2002).

During the 1860s gold and diamonds were discovered in the interior and for the first time Britain developed an interest in that area. The ensuing conflict between the British and the Dutch (Boers / Afrikaners) who had settled there, was a catalyst impulse for the growth of Afrikaner nationalism. Under the leadership of S. J. du Toit (Eerste Afrikaanse Taalbeweging; First African Language Movement) Afrikaans activism gained impetus. As

Afrikaans became a tool in the formation of an identity, the fight for the recognition of Afrikaans was not aimed only against English, but against Dutch as well. From 1860 onwards Afrikaans was increasingly used as a written language. In 1860 the Genootskap van Regte Afrikaners was formed in order to promote the production of, for example, an Afrikaans translation of the Bible, an Afrikaans national anthem and an Afrikaans newspaper.

However, the supporters of the Dutch language did not accept the loss of official recognition, which occured in 1822, and after much pressure Dutch was reintroduced in 1882 in the parliament of the British Cape Colony. In commemoration of this, a statue in honour of the Dutch language was erected in 1893, entitled 'De Overwinning der Hollandsche Taal'. During the Anglo-Boer War of 1899 the statue was partially destroyed by British troops, but after the war (in 1907), in a gesture of reconciliation, the British donated a replica of the original statue. Today the partly destroyed statue and the replica are still to be seen in the South African town of Burgersdorp.

The Anglo-Boer War (1899–1902) ended with the British annexation of the republics, and this irrevocably changed the language situation in South Africa. Under British rule an intense Anglicisation campaign was introduced and English became increasingly dominant in the business and industrial sphere. The major urbanisation of the late nineteenth century, with a massive influx of people from Europe, the USA and Australia, accompanied by the large-scale influx of black people into the mining areas, resulted in a unique mixture of foreign languages. Urban varieties of African languages also manifested themselves. A unique pidgin 'contact language' developed around the mines and in the urban areas, becoming known as 'Fanakalo' (Mesthrie 2002).

When the Union of South Africa was formed in 1910, combining the two former Boer republics and the British colonies of the Cape and Natal into one state, English and Dutch became the official languages. However, the British continued their attempts at Anglicising the Afrikaners in the conquered Boer republics. This caused an upsurge in Afrikaner resistance and stimulated a second movement in the activism for the recognition of Afrikaans (Tweede Afrikaanse Taalbeweging). The Afrikaans language, as a symbol of the Afrikaners' newly found identity and culture, played a central role in the development of the notion of an Afrikaner nation. This was also the beginning of the controversial attempts at gaining a position of dominance for the Afrikaans language, starting in 1914 when the National Party (NP) was founded. In the same year Afrikaans replaced Dutch in schools. In 1918 the Afrikaner Broederbond was established – an organisation consisting exclusively of white Afrikaans-speaking Protestant male members with the mission to promote the Afrikaans language and culture and Afrikaner interests. In order to co-ordinate the cultural leg of this organisation, the Federation of Afrikaans Cultural Organisations (FAK) was founded. By means of this powerful vehicle Afrikaans embarked on an organisation-driven *taalstryd* (language battle). Afrikaner ideology (*die Afrikaanse gedagte*) linked the Afrikaans language exclusively to white speakers of the language, while the coloured speakers were not regarded as belonging to 'the Afrikaner' (Francken and Renders 2005).

Afrikaans was not officially recognised until 1925 when it replaced Dutch (which had been used for almost 270 years – from 1652 to 1925 – as a written language in South Africa) as an official language. Zuid-Afrika became Suid-Afrika. From 1948 the Afrikaans word *apartheid* became synonymous with the new Nationalist government and its statutory implementation of separate development according to colour (roughly a division between 'black' and 'white'). The term 'black' was used to refer to the many different ethnic groups with a wide variety of languages, while the term 'white' roughly referred to the Afrikaans- and English-speaking white communities. However, in the South African context, the terms 'white' and 'black' changed from being neutral ethnic or racial categories into concepts charged with socio-political implications.

The Bantu Education Act, passed in 1953, had major consequences for linguistic development in South Africa. This law, controlling the syllabi and media of instruction, was a crucial factor in entrenching a permanent underclass of black people. The resistance against 'Bantu Education' and the language policy it imposed culminated in 1976 in the Soweto uprisings. During these uprisings schoolchildren revolted against the imposition of Afrikaans in 'black' schools. The unrest spread throughout the country and Afrikaans increasingly became associated with racism and known as 'the language of the oppressor'. As such the struggle against apartheid also became a struggle against Afrikaans, the dominant language of the oppressive régime.

However, Afrikaans is the home language of many coloured people too, who were victims of apartheid. Kaapse Afrikaans (Kaaps) spoken by the 'Cape coloured' community and the Cape Muslims is based on the linguistic varieties of the early slave and Khoikhoi communities in the Western Cape. For a very long time Afrikaans language purists denied this dialect a status worthy of being used for 'serious' literature. This was part of the Afrikaner ideology of racial purity – an ideology that promoted the notion of, in biblical tradition, a superior and chosen people. The coloured community of the Cape, and people supporting the recognition of Kaaps, became increasingly vociferous against the marginalisation and stigmatisation of this dialect. The production of literature in Kaaps became a way of protesting against the oppressive Afrikaner ideology and its language policies. Ironically the 'language of the oppressor' was used to protest against that very oppressor. For example, the coloured writer Adam Small produced verse written in Kaaps with incantating rhythms and repetitions, following in the tradition of black American protest poets. His poetry – strongly satirical and with a tone of bitterness – often transfers biblical situations as political metaphors onto the South African context. His acclaimed play, *Kanna hy kô hystoe* (1965), portrays a coloured family trapped in a working-class community, and their desperate need for a saviour.

In the 1980s and especially 1990s there was an upsurge in literary works capturing the lives of coloured people and their colourful Afrikaans dialect. The search for an identity is a prominent theme in this literature, as for example in Peter Snyders' conversational play, *Political Joke* (1983), set in an illegal drinking place (*sjebeen*). This play captures Snyders' view of the community: suffering, masked by humour and hints of recklessness. This play was followed in 2002 by *Political Joke 2*. Snyders is specifically known for his 'street poetry', reflecting the street dialect of the Kaapse Vlakte. Other works by Snyders within this linguistic category are *Brekfis met vier* (1981), *'n Ordinary mens* (1982), *'n Waarskynlike mens* (1992) and *Tekens van die tye* (2002). The publication of Abraham Phillips' *Die verdwaalde land* in 1992 was the start of the prose upsurge by coloured writers in the 1990s. This novel gives expression to the powerlessness and humiliation inflicted by apartheid on the coloured community. In his footsteps followed Karel Benjamin with *Staan uit die water uit!* (1996) and *Pastoor Scholls trek sy toga uit* (1999), examples which reflect the experiences of the coloured communities living in Cape Town's Goodwood and District Six. In 1995 the noteworthy novel *Vatmaar* by A. H. M. Scholtz was published. The author identifies this novel as 'a story of the coloured people of South Africa' and according to Francken and Renders (2005) this book, set in the early 1920s, is indeed 'the ultimate book of the coloured people'. Scholtz pronounces himself a supporter of Desmond Tutu and Nelson Mandela's post-apartheid 'rainbow nation' and calls for reconciliation. *Diekie vannie Bo-Kaap* (1997) by Zulfah Otto-Sallies is a depiction of the Cape Malay community and their typical language manifestations. The writer Joseph Daniel Marble grew up in the coloured townships of Johannesburg and his *Ek, Joseph Daniel Marble* (1999) describes his daily experiences with violence and gangs. He narrates how dangerous life can be in the townships, where only the strongest survive.

White writers have also dealt with the theme of the relationship between white and coloured Afrikaans speakers. Etienne van Heerden's *Toorberg* (1986) narrates the story of two families living together, but apart, on the farm 'Toorberg'. The farm belongs to the white family who has been living there in relative luxury for many decades. The coloured family has also been living on the farm for many generations but as workers, and in poverty. This division is symbolic of the two strands of Afrikaans speakers and their culture. The white family is on the verge of extinction while the coloured family is fertile. This novel, translated into English as *Ancestral Voices* (1993), thus comments on the future of the Afrikaans-speaker in the country.

The long struggle for South African democracy eventually led to the lifting of the ban on the ANC and the release of Nelson Mandela. In April 1994 the ANC won the country's first non-racial election and on 10 May 1994 Nelson Mandela was inaugurated as South Africa's first democratically elected President. At his inauguration Xhosa praise singers performed oral literature and Mandela recited (in English) the politically engaged poem 'Die Kind' by the Afrikaans poet, Ingrid Jonker. This mixture of cultures, languages and literary forms at this significant ceremony was a symbolic gesture of harmonious intercultural exchange. It also suggested the power and impact of language and literature. By giving prominence to an Afrikaans poet at his inauguration was also a linguistic reconciliatory gesture by Nelson Mandela towards the 'language of the oppressor' and its speakers.

In light of the fact that linguistic issues had always been closely related to political issues in South Africa, it came as no surprise that the political changeover brought about major linguistic changes for the country. With its new constitution (1996) and the Pan South African Language Board Act (1995), South Africa stands today in the forefront of promoting respect for other languages, multilingualism and the development of languages. According to Heugh (2002) this places the country at the cutting edge of international language-policy development. South Africa has become the country with the most official languages (eleven) in the world. These are Zulu, Xhosa, Afrikaans, English, Tswana, Sotho (previously known as South Sotho), Pedi (also known as North Sotho), Tsonga, Swati, Venda and Ndebele. The dynamic language scenario of South Africa is still changing. The last decade has seen a major influx of people from other African states such as Mozambique, Zimbabwe, Malawi and Nigeria, but also from different parts of Europe. However, most South Africans can communicate in more than one language, with English as the most commonly spoken in business and commerce. Despite the language tolerance in the country, many Afrikaans-speaking people regard Afrikaans as a threatened language within the new composition. The fear that the language will eventually disappear has brought along, as Francken and Renders (2005) suggest, a third language battle.

Because of the country's racial and language diversity, Nobel Peace Prize-winner Archbishop Desmond Tutu, in the euphoric aftermath of the transition from white minority to majority rule in 1994, coined the term 'the rainbow nation.' This term (also reflected in the five languages used in the national anthem) sounds a positive tone of hope for a future in which the more than 40 million South Africans can vanquish their differences and join in constructing a culturally rich society. Cultural, literary and linguistic exchanges have already started on many different levels. At the beginning of the twenty-first century the South African literary scene has become witness to significant literary attempts to bring Afrikaans and other South African languages, historically belonging to different camps, together. The Afrikaans author Antjie Krog has played a remarkable role in this regard. *Met woorde soos met kerse* (2002) is a collection of verse from various indigenous languages, translated by Krog into Afrikaans, often accompanied by illuminating introductions. Krog's other significant contribution is her translation of /Xam-poems from the texts by W. H. I. Bleek, L. C. Loyd and J. D. Lewis-Williams in her collection *Die sterre sê 'tsau'* (2004). Translations such as these have brought fascinating literature, in the past inaccessible to many South Africans, into a visible literary realm where it belongs. Such a multilingualism challenging the inseparability of language, culture and identity can, according to the South African linguist Neville Alexander (1992), play a vital role in achieving a new identity for all South Africans.

Annemie van Niekerk

Histories

Adhikari, M. (ed.) (1996), *Straatpraatjes: Language, Politics and Popular Culture in Cape Town, 1909–1922*, Cape Town: J. L. van Schaik.

Alexander, Neville (1992) 'A Language Policy for a Future South Africa', *Proceedings of the English Academy of Southern Africa Conference*, 1–3 July, Cape Town: University of Cape Town, pp. 154–62.

Besten, Hans den (2004), 'Where the Historian and the Creolist Meet: The Linguistic Analysis of "Quotations" and other Data in Cape Archives and in Travelogues', in Siegfried Huigen and Jean Kommers (eds), *Interpretations of Colonial Representations*, Saarbrücken: Nijmegen Studies in Development and Cultural Change, pp. 81–111.

Davids, A. (1990), 'Words the Cape Slaves Made: A Socio-Historical-Linguistic Study, *South African Journal of Linguistics* 8: 1–224.

Francken, Eep and Luc Renders (2005), *Skrywers in die strydperk. Krachtlijnen in de Zuid-Afrikaanse letterkunde*, Amsterdam: Uitgeverij Bert Bakker.

Hattersley, A. F. (1940), *Portrait of a Colony*, Cambridge: Cambridge University Press.

Heugh, Kathleen (2002), 'Recovering Multilingualism: Recent Language-Policy Developments', in R. Mesthrie (ed.), *Language in South Africa*, Cambridge: Cambridge University Press, pp. 238–47.

Huigen, Siegfried and Jean Kommers (eds) (2004), *Interpretations of Colonial Representations*, Saarbrücken: Nijmegen Studies in Development and Cultural Change.

Keegan, T. (1996), *Colonial South Africa and the Origins of the Racial Order*, Cape Town, David Philip.

Lanham, W. and K. Prinsloo (eds) (1978), *Language and Communication Studies in South Africa*, Oxford and Cape Town: Oxford University Press.

Marks, S. and S. Trapido (eds) (1987), *The Politics of Race, Class and Nationalism in Twentieth-Century South Africa*, London: Longman.

Mesthrie, Rajend (ed.) (2002), *Language in South Africa*, Cambridge: Cambridge University Press.

Roberge, Paul T. (2002), 'Afrikaans: Considering Origins', in R. Mesthrie (ed.), *Language in South Africa*, Cambridge: Cambridge University Press, pp. 79–103.

Slavery and Abolition

EAST INDIES

While studies in the history of slavery predominantly focus on the Atlantic trade in black slaves for the plantation economies in the Americas, it would be a mistake to ignore the Asian practices of slavery, serfdom and bonded or indentured labour, the feudal servants culture in traditional Asian societies, the large-scale use of cheap coolie labour after slavery was officially abolished, the trade in Indian and Indonesian coolies to the Caribbean in the latter part of the nineteenth century, or indeed their use in the plantations set up throughout the European colonies in India and South-East Asia.

It is not customary to talk of slavery in the Dutch East Indies, but – as is clear from the seven page article on Slavery in the *Encyclopaedie van Nederlandsch-Indie* – the practice certainly did exist, both in traditional Indonesian society and under European administration. Under the Dutch East India Company (VOC), slaves traditionally came from Bali and from the Papuan tribes in Irian Jaya (New Guinea), and until 1808 the colonial government itself kept slaves for labour of all kinds. In the Netherlands Indies slavery was officially abolished in May 1859. A total of 4,739 slaves were freed; and their owners indemnified to the tune of 784,668 guilders.

It was seen as part and parcel of indigenous feudal culture that Indonesian people of rank and distinction would have many servants at their disposal – a domestic practice that was quickly taken up by the Dutch colonisers, and as Multatuli explains in his novel *Max Havelaar*, the Dutchmen living in Batavia actually preferred their servants to come from the countryside, because that way, they would still be 'uncorrupted', that is, more docile and cheaper.

In the public sector, it was considered customary that village people would have to supply *corvee* labour for infrastructural works, such as the construction of Daendels' great *Postweg* across Java, the building of bridges, or large-scale agricultural works. This was not seen as slavery but as a traditional contribution, almost a tax in kind, which the colonial administration, like any feudal overlord, had every right to demand from its native Indonesian subjects.

After abolition, plantation labour was organised in the coolie system, which resulted in the mass recruitment of illiterate peasants from Java, or the importation of Chinese coolies from Singapore, for work in the large new plantations in the Deli province of Sumatra. Technically, these labourers were free to sign on, and they were also paid for their labour; so from a contractual point of view this was far better regulated than the former slave system. In actual fact, once he had signed on, a Javanese villager had no say whatsoever in where he was taken or what kind of work he would have to do. He could equally be taken to the plantations of Sumatra, or to the Caribbean, where to this day one can find descendants of Javanese coolies in Suriname. From those faraway lands, it was virtually impossible for a coolie to save enough money to pay for the return journey. Coolies were used for hard labour, and there were severe sanctions if they managed to flee the cruel treatment to which they were often subjected. The so-called *Cultuurpolitie* (agricultural police) actively patrolled the large Sumatra plantations and hunted down escapees for punishments which ranged from extensive beatings with rattan to hanging. In the meantime, the plantation management often made its coolies dependent on betting, loans, drink and opium, so as to force them to sign a new contract every time the old one ended.

A harrowing depiction of coolie life is given in the infamous Rhemrev report (ed. Breman) on the rampant abuses of coolies in the Deli plantations, and in the novel *Koelie* (*Coolie*, 1932) by Madelon Szekely-Lulofs, which, once it was translated into English, immediately attracted the attention of the ILO, who criticised labour conditions in the Dutch colonies. Breman and Szekely-Lulofs were merely following in the steps of the anti-colonial writer Multatuli, who wrote an important pamphlet about so-called 'Free Labor' (1870, American translation 1949), in which he sharply criticised the factual absence of freedom that was the reality of coolie labour.

Once slavery was abolished, it very quickly receded from people's memories. As a consequence, while many people in the Netherlands still know the popular nineteenth-century writer Hildebrand (Nicolaas Beets) as the author of the humorous *Camera Obscura* (1839), hardly anyone is aware that Beets was also an active campaigner for the Dutch Society for the Abolition of Slavery. Such blind spots and gaps dominate the collective memory of slavery amongst the Dutch. Allison Blakely's monograph, *Blacks in the Dutch World: The Evolution of Racial Imagery in a Modern Society* (1994) is the exception that confirms this rule.

It was authors such as Nicolaas Beets and Multatuli who raised the issue of slavery in Dutch public debate in the nineteenth century. And their contemporary van Hoevell, with his harrowing tale of the sale at auction of two young slave girls in Batavia, whose owner had meant to, but forgotten, to give them their freedom before she died. In the eighteenth century, Elisabeth Maria Post had done the same with her anti-slavery novel *Reinhart, of natuur en godsdienst* (1791–2). And in the twentieth century there was Albert Helman with his *De stille plantage* (1931). Today, again, it is writers who raise the issue of slavery, writers such as Frank Martinus Arion, Adriaan van Dis and Hugo Pos, who make it very clear that Dutch literature still has a job to do in the real world.

Reinier Salverda

THE DUTCH CARIBBEAN

As in other parts of the Caribbean, slavery was the dominant social and economic feature of the Dutch colonies in the New World until slave emancipation in 1863. Although slavery occurred in all of the Dutch possessions in the New World, the formal aspects of the slave system differed from one colony to the other.

Of the six Dutch islands in the Caribbean, only St Maarten and St Eustatius had a few plantations, while on Curaçao, Saba, Aruba and Bonaire an unfavourable climate and topography hindered the development of large-scale plantations. Here, small-scale holdings produced goods for local consumption and trading posts served shipping routes to Europe Africa, and the Americas. Curaçao and St Eustatius became important ports on the slave trade route. The few existing plantations held only a dozen slaves. The latter also worked in the salt marshes, boat yards or as gardeners or servants. As a result, the slave population had closer contact with whites than in most other New World slave societies. The conditions were also better overall: lighter work, a better climate and hence less need to acquire new slaves. As a result, the importance of the slave trade diminished over the years.

Historically, the main crop in Suriname was sugar cane. By the middle of the eighteenth century Suriname had become the first Caribbean colony to cultivate coffee. Later came the introduction of cotton. The harsh working conditions and high mortality rate created a constant need for new slaves. The death rate exceeded the birth rate among slaves, although this changed in later times because of improvements in their material conditions, and hence also in their physical well-being. By 1800, half the slave population had been born in Suriname. Up to the beginning of the nineteenth century, slaves accounted for 90 per cent of the population. At the start of the eighteenth century there were around 10,000 slaves on approximately 100 estates. In 1744 there were sixty-two slaves for every white person in the plantation area. While at the beginning of the slave period the authorities outlawed sexual relations between whites and blacks, the numerical imbalance encouraged white men to engage in forced sex with black female slaves. Many entered into a 'Surinamese marriage' (*Surinaams huwelijk*), a long-term relationship with a black or coloured woman. The children of these mixed unions were freed, as sometimes also happened with black male slaves. Together, this gave rise to a free coloured and black class.

With the emancipation of slaves happening elsewhere in the Caribbean, the abolition of slavery in the Dutch colonies gained prominence on the political agenda. The abolitionist movement was very limited in the Netherlands, as the West Indian colonies were of little interest to Dutch public opinion. Even abolitionists held the same stereotypes regarding slaves as did the partisans of slavery: black people were considered to be childish, lazy and unable to understand the implications of being free. For Dutch plantation owners, slavery was efficient, productive and profitable. In their eyes, there were no economic reasons for abolishing slavery. Although the decision formally to abolish slavery was taken in 1844, another eighteen years passed before emancipation was finally officially decreed on 9 July 1862 and effectively implemented on 1 July 1863. Issues such as the monetary compensation to slave owners, the revitalisation of the sugar economy, and the possible importation of contract labourers under government supervision slowed the emancipation process. Under the emancipation Act, each slave holder was awarded 300 guilders for every freed slave regardless of age, sex, mental or physical health. Almost 10 million guilders were paid out to slave owners from the surplus of the Netherlands West Indies. Although the abolition pertained to all the Dutch Caribbean its formal implementation differed in each colony.

In Suriname, 33,621 slaves were freed, approximately 55 per cent out of a total population of about 60,000. The emancipation Act required that each free slave sign a contract of apprenticeship with the colonial administration. This mandatory agreement implied a ten-year contract with an employer of the slave's choice, and was supervised by the state. On the economic level, emancipation caused the abandonment of many estates. By 1890, only fourteen sugar producing estates were left.

In the Dutch Antilles, 11,654 slaves were freed, a third of the 33,000 total population of the islands. No period of apprenticeship was introduced. On Aruba, which had no plantations, fewer than 500 slaves were freed. On St Maarten, the situation was complicated by the fact that in 1848 the slaves on the French part of the island had already been freed. This had led to a self-proclamation of freedom in the Dutch half. Negotiations between the planters and the colonial power showed that slavery effectively no longer existed on the island. Yet until the Emancipation Act of 1863 the situation officially continued unchanged. On Curaçao, local society was more heterogeneous than in Suriname. At the time of emancipation, half of the population consisted of free blacks while slaves accounted for 35 per cent of the island's population. Economically, the main concern was that a stagnating economy and limited agricultural land could not easily absorb the freed slaves nor provide work for them.

Patricia Krus

LITERARY WORKS
Dekker, Edouard Douwes [1860] (1982), *Max Havelaar*, Amherst, MA: University of Massachusetts Press.

Helman, Albert [1931] (1997), *De stille plantage: roman*, Schoorl: Conserve.

Luhofs, Madelon H. [1932] (1982), *Coolie*, Singapore: Oxford University Press.

McLeod, Cynthia (1996), *Ma Rochelle passée: welkom El Dorado*, Schoorl: Conserve.

Post, Elisabeth Maria (1791–2), *Reinhart, of natuur en godsdienst*, Amsterdam: Johannes Allart.

HISTORIES

Oostindië, Gert (ed.) (1995), *Fifty Years Later: Antislavery, Capitalism and Modernity in the Dutch Orbit*, Leiden: KITLV Uitgeverij.

— (ed.) (1999), *Het verleden onder ogen. Herdenking van de slavernij*, Den Haag: Uitgeverij Arena/Prins Claus Fonds.

— (2005), *Paradise Overseas: The Dutch Caribbean, Colonialism and its Transatlantic Legacies*, Oxford: Macmillan Caribbean.

Stipriaan, Alex van (1993), *Surinaams Contrast: roofbouw en overleven in een Caraïbische plantage kolonie 1750–1863*, Leiden: KITLV Uitgeverij.

— (1995), 'Suriname and the Abolition of Slavery', in Gert Oostindië (ed.), *Fifty Years Later: Antislavery, Capitalism and Modernity in the Dutch Orbit*, Leiden: KITLV Utigeverij, pp. 117–41.

Women's Histories

EAST INDIES – INDONESIA

A fascinating aspect of Dutch colonial history in Indonesia concerns the role and position of women in the former Dutch East Indies. During the seventeenth and eighteenth centuries – as was shown by Jean Gelman Taylor in *The Social World of Batavia* (1983) and by Leonard Blussé in *Strange Company* (1986) – Indonesian concubines (*nyai*), Chinese go-betweens and rich mestizo wives were often indispensable to the Dutch colonisers in running their empire. It is a theme one also finds in literature, in the nineteenth-century Indonesian folktale of Nyai Dasima, and again in the strong female characters portrayed by Indonesia's most important writer of the twentieth century, Pramoedya Ananta Toer.

Dutch women, on the other hand, made their appearance on the colonial stage mostly after the opening of the Suez canal in 1869, and were then usually dependent on the status, income and career of their husbands.

A remarkable number took to writing, and beginning with Mina Kruseman's feminist novel *Een Indisch Huwelijk* (*An Indies Marriage*, 1872), there is a significant line of Dutch women writers advocating emancipatory ideas for the colonies – from Augusta de Wit, Carry van Bruggen and Marie van Zeggelen in the early decades of the twentieth century, via Annie Salomons and Madelon Székely-Lulofs in the 1930s through to Hella Haasse, Beb Vuyk, Aya Zikken, Helga Ruebsamen and Marion Bloem in the post-war era.

However, Indonesian women had already begun to develop emancipatory ideas of their own. The most important figure is Kartini (1879–1904), who fought for the education of women and their liberation from the shackles of Javanese feudal traditions as much as Dutch colonial paternalism. Her 1910 posthumous *Door Duisternis tot Licht* (*Letters of a Javanese Princess*, 1921) have continued to inspire Indonesian women in their struggle for emancipation.

During the first half of the twentieth century, Dutch and Indonesian women, despite their shared aspirations, were set apart by their very different struggles for racial and sexual emancipation and equality under colonial conditions of the Dutch East Indies society.

In the 1920s there was a colonial debate about female labour, in which European notions clashed with Indonesian practices. Statistical data were collected on how much time Indonesian women spent working and what wages they earned, both in indigenous agriculture and on the large colonial plantations in Java.

In the domestic sphere, Javanese servants were handled in line with Dutch instruction manuals, and the role of the Dutch colonial women was defined as that of a wise but firm teacher of her servants/children, with a Western lifestyle modelled on an illusionary Netherlands in the tropics.

In the struggle for women's suffrage in the colonies, European women carried their 'white woman's burden' and considered themselves part and parcel of the Dutch colonial project; and they fought for their own voting rights, keeping a safe distance from the Indonesian women's movement. But the history of the women's struggle in Indonesia in the colonial era is defined most of all by the fierce verbal battles and political demonstrations of 1937, when the colonial government attempted to regulate family life through a new ordinance on marriage. The debate focused – and foundered – on the conflicting views of marriage and monogamy of the colonial government, of the Indonesian women's movement, and of the Islamic religious leaders who scored a memorable victory here.

The cultural battles in the colonies – over marriage, manners and morality, over relations, intimacy and sexual affairs just as much as over work, education, democracy and the law – show, again and again, how Western ideals and concepts of womanhood were in conflict with Indonesian views and colonial realities. Crossing the line was almost unthinkable, and Dutch novels strongly advised against mixed marriages, because in such a marriage the white woman would be reduced to the status of a 'native', without rights.

Today, there is the ongoing exploitation of Indonesian women in the sweatshops that produce cheap commodities for global companies and mass consumers in the West. And in the late 1990s, the Indonesian feminist, poet and philosopher Toety Herati Nurhadi was arrested simply for daring to hand out milk to the poor in Jakarta.

Reinier Salverda

THE DUTCH CARIBBEAN

The history of women in the Dutch Caribbean has aroused relatively little critical interest hitherto. Some attention has been paid to the position of female slaves within the wider context of slave societies. The main focus has been on the largest of the former Dutch Caribbean colonies, Suriname, to the detriment of the Dutch Antilles. Consequently, knowledge of women's histories and of issues of gender remains fragmentary. The position and role of women in the Dutch Caribbean have been greatly determined by the region's history of colonisation, slavery, indentured labour and migration. In Suriname, slavery introduced a skewed relationship between men and women within the white and black community, with major consequences for the relations between the different races and sexes. On the plantations female slaves worked primarily in the fields while the more skilled positions fell to male slaves. In the plantation household women slaves could become cooks, maids or housekeepers. With the rise of the cost of slaves and the end of the slave trade, the need to improve living conditions for slaves gained more importance, and female slaves were seen as valuable resources for reproductive purposes. Initially, the colonial authorities forbade sexual relations between whites and blacks. However, this rule was not respected due to the unequal sex ratio in the white planter class. White men forced sex upon black female slaves and eventually entered into long-term relationships with black or coloured women, a bond called *surinaams huwelijk* or 'Surinamese marriage'. The children of these unions were freed, giving rise to a free coloured and black class.

The majority of urban free men had a non-white partner, most of them free women. By 1811, there were three times more free black or coloured women than white women. Social pressure stopped many white men from marrying their non-white partner. An exception was Elisabeth Samson, who married a white man. The marriage was considered a scandal and considerably lowered the man's social status. Marriage was seen as a European institution. Concubinage was favoured by white and non-white men. Marriage entailed that the woman became subordinate to her husband and had no legal independence. As more coloured or black women obtained freedom by manumission or by birth, the range of professions available to them became more varied. In the 1811 census women registered as coloured worked as seamstresses, washerwomen, housekeepers, servants and landowners. Some free women achieved a comfortable economic status. For instance, Elisabeth Wilhelmina de Montel, daughter of a Sephardic Jew and a free black, eventually married a Frenchman. Her dowry included four slaves, goods and cash. Later she ran a coffeehouse and was the owner of thirty-one slaves.

Issues of relations between white and black women are as problematic in the Dutch Caribbean as in the rest of the region. In the plantation area white women were scarce, and most of them lived in the only urban centre in Suriname, Paramaribo. Relations between white women and black slaves are barely documented, with the exception of the infamous case of Alida, a female slave, and her owner, a white single woman, Susanna du Plessis. This story served as an example of the alleged sexual jealousy of white women toward their female slaves, and the subsequent ill treatment of the latter. Du Plessis allegedly had the breasts of her slave Alida cut off. Recent research, however, argues that this claim was exaggerated, and originated in the threat perceived by white male planters when faced with financially independent white women (Neus-van der Putten 2003).

In the post-emancipation period, the arrival of British Indian and Javanese indentured labourers fundamentally affected the make-up of local society. In the early years of indentured labour the lack of women of Indian or Chinese descent encouraged inter-racial relationships. Women of Hindustani background in the early years of arrival often had multiple relationships. In recent years more research has been undertaken on kinship and sexuality in Surinamese society, and on relations between men and women in the private and public sphere. In contemporary Suriname, women occupy the lower scale of the social hierarchy. The social class of women is determined by their male partners. This is particularly the case for upper-class women who attain their status by marriage. To this day the custom for men to maintain a sexual relationship outside marriage remains: a married man can have a spouse as well as an 'outside wife' (*buitenvrouw*). Researchers such as Gloria Wekker (1994) have underlined that Surinamese family structures, and sexuality in Suriname, are primarily gauged by Western standards and are consequently spoken of in pejorative terms, especially when it comes to matrifocal families that are usually presented as a typical Creole working-class phenomenon. The absence of written sources pertaining to previous eras also complicates research with regard to gender roles, perceptions of sexuality, and male–female relations. The custom of *matispelen*, a pattern of sexual behaviour involving multiple male and female partners, has been thought to be predominant among Creole working-class women, but Wekker claims this particular attitude towards sex has in fact been underresearched among other ethnic groups and among men. Moreover, behind a relaxed attitude to sexuality lies the problem of sexual harassment and intimidation, which goes back to the time of slavery and the post-emancipation era. The issue has been put on the political and social agenda in the past couple of decades as the need to root out sexual harassment in the work place has become more urgent.

Patricia Krus

SOUTH AFRICA

Since the early nineteenth century South African women have, broadly speaking, been subjected to two systems of patriarchy; the one has its origin in pre-capitalist indigenous societies and the other in European settler society. The intersecting of these systems, and the fact that the organisation of gender has all along been interwoven with political and economic transformations, complicate the mapping of both the past and present position of women in South Africa. This is made more complex by the division of South African women along sharp lines of culture, race and class. However, the pervasiveness of female subordination to men has given coherence to what might otherwise seem a bewildering range of variables.

In the pre-colonial era male appropriation of women's capacity to produce and reproduce was the axis on which South African societies turned. The gendered economy of the region was profoundly changed through colonisation. 'The Dutch read the southern region through Christian myths, assuming that the story of the Garden of Eden applied, and that Cape women were a reminder of man's Fall' (Daymond et al. 2003). The Khoi woman Sara Baartman in 1810 was taken to Europe as an ethnological curiosity and displayed in a cage as the 'Hottentot Venus'. After her death her body was preserved at the Musée de l'Homme in Paris as an emblem of 'primitive' sexuality. In 2002 her remains were ceremoniously returned to South Africa. (Daymond et al. 2003)

During the latter half of the nineteenth century 'hut taxes' imposed on the various African chiefdoms forced many rural men into wage labour. The growing mining and manufacturing industries created a migrant male labour system. Women became single-handedly responsible for homestead production in the native reserves. This put a strain on marriages and family structures. Women bore the brunt of the collision between settler and indigenous systems, as capitalist oriented European sexism was added to the patriarchal elements already present within pre-colonial society. By the early twentieth century the colonial authorities were implementing a dualistic legal system combining customary law with a capitalist-oriented legal system. This dualistic system preserved the outer form of the indigenous sex-gender system in a modern South Africa where the inner logic of the indigenous system had been destroyed. Missionary attempts to fight illiteracy created a split amongst indigenous women by creating a new literate élite. In *Missionaris* (1988), by the Afrikaans writer Elsa Joubert, an early nineteenth-century Dutch missionary in South Africa comes to realise the false foundation of his mission in bringing the Christian message to the Khoi people.

By the 1940s there was a rapid increase in women's flow from the reserves to urban areas. In order to survive economically and to maintain independence from men and the state, many women became involved in illicit liquor trading. Not only were these women discriminated against as women, but also as female members of a subjected race. The state increased its formal control over African women's mobility after 1948 through refined urban influx control measures and passes, such as the Population Registration Act (1950) and the Group Areas Act (1950).

Black women's response to colonial society followed diverse routes. Some saw prospects for freedom and emancipation in the new dispensation, for example through involvement in a market economy, Western-style education and the Church structures that proliferated in the early twentieth century. However, many women, especially from the older generation (supported by homestead heads), defended the traditional homestead system on which their status and security depended.

Despite attempts to preserve the traditional way of life, numerous African women became incorporated into colonial society. This mostly occurred through the institution of domestic service. Cock (in Walker 1990) indicates that black and white women's sharing of the intimate household space was blocked by the heightened awareness of racial, cultural and class differences. Consequently they could not operate as allies.

From the earliest days of Dutch settlement at the Cape, government was regarded as a male responsibility. White women's duties revolved around getting married, being submissive to male authority, supervising the household, bearing children and inculcating social norms. However, the simple but harsh pastoral economy of Boer society relied heavily on women's endurance and resourcefulness. The British, arriving in 1820, brought a sex-gender system along that categorised the private domestic domain as the realm of women, and the public domain of productive work and politics as the realm of men. Apart from being domestic, Victorian morals required women be modest and sexually pure. Even though these two systems started influencing one another within the southern African context, tension escalated between Afrikaner and British. For many Afrikaner women the Anglo-Boer War (1899–1902) brought extensive life changes: 27,000 people – mainly women and children – died in the British concentration camps and the peace treaty of 1902 was a major political defeat for the Afrikaners. Material losses, such as farms, homes, crops, cattle and so on, created rural impoverishment. This and the consequent proletarianisation encouraged the growth of Afrikaner nationalism and its ideology of the *volksmoeder* or 'mother of the nation'. This ideology valorised most gender conventions of the nineteenth century, but emphasised Afrikaner women's loyalty to male-dominated Afrikaner nationalism. The stress on the ideology of white supremacy and women's role in its preservation blurred class divisions amongst Afrikaners during a period when Afrikaner women were increasingly pulled into wage labour. Even though the ideology of female domesticity was extremely resilient, this new situation broadened the concept of 'women's sphere'. Many Afrikaner working-class women joined the Garment Workers' Union – one of the most militant unions during the inter-war years – and became prominent trade-union officials, emphasising the plea of the woman worker in an alienating industrial environment. With the flow of women into the urban and industrial sphere during the early twentieth century, the control over white women's sexuality was tightened up as a means of policing the boundaries of the white race. Walker (1990) explains that 'white male control over female sexuality thus operated to define men's relationships to other men as well as to women'.

The only political movement actively concerned with women's rights in the early twentieth century was the women's suffrage movement. However, as this was part of a bigger battle to uphold white power in the country, it was concerned only with the enfranchisement of white women, who received the vote in 1930.

On both sides of the racial divide women have played a double role in the history of gender relations in South Africa. On the one hand they have acted as agents of gender socialisation, reinforcing gender norms; on the other hand, many passively refused subjection. Resistance by black women, especially, was periodically visible, such as the 1913 campaign against pass laws and permits for African women. This paved the way for the establishment of the ANC Women's League (1913–14), still seen as a landmark in the development of the women's movement in South Africa. For most black women the struggle for women's rights was inseparable from the much larger campaign for equality. In 1954 the Federation of South African Women (1954–63) emerged and a 'women's charter' was adopted, identifying the women's movement as inherent to the national liberation movement. In 1956 the famous women's march against pass laws took place. Up to 20,000 women took part in the march to Pretoria – at that stage the largest crowd ever to have assembled at the Union Buildings. Despite the democratic elections of 1994, though, and the adoption of the constitution in 1996, all the subtle forms of gender discrimination influencing women's domestic and public lives have not yet been erased.

The corpus of South African literature (other than English) includes fascinating work dealing with women's history. Black women mainly published in English, but the novel *Unongxaki nezakhe* (1976) by Gertrude Belebesi is a Xhosa text, portraying the intermeshing of indigenous and colonial constraints on women. Many Afrikaans literary texts have dealt with gender issues, of which *Die swerfjare van Poppie Nongena* (1978) by Elsa Joubert is one of the most prominent. In this novel Joubert examines the hardships of a black South African woman during the period 1937 to 1976. This novel suggests the possible forging of a common consciousness between women from different classes and races. By the close of the 1980s, South African women had for the first time start writing openly about sexuality, including homoerotic experiences; these writers include Jeanne Goosen and Welma Odendaal.

By the end of the twentieth century numerous Afrikaans texts with female protagonists based on significant historical women, had been published. Some examples are Karel Schoeman's *Armosyn van die Kaap* (1999) dealing with the period 1451–1651; Schoeman's *Die wêreld van 'n slavin* (2001), covering the period 1652–1733; and Dalene Matthee's *Pieternella van die Kaap* (2000), based on the story of Krotoa (Eva), the Khoi woman who acted as van Riebeeck's interpreter, and her daughter Pieternella. E. K. M. Dido made her début in 1996 with the novel *Die storie van Monica Peters*, which is the first in a series of novels dealing with the lives of coloured women, battling with the political realities of a troubled South Africa. These novels are unique, because it is the first time in Afrikaans literature that the lives of coloured women are depicted by coloured women. *Agaat* (2004) by Marlene van Niekerk deals with the fascinating relationship between two South African women belonging to different race groups. White Milla Redelinghuys takes coloured Agaat Lourier into her childless home as surrogate child but also servant. The roles are reversed when Milla's health deteriorates and Agaat takes control. The story thus parallels the power reversal that marked the end of apartheid.

Annemie van Niekerk

LITERARY WORKS
Daymond, M. J. et al. (eds) (2003), *Women Writing Africa. The Southern Region*, Johannesburg: Witwaterst and University Press.
Debrot, Cola [1935] (1978), *Mijn zuster de negerin*, Amsterdam: De Bezige Bij.
McLeod, Cynthia (2004), *The Free Negress Elisabeth: Prisoner of Color*, trans. and ed. Sean F. Taylor and Monique S. Pool, Paramaribo: Waterfront Press.
Roemer, Astrid (1982), *Over de gekte van een vrouw*, Haarlem: In de Knipscheer.
Vianen, Bea (1969), *Sarnami, hai*, Amsterdam: Querido.
Vianen, Bea (1974), *Geen onderdelen*, Amsterdam: De Bezige Bij.

HISTORIES
Hoefte, Rosemarijn and Jean Jacques Vrij (2004), 'Free Black and Colored Women in Early Nineteenth-Century Paramaribo, Suriname', in David Barry Gaspar and Darlene

Clark Hine (eds), *Beyond Bondage: Free Women of Color in the Americas*, Urbana and Chicago, IL: University of Illinois Press, pp. 145–68.

Locher-Scholten, Elsbeth (2000), *Women and the Colonial State. Essays on Gender and Modernity in the Netherlands Indies 1900–1942*, Amsterdam: Amsterdam University Press.

Neus-van der Putten, Hilde (2003), *Susanna du Plessis: Portret van een slavenmeesteres*, Amsterdam: KIT Publishers.

Walker, Cheryl (ed.) (1990), *Women and Gender in Southern Africa to 1945*, Cape Town: David Philip Publishers.

— (1991), *Women and Resistance in South Africa*, Cape Town: David Philip Publishers.

Wekker, Gloria (1994), 'Of Mimic Men and Unruly Women: Family, Sexuality and Gender in Twentieth-Century Suriname', in Rosemarijn Hoefte and Peter Meel (eds), *Twentieth Century Suriname: Continuities and Discontinuities in a New World Society*, Leiden: KITLV Uitgeverij, pp. 174–97.

Other Europes

Clash of Civilisations

One wonders why, in the midst of debates about globalisation, the theme of the clash of civilisations should have emerged. The current wars and ethnic conflicts, especially across the region from the Mediterranean to the Far East, with, in the background, the emergence of new powers like China and India and the consolidation of religious and ethnic fundamentalist tendencies, when added to the drift of Africa towards chaos, may appear to confirm the agenda of the clash of civilisation. Yet, the situation is that there has been for some time now talk of a global culture, characterised by the intertwining of the local and the global and transnational economic, cultural, technological, ideological flows and 'scapes' (Appadurai in Featherstone 1990), already emergent since the beginning of modernism alongside a new cosmopolitan form of sociality. Furthermore the displacement and migration of people worldwide have brought to the fore the fact of diasporas and their transformative effects for cultures. So the view that cultures are being presented as distinct entities united by intrinsic differences that resist hybridisation and provoke conflict, a view currently associated with the position developed by Huntington (1993), needs to be interrogated in terms of relations of power and what is at stake in them. This geo-political dimension is explicit in Huntington when he claims that the world is, post Cold-War, riven not by economic or ideological wars but by conflicts that are increasingly cultural ones. The forces of the right everywhere have rushed to confirm his prognostic and align the new situation with the need to reconstitute civilisational blocs – Huntington identifies eight such blocs, based on mainly religion, with a mix of geography and language, elaborating previous classifications that already distinguished the Muslim, Hindu, Christian, Buddhist and Chinese worlds. The thrust of his thesis is that the USA in particular and the West should prepare militarily for 'national defence' and interventions. I am going to argue that the idea of the clash of civilisations not only gives a new lease of life to geopolitical entities like nations and race and the essentialisms that they assume; it obscures the fact that cultures are and have been historically interdependent and polyglot and it prevents one from imagining alternatives to current world problems by presenting either neo-liberal capitalism or neo-theological systems of thought as the only foundations for the 'good society'.

It is one of the important insights of postcolonial theory to have emphasised the diasporic and hybrid character of cultures. Said, for example, writes that 'all cultures are involved in one another; none is single and pure, all are hybrid, heterogenous, extraordinarily differentiated, and unmonolithic' (1993: xxix); he goes on to emphasise that 'Far from being unitary or monolithic or autonomous things, cultures actually assume more "foreign" elements, alterities, differences, than they consciously exclude' (1993). Similarly, Bhabha (1994) and others have emphasised the extent to which one of the effects of European colonialism has been to produce hybrid and hyphenated cultures that are at once Western and Asian or African, operating as assemblages that pluralise belonging and identities. The point is that the encounter between the imperial project of Europe and the societies it tried to subjugate and reconstitute has produced vernacular modernities. The evidence for the claim that a process of creolisation and hybridisation has produced recombinant cultures is clear at all levels of economic, political and cultural activities though it is especially striking in all the arts and in media technologies (Venn 2000). Here we can think of the novel or the cinema as particular modern forms and technologies of communication like radio and television and that have become universalised, with profound effects for how identities are constituted today, and how experiences from different parts of the world can be communicated to a worldwide public. Similarly, it is clear that musics and painting for generations now, and certainly with the spread of modernism, have mutated in all parts of the world as a result of cultural exchanges and transfers. This activity has contributed to the constitution of a transnational cosmopolitan public, who share particular knowledges and experiences and are able to communicate across other kinds of divide, such as religious differences, and indeed agree about goals and objectives that transcend national boundaries. An important aspect of the colonial encounter has also been the emergence of emancipatory projects and theoretical understanding that cut across ethnic and cultural differences to unite all of 'humanity' in the name of goals like socialism.

More recently, the term 'diaspora' has come to indicate this crossing of cultures locally and worldwide as well as to replace older terms like 'hybridity'. Indeed, one could extend the idea of diaspora to characterise the formation of cultures generally, in all periods and regions (Venn 2005). For it is the case that if one studies, say, the countries around the Mediterranean from Roman times to the end of the Arab colonisation of large areas of Southern Europe, one finds as extensive an exchange of knowledge, beliefs, customs, languages and artistic practices as one would find today in conditions of the global displacement of peoples. Similarly a history of India up to the Mughals shows a vitality in the process of exchange that affected all the cultures involved, leading to changes in language, religious beliefs, customs and technologies. Clearly, wars and conflicts were never absent from these regions. But they were not motivated by the apparently intrinsic and unsurmountable differences between cultures; many other factors played their part, chiefly to do with wealth and power – some things don't change. So, the re-emergence of a discourse about civilisations in conflict should alert us to be vigilant about the stratagems of power that ever seek to dissimulate its interest in ideologies of race and religious wars and the purity of cultures and origins.

A long history trails in the wake of the slippage in the idea of the clash of civilisations that produces an identity between religion and race and culture. In the period of modernity it must be associated with the emergence of occidentalism, that is to say, the co-articulation of colonialism, capitalism and a positivist, instrumentalist discourse of modernity in the worlding of the world as modern and globalised. From the nineteenth century, once imperialism entered a period of hegemonic consolidation, the modern project of the institution of an order that the conquering European powers sought to establish became transmuted into the idea of the 'civilising mission' of the West, a shift that thus endowed colonial occupation with a moral force, namely, that of bringing all the nations of the world within the perimeter of the 'humanisation' of societies that the project of modernity was supposed to deliver. For Kant, this universal history of nations was meant to happen through Europe taking charge of this mission of 'one day giving laws' to all the other continents (see Derrida 1997).

The same period saw the emergence of an idea of culture, tied both to the project of imperial governmentality (Venn 2000; Viswanathan 1989) and to the institution of the nation as a homogeneous entity. The birth of the nation-state as the territory of the modern form of governmentality required this assumption of the imagined community as homogeneous, united by common laws, common interest and a shared sense of identity. The idea of homogeneity rather than heterogeneity was necessary for instituting an order to which all segments of the population could be called in the name of the people, itself established as the foundation of political authority and law. Consent was premised on this, as was the idea of a democratic polity. What became erased in this move is the fact of the hetero-geneity of cultures. It is thus clear that the idea of civilisations as unitary entities united by ethnic or cultural identity is complicit with the concept of nation-state that emerged with modernity. The new demarcation of civilisations that Huntington proposes reterritorialises these unities, using religion and geography as markers; equally it erases a multiplicity of dif-ferences and distinctions, for example in lumping all states with a majority of Muslim pop-ulations in the same civilisational camp, as if the differences between Morocco and Pakistan were not as great as those between France and Australia. Not that these differ-ences should be a cause for inevitable conflict.

In the course of the Western imperial project then, concepts of race, nation, culture, civilisation and modernity became linked in a metonymic chain. This imaginary found its most coherent expression in the social Darwinist biopolitics that emerged in the wake of the theory of evolution, and that aligned the modern idea of linear progress and devel-opment with the struggle for survival of the fittest amongst nations, and the location of Europe or the West at the apex of civilisation. This biopolitics remains in the background of all the debates about the 'clash of civilisation', inciting the resurgence of the crudest racisms and archaic religious fanaticisms; its legacy lurks in the fantasised imaginings of ethnic cleansings. Today the 'civilising mission' has been appropriated by the forces of new empire in the name of capitalist liberal democracy, and is presented as the only alternative to permanent conflict arising from incommensurable religio-cultural differences. Huntington's claims fit only too well into the geo-political strategy of this new form of rule (Hardt and Negri 2000) and its imposition of a neo-liberal world order.

A different genealogy of this imaginary can be reconstructed if one takes account of a longer history of colonisation. Foucault, interestingly, in his studies of power, refers to the idea of 'race struggle' and 'state racism' which he examines by reference to the 'discourse of race war' ((2003) and its mutations over the centuries in Europe. He points out that mythico-religious discourses, and their narratives of promised emancipation or salvation, have historically proved to be a counter force to the power of sovereigns or despots who, having acquired power through the violence of conquest or invasion or misappropriations, have utilised the law and the history of the victors to conceal the instituting violence of their sovereignty under a discourse of ancestry and of good order. Yet, this discourse of race war in the context of colonialism operated as a counter-history, namely in providing grounds for a colonised people to oppose the attempts by the coloniser to re-present its sovereignty and its laws as legitimate:

> [I]n this history of races and of the permanent confrontation that goes on between races, beneath and through laws, we see the appearance, or rather the disappearance, of the implicit identification of people with monarch, and nation with sovereign, that the history of sover-eignty – and sovereigns – had made apparent. (2003)

Genealogy reveals several shifts in the form of sovereignty from the Roman to the European in mediaeval times and to the statist in the (post-Westphalian) period when a racist discourse begins to emerge which is used to preserve the sovereignty of the state. In the period of the modern form of governance, the magico-juridical rituals of the Indo-European form of representing power was replaced by medico-normalising techniques, inaugurating the age of modern bio-politics. With this shift 'from law to norm, from races in the plural to race in the singular, from the emancipatory project to a concern with purity, sovereignty was able to invest or take over the discourse of race struggle and reutilise it for its own strategy' (2003). Thus for Foucault the idea of race struggle, though it mutated into the state racism of Nazism in the twentieth century, has polyvalent associations with the history of a counter-history.

While Foucault's interest is the genealogy of concepts of sovereignty and biopolitics, I would point equally to the resilience of the counter-history he proposes, which complicates the debate about the 'clash of civilisations', not least because of slippages between the notions of race and nation and civilisation. In this respect one should mention two different kinds of development that seem to have converged in more recent times. On the one hand, social Darwinist biopolitics has become geneticised in socio-biology and informationalised, with consequences that are yet in process. On the other hand, counter-history, in the context of colonial resistance, took the form of strategies developed in the form of the ruses of the weak, such as mimicry and creative creolisation, as well as more subterranean and disguised stratagems for preserving ways of life that were threatened with rupture and extinction by occupying powers. Here one can mention Nandy's (1983) thesis that the assertion of Indian civilisation in the form of its traditions enabled the colonised Indians to resist the subjectifying intentions of British imperialism. Similar stratagems of resistance were developed by the Japanese as a way of both modernising, and thus Westernising, whilst preserving core elements of Japanese culture (Fukuzawa 1973; see also Venn 2005). Musics and rituals such as (amongst an endless list) *candoble* in Latin America or blues for African Americans are other examples. In relation to current conflicts, it is worth pointing out that elements of Islamic resistance to Western imperialism, taking the form of the refiguration of Islam in the nineteenth century, have followed a similar route, beginning with Islamic revivalism and reform in the eighteenth century, influenced by scholars like Ibn Abd al-Wahhab and Shah Wali Allah al-Dahlawi, to counter both Ottoman claim to leadership of the Muslim world as well as the rise of Europe as a world power. The idea of cleansing Islamic faith as part of resistance has, in conditions of global corporate capitalism and new imperialisms, mutated into contemporary Islamic fundamentalism. The idea of the clash of civilisations feeds these tendencies as well as lives off them.

A related point needs to be made: it is important to put on the agenda of the debate about civilisational conflict the problem of cultural difference and the politics of identity. It may appear that the politics of difference, expressed for instance in ideas of multiculturalism, or in disputes about the wearing of the *hijab*, are an index of intransigent and essential cultural rifts. However, it is well to remember that dominant groups, like settler-colonisers, whether a minority or not, did not feel the need to argue for multiculturalism or develop a politics of difference, since their way of life was not under threat. Quite the opposite. It is the context of exploitations and oppressions that were part of colonial régimes and are intrinsic to capitalism, and the associated denigration of non-European cultures, that produces such demands; they are part of the process of decolonising the mind and counter-hegemonic struggles. Against this one must set political visions shaped by ideas of convivial ways for a diversity of people to live together and counter-capitalist emancipation that have united people from quite different ethnic and religious background in the period of decolonisation, and continue to do so today. These are cosmopolitical movements, born out of a dissident or radical modernity, enriched by the diasporic translation of cultures, that fundamentally oppose and give the lie to the thesis of a clash of civilisations.

Couze Venn

LITERARY WORKS

Kureishi, Hanif (1998), *My Son the Fanatic*, London: Faber and Faber.

Maalouf, Amin (1983), *Crusades through Arab Eyes*, New York: Schocken Books.

— (1999), *Ports of Call*, London and New York: Harvill Press.

— (2000), *In the Name of Identity: Violence and the Need to Belong*, New York: Arcade Publishing.

Pamuk, Orhan (2004), *Snow*, New York: Vintage.

— (2005), *Istanbul: Memories and the City*, New York: Vintage.

HISTORIES

Borradori, Giovanna (2003), *Philosophy in a Time of Terror: Dialogues with Jurgen Habermas and Jacques Derrida*, Chicago, IL: University of Chicago Press.

Bhabha, Homi (1994), *The Location of Culture*, London: Routledge.

Derrida, Jacques (2001), *On Cosmopolitanism and Forgiveness*, trans. Mark Dooley and Michael Hughes, London: Routledge.

Featherstone, Mike (ed.) (1990), *Global Culture*, London: Sage.

Foucault, Michel (2003), *Society must be Defended*, trans. David Macey, New York: Picador.

Fukuyama, Francis (1992), *The End of History and the Last Man*, New York: Free Press.

Fukuzawa, Yukichi [1866] (1973), *An Outline of a Theory of Civilization*, Tokyo: Sophia University Press.

Hardt, Michael and Antonio Negri (2000), *Empire*, Cambridge, MA: Harvard University Press.

Huntington, Samuel P. (1993), 'The Clash of Civilizations?' *Foreign Affairs* 72 (3) (summer): 22–49.

— (1996), *The Clash of Civilizations and the Remaking of World Order*, New York: Simon and Schuster.

Lewis, Bernard (1993), *Islam and the West*, New York: Oxford University Press.

— (2002), *What Went Wrong?: The Clash between Islam and Modernity in the Middle East*, New York: Harper.

— (2003), *The Crisis of Islam: Holy War and Unholy Terror*, New York: Random.

Nandy, Ashis (1983), *The Intimate Enemy: Loss and Recovery of Self under Colonialism*, Bombay: Oxford University Press.

Qureshi, Emran and Michael A. Sells (eds) (2003), *The New Crusades*, New York: Columbia University Press.

Said, Edward (1993), *Culture and Imperialism*, London: Chatto and Windus.

Sen, Amartya (2006), *Identity and Violence: The Illusion of Destiny*, New York: Norton.

Venn, Couze (2000), *Occidentalism. Modernity and Subjectivity*, London: Sage.

Venn, Couze (2005), *The Postcolonial Challenge: Towards Alternative Worlds*, London: Sage.

Viswanathan, Gauri (1989), *Masks of Conquest*, London: Faber and Faber.

The Jewish Diaspora

(THE INSTANT TRANSUBSTANTIATION: HOW COLONISED JEWS BECAME COLONISERS)

It is now quite common to come across postcolonial Jewish and even postcolonial Israeli studies (Pappe 2006). This seems a very natural progress of the field. The European Jewish experience from the late Roman era up to the Holocaust is in many ways a trajectory of a minority's liberation from oppression. When a postcolonialist paradigm is applied to this history it is easy to see how the chronicles of the European Jews from the third or fourth century AD up to their emancipation in the nineteenth century can be depicted as a struggle against an internal colonialism (Adesanmi 2004). Moreover, although research on the topic has been scarce, there is enough evidence to point to a dialectal relationship developing between anti-Semitic theories and praxis on the one hand, and European colonialist policies, on the other. In short, the adoption of the postcolonialist perspective to European Jewish history and anti-Semitism is a refinement of the accepted narrative of Jewish victimhood in the period mentioned above.

However, a very important feature is missing from this new trend, and it is not likely to appear in the near future, given the global balances of power which influence knowledge production in the field of Jewish and Israeli studies. Most of these studies ignore the rapid transformation of the Jewish victims into victimisers – as individuals or as a new national Jewish collective within the Zionist and later Israeli contexts. We know that victims can become victimisers in the postcolonial world; we even, in rarer cases, have seen the colonised becoming the colonisers. But the former and latter cases are part of the research and the 'soul search' of postcolonial studies and ethics. However, this does not form a part of the ever-growing industry of postcolonial Jewish studies. In this article, I point to the missing component, and try to surmise why this lacuna has not been filled properly.

The transformation, in fact the transubstantiation, took place around the 1880s with the emergence of Zionism, in 1882, and the colonialist scramble for Africa a few years later. The more familiar case is Zionism. Until recently it was viewed as a successful liberation movement. Recent critical research, emerging in Israel itself, depicted Zionism as a colonialist project (Ram 1999). Seen from this perspective, Zionism transformed Jews from the colonised to the colonisers at an amazingly rapid pace. However, this critical view of Zionism has not yet been fused into the growing area of postcolonial Jewish studies, and is much more concerned with the effect of the colonialist past on contemporary Israel, and less with its implications for the historical view of Jews as the colonised or the victimised in the European chapter of their history.

While Zionism is, and will continue to be, a very popular subject matter for critical research, the less familiar and written-about case is that concerning the role played by individual Jews (prominent leaders in their own communities) in the European colonialist expansion of the late nineteenth century. These Jews could be found mainly in the civil service apparatus that first erected, and then maintained, the European colonialist empires in Asia and Africa. At times, the collective and individual transformations fused historically when Jewish German agronomes such as Otto Warburg, geographers such as Arthur Rupin, and Jewish British bankers such as the Rothschild and Moses Montifiorie, left the general imperial projects in which they were involved, for the sake of the more concrete colonialist Zionist enterprise.

It is difficult to give a learned explanation for the scholarly disregard of these transformations, since the phenomenon itself was ignored. On a very impressionist level, one would think that the objection to viewing Jews as colonialists derives from the same source that today inhibits European Jewish communities from criticising Israeli policy in the Palestinian-occupied territories. The ancient, and at times manipulated, fear of anti-Semitism is behind this reluctance, and may be at work here too. More precisely, in the case of postcolonial Jewish studies, the hesitation in including an analysis of the colonialist chapter in the history of the colonised is strongly connected to the Holocaust and its representations. The very short distance between emancipation and destruction in the history of European Jews created an ambivalence and obfuscation that even the flexibly hybrid typology of postcolonialism could not master. The immense catastrophe, and the manipulation of its memory, undermined not only the retrospective scholarly attempt to locate Jews within the postcolonial world, but more importantly, confused the anti-colonialists in their view of European Jewry. This ambivalence is still in place today in the very harsh and complex European Islamic attitudes towards Judaism in general, and Jews in Europe in particular.

Harsh or not, the rapid transformation of European Jews from the colonised to the colonisers is baffling, as is the absence of any discussion of the phenomenon within post-colonial Jewish studies. Reading back to the centre here is a very different exercise from the case of the more well-known subaltern groups liberated from one form or another of European oppression. Some scholars were aware of this, outside the frame of Jewish studies. That the inclusion of an article on the Jewish Diaspora in a straightforward postcolonial study or formulation requires caution and alertness was hinted at by Edward Said (1993), even during the heyday of his infatuation with the early twentieth-century cosmopolitan and humanist central European Jews whom he admired so much. Ella Shohat also attracted our attention, probably more than anyone else, to the intricacies of Jewish Diaspora in the shadow of Zionism, in her research on the Arab Jews (Shohat 2006). Others rooted more deeply Jewish experience within the colonialist context, but failed to explain when and how the transubstantiation took place (or for that matter, to discuss its moral ramifications).

Franz Fanon hovered around the question when he quoted Sartre's assertion that 'the Jews have allowed themselves to be poisoned by the stereotype that others have of them, and they live in fear that their acts will correspond to this stereotype . . . we may say that their conduct is perpetually overdetermined from the inside' (Ashcroft et al. 1995). But Fanon chose to be more ambivalent; he wrote 'The Jew can be unknown in his Jewishness, he is not wholly what he is. One hopes, one waits.' And also: 'He is a white man, but has no history of cannibalism.' All this Fanonian rhetoric was meant to conclude an internal discussion with himself about the question of whether the 'black man's fate is as that of the Jew's'. 'They are both hunted down', stated Fanon, but the Jews had always a chance, because they were an idea in the minds of people and in their own minds, while the black man, in the words of Fanon, knows that 'I am the slave not of the idea the people have of me, but of my appearance' (Ashcroft et al. 1995). Fanon's assertion that the postcolonial Jew would have a different fate from that of the 'black man' is indeed vindicated by the present realities in America, Africa and the Middle East.

The importance of Fanon's interest in the question is that in the twilight of colonialism he was the first to attract our attention to the rapid metamorphosis of a group so easily defined in the most basic parlance of postcolonialism as victim, oppressed, subaltern and what have you (in the binary entities on which postcolonialism rests), into the victimiser, the oppressor and above all, the coloniser. This process is the hidden tragedy of the Jewish question in our century. The spoken tragedy, the Holocaust, has redemption, whether in the form of Zionism, American Judaism or liberal Europeanism. The claim of so many Jewish collectives in this century to be part of the world that tried to destroy them, and at the same time to be a partner in the destruction of other worlds and cultures, is no less a tragedy than the Holocaust itself. And it poses not just questions of redemption but ques-tions of postcolonialist strategy; not just as an academic discipline, but as a moral, ethical and political posture vis-à-vis the history, the transition and the present reality of Judaism. By the latter, I am not referring only to Zionism and Israel, but also to the Western Jewish communities and their ambivalent position, foremost towards the Palestinians, but also towards the Arab societies and the Muslim world in general. They have (it is worth taking the risk to generalise) an impressive contemporary record when it comes to supporting oppressed groups in Africa and Asia.

That this recognition is missing from postcolonial Jewish studies can be seen in the way that in their principal *locus operandi*, the USA, these studies celebrate the Jewish immigrant to America as the template for new immigrants and minorities (interestingly and disturbingly, not for African American and Hispanic groups, but mainly for Asian immigrants). In some places, Jewish postcolonialist studies is described as the introductory course of initiation for the aspirant Asian American immigrant (whose ambition should be to become Jewish, or at least integrated as successfully as the Jews).

Future Agenda: whereas postcolonial Jewish studies may, so far, disappoint us in their treatment of Jewish colonialism, it has opened the way for a more comprehensive study of the Jewish experience in European history. Postcolonial studies de-essentialised the Jewish experience by stressing the heterogeneity of Jewish life and culture. This should help us when, and if, we choose to plunge into the question of what I call the transubstantiation of colonial roles. There were multiple ways in which the transition from internal colonialism to colonialism took place. Therefore, individual cases have to be examined in depth so that the dynamics, the ambivalence and final outcome of the process can be highlighted as a more general phenomenon. The wide geographic span of Jewish existence demands a more careful approach than the generalisation offered above, so as to delineate more mindfully the boundaries of that rapid transformation, indeed transubstantiation, which occurred around the end of the nineteenth century.

Although the recognition of a pluralist Jewish experience is one of the more positive aspects of the application of the postcolonialist paradigm to European Jewish history, this methodology was used mainly for inquiring about what postcolonial Jewish studies term as 'Jewish uniqueness'. The most recent work on this aspect is by Jonathan and Daniel Boyarin (2002). They assert that, viewed from the postcolonialist prism, the claim for Jewish uniqueness is not refuted, nor does the postcolonialist paradigm offer a way out. They challenge the national view of the Jewish diasporic experience as a condition of helplessness, and a pathology that must be overcome. Very much in the tradition of Walter Benjamin, Edward Said and others, they too view the diasporic Jewish posture as a unique source of power and strength (and by inference, the nationalisation of Jewish life as a potential point of weakness and dearth). Focusing on Jewish experience, their book forcefully argues that diasporic communities exercise a distinct form of cultural power in order to maintain themselves. There is a double merit in this approach. First, it allows us to juxtapose Jewish colonialism and Zionism with the diasporic condition in the same way that colonialism and colonised communities are usually collated. Secondly, this approach offers a universalisation of Jewish victimhood or exile, which can also be the departure point for understanding better the less gratifying chapters of modern Jewish history, as colonialists; or in the language of Jewish postcolonial studies, research can now focus on the Jewish 'way of maintenance', both in the diasporic, and in national/colonial, conditions.

Understanding the swift and dramatic transubstantiation from victim to victimiser, from colonised to coloniser, can be done as part of the general search for Jewish European existence as bordering between uniqueness and ordinariness, or between redemption and empowerment. Revisiting the Jewish past at its most crucial historical junctures (when victimhood ended and Jewish colonialism began) in a truly postcolonial hybrid manner may show us the way. It would require applying the same critical and merciless scrutiny

employed elsewhere, where postcolonialist realities disappointed as much as did the preceding colonialist chapters in a given place.

Conceding the *Sui Generis* Position: the idea of conceding an exclusive position for the
sake of hybridity, by relocating Jewish studies on the border between unique, and universal, human experiences has been strongly opposed by Jewish scholars. They demand a *sui
generis* historiographical and moral status for Jewish history in general, and for the chapter
of the Holocaust in particular. Morally and politically, a claim for exclusivity underwrites
the discipline of Jewish studies in Israel and in many American universities. But it has been
challenged successfully by general postcolonial studies, quite often in indirect ways. This
is particularly evident in the study of nineteenth-and twentieth-century cases of genocide.
If the ultimate victimiser of the Jews in modern times is universalised contextually, likewise, the transubstantiation of the victim into a coloniser can be examined in a similar way.

An extreme, but illuminating, example of such a course of action is the research that
emerged on Native Americans within the context of postcolonial studies. The mass killing
of Native Americans was, after years of denial, represented as genocide, committed by other
European groups who were themselves victims of internal colonialism, before arriving as settlers in the new continent. Lilian Friedberg (2000) adopts Raphael Lemkin's 1943 definition of 'genocide' (a term he coined), to point to the features in the general terminology
that apply to the case of the Native Americans, such as the undoubted demographic catastrophe that took place in the 150 years after European contact; the substantial acts of intentional killing; and the intentional culpability that led to cultural wastage of the survivors in
restricted reservations. Friedberg also draws parallels between the *Lebensraumpolitik* ideology and the moral justification of the genocidal drive in the USA. More crucially, persistent patterns of racism are still prominent in the United States today as part of the
postcolonial condition of Native Americans. Towards the end of the essay, like Fanon,
Friedberg insists that the Native American suffers a worse fate than the victims of Nazi
genocide. The argument becomes even harsher, and may be difficult to take for Jewish
readers. Friedberg insists that there is a key difference between the Jewish and American
holocausts: as awful as were the events of 1938–45, few would suggest that the Jewish population of the world faces extermination today. Yet the American holocaust is ongoing,
though now carried out primarily through extreme poverty and cultural despair. As for the
idea that this ultimately constitutes collective suicide, she quotes (2000) Ojibwe activist
and scholar Winona LaDuke:

> The survival of Native America is fundamentally about the collective survival of all human
> beings. The question of who gets to determine the destiny of the land, and of the people who
> live on it – those with the money or those who pray on the land – is a question that is alive
> throughout society . . . There is a direct relationship between the loss of cultural diversity and
> the loss of biodiversity.

One can agree or disagree with the comparative game of genocides, but one cannot ignore
the need to universalise all the genocides, and to point out the more subtle ways in which
some of them are carried out today. A similar willingness to tackle and universalise not only
the question of the uniqueness of the Jewish tragedy, but also of its transubstantiation, can
turn postcolonial Jewish studies into a worthy scholarly and moral project.

And indeed, as a final note, we can hope that the end result of such a journey to the
moment of transubstantiation, wherever it occurred, would dim the claim for uniqueness –
a claim that has been abused and exploited in order to justify the colonisation of Palestine.

One can understand the wish to maintain a more positive claim for Jewish uniqueness, which runs like a thread through contemporary postcolonial Jewish studies, mainly as a wish to respect the memory of the Holocaust. But it will not hold water in the future, and that is because of the extraordinary way in which the claim for *sui generis* victim-status was exercised for shielding Jewish colonialists and colonialism from universal criticism, and indeed for protecting it from a protracted anti-colonialist struggle. The cover-up of the colonisation of Palestine, and the displacement of its native population, which continues today, was mainly successful due to the claim for a *sui generis* position. It absolved Jewish communities from examining the destructive consequences of these actions and policies not only for the sake of the Palestinians themselves, but also for themselves, wherever they are located. Moreover, the employment of the *sui generis* shield blocked serious academic research into the current spurt of anti-Semitism within the new postcolonialist Jewish condition. It is clear now that such research in the future will have to be liberated from the manipulative narratives of anti-Semitism and the internal colonisation of the Jews, which prevent the colonialist chapters from being thrown into the discussion. A postcolonial perspective demands that the two chapters, of victimhood and colonisation, should be integrated into one dialectical study, not only for the sake of expanding our academic knowledge, but far more importantly, for the sake of peace and reconciliation in the Middle East, so needed in our postcolonial world.

Ilan Pappe

Literary Works

Amichai, Yehuda (1995), *Yehuda Amichai: A Life of Poetry, 1948–1994*, New York: Harper.

Appelfeld, Aharon [1939] (2005), *The Story of a Life*, London: Penguin/Hamish Hamilton.

Goldstein, Rebecca (2006), *Betraying Spinoza: The Renegade Jew who gave us modernity*, New York: Schocken Books.

Grossman, David (2002), *The Yellow Wind: With a New Afterword by the Author*, New York: Picador.

Oz, Amos [1982] (1983), *In the Land of Israel*, New York: Random House.

Ravikovitch, Dahlia (1989), *The Window: New and Selected Poems*, Riverdale-on-Hudson, NY: The Sheep Meadow Press.

Histories

Adesanmi, Pius (2004), ' "Nous les Colonisés": Reflections on the Territorial Integrity of Oppression', *Social Text* 22 (1): 35–58.

Ashcroft, Bill, Gareth Griffiths and Helen Tiffin (eds) (1995), *The Post-Colonial Studies Reader*, London; New York: Routledge.

Boyarin, Jonathan and Daniel Boyarin (2002), *Powers of Diaspora: Two Essays on the Relevance of Jewish Culture*, Minneapolis, MN: University of Minnesota Press.

Friedberg, Lilian (2000), 'Dare to Compare: Americanising the Holocaust', *American Indian Quarterly* 24 (3): 353–80.

Gelly, Alexander (1998), 'On the Myth of German-Jewish Dialogue: Sholem and Benjamin', *Jouvert: Journal of Post-colonial Studies* 3: 1–2.

Pappe, Ilan (ed.) (1999), *The Israel/Palestine Question*, London and New York: Routledge.

— (2006), 'The Exilic Homeland of Edward Said', *Interventions, The International Journal for Postcolonial Studies* 8 (1): 9–23.

Ram, Uri (1999), 'The Colonisation Perspective in Israeli Sociology', in Ilan Pappe (ed.), *The Israel/Palestine Question*, London and New York: Routledge, pp. 55–80.

Said, Edward (1993), *Representations of The Intellectual: The 1993 Reith Lectures*, New York: Pantheon Books.

Shohat, Ella (2006), *Taboo Memories, Diasporic Voices*, Durham, NC: Duke University Press.

Postcolonial Russia

Since the seventeenth century, Russia has expanded contiguously over large parts of the Eurasian continent, yet her territorial and demographic possessions have not been designated as colonies by mainstream scholarship. The cumulative contribution of Russian and foreign scholars discursively ignoring Russia's relentless acquisitions of non-Russian lands, and affixing in the authoritative historical narrative the image of Russian colonial innocence is one of the puzzles of modern history. It is partly explained by the difficulties of accommodating Russian colonialism within the postcolonial certitudes. First, Russia's colonies are not separated from the metropolis by a body of salt water. Second, instead of race, religion and nationalism have played key roles in Russian colonial affairs. Third, Russia's military conquests and subjugations of neighbouring countries have not been considered colonialist because in many cases both the exploiters and the exploited were white. *The Post-Colonial Studies Reader* (1995) edited by Bill Ashcroft, Garth Griffiths and Helen Tiffin does not devote a single chapter to Russia. In the relationship of Russians to other peoples, skin colour has only sporadically played a defining role; however, racism has intensified in the post-communist period. On certain occasions Russia has accommodated the darker-skinned people of Turkic and Mongol background, when they adopted the Russian identity. In Andrei Belyi's novel *St Petersburg* (1913), Apollon Apollonovich Ableukhov, a descendant of the 'Kyrgiz hordes' and a high-ranking Petersburg official, is a member of the Russian Orthodox Church and a devoted servant to the tsar. Similarly, Aleksandr Pushkin's partly African background did not prevent him from becoming the masthead poet of Russian romanticism. However, for reasons having to do with Russia's low prestige among the conquered peoples, few of them ever wished to assume the Russian identity in spite of a consistent policy of Russification. Finally, while the European colonial empires eventually accepted scholarship critical of their colonial misdeeds, Russian discourse remains impenetrable to postcolonial ideas. Russian intellectuals, scholars and the general public vigorously deny that tsarist Russia or its Leninist metamorphosis, the USSR, were colonial entities. In the early twenty-first century, the continuing war in Chechnya is viewed as a war against banditry and international terrorism rather than as a war of national liberation.

Russia usually overpowered a contiguous neighbour and first engaged in unsystematic looting, and then in reordering the economies of a new dependency to benefit the Russian economy, while promoting the use of the Russian language and imposing Russian political institutions on the conquered peoples. Unlike Britain and France, Russia had little to offer in terms of humanistic learning, technology or everyday culture: the Baltic rim, the partitioned Poland, and, after World War II, the remainder of Eastern and Central Europe were more advanced than the conqueror in these respects. The notorious transfer to Russia of entire factories from Germany, Poland, Czechoslovakia and Hungary after World War II symbolises the robbery syndrome that can be compared – *mutatis mutandis* – to the transfer of the Elgin Marbles to the British Museum.

Russia's expansion into territories with well-established non-Russian identities began with Ivan the Terrible's conquest of Kazan and Astrakhan (two Tatar strongholds inhabited by the indigenous Turkic peoples) in the late sixteenth century. Not even this early acquisition successfully underwent the process of assimilation, described by Michael Hechter in *Internal Colonialism* (1975). In the seventeenth century, Siberia was conquered: here the adversaries ranged from native tribes to Chinese emperors. The first were nearly wiped out, and the area was thinly resettled with Russians and prisoners belonging to other nationalities. In the post-Soviet period, a cultural uneasiness has been in evidence even in Siberia, as witnessed by the contemporary Russian nationalist Valentin Rasputin's nervous invocations of Russia in his Siberian tales. The eighteenth century marked a spectacular southern expansion in the area of the Black Sea and, for the first time in history, a major expansion into Europe. In the partitions of Poland, Russia acquired not only a large part of that nation but also Ukraine, Belarus and Lithuania. In the meantime, the Black Sea region became largely Russified and assimilated under Catherine I, owing to the extermination of Turkic Muslims and the flight of the remnants to the Ottoman Empire. This process enabled Nikolai Gogol's Chichikov to claim 'virgin territories' for his 'dead souls' in Gogol's famous novel of that title (1842). The nineteenth century was marked by the conquest of Central Asia and by numerous uprisings of the previously conquered and exploited peoples; each time the Russians managed to pacify them and hold onto their acquisitions. The Baltic fringe, the Caucasus and Eastern and Central Europe vigorously resisted Russian colonialism after they were conquered in the eighteenth and nineteenth centuries. Except for the Caucasus, they are now free; some are members of the European Union.

The 1917 revolution and the ensuing violent removal of the tsarist government did initially promise change in the subaltern status of non-Russians in the former Russian Empire, renamed the USSR and significantly transformed in terms of its ruling class. The abolition of *gubernias* (governorships) as administrative units and introduction of 'union republics', 'autonomous republics', 'autonomous regions' and 'autonomous areas' according to their ethnicity paved the way for future decolonisation. However, several of the 'autonomous republics' including Chechnya, Tatarstan and the whole of Siberia were incorporated into the Russian Soviet Republic, a decision which after the disintegration of the USSR brought about two Chechen wars, instability in Dagestan and demands for autonomy in Tatarstan, Tuva and, to a lesser extent, in parts of Siberia. Inside the USSR, the rule of terror and mass arrests were common by the late 1920s, along with a reimposition of Moscow's policies and the Russian language. Contrary to the well-entrenched myth, ethnic Russian losses in World War II were modest in comparison with the losses suffered by the western rim of the empire. It is also generally overlooked that Soviet Russia entered World War II as a friend and ally of Nazi Germany, and remained so for the first two years of the war, from September 1939 to June 1941.

As a result of the 1945 Yalta agreements, the Soviet Russian Empire took another large leap westward. All of Eastern Europe and portions of Central Europe became de facto colonies of Moscow, and between 1945 and 1989 were subservient to Moscow's interests in foreign and internal policies. Resistance was suppressed in territories occupied by the Red Army. The trajectory of this suppression has not yet been fully reconstructed, as countries liberated in 1989 lack the financial resources and access to Russian archives. Perhaps the most notorious case of the Russians' refusal to disclose the details of Moscow's colonialist policies is the so-called Katyn Affair, the 1940 prison-style execution of some 26,000 Polish officers and officials at Katyn and elsewhere.

The year 1945 marks the greatest triumph of Russian colonialism. Never before had Moscow exercised military and economic control over so vast a territory. Instant annexation of the newly acquired lands was impractical politically and linguistically, however, and only the Baltic countries and East Prussia were incorporated into the USSR. Like Britain's colonies, the Central and Eastern European countries were given a measure of autonomy in the day-to-day running of their domestic affairs. While investment capital went to the ethnically Russian territories (from the Bolshoi Ballet and the 'Soviet' Academy of Sciences in Moscow to sports facilities and financial institutions dispersed in Russian cities), the most polluting industries were built in the colonies. The resulting destruction of Uzbekistan's agricultural lands has been amply documented, and so has the pollution of Bashkortostan by nuclear waste, and consequences for the Kazakhs of the building of Baikonur.

In 1989, having exhausted themselves in enforcing unworkable economic policies and fending off numerous insurrections – Polish Solidarity being the most prominent – the Soviet Russian élites began to understand that change was inevitable. As the Soviet economic system neared collapse, the reformers tried to shore it up without relinquishing the empire. The last First Secretary of the Communist Party, Mikhail Gorbachev, tried the *perestroika* route, but it made the implosion of the communist system of governance even more obvious. Gorbachev's successor, Boris Yeltsin, did the right thing. On 8 December 1991 Yeltsin summoned Ukraine's Leonid Kravchuk and Belarus' Stanislau Shushkevich to a meeting during which the three leaders declared that the USSR had been dissolved and the Commonwealth of Independent States established instead. In addition to exposing the absence of legitimacy and legality in the Soviet system, the declaration turned out to be a major step in crippling Russian colonialism. The fourteen non-Russian Soviet republics and Soviet possessions in Central and Eastern Europe acquired sovereignty.

In 1991 the Russian Empire shrank demographically to half its size, or 151 million inhabitants. While the wealth remained in Russian hands, the break-up of the political and economic ties and the accompanying loss of prestige created difficulties for the metropolis. In 2003 the Russian Federation's GDP reached only 79.4 per cent of its 1990 level.

The year 1991 is celebrated as a victory in the non-Russian states of the former USSR, but Russian polls invariably show that the majority of Russians wish for the clock to be turned back. On 25 April 2005, in a nationally televised speech before the Russian Duma, Yeltsin's successor Vladimir Putin stated that the fall of the Soviet Union was 'the greatest geo-political catastrophe of the twentieth century'. This segment of Russia's authorising discourse was created shortly before Moscow's celebrations of the sixtieth anniversary of Soviet victory in World War II, and it reflects a continuing reliance on imperial vision in the politics of historical interpretation in Russia, as well as the incompleteness of Russia's decolonisation. While the victory belonged to the Soviet peoples (half of them non-Russian), the fruits of success are still assumed to belong to the Russians. At the outset of his presidency, Putin reverted to the default mode of Russian discourse by stressing the importance of great power status for Russia (*derzhavnost*), which in Russian circumstances goes hand in hand with holding onto the remaining colonies and cherishing neo-colonial ambitions toward what the Russians refer to as 'near abroad'.

The conditions under which the USSR was dissolved allowed the non-Russian Soviet republics either to claim a proportion of the USSR's wealth while at the same time assuming a proportion of the Soviet Union's debt, or to renounce all claims and be released from responsibility for debt. Since the governments of the new states had no financial resources (the money supply was controlled by Moscow), they were obliged to choose the second option. The Russian Federation thus became, de facto and de jure, the sole successor state to the Soviet Union. However, the Russian élites continue to refuse to accept the symbolic, let alone economic, responsibilities implied in the succession. The Russian government has repeatedly refused to issue even perfunctory apologies for Soviet crimes against non-Russian nationalities, from the Ukrainian famine to the Katyn Affair. Putin dismissed any notion of symbolic reparations by stating that the Eastern and Central Europeans owe gratitude to the Red Army for liberation from the Nazis. Yet the march of the Red Army toward Berlin did not have as its goal the liberation of Eastern Europe, but rather its subjugation to Moscow. The fact that post-Soviet Russia refuses to face up to its imperial history bodes ill for its future policies.

While the absence of symbolic apologies can be taken in stride, the problems facing those national groups which remained part of the Russian Federation go beyond symbolism. Russia's first foreign acquisition, Tatarstan on the Volga river, is typical of the fate of the non-Russian autonomous republics and regions within the federation. In 1992, under Boris Yeltsin's originally tolerant régime, a new Tatarstan constitution was adopted. In 1994, a power-sharing treaty between Russia and Tatarstan was signed, whereby Tatarstan defined itself as a 'sovereign state' whose citizenship entitled one to hold the citizenship of the Russian Federation. In 1994 the Tatarstan legislature decided to change the Cyrillic script (imposed on the Tatars by Stalin during World War II) back into Latin.

The destruction of Tatarstan's hopes and the hopes of other minority republics and regions came with the ascension to power of Vladimir Putin on 31 December 1999. He tightened Moscow's control over the autonomous republics, pressured the Tatars to reintroduce the Russian alphabet and abandon Latin, and cancelled Tatarstan's constitutional right to conduct independent economic policy. Tatarstan legislator Marat Galeev said that under Putin's federal reforms, Tatarstan has experienced 'an increase in unemployment, a reduction of its regional budget by almost half, and a decline in road construction by some 60 percent' (*Bigotry Monitor* 2003).

Not all resistance to colonialism within the Russian Federation was peaceful. The autonomous republic of Chechnya tumbled into a military insurrection. Chechnya was originally subjugated in 1859 after decades of fierce resistance. In 1839, Russian poet Mikhail Lermontov wrote 'A Lullaby' in which 'the evil Chechen' figures prominently and which has been required reading in Russian schools. In 1991, Chechen general, Dzhokhar Dudaev, declared Chechen independence, and the country was renamed Ichkeria. In 1994 Russia invaded Chechnya under the pretext that 'Chechen bandits' had plundered the property of peaceful Russians across the border. A university textbook of Russian history presents the war as Russia's answer to the provocations of the 'Chechen criminals' (Riabikin 1997). The war ended in 1996, and an agreement signed by General Aleksandr Lebed and the President of Ichkeria Aslan Mashkadov stipulated that Chechnya's final status be decided ten years later. Russia did not keep the truce and invaded again in 1999. The pretext for the invasion was provided by the explosions in the Moscow and Volgodonsk apartment blocks that killed 200 people. On 30 December 2003, the UPI reported that copies of a book linking Russia's FSB security service to apartment blasts in 1999 were seized by the Russian police.

The 1999 war never formally ended but was replaced by a partisan war. The last legally elected Chechen President, Aslan Mashkadov, was killed by Russians in 2005. In a report about the first Chechen war, Doctors Without Borders stated the following: 'We are involved in all the major conflicts in the world but we believe Chechnya is the most cruel war. We are in the field witnessing the systematic massacre of civilian villages which are flattened by a [Russian] strategy of reconquest in south Chechnya' (Reuters, 18 April 1996). The second war produced approximately 100,000 casualties, with torture and killings of civilians common. The Memorial human rights centre reported on 15 June 2005 that the beating of detainees and arrests of the rebels' relatives have become routine in the North Caucasus:

> 'What is going on in the North Caucasus with those detained on suspicion of terrorism – strange deaths, falls from the windows of prosecutor's offices, now the complaints . . . about beatings – is becoming a system', said Aleksandr Cherkasov of Memorial. (*Chechnya Weekly* 2005)

Efforts to retain Chechnya for the empire are related to the fact that as recently as 1991, this tiny republic produced 12 per cent of the entire Soviet GDP. More generally, the subjugation of Chechnya exemplifies the pattern of Russian colonialism and the methods of discouraging foreign commentary about it. First comes the development of a discourse exemplified by Lermontov's poem about 'the evil Chechen' in order to stir up the Russian population against the group slated for conquest. Then, as witnessed by Leo Tolstoy's story 'The Cossacks' (1862), the adversaries are divided into 'friendly' and 'hostile'. The subjugated are not given the chance to tell their story, while the Russians wield total power over the discourse. The resulting tendency to disregard Russia's continuing brutalities in the Caucasus (comparable with the final years of French rule in Algeria) prevents a more equitable version of history from emerging. Nicholas Riasanovsky, the émigré Russian author of *A History of Russia* widely used at American universities, inscribes the Chechen story in Russian history in carefree tones, as if it were a matter of ridding Russian life of banditry:

> 'In 1859 Bariatinsky captured the legendary Shamil . . . That event has usually been considered as the end of the fighting in the Caucasus, although more time had to pass before *order* could be fully established there. A large number of Moslem mountaineers *chose* to migrate to Turkey.' (Riasanovsky 2000; my italics)

Under Putin, journalists have been forbidden to visit the area; some have made clandestine journeys there. Russia's position as the imperial hegemon affords Russians wide access to foreign universities, libraries and willing listeners, thus creating what Edward Keenan has called 'the great mystifications' of Western historiography concerning Russia.

The perception of Chechnya as a brutalised colony that should be let free is still beyond the understanding of a majority of Russians. More broadly, the issue of granting autonomy to such regions as Tatarstan, Chechnya, Dagestan, Tuva, Bashkortostan, Yakutia or the Far East is not entertained by any political party. The Russians share Aleksandr Solzhenitsyn's belief that non-Russian lands became Russian possessions willingly. Under Putin it has been impossible to raise in Russian discourse the issue of the colonial advantage of Russians over the nations of the former Soviet Union.

There are writers, however, who indirectly try to deconstruct the empire. Foremost among them are Liudmila Petrushevskaia and Viktor Pelevin. The first has created images of Russian society under communism that make a mockery of imperial ideas and perceptions. The second has attacked the holy of holies of Russian imperial memory: World War II victory, the Red Army and Russia's worship of her literature. Petrushevskaia punctures the balloon of Russian self-importance by showing how the empire failed its women. Pelevin deconstructs the empire by liberating himself from Russia worship that dominated Russian literature from Pushkin to Solzhenitsyn. He refuses to genuflect before Russian history, and he is willing to let go of the pretensions to grandeur that so engage Russia's nationalist writers, journalists and politicians, as well as their kibitzers in the West.

The federation's demographic trends favour non-Russians over the Russians. The 2002 census showed that Russians made up 79.8 per cent of the population. In 1999, Sovietologist Paul Goble noted that the ethnic Russian population continued to shrink by half a million people a year, while the Islamic peoples' population was growing at a rate of 4 per cent a year; if the trends continued (and they have continued), by 2005 the federation's Islamic minority would reach 22 per cent. On 5 August 2005, *The Times* of London raised that figure to 23 million. It therefore appears that the federation is slated for instability. However, in spite of the actual and anticipated demographic changes, the grand narrative of Russian history is being passed on in the educational system and distributed abroad in an unchanged form. The politics of interpretation is still informed by the imperial vision. Russian history is yet to be recast in postcolonial terms.

Ewa Thompson

Literary Works

Belyi, Andrei [1913] (1959), *St Petersburg*, trans. John Cournos, New York: Grove.

Gogol, Nikolai [1842] (2004), *Dead Souls*, trans. Robert Maguire, New York: Penguin.

Lermontov, Mikhail (1965), *The Demon and Other Poems*, trans. E. Kayden, Yellow Springs, OH: Antioch Press.

Tolstoy, Leo [1862] (1967), *Great Short Works of Leo Tolstoy*, trans. Louise and Aylmer Maude, New York: Harper and Row.

Pelevin, Victor (1998), *A Werewolf Problem in Central Russia*, trans. Andrew Bromfield, New York: New Directions.

Petrushevskaia, Liudmila (1995), *Immortal Love*, trans. Sally Laird, London: Virago.

Rasputin, Valentin (1992), *Live and Remember*, trans. A. Bouis, Evanston, IL: Northwestern University Press.

Histories

Bigotry Monitor (2003), 'Union of Councils of Jews in the Former Soviet Union' (21 Feb.) 3: 8. www.fsumonitor.com/stories/022103Russia.shtml

Chechnya Weekly (2005), The 'Jamestown Foundation' (16 June) 6: 23.

Khazanov, A. M. (1995), *After the USSR: Ethnicity, Nationalism, and Politics in the Commonwealth of Independent States*, Madison, WI: University of Wisconsin Press.

Ob itogakh Vserossiiskoi perepisi naseleniia 2002 goda, an official Russian census survey available at <www.eastview.com/all_russian_population_census.asp> as of 1 July 2005.

Riabikin, C. (1997), *Noveishaia istoriia Rossii, 1991–1997: posobie dla uchitelei, starsheklassnikov, abiturientov i studentov*, Petersburg: Neva.

Riasanovsky, N. (2000), *A History of Russia*, 6th edn, Oxford: Oxford University Press.

Thompson, E. M. (2000), *Imperial Knowledge: Russian Literature and Colonialism*, Westport, CT: Greenwood.

Welcome to Hell: Arbitrary Detention, Torture, and Extortion in Chechnya (2000), New York: Human Rights Watch.

Postcolonial Sweden

Describing Sweden as postcolonial presents certain challenges: Sweden has largely taken the position of onlooker or marginal abetter in civilising missions; it never achieved any significant territorial expansion beyond Europe; and its neutrality during World War

II rendered the nation peripheral in the post-war arena of global power jostling. Nevertheless, as a European nation, Sweden's national identity has been formed in the context of the continent's post-Enlightenment intellectual and political traditions that spawned and justified various colonial ventures and racist policies, a process framed in Sweden, particularly in the nineteenth century, by a need to disavow the nation's loss of imperial greatness. Having battled for dominance with Denmark over the Baltic Sea area for centuries – and during its imperial high noon, lasting from the early 1600s until the early 1700s, Swedish territory covered Finland, Estonia, Latvia and parts of Russia and northern Germany, making the Baltic Sea a *mare nostrum* – in 1809 Sweden's imperial status was definitively lost when it was forced to surrender the last significant portion of its imperial territory to Russia: Finland, which had been joined to Sweden in a subordinate position since the 1200s. In a compensatory move, post-1809 Swedish historiography has treated the 1809 borders as fixed and eternal. Ignoring the historical fluidity of Sweden's borders and its constant flows of migration, this nationalistically inflected historiography has constructed a homogeneous and united Swedish nation, which has often resulted in limited tolerance for minorities like the aboriginal Sami, the Roma people or the Finnish people. Since the latter part of the twentieth century, however, Swedishness, as an idea and a lived practice, has been subjected to increased scrutiny. Sweden's entrance into the EU in 1995 and the ramifications of post-war labour and refugee immigration to the country on a scale exceeding that of many other European countries, prompting official declarations that Sweden is a multi-cultural nation, have occasioned a reckoning process as well as struggles over its national identity.

One controversial voice that has drawn attention to Swedish implication in European colonial projects is that of author Sven Lindqvist. In his celebrated travel narrative, *Exterminate All the Brutes* (1996), Lindqvist records the history of colonial brutalities that haunts contemporary European discourses of race and belonging. Among other things, he points to Sweden's participation in and complicity with European colonial projects and knowledge-production, like the involvement, if marginal, of Swedish missionaries, seafarers, traders and soldiers in the murderous exploitation of Congo under Leopold II, the backdrop for Conrad's *Heart of Darkness*. Mixing examples of colonial oppression with memories of the everyday violence lurking under the polished bourgeois surface of his Swedish childhood, he emphasises the connections between Europe's quiet drawing rooms and the cruelty and bloodiness of European colonialism. Swedish scholars, artists, missionaries and soldiers helped construct and maintain the West together with their European colleagues; Lindqvist maintains, 'Conrad would have been able to set his story using any of the peoples of European cultures' (1996).

Lindqvist's assertions resonate uneasily in a national imaginary predicated, since the mid-twentieth century, on ideas of equality, multiculturalism and solidarity with formerly colonised nations, expressed in, for instance, Sweden's aim to deliver 1 per cent of its GNP in foreign aid. Since the 1990s in particular, a number of scholars, authors and journalists have, however, begun the project of mapping the history of Swedish colonial involvement and its implications for present-day conceptions of Swedishness, recording evidence of, for example, Swedish attempts at entering the Atlantic slave trade, a brief colonial holding in the Caribbean, repression of minorities, and, acutely, the pervasive tendency to endow Swedishness with racial connotations, which has created the contrasting category of the stigmatised non-white 'immigrant' (*invandrare*), often used indiscriminately in media representations, for instance.

The Swedish state undertook colonial missions outside Europe between the 1600s and the mid-1800s, deploying its military forces and collaborating with tradesmen to promote trade and imperial expansion. Short-lived and unsuccessful, the projects included the colony 'New Sweden' in North America (1638–55); a slave-trading venture in Africa (1649–58); and the slave-trading port on the Caribbean island of Saint-Barthélémy (1784–1878). New Sweden was established in present-day Delaware, New Jersey and Pennsylvania, USA, as Swedish settlers procured land along the Delaware river, on which they built Fort Christina. The settlers traded with the Native Americans, exchanging fabrics, cooking utensils and tools for animal skins and corn. The colony was captured by the Dutch in 1655. During the same time period Swedes tried to enter the transatlantic slave trade through the establishment of the Africa Company, *Afrikakompaniet*, in 1649 with the mission to trade in slaves, gold and ivory. The company built the trading fort Karlsborg, or Carolusborg, on the Ghanaian coastline, which they lost to Denmark in 1658. A century later, another attempt to profit on the slave trade was made with the purchase of St Barthélémy from the French. The West India Company, *Västindiska Kompaniet*, was founded in 1786, and St Barthélémy was planned as a free port mainly for the sale of slaves. However, the Swedes' commercial ambitions failed. The island remained their one long-term Caribbean possession, where Swedish plantation owners subjected their slaves to the brutal conditions for which Caribbean plantations have become known. At its peak, the slave population consisted of around 2,500 people. Slavery was abolished in 1847, and the island, having become a financial liability, was sold back to the French in 1878 after a referendum in which the population (everyone but one) voted to belong to France (Sjöström in Granqvist 1999).

The Swedish state also employed colonising methods to expand its mainland territory and secure its borders. The state, early centralised, used the Church, educational institutions and military means to 'Swedify' and subdue local opposition and assimilate ethnic minorities. Finnish territory was acquired through crusades in the 1100s and 1200s; a cathedral was built in the Finnish coast town of Åbo (Finnish name Turku) in the 1200s; and a university was founded there in 1640, the third Swedish university established after Tartu (Dorpat) University in Estonia (1632) and Uppsala University (1477). The northern land of the nomadic, aboriginal Sami people, one of Sweden's five historical minorities, was similarly actively claimed from the 1600s onwards by the Swedish state in collaboration with the Church. The Sami, having herded their reindeer over a territory covering northern Norway, Sweden, Finland and Russia for thousands of years, had formally to recognise national borders in 1751, when the northernmost Swedish-Norwegian border was drawn. Although the Swedish nation-state has exploited the Sami's land, rich in natural resources like, timber and hydropower, the Sami have retained a measure of autonomy, much due to the Lapp Codicil of 1751, which gave them rights to traverse national borders with their reindeer and partly administer their own territory; land rights, however, remains a contested issue between the Sami and the Swedish state. From the late eighteenth until the early twentieth centuries the Sami came to be defined as a separate, primitive racial group, which resulted in paternalistic policies circumscribing the Sami's access to education, housing, choice of profession (they were deemed capable mainly of reindeer herding) and land ownership. This racial rhetoric ceased in official documents after 1945 (Lundmark 2002). In the 1970s, the Sami were recognised by the Swedish parliament as an indigenous people, and in 1993, a Sami parliament (*Sametinget*) was established. Sami languages were recognised as official minority languages in 2000, along with the languages of Sweden's four other historical minorities: Roma people, Jews, Finns and

Tornedalers. The special protection afforded the minority languages – Sami languages, Finnish, Meänkieli (the Finnish spoken by the Tornedalers, who live along the northern border), Romani and Yiddish – ensures their survival. Finnish, Meänkieli and Sami languages can be used in some municipalities in dealings with authorities.

The Roma came to Sweden in the 1500s, and until the mid-twentieth century, the Swedish state employed various harsh measures to expel them or contain them in its Finnish territory. Roma activists began fighting for rights to housing and education in the 1960s; considered unassimilable, Roma people were denied such rights until the 1970s. Particularly difficult for the Roma was World War II; a 1914 Swedish ban on Roma immigration was not eased in any way until 1954. The war also highlighted the status of Swedish Jews. Having resided in Sweden in more considerable numbers since the 1770s, Jews were given full citizenship rights in the 1880s, but were long reminded of their otherness, not least in 1933–42, when Sweden admitted few Jewish refugees. In 1942, finally, 750 Norwegian Jews were accepted; in 1943, Sweden famously received nearly the whole of the Danish Jewish population.

In tracing the role that 'race' has played in the formation of contemporary Swedishness, its use in the construction of the welfare state has been of particular concern. As discourses of racial biology and racial hygiene became widespread in Sweden by the end of the nineteenth century, scientists and social reformers concerned themselves with the qualities of the Swedish race, or *folk* (literally, 'people'); many of them saw in these discourses means for improving the *folk*, and thereby creating a better society. In 1922, the world's first state-run Institute for Racial Biology was established in Uppsala, with the mandate to classify the Swedish people; in the 1930s, its focus shifted to eugenics. During the 1930s, 1940s and 1950s, reformers became increasingly concerned with transforming a country still mired in poverty (Sweden did not become industrialised until the 1870s) through social change as well as biological intervention.

Some of the most vociferous advocates for such intervention were socialist and liberal reformers, like the internationally celebrated politician and diplomat Alva Myrdal and her husband, the economist Gunnar Myrdal. One measure widely deployed was sterilisation of individuals deemed mentally disabled or antisocial, a practice inspired by, among others, precedents in the US. Most of these were poor, working-class individuals or socially marginal 'travellers', who might have strayed from bourgeois norms for proper behaviour (or could potentially do so). The practice became increasingly infrequent with the welfare state's development from the 1960s onwards and was formally abolished in 1975; in the 1990s, it was brought to international attention and discussed widely as a national scandal and a tragedy for the affected people.

The Myrdals and other progressive thinkers were attempting to build a better and more just society. They helped draft a key concept of contemporary Swedish identity, its famous cradle-to-grave welfare system, which was given a name with domestic connotations, *folkhemmet*, literally, 'the people's home'. A Social Democratic concept, it aimed to even out social inequalities and provide opportunities for all citizens through a benevolent form of social engineering characterised by a strong commitment to solidarity and social justice at home and internationally. The implementation of this idea was enabled by a strong consensus regarding its basic values, expressed in the fact that the Social Democratic Party has been voted into power with only a few minor interruptions since 1932. With Sweden's entrance into the EU and with the Social Democratic Party's turn towards 'Third Way', neo-liberal policies in the 1990s, this consensus, crucial to the stability of the 'Swedish Model', has, however, been somewhat undermined.

As immigrants began entering this 'people's home' in large numbers after 1945, Sweden, in contrast to many other European countries, resisted the guest worker model. Immigrants were given nearly full citizenship rights, including the right to vote in local elections (from 1976), equal access to good housing, education and healthcare. Also, the development of a permanent American-style low-wage sector has been resisted. A driving force in such policies were the trade unions, which have played a central role in the implementation of many immigration and welfare policies, though their influence began waning in the 1990s.

Post-war immigration has contributed substantially to Sweden's population growth. At 16 per cent of the population, Sweden's number of residents with an immigrant background is one of the largest in the EU, relative to the country's total population (Schierup et al. 2006). The first post-war wave consisted of Finnish people, whose status in the early to mid-1900s approximated that of the Irish in Britain with regard to social status and economic conditions. Nordic countries have consistently provided the largest immigrant groups in Sweden. In the 1950s and 1960s, immigrants came in search of work from Southern Europe – Italy, Greece, and Yugoslavia – and Turkey. From 1972 onwards, when labour immigration was stopped at the request of the labour unions, besides family members reuniting, the new settlers have mainly consisted of refugees and asylum seekers, in the 1970s many Chileans and Christian Assyrians from Turkey; in the 1980s, Eritreans, Ethiopians, Iranians and Iraqis, including Kurds. By 2003, over 50 per cent of foreign citizens residing in Sweden hailed from countries outside of Europe, mainly Asia (Schierup et al. 2006). Since Sweden's entrance into the Schengen Agreement in 2001, and falling in line with EU policies, Swedish asylum policy has, however, become significantly more restrictive; immigration of any kind except family unification has been heavily curtailed.

Despite Swedish progressive policies, significant segregation along ethnic lines has occurred geographically and in the labour market, which is indicative of the still pervasive racialised division made between 'Swedes', predicated on a presumption of racial and cultural homogeneity, and the alien 'immigrants'. Some metropolitan suburban areas are dominated by low-income people of immigrant extraction, rendering them ghetto-like without, however, being hopeless slums; a certain proud 'suburban' identity has evolved. In terms of the labour market, scholars speak of a 'subordinated inclusion' (Mulinari and Neergard 2004): early on, labour unions implemented a practice whereby immigrant workers were included in the 'people's home' on condition that they not threaten the unions' (white, masculine) collective interests. The trade unions (LO) exercised veto rights over the labour recruitment process, allowing in specified numbers to manage labour shortages, for example. Hence, immigrants (and Swedish women) were treated as expendable labour and relegated to lower-status and lower-salaried jobs, which enabled Swedish (male) workers' upward social mobility.

As the importance of the nation-state has diminished for Sweden's self-conception with its EU membership, Swedishness as a cultural construct has gained in importance, resulting at times in a discourse of culturalism that restricts explanations of 'immigrants'' behaviour to their being culturally determined, disregarding differentiating factors like class and gender. But a reawakened awareness of the fluidity of Swedishness has been promoted by, for instance, a number of literary authors – together with a range of artists, journalists, scholars and politicians of immigrant and 'native Swedish' extraction – challenging the presumed homogeneity and fixity of the 1809 borders. Playing with the Swedish language, deemed so central to Swedish national identity, and drawing on diasporic modes that undo the easy binaries between the Swedish and foreign 'cultures', writers like Johannes Anyuru, Marjaneh Bakhtiari, Jonas Hassen Khemiri, Alejandro Leiva Wenger and Mohamed Omar represent – often satirically and playfully – the ambivalent kind of belonging that Swedishness can offer its visible minorities, simultaneously inclusive and divisive, while also asserting alternative (hi)stories of Swedishness.

Sheila Ghose

LITERARY WORKS

Andersson, Lena, *Du är alltså svensk?* (2004), Stockholm: Natur och Kultur.

— *Var det bra så?* (1999), Stockholm: Natur och Kultur.

Anyuru, Johannes (2003), *Det är bara gudarna som är nya*, Stockholm: Wahlström och Widstrand.

— *Omega* (2005), Stockholm: Wahlström och Widstrand.

Bakhtiari, Marjaneh (2005), *Kalla det vad fan du vill*, Stockholm: Ordfront.

Khemiri, Jonas Hassen (2003), *Ett öga rött*, Stockholm: Norstedt.

— *Montecore: En unik tiger* (2006), Stockholm: Norstedt.

Leiva Wenger, Alejandro (2001), *Till vår ära*, Stockholm: Bonniers.

Omar, Mohamed (2005), *Tregångare*, Stockholm: Ruin Förlag.

HISTORIES

Azar, Michael (2006), *Den koloniala bumerangen*, Eslöv: Brutus Östlings Bokförlag Symposion.

Broberg, Gunnar and Nills Roll-Hansen (eds) (c. 1996), *Eugenics and the Welfare State: Sterilization Policy in Demark, Sweden, Norway, and Finland*, East Lansing, MI: Michigan State University Press.

de los Reyes, Paulina, Irene Molina and Diana Mulinari (eds) (2002), *Maktens olika förklädnader: kön, klass och etnicitet i det postkoloniala Sverige*, Stockholm: Atlas.

Granqvist, Raoul (ed.) (1999), *Svenska överord: en bok om gränslöshet och begränsningar*, Stockholm/Stehag: Bruno Östlings Bokförlag Symposion.

Johansen, Jahn Otto (1990), *Zigenarnas Holocaust*, Stockholm/Stehag: Bruno Östlings Bokförlag Symposion.

Jonsson, Stefan (1993), *De andra: Amerikanska kulturkrig och europeisk rasism*, Stockholm: Norstedt.

Koblik, Steven (c. 1988), *The Stones Cry Out: Sweden's Response to the Persecution of Jews 1933–1945*, New York: Holocaust Library.

Lindqvist, Sven (1996), *Exterminate All the Brutes*, trans. Joan Tate, New York: Free Press.

Lundmark, Lennart (2002), *'Lappen är ombytlig, ostadig och obekväm . . .': Svenska statens samepolitik i rasismens tidevarv*, Umeå: Norrlands Universitetsförlag.

McEachrane, Michael and Louis Faye (2001), *Sverige och de Andra: postkoloniala perspektiv*, Stockholm: Natur och Kultur.

Mulinari, Diana and Anders Neergard (2004), *Den nya svenska arbetarklassen*, Umeå: Borea.

Petersen, Abby (1997), *Neo-Sectarianism and Rainbow Coalitions: Youth and the Drama of Immigration in Contemporary Sweden*, Aldershot: Ashgate.

Pred, Alan (2000), *Even in Sweden: Racisms, Racialized Spaces, and the Popular Geographical Imagination*, Berkeley, CA: University of California Press.

Schierup, Carl-Ulrik, Peo Hansen and Stephen Castles (2006), *Migration, Citizenship, and the European Welfare State: A European Dilemma*, Oxford: Oxford University Press.

Sellström, Tor (1999–2002), *Sweden and National Liberation in Southern Africa*, 2 Vols, Uppsala: Nordiska Afrikainstitutet.

Svanberg, Ingvar and Mattias Thydén (1992), *Tusen år av invandring: En svensk kulturhistoria*, Stockholm: Gidlund.

Taikon, Katarina (1963), *Zigenerska*, Stockholm: Wahlström och Widstrand.

Tamas, Gellert (2004), *Lasermannen: En berättelse om Sverige*, Stockholm: Ordfront.

Ålund, Aleksandra and Carl-Ulrik Schierup (1991), *Paradoxes of Multiculturalism: Essays on Swedish Society*, Aldershot: Avebury.

Turkey: Postcolonial discourse in a non-colonised state

Turkey has never been colonised and, except in the immediate aftermath of World War I (1918–22), has never been threatened by any Western country. Moreover, it had one of the most important empires of world history, the Ottoman Empire (Meeker 2002), which, until recently, was considered an imperial ruler both in the Arab world and in the Balkans. For a little over a decade, Arab and Balkan historians have proposed a much more nuanced and complex historical narrative of the Ottoman Empire (Karpat 2000).

Nevertheless, a new school of historiography, which draws fascinating parallels between the Ottoman administration of the nineteenth century in the Arab provinces, and Russian and Western colonial experiences, has provoked increasing interest among scholars (Kühn 2002). In such a context, how can one account for a strong postcolonial discourse in a country such as Turkey? Before answering this question, two facts must be kept in mind. First, although some scholars use conceptual and analytical tools and categories borrowed from subaltern studies in their intellectual production (*Toplum ve Bilim* 1999), in Turkey as in many other Middle Eastern countries, postcolonial theories and subaltern studies are rather weakly represented in academia. Second, mainstream anti-colonial discourses existed long before the emergence of subaltern studies among members of a more or less nationalist intelligentsia, whose sociological and intellectual profile has changed dramatically through the twentieth century. Understanding this intelligentsia requires a constant effort of contextualisation which takes into account both objective landmarks and nationalist subjectivities in Turkey.

There are three periods during which postcolonial discourses play a central role in Turkey: the Kemalist republic (1923–38); the period of radical protests and left-wing movements (the 1960s and 1970s); and the period following the Second Gulf War and the dissolution of the Soviet Union (1991–2006).

The Kemalist period: Kemalist Turkey had complex relations with the Ottoman legacy. On the one hand, the former peoples of the empire, who conducted a struggle for independence against Ottoman domination, were regarded as traitors to the state and to 'Turkishness'. The new state considered itself as the answer of the Turks to the claims formulated by the other ethnic and sectarian communities in Anatolia; but its policy towards Armenians, Greeks and Kurds clearly showed that these groups paid for the secessionist 'betrayal' of all the Christian and Muslim populations of the former empire. On the other hand, however, the Ottoman Empire was defined as a political power which had aimed at the suppression of the Turks themselves. Accordingly, under Ottoman rule, the Turks became alienated from their past. The last Ottomans, particularly, were described not only as the knights of mediaeval darkness, but also as the hired help of Western imperialism. Thus, the War of Independence was not only a struggle against the European powers which tended to destroy Turkey and 'Turkishness', but also a war of emancipation from the

Ottoman yoke. By extension, it was considered as the very prototype of anti-imperialist and anti-colonial wars.

The alliance of the Kemalist forces with the Soviet Union during the War of Independence (1919–22) explains why the Kemalist nationalist narrative used both national and international registers of legitimisation. While strongly opposed to the existence of an independent communist movement, the still weakly organised Kemalist state made extensive use of anti-imperialist and anti-colonial themes. In an obvious similarity with the discourses of the Komintern, it described itself as the avant-garde of the national liberation movements of the colonised peoples of Asia. Mustafa Kemal's famous speech (1933), announcing the 'awakening of the Eastern nations', and the 'death of imperialism and colonialism' on the earth, with the same certainty as he saw the 'rise of the sun' (Karal 1969), showed that years after his victory, he was still sensitive to the independence of Western dominated countries.

By the 1930s, the Turkish republic had already improved her relations with the European powers and refused to give open support to any national liberation movement in the world. Turkey had also openly adopted a policy of Westernisation, as the only way of wiping out the 'backward' aspects of Muslim-Ottoman civilisation. Although, sociologically, it was assumed that a Turk was, before everything else, an Anatolian Muslim, Mustafa Kemal paid no respect either to Islam or to the 'Asiatic traditions' that he criticised severely.

On the other hand, however, the Kemalist élite did not project itself in an exclusively national, Turkey-oriented framework. Like many other single-party régimes or party-states, it too was influenced by the Soviet and Italian régimes, and conceived itself as the agent of a universal and historical mission (Larsen 2001). Many former communist intellectuals, who had converted to Kemalism, emphasised the necessity of giving a universal sense to the Turkish revolution, and to creating a codified credo, which, while being comparable to the Soviet and Italian models, would also proffer its own mottos and symbols. This credo was meant to be at once national and international. In the aftermath of the 1929 economic crisis and the 1930 internal political turmoil, these intellectuals founded a largely state-sponsored review called *Kadro* (Türkes 1999), which tried to give a universal, that is, an extra-national value and dimension to the Kemalist experience. *Kadro* assumed that the future world would be profoundly anti-liberal and anti-democratic and would be structured around three main pillars: fascism, Bolshevism and Kemalism, of which the last was to show a new path to colonised countries and peoples (Süreyya 1932). Kemalism projected itself as a politically and economically non-liberal model applicable well beyond Turkey. In one of the introductory articles to the first issue of *Kadro*, Vedat Nedim Tör wrote (1932):

> The post-war economy has three pawns: (1) to build a communist economy in order to replace the capitalist one, as Russia tries to do it; (2) to save the capitalist economy, as the Society of the Nations tries to do it; (3) to replace the colonial economy by the national independent economy. This task belongs to the Republic of Turkey.

Burhan Asaf, another leading editor of *Kadro*, had the same orientation:

> By systematising her revolution, Turkey will become one of the leading nations of Asia. If Turkey . . . succeeds in getting the modern technology and creating a [class] conflict-free type of society, then the Turkish nation would become the nation that has contributed the most to the transformation of the twentieth century into the century of the emancipation of Asia and the emergence of an entirely new Asian nationalism. (1932)

Though *Kadro* was published for only three years, intellectuals (though not the state) continued to regard the Turkish situation as a postcolonial situation. They also treated the Kemalist régime as a, or even *the*, alternative to colonialism. These intellectuals would play a decisive role in the country's intellectual life in the 1960s, both as nostalgic references and as authentic followers of the Kemalist tradition.

The 1960s and 1970s – Western alliances and radicalisation: World War II, and the defeat of Italy, and later on, of Nazi Germany (which had considerable influence among some Kemalist intellectuals), came as serious blows to *Kadro*'s hopes of transforming Turkey into the third pillar of an anti-democratic world. The state-party system, led by Ismet Inönü, successor to Mustafa Kemal, who died in 1938, had no other choice than to accept a rapprochement with the Western bloc and with political pluralism. In spite of heavy criticism from the very weak Communist Party, Turkey reinforced ties with the United States during the 1950s. In a country where those in political power supported their Western allies and protectors against any anti-colonial movement in the world, including the Algerian War of Independence, the anti-colonial debate could have no intellectual or political currency.

The situation changed dramatically in the 1960s. The 1960 coup d'état, which led to the execution of Prime Minister Adnan Menderes and two of his ministers (and in contrast with many military coups around the world during this decade, brought more freedom in the field of expression), only marginally helped explain this change. The real reasons have to be sought elsewhere, starting with the revolutionary changes in the Middle East. While many Arab countries, such as Egypt under Gamal abd'al Nasser (which had been dismissed out of hand by the Kemalist tradition), became 'Third World' foci of radical anti-Western opposition, Turkey appeared little more than a simple subaltern member of the Western bloc which oppressed peoples all round the world. The long-lasting effects of Turkey's support for the Korea War, the emergence of a radical and strongly left-oriented workers' and students' movement during the 1960s, the feelings of solidarity with Palestine, reactions against the Vietnam War, the symbolic impact of anti-colonial wars in Africa; all provoked strong reactions in Turkey both against the Western bloc and against the pro-Western Turkish government. The 'linguistic turn' taken by the Kemalist faction after the death of Mustafa Kemal could but add symbolic resources to the massive reaction against what was perceived as colonialism. Until the end of the 1930s, 'colony' was described by the word *müstemleke*, an Arabic term, which included the sense of annexation and imperial expansion. By the 1960s, a new word defined this concept in Turkish: *sömürge*, which drew its sense from the verb *sömürmek*: to exploit.

During this period many Kemalist intellectuals adopted a left-oriented policy. According to the Turkish left, which was also influenced by the Chinese experience, Turkey was a 'semi-feudal, semi-colonised' country, which, in contrast to Mustafa Kemal's will, was reduced to under-development, and continued to be 'exploited' by the 'imperialist West'. The national struggle of 1919–22 had led to formal independence, but after Mustafa Kemal's death, independence had been betrayed from within. The country could find its way out of 'semi-colonialism' only through a second, and much more radical, national struggle that led, in its ultimate phase, to the establishment of a socialist régime. Many *Kadro* members, who were still alive, such as Sevket Süreyya Aydemir or Vedat Nedim Tör, became important figures for this new, anti-colonial discourse.

The second factor behind the re-actualisation of anti-colonial debates can be found in the emergence, during the 1960s and 1970s, of an almost 'subaltern' discourse emanating mainly from right-wing intellectuals. For these intellectuals (Cemil Meriç, Erol Güngör, Mehmed Dogan, Nurettin Topçu) Kemalism, Westernism and communism were the avatars of the same process of alienation, which operated through the destruction of the trust of the colonised or subordinated peoples, namely the Muslim and Turkish peoples of the world. The emergence of a Westernised élite class meant the colonisation of minds. Some left-wing intellectuals, such as Idris Küçükömer (1969), claimed that the Ottoman and Kemalist reforms constituted a process of 'alienation', which produced the domination of a Westernised bureaucracy over the people through the destruction of their cultural and social values. Such critics insisted on the fact that the programme of changing civilisation, and the coercive means used to achieve this aim, showed that the reformers (Young Ottomans and Young Turks, and later on Kemalists) interiorised the values and norms of the imperialist West and used them against their own population. Their reforms thus gave birth to a cultural rupture between the people and the military and bureaucratic élite.

The 1990s: The 1980s in Turkey were dominated by the consequences of a new military coup d'état (which took place on 12 September 1980). This coup paralysed intellectual life and repressed left-wing movements and intellectuals. By the end of the decade, events such as the political evolution in China, the fall of the Berlin Wall, and the disintegration of the Soviet Union, had deprived left-wing movements of their classical reference points, and pushed them into an intellectual vacuum. In the wake of the Second Gulf War (1991), many former left-wing militants switched to a new form of radical anti-Western discourse (Bozarslan 2004).

In the 1990s, while Kemalism became the country's 'transcendental system' (Copeaux 2002), with an unprecedented cult of personality, a new form of nationalism came to light, which brought together an assortment of left-wing, right-wing and Islamist intellectuals. This new nationalism reads the decline of the Ottoman Empire as the result of a colonial project conducted by the Western powers, which manipulated the minorities (specifically Greeks and Armenians) and aimed at the total destruction of Turkey and of 'Turkishness'. It alleges that a new form of 'world imperialism' (largely American and European) continues to manipulate the same elements as well as the Kurds (both inside and outside Turkey). The advocates of this theory interpret the Third Gulf War (2003) as a prelude to a much wider war that envisions the destruction of the nation-states of Turkey, Iran and Russia. This new nationalism considers the Turks as an oppressed class and an oppressed nation. Their external and internal enemies (Armenians, Greeks and Kurds) are seen as oppressive nations and classes, constituting an almost biological threat to 'Turkishness' (as argued often in periodicals such as *Turk Solu*, *Aydinlik*, *Türkistan* and *Ergenekon*).

This new anti-colonialist discourse is an exclusively state- and nation-based discourse and is used in order to disqualify any demand for democratisation, political liberalism and peaceful resolution of the Kurdish problem or recognition of the Armenian genocide. Any European call for broader democratic reforms is conceived as an imperialist inference, motivated by new colonial conspiracies. No wonder, then, that the omnipresence of an anti-colonialist discourse as inward policy, targeting 'internal enemies' as agents of 'external threats', and aimed at the 'besieged fortresses' of Turkey, goes hand-in-hand with the impossibility of postcolonial thought. Anti-colonialism thus becomes a tool for internal domination of the subaltern linguistic, religious and political groups and oppositions.

Translations into English by Hamit Bozarslan

Hamit Bozarslan

LITERARY WORKS

Agaoglu, Adalet (1997), *Curfew: A Novel*, Austin, TX: University of Texas Press.

— 'On the Changes of 1970–80 in the Turkish Novel' http://www.lightmillennium.org/2005_15th/aagaoglu_speech.html. [accessed 19 Nov. 2006].

Edib, Halide (1928), *The Turkish Ordeal*, New York and London: The Century Company.

Hikmet, Nazim (2002), *Beyond the Walls: Selected Poems*, London: Anvil Press.

Kemal, Yaşal [1955] (1961), *Memed, My Hawk*, trans. Edouard Roditi, London: Collins and Harvill Press.

Nesin, Aziz [1966] (1977), *Istanbul Boy*, trans. Joseph S. Jacobson, Austin, TX: University of Texas Press.

— (2001), *Memoirs Of An Exile*, Holladay, UT: SouthMoor Studios.

HISTORIES

Asaf, Burhan (1932), 'Asya', *Kadro* 3: 25–34.

Bozarslan, H. (2004) 'L'Anti-Américanisme en Turquie', *Le Banquet* 21: 61–72.

Copeaux, E. (2002), 'La Transcendance d'Atatürk', in C. Mayeur-Jouant (ed.), *Saints et héros du Moyen-Orient contemporain*, Paris: Maisonneuve-Larouse, pp. 121–35.

Karal, E. Z. (1969) *Atatürk'ten düşünceler*, Ankara: Is Bankasi.

Karpat, K. (ed.) (2000), *Ottoman Past and Today's Turkey*, Leiden, Boston, MA and Cologne: E. J. Brill.

Küçükömer, I. (1969), *Düzenin yabancilasmasi*, Istanbul: Ant Yayinlari.

Kühn, Thomas (2002), 'Ordering the Past of Ottoman Yemen', *Turcica* 34: 189–222.

Larsen, S. U. (ed.) (2001), *Fascism outside Europe. The European Impulse against Domestic Conditions in the Diffusion of Global Fascism*, New York: Columbia University Press.

Meeker, M. E. (2002), *A Nation of Empire: The Ottoman Legacy of Turkish Modernity*. Berkeley, Los Angeles, CA and London: University of California Press.

Nedim, V. (1932), 'Müstemleke iktisadiyatindan millet iktisadiyatina' ('From the Colonial to the National Economy'), *Kadro* 1: 8–11.

Süreyya (Aydemir), Sevket (1932), 'Inkilabin ideolojisi; millî kurtulus hareketlerinin ana prensipleri' ('The Ideology of the Revolution the main principles of the National Liberation Movement), *Kadro* 8: 6–12.

Toplum ve Bilim (Turkish review of social sciences: Istanbul) (1999), 'Osmanli: muktedirler ve mâdunlar' (The Ottomans: Power-holders and Subalterns): 93.

Türkes, M. (1999), 'The Ideology of the *Kadro* (Cadre) Movement: A Patriotic Leftist Movement in Turkey', in Sylvia Kedouri (ed.), *Turkey before and after Atatürk. Internal and External Affairs*, London: Frank Cass, pp. 92–119.

Portugal and its Colonies

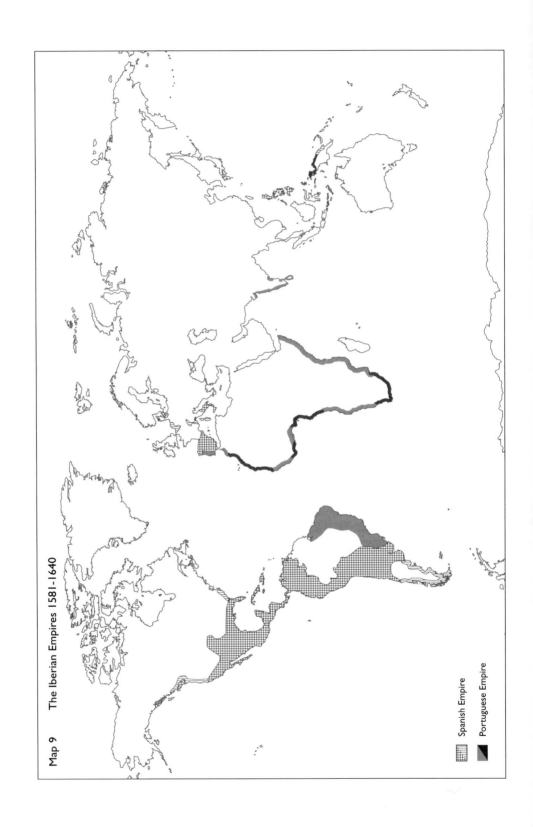

Map 9   The Iberian Empires 1581-1640

Spanish Empire

Portuguese Empire

Introduction: The Myths and Realities of Portuguese (Post)colonial Society

One of the standard clichés to circulate in Portugal, even after the fall of the New State régime in 1974, and the subsequent end of the Portuguese Empire, is that Portugal had a qualitatively different imperial experience from that of other European powers. Undoubtedly, every empire has its particularities – and Portugal was no exception. It was one of the first modern European nations to colonise outside the continent and lamentably among the last to relinquish its colonial possessions, five centuries later. It played a crucial role in opening up sea routes around the globe and was thus pivotal to the process that became known as the 'Discoveries'. The most troubling aspect of the national foregrounding of a belief that Portuguese colonialism was 'different' is the degree to which this normalises a profoundly ideological position. Portuguese imperial exceptionalism is often subtly underpinned by the conviction that Portugal was, in retrospect, somehow less immoral and less racist than other imperial powers. The lusotropical discourse discussed in one of the entries in this section in large part explains the persistence of that mindset. Of course, the problem with such normalising claims is that they often stand in the way of dealing with modern manifestations of racism and, unless challenged, allow for a colonising mentality to reconfigure.

Common versions of the Portuguese colonising myth include a belief that Portuguese men were particularly prone to miscegenation – often taken as evidence of a lack of racism. Gerald Bender's seminal work on Portuguese colonialism in Angola refutes, using sociological evidence, claims that the Portuguese were by their very essence more prone to miscegenation than any one else. Charles Boxer, to the chagrin of the dictator Salazar, pointed out that a nation whose colonial history is so steeped in the slave trade could hardly claim not to be racist. The miscegenation myth is really a claim to be giving something to the world. Portugal, as it were, was giving fathers away. The dubious notion that something is being given to those who are colonised functions as an attempted occlusion of the reality of something being taken away – be it land, commodities or human bodies. There are other rhetorical patterns in the apologetics machine of Portuguese colonialism that also seek to present rather base imperial designs in terms of acts of donation. These include the assertion that Portuguese imperialism was Christocentric – priests accompanying the caravels and assisting in the colonisation process were giving Christian salvation to the heathen. One of the most entrenched 'gifts' in the Portuguese imaginary was their language itself. The greatest gift they left to the colonies on departure was the language of Camões, the nation's epic poet whose poem *The Lusiads* celebrated in 1572 the early history of Portuguese colonial expansion.

The discourse of the Portuguese language being a gift to the colonised found resonance in the thought of Amílcar Cabral, one of lusophone Africa's foremost intellectuals and leader of the liberation movement of Guinea and Cape Verde in the 1960s until he was assassinated in 1973. He famously declared that the greatest gift the Portuguese coloniser had left was the Portuguese language. Like most of the leaders of the other liberation movements in lusophone Africa, Cabral saw Portuguese as the only language capable of fostering unity in the multilingual, multiethnic state he was fighting to bring into existence. The irony is that the Portuguese never made much effort to promulgate their language while in Africa, so that it fell onto the post-independence governments to render Portuguese a truly national language in the former colonies.

Despite a lack of concern prior to losing the colonies, there are profound sensitivities in postcolonial Portugal, at least among the chattering classes, regarding the need to protect their language in the former African colonies. When Mozambique, its former colony in south-east Africa, joined the Commonwealth in 1995, there was an outpouring of outrage among the Lisbon cultural élite. The former metropolis saw it as a betrayal of the gift of its language. Driven by the desire to keep the myth alive that the Portuguese language bears the essence of a fraternity – and that the language itself is the 'homeland', in the overcited words of Portugal's most important modernist poet, Fernando Pessoa – the Portuguese have been instrumental in the establishment of international bodies that celebrate 'lusofonia'.

In order to understand such mindsets in certain sectors of Portuguese (post)colonial society, it is important to realise the extent to which Portuguese colonialism generally felt insecure in relation to other colonial powers. The way in which Portugal came into being as a nation, as a renegade province that broke away from its more powerful neighbour to whom it owed vassalage, meant that from its very inception, it was always wary of what would become Spain. At various points in its history, crises occurred because of the imminence of a Spanish takeover of the Portuguese throne. In fact, for sixty years from 1580, Portugal was ruled by a succession of Spanish Felipes, until it reasserted its independence in 1640. During that time, its colonies fell under attack from the Dutch who invaded parts of Brazil and subsequently, in 1641, Angola, ostensibly because of the Netherlands' dispute with the Spanish monarch. A Brazilian expedition eventually recaptured Luanda for the Portuguese from the Dutch in 1648.

During the early phase of the imperial project, prior to 1580, Spain was Portugal's main rival in the colonial game. Alexander VI, the Spanish-born pope, had in 1493 divided the world up between the Iberian states, granting them rights over the territories they conquered. The following year modern diplomacy was effectively born through the Treaty of Tordesillas, which made changes to the papal bull, and marked the first state-to-state bilateral agreement of the modern era negotiated not under the auspices of the Vatican. The treaty gave Portugal a colonial monopoly over Africa as well as control of the easternmost part of South America.

The Portuguese imperial enterprise may be dated from 1415, when Dom João I led an expedition that conquered the North African city of Ceuta. The years that followed saw an intense rise in Portuguese interest in expansion. One of Dom João I's sons, Prince Henry the Navigator, is often considered to have been a driving force behind the age of maritime discoveries. Over the next hundred years, Portugal established a presence in Africa, South America and Asia.

The Portuguese imperial golden age was during the reign of Dom Manuel I. In fact, his predecessor, Dom João II, had a clear imperial vision for his country, and laid much of the groundwork for his cousin and successor's golden era. Dom Manuel I assumed the throne in 1495, a year after the Treaty of Tordesillas, and oversaw the establishment of a sea route to India, as well as the discovery of Brazil. The resultant wealth that flowed into the crown's coffers was squandered, leading to the economic difficulties that characterised the reign of his son, Dom João III. The installation of the Inquisition in Dom João III's reign aggravated the situation, since it provoked the flight of both capital and entrepeneurs from Portugal. His successor, his grandson, Dom Sebastião, who is discussed in more detail in another entry in this section, died heirless as the result of an ill-advised campaign of conquest in North Africa. His death, in 1578, led to the assumption of the Portuguese throne by Felipe II of Spain, who became Filipe I of Portugal in 1580. So ended the first cycle of Portuguese colonialism.

It would be another sixty years before Portugal regained its independence from a considerably weakened Spain. Over the next three centuries, the rules of the colonial game changed considerably, with the rise of other European colonising powers, notably for Portugal, the British and the French. The British had always claimed to be allies of the Portuguese, and several treaties of alliance were negotiated between the two powers because it was deemed to be in British interests to keep the power of Spain in check, by maintaining a foothold on the Iberian peninsula. As Spanish power waned, so did the British efforts to preserve friendly relations with Portugal. When France, under Napoleon, invaded the Iberian peninsula, one of the strangest episodes in imperial history occurred. In 1807, the court of Dona Maria I of Portugal transferred to the tropics. The Portuguese empire thus came to be ruled from Rio in Brazil. Britain arranged for the royal court to be transferred, and made little effort to hasten its return after expelling the French. Indeed, Dona Maria's successor, Dom João VI, was crowned King of the Portuguese Empire in Brazil and was reluctant to return to Portugal. Resentment at the British treatment of the Portuguese after they had 'liberated' them from the French led to a revolt in 1820. Dom João VI consented to return to Portugal the following year, leaving his son, Dom Pedro, in charge of Brazil. In an act of filial betrayal, Pedro declared Brazil independent in 1822, becoming its monarch.

Following the loss of Brazil, Portugal was plunged into a civil war, between those who subscribed to absolutism and those backing a more liberal cause. The liberal cause eventually prevailed, but during this period there was little consideration in the metropolis of what was left of the Portuguese colonies.

With the rise of modern colonialism, and the Scramble for Africa, Portugal was once again made aware of its insecurity as a colonial power. The Berlin Conference of 1884–5 established the priority of effective occupation over historical precedence as the determinant of European rights over African territory, to the detriment of Portugal. In 1890, Portugal clashed with Britain over jurisdiction of the Makololo territory in southern Africa, and following the issuance of an ultimatum from Lord Salisbury's government, Lisbon was forced to back down. The Ultimatum Crisis of 1890, as it became known, is often cited as one of the causes leading to the collapse of the monarchy in 1910, and the establishment in Portugal of a republic. The then king, Dom Carlos, was lampooned for acquiescing too quickly to British colonial demands, and anti-British sentiment, which had been present at least since Lord Beresford occupied Portugal following the expulsion of Napoleon, became more visible and channelled against the king and his successor. The ultimatum also taught the Portuguese that if they wanted to continue to be a colonial power, they would have to 'effectively occupy' their remaining five African colonies: the future nations of Angola, Mozambique, Guinea-Bissau, Cape Verde and São Tomé e Príncipe.

The Portuguese republic was initially characterised by instability. A coup in 1926 brought a military dictatorship to power. The dictatorship transformed into the Portuguese New State, a corporatist régime run autocratically by one of Portugal's most intransigent leaders, António de Oliveira Salazar. A professor at the University of Coimbra, he dominated Portuguese politics for the next forty years, until a stroke incapacitated him in 1968. A firm believer in Portugal's right to be a colonial power, he was responsible for a new constitution and a colonial act that legally discriminated on racial grounds.

As the tide turned against European colonialism following World War II, Salazar remained adamant that the colonies were an integral part of the Portuguese nation. As international pressure mounted, the Portuguese dictator renamed the colonies 'overseas provinces' in an effort to maintain that Portugal's imperial history was not a process of colonisation but rather the narrative of a pluricontinental nation. While Salazar engaged in banal sophistry in his foreign policy, he failed to notice the imminence of armed resistance in the African colonies.

In retrospect, 1961 was a decisive year heralding the eventual end of the Portuguese imperial enterprise. Not only did Nehru easily invade the remaining outposts of Portuguese territory in India, a violent uprising erupted in Angola. Salazar's response was to commit Portuguese troops to the colony in an ever-escalating conflict. Liberation movements soon took up arms in Mozambique and Guinea, drawing Portugal into a progressively more costly and futile conflict. The conscripted rank and file of the Portuguese armed forces became increasingly disillusioned with the régime at home and the war in Africa. In April 1974, they instigated the Carnation Revolution which brought an end to the New State, now headed by Marcello Caetano.

Over the next year, the revolutionary régime agreed to the independence of the remaining colonies. There were still those in Portugal, even among those who had risen to prominence following the Carnation Revolution, who believed the colonies could remain tied to Portugal in some kind of federation. This solution was not acceptable to the liberation movements, and total independence was definitively declared.

The subsequent history of lusophone Africa is not an altogether happy tale. Mozambique, Angola and Guinea-Bissau have all suffered from prolonged or intermittent civil wars, and where these have given way to civil society, it has generally been at the cost of jettisoning any aspiration to a more socially equitable system in favour of the brutality of the global market place, and the internal corruption that often implies.

Portugal very quickly transitioned to liberal democracy, and successfully applied to enter the European Economic Community. Indeed, for Portugal, in practical terms, postcolonial means European. For all the nostalgia for the lost empires, or the lusotropical mindset that is a vestige of the New State, Portugal's postcolonial moment arrived when it finally resolved the tension that Boaventura de Sousa Santos points to as its status of a 'calibanised Prospero'. It was a small country that chanced to be an imperial centre for a large and dispersed empire. Yet at the same time, it always felt itself to be at the margin of its own continent. In essence, it functioned as a semi-periphery. It was a coloniser that often felt colonised by larger European powers. By choosing Europe at the same time as it relinquished its colonies, Portugal has finally set itself on the path of exorcising its imperial ghosts.

Phillip Rothwell

LITERARY WORKS
Camões, Luís de (1997), *The Lusiads*, trans. Landeg White, Oxford and New York: Oxford
       University Press.
Pessoa, Fernando [1982] (1998), *The Book of Disquiet Composed by Bernardo Soares*, trans.
       Alfred MacAdam, Boston, MA: Exact Change.

HISTORIES
Bender, Gerald J. (1978), *Angola under the Portuguese: The Myth and the Reality*, Berkeley,
       CA: University of California Press.

Boxer, Charles R. (1963), *Race Relations in the Portuguese Colonial Empire, 1415–1825*, Oxford: Clarendon Press.

Cabral, Amílcar (1975), *Análise de Alguns Tipos de Resistencia*, 2nd edn, Lisbon: Seabra Nova.

Santos, Boaventura de Sousa (2002), 'Between Prospero and Caliban: Colonialism, Postcolonialism, and Inter-identity', *Luso-Brazilian Review* 39 (2): 9–43.

Saraiva, José Hermano (1997), *Portugal: A Companion History*, edited and expanded by Ian Robertson and L. C. Taylor, Manchester: Carcanet.

Anthropology and Ethnography of the Portuguese-speaking Empire

The history of Portuguese expansion and colonialism can be roughly divided into three distinct periods, marked by the importance of different geographical settings, trade routes and raw materials: India, Brazil and Africa, roughly corresponding to the fifteenth and sixteenth, seventeenth and eighteenth, and nineteenth and twentieth centuries respectively. For the purposes of this entry, only the last period will be considered – that which Clarence-Smith (1985) has called the 'Third Portuguese Empire'. It was during this period that colonialism as a modern project was implemented by the Portuguese authorities, and anthropological knowledge and practice as such emerged.

The turn to Africa – and the start of the Third Portuguese Empire – took place after the independence of Brazil in 1822. Portuguese expeditions in the 1840s and 1850s tried to map the African hinterland in order to claim sovereignty over large tracts of southern Africa between Angola on the Atlantic coast and Mozambique on the Indian Ocean coast. In the aftermath of the Berlin Conference (started in 1884), which carved up Africa for European colonialism, Britain issued an ultimatum to Portugal in 1890, demanding that Portuguese claims had to be based on effective occupation of the claimed territories. The last years of monarchy in Portugal and those of the first republic (1910–26) were marked by the effort to obtain actual control over the claimed African possessions. These efforts had economic as well as ideological motivations, both part of Portuguese modern nation-building (see Alexandre 2000). But Portuguese colonialism in its modern sense was developed mainly by the dictatorial régime established in 1926 (and which was to last in different shapes until 1974). In 1930, in the early stages of Salazar's régime, the Colonial Act was passed, proclaiming the need to bring indigenous peoples into Western civilisation and the Portuguese nation. Assimilation was proclaimed as the main objective, except for the colonies of Cape Verde (seen as an extension of Portugal), India and Macau (seen as having their own forms of 'civilisation'). In the colonies of mainland Africa, a distinction was made between white settlers, *assimilado*; and the indigenous, 'uncivilised' population.

Portuguese colonialism can be said to have been subaltern to other international and colonial powers; it was administered by a small semi-peripheral country, constituting a weak economic centre; it was sustained by a dictatorial political régime; and it lasted until 1975, later than other European colonialisms. Furthermore, the territories were dispersed and far apart. The weakness and underdevelopment of a colonial anthropology was certainly related to these factors and to Portugal's economic and political marginality on the international scene.

The last decades of the nineteenth century saw the emergence of anthropological practice in Portugal. In a period marked by economic crisis and the British ultimatum, the bourgeois élites openly expressed concern about what they called 'national decadence'. Literary and academic production revolved around the search for national identity, sought in popular, rural culture. Many authors concur with the notion that this focus on popular culture, the peasantry, folklore and ideas of tradition and authenticity help explain why a colonial anthropology never developed fully. João Leal (2000), following Stocking's (1982) typology, says that Portuguese anthropology was of the 'nation-building', not 'empire-building', sort. Other authors contest this idea, saying that the mainstream history of Portuguese anthropology establishes too neat a distinction between types of anthropology, namely cultural versus physical and national versus colonial, not seeing the connections between them in the representations and practices of the time (see Roque, 2001 and also Santos 2005). I believe that the construction of an Other in the colonial world was part of the process of constructing the Self in the homeland. This can be seen in the trajectory of influential anthropologists of the time, who did research on both national and colonial subjects. More important than these divides is the common weakness of anthropological production until the last quarter of the twentieth century: it was not up to date by international standards; it was not politically free; and it was ideologically permeated by the national messianic narrative of Portugal as the country of Discoveries.

Eusébio Tamagnini and Mendes Correia probably epitomise a first period, one of concern with the racial definition of the Portuguese, and opposed to miscegenation in the colonies. Tamagnini and Correia were the two main figures of the two schools of anthropology, respectively in Coimbra and Oporto. Their work – which never involved actual fieldwork – influenced a period from the late nineteenth century to the 1940s, and was mainly concerned with what today would be called 'physical anthropology', although the social, cultural and political concerns are quite obvious. Tamagnini's work, published from 1916 to 1949, was influenced by Broca and Topinard: he was looking for the anthropometric statistical averages among the Portuguese, wanting these to coincide with those of the average European. In the First National Congress of Colonial Anthropology in 1934 in Oporto (one year after the legislation of the Colonial Act), he was concerned with the 'dangers' of *mestiçagem* or miscegenation. In the Congress on the Portuguese World (held during the Portuguese World Expo that Salazar set up to promote Portuguese colonialism) he presented a study about the blood groups of the Portuguese and concluded that Portugal's population had been able to maintain 'relative ethnic purity'. In 1944 he was to acknowledge that he could not deny the existence of *mestiçagem* among a colonising people – although that should not allow one to place the Portuguese amongst the category of Negroid *mestiços*.

In the year following the 1926 dictatorial coup, Mendes Correia had called for the segregation of relapsing criminals, for the sterilisation of degenerates, and for the regulation of immigration and the banning of marriage for professional beggars. In 1932, he invited the president of the Brazilian Eugenics Organisation to give a conference in Oporto, during which he publicised the advantages of marriage within the same class or race and condemned *mestiçagem*. Based on a study of somatology and aptitude tests done with sixteen Cape Verdeans and six Macau *mestiços* who had come to the Colonial Expo of 1934 in Oporto, Mendes Correia concluded that miscegenation was a condemnable practice. In the plenary session, Tamagnini reminded his audience that 'the little repugnance that the Portuguese have regarding sexual approaches to elements of other ethnic origins is often presented as evidence of their higher colonising capacity', and asserted that 'it is necessary to change radically such an attitude' (Castelo 1999).

Besides the legal dispositions in the *Estatuto Político, Civil e Criminal dos Indígenas* of 1929, *Código do Trabalho dos Indígenas nas Colónias Portuguesas de África* of 1928, the constitution of 1933, the Colonial Act of 1930, and the Organic Charter of the Portuguese Colonial Empire of 1933, the régime encouraged initiatives to celebrate and exhibit empire: the Colonial Anthropology Congress of 1934 during the Colonial Expo, the Colonial Congress of 1940 and the Portuguese World Expo of 1940. Salazar's régime promoted a series of legal dispositions establishing the distinction between civilised peoples and indigenous populations. Simultaneously, propaganda stressed the cultural 'nationalisation' of the indigenous populations. The empire was progressively assimilated with the notion of nation (Thomaz 2001). At the same time that the *Estatuto . . . dos Indígenas* pointed to the 'respect' of native traditions, other items, whether in the Colonial Act or mostly in the *Código do Trabalho dos Indígenas das Colónias Portuguesas de África* (1928) stressed the efficient control of human resources in the colonies. Legal dispositions guaranteed, in practice, that the colonial administration and the colonists controlled the rights and labour of colonised peoples. The *Estatuto . . . dos Indígenas* lasted until 1961 and distinguished citizens from indigenous people, but both were 'Portuguese'.

The administration was supposed to identify the 'mores and customs' of the different ethnic groups in the empire. Colonial anthropologists did research work all over the empire, but mostly in Mozambique and Angola, for labour, economic and political reasons. A colonial knowledge was pursued by institutions such as the Sociedade de Geografia de Lisboa (SGL; which had been founded in 1875) or the Escola Superior Colonial, which prepared colonial administrators and civil servants; it was proposed by the SGL in 1883 but started de facto in 1906. It was to become a university institution in 1961, the only place with an anthropology course until the restoration of democracy. An autonomous research institution, Junta de Investigações do Ultramar, was active in promoting research on several colonial topics, including anthropology.

The 1950s and 1960s mark a turning point in colonial policy and also in anthropology. In 1953, a new law renamed the colonies as provinces. This was the result of international pressure for decolonisation in the post-World War II period and of the beginning of national liberation struggles in the colonies in the early 1960s. The international scene changed after the Bandung conference of 1955. The Lisbon régime was under pressure and started a campaign to legitimise the Portuguese presence in Africa. In 1961, when the African armed struggle for national liberation started, important legislation changes occurred: compulsory labour and the *Estatuto . . . dos Indígenas* were abolished. Anthropologist Jorge Dias worked in Africa against this backdrop. He broke away from Mendes Correia and his anthropobiology, was influenced by American cultural anthropology and, after joining the Escola Superior Colonial, he was invited by the Ministry of the Overseas to head the Missões de Estudo das Minorias Étnicas do Ultramar Português (Portuguese Overseas Ethnic Minorities' Research Missions). The missions had been proposed at the First Colonial Anthropology Congress in Oporto in 1934; and studied the Chope of southern Mozambique, Boers and Bushmen in southern Angola and, most of all, the Maconde of northern Mozambique, a study led by Dias. Dias' study of the Mozambican Maconde is a hallmark of the anthropology of the period. It followed the more up-to-date methods of social anthropological research. Besides his work on the Maconde (1964–70), he made secret reports from the field, which have been studied by Pereira (1986); and in them Dias is seen to be a reformist: he was critical of the régime's colonial errors and his official intention was to 'correct' them. Jorge Dias and his team (they were to found the Museum of Ethnology in line with a universalistic and not a strictly colonial conceptualisation) started what could be called a second, culturalist, period. Physical anthropology was no longer central. But Dias and his team did not become colonial anthropologists – they focused mainly on the ethnological tradition of studying Portuguese rural society. His public interventions did not dismiss the national narratives related to colonisation. What Dias did was to modernise them following the influence of Gilberto Freyre's lusotropicalism, a culturalist interpretation of the alleged humanistic and hybridising nature of both the colonisation of Brazil and modern Portuguese colonialism.

This is where we come full circle. The 1950s and 1960s were marked by the rhetoric of miscegenation and praise for the universalistic and multiracial nature of the Portuguese colonial endeavour, connecting it with the humanistic overtones of the Discoveries. This was achieved by the incorporation of lusotropicalism, a notion proposed by Brazilian sociologist Gilberto Freyre. *Um Brasileiro em Terras Portuguesas* is a collection of Freyre's speeches proffered between 1951 and 1952 during his journeys in the Portuguese colonies, as a guest of Portugal's Ministry of the Overseas. The work sums up the vision of a Portuguese way of creating a specific hybrid civilisation in the tropics through the processes of miscegenation. Tamagnini's and Mendes Correias' theses were no longer official; Freyre's was. And the production of the official brand of anthropology followed suit.

In 1974, the Portuguese dictatorship was over and in 1975 the colonies became independent, as a result of political changes in Portugal and the liberation movements in the colonies. In the mid-1980s Portugal joined the European Union and economic development led to a large increase in immigration from the ex-colonies. The democratic nation-state did not abandon the master national narrative based on the Discoveries and refashioned it in modern terms by means of promoting special ties with the ex-colonies and creating the notion of lusophony, largely equivalent to the better known francophony.

Contemporary anthropology in Portugal has severed the ties with pre-1974 anthropology. Today's anthropologists are either educated abroad or educated by those who returned to Portugal from exile after 1974. For the first time in its history, Portuguese anthropology is in tune with contemporary international trends. As a result, there has been a growing tendency towards compiling an anthropology of colonialism and empire. Many younger scholars are analysing the dispersed colonial anthropological production critically. At the same time, a growing number of anthropologists are studying the postcolonial situation in the ex-colonies and the processes of immigration to Portugal. Ironically, the 'colonial terrain' is at last being discovered.

Miguel Vale de Almeida

HISTORIES

Alexandre, Valentim (2000), *Velho Brasil, Novas Áfricas: Portugal e o Império (1808–1975)*, Porto: Afrontamento.

Castelo, Cláudia (1999), 'O Modo Português de Estar no Mundo'. O Luso-tropicalismo e a Ideologia Colonial Portuguesa (1933–1961), Oporto: Afrontamento.

Clarence-Smith, Gervase (1985), *The Third Portuguese Empire, 1825–1975: A Study in Economic Imperialism*, Manchester: Manchester University Press.

Dias, Jorge (1964–70), *Os Macondes de Moçambique*, 4 vols, Lisbon: Junta de Investigações do Ultramar.

Freyre, Gilberto (1955), *Um Brasileiro em Terras Portuguesas*, Lisbon: Livros do Brasil.

Leal, João (2000), 'A Antropologia Portuguesa entre 1870 e 1970: Um Retrato de Grupo', in J. Leal, *Etnografias Portuguesas (1870–1970): Cultura Popular e identidade nacional*, Lisbon: Dom Quixote, pp. 27–61.

Pereira, Rui (1986), 'Antropologia Aplicada na Política Colonial Portuguesa do Estado Novo', *Revista Internacional de Estudos Africanos* 4–5: 191–235.

Roque, Ricardo (2001), *Antropologia e Império: Fonseca Cardoso e a Expedição à Índia em 1895*, Lisbon: ICS.
Santos, Gonçalo Duro dos (2005), *A Escola de Antropologia de Coimbra*, 1885–1950, Lisbon: ICS.
Stocking, George (1982), 'Afterword: A View from the Center', *Ethnos* 47: 72–86.
Thomaz, Omar Ribeiro (2001), "'O Bom Povo Português': Usos e Costumes d'Aquém e d'Além-Mar', *Mana* 7 (1): 55–87.

FURTHER READING ON PORTUGUESE COLONIAL ANTHROPOLOGY
Bastos, Cristiana (2002), 'Um Centro Subalterno? A Escola Médica de Goa e o Império', in Cristiana Bastos, Miguel Vale de Almeida and Bela Feldman-Bianco (eds), *Trânsitos Coloniais: Diálogos Críticos Luso-Brasileiros*, Lisbon: ICS, pp. 133–50.
Bastos, Cristiana, Miguel Vale de Almeida and Bela Feldman-Bianco (eds) (2002), *Trânsitos Coloniais: Diálogos Críticos Luso-Brasileiros*, Lisbon: ICS.
Gallo, Donato (1988), *O Saber Português: Antropologia e Colonialismo*, Lisbon: Heptágono.
Margarido, Alfredo (1975), 'Le Colonialisme Portugais et l'Anthropologie', in J. Copans (ed.), *Anthropologie et Imperialisme*, Paris: Maspero, pp. 307–44.
Moutinho, Mário (1982), 'A Etnologia Colonial Portuguesa e o Estado Novo', in Mário Moutinho *O Fascismo em Portugal (Actas do Colóquio)*, Lisbon: A Regra do Jogo, pp. 415–42.
Pereira, Rui (1988), *Antropologia Aplicada na Política Colonial Portuguesa*, MA dissertation, Faculdade de Ciências Sociais e Humanas, Universidade Nova de Lisboa.
— (1998), 'Introdução à Reedição de 1998', in J. Dias (ed.), *Os Macondes de Moçambique*, Lisbon: CNCDP and IICT, pp. V–LII.
Pina-Cabral, João (1991), *Os Contextos da Antropologia*, Lisbon: Difel.
Thomaz, Omar Ribeiro (2002), *Ecos do Atlântico Sul. Representações sobre o terceiro Império Português*, Rio de Janeiro: Editora da UFRJ / FAPESP.
Vale de Almeida, Miguel (2004), *An Earth-Colored Sea. 'Race', Culture and the Politics of Identity in the Postcolonial Portuguese-speaking World*, Oxford and Providence: Berghahn Books.
— (2007), 'From Miscegenation to Creole Identity: Portuguese Colonialism, Brazil, Cape Verde', in Charles Stewart (ed.), *Creolization: History, Ethnography, Theory*, Walnut Creek, CA: Left Coast Press, pp. 108–32.

Anti-colonial Struggles

While Africa's other major colonial powers began decolonisation in the 1950s and 1960s, Portugal clung to its colonial empire, primarily due to its importance in sustaining the metropolis' underdeveloped economy. As cash crops began fuelling economic growth in the colonies during those decades, Portuguese immigration to Africa actually increased rapidly, especially in the white bastion of southern Africa. In this context, in Portugal's African colonies of Angola, Mozambique and Guinea-Bissau, activist organisations began developing and agitating for political change. Parties such as the Popular Movement for the Liberation of Angola (MPLA), the Front for the Liberation of Mozambique (FRELIMO), and the Union of the Peoples of Guinea and Cape Verde (PAIGC), organised protests and industrial action in urban areas within the colonies, only to be violently repressed by the colonial authorities. Following massacres by Portuguese forces in

Mozambique and Guinea-Bissau during 1960 and 1961, and the killing of tens of thousands of Africans after spontaneous revolts in Angola during 1961, political activists adopted strategies of rural guerrilla warfare launched from neighbouring countries.

While in Guinea-Bissau the PAIGC had been preparing for struggle under Amílcar Cabral's leadership since the 1950s, and in Mozambique FRELIMO was formed in 1962 as a united front against colonial rule under the leadership of Eduardo Mondlane, in Angola's case activists were from the start inexorably split between a number of mutually hostile political organisations. Agostinho Neto's MPLA was a metropolitan and cosmopolitan Marxist party, while Holden Roberto's National Front for the Liberation of Angola (FNLA) was an anti-communist and ethnically homogeneous group representing the interests of northern Angola. The FNLA was extremely hostile to the MPLA, especially after the anti-Lumumbist coup in their safe haven of the Republic of Congo. Jonas Savimbi then split from the FNLA in 1966 and created the National Union for the Total Independence of Angola (UNITA), which predominantly represented the ethnic interests of the southern Ovimbundu people. Though FRELIMO experienced numerous splits and internal conflict during the 1960s and 1970s it would remain the overwhelmingly dominant liberation organisation in Mozambique.

While the anti-colonial organisations used Eastern bloc weaponry to create liberated zones in which health services, education and communal markets were established, Portugal engaged in vicious counter-insurgency offensives with the financial backing of NATO. These often involved helicopter-borne troops, village militias and private fighting forces, the use of napalm, and the forced resettlement of thousands of villagers. Tens of thousands of Portuguese troops were deployed in the colonies, with even more Africans drafted into the colonial armies to combat the liberation forces. Nevertheless, the massive strain that the colonial wars placed on Portugal's society and economy contributed to the 1974 Carnation Revolution in Lisbon and subsequent decolonisation of the colonies under the auspices of the Armed Forces Movement. While in Mozambique and Guinea-Bissau power was transferred directly to FRELIMO and PAIGC, divisions remained in Angola and rapidly escalated into civil conflict as the Soviet bloc backed the MPLA, and the FNLA and UNITA secured support from China and the West.

David Robinson

HISTORIES

Birmingham, David (1992), *Frontline Nationalism in Angola and Mozambique*, London: James Currey.

Cann, John P. (1997), *Counter-Insurgency in Africa: The Portuguese Way of War 1961–1974*, London: Greenwood Press.

Chabal, Patrick (1983), *Amílcar Cabral: Revolutionary Leadership and People's War*, Cambridge: Cambridge University Press.

Ciment, James (1997), *Angola and Mozambique: Post-Colonial Wars in Southern Africa*, New York: Facts on File.

Lopes, Carlos (1987), *Guinea-Bissau: From Liberation to Independent Statehood*, London: Zed Books.

The Brazilian Independence Process

Unlike the other countries in Latin America struggling to extricate themselves from European colonial rule, the independence process in Brazil was relatively peaceful.

Dissatisfaction with the Portuguese government and discrimination against native-born Brazilians led to a series of revolts in various parts of Brazil in the eighteenth and early nineteenth centuries (most famously the Inconfidência Mineira of 1789 and the Conjuração Baiana of 1798), all of which were quashed by the army. The Portuguese King, Dom João VI, transported the Portuguese court to Rio de Janeiro in 1808 when he fled from Napoleon's invasion, a unique instance of a European monarch ruling the metropolis at a distance, from one of his colonies.

His arrival triggered a series of cultural developments: the founding of newspapers, the planting of the Botanical Garden and the construction of the National Library, theatres and opera houses. He also opened up the ports to trading with friendly nations. Dom João renamed his territories the United Kingdom of Portugal, Brazil and the Algarves in 1815, thus elevating Brazil's status. However, inequality in the regions and a perceived privileging of Portuguese nationals over Brazilians fuelled revolutionary temperaments and sparked revolts in Pernambuco in 1817.

In 1820 Dom João went back to Portugal to deal with the aftermath of the French invasion, leaving his eldest son Pedro (who supported the native Brazilians) as regent. The Brazilian élite did not wish to relinquish the autonomy they had gained during twelve years of self-government and urged Pedro to take control of the country. In January of 1822 Pedro was summoned back to Portugal by his father but he refused to return and subsequently, on 7 September that year, he declared Brazil's autonomy with the symbolic cry 'Independence or Death'.

The British, through diplomatic efforts and military assistance (including troops under Admiral Cochrane), helped control pockets of resistance, meaning that independence was achieved with relative speed, ease and lack of bloodshed. The change of governing power had little effect on the lives of the working people (slavery, for example was not affected), but it did afford the élites more economic and political independence. A constitutional charter was drawn up in 1824, but Brazil's independent status was recognised by Britain and Portugal officially only in 1825, and even then had to be bought for £1.4m and the promise to stop trading slaves.

Claire Williams

Literary Works

Almeida, Manuel Antonio de [1852] (1970), *Memórias de um Sargento de Milícias*, São Paulo: Cultrix.

Machado de Assis, Joaquim Maria [1881] (1970), *Memórias Póstumas de Brás Cubas*, São Paulo: Saraiva.

Ribeiro, João Ubaldo [1982] (1984), *Viva o Povo Brasileiro*, Rio de Janeiro: Nova Fronteira.

Histories

Bethell, Leslie (ed.) (1987), *Colonial Brazil*, Cambridge: Cambridge University Press.

Cavaliero, Roderick (1993), *The Independence of Brazil*, London: British Academic Press.

Holanda, Sérgio Buarque de [1936] (1997), *Raízes do Brasil*, São Paulo: Companhia das Letras.

Macauley, Neill (1986), *Dom Pedro: The Struggle for Liberty in Brazil and Portugal, 1798–1834*, Durham, NC: Duke University Press.

Schultz, Kirsten (2001), *Tropical Versailles: Empire, Monarchy and the Portuguese Royal Court in Rio de Janeiro 1808–1821*, New York: Routledge.

Amílcar Cabral

At a conference held in September 2004, to commemorate what would have been his eightieth birthday, over 100 scholars discussed Amílcar Cabral's impact on contemporary Africa. This revolutionary hero was born in Bafatá, Guinea, on 12 September 1924. In 1932, he moved with his family to Cabo Verde, where he was educated until 1950, when he won a scholarship to study at the Institute of Agronomy in Lisbon. Already influenced by his father's political views and by the effects of the colonial power's neglect of human rights and living conditions in Cabo Verde, Cabral read widely and discussed nationalism with fellow students from Portugal's other African colonies. In 1952, he returned to Bissau to work as an agricultural engineer, rather than staying on as a researcher in Lisbon. He organised a useful agricultural census of his country, but was exiled to Angola in 1955 for his political activities. On a visit home in 1956, he was instrumental in setting up a new political party, the Partido Africano para a Independência de Guiné-Bissau e Cabo Verde (PAIGC) and he also worked with Agostinho Neto towards the foundation of an Angolan liberation movement. He spoke out against the colonial system at every opportunity and encouraged party members to explain their struggle for independence and gain the support of the international arena. War broke out against the Portuguese army of occupation in Guinea in 1963 and Cabral trained and led the PAIGC forces to considerable success. He was assassinated in 1973, shortly after proclaiming that Guinea would see independence that year. A poet in his youth (publishing under the pseudonym Larbec), Cabral is remembered for his determination to mobilise and politicise his countrymen, his charismatic speeches and his innovative ideas about the importance of culture in the struggle for national liberation, defining it as 'simultaneously the fruit of a people's history and a determinant of history'.

Claire Williams

Literary Works

Augel, Moema Parente (1996), 'Guinea-Bissau', in Patrick Chabal et al., *The Postcolonial Literature of Lusophone Africa*, Evanston, IL: Northwestern University Press, pp. 165–78.
Cabral, Amílcar (1973), *Return to the Source: Selected Speeches*, New York: Monthly Review Press.
Chabal, Patrick (1985), 'Littérature et libération nationale. Le cas d'Amílcar Cabral', in Patrick Chabal et al., *Les Littératures Africaines de langue Portuguaise*, Paris: Fondation Caloute Gulbenkian, pp. 457–81.
Hamilton, Russell G. (1979), 'Lusophone African Literature: Amílcar Cabral and Cape Verdean Poetry', *World Literature Today*, 53 (1): 49–53.
Osório, Oswaldo (1984), *Emergência da Poesia em Amílcar Cabral: 30 poemas*, Praia: Grafedito.

Histories

African Identities (2006), Amílcar Cabral Special Issue, 4 (1).
Cabral, Amílcar (1980), *Unity and Struggle: Speeches and Writings*, trans. Michael Wolfers, selected by the PAIGC, London: Heinemann.
Chabal, Patrick (1983), *Amílcar Cabral: Revolutionary Leadership and People's War*, Cambridge: Cambridge University Press.

Davidson, Basil (1969), *The Liberation of Guiné: Aspects of an African Revolution* (foreword by Amílcar Cabral), Harmondsworth: Penguin.
Dhada, Mustafah (1993), *Warriors at Work: How Guinea Was Really Set Free*, Boulder, CO: University Press of Colorado.

The Carnation Revolution

The Carnation Revolution was a non-violent coup d'état that took place in Lisbon, Portugal on 25 April 1974 and resulted in the overthrow of the authoritarian dictatorship that had been in power for forty-eight years under António de Oliveira Salazar and his successor Marcelo Caetano. A group of army officers from the Movimento das Forças Armadas (Movement of Armed Forces), born in secrecy a year previously, led this bloodless revolution as they rallied around the ideals of a popular general António Spínola. In March 1974, the fascist government of the Estado Novo (New State) had fired General Spínola for insubordination following the publication in February of his book *Portugal and the Future* that argued in favour of colonial self-rule. As Portugal struggled to keep hold of her colonies in Africa, the war was taking a strong toll on the economic and social welfare of the country, causing a growing climate of unrest among the population.

The events of the peaceful overthrow of the dictatorial rule began on 24 April with the airing of the song that represented the country in the European Song Contest 'E Depois do Adeus' ('After Saying Goodbye'), alerting the rebel officers to start the revolution. The next morning, at 12.25 a.m., the national radio broadcast a banned protest folk song 'Grândola, Vila Morena' ('Grândola, Moorish Town'), which was the signal for the Movement of Armed Forces to take over strategic points of power in the country and principally in Lisbon (including the Salazar Bridge [later symbolically renamed the 25 April Bridge], the airport and train stations, the radio and television studios, and the government's police headquarters). Within six hours the dictatorial régime caved in leaving the governance of the country in the hands of the military officers. Thousands of civilians took to the streets on 25 April, despite the military urging them to stay home, and the 'Captains of April' put carnations in their gun barrels, replacing bullets with flowers as a symbol of victory and peace.

Kathryn Bishop-Sanchez

LITERARY WORKS
Antunes, António Lobo (1990), *Fado Alexandrino*, trans. Gregory Rabassa, New York: Grove Weidenfeld.
— (1995), *Act of the Damned*, trans. Richard Zenith, New York: Grove Press.
Barreno, Maria Isabel, Maria Teresa Horta and Maria Velho da Costa (1975), *New Portuguese Letters*, trans. Helen R. Lane, Garden City, NY: Doubleday.
Pires, José Cardoso (1986), *Ballad of Dogs' Beach*, trans. Mary Fitton, London: Dent.

HISTORIES
Bruce, Neil F. (1975), *Portugal, the Last Empire*, New York: Wiley.
Fields, Rona M. (1975), *The Portuguese Revolution and the Armed Forces Movement*, New York: Praeger.
Graham, Lawrence S. and Douglas L. Wheeler (1983), *In Search of Modern Portugal: The Revolution and its Consequences*, Madison, WI: University of Wisconsin Press.

Posadas, J. (1976), *The Portuguese Revolution: Selection of Articles*, London: Fourth International Publications.
Sobel, Lester A. (ed.) (1976), *Portuguese Revolution, 1974–76*, New York: Facts on File.

Charter Companies/*Prazos*

The origins of the *prazos da Coroa* can be traced back to the powerful positions reached by Portuguese individuals within African society in the lower Zambesi valley of the central regions of Mozambique in the sixteenth century. Formally land grants conferred by the Portuguese crown, in practice they were a type of chieftaincy headed by Afro-Portuguese families that involved a network of socio-economic relations embedded deeply in the local African culture.

During the seventeenth century, the crown relied increasingly on these families and on their private armies for its objective of establishing an effective colonial régime in the area. By the nineteenth century, intensive droughts, the escalating slave and ivory trades, and the Nguni invasions deeply affected the *prazo* system. It was restructured around a few centres of power dominated by dynasties of Indian origin, and around the conquests of Afro-Portuguese warlords and *chicunda* bands. During the last quarter of the nineteenth century, the *prazo* system, which had survived for centuries, was radically transformed by the new economic forces brought into the region through international commerce and as a result of the South African mining revolution. It was also altered as a consequence of the principle of effective occupation, agreed at the Berlin Conference.

Most of Mozambique, including the *prazos*, was granted to private commercial companies owned by foreign capital. These companies sought to attract foreign investment by 'pacifying' the region on behalf of Portugal, and by supplying a cheap African workforce through a system of taxation of the population and forced labour. The companies favoured a system of extensive labour emigration from their territories. Two large concessionary charter companies were established: the Moçambique Company, with an 1891 grant in the central region roughly between the Sabi and Zambesi rivers; and the Niassa Company, with an 1894 grant in the northern area between the Lurio and Rovuma rivers. The *prazos* along the Zambesi river fell under smaller plantation companies, which had to confront the enduring power of the old *prazo* holders. When the concessions ended, the last one being that of the Moçambique Company in 1941, for the first time in its history, Lisbon had direct administration of the entire country. However, the native and labour policy consolidated at the time of the companies, based on taxation of the African population and on the mobilisation of cheap African labour for internal plantations and public works or for foreign mining companies, radically shaped Portuguese colonial policy and practice in the following years.

Corrado Tornimbeni

HISTORIES
Isaacman, A. (1972), *Mozambique: The Africanisation of a European Institution, the Zambesi Prazos, 1750–1902*, Madison, WI: University of Wisconsin Press.
Newitt, M. (1995), *A History of Mozambique*, London: Hurst and Company.
Papagno, G. (1972), *Colonialismo e Feudalesimo. La Questione dei Prazos da Coroa nel Mozambico alla fine del XIX*, Torino: Einaudi.
Vail, L. and L. White (1980), *Capitalism and Colonialism in Mozambique*, London: Heinemann.

Creolisation and Creoleness

Creolisation is a term used to describe the cultural cross-fertilisation that occurred as a result of Portuguese colonial activity in different parts of the world, and which usually accompanied a process of racial mixing. Small pockets of creolised populations evolved in parts of the Indian Ocean and East and South-East Asia as a result of Portuguese commercial activity in the sixteenth century, and in the Atlantic, where they were very much a by-product of the slave trade between West Africa and Brazil. Creolisation took lasting linguistic forms in the Cape Verde islands and on the adjacent Guinean coast, with the emergence of a Creole language that became the lingua franca for commercial contact along parts of the West African coast and interior. Other Portuguese Creoles emerged in the islands of São Tomé, Príncipe and Ano Bom. If Creole languages never became as firmly entrenched in the larger mainland territories of the Atlantic Basin, such as Angola and Brazil, other forms of cultural cross-fertilisation occurred, especially in the major trading ports of Luanda, Benguela, Salvador, Recife, Rio de Janeiro and São Luís. They manifested themselves in degrees of religious syncretism, in aspects of social culture such as gastronomy, and in the infiltration of local lexical influences into the Portuguese language of the ruling élite of mixed African and European (and in the case of Brazil, Amerindian) descent. In Brazil, research into cultural creolisation is closely associated with the work of the social historian Gilberto Freyre (1900–87), and his theory of 'lusotropicalism'. In Angola, this élite straddled the border between the Lisbon-appointed administrators and the local native hierarchies, acting as middle men in the slave trade. This creolised population adopted Portuguese names and professed Catholicism, while often covertly observing local cultural mores. The Creoles of Luanda and Benguela had considerable influence in local affairs, dominating the civil service up until the third quarter of the nineteenth century. By this time, the Atlantic slave trade had ended, and Portugal formally set about imposing its sovereignty upon its African territories in the context of the 'Scramble for Africa' and the Congress of Berlin. As more Portuguese settlers entered Angola, the old Creole élite, some of whose members had aspired to independence for Angola in the wake of Brazilian independence in 1822, found itself politically marginalised, and it is no coincidence that, when Angolan nationalism emerged in the 1940s and 1950s, culminating in the formation of the Popular Movement for the Liberation of Angola (MPLA), many of the old Creole families threw in their lot with it. Creoleness, which suggests an identification with this mixed culture, has never been part of the rhetoric of Angolan nationalism, but there have always been writers whose works evoke the process and effects of creolisation in and around Luanda. Among others, these have included Alfredo Troni (1845–1904), Óscar Ribas (1909–2004), Mário António (1934–88), Luandino Vieira (1935–), Uanhenga Xitu (1929–), and more recently, José Eduardo Agualusa (1960-), whose novels and short stories also evoke the strong cultural links between Angola and Brazil.

David Brookshaw

LITERARY WORKS
Agualusa, José Eduardo (2002), *Creole*, trans. Daniel Hahn, London: Arcadia.
Chabal, Patrick et al. (1996), *The Postcolonial Literature of Lusophone Africa*, Evanston, IL: Northwestern University Press.
Hamilton, R. (1974), *Voices from an Empire: A History of Afro-Portuguese Literature*, Minneapolis, MN: University of Minnesota Press.

Xitu, U. (1988), *The World of 'Mestre' Tamoda*, trans. Annella McDermott, London: Readers International.

HISTORIES

Freyre, Gilberto (1961), *The Portuguese and the Tropics*, trans. Helen M. D'O. Matthew and F. de Mello Moser, Lisbon: Executive Committee for the Commemoration of the Vth Centenary of the Death of Prince Henry the Navigator.

Explorations and Discoveries

The concept of discovery has long been called into question for its Eurocentric bias, and particularly so at the time of the quincentenary of Columbus' first voyage, when Edmundo O'Gorman's (1951) alternative notion of the invention of America, *La idea del descubrimiento de América* (*The Invention of America*, 1961) became a banner under which people in several Latin American countries voiced their opposition to the celebration of the landing of the Europeans. A similar challenge later took place in India, which in 1998 refused to commemorate the arrival of the Portuguese in the East five centuries before. The term 'discovery' is nevertheless still used, but it is now often replaced by the notion of expansion, which better discloses the multiplicity of motives behind fifteenth- and sixteenth-century Iberian voyaging, namely a complex mix of desire for territorial growth achieved through military conquest, a certain spirit of holy crusade (religious expansion), and above all the urge for economic advancement through the finding of new markets beyond Europe. For its part, the concept of exploration is considerably less objectionable, for its stronger geographical and scientific connotations and its implications of intellectual curiosity.

Wedged between enemy Spain to the East and the vast ocean to the West, Portugal was the first Western European nation to absorb technical knowledge brought to the Iberian peninsula by the Arabs (in the fields of mathematics, geography, astronomy and nautical science), as well as by overland travellers, pilgrims and ambassadors, fishermen and merchants; and to put it to good practical use, by building ships capable of venturing into the oceans and developing sufficient navigational expertise to do so.

It is commonly believed that the great mind behind the age of Portuguese seafaring was Henry the Navigator. However, as Oliveira Marques (1972) points out, the prince was almost exclusively preoccupied with the military conquest of North Africa, and although he surrounded himself with the best Arab, Hebrew and European scholars of the time, thus gathering the indispensable technical know-how which finally enabled oceanic voyaging, it was his father, King John I, and the kings who succeeded him, who actively promoted most Portuguese voyages of exploration and conquest.

Portuguese oceanic voyaging and exploration developed in three principal areas: the African coasts and islands; the farther reaches of the Atlantic Ocean; and (at the turn of the century) the remote East. All major historians of Portugal devote much attention to this period of the country's history, but the most comprehensive and readable studies to date remain Damião Peres' *A History of the Portuguese Discoveries* (1960) and C. R. Boxer's *The Portuguese Seaborne Empire* (1969).

The age of Portuguese expansion began in 1415, with the capture of Ceuta, on the African side of the Strait of Gibraltar. But the proximity between the southern Portuguese and the northern African coasts meant that this expedition did not count as one of the great maritime voyages that came to demand increasing familiarity with sophisticated navigational instruments and accurate knowledge of the wind systems in the southern Atlantic.

Madeira was next, discovered by João Gonçalves Zarco and Bartolomeu Perestrelo; but the archipelago was neglected until the rival Spanish crown sent an expedition there, prompting the Portuguese to occupy the islands in 1419. In 1427, Diogo de Silves sighted at least two of the Azores islands. (Both archipelagos, which were uninhabited at the time of discovery, have remained part of Portugal since the early fifteenth century.) During the 1420s and 1430s, the main interest of Portuguese expeditions was to gain access to the legendary 'river of gold' on the western coast of Africa. In 1434, Gil Eanes first rounded Cape Bojador. The following year, the same pilot, accompanied by Gonçalves Baldaia, reached what they believed to be the famous river and named it Rio do Ouro. In 1441, Nuno Tristão reached Cape Blanco (in present-day Mauritania) and probably the mouth of the Senegal river. Diogo Gomes reached Guinea and Sierra Leone. Dinis Dias explored the Cape Verde islands, of which only Sal had previously been known. In the early 1460s the Portuguese arrived in the Gulf of Guinea and began to explore its coasts.

During King João II's reign, Diogo Cão first reached the coasts of present-day Gabon, Congo and Angola (in 1482) and later those of modern Namibia, which Bartolomeu Dias explored further during his 1487 voyage. The latter became one of the most auspicious voyages of the time because Dias finally succeeded in rounding the southern tip of Africa, naming it Cape of Good Hope in recognition of the possibilities it offered as it opened up a new route to India. Ten years later, Vasco da Gama departed from Lisbon following the same route; he again rounded the Cape, sailed on to Melinde (north of Mombasa, Kenya), there obtaining an Arab pilot who guided his fleet to India (May 1498). The ships returned to Portugal (in 1499) loaded with the Indian spices and other exotic luxury goods coveted by the Europeans, thus realising the dream of importing those by the cheaper and less dangerous maritime route. Another expedition to India was immediately prepared, under the command of Pedro Álvares Cabral. This expedition was to follow the same route as Vasco da Gama's but Cabral sailed further to south-west and reached the coast of Brazil, landing in a bay he named Porto Seguro, at Easter 1500. Ten days later the fleet sailed on to India, where it arrived in August 1500.

Meanwhile, sailing farther out into the Atlantic, in 1495, Pêro de Barcelos and João Fernandes Lavrador reached Greenland (Tiera del Larador), and in 1500 Gaspar Corte Real arrived in New Foundland (Tiera Nova de Corte Real), two destinations which the Portuguese very likely had already sighted in 1474. In the South Atlantic, further expedition began soon after the 1500 landing in Brazil: from 1501 the Brazilian coast was explored down to the River Plate.

By then the Portuguese were working towards establishing a firm presence in the East, obtaining permission to build fortresses on the East African coast, in Sofala (1505) and on the island of Mozambique (1507), in order to facilitate commerce with India. Having conquered Goa in 1510, they began building strongholds and factories on both Indian coasts, and later in Ceylon and in Malacca (Malaysia). Francisco Serrão reached the Moluccas in 1511. Jorge Álvares arrived in China in 1513, only fifteen years after Vasco da Gama's arrival in India. The Portuguese may have sighted the northern coast of Australia. Having explored Indonesia, they reached Timor in 1525. Portuguese private traders (including Mendes Pinto) entered Japan in 1543.

In the service of the rival Spanish crown, Portuguese Ferdinand Magellan reached Argentina and Chile and then crossed the Pacific Ocean, in search of a sea route to the Moluccas, which should procure for the Spanish crown the eastern spices that the Portuguese monarch was already enjoying.

The written records of the seafaring age (shipboard journals, shipwreck narratives, letters and chronicles) fulfilled not only the pragmatic function of informing the king and subsequent explorers, many also display incipient literary value. They all build up to the great epic poem of the Portuguese expansion, Luís de Camões' *The Lusiadas*, and to Fernão Mendes Pinto's extraordinary account of his travels, in which Maria Alzira Seixo identifies 'a specific dimension that we usually find only in the novel'. Most of the written records bear striking witness to many first encounters between the Portuguese and various local peoples, although there are marked differences between individual works. Azurara's *Chronicle of the Discovery and Conquest of Guinea*, for example, includes attractive descriptions of exotic locations, with the author occasionally paying attention to the most obvious signs of difference: nudity, diet, type of government (in the description of the islands of Tenerife and Palma). Pêro Vaz de Caminha, the scribe in Cabral's fleet, wrote King Manuel a delightful *Letter on the Finding of Brazil*, in which he hardly disguised his fascination with the nakedness and innocence of the indigenous people of Porto Seguro, subscribing in this way to some of the most common tropes of description of a paradisiacal existence. His remarks about the local Amerindians focused on their numbers and potential weapons, their skin colour, their body painting, their nudity and their diet, as well as their apparent friendliness and willingness to imitate the Portuguese in the ritual of the first mass celebrated ashore.

The most important literary text of the age of Portuguese voyaging is Camões' *The Lusiads* (1572), which many scholars (whether literary historians, like António José Saraiva, or cultural philosophers, like Eduardo Lourenço) have identified as the most powerful instrument in the definition of Portuguese cultural identity. This is mostly due to its intrinsic poetic quality, but also partly to the fact that the poem appeared just eight years before Portugal's temporary loss of independence to Spain, thus striking a particularly nationalistic chord. Inspired by dreams of imperial glory, *The Lusiads* constructs not only Vasco da Gama's voyage to India but also much of Portugal's history into myth, simultaneously praising the ideology of the Portuguese crown (expansion and evangelisation) in beautifully crafted epic lines. Nevertheless, the poem also contains a much discussed episode in which the Old Man of Restelo raises his solitary voice against the navigators' greed and temerity as they depart for India. Despite this awareness of potential moral failing associated with the expansion and of the heavy demands the imperial venture would impose on the tiny country, the overall theme of the poem remains the celebration of the splendour of Portuguese history. The real human cost of Portugal's oceanic voyaging was recorded in many shipwreck narratives individually published as loose pamphlets. Some of these episodes appear also in *The Lusiads*, their pathos adding force to the celebration of imperial grandeur. Most of those pamphlets were later collected by Gomes de Brito, in the mid-1730s, in *The Tragic History of the Sea*.

First published in 1614, but written before 1580 (the year generally considered to mark the end of the period of Portuguese expansion), Fernão Mendes Pinto's complex narrative of his seventeen-year travels in the East (during which he 'saw with [his] own eyes' Ethiopia, Mecca, southern Persia, India, Malacca, Siam, China, Japan and Sumatra, among other places) combines autobiography, travel writing and pure fiction. The author emphasises the primacy of empirical experience, which is a constant in the literature of this period. But in *Travels* the question of the encounter with other people stands out distinctively: unencumbered by panegyric preoccupations, Mendes Pinto reveals the humbling experience of a man who realises he has been living with people whose culture is far more dazzling than his. The city of Peking, in particular, fills him with admiration, due to its grandeur, cosmopolitanism and magnificence. Moreover, he recognises the elegance, tolerance and superior wisdom of the Chinese and Japanese, in contrast to the cruelty and profanity of his fellow Portuguese adventurers.

The most impressive of the contemporary texts on Portuguese voyaging, then, reveal a sometimes remarkable ability to recognise cultural difference, ranging from simple recording of basic dietary or clothing difference to some considerable interpretive efforts, including attempts to imagine how others may view the Portuguese. The Portuguese were in any case not exactly representative of all Europeans in this regard, given that their geographical position in Europe and their long cohabitation with Jews and Arabs in the Iberian peninsula may have better equipped them to deal with different cultures. This, however, did not preclude some amazing mistakes in interpretation, in which wishful thinking probably played a major part (for example, in Caminha's assumption that the Tupiniquins had no organised religion or government, thus being ready and willing to be converted and to accept Portuguese rule; or in Vasco da Gama's mistaking the Hindus for Christians).

Opening new routes via the Atlantic, the Indian and the Pacific oceans and reaching so many distant places were in themselves no small accomplishments. That this age of exploration and expansion should have given rise to a very protracted age of colonialism is much less admirable, to say the least. The other major Portuguese contributions to the shaping of the world as it then became known to the Europeans, however, is beyond dispute. As pilots' reports were used for the drawing of the first detailed maps of the routes and regions explored by the navigators, and as the written records of the great ocean voyages became known and avidly read, the world did acquire completely new dimensions in European eyes, and new tools for the interpretation of human existence came into being.

Isabel Moutinho

LITERARY WORKS

Azurara, Gomes Eannes de (1963), *The Chronicle of the Discovery and Conquest of Guinea*, trans. C. R. Beazley and Edgar Prestage, 2 vols, New York: Burt Franklin.

Brito, Bernardo Gomes de (1959), *The Tragic History of the Sea, 1589–1622*, and (1968) *Further Selections from The Tragic History of the Sea, 1559–1565*, trans. and ed. C. R. Boxer, Cambridge: Published for the Hakluyt Society at the University Press.

Camões, Luís de (1997), *The Lusiads*, trans. Landeg White, Oxford and New York: Oxford University Press.

Figueiredo, João R. (guest ed.) (2002), *Post-Imperial Camões, Portuguese Literary and Cultural Studies* 9, special issue.

Greenlee, W. B. (ed.) (1967), *The Voyage of Pedro Álvares Cabral to Brazil and India from Contemporary Documents and Narratives*, Nendeln: Kraus Reprint.

Pereira, Duarte Pacheco (1967), *Esmeraldo de Situ Orbis*, trans. and ed. G. H. T. Kimble, Nendeln: Kraus Reprint.

Pinto, Fernão Mendes (1989), *The Travels of Mendes Pinto*, trans. and ed. Rebecca D. Catz, Chicago, IL: University of Chicago Press.

Ravenstein, E. G. (ed.) (1963?), *A Journal of the First Voyage of Vasco da Gama, 1497–1499*, New York: Burt Franklin.

Seixo, Maria Alzira (1999), 'Wanderlust and Difference', in M. A. Seixo, A. P. Laborinho and M. J. Meria (eds), *A Vertigem do Oriente*, Lisbon and Macau: Cosmos and I.P.O, pp. 155–64.

HISTORIES

Albuquerque, Luís de, Justo Guedes and Gerlad Lombardi (eds) (c. 1990), *Portugal-Brazil: The Age of Atlantic Discoveries*, New York: Brazilian Cultural Foundation.

Bell, Christopher (1974), *Portugal and the Quest for the Indies*, London: Constable.

Boxer, C. R. (1969), *The Portuguese Seaborne Empire, 1415–1825*, London: Hutchinson.

Diffie, Bailey and George Winius (1977), *Foundations of the Portuguese Empire 1415–1580*, Minneapolis, MN: University of Minnesota Press.

Earle, T. F. and Stephen Parkinson (eds) (c. 1992), *Proceedings of the First Colloquium of the Centre for the Study of the Portuguese Discoveries*, Warminster: Aris and Phillips with the CNCDP.

Hower, Alfred and Richard A. Preto-Rodas (eds) (c. 1985), *Empire in Transition: The Portuguese World in the Time of Camões*, Gainesville, FL: University of Florida Press/Center for Latin American Studies.

Oliveira Marques, A. H. de (1972), *History of Portugal*, New York and London: Columbia University Press.

Peres, Damião (1960), *A History of the Portuguese Discoveries*, Lisbon: Comissão Executiva das Comemorações do Quinto Centenário da Morte do Infante D. Henrique.

Subrahmanyam, Sanjay (1997), *The Career and Legend of Vasco da Gama*, Cambridge: Cambridge University Press.

FRELIMO: Front for the Liberation of Mozambique

The Frente de Libertação de Moçambique (FRELIMO) was formed on 25 June 1962 after decades of political repression by Mozambique's colonial authorities, and the massacre of peaceful protesters at Mueda in northern Mozambique on 16 June 1960 led anti-colonial activists to form opposition parties in exile. A number of opposition groups united in the Tanganyikan capital Dar es Salaam to create FRELIMO as a political front and launched their guerrilla struggle in Mozambique in September 1964, attacking Portuguese outposts and politicising local populations. Political divisions and factional manoeuvring plagued FRELIMO throughout the 1960s, leading to many splits and expulsions. The assassination of FRELIMO President Eduardo Mondlane by letter bomb in February 1969 may have been connected to this internal rivalry. After Mondlane's death radical elements, led by Samora Machel, attained dominance within the party and expounded more explicitly Marxist political rhetoric.

While FRELIMO's guerrilla campaign continued to expand in the early 1970s, it was Portugal's 1974 Carnation Revolution that eventually led to Mozambican independence and brought FRELIMO, as the only major anti-colonial movement, to power. In the context of civil unrest and economic crisis precipitated by the flight of the majority of Mozambique's settler population, FRELIMO imprisoned thousands of political opponents in its first months of rule, though most were released by the early 1980s. The FRELIMO government subsequently embarked on ambitious national health and literacy campaigns, attempted to redress Mozambique's underdevelopment through Soviet-style industrialisation, and ensured multiracialism in government and the civil service. However, FRELIMO's intense hostility to traditional social structures and religion, and their collectivisation of agriculture, created resentment and ultimately resistance from elements of the rural population. FRELIMO's support for Zimbabwean nationalists and the African National Congress motivated economic and military destabilisation by the white régimes in South Africa and Rhodesia, resulting in the creation of the Resistência Nacional Moçambicana (RENAMO) in the late 1970s. With Rhodesian and then South African sponsorship RENAMO engaged in a brutal insurgency that became the FRELIMO government's main challenge until the mid-1990s.

Though outwardly unified, from the early 1980s divisions emerged within the FRELIMO leadership over issues of corruption, economics and the country's civil war. There are indications that President Machel's opponents attempted to remove him from power a number of times during the first half of the decade before he was finally assassinated in a 1986 plane crash. Following Machel's death, Joaquim Chissano assumed the presidency and marginalised Machel-loyalists within the government and armed forces. Chissano delayed negotiations with RENAMO, while hastening the liberalisation of the Mozambican economy and overseeing the introduction of a new democratic constitution in 1990. Following a 1992 peace agreement with RENAMO, FRELIMO emerged victorious in Mozambique's first general elections in 1994, and retained power in subsequent elections in 1999 and 2004. Chissano stepped down before the 2004 election, allowing Armando Guebuza to win the presidency. Though observers have declared Mozambique's elections to be reasonably free and fair, corruption has become institutionalised within the government and the separation between the FRELIMO party and Mozambican state remains inadequate.

David Robinson

HISTORIES

Cabrita, João M. (2000), *Mozambique: The Tortuous Road to Democracy*, Basingstroke: Palgrave.

Hall, Margaret and Tom Young (1997), *Confronting Leviathan: Mozambique since Independence*, London: Hurst and Company.

Manning, Carrie (2002), *The Politics of Peace in Mozambique: Post-Conflict Democratization 1992–2000*, London: Praeger.

Newitt, Malyn (1995), *A History of Mozambique*, Bloomington, IN: Indiana University Press.

Vines, Alex (1996), *RENAMO: From Terrorism to Democracy in Mozambique?*, London: James Currey.

FRETILIN and Xanana Gusmão

The Frente Revolucionária de Timor-Leste Independente – FRETILIN – arose in 1974, calling for an independent East Timor after four centuries of Portuguese colonial rule. Following the fall of Portugal's dictatorship on 25 April 1974, the process of withdrawal from the country's colonies would unravel with tragic consequences for the Timorese. As Portugal assumed the role of administrator of the territory whilst Timor's political leaders debated its future direction, FRETILIN set about an intensive campaign to raise national consciousness amongst the population. In contrast to its rivals (União Democrática Timorense (UDT) and APODETI), FRETILIN went out into the countryside, engaging with the rural population.

FRETILIN's leadership was made up largely of an educated élite fostered by the Portuguese. Xanana Gusmão, its future President, had received a seminary education, later entering into the lower échelons of the colonial civil service. Xanana's FRETILIN career began in the party's Department of Information and he became what the UDT saw as an unacceptable communist presence in East Timor. This communist threat was used to justify their coup in August 1975, which FRETILIN successfully resisted, and in its aftermath they saw no option but unilaterally to declare East Timor's independence in November 1975.

On 7 December, supposedly to intervene in a civil war that it had done much to instigate, Indonesia invaded East Timor. The Indonesian military hunted down FRETILIN members, killing many of them; and massacred many innocent civilians. From that date, FRETILIN led the resistance against the bloody Indonesian occupation, fighting a guerrilla war at home, and seeking international assistance abroad. Nicolau Lobato, FRETILIN's leader, was killed by Indonesian forces in December 1978, and it fell to Xanana Gusmão to reorganise both FRETILIN and its armed wing, FALINTIL. After his capture and imprisonment by the Indonesians in 1992, Xanana continued to direct FRETILIN policy, becoming a living symbol of the Timorese struggle for freedom. When the political landscape changed in Indonesia in 1998 with the fall of the country's dictator, General Suharto, it was to Xanana that people looked as the natural leader of an independent East Timor. The UN-sponsored referendum held in August 1999 saw the East Timorese voting for independence, despite violent intimidation at the hands of Indonesian-sponsored militias.

Xanana was released shortly after the referendum and became the President of East Timor after its formal independence on 20 May 2002. FRETILIN became the party of government, but its relationship with the President and its former leader has revealed tensions, with Xanana issuing veiled criticisms of those leading lavish lifestyles whilst Timor's population continues to lack basic necessities. As East Timor struggles to insert itself into global economic and political networks, it remains to be seen how FRETILIN will satisfy the competing demands of a people who were oppressed for several centuries by colonial powers, and those of a global economic structure that runs counter to many of the socialist beliefs that FRETILIN held during the fight for Timorese freedom.

Anthony Soares

LITERARY WORKS

Borja da Costa, Francisco (1976), *Revolutionary Poems in the Struggle against Colonialism: Timorese Nationalist Verse*, ed. Jill Jolliffe, Sydney: Wild and Woolley.

Cardoso, Luís (2000), *The Crossing: A Story of East Timor*, trans. Margaret Jull Costa, London: Granta.

Oliveira, Celso (2003), *Timor-Leste: Chegou a Liberdade (39 poesias para Timor Lorosa'e) Edição bilingue – português/inglês*, trans. and ed. Maria Teresa Carrilho, Lisbon: Soroptomist International: Clube Lisboa – Sete Colinas.

HISTORIES

Bentley, Peter and G. Carter Bentley (eds) (1995), *East Timor at the Crossroads*, London: Cassell.

Chomsky, Noam (2001), *A New Generation Draws the Line: Kosovo, East Timor and the Standards of the West*, London: Verso.

Hainsworth, Paul and Stephen McCloskey (eds) (2000), *The East Timor Question*, London: I. B. Tauris.

Taylor, John G. (1999), *East Timor: The Price of Freedom*, London: Zed Books.

The Frontline States

The Frontline States (FLS) was an informal alliance formed by southern Africa's independent black states in the late 1970s to co-ordinate the struggle for majority rule in the region and to compensate for their collective political and economic weakness. Military collaboration amongst the states always remained quite limited and predominantly bilateral in nature, though all suffered under South Africa's regional strategy of military and economic destabilisation. The formation of the FLS' sister organisation the South African Development Co-ordination Conference (SADCC) also enhanced regional economic integration from mid-1980. While eventually consisting of Angola, Botswana, Malawi, Mozambique, Namibia, Swaziland, Tanzania, Zambia and Zimbabwe, the origin of the FLS was in monthly consultations between Tanzanian President Nyerere and Zambian President Kuanda in the mid-1960s to promote economic co-operation. These meetings grew to include other presidents under the banner of the Mulungushi Club, and provided a diplomatic forum for the Angolan and Mozambican liberation movements. Following Portugal's 1974 revolution and the subsequent decolonisation of Angola and Mozambique, the southern African states created the FLS and were mandated by the Organisation of African Unity's (OAU) 1975 Dar es Salaam Declaration to support southern Africa's liberation movements. Though the FLS states possessed varying political and economic structures, its flexibility and efforts by Tanzanian President Nyerere to bridge divisions allowed the coalition to endure with common goals.

Upon its formation the FLS immediately provided support to the Zimbabwean liberation movements and committed itself to SWAPO's struggle against South African control in south-west Africa (Namibia). Though Zambia initially dissented over support for the MPLA in Angola's emerging civil conflict, this position shifted after the OAU's recognition of the MPLA in 1976. Rhodesia provided a particularly favourable environment for FLS intervention due to its geographical encirclement by the FLS nations and their influence on its liberation movements. The end of minority rule in Rhodesia was thus successfully achieved through sanctions, logistical support for Zimbabwean guerrillas, and the mobilisation of international mediation. In the process both Zambia and Mozambique suffered Rhodesian and South African counter-insurgency campaigns, which in the case of Mozambique developed into a seventeen-year civil war. Angola took the leading role in supporting SWAPO, though the FLS' more limited access to south-west African territory and the rapid internationalisation of Angola's civil conflict ensured that the FLS' primary role in the struggle always remained the leveraging of international diplomatic pressure on South Africa.

The FLS began providing military assistance to South Africa's African National Congress (ANC) from 1981, and Zimbabwe and later Tanzania intervened in Mozambique throughout the 1980s to protect SADCC's vital transport corridors from RENAMO guerrillas. In 1986 the FLS successfully pressured Malawi to co-operate against RENAMO by threatening economic sanctions, though it failed to coerce Zaire to cease support for UNITA in Angola. While Mozambique's 1984 Nkomati Accord with South Africa was viewed as a defeat by the FLS, during the late 1980s Mozambican rapprochement with South Africa and the West was influential in securing the FLS' goal of transition to majority rule in South Africa.

David Robinson

HISTORIES

Dreyer, Ronald (1994), *Namibia and Southern Africa: Regional Dynamics of Decolonization 1945–90*, London: Kegan Paul International.
Johnson, Phyllis and David Martin (eds) (1989), *Frontline Southern Africa*, Peterborough: Ryan Publishing.
Khadiagala, Gilbert M. (1994), *Allies in Adversity: The Frontline States in Southern African Security 1975–1993*, Athens, OH: Athens University Press.
Legum, Colin (1988), *The Battlefronts of Southern Africa*, New York: Africana Publishing Company.
Thompson, Carol (1985), *Challenge to Imperialism: The Frontline States in the Liberation of Zimbabwe*, Harare: Zimbabwe Publishing House.

Goa

The god Vishnu is believed to have created Goa, when, needing to purify himself on virgin soil after massacring an evil tribe, he threw his axe into the sea and commanded the waters to rise up around it. It appears several times in the Hindu epics with various names, all of which begin with the prefix 'go-', meaning cow, referring to its lush pastures. The territory lies on the east coast of India, from which it is separated by the Ghat mountain range. Its natural harbours and wide rivers made it an ideal base for trading, especially with the Arabian peninsula, and a desirable trophy for warring emperors who fought over it until the fifteenth century. In its heyday in the mid-fourteenth century travellers' accounts compared it to Rome for its beauty, size and wealth. Vasco da Gama's expedition reached Calicut in 1498, and twelve years later Afonso de Albuquerque led the Portuguese fleet in a first attempt to conquer Goa and turn it into Portugal's main spice trading port.

By 1543, the European invaders were able to expand their territory inland, as well as developing the port which became known as Goa Dourada (Golden Goa) due to its prosperity. The fortunes of Goa mirrored those of the Portuguese Empire: suffering coastal attacks from the British and Dutch, as well as from the Marathas inland. By the eighteenth century, dissatisfaction with Portuguese administrative rule from the distant metropolis was beginning to become more common and more violent. Only in 1812 was Goa represented in the Portuguese parliament. Under the Estado Novo (New State), civil liberties were suppressed along with local languages, and religious discrimination tolerated.

In 1928, the Goan National Congress (affiliated to the Indian National Congress) was founded by Dr Tristão de Braganza Cunha, to encourage independence or at least merging with India – which won its independence from Britain in 1947. Salazar, however, would not relinquish the Portuguese hold on Goa. In 1961 the Indian army invaded and liberated the territory in two days, without encountering much resistance. In 1987 Goa was officially designated India's twenty-fifth and smallest state, supplying three representatives to the Indian parliament.

Goa's culture reflects a blend of East and West, demonstrated in its language, cuisine, literature, art and architecture. The Catholic presence is still in evidence, through the colonial architecture of the seminaries and pilgrimages to the tomb of St Francis Xavier. Since being a hippy haven in the 1960s, the tourist industry has developed considerably. The beaches and growing eco-tourism holidays make Goa one of India's most popular resorts.

Claire Williams

LITERARY WORKS

Agualusa, José Eduardo (2001), *Um Estranho em Goa*, Lisbon: Cotovia.
Burton, Richard [1851] (1991), *Goa, and the Blue Mountains: Or, Six Months of Sick Leave*, London and Berkeley, CA: Richard Bentley and University of California Press.
Costa, Orlando da (1961), *O Signo da Ira*, Lisbon: Arcádia.
Devi, Vimala and Manuel de Seabra (eds) (1971), *A Literatura Indo-Portuguesa*, Lisbon: Junta de Investigações do Ultramar.
Nazareth, Peter (ed.) (1983), 'Goan Literature: A Modern Reader', *Journal of South Asian Literature* (winter – spring).

HISTORIES

Borges, Charles and Helmut Feldmann (1997), *Goa and Portugal: Their Cultural Links*, New Delhi: Concept.
Boxer, Charles (1984), *From Lisbon to Goa, 1500–1750: Studies in Portuguese Maritime Enterprise*, London: Variorum.
Portas, Catarina and Inês Gonçalves (2001), *Goa: História de um Encontro*, Coimbra: Almedina.
Scholberg, Henry (1982), *Bibliography of Goa and the Portuguese in India*, New Delhi: Promilla and Co.
Souza, Teotónio R. de (ed.) (1989), *Essays in Goan History*, New Delhi: Concept.
Subrahmanyam, Sanjay (1993), *The Portuguese Empire in Asia, 1500–1700: A Political and Economic History*, London: Longman.

Henry the Navigator

Prince Henry the Navigator (1394–1460) is mainly remembered in Portuguese history as the founder of an early fifteenth-century school of navigation in the city of Sagres, on the south-western tip of Portugal, and the inventor, albeit disputed, of the 'caravel'. The son of King João I of Portugal and Philippa of Lancaster, Henry lived at a time when Portugal had her eyes anxiously set on exploring lands across the sea and in particular along the coast of western Africa. Historically accurate facts and heroic legends merge in accounts surrounding Henry the Navigator, to the extent that it is nowadays almost impossible to distinguish myth from reality.

After the Portuguese successfully launched a crusade on Ceuta, North Morocco, and captured the port in 1415, Portugal began a seafaring enterprise that during Henry's lifetime would lead to the discovery of the Madeira islands (1420), the rounding of the Cape Bojador (1434), the discovery of Cape Verde (1455) and taking Portuguese explorers as far as Cape Palmas (today known as Liberia; 1459–60). In 1419, several years after the victory in Ceuta, King João made Henry governor of Portugal's southern coast. It is there that Henry is said to have established a base for sea exploration in the early 1420s, drawing a community of cartographers, navigators, geographers and shipbuilders to Sagres from all parts of Europe.

Behind the voyages of exploration was the desire to discover lands hitherto unknown beyond the much-feared Cape Bojador, along with the ambition of establishing greater trade relations in western Africa and the ongoing mission of converting Muslims to the Christian faith. In 1434, after the Portuguese had made some fifteen unsuccessful attempts, a squire by the name of Gil Eannes (on his second attempt) managed to pass the Cape Bojador, south of the Canaries, demystifying the existence of a 'sea of darkness' beyond the dreaded cape. Though Henry was the intellectual and financial force behind the explorations, ironically he did not participate in these voyages. He died in Sagres on the 13 November 1460 at the age of sixty-six.

Kathryn Bishop-Sanchez

LITERARY WORKS
Antunes, António Lobo [1988] (2002), *The Return of the Caravels: A Novel*, trans. Gregory Rabassa, New York: Grove Press.
Camões, Luís de [1552] (1952), *The Lusiads*, trans. William C. Atkinson, Harmondsworth and New York: Penguin.
Pessoa, Fernando [1934] (1992), *Message*, trans. Jonathan Griffin, intro. Helder Macedo, London: Menard Press.

HISTORIES
Boxer, Charles R. [1969] (1973), *The Portuguese Seaborne Empire 1415–1825*, Harmondsworth and New York: Penguin.
Elbl, Ivana (1991), 'Man of his Time (and Peers): A New Look at Henry the Navigator', *Luso-Brazilian Review* (winter) 28 (2): 73–89.
Russell, P. E. (1984), *Prince Henry the Navigator: The Rise and Fall of a Culture Hero*, Oxford: Clarendon Press.
Ure, John (1977), *Prince Henry the Navigator*, London: Constable.
Verlinden, Charles (1995), 'Prince Henry in Modern Perspective as Father of the "Descobrimentos"', in George D. Winius (ed.), *Portugal the Pathfinder*, Madison, WI: Hispanic Seminary of Mediaeval Studies, pp. 81–8.

Historiography

Portugal is often considered to be the oldest nation in Europe, dating its political existence from the moment when its first King, Dom Afonso Henriques, asserted the Portuguese county's independence from his mother and the Leonese and Castilian kingdom to which it then owed vassalage. The precise date of the nation's inception varies between 1139, 1143 and 1179 depending on whose recognition is deemed to be required for independence to come into effect (that of the young king, his Leonese relatives or the papacy, respectively). The earliest texts of Portuguese history, dating from the twelfth century, were collected and published by one of the most influential nineteenth-century historians, Alexandre Herculano, in his *Portugaliae Monumenta Historica* (1856). These include various fragments celebrating the feats of Portugal's first king that were transcribed in the Monastery of Santa Cruz in Coimbra and in the Abbey of Alcobaça. Their main ideological purpose was to assert the territorial independence of Portugal from its more powerful neighbour.

The *Chronicon Conimbricense*, dating from the early thirteenth century, begins to manifest an interest in the so-called 'reconquest' of the Iberian peninsula from the Moors. Several other chronica from the era have survived, including the *Chronicon Lamecense* and the *Chronicon Laurbanense*. The *Coroniqua de como Dom Payo Correa Mestre de Santiago de Castella Tomou este Reino do Algarve ao Moros*, published by Frei Joaquim de Santo Agostinho in 1792, and then later by Herculano, dates from the reign of Dom Dinis (1279–1325), and tells of the 'reconquest' of the southern parts of Portugal during the troubled reign of Dom Sancho II (1223–48) and his successor and effective deposer, Dom Afonso

III (1248–79). The *Breve Chronicon Alcobacense* dates from the fourteenth century and touches on the reign of Dom Afonso IV (1325–57), who is most remembered in the Portuguese imaginary for his execution, for reasons of political expediency, of Inês de Castro, the lover of his son and successor, Dom Pedro.

The fourteenth century saw the rise of hagiographies, principally from the monastic school in Alcobaça. A key event in the historiography of Portugal was King Dom Dinis' decision to have government documentation written in Portuguese. Another key event, dating from Dom Afonso IV's reign, was the edition in Portuguese of the *Crónica Geral de Espanha*, in 1344, a text inspired by the thirteenth-century text of the same name, which Alfonso X (the Wise) had commissioned. Luís Filipe Lindley Cintra (1951) considers this Portuguese text to mark the beginning of Portuguese historiography.

Often considered to be Portugal's first historian, Fernão Lopes (c. 1380–c. 1459) became the royal archiver and chronicler in 1434, a position created by Dom Duarte, who reigned from 1433 to 1438. Fernão Lopes held the post for the next twenty years. Part of his mandate was to write chronicles of the lives of previous kings. The royal chronicler became an essential part of the legitimisation of Portugal's second dynasty (the House of Aviz), which had come to power after two years of civil war in 1385. The civil war had been triggered because of a fear of Spanish influence over the Portuguese crown should the daughter of Dom Fernando accede to the throne. Eventually, the illegitimate son of Dom Pedro, João of Aviz (later Dom João I) was declared King. Fernão Lopes wrote histories of Dom Pedro and Dom Fernando, the two last kings of the previous dynasty, and of Dom João I, the founder of the House of Aviz, in such a way as to make João I appear to be the legitimate heir of Pedro, as Macedo and Gil (1998) have pointed out. Fernão Lopes thus provides a fascinating fifteenth-century example of how contemporaneous ideological needs inform the way history comes to be written.

Gomes Eanes de Zurara (c. 1410–74) succeeded Fernão Lopes as royal chronicler in 1454. He had already written an account of the Portuguese invasion of Ceuta (*Crónica da Tomada de Ceuta* [1449]), and one of the life of Prince Henry the Navigator (*Crónica dos Feitos do Infante Dom Henrique* [1453]). His account of Portugal's maritime activity up until 1453 was published under the title *Crónica dos Feitos da Guiné*. His chronicles changed the conception of the Portuguese nation away from an inward-looking consolidation of the royal house towards describing a dream of discovery and imperial expansion. Portugal was redefined in its historiography as an imperial nation in its own right rather than a nation born out of conflict with its more powerful neighbour.

A series of less celebrated chroniclers including Vasco Fernandes de Lucena succeeded Zurara to the prestigious post, which included responsibility for the collections at the Torre do Tombo, still one of Portugal's most important archives. Frei João Álvares, never a royal chronicler, was the unfortunate Infante Dom Fernando's confessor and confidant, and as such, wrote *Trautado da Vida e Feitos do Muito Vertuoso Sor Iffante Dom Fernando*, an account of the prince's capture and eventual death in 1443 in Fêz, North Africa.

The sixteenth century saw a still more marked shift towards the historical narration of the events of the imperial expansion. In particular, there were several celebrations of the discovery of the sea route to India as well as the fascinating and unique document, Pedro Vaz de Caminha's letter to Dom Manuel, dating from 1500, in which he relates to the Portuguese monarch the 'discovery' of what would become Brazil. João de Barros (c. 1496–1570) was contracted by royal authority to write about Portuguese activity in the Orient, something he did following the classical model of the *décadas*, of which he published three in his lifetime, with one published posthumously. These *décadas*, as their name suggests, related in ten volumes the occurrences over ten years in Portuguese Asia. His first *década* covered the feats of the Portuguese explorer Vasco da Gama. His style and interests were influenced by the Renaissance, and he was part of a concerted and ideologically loaded glorification of Portuguese greatness through imperial expansion.

Considered by Joaquim Veríssimo Serrão as one of Portugal's greatest historians of the sixteenth century, Fernão Lopes de Castanheda wrote the *História do Descobrimento e Conquista da Índia pelos Portugueses*, a multi-volume work the first part of which was published in Coimbra in 1551. Dealing with many of the same events as João de Barros, Castanheda's work predates that of Barros by a year. Gaspar Correia's *Lendas da Índia* is further surviving evidence of a sixteenth-century obsession with the discovery of the sea route to India, although the manuscript was itself only published in the second half of the nineteenth century. An interesting thing to note about the way the histories were written at the time is the extent to which they celebrated the nation as the hero, and not so much particular people (although individuals such as Vasco da Gama are singled out for praise). This is also a trait of Luís de Camões' epic celebration of the discovery of the sea route to India, *The Lusiads*. In it, it is the Portuguese nation that assumes the mantle of the hero. One of Camões' friends, Diogo do Couto (1542–1616), was named royal chronicler by Felipe II in 1595, one of the three Spanish monarchs to rule Portugal following the disaster of Alcácer Quibir and the death of Dom Sebastião. Couto continued writing *décadas*, and died in the Orient. His ironic tone contrasted with the epic tone of both Camões and Barros.

The most famous chronicler of the disaster of Alcácer Quibir, the battle in North Africa where Portugal lost its young and heirless king, Dom Sebastião, resulting in the Spanish takeover of the Portuguese throne for a period of sixty years, was Jerónimo de Mendonça. He wrote *Jornada de África*, an account of the military catastrophe that has been a principal source for subsequent literary reflections on the demise of the boy king, as well as contemporary literary rewritings such as Manuel Alegre's 1989 novel by the same name, which recounts the twentieth-century war for independence in Angola through a prism that includes the characters in Mendonça's original history.

Under the Spanish domination, one of the most important sources of a specifically Portuguese historiography was the Abbey of Alcobaça. Throughout the seventeenth century, a long succession of monks contributed to the huge opus, *Monarchia Lusitana* (the first part was actually published in 1597; the second part in 1609; and subsequent volumes followed throughout the century, including after the restoration of the Portuguese throne in 1640). One of its aims was to give an account of the history of the Portuguese nationality at a time of occupation by a foreign power, and in particular, using the Portuguese language at a time when Spanish was in the ascendancy. These 'monkish historians', as Charles Boxer (1969) terms them, were primarily responsible for the propagation of the belief that Christ appeared to Portugal's first King, Dom Afonso Henriques, at Ourique.

The eighteenth century saw a resurgence in Portuguese historiography, after the end of the Spanish occupation in the previous century. This was principally through the Royal Academy of History which was founded in 1720 by Dom João V, and was mandated to collect official documents. The academy folded in 1736, and was only reconfigured in 1940, in the heyday of Salazar's New State, as the Portuguese Academy of History. In the eighteenth century, memoirs and histories replaced chronicles as the mainstay of historiography. There was an increased interest in the study of Portuguese kings, particularly Dom Sebastião.

The nineteenth century saw the rise of Romanticism in Portugal, with its concerns for a national past and mediaeval essence. The triumph of liberalism in Portugal after years of civil war affected the ways in which history was written. The key figure of Portuguese history at the time was Alexandre Herculano (1810–77). He undertook a project to understand Portuguese history as a process of community formation and nation-building. Often considered Portugal's greatest historian, he was from a humble background and was self-taught. He fought the rise of absolutism in Portugal, and spent periods in exile in France and England. He essentially founded history as an academic discipline in Portugal, and wrote a monumental multi-volume work, *História de Portugal*, the first volume of which was published in 1846. He also wrote historical novels, including *Eurico, o Presbítero*, which celebrated the source of Portuguese greatness in the mediaeval age. His histories begin a profound questioning of the Portuguese imperial project.

The next great Portuguese historian, and the one who is often accused of writing a pessimistic portrait of the nation and its imperial history, was Oliveira Martins (1845–94). Linked to the Realist movement, Hegel's dialectism, positivism and socialist ideals, Oliveira Martins was damning of the results of Portuguese expansionism, and the nation's inability to accept a fate befitting its size. He rooted Portugal's loss of greatness in the disaster of Alcácer Quibir, and dated the nation's decline from the day Dom Sebastião was slain on the beaches of Africa.

Of the several serious historians of Portugal in the English language from the twentieth century, Charles Boxer stands out for both his prolific output and the rigour of his method. Among the first to question Portugal's claim to be an imperial paradise of racial harmony, particularly during the twentieth-century dictatorship of the New State, Boxer incurred the wrath of the Salazar régime, a credit to his scholarship. Other important English-language scholars include Kenneth Maxwell, whose work on the eighteenth-century enlightened dictator, Pombal, has become seminal, as has his study of the transition of Portugal from dictatorship to modern democracy in the 1970s. David Birmingham's and Gerald Bender's works on Angola, and Malyn Newitt's history of Mozambique, are key references that engage with the legacies of Portugal's colonialism in Africa. Patrick Chabal's edited volume on the history of postcolonial lusophone Africa is also an invaluable resource.

Phillip Rothwell

Literary Works

Alegre, Manuel (1989), *Jornada de África: Romance de Amor e Morte do Alferes Sebastião*, Lisbon: Dom Quixote.
Herculano, Alexandre (1980), *Eurico, o Presbítero*, Porto: Porto Editora.
Macedo, Helder and Fernando Gil (1998), *Viagens do Olhar: Retrospecção, Visão e Profecia no Renascimento Português*, Porto: Campo das Letras.

Histories

Bender, Gerald J. (1978), *Angola under the Portuguese: The Myth and the Reality*, Berkeley, CA: University of California Press.
Birmingham, David (1999), *Portugal and Africa*, New York: St Martin's Press.
— (2006), *Empire in Africa: Angola and its Neighbors*, Athens, OH: Ohio University Press.
Boxer, Charles (1969), *The Portuguese Seaborne Empire 1415–1825*, Harmondsworth: Penguin Books.
Caminha, Pedro Vaz de [1500] (1938), 'Letter to King Manuel', in William Brooks Greenlee (ed. and trans.), *The Voyage of Pedro Álvarez Cabral to Brazil and India from Contemporary Documents and Narratives*, London: Hakluyt Society, pp. 1–33.
Castanheda, Fernão Lopes de (1979), *História do Descobrimento e Conquista da Índia pelos Portugueses*, Porto: Lello.

Cintra, Luís Filipe Lindley (ed.) (1951), *Crónica Geral de Espanha de 1344*, Lisbon: n.p.

Chabal, Patrik (ed.) (2002), *A History of Postcolonial Lusophone Africa*, Bloomington, IN: Indiana University Press.

Herculano, Alexandre (1980), *História de Portugal*, Lisboa: Ulmeiro.

Lopes, Fernão (1979), *Crónica do Senhor Rei Dom Fernando Nono Rei destes Regnos*, Porto: Civilização.

— (1980), *Crónica de D. João I*, Lisbon: Seara Nova.

Maxwell, Kenneth (1995a), *Pombal: Paradox of the Enlightenment*, Cambridge: Cambridge University Press.

— (1995b), *The Making of Portuguese Democracy*, Cambridge: Cambridge University Press.

Newitt, Malyn (1981), *Portugal in Africa: The Last Hundred Years*, London: Hurst.

— (1995), *A History of Mozambique*, Bloomington, IN: Indiana University Press.

Prestage, Edgar (trans. and ed.) (1928), *The Chronicles of Fernao Lopes and Gomes Eannes de Zurara*, Watford: Voss and Michael.

Serrão, Joaquim Veríssimo (1962), *História Breve da Historiografia Portuguesa*, Lisbon: Verbo.

Zurara, Gomes Eanes de (1966), *Chronicle of the Discovery and Conquest of Guinea*, trans. Charles R. Beazley and Edgar Prestage, New York: Burt Franklin.

Independence Movements (Azores and Madeira)

When talking about the independence movements in the archipelagos of the Azores and Madeira, one must also reference the autonomous movements, as they are inextricably linked. However, it should be pointed out that it was in the aftermath of the 'Carnation Revolution' in Portugal that organised independence movements in the Azores and Madeira emerged. These were, nevertheless, linked not only to attempts at autonomy in both archipelagos since the 1820s, but they also reflected the global political anxieties of the 1970s.

Both the Azores and Madeira were strategic posts in the Portuguese colonial enterprise since their discovery and settlement in the early 1500s, providing Atlantic ports as well as marketable goods, such as wheat and wine, which raised revenue for the Portuguese crown. The island economies developed in such a way that the archipelagos depended on the importation of materials, such as foodstuffs, provoking an over-dependence on imports. Their isolation, compounded by food shortages and underdevelopment, alongside the taxation demands of the Portuguese mainland, meant that, from the nineteenth century onwards, a desire for some degree of administrative and political autonomy to channel the revenue generated by the archipelagos into public works, to ensure island development and survival, became a primary concern for both groups of islands. At the same time, emigration became an important escape-valve from the hardships of island life.

A limited degree of administrative autonomy had been granted in the 1830s, following a recognition of this need in the 1821 Carta Constitucional. This move also rewarded the key role that the two archipelagos had in the outcome of the civil war for the Portuguese throne. However, due to the precarious situation of the Portuguese economy, this administrative autonomy was revoked soon after. This pattern of being granted a degree of autonomy and then losing it due to the worsening political and economic crisis on the mainland would be repeated again and again until 1976, when both the Azores and Madeira were finally granted political and administrative autonomy. For instance, in 1895, the archipelagos gained a degree of self-government through the establishment of Juntas da Câmara in Funchal, Ponta Delgada, and, in 1898, in Angra do Heroísmo. However, this was taken away gradually, causing a worker's revolt in Madeira against taxation in 1931 that soon spread to the Azores. Although not independentist in character, the revolt shared the demands for autonomy and included the participation of political exiles in the archipelagos because of their opposition to the Estado Novo (New State). As a result, the little autonomy granted was taken away by the Portuguese government.

With the 1974 Carnation Revolution, both archipelagos finally saw a chance of achieving political and administrative autonomy through the process of democratisation, which resulted in the 1976 constitution. The autonomous movements had always stressed their membership of the Portuguese state when asking for political and administrative autonomy, or a degree of self-government. However, in the first few months after the Carnation Revolution, the increasing communist influence in Portuguese politics sparked off a conservative reaction in the archipelagos that mirrored events on the mainland. Two independence groups emerged – the FLA (Frente para a Libertação dos Açores), and the FLAMA (Frente para a Libertação de Madeira) – which had similar aims to the autonomous movements, but asked for the independence of the Azores and Madeira. These groups were sponsored by the CIA, encouraged by a small group of Madeiran and Azorean emigrants in the USA, who had seen that the previous autonomous attempts had not been successful and also feared a communist takeover in Portugal. These independence movements were very small and had very little support within the archipelagos. They should be understood in the context of the events of the Cold War. The USA wanted to safeguard their presence in the archipelagos. Since World War II, Portugal had allowed the USA to have military bases in the Azores. The threat of a communist takeover disappeared as the process of democracy solidified in Portugal. The approval of the 1976 constitution granted the level of autonomy that both archipelagos desired and that has been maintained until today. As a result, the independence movements disappeared almost overnight.

Carmen Maria Ramos Villar

HISTORIES

Aldritch, Robert and John Connell (1998), *The Last Colonies*, Cambridge: Cambridge University Press.

Melo Bento, Carlos (1993), *História dos Açores*, vol.1, Ponta Delgada: Empresa Gráfica Açoreana.

Mendonça, Luís (2000), *História dos Açores. Visão Geral (Sécs. XV–XX)*, Angra do Heroísmo: Nova Gráfica Ltd.

Nepamuceno, Rui (1994), *As Crises de Subsistência na História da Madeira*, Lisbon: Caminho.

Reis Leite, José Guilherme (1990), *Sobre a Autonomia dos Açores*, Ponta Delgada: Singo.

The Liberation Wars and Decolonisation in Portuguese-Speaking Africa

PORTUGAL IN AFRICA: A SPECIAL CASE?

Much of the debate around Portugal's African Empire – and its disintegration – is predicated on its uniqueness. Both pro- and anti-imperialists have argued that Portuguese Africa was in its imperial philosophy, anti-colonial ideology (and, of course, language) fundamentally different from the other European empires. In the twentieth century, Africa provided Portugal with a sense of national destiny which transcended its relative insignificance within Europe.

The principal philosopher of this 'Lusotropical' vision was the Brazilian writer Gilberto Freyre who in the 1940s and 1950s wrote of the quality of the Portuguese language itself as the essence of a unique *pax lusitania*. His best-known work, *O Mundo que os Português Criou* (1940) was enthusiastically adopted by the authoritarian Estado Novo (New State) of António de Oliveira Salazar as a semi-official statement of the country's imperial mission. Whatever mystical qualities may or may not have inhered in the Portuguese language, it had a major role in maintaining the separateness of the lusophone territories in Africa from their anglophone and francophone neighbours.

This separateness was deepened by the uniquely centralising character of Portugal's administrative and social policies in Africa. By linguistic necessity, the 'assimilated' élite from which the first generation of revolutionary leaders came, had their higher education in Portugal. There, they mixed not just with each other, but with Portuguese dissidents as well. This gave a unique tone to nationalism in lusophone Africa, linking it to anti-régime forces in the metropolis in a way wholly absent from the experience of the nationalist movements in British, French and Belgian Africa. Ironically, of course, this was a real but wholly unintended manifestation of the 'pluricontinentalism' that lay at the heart of Portugal's imperial philosophy.

Portugal was also unique among the European imperialists in Sub-Saharan Africa in its willingness to fight protracted colonial wars. Between 1961 and 1964 guerrilla campaigns began in the three continental territories of Angola, Guinea-Bissau and Mozambique and continued with varying degrees of intensity until the overthrow of the colonialist régime in Lisbon in the military coup of April 1974. Why did Portugal fight these wars? By most measures it was anything but a rational policy. Britain and France, both far better equipped to maintain Sub-Saharan empires by force, had acknowledged the winds of change in Africa by 1960 and planned their formal exits and even the parameters of their postcolonial relationships. Belgium, at the first suggestion of nationalist agitation in the Congo, arranged a hasty departure. Yet Portugal, itself virtually a Third World country with an impoverished underdeveloped economy and archaic social structure, opted to fight it out. Two explanations for this evident irrationality have been suggested.

By its own lights, Portugal did not have an 'empire' or even 'colonies'. From the early 1950s Portugal insisted that its African and other territories were 'overseas provinces' (*províncias ultramarinas*). In part this was a (wholly unsuccessful) device to divert international pressure, particularly from the United Nations, for movement towards colonial self-determination. But in part, too, it was a statement of the imperial philosophy outlined earlier. 'Independence' for Angola or Mozambique was, in this formulation, as meaningless as 'independence' for Lisbon or the Algarve. All were integral parts of the 'nation'. The presence of perhaps three quarters of a million European settlers in these African territories gave added force to this claim. For Portugal, therefore, the wars were not about confronting colonial uprisings but rather formed a single crusade to maintain the integrity of the nation.

In contrast to this explanation rooted in the irrationality of imperial delusion, the alternative interpretation of Portugal's determination to cling on in Africa suggests a 'rational' response to a fundamentally impossible set of circumstances. This view is rooted in neo-Marxist 'dependency theory'. Put briefly, it suggests that the African wars were an inevitable consequence of the fact that Portugal could not decolonise because it could not 'neo-colonise'. In this perspective, decolonisation by Britain, France and even Belgium was largely empty of economic meaning. The flags over their colonies could change without threatening their continued economic domination and control of the new 'independent' states. The structures of exploitation were in place and were strong enough to survive such essentially superficial political change. But Portugal had no such economic power. It was forced to retain formal control in its African territories precisely because of its own economic weakness, not in spite of it, as the necessary price of any economic advantage from Africa.

Wherever the balance lies in these alternative (though not necessarily mutually exclusive) interpretations, the wars that they set out to explain contributed to the sense of the exceptionalism of Portuguese Africa. For the African nationalists in the different lusophone territories the duration of these wars, along with a shared, loosely Marxist ideology (and the unifying pressure of the Portuguese language) generated a high level of mutual support. A joint co-ordinating body was set up, for example, which aided the advance of their case throughout and beyond Africa. All of this helped embed the idea of a single historic struggle in lusophone Africa while disguising the different origins and directions of the liberation movements in each territory.

ANGOLA: JOIA DA COROA

By general consensus, Angola was the jewel in Portugal's imperial crown. It had by far the largest number of European settlers (nearly half a million by the early 1970s). It also had enormous economic potential. Rich agricultural land provided the original attraction to settlers, but by the 1960s off-shore oil promised huge future wealth. Angola's cities, particularly the capital, Luanda, were diverse, culturally sophisticated centres which were in some respects more reminiscent of Latin America than Sub-Saharan Africa.

This cosmopolitanism was a factor in the development of the nationalist challenge, or at any rate one strand of it. The Popular Movement for the Liberation of Angola (MPLA) which launched the first of two separate attacks against Portuguese power at the beginning of 1961, was an urban-based organisation, led by mixed race (*mestiço*) intellectuals such as Agostinho Neto (independent Angola's first President) and Mário Andrade. It had been established in 1956 as an outgrowth of the Angolan Communist Party which itself had been founded as a cell of the Portuguese Party in the late 1940s. The MPLA's symbolic targets in 1961 were the installations of the secret police in the capital, and over the years its power base expanded among the Mbundu people who formed the greater part of the industrial working class of the Luanda region. From the outset, then, the MPLA was urban and internationalist in its political perspectives and affinities.

In March 1961, a few weeks after the MPLA action, a quite distinct strand of nationalist resistance ignited in the northern part of the country. There the Bakongo people, who provided the main workforce in the plantation economy of the region, launched a bloody uprising against the local Portuguese colonists. The initial outburst was largely spontaneous, but the movement which emerged from it evolved during the early 1960s into the National Front for the Liberation of Angola (FNLA). The FNLA was led by Holden Roberto who, reflecting the cross-border distribution of the Bakongo, was related by marriage to the Zairean dictator Mobutu Sese Seko. Portugal's initial brutal repression of these rebellions focused world attention on the anachronistic character of its imperial policies just at the time when elsewhere in Africa decolonisation was building an unstoppable momentum.

This fragmented armed struggle continued sporadically throughout the 1960s, but its initial intensity was not sustained. Despite the pronouncements of the guerrillas themselves (and the wishful thinking of their foreign supporters) the colonial state was never under critical threat in Angola. Fighting was desultory and restricted to sparsely populated regions. The most significant developments in fact took place within the divided nationalist movement itself. In 1966 Jonas Savimbi broke away from Roberto to form the National Union for the Total Independence of Angola (UNITA). Savimbi was from Angola's largest ethnic group, the Ovimbundu, who populate the country's central plateau, and he resented the Bakongo domination of the FNLA. His own movement was not at first a notable military success. While the MPLA had some support from the Soviet bloc and the FNLA could rely on supplies from Zaire (and, at least for a time, sympathy in Washington), UNITA had no foreign friends at the outset. The broader anti-colonial struggle was also vitiated by internal ideological and personality splits in the MPLA. Consequently, when the situation changed dramatically in Lisbon in 1974 there was little immediate sense of urgency over Angola. Day-to-day life, which for the greater part of the population had been largely untouched by the guerrilla war, initially continued much as before. Much more pressing concerns in other parts of Africa seemed to demand immediate attention from Lisbon.

For Angola, however, the interregnum was to prove a preliminary to sustained disaster. A joint agreement for the creation of a power-sharing government after independence was reached in January 1975, but it disintegrated within weeks. Portugal, desperate to extricate itself from the crisis – and unable to influence it in any significant sense – was determined to withdraw by the agreed date of November 1975. This left the MPLA in control of Luanda and Angola in a state of civil war.

Guinea-Bissau: the 'Furnace'

Uppermost in the African priorities of the Portuguese régime after April 1974 was Guinea-Bissau. The smallest of Portugal's mainland African colonies, Guinea had no settler community and provided virtually no economic benefit to the metropolis. But the war there posed the most sustained and serious challenge to Lisbon from its outbreak in 1963 until the 1974 revolution. Indeed, the very roots of that revolution could be traced back to this small west African territory.

The dominating personality of the liberation struggle in Guinea-Bissau was Amílcar Cabral. Significantly, Cabral himself was not Guinean, but a *mestiço* from the Cape Verde islands. The movement which he founded in 1956 and which later pursued the war against the Portuguese was the African Party for the Independence of Guinea and Cape Verde (PAIGC). The political leadership of the PAIGC was in fact largely Cape Verdean. The lower levels of the colonial bureaucracy had been occupied in large part by Cape Verdeans who thus formed an imported middle class in Guinea. As with the MPLA in Angola (in the formation of which Cabral himself had a hand), this *mestiço* intelligentsia constructed a liberation movement which was open to external ideological influences and adept at mobilising international support. Inevitably, though, ethnic tensions emerged in the movement between the African Guineans who fought the war and the Cape Verdeans who provided the political direction.

These tensions would lead, at the beginning of 1973, to the murder of Cabral himself. This did not, however, affect the pace of the war. In contrast to the campaigns in the other African territories, the intensity of the struggle in the forests and swamps of Guinea was unrelenting and continued largely unaffected by internal divisions within the PAIGC. To the Portuguese conscripts dispatched to fight there, Guinea was simply *o forno* (the furnace). Crucially, not only was the war in Guinea the fiercest in Africa, it was also, at least to those fighting it, the most pointless. The defence of Guinea, apparently against all logic, was both a statement of Portugal's 'pluricontinental' imperial policy and its nemesis. Guinea confronted the Lisbon régime with a critical dilemma. To allow it to slip from the 'Portuguese space' would be to breach the wall of imperial integrity. But the cost of maintaining it was, finally, the disintegration of the African Empire as a whole.

In September 1973, just a few months after Cabral's death, the PAIGC made a unilateral declaration of independence based on its control of 'liberated zones' and the restriction of the Portuguese to a few towns and fortified installations. To the fury of the Lisbon régime, a large majority of the United Nations General Assembly accepted the legitimacy of the new 'state'. Unsurprisingly, therefore, the post-coup administration in Lisbon sought urgently to resolve the Guinean situation. After a difficult series of talks, Guinea-Bissau's independence was formally recognised in September 1974. The one 'concession' that the Portuguese were able to secure from the PAIGC was the uncoupling of Cape Verde from the arrangement. There would be no bi-territorial state in the short term, and Cape Verde became independent in its own right the following year.

Mozambique: Relentless Advance

Mozambique was the last of the three main Portuguese territories in Africa to begin its armed struggle. The extent and impact of the fighting in Mozambique lay between the relative ineffectiveness of that in Angola and the intensity of that in Guinea-Bissau. The war in Mozambique began in 1964 with attacks on Portuguese government posts in the remote northern part of the country. These were mounted by the Front for the Liberation of Mozambique (FRELIMO). FRELIMO had emerged with the encouragement of Tanzania from a collection of smaller nationalist groupings and was led initially by Eduardo Mondlane, another urban intellectual. Its war effort benefited from the use of safe bases across the border in Tanzania where it had its headquarters, just as the PAIGC had its original base in independent Guinea-Conakry and the MPLA and FNLA had theirs in Congo-Brazzaville and Zaire respectively.

But like its sister movements, FRELIMO was also subject to considerable internal tensions, which contributed to Mondlane's assassination in somewhat mysterious circumstances in 1969. The schisms in FRELIMO were partly regional (with northern 'fighters' resentful at southern-dominated leadership) and partly ideological. As in Guinea, however, the armed struggle in Mozambique was not set back by the inter-factional violence. Mondlane was succeeded by Samora Machel who redoubled FRELIMO's commitment to Marxism. On the eve of the Lisbon coup FRELIMO, having survived a series of major Portuguese counter-offensives in the early 1970s, had extended the war southwards to threaten the showpiece Cabora Bassa hydro-electric scheme in the centre of the country and had come within striking distance of major urban centres.

Like the PAIGC in Guinea, FRELIMO showed no inclination to negotiate anything short of total independence with the new régime in Lisbon. In truth, of course, Portugal was in no position to resist this, having wholly lost the military initiative in Africa and now being forced to grapple with the barely manageable forces of revolutionary change in Portugal itself. Consequently, the People's Republic of Mozambique came into being in June 1975.

Portuguese-Speaking Africa: Still 'Special'?

The 'exceptionalism' of Portuguese imperialism in Africa, long conventional wisdom, has recently come under question. Now after three decades of postcolonial statehood, it is argued, Angola, Mozambique, Guinea-Bissau and the island microstates of Cape Verde and São Tomé e Príncipe should be seen in their African and regional contexts and not as members of a special category defined primarily by their shared imperial history. At the beginning of the twenty-first century, Angola is primarily a regional power in West Central Africa rather than a former Portuguese colony. Mozambique is part of the southern African region and surrounded by anglophone states. It is undergoing a form of linguistic Darwinism in which Portuguese may eventually be displaced by English (a process accelerated by Mozambique's Commonwealth membership). Guinea-Bissau has felt the same post-imperial magnetic force, though the attracting pole there has been francophone rather than anglophone.

For contemporary Portugal this process of dispersal has been difficult to come to terms with. There have been various attempts to nurture a post-imperial special relationship with the African territories, usually built around the Portuguese language. These, however, have had only limited success. The legacy of the long and destructive colonial wars and the post-independence convulsions that afflicted all three mainland territories have not been easily overcome. Moreover, Portugal has lacked the diplomatic and economic 'purchasing power' which has helped the other former imperial powers secure good postcolonial relationships. Colonial war on three fronts, therefore, may prove to have been the final manifestation of lusophone exceptionalism.

Norrie MacQueen

HISTORIES

Birmingham, D. (1992), *Frontline Nationalism in Angola and Mozambique*, London: James Currey.
Davidson, B. (1972), *In the Eye of the Storm: Angola's People*, Harmondsworth: Penguin.
— (1981), *No Fist is Big Enough to Hide the Sun: The Liberation of Guiné and Cabo Verde – Aspects of an African Revolution*, London: Zed Books.
MacQueen, N. (1997), *The Decolonization of Portuguese Africa: Metropolitan Revolution and the Dissolution of Empire*, London: Longman.
—— (1999), 'Portugal's First Domino: 'Pluricontinentalism' and Colonial War in Guiné-Bissau, 1963–1974', *Contemporary European History* 8 (2): 209–30.
Marcum, J. (1969), *The Angolan Revolution, Volume 1: The Anatomy of an Explosion, 1950–62*, Cambridge, MA: MIT Press.
— (1978), *The Angolan Revolution, Volume 2: Exile Politics and Guerrilla Warfare, 1962–76*, Cambridge, MA: MIT Press.
Munslow, B. (1983), *Mozambique: The Revolution and its Origins*, London: Longman.
Newitt, M. (1995), *A History of Mozambique*, London: Hurst.

Lusophone African Literature during Colonial Rule

In the early fifteenth century the Portuguese became the first Europeans to reach Sub-Saharan Africa. As a consequence, from West Africa through the offshore Cape Verde islands and eventually on the African east coast, Portuguese became the first European language with which native Africans had contact. Portuguese-based pidgins and Creoles were spoken by many Africans, including slaves taken to the Caribbean and the Americas. Early on there were also acculturated Africans who spoke and were literate in standard Portuguese. An outstanding example is that of Memba-a-Nzinga, who served from 1506 until 1540 as King of the Bakongo, an ethnic group native to the Congo-Angola region. In the early 1520s, using his Christian name, Afonso I, the Bakongo monarch wrote, in standard Portuguese, several letters to Dom Manuel, the King of Portugal. These letters, although friendly, complained of the immorality of Portuguese slave traders. With respect to literature per se, the renowned German Africanist, Janheinz Jahn, reveals in *Neo-African Literature: A History of Black Writing* that Afonso Álvares, who was born in Portugal to an African mother and a European father, wrote poems in Portuguese, three of which first appeared in print between 1613 and 1639. This revelation led Jahn to state that Álvares was probably the first person of African descent to write literary works in a European language.

In his historical study Jahn seeks to come to terms with what constitutes black writing and African literature. There are indeed numerous definitional concerns, with respect to individual works and a given literary corpus, based on language, race, ethnicity, nationality and a number of other categorisations. In considering what constitutes lusophone African literature, as well as who qualifies as one who produces literary works of, and not just about Angola, Cape Verde, Guinea-Bissau, Mozambique, and São Tomé and Príncipe, we deal, in the sections that follow, with several pertinent issues. By the mid-to late 1800s in the urban centres of the Portuguese colonies in Africa, there emerged an incipient literature produced by transcultural and acculturated, if not totally assimilated, black and mixed-race intellectuals. Moreover, with an increase in the number of Portuguese settlers, there emerged, starting in the 1930s, a relatively large body of works of prose fiction authored by Europeans. Many of these authors of fictional works about Africa labelled them 'colonial novels'. Titles such as *Princesa Negra: O Preço da Civilização em África* (*Black Princess: The Price of Civilisation in Africa*, 1932), by Luís Figueira, and *Terras do Nu e do Batuque* (*Lands of Nude People and Drumming*, 1933), by António de Aragão Paiva attest to the colonists' supposed civilising mission and to the prevailing exoticism of works directed at a European readership. Under António Salazar's New State régime the rather euphemistic *literature do ultramar* (literature of the overseas territories) came to be the official label applied to novels written by Portuguese settlers and, indeed, to some works authored by members of the indigenous élites in the colonies.

The following sections devoted to the individual former colonies assess the literary works and movements that emerged starting mainly in the post-World-War-II period, but with a few predecessors as early as the late nineteenth century. Most of these writers based their works on African or at least Creole social and cultural traditions. Whether black, mixed-race or white, the majority of these writers produced works of poetry and prose fiction with a perspective of cultural revindication, social protest and, increasingly, combativeness.

ANGOLA

In the late nineteenth century, in the city of Luanda, *filhos da terra* (sons and daughters of the homeland) constituted the literary generation. Among the most noteworthy members of this indigenous élite was Joaquim Dias Cordeiro da Matta, of Kimbundu ethnicity who, in 1887, published *Delírios* (*Ecstasies*), a collection of his poems, which unfortunately is lost, as is the manuscript of a novel he apparently wrote about Nzinga Mbandi, the legendary Queen of the Mbundu people. Héli Chatelain, a Swiss Protestant missionary who encouraged black and mixed-race Angolans to revindicate traditional culture, published, in 1894, *Folk-Tales of Angola*, a collection of traditional stories. Copies of this bilingual Kimbundu and English collection are still available. But it was not until 1934 that the first Angolan novel by a black or mixed-race author appeared. Its author was António Assis

Júnior; his *O Segredo da Morta: Romance de Costumes Angolanos* (*The Dead Woman's Secret: A Novel of Angolan Customs*) is considered by many to be Angola's first important fictional re-creation, in Portuguese, of indigenous cultural traditions.

Among other significant precursors or, according to some, founders of an authentic Angolan literature, is Castro Soromenho. Born in Mozambique to Portuguese parents, but raised from the age of one in rural Angola, during the 1950s and 1960s Soromenho authored several nativistic novels and collections of short stories in which, without being patronising or indulging in exotic depictions, he portrays local Bantu social and cultural traditions. Another significant writer is Tomás Vieira da Cruz, who was born in Portugal but spent most of his life in Angola, where he was known as the 'poet of the Mulatto muse'. A third precursor of importance is Óscar Ribas, born to a Kimbundu mother and Portuguese father, who wrote folkloric fiction that documented waning African traditions in such urban centres as Luanda.

It was, however, the founding of the Association of the Native Sons and Daughters of Angola in 1951, and the appearance of the first issue of *Mensagem* (*Message*), the group's cultural journal, that led to the formation of a co-ordinated literary movement. The founders and collaborators of this movement and journal were Viriato da Cruz, Mário Pinto de Andrade, Alda Lara, António Cardoso, António Jacinto, Mário António, João Abel, Antero Abreu, Henrique Abranches, Henrique and Mário Guerra, Tomás Jorge Vieira da Cruz, Arnaldo Santos, Boaventura Cardoso, Luandino Vieira and Agostinho Neto, the last of these being, of course, the liberation leader and poet who would become Angola's first President. Indeed, most of these black, mixed-race and white writers were political activists and members or supporters of the Movement for the Liberation of Angola (MPLA), founded in 1956. In sum, the generation of 1950 writers produced poetry, works of prose fiction and plays that expressed cultural revindication, social protest and combativeness. These works, many of which were issued clandestinely or in exile, constitute the true beginnings of an Angolan literature.

CAPE VERDE

For a number of reasons to do with the archipelago's geographical location, its settlement, and a number of other socio-historical factors, Cape Verde early gave rise to a Creole intellectual élite. Lusophone Africa's first co-ordinated literary movement emerged in Cape Verde. In 1936, in the city of Mindelo, on the windward island of São Vicente, a group of intellectuals founded *Claridade* (*Clarity*), a journal of arts and letters, nine issues of which would appear sporadically until 1960. Manuel Lopes, the journal's first Director, authored *Os Flagelados do Vento Leste* (*Victims of the East Wind*, 1959), considered to be a classic neo-realist novel about the drought-stricken archipelago. Another *Claridade* co-founder was Baltasar Lopes (da Silva), author of *Chiquinho* (1947), Cape Verde's first major novel. Both Manuel Lopes and Baltasar Lopes, using the pen-name Osvaldo Alcântara, wrote poetry. But it was Jorge Barbosa, the journal's third co-founder, who gained fame as Cape Verde's first poet of renown with the publication, in 1935, of a collection titled *Arquipélago*.

Due in part to the archipelago's comparatively high levels of secondary-school education and literacy, and despite a population that has never exceeded its current approximately half a million inhabitants, since the 1930s there has been a relatively large number of Cape Verdean writers. Along with those cited above, the works and their authors most likely included in the emerging canon of Cape Verdean literature are the following (listed according to earliest year of publication): *O Enterro de Nhá Candinha Sena* (*Miz Candinha*

Sena's Internment, 1957), António Aurélio Gonçalves; *Horas sem Carne* (*Hours without Flesh*, 1958), João Vârio; *Noti* (*Night*, 1964), Kaoberdiano Dambará (Felisberto Vieira Lopes); *Vida Crioula* (*Creole Life*, 1967); *Contra Mar e Vento* (*Against Sea and Wind*, 1972), Teixeira de Sousa; *Pão e Fonema* (*Bread and Phoneme*, 1974), Corsino Fortes; *Kordá Kaoberdi* (*Wake Up Cape Verde*, 1974), Kwame Kondé (Francisco Fragoso).

PORTUGUESE GUINEA

Now officially Guinea-Bissau, the small former Portuguese enclave located between Senegal and the Republic of Guinea, came under the colonial administration of Cape Verde. Indeed, many of Portuguese Guinea's minor government officials and civil servants were Cape Verdeans. But although Cape Verdean Creole became the second language of many members of Guinea's five ethnic groups, less than 2 per cent of the territory's indigenous population spoke and was literate in Portuguese. Consequently, with a small, assimilated or acculturated intellectual élite and few literary works by native-born writers came into being in Portuguese Guinea, the first work of prose fiction set in traditional Guinea is *Auá: Novela Negra* (*Auá: A Black Novella*, 1934), authored by Fausto Duarte, a Cape Verdean who lived many years in Portuguese Guinea, where he served as a functionary of the colonial administration.

António Baticã Ferreira, born in 1939, the son of a tribal chieftain, is perhaps the first native-born Guinean to produce literary works in Portuguese. Ferreira, who earned a degree in medicine in Switzerland, wrote verse in French as well as Portuguese. Several of his poems composed in Portuguese, but quintessentially Guinean, have been published in anthologies of lusophone African literature. Because of the changes brought about from the late 1950s with the emergence of a small but intense group of native-born militants under the leadership of Amílcar Cabral, the scene was set in the then colony for a home-grown generation of committed writers who would come of age just before or after 1974, the year in which Guinea-Bissau gained its independence.

MOZAMBIQUE

Starting in the first decade of the twentieth century, an occasional poem by a black or mixed-race Mozambican appeared in a newspaper and journal in the city of Lourenço Marques (today Maputo). *Livro da Dor* (*Book of Pain*, 1925), a collection of short stories by João Albasini, published by the author, was the first book-length project by a native-born Mozambican. It was, however, in post-World-War-II Mozambique that a literature of cultural revindication and incipient social protest came into being. Starting in the 1950s, José Craveirinha had a number of his poems published in newspapers and journals. In 1964 Craveirinha, born in Lourenço Marques to a Ronga mother and Portuguese father, published *Chigubo*, the first of two collections of his poems to appear in print prior to independence. Craveirinha is, of course, among lusophone Africa's most acclaimed poets. Another groundbreaking poet of that period is Noémia de Sousa, believed to be the first black or mixed-race female poet, not only of lusophone Africa, but of all of southern Africa. Noémia de Sousa is, in fact, one of only three females, among a total of fifty-five poets from twenty-three Sub-Saharan nations and colonies, with poems published in the anthology *Modern African Poetry* (1968). Another first with respect to Mozambican works in English translation is Luís Bernardo Honwana's *Nós Matámos o Cão Tinhoso*, published in Portuguese in 1964. The translation, titled *We Killed Mangy Dog and Other Mozambique Stories* (1969), is the first work by a lusophone writer to be published in the prestigious Heinemann's African Series. Other notable contributors to a nascent national literature during the final years of colonial rule are the poets Orlando Mendes, Rui Nogar and Marcelino dos Santos. Mendes is also the author of *Portagem* (*Toll Way*, 1965), a novel on race relations often compared with the South African Alan Paton's impassioned *Cry, the Beloved Country* (1948).

In the years just prior to independence, Mozambique's literary output, much of it clandestine, was characterised by overt political themes and anti-colonial combativeness. In the early 1970s, the Front of the Liberation of Mozambique (FRELIMO), at its headquarters in exile in Tanzania, issued two editions of *Poesia de Combate* (*Poetry of Combat*). Meanwhile, in Lourenço Marques, there were intellectuals and writers, including several Euro-Mozambicans, who sympathised with, even if they were not members of the liberation movement. Two such sympathisers were Rui Knopfli, a well-known poet, and Eugénio Lisboa, who, in 1971, founded a journal titled *Caliban*, in which were published poems, stories, drama fragments and essays by engaged Mozambican writers. These writers and their works helped to set the scene for the literary movement that would surge at the end of colonial rule.

São Tomé e Príncipe
São Tomé and Príncipe's first published writers were the poets Francisco Stockler (1839–84), Caetano da Costa Alegre (1864–90), and Marcelo Veiga (1892–1976). The first author of a prose fiction work is Viana de Almeida, born in 1903. His *Maiá Poçon: Contos Africanos* (*Maiá Poçon: African Stories*, 1937) depicts life on the coffee and cacao plantations of São Tomé and Príncipe, with their post-abolition contract workers from Cape Verde and Angola.

During colonial times, the two islands' major writers lived most of their lives in Portugal. Such was the case with Costa Alegre, Marcelo Veiga and Viana de Almeida. Francisco José Tenreiro (1921–63), without a doubt São Tomé and Príncipe's most outstanding writer and intellectual of the colonial period, also lived most of his short life in Portugal. Born on the island of São Tomé to an African mother and Portuguese father, he was sent while an adolescent to live in Lisbon. In Portugal he became a university professor of geography, a government deputy (the only politician of African descent to hold such a position during the colonial era), and a poet and literary essayist. Tenreiro's posthumously published *Coração em África* (*With My Heart in Africa*, 1964) contains poems that confirm Tenreiro's reputation as a proponent of Negritude and of what some have termed Mulattotude.

Three other acclaimed São Tomé and Príncipe poets who also spent years in Portugal as well as elsewhere in Europe are Tomás Medeiros, Maria Manuela Margarido and Alda Espírito Santo. An English translation of one of Alda Espírito Santos' poems appears in *Modern African Poetry*, mentioned above. Espírito Santo also has the distinction of being a co-founder of the Association of Writers of São Tomé and Príncipe and a force behind the nation's vibrant postcolonial literary movement.

Conclusions
Lusophone African writers, their works and the literary ambience they created in their homelands unquestionably played a significant role in the colonial period, particularly during the liberation struggle. Agostinho Neto, destined to be independent Angola's first President, became a poet of international acclaim. Samora Machel, Mozambique's first President, authored a few poems, which appear in *Poesia de Combate*, mentioned above. In his teens and early twenties, Amílcar Cabral, Cape Verde's and Guinea-Bissau's famous liberation leader, wrote and published about thirty poems. There were, indeed, a goodly

number of writers among the five former colonies' political activists. Thus, in postcolonial lusophone Africa many citizens are avid readers of their new nations' literary works, and significant numbers of young people aspire to be writers.

Russell G. Hamilton

LITERARY WORKS
Burness, Don (ed. and trans.) (1989), *A Horse of White Clouds: Poems from Lusophone Africa*, Athens, OH: Ohio University.
Ellen, Maria M. (ed.) (1988), *Across the Atlantic: An Anthology of Cape Verdean Literature*, North Dartmouth, MA: Southeastern Massachusetts University.
Honwana, Luís Bernardo (1969), *We Killed Mangy-Dog and Other Mozambique Stories*, trans. Dorothy Guedes, London: Heinemann.
Moore, Gerald and Ulli Beier (eds) (1968), *Modern Poetry from Africa*, Baltimore, MD: Penguin Books.
Neto, Agostinho (1974), *Sacred Hope*, trans. Marga Holness, Dar es Salaam: Tanzania Publishing House.
Vieira, José Luandino [1964] (1980), *Luuanda: Short Stories of Angola*, trans. Tamara Bender, London: Heinemann.
Wolfers, Michael (ed. and trans.) (1979), *Poems from Angola*, London: Heinemann.

HISTORIES
Hamilton, Russell G. (1975), *Voices from an Empire: A History of Afro-Portuguese Literature*, Minneapolis, MN: University of Minnesota Press.
— (1993), 'Portuguese-Language Literature', in Oyekan Owomoyela (ed.), *A History of Twentieth-Century African Literatures*, Lincoln, NE: University of Nebraska Press, pp. 240–84.
Jahn, Janheinz (1968), *Neo-African Literature: A History of Black Writing*, New York: Grove Press.
Moser, Gerald M. (1967), 'African Literature in Portuguese: The First Written, the Last Discovered', *African Forum* 2 (4): 78–98.
Moser, Gerald M. and Manuel Ferreira (1993), *A New Bibliography of the Lusophone Literatures of Africa*, London: Hans Zell.

Lusotropicalism, Race and Ethnicity

Notwithstanding the wide spectrum of existing interpretations of the historical meaning and ideological import of Lusotropicalism, a doctrine formulated in mid-twentieth century by the Brazilian sociologist and anthropologist Gilberto Freyre, scholars of the Portuguese-speaking world tend to agree on at least two basic points: the cultural roots of Freyre's intellectual project reach deep and it continues to cast long shadows. As Miguel Vale de Almeida has argued, all the elements of Freyre's differential characterisation of Portuguese colonialism may be found in pre-existing, as well as subsequent interpretations of Portuguese identity and colonial experience, in 'social sciences and literature, in official discourses, and in commonsense identity self-representations with amazing resilience and capacity to adapt to different political situations'. Lusotropicalist notions have been deployed in such recent high-profile contexts as a book-length 'conversation' between the President of Brazil, Fernando Henrique Cardoso, and the former President and Prime

Minister of Portugal, Mário Soares (*O Mundo em Português: um diálogo*), in which the interlocutors cite and endorse unquestioningly the central tenets of Freyre's doctrine: that 'the
Portuguese created a different world' and that its distinguishing features are 'an understanding of the Other . . . an ability to accept the Other . . . and a great curiosity about the
Other'.

The basic premise of Lusotropicalism was first sketched out by Freyre in his groundbreaking account of the formation of the Brazilian society, *The Masters and the Slaves*
(1933), where he diagnosed the 'singular disposition of the Portuguese to the hybrid, slave-
exploiting colonisation of the tropics . . . to be explained in large part by the ethnic or,
better, the cultural past of the people existing indeterminately between Europe and Africa'.
Freyre, a disciple of Franz Boas (at Columbia University, 1920–2), adopted his teacher's
progressive notion of cultural relativism as the enabling basis for his theorisation of the culturally distinct Portuguese colonisation of Brazil, as well as for his postulate that the practice of racial miscegenation, endemic to Brazilian slaveholding society, rather than
branding Brazilians irrevocably with the stigma of racial pathology, was both the essence
and the strongest point of the country's identity. As he wrote, praising the 'wealth of
balanced antagonisms' he described as characteristic of Brazilian culture, 'not that there
exist in the Brazilian, as in the Anglo-American, two enemy halves: the white and the
black, the master and the slave. . . . We are two fraternizing halves that are mutually
enriched with diverse values and experiences.'

Freyre carried over his interpretation of the Brazilian slaveholding society onto the
global ground of Portuguese colonialism in a series of lectures from the late 1930s, which
were gathered, revised and published in 1940 under the title *O Mundo que o Português Criou*
(*The World the Portuguese Created*). In this work he explored more extensively his claim
that it was Portugal's culturally specific 'vocation' to relate harmoniously to other cultures
and races, in particular to Africans. However, the true founding text of Lusotropicalism was
produced as the outcome of Freyre's grand tour throughout Portugal and its overseas
colonies, which he undertook at the invitation of Salazar's régime. Lasting from August
1951 to February 1952, the voyage encompassed, in addition to various regions of Portugal,
the island of Madeira, Portuguese Guinea (now Guinea-Bissau), Cape Verde, São Tomé,
Angola, Mozambique and Goa. In 1953, Freyre published two books, *Um Brasileiro em
Terras Portuguesas* (*A Brazilian in Portuguese Lands*), a collection of lectures given during
his trip, including the one read at the Vasco da Gama Institute in Goa, in which the
concept of Lusotropicalism was for the first time fully articulated, and *Aventura e Rotina*
(*Adventure and Routine*), a diary of the voyage subtitled 'Suggestions from a Journey in
Search of Portuguese Traits of Character and Action'. Less than a decade later, the
Lusotropicalist doctrine received its definitive form with the publication of *The Portuguese
and the Tropics*, an edition sponsored by the Portuguese government that appeared simultaneously in Portuguese, in English and in French at a time when European colonial powers
were rapidly divesting themselves of their overseas possessions. In this context, the international dissemination of Freyre's Lusotropicalist writings was meant to buttress Portugal's
continuing claim to its colonies by arguing for the profoundly transculturated (to the point
of becoming organically hybrid) character of the Portuguese presence in 'the tropics'.

As in his earlier works, in *The Portuguese and the Tropics* Freyre made a distinction
between Portuguese-style colonialism and that practised by other European colonial
powers, which he articulated through the metaphor of marriage. While other Europeans
contracted 'marriages . . . of convenience' with tropical territories and their inhabitants,
unions motivated exclusively by economic interest and never by love, the Portuguese, by

contrast, espoused the tropics through a unique configuration of 'convenience achieved through love'. Although Freyre did not address directly the political context in which his remarks were being widely publicised by Salazar's régime, the inescapable implication of his arguments was that the Portuguese and the Portuguese alone had deserved to avoid the traumatic experience of being forced to divorce their colonial consorts.

Given the latter-day co-optation of Freyre's ideas by Salazar's propagandists, it is worth recalling, as Cláudia Castelo (1998) has done in her comprehensive historical account, that their initial reception by the régime in the 1930s and 1940s was anything but positive. The modes of colonial ideology dominant at the time were incompatible with Freyre's insistence on the symbiotic fusion of distinct ethnocultural elements into a new, 'Lusotropical' civilisational complex. The dissemination of European cultural values in Africa and Asia presented itself to the régime as a one-way street, a process from which Portugal and the Portuguese should emerge unaffected by the potentially harmful (and not, as for Freyre, generally beneficial) influence of the tropics. Neither was the régime's eventual endorsement of Lusotropicalist ideology in full conformity with Freyre's ideas: it elided his insistence on 'balanced antagonisms' by stressing the sameness of globally disseminated Portugueseness over any notions of opposition and difference, and it transformed his strongly eroticised vision of intercultural and interracial symbiosis into a sanitised ideal of Christian brotherhood. It should be noted, however, that directions and contradictions inherent in Freyre's own work paved the way for this revisionist appropriation. As Cristiana Bastos (1998) has shown in her comparative analysis of Lévi-Strauss' *Tristes Tropiques* and Freyre's *Aventura e Rotina*, homogenisation of the Lusotropical continuum (diametrically opposed to Lévi-Strauss' privileging of alterity) became for the Brazilian anthropologist its centrally important condition of possibility.

The most trenchant early response to the propagation of Freyre's Lusotropicalist postulates came from the pen of Charles Ralph Boxer, an eminent historian and, since 1947, Camões Professor of Portuguese at King's College London, in a series of lectures delivered in 1962 at the University of Virginia and published a year later as *Race Relations in the Portuguese Colonial Empire 1451–1825*. While mentioning Freyre in a single, tangential footnote, Boxer was devastatingly direct in his denunciation of the historical falsehood perpetrated by Salazar's régime and its allies in Portuguese academia under the mantle of Lusotropicalist utopia: from his 'readiness to mate with coloured women' it did not follow 'that the Portuguese male had no racial prejudice'; notwithstanding the existence of 'respectable Indo-Portuguese married families', it was 'obvious that the system of household and domestic slavery which obtained in Golden Goa was not conducive to a wholesome family life'; 'slaves in Brazil were treated just as harshly as they were in the English, French and Dutch West-Indian colonies'; and so on.

Given the reliance of Freyre's Lusotropicalist interpretation of Portuguese colonialism and its consequences on a vast repository of literary and historical discourses of Portuguese national identity, any summary presentation of the relationship between lusophone literatures and Lusotropicalism can point only to a small selection of canonical references and postcolonial revisions. In the poetry of Portugal's national bard, Luís de Camões, himself one of those overseas explorers who 'acted as discoverers not only with their eyes but also with their sex organs' (Freyre 1984), two texts in particular have been repeatedly put into service of Lusotropical claims: his *endechas* to the dark-skinned slave Barbara, in which the poet praises her beauty and declares that, in spite of her name and colour, she is anything but a barbarian; and the Isle of Love episode in Canto Nine of *The Lusiads*. In the latter, Vasco da Gama's sailors returning from India are received on a magic island, created by their protectress Venus, by a bevy of lovely sea nymphs whom they promptly bed and, prior to their setting sail for Portugal, also wed. The episode, with its embedded prophecy of the Portuguese dominion over the Orient (presented to Gama by his own mythical consort, the sea goddess Tethys), can, in effect, be argued to constitute the original literary enactment of the Lusotropical scenario, in which sexual engagement is constitutive of, rather than accidental to colonial possession.

Freyre himself came rather slowly and grudgingly to his enshrinement of Camões in the pantheon of exemplary figures of Lusotropicalism he assembled in *The Portuguese and the Tropics*, favouring initially another literary 'distant precursor of the science to be defined as Luso-tropicology', Fernão Mendes Pinto, the author of the posthumously published travel memoir *Peregrinação* (translated into English as *The Travels of Mendes Pinto*, 1990). What may have made Mendes Pinto uniquely predisposed to empathise with and interpret tropical otherness was, according to Freyre, his rumoured identity as a New Christian and his consequent ability to draw on a culturally hybrid amalgam of competences complementing his 'Portuguese personality': 'Jewish perspicacy, Moorish astuteness and Jesuit subtleness', the last a reference to the writer's brief stint with the Society of Jesus.

Since the demise of their country's colonial empire, many Portuguese writers have entered into a critical dialogue with the ideological legacy crystallised in the doctrine of Lusotropicalism. Violently revisionary deconstruction of Lusotropicalist shibboleths is much in evidence in António Lobo Antunes' novel of the colonial war in Angola, *South of Nowhere*, whose Portuguese title, *Os Cus de Judas* (literally, 'Judas' asshole', meaning in common parlance 'a remote, forsaken place'), points to Antunes' rewriting of Lusotropicalism's foundational ethos of promiscuous heterosexual procreativity as a scatological and sexually dissident road to nowhere. In José Saramago's novel *The Stone Raft*, Portugal's and Iberia's role in the post-imperial world order is reimagined more assertively, as the Iberian peninsula becomes detached from the European subcontinent by a freak accident of nature and eventually comes to rest in the middle of the South Atlantic, halfway between Africa and South America. At the novel's closure, all female inhabitants of the thus reterritorialised Iberia simultaneously find themselves pregnant, as their homeland is fashioned into a sort of sexual and procreative utopia reminiscent of Camões Isle of Love. By contrast, the narrative testimony of the female protagonist of Lídia Jorge's novel *The Murmuring Coast*, who accompanies her soldier husband to Mozambique in the early years of the colonial war, disturbs the familiar male-authored scenario of the Portuguese marriage with the tropics in a more radical way, by placing Portuguese women's at the same time complicitous and oppositional relationship to the colonial project squarely at the centre of the novel's field of scrutiny.

Among lusophone African explicit or implicit responses to Freyre's doctrine, the writings by Cape Verdean intellectuals of the Claridade movement (1936–60) played a particularly prominent and complex role, beginning with their enthusiastic appropriation of Freyre's perspectives on racial miscegenation and interpenetration of cultures in the Brazilian context. For example, Baltasar Lopes' essay 'Uma experiência românica nos trópicos' ('A Romanic Experience in the Tropics') (*Claridade*, 1947), concentrated on linguistic aspects of Lusotropical transculturation, whose most advanced product appeared to be Cape Verdean Creole, a new, organically whole idiom that was an unquestionable offspring of Portuguese integration in the tropics. However, Freyre's own account of Cape Verde, published in *Aventura e Rotina* following his visit to the islands in October 1951, was a largely negative narrative, imbued with a disconcertingly severe spirit of criticism, in which the generalised use of Creole as a mother tongue among the Cape Verdean population emerged as the most visible and pernicious symptom of what Freyre diagnosed as the archipelago's 'lack of cultural character'. A heated debate inevitably issued, with writers such as Lopes and Gabriel Mariano taking Freyre to task for his view of the islands, and with Lopes' *Cabo Verde Visto por Gilberto Freyre* (*Cape Verde Seen by Gilberto Freyre*, 1956) as the most extensive attempt at refuting Freyre's erroneous interpretation of Cape Verde as untrue to and unworthy of the most cherished tenets of his own doctrine.

The lusophone African writer who may be most productively read against discourses of Lusotropicalist cultural ideology is arguably the Mozambican Mia Couto, whose works foreground complex entanglements of linguistic, cultural, racial and ethnic hybridity that at the same time re-enact and dismantle master narratives of Lusotropicalism. In novels such as *A Sleepwalking Night* and short story collections such as *Voices Made Night* (to name just two of several of Couto's works available in English), the writer's paradoxically deconstructive approach to the articulation of postcolonial Mozambican identity emerges as perhaps the most comprehensive counterdiscourse of the 'empire writing back' against the centuries of Lusotropical colonialist claims that became so momentously condensed in Gilberto Freyre's work.

Anna Klobucka

LITERARY WORKS

Antunes, António Lobo (1983), *South of Nowhere*, trans. Elizabeth Lowe, New York: Random House.

Camões, Luís de (1990), *Epic and Lyric*, trans. Keith Bosley, Manchester: Carcanet.

— (2002), *The Lusiads*, trans. Landeg White, Oxford: Oxford University Press.

Couto, Mia (1990), *Voices Made Night*, trans. David Brookshaw, Oxford: Heinemann.

— (2006), *A Sleepwalking Land*, trans. David Brookshaw, London: Serpent's Tail.

Jorge, Lídia (1995), *The Murmuring Coast*, trans. Natalia Costa and Ronald W. Sousa, Minneapolis, MN: University of Minnesota Press.

Pinto, Fernão Mendes (1990), *The Travels of Mendes Pinto*, trans. Rebecca D. Catz, Chicago, IL: University of Chicago Press.

Saramago, José [1986] (1996), *The Stone Raft*, trans. Giovanni Pontiero, New York: Harvest.

HISTORIES

Almeida, Miguel Vale de (2004), *An Earth-Colored Sea: 'Race', Culture and the Politics of Identity in the Postcolonial Portuguese-Speaking World*, New York and Oxford: Berghahn Books.

Bastos, Cristiana (1998), 'Tristes trópicos e alegres lusotropicalismos: das notas de viagem em Lévi-Strauss e Gilberto Freyre', *Análise Social* XXXIII (146–7), 415–32.

Boxer, C. R. (1963), *Race Relations in the Portuguese Colonial Empire 1415–1825*, Oxford: Clarendon Press.

Cardoso, Fernando Henrique and Mário Soares (1998), *O Mundo em Português: um diálogo*, Lisbon: Gradiva.

Castelo, Cláudia (1998), '*O modo português de estar no mundo*'. *O luso-tropicalismo e a ideologia colonial portuguesa (1933–1961)*, Porto: Afrontamento.

Freyre, Gilberto (1940), *O Mundo que o Português Criou*, Rio de Janeiro: Livraria José Olympio.

— (1961), *The Portuguese and the Tropics*, trans. Helen M. D'O. Matthew and F. de Mello Moser, Lisbon: Executive Committee for the Commemoration of the Vth Centenary of the Death of Prince Henry the Navigator.

Freyre, Gilberto (1971), _The Masters and the Slaves_, trans. Samuel Putnam, rev. edn, New
    York: Alfred A. Knopf.
— (1984), _Camões: Vocação de Antropólogo Moderno?_ São Paulo: Conselho da Comunidade
    Portuguesa do Estado de São Paulo.
Needell, Jeffrey D. (1995), 'Identity, Race, Gender and Modernity in the Origins of
    Gilberto Freyre's _Oeuvre_', _American Historical Review_ 100 (Feb.) (1): 51–77.

Samora Machel

Samora Moisés Machel was leader of the Frente de Libertação de Moçambique
(FRELIMO) from 1970, and President of Mozambique from independence in 1975 until
his death in 1985. Machel was born in 1933. As a child herding cattle, Machel was familiar with stories of his grandfather who fought with the Gaza Empire's army against the
Portuguese. Machel experienced directly the humiliations and injustices of colonialism.
In his home area Portuguese settlers had forced Africans off their lands. Machel was compelled to convert to Catholicism in order to take his fourth grade school exams. He chose
to study nursing; the only other options available to Africans were the priesthood or
manual labour. Machel worked in a health centre, while studying at night to continue his
training as a nurse.

In 1961 Machel attended a meeting with Eduardo Mondlane. His engagement in political discussions led to interrogations by the Portuguese secret police, the PIDE. In 1963
Machel was informed that the PIDE intended to arrest him. He escaped through Swaziland
to Botswana, where he travelled with a group of ANC militants to Tanzania. Joining
FRELIMO, Machel opted immediately for military training. On his return from Algeria he
became responsible for establishing a military training camp in Kongwa, Tanzania. Machel
spent much time at the front as well as in training camps, and in 1966 was appointed military commander of FRELIMO. Internal divisions in FRELIMO, regarding how to achieve
independence and what kind of society to construct afterwards, intensified after the assassination of Mondlane in 1969. Machel, who was firmly against racism, regionalism and trib-
alism, was elected leader of FRELIMO in 1970.

Machel's strengths in leadership and strategy enabled FRELIMO to defeat Portugal's
major military offensive, 'Gordian Knot'. After leading Mozambique to independence in
1975, Machel supported Zimbabwe's independence struggle. He allowed ZANU to operate
from Mozambique, played a crucial role in regional and international diplomacy towards
Rhodesia, and enforced UN sanctions against Rhodesia at great economic cost to
Mozambique. The Rhodesian and Portuguese security forces collaborated in establishing
the Mozambican National Resistance (RENAMO). After Zimbabwe's independence,
support transferred to South Africa and RENAMO's destabilisation of Mozambique
increased.

During the 1980s Machel struggled to build socialism, in the face of RENAMO's
intensified destruction and brutality against Mozambique's society and economy. Despite
the 1984 N'Komati Accord of Co-operation, RENAMO continued to receive support
from South Africa, as well as Malawi. On 19 October 1986, Machel was returning
from a meeting in Zambia discussing regional security when his aeroplane crashed near
Mbuzini in South Africa, killing all but nine passengers. Investigations have indicated that the crash was organised by South African forces, with internal help from
Mozambique.

Samora Machel was a man of the people. He had deep integrity and was firmly committed to overcoming corruption and abuse of power within the government and security forces of FRELIMO. He was a committed internationalist, a skilled diplomat and gifted orator. Machel's engagement with and understanding of socialism grew out of direct experience of the liberation war, and a deep understanding of the sufferings of ordinary Mozambicans.

Branwen Gruffydd Jones

LITERARY WORKS
Machel, Samora (1974a), *Mozambique: Sowing the Seeds of Revolution*, London: Committee for Freedom in Mozambique, Angola and Guiné.
— (1974b), *A Luta Continua: Antologia de Discursos do Presidente da Frelimo*, Porto: Afrontamento.
— (1975), *The Tasks Ahead: Selected Speeches*, New York: Afro American Information Service.
— (1977), *Le Processes de la révolution democratique populaire au Mozambique: Textes du Président du Frelimo 1970–1974*, Paris: editions L'Harmattan.
Munslow, Barry (ed.) (1985), *Samora Machel: An African Revolutionary. Selected Speeches and Writings*, trans. Michael Wolfers, London: Zed Books.

HISTORIES
Bragança, Aquino de (1977), 'La longue marche de Samora', *Afrique Asie* 133.
Cabrita, João M. (2005), *A Morte de Samora Machel*, Maputo: Edições Novafrica.
Christie, Ian (1988), *Machel of Mozambique*, Harare: Zimbabwe Publishing House.
Munslow, Barry (1983), *Mozambique: The Revolution and its Origins*, London: Longman.
Sopa, António (ed.) (2001), *Samora: Homen do Povo*, Maputo: Maguezo Editores.

Eduardo Mondlane

Eduardo Chivumbo Mondlane was the leader of the Frente de Libertação de Moçambique (FRELIMO) from its foundation in 1962 until his assassination in 1969. He was also a scholar, soldier and diplomat. Born in 1920, Mondlane's childhood was spent herding livestock, but on his mother's insistence he attended school. As a child Mondlane experienced the multiple oppressions of colonialism. His older brothers fled to South Africa to avoid forced labour, while as an African and Protestant his continuation to secondary school was barred. In 1945 with help from Methodist missionaries he went to secondary school in northern Transvaal, South Africa, then started a degree at the University of Witwatersrand. He helped to found the Núcleo dos Estudantes Secundários de Moçambique (NESAM), a cultural organisation which also provided a forum for political discussion. With the introduction of apartheid, Mondlane was expelled from South Africa; he and other NESAM leaders were arrested by the Portuguese secret police, the PIDE, and interrogated. Concluding that he was a threat to colonial rule, the authorities planned to send Mondlane to study in Portugal, to isolate him from fellow Africans. Although receiving a scholarship to study in America, Mondlane initially went to Lisbon. There he met other African anti-colonialists including Agostinho Neto and Amílcar Cabral. Continual harassment from the PIDE disrupted his studies and so, accepting the scholarship, he transferred to America. He studied sociology at Oberlin University, graduating in 1953, then completed his MA and doctorate at Northwestern University. During his studies he met his wife Janet, and they married in 1956. Mondlane's work for the UN Trusteeship Council gave him experience of African independence struggles, especially that of Tanzania, and he formed a lasting friendship with Julius Nyerere. His visit to Mozambique in 1961 convinced him to join the independence struggle and so he left the UN. While teaching at Syracuse University, he maintained contact with the three Mozambican parties formed in exile. A year later he was in Tanzania. Mondlane and Nyerere were influential in convincing the parties to form one united front. FRELIMO was founded in June 1962, with Mondlane elected as President. Mondlane recognised the necessity for armed struggle, given the character of the Portuguese fascist state and colonial rule, and led FRELIMO in preparing and launching the liberation war.

Mondlane's leadership of FRELIMO emphasised the importance of maintaining unity and overcoming ethnic chauvinism and racism. He believed passionately in the role of education in personal and collective liberation. Mondlane insisted that FRELIMO's struggle was not just against Portuguese rule, but for a new postcolonial society. While familiar with many revolutionary theories and struggles, Mondlane's socialism was rooted in the specific realities of the Mozambican peoples. He was a committed internationalist, taking seriously the need to support other African and anti-imperial struggles. On 3 February 1969, Mondlane was killed by a letter bomb, organised by the PIDE, allegedly in collaboration with German intelligence officers. Mondlane would have loved a university career; instead, abandoning a comfortable life in the West, he dedicated his life to the struggle for Mozambican independence.

Branwen Gruffydd Jones

LITERARY WORKS

Mondlane, Eduardo (1956), *Ethnocentrism and the Social Definition of Race as In-Group Determinants*, MA thesis, Evanston, IL: Northwestern University Press.
— (1964), 'The Development of Nationalism in Mozambique', in E. Mondlane, *Eduardo Mondlane*, London: PANAF, pp. 139–49.
— (1968), 'Race Relations and Portuguese Colonial Policy, with Special Reference to Mozambique', *Africa Today* 15 (1): 13–18.
— (1969), *The Struggle for Mozambique*, Harmondsworth: Penguin.
— (1982), 'Participation of Students in the Struggle for National Liberation', I: 107–13; 'Christian Missions Under Test', I: 168–9; 'The Role of the Church in Mozambique', I: 170–3; 'Development of Nationalism in Mozambique', II: 15–19; 'The Tribal Question in the Advanced Stage of the Struggle', II: 119–20; 'The Evolution of FRELIMO', II: 121; 'The Point of View of the US Government', III: 49–51; in A. de Bragança and I. Wallerstein (eds), *The African Liberation Reader* (3 vols), London: Zed Press.

HISTORIES

Cruz e Silva, Teresa (1998), 'The Influence of the Swiss Mission on Eduardo Mondlane (1930–1961)', *Journal of Religion in Africa* XXVIII (2): 187–209.
Manghezi, Nadja (1999), *O Meu Coração Está nas Mãos de Um Negro: Uma História da Vida de Janet Mondlane*, Maputo: Imprensa Universitária.
Saul, John S. (2005), 'Eduardo Mondlane and the Rise and Fall of Mozambican Socialism', *Review of African Political Economy* 32 (104–5): 309–15.
Shore, Herbert (1992), 'Remembering Eduardo: Reflections on the Life and Legacy of Eduardo Mondlane', *Africa Today* 39 (1–2): 35–52.

Various Authors (1999), *Estudos Moçambicanos*, no. 16, Special Issue on Eduardo Mondlane.

Moorish Portugal

In 711, the Moors invaded the southern part of the Iberian peninsula and defeated the Visigoths who had been settled for several centuries in the region. During their conquest northward, the Moors took all the main urban settlements in what is present-day Portugal, and reached the Pyrenees in 732. Other than a few small areas, the Moors ruled in the country until well into the twelfth century. The Moors were tolerant of their Christian and Jewish subjects and racial mixing took place throughout the land, while many people converted to Islam. The Moors fortified Lisbon early on in their occupation of the territory and held out against Christian attacks for over 400 years. In 1147, Christians led by Afonso Henriques recaptured Lisbon from the Moors, and Afonso Henriques became the self-proclaimed first King of Portugal, Afonso I, controlling most of the land except the southernmost strip of Portugal, the region known as *al-Gharb*, nowadays the Algarve. It was only in 1248 that the Moors were defeated in most of this region, and in 1272 King Afonso III expelled the Moors from their last stronghold, Faro. At this point Portugal's borders, very close to the ones of today, were firmly established under Christian monarchical rule. Similar to the situation in neighbouring Spain, the Moorish influence on Portugal is deep and widespread: Moorish architecture and designs are still found throughout Portugal in the form of monuments, fountains, bullrings, palaces and beautiful geometric gardens. Innumerable Moorish castles and fortresses add drama to many a Portuguese horizon. Moorish place-names are frequent in particular in central and southern Portugal, and terms and phrases derived from Arabic are common in the Portuguese spoken today, which includes some 1,000 words, mainly nouns, of Arabic descent. The Portuguese national song the *fado* also owes much to the influence of Moorish musicians and is traditionally performed for tourists and locals in restaurants in the Lisbon quarters of Alfama and Mouraria, longstanding settlements of the Moors. The exquisite tile-work known as the *azulejos* from the Arab term *azzeliz*, which can be found throughout Portugal, was originally introduced by the Moors and remains a strong testament to their presence in the country for over five centuries.

Kathryn Bishop-Sanchez

LITERARY WORKS
Bell, Aubrey F. G. [1925] (1967), *The Oxford Book of Portuguese Verse*, Oxford: Clarendon Press.
Carvalho, Mário de [1994] (1997), *A God Strolling in the Cool of the Evening*, trans. Gregory Rabassa, Baton Rouge, LA: Louisiana State University Press.
Saramago, José [1989] (1996), *The History of the Siege of Lisbon*, trans. Giovanni Pontiero, New York: Harcourt Brace.

HISTORIES
Kennedy, Hugh (1996), *Muslim Spain and Portugal: A Political History of Al-Andalus*, London and New York: Longman.
Nicolle, David (2001), *The Moors: The Islamic West 7th–15th Century AD*, Oxford: Osprey Military.
Read, Jan [1974] (1975), *Moors in Spain and Portugal*, Totowa, NJ: Rowman and Littlefied.

MPLA: Popular Movement for the Liberation of Angola

The MPLA's narrative of its own history claims it was founded in 1956. However, some recent historical studies suggest that 1960 was actually the year when the acronym MPLA first appeared as the designation for the Angolan independence movement. It was formed by Agostinho Neto, who united a number of smaller nationalist groups in Luanda. The new movement included organisations based outside Angola, such as the Anti-Colonial Movement composed mainly of Angolan students abroad. From 1961, the MPLA engaged in an armed struggle against the Portuguese colonial régime of the New State. The movement was riven from its inception by factionalism, as well as by its competition against rival liberation groups in Angola.

In April 1974, the Carnation Revolution in Portugal ended the thirteen-year anti-colonial struggle. A coalition government, set up by the Alvor Accords in January 1975, collapsed the same year, civil war broke out, a conflict which continued on and off until 2002. The MPLA, backed by Cuba and the Soviet Union, gained control of Luanda, defeating a rival bid for Angola's capital by the FNLA (National Front for the Liberation of Angola) in July 1975. In November of the same year, the MPLA declared Angola's independence unilaterally, as a one-party state. The FNLA eventually disintegrated. The other main rival to the MPLA, UNITA, did not.

The MPLA always presented itself as a multiracial nationalist project. The category of tribal ethnicity was considered by Neto to be harmful to the construction of a nation-state. Many MPLA activists, moreover, had studied abroad and came from socially advantaged Angolan families. Most of its leaders were of mixed racial background, whites or 'assimilated' blacks, overwhelmingly from urban areas. The movement was broadly supported by Mbundus (the nation's second largest ethnic group).

In 1962–3 two important founders of the movement, Mário Pinto de Andrade and Viriato da Cruz, vehemently disagreed with the direction in which Neto was taking the MPLA. Cruz ended up leaving the movement. Andrade remained but, in 1974, would lead with his brother what became known as the 'Active Revolt' against Neto's authoritarianism and the lack of democracy in the MPLA. Andrade was forced into exile.

After independence, the MPLA debated which political ideology to adopt. Opposed to what he considered the more progressive discourse of Neto, Nito Alves admired the Stalinist dictator of Albania, Enver Hoxha. In 1977, the most serious internal crisis of MPLA occurred, when Alves, supported by many young MPLA activists, attempted a coup on 27 May. The *nitistas* killed some close associates of Neto, leading to one of the darkest episodes in the history of the MPLA: the nationwide bloody persecution of the *nitistas*, which effectively eliminated any possibility of further dissent from within the ranks of the movement.

At its first congress, in December 1977, the MPLA adopted a Marxist-Leninist programme and became the 'MPLA-Labour Party'. Neto died in 1979 and José Eduardo dos Santos, an MPLA activist since 1961, became President of both the party and Angola.

In 1990, with the end of the Cold War, the MPLA abandoned its Marxist-Leninism, and at its third congress in December, adopted a social democratic ideology. In 1991, the MPLA revised Angola's constitution, declaring it a 'democratic, law-abiding state'. The cease-fire of the Bicesse Accords made possible the first free electoral process in September 1992. Despite the UN's supervision of the elections, UNITA, by now the MPLA's principal opponent in the civil conflict, did not recognise the victory of the MPLA and war restarted. At its fourth congress in 1998, acknowledging the failure of another attempt at peace, the Lusaka Protocol of 1994, the MPLA again declared war on UNITA. The war finally ended in 2002.

Hélia Santos

HISTORIES

Birmingham, David (2002), 'Angola', in P. Chabal (ed.), *A History of Postcolonial Lusophone Africa*, Bloomington, IN: Indiana University Press, pp. 137–84.

Bittencourt, Marcelo (1999), *Dos Jornais às Armas: Trajectórias da Contestação Angolana*, Lisbon: Veja.

Hodges, Tony (2001), *Angola from Afro-Stalinism to Petro-diamond Capitalism*, Bloomington, IN: Indiana University Press.

http://www.mpla-angola.org

Tali, Jean-Michel Mabeko (2001), *O MPLA perante Si Próprio: Dissidências e Poder de Estado: (1962–1977) Ensaio de História Política*, Luanda: Editorial Nzila.

Agostinho Neto

António Agostinho Neto, poet, doctor and revolutionary, was leader of the Movimento Popular de Libertação de Angola (MPLA) from 1962, and President of Angola from independence in 1975 until his death in 1979. Neto was born in 1922. His parents were both teachers, his father also a Methodist pastor. Neto completed secondary school in Luanda, and worked in the health services. He saved enough to travel to Portugal in 1947, to study medicine at the University of Coimbra, later receiving a scholarship from American Methodists. He graduated in 1958, then completed a further course in tropical medicine in Lisbon. While in Portugal, he met many other African anti-colonial nationalists, including Amílcar Cabral and Eduardo Mondlane. His activities connected to the promotion of African culture and independence, and democratic change in Portugal, led to repeated imprisonment during the 1950s. In 1959 he returned to Luanda with his Portuguese wife Maria Eugénia and their small son. Although practising medicine he remained politically active, and was arrested by the Portuguese secret police, the PIDE, in 1960. His arrest sparked a major demonstration in his home district, which was met with brutal repression by Portuguese forces. He was imprisoned and tortured in Lisbon and Cape Verde, and an international campaign led to his release in 1962. Neto was helped to escape from Portugal, made his way to Zaire and was elected leader of the MPLA. During the independence struggle Neto recognised the need for a broad front, uniting different groups against colonialism. He affirmed that the MPLA was an anti-colonial nationalist movement, refusing to allow Angola's struggle to become subordinate to the Sino-Soviet ideological conflict and refraining from publicly criticising either China or the Soviet Union. Under Neto's leadership the MPLA tried, unsuccessfully, to unite with the rival movements, the FNLA and UNITA. The MPLA suffered recurrent problems of internal division and factionalism, beginning in 1962 with Viriato da Cruz's split, then Daniel Chipenda's revolt in 1973, and continuing after independence with the 1977 coup attempt by Nito Alves' group. Neto survived these difficulties, remaining committed to anti-racism, independence, national unity and socialism. After independence, at the congress in 1977, Neto formally proclaimed the movement a Marxist-Leninist vanguard party, committed to building a socialist society. Neto responded to internal factionalism by tightening party discipline, and conducting widespread political education programmes. From

1978 power became increasingly centralised around the president. This was a consequence of the contradictions of socialist construction in an impoverished postcolonial society suffering from an ongoing civil war which was fuelled considerably by Western and South African support for MPLA's rivals. It has, however, also led to criticisms of authoritarian, dictatorial rule.

Neto was a poet of international acclaim, committed to cultural decolonisation. His poetry addressed the problems of Angola's peoples, their daily sufferings under colonial rule and their longing, hope and determination for independence and control over their lives and destiny. Some of his poems were regularly sung by MPLA soldiers during the liberation war and the subsequent civil war. His poetry has been translated into many languages. Neto died in 1979 in Moscow, where he was receiving treatment for cancer.

Branwen Gruffydd Jones

LITERARY WORKS

Neto, António Agostinho (1961), *Poemas*, Lisbon: Casa dos Estudantes do Império.
— (1974a), *Quem é o Inimigo? Qual é o Nosso Objectivo?*, Luanda: Edições Maria da Fonte.
— [1963] (1974b), *Sacred Hope*, trans. Marga Holness, Dar es Salaam: Tanzania Publishing House.
— (1979), *On Literature and National Culture*, Luanda: União dos Escritores Angolanos.
— (1985), *A Renúncia Impossível: Poemas Inéditos*, Luanda: União Dos Escritores Angolanos.

HISTORIES

Barradas, Acácio (ed.) (2005), *Agostinho Neto – Uma Vida Sem Tréguas 1922–1979*, Lisbon: Dinalivro.
Carreira, Iko (1996), *O Pensamento Estratégico de Agostinho Neto: Contribuição Histórica*, Lisbon: Publicações Dom Quixote.
Davidson, Basil (1972), *In the Eye of the Storm: Angola's People*, London: Longman.
Khazanov, Anatolii Mikhailovich (1986), *Agostinho Neto*, trans. Cynthia Carlile, Moscow: Progress Publishers.
Trigo, Salvato (ed.) (1989), *A Voz Igual: Ensaios Sobre Agostinho Neto*, Oporto: Fundação Eng. António de Almeida.

Orientalism in the Lusophone World

The reception of Edward Said's *Orientalism* in the lusophone world is understated to say the least. Indeed, mainstream critique makes very little reference to him and his important concepts. Nevertheless, his term's perspicacity allows us to see the phenomenon of Orientalism in a range of cultural expressions and forms of domination that occurred during the last decades of colonialism and the subsequent decades of independence, particularly in literature about and from Angola.

The search for a poetics of differentiation generally acts as a form of organising textuality in Angolan literature, providing a core example of Orientalist cultural practice in the lusophone context. At the centre of the production of imperial discourse, colonial Angola was the icon of utopian affirmation and contributed to the definition of Portugal's own identity internationally. During the colonial war, Angola's future leaders, fighting for independence, prepared an ideal society, one where the Other, multiple in ethnic terms, would justify a multicultural nation, representative of all the differences within its territory. This way of reading identity proved to be essentialist and insufficient to cope with the complexity of a post-independence system that evolved in the direction of social inequality and democratic deficit.

Ruy Duarte de Carvalho is an Angolan writer who embodies the recent transitions of his nation. He has depicted the changes between revolutionary utopia and postcolonial cultural heterotopias in Angola. His work permits the cross-reading of literature, ethnography, history and anthropology. Along with this innovative practice, he reads Angola and, in some ways, the world, from a place culturally located in the South of the country. Denying a strategy of generalisation, he chooses to follow what we could define as the localisation of the nation through a territorial delocalisation to the margins of the state.

His text that exemplifies this parody of Orientalist practice most is his enigmatic *Vou lá Visitar Pastores* (*I'm Going off to Visit Shepherds*, 1999), a travel narrative and ethnographic report, where the ambiguity of genres presents itself as a decisive value for the comprehension of personal and collective reading worlds. It is also highly inter-textual, addressing the author's work, Angolan cultures and literature, and other texts of various origins. In it, history becomes fiction and fiction rewrites history.

Ana Maria Mão-de-Ferro Martinho

LITERARY WORKS
Carvalho, R. D. (1999), *Vou lá Visitar Pastores*, Lisbon: Cotovia.

HISTORIES
Rabasa, Jose (2005), 'Colonial/Postcolonial', *Dispositio/n* 52 (XXV): 81–94.
Rothwell, Phillip (2004), *A Postmodern Nationalist: Truth, Orality and Gender in the Work of Mia Couto*, Lewisburg, PA: Bucknell University.
Said, Edward (2004), *Orientalismo*, Lisbon: Cotovia.
Sanches, M. R. (ed.) (2005), *Deslocalizar a Europa*, Lisbon: Cotovia.

Overseas Provinces/The Colonial Act

A military coup in Portugal on 28 May 1926 precipitated both the fall of the first republic and the rise of António Salazar's authoritarian régime, the Estado Novo (New State). Key nationalistic priorities for the Estado Novo included a reaffirmation of Portugal's imperial destiny and an administrative and economic consolidation of its overseas territories, which included Angola, Mozambique, the islands of Cape Verde and São Tomé and Príncipe, Guineau-Bissau, the enclaves of Goa, Diu and Damão in India, Timor in the Indonesian archipelago, and Macau in southern China. The Colonial Act of 8 July 1930, enacted by Salazar as interim Minister of the Colonies, established the legislative foundation for the Estado Novo's colonial policy. In so doing, it both asserted Portugal's political sovereignty over its overseas territories, in the face of growing anti-colonial sentiments internationally, and proclaimed the integration and interdependence of these territories with the metropolis and with each other. The Colonial Act also centralised administrative control of the territories within the state by restricting the autonomy of local government and foreign investors, nationalising economic development, regulating employment policy, and reiterating the terms by which the metropolis was to benefit economically from trade with its territories. Modified in 1935 and again in 1945, the

Colonial Act was in 1951 incorporated into the 1933 constitution in a symbolic effort to demonstrate to the international community that Portugal and its territories were linked by a mutual constitutional document. Following World War II, Portugal was confronted with growing criticism, particularly from the United Nations, regarding the legitimacy of its colonial empire. The New State responded in 1951 by amending the constitution so that the term 'colonies' was replaced by 'overseas provinces', thereby asserting that these territories, in fact, belonged to a single, united Portuguese nation, and that their populations, in theory, enjoyed the same rights as any Portuguese citizen. While this act of verbalism enabled Portugal, over the next few decades, to justify its colonial dominions in the eyes of an international community increasingly preoccupied with Cold War tensions, it could not mask the reality of social injustice, forced labour, and underdevelopment in its overseas territories. In fact, only a very small percentage of the colonial populations in 1951 enjoyed the status of *assimilado* or 'civilised', and with it the basic rights of citizenship.

Censorship and a highly centralised bureaucracy left little room for free expression or literary movements in the colonies during the New State. Moreover, Salazar's régime actively promoted, through prizes and other forms of support, a vein of colonial literature intended to exoticise and uphold the image of Portuguese Africa as a place of multiracial and patriotic harmony, much in line with the Lusotropicalist writings of Brazilian sociologist Gilberto Freyre. The novels of Henrique Galvão and Augusto Casimiro exemplify this nationalistic vision. Similarly, missionary and settler theatre in Mozambique and Angola promulgated the state's civilising mission. A more enlightened understanding of African culture may be found in the colonial writings of Fernando de Castro Soromenho, born in Mozambique to European parents.

Robert H. Moser

Literary Works

Chabal, Patrick (ed.) (1996), *The Post-Colonial Literature of Lusophone Africa*, Evanston, IL: Northwestern University Press.

Hamilton, Russell G. (1975), *Voices from an Empire: A History of Afro-Portuguese Literature*, Minneapolis, MN: University of Minnesota Press.

Mitras, Luís R. (2004), 'Theatre in Portuguese-Speaking African Countries', in M. Banham (ed.), *A History of Theatre in Africa*, Cambridge: Cambridge University Press, pp. 380–404.

Moser, Gerald (1969), *Essays in Portuguese-African Literature*, University Park, PA: Pennsylvania State University.

Soromenho, Fernando de Castro, [1949] (1979), *Terra Morta*, Lisbon: Livraria Sá da Costa Editora.

Histories

Birmingham, David (2003), *A Concise History of Portugal*, Cambridge: Cambridge University Press.

Duffy, James (1959), *Portuguese Africa*, Cambridge, MA: Harvard University Press.

Freyre, Gilberto (1961), *The Portuguese and the Tropics*, Lisbon: Executive Committee for the Commemoration of the 5th Centenary of the Death of Prince Henry the Navigator.

Machado, Diamantino P. (1991), *The Structure of Portuguese Society: The Failure of Fascism*, New York: Praeger.

Pinto, António Costa (ed.) (2003), *Contemporary Portugal: Politics, Society and Culture*, Boulder, CO: Social Science Monographs.

PAIGC: African Party for the Independence of Guinea-Bissau and Cape Verde

The Partido Africano para a Independência de Guiné-Bissau e Cabo Verde (PAIGC) was founded in 1956 by the revolutionary intellectual Amílcar Cabral with the aim of achieving independence from Portugal, at first by peaceful methods but later resorting to violence. In 1959, Portuguese troops killed fifty dock workers at a protest in Pidjiguiti, a brutal act which turned public opinion against the colonial power and helped boost support for the independence movement. Across the continent, nationalist parties were being formed to fight against European colonialism, and Portugal's 'overseas provinces' were not going to be left out. Armed warfare, undertaken by guerrillas in Guinea and by clandestine resistance in Cabo Verde, began in 1962 with an attack on the city of Praia. Full-scale war against Portugal was declared by Cabral in January 1963. The movement received arms and support from the USSR, Cuba and China. By 1967, the PAIGC controlled two thirds of the country so in 1968 the Portuguese stepped up their campaign with new Governor, António de Spínola, investing in the construction of infrastructure.

Despite the assassination of Cabral in 1973, and the lack of complete control of the territory, independence was declared on September 24 of that year and recognised by the United Nations in November. The military overthrow of the Portuguese government on 25 April 1974 led to the granting of independence on 10 October that year and Luís Cabral, Amílcar's brother, became the first President of Guinea-Bissau and Cabo Verde.

In 1980, amid accusations of corruption, João Bernardo Vieira demanded that the party be split between the countries, with himself ruling Guinea and Cabral leading the Cabo Verde government. The first multi-party elections were held in 1994, but civil war broke out in 1998. President Kumba Yala of the Social Renovation Party was ousted in a military coup in 2003. In 2004 the PAIGC was the largest single political party and it won 31.4 per cent of the popular vote. The following year, the PAIGC's presidential candidate lost narrowly to the independent candidate João Bernardo Vieira, who returned to the country after six years in exile.

Claire Williams

LITERARY WORKS
Barros, Filinto de [1990] (1999), *Kikia Matcho*, Lisbon: Caminho.
Sila, Abdulai (1995), *A Última Tragédia*, Bissau: Ku Si Mon.
Various (1977), *Mantenhas para quem Luta! A Nova Poesia da Guiné-Bissau*, Bissau: Conselho Nacional de Cultura.
Various (1978), *Antologia dos jovens poetas: momentos primeiros da construção*, Bissau: Conselho Nacional de Cultura.

HISTORIES
Aaby, Peter (1978), *The State of Guinea-Bissau: African Socialism or Socialism in Africa*, Uppsala: Scandinavian Institute of African Studies.
Cabral, Amílcar (1980), *Unity and Struggle: Speeches and Writings*, trans. Michael Wolfers, selected by the PAIGC, London: Heinemann.

Cabral, Vasco (1980), *1956–1980: 24 anos de luta*, Bissau: PAIGC.

Galli, Rosemary E. and Jocelyn Jones (1987), *Guinea-Bissau: Politics, Economics and Society*, London: Pinter.

Lopes, Carlos (1987), *Guinea-Bissau: From Liberation Struggle to Independent Statehood*, trans. Michael Wolfers, London: Zed.

Pepetela

Pepetela is the nom de plume of Artur Carlos Maurício Pestana dos Santos, born in 1941 in Benguela in Portuguese colonial Angola and one of the lusophone world's best-known, exciting and prolific novelists. He was awarded the prestigious Camões Prize in 1997. After studying in Portugal he travelled to Algeria where he qualified as a sociologist and became a founding member of the Centre for Angolan Studies. He joined the Movimento Popular de Libertação de Angola (MPLA), which fought for Angolan independence and has ruled the country ever since.

Pepetela's novels shadow the development of Angolan politics from the utopian ideals of the left-wing revolutionaries of the 1970s to a frequently comic critique of the petro-diamond capitalist kleptocracy of present-day Angola. He fought with the MPLA in the enclave of Cabinda, the setting for his novel *Mayombe*. Here, the Marxist guerrillas discuss the building of a brighter, non-tribal future for Angola, a home for Marx's New Man. Literature was central to nation-building projects in lusophone Africa and *Mayombe* might be seen as a myth about the birth of the nation whilst his other novels narrate the history and myths of the nation from pre-colonial times to today. For example, *Yaka* is a saga about a Portuguese settler family spanning the period from 1890 to the end of Portuguese rule in 1975. Perhaps his most complex novel, *A Geraçao da Utopia* (*The Generation of Utopia*) follows the protagonists from university in Portugal on the eve of the anti-colonial revolt, through the war in Angola, to a disillusioned former guerrilla diving for fish on a southern beach. In *The Return of the Water Spirit*, massive apartment blocks collapse in Kinaxixi square in Luanda, the dwellers miraculously escaping unharmed, whilst the 'heroine', Carmina, transforms herself from socialist functionary into an arms dealer. In his most recent novel, *Predadores* (*Predators*) Pepetela again fiercely mocks the present-day rulers, as the heroes of *Mayombe* and the disillusioned of *A Geraçao da Utopia* are now replaced by the murderous, philandering businessman gangster, Vladimiro Caposso, living in a sea of fellow sharks.

Igor Cusack

LITERARY WORKS

Pepetela (1992), *A Geraçao da Utopia*, Lisbon: Dom Quixote.

— [1980] (1996a), *Mayombe*, trans. Michael Wolfers, Oxford: Heinemann.

— [1984] (1996b), *Yaka*, trans. Marga Holness, Oxford: Heinemann.

— [1995] (2002), *The Return of the Water Spirit*, trans. Luís R. Mitras, Oxford: Heinemann.

— (2005), *Predadores*, Lisbon: Dom Quixote.

CRITICAL WORKS

Brookshaw, David (2000), 'Nation and Nation-Building: The Angolan Novels of Pepetela', in Charles M. Kelley (ed.), *Fiction in the Portuguese-Speaking World*, Cardiff: University of Wales, pp. 107–16.

Cusack, Igor (2004), '"Janus or Hydra": Pepetela, the New Man and the Construction of Angolan Masculinities', in Hilary Owen and Phillip Rothwell (eds), *Sexual/Textual Empires: Gender and Marginality in Lusophone African Literature*, Bristol: HIPLA, pp. 99–116.

Peres, Phyllis (1997), *Transculturation and Resistance in Lusophone African Narrative*, Gainesville, FL: University of Florida Press.

Rothwell, Phillip, (2004), 'Rereading Pepetela's *O Desejo de Kianda* after 11 September 2001: Signs and Distractions', *Portuguese Studies* 20: 195–207.

Postcolonial African Immigration to Portugal: African Mozambican Immigration

Portugal became an immigration destination for former Portuguese colonial subjects only in the 1970s, with the fall of Salazar's dictatorship and the independence of its former African colonies (Angola, Mozambique, Guinea-Bissau, Cape Verde and São Tomé e Príncipe). The Carnation Revolution of 25 April 1974 had a huge impact in Mozambique and in the other African Portuguese colonies. Increasingly, it became apparent that the Portuguese presence in Africa was coming to an end. Both *retornados* – the white Portuguese who had lived in the colonies and then returned to Portugal – and African immigrants, who had been part of the Portuguese colonial system as 'assimilated' subjects (those who condoned the colonist's behaviour, while rejecting their own culture), decided to restart their lives, mainly in the Lisbon metropolitan area.

African Mozambican immigration began both during the independence process and with the establishment of the FRELIMO government. In many respects, the euphoria which surrounded FRELIMO, around the time of the independence, was not shared in many districts and towns in Mozambique. As documented by Ribeiro (2000), the national struggle for liberation (1964–74) remained practically unknown to the majority of the urban inhabitants of Mozambique. The impact of FRELIMO's socialist ideology was deemed by some to be terrifying, while others celebrated it or saw its potential. However, shortly after the arrival of FRELIMO in Mozambique's cities, both the white and assimilated populations realised that their dreams and expectations were under threat. In essence, FRELIMO's socialist discourse regarding a new Mozambican society and the 'New Man' threatened their way of life. Parallel to this, the increasing degradation of health, educational, agricultural and justice structures caused by the rapid departure of a large number of white Portuguese professionals, teachers, doctors, lawyers and technicians had thrown the country into chaos, confusion and insecurity. As observed by Isaacman and Isaacman (1983), to a certain extent, Mozambique, like other former colonies, experienced massive problems due to colonialist neglect: massive illiteracy, poverty, unfamiliarity with democratic processes, racial and ethnic cleavages, obscurantism and, ultimately, the heritage of the Portuguese bureaucracy. Confronted by this undesirable situation, most assimilated African Mozambican families and individuals decided to take the difficult option of uprooting themselves from their homeland and emigrating to Portugal. In spite of being, socially and culturally, a silent 'community' in the context of Portuguese immigration, it is possible to outline three moments of African Mozambican immigration to Portugal.

The first moment of immigration goes from 1976 to 1977 (shortly after Mozambican independence on 25 June 1975), and was caused by anxiety concerning the economic, social and cultural reforms proposed by FRELIMO. The second moment of immigration encompasses the years from 1979 to 1983. Many Mozambican individuals and families saw themselves forced to depart from Mozambique due to hostile and degrading living conditions that resulted from the economic and political programme enacted by FRELIMO. The final stage covers the years from 1984 to 1989 and onwards. This period was characterised by a slow flow of immigration that was caused mainly by political as well as professional dissatisfaction and frustration.

Recent empirical evidence implies that African Mozambican immigration to Portugal is more a family affair than an individual project. In fact, even those who departed from Mozambique alone were usually connected with a family already based and settled in Portugal.

Many Mozambicans undertake their journey to the former metropolis, convinced that they will recover, on the one hand, their social status, and on the other hand, a lost golden past, as for them Portugal represents what Crites (1971) has referred to as 'the continuity of experience through time'. It comes to represent a safe place where they can shield their identities, and preserve hopes for a better future. Nonetheless, in Portugal, Mozambican immigrants have been unexpectedly confronted with an unfamiliar and diverse reality. This reality culturally and socially does not coincide with the Portugal they imagined: a Portugal reproduced and experienced in Africa. Consequently, post-imperial Portugal is, from their point of view, a space that does not accommodate their 'own' imposed history.

Sheila Khan

LITERARY WORKS

Adamodjy, Bahassan (2001), *Milandos de Um Sonho – A Euforia dos Sonhadores*, Lisbon: Quetzal Editores.

Chabal, Patrick et al. (1996), *The Postcolonial Literature of Lusophone Africa*, London: Hurst and Company.

Crites, S. (1971), 'The Narrative Quality of Experience', *Journal of the American Academy of Religion* 39: 291–311.

Hamilton, Russell (1984), *Literatura Africana, Literatura Necessária II – Moçambique, Cabo Verde, Guiné-Bissau, São Tomé e Príncipe*, Lisbon: Edições 70.

Laban, Michel (1998), *Moçambique – Encontro com escritores*, 3 vols, Porto: Fundação Engenheiro de Almeida.

HISTORIES

Isaacman, A. and B. Isaacman (1983), *Mozambique: From Colonialism to Revolution, 1900–1982*, Aldershot: Gower Publishing Company Limited.

Khan, Sheila (2003), *African Mozambican Immigrants – Narrative of Immigration and Identity, and Acculturation Strategies in Portugal and England*, doctoral dissertation, University of Warwick: Centre for Research in Ethnic Relations.

Newitt, M. (1995), *A History of Mozambique*, London: Hurst and Company.

Ribeiro, Gabriel (2000), *As representações sociais dos moçambicanos: do passado colonial à democratização – Esboço de uma cultura política*, Lisbon; Ministério dos Negócios Estrangeiros: Edição Do Instituto de Cooperação Portuguesa.

Rita-Ferreira, A. (1998), 'Moçambique pós-25 de Abril: Causas do êxodo da população de origem europeia e asiática'. *Actas da V Semana de Cultura Africana, Moçambique: Cultura e história de um país*, Coimbra: Universidade de Coimbra, Instituto de Antropologia, Centro de Estudos Africanos, pp. 121–69.

RENAMO

The Resistência Nacional Moçambicana (RENAMO) formed in Rhodesia in the late 1970s, following the ascendance of the Marxist FRELIMO party to power upon Mozambique's independence. FRELIMO's support of Zimbabwean nationalists provoked a covert war by Rhodesian security forces in central Mozambique, creating the context in which Mozambican dissidents formed RENAMO under Rhodesian sponsorship. The white Mozambican nationalist Orlando Cristina was amongst the first dissidents to operate from Rhodesia, taking control of Rhodesia's anti-FRELIMO radio station Voz da Àfrica Livre in 1976. RENAMO was founded in 1977 and trained by the Rhodesian SAS to create an indigenous counter-insurgency force in the tradition of the 'pseudo units' used during Kenya's Mau Mau rebellion and *Fletcha* units deployed in Angola. Cristina and the black Mozambican, André Matsangaissa, were RENAMO's original leaders, representing the wider combination of black anti-FRELIMO activists and white Mozambicans and Portuguese amongst RENAMO's supporters.

RENAMO guerrillas were initially deployed from Rhodesian territory, in collaboration with Rhodesian commandos, before permanent bases were established inside Mozambique in 1979. During Rhodesia's 1980 transition into Zimbabwe RENAMO's personnel were transferred to Phalaborwa in South Africa's Kruger National Park and Voz da Àfrica Livre was relocated to the Transvaal. Meanwhile, a FRELIMO government offensive decimated RENAMO's presence in Mozambique, and Afonso Dhlakama became RENAMO president following Matsangaissa's death in combat. Elements within the apartheid state subsequently rehabilitated RENAMO and covertly provided them with training, supplies, communications and intelligence throughout the 1980s. Orlando Cristina's desire for RENAMO to attain independence from South Africa led to his April 1983 assassination.

Under South African sponsorship RENAMO rapidly grew to a force of more than 20,000 fighters, many of whom were forcibly conscripted. By the mid-1980s RENAMO operated throughout Mozambique and had become renowned for its brutality and recruitment of child soldiers. The 1985 Gorongosa documents also revealed RENAMO's strategy revolved around destroying the Mozambican economy, in a campaign that ultimately claimed more than 100,000 lives. The 1984 Nkomati Accord between Mozambique and South Africa failed to halt South African support, though RENAMO was forced to diversify its support base, particularly amongst conservatives and the intelligence community in America. RENAMO also procured supplies from corrupt elements within the Mozambican armed forces. Following a number of failed negotiation attempts with the FRELIMO government, RENAMO experienced some factionalisation from 1986, possibly encouraged by Mozambican intelligence agents. A number of large-scale massacres by RENAMO in 1987, including an infamous incident at Homoíne, curtailed RENAMO's international support and forced it to return to negotiations from 1988.

Following Mozambique's 1992 peace agreement RENAMO demobilised its forces and became a political party, recruiting educated urbanites to represent it in parliament. RENAMO has subsequently failed to win government in Mozambique's 1994, 1999 or 2004 elections, but has remained Mozambique's only major opposition party. Afonso Dhlakama's dictatorial control over RENAMO has limited the party's effectiveness, and it has failed to represent a real alternative to the FRELIMO government. It retains a small militia, which has recently been accused of involvement in political violence and arms trafficking.

David Robinson

HISTORIES
Cabrita, João M. (2000), *Mozambique: The Tortuous Road to Democracy*, Basingstroke:
    Palgrave.
Manning, Carrie (2002), *The Politics of Peace in Mozambique: Post-Conflict Democratization
    1992–2000*, London: Praeger.
Minter, William (1994), *Apartheid's Contras: An Inquiry into the Roots of War in Angola and
    Mozambique*, London: Zed Books.
Newitt, Malyn (1995), *A History of Mozambique*, Bloomington, IN: Indiana University
    Press.
Vines, Alex (1996), *RENAMO: From Terrorism to Democracy in Mozambique?*, London:
    James Currey.

Salazar and the New State

António de Oliveira Salazar (1889–1970) was the dictator who ruled over Portugal and its colonial empire, comprising mainly the African colonies of Angola, Mozambique, Guinea-Bissau, Cape Verde and São Tomé e Príncipe, over several decades of the twentieth century. Salazar was a professor of finance and economics at the University of Coimbra and a conservative Catholic influenced by Charles Maurras and Pope Leo XIII when he became Portugal's Minister of Finance (1928–32) and then Prime Minister (1932–69). In the crucial years of 1932 to 1933 he argued in favour of a provisional dictatorship that ended up lasting four decades; the reactivation and growth of the Portuguese colonial project in Africa, as stated in the Colonial Act of 1933; and a new constitution for the Portuguese New State (Estado Novo). Salazar's brand of fascism, unlike Mussolini's in Italy or Hitler's in Germany, did not emphasise modernist industrialisation. On the contrary, his right-wing revolution, which was predicated on the criticism both of nineteenth-century Portuguese liberal movements under the monarchy and of the politically failed democratic First Republic (1910–26), took a clear anti-modernist stance, proposing a return to the rural virtues of the pre-nineteenth-century Ancien Régime and stressing God, Fatherland and Family (*Deus, Pátria e Família*). The representation of individuals in elections was stigmatised as artificial and an unnecessary importation of ideas foreign to Portugal; only 'natural' representation of native social formations like professional organisations was considered legitimate within Salazar's ideology of corporativism (*corporativismo*). The National Union (União Nacional), the party of all parties founded in 1930, became the régime's single autocratic political organ. Despite the dictator's academic background, Salazar's New State was by no means just an intellectual revolution. The alliance with the military, the creation of a political police, the reinforcement of censorship, and the establishment of a camp for political prisoners in Tarrafal (Cape Verde), were all facets of the institutionalised violence that became established practice in the New State. After the Spanish Civil War (1936–9), in which Salazar took the side of Franco against their common communist enemies, the dictatorship organised its most visible event to celebrate its accomplishments in renewing the 'Portuguese man' (Salazar's speeches and politics were explicitly addressed to men): the Great Exhibition of the Portuguese World in Lisbon in June 1940. Staunchly allied with the Catholic Church, Salazar insisted on maintaining Portugal's neutrality and on stressing its exceptionalism during World War II and its aftermath. The anachronistic Portuguese overseas empire, reaching 'from Minho [in northern Portugal] to Timor', the first and the last of Western Europe, deflected some of the international pressure to decolonise, and, despite the costly colonial wars fought in Angola, Mozambique and Guinea-Bissau since 1961, Salazar's New State survived his death until the very soldiers fighting for the empire overthrew it in the 1974 coup, bringing on a régime change for the metropolis and, one year later, independence for the five African colonies. Salazar has been a recurrent if diffused presence in some of the most celebrated works of Portuguese fiction published after democracy and decolonisation.

Victor J. Mendes

LITERARY WORKS

Antunes, António Lobo (2004), *The Inquisitors' Manual*, trans. Richard Zenith, New York: Grove.
Gersão, Teolinda (1982), *Paisagem Com Mulher e Mar ao Fundo*, Lisbon: O Jornal.
Jorge, Lídia (1995), *The Murmuring Coast*, trans. Natália Costa and Ronald W. Sousa, Minneapolis, MN: University of Minnesota Press.
Saramago, José (1991), *The Year of the Death of Ricardo Reis*, trans. Giovanni Pontiero, San Diego: Harcourt Brace Janovich.

HISTORIES

Cabrita, Felícia (1999), *Mulheres de Salazar*, Lisbon: Editorial Notícias.
Gil, José (1995), *Salazar: a Retórica da Invisibilidade*, Lisbon: Relógio d'Água.
Pinto, António Costa (1995), *Salazar's Dictatorship and European Fascism*, New York: Social Sciences Monographs, Boulder/Columbia University Press.
Rosas, Fernando (1994), *O Estado Novo (1926–1968)*, Vol. 7 of *História de Portugal* (ed. José Matoso), Lisbon: Estampa.
Salazar, António de Oliveira (1935–67), *Discursos e Notas Políticas*, Coimbra: Coimbra Editora.

Dom Sebastião

One of the most recurrent themes in Portuguese literature, culture and intellectual thought from 1580 onwards has been the messianic myth of the return of the lost King of Portugal, Dom Sebastião. Often described as the Portuguese version of the Arthurian legend, the history and fantasy surrounding Dom Sebastião have filled the Portuguese imagination from the moment that Sebastião was conceived in the womb of his mother, Dona Joana. Indeed, he acquired the soubriquet, 'the desired one', before he was even born. This was due to the high mortality rate among his father's eight siblings, which meant that Portugal's independence from Spain was under threat. With the death of Sebastião's father shortly before Sebastião's birth on 20 January 1554, Sebastião became the last feasible branch of the Portuguese royal House of Avis capable of producing offspring, and thus preventing the throne from falling into the hands of the Spanish. His grandfather, the monarch Dom João III, died three years later, leaving the Portuguese kingdom to the boy king, first under the regency of his grandmother, Dona Catarina, and then under the regency of his great-uncle, and, as fate would have it, successor to the throne, the Cardinal Dom Henrique.

The key point in the way that the Sebastião story came to be narrated was that the hopes of the nation's independence rested on Sebastião's fulfilment of his primary duty as a king – the provision of an heir to protect the nation's political independence. His mother left him shortly after his birth, to return to Spain, and he was educated principally under the tutelage of the Jesuits. At the age of fourteen, he took over the reigns of government, an adolescent driven by religious and imperial fervour, whose ambition was to conquer Moorish North Africa in the name of Christ.

As an infant, he suffered an affliction that affected his sex organs, from which it is assumed he did not recover. In any case, his intense hatred of women – the many accounts of his disdain or discomfort in their presence, or his insistence on washing his hands if he touched the same utensils as a woman had touched – may in large part explain his failure to marry. One thing we need to bear in mind is that many of the accounts of Sebastião's hatred of women or lack of virility were mediated through Spanish ambassadors to the Portuguese court, and doubtless, that colours them ideologically. The Spanish, after all, were set to be the primary beneficiaries of Sebastião's failure to produce offspring. Another interpretation of Sebastião's behaviour, generally elided by most Portuguese historians although the obvious has been stated more recently, is that he was homosexual. Whatever the truth of the matter, he continually thwarted his ministers' attempts to negotiate a marriage alliance for him, and surrounded himself with young sycophants who encouraged his obsession with conquering North Africa.

The result of his obsession with North Africa was the disaster of the Battle of Alcácer Quibir. Against the advice of his most experienced counsellors, the young king insisted on launching a campaign against the Moors, and on 4 August 1578, he was slain on the sands of Alcácer Quibir. Rumours quickly abounded in Portugal that, despite the military catastrophe, the young king was not, in fact, dead, and that he would return to restore glory to the Portuguese nation. Somehow, the rumours became fused with the prophetic doggerel verses of a man known as the Doodler (o Bandarra), or the shoemaker of Trancoso, Gonçalo Anes. His verses, which predated Sebastião, were sufficiently cryptic to be open to a multiplicity of interpretations. They foretold the return of a messiah king – subsequently deemed to be the lost King Sebastião.

In 1580, Felipe II of Spain asserted his right to rule Portugal, following the death of the Cardinal Dom Henrique. For the next sixty years, Portugal was ruled by Spanish monarchs, and during this time, the myth of Sebastião's return, as the messiah who would save the Portuguese from Spanish occupation, gained currency. The irony is, of course, that Sebastião himself was in no small part responsible for Felipe's accession to the Portuguese throne. If he had secured the succession before setting out on his foolhardy and disastrous endeavour, Portugal would not be waiting for the return of a Portuguese king.

Repeatedly, throughout subsequent Portuguese history, sebastianism surged at moments of national crisis. An interesting aspect of the myth is the manner in which Portuguese leaders have appropriated it as a means of consolidating or legitimising their power. They subtly cast themselves as the incarnation of Dom Sebastião. One of the most recent examples of this tendency was twentieth-century dictator Salazar, whose self-projection as a celibate saviour wedded to the Catholic nation resonated with whatever it was in the Portuguese collective imagination that predisposed Portugal to messianism. Of course, there have always been voices critical of the sebastianic trend, particularly in Portuguese literature.

The oldest, and by some accounts, most famous referencing of Dom Sebastião appears in the Portuguese national poem, *The Lusiads*, by Camões. The epic is dedicated to the young king who reigned at the time the poem was first published (1572). While *The Lusiads* celebrates Portuguese expansion, a project to which Sebastião was fanatically committed, it is interesting to note the warnings the poem contains against the ignoble and greedy side of imperialism that distracts the nation's attention away from domestic concerns and ultimately leads to disrepute. One example is the Old Man of Belém who warns the parting discoverers against 'the pride of power!' and the 'futile lust for that vanity known as fame'. While the critique is levelled against the discoverers of the Manueline Age, it does not take much imagination for it to be read as a veiled warning against the direction in which Sebastião was steering the nation.

Among the many plays, novels and poems that have interacted with sebastianism over the centuries, Almeida Garrett's 1843 *Brother Luiz de Sousa* is one of the most famous for its vehement critique through metaphor of a nation paralysed by a yearning for the return of what was lost on the shores of Alcácer Quibir. In the play, someone – assumed dead – does return from the battlefield many years later, and the consequences for all the characters in the play are catastrophic.

Portugal's foremost modernist poet, Fernando Pessoa, celebrated the young king's madness as the virtue of dreaming of a greater reality for his small nation in what many deem to be his response to *The Lusiads*, a 1934 collection of poems entitled *Message*. In contrast, José Régio's play *El-Rei Sebastião* (*King Sebastião*), first performed in 1948, characterises the monarch as a man driven by a hubristic ambition for perpetual fame and thus willing to sacrifice his own life and the welfare of his kingdom.

Following the Carnation Revolution of 1974, which brought the dictatorial régime of the New State to an end, and also heralded the demise of Portuguese colonialism, sebastianism has been revisited in many innovative forms by writers including Almeida Faria and Manuel Alegre. The former, in his short novel O *Conquistador* (*The Conqueror*), portrays a modern-day Sebastião, ironically characterised by his conquest of a variety of women, and simultaneously his vulnerability before them. The latter, in his novel *Jornada de África*, portrays the horrors and dilemmas of the Angolan war of independence fought by Portuguese soldiers who do not know why they have been sent to Africa. The cast of characters is drawn from Jerónimo de Mendonça's 1607 homonymous account (*Jornada de África*) of the disaster of Alcácer Quibir, and is a modern, and highly original, reinterpretation of the imperially doomed figure of Sebastião.

The fascination of the sebastianic myth still looms large in the Portuguese imaginary. Indeed, in 2004, Manoel de Oliveira, Portugal's leading film-maker, dramatised Régio's play, renaming it O *Quinto Império – Ontem como Hoje* (*The Fifth Empire – Yesterday like Today*). The new title points to the continuing fascination with bringing the past (the dead King Sebastião) into the present, and the ideological undercurrent that has always been at work when Sebastião comes into play – empire: either through a critique of its decadence or a lament of its demise.

Phillip Rothwell

LITERARY WORKS

Alegre, Manuel (1989), *Jornada de África: Romance de Amor e Morte do Alferes Sebastião*, Lisbon: Dom Quixote.

Camões, Luís de (1997), *The Lusiads*, trans. Landeg White, Oxford and New York: Oxford University Press.

Faria, Almeida (1990), O *Conquistador*, Lisbon: Caminho.

Garrett Almeida (1909), *The 'Brother Luiz de Sousa' of Viscount de Almeida Garrett: Done into English by Edgar Prestage*, London: Elkin Mathews.

Pessoa, Fernando (1992), *Message*, trans. Jonathan Griffin, London: Mernard.

Régio, José (1949), *El-Rei Sebastião: Teatro*, Lisbon: Brasília Editora.

HISTORIES
Boxer, Charles (1969), *The Portuguese Seaborne Empire 1415–1825*, Harmondsworth: Penguin Books.
Vitorino, Pedro, (1924), *O Sebastianismo na Iconografia Popular*, Porto: n.p.

Slavery and Abolition

Brazil received some 3.5 million slaves between roughly 1550 and 1850, nearly 40 per cent of all those imported into the Americas. African slaves provided the labour during the sugar boom in north-eastern Brazil between the middle of the sixteenth and middle of the seventeenth centuries. By the time sugar declined with the onset of competition from the Caribbean, African slavery was written into the fabric of Brazilian culture and society, for slaves were not only employed in the harvesting and production of sugar and in the domestic life of the planter's house, but were also found in all manner of manual labour and artisan activity in the towns; while slave women often had sexual relations with their masters, producing lighter-skinned offspring who either remained enslaved or were occasionally freed.

It took another boom in the first half of the eighteenth century for large-scale importation of African slaves to resume, when gold and other mineral deposits were discovered in the southern central region of Brazil, which came to be known as Minas Gerais. Many of the slaves came from Guinea, and already had experience of mining and metalwork, skills that were prized and exploited by the slaveowners. The gold boom spread westwards from Minas Gerais into the far interior of Brazil, but, by the last quarter of the century, had ended. Many miners cut their losses and retreated to the coast, abandoning their slaves who, along with slave maroons, or *quilombos*, formed isolated communities of 'free' Afro-Brazilians. Some of these have only recently been discovered, offering a valuable source of material for historians and anthropologists.

By the first quarter of the nineteenth century, a third major boom in coffee had began in the hinterland of Rio de Janeiro, and during the course of the century spread westwards into São Paulo. By this time, Brazil had gained its independence from Portugal. However, as a result of an Anglo-Brazilian treaty of 1827, whereby Britain recognised the country's independence, Brazil agreed to abolish the slave trade from Africa by 1830. This undertaking was given at a time when there had never been a greater need for slaves, and for this reason the slave trade continued illegally for a further twenty years, only eventually coming to an end in 1850 under mounting pressure from Britain. From this point on, successive governments took cautious steps to bring slavery to an end, a major landmark being the Law of Free Birth, eventually passed in 1871. However, it took another eighteen years before slavery was finally abolished in 1888. By this time, the old planters of the North-East had made the transition from slave to free labour, while the new, more technocratic coffee barons of São Paulo had invested in labour-saving machinery or European migrant labour, and no longer wanted to purchase increasingly expensive and elderly slaves. The large number of African slaves imported over such a long period of time explains the considerable impact of African culture on Brazilian life, which is still noticeable today.

David Brookshaw

HISTORIES
Bethell, L. (1970), *The Abolition of the Brazilian Slave Trade*, Cambridge: Cambridge University Press.

Boxer, C. (1962), *The Golden Age of Brazil*, Berkeley, CA: University of California Press.

Conrad, R. (1972), *The Destruction of Brazilian Slavery 1850–1888*, Berkeley, CA: University of California Press.

Degler, C. (1971), *Neither Black nor White: Slavery and Race Relations in Brazil and the United States*, New York: Macmillan.

Freyre, G. (1946), *The Masters and the Slaves*, New York: Alfred Knopf.

Toplin, R. B. (1972), *The Abolition of Slavery in Brazil*, New York: Atheneum.

Timor and Indonesia: Shared Currents

Two years after Indonesia's invasion of East Timor, Abílio Araújo, a fomer member of the East Timorese resistance movement published *Timor Leste: os loricos voltaram a cantar* (1977), in which he writes: 'Today it is some of the countries of the Third World that only yesterday were fighting for their independence that are now acting as new colonisers'. One of those new colonisers was Indonesia, a nation 'forged in the struggle against Dutch colonialism'. In the early sixteenth century, the island of Timor had been claimed by Portugal, whilst Holland had gained control of the archipelagos that would later become Indonesia. The Dutch later gained a foothold in the western half of Timor, and West Timor was formally integrated into Holland's overseas possessions following the Treaty of Lisbon in 1859. Dutch and Portuguese colonial policies differed, and East Timor developed cultural forms influenced by their Portuguese rulers. Nevertheless, the pre-colonial history of the island, when it existed as several kingdoms, meant that the various Timorese tribes – East and West – despite linguistic differences and distinct identities shared many cultural traits, some of which survived the presence of the Dutch and Portuguese. Therefore, when Indonesia's successful struggle for independence led to West Timor becoming part of the new Indonesian Republic, the western half of the island shared cultural elements with East Timor.

Following the rise to power in Indonesia of the dictator, Suharto, its own colonising impulses grew in intensity, expressed in the idea of a Greater Indonesia. Once Portugal began the process of decolonisation of its territories in 1974, Indonesia looked to make East Timor part of its republic and actively attempted to sabotage efforts by the East Timorese to assert their independence. Suharto, viewed as an enemy of communism, found Western powers willing to accept Indonesia's increasingly violent involvement in East Timor, which culminated in the invasion of 7 December 1975. Yet, despite the incredible cruelty of the Indonesian occupation, which is believed to have led to the deaths of a third of the population, the East Timorese are conscious of the fact that the primary responsibility lies with an Indonesian dictator who by 1977 had, according to Abílio Araújo, 'claimed more than a million lives of sons and daughters of the Indonesian Nation and has kept two hundred thousand political prisoners in concentration camps'. The East Timorese now enjoying independence do not blame ordinary Indonesians for the oppression that many of them also experienced, although their future relationship could be conditioned by the success or otherwise of bringing to justice those within the Indonesian régime responsible for the atrocities committed in East Timor. This search for justice is taking place in a postcolonial environment where the new country of East Timor is seeking to integrate itself into a global economy, and in which the West is once again looking to Indonesia as an important regional ally. Thus, justice may have to wait.

Anthony Soares

Histories

Carey, Peter (2005), 'Third-World Colonialism, the *Geração Foun* and the Birth of a New
    Nation: Indonesia through East Timorese Eyes, 1975–99', *Journal of Romance Studies*
    5 (1): 37–51.
Martin, Ian (2001), *Self-Determination in East Timor: The United Nations, the Ballot and
    International Intervention*, London and Boulder, CO: Lynne Rienner.
Ricklefs, Merle Calvin (1981), *A History of Modern Indonesia: c.1300 to the Present*,
    London: Macmillan.
Rutherford, Danilyn (2002), *Raiding the Land of the Foreigners: The Limits of the Nation on
    an Indonesian Frontier*, Princeton, NJ: Princeton University Press.
Vickers, Adrian (2005), *A History of Modern Indonesia*, Cambridge: Cambridge University
    Press.

UNITA: National Union for the Total Independence of Angola

UNITA was founded by Jonas Savimbi in 1966. Its charismatic leader had left the FNLA
(National Front for the Liberation of Angola) in 1964. UNITA received support from
Angola's largest ethnic group, the Ovimbundu. Initially a small underground movement,
it gradually grew to become the second party in Angola. In 1975, South Africa invaded
Angola from the South, supporting the armed struggle of UNITA. This support, together
with the US's monetary aid, lasted until the end of the Cold War, its goal being to weaken
the USSR's influence in the region.

Despite sanctions from the UN throughout the 1990s, UNITA managed to continue
with the armed struggle against the MPLA government. Until his death, Jonas Savimbi led
UNITA very autocratically. UNITA's fourth congress in 1985 gave Savimbi both command
of its armed forces as well as the presidency of the movement. His dictatorial style eventually led to dissent within the party which resulted in the breakaway movement 'UNITA-
Renovada' (UNITA-Renewed), founded by Eugénio Manuvakola and Jorge Valentim.

UNITA came second in the elections of 1992. With only 34 per cent of the votes,
UNITA refused to acknowledge the MPLA's victory and returned to civil war until 1994,
when it signed the Lusaka Protocol. Despite a relatively peaceful period between 1994 and
1998, UNITA's MPs did not enter the National Assembly before 1997. From the moment
the Lusaka Protocol was signed, Savimbi showed little willingness to comply with its goals.
His disdain for the accord was obvious through his absence from the signing ceremony, to
which he sent the then Secretary-General of UNITA, Eugénio Manuvakola, in his place.
In fact, UNITA would never hand in its heavy armaments nor did its troops retreat from
the battle fronts, two of the major points of the protocol. This led to the MPLA's decision
to declare war again at its fourth congress in 1998. The war continued until 2002, when
Savimbi was killed by government troops. Shortly thereafter, a ceasefire was signed in
Luanda, which lasts to this day.

Hélia Santos

Histories

Birmingham, David (2002), 'Angola', in P. Chabal (ed.), *A History of Postcolonial
    Lusophone Africa*, Bloomington, IN: Indiana University Press, pp. 137–84.
Hodges, Tony (2001), *Angola from Afro-Stalinism to Petro-diamond Capitalism*,
    Bloomington, IN: Indiana University Press.

Guedes, A. M. et al. (2003), *Pluralismo e Legitimação: a Edificação Jurídica Pós-colonial de Angola*, Coimbra: Almedina, Faculdade de Direito.
Guerra, João Paulo (2002), *Savimbi: Vida e Morte*, Lisbon: Bertrand.

Vasco da Gama

Born c. 1460 in Sines, and one of the heroes of the Portuguese 'Discoveries', Vasco da Gama's achievements are commemorated in all spheres of life: the names of streets, schools and scholarships, stamps, statues, football teams, even a crater on the moon. Little is known about his early life until he took to sea, when he fought off French attacks on the Portuguese trading points on the African coast. He was entrusted by Dom Manuel I with the mission to discover a route to the Indies that would enable the Portuguese to get involved in the spice trade. In the wake of Bartolomeu Dias, da Gama's small fleet of four ships embarked from Lisbon on 8 July 1497 and made its way down the West African coast and round the Cape of Good Hope. Travelling on up the East African coast, where the ships were able to take on supplies and fresh water, local pilots were employed to help them navigate across the Indian Ocean to Calicut, where they arrived on 20 May 1498.

Da Gama was also conscientious in his support of the Portuguese proselytising mission and he took priests on his voyages and punished those who were not amenable to conversion. In Calicut, he negotiated with the city's ruler to gain trading rights, and returned to Portugal to great acclaim and honour. The Monastery of the Jerónimos was built to commemorate the successful voyage and partly funded by profits from taxes on the imports of spices. On his second expedition in 1502, he captained twenty warships and used force rather than diplomacy to acquire trade concessions, guaranteeing that Portugal would reap rich rewards. Da Gama's third mission was to take up the viceroyalty of Goa, but he became ill soon after arriving there and died in 1524.

He is credited with joining the East and West and paving the way both for Portugal's maritime explorations and colonisation of territories in Africa and the Far East and the beginning of a global economy. Nevertheless in India (particularly Goa) he is associated with the beginning of an era of imperialism, violence and repression.

Claire Williams

LITERARY WORKS
Camões, Luís de [1572] (1980), *The Lusiads*, trans. William C. Atkinson, London: Penguin.
Carmelo, Luís (ed.) (1998), *Do Tamanho do Mundo*, Porto: Ataegina.
Medina, Miguel (1994), *Além do Mar*, Venda Nova: Bertrand.

HISTORIES
Braz de Oliveira, João [1892] (1971), *Os Navios de Vasco da Gama*, Lisbon: Agência-Geral do Ultramar.
Disney, Anthony and Emily Booth (eds) (2000), *Vasco da Gama and the Linking of Europe and Asia (Vasco da Gama Quincentenary Conference)*, Oxford: Oxford University Press.
Hart, Henry H. (1971), *Sea Road to the Indies: An Account of the Voyages and Exploits of the Portuguese Navigators, together with the Life and times of Dom Vasco da Gama, Capitão-Mor, Viceroy of India and Count of Vidigueira*, Westport, CT: Greenwood.
Subrahmanyam, Sanjay (1997), *The Career and Legend of Vasco da Gama*, Cambridge: Cambridge University Press.

Vakil, AbdoolKarim (1998), 'Vários Vascos de Gama', in Diogo Ramada Curto (ed.), *O Tempo de Vasco da Gama*, Lisbon: Comissão Nacional Para as Comemorações dos Descobrimentos Portugueses; Difel, pp. 353–78.

Women's Histories in the Lusophone Colonial and Postcolonial Worlds

Portuguese colonialism dates back to the golden era of the maritime expansion in the fifteenth century. The scientific advances of Prince Henry the Navigator and the maritime discoveries, most notably the sea voyage of Vasco da Gama to India (1497–8), led to Portugal's earliest contacts with the continent of Africa, as well as the first landfall in Brazil in 1500. Women's role in this enterprise was primarily reproductive. Conventional Portuguese nationalist iconography casts Henry the Navigator's mother, Philippa of Lancaster, as the divinely inspired womb of empire and the regenerative matrix of the modern nation. Over centuries that followed, the women with whom the Portuguese discoverers, settlers and colonisers made contact would come to act as the real matrices of empire in ways that literalised, often violently, the rhetorical maternity of empire attributed to Queen Philippa. One of the many impulses that drove Portugal's overseas expansion, in its various phases, was the need for this geographically small country, which had established its national land boundary with Spain in the fourteenth century, to acquire more land territory both for agricultural cultivation and the export of surplus population. The demographics of the colonial enterprise would therefore impact in profound and interrelated ways on the lived experiences and predominant cultural representations of women, both as colonisers and as colonised.

From the very earliest days of the maritime expansion, white Portuguese women were notable for their absence. Reared in strictly Catholic domestic environments and considered too fragile to contend with tropical conditions, they were closeted at home as the prized white bloodstock of pure Christian families. Very few became travelling companions and pioneering matriarchs overseas. Given this discourse of 'female deficit' in the colonies, both real and imagined, a pattern developed whereby Portuguese sailors, traders, colonial administrators and settlers formed liaisons with native African, Asian and South American indigenous women. As the pragmatics of territorial settlement and missionary christianisation placed a heavy emphasis on the populating of colonial space, a range of official, and unofficial cross-racial practices of reproduction developed in different parts of the empire at different times, according to the contingent needs of the Portuguese metropolis. At the same time, as C. R. Boxer indicates, in the seventeenth and eighteenth centuries, purity of blood and lineage remained preconditions for Portuguese men wishing to enter crown service, the military orders, the priesthood or municipal councils. Thus an important tension becomes discernible between legal family formation which still favoured union with pure-blooded, white élites and the pragmatics of population growth which sanctioned unofficial miscegenation born of concubinage outside marriage. The history of women's experiences under the Portuguese Empire has never been separable from that of race and ethnicity. Indeed, Portugal's much vaunted discourse of miscegenation was later to emerge as a specific distinguishing feature of the Portuguese Empire as distinct from the racial segregation endorsed by Anglo-Saxon, Protestant colonial systems.

As contemporary Portuguese postcolonial critics have pointed out, this has important implications for the way in which key terms of postcolonial criticism, such as 'hybridity' and 'ambivalence' come to be understood as materially raced and sexed concepts in the history of the Portuguese Empire. According to the sociologist, Boaventura de Sousa Santos (2002), 'The desire of the other, upon which Bhabha grounds the ambivalence of the representation of the coloniser, is not in this case a psychoanalytic phenomenon, nor is it doubled in language. It is physical, creative, and engenders creatures.' He continues:

> The existence of ambivalence or hybridity is, therefore, trivial as far as Portuguese postcolonialism is concerned. What is important is to understand the sexist rules of sexuality that usually allow the white man to sleep with the black woman, but not the white woman with the black man. In other words, Portuguese postcolonialism calls for a strong articulation with the question of sexual discrimination and feminism.

As Santos indicates, a particular image of 'Woman', as the eternal feminine matrix of Portuguese hybridity became central to the ways in which Portuguese colonialism represented its own continuity as natural, immutable, universal and divinely ordained. This was particularly true of the influential social theory that came to be known as 'Lusotropicalism' or 'Lusotropicology'. Developed by the Brazilian sociologist Gilberto Freyre in the mid-twentieth century and seeking to represent Brazil's racial mix as invigorating and regenerative, Lusotropicalism was deployed in the 1950s and 1960s as a social and cultural rationale for Portugal's continued colonial presence in Africa.

Portuguese Africa, the 'poor relation' of the lusophone colonies, had come to occupy the centre stage of empire in the late nineteenth century following Brazilian independence in 1822 and the abolition of slavery in 1888, effectively ushering in a modern 'second phase' of Portuguese colonial relations. The Scramble for Africa and the Conference of Berlin in 1884–5 pressured Portugal to undertake a more effective occupation of its colonial properties in the face of rivalry from other European colonial powers, notably Britain. In this process Portugal officialised its claims to Angola, Mozambique, Guinea Bissau, the Cape Verde Islands and the islands of São Tomé e Príncipe. The most intense, nationalistic and integrationist period of Portuguese colonialism in Africa and Asia began with the founding in 1933 of the totalitarian New State régime by António Oliveira Salazar. The Colonial Act of 1930 had already seen a tightening of racial categorisations in Portuguese Africa, and the constitution of 1933 specifically excluded all women and colonised indigenes from national citizenship. In the face of UN pressure and the increase of post-World War II decolonisation movements in neighbouring African countries, Salazarist Portugal remained irrevocably wedded to maintaining its empire in Asia and Africa and to justifying this internationally through recourse to Gilberto Freyre's raced and sexed discourses of Lusotropicalism.

Lusotropicalist theory was derived from a highly romanticised vision of the early discoverers' sexual encounters with native women, as well as the real mixed- race reproduction which slave masters visited upon slave women in Brazilian plantation life. In his later writings of the 1950s and 1960s, Freyre argued that the Portuguese Empire constituted a special, non-racist case, since the supposed racial affinities between the olive-skinned Portuguese and the tropical indigenes provided the 'natural' basis for racial intermixing and miscegenation, linking the Portuguese colonies across the globe in a non-racial, pan-Lusitanian family of empire, created and guided by the Christian civilising mission of the Portuguese. Central to this argument was the apolitical, naturalised status of gender and sexual relations. Where the 'Portuguese' in Freyre's theories were hegemonically male, the unacknowledged sex hierarchy inherent in Freyre's patriarchal scenario (permitting only white male relations with native women) effectively obscured the racism at the roots of

Lusotropicalism's 'whitening' process. Almeida (2004) aptly points out that 'sexual *hybris* naturalises power in the recesses of the libido, thus desocialising the processes of construction of gender and sexuality.' Lusotropicalism also masked women's specific histories of racial and sexual abuse under the Portuguese Empire since an idealised image of Brazilian slave miscegenation denied the sexually coercive situations in which mixed race populations were created.

Lusotropicalist propaganda notwithstanding, the period following World War II saw important stirrings of anti-colonial, anti-fascist, and African nationalist resistance across various cultural and political groupings in the Portuguese African colonies, predominantly among educated, urban coteries of white, left-wing, mixed race and assimilated intellectuals, including a number of women. In Mozambique, the *mestiça* Noémia de Sousa (1923–2003) became a prominent female opponent of colonialism, writing for the women's page of *O Brado Africano* (*The African Cry*) newspaper in the early 1950s as well as publishing a volume of poetry called *Sangue Negro* (*Black Blood*). De Sousa drew on her own mixed-race, assimilated background to deconstruct the premises of assimilation and to unmask the racism that Lusotropicalism concealed. Her contemporary, Alda do Espírito Santo, was also a pioneering figure for women's cultural and political liberation struggle on the island of São Tomé. Both of these women, and others, were involved in the work of the Casa dos Estudantes do Império (CEI) (*House of Students of the Empire*) in Lisbon in the 1950s. This was ostensibly a social meeting place for students from the African colonies but it became an important nucleus of political resistance. It was here that the male architects of Portuguese African decolonisation (most notably Agostinho Neto and Amílcar Cabral) carved out the theories and organisations (MPLA, FRELIMO and PAIGC) that would lead to the armed struggle for independence, beginning in Angola in 1961, spreading to Guinea-Bissau and Cape Verde in 1963 and Mozambique in 1964.

African women *guerrilhas* were actively engaged in armed combat on all fronts of the war. The length and ferocity of Portugal's colonial wars in Africa meant that the armed struggle for independence was progressively radicalised, discarding earlier classic African nationalist thinking to take on the non-racial, internationalist dimensions of Marxist-Leninist class struggle. The Marxist struggle for independence and the installation of state socialist régimes provided the educational and literary training ground for the women writers that emerged after independence. This generation includes Vera Duarte in Cape Verde; Domingas Samy in Guinea-Bissau; Lina Magaia, Lília Momplé and Pauline Chiziane in Mozambique; and Rosária da Silva in Angola. Some of these women were motivated to write primarily in support of the new Marxist-Leninist régimes. Lina Magaia became famous for her representation abroad of the FRELIMO/RENAMO conflict in Mozambique and her denunciation of South African destabilisation in *Dumba Nengue*. Lília Momplé tackled a similar topic in her novella *Neighbours*. Other women writers, such as Paulina Chiziane and Rosária da Silva in their novels *Niketche* and *Totonya*, and Domingas Samy in her short story collection *A Escola* evolved substantially beyond their Marxist roots, bringing challenging female perspectives to bear on sexual relations, body politics and the male-authored dialectics of modernity and tradition in family and kinship patterns. The critical review of Marxism's post-independence legacy for women has become more marked since the end of the Cold War, as the demise of the old nationalist pedagogies, particularly with the coming of democracy in Angola and Mozambique, has shaped women writers' changing perceptions of themselves. In the Cape Verdean archipelago, on the other hand, the fluidity that characterises national boundaries for migrant cultures has always been part of the picture. The construction of the immigrant 'between-space', as a negative dilemma of non-belonging in either colony or metropolis, is movingly rendered in the short stories of the Cape Verdean, Orlanda Amarílis.

Where postmodern, diasporic nation-spaces have unsettled the old liberal and Marxist concepts of unity and integration, one must also consider a literary group that receives relatively little attention in the postcolonial context, the white Luso-Africans who were first-, second- or even third-generation immigrants from Portugal to the colonies and who departed for Portugal following independence. For this group, the mobile boundaries of postcolonial nationhood express conflicted belongings and double-edged identifications that never correspond to the borders of the Marxist one-party state. As they continue to identify in significant if decentred ways with the countries of their birth, their ongoing sense of Africanness is not a matter of passports, visas or citizenship but rather entails affective and aesthetic ties expressed through personal, intimate discourses of memory and loss. A fine example of this is the 2002 poetry collection *Passaporte do Coração* (*Passport of the Heart*) by Ana Mafalda Leite who could be claimed by either Portuguese or Mozambican lyric traditions.

In a somewhat less ambiguous position stand those Portuguese metropolitan women writers who were, in some way, part of the colonial system and its late twentieth-century débâcle in Africa and Asia. Revisiting the events of the colonial war, and the realities of imperial history from a female perspective, these writers give a necessary counterpoint to the more prominent male genre of colonial war veteran memoirs. The best-known work in this category is Lídia Jorge's *The Murmuring Coast*. Derived partly from Jorge's observations as an officer's wife in Beira, Mozambique, this novel deals with women's implication in the violence of the colonial war, powerfully confronting the fact that postcolonial guilt, the inscription of historical memory and the narrative politics of colonial representation are as much women's responsibilities as they are men's. Explicitly deconstructing the national imperialist teleology that connects the twentieth-century colonial experiment with the fifteenth-century sons of Queen Philippa of Lancaster, Jorge denounces the sexist and racist costs of maritime expansion to show that the historically silenced 'wombs of empire' can and must finally talk back.

Hilary Owen

LITERARY WORKS

Beier, Ulli and Gerald Moore (ed.) (1963), *Modern Poetry from Africa*, Harmondsworth: Penguin African Library.

Bruner, Charlotte H. (ed.) (1993), *The Heinemann Book of African Women's Writing*, Oxford: Heinemann.

Chiziane, Paulina (2002), *Niketche. Uma História de Poligamia*, Lisbon: Caminho.

Jorge, Lídia [1988] (1995), *The Murmuring Coast*, trans. Natália Costa and Ronald W. Sousa, Minneapolis, MN: University of Minnesota Press.

Leite, Ana Mafalda (2002), *Passaporte do Coração*, Lisbon: Quetzal.

Magaia, Lina (1988), *Dumba Nengue, Run for your Life: Peasant Tales of Tragedy in Mozambique*, Intro. Allen Isaacman, trans. Michael Wolfers, Trenton, NJ: Africa World Press.

Momplé, Lília (2001), *Neighbours: The Story of a Murder*, trans. Richard Bartlett and Isaura de Oliveira, Oxford: Heinemann.

Samy, Domingas (1993), *A Escola*, Bissau: Author.

Silva, Rosária da [1988] (2005), *Totonya*, Luanda: BJLA.

Vera, Yvonne (ed.) (1999), *Opening Spaces: An Anthology of Contemporary African Women's Writing*, Oxford: Heinemann.

Histories

Almeida, Miguel Vale de (2004), *An Earth-Colored Sea: 'Race', Culture and the Politics of Identity in the Postcolonial Portuguese-Speaking World*, Oxford: Berghahn.

Anderson, Perry (1962), 'Portugal and the End of Ultra-Colonialism', *New Left Review* 15: 83–102; 16: 88–123; 17: 85–114.

Boxer, C. R. (1975), *Mary and Misogyny: Women in Iberian Expansion Overseas 1415–1815: Some Facts, Fancies and Personalities*, London: Duckworth.

Freyre, Gilberto (1961), *Portuguese Integration in the Tropics*, Lisbon: Tipografia Silva.

Madureira, Luís (1994), 'Tropical Sex Fantasies and the Ambassador's Other Death: The Difference in Portuguese Colonialism', *Cultural Critique* 28: 149–73.

Owen, Hilary and Phillip Rothwell (eds) (2004), *Sexual/Textual Empires: Gender and Marginality in Lusophone African Literature*, Lusophone Studies 2, Bristol: University of Bristol. Hispanic, Portuguese and Latin American Studies Dept.

Santos, Boaventura de Sousa (2002), 'Between Prospero and Caliban: Colonialism, Postcolonialism and Inter-identity', *Luso-Brazilian Review* 39 (2): 9–43.

Scott, Catherine V. (1995), *Gender and Development. Rethinking Modernization and Dependency Theory*, Boulder, CO: Lynne Riener.

Sheldon, Kathleen E. (2002), *Pounders of Grain: A History of Women, Work, and Politics in Mozambique*, Portsmouth: Heinemann.

Tétreault, Mary Ann (ed.) (1994), *Women and Revolution in Africa, Asia, and the New World*, Columbia, SC: University of South Carolina Press.

Urdang, Stephanie (1979), *Fighting Two Colonialisms: Women in Guinea-Bissau*, New York and London: Monthly Review Press.

— (1989), *And Still They Dance: Women, War, and the Struggle for Change in Mozambique*, London: Earthscan Publications.

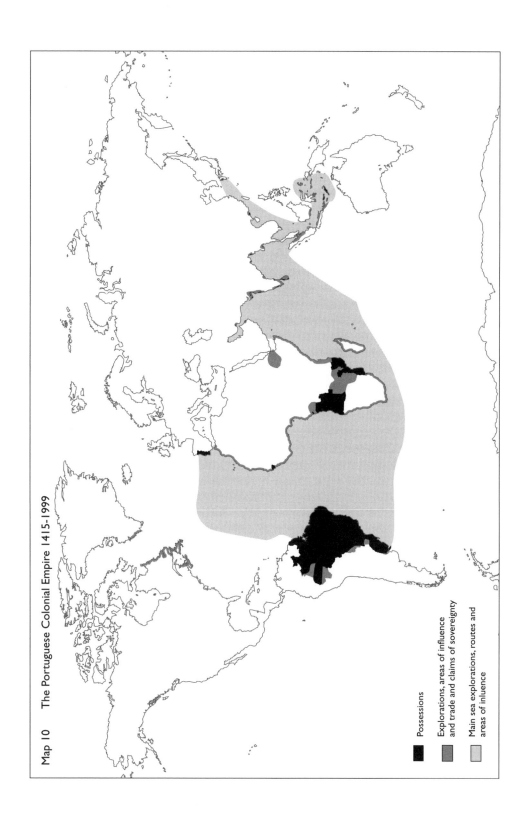

Map 10   The Portuguese Colonial Empire 1415-1999

■ Possessions

■ Explorations, areas of influence
   and trade and claims of sovereignty

   Main sea explorations, routes and
   areas of influence

Spain, Latin America and the Philippines

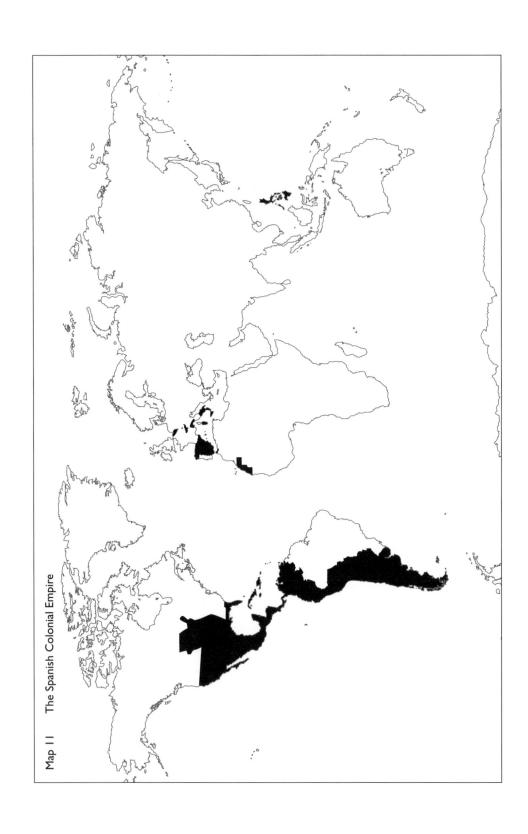

Map 11   The Spanish Colonial Empire

Spain and Latin America: Introduction

Two empires mobilised the first European expansion in America: Spain and Portugal. Both deployed unparalleled forces that resulted in the establishment of colonial rule in America, and the proliferation of Eurocentric modernities grounded in sixteenth-century mercantilism. Both failed to conceive of social and cultural encounters with the colonised except through the logic of possession, consumption, commodification and violence. In the case of Spain, this coercive logic was operative throughout the long period of the Reconquista (718–1492), when the military expansion of Christianity across the Iberian peninsula put to work a violent method of exterminating multicultural forms of society (Jewish and Muslim communities). Camouflaged under a spirit of 'crusade against unfaithful peoples', this forceful process of *reconquista* and political expansion culminated on 2 January 1492 with the fall of Granada (the last Muslim kingdom in the Iberian Peninsula), and had its greatest momentum nine months later, when Columbus first sighted the Indias Occidentales and the first Spanish settlement was established in the land of Hispañola on 12 October 1492. Twenty-nine years later, in 1521, Fernando de Magallanes reached the Western Pacific Islands, which in 1565 were incorporated into the Spanish Empire as the Philippines, a name coined by Ruy López de Villalobos in 1543, after Philip II then prince of Spain.

Imperial Spain built itself upon a structure of political, economic and theological power that claimed universal applicability and rendered any expression of difference invisible or subaltern. Not surprisingly, therefore, recent debates on the history of the colonisation of the Americas have often been informed by postcolonial theory, given the commitment of this late twentieth-century paradigm to both the historical destinies of the colonised and the dismantling of the colonising logic. And yet, as the twentieth century drew to an end, an erosion of Latin American local theorisations – empowered by the emergence of new historical actors such as social movements, indigenous movements and the women's movements – have challenged the theoretical reach of postcolonial theory by inviting us to think not only about the role of the Americas in relation to this conceptual paradigm but also in relation to its core discussion: the feasibility for alternative knowledges to interrupt imperial epistemic privileges.

To begin with, the extent to which in the Americas the colonial experience has a story of its own became evident. This is to say, we are dealing here with a story clearly different from that of the South-Asian realities that produced postcolonial theory, even when its primary thinkers write within the limits of a South–North discussion engaged from the perspective of US-based university departments (Edward Said, Gayatri Chakravorty Spivak, Partha Chatterjee and Homi Bhabha, for instance). For these creators of postcolonial discourses, the colonial experience has its inaugural moment in the eighteenth century, when Western European modernity and its ideology of nationalism (a European export to the rest of the world, in the words of Chatterjee) implanted an essential cultural difference between East and West.

From a Latin American perspective, however, the colonial experience begins in the sixteenth century (when the first European expansion 'turned the world upside down' as stated by Indian chronicler Felipe Guaman Poma de Ayala [1987]), and continues today under pervasive forms of perpetuation. In the late 1960s, it was the Mexican sociologist Pablo González Casanova (1992) who first reflected on this pervasiveness, identifying it as a form of *colonialismo interno* (internal colonialism). By this he meant the survival, in contemporary Latin American societies, of old structures of power that facilitate neo-colonial exploitations. In the 1970s, Bolivian sociologist Silvia Rivera Cusicanqui (1997) returned to González Casanova's concept of internal colonialism to develop an insurgent historiography in the Andean region in close collaboration with indigenous intellectuals committed to the production of decolonised knowledge in the region, but also to anti-colonial struggles. Later on, in 2000, Peruvian social scientist Aníbal Quijano advanced his theory of the 'coloniality of power', which locates the sources of present-day world power in the radicalisation of social, political and cultural relations. For Quijano, the most significant historical implication of the radicalised condition of social relations is 'the emergence of a Eurocentred capitalist colonial/modern world power'.

Interestingly enough, while Quijano's work on the coloniality of power had wide repercussions among Latin American postcolonial scholars in the North American academy, González Casanova remains a stranger to that readership; and Rivera Cusicanqui does not receive full credit for having first theorised the concept and, more importantly, for having associated it with current anti-colonial struggles in the Andes. In fact, Quijano doesn't even quote his predecessors when he refers to 'internal' colonisation in his celebrated essay entitled 'Coloniality of Power and Eurocentrism in Latin America' (a theoretical milestone for Latin American postcolonial scholars in the US). The whole situation clearly speaks about the conditions under which Latin American theorisations enter – or not – into metropolitan circuits of knowledge. When their creators produce theory in situ, from the perspective of the subalterns, and independent of metropolitan connections, their contributions to current debates remain relatively unknown. By the same token, it becomes evident that local Latin American theorisations on the colonial experience are primarily directed towards the creation of decolonising historiographies and are accomplished by the same actors who are making viable social and cultural transformations in the region and not, as in the case of postcolonial theory, by scholars committed to subaltern subjects while not really being part of them. This explains why, for postcolonial scholars, the 'mediation of knowledge via Europe and Western epistemologies' will not be a problem (Rodríguez 2005), while for Latin American decolonising writers, Western mediations will be conceived of as problematic, and indigenous and non-institutionalised thinkers (such as the above mentioned Indian chronicler Felipe Guaman Poma de Ayala, but also heterodox thinkers such as José Carlos Mariátegui, Fausto Reinaga or Gamaliel Churata) will be as relevant as academic ones.

In response to these particular circumstances, the selection of texts in this section differs from that in the other parts of this reader in two principal ways: (1) its emphasis on the cultural dimension of the colonial experience and its aftermath in Spain and its American, African and Asian empire; and, (2) its desire to see vital continuities of cultural history and anti-colonial resistance extending from the sixteenth and seventeenth centuries to the present. There is also a difference with standard histories of colonial Latin America, which tend to privilege Peru and Mexico, the seats of the two major viceroyalties in the early seventeenth century. Our selection and approach here suggests looking at the colonial experience more from the margins of the great viceroyalties – that is, from the point of view of that which is 'supplementary' to the usual account of Spanish colonialism. Our selection puts a special emphasis, first, on Bolivia, because of the crucial significance of its anti-colonial political, social and cultural movement today, and, second, on the Philippines, which has been all but ignored in accounts of Spanish colonialism, but which introduces an Asian dimension that is of utmost geopolitical relevance today. Our selection also relativises what one critic has called the 'colonial imposture', that is the gesture by the Creole élites in Latin America in the late eighteenth and early nineteenth centuries, to see themselves, rather than the indigenous and African peoples actually conquered and colonised by Spain and Portugal, as the victims of Spanish colonialism, and to identify Independence with their own interests and values. Going against the grain of that standard narrative of political Independence and nation formation, our selection pays attention to the agency of non-Creole subjects and peoples in the Hispanic Americas and Asian Pacific as central to the process of decolonisation, as much today as in the past.

The purpose of this introduction, therefore, is to present the reader with a comprehensive contextualisation of Latin American decolonising historiography and critique as it has taken shape in the course of more than five centuries of coloniality, including the achievements and failures to prevent its reproduction through conquest, colonisation, nationalism, capitalism, neo-colonialism and neo-liberalism. The first hint of this historiography arises from the meaning acquired by the history of the colonised peoples once it is investigated from the viewpoint of their own discourses, that is to say, within the framework of Amerindian cultural grammars. These grammars can be first accessed through the great historic-cosmogonic narratives that Gordon Brotherston calls 'the books of the Fourth World', and include texts such as the *Ayvu Rapyta* (*Origin of the Human Language*) of the Tupi-Guarani, the *Runa Indio* (*Huarochirí Manuscript*) of the Quechua, the *Nueva Corónica y Buen Gobierno* by Felipe Guamán Poma de Ayala, the *Popol Vuh* (*Book of Counsel*) of the K'iche-Maya and the *Books of Chilam Balam* ('Books of the Wizard-Jaguar') of the Maya; the *Amoxtli* (painted books) produced by Nahuatl *tlacuilos*; the *kipu* (knotted threads) produced by the Quechua and Aymara, and also through Andean textiles, as part of the materials produced before, during and after the Spanish Conquest, and available to contemporary readers after spectacular reconstructions and survivals.

The Western canon erroneously perceived these texts as myths, codex, museum curiosities, or vernacular expressions produced by primitive societies that had not achieved the greatness of civilisation through writing. And yet, recent studies (Arnold and Yapita 2004; Brotherston 1992; Gruzinski 1992, 1993; Rabasa 2002) have demonstrated that no Amerindian culture at the moment of the Conquest lacked writing. On the contrary, Amerindian cultures were saturated by writing, but since the scriptural systems at play were not alphabetic (as in the case of the pictographic writing of the *Amoxtli*, the hieroglyphic writing of the *Popol Vuh*, the knotted threads known as *kipu*, or the Andean textiles), it was easy for European phonocentrism to dismiss them as illiterate or irrational expressions. If, as an alphabet-oriented perspective would suggest, only by means of alphabetic writing can a given culture establish its capacity to be civilised, then any cultural formation perceived as *agrapha* would result in a non-culture, in a group of people with no human attributes, and without the capacity for self-reflection and symbolic representation. That is how imperial Spain (and its dominant cultural form: the colonial Baroque that John Beverley critically examines in this section) perceived the American indigenous peoples.

The contributions of Carlos López and Denise Arnold included in this section address all these complexities by paying attention to some of the most intriguing and fascinating Amerindian narratives: the *Popol Vuh*, and Andean textiles. In the first case, the author suggests that despite the manipulations of evangelisation, its reduction to Western alphabetic writing, and the arbitrariness of interpretation imposed by early twentieth-century anthropology and ethnography, ancient Amerindian narratives survive and challenge the monopoly of colonial chronicles of the conquest (Colombus, Cortés, Cabeza de Vaca, Bernal Díaz del Castillo, and so on) as well as their potential to give a comprehensive account of Amerindian histories. By reading them we learn that the Amerindian world, which Western Europe began to know of at the end of the sixteenth century by means of the work of missionaries and their native informants, was a coherent and compact universe perfectly able to produce knowledge, but also reflections on their colonial condition. In the case of the *Popol Vuh*, its final pages register the collapse suffered by the K'iche Maya as a result of the arrival of the Spaniards, and how this event distorted the internal logic of their world, demanding from its inhabitants various cultural adjustments that would violently eradicate the foundations that explained and conceptualised their realities. More importantly, López' work emphasises the political role that these ancestral traditions play for modern Mayans today, for whom the *Popol Vuh*, far from being an expression of the dead past, connects with the social practices that are involved in the resurgence of Maya culture and its decolonising struggles.

Denise Arnold's entry on Andean textiles brings the discussion of Amerindian scriptural systems through the various stages of their cultural and subversive functions. The reader learns that these textualities, mainly produced by women who 'weave' them, had the potential effectively to subvert colonial power by forging alternative forms of writing, textual authority and social memory. Arnold links the cultural action of 'weaving a textile' to the politics of 'waiving a communal history' deeply rooted in subversive memories and decolonising struggles. This notion of culture as a field of struggle is further discussed by Gonzalo Lamana. He takes up the idea that while Columbus' arrival in the Americas gave Spain the resources to lead the first global design, facilitated the rise of European world hegemony and caused the crushing of Amerindian cultures, native peoples did not play the role of victims. By whatever means, they struggled to destabilise the new order, transforming the colonial enterprise into a contested arena.

Also enacting a notion of culture as a battlefield, Dante Ambrosio's entry on Spanish-Christian Influences on Philippine Society and Culture explores the layers of complexity and syncretic appropriation of colonial structures that accompanied Spanish colonial rule in the Philippines. His historical account of more than three hundred years of colonial rule presents Filipino people as immersed in the process of being constructed primarily through modes of cultural and political resistance to colonising designs trying to reshape the islands according to their own material interests. From a different but complementary perspective, Jaime Balcos Veneracion's entry on the Philippines-Mexico Connection addresses one of the most challenging outcomes of the hispanisation of the Philippines. He demonstrates that while the Spanish Crown aimed at the 'hispanisation' of its colonies, more than two hundred years of Mexican-Philippine Galleon trade promoted a process of 'indigenisation' that affected all levels of social, cultural, political, and economic interaction. The entry on Marianisation in the Philippines by Evelyn Miranda covers another significant aspect of the lasting nature of the Spanish influence on the Philippines: religion. The specific role of literature as an instrument of culture and power in the Philippines is taken up by María Luisa Reyes, whose entry includes information that expands our historical knowledge on the islands and provides a comprehensive analysis of a literature that by the nineteenth century ceased to refer only to Philippine-born Spaniards to include Spanish and Chinese *mestizos*, and Hispanised *indios*.

Other entries in this section bring into focus the uninterrupted continuity of anti-colonial struggles in the Americas from the Conquest to the present. In the work of Juan

Antonio Hernández, but also in the first part of Arturo Arias' contribution, this continuity is examined from a Pan-Caribbeanist perspective centred on Marronage and Afro communities that began to revolt against forced labour imposed by the European colonial system as soon as the shock of the Conquest wore off. A challenge to the slave régime, these revolts – and their effects – are then contrasted with the Indigenous rebellions against colonial power that also burst immediately after the Conquest and have continued to challenge modern states and political modernity up until the present days. In both cases the most pervasive legacies of colonialism will remain a constant: patriarchy and racism.

John Beverley's entry on the Túpac Amaru Rebellion focuses on the most destabilising episode in the history of eighteenth-century colonial Spain, in which 2 million natives rose up against the viceroyalty of Peru demanding the elimination of the *mita* (system of forced labour), the *corregimiento* (district governance of Indians) and the *repartimiento* (system of land distribution), the three colonial institutions most directly responsible for the destruction of the indigenous communities in the Andean region. Beverley argues that Túpac Amaru's rebellion (as well as the parallel uprising led by Túpac Katari in what is today Bolivia) was the first of the great anti-colonial rebellions in modern history, and insinuates that in the Andes an Indian-centred society has historically posed a challenge to colonial and *criollo* politics.

Interestingly enough, as Arturo Arias suggests in the second part of his entry, three centuries after the first colonial encounters the advent of the first republics brought *criollos* and *mestizos* to power. With them, West European Enlightenment and liberal ideals inspired by the French Revolution emerged as leading forces that would shape the new republican states in their journey towards civilisation. There were sixteen newly created republics, with Mexico, Argentina and Brazil the most important centres of political, economic and cultural post-colonial life. It was precisely in reference to Mexico, that France coined the term 'Latin America' in the mid-1800s in an attempt to naturally justify its presence in the region (given the common 'Latin' origin of both cultures), but also to counter-balance the increasing US influence in the Americas, which had began soon after independence. The French occupation of Mexico lasted only five years (1862–67), ending with the execution of Maximilian of Hapsburg and the exaltation of liberalism in the figure of Benito Juárez. The 'Latin American' label, however, remained an inevitable cultural mark that even today many simply refuse to abandon.

Under *criollo* and *mestizo* rule, indigenous and African descendant subjects were seen as the agents of barbarism who had either to be exterminated or civilised. In the first years of the twentieth century, political Liberalism considered both populations as a 'biological problem' that was an obstacle to the progress of modern societies. The solutions that were then provided emerged from rationalising discourses bolstered by positivism, the pseudo-science of the late nineteenth century that scientifically proved the racial inferiority of Indians (in countries like Mexico, Peru, Bolivia or Guatemala) and/or Afro-descendants (in the Caribbean countries).

It was in the wake of the Mexican Revolution that a new political and cultural force emerged in Latin America: nationalism and its corollaries, mestizaje and indigenism. The contributions of Joshua Lund and Javier Sanjinés take their point of departure from several theses about the meaning and theoretical resonances of these key words in Latin Americanism. Lund concentrates on a meta-critical discussion of how a derivative term of mestizaje, *hibridez cultural* (cultural hybridity) entered both postcolonial theory (via Bhabha) as well as Latin American cultural theory (via García Canclini) without necessarily affecting each other, but nevertheless fully impacting the theoretical discussion of the 1990s.

The contribution of Javier Sanjinés addresses both the *mestizo* project of nation-building, as well as the cultural paradigm of indigenism within the historical framework of the two regions that produced the most intense debates on the 'national' subject: Mexico and the Andes. His work suggests that while mestizaje became the solution for diluting the barbarism of the Indian with the civilisation of the white population, indigenism was a lot more versatile. It could embody an official nationalistic rhetoric that sought to assimilate native cultures and traditions into modern, Westernised nations (as in the case of the Bolivian *letrados*), but it could also conceive of a unique, non-Western culture for Latin America (as in the case of Peruvian avant-garde indigenists Mariátegui, Orrego or Haya de la Torre).

Focused on this same historical period, Elizabeth Monasterios entries point out that side by side with the Peruvian avant-garde indigenism, an even more radical cultural intervention emerged in the Andes which is today still unacknowledged by trendy literary studies and cultural theory. What moved this intervention, making of it an 'Andean avant-garde', was a cultural project that, without necessarily breaking from Mariátegui, Orrego or Haya, operated from a position of radical alterity rooted in the conflicted space between colonising forces and decolonising wills. The authors who enacted such an intervention (mainly the Peruvians Gamaliel Churata and Alejandro Peralta, and the Bolivian Arturo Borda) shared the idea that indigenous peoples didn't need the mediation of any indigenist nor of any intellectual to make themselves viable, and that the day would come in which the Indo-American philosophical wealth would openly speak. For this to happen, they interrupted the representation of Indians through dominant frameworks of knowledge (indigenism and mestizaje), and let Amerindian cultural grammars to speak, converting the Andes in a site of defiant theoretical and epistemological debate.

In dialogue with these claims, Marcia Stephenson's contribution discusses the outbreak of indigenous mobilisation and cultural resurgence in the Bolivian Andes by examining the unprecedented thought of indigenous writer Fausto Reinaga (1906–44), who contested *mestizo-criollo* indigenism from the position of Indianism, a political and epistemological force of Indians fighting for their decolonisation. Stephenson stresses that this thinker, who encouraged a clear anti-colonial struggle, reclaimed indigenous historical knowledge as a site of resistance, critically examined the 'basics' of postcolonial discourse and insurgent nationalistic movements (Fanon, Gandhi, Malcolm X), and challenged the legacy of racism in left ideology, gave no place in his writings to the Indian woman. In this sense Reinaga's work (but also that of his predecessors) does not challenge patriarchal relations of power, inviting the reader to question gender subalternity from within decolonising perspectives.

John Beverley's entry on Calibán can be read as engaged in a dialogue with Reinaga's criticism of postcolonial discourse. First, Beverley claims that Roberto Fernández Retamar's celebrated essay 'Calibán' (1971) inaugurated postcolonial criticism in Latin America by building a character who challenges colonial epistemology from the position of a *masculine* mestizaje as the normative form of postcolonial identity. He then argues that at the bottom of this narrative lies a *criollo-mestizo* project that in spite of its decolonising agenda brings to light the central *aporia* of a representative cultural theory, which privileges representing marginal Others (women, Indians, and Afro-descendants) rather than legitimating their agency for cultural and political autonomy.

Beverley's radical criticism speaks of the conceptual conflictiveness of decolonising endeavours when a plurality of consciousness comes into consideration and when coloniality is challenged by non-hegemonic spheres of contestation. Denise Arnold's entry Colonialism and Popular Culture in the Andes addresses this latent conflict in *criollo-mestizo* Latin Americanism by addressing the scandal posed by indigenous popular practices. Marginalised since colonial times, popular culture has always challenged the hegemony of 'universal culture.' In the twentieth century, *criollo-mestizo* coloniality and neo-liberal politics have insistently distinguished belletristic traditions from 'handicraft' and 'folklore' in an attempt to keep subaltern populations apart from urban ones. Arnold's work observes that in many cases universal culture happily absorbs popular culture via the culture industry of expanding capitalism. But when popular culture becomes politically challenging (for instance in the Bolivia of Evo Morales), hegemonic culture quickly rearticulates its ruling position by reinforcing internal colonialism.

The underlying conflictivity of Latin American critical thought is furthermore discussed by Michael Handelsman, Julia Suárez Krabbe and Gustavo Verdesio. Their entries debate the questions and concerns that should be addressed when dealing over a critical thinking situated in a complex on-going process of affirmation, historical (re)construction and decolonisation. Finally, two entries, one by John Beverley on Spain, Modernity and Coloniality, the other by Julia Suárez Krabbe on Spanish Colonialism in a World Perspective, deal with the global logic of Spanish colonialism, providing the fundamental theoretical means to critically understand European modernity as a product of colonialism, and the modern world system we live in as its most refined outcome. Both entries make explicit a theme running through this section as a whole: that the Spanish conquest and colonisation of the New World was the condition of possibility for the later European colonial projects.

Elizabeth Monasterios

LITERARY WORKS

Ayvu Rapyta. Textos míticos de los Mbyá-Guaraní del Guairá (1997), Asunción: Biblioteca Paraguaya de Antropología.

Borda, Arturo (1966), *El Loco*, 3 vols, La Paz: Honorable Alcaldía Municipal de La Paz.

Churata, Gamaliel (1957), *El Pez de Oro. Retablos del Laykhakuy*, La Paz: Editorial Canata.

Cantares Mexicanos (1994), Facsimile edition of the anonymous manuscript conserved at the Biblioteca Nacional de México, ed. Miguel León-Portilla, Mexico City: Universidad Nacional Autónoma de México.

Códex Mendoza (1992), 4 vols, ed. Frances Berdan and Patricia Reiff, Berkeley, CA: University of California Press.

Dioses y hombres de Huarochirí. Narración quechua recogida por Francisco de Avila [c. 1598] (1966), ed. José María Arguedas and Pierre Duviols, Lima: Museo Nacional de Historia e Instituto de Estudios Peruanos.

Chilam Balam de Tazimin. (Manuscript) The Ancient Future of the Itza: The Book of Chilam Balam of Tisimin (1982), trans. and ed., Munro S. Edmonson, Austin, TX: University of Texas Press.

Fernández Retamar, Roberto 'Calibán' [1971] (1979), *Calibán y otros ensayos: Nuestra América y el mundo*, La Habana: Arte y Literatura.

Haya de la Torre, Víctor Raúl (1935), *¿A dónde va Indoamérica?*, 2nd edn, Santiago de Chile: Editorial Arcilla.

Mariátegui, José Carlos [1928] (1975), *Siete ensayos de interpretación de la realidad Peruana*, La Habana: Casa de las Américas.

Orrego, Antenor (2004), *Antenor Orrego: modernidad y culturas americanas: páginas escogidas*, ed. Eugenio Chang-Rodríguez, Lima: Fondo Editorial de Congreso del Perú.

Peralta, Alejandro (1926), *Ande*, Puno: Editorial Titikaka.

Popol Vuh. Las antiguas historias del Quiché (1953), ed. Adrián Recinos, México: Fondo de Cultura Económica.

HISTORIES

Arnold, Denise, and Juan de Dios Yapita (2004), 'The Nature of Indigenous Literatures in the Andes', in Mario J. Valdés and Djelal Kadir (eds), *Literary Cultures of Latin America. A Comparative History*, vol. 3, New York: Oxford University Press, pp. 385–414.

Bhabha, Homi K. (1994), *The Location of Culture*, London and New York: Routledge and Kegan Paul.

Bolívar, Simón [1819] (1984), 'Discurso pronunciado por el Libertador ante el Congreso de Angostura el 15 de febrero de 1918, día de su instalación', *Obras Completas*, 6: 148–71.

Brotherston, Gordon (1992), *Book of the Fourth World: Reading the Native Americas through their Literature*, Cambridge: Cambridge University Press.

Chasteen, John Charles (2001), *Born in Blood and Fire: A Concise History of Latin America*, New York: Norton.

Chatterjee, Partha (1986), *Nationalist Thought and the Colonial World, A Derivative Discourse*, London: Zed Books.

Cornejo Polar, Antonio (1978), 'El indigenismo y las literaturas heterogéneas: su doble estatuto socio-cultural', *Revista de Crítica Literaria Latinoamericana* 7–8: 7–21.

Dussel, Enrique (1995), *1492, The Invention of the Americas: Eclipse of the 'Other' and the Myth of Modernity*, trans. Michael D. Barber, New York: Continuum.

Fanon, Franz (1961), *Les Dammés de la terre*, Paris: Maspero.

Gandhi, Mahatma (1996), *Mahatma Gandhi: Selected Political Writings*, ed. Dennis Dalton, Indianapolis: Hackett Publishing Co.

González Casanova, Pablo (1992), 'Colonialismo interno. Una definición', *América Latina. Historia y Destino. Homenaje a Leopoldo Sea*, México: UNAM.

Gruzinski, Serge (1992), *Painting the Conquest: The Mexican Indians and the European Renaissance*, trans. Deke Dusinberre, Paris: Flammarion.

— (1993), *The Conquest of México: The Incorporation of Indian Society into the Western World, Sixteenth–Eighteenth Centuries*, trans. Eileen Corrigan, Cambridge: Polity Press.

Guamán Poma de Ayala, Felipe [c. 1613] (1987), *Nueva corónica y buen gobierno*, ed. John Murra, Rolena Adorno, and Jorge L. Urioste, Madrid: Historia 16.

Mignolo, Walter (1995), *The Darker Side of the Renaissance: Literacy, Territoriality and Colonisation*, Ann Arbor, MI: The University of Michigan Press.

Morales, Evo (2003), 'Bolivia, el poder del pueblo', *La Jornada*, 25 October.

Quijano, Aníbal (2000), 'Coloniality of Power and Eurocentrism in Latin America', *International Sociology* 15(2): 215–32.

Rabasa, José (2002), 'Pre-Columbian Pasts and Indian Presents in Mexican History', in Alvaro Félix Bolaños and Gustavo Verdesio (eds), *Colonialism Past and Present*, New York: SUNY Press, pp. 51–78.

Rama, Angel (1982), *Transculturación narrativa en América latina*, México: Siglo XXI.

Reinaga, Fausto (1978), *Indianidad*, La Paz: Imprentas Unidas.

Rivera Cusicanqui, Silvia (1997), 'Presentación', in Silvia Rivera Cusicanqui and Rossana Barragán (eds), *Debates Post Coloniales: Una introducción a los estudios de la subalternidad*, La Paz: Sierpe, pp. 11–19.

Rodríguez, Ileana (2005), 'Is There a Need for Subaltern Studies?', *Dispositio/N* 52: 43–62.

Said, Edward (1978), *Orientalism*, New York: Pantheon.

— (1989), 'Representing the Colonised: Anthropology's Interlocutors', *Critical Inquiry* 15: 205–25.

Spivak, Gayatri Chakravorty (1988), 'Can the Subaltern Speak?', in Cary Nelson and Lawrence Grossberg (eds), *Marxism and the Interpretation of Cultures*, Urbana, IL: University of Illinois Press.

The Andean Avant-Garde: A Latin American decolonising debate

Alongside twentieth-century avant-garde production, there emerged in the Andes an insurgent, anti-hegemonic and peripheral avant-garde yet to be acknowledged by current literary studies, which remains captivated by concepts of nationalism that prevent the thinking of a cultural, yet complex territoriality, as expressed in the idea of an Andean avant-garde. This movement emerged in Puno (Peru) around 1920, and shared the iconoclastic and renewing spirit emblematic to avant-garde writers. But unlike them, its language and its imaginary conveyed a powerful decolonising consciousness as well as a solid criticism of modernity.

Without necessarily breaking from the other 'vanguardists' that in the same years shocked the region, giving rise to the so-called Andean Indigenism (a movement mainly articulated under the influence of writers like González Prada, Mariátegui, Vallejo and Valcárcel), this distinct avant-garde resisted the attempt to understand the tragedy of indigenous peoples through European conceptual frames (Marxism being one of them), or from interpretations derived from the template of the mestizaje, clearly the *episteme* of the time. Understanding Andean cultures as realities historically torn by the effects of conquest, colonisation and twentieth-century forms of neo-colonisation, the members of this avant-garde conceived the legitimisation of an Andean reason, including its myths and rituals (that primitive past so stigmatised by narratives of modernity), as an act of emancipation from Spain as well as from the Latin American republican élites. Emphatically, however, they rejected any form of messianic indigenism, for it was not the triumph of a fossilised past but the construction of a time of insurgence informed by the past that they were looking for. Among those who enacted this movement, making it something different from Mariátegui and Vallejo's social 'vanguardisms', and also from the rhetoric of indigenism, the following writers stand out: the Peruvians Gamaliel Churata (1897–1969), Alejandro Peralta (1899–1965), and Uriel García (1891–1965); and the Bolivians Arturo Borda (1883–1953) and Carlos Medinaceli (1898–1949).

Deeply unconventional and anti-academic, with formidable scholarly abilities, the work of these writers performs an epistemological demolition of the Western teleological framework that steered the cultural life of their age, and resists the passing of time with astonishing creativity and originality. This unique cultural practice can be approached through a review of Gamaliel Churata's work after 1930, when the Orkopata Group that he had created ended its activities. This group was the epicentre of a peripheral Peruvian avant-garde that operated from the city of Puno and counted among its members indigenous poets as Inocencio Mamani and Eustaquio Aweranka. That is also the period when the *Boletín Titikaka* (*Titikaka Bulletin*, 1926–30), the group's main organ of diffusion, and the axle of Puno's avant-garde indigenism, ceased publication. Luis Alberto Sánchez once referred to this publication as 'the most curious and unusual of events in Peruvian literature' (Sánchez 1981).

In the Aymara language *Churata* means 'the chosen one', and 'Gamaliel Churata' was the pseudonym for Arturo Peralta. Churata was contemporaneous with a group of writers and artists known as the Generación Centenario, which included Uriel García, José Carlos

Mariátegui, José Sabojal, Luis Alberto Sánchez, and César Vallejo. Never organically associated with this group, Churata led a cultural counter-march that operated from the provincial city of Puno, which he named the 'Titikaka avant-garde'.

During his years of cultural activism in Puno, Churata had come to understand two
things that would orient his subsequent work: that Indians didn't need any indigenism nor
any intellectual to make themselves viable, and that the day would come in which 'the elu-
cidation of our Indoamerican philosophical tradition shall be confronted' (Churata 1957: 10).
Armed with this decolonising perception, and from a long exile in Bolivia (1932–64),
Churata devoted himself to finishing a monumental text which he had started writing in
1927 but completed only in 1957: *El pez de oro: retablos del laykhakuy* (*The Golden Fish:
Narratives of the Indian Wizard*). This book is a text deeply disruptive of the aesthetics of its
time. Five hundred pages of epistemological insurrection written in a multilingual style
that conforms to no established gender, and forges a protagonist who embodies the possibility of historic *pachacuti* ('change') in the Andes. With reference to this work, Marco
Thomas Bosshard has recently observed that this is a text that 'frightens', adding that the
marginalisation it suffered in the intellectual circles of Lima was due to the engagement of
its author with Andean indigenous cultures. According to Bosshard, 'The reader that
Churata addresses has perhaps existed for only two decades (this doesn't coincide with the
reader of José María Arguedas, but certainly with a reader like Arguedas).' It is in the light
of this provocative framework that contemporary readers can appreciate the impact of a
text that from its first page establishes that:

> the starting point of every literature lies in the language that sustains it. We Americans [from
> the Americas] don't have literature, philosophy, rights of people, public rights that are not
> contained in the vernacular languages . . . [and yet] we insist on writing by means of a lingua
> *non kuika*: the Hispanic one. And in so doing we scribble on it 'as Indians;' although not in
> Indian, which is a different thing. (Churata 1957: 9–10, my translation. I should alert the
> readers about the inherent linguistic and syntactic difficulty of *El Pez de Oro*, which makes
> translation an extremely challenging task. In translating I have tried as much as possible to
> preserve the integrity of a text that by all means resists linguistics domestication.)

This unsettling reflection on language enables Churata to question the authority of the
Inca Garcilaso de la Vega because 'he, who could and should have[written] in *Kheswa*, used
instead, and with such a Theresian grace! the language of his father, condemning his
mother's language to an interdiction short of being fatal' (Churata 1957: 11). Churata's critique of Garcilaso is based on the idea that for Andean subjects, Kheswa and Aymara play
a similar role to that of Latin and Greek for Greco-Romans, except that they are not repos-
itories of a 'classical knowledge' but of a 'classical sentiment of nature', of a cultural
grammar able to *express* (as opposed to the indigenist project of *representing*) the reality of
the Americas by provoking thoughts that 'in no time will become the politics and the aesthetics of its people' (Churata 1957: 10). Following this argument, Churata observes that
writing in the Andes at the fringes of an Andean cultural grammar shows 'how intercepted
Garcilaso carried the Indian within' and to what extent his writing subalternises his Indian
origin (Churata 1957).

This questioning of the colonial determinism that establishes uneven relations between
imperial languages and *lenguas kuikas* ('aboriginal ones'), also leads Churata to question cultural *mestizaje* as the possibility for a new national identity in the Andes. If Garcilaso was
an icon of the biological *mestizo*, how was it going to be viable to incorporate Indians in a

scheme that subalternised American languages? For Churata, the weakness of *Comentarios Reales* derives from the fact that in the metropolis, the germs of the conquered tend to dilute, producing what today's cultural theory would call transculturation from above. In contrast, when preserved within the conceptual frame of the aboriginal world, their potentiality is increased, motivating creative tensions between the Andean and the metropolitan culture. We can refer to these 'tensions' as forms of transculturation from below.

What better introduction to a Latin American decolonising historiography than these reflections on the subalternisation of indigenous languages and cultures? Furthermore, what better argument to embark on a theoretical reflection of the colonised condition of Latin-American literature? Churata himself begins this reflection by denouncing the absence of an Andean historiography in the midst of the twentieth century. In his opinion, this oblivion is not because of the non-existence of sources (there are, Churata insists, Guaman Poma de Ayala's work and the letters of Túpac Katari to Brigadier Segurola during the siege of La Paz in 1872), rather it is due to the lack of a disposition to assume the validity of those sources. Emphatically, Churata maintains that:

> . . . in the Americas, literary nobility cannot come from the colonial motherlands. Spanish colony constitutes the negation of the Americas' motherland; regardless of how much some gurus would say that not only do they give us definition in calling us Indians, but that Spain least conquered America inasmuch as it has invented it.
>
> It did not invent it! It has erased it! And we are the rough draft, Creoles and mestizos, for whom Spain is not worth a pit, and the Indian even less.
>
> [. . .] Nobody saw in the filthy Spanish of Guaman Poma or Tupac Katari the dialectic of an aesthetic, no critic tabulated the entanglement [*chaskadera*]; it was left for the spectacle of the indigenous market [*tantakatu*]. It was never thought that the aesthetic capacity of the Americas lies with the plebeian zones where American soul was confined.
>
> [. . .] The American world keeps itself reduced to the Indian silence, [but] that stillness will break one day, judging by the magnitude of this world and its expansive process, there is no doubt. However, it will be broken by the work of the Indian, which is the only thing with régimen in himself, with root and cosmos. (Churata 1957: 21, 25, 26)

We are certainly in the presence of a brutal emancipation of discourse regarding Western teleological frames. Bosshard is right in pointing out that Churata is writing 'exactly as Vallejo had demanded when he lamented the nonexistent "proper physiognomy" of American writers and observed the urgency of attaining in the Americas a spirit of one's own' (Vallejo 1927).

Together with a denunciation of the colonial legacy, there is, in *El pez de oro*, a great lucidity to foreseeing an eventual indigenous leadership, voiced in the idea that the silence that characterised Indians from colonial times 'will have to be broken one day, judging by the magnitude of this world and its process of expansion, there is no doubt. But it will be broken through the action of indigenous people, the only existence with a self-contained system, with roots and with cosmos' (Churata 1957: 26). Interestingly enough, Churata does not perceive in the members of the Andean avant-garde (mainly *mestizo* writers) those who will have a leading role in the indigenous momentum. In his opinion, this role will have to be played by the Indians themselves. This idea is clearly expressed on the last page of *El pez de oro*:

> We do not anticipate the number of centuries that this NEW BIRTH would require; however, we understand, that they will not be as many as 500 millennia – and even if they were – the

ones that would allow the Americans of the Americas to be and to express themselves in their lacteal language. Those poets of the Ayllu – the Orko-patas Mamani or Awaranka – are certainly anticipated facts . . . (Churata 1957: 26)

Distressed by what he saw as the lack of ethics in Western perceptions of the Americas, Churata fiercely attacks the utopia of progress, and the Hegelian thesis of American infantilism:

> The Americas, before flowering, must find their roots. Before gazing towards the Future, it must look at the Past; to take its own pulse without being candy-coated by stupidities such as that of its infantilism. There are no infantile universes . . . in cosmic phenomenology there is neither youth nor old age in anything or in anybody. By necessity, today's human being is the same as yesterday's. Here, in us, he must speak. In spite of the enthusiastic attempts of Ameghino and other paleontologists, the conclusion is that he has not appeared on American soil. We, too, are children of the 'vastness' of the sea: Wirakhochas. (26)

To this generic 'He' expelled from the philosophy of History, Churata dedicates all of his work. 'He', the *pez de oro* (a decolonised subject) should then be understood as an effort from inside literature to preserve the Andean reason, even when Churata suspects that the Ibero-American nations (including those in which still subsists an Amerindian sensibility) no longer understand their 'duties' once they are affected by the transfusion of the West, represented by migratory avalanches and the submissiveness to its civilising process (Churata 1957).

With this powerful widening of perception, Churata launched a decolonising debate that opened the door to critical theorisation of concepts such as mestizaje, hybridity, national identity and the condition of American subalternity in face of the Spanish metropolis; all this, accompanied by the suspicion that, as the twentieth century goes by, the Hispanic colonies, as well as the Spanish metropolis, will become colonies of other countries with higher digestive capacity. Churata's meticulous thinking resulted in an objectified awareness that in time, Hispanic cultures at large will be in tension with global relations of power which overall effects will change their cultures and societies in fundamental ways.

But Churata was not the only one who articulated this kind of thinking in his time, although he is undoubtedly the referential figure for the Andean Avant-Garde. In one way or another, he played a role in every one of its interventions: in Potosí (Bolivia), by partaking in the foundation of the literary movement 'Gesta Bárbara' (1918); in Puno by founding the Orkopata Group and by launching the *Boletín Titikaka* (1926–30); in Cuzco as an active member of the Resurgimiento Group led by Uriel Garcia; and in La Paz – where he produced thirty years of journalism between 1932 and 1964 – by empowering the 'olympically ignored Bolivian Avant-Garde, where writers such as Arturo Borda, Carlos Medinaceli and Andrés Cusicanqui used to gravitate' (Wiethüchter and Soldán 2002).

Today, we are at the dawn of the twenty-first century and still there is a dearth of any serious engagement with an organic study of these interventions. There are excellent discussions of Churata, Medinaceli and Borda (Bosshard; Diez de Medina 1957, Huamán 1994; Pantigoso 1999; Vilche 2000; Wiethüchter; and Soldán 2002; Zevallos 2002), but until we interconnect their work and appreciate them as the first local theorisation of the condition of coloniality to which the Andean cultures were subjected under the rule of the Spanish viceroyalty and the republican élites, we will be wasting our best opportunity to appreciate a decolonising debate proposed from within Latin America. What is most ironic is that this debate took place half a century before the emergence of postcolonial studies, when the questioning of the colonial *episteme* was considered to be a symptom of extravagance which stigmatised the audacious, and made him, or her, a subject of marginalisation from society, vanished from the paradise of critique.

Translations into English by Elizabeth Monasterios

Elizabeth Monasterios

LITERARY WORKS

Boletín Titikaka [1926–8] (2004), Arequipa: Universidad Nacional de San Agustín.

Borda, Arturo (1966), *El loco*, 3 vols, La Paz: Biblioteca Paceña. Honorable Alcaldía Municipal de La Paz.

Churata, Gamaliel (1957), *El pez de oro. Retablos del laykhakuy*, La Paz: Editorial Canata.

Gesta Bárbara (1952), *Cuadernos literarios*, Tupiza: Bolivia.

—— (1950), *Trigo, estaño y mar*, La Paz: Ultima Hora.

García, Uriel [1930] (1973), *El nuevo indio*, Lima: Editorial Universo.

Peralta, Alejandro (1926), *Ande*, Puno: Editorial Titikaka.

Sánchez, Luis Alberto (1981), *Indianismo e indigenismo en la literatura peruana*, Lima: Mosca Azul Editores.

Valcárcel, Luis E. [1927] (1972), *Tempestad en los Andes*, Lima: Editorial Universo.

Vallejo, César (1927), 'Contra el secreto profesional', *Variedades*, July 5, Lima.

HISTORIES

Angeles, L. César (2002), 'Entrevista a Marco Thomas Bosshard en torno a su libro Hacia una estética de la vanguardia andina. Gamaliel Churata entre el indigenismo y el surrealismo', http://www.andes.missouri.edu/andes/cronicas/CAL_bosshard.html

Beverley, John (2004), *Subalternidad y representación. Debates en teoría cultural*, Madrid: Iberoamericana.

Bhaba, Homi K. (1986), 'The Other Question: Difference, Discrimination and the Discourse of Colonialism', in Francis Barker, Peter Hulme and Margaret Iverson (eds), *Literature, Politics and Theory: Papers from the Essex Conference 1976–1984*, London: Methuen, pp. 148–72.

Castro-Klaren, Sara (2002), 'Writing with his Thumb in the Air. Coloniality, Past and Present', in A. F. Bolaños and G. Verdesio (eds), *Colonialism Past and Present. Reading and Writing about Colonial Latin America Today*, New York: SUNY Press, pp. 261–87.

Cornejo Polar, Antonio (1994), *Escribir en el aire. Ensayo sobre la heterogeneidad sociocultural en las literaturas andinas*, Lima: Editorial Horizonte.

Diez de Medina, Fernando (1957), 'Gamaliel Churata y el pez de oro', in eds *El Diario*, La Paz: Junio.

Dussel, Enrique [1992] (1995), *The Invention of the Americas. Eclipse of 'the Other' and the Myth of Modernity*, trans. Michael D. Barber, New York: Continuum.

— (2000), 'Europa, modernidad y eurocentrismo', in E. Lander (ed.), *La colonialidad del saber: eurocentrismo y ciencias sociales, perspectivas latinoamericanas*, Dinamarca: CLACSO. 246ff.

García Canclini, Néstor (1992), *Culturas híbridas. Estrategias para entrar y salir de la modernidad*, Buenos Aires: Paidós.

Grupo de Estudios Subalternos Latinoamericanos (1995), 'Founding Statement', in John Beverley, José Oviedo and Michael Arona (eds), *Debate in Latin America*, Durham, NC: Duke University Press.

Huamán, Miguel Angel (1994), *Fronteras de la escritura. Discurso y utopía en Churata*, Lima: Editorial Horizonte.

López Lenci, Yazmin (2005), 'Las vanguardias peruanas: la reconstrucción de continuidades culturales', *Revista de Crítica Literaria Latinoamericana* 62: 143–61.

Mariátegui, José Carlos [1928] (1975), *Siete ensayos de interpretación de la realidad Peruana*, Havana: Casa de las Américas.

Medinaceli, Carlos (1975), *La reivindicación de la cultura americana*, La Paz: Los Amigos del Libro.

— (1969), *Estudios críticos*, La Paz: Los Amigos del Libro.

Mignolo, Walter (1993), 'Colonial and Postcolonial Discourse: Cultural Critique or Academic Colonialism?, *Latin American Research Review* 28 (3): 120–34.

— (2000), 'Human Understanding and (Latin) American Interests – The Politics and Sensibilities of Geohistorical Locations', in Henry Schwarz and Sangeeta Ray (eds), *A Companion to Postcolonial Studies*, Oxford: Blackwell Publishers, pp. 180–201.

— (2005), 'Un paradigma otro: Colonialidad global, pensamiento fronterizo y cosmopolitanismo crítico', *Dispositio* 52: 127–46.

O'Gorman, Edmundo (1957), *La invención de América*, Mexico: FCE.

Pantigoso, Manuel (1999), *El ultraorbicismo en el pensamiento de Gamaliel Churata*, Lima: Universidad Ricardo Palma.

Reinaga, Fausto (1978), *Indianidad*, La Paz: Imprentas Unidas.

Spivak, Gayatri Chakravarty (1988), 'Can the Subaltern Speak?', in C. Nelson and L. Grossberg (eds), *Marxism and the Interpretation of Culture*, Urbana, IL: University of Illinois Press, pp. 217–313.

Unruh, Vicky (1994), *Latin American Vanguards: The Art of Contentious Encounters*, Berkeley, CA: University of California Press.

Vich, Cynthia (2000), *Indigenismo de vanguardia en el Perú. Un estudio sobre el Boletín Titikaka*, Lima: Pontificia Universidad Católica del Perú.

Vidal, Hernán (1993), 'The Concept of Colonial and Postcolonial Discourse. A Perspective from Literary Criticism', *Latin American Research Review* 28 (3): 113–19.

Wiethüchter, Blanca and Alba María Paz Soldán (2002), *Hacia una historia crítica de la literatura en Bolivia*, 2 vols, La Paz: PIEB.

Zevallos, Juan (2002), *Indigenismo y nación. Los retos a la representación de la subalternidad aymara y quechua en el Boletín Titicaca (1926–1930)*, Lima: IFEA and BCRP.

Andean Textiles

With the Spanish invasion of Cusco in 1532, new European forms of alphabetic writing for record keeping and cloth for Western dress were gradually established as the norm in urban centres, taking the place of traditional textiles. However, Andean textiles were to subvert colonial power in a number of ways: as alternative forms of text and writing, iconography, textual authority, history and social memory.

From the Toledan reforms of 1572 onward, in the context of the rebellion of Túpaq Amaru I, figuration in traditional textile designs was prohibited for fear of the religious and ideological messages encoded therein. Shortly thereafter, in 1584, in the aftermath of the

Third Lima Council, the Church carried out a holocaust of the knotted threads (called *kipu* in Quechua and *chinu* in Aymara), based on the same fears.

In spite of these colonising efforts, and in the absence of figuration, cultural messages were still encoded in the very structure of Andean textiles, in what Desrosiers (1997) considers the articulation of 'cultural logic' with 'textile logic'. No Spaniard could have imagined that the ideological values of these technical elements would continue to subvert colonial power.

Similarly the use of *kipus* as planning and recording instruments continued into the colonial and republican period, and even into modern times. First, after 1550, there was a transcultural recognition of their importance, then in the period post-1570, *kipus* were to serve Spanish power as a part of Toledan politics. The Spanish had proved their efficiency and accepted that the Indians could continue their use; *kipu* readers (or *kipukamayuq*) became notarial assistants, occupying an official role in the colonial administration in the elaboration of population counts, tributary records and accounting lists appended to administrative records. Finally, there was the more conflictive period post-1583, after the Third Lima Council. Despite those measures, the juridical use of *kipus* continued into the nineteenth century as a part of republican legal practices, while in some rural areas local leaders and heads of households continued to document on threads the populations, herds and land under their charge, organised according to regional patterns of social and political organisation, well into the twentieth century.

Many scholars argue that Andean textiles also constituted a regional form of symbolic writing that could be read in the different Andean languages. Others, such as Locke, suggest that this notion derives from a European neo-Platonic stance toward Andean textiles. The popular novel *Lettres d'une péruvienne* (1747), by Madame de Grafigny, portrays how an Inca princess captured by French pirates communicated with her Peruvian lover from Paris by using *kipus*. In his *Lettera Apologetica* (1750), the Italian Duque Sansevero di Sangro tried to decipher these codes according to a Roman alphabet, with a syllabic reading. A century later, in a publication of 1870, the French antiquarian Léon de Rosny reproduced the same drawings. These might have formed part of what Carmen Loza (1999) calls 'European *kipus*', especially the bulky nineteenth-century *quipolas*, still kept in some European museum collections as if they were Andean originals.

However, in the last decade, Laura Laurencich and others have suggested, on the basis of the controversial Micinelli-Clara documents found in Naples, that in the colonial period some rebel followers of the Jesuit Blas Valera tried to subvert the authority of the Spanish Church and crown by proving that the Incas had writing. To this end, they developed an alphabetic and syllabic reading of Andean textiles, with numerological significance, focusing on the *tocapu* boxed designs found on Inca tunics and mantles. The drawings of *kipus* attributed to Blas Valera seem to be those used as later sources by Sansevero di Sangro and Rosny.

Another function of Andean textiles is as maps of communal territory. The famous court case of the Coroma community (Oruro, Bolivia) versus some notorious North American collectors with underhand methods, achieved the return of many weavings, some from the sixteenth century, which community members associated with their ancestral spirits and land. This living quality of Andean textiles, still expressed in the corporeal language that weavers use, suggests that they were originally elaborated from parts of the dead.

In a more overtly subversive function, the weavers of Qero (Peru), developed a design repertory around the messianic myth of the Incas' return, as Incarriy, that serves as an alternative communal history to that taught at school. Similarly the textile repertory of the weavers of Choquecancha (Cusco, Peru), is based on the beheading of the Inca rebel Túpaq

Amaru II, in 1781; again the treatment of the head alludes to the Incarriy myth; of the seed that will grow anew. Weaving as a predominantly female activity is said to express an alternative voice to male political power and oratory. A brilliant young weaver in parts of southern Oruro (Bolivia) might elaborate once in a lifetime a special mantle that, by alluding to an Andean past, demonstrates an alternative state formation. In the Bolivian uprisings of 2000–5, Aymara women used their weavings to transport stones to the road blockades led by Felipe Quispe. This Aymara leader also used the visual language of his knitted jumpers to express the warlike mood of the times.

The unfamiliar design logic of Andean textiles underlies many examples of so-called 'modern art'. Braun (1993) and Paternosto (1996) argue that fragments of pre-Columbian Andean textiles that found their way into European museum collections, inspired artists such as Gauguin, Klee and others, as the basis of modernism in the Western world.

Denise Arnold

HISTORIES
Arnold, Denise Y. with Juan de Dios Yapita (2006), *The Metamorphosis of Heads*, Pittsburgh, PA: Pittsburgh University Press.
Braun, Barbara (1993), *Pre-Columbian Art and the Post-Columbian World: Ancient American Sources of Modern Art*, New York: Abrams.
Desrosiers, Sophie (1997), 'Lógicas textiles y lógicas culturales en los Andes', in T. Bouysse-Cassagne (ed.), *Saberes y memorias en los Andes. In Memoriam Thierry Saignes*, Lima: CREDAL-IFEA, pp. 325–49.
Loza, Carmen Beatriz (1998), 'Du bon usage del quipus face à l'administration coloniale espagnole (1550–1600)', *Population* 1–2: 139–60.
— (1999), '*Quipus* and *Quipolas* at the Museum für Völkerkunde, Berlin', *Baessler-Archiv*, Neue Folge (Berlin) XLVII: 39–75.
Paternosto, César (1996), *The Stone and the Thread. Andean Roots of Abstract Art*, Austin, TX: University of Texas Press.
Salomon, Frank (2004), *The Cord Keepers. Khipus and Cultural Life in a Peruvian Village*, Durham, NC and London: Duke University Press.
Seibold, Katherine E. (1992), 'Textiles and Cosmology in Choquecancha, Cuzco', in R. V. H. Dover et al. (eds), *Andean Cosmologies through Time. Persistence and Emergence*, Bloomington, IN: Indiana University Press, pp. 166–201.
Silverman, Gail (1998), *El tejido andino: un libro de sabiduría*, Lima: Fondo Editorial, Banco Central de Reserva del Perú.

Anti-Colonial Struggle in Latin America from the Conquista to the Present

When we consider the recent re-emergence of indigenous cultures in Latin America, we can still see the legacies of violence and racism grounded in the peculiar forms of Spanish and Portuguese colonisation endured by the native peoples, coupled with the effects on native peoples of the massive transportation of African slaves to the region. The terms of engagement between the supposedly 'white' ruling class and the dominated 'people of colour' (*mestizos*, indigenous people, mulattoes, people of African origin) were not substantially transformed after the region won independence from Spain and Portugal, due in good measure to the economic interests of both local élites and the neo-imperial powers that occupied the vacuum left by the Iberian empires.

In the conquest itself, indigenous peoples endured the destruction of their cities and their cultures, the rape of their women and the enslavement of their men, and in the fifty years following the event, they lost approximately six sevenths of their total population. Those who survived were forced to accommodate their perception of the world to new cultural and social realities.

The system of colonial domination established in the sixteenth century was characterised by excessive violence expressed through slavery, forced indigenous labour and terror. Colonial rule was enforced primarily through military means, and the Spaniards imposed an unhealthy respect for the arms they wielded in the New World. Indeed, one could argue that the *fuero militar*, a rule establishing that bearers of arms were not subject to civilian common law like ordinary citizens, served as a justification, centuries later, for the military dictatorships of the nineteenth and twentieth centuries. The forced labour imposed in the conquest and continued in colonialism remained a fixture of the Latin American economy long after the conquistadors, taking a variety of forms up to the middle of the twentieth century, when it was abolished in most countries.

The domination of the Spaniards and the Portuguese was cultural as well as military. Largely with the aid of the Holy Inquisition, they attempted to impose homogeneous linguistic and religious guidelines on the colonised. In these conditions, indigenous people could not manifest significant relations of power with European newcomers; they were not even permitted to tell their side of the story in a transformative manner, or to maintain their customs.

Such violent homogenisation was resisted by subaltern indigenous and Afro-Latino communities, who began to revolt as soon as the shock of the conquest wore off. In the 1560s, an Inca movement called Taki Onqoy (Dancing Sickness) preached the total rejection of Spanish religion and customs (note that 'Inca' is spelt 'Inka' by *quechua* speakers). Its leaders claimed that they were messengers from the native gods, and they prescribed a pan-Andean alliance to destroy Spanish power. The Spanish authorities seized these leaders, tortured them and expelled them from their communities. To prevent further insurrections, they mounted a new campaign against the last Inca holdout at Vilcabamba, which they defeated in 1572. There, they captured the last reigning Inca leader, Túpac Amaru, who had led a guerrilla resistance movement; then they tried him and beheaded him in Cusco, officially putting an end to the resistance of the conquest.

Throughout the Spanish colonial period, there were hundreds of indigenous revolts, most of which were small and isolated. Among the larger and most notable were those led by Canek in Yucatan (1761), by Túpac Amaru II in Peru (1780–3), and by Atanasio Tzul in Guatemala (1820). The most significant was the Túpac Amaru II rebellion, which took its name from the former Inca leader. The movement spread like wildfire throughout the Andes, leading to an analogous revolt by Túpac Katari in the area known today as Bolivia. The rebellion cost about 100,000 lives before it was crushed by the colonial military.

Some of the colonial rebellions were led by African slaves who fled their masters and formed independent communities, called *quilombos* in Brazil and *palenques* in the Caribbean. The largest slave revolt took place in Haiti (1791), leading to the death of most French colonists, and to the independence of the country; but the greatest of all *quilombos* was Palmares, a collection of fortified villages founded in the seventeenth century in the north-east territory of Brazil. Zumbi led the kingdom of Palmares, and resisted for over forty years before being defeated in 1695. He was so powerful that the colonial authorities felt obliged to display his head in public to dispel rumours of his immortality. He remains the most famous and beloved Afro-Brazilian hero to this day.

Another legacy of colonialism was patriarchy, the general principle of male domination. Spaniards and Portuguese were more rigidly patriarchal than most indigenous or African societies, and patriarchy structured all colonial institutions, including the Church. Iberian law and kinship relations were based on a logic related to property, which only men could own. People without property lacked honour, by definition. These policies ensured the economic and cultural marginalisation, not only of indigenous peoples and African slaves in Latin America, but also of women, whose struggles for equality may also be qualified as anti-colonialist movements.

In many parts of Latin America, independence from Iberia was won after long and bitter struggles that unravelled colonial rule, but these brought first *criollos*, and then *mestizos*, to power in the nineteenth century. Both groups were more ruthless and racist than peninsular Spaniards and Portuguese because of the insecurity generated by their own ambiguous racial identity, and this led to often contradictory policies. Thus, although the most important legacy of the liberal régimes ruled by *mestizos* was the suppression of slavery, they nonetheless also generated a climate of political oppression, keeping both indigenous peoples and newly liberated ex-slaves under similar conditions of subaltern disenfranchisement. What is more, in an effort to represent themselves as essentially white subjects, who had nonetheless overcome any traces of indigenous 'savagery', these leaders celebrated both the Spanish legacy and the Amerindian prehispanic past, while at the same time suppressing contemporaneous expressions of indigenous identities and cultures. Liberal élites even became advocates of the European discourse of the racial inferiority of their own native peoples, and they sponsored European immigration to 'whiten' their respective populations. Ironically, when the economies of the newly-formed countries reached ruin under the burden of debts owed to Britain and France, the Northern European countries, which were employing theories of white supremacy to justify their own colonial ventures and to disparage the former Spanish Empire, explained that Latin America's failures stemmed from the racial inferiority of its *criollo* and *mestizo* ruling classes.

The twentieth century saw the full-fledged emergence of neo-colonialism. In 1898, the United States declared war on Spain, and invaded Cuba and Puerto Rico, which began the North American nation's ongoing projection of military power into the Caribbean basin. The US also created Panama artificially after taking it from Colombia by force (1901), and built an inter-oceanic canal to control traffic between the Atlantic and Pacific oceans.

The US interventions solidified anti-colonial and anti-neo-colonial struggles in Latin America, and these new rebellions cut across boundaries of class, ethnicity and ideology. The first anti-colonial revolution that linked peasants and indigenous peoples in the twentieth century was led in Mexico (1910–20) by Emiliano Zapata and Francisco Villa, representatives of the poor peasant indigenous sector and poor northern ranchers. They joined forces with a marginalised provincial middle-class represented by Obregón and propertied provincial ranchers led by Carranza, in an unstable unity that overthrew the dictatorial régime (1911–14) and produced Mexico's modern constitution (1917) before degenerating into class in-fighting. Zapata and Villa – the true exponents of the anti-colonial struggle – were assassinated in 1919. Anti-colonial aspects of the original revolution were sacrificed to modern nationalist principles that attempted to homogenise disparate cultures under middle-class *mestizo* ideals. This led to the creation of a homogeneous national culture detrimental to the cultural autonomy of most indigenous groups, who were forced to identify with *mestizo* values and abandon their own.

The results of US foreign policy in Central America were also devastating to indigenous people. US marines landed in Nicaragua in 1909, and stayed until 1933, prompting

General Augusto César Sandino to take up arms and fight US neo-colonial power. From 1927 until 1933, he led Latin America's first modern guerrilla war, refusing to put down his arms until all US marines left Nicaraguan soil. Peace accords were signed in 1932, and Sandino became an ordinary citizen. General Anastasio Somoza, head of the Nicaraguan National Guard, orchestrated Sandino's assassination in February 1934, and took over the presidency two years later with US support. He and his two sons ruled Nicaragua until 1979, when a new liberation movement that took its name from Sandino, the Sandinista Front of National Liberation (FSLN) ended the Somozas' rule.

In El Salvador, economic factors – the 1929 Great Depression and the ensuing collapse of coffee prices – laid the groundwork for civil war. Starving peasants, including many indigenous peoples, launched a spontaneous insurrection in January 1932, on to which the Salvadoran Communist Party, led by Farabundo Martí, latched at the last minute. The masses, armed only with machetes, were no match for the army, which repressed the uprising with full force. It is estimated that as many as 30,000 men, women and children were killed during that month alone. Although Martí was tried and executed, his name, like Sandino's, became a symbol of resistance, and in the 1980s, a new guerrilla movement, the Farabundo Martí National Liberation Front (FMLN), fought the US-trained Salvadoran army to a standstill. A peace treaty ended the war in 1992.

Guatemala endured a long dictatorship under General Jorge Ubico (1931–44) until a broad political movement overthrew him. The US tolerated his fall, but tried to prevent the abolition of forced labour laws. When President Jacobo Arbenz attempted to create land reform modelled on the plan implemented by the US in Japan at the end of World War II, the Eisenhower administration ordered a covert military intervention that toppled the Guatemalan president in 1954. What followed was a succession of brutally repressive military régimes. The overthrow of Guatemalan democracy was the beginning of a new US interventionist approach. It angered major sectors of Latin America, which began to support radical measures to oppose the American presence in the continent.

Another point of departure for anti-colonial struggles was the Cuban revolution (1959). The US invasion of Guatemala in 1954, and its support of President Batista, transformed Fidel Castro into a powerful foe. He saw his struggle as a second wave of independence wars in Latin America, this time against US imperialism. Whereas Afro-Cubans and gays were originally oppressed under Castro's régime, a broader approach to anti-colonial and identity issues in the 1980s and 1990s enabled some Afro-Cubans to construct themselves as historical subjects, complicating official revolutionary narratives that had erased their voices.

The American response to the Cuban revolution revealed an ignorance of the interactions between global systems of oppression and local histories of resistance, particularly in the construction of subaltern subjectivities. For this reason, the US was caught by surprise by the revolution in Cuba, and by the many guerrilla movements seeking to emulate it throughout the continent during the 1960s. Among these, the Guatemalan resistance is particularly interesting because of the massive incorporation of Mayas, a first in the history of the continent. Indeed, the Maya struggle against racism helped forge the guerrilla-led peasant movements that exposed the disjunctions between Western and non-Western practices, by contesting the authority ascribed to Western parameters of modernity. The traditional revolutionary left saw themselves as the intellectual architects of an anti-imperialist revolution, and the American response indicated a similar reading of 'Marxist revolution', which could not be tolerated during the Cold War. The Mayas saw it differently. Poverty might have motivated their identification with the revolutionary process, but their larger goal was to eliminate colonial legacies co-existing with modernity in the region. This was 'the conspiracy within the conspiracy' that permitted Mayas to use the Guatemalan revolutionary process as a vehicle for an anti-colonial defence of their identity, and as a means for the future constitution of an alternative model of a nation free of colonial residues.

The 1980s saw the consolidation of major indigenous organisations throughout the continent. This occurred in part because of the example of Guatemala's Mayas and the leadership role played by Rigoberta Menchú, who was awarded the Nobel Peace Prize in 1992, but also because of the antagonistic relationship between neo-liberalism and indigenous politics.

Exemplary of this trend is the EZLN (Zapatista National Liberation Army), which came to the world's attention on 1 January 1994, in an uprising timed to coincide with the beginning of NAFTA (North American Free Trade Agreement). After the capture of San Cristóbal de las Casas, Subcomandante Marcos came out onto the balcony of the Municipal Palace and read a statement, the first *communique* from Chiapas:

> We are the product of five hundred years of struggle. We are the inheritors of the true builders of the nation . . . denied the most elementary preparation so that they can use us as cannon fodder and pillage the wealth of our country . . . But today we say: Ya Basta! Enough is enough.

The international circulation of the Zapatista struggles through the internet became one of the most successful examples of the use of computer communications by grassroots social movements. The indigenous character of the Zapatista rebellion also provoked new awareness, respect and study of the much broader phenomenon of indigenous revival and struggle.

At the beginning of the twenty-first century, indigenous people of the Andean subregion have successfully contested globalised neo-colonial practices. In Ecuador and Bolivia, they have consolidated political movements by contesting the free reign of globalised petroleum companies, whose pollution and extraction of natural gas were destroying the ecosystem and impoverishing the people. Mapuches in southern Chile and Argentina also became more radical in their claims to their ancestral territory, their demands for autonomy and the creation of indigenous reserves. In Bolivia, Evo Morales, a leader of the Bolivian Cocalero movement, has contested the American right to prohibit the cultivation of coca plants: 'After more than 500 years, we, the Quechuas and Aymaras, are still the rightful owners of this land. We, the indigenous people, after 500 years of resistance, are retaking the power.' In December 2005, Morales became the first indigenous person ever elected a president in Latin America since Mexico's Benito Juárez in the mid-nineteenth century. His main promise was to fight for Bolivia's control of its natural gas reserves, owned by Spain's Repsol and America's Exxon Mobil. He also redefined drug policies by insisting that the coca plant is sacred to Bolivians, and they have a right to cultivate it, without it necessarily becoming hostage to the illicit cocaine trade.

In this light, it would seem that as indigenous peoples in Latin America continue to eliminate colonial residues, their fate has taken a turn for the better. Nevertheless, the US 'war on terror' and 'war on drugs' targets them, and it remains to be seen if they will prevail in a region that America still considers its 'own back yard'.

Arturo Arias

HISTORIES
Chasteen, John Charles (2001), *Born in Blood and Fire: A Concise History of Latin American Studies*, New York and London: W.W. Norton.
Swanson, Philip (ed.) (2003), *The Companion to Latin American Studies*, London: Arnold.

Arturo Borda and the Andean Avant-garde

> When will human dignity burst?
> When will humiliation rebel? (*El loco*)

Easily the most irreverent and charismatic character of the Andean avant-garde, Arturo Borda (La Paz, 1883–1953) was known among his contemporaries by the nickname of *El Loco (The Madman)*, an implicit allusion to his preference for thinking about civilisation from the position of an alterity rooted in the conflicted space between colonising forces and decolonising wills. Widely known as a painter, he was also a journalist, a cineaste, an anarchist, and a social activist. In 1966, The honorable Alcaldía Municipal de La Paz posthumously published what we can appreciate today as the last work of the Andean decolonising saga: Arturo Borda's *El loco (The Madman)*. As in the case of Gamaliel Churata's *El Pez de Oro* (see pages 515–20 in this *Companion*), this is a text that frightens. Complex, unbearably irreverent with its time and its contemporaries, unclassifiable according to conventional parameters (it is not a novel or a diary, neither poetry, nor drama, ritual, nor essay, but it exhibits some features of each of these genres); multilingual, fragmented, without any pretension to being a finished work or even 'literature', *El loco* challenged everything that had been previously written in Bolivia. By exposing the colonial *episteme* in an epoch still co-opted by the Hispanic civilising impulse, *El loco* was immediately categorised as extravagant. To this feature one should add Borda's unsettling personality, which loudly accused his contemporaries of lending themselves to an intellectual servility (*pongueaje intelectual*) that cancelled out any possibility of social and historic dignity in the Americas. He also resisted being labelled as 'intellectual' or 'bohemian', types he saw as often serving to domesticate the disobedience expressed by means of artistic creation. Defiant of any form of domesticated language, Borda claimed for himself the status of a *lari*, an Aymara expression that alludes to people who knows no authority (*gente que no conoce autoridad*), an alteric existence openly opposed to hegemonic modernity.

With few exemptions (among them Carlos Medinacelli, one of the founders of Gesta Bárbara, the literary movement Churata helped to create in Potosí in 1918), Borda's work did not receive any critical attention nor was it included in any literary history or anthology. It was simply perceived as unacceptable. How could the lettered culture accept a character such as the protagonist of *El loco*, who lacks a proper name (we only know him by the appellation 'loco') and perceives himself as a symptom of the social experience of collective indignity? This *Madman*, besides rejecting modern Bolivian history, conceives its demolition, so that upon its ruins could be built a society other than the one imagined by Spanish colonised forces and the one imagined by the Creole élites who founded and led the American nations towards cultural and social alienation. To do so, he constructs himself as a 'demolisher of modernity', and from that epistemological site, articulates a project of radical cultural insubordination. Such a project is eloquently expressed in the beginning pages of *El Loco* which I reproduced in my own translation (stressing the fact that this is a text extremely difficult to translate because of its reliance on anti-conventional grammar and syntax):

> I have faith in my destiny: I know that I can make something out of myself. In something, I don't know what, I'll be the first and only one to do it; but my anguish is killing me, because I have no means of finding out where my strength lies; I cannot guess in what activity or which

faculty my triumph will be found. This is driving me crazy, and yet in the very depths of my existence the serene faith of victory is waiting. (*El loco*, I, 37)

Borda was not mistaken. He was indeed 'the first and the only one' to conceive in his time a radically decolonised writing. And yet, he lived tormented by not knowing exactly where to pinpoint the source of his strength. Perhaps it came from the decolonising project that inspired his work, or perhaps it arose from that extraordinary charge of indignation and fury with which he wanted to demolish everything, including the literary canon and the *mentira social* (social untruth). We can go so far as to think that Borda conceived what we can now properly call the last -ism of the avant-garde: demolitionism. What makes this Andean -ism so powerful and charged with theoretical validity, even today, is that besides the demolition of a colonised culture and society, it proposes the demolition of the perverse *mansedumbre de los subalternos* (subservient will of the subaltern). In Borda's own words: 'What's unbearable in all this is the vile subservience of the subalterns that allow themselves to be denigrated like hungry dogs. When will human dignity burst? When will humiliation rebel?' (*El loco*, 1, 79).

The Andean lettered élites were largely unable to dismantle the symbolic force that Borda's work (as well as Churata's) irradiated. Although a veil of silence was drawn over their writing, there was nothing to stop their proposals from breaking the weak discursive and ideological arena of lettered culture. In a cultural process that spans the second half of the twentieth century, the horizons of visibility opened by their interventions destabilised little by little the colonial rituals of dominant culture. Other languages, other histories and other protagonists began to populate the Andean cultural imaginary, producing an aesthetic legitimisation of territories so far perceived as degraded: a *yatiri* (Andean man of knowledge), an urban Indian, a *chola* (Indian woman residing in the city), a handful of coca leaves.

In the Andes, this momentum of cultural legitimisation was channelled in various ways. In some cases, it kept itself within the discursive limits of culture, creating situations in which modernity and coloniality were intellectually demolished by the action of insurgent writers (Borda and Churata being the best examples). In others, however, the impulse served as a complement to a more radical momentum of insurgence led by emancipated indigenous plebs. Insurgence, in this sense, resulted in social movements and mass rebellions such as those recently witnessed in Bolivia, in which thousands of Aymara and Quechua Indians – who since the 1970s had been politicising their ancestral cultures and producing their own narratives of insurgence – gave expression to the most important social movement in the political history of the last twenty years. Because of, literally 'burst human dignity, subverted humiliation (*reventada la dignidad humana, sublevada la humillación*), on the 22 January 2006, almost half a century after the immolation of the Inca Atahuallpa in Cajamarca, an Indian took command of an Andean nation. At the presidential ceremony of Evo Morales, the first Indian president in the Americas, nobody remembered Borda, Churata or their insurgent avant-gardism. There was no need to do so, since the 'silence of the subaltern' was not broken through the mediation of an intellectual committed to the Indian conflict, but as Churata once prophesied, by the indigenous people themselves and by their actions. If demolitionism demanded a time of dignity, that time seems to be the present, and it has not been reached through the linear progression of modernity – which can only conceive futurity in terms of going forward in the myth of progress – but throughout the time of insurgence, which heads to the future by embracing the past. Whether this time of insurgence will be able to interrupt the reproduction of

Western epistemologies of power, will depend on our time's commitment to re-orienting the course of history and culture.

Translations into English by Elizabeth Monasterios

Elizabeth Monasterios

Literary Works

Borda, Arturo (1966), *El loco*, 3 vols, La Paz: Biblioteca Paceña. Honorable Alcaldía Municipal de La Paz.
Gesta Bárbara (1950), *Trigo, estano y mar*, La Paz: Ultima Hora.
— (1952), *Cuadernos Literarios*, Tupiza: Bolivia.

Histories

El poder de la palabra. http://www.epdlp.com/pintor.php?id=3404 [accessed 16 Feb. 2007].
Lora, Guillermo (1993), 'El anarquismo en Borda', *Páginas de mi archivo*, La Paz.
Mendinaceli, Carlos (1969), *Estudios Críticos*, La Paz: Los Amigos del Libro.
— (1975), *La reivindicación de la cultura americana*, La Paz: Los Amigos del Libro.
— (1987), 'La personalidad y la obra de Arturo Borda', in Carlos Castañón Barrientos (ed.), *Taipip'unchaipi tutayarka*, La Paz: Los Amigos del Libro.
Saenz, Jaime (1979), *Vidas y muertes*, La Paz: Huayna Potosí.
Wiethüchter, Blanca and Alba María Paz Soldán (2002), *Hacia una historia crítica de la literatura en Bolivia*, 2 vols, La Paz: PIEB.

'Calibán'

The essay 'Calibán' by the Cuban writer and poet Roberto Fernández Retamar might be said, arguably, to have inaugurated postcolonial criticism as such in Latin America. Published originally in 1971 by the Cuban cultural journal *Casa de las Américas*, it rapidly became one of the key cultural manifestos of the Cuban revolution, along with Fidel Castro's 'Second Declaration of Havana' (1962) and Che Guevara's 'Socialism and Man in Cuba' (1969), setting the tone for a whole epoch of revolutionary militancy in the Americas.

The essay responds to two immediate circumstances: the so-called 'Padilla affair' in 1971, in which a prize-winning Cuban poet, Heberto Padilla, is repressed by the revolutionary government, causing widespread protest on the part of intellectuals previously sympathetic to the revolution; and the more or less simultaneous revelation that the journal *Mundo Nuevo* (*New World*), which brought together many prominent Latin American intellectuals, was secretly financed and controlled by the CIA as part of its campaign against the Cuban revolution.

'Calibán' belongs to the genre of what is called the 'national essay' in Latin American literature, and is itself a critical meditation on the national essay, as represented above all by three famous nineteenth-century writers: the Argentine Domingo Sarmiento, the Uruguayan José Enrique Rodó and the Cuban José Martí. The title refers, of course, to the character of Calibán in Shakespeare's comedy *The Tempest*. Shakespeare situates the play on an unknown island, supposedly in the Mediterranean, but clearly alluding to the islands revealed in the course of the colonisation of the New World and the Pacific, where Prospero has established himself as king with his daughter Miranda, in the process enslaving the native population, who are represented in turn by the contrasting figures of Ariel, a poet and 'creature of the air' and Calibán, a 'deformed', spiteful and rebellious slave. The name Calibán is Shakespeare's own anagram of 'cannibal', which in turn Retamar sees as having resulted from the conflation of 'caribe' and 'peoples of Can' – two of the names used to describe the inhabitants of the New World. The first part of the essay traces the genealogy in European cultural history of the figure of Calibán as symbolising the American 'Other' as barbarian or primitive (anticipating in this way Edward Said's idea of Orientalism). Retamar observes that the association Calibán/barbarian is, however, inverted in the 1960s by anglophone and francophone Caribbean intellectuals like George Lamming, Edward Baithwaite or Aimé Césaire to make Calibán the symbol of the post-colonial or anti-colonial intellectual.

But Retamar also has in mind a specifically Latin American precedent. That is Rodó's essay 'Ariel' (1900), written at the end of the nineteenth century as an attack on the emerging force of US imperialism and a reaffirmation of the singularity of a 'Latin' America. In that essay, Rodó identified Latin American civilisation with Ariel, that is, with the aesthetic principle, and the United States – because of its supposed materialism and brutality – with Calibán. Mass democracy in particular represented for Rodó *la entroniza-cion de Calibán* – the enthronement of Calibán.

In the new historical conjuncture inaugurated by the Cuban revolution, Retamar feels that 'our symbol is not Ariel, as Rodó thought, but Calibán'. In turn, Prospero becomes the symbol of colonialism as such, including the neo-colonialism of the United States. For Retamar, Ariel comes now to represent the 'Creole' or 'national' literary intellectual who nevertheless stands in the service of colonial or neo-colonial rule. Retamar mentions in this respect specifically Sarmiento, with his distrust of the *mestizo* and indigenous popula-tions of the continent, and his desire to Europeanise Argentina by a policy of racial 'whitening' (*blanqueamiento*). His more immediate target, however, is a group of literary intellectuals, including Borges, who in those years supported the US intervention in Vietnam and took a conservative position in Argentine politics, and the Mexican novel-ist Carlos Fuentes and the Uruguayan literary critic Emir Rodriguez Monegal, both liberal writers associated with the so-called 'boom' of the Latin American novel in the 1960s who turned against the Cuban revolution in the wake of the Padilla affair (both were also asso-ciated with the project of *Mundo Nuevo*). Retamar critiques the idea put forward by Monegal and Fuentes that the new Latin American novel is above all a 'formal' achieve-ment, without ideological implications; he sees this as a kind of neo-Arielism that cele-brates an élitist notion of art and literature over the political dynamism of the then quite dynamic revolutionary process in Latin America and the Third World generally. The essay concludes with a vision of the necessary coincidence between the process of decolonisa-tion in the Americas and socialism.

'Calibán' was a tremendously influential and widely debated manifesto. As noted above, it inaugurated or legitimised the postcolonial turn in Latin American literary and cultural criticism, However, more than thirty years later, it also shows some limitations in that regard. If for Aimé Césaire, in his rewriting of Shakespeare's play (*La tempête*), Calibán was a black worker, and Ariel a mulatto literary intellectual, for Retamar – faithful in this regard to the thought of Martí on the racial question in Cuba and the Americas – the image of Calibán was related to the familiar idea in Latin America of cultural and racial *mestizaje* as the normative form of postcolonial identity. It goes without saying that mes-*tizaje* is a concept that fits uncomfortably with projects for cultural affirmation or recov-ery of indigenous and Afro-American groups. As feminist critics noted too, Calibán represented for Retamar a *masculine* form of cultural heroism (the only woman who figures in the essay's list of 'the progeny of Calibán' was the Chilean singer Violeta Parra). Although the essay reflects the 'tricontinental' (Asia/Africa/Latin America) strategic perspective of the Cuban, as Retamar himself came to recognise, the equation of decolonisation and socialism in his essay was problematised with the collapse of the Soviet Union in 1989.

Retamar has returned several times to the idea of Calibán, correcting what he now considers overstatements in the original essay and seeking to find something like a postmodernist Calibán in the struggle of the new social movements in Latin America and the Caribbean against globalisation and neo-liberal hegemony. But the problem at the heart of the original essay remains: for Retamar, Calibán is the symbol of a new type of literary intellectual 'committed' to the cause of decolonisation. But the role of the literary intellectual and of literature itself was beginning to be called into question by the very process of decolonisation and radicalisation Retamar invoked in his essay; so the force of the figure points more in the direction of displacing the authority and centrality of the literary intellectual and the 'lettered city' as such.

John Beverley

LITERARY WORKS
Borges, Jorge Luis (1981), *Borges, a Reader: A Selection from the writings of Jorge Luis Borges*, ed. Emir Rodriguez Monegal and Alastair Reid, New York: Dutton.
Césaire, Aimé [1955] (1970), *Discours sur le colonialisme*, Paris: Présence Africaine.
Fernández Retamar, Roberto (1971), 'Calibán', *Casa de las Américas* 68: 124–51.
— (2000), *Todo Calibán*, La Habana: Letras Cubanas.
Fuentes, Carlos (1985), *Latin America: At War with the Past*, Toronto: CBC Enterprises.
Heberto Padilla (1969), *Fuera del juego*, Buenos Aires: Aditor.
Lamming, George (1966), 'Caribbean Literature: The Black Rock of Africa', *African Forum* 1 (4): 32–52.
Martí, José [1891] (1979), *Nuestra América*, Habana: Editorial de Ciencias Sociales.
Mundo Nuevo (1966–71), Paris: Instituto Latinoamericano de Relaciones Internacionales.
Rodó, José Enrique [1900] (1957), 'Ariel', México: Novaro.
Rodríguez Monegal, Emir (1993), *Obra crítica*, ed. Pablo Rocca y Homero Alsina Thevenet, Montevideo: Ediciones de la Plaza.
Said, Edward (1978), *Orientalism*, New York: Vintage Books.
Sarmiento, Domingo Faustino [1845] (1970), *Facundo: civilización y barbarie*, Buenos Aires: Espasa-Calpe.
Shakespeare, William [1623] (2002), *The Tempest*, ed. David Lindley, Cambridge and New York: Cambridge University Press.
Sklodowska, Elzbieta and Ben A. Heller (2000), *Roberto Fernández Retamar y los estudios latinoamericanos*, Pittsburgh, PA: IILI.

HISTORIES
Castro, Fidel [1962] (1997), *Segunda Declaración de la Habana*, New York: Pathfinder Press.
Guevara, Ernesto 'Che' [1965] (1969), 'Socialism and Man in Cuba', in Rolando Bonachea and Nelson Valdes (eds), *Che: Selected works of Ernesto Guevara*, Cambridge, MA and London: MIT Press, pp. 155–69.
Halperin Donghi, Tulio (1969), *Historia contemporánea de América Latina*, Madrid: Alianza Editorial.

Christian Influences on Philippine Society and Culture

Ferdinand Magellan reached the Philippines in 1521. Ruy Lopez de Villalobos gave it the name Filipinas in 1543 after King Philip II, then Prince of Spain. Twenty-five years later, in 1565, Miguel López de Legazpi began colonising the islands and became its first Spanish Governor-General. Spain thus gained a far-flung colony in the East which it governed from Mexico until 1821 and directly from Spain until 1898. More than 300 years of Spanish colonial rule left its indelible mark on the islands and its people. As the Spaniards tried to reshape the islands according to their wish, so did the natives according to their needs. Out of separate and independent family-based communities (*barangays*), a unitary colonial state was formed. From scattered settlements along rivers and coasts, provinces, towns and barrios were organised and established well into the interior with the church as the focal point. The native *datu* (chieftain), *babaylan* (shaman) and *bagani* (warrior) of the old *barangays* were replaced by a new set of officials, functionaries and social groups who were Spaniards at the top, richer native Indios and Chinese *mestizos* at the middle and poor Indios and Chinese at the lowest level. Belief in the Christian God bound the natives to the influential sway of the Spanish missionary priest who tried to wean them away from what he regarded as a pagan way of life. Christianised, they put their faith in this Christian God, subscribed to a Christian view of the world and observed Christian morality, rituals and ceremonies while adapting Christianity to their old faith, beliefs and practices. To fishing in communal fishing grounds and farming in communal farm lands were added new trades, professions and occupations based largely on private landownership and on export of crops to Europe. A new language and a new set of artistic and literary forms engaged the many languages in the islands and the native forms of art and oral literature to produce something that combined the elements of both. When the Spaniards left the Philippines in 1898 they left a world largely altered but not unrecognisable even to the natives who, by the time of the revolution of 1896, called themselves Filipinos.

During the Spanish period, Church and state shared rule over the archipelago. From the independent *barangays* they encountered in 1565, the Spaniards created a unitary state that included territories claimed by Muslim sultanates in Mindanao and Sulu. They established a highly centralised government based in the walled city of Intramuros in Manila. They governed an archipelago they divided into provinces, towns and barrios. The present Philippine political territory and administrative divisions remain almost identical to those established by the Spaniards. The Church itself divided the islands among the various religious orders – Augustinians, Franciscans, Dominicans, Jesuits, Recollects – and into archdioceses, dioceses and parishes which is how they remain divided today. The Church ran an organisation that paralleled the state administration down to the local level. It still wields vast influence in the political affairs of the country today.

Out of scattered settlements along rivers and coasts, the Spaniards created nucleated settlements with the church as the focal point. They introduced the European system of settlement based on the grid pattern of roads and clustering of buildings and houses around the church. This became the plaza complex of today which serves as the *bayan* or *centro* of every town. The natives were asked to live near the church in a process called *reducción*. When they protested the measure, the colonial administration and the Church resorted to the *cabecera-visita* system in which the main church was constructed in the *cabecera* while *visitas* or chapels were put up in outlying areas. In time, as the population grew, the *cabecera* became the town centre where the plaza complex was and out of the *visitas* sprang several barrios. Over a thousand stone churches were built during the colonial period through the combined effort of the Spaniards, the Chinese and the Indios. Four of these churches are now included among the UNESCO World Heritage sites. These churches still serve the religious needs of the people. Many of the older ones are in Bohol, Panay and Cebu in the Visayas and in Laguna, Pampanga, Bicol and the Ilocos provinces in Luzon. Almost every province has its own Spanish colonial church. It may no longer dominate the skyline but it still remains an imposing structure in the plaza complex in almost every town centre.

It was in Intramuros that the Spaniards built new structures never before seen in the islands. Aside from the walls and the fort that guarded the city, new structures for new institutions were constructed making use of stones, corals and wood. Intramuros remains the classic example of a Spanish colonial city, with church, government buildings and the houses of the rich and the powerful clustered around the church. It was from this core area facing Manila Bay that Manila expanded towards the interior to absorb other towns and cities into the National Capital Region of today. Lining the streets of every town centre were the large *bahay-na-bató* (stone houses) of the rich and the powerful. They were patterned after the local *bahay kubo* (nipa hut), only grander and more spacious, with the ground floor made of thick stone walls and the upper portion made of wood the better to cope with the frequent earthquakes that visited the islands. A number of schools and hospitals, the firsts of their kind, were built by the religious orders. One school, the Universidad de Santo Tomas (UST), founded by the Dominicans, will celebrate its quadricentennial in 2011. Ateneo de Manila (then called Ateneo Municipal) and Colegio de San Juan de Letran continue to provide education to Filipinos. Letran remained inside Intramuros, while UST and Ateneo eventually transferred to sites outside the city walls, as did two hospitals founded by the Franciscan fathers in the 1590s, the Hospital de San Juan de Dios (now in Pasay City) and the Hospital de San Lázaro (now in Sta Cruz, Manila).

Christianity provided the Spaniards with the glue with which to bind the Filipino people together. The missionary priests, while denouncing 'pagan' beliefs and practices, adapted some of the latter's features in proselytising in the same manner that the natives combined Christian and local religious elements in their practice of Christianity. Today's annual town or barrio fiesta held in honour of the patron saint is both a religious and a secular affair mixing entertainment, games, fairs, carnivals, beauty pageants, drinking, dining, dancing and loud music with masses, processions, mass weddings and other church services. It used to be a native thanksgiving ritual with a lot of merrymaking and drinking after each harvest. The Spanish friars appropriated it to attract the people to the church and turn them into converts and devotees. Each town or city has its unique way of celebrating fiestas showing how each adapted the foreign to the native. In Naga City in Camarines Sur, the image of Nuestra Señora de la Peñafrancia is transported during its September feast from one church to another in a fluvial procession. The Ati-atihan of Kalibo, Aklan which honours the Santo Niño every January was originally celebrated to commemorate the alleged Negrito or Ati handover of the Aklan lowland to Bornean *datus* centuries ago. This is the reason why participants paint themselves black like the Atis during the festival. In Obando, the old fertility rites became a Christian ritual dancing in May in honour of the town's patron saints, particularly Santa Clara, in which participants dancing in a procession ask for the saints' intercession so they may have a child or a partner in life.

The local population embraced the religious celebrations that came with Christianity, such as Christmas and Lent, but imbued their observance with their own beliefs and practices that even the Church could not but tolerate. Christmas was introduced as a purely religious affair celebrating the birth of Jesus Christ. But it has also become an occasion for the gathering of the expansive extended Filipino family which is rooted in the Austronesian bilateral kinship system. The expansion is a result as well of the *compadrazgo* system inaugurated by the Spaniards, in which the godparents and the godchildren became part of the family after every baptism, confirmation or wedding. Like Christmas, the New Year is welcomed by a family midnight meal but not before making loud noises to drive away bad spirits and doing whatever is believed to be necessary to bring good luck throughout the coming year. In March or April, the passion, death and resurrection of Jesus Christ are remembered during the forty-day Lenten season. A common practice during this time is the reading or chanting of the *pasyon*, the story of Jesus' passion, death and resurrection, and its re-enactment in a stage version called *senakulo*. Some scholars argue that the *pasyon* replaced the Tagalog epic *Bathala* (which spoke of a Supreme Being) and contributed much to the conversion and subjugation of natives, while others argue that the *payson* introduced an alternative perspective, which played a significant role in motivating natives during the revolution. As a way of atoning for their sins during this time, self-flagellants join street processions while others have themselves nailed to the cross on Good Friday. There are also a number of millenarian groups or religious cults spread throughout the archipelago whose teachings and practices were derived from or inspired by the Christian faith. Several have carved out their own niches in the sacred mountain of Banahaw in Laguna where pilgrims make their retreat during the season for spiritual renewal.

In the eighteenth and nineteenth centuries, Spain introduced economic reforms that changed not only the physical lay-out of the land but also its economic and social landscape. The reforms revolved around the cultivation of export crops bound for Europe: tobacco, sugar cane, abaca, coconuts. The present Philippine economy owes much to these reforms as it is still being propped up by these major export crops. Their production forced some regions to specialise in one crop and interact more closely with each other. The various types of produce were sent to Manila for distribution elsewhere. Manila thus strengthened its position as the administrative, business, financial, communications and transportation centre for inter-regional and global trade. Private landownership in the form of large haciendas deprived many peasants of their land but a robust export trade led to more changes – industrial, financial, institutional, infrastructural, educational, social and political. One result was the rise of an *ilustrado* (intelligent) class, children of Spanish, Chinese *mestizo* and 'Indio' parents who profited from the reforms and were thus able to send their children to universities in Manila and Europe. The *ilustrados* headed a propaganda movement in the 1880s which gave way to a separatist movement that heralded the 1896 Philippine revolution.

The rise of new social classes led to a culture and education that were more secular than in earlier centuries when the missionaries introduced Western art and literary forms in the process of spreading the word of God. However, the religious influence persisted, as in Gaspar Aquino de Belen's *Mahál na pasión ni Jesu Christong panginoón natin na tolâ* (*The Holy Passion of Our Lord Jesus Christ in Verse*), which came out in the early eighteenth century but is still being chanted during Lent today. There were also metrical romances derived from Spanish and Mexican mediaeval ballads, the most famous of which was Francisco Balagtas' *Florante at Laura* which some scholars regard as among the first attempts to expose tyranny in the country, even if the story was set in a foreign land. A poetical joust called *balagtasan*, named after the author of *Florante at Laura*, became popular as the local people proved more attuned to the spoken rather than the written word. Local painters, sculptors, writers, poets, musicians, dramatists and other artists found expressions for their art both in the demand of the Church in earlier times and in the rising need of the newly rich in later centuries of

Spanish rule. They mastered the art and literary forms introduced by the Spaniards, married them to local forms and produced works unique to the islands, like the aforementioned *balagtasans*, while giving vent to their deepest sentiments as an emerging nation.

The local élite, which included the more prosperous Indios and Chinese *mestizos*, tried their best to adapt to what was regarded as Spanish in order to belong; thus the adoption of manners and etiquette appropriate to the period's *alta sociedad* (high society). They adapted Spanish names and Hispanised their Indio and Chinese names just like the rest of the population, when the colonial government decreed surnames for all. Their attempts not to be different and to be well-acquainted with the latest in Europe were most noticeable at social gatherings where they rubbed shoulders with Spanish government and Church officials. During these occasions, they danced their own versions of *jota*, *pandanggo*, and other dances of Spanish, European or Mexican origin which eventually spread even to the lower classes and were later regarded as part of traditional Philippine folk dance. Hosts and guests alike wore the latest fashions adapted from those of Spain and the rest of Europe. They ate food of Spanish-Mexican origin like *adobo*, *menudo* and *lechón*, all of which has become part of the traditional fare at most Filipino celebrations.

Despite Spanish reluctance to teach Spanish to the natives, those who went to school were able to learn the language, as were the *ladinos* (native translators) of earlier centuries. It was through Spanish that the reformist aspirations were articulated. One of the more important works of the period was Gregorio Sanciangco's *El Progreso de Filipinas*. During the propaganda period of the 1880s, two novels that have since established themselves as classics of the local canon were produced by José Rizal: *Noli me tangere* and *El Filibusterismo*. The collective output of the newspaper *La Solidaridad*, edited first by Graciano Lopez-Jaena and later by Marcelo H. del Pilar belong to this category of nationalist writing. Likewise, many of the more important works of the Revolutionary government of General Emilio Aguinaldo were written in Spanish, among them the declaration of Philippine independence, the Philippine national anthem and the Malolos constitution.

By not teaching Spanish to the majority of natives and by preaching in local languages instead, the Church helped preserve parts of native culture. Lexicons compiled by the friars remain useful for students of Filipino culture of the period of first contact with the Spanish, as in Marcos de Lisboa's work on Bicol, Alfonso de Mentrida's Hiligaynon dictionary and Francisco de San Antonio's Tagalog vocabulary. Although language is still a problematic and emotional issue and Spanish is no longer spoken except by a very tiny minority, it is probably in the matter of language use that one finds the most widespread and useful Spanish influence. Almost every major Filipino language benefited from Spanish contact. Many Spanish words and expressions were incorporated into each local language over time. In some cases, the original meaning was preserved; in most cases, different connotations or even denotations evolved over time. One can speak or write an entire sentence in a Filipino language using recognisable Spanish words and yet remain Filipino in one's usage – *Kumusta ka?* (How are you?) or *Isara ang bintana* (Close the window). The individual words in such examples are almost all Spanish in origin: *como*, *estás*, *cerrar*, *ventana*; the only Filipino (Tagalog in this case) words are *ka* and *ang*. Yet the expressions are Filipino, not Spanish – a neat example.

Dante L. Ambrosio

LITERARY WORKS
Balagtas, Francisco [1838] (1927), *Florante at Laura: A Narrative Poem*, trans. George St Clair, Manila: Philippine Education Company, Inc.

Belen, Gaspar Aquino de [1704] (1990), *Mahál na pasión ni Jesu Christong panginoón natin na tolâ*, Quezon City: Ateneo de Manila University Press.

Francisco, José Mario C. (1994), *Sermones: Francisco Blancas de San José O.P.*, Quezon City: PULONG Sources for Philippine Studies, Ateneo de Manila University.

Lopez-Jaena, Graciano (1974), *Speeches, Articles and Letters*, trans. Encarnacion Alzona, Manila: National Historical Commission.

Paterno, Pedro Alejandro (1885), *Ninay (costumbres filipinas)*, Madrid: Imprenta de Fortanet.

Rizal, José P. [1887] (1996), *Noli me tangere*, trans. Ma. Soledad Lacson-Locsin, ed. Raul L. Locsin, Makati City: Bookmark.

— [1891] (1997), *El Filibusterismo: Subversion: A Sequel to Noli Me Tangere*, trans. Ma. Soledad Lacson-Locsin, ed. Raul L. Locsin, Makati City: Bookmark.

HISTORIES

Agoncillo, Teodoro A. [1960] (1990), *History of the Filipino People*, Quezon City: Garotech Publishing.

Alcina, Francisco I. [1668] (2002), *History of the Bisayan People in the Philippine Islands: Evangelisation and Culture at the Contact Period*, trans., ed and annot. Cantius J. Kobak and Lucio Gutierrez, Manila: UST Publishing House.

Blair, Emma H. and James A. Robertson (eds) (1903–9), *The Philippines Islands 1493–1898*, 55 vols, Cleveland, OH: Arthur H. Clark Co.

Chirino, P. Pedro [1890] (1969), *The Philippines in 1600*, trans. Ramon Echevarria, Manila: Historical Conservation Society.

Galende, Pedro G. and Rene B. Javellana (1993), *Great Churches of the Philippines*, Manila: Bookmark.

Ileto, Reynaldo C. (1979), *Pasyón and Revolution: Popular Movements in the Philippines, 1840–1910*, Quezon City: Ateneo de Manila University Press.

Morga, Antonio de [1609] (1990), *Historical Events of the Philippine Islands*, Manila: National Historical Institute.

Rafael, Vicente (1988), *Contracting Colonialism: Translation and Christian Conversion in Tagalog Society under Early Spanish Rule*, Quezon City: Ateneo de Manila University.

Robles, Eliodoro G. (1969), *The Philippines in the Nineteenth Century*, Quezon City: Malaya Books.

Colonial Baroque

The Baroque is the dominant cultural form of the Spanish and Portuguese colonial empires from the beginning of the seventeenth century to the mid-eighteenth century, when its hegemony begins to be displaced by Enlightenment models. Though it extends throughout the two empires, including their respective Asian and African possessions, it flourishes particularly strongly in the great American viceroyalties of Spain, centred on Mexico and Peru, and in the Minas Gerais region of colonial Brazil.

The ideological problematic of the Iberian colonial state in the seventeenth and eighteenth centuries differed from that of the period of the conquest in the sixteenth century in one important respect. The conquest was concerned with asserting what in Roman law was called *occupatio* – the right to seize and govern the lands of others. In the period of what historians call 'colonial stabilisation' in the seventeenth century, however, the problem was not so much to justify the territorial expansion of the empire, as to maintain its internal order and territorial integrity, preserving the metropolitan monopoly on trade and appointments. For that purpose, it was necessary to develop a colonial civil society in which the function of religion, art and literature would both temper and conceal the need to govern through a monopoly on the means of violence. The paradigmatic discourse of conquest and colonisation was the epic, the dominant form of colonial poetry in the sixteenth century (the greatest examples are perhaps the *Araucana*, about the conquest of Chile, and the *Lusiads*, about the formation of the Portuguese Empire). But the epic (and along with it the 'chronicles' of discovery and conquest) had lost its aesthetic and ideological force by the end of the sixteenth century. The Baroque rises up in its place, offering a mode of representation and self-expression in which the 'ordinary' activities of production, accumulation, government, religion and social reproduction – that is, the colonial state and civil society – could be represented and idealised.

The dominant formal characteristic of the Baroque style is complexity – in painting, sculpture and architecture, a taste for complex, flowing, richly gilded (often with gold in the interiors) surfaces, and turbulent dramatic compositions; in literature, a taste for allegory, complex syntax and word play (*conceptismo* and *culteranismo*). Following a tendency pioneered by the Italian Mannerists in the sixteenth century, the Baroque makes difficulty itself – *dificolta* – an aesthetic property. The often bewildering complexity, richness and variety of Baroque architecture, painting, music and literature, above all serve to 'astonish' – *deslumbrar*. That aesthetic effect is at the service of its political and ideological function.

The Baroque's dominant ideological characteristic is its connection to the world-view of the Counter-Reformation. The rise of the Baroque is in part the product of the insistence by the Jesuits (themselves founded as a 'modern' order) that the new forms of Renaissance literature and art, which had come under suspicion in the meetings of the Council of Trent in the mid-sixteenth century, could be recuperated and mobilised in the service of Catholicism and the emerging Catholic empires of Spain and Portugal. Implicit in this argument was a sense of the need to develop an effective cultural response to the Protestant Reformation, something that could re-energise Catholic spirituality and its political projects. That idea comes to fruition after the death of Philip II in 1598, leading in Spain (and to a lesser extent in Portugal, which had been absorbed by the Hapsburg monarchy at the time) to a liberalisation of cultural censorship and a tremendous explosion of literary and artistic invention that includes Cervantes' *Don Quixote*, the poetry of Camões, Góngora and Quevedo, the vast production of plays, numbering in the thousands, of the Spanish public theatre or *comedia*, and the body of novels that has come to be known as the Baroque picaresque. One powerful agent of Baroque culture was the system of colonial schools the Jesuits set up, where Baroque forms of writing such as the poetry of Luis de Góngora or the prose of Mateo Alemán were used as models of proper literary style and content in the place of the Classics.

The Baroque is above all an art of the state, a 'lyrical engineering of the human world', to borrow the expression of the Spanish cultural historian José Antonio Maravall, expressed in public buildings, churches, ceremonies of power, festivals. But there was a more private form of the Baroque too, especially evident in the practice of lyric poetry, which came to be, paradoxically, the central literary form of the colonial Baroque in particular. This is in sharp contrast to the situation in Spain itself in the seventeenth century, where the novel weighed more heavily. Fearing its secularising tendency, the Church and colonial authorities limited the publication and importation of novels in the colonies. They associated the novel in effect with an individualistic, proto-democratic ethos. It was not that merchant and manufacturing or artisan classes were lacking in the colonies – quite the contrary, immigration to 'New' Spain was often a means for a social mobility denied in the metropolis. But, perhaps because the problem of orthodoxy and legitimacy was all the more acute in the viceroyalties given their distance from the imperial centre and the extremely heterogeneous nature of the colonial populations, in both class and racial terms, the official colonial ethos was if anything even more *aristocratisant* than in Spain or Portugal.

The prohibition of the novel in the colonies has been over-emphasised in Latin American cultural history: many place names in the Americas, like California, derive from novels of chivalry that the conquistadores and their foot soldiers brought with them. We know that there was an ample contraband in novels: in spite of the prohibitions, the most popular and influential book in both Spain and its viceroyalties in the seventeenth century appears to have been Mateo Alemán's picaresque novel, *Guzmán de Alfarache*. And in the colonies proper, there are numerous novel-like texts, often showing a strong influence of the picaresque, such as *Los infortunios de Alfonso Ramírez*, which anticipates in some ways Defoe's *Robinson Crusoe*. Still, it is also true that there is no novel per se produced in the colonies until the end of the eighteenth century – critics usually point to the *Lazarillo de ciegos caminantes* (which is somewhere between a travel journal and a picaresque novel) as the first Latin American novel proper.

In both the Spanish and Portuguese courts and the colonial viceroyalties, art and politics are not yet regarded as clearly separate disciplines and activities. Secular literature (including history) – *letras humanas*, in the language of the day, as opposed to *letras sacras* – was seen as both a prerequisite for the formation of the statesman or clergyman, and as a form of expression of those in power. The equation (often an unstable one) was of the *letrado*, or writer-intellectual, with the *hidalgo*, or aristocrat. The regulations of 'purity of blood' (*limpieza de sangre*) meant that the top offices in the colonial administration were reserved for those who could claim in principle a title of nobility (though in practice the distinction between noble and commoner was often blurred). Relations between writers and the highest layers of the viceregal and ecclesiastical bureaucracy were often very close (the brilliant poetess and nun, Sor Juana Inés de la Cruz, was an intimate friend and confidante of the wife of the Spanish viceroy in Mexico, and wrote many 'occasional' sonnets to celebrate the quotidian events of the viceregal court like weddings, deaths, births or the installation of new authorities). The colonial institution that was perhaps most pertinent in this regard were the *certámenes*, or poetry competitions, in which the prize for a winning well-wrought sonnet in the style of, say, Góngora or Quevedo, could be an appointment as the secretary of the viceroy or the local bishop. The equation between the capacity to write and decipher complex literary creations and the capacity to exercise power becomes the foundation of what the modern critic Angel Rama called the institution of the 'lettered city '(*la ciudad letrada*) in subsequent Latin American history: the idea that literature itself is a practice in which power authorises itself, and that literary intellectuals (*letrados*) are somehow especially qualified to run the state, or advise those who do.

Baroque art depended on the patronage of the Church and state. But, by the same token, the nature of aristocratic and ecclesiastical power in the Iberian colonies itself depended on theatricality, ceremony, exhibitionism, splendour. Pomp, or the appearance of power, was not clearly separate from the substance of power: power was in a sense representation. One of the central Baroque allegorical images is that of the 'the great theatre of the world', and the colonial state and Church were themselves a kind of theatre of power or 'theatre-state', to borrow Clifford Geertz's term. The Baroque's particular visual and verbal alchemy constituted a kind of 'theory of magic accumulation' that masked the actual 'primitive accumulation of capital' (to recall Marx's phrase) in the colonies, making it appear harmonious with the religious and aristocratic assumptions of the colonial state.

There is a public Baroque in the colonies, represented, for example, by church architecture and sculpture and painting, certain forms of *mestizo* folk art, or the short allegorical plays the Jesuits developed, on the model of the Spanish auto *sacramental*, to teach Christian doctrine to indigenous communities. But, as noted, there is also a private, aristocratic Baroque that embodies the aristocratic fetish of a highly complex mode of art that is seen as noble or sublime precisely because it eludes the comprehension of both the colonised population – the *castas* – and at the same time the lower-class immigrants from Spain or Portugal, situating itself outside the value systems of money and market exchange as determinants of social power and status. In this regard, cultivation of literature and poetry in particular becomes a colonial form of what Pierre Bourdieu would call 'cultural capital': a way of discriminating between colonial élites and subaltern sectors.

The key product of Baroque culture is the modern system of Latin American cities itself, rising up around the viceregal courts, or more locally the 'captaincies' (*capitanías generales*). The Baroque articulates the colonial city as the apotheosis of history and thus of the colonial project itself: the text that is most illustrative in this regard is the *Grandeza Mejicana* by Bernardo de Balbuena of the early seventeenth century, a vast, book-long description in verse of the city of Mexico, built over the ruins of the former Aztec capital. The Iberian colonial system implied at the material level an enormous displacement of human and material resources in favour of the system of colonial cities, which were linked in turn to the European metropolis, but also at the cultural and political level a kind of 'ruralisation' of the countryside (because in the pre-Colombian era, even in the great empires of Mesoamerica and the Andes, the countryside was not just a region for the production of agricultural commodities, but also a space for cultural production and self-rule). Despite its function as an imperial and urbanising style, however, the Baroque has a very different sense of history from later European colonial projects, which tend to base themselves on a bourgeois-liberal notion of history as progress. History is seen as both a necessary condition for the expansion of the authority of the colonial régime, but also as a force of entropy and decay. The colonial Baroque thinks of itself as a form of 'modernity' (seeing the indigenous religions and social forms it abolishes or represses as barbaric or anachronistic), but it also seeks to ground itself in pre-modern representations of value and community, especially in its use of the pastoral.

The Baroque sense of history is linked to the idea of *desengaño* or disillusion, an experience that is both intellectual and spiritual. *Desengaño* invokes the paradoxical conjunction of the principle of submission to authority (the Church and state) with the practical ideal of the self-willed, autonomous individual. The quality of mind that is to synthesise these two aspects is *ingenio* – wit, or creative intelligence. Wit is seen primarily as a political virtue – the capacity to find or invent new solutions in a rapidly changing world; but it is to be learned primarily in the laboratory of poetry and art. Wit allows for both disillusion, a religious sense of the ultimate vanity of human desire and the things of the world, and innovation. It might be seen then as a kind of Catholic colonial version of Protestant 'interiority', on the one hand, and Machiavellian cunning and 'reason of state', on the other.

In evaluating the importance of the Baroque, it is pertinent to recall that at the end of the seventeenth century, at the height of viceregal culture, the Spanish and Portuguese colonies in the Americas were more or less at the same level of development and population density as what is today the United States. The gap between the two, especially in terms of economic development, begins to emerge in the later eighteenth century and widens after the colonies become formally independent from Spain in 1820–30. In that sense, the Baroque was a mature cultural formation. To borrow a distinction from the Indian historian Ranajit Guha, it represented a form of rule that was hegemonic, rather than simply dominant, as in the case of other colonial projects, for example, British rule in India. In that sense, it was 'accepted' by the lower classes and indigenous and African populations, and becomes also part of their culture in various hybrid forms (the Peruvian *letrado* Espinosa Medrano, for example, wrote plays based on the model of the Spanish Baroque *comedia* in Quechua).

Some of the highest achievements of Latin American art correspond to the Baroque. Sor Juana Inés de la Cruz is a towering figure, but there are many other important writers: the Peruvian Caviedes; the Brazilian Gregorio de Matos; Sor Juana's fellow Mexicans Ruiz de Alarcón and Siguenza y Góngora; the exiled Jesuit priest Rafael Landívar, whose *Rusticatio mexicana* is a description of the countryside of Central America written in Latin, poised intellectually and stylistically between the Baroque and the Enlightenment. There are the monumental religious installations, especially the monumental statues of the Prophets, in Minas Gerais, by the mulatto sculptor and architect Alejandinho, perhaps the greatest plastic artist Latin America has produced. In the same *mestizo* vein is the exquisite small church, mixing indigenous and rococo decorative elements on the outskirts of Puebla, in the shadow of an Aztec pyramid. Also part of the Baroque are the great churches and architectural complexes of Cuzco, Quito, old Havana, Potosi, Puebla; the painting of the Cuzco School; the cult of the Virgin of Guadalupe and her shrine on the outskirts of Mexico (and similar cults of the Virgin in every region of colonial Latin America); and the system of great libraries and universities (the first of which, San Marcos, in Lima, was founded more than a half a century before the Pilgrims set foot on Plymouth Rock).

The achievement of the Baroque period in colonial America has led to a wide-ranging discussion and debate about its significance for modern Latin America. According to one school – perhaps the dominant one – the colonial Baroque, because of its protean and hybrid nature, permitted a transculturation or syncretism between European and indigenous (and later Africa and Asiatic) elements. It provided a template in which the *criollo* and *mestizo* artists and writers of the colonies could begin to represent the American world they knew in ways that incorporated local elements and increasingly deviated from metropolitan models and assumptions, passing in this way from imitation or 'colonial mimicry', to borrow an expression from Homi Bhabha, to innovation. In this way, this school sees the Baroque as a 'proto-national' phenomenon, anticipating the rise of Latin American nationalism and the independence movements of the early nineteenth century. Indeed, there has been a strong tendency in modern Latin American cultural discourse to see the Baroque as the *essential* style of Latin American postcolonial identity, and many writers and artists have championed what they call a 'neo-Baroque'.

However, this celebration of the Baroque as a form of cultural nationalism may involve a misunderstanding. In historical terms, it is important to keep in mind the Baroque was a style *imposed* on the conquered populations of the continent. That is not to say that these populations, including indigenous peoples and Africans, did not contribute in many ways to its flourishing, but it is quite another thing to say that it is a style of colonial resistance. While it is undoubtedly the case that the Baroque art and literature was one of the places where a new, specifically 'American' *criollo-mestizo* sensibility begins to incubate and express itself in the colonies, it is also important to remember that the colonial upper and middle classes were by definition of a settler-colonial character, like the *pied noirs* of Algeria or the Boers of South Africa (in Latin American Spanish, *criollo* came to mean someone of European parentage, but born and raised in the colonies). It is not clear, therefore, that their demands for more autonomy, and their increasing sense of cultural isolation and difference from Spain and (less so in the case of Brazil) Portugal, were properly anti-colonial phenomena, or that formal political independence in the nineteenth century meant an end to colonialism as such. Seeing the *criollos*, and the new mixed or *mestizo* population, as the main cultural actors in the formation of a properly 'national' culture was (and is) at the expense of the exclusion or marginalisation of the populations that were actually colonised: the indigenous peoples and the African slaves. To posit the Baroque the cultural signifier of Latin America as such, then, would be in a sense to place the force of decolonisation in the continent, both in the past and the present, under essentially European auspices. At the same time, constructing the Baroque historically as in effect the 'waiting room' of the modern Latin American nation-state does not permit an understanding and appreciation of the Baroque on its own terms, that is, as a synchronic cultural-social formation with its own peculiar world-view, one that is quite different than the modernising teleology embodied in the postcolonial nation-state.

The persistence of the Baroque in Latin American cultural discourse and practice might be seen then as symptomatic of something like a cultural neurosis, linked to unresolved issues of cultural identity, authority and privilege – particularly having to do with class, gender, and race – still structured in some ways by colonial assumptions and epistemologies.

John Beverley

HISTORIES
Beverley, John (1993), 'On the Spanish Literary Baroque', in J. Beverley, *Against Literature*, Minneapolis, MN: University of Minnesota Press, pp. 47–68.
González Echevarría, Roberto (1993), *Celestina's Brood. Continuities of the Baroque in Spanish and Latin American Literature*, Durham, NC and London: Duke University Press.
Leonard, Irving (1959), *Baroque Times in Old Mexico*, Ann Arbor, MI: University of Michigan Press.
Maravall, José Antonio (1986), *Culture of the Baroque: Analysis of a Historical Structure*, trans. Terry Cochran, Minneapolis, MN: University of Minnesota Press.
Paz, Octavio (1990), *Sor Juana: Or, the Traps of Faith*, trans. Margaret S. Peden, Cambridge, MA: Harvard University Press.
Rama, Angel (1996), *The Lettered City*, trans. John Chasteen, Durham, NC and London: Duke University Press.

Colonialism and Popular Culture in the Andes

The subaltern status of popular culture in the Andes needs questioning. Under dominating and often homogenising influences, the powerful pressure to forget has often effaced the wider context of popular cultural practices. Both symbolic and real violence have also eradicated the former social and territorial groupings that gave rise to them. Many cultural practices were reshaped first by colonising Andean states above all the Inkas, then by the alienating effects of Spanish colonialism, followed by the colonising practices of nineteenth-century republican states forged around the making of monocultural and monolingual nations and their citizenship. Finally, the current subalternity of popular practices derives from the insistent internal coloniality of modern states in the twentieth century characterised by the homogenising effects of *mestizaje*. The same colonial experience generated conflicts over meanings and practices between social groups, defining differences between the city and rural areas, which in turn shaped popular practices, their production, reception and directions of change.

In the distant past of pre-subaltern days, these alternative territorial forms of cultural organisation came under the auspices of other institutions. For example, Inca ideology stressed work in agricultural and herding production as a ritual act through which individuals and groups contributed to the maintenance of the cosmos and the reproduction of society. In an ideology of hierarchical obligation and reciprocity between the Inca and groups under their dominion, the Inca and Coya gave food, drink and gifts to their subjects as payment for labour in agriculture or warfare. However, these exchanges in the field of production and cultural action were laced by the constant menace of real or symbolic violence, expressed in many war songs of the period. The forms of speech and dialogue of groups brought under Inca dominion were moulded in part by these gift-giving practices and their ritual acknowledgement, which extended new social ties fictively back to the local ancestors and gods. Inca institutional mechanisms of state power streamlined the local production of ceramics, weaving and other cultural artefacts within their extensive communication system of roads and way stations, as it did literary genres and their expression – the *wayñu* for example – forming a single cultural centre that extended from Ecuador to the Argentine region, and from the Amazon to the Pacific coast. Popular *wayñus* are songs and dances of courtship and marriage, once brought within the sphere of wider state obligations.

Aymara leaders exercised similar forms of institutional control by reciting before their subjects the words of the ancestors, their own genealogies and accomplishments in war. These past practices gave rise to the modern ones of libation making (*ch'alla*). In parts of Oruro (Bolivia), these still follow patterned 'pathways of social memory' back to the Inca gods in Cusco, and the ritual language used in these popular cultural forms is still defined by the boundaries of former Andean chiefdoms.

Under the Inca, Aymara literary forms that lauded the herds received state support. Guaman Poma de Ayala's popular seventeenth-century drawings and hybrid text illustrate typical feasts of the four quarters (*suyus*) where work and cultural performance went hand in hand; his terminology is not so different from that of today. Brotherston (1992) and others call our attention to the primary metaphor of herd organisation as the basis of Andean social organisation, and of literary pastoralism as the basis of Andean poetry, stories, drama and songs. Herding dances such as the *Kallawada* still characterise the great street fiestas of the barrios of La Paz.

With Inca colonisation, hybrid cultural forms combined Quechua with Aymara (and formerly Pukina) cultural practices. For example, the 'Dramas of the Death of the Inca Atawallpa' tend to be told in Quechua even in Aymara territories. With the Hispanic colony, Andean languages mingled with Spanish, and *parla* and *kuñtu* now described Andeanised versions of European folktales: 'The Fox and the Condor' or 'The Bearman', told in rural haciendas or urban meeting places.

Rowe and Schelling (1991) stress that the élitist tendency to perceive these popular songs, tales or oral histories as collective and anonymous creations is part of a romantic urban tendency to view the collective as authentic and the individual as alienating. In practice, individual modes of creation within regional repertoires and learning practices might describe the authorship issue more clearly. Similarly the common putdown of

Andean popular art in terms of the art versus handicrafts distinction fails to take into account the intention of the cultural producers themselves.

Other regional differences in popular practices are due to localised economic activities. The widespread 'Greasesucker' tales often emerge in contexts of extreme economic difference. The mining centres of La Paz, Potosí and Oruro tend to tell the tales of 'Snake Woman' and the underworld devils. For Abercrombie (1992), the great Carnival of Oruro (Bolivia) has combined rural and mining ideas of annual regeneration, animated by these devil spirits, with intense Christian ideas of the necessary expulsion of the devil as the 'Indian within'. This form of expiation served as a guiding icon of subaltern incorporation into *criollo* national values and controls, which was accompanied by xenophobia toward competing outside Western influences.

With Christian indoctrination in the colony, rites to the former ancestral mummy bundles were transferred to the new Catholic saints in the expanding circuits of patronal feasts. Other saints – Mama Copacabana, Santa Rosa of Lima, Taytacha Qoyllur Rit'i – replaced the former Andean sacred centres (*wak'a*) as miraculous pilgrimage sites. In Peru, the present June feast of Inti Raymi developed in the 1940s to celebrate civic pride in Cusco. But, according to Flores Ochoa, its powerful Inca roots acted like a generative *illa*-stone, animating its performance throughout the region in immense ritual-civic cycles of renewed Cusco-centric identity, inspired by indigenism. The notions of popular Catholicism or syncretism do not acknowledge the complex processes of cultural appropriations involved in these historical transformations. More recently, mystical tourism centred on Cusco has combined New Age with Incaic and Cusco-centric nostalgia, while further north, local identity draws on Moche, Chimu and Vicús artefacts from archaeological digs to create the paraphernalia of regional tourism.

Other facets of cultural appropriations are the portable altars of saints or *retablos* of Ayacucho (Peru), used originally for conversion, which became household instances of propitiation, and then, with 1940s indigenism, works of popular art developed by particular schools and artists. *Retablos* are still moulded from coloured earth, plaster and, importantly, potato paste, as the generative basis of a more magical *mise-en-scène*, even in the desacralised historical realist and customary schools with their scenes of popular life.

The Alasitas fair in La Paz, toward the end of January, where everything (money, professional diplomas, household pots and pans) takes a miniature *illa*-like form, centres on Ekeko, the regional thunder god, as an eclectic image of plenty for the bearer in the coming year. The popular handicrafts on sale, while serving these ritual functions, are also partial integrations into capitalism, peripheral activities brought into the marketing centre.

Throughout the Andes, games of chance, usually with some form of dice (*pichca* or 'fives' is an example) have a long history, being played in inter-seasonal transitions to direct human energies toward productive success. They are also played in wakes in the rite of passage between the living and the dead, to record the role a dead person played in his or her earthly labours. These games formerly served as part of a tournament economy, in the colonising transactions between the victor and the vanquished. They remind us of a region-wide (rather than simply subaltern) alternative to capitalist economic speculation, as well as of the shaping of an alternative aesthetics based on plenty that is still very much alive, especially in a precarious economic periphery.

Beyersdorff (1992) describes how, this time in complex textual transformations, written Catholic catechisms were disseminated in rural areas in the early colony, to be appropriated into local religious practices, and later collected as examples of Inca indigenous texts. Widespread Jesuit influence, based on the Testerian pedagogy of Mesoamerican experience, produced catechisms in glyphs for unlettered rural populations, who were to re-appropriate these prayers yet again as local forms of oratory for rain, while the glyphs have been viewed as indigenous Andean forms of writing. Even the language of the Resurrection and its remembrance through the host, was remoulded by local populations to suit their practices of warfare and regional ideas concerning salvation.

Another aspect of conflicting meanings and vying appropriations is how modern Andean nation-states have resorted to folklorism, based on a romantic view of rural peasant community life (*Gemeinschaft*), as one way of gaining hegemony over the diverse social and ethnic groupings in its interior. Rowe and Schelling's analysis of Latin American modernity suggests that this folkloric tendency aimed to establish authenticity banks, as safe categorisations of alternative cultures. In Peru and Bolivia this happened in the 1940s and 1950s, when folklore and nation-building coincided with the gradual demise of rural cultures amid waves of urban migrations. In those years, the state promotion of traditional music sought to create national rather than regional identities. In northern Chile, only recently has the destructive homogenising effect on local diversity of state patronage of folkloric dances from those years been questioned, and a new recognition of local variation re-established.

Meanwhile, the emerging urban barrios of rural migrants, faced with marginality by already established populations, forged alternative ethnic identities that gave rise in the 1980s to alternative national groupings (Quechua, Aymara). Barrio dance troops appropriated established urban choreographic forms as their own ethnic forms of expression. In later variants of these re-appropriations, students with rural backgrounds tend to perform the *tinku* war dance, wealthier groups perform the *caporales*, while older Aymaras dance the *morenada*, originally an *uru* dance that became associated with the march of Afro descendants to the Potosí mines. The *morenada* is also returning to rural areas to efface the local troops of flute players, as up-and-coming urban middle classes disseminate outward these performances of alternative ethnic power forged in the cities.

In school and university parades throughout the region, young dance troops vie with each other for supremacy, as they are shaped into citizens. In immense spectacles of nationhood, all of these dances are performed in Gran Poder in La Paz, or Carnival in Oruro, by competing urban and rural dance troops, anxious to be part of the Andean nations. At the same time, cultural centres such as La Paz inspire whole regions of neighbouring countries (Peru, Chile, Argentina) in music, dress and dance styles in wider multinational alternative identities, above all of Aymara nationhood.

The wider absorption of popular into mass culture, via the culture industry of expanding capitalism, has been another strategy by which former élites sought to control subaltern challenges. But while the pervasive invasion of Brazilian and Argentine television soap operas might contribute to the standardised repertoire of expanding capitalism, radio in indigenous hands has served to spread indigenous political ideologies (for example Katarism) and to create strong regional identities that finally challenged even the political power of conventional élites.

In the Andean region, the neo-liberal policies of multiculturalism were another controlling framework for the political and cultural absorption of indigenous alternatives (some would say alternative civilisations), permitting the recognition of difference but not its economic amelioration by a real redistribution of resources. Throughout Ecuador, Peru, Bolivia and Chile, a part of this intercultural recognition has been the inclusion in state policies of indigenous education, language teaching and common law, even of indigenous political authorities at a local level. However, the framing of this recognition in the ancestral ties of mediaeval land rights and cultural patrimony, even in the case of UNICEF's naming of entire regions (the Kallawaya healers and Uru-Chipaya 'water people') as world cultural patrimony, tends to limit indigenous horizons to the past, and so truncates their future.

Any posture that favoured the superior status of high art or high culture by the *criollo-mestizo* minorities, versus their popular alternatives, has only been able to control the school and university curriculum, or the contents of the mass media, through the political control of the police and the army, the law courts and the electoral courts. There, in the context of rampant capitalist globalisation, the common tendency toward lost contexts and histories, and a focus on the aesthetic rather than the socio-cultural holds sway. But once these pretensions have been seriously challenged politically, for instance in the Bolivia of Evo Morales, then a new set of hegemonic demands quickly takes their place.

As elsewhere, key moments of political rebellion have been contextualised by popular strategies. In the nineteenth century, it was common for rebellions to emerge out of Carnival festivities. In the great Aymara rebellions of 2000–5, the rural migrant strategies of 'fleas, skunks, and ants' were able to mobilise thousands spontaneously to sow the roads with stones, dig trenches or return canisters of tear gas against the deployed state violence of tanks and guns. Similarly, thousands of miners relocated in the 1980s in the city of El Alto were able to draw on their former union practices to provide the organising logic of certain rebellious districts of El Alto against the neo-liberal Bolivian state. They were backed by the solidarity of women herders using slingshots against the army, and the graffiti and colourful insults of the women artists of *mujeres creando*.

Finally, what relation has popular culture with populism? The uses of popular culture in the current populist politics of President Evo Morales in Bolivia certainly leaves an impression of déjà vu, when compared, say, to the Peruvian experience of populism in the early twentieth century. The play between opposing socialist and indigenous factions, with their different understandings of Andean collectivism, demands for self-determination, or nostalgia for recreating Tawantinsuyu, recall Mariátegui's socialism versus the Peruvian Comintern politics of national separations. Flores Galindo's account of *La agonía de Mariátegui* is also surprisingly relevant, of the frustration of trying to pursue a regional approach to political change when faced with ready-at-hand importations, in the present case from Cuba or Venezuela.

Evo Morales' drive to reinvent tradition in his inaugural ceremony in the ruins of Tiwanaku, or his opening of the Constituent Assembly (in the Bolivian capital of Sucre) with a pluricultural military march past, are important cultural re-appropriations within the auspices of an emerging plurinational state, but they are often accompanied by populist over-simplifications of Andean culture. While disseminating Morales' own brand of indigenous state power, these re-appropriations are also shaping new cultural stereotypes in the hands of urban politicians and party militants, difficult to reconcile with their historical precursors. Have the Indians 'found their Lenin', as Valcarcel asked in *Tempestad en los Andes* in 1927 at the height of neo-Incaism, or are they in danger of becoming the political objects of new forms of populist ideological domination, tinged with the familiar language of evangelical liberation?

Denise Arnold

LITERARY WORKS

Arnold, Denise Y. and Juan de Dios Yapita (2004), 'The Nature of Indigenous Literatures in the Andes', in M. Valdés and Djelal Kadir (eds), *Literary Cultures of Latin America: A Comparative History*, vol. 3, Oxford and New York: Oxford University Press, pp. 385–415.

Brotherston, Gordon (1992), *The Book of the Fourth World*, Cambridge: Cambridge University Press.
Rowe, William and Vivian Schelling (1991), *Memory and Modernity. Popular Culture in Latin America*, London: Verso.

HISTORIES
Abercrombie, T. A. (1992), 'El carnaval postcolonial en Oruro', *Revista Andina* 2: 279–325.
Beyersdorff, Margot (1992), 'Ritual Gesture to Poetic Text in the Christianisation of the Andes', *Journal of Latin American Lore* 19: 125–61.

Discovery and Conquest

Columbus' arrival in the Caribbean on 12 October 1492 started the process of discovery and conquest of America. The changes that the expedition unleashed would give Spain the resources to become the leader of the first global design, which, as North European nations developed it over the centuries, gave rise to European world hegemony and to the emergence of the Atlantic as a global centre of economic and political power. However, the changes were initially slow because the expeditions failed to achieve their goal: to sail westwards in order to reach India and China, which were the central commercial circuits of the world at that time. Sailing westwards was Spain's only option, given that the Turks controlled the West Mediterranean Sea and the Portuguese the route around Africa.

Discovery was followed by conquest, which was carried out, with a few exceptions, by private companies under royal licence. The way in which the colonial process unfolded varied depending on political and economic factors. In cases involving low population density and weak royal regulation, as in the Caribbean, the outcome was genocidal. In the twenty-seven years that the Spaniards remained in the islands their main economic activity was mining, which relied on the exploitation of the natives as a work force compelled to work in conditions of near-slavery. The result was the almost complete annihilation of the indigenous population and the consequent need to import slaves. This was done initially by raiding the coastal areas of Central America and northern South America; later, it was done largely by importing slaves from the west coast of Africa.

The situation was denounced by a loud minority from the Church in 1511; the ensuing debate reached all levels of Spanish society and lasted for years. Its high point was reached in the 1550–1 debates between Bartolomé de Las Casas and Juan Ginés de Sepúlveda. Concerned by the economic consequences of the decline in population (Indians paid taxes because they were vassals while slaves did not), and criticism from the Indian faction, the crown adopted the policy of protecting Indians. This policy went hand in hand with the conquest of the most advanced Amerindian polities, the Aztec and Inca empires, conquered by Hernán Cortés in 1519 and by Francisco Pizarro in 1532. Control over rich populations comprising several million inhabitants, under a highly developed political system, gave birth to the *encomienda* régime in its mature form. *Encomienda* grants gave conquerors the right to collect taxes from groups of native peoples; in exchange, *encomenderos* had to care for their Indians' conversion and well-being. In the case of resulting indirect rule, in which native lords secured the transfer of goods and labour to their Spanish lord, the population loss was, although still significant, much lower than in the Caribbean, in some instances less than 30 per cent.

While the conquests appear to testify to crushing European superiority, the situation was more complex. First, Amerindian empires were mosaics of different peoples, many of them ready to ally with the conquerors. In the 1521 final siege of the Aztec capital, for instance, the besiegers included about 800 Spaniards and some 50,000 Tlaxcalans. Second, the Spaniards were not always successful. When operating on territories not previously conquered by native empires, particularly in forests or areas of low aboriginal density and political centralisation, such as the Amazon, Chaco, north of Mexico, or south of Chile and Argentina, the outcome was sustained failure. Third, while the Spaniards' military superiority was uncontestable – native peoples had neither weapons that could penetrate the Spaniards' armour nor effective defensive gear against steel swords and firearms, nor experience of fighting cavalry – military superiority did not necessarily translate into cultural superiority.

Even if conquered, native peoples did not play the role of victims; they actively struggled to shape the new order, conditioning the Spaniards' colonial projects. These challenges were helped by the Spaniards' small numbers, which forced them to establish political alliances, and by their internecine conflicts, which opened room for manoeuvre – constant struggle between conquerors, royal officers and priests was common. The result was a contested field of religious, economic and political interactions.

In the political arena, the Spanish allies asked and most often obtained rewards that challenged their status as the vanquished, including exemptions from economic obligations and the award of nobility titles. More commonly, the Spanish need for indirect rule meant that the local leadership was entirely native; ethnic lords learned soon to manoeuvre between different Spanish interests and to exploit the benefits of a paternalistic royal legislation and a critical clergy. Their interventions could be spectacular. When, in 1560, the crown was debating whether to turn the *encomiendas* into perpetually inheritable properties, Peru's native peoples allied with critical sectors of the Church and made Philip II an astonishing offer: in exchange for running the colony on their own, supervised by priests, Andean lords offered to top *any* amount the Spanish *encomenderos* could offer.

The Spaniards also had to compete with native peoples in the economic arena. In all lucrative businesses, from trade to the production of coca or silk to mining or weaving, Indian communities and individuals sought to take advantage of the new opportunities that the colonial economy opened. Their profits allowed them more easily to fulfil their tribute payments, which also undermined the colonisers' ascendancy. In an ironic reversal of role, during much of the sixteenth century, the Spaniards often found themselves struggling to obtain the services of a scarce labour force, and to prevent the Indians from becoming successful competitors.

Christianisation was another contested terrain. Refusing to bow to the assumptions of superiority on the part of the Spanish clergy, native peoples established selective relations with the Christians' deity (or deities) and their representatives. They tapped into the potencies introduced by the Spaniards, while integrating them into their own religious field: for example, Mayans noticed the power with which Spaniards invested the cross, and included it in their own religious rituals. Such adaptations often frustrated the Spaniards and led to the repression of indigenous communities, as in the case of the Maya of Yucatán in the Franciscan missions. Since Christianity also grounded the Spanish colonial project in terms of an epistemology (a claim to know 'the Truth'), it was an additional terrain for intellectual contestation. The work of indigenous intellectuals, such as Guamán Poma or Alva Ixtlilxóchitl, shows a delicate balance that at once acknowledges the Spaniards' rules of recognition and subverts them by introducing other knowledges and meanings.

Gonzalo Lamana

Literary Works

Adorno, Rolena (2000), *Guaman Poma*, Austin, TX: University of Texas Press.
Mignolo, Walter (1995), *The Darker Side of the Renaissance*, Ann Arbor, MI: University of Michigan Press.
Pastor Bodmer, Beatriz (1992), *The Armature of Conquest*, Stanford, CA: Stanford University Press.
Rabasa, José (1993), *Inventing A-M-E-R-I-C-A*, Norman, OK: University of Oklahoma Press.
Seed, Patricia (1991), 'Failing to Marvel. Atahualpa's Encounter with the Word', *Latin American Research Review* 26 (1): 7–32.
Velazco, Salvador (2003), *Visiones de Anáhuac*, Guadalajara: University of Guadalajara.

Histories

Clendinnen, Inga (1987), *Ambivalent Conquests*, Cambridge: Cambridge University Press.
— (1991), 'Fierce and Unnatural Cruelty': Cortés and the Conquest of Mexico', *Representations* 33: 65–100.
Dussel, Enrique (1998), 'Beyond Eurocentrism. The World-System and the Limits of Modernity', in Frederic Jameson and Masao Miyoshi (eds), *The Cultures of Globalization*, Durham, NC: Duke University Press, pp. 3–31.
Lockhart, James (1992), *The Nahuas after the Conquest*, Stanford, CA: Stanford University Press.
Pietschmann, Horst (1989), *El estado y su evolución al principio de la colonización española de América*, México: Fondo de Cultura Económica.
Stern, Steve (1982), *Peru's Indigenous Peoples and the Challenge of Spanish Conquest*, Madison, WI: Wisconsin University Press.

Uriel García

Uriel García (Cusco 1891–1965) is the author of a book essential to calibrate the theoretical density of the Andean decolonising debate during the first decades of the twentieth century. With its avant-garde title, *El nuevo indio* (*The New Indian*, 1930), this text gives articulation to a decolonising impulse different from the one offered by Gamaliel Churata (the leading figure of the Andean Avant-Garde), and yet in dialogue with it. García insists on the idea that the continent occupied by Spain in the sixteenth century was not 'an unexplored jungle where Europe prolonged its history, but rather a historically precious milieu in possession of an immense vital force'. The conquerors, García points out, took possession of that world of immense vitality, which in spite of their victory singled them out as the defeated. The Indians, on their part, were pushed to defend furiously against that force, while being converted into *immigrants* (my emphasis) of the Incario in the new scene created by the conquest. The colonial enterprise, according to García's argument, is the history of that pain, of that 'infuriation' confronted with the Spanish desire for possession. That 'madness' – the struggle between two wills – produced the sprouting of a new human kind that García calls *el nuevo indio*.

No doubt we are dealing with a concept that takes the notion of mestizaje to a conceptual domain other than the one imagined by Vasconcelos in his celebrated *La raza cósmica* (*The Cosmic Race*, 1925). Here 'mestizaje' is no longer conceived from racial perspectives, but from the comprehension of a tragedy that reformulated history as well as the fate of its protagonists (Indians and Spaniards). Understood as a 'history forging' category, García's notion of mestizaje emerges as the possibility of the colonised entering with dignity a different and irreversible historical reality. For him, the colonial period is understood as a process of approximation or distance taken by Spaniards and Indians in relation to the *mestizo* reality of the Andes:

> The Indian that takes distance is a dead soul . . . He is the *ayllu* perched atop its mountain. But the Indian who audaciously shows his face to the painful reality and calmly confronts it, is the one who again masters the cathedral stones, the one who accepts the new idea and expresses it with his emotions, the one who reconquers the land with a decisive will. He is Garcilaso, Lunarejo, tupac Amaru. . . .Thus, the American *amestisamiento* that generates a new spirit that goes forward to the future conveys the serious problem of infusing in the Indian that juvenile soul to make of him a total *nuevo indio*. And into the singular case of our south Peruvian sierra, a vast zone of *indianidad*, the problem of culture also drags the social problem of the redemption of the Indian, a problem that as José Carlos Mariátegui states, affects mainly the young generations of the sierra, since it is the regionalist issue par excellence. (García 1973)

The proposition of mestizaje as a 'history forging' category, and the possibility of the colonised 'to enter with dignity a historical reality that is both distinct and irreversible', opened up unsuspected horizons of cultural reflection and anticipated proposals such as those put forth by García Canclini (2005), which would be heard in the last decades of the twentieth century. However, the cost of this rethinking of mestizaje, clearly formulated within a liberal ideological framework and compromised with the modern utopia of progress and the Indigenist project to 'educate' and 'redeem' the Indian, remains implicit. Gamaliel Churata, another writer deeply committed to this Andean debate, refused to pay this cost, arguing that the 'Garcilaso possibility' did not make viable a decolonised literature. Tenaciously, Churata insisted that in Garcilaso the seeds of the conquered get diluted, and therefore the only possible motherland that emerges is the one offered by the Spanish language and the Spanish metropolis. Openly opposed to García, Churata bets on the 'Huamán Poma possibility', where the strength and courage of the conquered is empowered, thus making possible the articulation of 'plebs' emancipated from the mental meridians generated in the Old World.

Translations into English by Elizabeth Monasterios

Elizabeth Monasterios

LITERARY WORKS
Boletín Titikaka [1926–8] (2004), Arequipa: Universidad Nacional de San Agustín.
García, Uriel [1930] (1973), *El nuevo indio*, Lima: Editorial Universo.

HISTORIES
Cornejo Polar, Antonio (1994), *Escribir en el aire. Ensayo sobre la heterogeneidad sociocultural en las literaturas andinas*, Lima: Editorial Horizonte.
García Canclini, Néstor [1992] (2005), *Hybrid Cultures: Strategies for Entering and Leaving Modernity*, trans. Christopher L. Chiappari and Silvia L. López, Minneapolis, MN: University of Minnesota Press.
Mariátegui, José Carlos [1928] (1975), *Siete ensayos de interpretación de la realidad Peruana*, Havana: Casa de las Américas.
Vasconcelos, José [1925] (1979), *The Cosmic Race*, Baltimore: Johns Hopkins University Press.

Vich, Cynthia (2000), *Indigenismo de vanguardia en el Perú. Un estudio sobre el Boletín Titikaka*, Lima: Pontificia Universidad Católica del Perú.

Zevallos, Juan (2002), *Indigenismo y nación. Los retos a la representación de la subalternidad aymara y quechua en el Boletín Titikaka (1926–1930)*, Lima: IFEA and BCRP.

Hibridación (Hybridity)

Hibridación refers to the mixing of discrete generic forms, often with the implication that such mixing will produce a new, 'hybrid', form. Sometimes called *hibridez*, hibridación is a massive concept. It holds special significance within a long-standing tradition of Latin Americanist thought and in recent years has become a key word in Latin American Cultural Studies. But *hibridación* extends well beyond that context, and its impact is felt in fields as disparate as botany and literary criticism, sociolinguistics and postcolonial studies.

Hibridación's first appearance in the Real Academia Española is in 1899, where it is rendered as a process, *la producción de híbridos*. A century later (1992) it takes on an ontological resonance, qualified with *seres* placed before *híbridos*. Tracking *híbrido* takes us to 1837, where it is associated with sexual reproduction – *procreado por dos distintas especies, como el mulo* – and linguistic formations – *voces formadas o compuestas de dos idiomas diferentes, como monóculo*. These two areas – the biological and philological sciences – will provide the conceptual context for hibridación until the twentieth century's so-called cultural turn in humanistic research. By 1899, the RAE discards the mule exemplification of *híbrido* and adds this comment: '*dícese de todo lo que es producto de elementos de distinta naturaleza*'. *Distinta naturaleza*: increasingly vague, *híbrido* now applies to all creatures that reproduce sexually and is full of euphemism, a quality that is unveiled when we turn to the more explicit etymology offered in the English context. A 'hybrid', the *Oxford English Dictionary* explains, comes to modern languages from the Latin, *ibrida*, and refers to the 'offspring of a tame sow and a wild boar'. The definitional narrative then calmly moves to this, somewhat bracing, assertion: 'hence, of human parents of different races, half-breed'.

The English sources list the first example of 'hybrid' in relation to human beings at 1630, from *The New Inn*, where Ben Jonson writes: 'She's a wild Irish born, sir, and a hybride.' In 1623, Cockeram writes of the adjectival 'hybridan', 'whose parents are of divers and sundry Nations'. The word would come into its own in the nineteenth century, in a number of national languages, through attempts to give scientific explanation to the proliferation of 'half-breeds' around the world. That is, hibridación makes its mark in terms of human culture in the area of race science.

The hybrid's early usage is nearly always inflected negatively; words residing around it in the OED include 'mongrel', 'grotesque', 'sickly', 'bastard' and 'monstrous'. In short, the rise of the 'hybrid' represented the emergence of a problem, quickly transformed into issues of 'race'. Robert Young, in his 1995 *Colonial Desire*, offers a critical history of the relations between hybridity, colonialism and race, especially in terms of how this relation still applies – sometimes in surprising ways – to theories of 'hybridity' in contemporary cultural criticism. Young illustrates hybridity's central yet inconsistent role in theories of race and practices of racism during the nineteenth century, particularly in the context of European colonial projects. *Hibridación*, in this scene, maintains its negative inflection. It is often invoked against the social and biological dangers of race-mixing and as an alleged proof for 'polygenesis', the idea that *homo sapiens* originally emerged out of a variety of local sources and that 'human families' are thereby naturally distinct. Polygenesis, in turn, served to justify slavery. *Hibridación* intervenes here through its association with sterility and the widely accepted theory that 'hybrid' humans would lose their ability to procreate. Paradoxically, hibridación – a theory of integration – would find its first political invocation as a defence of segregation. At the same time, *hibridación* could also make for a strong nation: Renan, or even Gobineau, understood all nations as essentially hybrid, and the English saw their country as a productive experiment in *hibridación*. In general, however, due to an increasingly separatist race science that presupposed real 'distance' between 'the races', *hibridación* between these races was hypothesised as the road toward a diminished capacity for reproductivity. Yet, in the context of rapid globalisation via the twin projects of imperial colonisation and national consolidation, the hypothesis flew in the face of a world's worth of evidence to the contrary. Nowhere was this fact more striking than in the hybrid nations that constituted the young republics of nineteenth-century Latin America.

Race articulates with *hibridación*, and it is important to underscore this history. But it is also important to recognise that hibridación's route into Latin Americanism is torturous, of multiple sources and influences. In terms of the generalised field of critical theory, a likely candidate for sparking the turn to *hibridación* is Mikhail Mikhailovitch Bakhtin. In *The Dialogic Imagination*, four essays left unpublished for four decades (until 1975), Bakhtin confronts us with his theory of the hybridisation of language. While a 'hybrid', in philological terms, refers to a single word whose root yields two different languages, Bakhtin's expansion of the very idea of languages into the social field – essentially understanding socially-coded ways of speaking as class languages, what he calls socio-linguistic consciousnesses – lends a new resonance to *hibridación*. Drawing upon the heteroglot utterance in narrative prose and, specifically, the novel, Bakhtin presents a concept of "hybridisation" that signals two things. First, hybridisation conventionally refers to the ways in which two merge into one. Differently-marked languages come together as a double-languaged discourse on the written page; the novel, then, provides the context within which they co-exist and – in their very cacophony – merge into a 'hybrid' literary language. Second, and crucially, the languages enter into struggle. If the hybridisation of language comes together at the novel, it is within this same hybridisation that social languages overcome – or not – their differences: 'a process teeming with future and former languages, with prim but moribund aristocrat-languages, with parvenu-languages and with countless pretenders to the status of language'. Two points follow. First, for Bakhtin, hybridisation is ambiguous, signalling a process that begets both fusion (coming together) and diffusion (multiplying languages through struggle). Second, there is a violence to hybridisation. And this is an old violence, rooted in the concept's association with race science: the production of 'mongrels' and 'half-breeds' first becomes a major object of scientific interest within the context of a strikingly intense struggle between classes of people, that of colonial domination. Through Bakhtin, we see how this violence can extend even to the basic level of language itself. The novel, the highest literary achievement of bourgeois civilisation, is impure, a mongrel.

Both violence and language – their nature, productivity and relations – are at stake in hibridación. One of the most influential contemporary exponents of the critical productivity that can emerge from the vicissitudes of these relations is Homi Bhabha. In a complex game of radical metonymy, Bhabha transfers the old 'dangers' of *hibridación* to a postcolonial – at once decolonising and diasporic – scene, turning it into the coloniser's nightmare. Like Bakhtin's, Bhabha's *hibridación* (which, for him, is more precisely 'hybridity') is ambivalent, moving in two opposing directions. Unlike Bakhtin's, Bhabha's cannot avoid the idea's explicitly racialised history. His hybridity is a mediator between colonial domination and its resistance. It has, moreover, a material referent: the colonial subject, described in his famous phrase as 'almost the same, but not quite . . . almost the same but not white'. Projects of colonial expansion and national consolidation produce a proliferation of these hybrid objects (artefacts, practices, people) that constantly slip past the colonial gaze and its desire for totalising power (in the words of Silviano Santiago (1978), its drive for 'unicity'), revealing it 'as something other than what its rules of recognition assert'. But Bhabha's hybridity is not reducible to objectification, the new object appearing in the wake of colonial violence, interrupting the smooth contours of an exterior sovereign power. Hybridity, in his sense, is also a splitting that represents the colonising authority's constant failure to produce a coherent and stable discourse of legitimation. Colonialism's hybrid voice – simultaneously attempting to assert its difference and its commonality – reveals its necessary recourse to violence: as Marx puts it, 'conquest, enslavement, robbery, murder, briefly force, play the greater part', and are always latent in the 'tender annals of Political Economy' that teach us the nature of the relations between exploiter and exploited. Bhabha, in turn, wants to teach us that force, the 'greater part', is already there, explicit in the colonial economies that underwrite the very hybrid enunciation of these 'tender annals'.

Between deconstruction and psychoanalytic literary criticism, Bhabha's 1980s essays on hybridity – at the leading edge of 'postcolonial studies' – are painstakingly (and sometimes painfully) wrought, and thus can be hard to understand. This fact, along with the proliferation of his vocabulary in the work of others, has led to suggestions or outright charges of quackery against Bhabha. On the bland side of these criticisms, some have noted the unhidden relationship between Bhabha's reading strategies and deconstruction, apparently implying that Bhabha's work is not easily convertible into political action. Beyond confusing deconstruction – essentially an analytic method – with a view of life (such as Marxism or Darwinism), this reading seems to ignore the precisely political critique of deconstruction implanted in Bhabha's innovation. His writings suggest that the gesture of reversal and displacement that defines the deconstructive act is most intensely practised and felt not within the Western canon; not even within its marginal texts; rather, it is felt in the margins of the world-system – the colonial outpost, the cosmopolitan slum – that is, the spaces of exception where the violence of bourgeois sensibilities, again to invoke Marx, 'goes naked'. And with Marx now conjured, it must be noted that Bhabha's most menacing and effective critics approach his work from a materialist perspective emerging out of various trajectories of the Marxist tradition. Two of the most convincing and important works that should always be read alongside Bhabha, especially by Latin Americanists, include Neil Larsen's *Determinations* (2001) and Shalini Puri's *The Caribbean Postcolonial* (2004).

The component parts of Bhabha's hybridity were more than familiar to Latin Americanists, and as his ideas began to catch on many wondered aloud what all the fuss was about. In particular, Silviano Santiago's theory (1978) of the *entre-lugar* – and other, less precise examples – seemed to capture exactly the critical gesture that suddenly appeared, through Bhabha, as a wild innovation. To understand the Latin Americanist reaction, which was often expressed with thinly-veiled irritation, we must remember that hibridación has a series of cognates representing nothing less than the central identitarian motif of the Latin American difference in world culture: *mestizaje*, transculturation, magical realism, borderlands and all the rest, are premised on the same structure of mixing that underwrites *hibridación's* critical gesture. Nobody has accused Bhabha of any intellectual property theft. But the resonance between regionally-inflected ideas, coupled with the absence of any Latin Americanist genealogy in Bhabha's sources (Bhabha's context is usually the British colonial experience), converted postcolonial theories of hibridación into the kindling for a fiery set of 1990s-era conversations around the circulation of ideas and their relation to neo-colonial power.

Latin America has a long history of references to something *like hibridación* punctuating essays, poems and political speeches. Limiting ourselves to the modern period, Humboldt, Bolívar, Bello, Sarmiento and nearly all of the great *próceres* speak to the special nature of Ibero-America in terms of its emergence out of a radical mixture: of races, languages, cultures, civilisations, political systems and so on. Already in 1950, for the great socio-critic Antonio Candido, Brazilian – and, by extension, Latin American – intellectual production was essentially hybrid, emerging between scientific and poetic discourse. But in terms of contemporary Latin Americanism, *hibridación* is ultimately associated with one name: Néstor García Canclini.

An Argentine-born urbanist whose decisive work on the relations between culture industries and globalisation emerges from his career in Mexican academia, García Canclini is the author of the renowned 1989 book *Culturas híbridas. Estrategias para entrar y salir de la modernidad*. Given their contemporaneity, it is striking how different García Canclini's hibridación is from Bhabha's. Whereas Bhabha is first and foremost a literary theorist mining texts for, as Jean Franco puts it, 'moments . . . when the struggle for interpretive power erupts', García Canclini is equally theoretical, yet more firmly grounded in the sociological and anthropological sciences and thus focused on the empirical processes of cultural exchange and social transformation. We must begin by noting, however, that the author himself has noted the slipperiness of *hibridación* and has wondered aloud at its utility vis-à-vis its more well-honed cognates (for example, *mestizaje*, transculturation, syncretism). In García Canclini's signature work, hibridación means far too much to detail in a single definition; its implications are at once empirical, methodological and critical. Nevertheless, reduced to its core conceptual significance, *hibridación* stands in as a nickname for one of García Canclini's other, more unwieldy key terms: multitemporal heterogeneity. As his subtitle indicates, García Canclini is concerned with the question of modernity in Latin America. In the same vein as previous theories of a heterogeneous modernity – those of Bloch, Williams, even Bhabha himself – García Canclini proposes that modernity is defined by a specific human relation with time; that there are many actual and potential models for the relations between human cultures and the temporal; and that in Latin America these temporal models, like everything else, are radically mixed. Latin American modernity, then, is not the one-way 'entrance' into that complex intersection between simultaneity and linearity known as 'modern time'. Rather, Latin American modernity is the palimpsestic layering of many times, and, above all, the interactions and mixing that happens between these layers of temporality. A peasant, in modern dress, guiding a horse-drawn cart, filled with industrially-produced 'local crafts', to a traditional marketplace where indigenous craftsmen mingle with urban brokers and cosmopolitan tourists, and where transactions will occur via gift-giving, barter, money, promises and many combinations of these and other forms of exchange: this is *hibridación*, the processes and circuits that define the mixing of entire strata of temporalities, the production of multitemporal heterogeneity.

Like Bhabha, García Canclini's influence has been spectacular, and his critics legion. Many argue that his model is the neo-liberalisation of cultural theory, giving new – and undue – credit to the market as a force of cultural innovation and thereby of (potential) political emancipation. García Canclini has addressed these criticisms, if not always with rigour, then at least with verve. Others have noted the teleological nature of his supposedly open-ended *hibridación*, which can resonate with the best and the worst of postmodernism. *Hibridación*, it is argued, simply explains what it already knows and, in so doing, it extracts the political from the cultural. Still others have attacked his conceptual coherence, both on grounds of epistemology (a problem that the author himself has conceded) and a surprising lack of historical consciousness. Regarding this last charge, many have questioned how García Canclini can confront us with a 'new' reading of the relations between culture and modernity in Latin America without seriously addressing precursors with nearly indistinguishable ideas: Vasconcelos, Mariátegui, Ortiz, Candido, Rama, Cornejo-Polar, even Borges and Paz, all come to mind, leading to a feeling of conceptual–historical vertigo in García Canclini's hibridación.

In an attempt to address his critics, García Canclini offers a kind of family tree of contemporary hybridity theory in the 2001 introduction to the re-edition of *Culturas híbridas*. Stretching all the way back to Pliny the Elder, he offers a cascade of citations from key thinkers of *hibridación*, from Bakhtin to Hannerz, from Hall to de la Campa. But this move makes the gaps in his specifically Latin Americanist genealogy even stranger. Two huge examples might appear here, thinkers that figure centrally in Latin American *hibridación*, and within the intellectual trajectory that García Canclini, and all Latin Americanist theoretically-oriented social science, is located. One is Manuel Gamio, Mexico's 'first' modern anthropologist, who, in his best-known work – the 1916 *Forjando patria. Pro-nacionalismo*, written smack in the middle of revolutionary stress – dedicates a chapter to a distinction between '*hibridación*' (foreign imposition and the artificial) and *mestizaje* (locally organic and authentic). The other – like Gamio, a student of Franz Boas – is Gilberto Freyre, author of the 1933 *Casa-grande e senzala*, indisputably the past century's most important (and controversial) interpretation of the relations between race and culture in Latin America. For Freyre, the special *características gerais da colonisação portuguesa do Brasil* is that this history represents the formation of a society that is, ultimately, *híbrida*. And while the term itself is only implicit for most of the book, Freyre's attention to the material hybridisations emerging out of circuits of social relations – between *casa-grande e senzala* – makes him a sorely missed reference in García Canclini's renovation of the term. And, recalling that *hibridación* normally resonates racially, there is also the unaddressed question of metaphors of 'mixed times' apparent in the liberal-positivist theories that were prominent throughout Latin America during the second half of the nineteenth century.

In the end, *hibridación* pertains to a complicated genealogy of theories of mixing that speak to the fundamental problems that emerge in the history of Latin American identity-formation. It has a dense conceptual history, evident in that *hibridación* and its extended family of terms slip around even in the hands of their most important theorists. García Canclini himself, after a modest attempt at differentiation between *hibridación* and *mestizaje*, a decade later abandons the distinction, speaking of good 'reasons to employ concepts of *mestizaje and* hybridisation' (my emphasis). And, of course, it is this flexibility that keeps *hibridación* relevant, allowing its impurifications to keep returning in new guises, enabling new questions for the study of Latin American cultures.

Joshua Lund

HISTORIES
Bakhtin, Mikhail Mikhailovitch [1935] (1975), *The Dialogic Imagination: Four Essays*, trans. Caryl Emerson and Michael Holquist, Austin, TX: University of Texas Press.

Bhabha, Homi (1994), *The Location of Culture*, London: Routledge.

Darwin, Charles [1859] (2004), *The Origin of Species by Means of Natural Selection*, New York: Barnes and Noble Classics.

Freyre, Gilberto [1933] (1992), *Casa-grande e senzala. Formação da família brasileira sob o regime da economia patriarcal*, Rio de Janeiro: Editora Record.

Gamio, Manuel [1917] (1992), *Forjando patria. Pro-nacionalismo*, México: Porrúa.

García Canclini, Néstor [1989] (2001), *Culturas híbridas. Estrategias para entrar y salir de la modernidad*, México: Grijalbo.

Gobineau, Joseph Arthur comte de (1853–5), *Essai sur l'inegalité des races humaines*, Paris: Firmin Didot.

Larsen, Neil (2001), *Determinations: Essays on Theory, Narrative and Nation in the Americas*, London: Verso.

Puri, Shalini (2004), *The Caribbean Postcolonial: Social Equality, Post-Nationalism, and Cultural Hybridity*, New York: Palgrave-Macmillan.

Santiago, Silviano [1971] (1978), 'O entre-lugar do discurso latino-americano', in S. Silviano, *Uma literatura nos trópicos*, São Paulo: Editora Perspectiva.

Young, Robert (1995), *Colonial Desire: Hybridity in Theory, Culture and Race*, London: Routledge.

Indigeneity

The word 'indigeneity' does not exist in Spanish. There is an expression that conveys a similar meaning: *lo indígena* (the indigenous), which is used to refer to peoples and things indigenous. However, these expressions are not interchangeable. They coincide in one point: both imply a question about what is indigenous – about what makes it possible that somebody or something be considered indigenous. Indigeneity, then, is the state of being indigenous (Onsman 2004). In short, it is a question about an essence, or a being. This is why it should not surprise anyone that 'indigeneity' often implies a certain degree of essentialism when it comes to defining what is indigenous and what is not. In this way, this concept reflects the weight and the influence of Western Metaphysics and its question about Being: about what makes something (or somebody) be what it is and not something else.

Indigeneity is mostly used in the United States, but similar expressions exist in other regions of the English-speaking world. For example, in Australia the term of preference is 'aboriginality'. Although the term is not interchangeable with 'indigeneity', it is used to refer to things indigenous and it implies, too, a question about an essence – a problematic use, according to Jennifer A. Martiniello (1999), who believes that these uses of 'aboriginality' hide, besides the essentialism inherent in the concept, the social processes through which real life aboriginality is produced.

In Latin America, as stated above, such an expression does not exist; but that does not mean that the question about what the indigenous is cannot be posed. Recently, the group GEAPRONA, led by Argentinean anthropologist Claudia Briones, has adopted the use of the term *aboriginalidad*, which they understand as 'a process and a framework for the alterisation of those populations whose ethnicity is mostly related to their autochthony' (GEAPRONA). Yet this is an isolated case, and the term is not broadly used either by Spanish-speaking academics or lay people. The most common expression to refer to the indigenous still is *lo indígena*.

As a category, then, 'indigeneity' can be seen from different epistemological and geopolitical perspectives. It all depends on both where the utterance is coming from and who is using it – it depends on the situation of enunciation from where it is uttered. Let us entertain several situations of enunciation. The concept can be used in the American academic world, where 'indigeneity' is commonly, if not universally (a high number of people within and outside academia are not familiar with the term) used, or in Latin America. In this geopolitical location, the indigenous can be viewed from several perspectives, but the predominant ones are the Criollo (and dominant society people in general, regardless of ethnic background) and the academic points of view. More recently, however, the Amerindians themselves have been using the expression *lo indígena* to advance their own political and social agendas.

This is so because the political climate, both at the international organisations (such as the United Nations) and in some social segments (especially the middle and upper-middle classes) of the central capitalist countries, has made it possible for indigeneity to become a legitimate concern. The United Nations proclamation of the years 1995–2004 as the International Decade of World Indigenous Peoples is just one example among many. Declarations like this are the consequence of the 'growing awareness that those values, knowledge, and priorities possessed by indigenous peoples may sustain an increasingly fragile planet' (Maaka and Fleras 2005). This is the international context in which several strong, and (sometimes) successful indigenous movements have developed, in the last decade or so, in different parts of Latin America. In Ecuador, the indigenous movement Pachacutik has been able to form an alliance with other forces and take Colonel Lucio Gutiérrez to the presidency in 2002. In Chiapas, Mexico, the Ejército Zapatista de Liberación Nacional (EZLN), represented by Subcomandante Marcos (a non-indigenous subject who speaks for the Amerindians), has changed, since 1994, the way dominant Mexican society views things indigenous. And finally, in Bolivia, an indigenous movement has been able to take their most representative leader, Evo Morales, to the presidency in 2005.

The fact that indigenous peoples themselves have been using the categories and concepts of *lo indígena*, 'indigeneity' and 'aboriginality' does not mean one should forget that all those terms are the product of colonialism: the peoples who are now called indigenous or aboriginal would not be called (and treated) so if there had not been foreign invaders who both deprived them of their lands and destroyed their societies.

Having said that, it is fair to acknowledge the usefulness of terms like 'indigeneity', regardless of their colonial origin. If not for any other reason, because of the need indigenous peoples from all over the world have to define themselves, either in relation to the nation-states where they live, or before the international organisations that could help them advance their cause. Thus, besides the academic discussion about what is indigenous, there is another, perhaps more pressing need for indigenous peoples today: to fit the definitions provided by international organisations such as the United Nations and the International Labor Organization. Both organisations establish three requirements in their definition of indigeneity, and they coincide in two of them: the claimants must be descendants of the peoples who populated the territory before the arrival of the colonisers; and they must prove a cultural continuity throughout time – that is, they must show they have preserved the customs and traditions of their ancestors. The main difference between the UN and the ILO is that the former requires that the indigenous populations are under the domination of a stronger, alien political power, while the latter considers self-identification a crucial element for the determination of indigeneity.

The consequences of these definitions for indigenous peoples from all over the world are multiple, and vary from case to case. Let us consider, for example, the case of Africa. For most of the peoples who claim to be indigenous in that continent, a strict definition is not desirable, due to the fact that in most modern African nation-states the oppressors today are not foreign powers but other peoples who were living in the continent before the arrival of European colonists. What all the indigenous African groups have in common is that their culture and way of life is different from that of the dominant society; and their culture is under threat, in some cases to the point of extinction (Lutz 2006). Most of these groups are hunter-gatherers (or former hunter-gatherers) and pastoralists, but there are other groups not characterised by their mode of production but by 'their small numbers, remote locale, lack of representation in political structures, and the extreme threat to their lands and lifestyles from governmental and international interests' (Nmehielle 2006).

In sum, although 'indigeneity' has a colonial (one might say an 'Orientalist') origin, its uses in the hands of indigenous peoples today are undeniably fruitful and it is very likely that in the (near?) future the term and its semantic range be shaped less by the powers that be than by the indigenous peoples themselves.

Gustavo Verdesio

HISTORIES
Brown, James N. and Patricia M. Sant (eds) (1999), *Indigeneity: Construction and Re/Presentation*, Commack, NY: Nova Science Publishers, Inc.
GEAPRONA. 'Proyectos' http://www.filo.uba.ar/contenidos/investigacion/institutos/ antropo/etnologia_etnografia/geaprona/proyecto.htm [accessed 20 November 2006].
Lutz, Ellen L. (2006), 'Beyond Indigeneity', *Cultural Survival* 30 (2) (summer): 4.
Maaka, Roger and Augie Fleras (eds) (2005), *The Politics of Indigeneity. Challenging the State in Canada and Aotearoa New Zealand*, Dunedin: University of Otago Press.
Martiniello, Jennifer (1999), 'Text and Transposition: Aboriginality, Representation, and Reappropriation', in James N. Brown and Patricia M. Sant (eds), *Indigeneity: Construction and Re/Presentation*, Commack, NY: Nova Science Publishers, Inc., pp. 159–76.
Nmehielle, Vincent O. (2006), 'Indigeneity in Africa', *Cultural Survival* 30 (2) (summer): 9.
Onsman, Andrys (2004), *Defining Indigeneity in the Twenty-First Century. A Case Study of the Free Frissians*, Lampeter: The Edwin Mellen Press.

Indigenismo and Mestizaje

Indigenismo (Indigenism) has been traditionally conceptualised as a broad current, which gained momentum during the 1920s and the 1930s, in the wake of the Mexican revolution, and which was manifested in the 'rediscovery' and revaluation of native cultures and traditions, as well as in the use of the Indian themes in literature and the visual arts, which are often articulated in terms of social protest. Yet, as Miguel León-Portilla wrote (1975), the official praise of the Indian heritage did not translate itself into forms of action which would really make possible the development of the indigenous communities. Indeed, Indians in Latin America have remained the principal victims of an official rhetoric which has sought to assimilate them into the modern nation.

We trace here the process by which both indigenismo and mestizaje became the dominant discourses elaborated by intellectuals from the beginning of the twentieth century.

Whether by postponing the social and political aspirations of the Indian component of society, or by co-opting its consciousness, men of letters such as the Mexicans José Vasconcelos and Manuel Gamio, and the Bolivians Alcides Arguedas and Franz Tamayo began a process of nation-building and modernisation.

If nineteenth-century Mexican positivists invoked the discourse of mestizaje as a means of articulating the perceived fragmentation of race and nation, the full significance of such an articulation became clear with José Vasconcelos' major works on mestizaje. During the 1920s, Vasconcelos (1882–1959) used 'the Indian' as a discursive formation in which the rhetorical deployment of the Indian served as the essential component in a system of representation. That system was mestizaje. In other words, mestizaje was underwritten by a discourse of race in which the racialised figure with which Vasconcelos was most obsessively preoccupied was the Indian (Lund 2006).

Both Vasconcelos and Manuel Gamio (1883–1960) diagnosed that the great threat to Mexican post-revolutionary nation-building was the ostensible lack of racial and linguistic unity. If Vasconcelos' formulation of mestizaje contained the basic concept of 'the cosmic race' (Vasconcelos 1979), which exhibited a remarkable tenacity during the twentieth century, we should be mindful of the fact that in Bolivia, even before the Mexican construction of a *mestizo* project, Alcides Arguedas (1879–1946), a prominent Criollo from La Paz, and one of the early *indigenista* novelists, published his *Pueblo enfermo* (*A Sick People*) (1937), which caused an enormous and not entirely favourable impact with the nation's élite. In his essay Arguedas assumed a mechanistic relation between man and environment, leading him to postulate a basically fatalistic vision of Bolivian reality. To be Indian, from this point of view, was to be stamped by fate, for the Indian's being had been marked by the purely mechanical and immutable action exerted on him by the high plateau of the Altiplano region. Geography thus influenced development negatively.

While the liberal élite apparently agreed with Arguedas' diagnosis, Franz Tamayo (1879–1956), Bolivia's foremost *mestizo letrado*, responded to the liberals' proposal for regeneration with *Creación de la pedagogía nacional* (*Creation of National Pedagogy*) (1975), a series of articles in which he sharply criticised the liberal impulse to imitate European pedagogical models indiscriminately. Tamayo argued that the nation's educational problems should not be addressed by contemplating European models, but only by looking to the vital strengths of Bolivia itself.

This exploration of Vasconcelos' and of Franz Tamayo's discourses on the autochthonous leads us to the relationship between the *indigenista* essay and the visual arts. In Mexico, the work of the *tres grandes* (Diego Rivera (1886–1957), José Clemente Orozco (1883–1949) and David Alfaro Siqueiros (1896–1974)) combined within the representational space of the mural formal elements of European high modernism (Futurism, Expressionism, Cubism) with the indigenous cultural components of a Mexico in the process of institutional consolidation after the devastating revolutionary war. Responding to the policy direction of José Vasconcelos, Minister of Public Education in the early 1920s, artists began painting monumental works of mural art in public buildings. Vasconcelean nationalism was given a regional and racial resonance by his theory of Latin American mestizaje. In this sense, Vasconcelean discourse became apparent in the integration of visual discourse to the public declamations of the *letrado*. But what was muted by Vasconcelos' inscription of the public significance of visual arts was the practice of the muralists themselves, those who actually executed the images that he lifted into the 'lettered' frame of reference. Diego Rivera, for example, followed and markedly developed nationalist themes through portrayals of Mexican popular culture and indigenous traditions that Vasconcelos found to be rather distasteful. Nevertheless, the 'lettered' mode of cultural production, resting on the prestige of literary authorship, was legible in the muralists' embrace of a popular (more precisely *indigenista*) aesthetic which they characterised as inimical to the reactionary bourgeois preference of those sacred spaces reserved for European traditions of landscape and portraiture (Campbell 2003).

As in Mexico, throughout the first half of the twentieth century, Tamayo's reflections on indigenismo and mestizaje remained intrinsic to the development of Bolivian discourse on the autochthonous as reflected in the plastic arts (Sanjinés 2004). A close look at the paintings of Cecilio Guzmán de Rojas (1899–1950), particularly at *Cristo Aymara* (*Aymara Christ*, 1939), one of the most prominent Bolivian paintings of the first half of the twentieth century, indicates that Guzmán de Rojas' stylised representations of the autochthonous, painted in accordance with upper-class 'good taste', are the best pictorial expressions of the discourse on mestizaje. Guzmán de Rojas, who started painting in 1919, influenced by the Spanish painter Romero de Torres, also painted stylised Indians, following the Peruvian José Sabogal's appeal to 'Incaism'.

Sabogal (1888–1956), whose most important painting is *The Indian Mayor of Chincheros: Varayoc* (1925), and who returned from Europe in 1919 with his new Fauvist-influenced *indigenista* style, dominated painting in Peru during the 1920s and 1930s. Sabogal influenced Guzmán de Rojas with his highly dignified and static *indigenista* figures. This was an art of academic formalism, which reproduced the hierarchical structure of society in a historical setting. Peruvian art critic Mirko Lauer (1967) suggests that the final achievement of this formalism 'was to make the undernourished muscular, the poor rich, the ragged luxurious, and to create in the public mind a division between the Andean people's past and their present'.

The more conservative state of Bolivian *indigenista* thought came in sharp contrast to the robustness of Peruvian indigenismo during the 1920s. The real divide was between those, like the Peruvian *indigenistas* we will see next, who wanted to create a unique, non-Western culture for Latin America and others, like the Bolivian *letrados*, who did not wish to depart from modern Western civilisation.

If the rethinking of the historical process was to create a new theoretical space for Latin America, the most creative mind, capable of rethinking Marxism, was that of the Peruvian *mestizo* thinker José Carlos Mariátegui (1895–1930).

Founder of *Amauta*, the most important Andean artistic journal of the times, José Carlos Mariátegui, author of the seminal *Siete ensayos de interpretación de la realidad peruana* (*Seven Interpretative Essays on Peruvian Reality*, 1928) took the Indian heritage as the source of cultural authenticity. In this sense, Mariátegui looked for 'cultural wholeness' as the 'praxis' – the integration of the abstract and the concrete, of the spiritual and the material – through which the regeneration of the indigenous communities and the revitalisation of Indian traditions would take place. Believing that the Inca state was a prototype of a socialist society, Mariátegui argued that the Indian peasantry rather than the industrial proletariat were the true revolutionary class in Latin America (Williamson 1992).

Mariátegui was also the key figure of Peru's literary vanguards. He coincided historically with the reformist and modernising dictatorship of Augusto Leguía (1919–33), who initiated social and educational reforms in order to eradicate the dissent of labour movements and student radicals that had emerged in the first two decades of the 1900s. Though the Leguía dictatorship stifled open intellectual and political exchange, Mariátegui gathered provincial intellectuals in the Peruvian capital, Lima, where they had been attracted by student reform activists. From Lima he published the journal *Amauta* (1926–30) to combat Leguía's plans to incorporate Peru's Indian population into upper-class Peruvian culture. Other Andean societies had no literary journal comparable to *Amauta*, nor any lasting regional vanguard magazine like the *Boletín Titikaka* (1926–30) of Peru's Puno province, which vigorously promoted the values of an autonomous indigenous culture (Unruh 1994).

From a postcolonial perspective, there are also clear epistemological differences between Mariátegui's thought and the writings of *letrados* promoting the autochthonous. While both Tamayo and Mariátegui revealed intellectual interest in Western thought, and coincided in their enthusiasm for Nietzsche, they appropriated the Western tradition in contrasting ways. While Tamayo worked within Schopenhauerian and Nietzschean global designs, without truly seeking the limits in their application to Bolivian culture, Mariátegui, on the other hand, moved inversely, from local histories to global designs. As a 'border thinker' (Mignolo 2000), not just a metropolitan thinker from the margin, Mariátegui encountered the limits of Marxism in the domain of Peruvian colonialism and racism.

Just as Mariátegui had done in his analysis of Peruvian reality during the 1920s, we also perceive in the Mexican anthropologist Guillermo Bonfil Batalla's essays the presence of indigenismo and mestizaje as nothing but an upper-class *letrado* discourse whose purpose was to justify the continued domination of the *mestizos*. The tensions between the 'universal' and the 'local' could not be better analysed than in Bonfil Batalla's perception that though Gamio's and Vasconcelos' constructions of mestizaje may have been different from the nineteenth-century endeavours to build the nation by dividing Western 'civilisation' from Amerindian 'barbarism', mestizaje remained under European disciplinary hegemony and implied a necessary temporal and spatial distinction between the West and the non-West. Bonfil Batalla (1935–91) counteracted this historicism by demonstrating that Gamio and Vasconcelos applied to Mexican mestizaje Western forms of interpretation and of representation. This historicism, according to Batalla, was just a local version of the same narrative that replaced 'Europe' with the *mestizo* as a locally constructed centre. In *México profundo. Una civilización negada* (*México Profundo. Reclaiming a Civilisation*, 1987), his critical view of mestizaje ran counter to the very notion that historical time is the measure of the cultural distance that is assumed to exist between the West and the non-West.

Finally, it should be noted that the linkage between indigenismo and mestizaje, where indigenismo is said to speak for indigenous subjects without including them, is being questioned by recent research (Favre 1998; Bigenho 2006). While a critique of Mexican and Andean indigenismo focuses on the exclusion of indigenous subjects from the *mestizo* project of nation-building, such an interpretation (Hale 1989; Knight 1990; Lund 2006; García-Pabón 1998; Rivera Cusicanqui 1993; Rossells 2004; Salmón 1997; Sanjinés 2004) is considered problematic 'because it remains within the essentialising binaries of Indian and non-Indian' and overlooks the other social changes that mark the period (Bigenho 2006). Challenging existing interpretations of how the Indian entered new creative spaces of *mestizo* production in writings and paintings of the period, there is apparently the need to explore the 'embodied *indigenismo*' (Bigenho 2006) of the actual practices of the sociocultural agents involved in the body politics of the time. However, more in-depth research in this direction is needed if we are to accept that the ties between mestizaje and nation-building are too narrow or incomplete.

Javier Sanjinés

Literary Works

Alegría, Ciro [1941] (1983), *El mundo es ancho y ajeno*, Madrid: Alianza Editorial.

Altamirano, Ignacio [1901] (1971), *El Zarco y Navidad en las montañas*, México: Editorial Porrúa.

Arguedas, Alcides [1919] (1988), *Raza de bronce*, Antonio Lorente Medina (ed.), Madrid: Colección Archivos.

Arguedas, José María [1971] (1988), *El zorro de arriba y el zorro de abajo*, Lima: Editorial Horizonte.

Azuela, Mariano [1915] (1997), *Los de abajo*, New York: Penguin Books.

Icaza, Jorge [1934] (1953), *Huasipungo*, Buenos Aires: Editorial Losada.

Matto de Turner, Clorinda [1889] (1994), *Aves sin nido*, Mexico: Colofón.

Histories

Arguedas, Alcides [1909] (1937), *Pueblo enfermo*, 3rd edn, Santiago de Chile: Ediciones Ercilla.

Bigenho, M. (2006), 'Embodied Matters: Bolivian Fantasy and Indigenismo', *The Journal of Latin American Anthropology* II (2): 267–93.

Bonfil Batalla, Guillermo (1987), *México Profundo: Reclaiming a Civilisation*, Austin, TX: University of Texas Press.

Campbell, Bruce (2003), *Mexican Murals in Times of Crisis*, Tucson, AZ: The University of Arizona Press.

Favre, Henri (1998), *El indigenismo*, México: Fondo de Cultura Económica.

García-Pabón, Leonardo (1998), *La patria íntima*, La Paz-Cochabamba: Plural/CESU.

Hale, Charles (1989), *The Transformation of Liberalism in Late Nineteenth-Century Mexico*, Princeton, NJ: Princeton University Press.

Knight, Alan (1990), 'Racism, Revolution and Indigenismo: Mexico, 1910–1940', in A. Helg (ed.), *The Idea of Race in Latin America, 1870–1940*, Austin, TX: University of Texas Press, pp. 71–114.

Lauer, Mirko (1967), *Introducción a la pintura peruana del siglo XX*, Lima: Centro de Estudios Culturales 'Bartolomé de las Casas'.

León Portilla, Miguel (1975), 'Aztecs and Navajos: A Reflection on the Right of Not Being Engulfed' (occasional paper, The Weatherland Foundation), New York, pp. 10–11.

Lund, Joshua (2006), *The Impure Imagination. Toward a Critical Hybridity in Latin America*, Minneapolis, MN: University of Minnesota Press.

Mariátegui, José Carlos [1928] (1979), *Siete ensayos de interpretación de la realidad peruana*, Caracas: Biblioteca Ayacucho.

Mignolo, Walter (2000), *Local Histories/Global Designs: Coloniality, Subaltern Knowledges and Border Thinking*, Princeton, NJ: Princeton University Press.

Tamayo, Franz [1910] (1975), *Creación de la pedagogía nacional*, 3rd edn, La Paz: Biblioteca del Sesquicentenario de la República.

Rivera Cusicanqui, Silvia (1993), 'La raíz: colonizadores y colonizados', in X. Albó and R. Barrios (eds), *Violencias encubiertas en Bolivia*, vol. 1, La Paz: Cipca/Ayuwiyiri, pp. 27–139.

Rossells, Beatriz (2004), 'Espejos y máscaras de la identidad: el discurso indigenista en las artes plásticas (1900–1950)', in A. R. Prada (ed.), *Estudios bolivianos 12: la cultura del pre-52*, La Paz: Instituto de Estudios Bolivianos/CIMA, pp. 297–400.

Salmón, Josefa (1997), *El espejo indígena: el discurso indigenista en Bolivia 1900–1956*, La Paz: Plural Editores/UMSA.

Sanjinés C., Javier (2004), Mestizaje *Upside-Down: Aesthetic Politics in Modern Bolivia*, Pittsburgh, PA: University of Pittsburgh Press.

Unruh, Vicky (1994), *Latin American Vanguards. The Art of Contentious Encounters*, Berkeley, CA: University of California Press.

Vasconcelos, José [1925] (1979), *The Cosmic Race*, Baltimore, MD: Johns Hopkins University Press.

Williamson, Edwin (1992), *The Penguin History of Latin America*, London: Penguin Books.

Latin American Critical Thought: A poetics of resistance and (re)construction

In 1961, Frantz Fanon wrote in his seminal book titled *Los condenados de la tierra* (*The Wretched of the Earth*) that 'decolonisation is really the creation of new men. But this creation does not receive its legitimacy from some supernatural power: the colonised 'thing' turns into a man during the very process through which he becomes liberated'. This brief commentary by Fanon captures what Latin American critical thought has been and what it continues to be: an ongoing process of struggle for decolonisation defined in terms of resistance and (re)construction – resistance from the conquest, on the one hand, and a long history of (re)construction projects on the other, that are laden with successes and failures, but which never lose sight of the ultimate goal of the 'creation of new men' who are unwavering in their struggle for liberation.

When bearing in mind that thought is ultimately an expression of language, one understands that the origins of language in the Americas – at least, symbolically – are to be traced back to 1532 when the Inca Atahuallpa and the Spanish conqueror Francisco Pizarro met; it was precisely at that moment in history when written language displaced orality as the only legitimate source of knowledge. This same legacy from that clash of cultures, often referred to today as the coloniality of knowledge and power, was analysed by Roberto Fernández Retamar in his 1971 essay, 'Calibán', in which he returned to Shakespeare's *The Tempest* to problematise colonial domination from a Caribbean perspective. In large part, for Fernández Retamar, this domination was based on the control of language, which was tantamount to having seized the power to name and categorise all things. In other words, through language one could control the fundamental structures of thought. According to Fernández Retamar:

> Our symbol is not Ariel . . . but rather Caliban. We *mestizos* who inhabit these very same islands where Caliban lived see this distinction very clearly: Prospero invaded the islands, killed our ancestors, enslaved Caliban and taught him his language to communicate with him. What else could Caliban do except use this same language – today he has no other – to curse him . . .? (1979)

More than three decades have passed since Fernández Retamar wrote the above words, and logically, during this time they have been subjected to innumerable readings and interpretations. Although it is true that at the present time one needs to rethink carefully such generalisations as 'we *mestizos*', a phrase that makes Afro-Caribbeans invisible, or that Latin America's Calibans have no other languages of their own, which in effect ignores the vitality and creativity of the indigenous languages, especially those from the Andean Region, it is important to reaffirm the validity of Fernández Retamar's reference to using the coloniser's language as a means of resistance. That is to say, the use of official language to 'curse' the master and the entire racist system that keeps him in power is a fundamental expression of rebellion. One will understand that, at times, during the more than 500 years of domination, 'to curse' has meant to denounce injustices, while on other occasions it has signalled a struggle to appropriate official language in order to open new horizons from which to think and imagine power relationships. Thus, along with resistance, one finds those 'new men', mentioned by Fanon, who instead of being satisfied by merely denouncing injustices, struggled for a liberation that continues to be predicated upon broad social and cultural changes, a liberation that today is understood by some as decoloniality rather than decolonisation (see Walsh 2005). Again, we situate Latin American critical thought in a complex ongoing process of affirmation and (re)construction, which is deeply informed by a language that is pluralist and polisemical, and which for some time now has been searching for more meaningful alternative grammars (see Franco 2006).

Clearly, this search has not been easy to carry out. A case in point is the Afro Cuban poet, Nicolás Guillén, who in 1938 offered a concise social and cultural portrait of the island of Guadaloupe in his poem titled 'Guadalupe W.I.':

> Blacks, toiling
> next to the steamer. Arabs, selling,
> the French strolling and resting,
> and the sun, burning.
> In the port the sea is at rest. The air roasts
> the palm trees . . . I shout: Guadalupe!, but no one answers.
> . . .

For those who might doubt that poetry – that is, literature in general – is a fertile ground for Latin American critical thought, this poem reveals the extent to which many poets continue contributing to the struggle for decolonisation. Besides representing through language the social hierarchy of Guadaloupe, what is of most interest here is the lack of communication and a system of fragmentation that has destroyed any possibility of a common identity founded on solidarity and justice. Upon shouting 'Guadalupe!', no one answers precisely because there is no notion of what Guadaloupe might be. On that island, while the sun burns, there are only blacks who toil, Arabs who sell, and the French who rest. In effect, such attempts to counter the absence of a common identity make up much of the history of Latin American critical thought.

From the many responses and proposals to achieve decolonisation elaborated in the Lettered City which Angel Rama interpreted years ago, and which the hegemonic powers of the colonial system still consider a periphery, two of particular importance had emerged by the 1960s to influence Latin America's intelligentsia. The first exemplary model who comes to mind is the Mexican writer, Alfonso Reyes, who commented that Latin America had arrived late to 'the banquet of civilisation', but who also insisted on 'the need for Latin America to adopt its historic mission and renounce its peripheral condition'. To realise this goal, Reyes wrote: 'I say before the tribunal of international thinkers . . . we recognize the right of universal citizenship that we have now conquered. We have reached adulthood. You will become accustomed to counting on us within the near future (Sánchez-Prado 2006). For his era, the above-mentioned recognition of universal citizenship which Latin Americans had conquered, especially through culture, was to be understood in terms of a supposed cultural autonomy that highlighted Latin America's ability to think with originality and creativity and which was equal to that of the best minds of Europe or the United States. In one fashion or another, what Reyes had declared was the culmination of a process of cultural maturation of the Latin American republics that dates back to the late eighteenth century. Nevertheless, today's readers who contemplate that intellectual tradition of the past would do well to remember that at no time was there doubt over the centrality and authority of Western Europe's traditions. In other words, the autonomy that Latin American intellectuals had so intensely championed was really conceived to confirm Latin America's successful integration into a modernity of development and progress modelled after that of Europe whose values and objectives had been adopted as its own (see Borges 1975 and Faber 2006).

Unlike these integrationist proposals whose intellectual foundation continued being the modernising project of Europe and the United States, one encounters the critical thought of Peru's José María Arguedas, who declared categorically in 1968, upon receiving the prestigious 'Inca Garcilaso de la Vega' Prize, that he was not acculturated. According to Arguedas:

> I had no other purpose than that of overturning . . . official Peruvian knowledge and art [with] the wealth of art and knowledge of a people considered degenerate . . . or 'strange' and 'impenetrable' but who, in reality, was . . . a great people, oppressed by social contempt, political domination and economic exploitation on its own soil where it had performed significant feats . . . . I am not acculturated; I am a Peruvian who proudly, like a happy demon speaks in Christian and in Indian, in Spanish and Quechua. (Arguedas 1971)

Clearly, the visceral identification that Arguedas felt, along with his insistence on breaking from a colonial system that refused to accept the authority and the equality of knowledge and thought produced by the Quechua nations, represents a different concept of what autonomy and the desired universal citizenship previously mentioned ought to be. In effect, more than a fusion or integration of values and traditions which ratified Europe as a civilising centre – and the basis of any cultural legitimacy that Latin America might acquire – the critical thought of Arguedas presaged an intercultural way of thinking that proposed to convert a process of resistance into one of (re)construction 'that is, the creation of radically different conditions of existence, knowledge, and power that might build distinct societies' (Walsh 2005). Similarly, Mabel Moraña (2006) has commented that Arguedas' declaration about not being acculturated illustrated that:

> he does not believe . . . in the death or universality of the subject, but rather in the proliferation of forms of subjectivity that are defined ethically and aesthetically in relation to the dominant powers: in their connections with the international centers, with the State and its institutions, with policies that regulate the uses of values, languages, traditions, and poetics.

In effect, Walsh and Moraña highlight a transitional moment in history in which people are debating about the virtues and advantages of either decolonisation or decoloniality; of course, that debate no longer pertains exclusively to an intellectual élite rooted in the traditional Academy, as exemplified by Alfonso Reyes. Other thinkers have emerged gradually and voiced their perspectives, especially since the turbulent 1960s. Women, Indians, blacks and other groups characterised as subalterns have assumed their respective forms of subjectivity, demonstrating that despite Gayatri Spivak's conclusion that the subalterns cannot speak, it has become apparent that not only can they speak, but they can also think.

Tránsito Amaguaña, Dolores Cacuango, Luis Macas and Juan García of Ecuador; Sub-Comandante Marcos of Mexico; Felipe Quispe of Bolivia; Manuel Zapata Olivella of Colombia; Nicomedes Santa Cruz of Peru are just a few examples of how Latin American critical thought is becoming more inclusive, and thus, there is a definite need to resignify what really constitutes critical thought and the meaning of being an intellectual in these times of globalisation.

For those Latin Americanists who work outside of the region, one of the most troubling aspects of the ways of today's market forces is what would appear to be an absolute acceptance of the centrality of the European/USA axis and the marginality of the rest of the world. Nestor García Canclini has observed, for example, that with respect to what is published in Spain each year, '70% is exported to Latin America, while a mere 3% of what is published there actually reaches Spain' (see Poblete 2006). To the extent that these figures are representative of the general production and distribution of Latin American publications in Latin America, one should not be surprised that many people outside the region still identify Latin American critical thought as something primarily relevant to local interests. In other words, Latin Americans think about Latin America, a particular region which 'continues to be a site where "case studies" are produced, rather than constituting a legitimate *locus* of theoretical enunciation' (Sánchez-Prado 2006).

Unfortunately, the diverse discourses described in terms of the World (for example, World Literature, World Languages, World Studies), the very same ones that the processes of globalisation tend to generate, have exacerbated the marginalisation of Area Studies. In higher education in the United States, for example, many scholars are reluctant to identify themselves as specialists in a particular area. Although the reference to the United States Academy might appear to be a digression, it does point to an entire network of influences and impositions that maintain Latin American critical thought – at least as it is studied in the Academy – in a position of dependence and inferiority.

However, when removing Latin American critical thought – or what traditionally has been considered to be thought – from the Academies anchored in the European disciplines of knowledge, one discovers that some sectors of Latin America are taking what was *resistance* to what Catherine Walsh has categorised as 'the creation of radically different conditions of existence, knowledge, and power that might contribute to the building of distinct societies' (2005). This is the context necessary to understand the meaning of the insistence upon Indianising the Q'aras in Bolivia, or the proposals for an Afro ethno-education elaborated from within local communities in Ecuador, for example. In effect, Rendón Wilka, that enigmatic and 'Other' character from *Todas las sangres*, a novel written by José María Arguedas, already had commented: '*Igual vemos, distinto entendemos*' ('We see similarly, we think differently'). There should be no doubt that Arguedas was already announcing through his literary character a new stage in the history of critical thought, a stage that has grown in strength, especially after 1990 (which marks throughout the Andean region a milestone in the gradual transition from resistance to the reconstruction of new forms of knowledge). Arguedas already understood the need to go beyond fashionable proposals for a national identity that was imagined in terms of cultural fusion and integration of diversity, but which really pointed to an illusory and masked mestizaje predicated upon yet one more process of whitening and westernising in Latin American history.

This resistance to cultural uniformity can be considered a prelude to what is now referred to as interculturality, or that 'process and social, political, ethical, and intellectual project that seize upon decoloniality as a strategy, action, and goal', according to Walsh (2005), who goes on to state:

> The concept of interculturality . . . is central to the (re)construction of an(other) critical thought, a critical thought of/from an(other) tradition, precisely . . . because it is conceived . . . from the lived experience of coloniality, that is, from the indigenous movement . . . [and] because it reflects a way of thinking not based on Eurocentric legacies or modernity; and . . . because it has its origin in the South, thus turning over the dominant geopolitics of knowledge that has had its center in the Global North.

It is worth noting that decoloniality as a socially inclusive process conceived to move societies closer to interculturality does not negate the importance of those intellectuals who traditionally have developed Latin American critical thought. However, it is now time to acknowledge that that tradition tended to be almost exclusively an intellectual practice of so-called high culture, and actually led to (dis)placing and (re)placing, consciously or not, important 'unlettered' social sectors that currently are demanding their own venues for self-representation. The emergence of these new actors and their respective agendas has brought into question the nature of a long history of representation in the Americas, be the latter one of legal and political matters, or that of thought and the construction of 'Other' imaginaries.

Consequently, it was not a mere coincidence that the Italian philosopher Gianni Vattimo commented during the Congreso sobre Latinidad, held in Quito during September 2006, that Latin Americans seem to be the ones most likely to create real alternatives of thought vis-à-vis those forces that would homogenise everything and everyone in a globalised hyper-reality that values media-driven images constructed for the market place more than life itself. It is in this sense that today, more than ever before, we have an urgent need for a new critical thought capable of taking resistance to (re)construction, and decolonisation to decoloniality. Perhaps this transition will establish the true centrality of Latin American critical thought, a tradition found deeply rooted in a world system where the local and the global converge, erasing each other, and in the process, open a space of hope for Latin American critical thought which can really become (an)other voice, both in terms of its production and its reception.

Michael Handelsman

LITERARY WORKS

Arguedas, José María (1971), *El zorro de arriba y el zorro de abajo*, 3rd edn, Buenos Aires: Editorial Losada.

—— [1964] (1973), *Todas las sangres*, Buenos Aires: Editorial Losada.

Borges, Jorge Luis (1975), *Other Inquisitions: 1937–1952*, Austin, TX: University of Texas Press.

Fernández Retamar, Roberto (1979), *Calibán y otros ensayos*, La Habana: Editorial Arte y Literatura.

Guillén, Nicolás (1947), *El son entero. Suma poética, 1929–1946*, Buenos Aires: Ediciones Catedra.

HISTORIES

Cornejo Polar, Antonio (1998), 'Mestizaje e hibridez: los riesgos de las metáforas. Apuntes', *Revista de Crítica Literaria Latinoamericana* XXIV 47: 7–11.

Faber, Sebastiaan (2006), 'Zapatero, a tus zapatos. La tarea del crítico en un mundo globalizado', in Ignacio M. Sánchez-Prado (ed.), *América Latina en la 'literatura mundial'*, Pittsburgh, PA: Instituto Internacional de Literatura Iberoamericana, pp. 117–46.

Fanon, Frantz (1980), *Los condenados de la tierra*, 6th edn, Mexico: Fondo de Cultura Económica.

Franco, Jean (2006), 'Nunca son pesadas/las cosas que por agua están pasadas', in Ignacio M. Sánchez-Prado (ed.), *América Latina en la 'literatura mundial'*, Pittsburgh, PA: Instituto Internacional de Literatura Iberoamericana, pp. 83–96.

Guillén, Nicolás [1938] (1990), *Summa poética*, Madrid: Ediciones Cátedra.

Moraña, Mabel (2006), 'Post-scriptum. "A río revuelto, ganancia de pescadores"', in Ignacio M. Sánchez-Prado (ed.), *América Latina en la 'literatura mundial'*, Pittsburgh, PA: Instituto Internacional de Literatura Iberoamericana, pp. 319–36.

Perus, Francoise (2006), 'La literatura latinoamericana ante La República Mundial de las Letras', in Ignacio M. Sánchez-Prado (ed.), *América Latina en la 'literatura mundial'*, Pittsburgh, PA: Instituto Internacional de Literatura Iberoamericana, pp. 147–82.

Poblete, Juan (2006), 'Globalización, mediación cultural y literatura nacional', in Ignacio M. Sánchez-Prado (ed.), *América Latina en la 'literatura mundial'*, Pittsburgh, PA: Instituto Internacional de Literatura Iberoamericana, pp. 271–306.

Ripoll, Carlos (1970), *Conciencia intelectual de América: Antología del ensayo hispanoamericano (1836–1959)*, 2nd edn, New York: Las Americas Publishing Company.

Sánchez-Prado, Ignacio M. (ed.) (2006), *América Latina en la 'literatura mundial'*, Pittsburgh, PA: Instituto Internacional de Literatura Iberoamericana.

Vidal, Hernán (2006), 'Derechos humanos y estudios literarios/culturales latinoamericanistas: perfil gnóstico para una hermenéutica posible (en torno a la propuesta de Pascale Casanova)', in Ignacio M. Sánchez-Prado (ed.), *América Latina en la 'literatura mundial'*, Pittsburgh, PA: Instituto Internacional de Literatura Iberoamericana, pp. 213–54.

Walsh, Catherine (ed.) (2006), *Pensamiento crítico y matriz (de)colonial (reflexiones latinoamericanas)*, Quito: Universidad Andina Simón Bolívar y Ediciones Abya-Yala.

Marianisation in the Philippines

Before the advent of Christianity, the archipelago that later became known as the Philippines was predominantly henotheistic. The early Filipinos worshipped the sun, moon, stars, animals and sites believed to be inhabited by *anitos* (the spirits of dead ancestors), such as rivers, springs, caves and mountains. They also worshipped Bathala/Maykapal as the deity who presided over the *anitos* and the lesser gods and goddesses of the environment. The early Filipinos propitiated their gods through rituals, offerings and sacrifices, and believed that afflictions were brought on by *anitos* whose habitats had not been properly respected. *Catalonans* or *babaylans* (festival leaders) officiated in rituals offering entrails of butchered animals, accompanied by drum-beating, especially after victorious wars. Such singing and dancing was common to all the tribes and *barangay* (clans) of the archipelago. When the Spanish *conquistadores* and missionaries brought Christianity to the region, various kinds of interactions developed over time between indigenous systems of belief and the rituals and icons of Christianity, chief among them the proliferation of Marian statues and images.

The history of Spanish colonialism in the Philippines is marked by resistance, such as the Tamblot revolt in Bohol province (1621), and the Tapar revolt in Panay province (1663). Other uprisings followed at regular intervals during the eighteenth and nineteenth centuries. However, they did not prevent the spread of Catholicism to the masses. As the new religion gained support in popular consciousness, Catholic beliefs and rituals became assimilated into indigenous forms of worship (Constantino 1975). At a later stage, the mixing of indigenous and Christian practices led to the first major religious movement that resisted Spanish rule in the Philippines, the Cofradia de San José. The movement was founded by Apolinario de la Cruz (Hermano Pule) in 1832, and soon developed branches in many towns in the provinces of Tayabas, Laguna, Batangas and Cavite.

It spread the belief that the *pasyon* (Passion of Christ) was an emblem of the suffering of indigenous peoples under Spanish rule. It interpreted the notion of salvation as the spiritual equivalent of political freedom (*kalayaan*), and it claimed that political as well as religious salvation could be attained if one had a pure and serene heart. Hermano Pule told his followers that he was in communion with Christ and the Virgin Mary, whose message to the movement was trust in God, and faith that salvation and freedom would follow (Ileto 1989). Hermano Pule was captured by the Spaniards in 1841 and executed. A revived brotherhood surfaced in the 1870s under the leadership of Januario Labios. He too, like Hermano Pule, claimed to be in communication with the Virgin, and encouraged his followers to fight for independence from Spain, trusting in the Virgin to give them freedom in this life and salvation thereafter (Ileto 1989).

Over the decades, as Christianity became more thoroughly indigenised among Filipinos, the religious expression of protest was transformed into a demand for equal rights for Filipinos within the Church. The demand for the Filipinisation of the clergy became an integral part of the nationalist format which culminated in the revolution (Constantino 1975). In August 1902, Isabelo de los Reyes, founder of the Union Obrera Democratica, proposed the founding of the Philippine Independent Church (Iglesia Filipina Independiente). The IFI membership consisted largely of peasants, both during the days of the republic and in succeeding years, chiefly because it was they who responded most directly to the merger of nationalist and religious idioms represented by the IFI. Its leader, Bishop Aglipay, preached the teachings of national heroes like Mabini, Rizal and Bonifacio, while also proclaiming that 'the Virgin at Balintawak is the Mother Country'. Eventually, this politicisation of religion brought about a separation between the IFI and the Catholic Church.

In the 1920s, Hermano Pule's *Cofradia* resurfaced as groups known as *colorums* (a corruption of the *et saecula saecolorum* used during Mass). Most members came from the peasantry and the urban poor. The *colorum* group in the province of Surigao, for example, combined religious devotion with devotion to the political patriot José Rizal (Constantino 1975). The culminating event in the long history of the Marianisation of the Philippines was the People Power revolution of 1986 which overthrew the régime of President Ferdinand Marcos. Among the huge mass of people gathered to protest against Marcos on the EDSA highway in Quezon City were nuns and priests who raised images of the Virgin to show their support for the rally. The nuns tried to stop government tanks, gave food and flowers to soldiers, and convinced military troops not to harm the people gathered at EDSA. It was also claimed that the pilot of an assault helicopter which had been ordered to drop bombs on the rebellious crowd saw an image of the Virgin in the sky, which made him abort the mission. A statue of the Virgin now stands at a spot where the protesters gathered in 1986. It symbolises the Filipino capacity for faith that the union of religious and political belief had a significant role to play in the liberation of the people from an oppressive régime.

Many examples can be cited to show the extent of Marianisation in the Philippines. A statue of the Virgin (now known as the Miraculous Lady of Piat), was brought to the

Philippines from Macau in 1604. Early Christianisation of the Eastern Region saw the Dominicans facing the hostile Itawes of Piat. By the bringing in of a Marian image, the Itawes were converted and Christianity spread across the region, especially after long seasons of drought came to an end – it was alleged – through the intercession of Marian veneration. An annual Sambali Festival honours the Piat-Virgin's conversion of hostile tribes to Christianity.

In 1626, a statue of the Virgin was brought from Acapulco to Manila by Governor Juan Niño de Tabora (Barcelona and Estepa 2004). In all subsequent galleon voyages, it became customary to keep a statue of the Virgin on board. It was claimed that its presence brought peace among sailors and ensured a safe voyage for ships. Other legends abound. An oil painting of the *Birhen ng Hapis* (Dolorous Virgin) was brought to Pakil Church from Laguna Lake by fishermen. The occasion is commemorated in a festival called the *Turumba* Festival. Yet another legend surrounds the worship of The Virgin of Peñafrancia, who is honoured with an annual festival (Gorospe and Javellana 1995).

As a nationwide devotional phenomenon, Filipinos continue to show their love for the Virgin through masses, novenas and other forms of festivities. Pre-Spanish rituals remain an intrinsic part of these celebrations. The indigenisation of Marian worship continues to be a prominent feature of Philippine culture after Independence.

Evelyn A. Miranda

HISTORIES

Agoncillo, Teodoro A. (1990), *History of the Filipino People*, Quezon City: Tala Publishing Services.

Barcelona, Mary Anne and Consuelo B. Estepa (2004), *Ynang Maria: A Celebration of the Blessed Virgin Mary in the Philippines*, Manila: Anvil Publishing.

Constantino, Renato (1975), *The Philippines: A Past Revisited*, Manila: Tala Publishing Services.

Gorospe, Vitaliano R. and Rene B. Javellana (1995), *Virgin of Peñafrancia: Mother of Bicol*, Manila: Bookmark, Inc.

Ileto, Reynaldo C. (1989), *Pasyon and Revolution: Popular Movements in the Philippines, 1840–1910*, Quezon City: Ateneo de Manila Press.

Jocano, F. Landa (1975), *Philippine Prehistory*, Quezon City: Philippine Center for Advanced Studies, University of the Philippines System.

Mercado, Monina (1980), *Antipolo: A Shrine to Our Lady*, Manila: Craftnotes, Inc. for Aletheia Foundation.

Phelan, John Leddy (1959), *The Hispanisation of the Philippines. Spanish Aims and Filipino Responses, 1565–1700*, Madison, WI: University of Wisconsin Press.

Vito, Iñigo (1997), *Turumba sa Birhen de los Dolores, Mga Kuwento, Alamat, Kasaysayan, Himala ng Birhen ng Hapis*, Quezon City: Echanis Press.

Marronage and Rebellion in the Hispano-American Caribbean

Marronage was the practice of active resistance that began, for all intents and purposes, with the conquest and colonisation of the Caribbean, at the beginning of the sixteenth century, and extended almost until the end of the nineteenth century in Cuba and Brazil. From the point of view of historiography and cultural anthropology, the great classics on the topic, notable for the holistic view they present, continue to be the works of José Luciano Franco and Richard Price. In the particular case of Venezuela, the contributions of Miguel Acosta Saignes, Federico Brito Figueroa, Jesús García and Angelina Poliak-Eltz have been fundamental for their understanding of the phenomenon in the land of Bolívar. In the Colombian Caribbean, María Borrego Plá, Anthony McFarlane and Nina de Friedemann have produced excellent investigations about the *palenqueros* of the region. Cuba has one of the most extensive and rich historiographic traditions regarding the issue: from the pioneering works of Villaverde in the nineteenth century, passing, in the twentieth century, to Fernando Ortiz and José Luciano Franco, and arriving at Deschamps Chapeaux, Duharte Jiménez and, more recently, the research of La Rosa Corzo on the palenques from the eastern part of the island. With regard to the Dominican Republic and Puerto Rico, the works of Moya Pons, García Arévalo and Nistal Moret have proved fundamental.

The hypothesis, proposed by José Juan Arrón, about the Taíno origins of the word *cimarrón* may be one of the most significant testimonies to the origins of *marronage* in the early stages of the conquest. This fact is connected to the well-known feats of cacique Enrique, in the mountains of Bahoruco, registered by Las Casas in his famous *Brevísima relación de la destrucción de las Indias*. Enrique's rebellion would be the theme of an important nineteenth-century novel from the Hispanic Caribbean: *Enriquillo* by Dominican Galván (1882). It was in the Bahoruco zone that, in subsequent centuries, a community of runaway slaves of African descent offered resistance to the colonial authorities until they had achieved a peace accord with them at the territory's border, divided between France and Spain, and Española Island. The word *cimarrón* may very well originate from the Taíno root *symara*:

> When the *símara* root is modified with the ending –n, a durative sign . . . *símaran* could be translated as arrow shot from the bow, escape from the dominion of man or, as Oviedo says, 'fugitive'. There, *símaran* equates to 'sylvan', 'of the jungle' or 'savage'; applied to non-cultivated plants, to 'runaway', 'rebellious' or 'ferocious' when applied to domesticated animals that become wild, and also to men, Indians first and blacks after, that run away and in their desperate escape searched for freedom far from the dominion of their master. (Arrón 1986)

The first communities of runaway slaves comprised indigenous peoples and slaves of African descent. As is well known, the colonial régime was able to divide indigenous people and Africans in later times. In any case, interactions between indigenous peoples and Africans, during an early stage of the mutual encounter, were repeated in 1552, in another of the most significant occurrences of massive *marronage* of the period: the rebellion of the 'Rey Miguel', in the western part of present-day Venezuela. At this point in the narrative, it might be useful to pause in order to clarify the definition of the concept of *marronage* and survey some of the debates that surround it.

Marronage was the word used to describe the escape (permanent or temporary slaves who toiled in the system of forced labour imposed by the European colonialism on American soil. Through the centuries, *marronage* assumed the most diverse forms. Academics refer to urban and maritime *maroons*, for example, in order to differentiate them from the most well-known forms of *marronage*: the escape of slaves to the mountains or to barely accessible areas outside the control of the colonial government. The size of *maroon* groups varied, from large and small bands, to powerful communities with dozens or hundreds (or in some cases, thousands) of integrated members, rather like the celebrated *quilombo* of the Paimares in colonial Brazil.

French slavery apologists have also introduced a distinction between *petit marronage* and *grand marronage* in order to differentiate individual from mass escapes, and also to separate forms of escape that did not threaten to create a complete rupture in the slavery system (*petit marronage*), from those that did (*grand marronage*). The slaves involved in *petit marronage* habitually remained in areas near the plantations. One of the traits that characterised *petit marronage* was its use as a tool of negotiation, with the intention of trying to obtain some improvement in working conditions. We now know that a clear distinction between *petit marronage* and *grand marronage* was, in some historical contexts, quite forced. The acts of *petit marronage*, while apparently inoffensive, were able to mask conspiracies against the colonial régime, or used to hide communications with communities of previously established *maroons*, as evidenced by the example of the slaves allied with Mackandal, in eighteenth-century Saint Domingue, to cite one of the most famous incidents, similar to what occurred in the celebrated *quilombo* of the Paimares in colonial Brazil (c. 1600), at an important crossroads in the slave trade between Africa and South America.

On the other hand, it is also worth emphasising that the communities produced by *grand marronage* received multiple names in colonial documents: *palenques*, *cumbes*, *cimarroneras*, *quilombos*, were the most common terms used to designate this type of social organisation. These communities developed in stages. A common pattern to this development included attempts to reproduce African forms of socio-cultural organisation in a Latin American context, and attempts to establish modes of production that might make the community self-sufficient.

Historiographic currents that have approached the question of *marronage* may be classified (extrapolating from a distinction proposed for Haiti by Michel Trouillot) into two major strands: the 'epic' and the 'banal'. The first of these discourses constructs a tradition of nationalist insurgency based on a romanticised image of the *cimarrón*. The second attempts, on the contrary, to explain acts of *marronage* ('desertions' is the unfortunate word used often in this discourse) as based on maltreatment, hunger or the attempt to reunite with a partner, family or friends. In the first characterisation, the *cimarrón* acquires traits of a pre-independence combatant or black guerrilla within the teleological narrative aimed at constructing a popular and nationalist symbol of communal identity. In the alternative (and 'banal') discourse of the revisionists, *marronage* is not endowed with any of the attributes of a politically rebellious subjectivity. It is no coincidence then that the revisionist discourse resembles the discourse of the apologists of slavery, who deny that slaves have the scope for autonomous action or political identity.

Currently it is impossible to reflect on *marronage* without having to deal with one of the most influential interpretive paradigms surrounding the topic, a proposal introduced two decades ago by Eugene Genovese. This paradigm (strongly influenced by the work of Hobsbawm on 'primitive rebels') characterises the socio-cultural practices of the communities of *maroons* as 'restorationist' or 'pre-political'. According to Genovese, the rural *maroons* attempted, with varying degrees of success, to reinstate or restore an African world within the territorial confines of colonialism in America, and remained on the margins of political modernity until the arrival of revolutionary ideas to the Caribbean from the Haitian revolution. His well-known essay, 'From Rebellion to Revolution', attempts to describe a process that develops from 'primitive' revolts to the kind of struggle seen in the bourgeois democratic project of the French Revolution. This process is described as connected to social stratification between slaves (house and country slaves, urban and plantation slaves) and the cultural differences between *criollos* and *bozales*, (that is, between slaves born in America and those born in Africa).

Despite its explicatory power, Genovese's paradigm subsumes *marronage* within the *telos* of a modernity aspiring to be homogeneous, or subordinated to the logic of a Hegelian-Marxist historicism. Studies on *marronage* lack the impulse to conceptualise the term beyond the logic proposed by Genovese, in a perspective analogous to that posed by Ranajit Guha in questioning the distinction between the political and the pre-political (a strategy initially used, as we have seen, by Eric Hobsbawm).

Revisionist historiographers question the notion of a causal relation between *marronage* and rebellion. The quantification of incidents of *marronage* in records written from the perspective of black nationalism has been thrown into doubt. It has been argued that communities of *maroons* were not as numerous as originally thought, nor as well-integrated as believed by some historians. In any case, it would seem that the revisionist historians underestimate – at times for ideological reasons – the symbolic impact of *palenques*, *cumbes* and *quilombos* (independent of their numbers) on those who remained enslaved in plantations. Furthermore, there exist documents that show how the very existence of *maroons* was capable of calling into question the ideological foundation of the slavery system. The most important example, cited by Genovese as the turning point of the rebellion against slavery, was the Haitian revolution. Certain official documents of the period are significant because they characterise this revolution as a vast instance of *marronage*. By implication, the very existence of *maroons* constituted, in and of itself, a challenge to the slavery régime, which was based on denying the humanity of the slave and his search for freedom.

Contemporary representations of *marronage*, both literary and cinematographic, do not claim to be exhaustive. In Cuban literature, the topic appears in two unique slave narratives written in the Spanish language which have survived into the present. One is the *Autobiografía* by Juan Francisco Manzano (1832), (which concludes with an act of *marronage* from the country to the city), and the other is the *Biografía de un cimarrón* (1962), written by Miguel Barnet and based on the oral narration of the former slave, Esteban Montejo. Both narratives present literary and historical criticism with diverse problems that are too complex to be surveyed here, except to indicate that they concern the authorship of the texts, and the question of their historical fidelity. Another interesting document is the *Diario del rancheador*, transcribed and published, in part, by Cirilo Villaverde, the author of *Cecilia Valdés*, towards the end of the nineteenth century. The *Diario of Francisco Estevez* documents the routine brutality of the boss of the *rancheadores* (groups of armed men trained in pursuing, capturing or killing *maroons*). In narrating Estevez' actions, as situated in the present-day Pinar del Río province, between 1837 and 1842, the diary evokes all the violence of the slavery régime and also served as the inspiration, during the mid-1970s, for one of the movies (*Rancheador*) of the Sergio Giral trilogy, which focuses on slavery in Cuba. Alejo Carpentier, in his novel about the Haitian revolution, *El reino de este mundo* (1949), represents the *cimarrón* Mackandal as a revolutionary symbol. Another text that is relevant in the context of the literature of the Cuban revolution is César Leante's novel *Los guerrilleros negros* (1979), in which *maroons* are represented as historical antecedents of the insurgency led by Fidel Castro. To complete this short enumeration, in films such as *La última cena* by Tomás Gutierrez Alea, the *cimarrón* is symbolised within the paradigm of the Hegelian dialectic of lordship and bondage. Giral's other two cinematographic works that engage the same topic also deserve mention: *El otro Francisco* (1975) and *Maluala* (1979). Finally, it is worth pointing out that in the case of contemporary Venezuelan literature, it is significant that two relatively recent novels, *Miguel de Buría* by Agudo (1991) and *El reino de Buría* by Arroyo (1993), have re-created the actions of a *cimarrón* leader from the first half of the sixteenth century. It remains to be acknowledged that a wide-ranging study that will take account of *marronage* in Hispanic Caribbean culture, while incorporating the most recent critical insights from Postcolonial and Subaltern Studies, has yet to be written.

Translations into English by William Ray Viestenz

Juan Antonio Hernández

HISTORIES

Acosta Saignes, Miguel (1967), *Vida de los esclavos negros en Venezuela*, Caracas: Hespérides.

Agudo Freites, Raúl (1991), *Miguel de Buría*, Caracas: Alfadil Ediciones.

Arroyo, Miguel (1993), *El reino de Buría*, Caracas: Monte Avila Editores Latinoamericana.

Arrón, José Juan y García Arévalo, Manuel (1986), *Cimarrón*, República Dominicana: Editora Amigo del Hogar.

Barnet, Miguel (1968), *Biografía de un cimarrón*, Buenos Aires: Editorial Galerna.

De las Casas, Bartolomé (1977), *Brevísima relación de la destrucción de Indias*, Madrid: Fundación Universitaria Española.

Deschamps Chapeaux, Pedro (1983), *Los maroons urbanos*, La Habana: Editorial de Ciencias Sociales.

Duharte Jiménez, Rafael (1992), *Rebeldía esclava en el Caribe*, Gobierno del México: Estado de Veracruz.

Fouchard, Jean (1981), *The Haitian Maroons: Liberty or Death*, New York: Edward W. Blyden Press.

Franco, José Luciano (1973), *Los palenques de los negros maroons*, Havana: Departamento de Orientación Revolucionaria del Comité Central del Partido Comunista de Cuba.

—— (1975), *La diáspora africana en el nuevo mundo*, Havana: Editorial de Ciencias Sociales.

Galván, Manuel (1996), *Enriquillo: leyenda histórica dominicana*, Madrid: Cultura Hispánica.

García, Jesús (1996), *Africanas, esclavas y cimarronas*, Caracas: Fundación Afroamérica.

Geggus, David (2002), *Haitian revolutionary studies*, Bloomington, IN: Indiana University Press.

Genovese, Eugene (1979), *From Rebellion to Revolution: Afro-American Slave Revolts in the Making of the Modern World*, Baton Rouge, LA: Louisiana University Press.

Guha, Ranajit (1994), *Elementary Aspects of Peasant Insurgency in Colonial India*, Oxford: Oxford University Press.

Hart, Richard (1984), *Esclavos que abolieron la esclavitud*, Havana: Casa de las Américas.

La Rosa Corzo, Gabino (2003), *Runaway Slave Settlements in Cuba: Resistance and Repression*, Chapel Hill, NC: University of North Carolina Press.

Leante, César (1979), *Los guerrilleros negros*, México: Siglo Veintiuno Editores.

Manzano, Juan Francisco (1975), *Autobiografía de un esclavo*, Madrid: Ediciones Guadarrama.

Moya Pons, Frank (1977), *Manual de historia dominicana*, Santo Domingo: Academia Dominicana de la Historia.

Pollak-Eltz, Angelina (2000), *La esclavitud en Venezuela: un estudio histórico-cultural*, Caracas: Universidad Católica Andrés Bello.

Price, Richard (ed.) (1996), *Maroon Societies: Rebel Slave Communities in the Americas*, Baltimore, MD: The Johns Hopkins University Press.

Trouillot, Michel-Rolph (1995), *Silencing the Past: Power and the Production of History*, Boston, MA: Beacon Press.

Villaverde, Cirilo (1982), *Diario del rancheador*, Havana: Letras Cubanas.

The Philippines–Mexico Connection

The 'Galeón de Manila', also known in Mexico as the 'Nao de Manila' or 'Galeón de Acapulco', was a symbol (but better analysed as the lifeline) of the more than 200 years of Philippine–Mexican relations during the period of Spanish colonial rule in Latin America and the Philippines (Schurz 1985). The galleon evolved through the centuries. It was basically a ship of Mediterranean provenance, but mated with the single mast Kogge ship adapted to the North Sea. The hybrid had been suited for Atlantic crossings, but changed to the more elegant ships of longer bows and taller sails that were better adapted to long trips across the Pacific (Braudel 1976). During the period of the galleon trade, it changed its design from smaller tonnages of 200–300 tons into something bigger reaching tonnages of 1,800–2,000, to allow heavier cargoes of exportable goods and weaponry. Certain place names in the Philippines suggest the deep influence galleons exerted. In Oriental Mindoro, a major district is called Puerto Galera, while the island of Capul, in eastern Samar, was alleged to have been named after Acapulco, as the first piece of land sighted by incoming galleons from Mexico, according to 'friar lore'. The Spanish galleons made a round trip between Acapulco and Manila twice a year: these trips were used to exchange goods between Spain, Mexico and Spain's Asian colony, and to bring European equipment and technology into the Philippines.

These exchanges are imprinted in the languages of both the former Spanish colonies. They cover the biological, cultural, social, economic and political aspects of the mutual influences between Mexico and the Philippines (Bernal 1968). At the biological level, the long voyage meant using long-lasting foodstuffs such as the *chicharrón* (deep-fried pig's skin) and the *tapa* (salted fish or meat), which were part of the culinary stock of the Filipino and the Mexican kitchen. Puebla in Mexico became known as the best supplier of the *bizcocho*, biscuits that could last the three month voyage of the galleon (Yuste 1997). Still eaten today, the *bizcocho* is a kind of small, square, dry bread widely favoured in the Philippines. The voyages of the galleon also transported and transplanted various flora and fauna useful for subsistence, such as the *camote*, *tomate*, chocolate, maize and varieties of chili from Mexico. The names of these food items became part of the Filipino vocabulary. From Manila came the 'mango de Manila', the coconut, and the by-products of the wild palm such as vinegar, tuba wine and various spices such as the *pimienta* (pepper), cloves and *canela* (cinnamon). Distilling of the tuba from coconuts became common in eastern Mexico, especially in the state of Jalisco and Guerrero (the latter was the site of the galleon port of Acapulco). 'Mango de Manila' is known in Mexico as a very good quality mango, while *sabong* (cockfighting) is a popular sport in Mexico matching the level of its popularity in the Philippines.

The Spaniards also brought along with their galleons diseases such as syphilis and small-pox (Braudel 1979). The latter devastated the Philippine population in the eighteenth century. To the credit of the explorer and scientist Balmis, in 1806, twenty-two Mexican children who had been inoculated against smallpox were brought to the Philippines to transfer the vaccine to local recipients (Colvin 2003). Fortunately for the Philippines, the effects of many of these European diseases, such as measles and the common cold, were not as bad as in Mexico. Although the population declined in the Philippines, the Filipinos were not as vulnerable because they had trade contacts with other Asians who might have introduced a certain degree of immunity even before the arrival of the Spanish. Not as many Filipinos were killed in the Philippines due to colonial exploitation as in Mexico. As there were no extensive silver and gold mines to be discovered in the Philippines, Filipinos were not subjected to as severe an imposition as that enforced in digging open mines in Mexico.

The Mexican influence may be gleaned from the transformation of such pre-colonial cultural markers in the Philippines such as the use of the *nganga* (chewing betel). Archaeological evidence has unearthed containers for the *apog* (lime) used for *nganga* among the human remains excavated in various neolithic sites. *Nganga* was important in preserving the teeth and suppressing mouth odour: the combination of lime, the *ikmo* plant leaves and ground betel nut helped in the removal of acids in the mouth. In pre-colonial times, and even at present, among some cultural minorities in the Philippines, the *nganga* has ritual value. A woman who accepts a man's proposal of marriage prepares the *nganga*, partly chews it, and then offers it to the man. This symbolic act is meant to indicate her love for the man and their oneness of purpose in life. A slight variation was seen by a nineteenth-century French traveller (M. J. Lannoy) to the Philippines who observed: 'When a young man has made his choice, his parents go to the family of the future bride, to whom they reveal the purpose of their visit, followed by an offer of betel (nganga). The acceptance of this present is always regarded as a certain sign of acquiescence . . .' (Lannoy 2003). With the galleon trade, the ingredient called *mascada* was added to the Philippine version of the *nganga*. While *mascada* is the Mexican form of chewing tobacco, in the Philippines it refers to the bar of sweetened tobacco sliced into thin pieces and mixed with the indigenous *nganga*, comprising ground betel nut, *ikmo* and lime. Since we know that tobacco arrived with the galleons from Mexico, this additional ingredient would indicate that it came as an influence from the outside and was not indigenous to the Philippines.

The process of modification and assimilation exemplified by this cultural marker (the *nganga*) is representative of the selective or limited manner in which Filipinos absorbed Spanish (or Mexican) influences. The beast of burden, the *carabao* (water buffalo) was not replaced by cattle, as in Mexico. The *carabao* provided milk and meat, while the sea provided the other staple element of the Filipino diet, fish. When not preserved as *tapa*, food was cooked in coconut oil, a readily available ingredient. In terms of cuisine, the Filipinos did not develop a liking or preference for the kind of food prevalent in Mexico, such as the *tortilla* and the *taco* (Arcos 1999).

Agriculture retained its focus on the cultivation of rice, the main staple in the Philippines even today. Maize, which came from Mexico, became a supplementary food item, but it did not displace rice. Even maize byproducts, such as the *tamales*, were transformed from being a cake made from corn (and wheat in northern Mexico) to one whose main ingredients are sticky rice and sugar. The Philippine *tamales* thus became a kind of Philippine *kakanin* (native delicacy). Bamboo and palm, which thrived very well in tropical Philippines, were the main construction materials for the traditional *nipa* hut (Arcos 1999). Weaving spliced bamboo rods into what was called *sawali* provided good materials for building walls. Bamboo was also used for stakes and fish pens for farming fish in lakes and rivers. These skills in weaving bamboo and rattan for fish traps, baskets and wall materials became the basis for a technology that also produced textiles such as the delicate *piña* cloth (from pineapple fibres), the *sinamay* (from maguey fibres) and the highly prized 'mantón de Manila' (from silk and sometimes cotton threads). The maguey was brought in from Mexico, an example of the adoption of an imported material for the production of local textiles. The other fibres used in the production of cordage and ropes (the *abaca*) became known as 'Manila hemp'. The same *abaca*, and hay from *palay* or rice was used in the manufacture of what became known as 'Manila envelopes' and 'Manila paper'.

The extent of Spanish domination in both countries could be seen in the way writing systems and languages were replaced. In the Philippines, the pre-colonial writing script called *baybayin* was replaced by Latinised characters. In Mexico, indigenous languages became dominated and even replaced by Spanish; in the Philippines, indigenous languages remained robustly in use by the general population. In the case of the Mangyans of Mindoro island and the Tagbanuas of Palawan, the *baybayin* script remains in use even today. Mexican influence was limited to the places around presidios and fortifications, as in Zamboanga and Cavite. In these places, a kind of pidgin Spanish called *chabacano* evolved, and it is still spoken by a good number of people there. It is interesting to note that in Mexico, *chabacano* means 'apricot'. The dictionary, however, refers to it as an adjective, defined as 'crude, coarse, vulgar' (Williams 1973). When anyone did something disagreeable or rude, he was described as someone like a Filipino: *es un punto filipino* means 'he is a scoundrel or a rogue' (Pelayo y Gross 1994). Yet the feeling could be mutual, since the Mexicans in the Philippines were called *guachinangos*, not much of a compliment. In Mexico, *guachinangos* are a kind of fish similar to carp and characterised by a big nose. On the other hand, the lasting relations between the two populations can be seen in the way a town in Pampanga was named Mexico, evidently to honour the soldier-mercenaries belonging to the Pampango troops that remained loyal to the Spanish crown until the revolution of 1896. It has been said that these Mexican mercenaries came from the Yaqui tribe of Sonora (Mexico), and were integrated into the colonial army (Parker 1911). It was perhaps in terms of a similar pattern of religiosity that the Mexicans and Filipinos resembled each other the most. 'Our Lady of Guadalupe' was declared by the Pope patroness for both countries, as former colonies of Spain (Phelan 1959; Nebel 1995). The presence of pre-colonial religious practices, with the priests and priestesses (called *babaylans* or *baylans*) had been an area of interest among the Spanish missionaries. The friars appropriated some of their rituals, such as feasts involving the offering of flowers to ancestors in caves and in burial places at the beginning of the rainy season. Now they are celebrated as the *flores de Mayo*, in which young girls offer flowers to the Virgin Mary. In Mexico, a similar 'maize festival' takes place in the city of Oaxaca in early May, in which girls offer flowers to the patron saint of corn, San Felipe de las Aguas.

The friars also took over the function of former priestesses as herbalists, and collected the names of plants used to cure diseases and ailments. By constructing churches on top of pre-colonial sites of worship, the friars literally buried evidence of the former religion. The best examples of this physical displacement may be found in Cholula, Mexico where the church to 'Our Lady of Remedies' was built on top of a pre-existing pyramid. The cathedral of Mexico City was likewise built on top of a former Aztec temple. The stones and foundations were recycled to construct new structures in the main city square, known as the *zocalo* (Riding 1984). In the Philippines, some examples of the same phenomenon may be cited: the Santa Ana Church built on top of a pre-colonial burial place, and the church similarly built on a place of worship at the town of Taytay, Morong province (Chirino 1969). Many images of the Holy Virgin and Christ sculpted in Mexico may be found as the objects of fanatical worship in the Philippines, among them, 'Our Virgin of Good Voyage' (Antipolo), in the province of Risal, and the Black Nazarene of Quiapo, a district in the city of Manila. On the other hand, the technique of sculpting such images apparently originated in the Philippines, specifically among the Chinese Filipino artisans. The ivory component used for the face and hands of the Virgin and of various saints was a practice that originated in the Philippines. In some statues found in Mexico there are also tell-tale signs of an oriental provenance, such as the introduction of lotus motifs (of Buddhist origin) in the pedestal on which the icons are mounted.

During the war of independence in Mexico, the image of 'Our Lady of Guadaloupe' was used as the banner of the revolution led by the priest Miguel Hidalgo. It was because of the fear of the same process (secular priests leading a revolution) occurring in the Philippines that the colonial authorities always looked with suspicion on the activities of men of the cloth. Out of this fear came the tragic execution of three priests in 1872, known as Gomburza (a portmanteau word for Mariano Gómez, José Burgos and Jacinto Zamora). The three were demanding equal treatment for native and foreign clergy in the administration of parishes, and were put to death because Spanish officials wanted to teach the natives a lesson in accepting a hierarchy based on the supposed racial superiority of the colonisers (Schumacher 2006). Instead of accepting this idea, Filipino intellectuals made the event of 1872 a rallying cry for revolution. Interestingly enough, the same rallying cry was invoked in 1986 by the Filipino people in what became known as the 'People Power Revolution'. In this latest use of religion for social and political change, images of the Virgin Mary were displayed prominently at the head of rallies and demonstrations to confront the tanks and weapons of the Marcos régime.

At the level of the economy, two terms of Mexican origin remain indicative of the Mexican connection in the Philippines: *palenque* and *tiangui*. It is not clear how *palenque*, which in Mexico refers to a temple complex at the border of Guatemala, came to mean 'market' in the Philippines. It can only be speculated that in the Philippines, the plaza complex of the sixteenth century already included a market just outside the Spanish-built church. But instead of using the Spanish word *mercado* to refer to a market, the Filipinos used *palenque*. The word *tiangui*, on the other hand, has a more definite Mexican genealogy, although some scholars suggest that it could also have come from the Chinese or Tagalog word *tingi* which refers to the retail purchases done by Filipinos as opposed to *pacquiao* (wholesale purchases). As used by Filipinos then and now, *tianguis* refers to rotating markets with ad hoc structures set up along beaches and main roads – with giant umbrellas or lean-tos protecting the retailers from the sun. The transactions in these markets are usually retail sales, involving light goods such as clothes, kitchen tools, children's toys and trinkets. Up to the end of the eighteenth century, traders moved from one town to another according to a definite schedule known as 'market day'.

The *tianguis* evolved in Mexico in the context of the Aztec Empire, which was a very different kind of political formation from the kinship organisation (*barangay*) that prevailed in the Philippines, which did not have overlords controlling huge chunks of the population. In a situation where big concentrations of population existed as in Mexico, markets could be used for the purpose of providing revenues for the state or as sources of supplies during war. There were professional merchants in pre-colonial Mexico – the *pochteca* (or *oztomeca* when they went to distant places). They were subject to regulations, with control of pricing and movement of goods. Even then, the establishment of definite places for the markets was an expression of the political power of the ruling élite (Carrasco 1983). In the Philippines, the words *banyaga* and *dayuhan* originally meant 'merchant'. In the course of time, these words became synonymous with foreigners, indicating that in the field of business and commerce, it was the foreigner (the Chinese, Indian and Arab) who established himself in the field as skilful, adept and capable. Colonial and postcolonial foreign influences are also seen in the various terms used for weights and measures and also those for lending or mortgage (such as *sangla*) and accounting. During pre-colonial times, trade and economic exchange were dominated by itinerant Chinese traders who brought in silk, porcelain and metal tools, in exchange for shells, beeswax, spices, bird's nests, pearls and *tripang*, a kind of sea cucumber found in the seas of the Sulu archipelago and Palawan (Ventura 1984). On the advent of Spanish colonialism, the Chinese were concentrated in a place designated for merchants and artisans, outside the walled city, which was called the *parian*. In Mexico, a similar place in the *zocalo* (main plaza) was established for the sale of products imported through the galleons. In the *parians*, the Chinese in Manila as well as those engaged in galleon trading used the silver and gold coins brought in from Mexico as the currency of choice. They were then called 'Mexican dollar' or '*pillar* dollar' until the eighteenth century. So lasting was this Mexican influence that even after the declaration of Mexican independence from Spain in 1821, the Mexican dollar continued to back up or guarantee the paper currency issued by Philippine banks. By then they were called *peso del aguila* or 'head dollar' (Lakowsky 1996). When sovereignty over the Philippines was transferred from Spain to the United States, the payment of the twenty million 'compensation' to the former, as indicated in the Treaty of Paris of 1898, was denominated in Mexican dollars.

The term *cacique*, of Mexican Aztec origin, refers to a local lord, and it gained currency in the Philippines as synonymous with the colonial enforcer as a 'big man', or an *encargado*, someone in charge of the lord's estates. The pre-colonial village headman was called a *datu*, a man respected by the community for his prowess in battle or his capacity to help another person in need. At the onset of colonial rule, the village headmen constituted the *principalia*, whose function was the collection of tributes for the foreign overlords. As collaborators of the colonisers, the *principalia* benefited through the titles they secured for themselves as well as the resources to buy land. As landowners, they received the title of *cacique*, which carried the same stature as their Mexican counterparts (Corpuz 1986).

However, there is also evidence of other, competing practices and terms that continued even with Spanish colonisation. When the colonisers arrived, they discovered that the inhabitants of the Philippines already had the framework of administration called the *barangay*. Originally referring to the ship in which, according to legend, the people had arrived in the various islands of the Philippines, the *barangay* eventually became synonymous with the system of social and political organisation headed by a *datu*. The Spaniards retained the term *barangay* and called the heads *cabezas de barangay*. It was in the imposition of higher overlords that the Spaniards introduced new terms: the *gobernadorcillo* to refer to the head of a *pueblo* (which consisted of several *barangays*); and the *alcalde mayor* to head a province consisting of various *pueblos*.

As the Philippines were governed by the Viceroyalty of New Spain (Mexico), we can expect to find ample evidence of Mexican influence in the field of higher political administration. For example, the budget for the Philippine bureaucracy came as a *real situado* (royal subsidy) from Mexico. However, as some historians have pointed out, this was a subsidy only on paper, since the money came from taxes on goods coming through the galleons in Acapulco. The customs duties were collected in Acapulco and the money thus collected was returned to Manila as the source of salaries for the officials of the government. The *real situado* served as an incentive for Spaniards to accept assignment in the far-flung Orient. Another incentive was provided by the stipulation that only those Spaniards who were based in the Philippines could actively participate in the galleon trade, but there were violations to the law (Yuste 1993).

Yet both Mexico and the Philippines were governed in a strictly centralised and highly bureaucratic manner. Today, both countries suffer from the after-effects of this Spanish inheritance. Not much innovation was allowed. Everything had to follow the laws as stipulated in the 'Recopilación de Leyes de los Reynos de las Indias'. The logic for this may be traced to the time when the Christian monarchs, Queen Isabella I and Ferdinand II tried to recover royal power from the various magnates and nobles who threatened to establish their own domains after ousting the Muslims from the Iberian peninsula. There was not much the monarchs could do then. Because of the quick reconquest that characterised the campaigns of the fifteenth century, land grants were awarded right and left and ad hoc administrative structures were set up. This gave the nobility which belonged to the military orders the power and economic clout to challenge the nascent national monarchy. The local nobles and even the military orders had private armies with whose might they could impose their will on the conquered populace. It took much effort on the part of the crown (steps such as establishing a national police organisation, local municipal systems and the election of Ferdinand II to the highest office of the military orders) to recover what it thought belonged to the king and queen by force of royal tradition.

Despite various petitions for titles of nobility, no other title except that of Marquiz del Valle de Oaxaca to Hernán Cortés, was granted by Spain either in Mexico or in the Philippines. Among the various governors-general, only the first, Miguel López de Legazpi came close to obtaining a title of nobility, getting the obscure title of Adelantado, similar to those possessed by the fifteenth-century conquerors of the Muslims in Navarra and País Vasco. In the Philippines, the accommodation of the crown to the colonisers, which were called *encomiendas*, did not refer to lands but only to the right of the individual colonisers to collect tributes from a certain number of villages and districts. And even in this case, the privilege was allowed only until the third generation, reckoning from the time of the first recipient. When the political set-up had been regularised, with the establishment of the towns and the provinces, the collection of tributes for the Real Hacienda (the king's coffers) became an activity that was allowed to run parallel to the official bureaucracy. All the lands that were not granted to individuals or whose owners had no heirs, reverted to the king (*realengas*), the basis for what became known later as the regalian principle of land ownership. In other words, under this principle, all public lands were lands of the king and only upon his permission (as shown by a title to the real property) could an individual make use of the land.

In summary, while the Spanish crown aimed at Hispanisation of its colonies in Mexico and the Philippines, what emerged was a creative appropriation of colonial influences by these subject peoples. Both colonies underwent a process of indigenisation of these influences such that in various ways, what eventually surfaced were original products that had become part and parcel of their local culture.

Jaime Balcos Veneracion

Literary Works

Lakowsky, Vera Valdes (1996), 'La plata: eslabón de las relaciones Mexicano-Filipinas', in *El Galeón de Manila*, México: JGH Editores.

Lannoy, M. J. [1849] (2003), *The Philippine Islands*, trans. Pura S. Castrence, Manila: National Historical Institute.

Ventura Fe. S. (1984), *Tianguis in Bulakan*, Manila: Centro Escolar University.

Histories

Arcos, María Fernanda García de los (1999), 'Geopolítica americana en los confines de Asia: el transplante de un modelo institucional', in *Perspectivas Históricas* 2 (4) (Jan.–July): 87–112.

Bernal, Rafael (1968), *México en Filipinas: estudio de una transculturisacion*, Serie Histórica No. 11, México: Instituto de Investigaciones Históricas UNAM.

Braudel, Fernand (1976), *The Mediterranean and the Mediterranean World in the Age of Philip II*, New York: Harper and Row.

Braudel, Fernand (1979), *Civilisation and Capitalism 15th–18th Century, vol. I: The Structures of Everyday Life: The limits of the Possible*, trans. Sian Reynolds, New York: Harper and Row.

Carrasco, Pedro (1983), 'Some Theoretical Considerations about the Role of the Market in Ancient Mexico', in Sutti Ortiz (ed.), *Economic Anthropology: Topics and Theories*, New York: University Press of America.

Chirino, Pedro [1604] (1969), *Relación de las Islas Filipinas*, Rome: Estevan Paulino.

Colvin, Tom (2003), *The Balmis Expedition of 1803–1898*, Malolos City: SAMPAKA Center for Bulakan Studies.

Corpuz, O. D. (1986), *Economic History of the Philippines*, Quezon City: University of the Philippines Press.

Cushner, Nicholas P. (1971), *Spain in the Philippines*, Quezon City: Ateneo de Manila University.

Nebel, Richard (1995), *Santa Maria Tonantzin Virgen de Guadalupe: continuadad y transformación religiosa en Mexico*, México: Fondo de Cultura Económica.

Pelayo y Gross, Ramon Garcia (1994), *Larousse Gran Diccionario Español-Inglés*, México: Ediciones Larousse.

Phelan, John Leddy (1959), *The Hispanisation of the Philippines: Spanish Aims and Filipino Responses, 1565–1700*, Madison, WI: University of Wisconsin Press.

Riding, Alan (1986), *Distant Neighbors: A Portrait of the Mexicans*, New York: Vintage Books.

Schumacher, John (2006), 'Burgos Manifesto', *Philippine Studies*, special issue, Quezon City: Ateneo de Manila University Institute of Philippine Culture.

Schurz, William Lytle (1985), *The Manila Galleon*, Manila: Historical Conservation Society.

Williams, Edwin B. (1973), *Diccionario Inglés–Español Español–Inglés*, New York: Bantam Books, Inc.

Yuste, Carmen (1993), 'Los comerciantes de la ciudad de México en la negociación transpacífica', in Leonor Ludlow and Jorge Silva Riquer (eds), *Los negocios y las ganancias de la colonia al México Moderno*, México: Instituciones de Investigaciones Históricas UNAM.

— (1997), 'Los tratos mercantiles transpacíficos de los comerciantes de la ciudad de México en el siglo XVIII', in Gemma Cruz Guerrero, et al., *El galeón de Manila un mar de historias*, México: JGH Editores.

The Popol Wuj

The Popol Wuj (this is the modern standard native spelling, but Popol Vuh is also a traditional variant) contains a wide array of tales produced by the cultures of the Maya, and later the K'iche', centuries before the arrival of the Spanish to the Amerindian continent. These works were composed between 500 and 2,000 years ago. The Popol Wuj begins with a group of narrations – in K'iche' called *tzij* – which deal with the creation of the universe, the life of man, and especially with the creation of the Maize Men. The next part comprises episodes (considered myths according to the Western canon) performed by religious–spiritual–mythical beings. In the third part of the book, the story of the origin and arrival of the Forefathers from Tulán (Toltecs) is told. They conquered and subjugated the native Mayan populations of the highlands, forced tributes from them, and then installed the dynasties and houses (political organisation) of K'umarcaaj, the capital of the K'iche' reign at the end of the fifteenth century. The K'iches are a mix of the Mayans and the Toltecs, and dominated the mountains of modern day Guatemala from approximately 1200 AD.

In 1524, Pedro de Alvarado took over K'umarcaaj (Utatlán), then burned it along with its key K'iche' leaders, and subjected the natives to forced dispersion, servitude and slavery. Along with these political and military measures, cultural artefacts were destroyed and native rituals and traditions were prohibited. This was the beginning of the colonisation and indoctrination of the indigenous peoples of the region within the scope of Eurocentric Christian doctrine. The Maya-K'iche' had had many ways of recording and perpetuating their knowledge, beliefs, traditions and social and ethical norms. The four primary ways of doing so was through murals and stelae, through their ceramic artefacts, through the *wujs* (mistakenly called codexes by the Spanish), and through their ritual drama-dances. In addition, many traditions were contained in their religious ceremonies and prayers. The *wujs* were fashioned with the bark of the *ámate* (a vegetable native to the region), and prepared in sheets, approximately 30 centimetres wide and 120–60 centimetres long, which were folded like an accordion. In each of these segments the scribes crafted their knowledge and traditions through an elaborate style of hieroglyphs and math symbols. The *wujs* were then conserved in special places, presumably under the custody of religious leaders.

When the Spanish invaded the region, they dedicated themselves systematically to destroying the *wujs* because they preserved the idolatry and 'erroneous beliefs taught by the devil'. The most well documented example of this ethnocide was the burning of the Códices by Bishop Fray Diego de Landa, in Maní (Yucatán) in 1562. The natives hid what they could of the tales from these narrations, and tried to preserve their traditions of worship, as well as oral history in secret. In the 1550s, in Santa Cruz del Quiché, a town constructed about a mile from the ruins of K'umarcaaj, someone wrote a compilation of the K'iche's *tzijs* which were found in distinct places – not only *wujs* – at the moment of the Spanish invasion, composed in Western style (Latin characters, paper and ink). We do not know if this was a single and unique version, or one of many copies; we also do not know why they were written in this way. What is certain is that these texts were selected and set down in a certain sequence that did not exist as such prior to 1524; the content, however, is of the pre-colonial era. Thus, the coercive colonial act shaped a fixed compendium of the narrations within the structures of the Western textual format. It remains unknown if, as a result of an intentional effort, or by mere coincidence, this anthology is what allowed the *tzijs* to survive colonial and neo-colonial conditions.

Around 1701–3, the Dominican friar Francisco Ximénez, while at the church of San Pablo Chuilá, in Chichicastenango, obtained one of the versions of this antique manuscript, laboriously copied the K'iche' text, and translated it into Spanish. His intention was to learn in detail about native customs, and then find an efficient way to eradicate them. This was part of the aim of dominating the subjectivity of the colonised individuals, such that they became tame and useful in relation to the interests of the metropolis. Even though Father Ximénez took steps to ease some of the maltreatment suffered by indigenous peoples, he also zealously fulfilled his mission of making them forget their own traditions, teachings and wisdom.

Ximénez' manuscript was virtually unknown during the rest of the colonial period. During the mid-nineteenth century, after the establishment of the modern state of Guatemala, two Europeans who travelled the world as scientific ambassadors found the manuscript at the library of the University of San Carlos, Guatemala, where it was placed in the year 1830. In 1857, Carl Scherzer published in Vienna the translation into Spanish made by Ximénez, and in Paris in 1861 the Abbé Charles Brasseur de Bourbourg published a copy of the K'iche' text along with a French translation. Brasseur gave these texts the name Popol Vuh, and it was from that point on that this work began to be transformed into an object of intellectual curiosity in the West. Despite such acclaim in Europe, in Guatemala only the members of the Ladino élite class (Ladinos are people of mixed blood) were familiar with these texts, and in the rest of the Americas the Popol Vuh remained completely unknown. At the end of the nineteenth century, the manuscript, which was part of Brasseur's personal library, was bought by the North American collector Edward E. Ayer, who in 1909 donated it to the Newberry Library in Chicago, where it can be found today.

In 1947, with the publication of the translation into Spanish by Adrián Recinos, edited by the Fondo de Cultura de Mexico, the Popol Wuj emerged from the veil of obscurity under which it had lain since its first emergence in a Western format. In 1950, Sylvanus Morley and Delia Goetz translated Recinos' work into English, opening the door to this work for an English-speaking audience. In 1955, Dora Burgess and Patricio Xec made a bilingual edition (K'iche'–English), as part of the evangelical Church activities in Guatemala. That, and later translations by Munro Edmonson (1971), and Dennis Tedlock (1985) have given the Popol Vuh wider circulation in the USA, especially in academic settings.

Around 1945, Don Adrián Inés Chávez, a teacher by profession and a native K'iche' speaker, began the significant task of decolonising the phonetic spelling of his native tongue. Chávez noticed that phonetic transcripts done by the sixteenth-century scribes and Father Ximénez had transmitted many errors: colonisation thus left the wrong kind of imprint on the Popol Wuj, according to Chávez. To remedy the situation, he copied the text at the Newberry Library, then rewrote it in a phonetic form that fitted the meaning as understood by native K'iche' speakers, and then went on to translate this into Spanish. His edition was published in 1979. It highlighted the need to correct the distortions imposed on the language in the colonial transcription of the Popol Wuj, and the educational role the work could play in the process of regaining Mayan pride.

This endeavour was developed in the midst of a vast social movement to regain indigenous rights, characterised by a new awareness of cultural and ethnic identity. The Creole–Ladino élite – sheltered by Cold War politics and by neo-liberal economic expansion – unleashed a civil war that went on to become a genocide (more than 80 per cent of the victims were indigenous, 93 per cent of the crimes were committed by members of the armed forces or by paramilitary groups, 3 per cent by the guerrilla movement and the rest unidentified, according to CEH 1999). On top of this, there was vigorous activity on behalf of several fundamentalist evangelical Churches, especially the Pentecostal Church, which worked in collaboration with dictator Efraín Ríos Montt. Protestant churches began to develop in Guatemala in 1873 (under the government of Justo Rufino Barrios) along with the capitalist neo-colonisation project which aimed to 'liberalise' the country by attacking the conservative Catholic Church. However, it was not until the 1960s and the fight against communism that these Churches gained sufficient force through foreign sponsors. The Pentecostals not only justified the crimes committed by the Civil Defense Patrol (PAC or death squads) through their doctrine, but they also dedicated themselves to the neo-evangelisation which sought to reconvert Catholic natives to evangelical doctrine. A central concern of the evangelical fundamentalists was to eradicate the remnants of pre-colonial rituals and traditional beliefs. According to Similox Salazar (in *Memorias* 1999), a very small percentage of the churches in Guatemala were not fundamentalist or conservative. The combined effect of political-military actions and ideological-religious interventions contributed to the struggle for the realisation of Mayan cultural awareness.

Thus, the ancestral oral traditions of indigenous communities were gradually revitalised, along with the practices of the *aj'quij* (spiritual guides). The effects of this process were reflected in two conferences about the Popol Wuj, one held in 1979 in Santa Cruz del Quiché, and the other held in Quetzaltenango in 1999. The first conference took place while campaigns of extermination were in their early stages; the second took place shortly after peace was declared. During the second conference, the difference between how K'iche' intellectuals treated the Popol Wuj and how it was treated by foreign scholars was especially noticeable. For the natives, the texts have a central role to play in the fight to end the remnants of Spanish colonisation. They are instruments of decolonisation for modern times (Sotero Chunuj, in *Memorias* 1999). For modern Mayans, the Popol Wuj is an important philosophical reference tool with which to confront the cultural and economic adversities of the post-industrial capitalist model. Ideas concerning harmony, solidarity and respect for nature and life are key values found in the Popol Wuj (in *Memorias* 1999, see Montejo; Matul; Sac; Batzibal Tunal). For foreign academics, the Popol Wuj is a literary or anthropological work of reference; for the K'iches, it connects social, political and cultural practices of the past to the resurgence of the Mayan peoples today.

Comparing the documents from these conferences with all other academic works on the Popol Wuj, it is clear that the Popol Wuj has yet to be put under the spotlight in debates about the internal and external neo-colonial realities of the Mayans and of other indigenous groups. *The Book of the Fourth World*, by Gordon Brotherstone, distinguishes itself from the kind of Western perspective which ignores native texts that do not fit within its parameters; and in *Los Popol Wuj y sus epistemologías* (1999), I propose a decolonisation of the Popol Wuj at the ideological level.

This leads us to the notion that, somehow, a museum-like ambience still predominates in the realm of the academic approach to native texts. However, texts such as the Popol Wuj are not mere literary works; rather, they are part of a dynamic socio-cultural process still in full development. They are not testimonies of an extinguished past; instead, they are components of a reality that also involves the intellectual who reflects upon the discourses developed before and during the postcolonial/ neo-colonial era.

Within the realm of works in the English language, books such as those by José Rabasa and Walter Mignolo address the issue of neo-colonisation in disciplines such as history, political sciences or sociology; however, the repercussions of neo-colonialism in relation to Mayan realities is most prominent in the Menchú–Stoll controversy. The testimony of Rigoberta Menchú touches on two extremes of Mayan reality: the roots of the outlook on reality related through the Popol Wuj, and the connection between those discourses and the social practices of indigenous communities. The controversy unleashed by the 'exposé' of David Stoll (Warren 1998) had repercussions within English-speaking academic circles, but did not make an impact in Mayan communities or anywhere else in Latin America.

In other words, an analytical corpus (critical and theoretical) has yet to develop for these emerging discourses within the cultural and cosmogonic traditions that trace back their origins to the precolonial *tzijs*, which will further the epistemological and philosophical task of decolonisation that Adrián Chávez has been working on for over half a century.

Carlos M. López

LITERARY WORKS AND AUTOBIOGRAPHIES

Asturias, Miguel Angel (1993), *Men of Maize*, trans. Gerald Martin, Pittsburgh, PA: University of Pittsburgh Press.

Bisarro Ujpán, Ignacio and James D. Sexton (1985), *Campesino: The Diary of a Guatemalan Indian*, Tucson, AZ: University of Arizona Press.

Menchú, Rigoberta (1983), *I, Rigoberta Menchu: An Indian Woman in Guatemala*, London: Verso.

Menchú, Rigoberta and Dante Liano (2004), *The Girl from Chimel: Tales from a Mayan Village*, Tadworth: Acorn.

Tecú Osorio, Jesús (2002), *Memoria de las masacres de Río Negro*, Rabinal and Baja Verapaz: n.p.

HISTORIES

('Histories' in the conventional sense do not yet exist. Mayan-K'iches are just starting to rewrite history from a new perspective.)

Brotherston, Gordon (1993), *Book of the Fourth World: Reading the Native Americas through their Literature*, Cambridge: Cambridge University Press.

Burgess, Dora M. de and Patricio Xec (1955), *Popol Wuj*, Quetzaltenango: El Noticiero Evangélico.

Comisión para el Esclarecimiento Histórico (CEH) [1999] (2005), *Guatemala, Memoria del silencio*, CD-ROM by the Asociación Americana para el Avance de las Ciencias, Guatemala: F&G Editores.

Chávez, Adrián Inés (1979), *Pop Wuj*, México: Ediciones de La Casa Chata.

Edmonson, Munro S. (1971), *The Book of Counsel: The Popol Vuh of the Quiche Maya of Guatemala*, Middle American Research Institute Publication 35, New Orleans, LA: Tulane University Press.

López, Carlos M. (1999), *Los Popol Wuj y sus epistemologías. Las diferencias, el conocimiento y los ciclos del infinito*, Quito: Ediciones Abya-Yala.

Memorias del •• Congreso Internacional sobre el Pop Wuj (1999), Quetzaltenango: Centro de Estudios Mayas Adrián Inés Chávez – TIMACH. (The two dots mean '2' in the Mayan numerical system. The authors wanted to preserve their cultural identity.)

Stoll, David (2000), *Rigoberta Menchu and the Story of all Poor Guatemalans*, New York: HarperCollins.

Tedlock, Dennis (1986), *Popol Vuh. The Mayan Book of the Dawn of Life*, New York: Simon and Schuster.

Warren, Kay B. (1998), *Indigenous Movements and their Critics: Pan-Maya Activism in Guatemala*, Princeton, NJ: Princeton University Press.

Postcoloniality and Alternative Histories: Latin America

The independence movements taking place in the first half of the nineteenth century in the Spanish and Portuguese colonies were tied to European imperial conflicts over economical and political control of the 'new' territories and the Atlantic circuit. They materialised simultaneously with French usurpation of power in Spain and Portugal in 1807–8. The Creoles (people of Spanish and Portuguese descent born in the colonies, and second to Europeans in the social/racial hierarchy of the colonies) initiated the struggles for independence as a consequence of an obvious weakening of the colonial powers, and of an accumulated discontent with their marginalisation by Spaniards and Portuguese born in the Iberian peninsula and living in the colonies. The idea of 'Latin' America started to emerge after the decline of the Spanish and Portuguese empires from the mid-nineteenth century and the rise of the British, Dutch, French and US empires in the second half of the nineteenth century. The division of America into 'Anglo-Saxon' and 'Latin' reflected the geo-political struggles between France and the US to gain control over these territories. In this context, France alluded to the idea of Latinité to justify its involvement in America, referring to its linguistic connection with Hispanic and lusophone territories. In postcolonial Latin America this idea was to metamorphose into the idea of a transnational Creole identity (Mignolo 2005).

Likewise, Latin America evolved into an idea among postcolonial Creole and Mestizo élite populations who identified with European descent and histories, and continued to find inspiration in French republican ideas, British ideas of liberalism and ideas of self-rule learned from the North American struggle for independence. The indigenous and African-descent populations were still thought to be racially and epistemically inferior, and were excluded from having a part in official history. As in Europe and in the US, history was 'white', Christian and male and, as such, started with the 'discovery' of America. The natural consequence of these assumptions was the belief that the only way possible for the course of history to unfold was toward European modernity, civilisation and progress. Latin America, as an extension of Europe, was the domain of the 'Latin' race (not of the American Indian, not of those of African descent). Latin American 'backwardness' could be corrected if it followed after Europe. In this manner, the colonial conception of America as a continent across which Europe could naturally extend was never called into question. Postcolonial Latin America thus took shape reproducing and adapting colonial hierarchies and social organisation to fit the interests of the new élites, that is, through 'internal colonialism'. The idea of purity of blood, which had been brought to the 'new' continent from Spain and Portugal, now became fundamental for the hierarchical social–racial differentiation that justified Creole domination over other groups. In this hierarchy, Creoles were followed by Mestizos (Indo-European descent), Mulattos (Afro-European descent), Indios (descendants of the indigenous population), Zambos (Afro-Indian descent) and Negroes (Afro descent). As Walter Mignolo has noted, Creole identity emerged in a double way; as geo-political consciousness in relation to Europe, and as racial consciousness in relation to the other populations in the colonies. The questions and concerns among the Creoles were thus very different from those of the Afro-descendent and indigenous peoples. The Creole/Mestizo experience is marked by its participation in colonial and imperial projects and, at the same time, being imperial and colonial subjects, the suppressed colonial histories of the people of Afro-descent are more entrenched with the African diaspora, slavery and *cimarronismo*; and the stories of Mesoamerican and Andean indigenous peoples are more determined by the population's relation, rebellion and resistance to Spanish institutions and settlements.

The imperial power of the US in Latin America started to take shape with the Spanish–American War in the late nineteenth century. In this period, the US gained political, economic and military control over Cuba, Panama and Puerto Rico. The Roosevelt corollary to the Monroe Doctrine, which stated the 'right' of the US to intervene in Latin

American countries, can be said to mark the transition from European to US dominance. At the same time, it marks the will to establish clear-cut boundaries between 'Latin' and 'Anglo-Saxon' America. Nevertheless, in practice these boundaries start to blur from the very moment of their inception namely because one of the effects of US imperial activity in Latin America has been an increase in the Latino population in the US (Mignolo 2005). The singularity of this phenomenon is maybe best illustrated in Chicana activism, scholarship and literature. By the end of the nineteenth century and the beginning of the twentieth, critical reflections on the colonial and geo-political idea of Latin America were concerned with the colonial legacy and the inceptions of new colonialisms, and involved a search for understandings of history and society based on different logics from the ones dictated from European thought, and reproduced by Creoles and Mestizos. Among these contributions, which were to be taken up repeatedly in Latin American postcolonial thought, is José Martí's *Nuestra America* (1891) and José Carlos Mariátegui's adaptation of Marxism into a proposal of 'revolutionary indigenism' (*Seven Interpretative Essays on Peruvian Reality*, 1928). Marxism also inspired Sergio Bagú's conceptualisation of 'dependent capitalism' in 1949 (*Economía de la sociedad colonial*), which was to be significant in the development of dependency theory in the 1960s that saw a direct relationship between the 'underdevelopment' of 'Third World' countries and their economic dependency on 'First World' countries. The critical ideas of the twentieth century, such as those in Leopoldo Zea's *América en la historia* (1958) and Edmundo O'Gorman's *The Invention of America* (1961), were also inclined to revise and discuss national and sub-continental identity. The term 'internal colonialism', coined by Rodolfo Stavenhagen and Pablo González Casanova in the 1960s, was to be of special concern through the 1980s for scholars such as Silvia Rivera Cusicanqui and Xavier Albó. From the increasing relevance of the social sciences, together with an interest in those past and present histories which were suppressed by the colonial and Creole narrations, attempts were made to elaborate ideas through which the colonial legacies of epistemological and economic dependency could be overcome. In the 1970s, a 'philosophy of liberation' (Enrique Dussel) and a 'sociology of liberation' (Orlando Fals-Borda) emerged as part of these efforts.

The concerns about the epistemic aspects of colonialism and the colonial legacy as inherent parts of economical and political coloniality grew, and continues to inform postcoloniality in contemporary Latin America. Immanuel Wallerstein's idea of the modern world system has been complemented by pointing at how modernity would never have been possible without its 'darker side': coloniality. Thus, increasing emphasis is laid in locating the sixteenth century as a constitutive moment of the modern/colonial world system. In this respect, Latin American postcolonial criticism differs from other postcolonial traditions which emphasise the eighteenth century as a decisive moment.

Maybe the most influential concept to have come from this perspective is that of the 'coloniality of power', an idea developed by Aníbal Quijano (2000), which refers to the ways in which the power matrix that was constituted with the 'discovery' of America, in which race came to play a decisive role, continues to be the dominant organising principle of social relations on a global scale. However diverse, all social practices and intersubjective relations in the world must pass through this colonial sphere of value orientation and organisation of the whole. From this idea emerge derivative concepts such as the 'coloniality of knowledge' and the 'coloniality of being' which are followed by an increasing interest in looking at 'Other', silenced histories and, through these, to emphasise the local character of official history, and to seek in diverse ways to revise and rethink not only history but also the future of the 'colonial difference' (Mignolo 2005). The 'colonial difference' refers to the epistemic importance of a person's situation and situatedness in the world. To think from the colonial difference is thus to think from a position which is given by coloniality, but also to assume and realise this difference in one's thinking. Coloniality not only suppressed and sought to erase epistemologies different from the Eurocentric, it simultaneously created the possibility of thinking from the colonial difference, that is, of 'border thinking'. Border thinking entails an epistemology placed in the excluded and suppressed side of modernity/coloniality from which the possibility of decolonising knowledge materialises (Mignolo 2005).

Border thinking has existed since the sixteenth century, and is to be found in many different manifestations and spheres in Latin America. Maybe the best known and the oldest example is Guaman Poma's *The First New Chronicle and Good Government* (1615), a source that continues to have an important position in Latin American intellectual works. *Katarismo* in Bolivia, *inter-culturalidad* in Ecuador and *Zapatismo* in Chiapas are expressions of border thinking from the indigenous colonial difference, while the ideas of the Process of Black Communities in the Colombian Pacific exemplify border thinking from the Afro-descendent colonial difference, and Chicana thinking from the US-Mexican-indigenous-female colonial difference. As practice and analytical category, border thinking transcends the modern/colonial hierarchical division between orality and literacy, which implies the division between doxa and scientific knowledge (Castro-Gómez 2005). This distinction has determined the validity of knowledge and its scientificity, and the ways in which orally transmitted knowledge, which continues to be important in knowledge production among non-élites in Latin America, is analysed in the social sciences and the humanities. However, the difference between orality and literacy is not only one of form, but also one of epistemology. It also implies a distinction in which orality and doxa belong to the past, and literacy and science to the present. Furthermore, it places the past behind, literally as past. In contrast, to many indigenous peoples in Latin America, the past is continually present in as much as it enables both present and future. Invoking the past through words is thus not only a retelling of past events, but also the (past/present) act of opening future paths (Rivera Cusicanqui 1993). Conversely, the deliberate silencing of specific histories that have determined negative events can serve to prevent the possibility of these events taking place again (Espinoza Arango 1995).

The renewed interest in alternative histories is, thus, from a postcolonial viewpoint, interconnected with the practice of epistemic resistance, with the struggles of social movements, and the reconstruction of knowledge under way after the decline and fall of colonialism. A short description of such initiatives reveals their complexity, and forms an example of an alternative history. The Peasant University of Resistance in Colombia is a project undertaken by ten different Colombian social movements (peasants, Afro-Colombian and indigenous ethnic groups) embroiled in the Colombian war, facing persecution, killings, harassment, food and medicine shortages and continuous efforts at displacing them. These communities refuse to co-operate with either of the armed actors in the war, and share the understanding that their practical needs go hand-in-hand with other needs of a philosophical or epistemological nature. Thus, alimentary, health and medical self-supply, education and the developing of communication media which do not distort information are practical needs which can only be met satisfactorily if they are grounded on modes of organisation, thinking and living which are consistent with a way of life based on resistance and solidarity. Hence, they work together in the framework of the university, sharing different modes of knowledge and searching for constructions of society alternative to the dominant, modernity/coloniality-based framework. This implies meeting the needs of situations resulting from a history of violent oppression, from the struggle for attaining independence from liberal market forces, and for access to education which respects and includes their cultural and ethnic identities and knowledge.

With the Peasant University, the communities seek to create a space of theoretical and practical education where the main objective is to complement and build upon each other's knowledge. Emphasis is placed on practice-oriented knowledge, which is always at the service of resistance and not on knowledge derived from the dominant modern Eurocentric understanding of science, development and justice. Participation in this university has no cost, is not career-oriented, and does not entail either a staff of 'experts' or a campus. Instead, the different communities involved take turns in hosting the university's sessions, held once or twice a year. Knowledge construction and sharing is regarded as an ongoing process, and everyone has something to learn and some knowledge to share. The university deals with the following four different 'alternative lines of work' which have been identified by the communities: agro-alimentary issues, health, education and communication, and the realm of the juridical-philosophical.

The legacy of practice-oriented ideas such as the ones associated with Orlando Fals-Borda and Enrique Dussel are an important component of the process of resistance to the coloniality of power in Latin America. The blurring of the division between theory and practice, doxa and scientific knowledge, is most visible in the close relationship between social movements and scholars. For example, the work of Catherine Walsh and Chucho García (2002) with the Afro-Ecuadorian movement explores Afro-Ecuadorian intellectual practices such as 'unlearning the learnt and relearning one's own knowledge', the relationship between territory and identity, resignification as an organisational strategy, and the role of ancestrality in thinking and acting processes. In a similar vein, Pablo Dávalos (2002) seeks to reach an understanding of how Ecuadorian indigenous social movements elaborate their notions of meaning, their fields of theoretical validation, and their most immediate discourses and practices. This is done through the Intercultural University of the Indigenous Peoples and Nationalities. Finally, Teresa Basile (2002) analyses the case of the Popular University of the Mothers of the May Square exploring issues concerning the linking of pedagogical practices with social transformation, on experience-grounded knowledge and its political dimensions, on knowledge which articulates theory and practice, and on suffering as a source of knowledge.

Julia Suárez Krabbe

LITERARY WORKS
Arguedas, José María (1961), *Deep Rivers*, New York: Longitude.
Asturias, Miguel Angel [1949] (1995), *Men of Maize*, Pittsburgh, PA: University of Pittsburgh Press.
Barnet, Miguel [1968] (1994), *Biography of a Runaway Slave–Esteban Montejo*, Willimantic, CT: Curbstone Press.
Cisneros, Sandra (1987), *My Wicked, Wicked Ways*, Bloomington, IN: Third Woman Press.
García Márquez, Gabriel [1967] (2000), *One Hundred Years of Solitude*, London: Penguin Books.
Jesus, Carolina Maria de (1966), *Child of the Dark*, New York: E. P. Dutton.

HISTORIES
Basile, Teresa (2002), 'La Universidad Popular de las Madres de Plaza de Mayo: emergencia de nuevas prácticas en cultura y poder en la Argentina de la posdictadura', in

D. Mato (ed.), *Estudios y otras prácticas intelectuales latinoamericanas en cultura y poder*, Caracas: CLACSO, CEAP, FACES, Universidad Central de Venezuela, pp. 67–78.

Castro-Gómez, Santiago (2005), *La Hybris del Punto Cero. Ciencia, raza e ilustración en la Nueva Granada (1750–1816)*, Bogota: Editorial Pontificia Universidad Javeriana.

Dávalos, Pablo (2002), 'Movimiento indígena ecuatoriano: construcción política y epistémica', in D. Mato (ed.), *Estudios y otras prácticas intelectuales latinoamericanas en cultura y poder*, Caracas: CLACSO, CEAP, FACES, Universidad Central de Venezuela, pp. 90–8.

Espinoza Arango, Mónica (1995), *Convivencia y poder político entre los andoques*, Bogota: Editorial Universidad Nacional.

Mignolo, Walter D. (2005), *The Idea of Latin America*, Oxford: Blackwell.

Rivera Cusicanqui, Silvia (1993), 'La raíz: colonisadores y colonisados', in Albó and R. Barrios (eds), *Violencias encubiertas en Bolivia, 1: cultura y política*, La Paz: CIPCA-Aruwiyiri, pp. 25–139.

Peasant University of Resistance, working-papers in Spanish at http://www.nodo50.org/tortuga/article.php3?id_article=4858 [accessed April 2007].

Quijano, Aníbal (2000), 'Colonialidad del poder, eurocentrismo y América Latina', in E. Lander (ed.), *La colonialidad del saber: eurocentrismo y ciencias sociales. Perspectivas latinoamericanas*, Buenos Aires: CLACSO, pp. 201–46.

Walsh, Catherine and Juan García (2002), 'El pensar del emergente movimiento afro-ecuatoriano. Reflexiones (des)de un proceso', in D. Mato (ed.), *Estudios y otras prácticas intelectuales latinoamericanas en cultura y poder*, Caracas: CLACSO, CEAP, FACES, Universidad Central de Venezuela, pp. 318–26.

Fausto Reinaga and the Revitalisation of the Indianista Movement in the Andes

Over the past three decades, the Andean region has witnessed the resurgence of indigenous mobilisation. This organisation is taking place on local, national and transnational fronts. Indigenous peoples insistently foreground the critical relationship between the struggle for territorial rights and the revitalisation of native historical memory. For indigenous peoples, the right to exercise political and cultural control over their own territory signifies the ability to 'exercise jurisdiction over the concrete, historical manifestation of one's own place of culture, one's own system of knowledge, one's own epistemic structure and the mode of praxis that is linked to such belonging' (Varese 2003).

Fausto Reinaga (Bolivia, 1906–94) was one of the most influential and controversial early theorists of indigenous mobilisation throughout the region. Among his numerous books and articles, three volumes in particular impacted greatly on young indigenous activists of the 1970s and 1980s: *La revolución india* (*Indian Revolution*, 1969), *Manifesto del partido indio de Bolivia* (*Manifesto of the Indian Party of Bolivia*, 1970), and *Tesis india* (*Indian Thesis*, 1971). In his prologue to *Indian Thesis*, Peruvian essayist and political leader, Guillermo Carnero Hoke, declared Bolivia to be the revolutionary capital of Indian America due to the unprecedented publications of Fausto Reinaga and the ongoing rebellion of the Aymara masses. Reinaga's writings delineated a theory of social revolution rooted in the historical and material context of the Andes. His thought led to numerous offshoots from his own Indian Party of Bolivia, including the Tupak Katari Indian Movement, the Julian Apasa University Movement, the Tupak Katari Revolutionary

Movement, and Felipe Quispe's Red Ayllu Offensive. While inspiring to a new generation of indigenous leaders and intellectual-activists, Reinaga was subjected to attempted marginalisation by many prominent figures of the political left and right who dismissed him as a belligerent upstart. Others disparaged Reinaga by labelling him a racist because of his passionately expressed anti-white sentiments. Later book titles such as *La podredumbre criminal del pensamiento europeo* (*The Criminal Putrefaction of European Thought*, 1982) and *Europa prostituta asesina: Congreso mundial de los intelectuales del tercer mundo* (*Europe, Murderous Prostitute: World Congress of Third World Intellectuals*, 1984) convey a sense of the combative style in which he generally wrote. Although Reinaga's work from these years is not without contradictions and tensions, indigenous activists claim that he continues to be a major source of influence in the present (Hurtado 1986).

According to his biographer, Gonzalo Humberto Mata, Reinaga was born in Macha, Potosí, where he spent the first sixteen years of his life working as a herder, wood cutter and miner. Due to his humble origins, he was first admitted to school on a conditional basis, although later he became an honours student (Mata 1968). The young man persevered at his studies, overcoming the racial prejudices of the time to become eventually a professor of philosophy, a lawyer, politician, diplomat, journalist and congressman.

Reinaga's *Indian Revolution* appeared two years after the assassination of Ernesto 'Che' Guevara, a critical political conjuncture in contemporary Bolivian history. The timing of Reinaga's publication was especially meaningful because it arrived on the scene at a time when the political left was dominated by a revolutionary working-class consciousness, exemplified best by Bolivia's militant labour unions. *Indian Revolution* disrupted this trend with its claim that an analysis of class alone was insufficient for understanding the legacy of racism that still pervades Bolivia's social, cultural and economic institutions. Reinaga proclaimed the need to broaden left ideology by recuperating race as a category of analysis and by incorporating a critique of colonialism into revolutionary consciousness. Taking his cue from the Black Power Movement in the USA, he wrote: 'It would be an aberration if blacks, rather than calling themselves blacks, preferred to be called peasants' (Reinaga 1969). Reinaga argued that 'whites' in Bolivia, and in that category he included *mestizos* and those who 'act white', are terrified of Indians self-identifying as Indians: 'By calling him "comrade peasant" they believe that they can erase from the Indian's memory what they have done to him in four centuries . . . they are trying to introduce with the name "campesino" another being, not the Indian.' Thus, he asserted, the Indian's problem was not assimilation, it was liberation: 'It is not a class problem (of a peasant class), it is a problem of race, of spirit, of culture, of a people, of a Nation.' Methodologically, Reinaga turned away from Marx and Lenin to look, instead, to Third World intellectuals and leaders of nationalist movements who expressed a clear anti-colonial position.

Of particular interest to Reinaga in these early writings were proponents of insurgent nationalist movements, including such prominent figures as Patrice Lumumba, Franz Fanon, Mohandas Karamchand Gandhi, Malcolm X and Stokely Carmichael. He included in *Indian Revolution* lengthy quotes from these and other writers to argue that the Third World needs to forge a path in contradistinction to that of Europe. Not only has Europe been unable to resolve the problems besetting the Third World, it has been the primary agent of oppression and genocide. Reinaga was particularly interested in Fanon's analysis of how the process of decolonisation must necessarily be violent. For example, in *The Wretched of the Earth*, Fanon noted that decolonisation inevitably brings about the meeting of two opposing forces: 'The naked truth of decolonisation evokes for us the searing bullets and bloodstained knives which emanate from it. For if the last shall be first, this will only come to pass after a murderous and decisive struggle between the two protagonists' (Fanon 1963). This dynamic of two opposing forces that must eventually collide underlies Reinaga's vision of the Indian revolution, which becomes synonymous with the revolution of the Third World and the struggle to destroy the sway that Europe holds over it.

Reinaga's writings revealed how the violence of colonialism works implicitly and explicitly to eradicate any and all manifestations of indigenous identity, and they document the painful battle to affirm indigenous agency. It is an urgent project, one that is succinctly expressed in his emblematic phrase: 'The Indian Revolution is a matter of life or death' (*Ser o no Ser*). This critical discursive stance predicated in binary oppositions gave rise to one of Reinaga's fundamental convictions that there exists not one but two Bolivias: 'a Bolivia that is Europeanised and *mestizo*, and another Bolivia that is Indian and autochthonous'. This was not a particularly new idea, as writers such as Alcides Arguedas, among others, had long lamented Bolivia's fragmentation along racial and cultural lines. Nevertheless, this racial divide served as a vital nexus of power and knowledge whereby social and political élites reinscribed their own position of privilege. In contrast, Reinaga refuted the prevailing politics of cultural assimilation, by *affirming* the vision of a divided Bolivian society. Javier Hurtado has suggested that herein lies much of the importance of Reinaga's work because he reopened the discussion on the problem of the Indian. Reinaga embraced the name 'Indian' precisely because this was the word that had been used to dominate, oppress and exterminate indigenous peoples from the conquest to the present. Although the coloniser had created the binary Indian/*criollo-mestizo*, indigenous peoples needed to transform the same oppositional framework into a radical political and epistemological stance. Reinaga's appropriation of difference enabled him to emphasise the fact that if the history of the binary 'Indian/*mestizo-criollo*' had been a repository of colonising practices, it could also be a repository of *decolonising* practices (hooks 1990).

This political and epistemological movement to recuperate the name 'Indian' is what Reinaga designated as *indianismo*, a term he distinguished from *indigenismo*. For Reinaga, Indianismo was a revolutionary political force of Indians fighting for their liberation, while Indigenismo was a movement comprised of whites and *mestizos* calling for the assimilation of Bolivia's indigenous peoples (1971).

Reinaga believed that this revolutionary struggle was necessarily tied to the recuperation of native historical memory. In order for Indians to be agents of history, he argued, they first had to learn about their own past. In both *Indian Revolution* and *Indian Thesis*, he included lengthy accounts of historical figures who actively resisted colonial domination. For example, Reinaga was one of the first to call attention to the continued relevance of Aymara leaders such as Túpac Katari (eighteenth century) and Zárate Willka (nineteenth century), and to significant events such as the uprising and massacre of Indians at Jesús de Machaca (twentieth century). This concern for native memory and history led him to examine rural education and the impact it had on indigenous students. The rural school, he argued, rather than practise Paulo Freire's pedagogy of the oppressed, employed the pedagogy of the oppressor. Instead of education as the practice of liberation, it was the practice of slavery. This pedagogy requires that Indians become the object of colonial history rather than the subject of their own history (1971). First subjugated and colonised, the lettered Indian who unquestioningly assimilates Western ideas is by definition dead to himself and to his community. The primary function of rural schools is to ensure that this process takes place smoothly by eradicating alternative ways of thinking. Reinaga thus reclaimed indigenous historical knowledge as a radical site of resistance where indigenous peoples can affirm and sustain their agency. This knowledge would empower indigenous peoples, he argued, and unleash a heretofore unknown force, one more dangerous than that of nuclear power: 'the force of hatred and hunger. Four centuries of hunger and hatred' (1970).

In the context of Reinaga's Indianismo, the word 'Inca' acquired important significance, representing human nature that is an outgrowth of the Andean social contract: don't lie, don't steal, don't exploit others. He contended that Inca human nature is the enduring legacy of a revolutionary, historical consciousness embodied today in those who rise up off their knees and stand together to face their oppressors (1969). Reinaga asserted that this revolutionary consciousness would take on unprecedented force and spill over national boundaries. He introduced his notion of internationalisation of the Indian movement when he foresaw the formation of a revolutionary Indian Party of America (1971). Reinaga's call for an international Indian Party that posits shared political and ethical ties between diverse indigenous peoples anticipated the more recent transnational indigenous movement that similarly calls for native peoples to form a united front against the colonising violence of Western civilisation. With regard to the transnational indigenous movement, Mexican anthropologist Guillermo Bonfil Batalla notes:

> By introducing into its discourse, the notion of a single, common civilisation, the Indian Movement positions cultural differences between itself and the West on a different level: it becomes a global confrontation of two civilisations, two civilising projects. In this manner, it no longer is a matter of each individual indigenous nation struggling in isolated fashion and from an unequal and inferior position against the strength and prevailing tendencies of the surrounding national societies. Rather, it is a general movement in which all indigenous peoples participate, transcending their cultural differences to emphasise instead their common struggle. (1991)

Reinaga's numerous publications resonated in the official public sphere and alarmed lettered élites from both sides of the political spectrum. The fiery register in which he wrote provoked angry responses among the Bolivian intelligentsia, and members of the left and the right attempted to silence his pen. Through the practice of strategic essentialism, Reinaga mounted an attack against the legacy of colonial domination and racism that continues to pervade the Andean region (see Spivak 1988 on 'strategic essentialism'). Writing with urgency and rage, he forged an intellectual space of resistance to the prevailing politics of assimilation and genocide. By deploying a differential consciousness, Reinaga laid the foundation for the Indianista movement of the second half of the twentieth century.

Although Reinaga's work attempted to forge a space for the construction of a revolutionary indigenous subject at the intersections of history, philosophy and political economy, one of the questions still to be considered concerns the place of the indigenous woman in his conceptual framework. What the reader discovers is that, for the most part, the indigenous woman is noticeable primarily as an absence. With few exceptions, the Indian woman occupied no place in his writings as a flesh and blood historical presence. Although Reinaga devoted a few paragraphs to the heroic struggle and martyrdom of Micaela Bastidas and Bartolina Sisa (eighteenth century), these are the only women who emerge as historical actors in the pages of his books. Generally speaking, the Indian woman is, in his words, 'an open wound that breaks your heart'. Her life moves forward as if responding to instinct alone: 'She procreates and works; she works and procreates. That is the Indian woman' (1969). She is always only the victim of the violence of colonialism, repeatedly raped by the masters as the Indian male is forced to stand by silently without protest. In his writings, the Indian woman takes on meaning as a symbol of the virginal 'true' essence of the lost utopia (Alarcón 1990). Ironically, even as Reinaga historicised the material struggle for the insertion of male indigenous subjectivity, he negated the subjectivity of the indigenous woman in all of her historical complexity by relegating her to the domain of the symbolic. Although Reinaga's writings construct an oppositional discursive space, they also reproduce patriarchal power relations that ultimately legitimate his own interests and political objectives (Hoskins 2000). The concern then is that in Reinaga's male-centred oppositional framework, it becomes difficult if not impossible to 'pluralise the racialised body' by reclaiming and redefining the indigenous woman's experience through the 'reappropriation of "the" native woman' on her own terms (Alarcón 1990).

In Bolivia, indigenous activists, such as the women of the NGO 'The Organisation of Aymara Women of Kollasuyu [Bolivia]' (OMAK), contend that Andean women used to exercise authority in the community, and many continue to do so (Flores et al. 1990). Nevertheless, following the 1952 revolution, the system of political parties and the rural syndicalisation of peasant communities was promoted over Andean forms of governance. Women and community elders were edged out of leadership roles under the guise of 'modernising' indigenous political structures.

The 1980s witnessed a resurgence in indigenous movements dedicated to the reconstitution of native community structures, with one of the goals being to replace the syndicate system of leadership with traditional Andean forms of governance. The women of OMAK argue, however, that even in the current struggle taking place in Bolivia for the right to autonomy and self-determination, the men continue to be the privileged half.

María Eugenia Choque and Guillermo Delgado-P. co-authored a paper that came out of a series of conversations they had regarding the vital roles that indigenous women play today in the transformation and strengthening of the indigenous movement in local and transnational contexts. According to the authors, the indigenous woman's struggle takes place on many fronts, including challenging male-only leadership, demanding the right to education, acquisition of human rights and access to better health care. Indigenous women exercise their autonomy by examining their cultural traditions to reclaim the authority and leadership they once had.

One method of analysis has been to re-examine traditional stories and sayings that highlight women in leadership roles and as agents of history. Choque and Delgado emphasise the need to recover important teachings that can stimulate the debate on the role of indigenous women in the Andean community. For example, the saying '*Qhari sapa ma' atinmanchu*' or 'Males are incapable by themselves' is one illustration of the way by which indigenous women 'renarrativise their search for power'. Although some male leaders have attempted to dismiss this work, arguing that it is only a cultural enterprise and thus not engaged with the real struggle, indigenous women insist on the political relationship between the revitalisation of alternative histories that include both men and women, and the formation of a contestatory Andean cultural politics located in the collaborative context of the community. In this way they reclaim an Indianismo which emphasises the transformative agency of indigenous men *and* women.

Marcia Stephenson

Histories

Alarcón, Norma (1990), 'Chicana Feminism: In the Tracks of "the" Native Woman', *Cultural Studies* 4 (3): 248–56.

Bonfil Batalla, Guillermo (1991), *Pensar nuestra cultura*, México: Alianza Editorial.

Choque Quispe, María Eugenia, and Guillermo Delgado P. (2000), 'Indigenous Women and Transnational Struggles: Notes on Renarrativized Social Memory',

Working Paper no. 32, Santa Cruz: Chicano/Latino Research Center, University of California.

Fanon, Frantz (1963), *The Wretched of the Earth*, trans. Constance Farrington, New York: Grove Press.

Flores T., F. G. Andrea and V. Arminda (1990), 'Bolivia: Women in the Andean World. We Aymaran [sic] Women', in *Indigenous Women on the Move*, Copenhagen: IWIGIA Document no. 66, 9–13.

hooks, bell (1990), *Yearning: Race, Gender, and Cultural Politics*, Boston, MA: South End.

Hoskins, Te Kawehau Clea (2000), 'In the Interests of Maori Women? Discourses of Reclamation', in Alison Jones, Phyllis Herda and Tamasailau M. Suaalii (eds), *Bitter Sweet: Indigenous Women in the Pacific*, Dunedin: University of Otago Press, pp. 33–48.

Hurtado, Javier (1986), *El katarismo*, La Paz: Hisbol.

Mata, Gonzalo Humberto (1968), *Fausto Reinaga: Akapi Jacha'j*, La Paz: Ediciones Partido Indio de Bolivia.

Reinaga, Fausto (1969), *La revolución india*, La Paz: Ediciones Partido Indio de Bolivia.

— (1970), *Manifiesto del partido indio de Bolivia*, La Paz: Ediciones Partido Indio de Bolivia.

— (1971), *Tesis india*, La Paz: Ediciones Partido Indio de Bolivia.

— (1982), *La podredumbre criminal del pensamiento europeo*, La Paz: Renovación.

— (1984), *Europa prostituta asesina: Congreso mundial de los intelectuales del tercer mundo*, La Paz: Comunidad Amaútica Mundial.

Spivak, Gayatri (1988), 'Subaltern Studies: Deconstructing Historiography', in Ranajit Guha and Gayatri Chakravorty Spivak (eds), *Selected Subaltern Studies*, New York and Oxford: Oxford University Press, pp. 3–32.

Varese, Stefano (2003), 'Indigenous Epistemologies in the Age of Globalisation', in J. Poblete (ed.), *Critical Latin American and Latino Studies*, Minneapolis, MN: University of Minnesota Press, pp. 138–53.

The Role of Literature in Filipino Resistance to Spanish Colonialism

From 1521 to 1898, Catholic religious orders, Spanish officials and local chieftains dominated the Spanish colonial order in the Philippines. Under a feudal system, *barangays* were subjugated under the *encomiendas*, awarded as royal grants, within which tributes were collected, *corvée* labour was enforced and native soldiers were conscripted. The friars were ensured great powers by the union of Church and state, allowing them dominion over the spiritual, economic, political and social life of the natives, not only in vast landed estates owned by the religious orders, but also at all levels of government. Under *frailocracia*, religious orders interfered in running the colonial government even as they administered the census, taxation, schools and public works.

Between 1621 and 1655, Filipinos were conscripted in large numbers to work in forests felling timber and building ships. Eventually, revolts began breaking out sporadically all over the country against abuse, forced labour, land-grabbing and arbitrary practices. These included popular uprisings by millenarian movements. Between the sixteenth century and the middle of the eighteenth century, the Philippines were isolated from the rest of the world, and the natives knew of Europe only through their contact with the Spanish colonisers.

From the sixteenth century, the Manila–Acapulco trade yielded revenues for the central colonial government. In 1785, the establishment of the Real Compania de Filipinas further consolidated the trade which eventually connected the Philippines to the outside world. From 1812 trade was largely replaced by large-scale cultivation of export crops. The exploitation of natives under the *hacienda* system forced them to produce export crops like sugar, hemp, tobacco and coconut. The arbitrary expansion of friar estates through fraudulent surveys and through exorbitant land rent added to native suffering. Spanish rule also saw improvements in transportation and communications. These forced ever-increasing numbers of natives to build roads, ports and bridges. On the positive side, such work provided better access between cities and the countryside, and made contact among oppressed natives easier.

Local native chiefs (the *principalia*) enjoyed a certain degree of economic prosperity either as small landowners or leaseholders on friar estates; through Spanish officials; as traders; through commerce with factories, shipping or banking firms. Beginning in 1766, direct trade with Spain allowed the repercussions of political events in Spain and Europe to be felt more quickly in the Philippines. Moreover, many officials of liberal persuasion were brought to the Philippines whose anti-clericalism resonated with native resentment at the abuses perpetrated by the friars. The opening of the Suez Canal in 1869 accelerated economic and political contacts between Europe and the Philippines. This allowed liberal ideas to reach educated Filipinos more readily than in the previous 300 years.

After three centuries of colonisation, a royal decree of 1863 provided for a complete educational system, opening new opportunities to the nascent native middle class. From this system emerged the writers of the Reform or Propaganda Movement who were active from the 1870s to the 1890s; and the leaders of the anti-Spanish Philippine Revolution of 1896 and the Philippine–American War of 1898. They used literature not for propagating or celebrating the Christian religion brought to them by the Spanish but for a change in the concept of the 'Filipino', which by the nineteenth century had ceased to refer only to Philippine-born Spaniards and now included Spanish and Chinese *mestizos* and Hispanised *indios*.

If the Spanish had chosen, the Spanish language could have served as the bridge for bringing into the Philippines the cultural wealth of the Spanish Renaissance. However, the language was not taught to the natives, for practical and evangelical reasons. Throughout the eighteenth and nineteenth centuries, the clergy and the colonial administration advised against spreading Spanish among the natives so as to insulate them from subversive ideas that might otherwise come in from Europe, especially France. Nevertheless, the number of highly educated *indios* and *mestizos* (known as the *ilustrados*) increased during the nineteenth century as the now relatively prosperous *principalia* began to send their children in greater numbers to the colonial colleges and universities, or to Spain, for higher education. Among the more prominent Filipinos to be educated in the Philippines were Father Pedro Pelaez, who joined the secularisation movement in the 1860s and later, the priests Father Burgos, Gomez and Zamora. They spoke out in favour of the secularisation and Filipinisation of Philippine parishes. In 1872 they were accused of leading the Cavite Mutiny, alleged to have attempted to overthrow the Spanish colonial régime, and therefore condemned and hanged (and thus martyred). In Philippine history books, the martyrdom of these priests marks the beginning of the Philippine struggle for independence and nationalism, the first of its kind in South-East Asia.

The *principalia*, who had enjoyed a certain degree of economic prosperity under Spanish rule, were also subjected to oppressive demands by the exploitative colonial régime, such as arbitrary increases in quotas of agricultural production, tribute collection and high rates of interest in loans. Inability to keep up with these economic pressures led to bankruptcy, confiscation of property or ejection from leaseholds. By the second half of the nineteenth century, despite Spanish attempts to keep the Philippines 'a cloistered colony', many Filipino intellectuals had awakened to the need to register their opposition to the colonial order (Tiongson 1994). A century earlier, in _Florante at Laura_, by Francisco Baltazar, patriotism made an appearance through the speeches assigned to the character of Florante. They were the first seeds of nationalism sown among local readers by Filipino _ilustrados_, even though the role of the Spanish priest as a literary dictator went almost unchallenged through three centuries of Spanish rule.

Over time, the harvest of writers in Spanish and Tagalog became bountiful. It included José Rizal (1861–96), the country's national hero, and Marcelo H. del Pilar (1850–96), who were assimilationists, and the more radical Emilio Jacinto (1875–99) and Andres Bonifacio (1863–96), who were separatists. The position of Rizal and del Pilnar as _ilustrados_ and middle-class intellectuals implicated them in the entire colonial system of power relations from which they could not divorce themselves during regional and national crises.

The Propaganda Movement was reformist in nature. The intelligentsia, led by Rizal, advocated changes in colonial policy that would bring Spain and her colony into closer harmony. When that failed, the struggle turned to the Revolutionary Movement of the 1890s, led by the Katipunan (the secret society that toppled Spanish rule), founded by Bonifacio and later led by Emilio Aguinaldo. The Reform Movement was said to have benefited from the discursive and didactic tradition of the missionary writers. It emerged with the goal of exposing friar oppression and asserting the right of the Filipinos to be treated as citizens of Spain, even as it also emphasised love for the native land. In the counter-hegemonic literature of reform and revolution, the homeland was not just an 'imagined' community; it was where one lived, endured and suffered. It was self-evident to the reformists and revolutionaries that Philippine society could not develop or modernise so long as the people were dominated by oppressive Spanish colonial structures. Literature could be used as a weapon against continued enslavement. The central questions that underpinned the literature of reform and revolution involved the conceptualisation of the idea of 'nation'. Who constitutes the nation? Whose interest should define the nation? The reformist and revolutionary literature articulated an ideal of Filipino nationhood based on the people's right to self-determination.

Philippine literature fought for the people's self-recognition via an imagined community, in tropes that prefigured a self-reliant and self-actualised national space. Gregorio Sancianco's treatise on Philippine problems, _El Progreso de Filipinas_ (_The Progress of Filipinas_, 1881), is said to have inspired José Rizal to write 'Sobre la indolencia de los Filipinos' ('On the Indolence of Filipinos', 1889), which defended the Filipinos' alleged 'laziness' in the face of Spanish exploitation. The essays that Rizal published in _La Solidaridad_ between 1889 and 1890 reveal his wit, versatility and humour, as for example, in 'Por Telefeno' ('The Telephone'), 'La vision de Fray Rodriguez' ('The Vision of Fr Rodriguez'), 'Su Excellencia, Senor Don Vicente Barrantes' ('His Excellency, Sir Don Vicente Barrantes'), and 'Filipinas dentro cien anos' ('The Philippines within a Century'). Rizal's first novel, in Spanish, _Noli me tangere_ (1887), narrates the life of a young Filipino, Ibarra, who has obtained a university education in Europe and comes back to the Philippines full of the zeal and idealism of a dedicated reformist. His second novel, _El filibusterismo_ (1891), the sequel to _Noli_, is about how a mysterious stranger named Simoun tries to hasten the downfall of the Spanish colonial régime by abetting the corruption of friars and colonial officials, and instigates an armed rebellion among the natives. These novels are considered the 'most important literary works produced by a Filipino writer, animating Filipino consciousness to this day, setting standards no Filipino writer can ignore' (Mojares 1983).

M. H. del Pilar, wrote *Dasalan at Tocsohan* (*Manual of Prayers and Jokes/Temptations*, c. 1888), a satire on the friars' hypocrisy, licentiousness and greed, which consists of parodies of the Sign of the Cross, the Act of Contrition, the Lord's Prayer, the Hail Mary and the catechism. He also wrote political tracts that characterised the friars as exploitative and oppressive, such as *La soberania monacal en Filipinas* (*The Monastic Supremacy in the Philippines*, 1888), and *La frailocracia Filipinas* (*The Philippine Friarcracy*, 1889). M. H. del Pilar was well-versed in the art of poetic jousting (called *duplo*) before he assumed the post of editor of *La Solidaridad*. The long poem *Sagot ng Espanya sa hibik ng Pilipinas* (*The Response of Spain to the Pleas of the Philippines*) was a reply to Hermenegildo Flores' *Hibik ng Pilipinas sa Inang Espanya* (*The Plea of the Philippines to Mother Spain*), which portrayed the exploitation of natives under the *frailocracia*. As a parodist, del Pilar was at his best in *Ang Pasyong dapat ipag-alab ng taong baba sa kalupitan ng fraile* (*The Passion Story that Ought to Inflame the Hearts of Persons Subjected to the Cruelty of Friars*), where he uses popular 'sacred' forms for his anti-friar attacks. In poems such as the fragment 'Dupluhan', del Pilar gave a subversive patriotic content to the form of the *duplo*. Of this adaptation Lumbera writes:

> The poet did not need to start from scratch: he only needed to take over and renovate what was already available. This was what the missionaries did when they came in the sixteenth century and were in need of a bridge by which to reach the natives. Del Pilar's insight was to turn the missionary tactics against the friars – to use old forms to propagate new attitudes. (Lumbera 1986)

Among the leaders of the Propaganda Movement was Graciano López Jaena who, like del Pilar, subverted religious tradition in Philippine literature for anti-clerical satires. López Jaena was forced to flee to Spain because he had enfuriated the friars with his satirical piece, *Fray botod* (*Friar Potbelly*, c. 1889). The newspaper *La Solidaridad* broadcasted the views of the movement. The paper was founded 'to fight all forms of reaction, to impede all retrogression, to hail and accept all liberal ideas, and to defend all progress'. It has been said that in the pages of *La Solidaridad* the genre of the essay became the most significant contribution to Philippine literature in Spanish.

The effect of any literary work on its audience is mediated by the historical circumstances of its reception. It was the martyrdom of the three priests that inspired Rizal in his fight for reforms, and made him dedicate his second novel, *El filibusterismo*, to their martyrdom; it was Rizal's writings that inspired Bonifacio to organise the Katipunan which would finally topple Spanish colonial rule in the Philippines; and it was through Bonifacio that Rizal's literary works were to be popularised. The literature of reform and revolution, at once hybrid and creative, focused Filipino awareness of their plight under Spanish rule on the affirmation of the national identity of a distinct and historically evolved community. The fact that many reformist works were written in Spanish can be said to show how the language became an instrument for 'writing back' to the Spanish Empire. Rizal, for example, used the Spanish language to speak on behalf of the Philippines. His last poem, 'Mi último adios' ('My Last Farewell') written in Spanish, shortly before his execution, overflows with love for his native land.

By the end of the nineteenth century, many members of the intelligentsia who had been part of the Propaganda Movement realised that their efforts had not brought about changes in colonial policy. Lumbera remarks:

The shift from Spanish to Tagalog as the language of the nationalist movement signaled more than a change of medium; it was above all a shift in tactics. A new audience was being addressed – the Filipino masses rather than Spanish liberals and fellow native intellectuals. This meant that reformism had been abandoned and the revolution had begun. (Lumbera and Lumbera 2005)

By the late 1890s, the oppressed lower classes saw the time was ripe for revolution.

The Katipunan used Tagalog (spoken in Manila and surrounding provinces) as its official language. Consequently, Tagalog came to be associated with nationalism, and the literature that was written in it during the years to come would highlight the nationalist cause. The Katipunan leaders Andres Bonifacio and Emilio Jacinto used Tagalog to advantage as a tool for organising and awakening the masses. *Katapusang hibik ng Pilipinas* (*The Ultimate Plea of the Philippines*) refers back to Flores' *Hibik* and del Pilar's *Sagot*, and builds on the situation implied in the two earlier poems, where a desperate daughter appeals to her mother for help. Bonifacio's poem establishes a final break from reformism by making the daughter renounce 'negligent and perfidious' Mother Spain.

Revolutionary essayists were more polemical and exhortative than their other reformist colleagues. Bonifacio's *And dapat mabatid ng mga Tagalog* (*What the Tagalog Should Know*) is in the form of a straightforward account of how Spain had damaged the Philippines, which urges people to revolt. Jacinto's essays, collected in *Liwanag at dilim* (*Light and Darkness*, 1896), expound on the libertarian doctrines of the Katipunan. *Ang ningning at ang liwanag* (*Glitter and Light*), for example, urges people to be wary of appearances because treason and perversity seek glitter to hide the truth, while sincerity and honesty allow themselves to be seen confidently by the light of the day. The poems of Flores, del Pilar and Bonifacio gave poetry a role in the creation of the Filipino nation. Three hundred years of Spanish colonial régime ended in 1898; but Philippine independence lasted only very briefly, as the United States soon invaded the country. Independence from American dominance becomes part of another narrative of struggle for independence.

Maria Luisa T. Reyes

LITERARY WORKS

Del Castillo, Teófilo y Tuazon and Bueneventura S. Medina, Jr (1972), *Philippine Literature: From Ancient Times to the Present*, Quezon City: Philippines: Del Castillo.

Lumbera, Bienvenido L. (1986), *Tagalog Poetry 1570–1898: Tradition and Influences in its Development*, Quezon City: Ateneo de Manila University Press, pp. 138–49.

Lumbera, Bienvenido and Cynthia Nograles Lumbera (2005), *Philippine Literature: A History and Anthology*, Pasig City: Anvil Publishing, Inc.

Medina, Jr, Buenaventura S. (1974), *Confrontations: Past and Present in Philippine Literature*, Manila: National Book Store, Inc.

Mojares, Resil B. (1983), *Origins and Rise of the Filipino Novel: A Generic Study of the Novel until 1940*, Diliman: University of the Philippines University Press, pp. 137–50.

Tiongson, Nicanor G. (1994), 'The Spanish Colonial Tradition', in *CCP Encyclopedia of Philippine Art*, Manila: Cultural Center of the Philippines, vol. IX, pp. 62–9.

HISTORIES

Alzona, Encarnacion (1932), *History of Education in the Philippines, 1565–1930*, Manila: University of the Philippines Press.

Agoncillo, Teodoro A. (1956), *The Revolt of the Masses: The Story of Bonifacio and the Katipunan*, Quezon City: University of the Philippines Press.

Agoncillo, Teodoro A. and Milagros C. Guerrero (1960), *A History of the Filipino People*, Quezon City: R.P. Garcia.

Constantino, Renato, with the collaboration of Letisia R. Constantino (1975), *The Philippines: A Past Revisited*, Manila: Renato Constantino.

Ileto, Rafael Clemena (1979), *Pasyon and Revolution: Popular Movements in the Philippines, 1840–1910*, Quezon City: Ateneo de Manila University Press.

Rafael, Vicente L. (1988), *Contracting Colonialism: Translation and Christian Conversion in Tagalog Society under Early Spanish Rule*, Quezon City: Ateneo de Manila University Press.

San Juan, Jr, Epifanio E. (1998), 'Interrogations and Interventions: Who Speak for Whom?', E. E. San Juan, *Beyond Postcolonial Theory*, New York: St. Martin's Press, pp. 21–52.

Spain, Modernity and Colonialism

The 'discovery' and conquest of the New World by Spain after 1492, along with the colonisation of the Atlantic islands, the west coast of Africa, and northern Brazil by the Portuguese, inaugurated the modern world system as such. However, the great European colonial projects (the Dutch, British, French, German, Danish, Flemish, North American, and so on) often had at their core one or another version of the Black Legend – the notion, advanced especially during the Enlightenment, that the Spanish conquest of the Americas in the sixteenth century was not only cruel but anachronistic. Thus, these projects justified themselves in the name of a 'modernity' that they supposedly represented vis-à-vis Spain, on the one hand, and the populations they were submitting to their rule, on the other.

However, the disavowal or marginalisation of the role of Spain and Portugal in the formation of the modern world system from 1492 through to the end of the seventeenth century is itself part of the ideology of colonialism (it would come to justify, for example, the military conquest and occupation by the rising American state of parts of Mexico; and to Napoleon the occupation of Spain itself in the wake of the French Revolution). European modernity is itself a product of colonialism. There is no modernity without colonialism, and vice versa, no colonialism without modernity. Both modernity and the colonial world originate together in the sixteenth century with the 'discovery' and conquest by Spain and Portugal of what came to be (mis)named 'America'. The great territorialities of Antiquity and the Middle Ages, like the Holy Roman Empire, did not constitute economically or legally a world system. The conditions for the formation of a world market include then not only the circumnavigation of the globe and 'discovery', but also the subjection to forced labour and the genocide of the Indian populations of the Americas, and the imposition of the slave system in Africa and the Atlantic and the trans-Caribbean. Spanish/Portuguese colonial rule in Africa, Asia and the Americas should therefore be seen as a form of (colonial) modernity, rather than its antithesis: a non-capitalist, Catholic modernity, founded on the absolutist state, colonial conquest, and mercantilist economics.

The Renaissance in its different, sometimes contradictory manifestations (the Reformation and Counter-Reformation, secular humanism, the Baroque, the rise of the vernacular national literatures and the sciences) is the cultural form, and an aspect of the self-justification, of European colonialism. Capitalism is its economic form. Though Spanish and Portuguese colonial rule in the Americas is not capitalist, or more specifically is contained within its pre-industrial, mercantilist phase, the extraction of vast amounts of wealth from their American and Atlantic colonies – initially in the form of precious metals, later of agricultural commodities like sugar – is a crucial aspect of the 'primitive accumulation' of capital (Marx) that allowed the nascent trading and industrial economies of Northern Europe to consolidate themselves in the late sixteenth and seventeenth centuries.

The legal basis of the modern colonial system is the Roman concept of *occupatio* (which, as a specifically colonial or external form of rule, was distinguished from the incorporation of other lands and people into the state itself). As Machiavelli recognised, Spain under the Catholic kings, Columbus' patrons, was the first European nation to constitute itself as a 'state' in the modern sense – that is, as a demarcated, sovereign, self-contained, non-theological and non-feudal territorial order. The shift away from mediaeval forms of territoriality and citizenship towards the modern nation-state was a necessary precondition for the emergence of the colonial world order as such, in the sense that only as a result of the demarcation of clear 'national' territorialities did the question of the right of conquest and occupation come into focus as a matter of international law; *jus inter gentes* (law among nations) rather than *jus gentium* (the law, or rights of a people or nation) – or religious 'crusades.' More particularly, what comes to be elaborated in the sixteenth century by thinkers connected to the colonial enterprise of Spain like Vitoria as *jus publicum Europaeum* (the law of the relations between states in Europe) sets the basis for presumption of the right of European states to occupy the lands of and govern other peoples, specifically those of the New World (although Vitoria himself did not hold that Spain or the other European states had a right of occupation of 'discovered' territories). The appointment in 1569 of Francisco de Toledo as Viceroy of Peru by Philip II of Spain marks the first time a European state creates a legally constituted government to rule over an overseas territory.

Though many aspects of the Spanish and Portuguese empires are quasi-feudal and religious in character (and some others are inheritances of Islamic models of territorial occupation and rule) – for example, the aristocratic doctrine of 'purity of blood' as a requirement for positions of authority in the colonial administration; or the principle of converting the native populations to Catholicism; or the granting of *encomiendas* (land grants) – the empires were also founded on a highly centralised and relatively effective secular and ecclesiastical bureaucracy, which sought, especially in the case of the Spanish colonies, to control all details of life, from local market prices to sexual practices to forms of spirituality.

The defeat of the Spanish Armada in 1588 marks in historical retrospect a shift of momentum of the colonial dynamic from Spain and Portugal to Northern Europe, and especially to Holland and England. But the Dutch and English essentially build on the world system and its structuring assumptions and institutions already put in place by the Iberian colonial project, which establishes the pattern for the administrative and military disciplinary and control structures of future colonialisms, though each will have its own specific national character. The great difference is that, against its own intentions, the Spanish and Portuguese colonial project results in the death of most of the indigenous population of the Americas (an estimated 90 per cent die off in the century following 1492, mainly from the spread of infectious diseases among defeated, and often demoralised and overworked populations), whereas in other colonial projects, such as the British occupation of India or the partition of Africa, the native population survives colonisation more or less intact. But it is above all the 'right' to colonise that the states will inherit from the Spanish, along with other basic features of the colonial relation that are still with us today: structural racism; military domination; unequal economic exchange; repressive paternalism.

Spain's American colonies become independent in the early nineteenth century (with the exception of Cuba and Puerto Rico); and Brazil becomes a sovereign nation by the mid-nineteenth century. But independence, which is the product of the Creole settler middle and upper classes rather than the colonised native populations and the slaves, does not mark the end of the colonial relation as such. Rather, colonial assumptions continue to dominate the structuring ideologies and institutions of the new republics. New colonial projects emerge in the nineteenth century from Britain, the USA and France (the idea of 'Latin' America itself was a product of the French effort to establish a colonial presence in the region in the nineteenth century, in competition with the United States and Britain). The year 1898, and the loss of Spain's remaining empire (except for its African enclaves) to the USA in the Spanish-American war marks the nadir of Spanish colonialism, but also the definitive conquest of the Indians of North America, the completion of the partition of Africa, and the emergence of new colonial or semi-colonial powers: the USA, Japan, Germany.

John Beverley

HISTORIES
Chomsky, Noam (1993), *Year 501: The Conquest Continues*, Boston, MA: South End Press.
Dussel, Enrique (1995), *The Invention of the Americas: Eclipse of 'the Other' and the Myth of Modernity*, trans. Michael D. Barber, New York: Continuum.
Las Casas, Bartolomé de (1967), *Apologética historia sumaria*, ed. Edmundo O'Gorman, 2 vols, Mexico: UNAM.
— [1537] (1975), *Del único modo de atraer a todos los pueblos a la verdadera religión*, Mexico: Fondo de Cultura Económica.
— [1875] (1986), *Historia de las Indias*, Caracas: Biblioteca Ayacucho.
— [1552] (2003), *Brevísima relación de la destrucción de las Indias*, Madrid: Cátedra.
Machiavelli, Niccolo [1513] (2005), *The Prince*, intro. William J. Connell, Boston, MA: Bedford St Martin's.
Mignolo, Walter (2005), *The Idea of Latin America*, London: Blackwell.
Schmitt, Carl (2003), *The Nomos of the Earth*, trans. G. L. Ulmen, New York: Telos Press.
Sepúlveda, Juan Ginés de [1574] (1984), *Demócrates Segundo o de las justas causas de la guerra contra los indios*, Madrid: Instituto Francisco Vitoria.
Vitoria, Francisco de (1951), *La conquista de América y el descubrimiento del moderno derecho internacional*, Buenos Aires: Editorial Guillermo Kraft.
— [1532] (1992), *Doctrina sobre los indios* (facsimile), Salamanca: Editorial San Esteban.

Spanish Colonialism in a World Perspective

Spanish colonialism extended historically between 1492 with the 'discovery' of America, and ended with the final colonies in northern Africa becoming independent of colonial administration after UN pressure in 1976. Territorially, it covered vast areas of America, Morocco (from 1860) and western Sahara (from 1884), Spanish Guinea (1884–1968) and the Philippines (1521–1898). The initial travels of Columbus were aimed at finding an alternative access for Spain to the Asian commercial circuits and markets. With Amerigo Vespucci's realisation that the lands to which Columbus had arrived were not on the Asian continent, in 1502, the formation of the Atlantic commercial circuit was initiated. The Atlantic commercial circuit connected the two existing commercial circuits in the

Americas, Anáhuac (today's Central America) and Tawantinsuyu (large parts of today's South America) with the eight commercial circuits existing in Europe, Africa and Asia. An additional circuit was established in 1571, which connected the Americas, especially from the Pacific coast of Mexico, with the Philippines and China. In this manner, Spanish colonialism had decisive effects in the integration of the world system, understood in a literal sense as encompassing all areas of the globe (Mignolo 2000; Bjork 1998).

Postcolonial efforts at studying Spanish colonialism in a world perspective share the general interest of decentring Europe and breaking the historical line chaining Greece, Rome, Christianity and modern Europe into a constitutive narrative of modernity and globalisation. Additionally, they aim at achieving a change not only in the contents of the discussions in the social sciences and the humanities, but also in the terms of these discussions. These efforts are thus relevant in the context of the production of an epistemological change on which theory and action can be based. By shifting from an analytic perspective which bases itself on a Euro-centred narrative of modernity and globalisation to a global one, several important insights are gained concerning modern subjectivity, capitalism, law and science. The idea is not one of denying other central processes that took place prior to and after Spanish colonialism or in other areas of the world, but rather to widen our knowledge of factors which were contingent to it which can only be conceptualised by thinking from the Latin American critical perspective. From this perspective, the period between 1492 and Spanish and Portuguese colonialism in the seventeenth-century constitutes what we might call the period of the First Modernity, which developed into a Second Modernity of Northern Europe that starts at the end of the seventeenth century, and whose central developments are the Industrial Revolution and the Enlightenment. The period of First Modernity includes Europe's hegemony over the Atlantic, a crucial phenomenon in the transition to the Second Modernity, where it will have achieved a position as a geo-political centre (Dussel 2004). With Spanish colonialism and the 'invention' of America, a complex set of processes were initiated which had profound impact on the constitution of the modern/colonial world system, and whose range extended from processes of subjectivisation and identity to the economical, social and epistemic ordering of the world. The world system is conceptualised as 'modern/colonial' because the 'coloniality of power' – not colonial power – (Quijano 2000) is the often neglected side of modernity. The notion of the coloniality of power concerns the entanglement of a diversity of global hierarchies of class and labour (including the international division of labour), capital, social organisation, gender, sexuality, spirituality, knowledge and language which, with the 'discovery' of America, are articulated around the idea of race (Quijano 2000).

The Spanish 'discovery' of America brought with it several epistemological changes decisive to the development of modern ways of knowing and ordering the world and its inhabitants through the construction of notions like rationality, objectivity, race and gender. One of these changes regards the ways in which the world was envisioned in cartography. Before 1492, the ethnic and the geometric centre of most maps was the same, that is, the place of observation was drawn into the maps. With the conquest of America, European cartographers started to apply the mathematisation of perspective, which implied the non-visibility of the place of observation and the adoption of a universal view of space (Mignolo 2005). This point of view – from no point of view – was an effect of the Spanish desire to control the Atlantic circuit and eradicate the cosmologies of its colonies. Thus, the cartographical organisation of the world came to obey an idea through which an 'unobserved observer's sovereign view' orders space into geographical continents and geo-political empires (Castro-Gómez 2005). In the realm of ethics and law, the epistemological change is illustrated with the idea of 'rights of people', which was at the centre of the Valladolid debates on the nature of the humanity of the Amerindians between Ginés de Sepúlveda and Bartolomé de las Casas during 1550 and 1551 (the humanity of African slaves was not discussed). The final prevalence of Sepúlveda's ideas of order (which were based on attributing rationality or degrees of rational capacity to the different 'races') over those of las Casas (which were based upon the idea of spiritual perfection) paved the way for the development of the centralising state and for the expansion of mercantilism based on colonial exploitation (Wynter 2003). Francisco de Vitoria's thought and the debates in the School of Salamanca on natural law, human rights, justice, sovereignty and 'just' war also played a role in the re-articulation of 'the racial imaginary' during this period. This re-articulation was concerned with the problems faced in the re-ordering of the European (and especially of the Iberian) world in light of its colonising culture. Vitoria's theologically-based formulation of the *ius gentium* is regarded as the first attempt to formulate a legal document that was to have an international impact. These ideas were to be reformulated in the eighteenth century – with a characteristic absence of concern with colonial questions – as a now secular document on the rights of men and of citizens (Mignolo 2000). In both cases, ideas such as rationality and private property were discussed, and in both cases an ontological construction of humanity took place (Wynter 2003).

According to Enrique Dussel (1995), during the period of First Modernity several processes were under way which would be decisive in the development of a modern subjectivity that culminates in 1636 with the Cartesian *Discourse on Method*. One such feature concerns the 'invention' of the Asian in the Americas (O'Gorman 1991), that is, the failure to realise, from 1492 to 1502, that what Columbus had 'discovered' was not Asia. This misrecognition was significant because it implied that the (American) Indians were not discovered as the Other, but as the Same – the Asian. A second feature concerns the proper 'discovery' of the 'New World', between 1502 and 1520, which triggered the existential experience of an Occidental Europe as the centre of history. There was a transition from a polycentric world to the constitution of Europe as a 'discovering universality'; the whole idea of a New World implied the equally important discovery of an Old World and this, by extension, meant the ontological realisation of a planetary world and the justification of the Old imposing its development on the New. In this way, America is discovered as the site onto which the same is projected; what Dussel names *encubrimiento* (*Entdeckungen*: covering over). These processes give place to a third feature in the development of modern subjectivity: the 'I conquer' that negates and seeks to erase the Other through exploitation and violence. This ego is complemented by a fourth factor: the colonisation of the life-world of the Other through an erotic, pedagogical, cultural, political, labouring and bureaucratic practice of assimilation. These features were founded in religion and were part and parcel of belief in a divine mission which, at the same time, gave place to a fifth feature, the spiritual conquest which, in a strictly formal sense, took place between the 1520s and the 1550s or the 1570s. A final feature concerns the idea of an 'encounter' between two worlds or cultures, which covers over the asymmetry in the relationship and hides the domination exercised by the European modern ego upon the life-worlds of other peoples, denying the value of their ideas, knowledge and ways of life.

All these factors were decisive in the formation of a modern subjectivity understood not only as a European bourgeois subjectivity, but also as the Hispanic colonial subjectivity which emerged in conjunction with a discourse of the purity of blood (Castro-Gómez 2005). Prior to the period of First Modernity, the Christian hierarchical conceptualisation of the world was organised according to an attributed origin from Noah's children. Thus,

Ham's descendants were to be found in Africa, Shem's in Asia and Japheth's in Europe. The 'discovery' of a fourth continent posed new problems to be solved in the context of this taxonomy. In the sixteenth century, intellectuals from France and Italy started to conceptualise America as the extension of Japheth's territory, which then was seen as the place where the superior Christian, white, European population could naturally extend (Mignolo 2000). The local European discourse of purity of blood, rooted in the Christian aristocratic mentality of the Middle Ages became, with Spanish and European colonial expansion, the first universalist discourse through which the global population was classified and ordered according to the place they occupied in the international division of labour, namely the discourse of race. From these classifications emerged historically new social identities such as American Indian, Negro, Mestizo, Mulatto; and existing classifications such as Spaniard and European were reordered (Quijano 2000). The discourse of the purity of blood is, hence, conceptualised as being the Occidentalism of the First Modernity, preceding the Orientalism conceptualised by Edward Said, which belongs to the period of Second Modernity (Mignolo 2000, 2005). Both Occidentalism and Orientalism are subjectivisation processes which cannot be disentangled from economical, social, political and military processes, nor from the epistemic fundaments of colonialism in the periods of the First and the Second Modernity (Castro-Gómez 2005).

The fact that Spanish men arrived with specific notions of gender and sexuality in places where there were very few Spanish women had decisive effects on the social, political and economical organisation of the modern/colonial world system, and played a determining role in the colonisation of the life-worlds of the colonised (Silverblatt 1987). Dussel's 'I conquer', a phallic ego, is a deeply gendered ego that exploits or kills the Indian man and has sex with the Indian, and later also the African woman. The eroticism practised by this phallic ego in the colonies was part of a practice of domination of the body through the sexual colonisation of women and the imposition of forced labour upon men (Dussel 1995). In Europe, the legacy of Sepúlveda's theories of order based on hierarchies of rational capacity attributed to the different 'races' were central to the development of the centralising state in the period of First Modernity. White, Christian and adult males were regarded as embodying reason, order and agency, while degrees of infantilism and femininity were attributed to non-whites according to their race/colour. Concurrently, the public and private spheres of social life were constructed as spheres which ordered inter-subjective relations in gendered, normative terms through the coloniality of power (Santiago-Valles 2003). During the period of First Modernity regulation, control and repression of previously semi-autonomous spaces of women took place on both sides of the Atlantic concurrent with the widespread practice of the rape of Indian and African-descended women. This sexual violence, which continues to exist today – most notably in the context of human trafficking – was, and remains, a racialised and gendered form of violence embedded in the coloniality of power: its mere existence rests on the assumption that these women were not of the same racialised gender as 'white' women (Santiago-Valles 2003). Thus, ideas of race and gender merged into new hierarchical notions that produced the new patriarchal orderings that were constitutive of the modern/colonial world system (Grosfoguel 2007). On the geo-political European side, the development took shape under the configuration of the private sphere, which was to be a male preserve, which also purported to supply the natural and moral basis for the constitution of the modern family (Santiago-Valles 2003).

Spanish colonialism and the 'discovery' and creation of America also had repercussions in the material relationships that were decisive in the consolidation of capitalism. With Spanish colonialism, all the existing forms of control and exploitation of labour – spanning from slavery to reciprocity – were articulated around the capital-salary relationship and the global market. Through this articulation, they assumed a new historical and sociological nature; they were now to produce goods for a global market, and this new articulation led to the development of new historical and structural characteristics (Quijano 2000). The place of a person in the division of labour was determined by his and her race and thus, the previously non-racialised slavery became increasingly 'black'. The same racial criteria were deployed by Europe during the period of the Second Modernity upon its colonies, where additional social/racial identities thereby emerged. This naturalised distribution of labour according to racial categories determined the social geography of capitalism and has proven to be a long-lived 'exploitation/domination technology', constituted through the coloniality of power (Quijano 2000).

Postcolonial studies of Spanish colonialism from a world perspective carry with them several implications. These concern, first, a rupture of the historical and temporal line which organises all other histories and temporalities into one universal history in which Europe is both the geographical centre and the culmination of time. Second, the idea of a world system as constituted by the entanglement of multiple hierarchies overcomes the Marxist idea of infrastructure and superstructure inasmuch as it places subjectivity and the social imaginary as being both constitutive of and constituted by the world system. In extension of the above, a third implication is that the division between culture and political-economy, which obstructs the understanding of the complexity of the world system, is overcome. Instead, it underscores the misleading effects of calling today's world system 'capitalist' insofar as this label refers to processes occurring in the economic realm: thus the use of the label modern/colonial world system. Fourth, this perspective calls forth struggles which take into account the complex entanglement of hierarchies in the modern/colonial world system (Grosfoguel 2007). Simultaneously, it draws upon theories developed by social movements in the context of their struggles and evolves around networks of Latin American activists and academic intellectuals that seek to reorder and subvert the hierarchy between lettered and non-lettered knowledge and to counter all forms of modern/colonial epistemic violence (Flórez-Flórez 2005). Finally, these studies have carried with them an epistemological change that sheds light on how processes, ideas and actions are entangled in coloniality. Thereby emerge related concepts such as 'coloniality of knowledge' (Lander 2000), being, truth and freedom (Wynter 2003) which are constitutive of and important to the world system and concern modern/colonial processes conceptualised from the less and less silenced and subalternised colonial side of the modern/colonial whole, from the 'colonial difference' (Mignolo 2000).

Julia Suárez Krabbe

HISTORIES

Bjork, Katharine (1998), 'The Link that Kept the Philippines Spanish: Mexican Merchant Interests and the Manila Trade, 1571–1815', *Journal of World History* 9 (1): 25–50.

Castro-Gómez, Santiago (2005), *La Hybris del Punto Cero. Ciencia, raza e ilustración en la Nueva Granada (1750–1816)*, Bogotá: Editorial Pontificia Universidad Javeriana.

Dussel, Enrique [1992] (1995), *The Invention of the Americas. Eclipse of 'the Other' and the Myth of Modernity*, trans. Michel D. Barber, New York: Continuum.

— (2004), 'La China (1421–1800) (razones para cuestionar el eurocentrismo)' http://www.afyl.org/articulos.html

Flórez-Flórez, Juliana (2005), 'Aportes postcoloniales (latinoamericanos) al estudio de los movimientos sociales', *Tabula Rasa* 3: 76–93.

Grosfoguel, Ramón (forthcoming), 'Decolonising Political-Economy and Post-Colonial Studies: Transmodernity, Border Thinking, and Global Coloniality', in R. Grosfoguel, J. D. Saldívar and N. Maldonado Torres (eds), *Unsettling Postcoloniality: Coloniality, Transmodernity and Border Thinking*, Durham, NC: Duke University Press. Reprint of 2006 Spanish version: 'La descolonización de la economía-política y los estudios poscoloniales: transmodernidad, pensamiento fronterizo y colonialidad global', *Tábula Rasa* 4: 17–48.

Lander, Edgardo (2000), 'Ciencias sociales: saberes coloniales y eurocéntricos', in E. Lander (ed.), *La colonialidad del saber: eurocentrismo y ciencias sociales. Perspectivas latinoamericanas*, Buenos Aires: CLACSO, pp. 11–40.

Mignolo, Walter D. (2000), *Local Histories/Global Designs: Coloniality, Subaltern Knowledges, and Border Thinking*, Princeton, NJ: Princeton University Press.

—— (2005), *The Idea of Latin America*, Oxford: Blackwell.

O'Gorman, Edmundo [1957] (1991), *La invención de América. Investigación acerca de la estructura histórica del nuevo mundo y del sentido de su devenir*, México: Fondo de Cultura Económica.

Quijano, Aníbal (2000), 'Colonialidad del poder, eurocentrismo y América Latina', in E. Lander (ed.), *La colonialidad del saber: eurocentrismo y ciencias sociales, Perspectivas latinoamericanas*, Buenos Aires: CLACSO, pp. 201–46.

Santiago-Valles, Kelvin (2003), ' "Race", Labour, "Women's Proper Place", and the Birth of Nations. Notes on Historicising the Coloniality of Power', *New Centennial Review* 3 (3): 47–68.

Silverblatt, Irene (1987), *Moon, Sun, and Witches. Gender Ideologies and Class in Inca and Colonial Peru*, Princeton, NJ: Princeton University Press.

Wynter, Sylvia (2003), 'Unsettling the Coloniality of Being/Power/Truth/Freedom Towards the Human, after Man, its Overrepresentation – An Argument', *New Centennial Review* 3 (3): 257–337.

The Túpac Amaru Rebellion

The Túpac Amaru Rebellion, an Indian-led movement that spread across the southern highlands of what is today Andean Peru and Bolivia between 1780 and 1782, was the first of the great anti-colonial rebellions in the modern world (the American revolution of 1776, which preceded and may in part have influenced it, was not properly speaking a rebellion by a colonised population, but rather an uprising of European, mainly British settlers, against political domination by the British crown). At its height in early 1781, the rebellion affected a territory ranging from southern Colombia to northern Argentina, and came very close to defeating Spanish colonial rule in South America.

The rebellion takes its name from its leader, José Gabriel Condorcanqui, Túpac Amaru, who was a prominent *cacique* from the Cuzco area, one of the descendants of the Inca aristocracy given a special role by the Spanish authorities as intermediaries between themselves and semi-autonomous communities of the so-called 'republic of Indians'. Condorcanqui claimed to be a direct descendant of the last of the great Inca kings, Túpac Amaru, beheaded by the Spanish in 1572, and took his name, calling himself Túpac Amaru II. The immediate cause of the rebellion lay in grievances caused by a series of modernising reforms of the colonial administration implemented by the Bourbon monarchy in Spain under Charles III (1759–88), centralising administrative and economic control and placing heavier tax and labour burdens on both the Indian and Creole populations. The focus of discontent was the main representative of the crown in Peru, the *visitador general* José Antonio Areche.

Ideologically, the rebellion was complex. At one level, it expressed simply a demand on the Spanish authorities for changes and reforms within the structure of colonial rule, often speaking in the name of the king himself, for example. At another, it envisioned an overthrow of European rule, and something like a restoration of the pre-conquest Inca empire, the Tahuantinsuyo. Túpac Amaru's claim to be the legitimate descendant of the Inca suggested the possibility of an aristocratic state similar to the one envisioned in the sixteenth century by the *mestizo* writer, Inca Garcilaso de la Vega, who saw the Incas as sharing rule with the Spanish aristocracy. But there were also strong millenarian, proto-Jacobin and even proto-communist elements in the rebellion. In the main, the soldiers of the Tupamarista armies were poor Indian peasants, artisans and women, who saw the rebellion not so much as a question of reforms or power sharing but as an opportunity to 'turn the world upside down'. The restoration of the Inca Empire meant for them the possibility of an egalitarian society, based economically on the Inca communal agricultural system, the *ayllu*, and one without *castas* (racial divisions), rich and poor, or forced labour in *haciendas*, mines and factories, particularly the dreaded textile mills.

The disturbances that led up to the rebellion broke out first in the southern city of Arequipa in early 1780, but its main focus later in the year was the region in and around the old Inca capital of Cuzco. The movement's leadership was heterogeneous, including besides Túpac Amaru himself and his immediate family, – his wife Micaela was a brilliant military strategist in her own right – other *caciques, mestizos*, Creoles, even a few priests and Spaniards. At the height of the rebellion in early 1781, Túpac Amaru's armies controlled most of the Andean region of Peru, and had entered into an alliance with a parallel uprising led by Túpac Katari of Aymara-speaking Indians in the region around the Lake Titicaca and the city of La Paz, in what is today Bolivia.

Against his wife's advice, however, Túpac Amaru hesitated to attack Cuzco itself. Finally, in January 1781, he mounted a siege of Cuzco, but the effort came too late, and he was unable to take the city. The rebellion lost momentum; internal divisions began to appear. The Spanish launched a successful counter-offensive, bringing in troops from the coast. Túpac Amaru, along with his wife and other leaders of the rebellion were captured and brought in chains to Cuzco in April 1781, where, in the presence of the hated *visitador* Areche, they were executed in the central plaza. Túpac Amaru's tongue was cut off; then he was tied to four horses to be pulled apart. When this failed, Areche ordered him beheaded and his body cut into pieces; these were later exhibited throughout the towns of the region.

The rebellion did not end with Túpac Amaru's capture and execution; but it gradually began to break apart, and the Spanish were able to suppress the last pockets of resistance by the end of 1782. What followed was something like a 'second' conquest of the Andes, beginning with a destruction of all vestiges of the neo-Inca nationalism that underlay the rebellion, including a prohibition on the use of Quechua. Túpac Amaru is often represented in official Latin American histories as a forerunner of the independence movement led by Simon Bolivar and the Creole élites in the first quarter of the nineteenth century. But had the rebellion he led triumphed, it would have resulted in an entirely different state and society from what Latin America became after independence – one that would have been Indian-centred and probably more egalitarian than the new nation-states created and dominated by the Creoles. Such an outcome would have had, in turn, an enormous positive impact on the Haitian revolution and on Indian resistance throughout the Americas.

John Beverley

LITERARY WORKS

Arguedas, José María (1962), *Túpac Amaru Kanaq Taytanchisman: haylli-taki. A nuestro padre creador Túpac Amaru: himno-canción*, Lima: Ediciones Salquantay.

Morante, Luis Ambrosio (1924), *Túpac-Amaru, drama en cinco actos, año de 1821*, Buenos Aires: Coni.

HISTORIES

Arnold, Denise (1992), 'Introducción', in D. Arnold (ed.), *Hacia un orden andino de las cosas: tres pistas de los Andes meridionales*, La Paz: Hisbol, pp. 13–30.

Cieza de León, Pedro de [1553] (1971), *La Crónica del Perú*, Bogota: Ediciones de la Revista Ximénez de Quesada.

Cornejo Bouroncle, Jorge (1963), *Túpac Amaru, la revolución precursora de la emancipación continental*, Cuzco: H. G. Rozas.

Flores Galindo, Alberto (1976), *Túpac Amaru II: sociedad colonial y sublevaciones populares*, Lima: Retablo de Papel Ediciones.

— (1986), *Buscando un Inka: identidad y utopía en los Andes*, Havana: Casa de las Américas.

González del Riego, Delfina (2001), *Túpac Amaru en debate: estudio bibliográfico crítico*, Lima: Biblioteca Nacional del Perú, Fondo Editorial.

Johnson, Lyman L. (ed.) (2004), *Death, Dismemberment, and Memory: Body Politics in Latin America*, Albuquerque, NM: University of New Mexico Press.

Robins, Nicholas A. (2002), *Genocide and Millennialism in Upper Peru: The Great Rebellion of 1780–1782*, Westport, CT: Praeger.

Thomson, Sinclair (2002), *We Alone Will Rule: Native Andean Politics in the Age of Insurgency*, Madison, WI: University of Wisconsin Press.

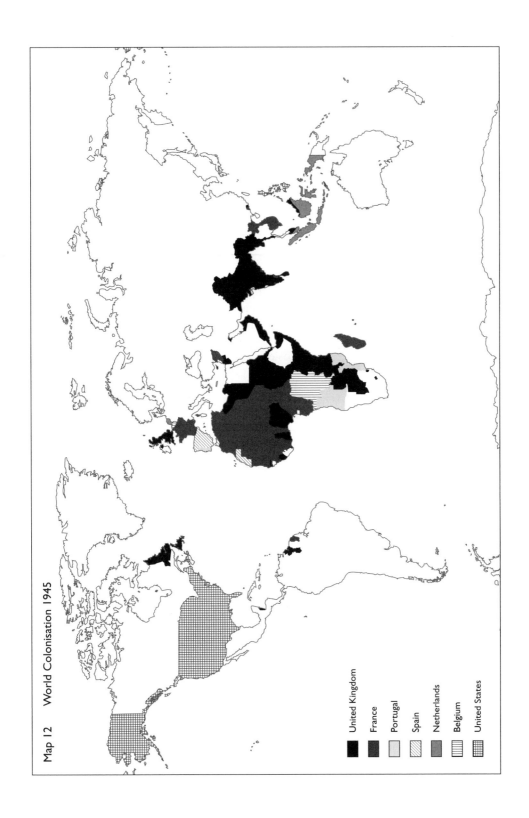

Map 12   World Colonisation 1945

United Kingdom

France

Portugal

Spain

Netherlands

Belgium

United States

Alphabetical List of Contributors

Ahmida, Ali Abdullah	University of New England
Alessi, J. P.	Colorado Springs
Allofs, Luc	Museum of Aruba
Ambrosio, Dante L.	University of the Philippines
Andall, Jacqueline	Bath University
Appama, Priscilla R.	Université de Franche-Comt
Arias, Arturo	University of Texas, Austin
Arnold, Denise	Instituto de Lengua y Cultura Aymara
Austen, Ralph A.	University of Chicago
Badenberg, Nana	Basle
Barclay, Fiona	University of Glasgow
Barth, Boris	Universität Konstanz
Becker, Frank	Universität Münster
Ben-Ghiat, Ruth	New York Unversity
Berman, Nina	Ohio State University
Beverley, John	University of Pittsburgh
Bishop-Sanchez, Kathryn	Wisconsin University
Bojsen, Heidi	Roskilde University
Botofte, John	Brussels
Bozarslan, Hamit	EHESS
Braeckman, Colette	Brussels
Bregnsbo, Michael	University of Southern Denmark
Brookshaw, David	Bristol University
Burdett, Charles	Bristol University
Bührer, Tanja	Universität Bern
Campbell, Aisling	Liverpool University
Chafer, Tony	University of Portsmouth
Conrad, Sebastian	European University Institute, Florence
Corcoran, Patrick	Roehampton University
Cornélis, Sabine	Royal Museum of Central Africa
Couttenier, Maarten	Katholieke Universiteit Leuven
Cresti, Federico	University of Catania
Crowley, Patrick	University College Cork
Cusack, Igor	Birmingham University
Deutsch, J.-G.	University of Oxford
Dh'aen, Theo	Leuven University

Doomernik, Jeroen   University of Amsterdam
Doumanis, Nicholas   University of South Wales

Fihl, Esther   Copenhagen University
Forsdick, Charles   Liverpool University
Fraiture, Pierre-Philippe   University of Warwick
Fuller, Mia   University of California at Berkeley

Geulen, Christian   Universität Koblenz-Landau
Ghose, Sheila   New York University
Griffiths, Claire   University of Hull
Grosse, Pascal   Charité Berlin

Halen, Pierre   Paul Verlaine-Metz University
Hamilton, Russell   Vanderbilt University
Handelsman, Michael   University of Tennessee
Hansen, Klaus Georg   Nuuk
Harrison, Nicholas   King's College London
Hernández, Juan Antonio   Cornell University
Heyden, Ulrich van der   Humboldt Universität zu Berlin
Høiris, Ole   Aarhus University
Honold, Alexander   Universität Basel
Hunt, Nancy Rose   Michigan University
Hvenegård-Lassen, Kirsten   Roskilde University

Iyob, Ruth   Washington University

Jensen, Lars   Roskilde University
Johansen, Pia Krüger   Roskilde University
Jones, Branwen Gruffydd   Aberdeen University

Kagan, Richard C.   Hamline University
Khan, Sheila   University of Manchester
Klobucka, Anna   University of Massachusetts
Krabbe, Julia Suárez   Roskilde University
Krus, Patricia   Unversity of Stirling
Kundrus, Birthe   Hamburger Institut für
                                       Sozialforschung

Laak, Dirk van   Universität Giessen
Labanca, Nicola   University of Siena
Lamana, Gonzalo   University of Pittsburgh
Langgård, Karen   University of Greenland
Lewerenz, Susann   Hamburg
Lombardi-Diop, Cristina   American University in Rome
Lopéz, Carlos M.   Marshall University
Lund, Joshua   University of Pittsburgh

Macdonald, Amanda	University of Queensland
MacQueen, Norrie	Dundee University
Mai, Nicola	London Metropolitan University
Majumdar, Margaret A.	University of Portsmouth
Marechal, Philippe	Royal Museum of Central Africa
Marsh, Kate	Liverpool University
Marshall, Bill	University of Glasgow
Martinho, Ana Maria Mão-de Ferro	Lisbon Nova University
Martone, Eric	Waterbury
McCusker, Maeve	Queen's University Belfast
Mealor, Cheralyn	Aarhus University
Mélice, Anne	Liège University
Mendes, Victor J.	University of Massachusetts
Meuwese, Mark	Winnipeg University
Miranda, Evelyn A.	University of the Philippines
Moe, Nelson	Barnard College
Monasterios, Elizabeth	University of Pittsburgh
Moser, Robert	Georgia University
Moutinho, Isabel	La Trobe University
Moyd, Michelle	Cornell University
Mülhahn, Klaus	Indiana University
Munro, Martin	University of the West Indies
Murphy, David	University of Stirling
Murdoch, H. Adlai	University of Illinois
Negash, Tekeste	Dalarna University
Niekerk, Annemie van	
Ní Loingsigh, Aedín	University of Edinburgh
Ó Ciosáin, Éamon	National University of Ireland
Olsen, Nanna Folke	Copenhagen
Owen, Hilary	Manchester University
Pappe, Ilan	Haifa University
Past, Mariana	Dickinson College
Penny, Glenn H.	University of Iowa
Raedt, Thérèse de	Utah University
Reid, Victoria	Liverpool University
Reyes, Luisa T.	University of the Philippines
Ringrose, Priscilla	Trondheim University
Robinson, David	University of Western Australia
Rosenhaft, Eve	University of Liverpool
Rothwell, Phillip	Rutgers University
Rønsager, Mette	Copenhagen University
Rutgers, Wim	University of Aruba
Salhi, Kamal	University of Leeds

Salverda, Reinier	University College, London; Fryske Akademy
Sanjinés, Javier C.	University of Michigan
Santos, Hélia	Coimbra University
Schubert, Michael	Universität Osnabrück
Scott, William R.	Lehigh University
Sebald, Peter	Berlin
Sebro, Louise	Lund University
Shilton, Siobhán	Bristol University
Shipway, Martin	Birkbeck College, University of London
Soares, Anthony	Belfast University
Sòrgoni, Barbara	Università Federico II
Spaas, Lieve	Kingston University
Stacey, Pascale	Liverpool University
Stafford, Andy	University of Leeds
Stecher-Hansen, Marianne	University of Washington
Stephenson, Marcia	Purdue University
Thode-Arora, Hilke	Auckland/Berlin
Thompson, Ewa	Rice University
Thomson, Claire	University College, London
Tornimbeni, Corrado	Bologna University
Triulzi, Alessandro	Istituto Orientale, Naples
Tyre, Stephen	University of St Andrews
Vale de Almeida, Miguel	Lisbon University
Veneracion, Jaime	University of the Philippines
Venn, Couze	Nottingham Trent University
Verdesio, Gustavo	University of Michigan
Villar, Carmen Maria Ramos	Sheffield University
Walther, Daniel J.	Wartburg College
Werkmeister, Sven	Humboldt Universität zu Berlin
Wildenthal, Lora	Rice University
Williams, Claire	Liverpool University
Wolsgård, Lasse	Copenhagen
Woodhull, Winifred	University of California
Yervasi, Carina	Swarthmore College
Zeller, Joachim	Berlin
Zeuske, Michael	Universität zu Köln
Zimmerer, Jürgen	University of Sheffield

Select Index of Authors and Works Cited, including Journals

Subject Index